lonely

England

Newcastle &
Northeast England
p601

Lake District
& Cumbria
p563

Yorkshire
p473

Manchester, Liverpool
& Northwest England
p527

Birmingham &
the Midlands
p391

Cambridge &
East Anglia
p353

Oxford & the
Cotswolds
p177

London
p55

Bristol,
Bath &
Somerset
p221

Hampshire,
Wiltshire &
Dorset
p257

Canterbury &
Southeast England
p143

Devon,
Cornwall & the
Isles of Scilly
p293

Berry, Joe Bindloss, Fionn Davenport,
Ham, Damian Harper, Catherine Le Nevez

Contents

LOWER SLAUGHTER P197

GORDON BELL/SHUTTERSTOCK ©

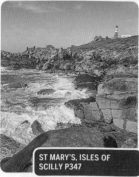

ST MARY'S, ISLES OF SCILLY P347

KATH WATSON/SHUTTERSTOCK ©

Contents

SPECIAL FEATURES

Contents

ON THE ROAD

DOVER CASTLE P157

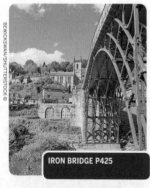

IRON BRIDGE P425

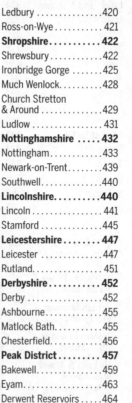

NORTH YORK MOORS
NATIONAL PARK P492

Contents

COVID-19

We have re-checked every business in this book before publication to ensure that it is still open after 2020's COVID-19 outbreak. However, the economic and social impacts of COVID-19 will continue to be felt long after the outbreak has been contained, and many businesses, services and events referenced in this guide may experience ongoing restrictions. Some businesses may be temporarily closed, have changed their opening hours and services, or require bookings; some unfortunately could have closed permanently. We suggest you check with venues before visiting for the latest information.

Right: Stow-on-the-Wold (p198), the Cotswolds

WELCOME TO

England

I was born in London but grew up in Australia, from where England seemed to glow over a distant horizon. England was my go-to for journalism, comedy, music and films. When I moved back as an adult, I walked, drove, cycled, and rode trains across the length and breadth of the country, lapping up the places I'd dreamed of seeing: historic sites, museums, cities, villages and iconic landscapes. This country has shaped the world we live in, but it is also continually renewed by the world that comes to see it.

By Tasmin Waby, Writer
For more about our writers, see p704

NIGEL JARVIS/SHUTTERSTOCK ©

England

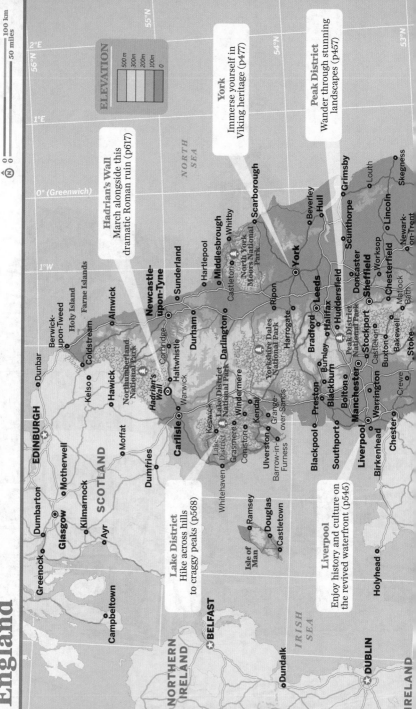

Hadrian's Wall
March alongside this dramatic Roman ruin (p617)

York
Immerse yourself in Viking heritage (p477)

Peak District
Wander through stunning landscapes (p457)

Lake District
Hike across hills to craggy peaks (p568)

Liverpool
Enjoy history and culture on the revived waterfront (p545)

ELEVATION

500m
300m
200m
100m
0

100 km
50 miles

56°N
2°E
55°N
1°E
0° (Greenwich)
1°W
54°N
53°N

NORTH SEA
IRISH SEA

SCOTLAND
NORTHERN IRELAND
IRELAND

EDINBURGH
Dunbar
Motherwell
Dumbarton
Greenock
Glasgow
Kilmarnock
Ayr
Campbeltown

Berwick-upon-Tweed
Holy Island
Farne Islands
Kelso
Coldstream
Hawick
Moffat
Dumfries
Alnwick
Northumberland National Park
Hadrian's Wall
Warwick
Corbridge
Haltwhistle
Carlisle
Newcastle-upon-Tyne
Sunderland
Durham
Hartlepool
Middlesbrough
Darlington
Whitby
Scarborough
Castleton
North York Moors National Park
Ripon
Harrogate
York
Beverley
Hull
Grimsby
Louth
Skegness
Lincoln
Newark-on-Trent
Scunthorpe
Worksop
Doncaster
Chesterfield
Matlock
Bath
Sheffield
Leeds
Bradford
Halifax
Huddersfield
Burnley
Blackburn
Bolton
Stockport
Manchester
Warrington
Crewe
Stoke
Buxton
Bakewell
Castleton
Peak District National Park
Yorkshire Dales National Park
Keswick
Grasmere
Windermere
Coniston
Kendal
Ulverston
Grange-over-Sands
Barrow-in-Furness
Whitehaven
Lake District National Park
Preston
Blackpool
Southport
Liverpool
Birkenhead
Chester
Isle of Man
Ramsey
Douglas
Castletown

BELFAST
DUBLIN
Dundalk
Holyhead

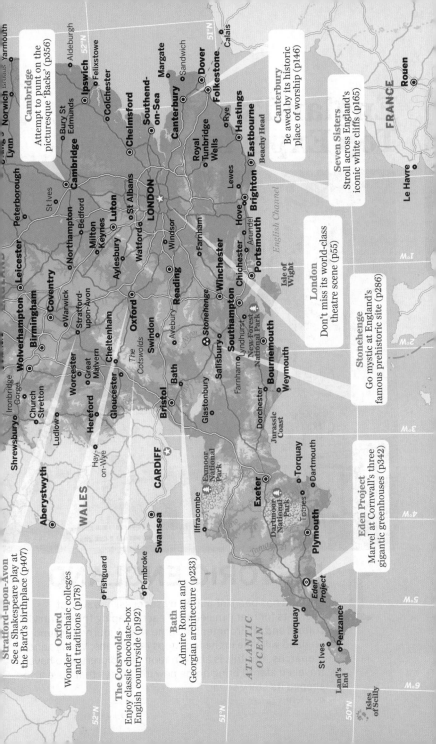

Stratford-upon-Avon
See a Shakespeare play at the Bard's birthplace (p407)

Oxford
Wonder at archaic colleges and traditions (p178)

The Cotswolds
Enjoy classic chocolate-box English countryside (p192)

Bath
Admire Roman and Georgian architecture (p233)

Eden Project
Marvel at Cornwall's three gigantic greenhouses (p342)

Stonehenge
Go mystic at England's famous prehistoric site (p286)

London
Don't miss its world-class theatre scene (p55)

Seven Sisters
Stroll across England's iconic white cliffs (p165)

Canterbury
Be awed by its historic place of worship (p146)

Cambridge
Attempt to punt on the picturesque 'Backs' (p356)

FRANCE

WALES

CARDIFF

ATLANTIC OCEAN

English Channel

Isles of Scilly

England's Top Experiences

SAIOT/SHUTTERSTOCK ©

1 HISTORIC ENGLAND

England has been inhabited by successive waves of migrants for many millennia – each shaping the country's culture and environment in some way. A journey around England will take in the footsteps of Romans, Vikings and monarchs. But this is also a nation of explorers who have travelled afar to bring home new influences that have also shaped its story so far.

Above: Tower Bridge (p78), London

Tower of London

Europe's best-preserved medieval fortress and one of Britain's best-known attractions, this 1000-year-old landmark has served as a palace, a prison, an arsenal and a mint. Today it's home to the spectacular Crown Jewels; the legendary Beefeaters, with their distinctive red uniforms; and ravens that are attributed with mythical powers. p76

British Museum

In the varied (and occasionally controversial) collection of the British Museum in London, you'll see some of the world's greatest treasures, and learn a little more about how England sees the world today. p68

Canterbury Cathedral

The fulcrum of the Anglican Church and a place of worship for more than 15 centuries, Canterbury Cathedral's intricate tower dominates the city's skyline. At its heart lies a 12th-century crime scene, where Archbishop Thomas Becket was put to the sword after disagreements with the king. p146

CITY LIFE

2

English cities made famous by films, TV, music and art loom large in the imagination. Each is unique, from distinctive city skylines to the culture of the people who make these thriving metropolises home. Tick off all the must-see sights in London, but also leave time to soak up the distinctive character of England's other great cities.

COWARDLION/SHUTTERSTOCK ©

CHRIS LAWRENCE TRAVEL/SHUTTERSTOCK ©

Bristol

The industrial history of this former port city has been reclaimed by a counterculture vibe, thriving music and street-art scenes (made famous by the mischievous political muralist, Banksy). Stay a few days and you'll find a wealth of art collectives, cafes and small festivals that bring out the city's best. p222

Above left: M Shed (p226), Bristol

Liverpool

The reborn water-front at Albert Dock houses top museums – the Merseyside Maritime Museum and the International Slavery Museum ensure the good and bad sides of Liverpool's history are not forgotten, while the Tate Liverpool and the Beatles Story celebrate pop culture and the city's musical sons. p545

Above top: Tate Liverpool (p549)

Cambridge

One of the two most famous English university cities, a visit to Cambridge is best spent wandering historic colleges, marvelling at the intricate vaulting of King's College Chapel, then taking a punt (flat-bottomed boat) under the bridges of the picturesque River Cam. p356

Above: River Cam and the Backs (p360)

3 EPIC COASTLINES

England's coasts are as varied as its history, and the civilisations that have grown up in each region are shaped by these landscapes. From the wide, watery Broads of East Anglia to the south-facing cliffs of Sussex and the ancient Celtic kingdom of Cornwall, each deserves a proper visit for its unique mystery and beauty.

Cornwall

Cornwall's dramatic coastline shelters a string of cliffs, coves and peninsulas – with stunning views at every turn. Get exploring, whether it's to swim, surf or to gobble up delectable seafood at a seaside shack. p319

Below left: Land's End (p334), Cornwall

Seven Sisters Cliffs

An epic four-mile rollercoaster walk along sheer white chalk cliffs rollicking along the Sussex coast – overlooking the English Channel – is breathtaking, in every sense. p165

Top right: Seven Sisters Cliffs

North Norfolk

Although a seemingly sleepy section of coastline, North Norfolk's sandy beaches and marshes attract a rich concentration of birdlife, including plovers, curlews and brent geese. It's also home to stately houses and quaint seaside towns. p379

Right: Cromer (p382), Norfolk

4 COUNTRY JAUNTS

ALEXEY FEDORENKO/SHUTTERSTOCK ©

Hiring a car and driving through gorgeous English landscapes, visiting quaint villages and epic castles is a highlight no matter what the season. Off the main roads you can meander down narrow lanes of hedgerows and stop to watch the sun set or a bird of prey gliding in the sky above.

Above: Clapper Bridge, Postbridge (p316), Dartmoor National Park

Northumberland Coast

Charming, castle-crowned villages are dotted around this wild and remote region. In winter you may find yourself the only visitor from out of town, and guaranteed a friendly welcome for it. p625

Dartmoor National Park

Driving on Dartmoor is like being inside a feature film, with 360-degree views of the moor's shifting mists and stark, otherworldly nature. Stop at rustic pubs or walk the forested gorges of moss-covered trees. p311

Cotswolds

These quintessential English villages of rose-clad cottages and honey-coloured stone demand a convertible car and wicker picnic basket. Book to stay in one of the tastefully decorated boutique hotels in the region. p192

5 STATELY HOMES

Britain's best stately homes have proudly hosted royalty, prime ministers, famous actors and poets. Some are examples of architectural brilliance, others hide scandalous stories you'll only learn about on a guided tour.

Blenheim Palace

Famously Winston Churchill's birthplace, Blenheim is one of England's greatest stately homes. After you explore the palace, leave time to wander the magnificent 2000-acre garden. p191

Top left: Blenheim Palace

Castle Howard

Starring in a host of period dramas, including the 1980s TV version of Evelyn Waugh's *Brideshead Revisited*, this baroque edifice in North Yorkshire is one of the world's most beautiful buildings. p485

Above left: Castle Howard

Chatsworth House

A treasure trove of heirlooms and works of art, this quintessential stately home sits in 25 sq miles of grounds and ornamental gardens. p460

Above right: Chatsworth House gates

6 ENGLAND ON A PLATE

SUBSTANCEPRODUCTIONS/SHUTTERSTOCK ©

Afternoon Tea

In England tea is quietly brewed in a pot, preferably silver-plated, and ritualistically poured into fine bone-china cups on saucers. It's then served with a side of scones and cream, fruit cake or feather-light cucumber sandwiches. p650

Top left: Scones with jam and cream

Sunday Pub Lunch

Ideally eaten in a cosy country pub that has remained unchanged for 100-plus years, the Sunday pub lunch is almost always a roast (beef, pork, or a nut-roast if you prefer) served with gravy, vegetables and Yorkshire pudding, washed down with a tap beer. p649

Left: Roast meal with Yorkshire pudding

AMY LAUGHINGHOUSE/SHUTTERSTOCK ©

Modern Gastronomy

Once an afterthought, eating out is now a highlight of a visit here thanks to a combination of experimental chefs, a resurgence in quality locally sourced ingredients, and the wild popularity of cooking shows – from Jamie Oliver's breakout career in the naughties to the *Great British Bake Off* today. The English have embraced food culture with both arms and are holding tight. Your tastebuds will be happy they did!

Beyond big cities – where you're spoiled for epicurean delights – England's best foodie destinations can be found all over the country: from tiny Bray just outside London, to beautiful Cartmel and medieval Ludlow (p432) in the north.

7 ANCIENT HISTORY

England is littered with historic sites to explore, from neolithic stone circles to Anglo-Saxon burial mounds, where you're cast back to an era characterised by myth and mystery. Roman ruins run the length of the country – villas, baths, mosaic floors and amphitheatres tell the story of a thriving empire, from London to Chester and beyond to Hadrian's Wall.

Stonehenge

Visitors have been drawn to this myth-laden ring of boulders for more than 5000 years, and we still don't know quite why it was built. Nearby Avebury Stone Circle is equally beguiling and atmospheric. p286

Below left: Stonehenge

Roman Relics

Be it in the ancient baths in Bath (p233), an amphitheatre in Cirencester or marvelling at mosaics in Chichester, you're never far from England's Roman past beneath your feet.

Top right: Roman Baths (p233), Bath

Hadrian's Wall

This 2000-year-old procession of abandoned forts, garrisons and towers marches across the wild landscape of northern England, marking an edge-of-empire barrier against the Celts to the north. p617

Right: Housesteads Roman Fort (p619), Hadrian's Wall

8 CONTEMPORARY CULTURE

ARCHITECT: NICHOLAS GRIMSHAW; IMAGE: NICOLE KWIATKOWSKI/SHUTTERSTOCK

Modern England is a powerhouse of culture and creativity. There's something about this tightly populated country with its unique blend of colonial diaspora, who now call England home, that continues to incubate fresh ideas and global trends. Make time in your schedule to explore its music venues, street art and art galleries, and seek out its distinctive designers, the latest writers and up-and-coming performers.

Fashion Icons

Yes, recognisable British labels like Burberry and Vivienne Westwood are loved, but England's fashion icons are everywhere, from vintage up-cycling market stores to up-and-coming independent designers in Brighton's North Lanes. p171

Art & Artists

England is popping with contemporary art galleries, from London's iconic Tate Modern (p79) to regional show stoppers like Newcastle's BALTIC. Its artists and arts scene will never stop inspiring.

Sustainable Futures

The gigantic hemispherical greenhouse of the Eden Project is one of many ambitious self-made projects connecting people with the natural world, exploring ways to build a greener future today. p342

Above: Concert at the Eden Project

Need to Know

For more information, see Survival Guide (p677)

Currency
Pound sterling (£)

Language
English

Visas
Many nationalities do not require a visa to visit the UK. Check online at www.gov.uk/check-uk-visa.

Money
Contactless payments encouraged; credit cards widely accepted.

Mobile Phones
The UK uses the GSM 900/1800 network, which covers the rest of Europe, Australia and New Zealand. It's recommended you get a UK SIM card on arrival unless you have a good data roaming plan.

Time
Greenwich Mean Time (GMT/UTC); British Summer Time (BST/UTC+1) runs from the last Sunday in March until the last Sunday in October.

When to Go

Carlisle
GO May–Sep

York
GO May–Sep

Liverpool
GO May–Sep

Norwich
GO May–Sep

London
GO Any time

Exeter
GO Apr–Sep

High Season
(Jun–Aug)

➡ Weather at its best. Accommodation rates high, particularly in August (school holidays).

➡ Carparks busy, especially in seaside areas, national parks and popular cities, such as Oxford, Bath and York.

Shoulder
(Easter–May, Sep & Oct)

➡ Crowds reduce.

➡ Weather often good: March to May sun mixes with sudden rain; September and October can feature balmy autumn days.

Low Season
(Nov–Easter)

➡ Wet and cold is the norm. Snow can fall, especially up north.

➡ Opening hours reduced October to Easter; some places shut for the winter. Major sights (especially in London) open all year.

PLAN YOUR TRIP NEED TO KNOW

Useful Websites

Visit England (www.visit england.com) Official tourism website.

Lonely Planet (www.lonely planet.com/england) Destination information, hotel bookings, traveller forum and more.

Traveline (www.traveline.info) Excellent portal site for public transport around England.

British Arts Festivals (www.artsfestivals.co.uk) Lists festivals – art, literature, dance, folk and more.

What's On Stage (www.whats onstage.com) Up to date theatre information across England

Important Numbers

England (and UK) country code	✆44
International access code	✆00
Emergency (police, fire, ambulance, mountain rescue or coastguard)	✆112 or ✆999

Exchange Rates

Australia	A$1	£0.54
Canada	C$1	£0.56
Eurozone	€1	£0.87
Japan	¥100	£0.75
New Zealand	NZ$1	£0.51
USA	US$1	£0.72

For current exchange rates, see www.xe.com.

Daily Costs

Budget: Less than £55

➡ Dorm beds: £15–30

➡ Cheap meals in cafes and pubs: £7–11

➡ Long-distance coach: £15–40 (200 miles)

Midrange: £55–120

➡ Double room in a midrange hotel or B&B: £65–130 (London £100–200)

➡ Main course in a midrange restaurant: £10–20

➡ Long-distance train: £20–80 (200 miles)

Top End: More than £120

➡ Four-star hotel room: from £130 (London from £200)

➡ Three-course meal in a good restaurant: around £40

➡ Car rental per day: from £35

Opening Hours

Opening hours may vary throughout the year, especially in rural areas where many places have shorter hours, or close completely, from October or November to March or April.

Banks 9.30am–4pm or 5pm Monday to Friday; some open 9.30am–1pm Saturday

Pubs & bars noon–11pm Monday to Saturday (some till midnight or 1am Friday and Saturday), 12.30pm–11pm Sunday

Restaurants lunch noon–3pm, dinner 6pm–9pm or 10pm (later in cities)

Shops 9am–5.30pm or 6pm Monday to Saturday, often 11am–5pm Sunday

Arriving in England

Heathrow Airport Heathrow Express train (£25, 15 minutes) is the fastest link to London; Piccadilly line on the London Underground (£6, one hour) is slower but cheaper. Services run from around 5am to midnight. At other times catch the N9 night bus (£1.50, 1¼ hours) or a taxi (£50 to £100).

Gatwick Airport Trains to central London £10 to £20; hourly buses to central London around the clock from £8; taxi £100.

St Pancras International Arrival point for Eurostar trains to/from Europe, with Underground/bus connections across London.

Getting Around

Transport within England can be expensive; local buses serve most remote parts of the country. For timetables, check out www.traveline.info.

Car Useful for travelling at your own pace, or for visiting regions with minimal public transport. Car hire available in every city.

Train Relatively expensive, with extensive coverage and frequent departures throughout most of the country.

Bus Cheaper and slower than trains; useful for more remote places that aren't serviced by rail.

For much more on **getting around**, see p685

First Time England

For more information, see Survival Guide (p677)

Checklist

➡ Check your passport expiration date (you should have at least six months validity after your return)

➡ Check current entry requirements, eg vaccinations

➡ Make bookings (sights, accommodation, travel)

➡ Check airline baggage restrictions

➡ Inform your credit-/debit-card company of your travel plans

➡ Organise the correct level of travel insurance

➡ Check mobile (cell) phone compatibility, unlock it to use a local SIM

What to Pack

➡ UK electrical plug adaptor

➡ Umbrella – because the rumours about the weather are true

➡ Waterproof jacket – because sometimes the umbrella is not enough

➡ Comfortable walking shoes

➡ Warm socks, just in case

Top Tips for Your Trip

➡ At major London airports, tickets for express trains into central London are usually substantially more than local, slower transport.

➡ The best way to get local currency is from an ATM, known colloquially in England as a 'cash point'.

➡ If staying more than a few days in London get an Oyster Card, fees for using your contactless bankcard can add up.

➡ Be on guard as pickpockets lurk in the more crowded tourist areas, especially in London.

➡ Pre-book your must-see major attractions ahead of your visit as tickets can sell out.

➡ The unpredictable English weather makes a lightweight, waterproof jacket a must-have item.

What to Wear

Sunscreen and a rain jacket (even in summer) are essential items – you're bound to use both, possibly on the same day. For sightseeing, comfortable shoes will make or break a trip; if you plan to enjoy Britain's great outdoors, hiking gear is required in higher/wilder areas, but not for casual strolls in the countryside.

Take note that some bars and restaurants have dress codes banning jeans, T-shirts and trainers (sneakers or runners). You'll almost never feel over-dressed in England, so pack your best threads and dress to impress, if it pleases you.

Sleeping

Accommodation in England ranges from low-cost options like camping (many have pre-prepared glamping options including bedding), hostels and single rooms in pubs and inns, to classic (and sometimes eccentric) B&Bs and guest-houses, recognised hotel chains, and high-end luxury options that deliver all the hospitality you'd expect at different price points. For something more unusual, look into 'bothies' in wilder locations (BYO sleeping bag!), or consider hiring a canal boat for a break on a rural waterway.

Money

ATMs (usually called 'cash points' in England) are common in cities and even small towns. Withdrawals from some ATMs are subject to a small charge, but most are free (look for 'Free Cash'). Check how much your home bank charges for withdrawing money overseas and ask about options. Watch out for tampered ATMs; one ruse by scammers is to attach a card-reader or minicamera.

Bargaining

A bit of mild haggling is acceptable at flea markets and antique shops, but everywhere else you're expected to pay the advertised price.

Tipping

In England you're not obliged to tip if the service or food was unsatisfactory (even if it's been automatically added to your bill as a 'service charge'), but few Brits would dare to argue it!

Restaurants 12.5% in restaurants and teahouses with table service (usually added to your bill), 15% at smarter restaurants.

Pubs & bars Not expected if you order drinks (or food) and pay at the bar; usually 10% if you order at the table and your meal is brought to you.

Taxis Usually 10%, or rounded up to the nearest pound, especially in London.

TUPUNGATO/SHUTTERSTOCK ©

Pub on London's Portobello Rd (p100)

Etiquette

Manners The English have a reputation for being polite, and good manners are considered important in most situations. When asking directions, 'Excuse me, can you tell me the way to...' is better than 'Where's...'

Queues In England, queuing ('standing in line') is sacrosanct, whether to board a bus, buy tickets at a kiosk or enter the gates of an attraction. Any attempt to 'jump the queue' will result in very quiet tut-tutting and hard stares – which is about as angry as most locals get in public.

Escalators If you take an escalator (especially at London Tube stations) or a moving walkway (eg at an airport) be sure to stand on the right, so folks can pass on the left – or expect to be told off.

Eating

Book ahead for restaurants, especially at weekends. High profile restaurants should be booked at least a couple of months in advance.

Restaurants England's restaurants range from cheap-and-cheerful to Michelin-starred, and cover every cuisine you can imagine.

Cafes Open during daytime (rarely after 6pm), cafes are good for a casual breakfast or lunch, or just a tea or coffee.

Pubs Most of England's pubs serve reasonably priced meals; many can compete with restaurants on quality.

What's New

England stepped into a post-EU era slightly less confident than when the Brexit referendum was accepted. The coronavirus pandemic amplified tensions between the north and south and between Wales, Scotland and England, as well as halting inbound tourism. The mood: tentatively optimistic or pessimistic – depending on whom you ask.

Social Distancing

The global pandemic saw changes implemented in 2020 to reduce the risk of virus transmission, and many may remain. Pre-booking tickets – even for free-of-charge events and sights – allows better management of crowding in tourist hotspots. Timed entry and fewer walk-in-only restaurants is left to chance and a wise maxim applies more than ever: life belongs to the organised.

Living Greener

England is getting closer to weaning itself off single-use plastics by first banning non-degradable straws, stirrers and cotton buds. Zero-waste grocery stores are popping up all over the country, and big chains are moving to plastic-free aisles where shoppers bring their own containers to fill up on staples. Vegan dining went mainstream, rural stays offer food foraging tours, and minimal-waste cooking is trending at high-end restaurants.

Museums Revisited

The Black Lives Matter movement began as a response to police brutality in the USA but England is also coming to terms with its own history. Colonial statues came down in 2020 – some forcibly, others quietly. Museum curation notes were reviewed and school curricula scrutinised. The Wellcome Collection (p98) in London is one of many institutions reshaping its exhibits. A Commission for Diversity in the Public Realm was established by London mayor Sadiq Kahn to consult on the future of landmarks, including murals, street names and other memorials.

Rewilding England

England signed the UN Leaders' Pledge for Nature, committing an extra 400,000

WHAT'S HAPPENING IN ENGLAND

Tasmin Waby, Lonely Planet writer

England is currently contemplating its place in the world, the legacies of its colonial past and what story it will write into the future. The end of its 47-year long EU membership in 2021 left many questions about its trade and political alliances as yet unanswered.

With air fleets grounded and businesses temporarily closed by Covid-19, the country took a collective moment to slow down and reprioritise. Meanwhile, green initiatives such as better cycling infrastructure were pushed forward by local governments.

The British government also committed to reversing biodiversity loss and many hoped the Covid-19 pandemic would be a cause for reinventing the economy on more sustainable lines, as the country recovers from the devastating impacts. One thing is certain: the only constant is change.

hectares of English countryside to be protected for biodiversity by 2030 while individual groups were implementing re-wilding projects on private land across the country. Existing National Parks, and Areas of Outstanding Natural Beauty (AONB) comprise approximately 26% of land in England.

Slower Ways

The opening of the England Coast Path (p41), a major project to define a walkable route around the full coastline of England, is one of many ways the English have embraced 'slow travel' since Covid-19 hit. Social enterprise Urban Good (www.urban good.org) published maps of London's best streets, and people are reclaiming pre-existing footpaths between neighbouring villages hoping to create daisy-chain routes for long distance journeys across the country.

Dark Skies Festivals

An interest in astrotourism continued to gather pace in the early 21st century, with campaigns to reduce light pollution so as to better appreciate the sky above us. In England a new breed of winter festival has popped up, focused on all things starry nights. Kicking off in the North York Moors during February – the coldest and darkest month of the year – Dark Skies festivals are also scheduled for Northumberland and the South Downs.

Bike-packing King Alfred's Way

This new 220-mile off-road cycling route (www.cyclinguk.org/king-alfreds-way) traces millennia of English history, connecting iconic sites including Stonehenge, Avebury Stone Circle, Iron Age hill forts, and Winchester and Salisbury Cathedrals. Named after the King of Wessex, Alfred the Great, the circular trail starts and ends at his statue in Winchester, where he is buried. It includes gravel road, so travellers will need to hire an off-road bike and pre-book accommodation along the way.

FAST FACTS

Food trend: Zero waste

Highest mountain: Scafell Pike, 978m

Average age: 40.3 years

Population: 56.2 million

population per sq km

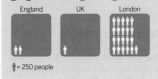

England | UK | London

👤 ≈ 250 people

A dedicated guidebook covers all such details.

DIY Gin

From Plymouth to North Yorkshire, gin distilleries have started to offer visitors 'distil your own' experiences to complement tastings and behind-the-scenes tours. Talk about the ultimate travel souvenir: from botanical to citrus to chocolate flavours, you'll learn how to blend your very own signature gin at a number of boutique distilleries, starting with Plymouth Gin Distillery (p309).

Accommodation

Find more accommodation reviews throughout the On the Road chapters (from p53)

PRICE RANGES

We quote prices for a double room with private bathroom in high season. But be aware – dynamic pricing means one room will cost more, or less, depending on demand. Hotels in London are more expensive than the rest of the country, so these have different price ranges.

£ less than £65 (London £100)

££ £65–£130 (London £100–£200)

£££ more than £130 (London £200)

Accommodation Types

B&Bs & guesthouses Small, family-run houses generally provide good value. More luxurious versions are similar to boutique hotels.

Bothies & bunkhouses Usually a simple stone or wood building with a communal sleeping area, plus stoves for self-catering. BYO sleeping bag.

Camping From farmer's fields to proper sites with facilities; an increasing number of places offer fully catered glamping in bell tents.

Hostels There's a good choice of both big brand and independent hostels, many housed in rustic and/or historic buildings. These are popular with families and groups.

Hotels English hotels range from half-a-dozen rooms above a pub to restored country houses and castles, with commensurate rates.

Houseboats Rent a canal boat and you can explore a section of rural waterway for a quintessential English break.

Pubs & inns Cosy country pubs and coaching inns often offer lodgings from the basic to almost luxurious.

University rooms Inexpensive, functional single bedroom accommodation and self-catering flats available over summer.

Best Places to Stay

Best on a Budget

Low cost doesn't translate to a lesser experience at many of England's budget digs. These all deliver on simple comforts, atmosphere and location, but without breaking your bank account.

➡ NQ1 (p536), Manchester

➡ Tune Hotel (p550), Liverpool

➡ Vintage Vardos (p317), North Devon

➡ Hebden Bridge Hostel (p517), West Yorkshire

➡ Igloo Hybrid Hostel (p435), Notthinghamshire

Best Eccentric Stays

One thing England does well is eccentricity. These quirky stays mix history with modern flourishes to create comfortable and highly photographable rooms to snuggle down in for the night.

➡ Rum Doodle (p571), the Lake District

➡ Covenstead (p248), Glastonbury

➡ 16a (p261), Winchester

➡ La Rosa Hotel (p499), Whitby

➡ 40 Winks (p113), London

Best for Families

Families looking for accommodation with enough room for children, and that entertains them at the same time, will love this list. Choose between a luxury castle or sleeping by the beach in a ramshackle camping ground – you'll remember these stays fondly.

➡ Otterburn Castle Country House Hotel (p624), Northumberland National Park

➡ Lumley Castle (p614), Durham

➡ Deepdale Backpackers & Camping (p387), Norfolk

➡ Henry's Campsite (p338), Cornwall

➡ Whitby YHA (p499), North Yorkshire

Best for Solo Travellers

Whether you're travelling in London or the countryside, the place you sleep can make all the difference when it comes to meeting fellow travellers as well as locals. Pubs, inns, hostels and small B&Bs are your best options.

➡ Wasdale Head Inn (p583), the Lake District

➡ Gurnard's Head (p334), Cornwall

➡ Generator (p108), London

➡ Kipps (p170), Brighton

➡ Hull Trinity Backpackers (p523), Yorkshire

DANNY FIELDING/SHUTTERSTOCK ©

Wasdale Head Inn (p583)

PLAN YOUR TRIP ACCOMMODATION

Booking

In the high season (which includes holiday periods like Christmas and Easter), it's best to book your accommodation a few months ahead to avoid disappointment. Larger booking sites will have availability at the last minute, but you'll miss out on the best options, and likely pay more for the privilege.

Lonely Planet (www.lonelyplanet.com/england/hotels) Find independent reviews, as well as recommendations on the best places to stay – and then book them online.

Bed & Breakfast Nationwide (www.bedandbreakfastnationwide.com) B&B listings.

Cottages.com (www.cottages.com) Holiday cottage rentals.

National Trust (www.nationaltrust.org.uk/holidays) Holiday rentals in historic National Trust properties.

Stilwell's (www.stilwell.co.uk) Holiday cottage rentals.

University Rooms (www.universityrooms.co.uk) Summer accommodation in university student halls.

Self-Contained Accommodation

If you want to base yourself in one place and have a little more privacy, renting for a week can be ideal. Choose from small apartments in cities or quaint old houses (called 'cottages', whatever the size!) in country areas. Cottages for four people start from £300 in high season. Rates fall in the low season and there's also often more options to book a half-week or long weekend.

Month by Month

January

After the festivities of Christmas and New Year's Eve, the first few weeks of the year can feel like a bit of an anticlimax – never helped by the often bad weather.

 London Parade

The New Year's Day Parade (www.londonparade.co.uk) in London is one of the biggest events of its kind in the world, featuring marching bands, street performers, classic cars, floats and displays winding their way through the streets.

Chinese New Year

Late January or early February sees London's China-town snap, crackle and pop with fireworks, a colourful street parade, lion dances and dim sum aplenty.

February

The country may be scenic under snow and sunshine, but is more likely to be grey and gloomy. Festivals and events to brighten the mood are still thin on the ground.

Jorvik Viking Festival

In chilly mid-February, the ancient Viking capital of York becomes home once again to invaders and horned helmets galore, with the intriguing addition of longship races. (p481)

Dark Skies Festival

Stargazing, deep space virtual reality, ghost walks, night-running, zip-lining in the dark, yoga and mindfulness, and Aurora hunting are among the night-time experiences at this week-long festival (www.dark skiesnationalparks.org.uk) in the North York Moors and Yorkshire Dales.

Six Nations Rugby Championship

This highlight of the rugby calendar (www.rbs6 nations.com) runs from late January to March, with the England team playing its home matches at London's Twickenham stadium.

March

Spring starts to show itself, with daffodil blooms brightening up the month. Hotels and inns offer special weekend rates to tempt people out from under their duvets.

University Boat Race

An annual institution (since 1856), this race is held in late March/early April down the River Thames in London between the rowing teams from Cambridge and Oxford Universities. (p105)

April

The weather is looking up, with warmer and drier days bringing out the spring blossoms. Sights and attractions that closed for the low season open up around the middle of the month or at Easter.

Grand National

Half the country has a flutter on the highlight of the three-day horse race meeting at Aintree: a steeple-chase with a testing course and high jumps. Held on a Saturday in April. (p550)

🏃 London Marathon

Super-fit athletes, both local and international, cover 26.2 miles in just over two hours. Others dress up in daft costumes and take considerably longer (www.virginmoneylondon marathon.com).

🎭 Stratford Literary Festival

The top event on the cultural calendar in William Shakespeare's home town attracts big hitters from the book world for a week of debates, author events, workshops and humour. (p410)

May

With sunny spring days, the calendar fills with more events. Two public holidays (the first and last Mondays of May) mean road traffic is very busy over the adjoining long weekends.

🎭 Padstow May Day

Known locally as 'Obby 'Oss Day, the north Cornish town of Padstow celebrates its ancient pagan spring festival on 1 May, featuring two rival 'osses that swirl through the crowds to the town's maypole. (p324)

🎭 Brighton Festival

A lively three-week arts fest takes over the streets of buzzy south-coast resort Brighton during May. Alongside the mainstream performances there's a festival 'fringe' as well. (p169)

☆ FA Cup Final

The highlight of the football season for over a century. Throughout winter, teams from all of England's football divisions have been battling it out in a knockout tournament, culminating in this heady spectacle at Wembley Stadium. Held in early May.

🎭 Chelsea Flower Show

The Royal Horticultural Society flower show in late May is the highlight of the gardener's year. Top garden designers take gold, silver and bronze medals (and TV accolades), while the punters take the plants in the last-day giveaway. (p105)

☆ Glyndebourne

From late May till the end of August, this open-air festival (www.glynde bourne.com/festival) of world-class opera enlivens the pastoral surroundings of Glyndebourne House in East Sussex.

🏃 Keswick Mountain Festival

A long weekend in late May in the heart of the Lake District is dedicated to celebrating all things outdoor-related, from outdoor activities and celebrity speakers to live music and sporting events. (p584)

June

You can tell it's almost summer because June sees the music-festival season kick off properly, while sporting events fill the calendar.

☆ Derby Week

Horse racing, people watching and clothes spotting are on the agenda at this week-long race meeting (www.epsomderby.co.uk) in Epsom, Surrey, in early June.

🎭 Cotswold Olimpicks

Welly wanging, pole climbing and shin kicking are the key disciplines at this traditional Gloucestershire sports day in early June, held each year since 1612. (p202)

☆ Isle of Wight Festival

Originally held from 1968 to 1970 during the high point of hippie counterculture, this musical extravaganza was resurrected in 2002. Today it attracts top bands, especially from the indie and rock fraternities. Held in mid-June. (p267)

☉ Trooping the Colour

Military bands and bearskinned grenadiers march down London's Whitehall in this mid-June martial pageant to mark the monarch's birthday. (p105)

☆ Royal Ascot

It's hard to tell which matters more – the fashion or the fillies – at this highlight of the horse-racing year, held in mid-June at Berkshire's Royal Ascot racetrack. Expect top hats, designer frocks and plenty of frantic betting. (p217)

🎭 Broadstairs Dickens Festival

Charles Dickens, one of England's best-known writers, is celebrated at this literary festival in the town where he spent his summers and based many of his novels. (p154)

☆ Wimbledon Lawn Tennis Championships

Correctly titled the All England Club Championship, and the best-known grass-court tennis tournament in the world, Wimbledon attracts all the big names. Held in late June. (p133)

☆ Glastonbury Festival

England's favourite music festival held (nearly) every year on a dairy farm in Somerset in late June. Invariably muddy and still a rite of passage for every self-respecting British music fan. (p248)

☆ Meltdown Festival

In late June, London's Southbank Centre hands over the curatorial reigns to a legend of contemporary music (David Bowie, Morrissey, Patti Smith) to pull together a full program of concerts, talks and films.

☆ Royal Regatta

In late June or early July, boats of every description take to the water for an upper-crust river regatta at Henley-on-Thames. (p218)

☆ Pride

The big event on the LGBT+ calendar is a technicolour street parade through London's West End, culminating in a concert in Trafalgar Sq. Late June or early July. (p105)

☆ Aldeburgh Festival

Founded by composer Benjamin Britten in 1948, this exploration of classical music is East Anglia's biggest festival, taking in new, reinterpreted and rediscovered pieces, and extending into the visual arts. (p377)

July

This is it: summer, with weekly festivals and county shows. Schools break up at the end of the month, so there's a holiday tingle in the air, dulled only by busy Friday-evening roads.

☆ Camp Bestival

A family-focused music and camping festival with performances, DJs, activities and moonlight cinema for kids of all ages (www.campbestival.net) held at Lulworth Castle, Dorset.

☆ Great Yorkshire Show

The charming town of Harrogate plays host to one of England's largest county shows. Expect Yorkshire grit, Yorkshire tykes, Yorkshire puddings, Yorkshire beef... (p488)

☆ Latitude Festival

Popular and eclectic festival held near the lovely Suffolk seaside town of Southwold, with top names from the alternative-music scene complemented by theatre, cabaret and literary events. Held in mid-July. (p378)

☆ Cowes Week

The country's biggest yachting spectacular hits the choppy seas around the Isle of Wight in late July. (p267)

☆ Womad

In late July, roots and world music take centre stage at this global festival (www.womad.org), held in Charlton Park near Malmesbury.

August

Schools and colleges are closed, parliament is in recess, the sun is shining and England is in a holiday mood.

☆ Robin Hood Festival

Over a week in August, the Sherwood Forest National Nature Reserve hosts a celebration of its legendary bandit, with medieval re-enactments, archery lessons and much merriment. (p438)

☆ Notting Hill Carnival

A multicultural, Caribbean-style street carnival in late August in London's district of Notting Hill. Steel drums, dancers and outrageous costumes. (p105)

☆ Reading Festival

England's second-oldest music festival. Originally a rock fest, it veers a bit more towards pop these days, but it's still a good bet for big-name bands. Happens in late August. (p218)

☆ Leeds Festival

Leeds' major music festival, and the northern sister of the festival in Reading. The two festivals are held on the same late-August weekend, with the same line-up. If artists play Reading on the Friday, they'll play

Top: Glastonbury Festival (p248)

Bottom: Royal Ascot (p217)

Leeds on Saturday, and vice versa. (p510)

⚐ Manchester Pride

One of England's biggest celebrations of love and life for the whole queer rainbow happens in late August in Manchester. (p535)

☆ International Beatleweek

Held in the last week of August, the world's biggest tribute to the Beatles features six days of music, exhibitions, tours and memorabilia sales in Liverpool. (p550)

September

The first week of September feels more like August, but then schools open up again and motorway traffic returns to normal. Good weather is still a chance.

☆ International Birdman

In the first weekend in September, competitors dressed as batmen, fairies and flying machines join in an outlandish celebration of self-powered flight (www.bognorbirdman.com) at West Sussex' Bognor Regis. So far no one's got near the hallowed 100m goal.

☆ World Gurning Championships

Gurning is face-pulling, and this has to be one of the weirdest events of the year (www.egremontcrab-fair.com). Elastic-faced contestants come to Egremont in Cumbria in mid-September every year, contorting their features in

a bid to pull the most grotesque expressions.

🏃 Great North Run

Britain's biggest marathon is in London, but the Great North Run (www.greatrun. org/great-north-run) in Tyneside in September is the biggest half-marathon in the world, with the greatest number of runners of any race over this distance.

October

Leaves turn golden-brown, the weather begins to get colder, and days shorter. Sights and attractions start to shut down for the low season, and accommodation rates drop.

⚔ Falmouth Oyster Festival

The West Country port of Falmouth hosts this event (www.falmouthoysterfes-tival.co.uk) to mark the start of the traditional oyster-catching ('dredging') season, and to celebrate local food from the sea and farmland of Cornwall.

☆ Horse of the Year Show

The country's major indoor horse show (www. hoys.co.uk), with dressage,

showjumping and other equine activities. Held in early October at the NEC arena near Birmingham.

📚 Cheltenham Literature Festival

Established in 1949, the world's longest-running books-focused festival showcases the biggest names in literature over 10 days in autumn. (p208)

November

The weather's often cold and damp, suitably sombre for Remembrance Day, while Guy Fawkes Night sparks up some fun.

🎆 Guy Fawkes Night

Also called Bonfire Night and Fireworks Night (www.bonfirenight.net), 5 November sees fireworks filling the country's skies in commemoration of a failed attempt to blow up parliament in 1605. Effigies of Guy Fawkes, the leader of the Gunpowder Plot, often burn on bonfires.

🎆 Flaming Tar Barrels

Boisterous locals of Ottery St Mary carry flaming tar barrels through packed-out streets on 5 November, while paramedics and health-and-safety officials watch on in horror.

◉ Remembrance Day

On 11 November, red poppies are worn and wreaths are laid in towns and cities around the country. The day (www.poppy.org.uk) commemorates military personnel killed and injured in the line of duty, from the world wars to modern conflicts.

☆ World's Biggest Liar Contest

Another whacky event, and it's Cumbria again. Fibbers from all walks of life go head-to-head in a battle of mid-November mendacity at the Bridge Inn (www. santonbridgeinn.com) in Wasdale.

December

Schools break up around mid-December. Many towns and cities hold Christmas markets, ideal places for browsing Christmas presents with a cup of mulled wine.

🎆 New Year Celebrations

On 31 December, fireworks and street parties happen in town squares across the country, lighting up the nation to welcome in the New Year.

Itineraries

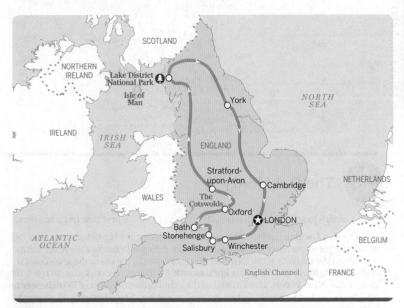

 **Essential England**

Just over a week is long enough to tick off many of England's highlights. This tour takes in a dozen of the nation's top sights, from London to the Lakes.

Start with a full day in the nation's capital, **London**, simply walking the streets to admire the world-famous sights: Buckingham Palace, Tower Bridge, Trafalgar Sq and more. Then head southwest for one or both of the grand cathedral cities of **Winchester** and **Salisbury**. Next stop: ancient history – the iconic megaliths of **Stonehenge**.

A short hop northwest leads to the beautiful city of **Bath**, for Roman history and fabulous Georgian architecture. Then cruise across the classic English countryside of the Cotswolds to reach that ancient seat of learning, **Oxford**. Not far away is **Stratford-upon-Avon**, for everything Shakespeare.

Next, strike out north for the **Lake District**, one of the country's most scenic areas, then across to **York** for Viking remains and the stunning Minster. End your trip with a visit to **Cambridge**, England's other great university city. Then a final day back in **London**, immersed in galleries, museums, parks, street markets, West End shows or East End cafes – or whatever takes your fancy.

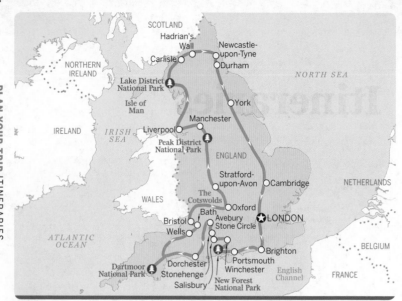

The Full Monty

4 WEEKS

With a month to spare, you can enjoy a trip taking in all the best that England offers.

Kick off in **London**, and spend a couple of days seeing the big-ticket attractions, but make time for exploratory saunters as well – along the south bank of the River Thames, or through the markets of the East End. Next, go down to the sea at the artsy coastal resort of **Brighton**; then west, via **Portsmouth** for the historic dockyard, to reach the picturesque **New Forest**. Head inland to the grand cathedral cities of **Winchester** and **Salisbury**, and on to England's best-known ancient site, **Stonehenge**, and nearby **Avebury Stone Circle**.

Onwards into deepest Wessex, via Thomas Hardy's hometown, **Dorchester**, to reach the wide and wild expanse of **Dartmoor National Park**. Then it's time for yet another historic city, **Wells**, with its beautiful cathedral, en route to the Georgian masterpiece of **Bath** and the southwest's big little city, **Bristol**. Next comes the classic English countryside of the **Cotswolds**, with a pause at delightful Stow-on-the-Wold, and maybe Broadway or Chipping Campden, before reaching **Oxford**, England's oldest university city. Not far away is Shakespeare Central at **Stratford-upon-Avon** – plan ahead to see a cutting-edge production by the RSC. Continue journeying north via the heather-clad moors and tranquil limestone dales of the **Peak District** to reach England's second major city, **Manchester**, and neighbouring cultural crossroads **Liverpool**.

Then it's back to the wilds again with a short hop to the scenic wonders of the **Lake District**. From the sturdy border town of **Carlisle**, follow the ancient Roman landmark of **Hadrian's Wall** all the way to revitalised city **Newcastle-upon-Tyne**. Then it's into the final leg, south via **Durham** and its world-class cathedral, and then **York** for its Viking remains and stunning minster, to reach England's other great seat of learning, **Cambridge**. From here it's a hop back to **London**, to use up the last few days of your grand tour, taking in its many highlights.

The Wild Side
2 WEEKS

This is a tour through the best of England's natural landscape, the inspiration for generations of poets, writers and composers. Put on your hiking boots as we meander through some of the country's finest national parks and open countryside.

Start at the spectacular Roman remains of **Hadrian's Wall**, one of England's finest reminders of the classical era, where you can explore the ancient forts and stride beside the ramparts centurion-style. Then continue into Cumbria for the high peaks of the **Lake District National Park**, once the spiritual home of Wordsworth and the Romantic poets, now a magnet for outdoor enthusiasts, with hikes for all abilities, plus cosy inns and country hotels.

Travelling east from the Lakes carries you across the Pennines – the chain of hills known as the backbone of England – to reach the green hills and valleys of the **Yorkshire Dales National Park**. Nearby are the moors around **Haworth** – inspiration for Emily Brontë's *Wuthering Heights*.

Travel south through the hills and dales of the **Peak District National Park** – stopping off to explore the great park around Chatsworth House if time allows – then through central England, via Elgar's beloved **Malvern Hills**, to reach the classic English countryside of the **Cotswolds**. Then continue southwards to enjoy the epic emptiness of **Salisbury Plain**, home to **Stonehenge** and other archaeological intrigues. Nearby is **Avebury**, England's other great stone circle. A few miles more and you're on Dorset's spectacular fossil-ridden **Jurassic Coast**.

Head further west to take in the lush farmland of Devon and the heathery hills and sandy coves of **Exmoor National Park**, then it's on to the eerie granite tors of **Dartmoor National Park**, which offers some of the country's most bleakly beautiful views. Next stop: **Cornwall**, for pretty ports, gorse-clad cliffs and sparkling bays. Finish this bucolic excursion at **Land's End**, where the English mainland finally runs out of steam and plunges headlong into the restless ocean.

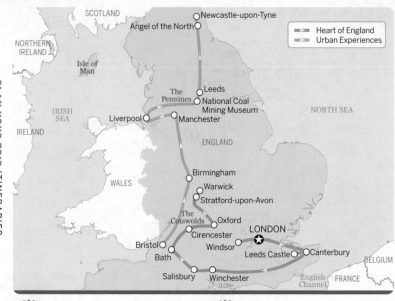

2 WEEKS Heart of England

Journey through the country's heartland, taking in castles, cathedrals and picturesque medieval towns and villages.

Start in **London** with its famous landmarks. Further afield the gorgeous gardens at Kew, Eton College and **Windsor Castle** are more must-see sights. Beyond the capital lies old England proper, especially around the market towns of Kent, where **Canterbury Cathedral** and **Leeds Castle** are top historic sights. Then loop through Sussex and into Hampshire, where **Winchester**, the ancient capital, boasts another fine cathedral. Nearby **Salisbury** jostles for prominence, with its famous cathedral spire dominating the landscape.

Out to the west, **Bath** is crammed with landmark Georgian architecture, while the picture-perfect **Cotswolds** conceal a host of pretty towns and villages, such as Northleach, Wantage and Cirencester, as well as stately home Blenheim Palace. On to picturesque **Oxford**, crammed with college buildings carved from honey-coloured stone, and **Stratford-upon-Avon**, the home of Shakespeare, leaving just enough time to top up on English history at stunning **Warwick Castle**.

8 DAYS Urban Experiences

Outside of London, England's provincial cities provide a vibrant counterpoint to the country's tranquil coast and countryside.

Start in **Bristol**, a thriving regional capital famed for its engineering heritage and lively cultural scene. Then to **Birmingham**, in the heart of the Midlands, now a byword for successful urban renewal. Continue north to **Manchester**, famous for its music and football team, where architectural highlights include the Imperial War Museum North. Nearby **Liverpool** has reinvented itself as a cultural capital with its redeveloped historic waterfront, Albert Dock.

Cross the Pennines to **Leeds**, the 'Knightsbridge of the North', where once-rundown factories and abandoned warehouses are now loft apartments and designer boutiques. But don't forget the past: go underground at the nearby **National Coal Mining Museum**. Further north is **Newcastle-upon-Tyne** and neighbouring Gateshead, former kings of coal, ships and steel, where heavy industries have given way to art and architecture. Conclude your urban tour with a visit to England's best-known public art, the iconic **Angel of the North**.

Top: Birmingham
Museum & Art Gallery
(p395)

Bottom: Cirencester
(p193), the Cotswolds

MO WU/SHUTTERSTOCK ©

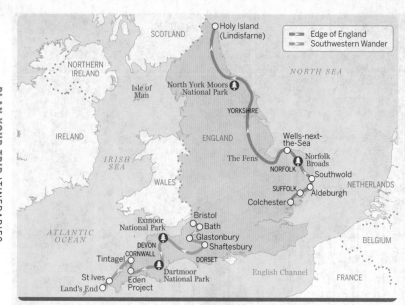

Edge of England
Southwestern Wander

Edge of England
2 WEEKS

If you like the outdoors, and prefer flocks of birds to crowds of people, try this backwater route along England's eastern fringe.

Start in **Colchester**, with its magnificent castle, then visit sleepy **Suffolk**, where quaint villages and market towns dot the landscape. Along the coast you'll discover wildlife reserves, shingle beaches, fishing ports such as **Aldeburgh**, and the delightfully retro seaside town of **Southwold**. Things get even quieter in Norfolk, especially around the misty lakes and windmill-lined rivers of the **Norfolk Broads**. For beach strolls or historic country pubs head for the coastal villages near **Wells-next-the-Sea**.

North of Norfolk lies the eerie, flat landscape of the **Fens**, now a haven for otters and birdlife. Then it's north again into Yorkshire to the heather-clad **North York Moors**, where humpbacked hills roll all the way to the coast to drop dramatically into the choppy waters of the North Sea. Round things off with a stroll between the castles of Bamburgh and Dunstanburgh on the wild Northumberland Coast, finishing your tour at the historic island priory of **Holy Island (Lindisfarne)**.

Southwestern Wander
2 WEEKS

The southwest of England takes a bit of effort to reach but repays in full with a rich green landscape dotted with hills and moors, surrounded by glittering seas.

Start in the historic university city of **Bristol**, factoring in the M Shed museum, a walk around the harbour and a visit to Brunel's groundbreaking steamship, SS *Great Britain*. Detour to beautiful **Bath** to wander around the Royal Crescent and Roman Baths. Saunter to **Glastonbury** – famous for its annual music festival, ruined abbey and many mystical legends. Continue south into Dorset, where highlights include picturesque **Shaftesbury**.

Head west to **Exmoor National Park**, then onwards into Devon, where there's a choice of coasts, as well as **Dartmoor National Park**, with the highest and wildest hills in southern England. Cross into Cornwall to explore the biodomes of the **Eden Project**. Nearby, but in another era entirely, **Tintagel Castle** is the legendary birthplace of King Arthur. Next visit the galleries of **St Ives**, before concluding at **Land's End**, where the English mainland comes to a final full stop.

Windermere (p568), the Lake District

Plan Your Trip
The Great Outdoors

What's the best way to slow down, meet the locals and get off the beaten track? Simple: get out to the English countryside. Beautiful green spaces are surprisingly accessible in England, by train, bus or car. Whether it's forests, rivers, canals, heaths or moors to visit, you're spoiled for options in every corner of the country.

Best Hiking & Walking

Best Long-Distance Walks
Coast to Coast, Hadrian's Wall Path, South West Coast Path

Best Areas for Short Walks
Lake District, Yorkshire Dales, Cotswolds, Dartmoor

Best for Coast Walks
Northumberland, Devon & Cornwall, Norfolk & Suffolk, Dorset

Best Time to Go
Summer (Jun–Aug) The best time for walking: weather usually warm and hopefully dry; plenty of daylight, too.

Late spring (May) and early autumn (Sep) The seasons either side of summer can be great for walking: fewer crowds; days often mild and sunny.

Best Maps for Walking
Ordnance Survey (UK's national mapping agency) Explorer series 1:25,000 scale.

Harvey Maps (specially designed for walkers) Superwalker series 1:25,000 scale.

Hiking & Walking

England is covered in a vast network of footpaths, many of which are centuries old, dating from the time when walking was the only way to get from farm to village, from village to town, from town to coast, or valley to valley. Any walk you do today will incorporate these historic paths. Even England's longest walks simply link up these networks of many shorter paths. You'll also sometimes walk along bridleways, originally for horse transport, and old unsurfaced roads called byways.

Nearly all footpaths in England are 'rights of way' – public paths and tracks across private property. Even though most land in England is privately owned, from tiny cultivated areas to vast mountain ranges, a right of way across the land cannot be overruled by the owner. If there is a right of way, you can follow it through fields, woods, pastures, paddocks, even farmhouse yards, as long as you keep to the correct route and do no damage.

Generally speaking, the lower and more cultivated the landscape, the easier the walking, with clear paths and signposts – ideal for beginners. In mountain and moorland areas, if the route is popular there will be a path (although sometimes this is faint), but not many signposts. If the route is rarely trodden, there may be no visible path at all, and absolutely no signposts, so you'll need to know what you're doing – take a detailed map and compass for navigation.

Best Walking Areas

Although you can walk pretty much anywhere in England, some areas are better than others. Some are suitable for short walks of a couple of hours, others for longer all-day outings.

Dartmoor
In England's southwest, Dartmoor National Park boasts the highest hills for miles around, dotted with weathered granite outcrops known as tors. Much of the landscape is devoid of trees and surprisingly wild. Below the hills, valleys cut into the edges of the moor, perfect for picnics and riverside strolls in summer.

Lake District
England's most popular walking area, the Lake District offers high peaks, endless views, deep valleys and, of course, beautiful lakes. Protected by the Lake District National Park (and often abbreviated to simply the 'Lakes' or 'Lakeland', but never, ever the 'Lakes District'), it is loved by walkers, partly because of the landscape, and partly because of the history; thanks to poet Wordsworth and his Romantic chums, this is where walking for pleasure really began.

Peak District
Despite the name, the Peak District has very few peaks. But there are plenty of hills, valleys and moors, making it a favoured walking area in northern England. Protected as a national park, the landscape falls into two zones: the south is mainly farmland, cut by limestone valleys; in the north are high peaty moors with rocky outcrops, and a more austere character.

Yorkshire Dales

With rolling hills, wild moors, limestone outcrops and green valleys cut by scenic streams, the Yorkshire Dales National Park is another of England's most popular walking areas. Paths are a little gentler and conditions a little less serious than in the Lake District, with the happy addition of some delightful villages nestling in the dales – many with pubs and tearooms providing refreshments for walkers.

Southwest Coast

Cornwall and Devon enjoy the best of the English climate and some of the finest coastal scenery in the country – but the rugged landscape means tough days on the trail. Thanks to those beautiful rivers flowing down steep valleys to the sea, you're forever going up or down. The coastline in neighbouring Dorset – known as the Jurassic Coast thanks to the proliferation of fossils – is less arduous and another great area for seaside walks.

North Downs & South Downs

Between London and the south coast (and within easy reach of both), the North and South Downs are two parallel ranges of broad chalky hills. On the map, the North Downs appear hemmed-in by motorways and conurbations, but while this area can never be described as wilderness, the walking here is often unexpectedly tranquil. The South Downs are higher, and not so cramped by urban expansion, with more options for walks, and a landscape protected by England's newest national park.

Cotswolds

One of the most popular areas for walkers in southern England, the Cotswold Hills offer classic English countryside, where paths meander through neat fields, past pretty villages with cottages of honey-coloured stone. The eastern side of the Cotswolds tends to be a gentler landscape, while the paths undulate more on the western side, especially along the Cotswold Escarpment – although the views are better here.

Exmoor

Just to the north of Dartmoor, and sometimes overshadowed by its larger neighbour, southwest England's other national park is Exmoor. Heather-covered hills cut by deep valleys make it a perfect walking area, edged with the added bonus of a spectacular coastline of cliffs and beaches.

Long Distance Trails

England Coast Path

➡ 2800 miles; www.nationaltrail.co.uk/england-coast-path

Opening in sections, when it's complete this will be officially the longest trail in the country – an epic, round-England trek that (even for the fittest walkers) is likely to require the best part of a year to complete.

South West Coast Path

➡ 630 miles; 8-10 weeks; www.southwestcoastpath.com

A roller-coaster romp around England's southwest peninsula, past beaches, bays, shipwrecks, seaside resorts, fishing villages and clifftop castles. Given its length, most walkers do it in sections: the two-week stretch between Padstow and Falmouth around Land's End is most popular.

Hadrian's Wall Path

➡ 84 miles; 7-8 days; www.nationaltrail.co.uk/hadrianswall

A footpath following the world-famous Roman structure across northern England, via forts, castles, ramparts and battlements, and giving the Coast to Coast a run for its money in the popularity stakes.

WEATHER WATCH

While enjoying your walking in England, it's always worth remembering the fickle nature of English weather. The countryside can appear gentle and welcoming, and often is, but sometimes conditions can turn nasty – especially on higher ground. At any time of year, if you're walking on the hills or open moors, it's vital to be well equipped. You should carry warm and waterproof clothing (even in summer), a map and a compass (that you know how to use), some water and food (particularly high-energy food). If you're really going off the beaten track, leave details of your route with someone.

Walking at Hadrian's Wall (p617)

WALKING WEBSITES

Ramblers (www.ramblers.org.uk) The country's leading organisation for walkers.

Ordnance Survey (www.ordnance-survey.co.uk) The UK's official map-making organisation; buy printed paper maps, or download them to your phone.

National Trail (www.nationaltrail.co.uk) Good resource for planning longer routes.

Pennine Way

➡ 268 miles; 14-21 days; www.nationaltrail.co.uk/pennineway

The granddaddy of them all, an epic trek along the mountainous spine of northern England, via some of the highest, wildest landscapes in the country. Even in the summer, the elements can be dire, and many walkers find it an endurance test – but not one without rewards.

Dales Way

➡ 85 miles; 6 days; www.dalesway.org.uk

A non-strenuous walk through the delightful Yorkshire Dales, via some of the most scenic valleys in northern England, ending at Windermere in the Lake District.

South Downs Way

➡ 100 miles; 7-9 days; www.nationaltrail.co.uk/southdowns

A sweeping hike through southeast England, along an ancient chalky highway from Winchester to the sea, mostly following a line of rolling hills, meaning big skies and wonderful views, plus picture-perfect villages and prehistoric sites.

Coast to Coast

➡ 190 miles; 12-14 days; www.wainwright.org.uk/coasttocoast.html

Also known as Wainwright's Coast to Coast (after the man who devised it), this is not a national trail, but it is England's number-one long-distance route for locals and visitors alike – through three national parks via a spectacular mix of valleys, plains, mountains, dales and moors.

bike trail centres where specially built single-track trails wind through forests. Options at these centres vary from delightful dirt roads ideal for families to gnarly rock gardens and precipitous drop-offs for hard-core riders, all classified from green to black in ski-resort style.

➡ **www.sustrans.org.uk** Details of Britain's national network of cycling trails.

➡ **www.forestryengland.uk/cycling** Guide to forest cycling and mountain-biking trails in England.

Horse Riding

If you want to explore the hills and moors but walking or cycling is too much of a sweat, seeing the wilder parts of England from horseback is highly recommended. In rural areas and national parks such as Dartmoor and Northumberland, riding centres cater to all levels of proficiency, with ponies for kids and beginners, and horses for the more experienced.

➡ **British Horse Society** (www.bhs.org.uk) Lists approved riding centres offering day rides or longer holidays on horseback.

Windsurfing, Devon (p295)

Cycling & Mountain Biking

A bike is the perfect mode of transport for exploring England's towns and countryside. There is a vast network of cycleways called the National Cycle Network, as well as quiet country lanes winding through fields and peaceful villages, ideal for cycle touring. You can cruise through gently rolling landscapes or for the more serious cyclist there are popular hilly regions with steep ascents and swooping downhill sections.

In cities you'll find local bike share schemes (such as BTN, www.btnbikeshare.com) as well as bike rental stores where a multi-day hire gives you time to cycle from place to place, perhaps linking up a cycle tour with a train return if you want. Many B&Bs, especially along major cycle routes, are cyclist-friendly. All you need is a map and a sense of adventure.

Mountain bikers can go further into the wilds on the tracks and bridleways that criss-cross Britain's hills and high moors, or head for the many dedicated mountain-

Surfing & Windsurfing

England may not seem an obvious destination for surfing, but conditions are surprisingly good and the large tidal range often means a completely different set of breaks at low and high tides. If you've come from the other side of the world, you'll be delighted to learn that summer water temperatures in southern England are roughly equivalent to winter temperatures in southern Australia (ie you'll still need a wetsuit). It's easy enough to hire boards and wetsuits at major surfing spots.

Top of the list are the Atlantic-facing coasts of Cornwall and Devon (Newquay is surf central, with all the trappings from Kombi vans to bleached hair), and there are smaller surf scenes elsewhere, notably Norfolk and Yorkshire in eastern England.

Windsurfing is hugely popular all around the coast. Top areas include Norfolk, Suffolk, Devon and Cornwall, and the Isle of Wight.

HWA CHO YI/SHUTTERSTOCK ©

Top: Cycling in the Peak District National Park (p459)

Bottom: Seven Sisters Cliffs (p165), South Downs National Park

MORE OUTDOORS ACTIVITIES

If you're looking for something a bit different to the usual hiking and biking, here are a few more esoteric activities you could try:

Archery The heyday of the English longbow is long gone, but archery remains a popular sport. Find a club through www.archerygb.org.

Coasteering A cross between rock climbing, scrambling and diving, usually followed by a plunge into the sea. Often offered by outdoor activity providers in Devon and Cornwall.

Ghyll scrambling Like coasteering, only along river gorges – it's especially popular in Yorkshire and Cumbria.

Orienteering This popular pastime involves navigating your way around a preset course using a map and compass, competing either against the clock or other teams. A variant is geocaching (www.geocaching.com), where you use GPS to find hidden boxes – Dartmoor has loads, but you'll find them in other locations, too.

Rock climbing England has a long history of rock climbing and mountaineering. The main areas include the Lake District, the Peak District and Yorkshire, plus the sea cliffs of Devon and Cornwall. The UK Climbing website (www.ukclimbing.com) has plenty of useful information.

Stand-up paddle boarding SUP has become a popular sport, and is a great way to explore England's coasts, rivers and waterways. Contact www.bsupa.org.uk for details of where you can do it.

Wild swimming A selection of Britain's lakes and rivers are open to swimmers, although temperatures can be bracing. Contact www.outdoorswimmingsociety.com.

➡ **www.ukwindsurfing.com** Good source of info on windsurfing.

➡ **www.surfingengland.org** Listings of approved surf schools, courses, competitions and more.

➡ **www.britishcanoeing.org.uk** Lists approved canoeing centres in England.

Sailing & Boating

The south coast of England, with its superb scenery and challenging winds and tides, is one of Europe's most popular yachting areas, while the English canals offer a classic narrow-boating experience. Beginners can take a Royal Yachting Association training course in yachting or dinghy sailing at many sailing schools around the coast. Narrow boating only requires a quick introductory lesson at the start of the trip and you're away.

➡ **www.rya.org.uk** The Royal Yachting Association's website.

➡ **www.canalholidays.com** For more info on narrow boats and lessons.

Canoeing & Kayaking

Southwest England's coast, with its sheltered inlets and indented shoreline, is ideal for sea kayaking, while inland lakes and canals across the country are great for canoeing. Although tame by comparison with alpine torrents, the turbulent spate rivers of the Lake District, Northumberland and Devon offer challenging whitewater kayaking.

Equipment rental and instruction are readily available in major centres such as Cornwall, Devon and the Lake District.

Plan Your Trip
Family Travel

England is an interesting destination for children of any age, although teens may get more out of the historic attractions. Travel times are short and there is plenty to distract youngsters, from animal encounters to excellent playgrounds, museums for kids, and opportunities to dress-up and make-believe.

Keeping Costs Down

Accommodation
Look for 'family rooms' at budget hotels and YHAs. They often sleep up to four people, which saves enormously and compares favourably to the cost of renting an entire flat or cottage for a night.

Transport
Kids up to age 11 travel for free on city public transport. Fares on inter-city routes are often nominal if combined with a full-fare adult ticket.

Eating
Most chain restaurants – and many independent ones too – offer excellent-value children's menus. Admittedly the dishes are usually fairly unadventurous and monotonous (typically a pasta dish, chicken nuggets, corn on the cob...) but they usually come with a drink and dessert.

Activities
England's parks, gardens and green spaces are plentiful and free to visit, many with specific play areas for children to get some climbing, sliding and swinging time.

Children Will Love...

Fresh-Air Fun

Conkers, Leicestershire (p454) Play indoors, outdoors or among the trees in the heart of the National Forest.

Puzzlewood, Forest of Dean (p210) A wonderful woodland playground with maze-like paths, weird rock formations and eerie passageways to offer a real sense of discovery.

Bewilderwood, Norfolk (p385) Zip wires, jungle bridges, tree houses, marsh walks, boat trips, mazes and all sorts of old-fashioned outdoor adventure.

Lyme Regis & the Jurassic Coast, Dorset (p280) Guided tours show you how to find your very own prehistoric fossil.

Secretly Educational

We the Curious, Bristol (p227) One of the best interactive science museums in England, covering space, technology and the human brain.

Jorvik Viking Centre, York (p480) An excellent smells-and-all Viking settlement reconstruction.

Natural History Museum, London (p85) Animals everywhere! Highlights include the life-size blue whale and the animatronics dinosaurs.

National Space Centre, Leicester (p447) Space-suits, zero-gravity toilets and mini-astronaut training – all guaranteed to fire up little minds.

Animal Encounters

London Wetland Centre, London (p105) Break out the binoculars to spy bitterns, black swans, herons and kingfishers.

Longleat, Wiltshire (p288) Pretend you're driving across the savannah at this Wiltshire country estate, surrounded by rhinos, giraffes, elephants and lions.

Whitby Coastal Cruises, Yorkshire (p498) If you're lucky, you'll spot minke, sei and fin whales off the north coast.

Scilly Seal Snorkelling, St Martin's, Isles of Scilly (p350) Don your fins and swim with playful grey seals off the island of St Martin's.

Region by Region

London

Tired of London? Impossible! There is an abundance of world-class attractions just for children here, as well as activities that'll please the whole family. Top kids picks include Hamleys (p133) and the Diana, Princess of Wales Memorial Playground (p92) – not to mention watching the buskers of Covent Garden or the horses at Buckingham Palace (p72). Plenty of top kids' days out can be done for next to nothing, with free entry and free public transport.

Canterbury & Southeast England

Seaside resorts like Brighton (p167) and Margate (p151) feel like a time warp to the iPad generation, but who doesn't love a rickety rollercoaster and swooping seagulls? History lovers won't want to leave Dover (p157) or Leeds (p151) castles so allow plenty of time to linger.

Oxford & the Cotswolds

Begin your tour of this vast region with a half-day at the Harry Potter film studios (p213). Other highlights include Windsor Great Park (p216), the Roald Dahl Museum (p212) in Great Missenden and, of course, the historic colleges of Oxford (p178). The Cotswold countryside is dotted with neolithic and Roman historic sites, too.

Bristol, Bath & Somerset

From the neolithic village recreation at Stonehenge (p286) to the Regency architecture of Bath (p233), and Roman ruins to boot, there's something for every age group here. Teens might get inspired to change the world after a visit to the spot where Bristol slaver Edward Colston's statue was torn down in 2020.

Devon, Cornwall & the Isles of Scilly

Best enjoyed in the summer, the most dramatic beaches in England are found on the southwest coast (p319). When the wintery weather hits (a feature of summer in England as well as winter), swap splashing in the ocean for combing the beach for fossils, shells and heart-shaped rocks.

Birmingham & the Midlands

Even little legs will enjoy an outdoors adventure in the Peak District (p457) where former railways have been converted to traffic-free cycle routes, making this a perfect family cycling (and walking) spot. Stratford-upon-Avon (p407) ticks all the boxes for literature and history touring.

Yorkshire

Pack your best historic dress-ups when heading to Yorkshire (p473), a region rich with fortified castles to play-act as lords, knights or rival armies coming to loot and plunder. Check calendars for specific activities for children like historic re-enactments celebrating York's Norse heritage or falconry displays.

Manchester, Liverpool & Northwest England

Prep the kids for a trip to Liverpool (p545) by playing them the Beatles back catalogue. There's plenty of industrial history to observe, too, including the canal network, plus excellent museums and galleries.

The Lake District & Cumbria

The Lake District (p568) is outdoor activities central. Adventurous older children and teens will be delighted by the mountain biking and zip wires, while youngsters can get lost in the magic of Beatrix Potter stories come to life (p578).

Good to Know

Look out for the 🚼 icon for family-friendly suggestions throughout this guide.

People are fairly tolerant of children, but not overly forgiving of misbehaviour in places mostly suitable for adults, for example upmarket restaurants, quiet performance spaces or small boutique B&Bs.

Breastfeeding in public is acceptable, but not often witnessed. Change tables are available at some public toilets, but not all – bring your own change mat and expect to be using the floor or the back of your car more than you'd hope.

England's accessibility challenges for travellers with special needs include children – towns often have very narrow and uneven footpaths and most London Tube stations lack ramps or lifts. This often means carrying your pram, bags and an exhausted toddler up several flights of stairs. Luckily it doesn't take much for someone to step in and lend a hand. The Brits are well mannered like that.

Western safety standards and expectations apply here, such as using seatbelts and child seats in cars, or having a lockable brake on your stroller – but it can seem like no one enforces the rules, it's up to you to manage your risk taking. Ideally you'll bring your own equipment from home.

Useful Resources

BBC CBeebies (www.bbc.co.uk/cbeebies) Packed with information, activities and games, plus a local iPlayer with British kids' shows.

Horrible Histories (www.horrible-histories.co.uk) Books and shows that make British history accessible, memorable and funny!

Mumsnet (www.mumsnet.com) No-nonsense advice from a gang of UK mothers.

Lonely Planet Kids (www.lonelyplanet.com/kids) Loads of activities and great family travel blog content.

Visit England (www.visitengland.com) Official tourism website for England, with lots of useful info for families.

Kids' Corner

Say What?

Hello	Ay-up (Yorkshire slang)
Goodbye	Cheerio (London slang)
Thank you	Cheers (English slang)
It's cold	It's a bit parky (English slang)

Did You Know? ℹ️

- The Thames is the longest river in England at 215 miles.

Have You Tried?

COMPOSEDPIX/SHUTTERSTOCK ©

Cheese Rolling
Annual contest in Gloucestershire

Regions at a Glance

From the multicultural melting pot of London to the lonely spiritual outpost of Holy Island (Lindisfarne), England's regions offer a kaleidoscope of experiences. Southern England is where you'll find the archetypal English countryside of lush meadows, thatched cottages and games of cricket on the village green. The southwestern counties of Devon and Cornwall are wilder in nature, known for their surf beaches and seafood restaurants. Lovers of moor and mountain will be spoilt for choice in the Lake District and Peak District, while those who prefer gritty industrial heritage and lively nightlife will enjoy the northern cities of Manchester, Liverpool and Newcastle. And bang in the middle is Yorkshire, with everything from the gorgeous city of York to the rolling hills of the Yorkshire Dales.

London

History
Entertainment
Culture

Historic Streets

London's ancient streets echo with the footfalls of monarchs, poets, sinners and saints from the Tower of London to Westminster Abbey, and coaching inns that once served Dickens, Shelley, Keats and Byron.

Music, Theatre & Sport

Endless distractions await in London, be it world-class theatres; clubs, bars and pubs; or stunning historic opera houses and music halls. Sports fans know to book ahead to enjoy the spectacle at Wimbledon, Lord's or Wembley.

Museums & Galleries

While the British Museum is the big crowd-puller, the capital has museums and galleries of every shape and size, like the V&A and the Tate. Many are free, but book ahead.

p55

Canterbury & Southeast England

Cathedral
History
Art

Canterbury Cathedral

A major reason to visit southeast England, this is one of the most holy places in Christendom. Write your own Canterbury tale as you explore its atmospheric chapels, cloisters and crypts.

Invasion Heritage

A gateway to the Continent, the southeast is studded with castles and fortresses, the 1066 battlefield, and Dover's secret wartime tunnels.

The South Coast

England's south coast towns have a faded, genteel grandeur and thriving artistic scene: from Brighton's eccentric shops to Margate's Turner Contemporary gallery and Folkestone's art installations.

p143

Oxford & the Cotswolds

Architecture
Stately Homes
Villages

University Colleges

Oxford's architecture will always impress, whether you admire the legendary 'dreaming spires' or gaze up at the fantastic gargoyles on college facades.

Blenheim Palace

Favoured by the rich and powerful for centuries, this region is scattered with some of the finest country houses in England. Top of the pile is the baroque masterpiece of Blenheim Palace, birthplace of Sir Winston Churchill.

Cotswold Villages

Dotted with picturesque 'chocolate box' scenes of stone cottages, thatched roofs and cobbled lanes, the villages of the Cotswolds provide a charming dreamscape of rural England.

p177

Bristol, Bath & Somerset

History
Culture
Outdoors

Historic Buildings

Get lost in Bath's beautiful architecture, from the Roman Baths to gorgeous Georgian houses. Marvel at Bristol's M Shed museum and the gothic Wells Cathedral.

Culture

Join a walking tour of Bristol's street-art history, soak up the counter-culture vibes in Glastonbury then swan through Jane Austen's Bath.

Outdoor Adventure

Cycle, walk or stargaze in Exmoor; get rock climbing in Cheddar Gorge; hike to the top of Glastonbury Tor and take in the views; then swim in the open-air pools at Thermae in Bath or the Bristol Lido.

p221

Hampshire, Wiltshire & Dorset

History
Coast
Cool Camping

Mythological Sites

The area is rich with ritual sites and home to England's most important archaeological site, Stonehenge.

Coastal Exploration

Fossil-hunting walks take you through 185 million years of geological history on Unesco-listed Jurassic Coast. The Isle of Wight has a 67-mile coast path to tackle.

Cool Camping & Hotels

Options abound for cool camping and contemporary glamping sites in farmers' fields or overlooking the ocean. Hip hotels here, such as the Pig, are really restaurants with kitchen gardens and rooms to stay.

p257

Devon, Cornwall & the Isles of Scilly

Food & Drink
Beaches
Island Hopping

Epicurean Delights

Seafood enclaves like Salcombe, Padstow and Port Isaac brim with wharf-side shacks and fine dining. Chase these ocean delights down with a lush Cornish ice-cream or a boutique gin from Plymouth's own distillery.

Beaches

England's south-west peninsula juts determinedly into the Atlantic, fringed by an almost endless chain of sandy beaches, from the picturesque scenery of Kynance Cove to the rolling surf of Newquay.

Island Hopping

Explore the Isles of Scilly – the Cornish archipelago with a touch of the Med – by hopping on and off ferries, camping and sea swimming.

p293

Cambridge & East Anglia

Architecture
Coastline
Waterways

Historic Churches

From the magnificent cathedrals of Ely and Norwich to Cambridge's King's College Chapel, Trinity's Great Court and the New Court at St John's, East Anglia's architectural splendour is second to none.

Seaside Resorts

With wide sandy beaches, excellent seafood, delightful old pubs, historic villages and seaside resorts like Southwold and Cromer, the coastline of East Anglia is rich and varied.

The Broads

The Norfolk and Suffolk Broads are a tranquil haven of lakes and meandering rivers, and an ideal spot for boating, birdwatching, canoeing, cycling or walking.

p353

Birmingham & the Midlands

Activities
History
Food & Drink

Hiking & Biking

The Peak District National Park, Shropshire Hills, Malvern Hills, Offa's Dyke Path, Tissington Trail and Pennine Cycleway all make this region great for hiking and biking.

Stately Homes

Grand houses including Haddon Hall, Burghley House and especially Chatsworth promise sprawling landscaped gardens and grand interiors full of priceless heirlooms.

Global Gastronomy

Birmingham's vibrant eating scene ranges from street food to Michelin-starred Indian, while the tiny town of Ludlow is rich with small and independent producers.

p391

Yorkshire

Activities
Food & Drink
History

Outdoor Pastimes

With rolling hills, scenic valleys, high moors and a cliff-lined coast, all protected by two of England's best-loved national parks, Yorkshire is a natural adventure playground.

Roast Beef & Real Ale

Yorkshire beef and lamb are highly sought after, while the famous Theakston's and Black Sheep Breweries of Masham turn out excellent real ales.

Ancient Abbeys

From York's Roman and Viking heritage and the medieval abbeys of Rievaulx, Fountains and Whitby to the industrial archaeology of Leeds, Bradford and Sheffield, Yorkshire allows you to explore several of Britain's most important historical narratives.

p473

Manchester, Liverpool & Northwest England

History
Sport
Seaside Resorts

Museums

The northwest's collection of heritage sites, including the wonderful People's History Museum in Manchester, is testament to the region's rich history.

Football

Two cities, Liverpool and Manchester, give the world four famous clubs, including the two most successful in English history. The National Football Museum in Manchester is just another reason for football fans to visit this region.

Seaside Towns

The epitome of the classic English seaside resort just keeps on going, thanks to the rides of the Blackpool Pleasure Beach amusement park, where adrenalin junkies can always find a fix.

p527

The Lake District & Cumbria

Scenery
Activities
Literature

Lakes & Fells

The most mountainous part of England, home to humpbacked hills and countless scenic lakes. Some lakes are big and famous – Windermere, Coniston, Ullswater – while others are smaller and hidden away.

Hiking

Casual strollers find gentle routes, while serious hikers hit the high fells – including Helvellyn, Skiddaw, Blencathra and England's highest mountain, Scafell Pike.

Romantic Writers

The beauty of the Lake District famously moved William Wordsworth to write his odes, and visiting landmarks like Dove Cottage, Rydal Mount and his childhood home in Cockermouth is among the region's draws.

p563

Newcastle & Northeast England

History
Landscapes
Castles

Hadrian's Wall

One of the greatest feats of Roman engineering, this potent symbol of imperial power strides for over 70 miles across the neck of England, from Tyneside to the Solway Firth.

Northumberland National Park

If it's widescreen vistas you're after, the broad moors, stone villages and expansive views of England's most northerly national park always deliver. It's also the heart of England's biggest dark-sky park.

Alnwick Castle

Northumberland is dotted with some of Britain's finest castles, including the coastal fortresses of Bamburgh and Dunstanburgh, but Alnwick – setting for the Harry Potter movies – is the most famous.

p601

On the Road

AT A GLANCE
POPULATION

8.8 million

OLDEST CHURCH
St Bartholomew-the-Great (founded in 1123; p79)

BEST FOOD MARKET
Borough Market (p134)

BEST COCKTAIL BAR
Connaught Bar (p123)

BEST TRADITIONAL PUB
Holly Bush (p127)

WHEN TO GO

Mar–May Colour returns with daffodils, cherry blossoms and wisteria in bloom.

Jun–Sep Parks fill with sunbathers and picnics, and the city is busy with summer festivals.

Oct–Dec Halloween, Guy Fawkes Night and Christmas promise parties, decorations, fireworks, and possibly a whisper of snow.

The Shard (p85) and London skyline

London

Immersed in history, London's rich seams of eye-opening antiquity are everywhere, with landmarks like the Tower of London, Westminster Abbey and the Palace of Westminster. These are juxtaposed with modern icons like the Shard, the Gherkin and Tate Modern. London is also a city of ideas and the imagination – whether it's theatrical innovation, contemporary art, music, writing, cutting-edge design or culinary adventure. Throw in charming parks, historic neighbourhoods, leafy suburbs and tranquil riverbanks and you have, quite simply, one of the world's great metropolises.

History

London first came into being as a Celtic village near a ford across the River Thames, but the city only really took off after the Roman conquest in 43 CE. The invaders enclosed their 'Londinium' in walls that still find refrain in the shape of the City (with a capital 'C') of London today.

By the end of the 3rd century CE, Londinium was home to some 30,000 people. Internal strife and relentless barbarian attacks wore the Romans down, however, and they abandoned Britain in the 5th century, reducing the settlement to a sparsely populated backwater. The Saxons moved in next, their 'Lundenwic' prospering and becoming a large, well-organised town.

As the city grew in importance, it caught the eye of Danish Vikings who launched numerous invasions. In 1016 the Saxons, finally beaten down, were forced to accept the Danish leader Knut (Canute) as King of England, after which London replaced Winchester as capital. In 1042, the throne reverted to the Saxon Edward the Confessor, who built Westminster Abbey.

The Norman Conquest of 1066 saw William the Conqueror march into London, where he was crowned king. He built the White Tower (the core of the Tower of London), negotiated taxes with the merchants, and affirmed the city's right to self-government. From then until the late 15th century, London politics were largely taken up by a three-way power struggle between the monarchy, the Church and city guilds.

An uneasy political compromise was reached between the factions, and the city expanded rapidly in the 16th century under the House of Tudor. In a rerun of the disease that wiped out half of London's population between 1348 and 1350, the Great Plague struck in 1665, and by the time the winter cold arrested the epidemic, 100,000 Londoners had perished.

The cataclysm was followed by further devastation when the Great Fire of 1666 sent the city skywards. One upshot of the conflagration was a blank canvas for master architect Sir Christopher Wren to build his magnificent churches. Despite these setbacks, London continued to grow, and by 1700 it was Europe's largest city, with 600,000 people. An influx of foreign workers brought expansion to the east and south, while those who could afford it headed to the more salubrious environs of the north and west.

Georgian London saw a surge in artistic creativity, with the likes of Dr Johnson, Handel, Gainsborough and Reynolds enriching the city's culture, while architects fashioned an elegant new metropolis. In 1837, 18-year-old Victoria began her epic reign, as London became the fulcrum of the British Empire. The Industrial Revolution saw the building of new docks and railways (including the first underground line in 1863), while the Great Exhibition of 1851 showcased London to the world. During the Victorian era, the city's population mushroomed from just over two million to 6.6 million.

Although London suffered a relatively minor bruising during WWI, it was devastated by the Luftwaffe in WWII, when huge swaths of the centre and East End were flattened and 32,000 people were killed. Ugly housing and low-cost developments followed, but prosperity gradually returned to the city, and creative energy bottled up in the postwar years was suddenly unleashed. In the 'Swinging Sixties', London became the capital of cool in fashion and music – a party followed morosely by the austere 1970s.

Since then the city has surfed up and down the waves of global fortunes, hanging on to its position as the world's leading financial centre. In 2000, the modern metropolis won its first mayor of London, an elected role covering the City and all 32 urban boroughs. Bicycle-riding Boris Johnson was elected in 2008, and retained his post in the 2012 mayoral election. In August 2011, numerous London boroughs were rocked by riots characterised by looting and arson, triggered by the controversial shooting of a man by police in Tottenham.

Both the Olympics and the Queen's Diamond Jubilee concocted a splendid display of pageantry for London in 2012. New overground train lines opened, a cable car was flung across the Thames and a once rundown and polluted area of East London was regenerated for the Olympic Park.

Since the Olympics, the city has changed leadership, with Labour politician Sadiq Khan taking over as mayor from Boris Johnson. Scores of new high-rise buildings transformed the London skyline, most notably on the South Bank. Another key development has been the Crossrail, the

LONDON IN...

Two Days

Begin with the West End's big-draw sights: Westminster Abbey, then Buckingham Palace (p72) for the Changing of the Guard. Walk up the Mall to Trafalgar Square (p69) for its architectural grandeur and photo-op views down Whitehall, then take a spin round the National Gallery (p69). In the afternoon, hop over to the South Bank for a ride on the London Eye (p83) and a visit to the Tate Modern (p79), followed by an evening performance at Shakespeare's Globe (p83).

On day two, spend the day wandering around the marvellous British Museum (p68), followed by a spot of shopping around Covent Garden and Oxford St, then dining and bar hopping in Chinatown and Soho.

Four Days

On day three, head for London's finance-driven heart in the City, home to the sprawling and ancient Tower of London (p76). Spend the morning watching the Beefeaters and resident ravens preen and strut, and then marvel at the Crown Jewels. When you're finished, admire the iconic Tower Bridge (p78) from the banks of the Thames or through the glass floors of the walkways connecting the two towers. While away the rest of the day exploring the street art and shopping of the East End, with visits to Brick Lane and Spitalfields Market (p134).

On day four, hop on a boat from any central London pier and make your way down to Greenwich with its world-renowned architecture and links to time, the stars and space. Start your visit at the legendary Cutty Sark (p100), a star clipper during the tea-trade years, and have a look into the National Maritime Museum (p99). Stroll up through Greenwich Park all the way to the Royal Observatory (p99). Head back to South Bank and Southwark by ferry for a show or a film at one of its iconic theatres (p129).

Seven Days

With a few extra days, you'll have time to explore some of London's other neighbourhoods. On day five, head for North London, with a morning at Camden Market (p134), a visit to Highgate Cemetery (p98) and a walk over Hampstead Heath (p97). On day six, explore the famous Portobello Road Market (p100) in Notting Hill, then spend the rest of the day with chic shopping in Knightsbridge, or visiting the museums of South Kensington, such as the Natural History Museum (p85) and the Science Museum (p89). On day seven, head out to West London, where you'll discover the delightful green spaces of Kew Gardens and Richmond Park and the grand palace of Hampton Court (p101).

capital's large and costly construction project, which will add a new east–west train line that promises to ease travel time and congestion for city commuters. But what lasting impact the Covid-19 pandemic coupled with Brexit will have on this great city's future remains to be seen.

◉ Sights

◉ West End

★ **Westminster Abbey**   CHURCH
(Map p64; ☎ 020-7222 5152; www.westminster-abbey.org; 20 Dean's Yard, SW1; adult/child £24/10, half-price Wed 4.30pm; ◷ 9.30am-3.30pm Mon, Tue, Thu & Fri, to 6pm Wed, to 3pm Sat May-Aug, to 1pm Sat Sep-Apr; Ⓤ Westminster) A splendid mixture of architectural styles, Westminster

Abbey is considered the finest example of Early English Gothic. It's not merely a beautiful place of worship – the Abbey is still a working church and the stage on which history unfolds. For centuries, the country's greatest have been interred here, including 17 monarchs from King Henry III (1272) to King George II (1760). Much of the Abbey's architecture is from the 13th century, but it was founded much earlier, in 960 CE.

Every monarch since William the Conqueror has been crowned here, with the exception of a couple of Eds who were either murdered (Edward V) or abdicated (Edward VIII) before the magic moment. Never a cathedral (the seat of a bishop), Westminster Abbey is what is called a 'royal peculiar', administered by the Crown.

Continued on p65

London Highlights

1 British Museum (p68)
Marvelling at the epoch-spanning collections of the nation's flagship museum.

2 Tower of London (p76)
Viewing the dazzling Crown Jewels in this thousand year-old fortress.

3 St Paul's Cathedral (p75)
Reaching for the heavens inside and outside on that iconic dome.

4 Tate Modern (p79)
Exploring London's architecturally distinctive art museum.

5 Hampstead Heath (p97)
Wandering the paths and

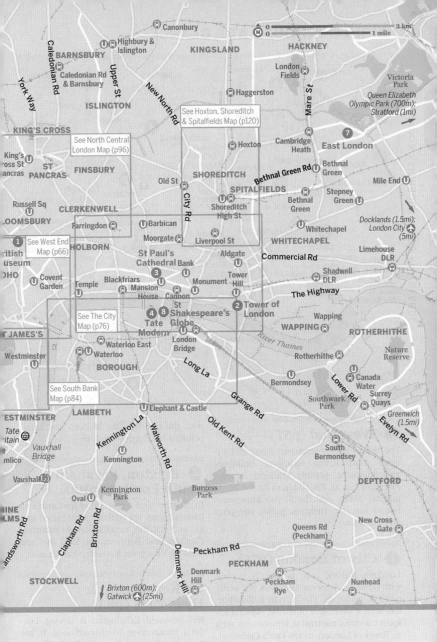

woodlands of North London's green space.

6 Kew Gardens (p101) Stepping into a miniature rainforest inside the subtropical Palm House.

7 East London (p119) Snapping street art, vintage shopping and indulging in innovative dining.

8 Shakespeare's Globe (p83) Seeing one of the Bard's

plays or taking a guided tour of the replica theatre.

9 Regent's Park (p98) Watching the world pass by in one of London's loveliest parks.

NEIGHBOURHOODS AT A GLANCE

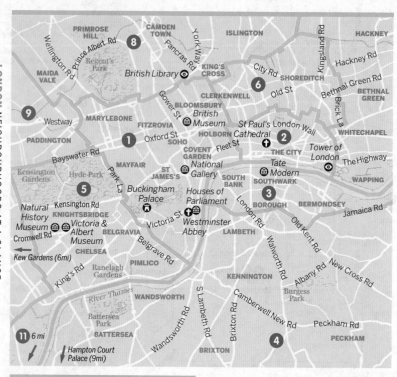

❶ West End (p57)

The West End encompasses many of London's most iconic locations, buildings and museums, notably Trafalgar Square, Piccadilly Circus, Buckingham Palace, Westminster Abbey and the British Museum – not to mention theatres, parks, shopping and nightlife.

❷ City of London (p75)

London's historic core is usually packed with office workers on weekdays but eerily quiet at weekends. The current millennium has seen a profusion of daring skyscrapers sprout, a visual contrast to famous sites such as Tower of London and St Paul's Cathedral.

❸ South Bank (p79)

South Bank is a must-visit area for art lovers, theatre-goers and architecture buffs, with the creative Tate Modern and iconic brutalist buildings to explore.

❹ Brixton, Peckham & South London (p100)

In Brixton and Peckham, Afro-Caribbean haunts bump up against pocket-sized eating and drinking venues. Sample suburban Clapham and Battersea for local life, and Dulwich Village for a country-hamlet vibe.

❺ Kensington & Hyde Park (p85)

Well-groomed Kensington is among London's handsomest neighbourhoods. It has three fine museums – the V&A, Natural History Museum and Science Museum – plus excellent dining and shopping, graceful parklands and grand period architecture.

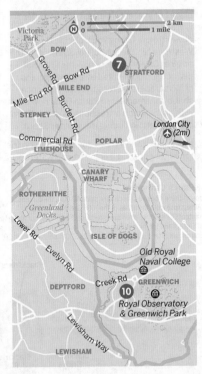

❾ West London (p100)

Come for Portobello Road Market, the Design Museum, historic cinemas, lush parkland, grand mansions and imposing churches. Stay for the superb pubs and clubs, diverse shopping and global eats.

❿ Greenwich (p99)

Regal historic Greenwich complements its riverside village feel with grand architecture, bustling weekend markets, grassy parklands and cosy riverside pubs.

⓫ Richmond, Kew & Hampton Court (p101)

Visit London's leafy, riverside region to get lost in Kew Gardens, deer-spot in Richmond Park, traipse around Wimbledon Common and down a pint waterside as the sun sets on the Thames.

❻ Clerkenwell, Shoreditch & Spitalfields (p93)

Historic city-fringe neighbourhoods best known for culture and nightlife. Shoreditch and Hoxton long ago replaced Soho and Camden as London's hippest party spots.

❼ East London (p94)

Interesting museums and galleries, excellent pubs, canal-side dining, punctuated by street art and vintage stores.

❽ North London (p95)

Head east from Camden's famous market and unrivalled music scene to check out the transformed King's Cross Station area. Then take in the green spaces at Hampstead Heath and Regent's Park.

The River Thames

A FLOATING TOUR

London's history has always been determined by the Thames. The city was founded as a Roman port nearly 2000 years ago and over the centuries since then many of the capital's landmarks have lined the river's banks. A boat trip is a great way to experience the attractions.

There are piers dotted along both banks at regular intervals where you can hop on and hop off the regular services to visit

places of interest. The best place to board is Westminster Pier, from where boats head downstream, taking you from the City of Westminster, the seat of government, to the original City of London, now the financial district and dominated by a growing band of skyscrapers. Across the river, the once shabby and neglected South Bank now bristles with as many top attractions as its northern counterpart, including the slender Shard.

In our illustration we've concentrated on the top highlights you'll enjoy from a waterborne

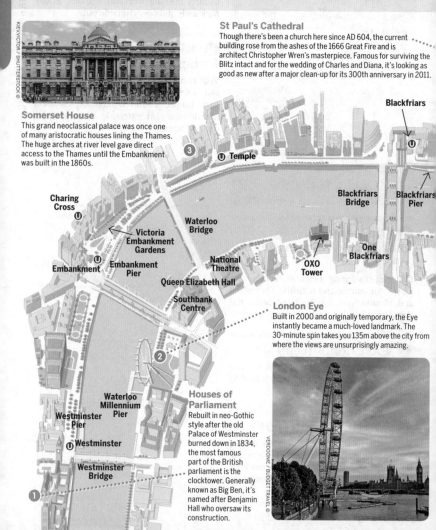

St Paul's Cathedral
Though there's been a church here since AD 604, the current building rose from the ashes of the 1666 Great Fire and is architect Christopher Wren's masterpiece. Famous for surviving the Blitz intact and for the wedding of Charles and Diana, it's looking as good as new after a major clean-up for its 300th anniversary in 2011.

Blackfriars

Somerset House
This grand neoclassical palace was once one of many aristocratic houses lining the Thames. The huge arches at river level gave direct access to the Thames until the Embankment was built in the 1860s.

Temple

Charing Cross

Blackfriars Bridge

Blackfriars Pier

Victoria Embankment Gardens

Waterloo Bridge

Embankment

Embankment Pier

National Theatre

OXO Tower

One Blackfriars

Queen Elizabeth Hall

Southbank Centre

London Eye
Built in 2000 and originally temporary, the Eye instantly became a much-loved landmark. The 30-minute spin takes you 135m above the city from where the views are unsurprisingly amazing.

Waterloo Millennium Pier

Westminster Pier

Westminster

Houses of Parliament
Rebuilt in neo-Gothic style after the old Palace of Westminster burned down in 1834, the most famous part of the British parliament is the clocktower. Generally known as Big Ben, it's named after Benjamin Hall who oversaw its construction.

Westminster Bridge

vessel. These are, from west to east, the ① Houses of Parliament, the ② London Eye, ③ Somerset House, ④ St Paul's Cathedral, the ⑤ Tate Modern, ⑥ Shakespeare's Globe, the ⑦ Tower of London and ⑧ Tower Bridge.

In addition to covering this central section of the Thames, boats can also be taken upstream as far as Kew Gardens and Hampton Court Palace, and downstream as far as Greenwich and the Thames Barrier.

BOAT HOPPING

Thames Clippers hop-on/hop-off services are aimed at commuters but are equally useful for visitors, operating every 15 minutes on a loop from piers at Westminster, Embankment, Waterloo, Blackfriars, Bankside, London Bridge and the Tower. Oyster cardholders get a discount off the boat ticket price.

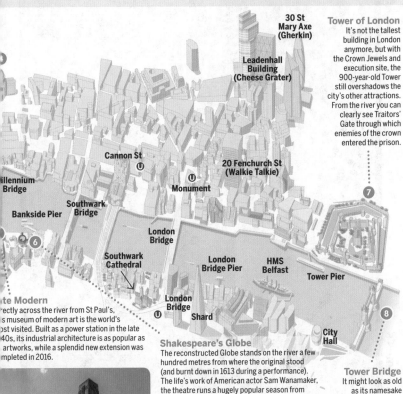

30 St Mary Axe (Gherkin)

Leadenhall Building (Cheese Grater)

Tower of London
It's not the tallest building in London anymore, but with the Crown Jewels and execution site, the 900-year-old Tower still overshadows the city's other attractions. From the river you can clearly see Traitors' Gate through which enemies of the crown entered the prison.

Cannon St Ⓤ

20 Fenchurch St (Walkie Talkie)

Ⓤ Monument

⑦

Millennium Bridge

Southwark Bridge

Bankside Pier

London Bridge

⑥

Southwark Cathedral

London Bridge Pier

HMS Belfast

Tower Pier

London Bridge Ⓤ

Tate Modern
Directly across the river from St Paul's, this museum of modern art is the world's most visited. Built as a power station in the late 1940s, its industrial architecture is as popular as the artworks, while a splendid new extension was completed in 2016.

Shard

City Hall

⑧

Shakespeare's Globe
The reconstructed Globe stands on the river a few hundred metres from where the original stood (and burnt down in 1613 during a performance). The life's work of American actor Sam Wanamaker, the theatre runs a hugely popular season from April to October each year.

PRES PANAYOTOV / SHUTTERSTOCK ©

Tower Bridge
It might look as old as its namesake neighbour but one of the world's most iconic bridges was only completed in 1894. Not to be confused with London Bridge upstream, this one's famous raising bascules allowed tall ships to dock at the old wharves to the west and are still lifted up to 1000 times a year.

Westminster & St James's

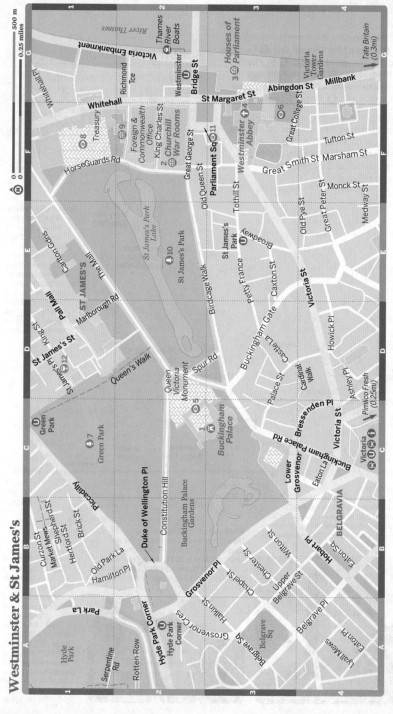

0 — 500 m
0 — 0.25 miles

River Thames

Thames River Boats

Victoria Embankment

Houses of Parliament 3

Westminster Bridge St

St Margaret St

Abingdon St

Millbank

Tate Britain (0.3mi)

Victoria Tower Gardens

Whitehall

Treasury

Foreign & Commonwealth Office

Churchill War Rooms 2

Horse Guards Rd

9

8

King Charles St

Great George St

Old Queen St

Parliament Sq 11

Westminster Abbey 4

6

Great College St

Tufton St

Great Smith St Marsham St

Tothill St

Great Peter St

Monck St

Medway St

Old Pye St

St James's Park

Broadway

St James's Park Lake

10

Birdcage Walk

Caxton St

Petty France

Victoria St

Howick Pl

Ashley Pl

Pimlico Fresh (0.25mi)

ST JAMES'S

Pall Mall

Carlton Gdns

The Mall

Marlborough Rd

St James's St

St James's Pl 12

Green Park

Queen's Walk

Buckingham Gate

Castle La

Palace St

Cardinal Walk

Bressenden Pl

Victoria St

Victoria

Green Park 7

Queen Victoria Monument

Spur Rd

5

1

Buckingham Palace

Lower Grosvenor Pl

Buckingham Palace Rd

Eaton La

Piccadilly

Duke of Wellington Pl

Constitution Hill

Buckingham Palace Gardens

BELGRAVIA

Eaton Sq

Hobart Pl

Curzon St

Market Mews

Shepherd St

Hertford St

Brick St

Old Park La

Hamilton Pl

Park La

Hyde Park Corner

Grosvenor Pl

Grosvenor Cres

Halkin St

Wilton St

Chester St

Chapel St

Upper Belgrave St

Belgrave St

Belgrave Sq

Belgrave Pl

Lyall Mews

Eaton Pl

Hyde Park

Serpentine Rd

Rotten Row

Westminster & St James's

Continued from p57

At the heart of the Abbey is the beautifully tiled **sanctuary**, the stage for coronations, royal weddings and funerals. Architect George Gilbert Scott designed the ornate **High Altar** in 1873. In front of the altar is the **Cosmati Pavement**, dating to 1268. It has intricate designs of small pieces of stone and glass inlaid into plain marble, which symbolise the universe at the end of time (an inscription claims the world will end after 19,683 years). At the entrance to the lovely **Chapel of St John the Baptist** is a sublime translucent alabaster *Virgin and Child*, placed here in 1971.

The most sacred spot in the Abbey is the **shrine of St Edward the Confessor**, which lies behind the High Altar; access is restricted to guided tours to protect the fragile 13th-century flooring. King Edward, long considered a saint before he was canonised, was the founder of the Abbey, and the original building was consecrated a few weeks before his death in 1066. Henry III added a new shrine with Cosmati mosaics in the mid-12th century where the sick prayed for healing – and also chipped off a few souvenirs to take home.

The **Quire** (choir), a stunning space of gold, blue and red Victorian Gothic decoration above a black-and-white chequerboard tiled floor, dates to the mid-19th century. It sits where the original choir for the monks' worship would have been but bears little resemblance to the original. Nowadays, the Quire is still used for singing, but its regular occupants are the Choir of Westminster Abbey – about 30 boys and 12 'lay vicars' (men) who sing the daily services and evensong (5pm on weekdays except Wednesday and 3pm on weekends).

Henry III began work on the new Abbey building in 1245 but didn't complete it; the Gothic nave was finished under Richard II in 1388. Henry VII's magnificent Perpendicular Gothic–style **Lady Chapel**, with an impressive fan-vaulted ceiling and tall stained-glass windows, was completed after 13 years of construction in 1516.

Opened in 2018, the **Queen's Diamond Jubilee Galleries** (timed tickets, an additional £5) are a new museum and gallery space located in the medieval triforium, the arched gallery above the nave. Among its exhibits are the death masks and wax effigies of generations of royalty, armour and stained glass. Highlights are the graffiti-inscribed chair used for the coronation of Mary II, the beautifully illustrated manuscripts of the *Litlyngton Missal* from 1380 and the 13th-century Westminster Retable, England's oldest surviving altarpiece.

At the western end of the nave near the **Tomb of the Unknown Warrior**, killed in France during WWI and laid to rest here in 1920, is St George's Chapel, which contains the rather ordinary-looking **Coronation Chair**, upon which every monarch since the early 14th century has been crowned (apart from joint monarchs Mary II and William III, who had their own chairs fashioned for the event in 1689).

Apart from the royal graves, keep an eye out for the many famous commoners interred here, especially in **Poets' Corner**, where you'll find the resting places of Geoffrey Chaucer, Charles Dickens, Thomas Hardy, Alfred Tennyson, Samuel Johnson and Rudyard Kipling, as well as memorials to the other greats (William Shakespeare, Jane Austen, the Brontë sisters etc). Another set of illustrious stones is in **Scientists' Corner** near the north aisle of the nave, including the final resting places of Sir Isaac Newton, Charles Darwin and the ashes of Stephen Hawking.

Downloadable audio guides are included in the ticket price, but to get more out of your visit, join a 90-minute **verger-led tour** (an additional £7), which includes some 'VIP access', such as Edward's shrine and getting to sit in the Quire stalls.

West End

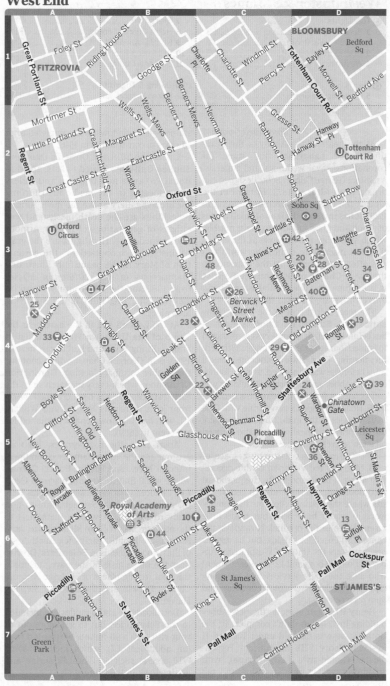

BLOOMSBURY

FITZROVIA

SOHO

ST JAMES'S

Green Park

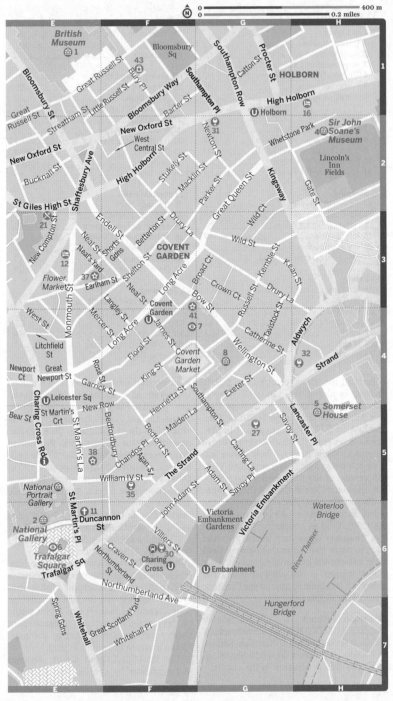

0   400 m
0   0.2 miles

E

British Museum 1

Great Russell St

Bloomsbury Sq

43

Great Russell St

Little Russell St

Bloomsbury Way

Bloomsbury Pl

Southampton Row

Procter St

Catton St

HOLBORN

Great Russell St

Streatham St

New Oxford St

Barter St

High Holborn

Holborn 16

Whetstone Park

Sir John Soane's Museum 4

New Oxford St

West Central St

Newton St

Lincoln's Inn Fields

Bucknall St

Shaftesbury Ave

High Holborn

Stukely St

31

Macklin St

Parker St

Great Queen St

Kingsway

Gate St

St Giles High St

21

Endell St

Betterton St

Drury La

Wild Ct

Wild St

New Compton St

12

Shorts Gdns

Neal St

Shelton St

COVENT GARDEN

Long Acre

Broad Ct

Crown Ct

Russell St

Kemble St

Kean St

Drury La

Flower Market 37

Earlham St

Neal St

Bow St

Tavistock St

Catherine St

Aldwych

West St

Monmouth St

Langley St

Mercer St

Long Acre

Covent Garden 41

James St

7

Wellington St

32

Strand

Litchfield St

Floral St

Covent Garden Market

8

Exeter St

Somerset House 5

Newport Ct

Great Newport St

Rose St

King St

Garrick St

Southampton St

Henrietta St

Maiden La

Lancaster Pl

Savoy St

Leicester Sq

St Martin's Crt

New Row

Bedfordbury

Bedford St

Chandos Pl

Agar St

The Strand

Carting La

27

Savoy Pl

Charing Cross Rd

Bear St

St Martin's La

38

William IV St

35

John Adam St

Adam St

Victoria Embankment

Waterloo Bridge

National Portrait Gallery

St Martin's Pl

11

Duncannon St

Villiers St

Victoria Embankment Gardens

River Thames

National Gallery 2

6

Trafalgar Square

Trafalgar Sq

Craven St

Northumberland St

30

Charing Cross

Embankment

Spring Gdns

Whitehall

Northumberland Ave

Great Scotland Yard

Whitehall Pl

Hungerford Bridge

F   **G**   **H**

West End

Parts of the Abbey complex are free to visitors, including the Cloisters, Chapter House and the 900-year-old **College Garden** (Map p64; off Great College St, SW1; ⊙10am-4pm Tue-Thu) FREE. The octagonal **Chapter House** dates from the 1250s and was where the monks would meet for daily prayer and their job assignments, before Henry VIII's suppression of the monasteries some three centuries later. To the right of the entrance to Chapter House is what's claimed to be the oldest door in Britain – it's been there since the 1050s. Used as a treasury, the crypt-like **Pyx Chamber** dates from about 1070 and takes its name from boxes that held gold and silver to be tested for purity to make coins.

Photography is not allowed inside the Abbey but is permitted around the Cloisters. Pre-booking tickets required.

★ **British Museum**   MUSEUM
(Map p66; ☑ 020-7323 8000; www.britishmuseum.org; Great Russell St, WC1; ⊙10am-5pm (last entry 3.30pm); Ⓤ Tottenham Court Rd or Russell Sq) FREE The British Museum is the country's most popular museum (around 5.8 million visitors annually) and one of the world's oldest (opened in 1759). Don't miss the **Rosetta Stone**, the key to deciphering Egyptian hieroglyphics (head upstairs for the **Egyptian mummies**); the controversial **Parthenon sculptures**, taken from Athens' Acropolis by Lord Elgin (British ambassador to the Ottoman Empire); and the vast Etruscan, Greek, Roman, European, Asian and Islamic galleries. Other must-see items include the Anglo-Saxon **Sutton Hoo Ship Burial** relics and the **winged bulls from Khorsabad**.

It's been acknowledged work needs to be done on the Americas collection.

Begun in 1753 with a 'cabinet of curiosities' sold to the nation by physician and collector Sir Hans Sloane, the collection mushroomed over the ensuing years through acquisitions, bequests and the indiscriminate plundering of the empire. The grand Enlightenment Gallery was the first section of the redesigned museum to be built in 1823.

The light-filled **Great Court**, restored and augmented by architect Norman Foster in 2000, has a spectacular glass-and-steel roof. In the centre is the **Reading Room** (currently closed while the museum reworks this room since its books went to the British Library), where Karl Marx researched and wrote *Das Kapital;* Virginia Woolf and Mahatma Gandhi were also cardholders. See more on p74.

Due to Covid-19 restrictions on numbers at the time of research, it's imperative that you book your visit ahead of time. Audio guides aren't available, so pre-download the audio introductions to each of the galleries and listen on your own device via iTunes or Google Play. There's also a one-hour Highlights tour map of the blockbusters of the collection.

⭐**Trafalgar Square**   SQUARE
(Map p66; U Charing Cross or Embankment) Opened to the public in 1844, Trafalgar Sq is the true centre of London, where rallies and marches take place, tens of thousands of revellers usher in the New Year and locals congregate for anything from communal open-air cinema and Christmas celebrations to political protests. It is dominated by the 52m-high **Nelson's Column**, guarded by four **bronze lion statues**, and ringed by many splendid buildings, including the National Gallery and the church of **St Martin-in-the-Fields** (Map p66; ☎ 020-7766 1100; www.stmartin-in-the-fields.org; ⊗ 8.30am-6pm Mon-Fri, from 9am Sat & Sun).

⭐**National Gallery**   GALLERY
(Map p66; ☎ 020-7747 2885; www.nationalgallery.org.uk; Trafalgar Sq, WC2; ⊗ 11am-6pm Sat-Thu, to 9pm Fri; U Charing Cross) **FREE** With more than 2300 European masterpieces in its collection, this is one of the world's great galleries, with seminal works from the 13th to the mid-20th centuries, including masterpieces by Leonardo da Vinci, Michelangelo, Titian, Vincent van Gogh and Auguste Renoir. Many visitors flock to the eastern rooms on the main floor (1700–1930), where works by British artists such as Thomas Gainsborough, John Constable and JMW Turner, and Impressionist and post-Impressionist masterpieces by Van Gogh, Renoir and Claude Monet await. Pre-booking required.

⭐**Houses of Parliament**   HISTORIC BUILDING
(Map p64; Palace of Westminster; ☎ tours 020-7219 4114; www.parliament.uk; Parliament Sq, SW1; U Westminster) A visit here is a journey to the heart of UK democracy. The Houses of Parliament are officially called the Palace of Westminster, and its oldest part is 11th-century **Westminster Hall**, one of only a few sections that survived a catastrophic 1834 fire. The rest is mostly a neo-Gothic confection built over 36 years from 1840. Tours inside were suspended at the time of research and online tours were the only option.

The palace's most famous feature is its clock tower, Elizabeth Tower (better known as **Big Ben**), covered in scaffolding until restoration works are finished in 2021.

Parliament is split into two houses. The green-hued **House of Commons** is the lower house, where the 650 elected Members of Parliament (MPs) sit. Traditionally the home of hereditary blue bloods, the scarlet-decorated **House of Lords**, with around 800 members, now has peers appointed through various means. Both houses debate and vote on legislation, which is then presented to the Queen for her Royal Assent (in practice, this is a formality; the last time Royal Assent was denied was in 1707). At the annual State Opening of Parliament in May or June, the Queen takes her throne in the House of Lords, having arrived in the gold-trimmed Irish State Coach from Buckingham Palace (her crown travels alone with equerries in Queen Alexandra's State Coach).

Visitors are welcome on Saturdays year-round and on some weekdays during parliamentary recesses (which includes Easter, summer and Christmas). If tours are running again, choose either a **self-guided audio tour** in one of nine languages lasting about 75 minutes or a much more comprehensive 90-minute **guided tour** of both chambers, Westminster Hall and other historic buildings (in English only). Tack on **afternoon tea** (an additional £30) in a riverside room in the House of Commons. It's best to book online far in advance (check the changing schedules), which also shaves a few pounds off the price. Otherwise, buy tickets from the office in front of Portcullis House on Victoria Embankment. UK residents can approach their MPs to arrange a free tour.

Residents and visitors can watch debates, Prime Minister's Question Time and Ministerial Question Time from the public galleries for free. Check the schedule online and book in advance when possible; queues can be long. Public access to the Houses of Parliament is via the Cromwell Green

The British Museum

A HALF-DAY TOUR

The British Museum, with almost eight million items in its permanent collection, is so vast and comprehensive that it can be daunting for the first-time visitor. To avoid a frustrating trip – and getting lost on the way to the Egyptian mummies – set out on this half-day exploration, which takes in some of the museum's most important sights. If you want to see and learn more, download the British Museum audio guide app to your phone pre-arrival.

A good starting point is the **1 Rosetta Stone**, the key that cracked the code to ancient Egypt's writing system. Nearby treasures from Assyria – an ancient civilisation centred in Mesopotamia between the Tigris and Euphrates Rivers – including the colossal **2 Winged Bulls from Khorsabad**, give way to the **3 Parthenon Sculptures**, high points of classical Greek art that continue to influence us today. Be sure to see both the sculptures and the

Winged Bulls from Khorsabad
This awesome pair of alabaster winged bulls with human heads once guarded the entrance to the palace of Assyrian King Sargon II at Khorsabad in Mesopotamia, a cradle of civilisation in present-day Iraq.

Parthenon Sculptures
The Parthenon, a white marble temple dedicated to Athena, was part of a fortified citadel on the Acropolis in Athens. There are dozens of sculptures and friezes with models and interactive displays explaining how they all once fitted together.

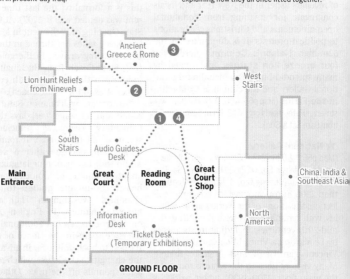

GROUND FLOOR

Bust of Pharaoh Ramesses II
The most impressive sculpture in the Egyptian galleries, this 725kg bust portrays Ramesses the Great, scourge of the Israelites in the Book of Exodus, as great benefactor.

Rosetta Stone
Written in hieroglyphic, demotic (cursive ancient Egyptian script used for everyday) and Greek, the 762kg stone contains a decree exempting priests from tax on the first anniversary of young Ptolemy V's coronation.

monumental frieze celebrating the birth of Athena. En route to the West Stairs is a huge ④ **Bust of Pharaoh Ramesses II**, just a hint of the large collection of ⑤ **Egyptian mummies** upstairs. (The earliest, affectionately called Ginger because of its wispy reddish hair, was preserved simply by hot sand.) The Romans introduce visitors to the early Britain galleries via the rich ⑥ **Mildenhall Treasure**. The Anglo-Saxon ⑦ **Sutton Hoo Ship Burial** and the medieval ⑧ **Lewis Chessmen** follow.

EATING OPTIONS

Court Cafe At the northern end of the Great Court; takeaway counters with salads and sandwiches; communal tables.

Gallery Pizzeria Out of the way off Room 12; quieter; children's menu available.

Great Court Restaurant Upstairs overlooking the former Reading Room; sit-down meals.

Lewis Chessmen
The much-loved 78 chess pieces portray faceless pawns, worried-looking queens, bishops with their mitres turned sideways and rooks (or castles) as 'warders', gnawing away at their shields.

Sutton Hoo Ship Burial
This unique grave of an important (but unidentified) Anglo-Saxon royal has yielded drinking horns, gold buckles and a stunning helmet with face mask.

MAVRITSINA IRINA/SHUTTERSTOCK ©

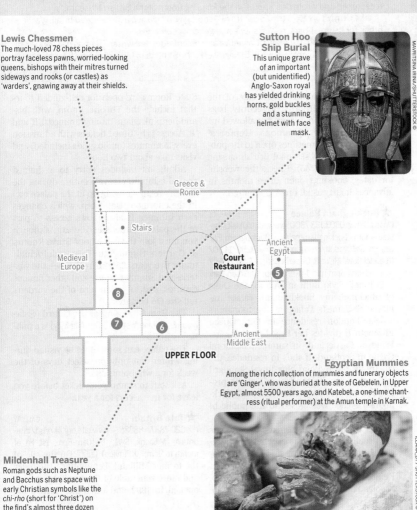

Greece & Rome

Stairs

Medieval Europe

Court Restaurant

Ancient Egypt ⑤

⑧

⑦ ⑥

Ancient Middle East

UPPER FLOOR

Egyptian Mummies
Among the rich collection of mummies and funerary objects are 'Ginger', who was buried at the site of Gebelein, in Upper Egypt, almost 5500 years ago, and Katebet, a one-time chantress (ritual performer) at the Amun temple in Karnak.

ILEANA_BT / SHUTTERSTOCK ©

Mildenhall Treasure
Roman gods such as Neptune and Bacchus share space with early Christian symbols like the *chi-rho* (short for 'Christ') on the find's almost three dozen silver bowls, plates and spoons.

LOCAL KNOWLEDGE

SOHO

London's most bohemian neighbourhood was once pastureland; the name Soho is thought to have evolved from a hunting cry. While the centre of London nightlife has shifted east, and Soho has recently seen landmark clubs and music venues shut down, the neighbourhood still comes into its own in the evenings and remains a proudly LGBT+ friendly district. During the day you'll be charmed by the area's sheer vitality.

At Soho's northern end, leafy **Soho Sq** (Map p66; Ⓤ Tottenham Court Rd or Leicester Sq) is the area's back garden. It was laid out in 1681 and originally called King's Sq; a statue of Charles II stands in its northern half. In the centre is a tiny half-timbered mock-Tudor cottage built as a gardener's shed in the 1870s. The space below it was used as an underground bomb shelter during WWII.

South of the square is **Dean St**, lined with bars and restaurants. No 28 was the home of Karl Marx and his family from 1851 to 1856; they lived here in extreme poverty as Marx researched and wrote *Das Kapital* in the Reading Room of the British Museum.

Old Compton St is the epicentre of Soho's gay village. It's a street loved by all, gay or other, for its great bars, risqué shops and general good vibes.

Seducer and heart-breaker Casanova and opium-addicted writer Thomas de Quincey lived on nearby **Greek St**, while the parallel **Frith St** housed Mozart at No 20 for a year from 1764.

entrance on the southwestern side of the building. Expect airport-style security; bags larger than carry-on size are not allowed in.

The **House of Commons Members' Dining Room** is sometimes open to the public for set meals of seasonal British cuisine (lunch/dinner £45/55). Check the website for dates; bookings open three months in advance. Smart casual dress is required.

★**Buckingham Palace** PALACE
(Map p64; ☏ 0303 123 7300; www.rct.uk/visit/the-state-rooms-buckingham-palace; Buckingham Palace Rd, SW1; adult/child/under 5yr £26.50/14.50/free, incl Royal Mews & Queen's Gallery £49/26.50/free; ⊙ 9am-6pm mid-Jul–end Sep; Ⓤ Green Park or St James's Park) Built in 1703 for the Duke of Buckingham, Buckingham Palace replaced St James's Palace as the monarch's official London residence in 1837. Queen Elizabeth II divides her time between here, Windsor Castle and, in summer, Balmoral Castle in Scotland. If she's in residence, the square yellow, red and blue Royal Standard is flown; if not, it's the Union Flag. To protect the wellbeing of visitors and staff, Buckingham Palace was closed to the public in 2020 until further notice.

The 19 lavishly furnished State Rooms are usually open to visitors when Her Majesty is on holiday from mid-July to September. Hung with artworks by the likes of Rembrandt, Anthony van Dyck, Canaletto, Nicolas Poussin and Johannes Vermeer, the State Rooms are open for self-guided tours that include the **Throne Room**, with his-and-her pink chairs monogrammed 'ER' and 'P'. Access is by timed tickets with admission every 15 minutes (audio guide included) and visits take about two hours.

Admission includes entry to a themed special exhibition (royal couture during the Queen's reign, growing up at the palace etc) in the enormous **Ballroom**, which changes each summer. It also allows access to part of the palace gardens as you exit, although you must join the three-hour **State Rooms & Garden Highlights Tour** (adult/child/under five years £35/21/free) to see the wisteria-clad Summer House and other famous features, and to get an idea of the garden's full size (16 hectares).

The 11am **Changing of the Guard** (⊙ daily Jun & Jul, Mon, Wed, Fri & Sun Aug-May) is a public institution.

The palace can sometimes be visited during winter, but only on select days of the week for a whopping £85.

Ask staff to stamp your ticket before you leave for free access for a year.

★**Tate Britain** GALLERY
(☏ 020-7887 8888; www.tate.org.uk/visit/tate-britain; Millbank, SW1; ⊙ 10am-6pm, 1st Fri of month to 9pm; Ⓤ Pimlico) FREE On the site of the former Millbank Penitentiary, the older and more venerable of the two Tate siblings opened in 1892 and celebrates British art

from 1500 to the present, including pieces from William Blake, William Hogarth, Thomas Gainsborough, John Constable and Joshua Reynolds, as well as vibrant modern and contemporary pieces from Lucian Freud, Barbara Hepworth, Gillian Ayres, Francis Bacon and Henry Moore. The stars of the show are, undoubtedly, the light-infused visions of JMW Turner in the **Clore Gallery**.

After Turner died in 1851, his estate was settled by a decree declaring that whatever had been found in his studio – 300 oil paintings and about 30,000 watercolours and sketches – would be bequeathed to the nation. The collection here constitutes a grand and sweeping display of his work, including classics such as *The Field of Waterloo* and *Norham Castle, Sunrise*.

Tate Britain is also home to seminal works from the Pre-Raphaelites, including William Holman Hunt's *Strayed Sheep*, John William Waterhouse's sculpture *Hylas Surprised by the Naiades*, *Christ in the House of His Parents* by John Everett Millais and Edward Burne-Jones' *The Golden Stairs*. Look out also for Francis Bacon's *Three Studies for Figures at the Base of a Crucifixion*.

The gallery hosts the prestigious and often controversial **Turner Prize** from October to early January every year (adult/child £13/free), plus a programme of ticketed exhibitions that changes every few months; consult the website for what's on.

Quick 15-minute **Art in Focus talks** on a selected work take place every Tuesday, Thursday and Saturday at 1.15pm; the piece under the microscope changes monthly, so check online or ask at the visitor information desk. Free 45-minute **themed guided tours** are held four times a day, and the 3pm slot is invariably on the work of JMW Turner. Both tours are free; booking is not required.

On the first Friday of each month, **Late at Tate Britain** means the gallery stays open until 9.30pm.

⭐ **Wallace Collection**   GALLERY
(Map p114; ☑ 020-7563 9500; www.wallace collection.org; Hertford House, Manchester Sq, W1; ⊙10am-4pm; Ⓤ Bond St) **FREE** Arguably London's finest smaller gallery, the Wallace Collection is an enthralling glimpse into 18th-century aristocratic life. The sumptuously restored Italianate mansion houses a treasure trove of 17th- and 18th-century paintings, porcelain, artefacts and furniture collected by generations of the same family and bequeathed to the nation by the widow of Sir Richard Wallace (1818–90) on the condition it remain displayed in the same fashion.

⭐ **Churchill War Rooms**   MUSEUM
(Map p64; ☑ 020-7416 5000; www.iwm.org.uk/ visits/churchill-war-rooms; Clive Steps, King Charles St, SW1; adult/child £23/11.50; ⊙9.30am-6pm; Ⓤ Westminster) Former Prime Minister Winston Churchill helped coordinate the Allied resistance against Nazi Germany on a Bakelite telephone from this underground complex during WWII. The **Cabinet War Rooms** remain much as they were when the lights were switched off in 1945, capturing the drama and dogged spirit of the time, while the modern multimedia **Churchill Museum** affords intriguing insights into the life and times of the resolute, cigar-smoking wartime leader.

Tickets are slightly cheaper if booked online and come with priority entry to beat the ever-present queue.

⭐ **Royal Academy of Arts**   GALLERY
(Map p66; ☑ 020-7300 8000; www.royalacademy. org.uk; Burlington House, Piccadilly, W1; ⊙10am-6pm; Ⓤ Green Park) **FREE** Britain's oldest society devoted to fine arts was founded in 1768 and moved here to Burlington House a century later. For its 250th birthday in 2018, the RA gave itself a £56-million makeover. Its collection of drawings, paintings, architectural designs, photographs and sculptures by past and present Royal Academicians, such as Sir Joshua Reynolds, John Constable, Thomas Gainsborough, JMW Turner, David Hockney and Tracey Emin, has historically been male-dominated, but this is slowly changing.

⭐ **Sir John Soane's Museum**   MUSEUM
(Map p66; ☑ 020-7405 2107; www.soane.org; 13 Lincoln's Inn Fields, WC2; ⊙10am-5pm Thu-Sat; Ⓤ Holborn) **FREE** This museum is one of the most atmospheric and fascinating in London. The Georgian building was the beautiful, bewitching home of architect Sir John Soane (1753–1837), which he bequeathed to the nation through an Act of Parliament on condition that it remain untouched after his death and free to visit. It's brimming with Soane's vast collection of art and archaeological

GETTING HIGH IN LONDON

Not so long ago, getting a good view of London was a near-impossible endeavour. Beyond joining the tourists on the London Eye (p83), dining at City Social (p116) involved a lot of forward planning. Things are a lot more democratic these days and, well, the sky's the limit.

The 72nd-floor open-air platform of the Shard (p85) is as high as you'll get in Europe. The lush interior Sky Garden (p79) is free with a forward booking. For all-night dining head for the 40th-floor location of Duck & Waffle (p116). For drinks we love **Radio Rooftop Bar** (Map p66; ☑020-7395 3440; https://radiorooftop.com/london; 10th fl, ME London, 336-337 The Strand, WC2; ☑7am-1am Mon-Wed, to 2am Thu-Sat, to midnight Sun; Ⓤ Temple or Covent Garden), Frank's at Peckham Levels (p117) or Seabird at Hoxton Southwark (p109). And the **5th View** (Map p66; ☑020-7851 2433; www.5thview.com; 5th fl, Waterstones Piccadilly, 203-206 Piccadilly, W1; mains £10-12; ☑9am-9.30pm Mon-Sat, noon-5pm Sun; 🛜; Ⓤ Piccadilly Circus) atop Waterstones bookshop in Piccadilly is an option for afternoon tea.

purchases, as well as intriguing personal effects and curiosities. The house-museum represents his exquisite and eccentric tastes, persuasions and proclivities.

London Transport Museum MUSEUM
(Map p66; ☑020-7379 6344; www.ltmuseum.co.uk; Covent Garden Piazza, WC2; adult/child £18.50/free; ☑10am-6pm; ♿; Ⓤ Covent Garden) Housed in Covent Garden's former flower-market building, this captivating museum looks at how London developed as a result of better transport. It's stuffed full of horse-drawn omnibuses, vintage Underground carriages with heritage maps, and old double-decker buses (some of which you can clamber through, making this something of a kids' playground). The **gift shop** also sells great London souvenirs such as retro Tube posters and pillows made from the same fabric as the train seats.

Madame Tussauds MUSEUM
(Map p114; ☑0870 400 3000; www.madame-tussauds.com/london; Marylebone Rd, NW1; adult/child 4-15yr £35/30; ☑10am-6pm; Ⓤ Baker St) It may be kitschy and pricey, but Madame Tussauds makes for a fun-filled day. There are photo ops with your dream celebrity (be it Daniel Craig, Lady Gaga, Benedict Cumberbatch, or Audrey Hepburn), the Bollywood gathering (starring studs Hrithik Roshan and Salman Khan) and the Royal Appointment (the Queen, Harry and Meghan, William and Kate). Book online for much cheaper rates and check the website for seasonal opening hours.

★ **Somerset House** HISTORIC BUILDING
(Map p66; ☑020-7845 4600; www.somersethouse.org.uk; The Strand, WC2; ☑10am-7pm; Ⓤ Temple) Designed in 1775 for government departments and royal societies – perhaps the world's first office block – Somerset House now contains galleries, restaurants and cafes that encircle a lovely open courtyard and extend to an elevated sun-trap terrace. The **Embankment Galleries** are devoted to temporary exhibitions (usually related to photography, design or fashion). In summer, the grand courtyard hosts open-air live performances, dancing fountains for kids to cool off in and the Film4 Summer Screen (p105); there's an atmospheric ice-skating rink in winter.

No 10 Downing Street HISTORIC BUILDING
(Map p64; www.number10.gov.uk; 10 Downing St, SW1; Ⓤ Westminster) The official office of British leaders since 1735, when King George II presented No 10 to 'First Lord of the Treasury' Robert Walpole, this has also been the prime minister's London residence since the late 19th century. For such a famous address, No 10 is a small-looking Georgian building on a plain-looking street, hardly warranting comparison with the White House, for example. Yet it is actually three houses joined into one and boasts roughly 100 rooms plus a 2000-sq-metre garden.

Charles Dickens Museum MUSEUM
(Map p96; ☑020-7405 2127; www.dickensmuseum.com; 48-49 Doughty St, WC1; adult/child £9.50/4.50; ☑10am-5pm Fri-Sun; Ⓤ Russell Sq or Chancery Lane) The prolific writer Charles Dickens lived with his growing family in this handsome four-storey Georgian terraced

house for a mere 2½ years (1837–39), but this is where his work really flourished, as he completed *The Pickwick Papers*, *Nicholas Nickleby* and *Oliver Twist* here. Each of the dozen rooms, some restored to their original condition, contains various memorabilia, including the study where you'll find the desk at which Dickens wrote *Great Expectations*.

St James's Park PARK
(Map p64; www.royalparks.org.uk/parks/st-jamess-park; The Mall, SW1; ⊙5am-midnight; ⒰St James's Park, Green Park) At 23 hectares, St James's is the second-smallest of the eight royal parks after **Green Park** (Map p64; www.royalparks.org.uk/parks/green-park; ⊙5am-midnight; ⒰Green Park). But what it lacks in size it makes up for in grooming, as it is the most manicured green space in London. It has brilliant views of the London Eye, Westminster, St James's Palace, Carlton House Terrace and Horse Guards Parade; the picture-perfect sight of Buckingham Palace from the **Blue Bridge** spanning the central lake is the best you'll find.

City of London

★**St Paul's Cathedral** CATHEDRAL
(Map p76; ☑020-7246 8357; www.stpauls.co.uk; St Paul's Churchyard, EC4; adult/child £17/7.20; ⊙8.30am-4.30pm Mon-Sat; ⒰St Paul's) Towering over diminutive Ludgate Hill in a superb position that's been a place of Christian worship for more than 1400 years (and pagan before that), St Paul's Cathedral is one of London's most magnificent buildings. For Londoners, the vast dome is a symbol of resilience and pride, standing tall for more than 300 years. Viewing architect Sir Christopher Wren's masterpiece from the inside and climbing to the top for sweeping views of the capital is a celestial experience.

Following the destructive Great Fire of London in 1666, which burned 80% of the city, Wren designed St Paul's to replace the old church, and it was built between 1675 and 1710. The site is ancient hallowed ground, with four other cathedrals preceding Wren's English baroque masterpiece, the first dating from 604 CE.

The cathedral dome, inspired by St Peter's Basilica in the Vatican, is famed for surviving Luftwaffe incendiary bombs in the 'Second Great Fire of London' of December 1940, becoming an icon of London resilience during the Blitz. North of the church is the simple **People of London Memorial**, honouring the 32,000 civilians killed.

Inside, rising more than 85m above the floor, the dome is supported by eight huge columns. It actually consists of three parts: a plastered brick inner dome, a nonstructural lead outer dome visible on the skyline and a brick cone between them holding it all together. The walkway around its base, accessed via 257 steps from a staircase on the western side of the southern transept, is called the **Whispering Gallery**. A further 119 steps brings you to the exterior **Stone Gallery**, your first taste of the city vistas, and 152 iron steps more bring you to the **Golden Gallery** at the very top, with unforgettable views of London.

The **crypt** has memorials to around 300 of Britain's great and the good, including the Duke of Wellington and Vice Admiral Horatio Nelson, whose body lies directly below the dome. But the most poignant is to Wren himself. On a simple tomb slab bearing his name, part of a Latin inscription translates as: 'If you seek his monument, look around you'.

> ### ⓘ LONDON TOP TIPS
>
> ➡ London is huge – organise your visit by neighbourhood to avoid wasting time (and money) on transport.
>
> ➡ An Oyster Card is a cheaper and convenient way to use public transport, but you can also pay by contactless bank cards and smart phones.
>
> ➡ Note that a large number of places are now cashless.
>
> ➡ Walk – it's free and the best way to discover central London.
>
> ➡ For last minute West End performances check out standby ticket options, which you buy on the day at the venue or from the booth on Leicester Sq.
>
> ➡ To treat yourself to fine dining without breaking the bank, opt for lunch rather than dinner, or try for pre- or post-theatre dinner deals.
>
> ➡ Book online for ticketed attractions to save money and skip queues.
>
> ➡ Download local apps for taxis (Gett), public transport (CityMapper) and theatre tickets (TodayTix).

The City

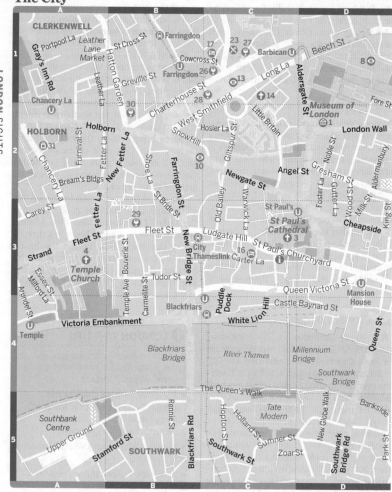

There's no charge to attend a service, but not all areas of the cathedral are accessible. To hear the cathedral choir, attend the 11.30am Sunday Eucharist or Evensong (5pm Monday to Saturday and 3.15pm Sunday), but check the website as a visiting choir may appear for the latter.

Book tickets online in advance for a slight discount and faster entry. Admission includes an audio guide. Free 1½-hour guided tours depart four times a day (10am, 11am, 1pm and 2pm); reserve a place at the tour desk, just past the entrance. About three times a month, one-hour tours (£8) visit the Geometric Staircase, Great

Model and astonishing library (closed for renovations until at least spring 2021), and include impressive views down the nave from above the Great West Doors; check online for timings.

★ Tower of London   HISTORIC SITE
(Map p76; ☎ 020-3166 6000; www.hrp.org.uk/tower-of-london; Petty Wales, EC3; adult/child £25/12.50; ⏰ 9am-4.30pm, from 10am Sun & Mon; Ⓤ Tower Hill) The unmissable Tower of London offers a window into 1000 years of gruesome and compelling history. A former royal residence, treasury, mint, armoury and zoo, it's perhaps most remembered as the

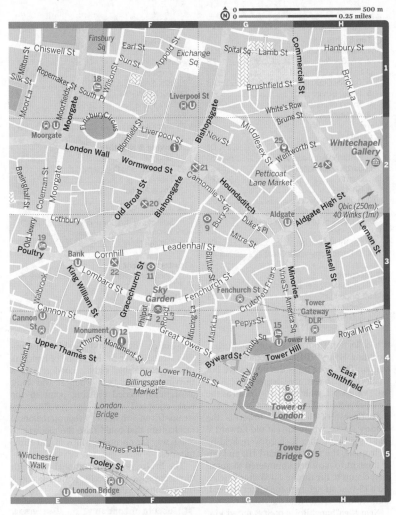

prison where a king, three queens and many nobles met their deaths. The immaculately dressed Yeomen Warders (better known as the Beefeaters), who live on site, protect the spectacular Crown Jewels, containing the biggest diamonds in the world, and lead tours of the Tower, as soothsaying resident ravens flit overhead.

The Tower of London is a densely packed history-laden site, so expect to spend at least half a day. To get your bearings, take one of the entertaining (and free) **guided tours** with the Yeomen Warders; the 45-minute-long tours leave every 30 minutes from the bridge near the main entrance until

3.30pm (2.30pm in winter). For a quick visual overview, see p85.

Most visitors head straight to the Waterloo Barracks, which contains the **Crown Jewels**, including the platinum crown of the late Queen Mother, set with the 106-carat Koh-i-Nûr (Persian for 'Mountain of Light') diamond, and the Imperial State Crown, worn by the monarch at the State Opening of Parliament. Slow-moving walkways slide wide-eyed visitors past the collection.

Started in the 1070s by William the Conqueror, the striking **White Tower** is London's oldest building, with solid Norman architecture and four turrets. On the entrance floor

The City

is a collection from the **Royal Armouries**, including Henry VIII's commodious suit of armour. One floor up is the impressive but unadorned 11th-century **Chapel of St John the Evangelist**, which was once used as the national record office.

Southwest of the White Tower is the **Bloody Tower**, where 12-year-old Edward V and his little brother Richard were held by their uncle, the future Richard III, and later thought to have been murdered to annul their claims to the throne. Sir Walter Raleigh did a 13-year stretch here too under James I, and wrote his *Historie of the World*.

Near the Chapel Royal of St Peter ad Vincula stood the Tower Green **scaffold**, where nobles such as Anne Boleyn and Catherine Howard (Henry's second and fifth wives) were beheaded.

Look out for the Tower's famous ravens, which legend says could cause the Tower, and therefore the kingdom, to collapse should they leave (a spare bird is kept in the aviary, and their wing feathers are clipped in case they get any ideas).

Book online in advance for cheaper rates.

★ **Tower Bridge**   BRIDGE
(Map p76; ☑ 020-7403 3761; www.towerbridge. org.uk; Tower Bridge, SE1; Ⓤ Tower Hill) With its

neo-Gothic towers and sky-blue suspension struts, Tower Bridge is one of London's most recognisable sights. London was a thriving port in 1894 when it was built as a much-needed crossing point in the east, equipped with a then-revolutionary steam-driven bascule (counterbalance) mechanism that could raise the roadway to make way for oncoming ships in just three minutes.

The bridge is still operational, although these days it's electrically powered; check the website for lift times.

★ **Museum of London**   MUSEUM
(Map p76; ☑ 020-7001 9844; www.museumof london.org.uk; 150 London Wall, EC2; ⊙ 10am-6pm; Ⓤ Barbican) **FREE** Romp through 450,000 years of London history at this entertaining and educational museum, one of the capital's finest. Exhibiting everything from a mammoth's jaw circa 200,000 BCE to Oliver Cromwell's death mask and the desperate scrawls of convicts on a cell from Wellclose Prison, interactive displays and reconstructed scenes transport visitors from Roman Londinium and Saxon Lundenwic right up to the 21st-century metropolis. Free themed tours are offered daily; check at reception for timings and topics.

★ Sky Garden   VIEWPOINT

(Map p76; ☑020-7337 2344; https://skygarden. london; 20 Fenchurch St, EC3; ⊙10am-6pm Mon-Fri, 11am-9pm Sat & Sun; Ⓤ Monument) FREE The ferns, fig trees and purple African lilies that clamber up the final three storeys of the 'Walkie Talkie' skyscraper are mere wallflowers at this 155m-high rooftop garden – it's the extraordinary 360-degree views of London that make this vast, airport-terminal-like space so popular. The Sky Garden has front-row seats overlooking the Shard (p85) and vistas that gallop for miles east and west. Visits must be booked online in advance, and tickets run out quickly.

Monument to the
Great Fire of London   MONUMENT

(Map p76; ☑020-7403 3761; www.themonument. org.uk; Fish St Hill, EC3; adult/child £5/2.50, incl Tower Bridge Exhibition £12/5.50; ⊙9.30am-5.30pm; Ⓤ Monument) Designed by Christopher Wren, this immense Doric column of Portland stone is a reminder of the Great Fire of London in 1666, which destroyed 80% of the city. It stands 62m high, the distance from the bakery in Pudding Lane where the fire is thought to have started. Although Lilliputian by today's standards, the Monument towered over London when it was built. Climbing up the column's 311 spiral steps still provides great views thanks to its central location.

The garden space includes a restaurant, a brasserie and three bars with varying opening times. If tickets have sold out, you can reserve a table at one of them to gain access, though you will have to order something.

Barbican   ARCHITECTURE

(Map p76; ☑020-7638 4141; www.barbican.org. uk; Silk St, EC2; Ⓤ Barbican) The architectural value of this sprawling post-WWII brutalist housing estate divides Londoners, but the Barbican remains a sought-after living space as well as the City's preeminent cultural centre. Public spaces include a quirky **conservatory** (☑0845 120 7500; Level 3; ⊙noon-5pm Sun) FREE and the Barbican Centre theatres, cinema and two art galleries: **Barbican Art Gallery** (☑020-7638 8891; Level 3; ⊙noon-6pm Mon & Tue, to 9pm Wed-Fri, 10am-9pm Sat, to 6pm Sun) and **The Curve** (☑020-7638 8891; Level 1; ⊙11am-8pm Sat-Wed, to 9pm Thu & Fri) FREE. Navigating the Barbican, designed to be a car-free urban neighbourhood, requires reliance on a network of elevated paths that didn't quite come to fruition. Find your bearings on an **architecture tour** (adult/child £12.50/10).

St Bartholomew the Great   CHURCH

(Map p76; ☑020-7600 0440; www.greatstbarts. com; W Smithfield, EC1; ⊙10am-4pm Mon-Wed, Fri & Sat, 10am-1pm Thu, 1-6pm Sun; Ⓤ Barbican) FREE Dating from 1123, St Bartholomew the Great is one of London's oldest churches. The Norman arches and profound sense of history lend this holy space an ancient calm, and it's even more atmospheric when entered through the restored 13th-century half-timbered gatehouse. The church was originally part of an Augustinian priory but became the parish church of Smithfield in 1539 when Henry VIII dissolved the monasteries.

Gherkin   NOTABLE BUILDING

(Map p76; www.thegherkinlondon.com; 30 St Mary Axe, EC3; Ⓤ Aldgate) Nicknamed 'the Gherkin' for its distinctive shape, 30 St Mary Axe remains the City's most intriguing skyscraper, despite the best efforts of the engineering individualism that now surrounds it. It was built in 2003 by architect Norman Foster, with a futuristic exterior that has become an emblem of modern London. The top floors of the building, once a private members' club, are now open to the public as a **bar-restaurant** (Map p76; ☑0330 107 0816; https://searcysatthegherkin.co.uk; ⊙11am-10pm Mon-Sat, 10am-4pm Sun).

◉ South Bank

★ Tate Modern   GALLERY

(Map p84; ☑020-7887 8888; www.tate.org.uk; Bankside, SE1; ⊙10am-6pm Sun-Thu, to 10pm Fri & Sat; Ⓤ Southwark) FREE One of London's most amazing attractions, this outstanding modern- and contemporary-art gallery is housed in the creatively revamped Bankside Power Station. A spellbinding synthesis of modern art and capacious industrial brick design, Tate Modern has been extraordinarily successful in bringing challenging work to the masses, both through its free permanent collection and fee-charged big-name temporary exhibitions. The stunning **Blavatnik Building**, with a panoramic 10th-floor viewing terrace, opened in 2016, increasing the available exhibition space by 60%.

Tower of London

TACKLING THE TOWER

Although it's usually less busy in the late afternoon, don't leave your assault on the Tower until too late in the day. You could easily spend hours here and not see it all. Start by getting your bearings on one of the Yeoman Warder (beefeater) tours; they are included in the cost of admission, entertaining and the easiest way to access the ❶ **Chapel Royal of St Peter ad Vincula**, which is where they finish up.

When you leave the chapel, the ❷ **Scaffold Site** is directly in front. The building immediately to your left is Waterloo Barracks, where the ❸ **Crown Jewels** are housed. These are the absolute highlight of a Tower visit, so keep an eye on the entrance and pick a time to visit when it looks relatively quiet. Once inside, take things at your own pace. Slow-moving travelators shunt you past the dozen or so crowns that are the treasury's centrepieces, but feel free to double-back for a second or even third pass.

Allow plenty of time for the ❹ **White Tower**, the core of the whole complex, starting with the exhibition of royal armour. As you continue onto the 1st floor, keep an eye out for ❺ **St John's Chapel**.

The famous ❻ **ravens** can be seen in the courtyard south of the White Tower. Next, visit the ❼ **Bloody Tower** and the torture displays in the dungeon of the Wakefield Tower. Head next through the towers that formed the ❽ **Medieval Palace**, then take the ❾ **East Wall Walk** to get a feel for the castle's mighty battlements. Spend the rest of your time poking around the many other fascinating nooks and crannies of the Tower complex.

BEAT THE QUEUES

➡ Buy tickets online, avoid weekends and aim to be at the Tower first thing in the morning, when queues are shortest.

➡ The London Pass (www.london pass.com) allows you to jump the queues and visit the Tower (plus some other 80 attractions) as often as you like.

Chapel Royal of St Peter ad Vincula
This chapel serves as the resting place for the royals and other members of the aristocracy who were executed on the small green out front. Several other historical figures are buried here too, including St Thomas More.

Scaffold Site
Seven people, including three queens (Anne Boleyn, Catherine Howard and Jane Grey), lost their heads here during Tudor times, saving the monarch the embarrassment of public executions on Tower Hill. The site features a rather odd 'pillow' sculpture by Brian Catling.

Dry Moat

Beauchamp Tower

Coins & Kings display

Main Entrance

Middle Tower

Byward Tower

Bell Tower

White Tower
Much of the White Tower is taken up with an exhibition on 500 years of royal armour. Look for the virtually cuboid suit made to match Henry VIII's bloated 49-year-old body, complete with an oversized armoured codpiece to protect, ahem, the crown jewels.

FLIK47 / GETTY IMAGES ©

EXECUTION SITE MEMORIAL BY BRIAN CATLING

CHRISDORNEY / SHUTTERSTOCK ©

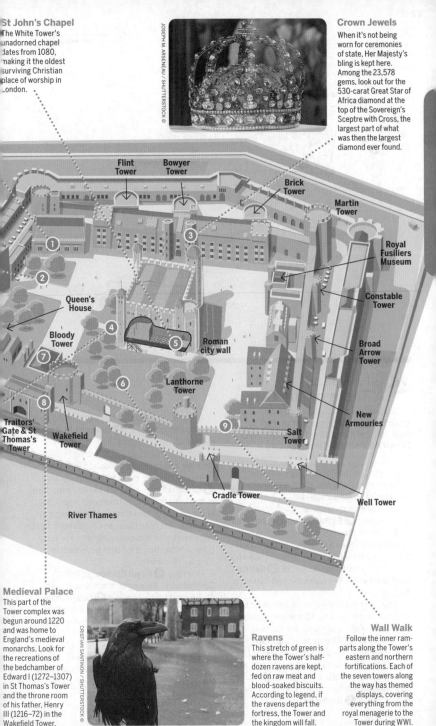

St John's Chapel
The White Tower's unadorned chapel dates from 1080, making it the oldest surviving Christian place of worship in London.

Crown Jewels
When it's not being worn for ceremonies of state, Her Majesty's bling is kept here. Among the 23,578 gems, look out for the 530-carat Great Star of Africa diamond at the top of the Sovereign's Sceptre with Cross, the largest part of what was then the largest diamond ever found.

JOSEPH M. ARSENEAU / SHUTTERSTOCK ©

Flint Tower

Bowyer Tower

Brick Tower

Martin Tower

Royal Fusiliers Museum

Constable Tower

Queen's House

Bloody Tower

Roman city wall

Broad Arrow Tower

Lanthorne Tower

New Armouries

Traitors' Gate & St Thomas's Tower

Wakefield Tower

Salt Tower

Cradle Tower

Well Tower

River Thames

Medieval Palace
This part of the Tower complex was begun around 1220 and was home to England's medieval monarchs. Look for the recreations of the bedchamber of Edward I (1272–1307) in St Thomas's Tower and the throne room of his father, Henry III (1216–72) in the Wakefield Tower.

CRISTIAN SANTINON / SHUTTERSTOCK ©

Ravens
This stretch of green is where the Tower's half-dozen ravens are kept, fed on raw meat and blood-soaked biscuits. According to legend, if the ravens depart the fortress, the Tower and the kingdom will fall.

Wall Walk
Follow the inner ramparts along the Tower's eastern and northern fortifications. Each of the seven towers along the way has themed displays, covering everything from the royal menagerie to the Tower during WWI.

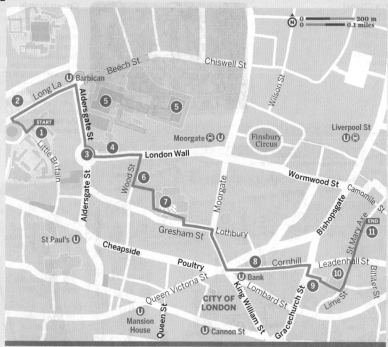

🏃 City Walk
A Taste of the City

START ST BARTHOLOMEW THE GREAT
END 30 ST MARY AXE (THE GHERKIN)
LENGTH 1.2 MILES; THREE HOURS

The City of London has as a huge wealth of history in its square mile, and this walk picks out just a few of its many highlights.

Start by exploring the wonderful 12th-century ❶ **St Bartholomew the Great** (p79), whose atmospheric interior has been used frequently as a film set. Head through the Tudor gatehouse and turn right towards the colourful Victorian arches of ❷ **Smithfield Market** (p134), London's last surviving meat market.

Head northeast along Long Lane and take a right at Aldersgate St. Follow the roundabout to the right and nip up the stairs (or take the lift) to the ❸ **Museum of London** (p78). After exploring the museum's excellent free galleries turn left onto the highwalk and pause to examine the ruins of the ❹ **Roman city walls** and behind them the distinctive towers of the ❺ **Barbican** (p79).

Descend from the highwalk and cross over to Wood St to find the ❻ **tower of St Alban** (1698), all that's left of a Wren-designed church destroyed in WWII bombing in 1940. Turn left into Love Lane and right into Aldermanbury – the impressive 15th-century ❼ **Guildhall** is on your left, behind a modern extension. Crossing its courtyard – note the black outline of the Roman amphitheatre – continue east onto Gresham St, taking a right into Prince's St and emerging onto the busy Bank intersection lined with neoclassical temples to commerce.

From the ❽ **Royal Exchange**, follow Cornhill and take a right down Gracechurch St. Turn left into wonderful ❾ **Leadenhall Market** (p134), roughly where the Roman forum once stood. As you leave the market's far end, ❿ **Lloyd's of London** displays its innards for all to see. Turn left onto Lime St for ⓫ **30 St Mary Axe** (the Gherkin; p79). Built nearly 900 years after St Bartholomew the Great, it's a tangible testimony to the city's ability to constantly reinvent itself.

The 200m-long building, made of 4.2 million bricks, is an imposing sight, and was designed by Swiss architects Herzog and de Meuron, who scooped the prestigious Pritzker Architecture Prize in 2001 for their transformation of the former power station. Significant achievements include leaving the building's central 99m-high chimney, adding a two-storey glass box onto the roof and turning the cavernous Turbine Hall into a dramatic exhibition space. Herzog and de Meuron also designed the later 10-storey Blavatnik Building extension.

Tate Modern's permanent collection is free to visit and is arranged by both theme and chronology on levels 2 and 4 of the riverside Natalie Bell Building and on levels 0, 3 and 4 of the Blavatnik Building. More than 60,000 works of the permanent collection are on constant rotation, and the curators have at their disposal paintings by Georges Braque, Henri Matisse, Piet Mondrian, Andy Warhol, Mark Rothko and Jackson Pollock, as well as pieces by Joseph Beuys, Barbara Hepworth, Damien Hirst, Rebecca Horn and Claes Oldenburg.

Don't miss sublime city views from the 10th-floor Viewing Level of the Blavatnik Building and the view of the River Thames and St Paul's Cathedral from the 6th-floor cafe in the Natalie Bell Building. Head to the level 4 bridge connecting the two buildings to get a lofty view of Turbine Hall.

Free guided tours of sections of the permanent collection depart at noon, 1pm and 2pm daily. To visit the sister museum Tate Britain (p72), hop on the RB2 riverboat service from Bankside Pier (Map p84; www.thames clippers.com; one way adult/child £8.70/4.35).

★ **Shakespeare's Globe**   THEATRE
(Map p84; ☑ 020-7401 9919; www.shakespeares globe.com; 21 New Globe Walk, SE1; tour adult/ child £17/10; ⊙ box office 10am-6pm; Ⓤ Blackfriars or London Bridge) The reconstructed Shakespeare's Globe was designed to resemble the 16th-century original as closely as possible, constructed with 600 oak pegs (there's not a nail or screw in the house), specially fired Tudor-style bricks and a circular thatch roof that leaves the theatre's centre – and the groundlings watching the performance – vulnerable to the elements. Guided tours take in the architecture and give access to the exhibition space, with displays on Shakespeare, life in Bankside and theatre in the 17th century.

Shakespeare wrote for both outdoor and indoor theatre, and outside the Globe's April to October season, the Sam Wanamaker Playhouse – an indoor Jacobean-style theatre – puts on year-round performances.

★ **London Eye**   VIEWPOINT
(Map p84; www.londoneye.com; near County Hall, SE1; adult/child from £24.50/22; ⊙ 10am-8.30pm, reduced hours in low season; Ⓤ Waterloo or Westminster) Standing 135m high in a fairly flat city, the London Eye is the world's largest cantilevered observation wheel and affords views 25 miles in every direction (as far as Windsor Castle), weather permitting. Each ride – or 'flight' – takes a gracefully slow 30 minutes. The London Eye is the focal point of the capital's midnight New Year's Eve fireworks display and one of the UK's most popular tourist attractions; book tickets online in advance for a slight discount or fast-track entry to jump the queue.

★ **Southbank Centre**   ARTS CENTRE
(Map p84; ☑ 020-3879 9555; www.southbank centre.co.uk; Belvedere Rd, SE1; ⊙ 10am-11pm; ♿; Ⓤ Waterloo) Southbank Centre, Europe's largest space for performing and visual arts, is made up of three brutalist buildings that stretch across seven riverside hectares: Royal Festival Hall (p132), Queen Elizabeth Hall (p132) and Hayward Gallery (⊙ 11am-7pm Mon-Sat 10am-6pm Sun). With cafes, restaurants, shops and bars, this complex is always a hub of activity, from the singing lift up to the 6th floor to teenage skateboarders doing tricks in the Undercroft. In summer, the fountains and artificial beach on the waterfront are a hit with youngsters.

★ **Southwark Cathedral**   CATHEDRAL
(Map p84; ☑ 020-7367 6700; www.cathedral.south wark.anglican.org; Montague Cl, SE1; ⊙ 9am-5pm Mon-Fri, 9.30am-3.45pm & 5-6pm Sat, 12.30-3pm & 4-6pm Sun; Ⓤ London Bridge) Southwark Cathedral, a mostly Victorian construction but with a history dating back many centuries earlier, was the nearest church to what was once the only entry point into the city, London Bridge. The cathedral is relatively small, but the Gothic arched nave is impressive, as is the 16th-century saint-filled High Altar Screen. Tombs and memorials are scattered throughout (follow the one-way system), including the tomb of John Gower and an alabaster Shakespeare Memorial. Evensong takes place at 5.30pm on weekdays, 4pm on Saturdays and 3pm on Sundays.

South Bank

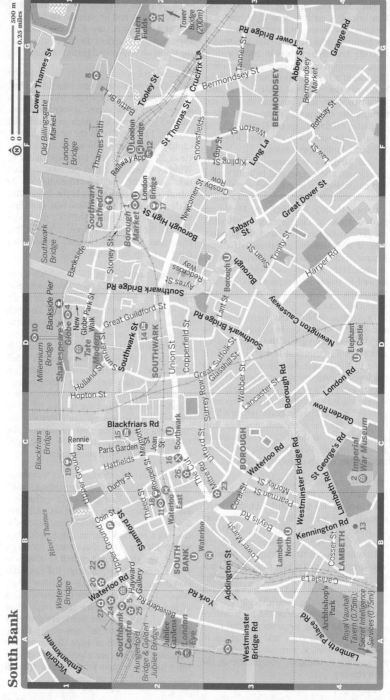

500 m
0.25 miles

River Thames

Victoria Embankment

Waterloo Bridge

Blackfriars Bridge

Millennium Bridge

Southwark Bridge

London Bridge

Tower Bridge (200m)

Lower Thames St

Old Billingsgate Market

London Bridge

Thames Path

Bankside Pier

Shakespeare's Globe

Bankside

Southwark Bridge

Railway App

London Bridge

Tooley St

Potters Fields

Crucifix La

Battle Bri La

St Thomas St

BERMONDSEY

Tanner St

Tower Bridge Rd

Grange Rd

Abbey St

Bermondsey Market

Rothsay St

Law St

Bermondsey St

Guy St

Snowsfields

Weston St

Long La

Kipling St

Crosby Row

Newcomen St

Great Dover St

Southwark Cathedral

Borough Market

Borough High St

Stoney St

Ayres St

Redcross Way

Tabard St

Trinity St

Swan St

Harper Rd

Great Guildford St

New Globe Walk

Sumner St

Holland St

Hopton St

Southwark St

Southwark Bridge Rd

SOUTHWARK

Union St

Copperfield St

Great Suffolk St

Glasshill St

Lant St

Borough

Newington Causeway

Elephant & Castle

London Rd

Borough Rd

Webber St

Lancaster St

Surrey Row

Garden Row

Blackfriars Rd

Rennie St

Paris Garden

Hatfields

Duchy St

Upper Ground

Coin St

Stamford St

Upper Ground

Meymott St

Joan St

Roupell St

Theed St

Waterloo East

The Cut

Waterloo Rd

Southwark

BOROUGH

Waterloo Rd

Imperial War Museum

St George's Rd

Westminster Bridge Rd

Lambeth Rd

Cosser St

Kennington Rd

Lambeth North

LAMBETH

Carlisle La

Royal Vauxhall Tavern (0.75mi); Secret Intelligence Services (0.75mi)

Lambeth Palace Rd

Archbishop's Park

Westminster Bridge Rd

York Rd

Addington St

Lower Marsh

Baylis Rd

Waterloo

SOUTH BANK

Pearman St

Morley St

Coral St

Hungerford Bridge & Golden Jubilee Bridge

Jubilee Gardens

London Eye

Belvedere Rd

Hayward Gallery

Southbank Centre

Waterloo Rd

South Bank

⊙ Top Sights
1 Borough Market E2
2 Imperial War Museum C4
3 London Eye A2
4 Shakespeare's Globe D1
5 Southbank Centre A2
6 Southwark Cathedral E1
7 Tate Modern D1

⊙ Sights
8 HMS Belfast G1
9 London Dungeon A3
10 Millennium Bridge D1
11 Roupell St B2
12 Shard F2

⊙ Activities, Courses & Tours
13 London Bicycle Tour B4

⊙ Sleeping
14 CitizenM London Bankside D2
15 Hoxton Southwark C2
Shangri-La Hotel at the Shard ...... (see 12)

⊗ Eating
16 Anchor & Hope C2
Padella .... (see 1)
Skylon .... (see 25)

⊙ Drinking & Nightlife
17 George Inn E2
18 Kings Arms B2
19 Lyaness C1
Queen Elizabeth Hall Roof
Garden .... (see 24)
Seabird .... (see 15)

⊙ Entertainment
20 BFI Southbank B1
21 Bridge Theatre G2
22 National Theatre B1
23 Old Vic B3
24 Queen Elizabeth Hall A1
25 Royal Festival Hall A2
26 Young Vic C2

⊙ Shopping
27 Southbank Centre Book Market A1

London Dungeon AMUSEMENT PARK
(Map p84; ☎0333 321 2001; www.thedungeons.
com/london; County Hall, Westminster Bridge Rd,
SE1; adult/child £30/24; ⊙10am-4pm; ⓤWater-
loo or Westminster) A scary tour of London's
gruesome history awaits. Expect darkness,
sudden loud noises, flashing lights, squirts
of unspecified liquid and unpleasant smells
as you shuffle through themed rooms where
actors, often covered in fake blood, tell
creepy stories and goad visitors. It's spooky,
interactive and fun if you like jumping out
of your skin. Pre-booking tickets online is essential. It takes around 90 minutes to work
your way through. Not suitable for young
children.

Shard VIEWPOINT
(Map p84; ☎0844 499 7111; www.theview
fromtheshard.com; Joiner St, SE1; adult/child from
£25/20; ⓤLondon Bridge) Puncturing the skies
above London, the dramatic splinter-like
form of the Shard has become an icon of
the city and is one of the tallest buildings
in Europe. The scene from the 244m-high
viewing platforms on floors 69 and 72 is like
none other in town, but it comes at an equally lofty price; book online in advance for a
potential discount. Premium tickets come
with a good-weather guarantee, meaning
you might be able to return for free. Check
online for opening hours, which vary depending on events.

HMS Belfast SHIP
(Map p84; www.iwm.org.uk/visits/hms-belfast;
Queen's Walk, SE1; adult/child £19/9.50; ⊙10am-
4pm; ⓤLondon Bridge) HMS *Belfast* is a
magnet for kids of all ages. This large, light
cruiser – launched in 1938 – served in WWII,
helping to sink the Nazi battleship *Sand*
shelling the Normandy coast on D-Day, and
in the Korean War. Its 6in guns could bom-
bard a target 12 miles distant. Displays offer
great insight into what life on board was
like, in peacetime and during military en-
gagements. Excellent audio guides, included
in the admission fee, feature anecdotes from
former crew members.

⊙ Kensington & Hyde Park

★**Natural History Museum** MUSEUM
(Map p86; www.nhm.ac.uk; Cromwell Rd, SW7;
⊙10am-5.50pm; ⓐ; ⓤSouth Kensington) FREE
On a vast 5.7 hectare plot and housing 80
million specimens, this colossal and magnificent building is infused with the irrepressible Victorian spirit of collecting, cataloguing
and interpreting the natural world. The
Dinosaurs Gallery (Blue Zone) is a must
for children, who gawp at the animatronic
T-rex. Adults will love the intriguing Treasures exhibition in the **Cadogan Gallery**
(Green Zone), which displays a host of un-
related objects, each telling its own unique

Knightsbridge, South Kensington & Chelsea

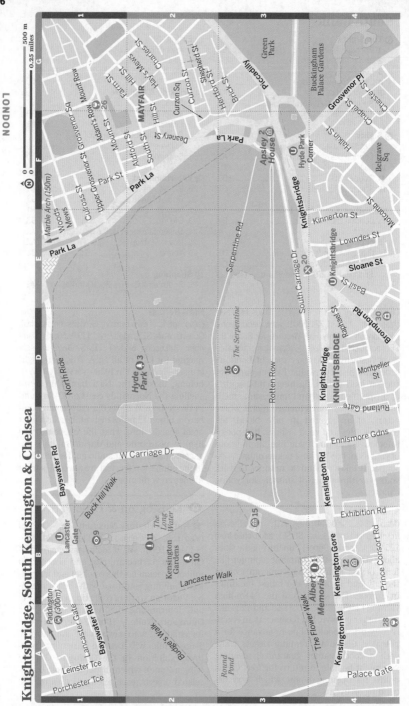

500 m
0.25 miles

Marble Arch (150m)
Paddington (300m)

MAYFAIR

Mount Row
Adam's Row
Farm St
Hill St
Hay's Mews
Charles St
Grosvenor Sq
Culross St
Upper Grosvenor St
Mount St
Aldford St
South St
Deanery St
Hill St
Curzon St
Shepherd St
Curzon Sq
Hertford St
Brick St
Shepherd St
Piccadilly
Green Park
Buckingham Palace Gardens
Grosvenor Pl
Chester St
Chapel St
Halkin St
Belgrave Sq

Park La
Park La
Park La

Apsley House
Hyde Park Corner
Knightsbridge

Kinnerton St
Lowndes St
Sloane St
Basil St
Motcomb St

Woods Mews

North Ride

Hyde Park

The Serpentine

Serpentine Rd

South Carriage Dr

Knightsbridge
KNIGHTSBRIDGE

Rotten Row

Rutland Gate
Montpelier St
Raphael St
Brompton Rd
Ennismore Gdns
Kensington Rd

Bayswater Rd

W Carriage Dr

Buck Hill Walk

The Long Water

Kensington Gardens

Lancaster Walk

Lancaster Gate
Lancaster Gate

Exhibition Rd

Kensington Gore

Albert Memorial

The Flower Walk

Kensington Rd
Kensington Rd

Prince Consort Rd

Leinster Tce
Porchester Tce

Bayswater Rd
Bayswater Rd

Budge's Walk

Round Pond

Palace Gate

LONDON

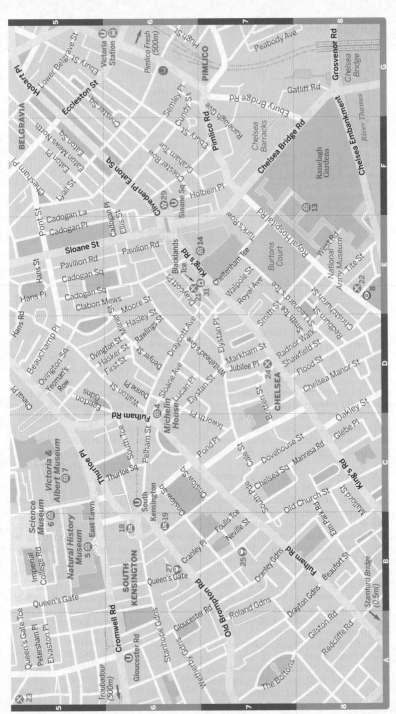

Knightsbridge, South Kensington & Chelsea

story, from a chunk of moon rock to a dodo skeleton.

Also in the Green Zone, the **Mineral Gallery** is a breathtaking display of architectural perspective leading to the **Vault**, where you'll find the **Aurora Collection** of almost 300 coloured diamonds. In the Orange Zone, the vast **Darwin Centre** focuses on taxonomy, showcasing 28 million insects and six million plants in a giant cocoon; glass windows allow you to watch scientists at work.

At the centre of the museum is **Hintze Hall**, which resembles a cathedral nave – quite fitting, as it was built in a time when the natural sciences were challenging the biblical tenets of Christian orthodoxy. The colossal blue whale skeleton you see on entering the hall has replaced the famous cast of a diplodocus skeleton (nicknamed Dippy), which has gone on a long tour of the UK. The transfer itself was a painstaking engineering project, disassembling and preparing the whale's 4.5 tonnes of bones for reconstruction in a dramatic diving posture that greets museum visitors.

The NHM hosts regular exhibitions (admission fees apply), some of them on a recurrent basis. **Wildlife Photographer of the Year** (adult/child £13.95/8.25, family £29-39.50; ◎ Oct-Dec), for example, with its show-stopping images, has been going since 1964.

A slice of English countryside in SW7, the beautiful **Wildlife Garden** (April to November), next to the West Lawn, encompasses a range of British lowland habitats, including a meadow with farm gates and a bee tree where a colony of honey bees fills the air.

The museum is transforming its outdoor spaces, enlarging the Wildlife Garden and creating a piazza in the eastern grounds.

From Halloween to January, a section of the museum by the East Lawn is transformed into a glittering and highly popular **ice rink**, complete with a hot-drinks stall. Book your slot well ahead.

More than five million visitors head to the museum each year, so queues can often get long, especially during the school holidays. Avoid the queues at the congested main Cromwell Rd entrance by aiming for the Exhibition Rd entrance round the corner.

The best time to come on weekdays is after 2pm when school groups leave; at weekends it's best to arrive as soon as it opens.

★**Victoria & Albert Museum**   MUSEUM
(V&A; Map p86; ☎ 020-7942 2000; www.vam. ac.uk; Cromwell Rd, SW7; ◎10am-5.45pm Sat-Thu, to 10pm Fri; ⏺ South Kensington) FREE The Museum of Manufactures, as the V&A was

known when it opened in 1852, was part of Prince Albert's legacy to the nation in the aftermath of the successful Great Exhibition of 1851. It houses the world's largest collection of decorative arts, from Asian ceramics to Middle Eastern rugs, Chinese paintings, Western furniture, fashion from all ages and modern-day domestic appliances. The (ticketed) temporary exhibitions are another highlight, covering anything from David Bowie to Mary Quant retrospectives, car design, special materials and trends. See more on p90.

⭐**Science Museum**   MUSEUM
(Map p86; ☑0333 241 4000, 020-7942 4000; www.sciencemuseum.org.uk; Exhibition Rd, SW7; ◉10am-6pm, last entry 5.15pm; 👪; Ⓤ South Kensington) FREE This scientifically spellbinding museum will mesmerise adults and children alike, with its interactive and educational exhibits covering everything from early technology to space travel. On the ground floor, a perennial favourite is **Exploring Space**, a gallery featuring genuine rockets and satellites and a full-size replica of the *Eagle,* the lander that took Neil Armstrong and Buzz Aldrin to the moon in 1969. The **Making the Modern World Gallery** next door is a visual feast of locomotives, planes, cars and other revolutionary inventions.

⭐**Hyde Park**   PARK
(Map p86; www.royalparks.org.uk/parks/hyde-park; ◉5am-midnight; Ⓤ Marble Arch, Hyde Park Corner, Knightsbridge, Queensway) Hyde Park is central London's largest green space, expropriated from the church in 1536 by Henry VIII and turned into a hunting ground and later a venue for duels, executions and horse racing. The 1851 Great Exhibition was held here, and during WWII the park became a vast potato field. These days, it's a place to stroll and picnic, boat on the **Serpentine lake** (Map p86; ☑020-7262 1330; Ⓤ Lancaster Gate, Knightsbridge), or catch a summer concert or outdoor film during the warmer months.

⭐**Kensington Palace**   PALACE
(Map p92; www.hrp.org.uk/kensington-palace; Kensington Gardens, W8; adult/child £21.50/10.70, cheaper weekdays after 2pm; ◉10am-6pm, to 4pm Nov-Feb; Ⓤ High St Kensington) Built in 1605, Kensington Palace became the favourite royal residence under William and Mary of Orange in 1689, and remained so until George III became king and relocated to Bucking-

ham Palace. Today, it remains a residence for high-ranking royals, including the Duke and Duchess of Cambridge (Prince William and his wife Kate). A large part of the palace is open to the public, however, including the King's and Queen's State Apartments.

Royal Albert Hall   HISTORIC BUILDING
(Map p86; ☑0845 401 5034, box office 020-7589 8212; www.royalalberthall.com; Kensington Gore, SW7; tours adult/child from £14.25/7.25; ◉tours from 10am; Ⓤ South Kensington) Built in 1871, thanks in part to the proceeds of the 1851 Great Exhibition organised by Prince Albert (Queen Victoria's husband), this huge, domed, red-brick amphitheatre, adorned with a frieze of Minton tiles, is Britain's most famous concert venue and home to the BBC's Promenade Concerts (the Proms) every summer. To find out about the hall's intriguing history and royal connections, and to gaze out from the Gallery, book an informative one-hour front-of-house **grand tour** (Map p86; ☑020-7589 8212; adult/child £14.25/7.25; ◉hourly 9.30am-4.30pm Apr-Oct, 10am-4pm Nov-Mar), operating most days.

⭐**Apsley House**   HISTORIC BUILDING
(Map p86; ☑020-7499 5676; www.english-heritage. org.uk/visit/places/apsley-house; 149 Piccadilly, Hyde Park Corner, W1; adult/child £10.50/6.30, with Wellington Arch £13.60/8.20; ◉11am-5pm Wed-Sun Apr-Oct, 10am-4pm Sat & Sun Nov-Mar; Ⓤ Hyde Park Corner) This stunning house, containing exhibits about the Duke of Wellington, who defeated Napoleon Bonaparte at Waterloo, was once the first building to appear when entering London from the west and was therefore known as 'No 1 London'. Wellington memorabilia, including the Duke's death mask, fills the **basement gallery**, while an astonishing collection of china and silver, and paintings by Velasquez, Rubens, Van Dyck, Brueghel, Murillo and Goya awaits in the 1st-floor **Waterloo Gallery**, which runs the length of the building's west flank.

Kensington Gardens   PARK
(Map p86; ☑0300 061 2000; www.royalparks. org.uk/parks/kensington-gardens; ◉6am-dusk; Ⓤ Queensway or Lancaster Gate) A delightful collection of manicured lawns, tree-shaded avenues and basins immediately west of Hyde Park, the picturesque expanse of Kensington Gardens is technically part of Kensington Palace, located in the far west of the gardens. The large **Round Pond** in front of the palace is enjoyable to amble around.

Victoria & Albert Museum

HALF-DAY HIGHLIGHTS TOUR

The art- and design-packed V&A is vast: we have devised an easy-to-follow tour of the museum highlights to help cover some signature pieces while also allowing you to appreciate some of the grandeur of the museum architecture.

Enter the V&A by the main entrance off Cromwell Rd and immediately turn left to explore the Islamic Middle East Gallery and to discover the sumptuous silk-and-wool **1 Ardabil Carpet**. Among the pieces from South Asia in the adjacent gallery is the terrifying automated **2 Tipu's Tiger**. Continue to the outstanding **3 Fashion Gallery** with its displays of clothing styles through the ages. The magnificent gallery opposite houses the **4 Raphael Cartoons**, large paintings by Raphael used to weave tapestries for the Vatican. Take the stairs to level 2 and the Britain 1500–1760 Gallery; turn

Raphael Cartoons
These seven drawings by Raphael, depicting the acts of St Peter and St Paul, were the full-scale preparatory works for seven tapestries that were woven for the Sistine Chapel in the Vatican.

Fashion Gallery
With clothing from the 18th century to the present day, this circular and chronologically arranged gallery showcases evening wear, undergarments and iconic fashion milestones, such as 1960s dresses designed by Mary Quant.

Great Bed of Ware
Created during the reign of Queen Elizabeth I, its headboard and bedposts are etched with ancient graffiti; the 16th-century oak Great Bed of Ware is famously name-dropped in Shakespeare's *Twelfth Night*.

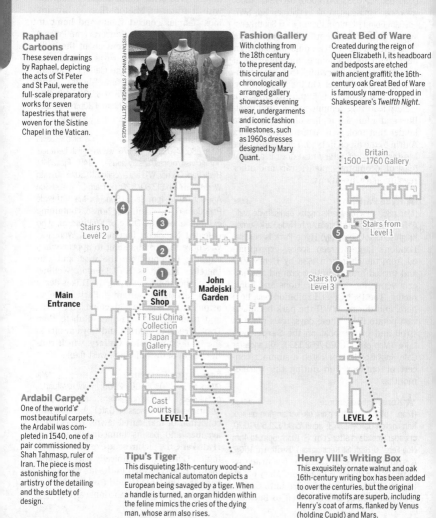

TRISTAN FEWINGS / STRINGER / GETTY IMAGES ©

Ardabil Carpet
One of the world's most beautiful carpets, the Ardabil was completed in 1540, one of a pair commissioned by Shah Tahmasp, ruler of Iran. The piece is most astonishing for the artistry of the detailing and the subtlety of design.

Tipu's Tiger
This disquieting 18th-century wood-and-metal mechanical automaton depicts a European being savaged by a tiger. When a handle is turned, an organ hidden within the feline mimics the cries of the dying man, whose arm also rises.

Henry VIII's Writing Box
This exquisitely ornate walnut and oak 16th-century writing box has been added to over the centuries, but the original decorative motifs are superb, including Henry's coat of arms, flanked by Venus (holding Cupid) and Mars.

left in the gallery to find the **⑤ Great Bed of Ware**, beyond which rests the exquisitely crafted artistry of **⑥ Henry VIII's Writing Box**. Head up the stairs into the Ironwork Gallery on level 3 for the **⑦ Hereford Screen**. Continue through the Ironwork and Sculpture Galleries and through the Leighton Corridor to the glittering **⑧ Jewellery Gallery**. Exit through the Stained Glass Gallery, at the end of which you'll find stairs back down to level 1.

LAPAS77 / SHUTTERSTOCK ©

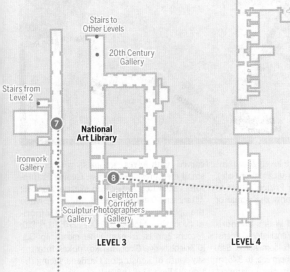

Stairs to
Other Levels

20th Century
Gallery

Stairs from
Level 2

⑦

**National
Art Library**

Ironwork
Gallery

⑧

Leighton
Corridor

Sculptur Photographers
Gallery Gallery

LEVEL 3

LEVEL 4

Jewellery Gallery
The beautifully illuminated Jewellery Gallery has a stunning collection of items from ancient Greece to the modern day, including a dazzling gold Celtic breastplate, art-nouveau jewellery and animals fashioned by Fabergé.

©AID KORNSILAPA / SHUTTERSTOCK ©

Hereford Screen
Designed by George Gilbert Scott, this awe-inspiring choir screen is a labour of love, originally fashioned for Hereford Cathedral. It's an almighty conception of wood, iron, copper, brass and hardstone, and there were few parts of the V&A that could support its great mass.

Notting Hill & Baywater

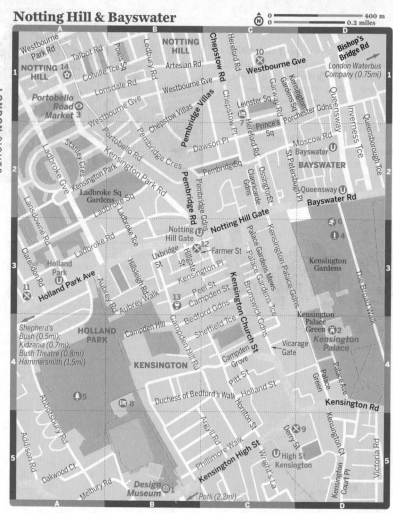

Also worth a look are the lovely fountains in the **Italian Gardens** (U Lancaster Gate), believed to be a gift from Prince Albert to Queen Victoria; they are now the venue of a cafe.

The **Diana, Princess of Wales Memorial Playground** (Map p92; Kensington Gardens; ☉10am-7.45pm May-Aug, to 6.45pm Apr & Sep, to 5.45pm March & Oct, to 4.45pm Feb, to 3.45pm Nov-Jan; ☒; U Queensway), in the northwest corner of the gardens, has some pretty ambitious attractions for children. Next to the playground stands the delightful **Elfin Oak** (Map p92), a 900-year-old tree stump

carved with elves, gnomes, witches and small creatures. To the east, George Frampton's celebrated **Peter Pan statue** (Map p86; U Lancaster Gate) is close to the lake, while the opulent and elaborate **Albert Memorial** (Map p86; ☑ tours 0300 061 2270; tours £10; ☉ tours 2pm 1st Fri every other month, Apr-Oct; U Knightsbridge, Gloucester Rd) pokes into the sky south of Kensington Gardens, facing the Royal Albert Hall (p89).

Chelsea Physic Garden   GARDENS
(Map p86; ☑ 020-7352 5646; www.chelseaphysic garden.co.uk; 66 Royal Hospital Rd, SW3; adult/

Notting Hill & Bayswater

child under 15/family £9.50/8.50/37; ◷ Mon-Fri & Sun 11am-5pm, to 4pm Nov-Feb; U Sloane Sq) You may bump into a wandering duck or two as you enter this walled pocket of botanical enchantment, established by the Apothecaries' Society in 1673 for students working on medicinal plants and healing. One of Europe's oldest of its kind, the small grounds are a compendium of botany, from carnivorous pitcher plants to rich yellow flag irises, a cork oak from Portugal, the largest outdoor fruiting olive tree in the British Isles and rare trees and shrubs.

Royal Hospital Chelsea   MUSEUM
(Map p86; ✎ tours 020-7881 5493; www.chelsea-pensioners.co.uk; Royal Hospital Rd, SW3; ◷ grounds 10am-5pm, Great Hall 10am-noon & 2-4pm, museum 10am-4pm Mon-Fri; U Sloane Sq) FREE Designed by Christopher Wren, this superb structure was built in 1692 to provide shelter for ex-servicemen. Since the reign of Charles II, it has housed hundreds of war veterans, known as Chelsea Pensioners. They're fondly regarded as national treasures, and cut striking figures in the dark-blue greatcoats (in winter) or scarlet frock coats (in summer) that they wear on ceremonial occasions.

Serpentine Gallery   GALLERY
(Map p86; ✎ 020-7402 6075; www.serpentinegalleries.org; Kensington Gardens, W2; ◷ 10am-6pm Tue-Sun; U Lancaster Gate or Knightsbridge) FREE This gallery is one of London's most important contemporary-art galleries. Damien Hirst, Andreas Gursky, Louise Bourgeois, Gabriel Orozco, Tomoko Takahashi and Jeff Koons have all exhibited here. A leading architect (who has never built in the UK) is annually commissioned to build a new 'Summer Pavilion' nearby, open from June to October. The galleries run a full program of readings, talks and workshops. Sister space the Serpentine Sackler Gallery, designed by Zaha Hadid, is a few minutes away over the bridge.

◉ Clerkenwell, Shoreditch & Spitalfields

★**Whitechapel Gallery**   GALLERY
(Map p76; ✎ 020-7522 7888; www.whitechapelgallery.org; 77-82 Whitechapel High St, E1; ◷ 11am-6pm Tue, Wed & Fri-Sun, to 9pm Thu; U Aldgate East) FREE A firm favourite of art students and the avant-garde cognoscenti, this ground-breaking gallery doesn't have a permanent collection but is devoted to hosting edgy exhibitions of contemporary art. It made its name by staging exhibitions by both established and emerging artists, including the first UK shows by Pablo Picasso, Jackson Pollock, Mark Rothko and Frida Kahlo. The gallery's ambitiously themed shows change every couple of months (check online) and there's also often live music, talks and films on Thursday evenings.

Museum of the Home   MUSEUM
(Map p120; ✎ 020-7739 9893; www.museumofthehome.org.uk; 136 Kingsland Rd, E2; ◷ 10am-5pm Tue-Sun; U Hoxton) FREE These beautiful ivy-clad brick almshouses (closed until 2021 for renovations at the time of research), were built in 1714 as a home for poor pensioners. Two rooms have been furnished to show how residents lived in the 1770s and 1880s, atmospherically lit by candles and the original gas lamps. The attention to detail is impressive, down to the vintage newspaper left open on the breakfast table.

★**Dennis Severs' House**   HISTORIC BUILDING
(Map p120; ✎ 020-7247 4013; www.dennissevershouse.co.uk; 18 Folgate St, E1; day/night £10/15; ◷ noon-2pm & 5-9pm Mon, 5-9pm Wed & Fri, noon-4pm Sun; U Liverpool St) This extraordinary

Georgian house is set up as if its occupants – a family of Huguenot silk weavers – have just walked out the door. Each of the 10 rooms is stuffed with the minutiae of everyday life from centuries past: half-drunk cups of tea, emptied but gleaming wet oyster shells and, in perhaps unnecessary attention to detail, a used chamber pot by the bed. It's more an immersive experience than a traditional museum; explorations of the house are conducted in silence.

Old Truman Brewery   HISTORIC BUILDING
(Map p120; ☑020-7770 6000; www.truman brewery.com; Brick Lane, E1; Ⓤ Shoreditch High St) Founded here in the 17th century, Truman's Black Eagle Brewery was, by the 1850s, the largest brewery in the world. Spread over a series of brick buildings and yards straddling both sides of Brick Lane, the complex is now completely given over to edgy markets, pop-up fashion stores, vintage clothes shops, cafes and bars – it's at its busy best when market stalls are set up on Sundays.

Beer may not be brewed here any more, but it certainly is consumed.

◉ East London

★Museum of London Docklands   MUSEUM
(☑020-7001 9844; www.museumoflondon.co. uk/docklands; West India Quay, E14; ⊘10am-6pm; ⓊDLR West India Quay) FREE Housed in an 1802 warehouse, this educational museum combines artefacts and multimedia displays to chart the history of the city through its river and docks. The best strategy is to begin on the 3rd floor and work your way down through the ages. Perhaps the most illuminating and certainly the most disturbing gallery is London, Sugar and Slavery, which examines the capital's role in the transatlantic slave trade.

★Columbia Road Flower Market   MARKET
(Map p120; www.columbiaroad.info; Columbia Rd, E2; ⊘8am-3pm Sun; ⓊHoxton) A wonderful explosion of colour and life, this weekly market sells a beautiful array of flowers, pot plants,

---

LONDON FOR (ALMOST) FREE

Sights It usually costs nothing to visit the Houses of Parliament (p69) if you're going to watch debates. Another institution of public life, the Changing of the Guard at Buckingham Palace (p76), is free to watch. For one weekend in September, Open House London (p105) opens the doors to some 850 buildings for free.

Museums & Galleries The permanent collections of all state-funded museums and galleries are open to the public free of charge. They include the V&A (p88), Tate Modern (p79), British Museum (p68) and National Gallery (p69). The Saatchi Gallery (Map p86; www.saatchigallery.com; Duke of York's HQ, King's Rd, SW3; ⊘10am-6pm; ⓊSloane Sq) FREE is also free.

Views Why pay good money when some of the finest viewpoints in London are free? Head up to Level 10 of Switch House at Tate Modern (p79) or the Sky Gardens atop the Walkie Talkie (p78).

Concerts A number of churches usually offer free lunchtime classical music concerts. Try St Martin-in-the-Fields (p69), St James's Piccadilly (Map p66; ☑020-7734 4511; www.sjp.org.uk; 197 Piccadilly, W1; ⊘8am-8pm; ⓊPiccadilly Circus), Temple Church (Map p76; ☑020-7353 3470; www.templechurch.com; King's Bench Walk, EC4; adult/child £5/3; ⊘10am-4pm Mon, Tue, Thu & Fri, 2-4pm Wed, hours & days vary; ⓊTemple) and St Alfege Church (☑020-8853 0687; www.st-alfege.org; Greenwich Church St, SE10; ⊘11am-4pm Mon-Sat, from noon Sun; ⓊCutty Sark).

Walks Walking around town is possibly the best way to get a sense of the city and its history. Roam through Hampstead Heath (p97) in North London, follow the Thames along the South Bank, or just walk from A to B in the compact West End.

Low-Cost Transport Bike-share your way around through Santander Cycles (p139) – the access fee is £2 for 24 hours; bike hire is then free for the first 30 minutes. Travel as much as you like on London Transport with a one-day Travelcard or an Oyster Card.

REGENT'S CANAL

The towpath of the tranquil **Regent's Canal** (Map p128; https://canalrivertrust.org.uk/enjoy-the-waterways/canal-and-river-network/regents-canal) makes an excellent shortcut across North London, either on foot or by bike. In full, the ribbon of water runs 9 miles from Little Venice (where it connects with the Grand Union Canal) to the Thames at Limehouse.

You can make do with walking from Little Venice to Camden Town in less than an hour, passing Regent's Park and London Zoo, as well as beautiful villas designed by architect John Nash and redevelopments of old industrial buildings. Allow 25 to 30 minutes between Little Venice and Regent's Park, and 15 to 20 minutes between Regent's Park and Camden Town. There are plenty of well-signed exits along the way.

If you decide to continue on, it's worth stopping at the **London Canal Museum** (☑020-7713 0836; www.canalmuseum.org.uk; 12-13 New Wharf Rd, N1; adult/child £5/2.50; ⊙10am-4.30pm Fri-Sun; Ⓤ King's Cross St Pancras) in King's Cross to learn more about the canal's history. Shortly afterwards you'll hit the 878m-long Islington Tunnel and have to take to the roads for a spell. After joining the path again near Colebrooke Row, you can follow the water all the way to the Thames at Limehouse Basin, or divert on to the Hertford Union Canal at Victoria Park and head to Queen Elizabeth Olympic Park.

bulbs, seeds and everything you might need for the garden. It's a lot of fun and the best place to hear proper Cockney barrow-boy banter ('We got flowers cheap enough for ya muvver-in-law's grave' etc). It's popular, so go as early as you can, or later on when the vendors sell off cut flowers cheaply.

★ **Queen Elizabeth Olympic Park**   PARK
(www.queenelizabetholympicpark.co.uk;   E20; Ⓤ Stratford) The glittering centrepiece of London's 2012 Olympic Games, this vast 227-hectare expanse includes the main Olympic venues as well as playgrounds, walking and cycling trails, gardens and a diverse mix of wetland, woodland, meadow and other wildlife habitats – an environmentally fertile legacy for the future. The main focal point is London Stadium (p132), now the home ground for West Ham United FC.

ArcelorMittal Orbit   TOWER
(☑0333 800 8099; www.arcelormittalorbit.com; 3 Thornton St, E20; adult/child £12.50/7.50, with slide £17.50/12.50; ⊙11am-3pm Mon-Fri, 10am-7pm Sat & Sun; Ⓤ Stratford) Turner Prize–winner Anish Kapoor's 115m-high, twisted-steel sculpture towers strikingly over the southern end of Queen Elizabeth Olympic Park. In essence it's an artwork, but at the 80m mark it also offers an impressive panorama from a mirrored viewing platform, which is accessed by a lift from the base of the sculpture (the tallest in the UK). A dramatic tunnel slide running down the tower is the world's highest and longest, coiling 178m down to ground level.

Victoria Park   PARK
(www.towerhamlets.gov.uk/victoriapark; Grove Rd, E3; ⊙7am-dusk; Ⓤ Hackney Wick) The 'Regent's Park of the East End', this 86-hectare leafy expanse of ornamental lakes, monuments, tennis courts, flower beds and lawns was opened in 1845. It was the first public park in the East End, given the go-ahead after a local MP presented Queen Victoria with a petition of 30,000 signatures. It quickly gained a reputation as the 'People's Park' when many rallies were held here.

**Viktor Wynd Museum
of Curiosities, Fine Art
& Natural History**   MUSEUM
(☑020-7998 3617; www.thelasttuesdaysociety.org; 11 Mare St, E8; £8; ⊙noon-11pm Wed-Sat, to 10pm Sun; Ⓤ Bethnal Green) Museum? Art project? Cocktail bar? This is not a venue that's easily classifiable. Inspired by Victorian-era cabinets of curiosities, Wynd's wilfully eccentric collection includes stuffed birds, pickled genitals, two-headed lambs, shrunken heads, a key to the Garden of Eden, dodo bones, celebrity excrement and a gilded hippo skull that belonged to Pablo Escobar. A self-confessed 'incoherent vision of the world displayed through wonder'; make of it what you will. Or stop by for a cocktail at the bar upstairs.

◉ North London

★ **British Library**   LIBRARY
(Map p96; ☑0330-333 1144; www.bl.uk; 96 Euston Rd, NW1; ⊙9.30am-8pm Mon-Thu, to 6pm Fri, to 5pm Sat, 11am-5pm Sun; Ⓤ King's Cross

North Central London

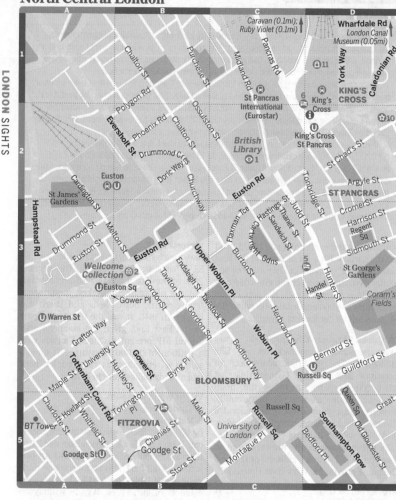

Caravan (0.1mi);
Ruby Violet (0.1mi)

Wharfdale Rd
London Canal
Museum (0.05mi)

North Central London

St Pancras) **FREE** Consisting of low-slung red-brick terraces and fronted by a large piazza with an oversized statue of Sir Isaac Newton, Colin St John Wilson's British Library building is an architectural wonder. Completed in 1998, it's home to some

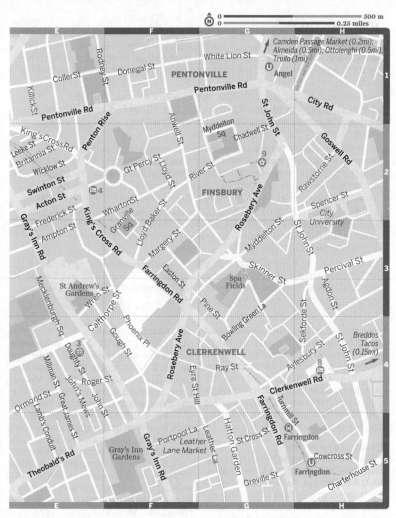

of the greatest treasures of the written word, including the *Codex Sinaiticus* (the first complete text of the New Testament), Leonardo da Vinci's notebooks and two copies of the Magna Carta (1215).

★ ZSL London Zoo   ZOO

(Map p128; ☎ 0344-225 1826; www.zsl.org/zsl-london-zoo; Outer Circle, Regent's Park, NW1; depending on date, adult £25-32.50, child £16-20.50; ☺ 10am-6pm Apr-Aug, to 5pm mid-Feb–Mar, Sep & Oct, to 4pm Nov–mid-Feb; ♿; ☐ 88, 274) Opened in 1828, London Zoo is the oldest in the world. The emphasis nowadays is firmly on conservation, breeding and education,

with fewer animals and bigger enclosures. Highlights include Land of the Lions, Gorilla Kingdom, Night Life, Penguin Beach and the walk-through In with the Lemurs . There are regular feeding sessions and talks; various experiences are available, such as Keeper for a Day; and you can even spend the night in one of nine Gir Lion Lodge cabins.

★ Hampstead Heath   PARK

(www.cityoflondon.gov.uk/things-to-do/green-spaces/hampstead-heath; ⓤ Hampstead Heath or Gospel Oak) Sprawling Hampstead Heath, with its rolling woodlands and meadows,

LONDON'S LIDOS

The capital's long-running love of outdoor bathing has enjoyed a resurgence in recent years, and its lovely lidos (outdoor pools) are busier than ever. You'll see Londoners taking to the water in pretty much all weathers – even, for the real diehards, the middle of winter.

Serpentine Lido (Map p86; 020-7706 3422; Hyde Park, W2; adult/child/family £4.80/1.80/12, after 4pm adult/child/family £4.10/1.10/9; 10am-6pm Jun-early Sep, Sat & Sun May; Hyde Park Corner, Knightsbridge) Perhaps the ultimate London pool is inside the Serpentine lake.

Hampstead Heath Ponds (www.cityoflondon.gov.uk/things-to-do/green-spaces/hampstead-heath/activities-at-hampstead-heath; Hampstead Heath, NW5; adult/child £4/1; from 7am, closing times vary with season; Hampstead Heath) Set in the midst of the gorgeous heath, the brown waters of Hampstead's three bathing ponds (men's, women's and mixed) offer a bracing dip. The water's tested daily, so don't be deterred by the colour.

London Fields Lido (020-7254 9038; www.better.org.uk/leisure-centre/london/hackney/london-fields-lido; London Fields West Side, E8; adult/child £5/3; 6.30am-9pm; London Fields) Built in the 1930s but abandoned by the '80s, this heated 50m Olympic-size outdoor pool reopened in 2006.

London Aquatics Centre (020-8536 3150; www.londonaquaticscentre.org; Carpenters Rd, E20; adult/child from £5/3; 6am-10.30pm; Stratford) Not strictly a lido as it's inside, but Zaha Hadid's award-winning Aquatics Centre, built for the 2012 Olympics, is worth mentioning for its fabulous, undulating architecture.

feels a million miles away – despite being about 3.5 miles from Trafalgar Sq. It covers 320 hectares and is home to about 180 bird species, 25 species of butterflies, grass snakes, bats and a rich array of flora. It's a wonderful place for a ramble, especially to the top of **Parliament Hill** (Hampstead Heath, Gospel Oak), which offers expansive views across flat-as-a-pancake London.

★**Highgate Cemetery** CEMETERY
(020-8340 1834; www.highgatecemetery.org; Swain's Lane, N6; adult/child £4/free; 10am-5pm Mar-Oct, to 4pm Nov-Feb; Archway) A Gothic wonderland of shrouded urns, obelisks, broken columns, sleeping angels and Egyptian-style tombs, Highgate is a Victorian Valhalla spread over 20 wonderfully wild and atmospheric hectares. On the eastern side, you can pay your respects to the graves of Karl Marx and Mary Ann Evans (better known as novelist George Eliot). The real highlight, however, is the overgrown **West Cemetery**, which can only be visited on a **guided tour** (020-8340 1834; www.highgatecemetery.org; Swain's Lane, N6; adult/child £12/6; 1.45pm Mon-Fri, every 30min 10.30am-3pm Sat & Sun Nov-Feb, to 4pm Sat & Sun Mar-Oct; Archway). Tours of the East Cemetery (adult/child £8/4) depart at 2pm some Saturdays.

★**Wellcome Collection** MUSEUM
(Map p96; 020-7611 2222; www.wellcomecollection.org; 183 Euston Rd, NW1; 10am-6pm Tue, Wed & Fri-Sun, to 9pm Thu; Euston Sq or Euston) FREE Under a new director Melanie Keen (appointed in 2019), Wellcome Collection committed to addressing the challenges of its less enlightened beginnings. The museum focuses on the interface of art, science and medicine. At its heart is Sir Henry Wellcome's collection of (at times controversial) medical curiosities (saws for amputation, forceps through the ages, sex aids and amulets...). Beyond the permanent galleries, there are absorbing temporary exhibitions, plus a great cafe and a fantastic shop.

Regent's Park PARK
(www.royalparks.org.uk/parks/the-regents-park; 5am-dusk; Regent's Park or Baker St) The largest and most elaborate of central London's many Royal Parks, Regent's Park is one of the capital's loveliest green spaces. Among its many attractions are London Zoo (p97), Regent's Canal (p95), an ornamental lake, and sports pitches where locals meet to play football, rugby and volleyball. **Queen Mary's Gardens**, towards the south of the park, are particularly pretty, especially in June when the roses are in bloom. Performances take place here in an **open-air theatre** (0333 400 3562; www.openair

theatre.org; ⊙ May-Sep; 🚻; U Baker St) during summer.

Abbey Road Studios   HISTORIC BUILDING
(☏020-7266 7000; www.abbeyroad.com; 3 Abbey Rd, NW8; U St John's Wood) Beatles aficionados can't possibly visit London without making a pilgrimage to this famous recording studio in St John's Wood. The studios themselves are off-limits, so you'll have to content yourself with examining the decades of fan graffiti on the fence outside. Stop-start local traffic is long accustomed to groups of tourists lining up on the zebra crossing to re-enact the cover of the fab four's 1969 masterpiece *Abbey Road*. In 2010 the crossing was rewarded with Grade II heritage status.

For a strangely engrossing real-time view of the crossing, hit the 'Visit' tab for the webcam on the studio's website; you can even find your own crossing shot by punching in your time. To reach Abbey Road Studios, take the tube to St John's Wood, cross the road, follow Grove End Rd to its end and turn right. Don't do what some disappointed fans do and head to Abbey Rd Station in West Ham in London's distant East End – it's no relation to the true site and miles off course. There are at least 10 Abbey Rds in London, adding to confusion.

Primrose Hill   PARK
(Map p128; U Chalk Farm) On summer weekends, Primrose Hill park is absolutely packed with locals enjoying a picnic and the extraordinary views over the city skyline. Come weekdays, however, and there are mostly just dog walkers and nannies. It's a lovely place to enjoy a quiet stroll or an alfresco lunch.

⊙ Greenwich

★ National Maritime Museum   MUSEUM
(☏020-8312 6565; www.rmg.co.uk/national-maritime-museum; Romney Rd, SE10; ⊙10am-5pm; 🚻; U Cutty Sark) FREE Narrating the long, briny and eventful history of seafaring Britain, this excellent museum has three floors of engrossing exhibits. Highlights include JMW Turner's huge oil painting *Battle of Trafalgar* (1824), the 19m-long gilded state barge built in 1732 for the prince of Wales, and the colourful figureheads installed on the ground floor. Families will love the children's galleries, as well as the Great Map splayed out near the upper-floor cafe.

On the 1st floor, **Atlantic Worlds** and **Traders** look back on Britain's role in the transatlantic slave trade and commerce with the East in the 19th century. One floor up, **Nelson, Navy, Nation** focuses on the history of the Royal Navy during the conflict-ridden 17th century and even includes the coat in which Nelson was fatally wounded during the Battle of Trafalgar, with a musket-ball hole in the left shoulder. The **Exploration Wing**, opened in 2018, contains four galleries: Pacific Encounters, Polar Worlds, Tudor and Stuart Seafarers, and Sea Things, devoted to indigenous maritime civilisations, European exploration and human endeavour.

★ Royal Observatory   MUSEUM
(☏020-8312 6565; www.rmg.co.uk/royal-observatory; Greenwich Park, Blackheath Ave, SE10; adult/child £16/8; ⊙10am-5pm Sep-Jun, to 6pm Jul & Aug; U Greenwich or Cutty Sark) Rising like a beacon of time atop **Greenwich Park** (www.royalparks.org.uk/parks/greenwich-park; ⊙6am-sunset; U Greenwich, Maze Hill or Cutty Sark), the Royal Observatory is home to the prime meridian (longitude 0° 0' 0"). Tickets include access to the Christopher Wren–designed **Flamsteed House** (named after the first Royal Astronomer) and the **Meridian Courtyard**, where you can stand with your feet straddling the eastern and western hemispheres. You can also see the Great Equatorial Telescope (1893) inside the onion-domed **observatory** and explore space and time in the **Weller Astronomy Galleries**.

In a small brick structure next to the Meridian Courtyard, the astonishing **camera obscura** projects a live image of Queen's House – as well as the people moving around it and the boats on the Thames behind – onto a table. Enter through the thick, light-dimming curtains and close them behind you to keep the room as dark as possible.

Night-sky shows are projected daily on the inside of the roof of the **Peter Harrison Planetarium** (☏020-8858 4422; www.rmg.co.uk/whats-on/planetarium-shows; adult/child £10/5; 🚻).

The Royal Observatory was built by order of Charles II in 1675 to help solve the riddle of longitude. In 1884, Greenwich was designated as the prime meridian of the world, and Greenwich Mean Time (GMT) became the universal measurement of standard time.

★ Old Royal
Naval College   HISTORIC BUILDING
(https://ornc.org; SE10; ⊙8am-11pm; Ⓤ Cutty Sark) FREE Home to the University of Greenwich and Trinity Laban Conservatoire of Music and Dance, the Christopher Wren–designed Old Royal Naval College is a masterpiece of baroque architecture. The sprawling grounds are open to the public, as well as the recently restored Painted Hall (✆ 020-8269 4799; www.ornc.org; adult/child £12/free; ⊙10am-5pm), nicknamed the 'Sistine Chapel of the UK' and covered from floor to ceiling with extraordinary 18th-century art, and the neoclassical Chapel of St Peter and St Paul (✆ 020-8269 4788; ⊙10am-5pm) FREE. Tours of the grounds are included in the price of the Painted Hall ticket.

Queen's House   GALLERY
(✆ 020-8312 6565; www.rmg.co.uk/queenshouse; Romney Rd, SE10; ⊙10am-5pm; Ⓤ Cutty Sark) FREE Designed by architect Inigo Jones, Queen's House was the UK's first classical building, and it's as enticing for its form as for its art collection. Many pieces on display are portraits and have an unsurprising maritime bent; don't miss the iconic *Armada Portrait of Elizabeth I*, which depicts the queen in a vibrantly coloured lace and jewelled gown and commemorates the failed invasion of England by the Spanish in 1588. It's in the immaculately restored Queen's Presence Chamber on the 1st floor.

Cutty Sark   SHIP
(✆ 020-8312 6565; www.rmg.co.uk/cuttysark; King William Walk, SE10; adult/child £15/7.50; ⊙10am-5pm; Ⓤ Cutty Sark) The last of the great clipper ships to sail between China and England in the 19th century, the *Cutty Sark* was launched in 1869 and carried almost 4.5 million kg of tea in just seven years of service. Nearly a century later, it was dry-docked in Greenwich and opened to the public. Films, interactive maps, illustrations and props give an idea of what life on board was like. Book online.

◉ Brixton, Peckham
& South London

★ Imperial War Museum   MUSEUM
(Map p84; ✆ 020-7416 5000; www.iwm.org.uk; Lambeth Rd, SE1; ⊙10am-6pm; Ⓤ Lambeth North) FREE Fronted by an intimidating pair of 15in

naval guns and a piece of the Berlin Wall, this riveting museum is housed in what was the Bethlem Royal Hospital, a psychiatric facility also known as Bedlam. Although the museum's focus is on military action involving British or Commonwealth troops, largely during the 20th century, it also covers war in the wider sense. Must-see exhibits include the state-of-the-art First World War galleries and Witnesses to War in the forecourt and atrium.

In Witnesses to War, you'll find huge remnants of war, from a Battle of Britain Spitfire and a towering German V-2 rocket to a Reuters Land Rover damaged by rocket attack in Gaza in 2006.

The 1st-floor exhibition Turning Points: 1934–1945 takes a look at WWII through a series of poignant objects, including the casing made for the 'Little Boy' atomic bomb and a trunk sent by Jewish parents to their children who had already escaped from Nazi persecution to the UK. Peace and Security: 1945–2014 on the 2nd floor dives into more recent events. The 3rd floor is given over to Curiosities of War, a mix of unexpected creations and artefacts from times of conflict, and temporary exhibitions.

One of the most challenging sections is the extensive and harrowing The Holocaust exhibition (not recommended for children under 14); its entrance is on the 4th floor.

◉ West London

★ Portobello Road Market   MARKET
(Map p92; www.portobellomarket.org; Portobello Rd, W10; ⊙9am-6pm Mon-Wed, to 7pm Fri & Sat, to 1pm Thu; Ⓤ Notting Hill Gate or Ladbroke Grove) Lovely on a warm summer's day, Portobello Road Market is an iconic London attraction with an eclectic mix of street food, fruit and veg, antiques, curios, collectables, fashion and trinkets. The shops along Portobello Rd open daily and the fruit-and-veg stalls (from Elgin Cres to Talbot Rd) only close on Sunday. But while some antique stalls operate on Friday, the busiest day by far is Saturday, when antique dealers set up shop (from Chepstow Villas to Elgin Cres).

★ Design Museum   MUSEUM
(Map p92; ✆ 020-3862 5900; www.designmuseum.org; 224-238 Kensington High St, W8; ⊙10am-6pm, to 8pm or 9pm 1st Fri of month;

U High St Kensington) FREE Relocated from its former Thames location to a stunning new £83-million home by Holland Park in 2016, this slick museum is dedicated to design's role in everyday life. Its permanent collection is complemented by a revolving program of special exhibitions, and it's a crucial pit stop for anyone with an eye for recent technology or contemporary aesthetics. Splendidly housed in the refitted former Commonwealth Institute (which opened in 1962), the lavish interior – all smooth Douglas fir and marble – is itself a design triumph.

◉ Richmond, Kew & Hampton Court

★ Kew Gardens   GARDENS
(Royal Botanic Gardens, Kew; www.kew.org; Kew Rd, TW9; adult/child £17.50/5.50; ⊙10am-7pm Apr-Sep, to 6pm Mar & Oct, closes earlier rest of year; 🚢 Kew Pier, 🚉 Kew Bridge, U Kew Gardens) In 1759 botanists began rummaging around the world for specimens to plant in the 3-hectare Royal Botanic Gardens at Kew. They never stopped collecting, and the gardens, which have bloomed to 121 hectares, provide the most comprehensive botanical collection on earth (including the world's largest collection of orchids). A Unesco World Heritage Site, the gardens can easily devour a day's exploration; for those pressed for time, the Kew Explorer (📞020-8332 5648; www.kew.org/kew-gardens/whats-on/kew-explorer-land-train; tours adult/child £5/2; ⊙10.30am-3.30pm) hop-on/hop-off road train takes in the main sights.

Don't worry if you don't know your golden slipper orchid from your fengoky; a visit to Kew is a journey of discovery for everyone. Highlights include the enormous, steamy early Victorian Palm House (face covering required), a hothouse of metal and curved sheets of glass; the impressive Princess of Wales Conservatory; the red-brick 1631 Kew Palace (www.hrp.org.uk/kewpalace; ⊙10.30am-5.30pm Apr-Sep), formerly King George III's country retreat; the celebrated Chinese Pagoda, designed by William Chambers in 1762; the Temperate House, the world's largest ornamental glasshouse; and the very enjoyable Treetop Walkway, where you can survey the tree canopy from 18m up in the air.

A lattice fashioned from thousands of pieces of aluminium illuminated with hundreds of LED lights, the 17m-high Hive mimics activity within a real beehive. Opened in 2016, the 320m-long Great Broad Walk Borders is the longest double herbaceous border in the UK. The idyllic, thatched Queen Charlotte's Cottage (⊙11am-4pm Sat & Sun Apr-Sep) in the southwest of the gardens was popular with 'mad' George III and his wife; the beautiful carpets of bluebells around here are a draw in spring. Several long vistas (Cedar Vista, Syon Vista and Pagoda Vista) are channelled by trees from vantage points within Kew Gardens. An interactive Children's Garden the span of 40 tennis courts was added in 2019.

Check the website for a full list of activities at Kew, including free one-hour walking tours (daily), photography walks, theatre performances, outside cinema as well as a host of seasonal events and things to do.

Kew Gardens is easily reached by tube, but you might prefer to take a cruise on a riverboat with Thames River Boats (Map p64; 📞020-7930 2062; www.wpsa.co.uk; Westminster Pier, Victoria Embankment, SW1; adult/child Kew 1-way £15/7.50, return £22/11, Hampton Court 1-way £19/9.50, return £27/13.50; ⊙10am-4pm Apr-Oct; U Westminster).

★ Hampton Court Palace   PALACE
(www.hrp.org.uk/hamptoncourtpalace; Hampton Court Palace, KT8; adult/child £24.50/12.20; ⊙10am-6pm Apr-Oct, to 4.30pm Nov-Mar; 🚢 Hampton Court Palace, 🚉 Hampton Court) Built by Cardinal Thomas Wolsey in 1515 but coaxed from him by Henry VIII just before Wolsey (as chancellor) fell from favour, Hampton Court Palace is England's largest and grandest Tudor structure. It was already one of Europe's most sophisticated palaces when, in the 17th century, Christopher Wren designed an extension. The result is a beautiful blend of Tudor and 'restrained baroque' architecture. You could easily spend a day exploring the palace and its 24 hectares of riverside gardens, including a 300-year-old maze. See more on p102.

Richmond Park   PARK
(📞0300 061 2200; www.royalparks.org.uk/parks/richmond-park; ⊙7am-dusk; U Richmond) At almost 1000 hectares (the largest urban parkland in Europe), this park offers everything

Hampton Court Palace

A DAY AT THE PALACE

With so much to explore in the palace and seemingly infinite gardens, it can be tricky knowing where to begin. It helps to understand how the palace has grown over the centuries and how successive royal occupants embellished Hampton Court to suit their purposes and to reflect the style of the time.

As soon as he had his royal hands upon the palace from Cardinal Thomas Wolsey,

Henry VIII began expanding the **1 Tudor architecture**, adding the **2 Great Hall**, the exquisite **3 Chapel Royal**, the opulent Great Watching Chamber and the gigantic **4 Tudor kitchens**. By 1540 it had become one of the grandest and most sophisticated palaces in Europe. James I kept things ticking over, while Charles I added a new tennis court and did some serious art-collecting, including pieces that can be seen in the **5 Cumberland Art Gallery**.

OPEN FOR INSPECTION

The palace was opened to the public by Queen Victoria in 1838.

Tudor Kitchens

These vast kitchens were the engine room of the palace, and had a staff of 200 people. Six spit-rack-equipped fireplaces ensured roast meat was always on the menu (to the tune of 8200 sheep and 1240 oxen per year).

7 The Maze

Around 150m north of the main building
Created from hornbeam and yew and planted in around 1700, the maze covers a third of an acre within the famous palace gardens. A must-see conclusion to Hampton Court, it takes the average visitor about 20 minutes to reach the centre.

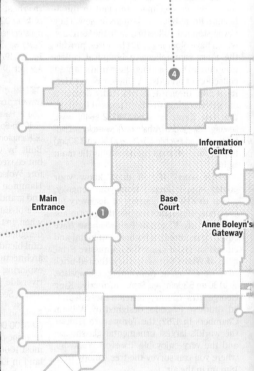

Information Centre

Main Entrance

Base Court

Anne Boleyn's Gateway

Tudor Architecture

Dating to 1515, the palace serves as one of the finest examples of Tudor architecture in the nation. Cardinal Thomas Wolsey was responsible for transforming what was originally a grand medieval manor house into a stunning Tudor palace.

PETER FIELDS / ALAMY STOCK PHOTO ©

KIEVVICTOR / SHUTTERSTOCK ©

After the Civil War, puritanical Oliver Cromwell warmed to his own regal proclivities, spending weekends in the comfort of the former Queen's bedroom and selling off Charles I's art collection. In the late 17th century, William and Mary employed Christopher Wren for baroque extensions, chiefly the William III Apartments, reached by the **6 King's Staircase**. William III also commissioned the world-famous **7 maze**.

TOP TIPS

➡ Ask one of the red-tunic-garbed warders for anecdotes and information.

➡ Tag along with a themed tour led by costumed historians or do a dusk-till-dawn sleepover at the palace.

➡ Grab one of the audio tours from the Information Centre.

The Great Hall
This grand dining hall is the defining room of the palace, displaying what is considered England's finest hammer-beam roof, 16th-century Flemish tapestries that depict the story of Abraham, and some exquisite stained-glass windows.

Chapel Royal
The blue-and-gold vaulted ceiling was originally intended for Christ Church, Oxford, but was installed here instead; the 18th-century oak reredos was carved by Grinling Gibbons. Books on display include a 1611 first edition of the King James Bible, printed by Robert Barker.

The King's Staircase
One of five rooms at the palace painted by Antonio Verrio and a suitably bombastic prelude to the King's Apartments, the overblown King's Staircase adulates William III by elevating him above a cohort of Roman emperors.

Chapel
Court Garden

2

3

Clock
Court

5

Fountain
Court

6

GORDON BELL / SHUTTERSTOCK ©

Cumberland Art Gallery
The former Cumberland Suite, designed by William Kent, has been restored to accommodate a choice selection of some of the finest works from the Royal Collection.

from formal gardens and ancient oaks to unsurpassed views of central London 12 miles away. It's easy to flee the several roads slicing up the rambling wilderness, making the park perfect for a quiet walk or a picnic, even in summer when Richmond's riverside heaves. Coming from Richmond, it's easiest to enter via Richmond Gate or from Petersham Rd.

Strawberry Hill HISTORIC BUILDING
(☑020-8744 1241; www.strawberryhillhouse.org.uk; 268 Waldegrave Rd, TW1; adult/child free; ☉house 11am-4pm Sun-Thu, garden 10am-4pm Sun-Thu; ℝStrawberry Hill, ⓊRichmond Station) With its snow-white walls and Gothic turrets, this fantastical and totally restored 18th-century creation in Twickenham is the work of art historian, author and politician Horace Walpole. Studded with elaborate stained glass, the building reaches its astonishing apogee in the gallery, with its magnificent papier-mâché ceiling. For the full magic, join a twilight tour (£25). Last admission to the house is one hour before closing time.

👉 Tours

★**Guide London** TOURS
(Association of Professional Tourist Guides; ☑020-7611 2545; www.guidelondon.org.uk; half-/full-day tours £176/288) Hire a prestigious Blue Badge Tourist Guide, knowledgeable guides who have studied for two years and passed a dozen written and practical exams to do their job. They can tell you stories behind the sights that you'd only hear from them or whisk you on a themed tour (eg Royalty, the Beatles, museums, parks). Go by car, public transport, bike or on foot.

For private tours by car, driver guides typically charge £405 for a half day and £585 for a full day.

★**London Waterbus Company** CRUISE
(☑07917 265114; www.londonwaterbus.com; Browning's Pool, Warwick Cres W2; tours adult/child 1-way £12/9; ☉hourly 10am-5pm Apr-Oct, weekends only & less frequent departures other months; ⓊWarwick Avenue, Camden Town) These enclosed barges take enjoyable 50-minute trips on Regent's Canal between Little Venice and Camden Lock, passing by Regent's Park and stopping at London Zoo. Fewer departures go outside high season; check the website for schedules. One-way tickets (adult/child £32/25 from Little Venice or £30/22 from Camden Lock) include zoo entry and allow

passengers to disembark within the zoo grounds. Buy tickets on board.

Look Up London CULTURAL
(https://lookup.london; per person £15-30) Walking tours include secrets of Bermondsey, Soho, Greenwich and the City plus a Feminist Jack the Ripper tour that tells the stories of the women involved in this bloody chapter of London's history. Group sizes are kept small. Tours go for one to two hours. Also does online tours.

Black History Walks HISTORY
(www.blackhistorywalks.co.uk; 2hr tours £10) Learn a little of London's 2000 years of black history in Soho, St Paul's and Notting Hill, to name a few locations where these informative, paradigm-shifting tours are run. Also runs online seminars.

Alternative London CULTURAL
(www.alternativeldn.com; per person from £18) Avoiding the obvious headline London sites, these small-group cycling and walking tours cover themes such as street art, culinary experiences and craft-beer spots, mainly around East London.

London Bicycle Tour CYCLING
(Map p84; ☑020-7928 6838; www.londonbicycle.com; 74 Kennington Rd, SE11; tour incl bike adult/child from £34.95/28.95, bike hire per day £24; ⓊLambeth North) Three-hour tours begin in Lambeth and take in London's highlights on both sides of the river; the classic tour is run in six languages. A night ride is available. You can also hire traditional or specialty bikes, such as tandems and folding bikes, by the hour or day.

Unseen Tours WALKING
(☑07514 266774; https://unseentours.org.uk; tours £15) 🖉 See London from an entirely different angle on one of these award-winning neighbourhood tours led by the London homeless (60% of the tour price goes to the guide). Tours cover Covent Garden, Soho, Brick Lane, Shoreditch and London Bridge.

Big Bus Tours BUS
(☑020-7808 6753; www.bigbustours.com; tours adult/child/family £39/29/107; ☉every 5-20min 8.30am-6pm Apr-Sep, to 5pm Oct & Mar, to 4.30pm Nov-Feb) Globally recognised bus touring group with informative commentaries in 12 languages. Hop-on hop-off along four bus routes. The ticket includes a free river cruise with City Cruises and three thematic walk-

ing tours. The ticket is valid for 24 hours; for a small additional charge you can upgrade to the 48-hour 'premium' ticket.

London Mystery Walks — WALKING
(☎07957 388280; www.tourguides.org.uk; per person from £15) Get spooked with London's ghost stories or serial killer Jack the Ripper–themed walking tours. For something more nourishing, try VIP chocolate or gelato tours (£40). Book in advance.

✿ Festivals & Events

The Boat Race — ROWING
(www.theboatrace.org; ⊘ late Mar/early Apr) A grudge match held annually since 1829 between the rowing crews of Oxford and Cambridge universities. Surging upstream between Putney and Mortlake, the event (which included a female crew boat race for the first time in 2015) draws huge crowds along the river.

Chelsea Flower Show — HORTICULTURE
(☎020-3176 5800; www.rhs.org.uk/chelsea; Royal Hospital Chelsea, Royal Hospital Rd, SW3; tickets £39.75-92.75; ⊘ May; Ⓤ Sloane Sq) Held at the lovely Royal Hospital Chelsea, this is arguably the world's most renowned horticultural show, attracting green fingers from all four corners of the globe.

Trooping the Colour — PARADE
(www.householddivision.org.uk/trooping-the-colour; Horse Guards Parade, SW1; ⊘ Jun; Ⓤ Westminster or Charing Cross) Celebrating the Queen's official birthday (her actual birthday is in April), this ceremonial procession of troops, marching along the Mall for their sovereign's inspection, is pageantry overload, featuring 1400 officers and personnel on parade, plus 200 horses and 400 musicians from 10 bands.

The parade can be watched from the street, but to get closer to the action, enter an online draw to sit in the stands in Horse Guards Parade (Map p64). The ballot opens in January (£40 per person if you're successful). Smart casual dress is required.

Pride — LGBT+
(www.prideinlondon.org; ⊘ late Jun/early Jul) The LGBT+ community paints the town pink in this annual extravaganza, featuring a smorgasbord of experiences, from talks to live events, and culminating in a huge parade across London.

LONDON WETLAND CENTRE

One of Europe's largest inland wetland projects, this 42-hectare centre (☎020-8409 4400; www.wwt.org.uk/wetland-centres/london; Queen Elizabeth's Walk, SW13; adult/child/family £13/8/36; ⊘ 9.30am-5.30pm, to 4.30pm Nov-Feb; ℝ Barnes, Ⓤ Hammersmith) run by the Wildfowl & Wetlands Trust was transformed from four Victorian reservoirs in 2000 and attracts some 140 species of birds, as well as frogs, butterflies, dragonflies and lizards, plus a thriving colony of watervoles. The glass-fronted observatory affords panoramic views over the lakes, while meandering paths and boardwalks lead visitors through the watery habitats of black swans, Bewick's swans, geese, red-crested pochards, sand martins, coots, bitterns, herons and kingfishers.

Film4 Summer Screen — FILM
(☎0333 320 2836; www.somersethouse.org.uk; Somerset House, Strand, WC2; tickets from £19; ⊘ Aug; Ⓤ Temple) For two weeks every summer, Somerset House (p74) turns its stunning courtyard into an open-air cinema and screens an eclectic mix of film premieres, cult classics and popular requests. Pack a picnic and blankets or cushions to cover the hard ground (or pre-order them with your entry tickets for an extra fee).

Notting Hill Carnival — CARNIVAL
(www.nhcarnival.org; ⊘ Aug) Every year, August ends with a long bank-holiday weekend, and West London echoes to the ska, reggae, R&B, dancehall and soca sounds of the Notting Hill Carnival. Launched in 1964 by an Afro-Caribbean community keen to celebrate its culture and traditions, it has grown to become Europe's largest street festival (over two million people) and a highlight of London's calendar.

Open House London — CULTURAL
(☎020-7383 2131; https://openhouselondon.open-city.org.uk; ⊘ Sep) The annual two-day Open House London event during the third weekend of September sees over 800 buildings open to the public. Open House London is run by Open City, a charity promoting cities with a year-round programme of events and initiatives, including talks and architectural

ELROCE/SHUTTERSTOCK ©

1. Tower of London (p76) 2. Hampton Court Palace (p101)
3. Windsor Castle (p216) 4. Buckingham Palace (p72)

Royal London

IR STONE/SHUTTERSTOCK ©

Along with Stonehenge and Big Ben, the current monarch, Queen Elizabeth II, is one of the most potent symbols of England. Pretty much anything connected to the country's royal heritage is a guaranteed attraction – especially the capital's fine collection of palaces and castles.

The Tower of London

The Tower of London (p76) has a 1000-year-old history and foundations that date back to Roman times. Over the centuries it's been a royal residence, a treasury, a mint, a prison and an arsenal. Today it's home to the spectacular Crown Jewels, as well as red-coated Beefeaters and ravens attributed with mythical power.

Windsor Castle

Although not actually in London, Windsor Castle (p216) is near enough to visit on a day trip. This is the largest and oldest occupied fortress in the world, an astounding edifice of defensive walls, towers and battlements, used for state occasions and as the Queen's weekend retreat.

Buckingham Palace

Buckingham Palace (p72) has been the monarch's London residence since 1837, and the current Queen divides her time between it, Windsor Castle and Balmoral in Scotland. If she's at home, the 'Royal Standard' flag flies on the roof. If she's away on her summer holiday, you can take a tour to see inside. Either way, don't miss the famous Changing of the Guard.

Hampton Court Palace

Hampton Court Palace (p101) is England's largest and grandest Tudor structure, used by King Henry VIII as a riverside hideaway. After admiring the grand interior, you can relax in the extensive gardens, but don't get lost in the 300-year-old maze.

tours on foot, by boat and bike to various parts of London.

London Film Festival · FILM

(www.bfi.org.uk/lff; ⊙ Oct) The city's premier film event attracts big overseas names and you can catch as many as 350 British and international films in venues across the city before their cinema release.

🛏 Sleeping

🛏 West End

YHA London Oxford Street · HOSTEL £

(Map p66; ☑ 020-7734 1618; www.yha.org.uk/ hostel/yha-london-oxford-street; 14 Noel St, W1; dm £18-36, tw £50-90; 🛜; Ⓤ Oxford Circus) The most central of London's seven YHA hostels is also one of the most intimate with just 104 beds in 36 rooms. The excellent shared facilities include a fuchsia-coloured kitchen and a bright, funky lounge. Dormitories have two solid bunk beds, and there are doubles and twins. The in-house shop sells coffee and beer. Free wi-fi in common areas.

Generator London · HOSTEL £

(Map p96; ☑ 020-7388 7666; https://staygenerator .com/hostels/london; 37 Tavistock Pl, WC1; dm/r from £11/61; �│🛜; Ⓤ Russell Sq) With its industrial lines and hip decor, the huge Generator (it has more than 870 beds) is one of central London's grooviest budget spots. The bar, complete with pool tables, stays open until 3am and there are frequent themed parties. Dorm rooms have between four and 13 beds; backing it up are twins and triples.

Jesmond Hotel · B&B ££

(Map p96; ☑ 020-7636 3199; www.jesmond hotel.org.uk; 63 Gower St, WC1; s/d/tr/q from £80/105/140/160; @🛜; Ⓤ Goodge St) The 15 guestrooms at this popular, family run Georgian-era B&B in Bloomsbury are basic but clean and cheerful (four are with shared bathroom); there's a small, pretty garden out back, and the prices are very attractive indeed. There's also laundry service and good breakfasts for kicking off your London day. Location is highly central.

★ Haymarket Hotel · HOTEL £££

(Map p66; ☑ 020-7470 4000; www.firmdalehotels. com/hotels/london/haymarket-hotel; 1 Suffolk Pl, off Haymarket, SW1; r/ste £350/550; �│🛜🌐🌐; Ⓤ Piccadilly Circus) With the trademark colours and lines of hotelier/designer duo Tim and Kit Kemp, in a converted building designed by John Nash, the Haymarket is scrumptious, with hand-painted Gournay wallpaper, signature fuchsia and green designs in the 50 different guest rooms – 206 has windows on two sides – a sensational 18m pool, an exquisite library lounge, and original artwork.

★ Ritz London · LUXURY HOTEL £££

(Map p66; ☑ 020-7493 8181; www.theritzlondon. com; 150 Piccadilly, W1; r/ste from £650/1500; 🅿🌐@🛜; Ⓤ Green Park) What can you say about a place that has lent its name to the English lexicon? This 136-room hotel, opened by the eponymous César in 1906, has a spectacular position overlooking Green Park and is supposedly the Royal Family's home away from home. (It is very close to the palace.) All rooms have Louis XVI–style interiors and antique furniture.

Covent Garden Hotel · BOUTIQUE HOTEL £££

(Map p66; ☑ 020-7806 1000; www.firmdalehotels. com/hotels/london/covent-garden-hotel; 10 Monmouth St, WC2; d/ste from £360/550; 🌐@🛜; Ⓤ Covent Garden) This gorgeous and discreet 58-room boutique hotel housed in a former French hospital features antiques; sumptuous bright fabrics; and quirky bric-a-brac to mark its individuality. There's an excellent bar-restaurant off the lobby and two stunning guest lounges with fireplaces (note the beautiful marquetry desk) on the 1st floor, which come into their own in the winter.

Rooms on the ground floor (such as rooms 3, 5 and 8) are larger and have higher ceilings. The Asian touches in room 4 are fetching.

Rosewood London · HOTEL £££

(Map p66; ☑ 020-7781 8888; www.rosewoodhotels. com/en/london; 252 High Holborn, WC1; d/ste from £440/1100; 🅿🌐@🛜🌐; Ⓤ Holborn) What was once the grand Pearl Assurance building (dating from 1914) now houses the stunning Rosewood hotel, where an artful marriage of period and modern styles, thanks to designer Tony Chi, can be found in its 262 rooms and 45 suites. British heritage is carefully woven throughout the bar, restaurant, lobby and even the housekeepers' uniforms.

Hazlitt's · HERITAGE HOTEL £££

(Map p66; ☑ 020-7434 1771; www.hazlittshotel. com; 6 Frith St, W1; s/d/ste from £200/230/600; 🌐🛜; Ⓤ Tottenham Court Rd) Built in 1718 and comprising four original Georgian houses, this Soho gem was the one-time home of essayist William Hazlitt (1778–1830). The 30 guest rooms are furnished with original antiques from the appropriate era and boast a profusion of seductive details, including panelled walls, mahogany four-poster beds, antique desks, Oriental carpets, sumptuous fabrics and fireplaces in every room.

🛏 City of London

London St Paul's YHA
HOSTEL **£**

(Map p76; 📞 020-7236 4965; www.yha.org.uk; 36 Carter Lane, EC4; dm/d from £20/70; 📶; Ⓤ St Paul's) Housed in the former boarding school for St Paul's Cathedral choir boys, this 213-bed hostel has notable period features, including Latin script in a band around the exterior. There's no kitchen, no lift and no en-suite rooms, but there is a comfortable lounge, a licensed cafe and all new beds with USB ports.

★ CitizenM
Tower of London
DESIGN HOTEL **££**

(Map p76; 📞 020-3519 4830; www.citizenm.com/destinations/london/tower-of-london-hotel; 40 Trinity Sq, EC3; r from £170; 🕸@📶; Ⓤ Tower Hill) Downstairs it looks like a rich hipster's living room, with well-stocked bookshelves, kooky art like Warhol's *Reigning Queens* and Beefeater bric-a-brac. The 370 rooms are compact but well-designed, with an iPad controlling curtains, the TV and even the shower lighting. It's worth paying an extra £20 for the extraordinary Tower views, although they're even better from the two-level 7th floor bar.

★ The Ned
HERITAGE HOTEL **£££**

(Map p76; 📞 020-3828 2100; www.thened.com; 27 Poultry, London, EC2; r £230-400; 🕸@📶🐾; Ⓤ Bank) What was until recently the Midland Bank, designed by Sir Edwin 'Ned' Lutyens in 1924, has metamorphosed into a splendid butterfly with 250 rooms over nine floors. Choose a 'Cosy' room (there are a dozen different types) facing Queen Victoria St. The Ned counts a full seven restaurants in the erstwhile Grand Banking Hall, where there is daily live music.

The spa with enormous swimming pool, sauna and hammam in the basement is a delight. Beg, borrow or steal to get into the Vaults lounge and its adjacent bar with 3000 original safe-deposit boxes.

South Place
HOTEL **£££**

(Map p76; 📞 020-3503 0000; www.southplacehotel.com; 3 South Pl, EC2; d/ste from £232/740; 🕸📶🐾; Ⓤ Moorgate) A hip, design-led hotel, South Place impresses at every turn. From the art-filled lobby and espionage-inspired theme (a Russian spy ring was once located in this area) to the Michelin-starred Angler (Map p76; 📞 020-3215 1260; www.anglerrestaurant.com; mains £32-38; ⏱ noon-2.30pm & 6-10pm Mon-Sat, 6-10pm Sun) seafood restaurant and 80 beautifully laid-out rooms – every detail has been carefully considered. There are even cheeky hangover cures and sex kits alongside the British products in the luxurious minibar.

🛏 South Bank

★ Hoxton Southwark
HOTEL **££**

(Map p84; 📞 020-7903 3000; https://thehoxton.com/london/southwark; Blackfriars Rd, SE1; r £140-300; 🕸@📶🐾; Ⓤ Southwark) This latest feather in the now three-plumed Hoxton cap counts 192 retro-styled rooms (antique radios, rotary telephones) and fabulous artwork displayed in every nook and cranny. Like its sisters the Hoxton Southwark offers stylish yet affordable accommodation in rooms that vary enormously in size and comfort; try Cosy room 419 or the bigger Roomy 408 looking onto a churchyard.

The lobby bar is always buzzy but the destination outlet here is the rooftop Seabird bar and restaurant, with unmatchable views.

CitizenM
London Bankside
BOUTIQUE HOTEL **££**

(Map p84; 📞 020-3519 1680; www.citizenm.com/destinations/london/london-bankside-hotel; 20 Lavington St, SE1; r £109-325; 🕸@📶; Ⓤ Southwark) If citizenM had a motto, it would be 'Less fuss, more comfort'. The hotel has done away with things it considers superfluous like room service and reception and instead has gone all out on mattresses and bedding, and state-of-the-art technology (everything from mood lighting to TV is controlled through a tablet computer and you unlock the door with your phone).

Shangri-La Hotel at the Shard
HOTEL **£££**

(Map p84; 📞 020-7234 8000; www.shangri-la.com/london/shangrila; 31 St Thomas St, SE1; d/ste from £500/1000; 🕸@📶🐾; Ⓤ London Bridge) Unsurprisingly for a hotel occupying levels 34 to 52 of the Shard, there are breathtaking

Where to Stay in London

Hampstead
Heath

West End

In the heart of London: big-ticket sights; vibrant Soho nightlife; excellent restaurants, shopping and entertainment.

Best For A city break; LGBT+ travellers

Transport Excellent transport connections

Price Varies, mostly midrange

Regent's
Park

British
Museum

The West End

St Paul
Cathedra

Covent
Garden

Piccadilly
Circus

Tat
Mode

Hyde
Park

**Kensington &
Hyde Park**

South Bank

Victoria &
Albert
Museum

Buckingham
Palace

Westminster
Abbey

**Kensington
& Hyde Park**

Outstanding museums, galleries and parklands. Beautiful buildings and boutique hotels.

Best For First timers

Transport Well connected but busy with tourists

Price Mostly Top End

Tate
Britain

South Bank

Big ticket sights, great dining and decent accommodation options, but as a neighbourhood it lacks character.

Best For A central location

Transport Well connected by Tube and bus

Price Mostly midrange

Clerkenwell, Shoreditch & Spitalfields

Unique shopping, excellent pubs and bars, outstanding dining, and destination hotels.

Best For City breaks

Transport Well connected by trains and buses

Price Mostly Midrange

East London

Local life: vintage stores, indie markets, street art, small bars and great restaurants.

Best For A city break; shoppers and foodies.

Transport Not well served by the Tube.

Price Mostly midrange

City of London

Historic buildings and major sights; quiet on weekends. Surprising number of excellent bars, restaurants and accommodation options.

Best For Weekend visitors

Transport Well connected to the Thames and West End

Price Mostly top-end

Greenwich

Packed with great sights and with a grand holiday vibe, but lacking in decent dining or accommodation options. Look for private apartment rentals

Best For A retreat for families

Transport Well connected by train

Price Midrange

views everywhere you look in the 202-room Shangri-La: be it the floor-to-ceiling windows in the bedrooms, the panoramic bathrooms (you've never had such a good view while having a bath), the Skypool, the bar or the restaurant. The decor is a stylish blend of Chinese influence and modern.

The Shard's tapering shape puts the suites on lower floors, and each guest room is slightly different in design. Rooms are the latest in comfort and technology, with Nespresso coffee machines, a pillow menu and imported Japanese toilets (with a mind-boggling array of options).

🛏 Kensington & Hyde Park

★ Number Sixteen HOTEL £££
(Map p86; ✆ 020-7589 5232; www.firmdalehotels.com/hotels/london/number-sixteen; 16 Sumner Pl, SW7; s/d from £200/£300; ❄@🐾🐕; Ⓤ South Kensington) With uplifting splashes of colour, choice art and a sophisticated-but-fun design ethos, Number Sixteen is simply ravishing. There are 41 individually designed rooms, a cosy drawing room, library and honesty bar. And wait till you see the idyllic, long back garden set around a pond stocked with koi or sit down for breakfast in the light-filled conservatory.

Great amenities for families, too. Lovely room 209 looks down to Sumner Pl.

Ampersand Hotel DESIGN HOTEL £££
(Map p86; ✆ 020-7589 5895; https://ampersandhotel.com; 10 Harrington Rd, SW7; s/d from £170/£216; ❄@🐾🐕; Ⓤ South Kensington) It feels light, fresh and bubbly in the Ampersand, where smiling staff wear denims, waistcoats and ties rather than impersonal dark suits. The common rooms are colourful and airy, and the 111 stylish guest rooms are decorated with wallpaper designs celebrating the nearby arts and sciences of South Kensington's museums.

Deluxe studio 117 has two large windows looking to the street and a separate shower and toilet.

🛏 Clerkenwell, Shoreditch & Spitalfields

★ Hoxton Shoreditch HOTEL ££
(Map p120; ✆ 020-7550 1000; www.thehoxton.com/london/shoreditch/hotels; 81 Great Eastern St, EC2; r £109-260; ❄🐕; Ⓤ Old St) In the heart of hip Shoreditch, this sleek hotel takes the low-cost airline approach to selling its rooms – book long enough ahead and you might pay just £109. The 210 renovated rooms are small but stylish, with TVs, desks, fridges with complimentary bottled water and milk, and breakfast (orange juice, granola, yoghurt and banana) in a bag delivered to your door.

CitizenM
London Shoreditch DESIGN HOTEL ££
(Map p120; www.citizenm.com/destinations/london/london-shoreditch-hotel; 6 Holywell Lane, EC2; r £119-300; ❄@🐕; Ⓤ Shoreditch High St) CitizenM's winning combination of awesome interior design and a no-nonsense approach to luxury (yes to king-sized beds and high-tech pod rooms; no to pillow chocolates and room service) is right at home in Shoreditch. Rates at the 216 rooms are just right, and the convivial 24hr lounge/bar/reception on the ground floor always seems to be on the right side of busy.

★ Rookery HERITAGE HOTEL £££
(Map p76; ✆ 020-7336 0931; www.rookeryhotel.com; 12 Peter's Lane, Cowcross St, EC1; d/ste from £249/650; ❄🐕; Ⓤ Farringdon) This charming warren of 33 rooms has been built within a row of 18th-century Georgian townhouses and fitted out with period furniture (including a museum-piece collection of Victorian baths, showers and toilets), original wood panelling shipped over from Ireland and artwork selected by the owner. Highlights include the small courtyard garden and the library with its honesty bar and working fireplace.

Zetter Hotel BOUTIQUE HOTEL £££
(Map p96; ✆ 020-7324 4444; www.thezetter.com; St John's Sq, 86-88 Clerkenwell Rd, EC1; d from £210, studio £300-438; ❄🐕; Ⓤ Farringdon) 🌿 The Zetter Hotel is a temple of cool minimalism with an overlay of colourful kitsch on Clerkenwell's main thoroughfare. Built using sustainable materials on the site of a derelict office block, its 59 rooms are spacious for this area. The rooftop studios are the real treat, with terraces commanding superb views. There is a hot-drink station on every floor for guests' use.

🛏 East London

Qbic DESIGN HOTEL £
(✆ 020-3021 3300; https://qbichotels.com/london-city; 42 Adler St, E1; r £54-100; Ⓟ❄@🐾🐕; Ⓤ Aldgate East) 🌿 There's a modern feel to this snappy hotel, with white tiling,

neon signs, vibrant art and textiles and a pool table in the lobby. Its 171 rooms are sound-insulated, mattresses are excellent and rainforest showers powerful. Prices vary widely depending on when you book, and the cheapest rooms are windowless.

★ 40 Winks
B&B **££**

(⟋020-7790 0259; www.40winks.org; 109 Mile End Rd, E1; s/d/ste £115/185/280; ☏; Ⓤ Stepney Green) Short on space but not on style, this 300-year-old townhouse in Stepney Green oozes quirky charm. There are just two bedrooms (a double and a compact single) that share a bathroom – or you can book both as a spacious suite. Owned by a successful designer, the rooms are uniquely and extravagantly decorated with an expert's eye.

🛏 North London

★ Clink78
HOSTEL **£**

(Map p96; ⟋020-7183 9400; www.clinkhostels.com/london/clink78; 78 King's Cross Rd, WC1; dm/r from £16/65; @☏; Ⓤ King's Cross St Pancras) This fantastic 630-bed hostel is housed in a 19th-century magistrates' courthouse where Charles Dickens once worked as a scribe and members of the Clash stood trial in 1978. It features pod beds (including overhead storage space) in four- to 16-bed dormitories. There's a top kitchen with a huge dining area and a busy bar – Clash – in the basement.

Great Northern Hotel
HISTORIC HOTEL **£££**

(Map p96; ⟋020-3388 0800; www.gnhlondon.com; King's Cross Station, Pancras Rd, N1; r from £180; ✳@☏; Ⓤ King's Cross St Pancras) Built as the world's first railway hotel in 1854, the GNH is now an 88-room boutique hotel in a classic style reminiscent of luxury sleeper trains. Exquisite artisanship is in evidence everywhere. And in addition to the two lively bars and a restaurant, there's a 'pantry' on every floor, from which you can help yourself to hot or cold drinks and snacks.

Rooms come in three categories. Guests have access to a nearby gym with large swimming pool.

🛏 West London

Safestay Holland Park
HOSTEL **£**

(Map p92; ⟋020-7870 9626; www.safestay.com/london-kensington-holland-park; Holland Walk, W8; dm/r from £12.50/70; ☏; Ⓤ High St Kensington,

Holland Park) This upbeat and well-run place has taken over a long-serving YHA hostel with over 300 beds. With a bright (fuchsia) and bold design, the hostel has dorm rooms with four to 21 bunk beds and twins with a single bunk, free wi-fi in the lobby and a fabulous location in the Jacobean east wing of Holland House in Holland Park.

There's a large and very comfortable bar and restaurant downstairs with mains from £6, a pool room and garden.

New Linden Hotel
BOUTIQUE HOTEL **££**

(Map p92; ⟋020-7221 4321; www.newlinden.co.uk; 59 Leinster Sq, W2; s/d from £90/128; ☏; Ⓤ Bayswater) The Buddha bust in the lobby sets the zen tone for this light, airy and beautifully designed option located between Westbourne Grove and Notting Hill. Some of the 50 rooms (eg room 108 with a small balcony) are on the small side due to the Georgian building's quirky layout, but they feel cosy rather than cramped. Staff are charming, too.

Check out the gorgeous wooden door leading to the lounge. There's a lift, too.

🍴 Eating

🍴 West End

★ Kanada-Ya
RAMEN **£**

(Map p66; ⟋020-7240 0232; www.kanada-ya.com; 64 St Giles High St, WC2; mains £11-13; ⊙ noon-3pm & 5-10.30pm Mon-Sat, to 8.30pm Sun; Ⓤ Tottenham Court Rd) In the debate over London's best ramen, we're still voting for this one. With no reservations taken, queues can get impressive outside this tiny and enormously popular canteen, where ramen cooked in *tonkotsu* (pork-bone broth) draws in diners from near and far. The noodles arrive at just the right temperature and hardness, steeped in a delectable broth and rich flavours.

Mildreds
VEGETARIAN **£**

(Map p66; ⟋020-7494 1634; www.mildreds.co.uk; 45 Lexington St, W1; mains £12-13; ⊙ 11am-11pm Mon-Sat, to 10pm Sun; ☏🖉; Ⓤ Oxford Circus or Piccadilly Circus) One of the West End's most enduringly popular vegetarian restaurants, Mildreds is crammed at lunchtime: you can't be shy about sharing a table in the skylit dining room. Expect the likes of pumpkin gnocchi (boiled and fried) with pumpkin sauce and *pangrattato* (fried breadcrumbs), halloumi and harissa burgers and Levantine

Marylebone

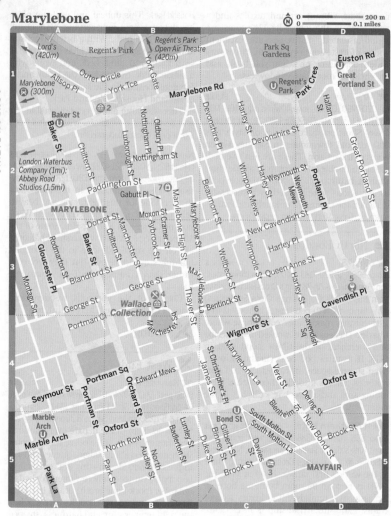

Chick'n kebabs. There are also vegan and gluten-free options.

So popular has Mildred's become, there are now branches in Dalston, Camden and King's Cross.

★Palomar   ISRAELI ££

(Map p66; ☎020-7439 8777; www.thepalomar. co.uk; 34 Rupert St, W1; mains £14-16; ☺6-10pm Mon-Wed, 12.30-2.30pm & 6-10pm Thu-Sun; ☎; ⓤPiccadilly Circus) Packed and praised from the day it opened, Palomar is a wonderful Israeli/Levantine restaurant with the look of a 1930s diner and the constant theatre of expert chefs whipping up magic behind

the central zinc bar. Unusual dishes such as date-glazed octopus with harissa will blow you away, as will slow-cooked Tel Aviv seafood and beetroot labneh with parsley vinaigrette.

It's usually possible to get one or two of the 16 bar stools at shortish notice for lunch, but book further ahead for a table in the 40-seat dining room, or for dinner.

★Kiln   THAI ££

(Map p66; www.kilnsoho.com; 58 Brewer St, W1; dishes £4.50-14; ☺noon-3pm & 5-11pm Mon-Thu, noon-11pm Fri & Sat, to 10pm Sun; ⓤPiccadilly Circus) Crowned the UK's best restaurant

Marylebone

in 2018, this tiny Thai grill cooks up a storm in its long, narrow kitchen, overseen by diners on their stools. The short menu rides the small-plates wave and works best with a few friends so you can taste a greater variety. The beef-neck curry is phenomenal, as are the claypot-baked glass noodles.

Bar Shu   SICHUAN ££
(Map p66; ☑020-7287 6688; http://barshurestaurant.co.uk; 28 Frith St, W1; mains £11-23; ��noon-10pm Sun-Thu, to 11.30pm Fri & Sat; Ⓤ Piccadilly Circus or Leicester Sq) You might think Bar Shu – adorned with slatted blinds, latticed woodwork and tasselled lanterns – was a sweet-and-sour honeytrap for Soho tourists; but you'd be missing out on possibly the best Sichuan food in London. The *ma-po* tofu ('pockmarked grandmother's tofu', reputedly Chairman Mao's favourite) is the best we've ever had: all funky fermented beans, chilli oil, pork and fresh beancurd.

There's a wide disparity in dish pricing; while simple choices such as the *ma-po* or 'ants climbing trees' (a classic stir-fried cellophane-noodle dish) come in at around £10, you'll be in for a shock if you order sea cucumber, abalone or crab without checking the prices first.

Barrafina   TAPAS ££
(Map p66; ☑020-7440 1456; www.barrafina.co.uk; 26-27 Dean St, W1; basic tapas £4-7, larger plates £9-20; ☑noon-3pm & 5-10pm Mon-Sat, 1-8pm Sun; Ⓤ Tottenham Court Rd) Tapas are always better value in Spain than in London (even more so when complimentary with drinks, as is traditional), but the exceptional quality at Barrafina justifies the extra expense. Along with *gambas al ajillo* (prawns in garlic), there are more unusual items, such as tuna tartare and grilled quail with alioli, plus a wonderful changing menu of specials.

Customers sit along the bar facing the busy chefs, so it's not a good choice for groups (and the maximum party size is four).

Yauatcha   DIM SUM ££
(Map p66; ☑020-7494 8888; www.yauatcha.com; 15-17 Broadwick St, W1; mains £15-30, dim sum £8-10; ☑noon-1am Mon-Sat, to midnight Sun; Ⓤ Tottenham Court Rd or Oxford Circus) London's glamorous Michelin-starred dim sum restaurant has a ground-floor dining room that's a blue-bathed oasis of calm amid the chaos of Berwick Street Market; downstairs is smarter, with constellations of 'star' lights. Lobster dumplings with *tobiko* (flying-fish roe) exemplify the refined dim sum, while spicy steamed bass with pickled chilli is just one of the more substantial options.

The Soho Lunch (£28 per person for at least two) is a great-value introduction to its divine dim sum. Unusually, Yauatcha also produces delicate cakes, macarons and other sweet delights.

★ **Foyer & Reading Room at Claridge's**   BRITISH £££
(Map p114; ☑020-7107 8886; www.claridges.co.uk; Brook St, W1; afternoon tea £70, with champagne £80-90; ☑7am-10pm Mon-Sat, from 8am Sun, afternoon tea 2.45-5.30pm; ☎; Ⓤ Bond St) Refreshing the better sort of West End shopper since 1856, the jaw-dropping Foyer and Reading Room at Claridge's (Map p114; ☑020-7629 8860; www.claridges.co.uk; Brook St, W1; r/ste from £450/780; ✳@☎☀; Ⓤ Bond St), refulgent with art-deco mirrors and a Dale Chihuly glass sculpture, really is a memorable dining space. Refined food is served at all mealtimes, but many choose to nibble in best aristocratic fashion on the finger sandwiches and pastries of a classic afternoon tea.

Smart attire is always required.

LONDON EATING

★ **Spring**   BRITISH £££

(Map p66; ☎020-3011 0115; www.springrestaurant.co.uk; New Wing, Somerset House, Lancaster Pl, WC2; mains £29-33, 2-/3-course lunch £29/32; ◷noon-2.30pm & 5.30-10pm Mon-Sat; Ⓤ Temple) 🍴 White walls, ball chandeliers and columns are offset by the odd blossom in this restored Victorian drawing room in Somerset House (p74). Award-winning Australian chef Skye Gyngell leads a team dedicated to sustainability – no single-use plastic – and an early-evening scratch menu (£25 for three courses) using food that would otherwise be wasted. Desserts are legendary.

Pollen Street Social   EUROPEAN £££

(Map p66; ☎ 020-7290 7600; www.pollenstreetsocial.com; 8-10 Pollen St, W1; mains £41-44; ◷ noon-2.30pm & 6-10pm Mon-Sat; Ⓤ Oxford Circus) Chef Jason Atherton's cathedral to haute cuisine (Michelin-starred within six months of opening) is a worthy splurge, especially for those in search of the best produce in these islands. It's expensive, but if you fancy trying Braehead pheasant with chestnut gnocchi or roasted Cornish cod with salt-baked vegetables without overspending, the three-course lunch menu (£40) is excellent value.

✖️ **City of London**

Simpsons Tavern   BRITISH £

(Map p76; ☎020-7626 9985; www.simpsonstavern.co.uk; Ball Ct, 38½ Cornhill, EC3; mains £9.75-15.80; ◷8.30-10.30am Tue-Fri & noon-3.30pm Mon-Fri; Ⓤ Bank) 'Old school' doesn't even come close to describing Simpsons, a City institution since 1757. Huge portions of traditional British grub are served to diners in dark-wood and olive-green booths. Save space for the tavern's famous stewed-cheese dessert.

★ **Duck & Waffle**   BRITISH ££

(Map p76; ☎020-3640 7310; www.duckandwaffle.com; Heron Tower, 110 Bishopsgate, EC2; mains £14-44; ◷24hr; ☎; Ⓤ Liverpool St) London tends to have an early bedtime, but Duck and Waffle is the best restaurant that's ready to party all night. Survey the kingdom from the highest restaurant in town (on the 40th floor) over a helping of the namesake dish: a fluffy waffle topped with a crispy leg of duck confit and a fried duck egg, drenched in mustard-seed maple syrup.

City Social   BRITISH £££

(Map p76; ☎020-7877 7703; www.citysociallondon.com; Tower 42, 25 Old Broad St, EC2; mains £26-37; ◷noon-2.30pm & 6-10.30pm Mon-Fri, 5-10.30pm Sat; Ⓤ Bank) City Social pairs sublime skyscraper views from its 24th-floor digs with delicate Michelin-starred cuisine. The interior is all art-deco inspired low-lit glamour. If you don't want to splash out on the full menu, opt for the bar, Social 24, which has longer hours and a compelling menu of nibbles (don't miss the goats'-cheese churros with locally sourced truffle-infused honey).

Bookings are essential; expect airport-style security before you can get in the lift.

✖️ **South Bank**

★ **Padella**   ITALIAN £

(Map p84; www.padella.co; 6 Southwark St, SE1; dishes £4-12.50; ◷noon-3.45pm & 5-10pm Mon-Sat, to 9pm Sun; ☏; Ⓤ London Bridge) Come hungry for the best pasta this side of Italy. Padella is a small, energetic bistro specialising in handmade noodles, inspired by the owners' extensive culinary adventures. The portions are small, which means that you can (and should!) have more than one dish. Download the WalkIn app to join the queue virtually to dine here then head to the market or pub.

Anchor & Hope   GASTROPUB ££

(Map p84; ☎020-7928 9898; www.anchorandhopepub.co.uk; 36 The Cut, SE1; mains £12.40-19.40; ◷5-10pm Mon, from 11am Tue-Sat, 12.30-3.15pm Sun; Ⓤ Southwark) Started by former chefs from nose-to-tail pioneer St John (p118), the Anchor & Hope is a quintessential gastropub: elegant but not formal, serving utterly delicious European fare with a British twist. The menu changes daily, but it could include grilled sole served with spinach, or roast rabbit with green beans in a mustard-and-bacon sauce. Bookings taken for Sunday lunch only.

Skylon   EUROPEAN £££

(Map p84; ☎020-7654 7800; www.skylon-restaurant.co.uk; 3rd fl, Royal Festival Hall, Southbank Centre, Belvedere Rd, SE1; mains £16.50-34; ◷noon-10pm Mon-Fri, 11.30am-3pm & 5-10pm Sat, 11.30am-10pm Sun; ☎📶; Ⓤ Waterloo) Named after the original structure in this location for the 1951 Festival of Britain, Skylon brings the 1950s into the modern era, with retro-futuristic decor (cool then, cooler now) and a season-driven menu of contemporary British cuisine. But its biggest selling point might be the floor-to-ceiling windows that bathe you in magnificent views of the Thames and the city.

🍴 Brixton, Peckham & South London

Peckham Levels FOOD HALL £
(https://peckhamlevels.org; 95a Rye Lane, SE15; ⊙10am-11pm Mon-Wed, to 1am Thu-Sat, to midnight Sun; 🚇Peckham Rye) A few floors below famous **Frank's** (http://boldtendencies.com/franks-cafe; 10th fl, 95a Rye Lane, SE15; ⊙5-11pm Tue & Wed, from 2pm Thu & Fri, 11am-11pm Sat & Sun mid-May–mid-Sep), Peckham Levels is the place to go if you want to drink in a former car park year-round. The first five floors are filled with small business coworking spaces, so head straight to the 6th floor for a delightful mix of street-food stalls and bars with enclosed weather-proof views toward London's skyscrapers.

Kudu SOUTH AFRICAN ££
(☑020-3950 0226; www.kuducollective.com; 119 Queen's Rd, SE15; dishes £8.50-18; ⊙6-10pm Wed-Sun; 🚇Queens Rd Peckham) Northeast of Peckham's core, this family run neighbourhood restaurant is worth the venture. Decorated with dusky pink and exposed-brick walls and blue velvet banquettes, Kudu presents South African flavours with inventive ingredients on delicate sharing plates. The menu can do no wrong, so order as much as you can: pig's-head tortellini, Parmesan churros with brown crab mayo and the signature pot-baked kudu bread.

⭐**Chez Bruce** FRENCH £££
(☑020-8672 0114; www.chezbruce.co.uk; 2 Bellevue Rd, SW17; 3-course lunch/dinner from £39.50/60; ⊙noon-2.30pm & 6-9.30pm Mon-Thu, noon-2.30pm & 6-10pm Fri & Sat, 12.30-3.30pm Sun; 🚇Wandsworth Common) Far off the usual tourist track, the phenomenal Chez Bruce, opposite leafy Wandsworth Common, has been in business for more than two decades. Despite its Michelin star, the atmosphere remains less pretentious than at other fine-dining establishments, and tables are filled with well-heeled locals. Dishes rotate frequently, but duck is often the star of the menu.

🍴 Kensington & Hyde Park

Pimlico Fresh CAFE £
(☑020-7932 0030; 86 Wilton Rd, SW1; mains from £3.50; ⊙7.30am-7.30pm Mon-Fri, 9am-6pm Sat & Sun; 🚇Victoria) This chirpy two-room cafe will see you right, whether you need breakfast (French toast, bowls of porridge laced with honey, banana, maple syrup or yoghurt; £3.50), lunch (home-made quiches and soups, 'things' on toast) or just a good old latte and cake.

Rabbit MODERN BRITISH ££
(Map p86; ☑020-3750 0172; www.rabbit-restaurant.com; 172 King's Rd, SW3; mains £6-20; ⊙noon-9pm Tue-Sat, noon-8pm Sun; 🍴; 🚇Sloane Sq) Three brothers grew up on a farm. One became a farmer, another a butcher, while the third worked in hospitality. So they pooled their skills and came up with Rabbit, a breath of fresh air in upmarket Chelsea. The restaurant rocks the agri-chic look, and the creative, seasonal and oft-changing Modern British menu is fabulous.

⭐**Dinner by Heston Blumenthal** MODERN BRITISH £££
(Map p86; ☑020-7201 3833; www.dinnerby heston.com; Mandarin Oriental Hyde Park, 66 Knightsbridge, SW1; 3-course set lunch £48, mains £44-52; ⊙noon-2.15pm & 6-9.30pm Sun-Wed, noon-2.30pm & 6-10pm Thu-Sat; 🛜; 🚇Knightsbridge) With two Michelin stars, sumptuously presented Dinner is a gastronomic tour de force, taking diners on a journey through British culinary history (with inventive modern inflections). Dishes carry historical dates to convey context, while the restaurant interior is a design triumph, from the glass-walled kitchen and its overhead clock mechanism to the large windows looking onto the park. Book ahead.

⭐**Gordon Ramsay** FRENCH £££
(Map p86; ☑020-7352 4441; www.gordonramsay restaurants.com/restaurant-gordon-ramsay; 68 Royal Hospital Rd, SW3; 3-course lunch/dinner £70/130; ⊙noon-2.15pm & 6.30-9.45pm Mon-Fri; 🛜🍴; 🚇Sloane Sq) One of Britain's finest restaurants and London's longest-running with three Michelin stars (held since 2001), this is hallowed turf for those who worship at the altar of the stove. The blowout Menu Prestige (£160) is seven courses of perfection, also available in vegetarian form (£160); a three-course vegetarian menu

(£130) is also at hand. Smart dress code (enquire); reserve early.

For unstoppable enthusiasts, masterclasses with Chef de Cuisine Matt Abé are also available.

★ **Five Fields**   MODERN BRITISH £££
(Map p86; ☑ 020-7838 1082; www.fivefieldsrestaurant.com; 8-9 Blacklands Tce, SW3; tasting menus £90-110; ⊙ noon-2pm Thu-Sat, 6.30-10pm Tue-Sat; 🐾; ⓤ Sloane Sq) The inventive British prix fixe cuisine, consummate service and enticingly light and inviting decor are hard to resist at this triumphant Chelsea restaurant – now with a Michelin star – but you'll need to plan early and book way up front. No children under 12.

Launceston Place   MODERN BRITISH £££
(Map p86; ☑ 020-7937 6912; www.launceston place-restaurant.co.uk; 1a Launceston Pl, W8; mains £22-34, tasting menus £79, 'early dinner' 3-course set menu £40; ⊙ noon-2.30pm & 5-10pm Wed-Sat, noon-3.30pm & 6.30-9pm Sun; 🐾🖊; ⓤ Gloucester Rd or High St Kensington) This exceptionally handsome, superchic Michelin-starred restaurant is almost anonymous on a picture-postcard Kensington street of Edwardian houses. Prepared by London chef Ben Murphy, dishes occupy the acme of gastronomic pleasures and are accompanied by an award-winning wine list. The adventurous will aim for the eight-course tasting menu (£85; vegetarian and vegan versions available).

✖️ Clerkenwell, Shoreditch & Spitalfields

★ **Breddos Tacos**   TACOS £
(☑ 020-3535 8301; www.breddostacos.com; 82 Goswell Rd, EC1; tacos from £5, mains £7.50-17; ⊙ noon-3pm & 5-11pm Mon-Fri, noon-11.30pm Sat; 🖊; ⓤ Old St or Farringdon) Started in an East London car park in 2011, Breddos found its first permanent home in Clerkenwell, dishing out some of London's best Mexican grub. Grab some friends and order each of the eight or so tacos, served in pairs, on the menu: fillings vary, but past favourites include confit pork belly, and veggie-friendly mole, queso fresco and egg.

Boiler House Food Hall   MARKET £
(Map p120; https://theboilerhouse.org/conscious-market; Old Truman Brewery, 152 Brick Lane, E1; dishes £5-12; ⊙ 11am-6pm Sat & Sun; 🖊; ⓤ Shoreditch High St) More than 50 plant-based food stalls and ethical retail brands pitch up in the Old Truman Brewery's high-ceilinged boiler room at the weekend. Munch on the likes of cauliflower 'wings', vegan hot dogs, barbecue seitan brisket sandwiches, and 'tofish' and chips.

★ **Smoking Goat**   THAI ££
(Map p120; www.smokinggoatbar.com; 64 Shoreditch High St, E1; dishes £4-29; ⊙ noon-9pm Mon-Sun; ⓤ Shoreditch High St) Trotting in on one of London's fleeting flavours of the week, Smoking Goat's modern Thai menu is top notch. The industrial-chic look of exposed brick, huge factory windows and original parquet floors surround the open kitchen. It's a tough place for the spice-shy; cool down with a cold one from the exquisite cocktail list. Don't miss the smoked five-spice chicken.

St John   BRITISH ££
(Map p76; ☑ 020-7251 0848; www.stjohnrestaurant.com; 26 St John St, EC1; mains £17-26.50; ⊙ noon-3pm & 6-11pm Mon-Fri, 6-11pm Sat, 12.30-4pm Sun; ⓤ Farringdon) Around the corner from London's last remaining meat market, St John is the standard-bearer for nose-to-tail cuisine. With whitewashed brick walls, high ceilings and simple wooden furniture, it's surely one of the most humble Michelin-starred restaurants anywhere. The menu changes daily but is likely to include the signature roast bone marrow and parsley salad.

Yuu Kitchen   ASIAN ££
(Map p76; ☑ 020-7377 0411; www.yuukitchen.com; 29 Commercial St, E1; dishes £5-10; ⊙ 6-10pm Tue-Fri, noon-10pm Sat, noon-5pm Sun; 🖊; ⓤ Aldgate East) Manga images pout on the walls and birdcages dangle from the ceiling at this fun, relaxed place. Dishes are either bite-sized or designed to be shared, and while the focus is mainly Asian, some dishes from further along the Pacific Rim pop up, too. Hence Filipino *lechon kawali* (slow-braised pork belly) sits alongside Vietnamese rolls and show-stopping *bao* (Taiwanese steamed buns).

Poppie's   FISH & CHIPS ££
(Map p120; ☑ 020-7247 0892; www.poppies fishandchips.co.uk; 6-8 Hanbury St, E1; mains £12-17; ⊙ 11am-11pm Mon-Sat, to 10.30pm Sun; ⓤ Liverpool St) This glorious recreation of a

1950s East End chippy comes complete with wait-staff in pinnies and hairnets, and Blitz memorabilia. As well as the usual fishy suspects, it does old-time London staples – jellied eels and mushy peas – plus kid-pleasing, sweet-tooth desserts (sticky toffee pudding or apple pie with ice cream), and there's a wine list.

★**Hawksmoor Spitalfields** STEAK £££
(Map p120; ✆020-7426 4850; www.the hawksmoor.com; 157a Commercial St, E1; mains £15-60; ☺noon-3pm & 5-10.30pm Mon-Fri, noon-10.30pm Sat, noon-9pm Sun; ☎; ⓤShoreditch High St) You could easily miss Hawksmoor, discreetly signed and clad in black brick, but dedicated carnivores will find it worth seeking out. The dark wood and velvet curtains make for a handsome setting in which to gorge yourself on the best of British beef. The Sunday roasts (£22) are legendary, but it's *the* place in London to order a steak.

✘ **East London**

★**Barge East** BRITISH ££
(✆020-3026 2807; www.bargeeast.com; River Lee, Sweetwater Mooring, White Post Ln, E9; small plates £7-8.50, mains £14-19; ☺5-11pm Mon-Thu, noon-11.30pm Fri, 10am-10.30pm Sat, 11am-10.30pm Sun; ⓤHackney Wick) Moored along the River Lee in Hackney Wick is the *De Hoop*, a 100-tonne barge that sailed from Holland to offer seasonal fare and delicious drinks with waterside views. Small plates like nduja scotch eggs with black garlic or large dishes of Szechuan aubergine with cashew cream wash down splendidly with cocktails like the Earl Grey–based East London iced tea.

Berber & Q NORTH AFRICAN ££
(✆020-7923 0829; www.berberandq.com; 338 Acton Mews, E8; mains £13-18; ☺6-11pm Tue-Fri, 11am-3pm & 6-11pm Sat & Sun; ⓤHaggerston) A mouth-watering barbecue smell greets you as you enter under the railway arches into this very cool Berber-style grill house. Lamb shawarma (kebab) is meltingly tender, while piquant treats include dukkah-crusted lamb nuggets, wood-roasted prawns with garlic confit, spiced beef *kofte*, and vegetarian-friendly shiitake- and oyster-mushroom kebab with porcini tahini.

Corner Room MODERN BRITISH ££
(✆020-7871 0460; www.townhallhotel.com; Patriot Sq, E2; mains £14-26, 5-course dinner £39; ☺noon-2.30pm & 6-9.45pm; ⓤBethnal Green) Tucked away on the 1st floor of the Town Hall Hotel, this relaxed industrial-chic restaurant serves expertly crafted dishes with complex yet delicate flavours, highlighting the best of British seasonal produce, with a French touch.

Bistrotheque MODERN BRITISH ££
(✆020-8983 7900; www.bistrotheque.com; 23-27 Wadeson St, E2; mains £14-31, 3-course early dinner £25; ☺6-10.30pm Mon-Fri, 11am-4pm & 6-10.30pm Sat & Sun; ⓤBethnal Green) This unmarked warehouse conversion ticks all the boxes of a contemporary upmarket London bistro (the name made more sense when there was a club-like cabaret space downstairs). The food and service are uniformly excellent. One of the best weekend brunch spots in Hackney.

★**Silo** BRITISH £££
(✆020-7993 8155; https://silolondon.com; Unit 7, Queen's Yard, E9; 6-course tasting menu £50, brunch dishes £7.50-11.50; ☺6-10pm Tue-Fri, 11am-3pm & 6-10pm Sat, 11am-3pm Sun; ⓤHackney Wick) ✈ Brighton's Silo, the world's first zero-waste restaurant, has moved to Hackney Wick. Here, trailblazing chef Doug McMaster fashions lesser-loved ingredients and wonky produce into the likes of beetroot prune with egg yolk fudge or Jerusalem artichoke in brown butter. The canalside space – where everything down to the lampshades is upcycled – is as gorgeous as the dishes on the ever-changing menu.

✘ **North London**

★**Ruby Violet** ICE CREAM £
(✆020-7609 0444; www.rubyviolet.co.uk; Midlands Goods Shed, 3 Wharf Rd, N1; 1 scoop £3; ☺11am-7pm Mon & Tue, to 10pm Wed-Sun; ⓤKing's Cross St Pancras) Ruby Violet takes ice cream to the next level: flavours are wonderfully original (masala chai, raspberry and sweet potato) and toppings and hot sauces are shop-made. Plus, there's Pudding Club on Friday and Saturday nights, when you can dive into a mini baked Alaska or hot chocolate fondant. Eat in or sit by the fountain on Granary Sq.

Hoxton, Shoreditch & Spitalfields

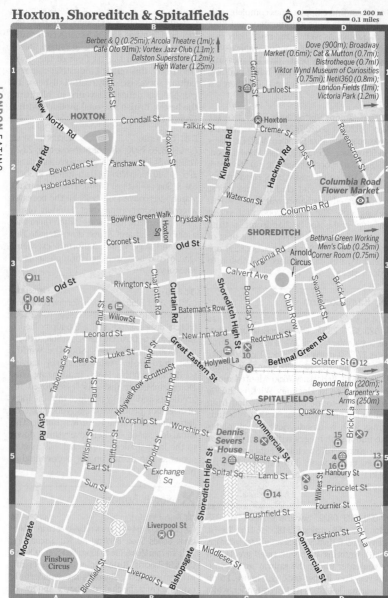

Chin Chin Labs ICE CREAM **£**
(Map p128; ☑07885 604284; www.chinchinlabs.com; 49-50 Camden Lock Pl, NW1; ice cream from £4.95; ◷noon-7pm; ⓊCamden Town) This is food chemistry at its absolute best. Chefs prepare the ice-cream mixture and freeze it on the spot by adding liquid nitrogen. Flavours change regularly and match the seasons (tonka bean, Valrhona chocolate, burnt-butter caramel or pandan leaf, for instance). The dozen toppings and sauces are equally creative. Try the ice-cream sandwich (£5.65): ice cream wedged inside gorgeous brownies or cookies.

Hoxton, Shoreditch & Spitalfields

Hook Camden Town   FISH & CHIPS £
(Map p128; ☏020-7482 0475; www.hookrestau
rants.com; 63-65 Parkway, NW1; mains £11-17;
⊙noon-3pm & 5.30-9pm Mon, to 10pm Tue-Thu,
to 10.30pm Fri & Sat, to 9pm Sun; 🚼; Ⓤ Camden
Town) 🌱 In addition to working entirely
with sustainable small fisheries and local
suppliers, Hook makes all its sauces on-
site and wraps its fish in recycled materials, supplying diners with extraordinarily
fine-tasting morsels. Totally fresh, the fish
arrives in panko breadcrumbs or tempura
batter, with seaweed salted chips. Wash it
down with craft beer, wines and cocktails.
There's also a great kids' menu.

★**Ottolenghi**   MEDITERRANEAN ££
(☏020-7288 1454; www.ottolenghi.co.uk; 287
Upper St, N1; breakfast £5.90-12.50, mains lunch/
dinner from £16.50/10; ⊙8am-10.30pm Mon-Sat,
9am-7pm Sun; 🍽; Ⓤ Highbury & Islington) Mountains of meringues tempt you through the
door of this deli-restaurant, where a sumptuous array of baked goods and fresh salads
greets you. Meals are as light and bright as
the brilliantly white interior design, with a
strong influence from the eastern Mediterranean. Mains at lunch are full platters and
include two salads.

Trullo   ITALIAN ££
(☏020-7226 2733; www.trullorestaurant.com;
300-302 St Paul's Rd, N1; mains £16.50-24;
⊙12.30-2.45pm & 6-10.15pm Mon-Sat, to 9.15pm
Sun; Ⓤ Highbury & Islington) Trullo's daily
homemade pasta is delicious (pappardelle,
fettuccine), but the main attraction here is
the charcoal grill, which churns out the likes
of succulent Italian-style pork chops, lamb
rump and fish. The all-Italian wine list is
brief but well chosen. Service is excellent,

although dinner time can get packed. Book
well in advance.

Caravan   INTERNATIONAL ££
(☏020-7101 7661; www.caravanrestaurants.co.uk; 1
Granary Sq, N1; small plates £7.50-9, mains £17.50-
19; ⊙8am-10.30pm Mon-Fri, 10am-10.30pm Sat,
to 4pm Sun; 🍽🌱; Ⓤ King's Cross St Pancras)
Housed in the lofty Granary Building, the
King's Cross redevelopment's first tenant is
a vast industrial-chic destination for tasty
fusion bites from around the world. You
can opt for several small plates to share tapas-style, or stick to main-sized dishes. The
outdoor seating area on Granary Sq is especially popular on warm days, and cocktails
are popular regardless of the weather.

✖ Greenwich

Marcella   ITALIAN ££
(☏020-3903 6561; https://marcella.london; 165a
Deptford High St, SE8; mains £12-16; ⊙noon-
2.30pm & 6-10pm Wed-Thu, to 10.30pm Fri & Sat,
noon-4pm Sun; 🌱; ® Deptford) If you avoid
pasta restaurants because you think you
can make it just as easily at home, Marcella
is here to prove you wrong. Perfect house-
made pasta comes with seasonally changing
sauces in simple but delicious combinations.
Starters are equally tasty (the house ricotta
is creamy heaven), as are the generously
large fish- and meat-based mains, made to
share.

✖ West London

Potli   INDIAN £
(☏020-8741 4328; www.potli.co.uk; 319-321 King
St, W6; weekday 1-/2-course set lunch £7.95/10.95,
weekend 3-course set lunch £14.95, mains £8-15;
⊙noon-2.30pm & 6-10.15pm Mon-Thu, noon-3pm

& 5.30-10.30pm Fri & Sat, noon-10pm Sun; ⌚; Ⓤ Stamford Brook or Ravenscourt Park) With its scattered pieces from Mumbai's Thieves Market, Indian-market-kitchen/bazaar cuisine, homemade pickles and spice mixes, plus an accent on genuine flavour, tantalising Potli deftly captures the aromas of a culinary home. Downstairs there's an open kitchen, and service is friendly. But it's the alluring menu – where flavours are teased into a rich and authentic Indian culinary experience – that's the real crowd-pleaser.

Dishoom
INDIAN ££

(Map p92; ☎ 020-7420 9325; www.dishoom.com/kensington; 4 Derry St, W8; ⊙ 8am-11pm Mon-Fri, from 9am Sat & Sun; ⌚; Ⓤ High St Kensington) Dishy Dishoom is not only a delightful art-deco-style treat and a delicious picture to behold, but also serves some of the finest Indian food in London. Staff at this new Kensington branch of the famous restaurant are also first rate, though you may have to wait in the evening (no reservations for groups of less than six after 6pm).

Wallace Restaurant
EUROPEAN ££

(Map p114; ☎ 020-7563 9505; www.peytonand byrne.co.uk/venues/wallace-restaurant; Hertford House, Manchester Sq, W1; mains £20-24; 3-course set menu £35; ⊙ 10am-5pm Sun-Thu, to 11pm Fri & Sat; Ⓤ Bond St) Run by an outfit with broader catering experience, the Wallace Collection's (p73) cafe-restaurant is a notch above what you'd expect from a museum. Equally good for a daytime coffee and pastry, an evening drink, or a more substantial French-inspired meal, it's in the covered, candy-pink-and-white central courtyard. Even potted plastic bay and Japanese maple trees don't detract from the civilised atmosphere.

Afternoon tea is served daily between 2.30pm and 4.30pm. It's £19 per person, or £27 if you'd like a glass of bubbles with your Coronation chicken sandwiches.

★ Flat Three
INTERNATIONAL ££

(Map p92; ☎ 020-7792 8987; www.flatthree. london; 120-122 Holland Park Ave, W11; mains £18-36; ⊙ noon-2.30pm Fri & Sat, 6-9.30pm Tue-Sat; ⌚🅿; Ⓤ Holland Park) With pronounced Japanese, Korean and Scandinavian inflections, this lovely downstairs Holland Park restaurant is full of surprises and creative discoveries. Juliana and her team have crafted something delectable in the kitchen, matched by a natural, simple and appealing dining space.

Vegans will find themselves well looked after, too. The five-course menu is excellent, while superb cocktails add the final touch.

Geales
SEAFOOD ££

(Map p92; ☎ 020-7727 7528; www.geales.com; 2 Farmer St, W8; mains £10-14, set meal from £22; ⊙ noon-3pm Fri, 6-11pm Mon-Fri, noon-11pm Sat & Sun; ⌚; Ⓤ Notting Hill Gate) Frying on Farmer St since 1939 – a bad year for the European restaurant trade – Geales has endured, despite its quiet location tucked away on a street corner behind Notting Hill Gate. The succulent fish in crispy batter is a fine catch, but the fish pie and rich mushy peas are also worth angling for, with jam roly poly and custard for pudding.

Farmacy
VEGAN ££

(Map p92; ☎ 020-7221 0705; www.farmacylondon. com; 74 Westbourne Grove, W2; £15-16.50; ⊙ 9am-5pm & 6-10pm Mon-Fri, 9am-4pm & 6-10pm Sat, 9am-4pm & 6-9.30pm Sun; ⌚🅿; Ⓤ Bayswater) 🍃 Pricey and well in step with dining trends, Farmacy aims squarely at wholesome, organic, gluten-free, vegan detoxing. For breakfast (Monday to Friday, brunch at weekends), size up a healthy choice of chickpea pancake 'omelettes', avocado on sourdough toast and buckwheat granola with fruit and almond milk. Walnut, beetroot and mushroom burgers or meat-free lasagne are on the lunch menu.

✖ Richmond, Kew & Hampton Court

★ Gelateria Danieli
GELATO £

(☎ 020-8439 9807; www.gelateriadanieli. com; 16 Brewers Lane, TW9; ice cream from £3; ⊙ 10am-6pm, from 11am Sun, open later in summer; ® Richmond, Ⓤ Richmond) Stuffed away down delightful narrow, pinched and flagstone-paved Brewer's Lane off Richmond Green, this tiny gelateria is a joy, and often busy. The handmade ice cream arrives in some two dozen lip-smacking flavours, from Bakewell Tart pudding to pistachio, walnut and tiramisu to pinenut and chocolate, scooped into small tubs or chocolate and hazelnut cones. There are milkshakes (£5) and coffee too.

★ Petersham Nurseries Cafe
MODERN EUROPEAN £££

(☎ 020-8332 8665; www.petershamnurseries. com; Church Lane, off Petersham Rd, TW10; mains

£24-30; ⊘ cafe noon-5pm Tue-Sun; Ⓤ Richmond) In a greenhouse at the back of the fabulously located Petersham Nurseries is this award-winning cafe straight out of the pages of *The Secret Garden*. The confidently executed cuisine includes organic ingredients harvested from the nursery gardens and produce adhering to Slow Food principles. Seasonal dishes include chargrilled monkfish, sage pork chops and veggie tagine. Booking in advance is essential.

Glasshouse   MODERN EUROPEAN £££

(☑020-8940 6777; www.glasshouserestaurant. co.uk; 14 Station Pde, TW9; 3-course lunch/dinner from £40/57.50; ⊘noon-12.30pm & 6.30-9.30pm Tue-Thu, noon-2.30pm & 6.30-10.30pm Fri & Sat, 12.30-4pm Sun; 🕿; ℝKew Gardens, ⓊKew Gardens) A day at Kew Gardens finds a perfect conclusion at this Michelin-starred gastronomic highlight. The glass-fronted exterior envelops a delicately lit, low-key interior, where the focus remains on divinely cooked food. Diners are rewarded with a seasonal, consistently accomplished menu from chef Gregory Wellman that combines English mainstays with modern European innovation.

 ## Drinking & Nightlife

West End

⭐ **Connaught Bar**   COCKTAIL BAR

(Map p86; ☑020-7499 7070; www.the-connaught. co.uk/mayfair-bars/connaught-bar; Connaught Hotel, Carlos Pl, W1; ⊘11am-1am Mon-Sat, to midnight Sun; 🕿; ⓊBond St) Drinkers who know their stuff single out the travelling martini trolley for particular praise, but almost everything mixed at the silver-and-platinum-toned bar at this iconic Mayfair hotel, built as the Coburg in 1815, gets the nod. You'll enjoy lavish art-deco design, faultless service, and some of the best drinks in town. Classic and reimagined cocktails range from £12 to £21.

⭐ **American Bar**   COCKTAIL BAR

(Map p66; ☑020-7836 4343; www.fairmont.com/ savoy-london/dining/americanbar; Savoy Hotel, Strand, WC2; ⊘11.30am-midnight Mon-Sat, from noon Sun; 🕿; ⓊTemple, Charing Cross or Embankment) Home of the Lonely Street, Concrete Jungle and other house cocktails named after iconic songs collected in the 'Savoy Songbook', this seriously dishy American Bar is a London icon, with soft blue furni-

ture, gleaming art-deco lines and live piano jazz from 6.30pm nightly. Cocktails start at £20 and peak at a stupefying £5000 (for the Sazerac, containing cognac from 1858).

Artesian   COCKTAIL BAR

(Map p114; ☑020-7636 1000; www.artesian-bar. co.uk; Langham Hotel, 1c Portland Pl, W1; ⊘11am-1am Mon-Wed, to 2am Thu-Sat, to midnight Sun; 🕿; ⓊOxford Circus) For a dose of colonial glamour with a touch of Oriental elegance, the sumptuous (often crowded) bar at the Langham hits many marks. Its cocktails (from £20) have won multiple awards, and the bar itself has been acclaimed the world's best. Its name acknowledges the 360ft-deep well beneath the hotel and, metaphorically, the immaculately designed 'source of indulgence' to be found within.

Sketch   COCKTAIL BAR

(Map p66; ☑020-7659 4500; www.sketch. london; 9 Conduit St, W1; ⊘7am-2am Mon-Fri, 8am-2am Sat, 8am-midnight Sun; ⓊOxford Circus) Merrily undefinable, Sketch has all at once a two-Michelin-starred restaurant, a millennial-pink dining room lined with nonsensical cartoons by British artist David Shrigley, a mystical-forest-themed bar with a self-playing piano, and toilets hidden inside gleaming white egg-shaped pods. We don't know what's happening either, but we're here for it.

Dukes London   COCKTAIL BAR

(Map p64; ☑020-7491 4840; www.dukeshotel.com/ dukes-bar; Dukes Hotel, 35 St James's Pl, SW1; ⊘2-11pm Mon-Sat, 4-10.30pm Sun; 🕿; ⓊGreen Park) Superb martinis and a gentlemen's-club-like ambience are the ingredients of this classic bar, where white-jacketed masters mix up perfect preparations. James Bond fans should make a pilgrimage here: author Ian Fleming used to frequent the place, where he undoubtedly ordered his drinks 'shaken, not stirred'. Smokers can ease into the secluded **Cognac and Cigar Garden** to enjoy cigars purchased here.

Swift   COCKTAIL BAR

(Map p66; ☑020-7437 7820; www.barswift.com; 12 Old Compton St, W1; ⊘3pm-midnight Mon-Sat, to 10.30pm Sun; ⓊLeicester Sq or Tottenham Court Rd) A favourite Soho drinking spot, Swift has a sleek, candlelit upstairs bar for walk-ins seeking a superior cocktail before dinner or the theatre, and a bookings-only downstairs bar (open from 5pm) offering more than

LGBT+ LONDON

The West End, particularly Soho, is the visible centre of LGBT+ London, with venues clustered around Old Compton St and its surrounds, but there are queer-friendly venues scattered all over the capital.

Heaven (Map p66; ☑ 020-7930 2020; www.heavennightclub-london.com; Villiers St, WC2; ☺ 11pm-5am Mon, to 4am Thu & Fri, 10.30pm-5am Sat; Ⓤ Embankment or Charing Cross) Encouraging hedonism since 1979, when it opened on the site of a former roller disco, this perennially popular mixed/gay bar under the Charing Cross arches hosts excellent gigs and club nights, and has hosted New Order, The Birthday Party, Killing Joke and many a legendary act. Monday's mixed party Popcorn offers one of the best weeknight's clubbing in the capital.

The celebrated G-A-Y takes place here on Thursday (G-A-Y Porn Idol), Friday (G-A-Y Camp Attack) and Saturday (plain ol' G-A-Y).

Duke of Wellington (Map p66; ☑ 020-7439 1274; www.dukeofwellingtonsoho.co.uk/london; 77 Wardour St, W1; ☺ noon-midnight Mon-Sat, to 11.30pm Sun; ☎; Ⓤ Leicester Sq) This twin-floored pub off Old Compton St attracts a bearded, fun-loving gay crowd, welcoming friendly comers of all persuasions. A classic jumping-off point for wilder Soho nights, it spills onto the pavement in the warmer months, hosting free DJ after-parties when 'divas' such as Mariah Carey and Celine Dion are performing in town.

Royal Vauxhall Tavern (☑ 020-7820 1222; www.vauxhalltavern.com; 372 Kennington Lane, SE11; ☺ 7pm-midnight Mon-Thu, to 4am Fri, 9pm-4am Sat, 4-10.30pm Sun; Ⓤ Vauxhall) A gay landmark, the welcoming Royal Vauxhall Tavern is one of the city's most loved cabaret and performance venues, and there's something on every night of the week. Saturday's Duckie, dubbed a rock-and-roll honky tonk, is the club's signature queer performance.

Bethnal Green Working Men's Club (☑ 020-7739 7170; www.workersplaytime.net; 42-44 Pollard Row, E2; ☺ pub 6pm-late Wed-Sat, club hours vary; Ⓤ Bethnal Green) As it says on the tin, this is a true working men's club. Except that this one has opened its doors and let in all kinds of off-the-wall club nights, including trashy burlesque, LGBT+ shindigs, retro nights, beach parties and bake-offs. Expect sticky carpets, a shimmery stage set and a space akin to a school-hall disco.

Two Brewers (☑ 020-7819 9539; www.the2brewers.com; 114 Clapham High St, SW4; ☺ 5pm-2am Sun-Wed, to 3am Thu, to 4am Fri & Sat; Ⓤ Clapham Common) Two Brewers endures as one of the best London gay bars outside the LGBT+ villages of Soho and Vauxhall. There's cabaret, bingo or karaoke most nights of the week, and the venue is a full-on dancing madhouse on weekends. ID is required for entry, and there's often a cover charge.

Dalston Superstore (☑ 020-7254 2273; www.dalstonsuperstore.com; 117 Kingsland High St, E8; ☺ 5pm-2am Mon, noon-2am Tue-Fri, noon-3am Sat, 10am-2am Sun; Ⓤ Dalston Kingsland) Bar, club or diner? Gay, lesbian or straight? Dalston Superstore is hard to pigeonhole, which we suspect is the point. This two-level industrial space is open all day but really comes into its own after dark when there are club nights in the basement.

250 whiskies, art-deco-inspired sofas, and live blues and jazz from 9pm on Fridays and Saturdays. Bar snacks include oysters and olives.

Princess Louise   PUB
(Map p66; ☑ 020-7405 8816; 208 High Holborn, WC1; ☺ 11am-11pm Mon-Fri, from noon Sat, noon-6.45pm Sun; Ⓤ Holborn) The gorgeous ground-floor saloon of this Sam Smith's pub, dating from 1872, boasts pressed-tin ceilings, handsome tiling, etched mirrors and 'snob screens', and a stunning central horseshoe bar. The original Victorian wood partitions provide plenty of private nooks, and typical pub food is served from noon to 2.30pm Monday to Friday, and 6pm to 8.30pm Monday to Thursday (mains £8 to £12).

Terroirs   WINE BAR
(Map p66; ☑ 020-7036 0660; www.terroirswinebar.com; 5 William IV St, WC2; ☺ noon-11pm Mon-Sat; ☎; Ⓤ Charing Cross) This food-friendly wine bar near Charing Cross has a fantastic

selection of Old and New World wines, with plenty by the glass and available for takeaway. Food isn't an afterthought either, with small plates such as burrata with clementine, radicchio and pine nuts augmented by a couple of mains (perhaps lamb rump with black-cabbage pesto and aubergine) and charcuterie platters.

Dog & Duck   PUB

(Map p66; ☑ 020-7494 0697; www.nicholsonspubs.co.uk; 18 Bateman St, W1; ⊙11.30am-11pm Mon-Wed, to 1am Thu-Sat, noon-10.30pm Sun; Ⓤ Tottenham Court Rd) With a fine array of real ales and some stunning Victorian glazed tiling and pressed-tin ceilings adorning its intimate interior, the Dog & Duck has attracted an eclectic crowd since opening its doors around 1734 – including John Constable, Dante Gabrielle Rossetti, George Orwell and Madonna. Intriguing pies such as boar and chorizo and wild game reward the curious.

into the sleek mod furniture at this hotel bar (p109), where floor-to-double-height-ceiling bookcases and pop-art portraits of the Queen overlook the Tower of London just across the street. The standard drinks menu doesn't stray into groundbreaking territory, but the wrap-around outdoor balcony provides unforgettable sundowner views.

Ye Olde Cheshire Cheese   PUB

(Map p76; ☑ 020-7353 6170; Wine Office Ct, 145 Fleet St, EC4; ⊙noon-11pm Mon-Sat; ⓇCity Thameslink, Ⓤ Blackfriars) Rebuilt in 1667 after the Great Fire, this is one of London's most famous – and most crowded – pubs. It has strong literary connections, with Mark Twain, Sir Arthur Conan Doyle and Charles Dickens on the list of regulars. The gloomy interior, narrow passageways and convoluted layout add to its appeal, but surly staff and tight quarters will force you to move on quickly.

🍴 City of London

⭐ Nickel Bar   COCKTAIL BAR

(Map p76; ☑ 020-3828 2000; www.thened.com/restaurants/the-nickel-bar; 27 Poultry, EC2; ⊙8am-2am Mon-Fri, 9am-3am Sat, to midnight Sun; 🔊; Ⓤ Bank) There's something *Great Gatsby*–ish about the Ned (p109) hotel: the elevated jazz pianists, the vast verdite columns, the classy American-inspired cocktails. Of all the public bars inside this magnificent former banking hall, the Nickel Bar soaks up the atmosphere best. Inspired by the glamorous art-deco saloons and the ocean-liner-era elegance, this is timeless nightcap territory.

⭐ Oriole   COCKTAIL BAR

(Map p76; ☑ 020-3457 8099; www.oriolebar.com; E Poultry Ave, EC1; ⊙6pm-2am Tue-Sun, to 11pm Mon; Ⓤ Farringdon) Down a darkened alley through the eerie evening quiet of Smithfield Market is an unlikely spot for one of London's best cocktail bars, but the journey of discovery is the theme at speakeasy-style Oriole. The cocktail menu, divided into Old World, New World and the Orient, traverses the globe, with out-of-this-world ingredients including clarified octopus milk, strawberry tree curd and slow-cooked chai palm.

cloudM   ROOFTOP BAR

(Map p76; ☑ 020-3519 4830; www.citizenm.com/cloudm-tower-of-london; 40 Trinity Sq, citizenM Tower of London, EC3; ⊙7am-1am Mon-Fri, 3pm-1am Sat, to midnight Sun; 🔊; Ⓤ Tower Hill) Settle

🍴 South Bank

⭐ Seabird   ROOFTOP BAR

(Map p84; ☑ 020-7903 3050; https://seabird london.com; Hoxton Southwark, 40 Blackfriars Rd, SE1; ⊙noon-midnight Mon-Thu, to 1am Fri, 11am-1am Sat, to midnight Sun; Ⓤ Southwark) South Bank's latest rooftop bar might also be its best. Atop the new Hoxton Southwark (p109) hotel, sleek Seabird has palm-filled indoor and outdoor spaces where you can spy St Paul's from the comfort of your wicker seat. If you're hungry, seafood is the speciality, and the restaurant claims London's longest oyster list.

⭐ Kings Arms   PUB

(Map p84; ☑ 020-7207 0784; www.thekings armslondon.co.uk; 25 Roupell St, SE1; ⊙11am-11pm Mon-Sat, noon-10.30pm Sun; Ⓤ Waterloo) Set on old-school Roupell St (Map p84; Roupell St, SE1; Ⓤ Waterloo), this charming backstreet neighbourhood boozer serves up a rotating selection of traditional ales and bottled beers. The after-work crowd often makes a pit stop here before heading to Waterloo station, spilling out onto the street at peak hours. The farmhouse-style room at the back of the pub serves decent Thai food.

George Inn   PUB

(Map p84; ☑ 020-7407 2056; www.national trust.org.uk/george-inn; 77 Borough High St, SE1; ⊙11am-11pm Mon-Thu, to midnight Fri & Sat, noon-10.30pm Sun; Ⓤ London Bridge) This magnificent galleried coaching inn is the last of its kind in London. The building, owned by the National Trust, dates from 1677 and is mentioned in Charles Dickens' *Little Dorrit*. In the evenings, the picnic benches in the huge cobbled courtyard fill up (no reservations); otherwise, find a spot in the labyrinth of dark rooms and corridors inside.

Lyaness
COCKTAIL BAR

(Map p84; ☎020-3747 1063; https://lyaness.com; Sea Containers, 20 Upper Ground, SE1; ⊙4pm-1am Mon-Wed, noon-2am Thu-Sat, to 12.30am Sun; ☏; ⓊSouthwark) Six months after Dandelyan was named the best bar in the world, renowned mixologist Ryan Chetiyawardana closed it down. Reincarnated in that space with much the same atmosphere and modus operandi is Lyaness. The bar prides itself on unusual ingredients; look out for vegan honey, whey liqueur and onyx, a completely new type of alcohol.

⚑ Kensington & Hyde Park

Anglesea Arms
PUB

(Map p86; ☎020-7373 7960; www.angleseaarms. com; 15 Selwood Tce, SW7; ⊙11am-11pm Mon-Sat, to 10.30pm Sun; ⓊSouth Kensington) Seasoned with age and decades of ale-quaffing patrons (including Charles Dickens, who lived on the same road, and DH Lawrence), this old-school pub boasts considerable character and a strong showing of beers and gins (over two dozen), while the terrace out front swarms with punters in warmer months. Arch-criminal Bruce Reynolds masterminded the 1963 Great Train Robbery over drinks here.

K Bar
COCKTAIL BAR

(Map p86; ☎020-7589 6300; www.townhouse kensington.com/k-bar; Town House, 109-113 Queen's Gate, SW7; cocktails £10; ⊙4pm-midnight Mon-Thu, to 1am Fri, noon-1am Sat, to 11pm Sun; ☏; ⓊSouth Kensington) In a part of town traditionally bereft of choice, the K Bar is a reassuring presence. A hotel bar maybe, but don't let that stop you – the place exudes panache with its leather-panelled and green-marble counter bar, smoothly glinting brass, oak walls and chandeliers, drawing a cashed-up crowd who enjoy themselves. Cocktails are prepared with as much class as the ambience.

Queen's Arms
PUB

(Map p86; www.thequeensarmskensington. co.uk; 30 Queen's Gate Mews, SW7; ⊙noon-11pm; ⓊGloucester Rd) Just around the corner from the Royal Albert Hall is this blue-grey-painted godsend. Located in an adorable cobbled-mews setting off bustling Queen's Gate, the pub beckons with a cosy interior, welcoming staff and a right royal selection of ales – including selections from small, local cask brewers – and ciders on tap. In warm weather, drinkers stand outside in the mews (only permitted on one side).

⚑ Clerkenwell, Shoreditch & Spitalfields

★ Nightjar
COCKTAIL BAR

(Map p120; ☎020-7253 4101; https://barnightjar. com; 129 City Rd, EC1V; music cover £5-8; ⊙6pm-1am, to 2am Thu, to 3am Fri & Sat; ⓊOld St) Behind a nondescript, gold-knobbed door just north of the Old Street roundabout is this bona fide speakeasy, pouring award-winning libations from a four-section menu that delineates the evolution of the cocktail. Leather banquettes, brick-walled booths and art-deco liquor cabinets stocked with vintage spirits set the perfect scene for jazz and blues acts that take the stage nightly at 9.30pm.

★ Discount Suit Company
COCKTAIL BAR

(Map p76; ☎020-7247 8755; www.discountsuit company.co.uk; 29a Wentworth St, E1; ⊙5pm-midnight Mon-Thu, 2pm-1am Fri & Sat, 5-11pm Sun; ⓊAldgate East) Tucked away like a hidden seam, Discount Suit Company is one of the city's finest speakeasies – though on weekends you'll see that this closet-sized space is no secret. Superb, reasonably priced concoctions (a rarity in this area) are created behind the bar, originally a storeroom for the suit company above. Superfriendly staff and mixologists who'll happily go off-piste seal the deal.

★ Fabric
CLUB

(Map p76; ☎020-7336 8898; www.fabriclondon. com; 77a Charterhouse St, EC1; ⊙11pm-7am Fri, to 8am Sat, to 5.30am Sun; ⓊFarringdon) The monarch of London's after-hours scene, Fabric is a huge subterranean rave cave housed in a converted meat cold store. Each room has its own sound system, which you'll really feel in Room One – it has a 'bodysonic' vibrating dance floor that's attached to 450 bass shakers, which emit low-end frequencies so the music radiates into your muscles just by standing there.

★ **Fox & Anchor** PUB

(Map p76; ☑020-7250 1300; www.foxandanchor.com; 115 Charterhouse St, EC1; ☺7am-11pm, from 8.30am Sat, from 11am Sun; ☏; Ⓤ Barbican) Behind the Fox & Anchor's wonderful 1898 art-nouveau facade is a stunning traditional Victorian boozer, one of the last remaining market pubs in London that's permitted to serve alcohol before 11am. Fully celebrating its proximity to Smithfield Market, the grub is gloriously meaty. Only the most voracious of carnivores should opt for the City Boy Breakfast (£19.50).

Ye Olde Mitre PUB

(Map p76; www.yeoldemitreholborn.co.uk; 1 Ely Ct, EC1; ☺11am-11pm Mon-Fri; ☏; Ⓤ Farringdon) A delightfully cosy historic pub with an extensive beer selection, tucked away in a backstreet off Hatton Garden, Ye Olde Mitre was originally built in 1546 for the servants of Ely Palace. There's no music, so rooms echo only with amiable chit-chat. Queen Elizabeth I danced around the cherry tree by the bar, or so they say.

🍸 East London

Dove PUB

(☑020-7275 7617; www.dovepubs.com; 24-28 Broadway Market, E8; ☺noon-11pm, from 11am Sat; ☏; Ⓤ London Fields) The Dove has a rambling series of wooden floorboard rooms and a wide range of Belgian Trappist, wheat and fruit-flavoured beers. Drinkers spill on to the street in warmer weather, or hunker down in the low-lit back room with board games when it's chilly. Pub meals with good vegetarian options are available, too.

Cat & Mutton PUB

(☑020-7249 6555; www.catandmutton.com; 76 Broadway Market, E8; ☺noon-11pm Mon, to midnight Tue-Thu, to 1am Fri, 10am-1am Sat, noon-11.30pm Sun; Ⓤ London Fields) At this fabulous Georgian pub, Hackney locals sup pints under the watchful eyes of hunting trophies, B&W photos of old-time boxers and a large portrait of Karl Marx. If it's crammed downstairs, head up the spiral staircase to the comfy couches. Weekends get rowdy, with DJs spinning their best tunes until late.

Netil360 ROOFTOP BAR

(www.netil360.com; 1 Westgate St, E8; ☺noon-8.30pm Wed & Sun, to 10.30pm Thu-Sat Apr-Dec; ☏; Ⓤ London Fields) Perched atop Netil House, this uberhip rooftop cafe-bar offers incredible views over London, with brass telescopes enabling you to get better acquainted with workers in 'the Gherkin' building. In between drinks you can knock out a game of croquet on the Astroturf, or perhaps book a hot tub for you and your mates to stew in.

High Water COCKTAIL BAR

(☑020-7241 1984; www.highwaterlondon.com; 23 Stoke Newington Rd, N16; ☺4.30pm-2am Mon-Thu, 3.30pm-3am Fri & Sat, 3.30pm-2am Sun; ☒ Dalston Kingsland) Table service is offered at this narrow, brick-walled bar – but if you like to indulge in conversations with complete strangers, we suggest grabbing a seat at the bar. That way you can interrogate the charming staff about what corners of their largely self-devised cocktail list will best cater to your taste, and then watch them concoct it.

Carpenter's Arms PUB

(☑020-7739 6342; www.carpentersarmsfreehouse.com; 73 Cheshire St, E2; ☺4-11.30pm Mon-Thu, noon-midnight Fri & Sat, noon-10.30pm Sun; ☏; Ⓤ Shoreditch High St) Once owned by infamous gangsters the Kray brothers (who bought it for their old ma to run), this chic yet cosy pub has been beautifully restored and its many wooden surfaces positively gleam. A back room and small yard provide a little more space for the convivial drinkers. There's a huge range of draught and bottled beers and ciders.

🍸 North London

★ **Holly Bush** PUB

(☑020-7435 2892; www.hollybushhampstead.co.uk; 22 Holly Mount, NW3; ☺noon-11pm Mon-Sat, to 10.30pm Sun; ☏🍴☺; Ⓤ Hampstead) This beautiful Grade II–listed Georgian pub boasts a splendid antique interior, with open fires in winter. It has a knack for making you stay longer than you planned. Set above Heath St, in a secluded hilltop location, it's reached via the Holly Bush Steps.

Edinboro Castle PUB

(Map p128; ☑020-7255 9651; www.edinborocastlepub.co.uk; 57 Mornington Tce, NW1; ☺noon-11pm Mon-Sat, to 10.30pm Sun; ☏; Ⓤ Camden Town) Large and relaxed, the Edinboro offers a fun

Camdon Town

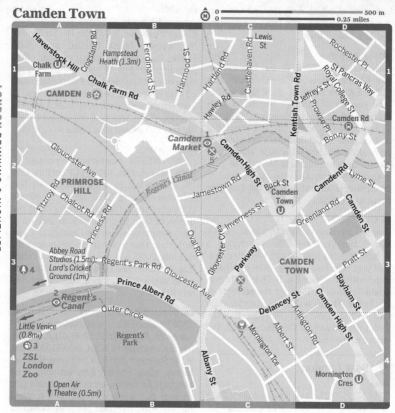

Camden Town

◎ Top Sights

◎ Sights

✕ Eating

◎ Drinking & Nightlife

◎ Entertainment

atmosphere, a fine bar and a full menu. The highlight, however, is the huge beer garden, complete with warm-weather barbecues and decorated with coloured lights on long summer evenings. Patio heaters appear in winter.

▼ Greenwich

Old Brewery PUB
(☎020-3437 2222; www.oldbrewerygreenwich. com; Pepys House, Old Royal Naval College, SE10; ⊙10am-11pm Mon-Sat, to 10.30pm Sun; ☎; Ⓤ Cutty Sark) On the grounds of the Old Royal Naval College (p100), the Old Brewery once housed Greenwich Meantime, one of London's earliest craft breweries. Now owned by Young's pub company, it serves decent pub food and a range of beers, best enjoyed in the huge beer garden.

Cutty Sark Tavern PUB
(☎020-8858 3146; www.cuttysarkse10.co.uk; 4-6 Ballast Quay, SE10; ⊙11.30am-11pm Mon-Sat, noon-10.30pm Sun; ☎; Ⓤ Cutty Sark) ✐ Housed in a delightful bow-windowed, wood-beamed Georgian building directly on the Thames,

this 200-year-old tavern is one of the few independent pubs left in Greenwich. Half a dozen cask-conditioned ales on tap line the bar, there's an inviting riverside seating area opposite and an upstairs dining room looking out on to glorious views.

Greenwich Union PUB
(☎020-8692 6258; www.greenwichunion.com; 56 Royal Hill, SE10; ⊘noon-11pm Mon-Thu, from 11.30am Fri & Sat, 11.30am-10.30pm Sun; 🛜; Ⓤ Greenwich) The award-winning Union plies a handful of local microbrewery beers (it used to be owned by Greenwich-based Meantime Brewery) and a strong list of ales, plus bottled international brews. It's a handsome place with a welcoming long, narrow bar leading to a conservatory and beer garden at the back.

Trafalgar Tavern PUB
(☎020-3887 9886; www.trafalgartavern.co.uk; Park Row, SE10; ⊘noon-11pm Mon-Thu, to 1am Fri, 9am-1am Sat, to 11pm Sun; Ⓤ Cutty Sark) This elegant tavern, with crystal chandeliers, nautical decor and big windows overlooking the Thames, is steeped in history. Dickens apparently knocked back a few here – and used it as the setting for the wedding-breakfast scene in *Our Mutual Friend* – and Prime Ministers William Gladstone and Benjamin Disraeli used to dine on the pub's celebrated whitebait.

📍 West London

⭐**Troubadour** BAR
(☎020-7341 6333; www.troubadourlondon.com; 263-267 Old Brompton Rd, SW5; ⊘cafe 9am-midnight, club 8pm-12.30am or 2am Mon-Sat, to 11.30pm Sun; 🛜; Ⓤ Earl's Court) On a comparable spiritual plane to Paris' Shakespeare and Company bookshop, this eccentric, time-warped and convivial boho bar-cafe has been serenading drinkers since 1954. Adele, Ed Sheeran, Joni Mitchell, Jimi Hendrix and Bob Dylan have performed here, and there's still live music (largely jazz and folk) most nights downstairs. A wide-ranging wine list, Sunday roasts and a pleasant rear garden complete the picture.

Windsor Castle PUB
(Map p92; ☎020-7243 8797; www.thewindsor castlekensington.co.uk; 114 Campden Hill Rd, W11; ⊘noon-11pm Mon-Sat, to 10.30pm Sun; 🛜; Ⓤ Notting Hill Gate) This classic tavern on the brow of Campden Hill Rd has history, nooks and

charm on tap. Alongside a decent beer selection and a solid gastropub-style menu, it has a historic compartmentalised interior, a roaring fire (in winter), a delightful beer garden (in summer) and affable regulars (all seasons). In the old days, Windsor Castle was visible from the pub, hence the name.

🍸 Richmond, Kew & Hampton Court

City Barge PUB
(☎020-8994 2148; www.metropolitanpubcompany.com/our-pubs/the-city-barge; 27 Strand on the Green, W4; ⊘noon-11pm Mon-Thu, to midnight Fri, 10am-midnight Sat, 10am-10.30pm Sun; 🛜; Ⓤ Gunnersbury) In a line of small riverside cottages facing wooded Oliver's Island (where Cromwell is alleged to have taken refuge), this excellent pub looks straight onto the muddy Thames. Its lineage to the 14th century would make it one of London's most ancient pubs. There are three open fires, drinkers spill outside in clement weather and a fine gastropub menu has taken hold.

White Cross PUB
(☎020-8940 6844; www.thewhitecrossrichmond.com; Water Lane, TW9; ⊘10am-11pm, to 10.30pm Sun; 🛜; Ⓤ Richmond) The riverside location and fine food and ales make this bay-windowed pub – on the site of a former friary – a winner. There are entrances for low and high tides, but when the river is at its highest, Cholmondeley Walk along the Thames floods and the pub is out of bounds to those not willing to wade. Wellies are provided.

⭐ Entertainment

Theatre

Donmar Warehouse THEATRE
(Map p66; ☎020-3282 3808; www.donmarware house.com; 41 Earlham St, WC2; Ⓤ Covent Garden) The 250-seat Donmar Warehouse is London's 'thinking person's theatre'. With new artistic director Michael Longhurst, works in progress are more provocative and less celebrity-driven than traditional West End theatre.

Almeida THEATRE
(☎020-7359 4404; www.almeida.co.uk; Almeida St, N1; tickets £10-42.50; Ⓤ Highbury & Islington) Housed in a Grade II–listed Victorian building, this plush 325-seat theatre can be relied on for imaginative programming. Its emphasis is on new, up-and-coming talent. For

theatre-goers aged 25 and under, £5 tickets (two per person) are available for select performances.

★ Bush Theatre
THEATRE

(☑ 020-8743 5050; www.bushtheatre.co.uk; 7 Uxbridge Rd, W12; ⊙ 10am-11pm Mon-Sat; Ⓤ Shepherd's Bush) Located in the former Passmore Edwards Public Library building, this West London theatre is renowned for encouraging new writing. Its success since 1972 is down to strong plays from the likes of Jonathan Harvey, Conor McPherson, Stephen Poliakoff, Caroline Horton and Tanya Ronder. The Holloway Theatre is the main space; the Studio is the smaller, 70-seat venue. There's an excellent cafe and bar (⊙ 10am-11pm Mon-Sat; ☎).

National Theatre
THEATRE

(Map p84; ☑ 020-7452 3000; www.national theatre.org.uk; Upper Ground, SE1; Ⓤ Waterloo) The nation's flagship theatre delivers up to 25 shows every year across its three venues inside this brutalist block. Even if you're not here for a show, you can explore the foyers, which contain a bookshop, restaurants, bars and exhibition spaces. Get behind the scenes on a tour, including going backstage, a deep-dive into the building's architecture and an experience with the costume team.

Royal Court Theatre
THEATRE

(Map p86; ☑ 020-75655000; www.royalcourttheatre. com; Sloane Sq, SW1; tickets £12-38; Ⓤ Sloane Sq) Equally renowned for staging innovative new plays and old classics, the Royal Court is among London's most progressive theatres and has continued to foster major writing talent across the UK for over 60 years. There are two auditoriums: the main Jerwood Theatre Downstairs and the much-smaller studio Jerwood Theatre Upstairs.

Old Vic
THEATRE

(Map p84; ☑ 0344 871 7628; www.oldvictheatre. com; The Cut, SE1; Ⓤ Waterloo) This 1000-seater nonprofit theatre celebrated its 200th season in 2018 and continues to bring eclectic programming occasionally bolstered by big-name actors, such as Daniel Radcliffe.

Young Vic
THEATRE

(Map p84; ☑ 020-7922 2922; www.youngvic.org; 66 The Cut, SE1; ⊙ box office 10am-6pm Mon-Sat; Ⓤ Southwark) This groundbreaking theatre is as much about showcasing and discovering new talent as it is about people discovering theatre. The Young Vic features actors, directors and plays from across the world, many tackling contemporary political and cultural issues, such as the death penalty, racism or corruption, and often blending dance and music with acting.

Bridge Theatre
THEATRE

(Map p84; ☑ 0333 320 0051; https://bridgetheatre. co.uk; 3 Potters Fields Park, SE1; Ⓤ London Bridge) Opened in 2017 and London's first new major theatre in 80 years, Bridge Theatre seats 900 in a cool, modern space and focuses on new productions, with the occasional classic thrown in.

Arcola Theatre
THEATRE

(☑ 020-7503 1646; www.arcolatheatre.com; 24 Ashwin St, E8; Ⓤ Dalston Junction) Dalston's a fair schlep from the West End, but drama buffs still flock to this innovative theatre for its adventurous and eclectic productions. A unique annual feature is Grimeborn, an opera festival focusing on lesser-known or new works – it's Dalston's answer to East Sussex's world-famous Glyndebourne opera festival, taking place around the same time (August).

Live Music

★ Royal Albert Hall
CONCERT VENUE

(Map p86; ☑ 0845 401 5034; 020-7589 8212; www.royalalberthall.com; Kensington Gore, SW7; Ⓤ South Kensington) This splendid Victorian concert hall hosts classical music, rock and other performances, but is famously the venue for the BBC-sponsored Proms. Booking is possible, but from mid-July to mid-September Promenaders queue for £5 standing tickets that go on sale one hour before curtain-up. Otherwise, the box office and prepaid-ticket collection counter are through door 12 (south side of the hall).

★ Scala
LIVE MUSIC

(Map p96; ☑ 020-7833 2022; www.scala.co.uk; 275 Pentonville Rd, N1; cover £10-35; Ⓤ King's Cross St Pancras) Opened in 1920 as a cutting-edge golden-age cinema, Scala slipped into porn-movie territory in the 1970s, only to be reborn as a club and live-music venue in the early 2000s. It's one of the top places in London to catch an intimate gig and is a great dance space, too, hosting a diverse range of club nights.

★ Ronnie Scott's
JAZZ

(Map p66; ☑ 020-7439 0747; www.ronnie scotts.co.uk; 47 Frith St, W1; ⊙ 6pm-3am Mon-Sat, noon-4pm & 6.30pm-midnight Sun;

U Leicester Sq or Tottenham Court Rd) Ronnie Scott's jazz club opened in 1959 and became widely known as Britain's best, hosting such luminaries as Miles Davis, Charlie Parker, Ella Fitzgerald, Count Basie and Sarah Vaughan. The club continues to build upon its formidable reputation by presenting a range of big names and new talent. Book in advance, or come for a more informal gig at **Upstairs @ Ronnie's**.

Roundhouse   CONCERT VENUE
(Map p128; ☑ 0300 678 9222; www.roundhouse. org.uk; Chalk Farm Rd, NW1; U Chalk Farm) Built as a railway repair shed in 1847, this unusual Grade II–listed round building became an arts centre in the 1960s and hosted legendary bands before falling into near-dereliction in 1983. Its 21st-century resurrection as a creative hub has been a great success and it now hosts everything from big-name concerts to dance, circuses, stand-up comedy, poetry slams and improvisation.

O2 Academy Brixton   LIVE MUSIC
(☑ 020-7771 3000; https://academymusicgroup. com/o2academybrixton; 211 Stockwell Rd, SW9; U Brixton) The O2 hosts club nights and gigs galore inside a 1920s art-deco theatre with a nearly 5000-person capacity. The sloped floor guarantees good views, though if you aren't dancing enough, the ground, sticky with beer spills, may glue you into place.

Cafe Oto   LIVE MUSIC
(www.cafeoto.co.uk; 18-22 Ashwin St, E8; ☉ 9.30am-late; ☎; U Dalston Junction) Dedicating itself to promoting experimental and alternative musicians, this is Dalston's premier venue for music nerds to stroke their proverbial beards while listening to electronic bleeps, Japanese psychedelica or avant-folk. Set in a converted print warehouse, it's one of London's most idiosyncratic live-music venues. When there are no gigs on, it's open as a cafe-bar.

Vortex Jazz Club   JAZZ
(☑ 020-7254 4097; www.vortexjazz.co.uk; 11 Gillett Sq, N16; ☉ 8pm-midnight; ℝ Dalston Kingsland) With a fantastically varied menu of jazz, the Vortex hosts an outstanding line-up of musicians, singers and songwriters from the UK, the US, Europe, Africa and beyond. It's a small venue so make sure you book if there's an act you particularly fancy.

Cinemas

★ **Prince Charles Cinema**   CINEMA
(Map p66; ☑ 020-7494 3654; www.princecharles cinema.com; 7 Leicester Pl, WC2; U Leicester Sq) The last independent theatre in the West End, Prince Charles Cinema is universally loved for its show-anything attitude. Singalongs and quote-a-longs (*Frozen*, *Elf* and *The Rocky Horror Picture Show* are perennial faves), all-nighter movie marathons (including PJ parties), and anniversary and special-format screenings regularly grace its listings. Arriving in costumed character is encouraged.

Electric Cinema   CINEMA
(Map p92; ☑ 020-7908 9696; www.electric cinema.co.uk; 191 Portobello Rd, W11; adult £17.50-45, child £10; U Ladbroke Grove) Having notched up its centenary in 2011, the Electric is one of the UK's oldest cinemas, now updated. Avail yourself of the luxurious leather armchairs, sofas, footstools and tables for food and drink in the auditorium, or select one of the six front-row double beds! Tickets are cheapest on Mondays.

BFI Southbank   CINEMA
(Map p84; ☑ 020-7928 3232; https://whatson.bfi. org.uk; Belvedere Rd, SE1; ☉ 9.45am-11pm; U Waterloo) Tucked almost out of sight under the arches of Waterloo Bridge, the British Film Institute contains four cinemas that screen thousands of films each year (many art-house), a gallery devoted to the moving image, and a mediatheque where you can watch movie and TV highlights from the BFI National Archive.

Comedy

Comedy Store   COMEDY
(Map p66; ☑ 0844 871 7699; www.thecomedystore. co.uk; 1a Oxendon St, SW1; U Piccadilly Circus) This is one of the first (and some say one of the best) comedy clubs in London. The Comedy Store Players take the stage on Wednesday and Sunday nights, with the wonderful Josie Lawrence, a veteran of the scene, plus special guest comedians. On Thursdays, Fridays and Saturdays, Best in Stand Up features the best of London's comedy circuit.

Soho Theatre   COMEDY
(Map p66; ☑ 020-7478 0100; https://sohotheatre. com; 21 Dean St, W1; tickets £8-25; U Tottenham Court Rd) The Soho Theatre has developed a superb reputation for showcasing new comedy-writing talent as well as drama. It hosts top stand-up and sketch-based comedians,

SPORTING LONDON

You're very unlikely to land tickets to the FA Cup Final at Wembley Stadium or front-row seats for the Wimbledon finals, but there are plenty of ways to enjoy sport in London. You could find yourself watching the Oxford–Cambridge boat race (p105), cheering runners at the London Marathon or catching some park cricket in summer – there's lots on offer. Why not check out the impressive facilities in the Queen Elizabeth Olympic Park (p95), which hosts the (former Olympic) London Stadium, the stunning Aquatics Centre and the cutting-edge Velodrome.

Alternatively, take a tour of one of the capital's great sporting stadia:

Lord's (☑ 020-7616 8500; https://apps.lords.org/lords/tours-and-museum; St John's Wood Rd, NW8; tours adult/child £25/16; ⊙ 4-6 tours daily; Ⓤ St John's Wood) The hallowed 'home of cricket', with a fascinating museum.

Wimbledon Lawn Tennis Museum (☑ 020-8946 6131; www.wimbledon.com/museum; Gate 4, Church Rd, SW19; adult/child £13/8, museum & tour £25/15; ⊙ 10am-5pm, last admission 4.30pm; ⓡ Wimbledon, ⓡ Wimbledon, Ⓤ Wimbledon, Ⓤ Southfields) Chart the history of lawn tennis, and see Centre Court from the 360-degree viewing box.

Wembley Stadium (☑ 0800 169 9933; www.wembleystadium.com; tours adult/child £19/12; Ⓤ Wembley Park) The city's landmark national stadium, used for football test matches and mega concerts.

Twickenham Stadium (☑ 020-8892 8877; www.englandrugby.com/twickenham; 200 Whitton Rd, Twickenham, TW2; tours adult/child £25/15; ⓡ Twickenham, Ⓤ Hounslow East) London's famous rugby union stadium, used for international test matches.

London Stadium (☑ 020-8522 6157; www.london-stadium.com; Queen Elizabeth Olympic Park, E20; tours adult/child £19/11; ⊙ tours 10am-4.15pm, to 4.45pm Sat; Ⓤ Pudding Mill Lane) Built as the centrepiece stadium for the 2012 Olympics and now home to West Ham United FC.

Arsenal Emirates Stadium (☑ 020-7619 5003; www.arsenal.com/tours; Hornsey Rd, N7; self-guided tours adult/child £25/16, guided tours £40/20; ⊙ 10am-5pm Mon-Fri, 9.30am-6pm Sat, 10am-4pm Sun; Ⓤ Holloway Rd) Offers both self-guided tours or tours led by former Arsenal players.

Stamford Bridge (☑ 0371 811 1955; www.chelseafc.com; Stamford Bridge, Fulham Rd, SW6; tours adult/child £24/15; ⊙ museum 9.30am-6.30pm Jul & Aug, to 5.30pm Apr-Jun, to 5pm Sep-Mar; tours 10am-5pm Jul & Aug, to 4pm Apr-Jun, to 3pm Sep-Mar; Ⓤ Fulham Broadway) Home of Chelsea FC.

plus cabaret. At the time of research you could watch previous shows online.

Classical Music

★ **Wigmore Hall** CLASSICAL MUSIC
(Map p114; ☑ 020-7935 2141; www.wigmore-hall.org.uk; 36 Wigmore St, W1; Ⓤ Bond St) Wigmore Hall, built in 1901 as a piano showroom, is one of the best and most active classical-music venues in town, with more than 460 concerts a year. This isn't just because of its fantastic acoustics, beautiful Arts and Crafts–style cupola over the stage and great variety of concerts, but also because of the sheer quality of the performances.

Royal Festival Hall CONCERT VENUE
(Map p84; ☑ 020-3879 9555; www.southbankcentre.co.uk/venues/royal-festival-hall; Southbank Centre, Belvedere Rd, SE1; ☎; Ⓤ Waterloo) The 2700-capacity Royal Festival Hall is one of the best places in London to hear modern and classical music, poetry and spoken-word performances. The hall has four resident orchestras, including the London Philharmonic Orchestra and the London Sinfonietta.

Queen Elizabeth Hall LIVE PERFORMANCE
(Map p84; ☑ 020-3879 9555; www.southbankcentre.co.uk/venues/queen-elizabeth-hall; Southbank Centre, Belvedere Rd, SE1; Ⓤ Waterloo) Queen Elizabeth Hall has a full programme

of gigs, chamber orchestras, dance performances and opera throughout the year, on
a smaller scale than the nearby Royal Festival Hall that's also part of Southbank Centre
(p83). The space reopened in 2018 after a
three-year refurb. In summer, don't miss the
plant-strewn cafe-bar on the roof (☺noon-
9pm Apr–mid-Jun & Sep-Oct, 10am-10.30pm
mid-Jun–Aug).

Sport

**Wimbledon
Championships**   SPECTATOR SPORT
(☎020-8944 1066; www.wimbledon.com; Church
Rd, SW19; grounds £8-25, tickets £33-225; ▣493,
Ⓤ Southfields) For a few weeks each June and
July, the sporting world's attention is fixed
on the quiet southern suburb of Wimbledon,
as it has been since 1877. Most show-court
tickets for the Wimbledon Championships
are allocated through public ballot, appli-
cations for which begin in early August of
the preceding year and close at the end of
December.

Opera & Dance

Royal Opera House   OPERA
(Map p66; ☎020-7304 4000; www.roh.org.uk; Bow
St, WC2; ☺gift shop & cafe from 10am; Ⓤ Covent
Garden) Opera and ballet have a fantastic
setting on Covent Garden Piazza, and a
night here is a sumptuous affair. Although
the programme has modern influences, the
main attractions are still the classic productions with their world-class performers. A
three-year, £50-million revamp finished in
October 2018, with new areas open to the
non-ticketed public for the first time, including the cafe and bar.

Sadler's Wells   DANCE
(Map p96; ☎020-7863 8000; www.sadlerswells.
com; Rosebery Ave, EC1; Ⓤ Angel) A glittering
modern venue that was first established
in 1683, Sadler's Wells is the most eclectic
modern-dance and ballet venue in town,
with experimental dance shows of all
genres and from all corners of the globe.
The Lilian Baylis Studio stages smaller
productions.

English National Opera   OPERA
(ENO; Map p66; ☎020-7845 9300; www.eno.
org; St Martin's Lane, WC2; Ⓤ Leicester Sq) The
English National Opera is celebrated for
making opera modern and more accessible, as all productions are sung in English. It's based at the impressive London

Coliseum, built in 1904 and lovingly
restored a century later. The English
National Ballet also holds regular performances at the Coliseum. Tickets range
from £12 to £125.

Barbican Centre   PERFORMING ARTS
(Map p76; ☎020-7638 8891; www.barbican.org.
uk; Silk St, EC2; ☺box office 10am-9pm Mon-
Sat, noon-8pm Sun; Ⓤ Barbican) You'll get as
lost in the astounding programme as you
will in the labyrinthine brutalist building. Home to the London Symphony Orchestra, the BBC Symphony Orchestra
and the Royal Shakespeare Company,
the Barbican Centre is the City's premier
cultural venue. It hosts concerts, theatre
and dance performances, and screens indie films and Hollywood blockbusters at
the cinema on Beech St.

🛍 Shopping

🛍 West End

★**Fortnum & Mason**   DEPARTMENT STORE
(Map p66; ☎020-7734 8040; www.fortnumand
mason.com; 181 Piccadilly, W1; ☺10am-9pm Mon-
Sat, 11.30am-6pm Sun; Ⓤ Green Park or Piccadilly Circus) With its classic eau-de-nil (pale
green) colour scheme, the 'Queen's grocery
store' (established in 1707) refuses to yield
to modern times. Its staff – both men and
women – still wear old-fashioned tailcoats,
and its glamorous food hall is supplied
with hampers, marmalade and speciality
teas. Stop for a spot of afternoon tea at the
Diamond Jubilee Tea Salon, visited by
Queen Elizabeth II in 2012.

★**Foyles**   BOOKS
(Map p66; ☎020-7434 1574; www.foyles.co.uk;
107 Charing Cross Rd, WC2; ☺9.30am-9pm Mon-
Sat, noon-6pm Sun; Ⓤ Tottenham Court Rd) London's most legendary bookshop, where you
can find even the most obscure titles. Once
synonymous with chaos, Foyles got its act together and now this carefully designed store
is a joy to explore. The cafe is on the 5th
floor, plus a small gallery for art exhibitions.
Grant & Cutler, the UK's largest foreign-
language bookseller, is on the 4th floor.

Hamleys   TOYS
(Map p66; ☎0371 704 1977; www.hamleys.com;
188-196 Regent St, W1; ☺10am-9pm Mon-Fri, from
9.30am Sat, noon-6pm Sun; ♿; Ⓤ Oxford Circus) The biggest and oldest toy emporium

LONDON'S MARKETS

Perhaps the biggest shopping draw for visitors is the capital's famed markets. A treasure trove of small designers, unique jewellery pieces, original framed photographs and posters, colourful vintage pieces and bric-a-brac, they are the antidote to impersonal, carbon-copy shopping centres.

Camden Market (Map p128; www.camdenmarket.com; Camden High St, NW1; ☉ 10am-late; Ⓤ Camden Town, Chalk Farm) London's busiest and best-known market may have stopped being cutting-edge several thousand cheap leather jackets ago, but it remains one of London's most popular attractions. There are three main market areas – Buck Street Market, Camden Lock Market and Stables Market – extending most of the way from Camden Town tube station to Chalk Farm tube station. You'll find a bit of everything: clothes (of varying quality) in profusion, bags, jewellery, arts and crafts, candles, incense and myriad decorative bits and pieces.

Sunday Upmarket (Map p120; ☑ 020-7770 6028; www.sundayupmarket.co.uk; Old Truman Brewery, 91 Brick Lane, E1; ☉ 11am-5.30pm Sat, 10am-6pm Sun; Ⓤ Shoreditch High St) Open all weekend, this lively market in the Old Truman Brewery offers a mix of young designers, food stalls in the Boiler House, antiques and bric-a-brac, and a huge range of vintage clothes in the basement across the street.

Old Spitalfields Market (Map p120; www.oldspitalfieldsmarket.com; Commercial St, E1; ☉ 10am-8pm, to 6pm Sat, to 5pm Sun; Ⓤ Liverpool St, Shoreditch High St, Aldgate East) Traders have been hawking their wares here since 1638 and it's still one of London's best markets. Sundays are the biggest and best days, but Thursdays are good for antiques and Fridays for independent fashion. There are plenty of food stalls too.

Smithfield Market (Map p76; ☑ 020-7248 3151; www.smithfieldmarket.com; Charterhouse St, EC1; ☉ 2-10am Mon-Fri; Ⓤ Farringdon) This is central London's last surviving meat market, and though most of the transactions today are wholesale, visitors are invited to shop too; arrive before 7am to see it in full swing. The market has been at this location since the 12th century, but the current colourful building was designed in 1868 by Horace Jones.

Leadenhall Market (Map p76; www.leadenhallmarket.co.uk; Gracechurch St, EC3; ☉ public areas 24hr; Ⓤ Bank) The ancient Romans had their forum on this site, but this covered shopping arcade harks back to the Victorian era, with cobblestones underfoot and 19th-century ironwork linking its shops, restaurants and pubs. The market appears as Diagon Alley in *Harry Potter and the Philosopher's Stone*.

Borough Market (Map p84; https://boroughmarket.org.uk; 8 Southwark St, SE1; ☉ full market 10am-5pm Wed & Thu, to 6pm Fri, 8am-5pm Sat, limited market 10am-5pm Mon & Tue; Ⓤ London Bridge) Located in this spot since the 13th century (possibly since 1014), 'London's Larder' is always overflowing with food lovers, gastronomes and Londoners in search of dinner inspiration. The full market runs from Wednesday to Saturday, but some traders and takeaway stalls also open Mondays and Tuesdays.

Brick Lane Market (Map p120; ☑ 020-7364 1717; www.visitbricklane.org; Brick Lane, E1; ☉ 10am-5pm Sun; Ⓤ Shoreditch High St) Spilling out into its surrounding streets, this irrepressibly vibrant market fills a vast area with household goods, bric-a-brac, secondhand clothes, cheap fashion and ethnic food.

Greenwich Market (www.greenwichmarket.london; College Approach, SE10; ☉ 10am-5.30pm; Ⓤ Cutty Sark) This small market has a different theme every day. On Tuesdays, Thursdays and Fridays, you'll find vintage, antiques and collectables. Wednesdays, Fridays and weekends are the best days for artists, indie designers and crafts.

South Bank Book Market (Map p84; Queen's Walk, SE1; ☉ 11am-7pm, shorter hours in winter; Ⓤ Waterloo) Prints and secondhand books under the arches of Waterloo Bridge.

in the world, Hamleys houses six floors of fun for kids of all ages, from the basement's Star Wars and Harry Potter collections up to Lego World, a sweet shop and tiny cafe on the 5th floor. Staff on each level have opened the packaging and are playing with everything from boomerangs to bubbles. Kids will happily spend hours here planning their Santa letters.

Liberty — DEPARTMENT STORE
(Map p66; ☑ 020-7734 1234; www.libertylondon.com; Regent St, entrance on Great Marlborough St, W1; ☉ 10am-8pm Mon-Sat, 11.30am-6pm Sun; 📶; Ⓤ Oxford Circus) One of London's most recognisable shops, Liberty department store has a white-and-wood-beam Tudor Revival facade that lures shoppers in to browse luxury contemporary fashion, homewares, cosmetics and accessories, all at sky-high prices. Liberty is known for its fabrics and has a full haberdashery department; a classic London gift or souvenir is a Liberty fabric print, especially in the form of a scarf.

★ Daunt Books — BOOKS
(Map p114; ☑ 020-7224 2295; www.dauntbooks.co.uk; 83 Marylebone High St, W1; ☉ 9am-7.30pm Mon-Sat, 11am-6pm Sun; Ⓤ Baker St) An original Edwardian bookshop, with oak panels, galleries and gorgeous skylights, Daunt is one of London's loveliest bookshops. There are several Daunt outlets but none as gorgeous as this. Browse its travel, general fiction and nonfiction titles over two floors.

Blade Rubber Stamps — ARTS & CRAFTS
(Map p66; ☑ 020-7831 4242; www.bladerubberstamps.co.uk; 12 Bury Pl, WC1; ☉ 10.30am-6pm Mon-Sat, 11.30am-4.30pm Sun; Ⓤ Holborn) This specialist stationary shop stocks just about every wooden-handled rubber stamp you care to imagine: from London icons like phone boxes and the Houses of Parliament to landscapes, planets, rockets and Christmas stamps. You can have one made to your design or DIY with a stamp-making kit. They make excellent lightweight gifts!

Sister Ray — MUSIC
(Map p66; ☑ 020-7734 3297; www.sisterray.co.uk; 75 Berwick St, W1; ☉ 10am-8pm Mon-Sat, noon-6pm Sun; Ⓤ Oxford Circus or Tottenham Court Rd) A stalwart of the Soho record-shop scene, specialising in a collection that BBC 1's John Peel would be proud of: innovative, experimental and indie music. Staff are knowledgeable, and the tunes are banging (that means good, not painful).

🔒 City of London

London Silver Vaults — ANTIQUES
(Map p76; ☑ 020-7242 3844; https://silvervaultslondon.com; 53-64 Chancery Lane, WC2; ☉ 9am-5.30pm Mon-Fri, to 1pm Sat; Ⓤ Chancery Lane) For one of London's oddest shopping experiences, pass through security and descend 12m into the windowless subterranean depths of the London Silver Vaults, which house the largest collection of silver for sale in the world. The 30-odd independently owned shops, each entered through thick bank-safe-style doors, offer vintage Victorian and Georgian silver, cufflinks, candleholders, goblets and much more.

🔒 Kensington & Hyde Park

★ John Sandoe Books — BOOKS
(Map p86; ☑ 020-7589 9473; www.johnsandoe.com; 10 Blacklands Tce, SW3; ☉ 9.30am-6.30pm Mon-Sat, 11am-5pm Sun; Ⓤ Sloane Sq) Steeped in literary charm and a perfect antidote to impersonal book superstores, this three-storey bookshop in an 18th-century premises inhabits its own universe. A treasure trove of literary gems and hidden surprises, it's been in business for over six decades. Loyal customers swear by it, and knowledgeable booksellers spill forth with well-read pointers and helpful advice.

Illustrated books that are hard to find elsewhere are a particular strong point, as are privately published works that larger bookshops would pass on. Should you have the money and the inclination, staff can even help you create your own personal home library.

★ Harrods — DEPARTMENT STORE
(Map p86; ☑ 020-7730 1234; www.harrods.com; 87-135 Brompton Rd, SW1; ☉ 10am-9pm Mon-Sat, 11.30am-6pm Sun; Ⓤ Knightsbridge) Garish and stylish in equal measure, perennially crowded Harrods is an obligatory stop for visitors, from the cash-strapped to the big spenders. The stock is astonishing, as are many of the price tags. Many visitors don't make it past the ground floor where designer bags, myriad scents from the perfume hall and the mouthwatering counters of the food hall provide plenty of entertainment.

Conran Shop — DESIGN
(Map p86; ☑ 020-7589 7401; www.conranshop.co.uk; Michelin House, 81 Fulham Rd, SW3; ☉ 10am-6pm Mon, Tue & Fri, to 7pm Wed & Thu, to 6.30pm

Sat, noon-6pm Sun; U South Kensington) The original design store (going strong since 1987), the Conran Shop is a treasure trove of beautiful things – from radios to sunglasses, kitchenware to children's toys and books, bathroom accessories to greeting cards. Browsing bliss. Spare some time to peruse the magnificent art nouveau/deco **Michelin House** the shop is housed in.

Clerkenwell, Shoreditch & Spitalfields

Libreria BOOKS
(Map p120; https://libreria.io; 65 Hanbury St, E1; ⊙10am-6pm Tue & Wed, to 8pm Thu-Sat, 11am-6pm Sun; U Aldgate East) Mismatched vintage reading lamps spotlight the floor-to-ceiling canary-yellow shelves at this delightful indie bookshop, where titles are arranged according to themes like 'wanderlust', 'enchantment for the disenchanted', and 'mothers, madonnas and whores'. Cleverly placed mirrors add to the labyrinthine wonder of the space, which is punctuated with mid-century furniture that invites repose and quiet contemplation.

Rough Trade East MUSIC
(Map p120; ✆020-7392 7788; www.roughtrade. com; Old Truman Brewery, 91 Brick Lane, E1; ⊙9am-9pm Mon-Thu, to 8pm Fri, 10am-8pm Sat, 11am-7pm Sun; U Shoreditch High St) It's no longer directly associated with the legendary record label (home to the Smiths, the Libertines and the Strokes, among others), but this huge record shop is still tops for picking up indie, soul, electronica and alternative music. In addition to an impressive selection of CDs and vinyl, it also dispenses coffee and stages gigs and artist signings.

East London

★**Broadway Market** MARKET
(www.broadwaymarket.co.uk; Broadway Market, E8; ⊙9am-5pm Sat; ☐394) There's been a market down here since the late 19th century, but the focus these days is artisanal food, handmade gifts and unique clothing. Boutique shops along both sides of the street (open seven days a week) do a roaring trade with coffee-drinking shoppers. Stock up on edible treats then head to **London Fields** (Richmond Rd, E8; U London Fields) for a picnic.

Beyond Retro VINTAGE
(✆020-7729 9001; www.beyondretro.com; 110-112 Cheshire St, E2; ⊙11am-7pm Mon-Sat, 11.30am-6pm Sun; U Shoreditch High St) A huge selection of vintage clothes, including wigs, shoes, jackets and sunglasses, expertly slung together in a lofty warehouse.

North London

★**Camden Passage Market** ANTIQUES
(www.camdenpassageislington.co.uk; Camden Passage, N1; ⊙9am-6pm Wed & Sat; U Angel) Not to be confused with Camden Market (p134), Camden Passage is a pretty cobbled lane in Islington lined with antique stores, vintage-clothing boutiques and cafes. Scattered along the lane are three not-so-separate market areas. The main market days are Wednesday and Saturday, though some open on Thursday, Friday and Sunday as well, and the shops are open all week.

Harry Potter Shop at Platform 9¾ GIFTS & SOUVENIRS
(Map p96; ✆020-3427 4200; www.harrypotter platform934.com; King's Cross Station, N1; ⊙8am-10pm Mon-Sat, 9am-10pm Sun; U King's Cross St Pancras) Pottermania refuses to die down and Diagon Alley remains impossible to find, but if you have junior witches and wizards seeking a wand of their own, take the family directly to King's Cross Station. This little wood-panelled store also stocks jumpers sporting the colours of Hogwarts' four houses (Gryffindor having pride of place) and assorted merchandise, including, of course, the books.

ℹ Information

DANGERS & ANNOYANCES
London is a fairly safe city for its size, but exercise common sense.

➡ Occasional terror attacks have afflicted London over the last few decades, but risks to individual visitors are remote.

➡ Keep a hand on your handbag/wallet, especially in bars and nightclubs, and in crowded areas such as the Underground.

➡ Be discreet with your tablet/smartphone – snatch-and-run happens all too often.

➡ When crossing the road look out for silent high-speed cyclists.

➡ Victims of rape and sexual abuse can contact **Rape Crisis England & Wales** (✆0808 802 9999, www.rapecrisis.org.uk); anyone in emotional distress contact **Samaritans** (✆116 123 toll-free, 24 hours; www.samaritans.org).

EMERGENCY

London area code	☏ 020
International access code	☏ 00
Police, fire or ambulance emergency	☏ 999
Non-emergency police	☏ 101

INTERNET ACCESS

➡ Virtually every London hotel provides free wi-fi now.

➡ Numerous cafes and restaurants offer free wi-fi to customers, as do cultural venues such as the Barbican or the Southbank Centre.

➡ Street level wi-fi access is available in some areas, look for signs.

➡ Major train stations, airport terminals and some of the 270 Underground stations and 79 Overground stations offer free wi-fi (though signals are often weak).

MEDICAL SERVICES

A number of London hospitals have 24-hour accident and emergency departments. However, in an emergency just call an ambulance.

Charing Cross Hospital (☏ 020-3311 1234; www.imperial.nhs.uk/charingcross; Fulham Palace Rd, W6; Ⓤ Hammersmith) Hammersmith

Chelsea & Westminster Hospital (☏ 020-3315 8000; www.chelwest.nhs.uk; 369 Fulham Rd, SW10; 🚍 14 or 414, Ⓤ South Kensington, Fulham Broadway) Fulham

Guy's & St Thomas' Hospital (☏ 020-7188 7188; www.guysandstthomas.nhs.uk; Westminster Bridge Rd, SE1; Ⓤ Waterloo or Westminster) Waterloo

Royal Free Hospital (☏ 020-7794 0500; www.royalfree.nhs.uk; Pond St, NW3; Ⓤ Belsize Park, Hampstead Heath) Hampstead

Royal London Hospital (☏ 020-7377 7000; www.bartshealth.nhs.uk; Whitechapel Rd, E1; Ⓤ Whitechapel) Whitechapel (includes children's hospital)

University College London Hospital (☏ 020-3456 7890; www.uclh.nhs.uk; 235 Euston Rd, NW1; Ⓤ Warren St or Euston Sq) Euston

TOURIST INFORMATION

Visit London (www.visitlondon.com) has info on special events, tours, accommodation, eating, theatre, shopping etc.

ℹ Getting There & Away

AIR

The city has six airports: Heathrow, which is the largest, to the west; Gatwick to the south; Stansted to the northeast; Luton to the northwest; London City in the Docklands and London Southend. For details of London's airports, see p684.

BUS

Victoria Coach Station (Map p86; 164 Buckingham Palace Rd, SW1; Ⓤ Victoria) Long-distance and international buses arrive and depart from Victoria Coach Station, close to the Victoria Tube and rail stations.

TRAIN

Main national rail routes are served by a variety of private train-operating companies. Tickets are not cheap, but if you book ahead you can get better deals. If you're planning to do a lot of train travel, look into the cost of a Rail Card and how much you may save, especially if travelling in a family group. Check the website of **National Rail** (www.nationalrail.co.uk) for timetables, fares and Rail Cards.

Eurostar (www.eurostar.com) High-speed passenger rail service linking London St Pancras International with Paris, Brussels, Amsterdam and Marseilles, with up to 19 daily departures. Fares vary greatly, from £29 for a one-way standard-class ticket to around £245 each way for a fully flexible business premier ticket (prices based on return journeys). Sign up to Eurostar social media channels or email to get notifications of special deals and sales.

ℹ Getting Around

TO/FROM THE AIRPORTS
Heathrow

The Underground, commonly referred to as 'the Tube', is the cheapest way of getting anywhere from Heathrow (approximately one hour) and trains depart every three to nine minutes. It runs from just after 5am to 11.45pm (11.28pm Sunday); to the airport it runs from 5.47am to 12.32am (11.38pm Sunday). The Tube runs all night Friday and Saturday on this line, with reduced frequency. Buy a local Oyster card (reusable charge card) at Heathrow Tube station. The ticket machines are fairly simple to use and issue cards for £5 (refundable when you return them on departure).

Heathrow Express (www.heathrowexpress.com; one way/return £25/37, children free; 🛜), every 15 minutes, and **Heathrow Connect** (☏ 0343 222 1234; www.tfl.gov.uk; adult single/open return £10.20/12.50), every 30 minutes, trains link Heathrow with Paddington train station. Heathrow Express trains take a mere 15 minutes to reach Paddington. Trains on each service run from around 5am to between 11pm and midnight.

National Express (www.nationalexpress.com) coaches (one way from £6, 40 to 90 minutes, every 30 minutes to one hour) link Heathrow

ⓘ OYSTER CARD

The cheapest way to get around London is with an Oyster Card, a smart card on which you store credit as well as Travelcards valid for periods from a day to a year. Oyster Cards are valid across the entire public transport network in London, and fares are lower than standard ones. If you make several journeys in a day, the total is capped at the appropriate Travelcard rate (peak or off-peak).

Oyster Cards can be bought (£5 refundable deposit required) and topped up at any Underground station, travel information centre or shop displaying the Oyster logo. To get your deposit back along with any remaining credit, simply return your Oyster Card at a ticket booth.

All you need to do when entering a station is touch your card on a reader (which has a yellow circle with the image of an Oyster Card on it) and then touch again on your way out. For bus journeys, you only need to touch once upon boarding. Note that some train stations don't have exit turnstiles, so you will need to tap out on the reader before leaving the station; if you forget, you will be hugely overcharged.

Contactless payment cards (which do not require chip and pin or a signature) are subject to the same Oyster fares, but foreign visitors should bear in mind the cost of card transactions.

Central bus station with Victoria coach station. The first bus leaves Heathrow Central bus station (at Terminals 2 and 3) at 4.20am, with the last departure at 10.05pm. The first bus leaves Victoria at 1am, the last at around midnight.

If you arrive very late, the **N9 bus** (£1.50, 1¼ hours, every 20 minutes) connects Heathrow Central bus station (and Heathrow Terminal 5) with central London, terminating at Aldwych.

A metered black-cab trip to/from central London will cost between £50 and £100 and take 45 minutes to an hour, depending on traffic.

Ride-share services, such as Uber, require organising a meeting point near the airport exit directly with your driver; problematic if you're relying on airport wi-fi.

Gatwick

National Rail (www.nationalrail.co.uk) Regular train services to/from London Bridge (30 to 45 minutes, every 15 to 30 minutes), London King's Cross (55 minutes, every 15 to 30 minutes) and Victoria (30 to 50 minutes, every 10 to 15 minutes) run almost all night. Fares vary depending on the time, route, company (Southern or Thameslink) and class you take. Ticket machines are near the airport exit to the train station or pay with an Oyster Card, or contactless payment card.

Gatwick Express (www.gatwickexpress.com; one-way/return adult £19.90/36.70, child £9.95/18.35, under 5yrs free) Trains run every 15 minutes from the station near the Gatwick South Terminal to Victoria. From the airport, there are services between 6am and 11pm. From Victoria, they leave between 5am and 10.44pm. The journey takes 30 minutes; book online for the slightly cheaper fares.

National Express (www.nationalexpress.com) Coaches run throughout the day from Gatwick to Victoria coach station (one way from £10). Services depart hourly around the clock. Journey time is between 80 minutes and two hours, depending on traffic.

EasyBus (www.easybus.com) Runs 13-seater minibuses to Gatwick every 15 to 20 minutes on several routes, including from Earl's Court/West Brompton and Victoria coach station (one way from £2 if you book ahead online). The service runs around the clock. The journey time averages 75 minutes; it must be booked in advance.

Taxi A metered black-cab trip to/from central London costs around £100 and takes just over an hour. Minicabs or ride-share taxis are usually, but not always, cheaper.

Stansted

Stansted Express (☑ 0345 600 7245; www.stanstedexpress.com; one-way/return £19.40/30.70) Rail service (45 minutes, every 15 to 30 minutes) linking the airport with Liverpool St station via Tottenham Hale (which also has good Tube connections). From the airport, the first train leaves at 5.30am, the last at 12.30am. Trains depart Liverpool St station from 4.40am (on some days at 3.40am) to 11.25pm.

National Express (www.nationalexpress.com) Coaches run around the clock, offering 200 services per day.

Airbus A6 (☑ 0871 781 8181; www.national express.com; one way from £10) Runs to Westminster (around one hour to 1½ hours, every 20 minutes) via Marble Arch, Paddington, Baker St and Golders Green. **Airbus A7** (☑ 0871 781 8181; www.nationalexpress.com; one way from

£10) also runs to Victoria coach station (around one hour to 1½ hours, every 20 minutes), via Waterloo and Southwark. **Airbus A8** (☎ 0871 781 8181; www.nationalexpress.com; one way from £7) runs to Liverpool St station (60 to 80 minutes, every 30 minutes), via Bethnal Green and Shoreditch High St. **Airbus A9** (one-way from £7, 50 minutes) goes to London Stratford.

Airport Bus Express (www.airportbusexpress. co.uk; one-way from £8) Runs every 30 minutes to Victoria coach station, Baker Street, Liverpool St and London Stratford.

EasyBus (www.easybus.com) Runs services to Victoria coach station via Waterloo station every 15 minutes, or Liverpool St station via London Stratford. The total journey to central London (one-way from £2) takes 1¾ hours.

Terravision (www.terravision.eu) Coaches link Stansted to Liverpool St station (one-way from £7, 75 minutes) and Victoria coach station (from £7, two hours) every 20 to 40 minutes between 6am and 1am.

London City

Docklands Light Railway (DLR; www.tfl.gov. uk/dlr) stops at the London City Airport station (zone 3). Trains depart every eight to 10 minutes from just after 5.30am to 12.15am Monday to Saturday, and 7am to 11.15pm Sunday. The journey to Bank takes just over 20 minutes.

Luton

National Rail (www.nationalrail.co.uk) Has 24-hour services (one-way from £16.70, 35 to 50 minutes, regular departures during peak times) from London St Pancras International to Luton Airport Parkway station, from where an airport shuttle bus (one-way/return £2.40/3.80, half-price for five- to 15-year-olds, kids under five ride for free) will take you to the airport in 10 minutes. Cash or contactless payment cards are accepted on the shuttle bus.

Airbus A1 (www.nationalexpress.com; one way if booked online from £7) Runs over 60 times daily around the clock to Victoria coach station, via Portman Sq, Baker St, St John's Wood, Finchley Rds and Golders Green. It takes around one to 1½ hours.

Green Line Bus 757 (Map p86; ☎ 0344 800 4411; www.greenline.co.uk; one way/return £11.50/17.50) Runs to Luton Airport from Victoria coach station every 30 minutes on a 24-hour service via Marble Arch, Baker St, Finchley Rd and Brent Cross. The journey takes 75 to 90 minutes.

London Southend

Trains run to/from a purpose-built station at the airport (adult/child £17.80/8.90), making connecting to London Liverpool St or Stratford station an easy one-hour journey. Six trains run per hour during peak times, fewer off-peak. The first train from Liverpool St leaves at 4.30am to meet early-morning flight departures, and the last train leaves at 11.59pm.

Flight delays or any procrastinating will mean you're in a fix after midnight. It's either an expensive taxi ride (£110, but can be split with others, of course) or an airport hotel. Phone **Andrews Taxis** (01702 200 000), currently the only option at this hour.

BICYCLE

London's main cycle-hire scheme is called **Santander Cycles** (☎ 0343 222 6666; www.tfl. gov.uk/modes/cycling/santander-cycles). The bikes have proven as popular with visitors as with Londoners.

The idea is simple: pick up a bike from one of the 750 (and counting) docking stations dotted around the capital; cycle; drop it off at another docking station.

The access fee is £2 for 24 hours. All you need is a credit or debit card. The first 30 minutes are free; it's £2 for any additional period of 30 minutes, to keep you regularly docking the bikes.

You can take as many bikes as you like during your access period (24 hours), leaving five minutes between each trip.

The pricing structure is designed to encourage short journeys rather than longer rentals; for those, go to a hire company. You'll also find that although easy to ride, the bikes only have three gears and are quite heavy. You must be aged 18 to buy access and at least 14 to ride a bike.

Alternatively, Uber's bike-share scheme **Jump** (www.jump.com) has been superseded by **Beryl Bikes** (https://beryl.cc/bikeshare/london) and **Lime Scooters** (www.li.me/en-us/home). There's likely to be an even newer option for cycling, scootering, e-biking or hovercrafting by the time you visit.

CAR

London has a congestion charge in place to reduce the traffic and pollution in the city centre. The charge zone begins at Euston and Pentonville Rds to the north, Park Lane to the west, Tower Bridge to the east, and Elephant and Castle and Vauxhall Bridge Rd to the south. As you enter the zone, you will see a large white 'C' in a red circle on signs and painted on the road.

If you enter the zone between 7am and 6pm Monday to Friday (excluding public holidays), you must pay the £11.50 charge (payable in advance or on the day) or £14 on the first charging day after travel to avoid receiving a fine (£160, or £80 if paid within 14 days).

In addition, if your car is not a new cleaner greener model, the Ultra Low Emission Zone (ULEZ) charge needs to be paid in the same zone 24/7. You can pay online or over the phone. For full details, see the TFL website (www.tfl.gov.uk).

PUBLIC TRANSPORT
Boat

Several companies operate along the River Thames; only **Thames Clippers** (www.thamesclippers.com; one way adult/child £8.70/4.35) really offers commuter services, however. It's fast, pleasant and you're almost always guaranteed a seat and a view. All boats are fully wheelchair-accessible and all piers are wheelchair-accessible apart from Cadogan Pier, Wandsworth Riverside Quarter Pier and London Bridge City Pier.

Thames Clippers boats run regular services between Embankment, Waterloo (London Eye), Blackfriars, Bankside (Shakespeare's Globe), London Bridge, Tower Bridge, Canary Wharf, Greenwich, North Greenwich and Woolwich piers from 6.28am to 11.38pm (from 8.10am to 11.20pm on weekends).

Thames Clippers River Roamer tickets (adult/child £17.80/8.90) give the freedom to hop on and off boats on most routes all day. Book online for the discounted fare; only piers with a ticket booth accept cash payments.

You can also get a discount if you're a pay-as-you-go Oyster Card holder or Travelcard holder (paper ticket or on Oyster Card). Children under five travel free on most boats.

Between April and October, Hampton Court Palace can be reached by boat on the 22-mile route along the Thames from Westminster Pier in central London (via Kew and Richmond). The trip can take up to four hours, depending on the tide. Boats are run by **Westminster Passenger Services Association** (www.wpsa.co.uk; one-way/return adult £19/27, child £9.50/13.50).

The London Waterbus Company (p104) runs canal boats between Camden Lock and Little Venice.

Bus

London's ubiquitous red double-decker buses afford great views of the city, but be aware that the going can be slow, thanks to traffic jams and dozens of commuters getting on and off at every stop.

There are excellent bus maps at every stop detailing all routes and destinations served from that particular area (generally a few bus stops within a two- to three-minute walk, shown on a local map).

Bus services normally operate from 5am to 11.30pm. Many bus stops have LED displays listing bus arrival times, but downloading an app such as Citymapper to your smartphone is the most effective way to keep track of when your next bus is due.

Almost all buses are now wheelchair- and pram-accessible, lowering to the pavement with an automated ramp facility – you'll need to board at the middle doors and touch on with your Oyster Card when you can. Other passengers are mostly patient and courteous when assisting people on and off the bus with items like prams or large suitcases.

Cash cannot be used on London's buses. You must pay with an Oyster Card, Travelcard or a contactless payment card. Bus fares are a flat £1.50, no matter the distance travelled. If you don't have enough credit on your Oyster Card for a £1.50 bus fare, you can make the journey (and go into the black) but must top up your credit before your Oyster Card will work again.

Children aged under 11 travel free; 11- to 15-year-olds travel half-price if registered on an accompanying adult's Oyster Card on the Young Visitor Discount (register at Zone 1 or Heathrow Tube stations).

➡ More than 50 night-bus routes (prefixed with the letter 'N') run from around 11.30pm to 5am.

➡ There are also another 60 bus routes operating 24 hours; the frequency decreases between 11pm and 5am.

➡ Oxford Circus, Tottenham Court Rd and Trafalgar Sq are the main hubs for night routes.

➡ Night buses can be infrequent and stop only on request, so remember to ring for your stop.

Underground, DLR & Overground

The London Underground ('the Tube'; 11 colour-coded lines) is part of an integrated-transport system that also includes the Docklands Light Railway (DLR; www.tfl.gov.uk/dlr; a driverless train operating in the eastern part of the city) and Overground network (mostly outside of Zone 1 and sometimes underground). Despite the never-ending upgrades and 'engineering works' requiring weekend closures and escalators out of action, it is overall the quickest and easiest way of getting around the city.

The Tube runs roughly 5am to 1am, but when your last train departs varies by line and the day of the week. Apps like TfL Go (www.tfl.gov.uk/maps_/tfl-go) and CityMapper (www.citymapper.com) will give you the most up-to-date information. Several lines (the Victoria and Jubilee lines, plus most of the Piccadilly, Central and Northern lines) run all night on Friday and Saturday to get revellers home (on what is called the 'Night Tube', with trains every 10 minutes or so. Fares are off-peak.

During weekend closures, schedules, maps and alternative route suggestions are posted in every station, and staff are at hand to help redirect you.

Some stations, most famously Leicester Sq and Covent Garden, are much closer in reality than they appear on the map.

Not all Tube stations are fully step-free and are therefore inaccessible to travellers with prams, wheelchairs and even heavy luggage. Stops that have lifts are marked on the Tube map with a wheelchair symbol so you can plan your journey accordingly. Station staff will assist with a portable ramp to enable wheelchair users to board trains safely.

TAXI
Black Cabs

The black cab is as much a feature of the London cityscape as the red double-decker bus. Licensed black-cab drivers have The Knowledge, acquired over three to five years of rigorous training and a series of exams. They are supposed to know 25,000 streets within a 6-mile radius of Charing Cross/Trafalgar Sq and the 100 most-visited spots of the moment, including clubs and restaurants.

➡ Cabs are available for hire when the yellow sign above the windscreen is lit; just stick your arm out to signal one.

➡ All are supposed to be wheelchair-accessible but experiences reported on the ground belie this claim.

➡ Fares are metered, with the flagfall charge of £2.60 (covering the first 235m during a weekday), rising by increments of 20p for each subsequent 117m.

➡ Fares are more expensive in the evening and overnight.

➡ You can tip taxi drivers up to 10%, but most Londoners simply round up to the nearest pound.

➡ Apps such as **Gett** (https://gett.com) use your smartphone's GPS to locate the nearest black cab. You only pay the metered fare.

➡ **ComCab** (☏ 020-7908 0271; www.com-cab-london.co.uk) operates one of the largest fleets of black cabs in town.

Minicabs

➡ Minicabs, which are licensed, are (usually) cheaper competitors to black cabs.

➡ Unlike black cabs, minicabs cannot legally be hailed on the street; they must be hired by phone or directly from one of the minicab offices (every high street has at least one).

➡ Minicabs don't have meters; there's usually a fare set by the dispatcher. Make sure you ask before setting off.

➡ Your hotel or host will be able to recommend a reputable minicab company in the neighbourhood. Alternatively, phone a large 24-hour operator such as **Addison Lee** (www.addison lee.com).

➡ Ride-share apps such as **Uber** (www.uber. com) allow you to book a ride easily

⭐

POPULATION
Kent: 1,846,000

OLDEST CASTLES
Pevensey Castle,
Leeds Castle, Dover
Castle, Arundel
Castle

BEST VIEWS
Box Hill (p173)

BEST SEAFOOD
Angela's (p152)

BEST PUB
Fordwich Arms
(p149)

📅

WHEN TO GO

Apr & May The
hiking season com-
mences for tackling
the South Downs
Way.

Jun Visitors revel in
frilly Victoriana at
the Dickens Festival
in Broadstairs.

Jul & Aug Perfect
weather for hitting
the glorious beaches
of Thanet in East
Kent.

Christ Church Gate, Canterbury Cathedral (p148)
ROBERT MULLAN/SHUTTERSTOCK ©

Canterbury & Southeast England

Rolling chalk hills, venerable Victorian resorts, fields of hops and grapes: welcome to England's sunny southeast, four soothing counties' worth of country houses and fairy-tale castles, accompanied by lots of fine food and drink. That fruit-ripening sun also warms a string of seaside towns and beaches wedged between formidable chalk cliffs. There's something for everyone here, from the medieval quaintness of Sandwich to the bohemian spirit of hedonistic Brighton.

England's spiritual heart is Canterbury; its cathedral and ancient World Heritage–listed attractions are essential viewing, while the southeast is also pockmarked with reminders of darker days: the region's position as the front line against Continental invaders has left a wealth of relics of more turbulent times.

INCLUDES

Canterbury & Southeast England Highlights

1 Brighton & Hove (p167) Shopping, tanning and partying in the hedonist capital of the southeast.

2 Canterbury Cathedral (p146) Making a pilgrimage to one of England's most important religious sites.

3 Dover Castle (p157) Delving into the atmospheric WWII tunnels beneath this sprawling castle.

4 Rye (p159) Ambling around the lanes of one of England's prettiest towns.

5 RHS Garden Wisley (p165) Wandering among flowers, bushes, trees and superb horticultural vistas.

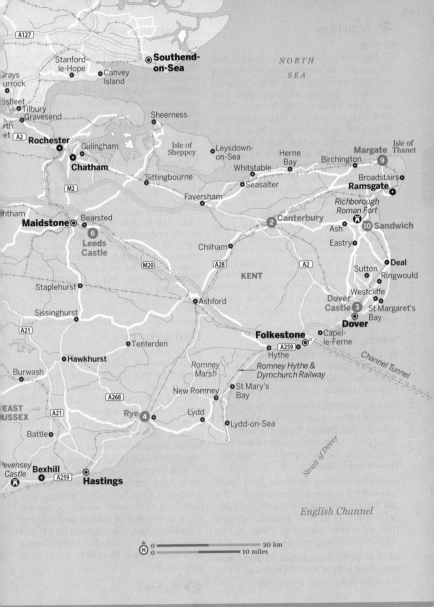

6 Leeds Castle (p151)
Getting into exploration mode at this moated marvel.

7 Beachy Head (p165)
Scrambling up this spectacular headland with its icing-sugar-white chalk cliffs.

8 Chichester (p174)
Discovering Roman remains and an excellent art gallery in this historic cathedral city.

9 Margate (p151) Getting down with the hipsters in the art capital of the southeast.

10 Sandwich (p156)
Becoming hopelessly lost in a maze of crooked medieval streets.

🏃 Activities

Cycling

Finding quiet roads for cycle touring may take a little extra perseverance in the southeast of England, but the effort is richly rewarded. Long-distance routes that form part of the National Cycle Network (NCN; www.sustrans.org.uk/national-cycle-network) include the Downs & Weald Cycle Route (110 miles; NCN Routes 2, 20 and 21) from London to Brighton and on to Hastings, and the Garden of England Cycle Route (172 miles; NCN Routes 1 and 2) from London to Dover and then Hastings.

You'll also find less demanding routes on the NCN website. Meanwhile there are plenty of uppers and downers to challenge mountain bikers on walking trails such as the South Downs Way National Trail (100 miles), which takes between two and four days to complete. The Devil's Punchbowl and Box Hill in Surrey are both very popular with cyclists, while the 32-mile Viking Coastal Trail around the Isle of Thanet is breezy and delightful.

Walking

Two long-distance trails meander steadily westward through the region, and there is no shortage of shorter ambles to match your schedule, stamina and scenery wish list.

South Downs Way National Trail (www.nationaltrail.co.uk/south-downs-way) This 100-mile trail through England's newest national park is a beautiful roller-coaster walk along prehistoric drove roads between Winchester and Eastbourne.

North Downs Way National Trail (www.nationaltrail.co.uk/north-downs-way) This 153-mile walk begins near Farnham in Surrey, but one of its most beautiful sections runs from near Ashford to Dover. A loop takes in Canterbury near its end.

1066 Country Walk Heads 32 miles from Pevensey Castle to Rye and serves as a continuation of the South Downs Way.

KENT

Kent isn't known as the Garden of England for nothing. Within its largely sea-lined borders extends a fragrant landscape of gentle hills, fertile farmland, cultivated country estates and fruit-laden orchards. It could also be described as the beer garden of England as it produces the world-renowned Kent hops and some of the country's finest ales, as well as wines from numerous vineyards. At its heart is spellbinding Canterbury, crowned by its enthralling cathedral. You'll also find beautiful coastal stretches dotted with beach towns, villages and some riveting landscapes, from old-school Broadstairs to gentrified Whitstable, the hip old quarter of Margate and the magnificent white cliffs of Dover.

❶ Getting There & Away

Kent is very well connected to London, with two high-speed lines linking the north Kent coast and East Kent to the capital. Connections with East Sussex could be better (there's no Canterbury–Brighton coach for instance), but are still reasonably good. Ferries from Dunkirk and Calais (France) tie up at Dover, Kent's last cross-Channel passenger port, and hundreds of cruise ships call in at the town's Western Docks. The Channel Tunnel, which emerges from the chalky ground near Folkestone, is a major gateway to the Continent.

Canterbury

📞 01227 / POP 55,240

One of southern England's top attractions, Canterbury tops the charts for English cathedral cities. Many consider the World Heritage–listed cathedral that dominates its centre to be one of Europe's finest, and the town's narrow medieval alleyways, riverside gardens, ancient city walls and England's largest surviving medieval gateway (www.onepoundlane.co.uk/westgate-towers; St Peter's St; adult/concession/child £4/3/2; ⊘11am-4pm) are a joy to explore. But Canterbury isn't a museum showcase – it's a bustling, busy place with an energetic student population and a wide choice of pubs, restaurants and independent shops. Book ahead for the best hotels and eateries: pilgrims may no longer flock here in their thousands, but tourists certainly do.

◎ Sights

★ Canterbury Cathedral   CATHEDRAL

(www.canterbury-cathedral.org; adult/concession/child £12.50/10.50/8.50, tours adult/child £5/4, audio guide £4/3; ⊘10am-4.30pm Mon-Sat, 12.30-4.30pm Sun) A rich repository of more than 1400 years of Christian history, the Church of England's crown jewel is a truly extraordinary place and an astonishing spectacle. This Gothic cathedral, the highlight of the

Canterbury

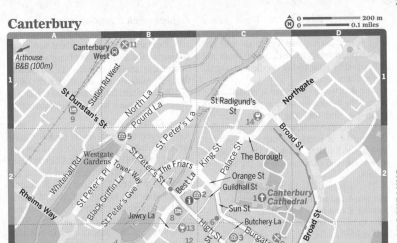

Canterbury

◎ Top Sights
1 Canterbury Cathedral............................C2

◎ Sights
2 Beaney House of Art & Knowledge.......B2
3 Roman Museum.....................................C3
4 St Augustine's Abbey............................D3
5 West Gate Towers..................................B2

✚ Activities, Courses & Tours
6 Canterbury Guided Tours......................C2
7 Canterbury Historic River Tours...........B2

🛌 Sleeping
8 ABode Canterbury...................................B2
9 House of Agnes.......................................A1

✘ Eating
10 Chapter...C3
11 Goods Shed...B1
12 Tiny Tim's Tearoom................................B3

🍷 Drinking & Nightlife
13 Foundry Brewpub....................................B3
14 Parrot..C1

city's World Heritage sites, is southeast England's top tourist attraction and a holy place of worship. It's also the site of one of English history's most notorious murders: Archbishop Thomas Becket met his maker here in 1170. Allow at least two hours to do the cathedral justice.

The cathedral is an overwhelming edifice crammed with enthralling stories, arresting architecture and a very real and enduring sense of spirituality – although visitors can't help but pick up on ominous undertones of violence and bloodshed that whisper from its walls.

This ancient structure is packed with monuments commemorating the nation's battles. Also here are the grave and heraldic tunic of one of the nation's most famous warmongers, Edward the Black Prince (1330–76). The spot in the northwest transept where Becket met his grisly end has drawn pilgrims for more than 800 years and is marked by a flickering candle and a striking modern altar.

The doorway to the crypt is alongside the altar. This cavernous space is the cathedral's highlight, and the only survivor from the devastating fire in 1174 (just four years after the murder of Becket), which destroyed the rest of the building. Look for the amazingly well-preserved carvings among the forest of pillars.

The wealth of detail in the cathedral is immense and unrelenting, so it's well worth joining a one-hour tour (three daily, Monday to Saturday) or taking a 40-minute self-guided audio tour.

Roman Museum
MUSEUM

(www.canterburymuseums.co.uk; Butchery Lane; adult/concession/child £9/6/free; ⊙10am-5pm) This subterranean archaeological site affords fascinating insights into everyday life in Canterbury almost two millennia ago. Stroll a reconstructed Roman marketplace and rooms, including a kitchen, and examine Roman mosaic floors. Almost everything you see here was only discovered after WWII bombs engaged in impromptu excavation. A highlight is the almost entirely intact Roman soldier's helmet dating from Caesar's invasion, unearthed near the village of Bridge in 2012. It's the most complete example ever found in the UK.

Beaney House of Art & Knowledge
MUSEUM

(www.canterburymuseums.co.uk; 18 High St; ⊙museum 10am-5pm Tue-Sat, 11am-4pm Sun; ⊕) **FREE** This mock-Tudor edifice is the grandest on the main shopping thoroughfare, if not the most authentic. Formerly called the Royal Museum & Art Gallery, it has housed Canterbury's main library, a museum and an art gallery since 1899 – its current name is in honour of the 19th-century benefactor who funded the original building. In addition to the city's main library and the tourist office (p150), the mixed bag of museum exhibits is worth half an hour between the main sights.

St Augustine's Abbey
RUINS

(EH; www.english-heritage.org.uk; Longport; adult/concession/child £7.90/7.10/4.70; ⊙10am-6pm Apr-Sep, to 5pm Oct, to 4pm Sat & Sun Nov-Mar) An integral but often overlooked part of the Canterbury World Heritage Site, St Augustine's Abbey was founded in AD 598, marking the rebirth of Christianity in southern England. Destroyed during Henry VIII's Dissolution of the Monasteries in the 16th century, and later requisitioned as a royal palace and for a period serving as a jail and a school, only forlorn ruins remain today. A small museum and a free audio guide underline the site's importance and put flesh back onto its now-humble bones.

Tours

Canterbury Historic River Tours
BOATING

(☑07790 534744; www.canterburyrivertours.co.uk; King's Bridge; adult/concessions/child £12.50/11.50/7; ⊙10am-5pm Mar-Oct) Knowledgeable guides double as energetic oarsmen on these fascinating, multi-award-winning River Stour minicruises, which depart from King's Bridge.

Canterbury Guided Tours
WALKING

(☑01227-459779; www.canterburyguidedtours.com; adult/concession/child from £8/7.50/6.50; ⊙11am Feb-Oct, plus 2pm Jul-Sep) Ninety-minute walking tours led by professional green-badge guides leave from opposite the Canterbury

---

THE CANTERBURY TALES

If English literature has a father figure, then it is Geoffrey Chaucer (1342–1400), the first English writer to introduce characters – rather than 'types' – into fiction, doing so to greatest effect in his best-known work, *The Canterbury Tales*.

Written between 1387 and his death, in the hard-to-decipher Middle English of the day, Chaucer's Tales is an unfinished series of 24 vivid stories told by a party of pilgrims journeying between London and Canterbury. Chaucer successfully created the illusion that the pilgrims, not Chaucer (though he appears in the tales as himself), are narrating the stories, which gave him unprecedented freedom as an author. *The Canterbury Tales* remains one of the pillars of the literary canon, but more than that, it's a collection of rollicking good yarns of adultery, debauchery, crime and edgy romance, stuffed with Chaucer's perceptive and witty observations about human nature.

Cathedral entrance. Tickets can be purchased from the tourist office and online.

Sleeping

★ABode Canterbury
BOUTIQUE HOTEL ££

([📞]01227-766266; www.abodecanterbury.co.uk; 30-33 High St; r from £74; [📶]) The 72 rooms at this super-central hotel, the only boutique hotel in town, are graded from 'comfortable' to 'fabulous' (via 'enviable'), and for the most part live up to their names. They come with features such as handmade beds, chesterfield sofas, tweed cushions and beautiful modern bathrooms. There's a splendid champagne bar, restaurant and tavern, too.

★Pig at Bridge Place
HOTEL ££

([📞]01227-830208; www.thepighotel.com/at-bridge -place; Bourne Park Rd, Bridge; d/lodge from £109/305; [📶]) Oozing character and charmingly nestled in the Nailbourne Valley, 4 miles southeast of Canterbury, this delightfully restored period house (and former rock venue – Led Zeppelin played here) is one of a litter of seven Pig hotels across the UK. Rooms range from titchy with an imposing four-poster bed to fully equipped lodges for families. Expect much wood panelling, fireplaces and a superb restaurant.

Each room comes with a stocked larder. Prices rise at weekends.

House of Agnes
HOTEL ££

([📞]01227-472185; www.houseofagnes.co.uk; 71 St Dunstan's St; r incl breakfast £70-145; [📶]) This rather wonky 13th-century beamed inn, mentioned in Dickens' *David Copperfield*, has eight themed rooms bearing names such as 'Marrakesh' (Moorish), 'Venice' (carnival masks), 'Boston' (light and airy) and 'Canterbury' (antiques, four-poster, heavy fabrics). If you prefer your room to have straight lines and right angles, there are eight less exciting, but no less comfortable, 'stable' rooms in the garden annexe.

Arthouse B&B
B&B ££

([📞]07976 725457; www.arthousebandb.com; 24 London Rd; r from £75; [P][📶]) Housed in a 19th-century fire station, the stylishly designed and quirky ambience at this light and bright choice is a welcome relief. The whole effect is good-looking and distinctive, with contemporary and comfortable double rooms. There's also a two-bedroom red-brick fireman's cottage that sleeps four.

Eating

Tiny Tim's Tearoom
CAFE £

(www.tinytimstearoom.com; 34 St Margaret's St; mains £6-10.50, afternoon tea £18.95; [⊘]9.30am-5.30pm Mon-Sat, 10.30am-4.30pm Sun) It's no mean feat to be declared 'Kent Tearoom of the Year', an accolade awarded to this swish 1930s cafe in 2015. It offers hungry shoppers big breakfasts packed with Kentish ingredients, and tiers of cakes, crumpets, cucumber sandwiches and scones plastered in clotted cream. On busy shopping days you're guaranteed to queue for a table.

Chapter
ITALIAN £

([📞]01227-809198; www.chaptercanterbury.co.uk; 11-12 Burgate; mains around £8, 2/3-course brunch menu £35/39; [⊘]noon-3pm & 5-10pm Mon-Wed, noon-10pm Thu & Fri, 11am-10pm Sat, 11am-8pm Sun; [📶]) You literally seem to eat your dinner off the floor in this place – the tables are made of what looks like squares of reclaimed parquet flooring. Thankfully there's a plate between that and the very authentic Italian fare – a brief menu of simple, flavour-packed sourdough pizzas. The bottomless Saturday brunch is a popular blowout, with limitless drink.

★Goods Shed
MARKET ££

([📞]01227-459153; www.thegoodsshed.co.uk; Station Rd West; mains £17.50-20; [⊘]market 9am-7pm Tue-Sat, to 4pm Sun, restaurant noon-2.30pm & 6pm-midnight Tue-Fri, 8am-9.30pm Sat, 9am-3pm Sun) Aromatic farmers market, food hall and fabulous restaurant rolled into one, this converted warehouse by Canterbury West train station is a hit with everyone from itinerant self-caterers to sit-down gourmands. The chunky wooden tables sit slightly above the market hubbub, but in full view of its appetite-whetting stalls. Daily specials exploit the freshest farm goodies the Garden of England offers.

★Fordwich Arms
BRITISH £££

([📞]01227-710444; www.fordwicharms.co.uk; King St, Fordwich; mains £30-32, tasting menu £75, set lunch/dinner £35/50; [⊘]noon-2.30pm & 6-9pm Tue-Sat, noon-4pm Sun; [📶]) By the River Stour in England's smallest town (population 400), this pub is elevated by both views from the riverside terrace and a twinkling Michelin star. With its 1930s bar, the restaurant, under the leadership of head chef Daniel Smith, has caused a Kentish stir. Each dish is a work of art, employing fresh creativity and locally sourced ingredients.

Expect such delightful choices as rock oysters and mignonette dressing; line-caught turbot, mussels, cabbage, smoked bacon and *vin jaune;* or roast duck with parsnip, pickled walnut and quince. Vegetarian menus are also available. The home-baked bread with home-churned butter is very moreish. Fordwich is 3.5km east of Canterbury, south of the A28.

 ## Drinking & Nightlife

Foundry Brewpub MICROBREWERY
(www.thefoundrycanterbury.co.uk; White Horse Lane; ⊙noon-midnight Mon-Sat, to 6pm Sun) Canterbury's brewpub pumps out award-winning craft beers in the industrial setting of the former foundry where New York's first streetlights were made. It also stocks a wide range of local and national ales and ciders, serves light snacks and meals, and distils its own gin and rum.

Parrot PUB
(www.parrotcanterbury.co.uk; 1-9 Church Lane; ⊙noon-11pm Mon-Sat, to 10.30pm Sun; 🛜) Flung up in 1370 on Roman foundations, Canterbury's oldest boozer has a snug, beam-rich, slightly upmarket pub downstairs and a much-lauded dining room (with vegetarian and vegan choices) upstairs, beneath yet more ageing oak. Many a local ale is pulled in both spaces.

❶ Information

Tourist Office (☑ 01227-862162; www.canterbury.co.uk; 18 High St; ⊙9am-6pm Mon-Wed & Fri, to 8pm Thu, to 5pm Sat, 10am-5pm Sun; 🛜) Located in the Beaney House of Art & Knowledge (p148). Staff can help book accommodation, excursions and theatre tickets.

❶ Getting There & Away

BUS

The city's **bus station** (St George's Lane) is just within the city walls. Canterbury connections:
Dover (£5.70, 34 minutes, three hourly)
London Victoria (National Express; £11, two hours, hourly)
Margate (£5.70, one hour, two hourly)
Ramsgate (£5.70, 45 minutes, hourly)
Sandwich (£4.40, 40 minutes, three hourly)
Whitstable (£5.20, 30 minutes, every 10 minutes)

TRAIN

There are two train stations: Canterbury East for London Victoria, and Canterbury West for London's Charing Cross and St Pancras stations. Canterbury connections:
Broadstairs (£6.20, 25 minutes, half-hourly) Runs mainly from Canterbury West train station, with some from Canterbury East.
Dover Priory (£8.90, 28 minutes, half-hourly) Runs from Canterbury East train station.
London St Pancras (£34.70, one hour, hourly) High-speed service.
London Victoria and Charing Cross (£5.80, 1¾ hours, two hourly)

Whitstable

📞 01227 / POP 32,100

Perhaps it's the oysters harvested since Roman times? Maybe it's the weatherboard houses and shingle beach? Or perhaps it's the pleasingly old-fashioned main street with petite boutiques, art galleries, been-there-forever outfitters and emporia of vintage frillies? Most likely it's for all of these reasons that Whitstable has become a bit of a weekend magnet for metropolitan types seeking refuge from the city hassle. It's also a simple day trip from Canterbury, to which it is linked by regular local bus.

For a week in late July, the town hosts the **Whitstable Oyster Festival** (www.whitstableoysterfestival.co.uk; ⊙late Jul), a seafood, arts and music extravaganza offering a packed schedule of events, from history walks, crab catching and oyster-eating competitions to a beer festival and traditional 'blessing of the waters'.

✗ Eating

Wheelers Oyster Bar SEAFOOD ££
(☑ 01227-273311; www.wheelersoysterbar.com; 8 High St; dozen oysters from £12, mains from £7.50; ⊙10am-4pm Thu-Sun) Squeeze onto a stool by the bar, or into the four-table Victorian dining room of this baby-blue and pink restaurant, then choose from the seasonal menu and enjoy the best seafood in Whitstable. This place knows its stuff, as it's been serving oysters since 1856. Bookings are crucial unless you're travelling solo. Cash only.

Samphire MODERN BRITISH ££
(☑ 01227-770075; www.samphirewhitstable.co.uk; 4 High St; mains £9-20; ⊙8am-9.30pm Sun-Tue & Thu, 9am-9.30pm Wed, 8am-10pm Fri & Sat) The shabby-chic jumble of tables and chairs, big-print wallpaper and blackboard menus create the perfect stage for meticulously crafted mains containing East Kent's most flavour-packed ingredients. An

DON'T MISS

LEEDS CASTLE

An immense moated pile just east of Maidstone, Leeds Castle (www.leeds-castle.com; adult/concession/child £27/25/18.50; ⊙10am-6pm Apr-Sep, to 5pm Oct-Mar; 🐾) is, for many, the world's most romantic castle, and it's certainly one of the most visited in Britain. Positioned stoutly on two islands, the formidable and hefty bastion is known as something of a 'ladies castle', because – during its 1000 years of history – it has been home to a who's who of medieval queens, most famously Henry VIII's first wife, Catherine of Aragon.

The castle was transformed from fortress to lavish palace over the centuries, and its last owner, the high-society hostess Lady Baillie, used it as a princely family home and party pad to entertain the likes of Errol Flynn, Douglas Fairbanks and John F Kennedy.

The castle's vast estate offers enough attractions of its own to justify a day trip: peaceful walks, a duckery, aviary, and falconry displays. You'll also find possibly the world's sole dog-collar museum, plenty of kids' attractions and a hedge maze, overseen by a grassy bank from where fellow travellers can shout encouragement or misdirections.

Since Lady Baillie's death in 1974, a private trust has managed the property. This means that some parts of the castle are periodically closed for private events.

Trains run from London Victoria to Bearsted, where you catch a special shuttle coach to the castle.

interesting side dish is its namesake samphire, an asparagus-like plant that grows on sea-sprayed rocks and cliffs, often found on menus in these parts.

★ **Sportsman Pub**   BRITISH £££
(www.thesportsmanseasalter.co.uk; Faversham Rd, Seasalter; five-course tasting menu £60; ⊙restaurant noon-2pm & 7-9pm Tue-Sat, 12.30-2.45pm Sun) The anonymous village of Seasalter, 4 miles west of Whitstable, would barely deserve mention without the deceivingly ramshackle Sportsman Pub, decorated with a Michelin star (held for 12 years). Local ingredients from sea, marsh and woods are crafted by Whitstable-born chef Stephen Harris into taste-packed Kentish creations that have food critics drooling.

🛍 Shopping

Chappell Contemporary   ART
(📞01227-637329; www.chappellcontemporary.com; 30 Oxford St) This cool art gallery primarily displays bold, colourful, edgy and exciting silk screen prints, lithographs and etchings from established and up-and-coming British artists.

ℹ Information

There is no tourist information office in Whitstable, though you can glean info from the **Whitstable Community Museum & Gallery** (📞01227-264742; www.whitstablemuseum.org; 5 Oxford St; adult/concession/child £3/2/free;

⊙10.30am-4.30pm Thu-Sat, 10.30am-4.30pm Wed-Sat during school holidays).

ℹ Getting There & Away

BUS
Whitstable has connections to Canterbury (£5.20, 30 minutes, every 10 minutes) and London Victoria (£12.60, two hours, daily).

TRAIN
Whitstable has the following connections:
London St Pancras (£32.10, 80 minutes, hourly)
London Victoria (£25.30, 80 minutes, hourly)
Margate (£7.90, 20 minutes, twice hourly)
Ramsgate (£10.30, 36 minutes, twice hourly)

Margate
📞01843 / POP 65,000

A popular resort for more than two centuries, Margate's late-20th-century slump was long and bleak as British holidaymakers ditched Victorian frump for the carefree *costas* of Spain. But this grand old seaside resort, with fine-sand beaches, artistic associations and the famous Dreamland (www.dreamland.co.uk; Marine Tce; entry £5, rides £1.50-5; ⊙10am-6pm, days vary throughout the year; 🐾) amusement park, has bounced off the bottom, re-emerging with a new and fashionable nickname: Shoreditch-on-Sea, in honour of the London hipster ghetto. Major cultural regeneration projects, including the

WORTH A TRIP

CHATHAM HISTORIC DOCKYARD

On the riverfront in Chatham, **Chatham Historic Dockyard** (☑ 01634-823800; https://thedockyard.co.uk; Dock Rd; adult/concession/child £25/22.50/15; ☉ 10am-6pm Apr-Oct, to 4pm mid-Feb–Mar & Nov), a candidate for Unesco World Heritage status, occupies a third of what was once the Royal Navy's main dock facility. It is possibly the most complete 18th-century dock in the world and has been transformed into a maritime museum examining the Age of Sail. Exhibits include well-restored ships, exhibitions on a variety of shipbuilding themes and a working steam railway.

spectacular Turner Contemporary art gallery, are reversing the town's fortunes, and a bevy of superb restaurants adds to the boho cafes and carefully curated junk emporia of the rejuvenated old town.

◉ Sights

★ **Turner Contemporary**   GALLERY
(☑ 01843-233000; www.turnercontemporary.org; Rendezvous; ☉ 10am-5pm Wed-Sun) **FREE** This blockbuster contemporary art gallery, bolted together on the site of the seafront guesthouse where master painter JMW Turner used to stay, is one of East Kent's top attractions. The opinion-cleaving architecture – 'alien, brutal and bleak' was one assessment – may leave you cold, but the artwork is riveting, while the sea view from the floor-to-ceiling windows allows you to fully fathom the very thing Turner loved so much about Margate – the sea, sky and refracted light of the north Kent coast.

The gallery attracts top-notch contemporary installations by high-calibre artists such as Tracey Emin (who grew up in Margate) and Alex Katz. When you're finished with the art, culinary creations await in the cafe, and the gift shop is excellent. At the time of writing, the gallery was closed for refurbishment and was due to reopen in 2021, in time to mark its 10th anniversary with a special programme of exhibitions and events.

Shell Grotto   CAVE
(www.shellgrotto.co.uk; Grotto Hill; adult/child £4.50/2; ☉ 10am-5pm Apr-Oct, 11am-4pm Sat & Sun Nov-Mar) Margate's unique attraction is a mysterious subterranean grotto, discovered in 1835. It's a claustrophobic collection of rooms and passageways embedded with 4.6 million shells arranged in symbol-rich mosaics. It has inspired feverish speculation over the years – some think it a 2000-year-old pagan temple or a secret meeting place for cultists, while others see an elaborate 19th-century hoax. Either way, it's a one-of-a-kind spot.

🛏 Sleeping

★ **Reading Rooms**   B&B £££
(☑ 01843-225166; www.thereadingroomsmargate.co.uk; 31 Hawley Sq; r incl breakfast £190; ☎) Occupying an unmarked 18th-century Georgian town house on a tranquil square just five minutes' walk from the sea, this luxury two-bedroom boutique B&B is an elegant treat. Antique white-painted rooms with waxed wooden floors and beautiful French antique reproduction furniture contrast with the 21st-century bathrooms fragrant with luxury cosmetics. Breakfast is served in your room. Bookings essential.

No children or pets. There is no bell, just a door knocker.

✗ Eating

★ **Peter's Fish Factory**   FISH & CHIPS £
(12 The Parade; fish & chips from £4.75; ☉ 11am-11pm) The queues for this super-popular place – frying up for decades – go round the block, so get in line and wait for some first-rate and very fresh fish and moreish chips. If there's space, grab one of the outside tables, or take away and munch on the move around Margate.

★ **Angela's**   SEAFOOD ££
(☑ 01843-319978; www.angelasofmargate.com; 21 The Parade; mains £12-21; ☉ noon-2.30pm & 5.45-10pm Tue-Sat) 🖉 Simple white-fronted Angela's casts its net wide over local and visiting diners seeking top-notch seafood. Built on a sustainable ethic and run by lovely staff, the restaurant serves delightful goodies from the brine. The menu changes daily but expect options like smoked haddock chowder, Whitstable rock oysters, mussels with cider and garlic, or ray wing with leek, rosemary and smoked paprika.

Sit outside in the sea breeze or fold in your elbows and squeeze inside.

Hantverk & Found JAPANESE **££**
(☑ 01843-280454; www.hantverk-found.co.uk; 18 King St; set menu from £20; ☺ noon-4pm & 6.30-9.30pm Thu, to 11pm Fri, noon-11pm Sat, noon-4pm Sun) Hantverk & Found serves up seafood with imagination, flair and a Japanese focus, whether as bento or kaiseki menus or takeaway sushi. With a titchy bar, the dining space is simple and understated, the ingredients Kent-sourced wherever possible, and it doubles as a commissioning gallery with regularly changing shows of top-quality art.

Shopping

Margate Bookshop BOOKS
(☑ 01843-639660; www.themargatebookshop.com; 2 Market Pl; ☺ 10am-5pm Tue-Sat, to 4pm Sun) This mint-coloured cutesy bookshop is a small and intimate book-lined space, with cups of coffee brewed up behind the till, bookish staff, a browse-worthy selection of titles – many from independent publishers – and a writer's room upstairs (day pass £5) if you feel those sudden and irrepressible literary urges.

❶ Information

Tourist Office (☑ 01843-577637; www.visitthanet.co.uk; Droit House, Stone Pier; ☺ 10am-5pm daily Easter-Oct, Tue-Sat Nov-Easter) In the building with the clock tower obliquely opposite the Turner Contemporary by the harbour, the helpful tourist office hands out *Isle,* a glossy magazine crammed with Thanet listings, published twice a year, and a free quarterly newspaper called the *Mercury,* containing all the latest happenings.

❶ Getting There & Away

BUS
Departure and arrival points for local buses are Queen St and adjacent Cecil St. Margate connections:
Broadstairs (Thanet Loop Bus; £2.30, 22 minutes, up to every 10 minutes)
Canterbury (£5.70, one hour, two hourly)
London Victoria (National Express; from £8.60, three hours, seven daily)
Ramsgate (Thanet Loop Bus; £2.90, 30 minutes, up to every 10 minutes)

TRAIN
The train station is just a few steps from the beach. There are hourly services to London Victoria (£25.80, 110 minutes) and a high-speed

service to London St Pancras (£28.20, 1½ hours) that runs twice hourly.

❶ Getting Around

The 32-mile Viking Coastal Trail cycling route loops around the Isle of Thanet (p153), embracing Ramsgate, Broadstairs and Margate, as well as dramatic scenery, bays, beaches, coves, churches and sleepy rural villages. The **Bike Shed** (☑ 01843-423193; www.thebikeshedkent.co.uk; 71 Canterbury Rd; 1/5 hours £5/20; ☺ 9am-5pm Tue-Sat) hires out good-looking, powder-blue, British-built Pashley parabikes. Kid's bikes also available. The bike collection point is at Margate train station.

Broadstairs

☑ 01843 / POP 25,000
While its bigger, brasher neighbours seek to revive and regenerate themselves, quaint little Broadstairs quietly gets on with what it's done best for the past 150 years – wowing visitors with its tight sickle of coarse sand (Viking Bay) and shallow, sun-warmed sea. Charles Dickens certainly thought it an agreeable spot, spending most summers here between 1837 and 1859. The resort now plays the Victorian nostalgia card at every opportunity, but this is a minor distraction for the fine-weather crowds that descend from London in search of sun, sand and surf.

ISLE OF THANET
You won't need a wetsuit, a ferry or snorkel to reach the Isle of Thanet and its towns of Margate, Ramsgate and Broadstairs: the 2-mile-wide Wantsum Channel, which divides the island from the mainland, silted up in the 16th century, transforming the East Kent landscape forever. In its island days, Thanet was the springboard for several epochal episodes in English history. It was here that the Romans kicked off their invasion in the 1st century BC, landing at Pegwell Bay south of present-day Ramsgate (a large Roman fort from 55 to 50 BC has been recently excavated here) and where St Augustine landed in AD 597 to launch his conversion of the pagans. If global warming forecasts are right, Thanet could once again be an island by the end of the century.

◉ Sights

Dickens House Museum MUSEUM
(www.dickensfellowship.org; 2 Victoria Pde; adult/
child £3.75/2.10; ⊙1-4.30pm Easter–mid-Jun &
mid-Sep–Oct, 10am-4.30pm mid-Jun–mid-Sep,
1-4.30pm Sat & Sun Nov) This quaint museum
is Broadstairs' top indoor attraction and
the former home of Mary Pearson Strong –
Dickens' inspiration for the character of Bet-
sey Trotwood in *David Copperfield*. Diverse
Dickensiana on display includes letters from
the author.

☼ Festivals & Events

Dickens Festival CULTURAL
(www.broadstairsdickensfestival.co.uk; ⊙mid-Jun)
Broadstairs' biggest bash, this week-long
festival culminates in a banquet and ball in
Victorian fancy dress.

⌂ Sleeping & Eating

Bay Tree Hotel HOTEL **££**
(☑01843-862502; www.baytreebroadstairs.co.uk;
12 Eastern Esplanade; s/d from £70/130) Whichever way you turn, you bump into a framed
Harry Potter poster at this lovingly refurbished 10-room hotel overlooking Stone Bay,
run by friendly staff. Most of the tastefully
furnished rooms have sea views and one
has a balcony; there's a cosy library and bar
downstairs and a comfortable living room.
The restaurant serves all meals, including
afternoon tea.

Morelli's GELATO **£**
(☑01843-862500; www.facebook.com/morellis
gelatouk; 14 Victoria Pde; gelato from £2; ⊙8am-
5.30pm Mon-Fri, to 8pm Sat & Sun) When the sun
is radiant, head here. Facing straight onto
Viking Bay, Morelli's is a Broadstairs gelato
institution. With its pronounced retro look,
it has been serving tubs, cones and glasses of
ice cream to families clustered around Formica tabletops since 1932, or for takeaway to
tots and adults alike.

★**Wyatt & Jones** BRITISH **££**
(☑01843-865126; www.wyattandjones.co.uk; 23-
27 Harbour St; mains £6-21; ⊙9am-8.30pm Wed &
Thu, to 9.30pm Fri & Sat, to 4pm Sun) Broadstairs'
best gastronomical offering is this contemporary British restaurant just a few steps off
the beach. Savour unashamedly local dishes
such as Whitstable oysters, local sea trout,
mussels and chips, or a day-launching breakfast in an uncluttered interior of gun-metal
blue and scratched timber floors. Then admire your expanding waistline in the retro
mirror wall.

☼ Drinking & Nightlife

Chapel Bar & Bookshop BAR
(www.chapelbroadstairs.com; 44-46 Albion St;
⊙4pm-1am Mon-Wed, noon-2am Thu-Sat, noon-
1am Sun; ☜) Bar. Bookshop. Chapel. Cafe.
Books for hymn and her: booze as your
browse through this endearing two-floor
space – stuffed to its holy rafters with literature – meditate on God, or just sit for a coffee and unwind amid all the literary charm.

LOCAL KNOWLEDGE

HOPS & VINES

Both Kent and Sussex produce some of the most delicious ales in the UK, and the southeast's wines are even outgunning some traditional continental vintners.

Kent's **Shepherd Neame Brewery** (☑01795-542016; www.shepherdneame.co.uk; 10
Court St, Faversham; tours £14; ⊙tours 2pm daily) is Britain's oldest and cooks up aromatic ales brewed from Kent-grown premium hops. Sussex's reply is **Harveys Brewery**
(☑01273-480209; www.harveys.org.uk; Bridge Wharf; ⊙9am-5pm), which perfumes Lewes'
town centre with a hop-laden scent. Book well in advance for tours of either brewery.

Thanks to warmer temperatures and determined winemakers, English wine, particularly of the sparkling variety, is also developing a strong fan base all of its own.
Award-winning vineyards exist in both Sussex and Kent, where the chalky soils are lik-
ened to France's Champagne region. Many vineyards now offer tours and wine tastings.
Two of the most popular are **Biddenden Vineyards** (☑01580-291726; www.biddenden
vineyards.com; Gribble Bridge Lane; £1 donation to charity, tours £10; ⊙10am-5pm Mon-Sat,
11am-5pm Sun, tours Sat Apr-Sep), 1 mile due south along the A262 from the village of Biddenden, and **Chapel Down Vinery** (☑01580-766111; www.chapeldown.com; Small Hythe,
Tenterden; tours £20; ⊙tours daily Mar-Nov), located 2.5 miles south of Tenterden on the
B2082.

Located in the former St Mary's Chapel (1601), with an excellent range of craft beer at hand.

❶ Getting There & Away

BUS

Broadstairs connections include the following:

Canterbury (£5.70, 1½ hours, twice hourly)

London Victoria (National Express; from £9, 3¼ hours, seven daily)

Margate (Thanet Loop Bus; £2.30, 22 minutes, up to every 10 minutes)

Ramsgate (Thanet Loop Bus; £1.80, 14 minutes, up to every 10 minutes)

TRAIN

Broadstairs is connected to London Victoria (£25.80, two hours, hourly) and by high-speed service to London St Pancras (£34.70, 80 minutes to two hours, twice hourly).

Ramsgate

📞 01843 / POP 40,400

The most varied of Thanet's towns, Ramsgate has a friendlier feel than rival Margate and is more vibrant than quaint little Broadstairs. A forest of masts whistles serenely in the breeze below the handsomely curved walls of Britain's only royal harbour, and the seafront is surrounded by bars and cosmopolitan street cafes. Just one celebrity chef away from being labelled 'up and coming', Ramsgate retains a shabbily undiscovered charm, with its sweeping, environmentally sanctioned Blue Flag beaches and some spectacular Victorian architecture making it well worth the visit. August sees experimental music bands performing in the two-day (and free) Contra Pop Festival on Ramsgate Beach.

◉ Sights

Spitfire & Hurricane Memorial Museum
MUSEUM

(www.spitfiremuseum.org.uk; Manston Rd; ⊙10am-5pm Mar-Oct, to 4pm Nov-Feb) FREE Around 4 miles northwest of Ramsgate's town centre, at Manston Airport, this purpose-built museum stores two WWII planes: a Spitfire and a Hurricane. Both look factory-fresh but are surprisingly delicate and so, sadly, there's no clambering aboard, though you can have a go in a rather amateurishly built simulator (£30 for 30 minutes). Gathered around the planes are myriad flight-associated exhibits, many relating to Manston's role as an

DOWN HOUSE

Charles Darwin's home from 1842 until his death in 1882, **Down House** (EH; www.english-heritage.org.uk; Luxted Rd, Downe; adult/concession/child £14.50/13.10/8.70; ⊙10am-6pm Apr-Sep, to 5pm Oct, 10am-5pm Sat & Sun Nov-Mar) witnessed the development of Darwin's theory of evolution by natural selection. The house and gardens have been restored to look much as they would have in Darwin's time, including the study where he undertook much of his reading and writing, the drawing room where he tried out some of his indoor experiments, and the gardens and greenhouse where some of his outdoor experiments are recreated.

There are three self-guided trails in the area, where you can follow in the great man's footsteps. Take bus 146 from Bromley North or Bromley South railway station, or service R8 from Orpington.

airfield during the Battle of Britain, when many Spitfires were based here.

The museum has a decent cafe with views of the airstrip. Take bus 38 or 11 from King St and ask the driver to drop you as near as possible.

🍴 Sleeping & Eating

Glendevon Guesthouse
B&B ££

(📞01843-570909; www.glendevonguesthouse. co.uk; 8 Truro Rd; s/d from £52.50/70; 🅿🛜) 🌿 Run by energetic and knowledgeable hosts, this comfy guesthouse takes the whole eco-friendly thing seriously, with guest recycling facilities, eco-showers and energy-saving hairdryers. The hallways of the grand Victorian house, a block back from the seafront, are decorated with works by local artists. All six rooms and apartments have kitchenettes, and breakfast (£12.50) is convivially taken around a communal table.

Royal Harbour Hotel
BOUTIQUE HOTEL ££

(📞01843-591514; www.royalharbourhotel.co.uk; 10-12 Nelson Cres; s/d from £70/110; 🛜) Occupying two Regency town houses on a glorious seafront crescent, this boutique hotel feels enveloped in warmth and quirkiness – an eclectic collection of books, magazines, games and artwork line the hotel. Rooms

DON'T MISS

CHARTWELL

The home of Sir Winston Churchill from 1924 until his death in 1965, Chartwell (NT; www.nationaltrust.org.uk; Westerham; adult/child £17.25/8.60; ☺11.30am-5pm Mar-Oct) offers a breathtakingly intimate insight into the life of England's famous cigar-chomping bombast. This 19th-century house and its rambling grounds have been preserved much as Winnie left them, full of books, pictures, maps and personal mementos. Churchill was also a prolific painter and his now extremely valuable daubings are scattered throughout the house and fill the garden studio. Chartwell is 6 miles west of Sevenoaks.

Transport options are very limited without a car; it's best to have your own set of wheels. Take a taxi from the nearest train station Edenbridge (4 miles), accessible from London Victoria (£10).

range from tiny singles to country-house-style four-poster suites, most with postcard views over the forest of masts below. All are perfectly appointed with bags of character.

★ **Royal Victoria Pavilion**   PUB FOOD £
(www.jdwetherspoon.com; Harbour Pde; mains £5-11; ☺8am-midnight Sun-Thu, to 1am Fri & Sat; 🛜) The old pavilion has sat on Ramsgate seafront like an upturned boat since 1904, its grand architecture, based on the Little Theatre at Versailles, a vacant symbol of the British seaside's bygone glory days. The hall was brought spectacularly back to life by Wetherspoons (it's the chain's biggest) and is now a place to eat that packs a wow factor.

ℹ Information

Tourist Office (☎01843-598750; www. ramsgatetown.org; Customs House, Harbour Pde; ☺10am-4pm) A small, staffed visitor centre with out-of-hours brochure stands.

ℹ Getting There & Away

BUS

Ramsgate has the following bus connections:
Broadstairs (Thanet Loop Bus; £1.80, up to every 10 minutes)
London Victoria (National Express; from £9.20, three hours, six daily)

Margate (Thanet Loop Bus; £2.30, 29 minutes, up to every 10 minutes)
Sandwich (£3.40, 28 minutes, hourly)

TRAIN

Ramsgate has many services to London Victoria (£25.80), London St Pancras (£34.70) and London Charing Cross (£34.70). Journey times range from 1¼ to two hours. There are also services to Sandwich (£5.40, 12 minutes, hourly) and Dover (£10.60, 35 minutes, two hourly).

Sandwich

☑ 01304 / POP 5000

As close as you'll get to a living museum, Sandwich was once England's fourth city (after London, Norwich and Ipswich). It can be hard to grasp this as you wander its drowsy medieval lanes, discovering its ancient churches, Dutch gables, crooked peg-tiled roofs and overhanging timber-framed houses. Once a port to rival London, Sandwich began its decline when the entrance to the harbour silted up in the 16th century, and this once-vital gateway to and from the Continent spent the next 400 years retreating into quaint rural obscurity. Preservation is big here today, with huge local interest in period authenticity. In the town's historic core, unlisted buildings are few and far between.

⊙ Sights

Sandwich's web of medieval and Elizabethan streets is perfect for ambling through and getting pleasantly lost (as many do). Strand St in particular has one of the country's highest concentrations of half-timbered buildings. Ornate brickwork on some houses betrays the strong influence of 350 Protestant Flemish refugees (referred to as 'the Strangers') who settled in the town in the 16th century at the invitation of Elizabeth I. The tiny **Empire Cinema** (☎01304-620480; www.empiresandwich.co.uk; Delf St) is preserved as an art deco museum piece and the 1920s garage deals more in classic cars than modern vehicles.

Sandwich Quay   WATERFRONT
Several attractions line the River Stour. The cute little flint-chequered Barbican tollgate was built by Henry VIII and controls traffic flow over the river's only road bridge. Nearby rises Fishergate, built in 1384 and once the main entrance to the town, through which goods from the

Continent and beyond passed. On fair-weather days, hop aboard the Sandwich River Bus (07958-376183; www.theriverbus.co.uk; The Quay; adult/child 30min trip £7/5, seal spotting £20/14; 11am-6pm Thu-Sun Apr-Sep, Sat & Sun Oct-Mar) beside the toll bridge for seal-spotting trips along the River Stour and out into Pegwell Bay.

Guildhall Museum   MUSEUM
(www.sandwichguildhallmuseum.co.uk; Guildhall, Cattle Market; 10am-4pm Wed-Sun) FREE
Sandwich's small but thorough museum is a good place to start exploring the town. The exhibition space was fully renovated in 2017 to house a copy of the Magna Carta, accidentally discovered in Sandwich's archives in 2015. Other exhibitions examine the town's rich past as a Cinque Port (p162), its role in various wars, and the gruesome punishments meted out to felons, fornicators and phoney fishers.

Sleeping

Bell Hotel   HOTEL ££
(01304-613388; www.bellhotelsandwich.co.uk; Sandwich Quay; d/f from £75/85; P) Today the haunt of celebrity golfers, the Bell Hotel has been sitting on the town's quay since Tudor times, though much of the remaining building is from the 19th century. A splendid sweeping staircase leads to luxurious rooms, some with pretty quay views. The Old Dining Room restaurant is one of East Kent's poshest nosh spots.

ⓘ Information

Tourist Office (www.open-sandwich.co.uk; Guildhall, Cattle Market; 10am-5pm) Located in the historic Guildhall.

ⓘ Getting There & Away

BUS

Buses go to Ramsgate (£3.40, 25 minutes, hourly), Dover (£4.20, 80 minutes, two hourly) and Canterbury (£4.40, 40 minutes, three hourly).

TRAIN

Trains run to Dover Priory train station (£7.80, 22 minutes, hourly), Ramsgate (£5.40, 12 minutes, hourly) and London St Pancras (£34.70, 1½ hours, hourly).

Dover

01304 / POP 31,000

One of the Cinque Ports (p162), Dover has certainly seen better days. Its derelict postwar architecture and shabby town centre is a rather uninspiring introduction to England for travellers arriving on cross-Channel ferries and cruise ships, most of whom breeze through speedily. But the town has a couple of redeeming, stellar attractions. The port's vital strategic position so close to mainland Europe gave rise to an important and sprawling hilltop castle, embedded with some 2000 years of history. The spectacular white cliffs, as much a symbol of English wartime resilience as Winston Churchill or the Battle of Britain, rear in chalky magnificence to the east and west.

ⓞ Sights

Dover Castle   CASTLE
(EH; 03703-331181; www.english-heritage.org.uk; adult/concession/child £17/15.30/10.20; 10am-6pm Apr-Jul & Sep, 9.30am-6pm Aug, to 5pm Oct, 10am-4pm Sat & Sun Nov-Mar; P) Occupying top spot, literally and figuratively,

---

THE WHITE CLIFFS OF DOVER

Immortalised in song, film and literature, the iconic white cliffs of Dover are embedded in the national consciousness, forming a big 'Welcome Home' sign to generations of travellers and soldiers. The cliffs rise to 100m in height and extend either side of Dover, but the best bit is the 6-mile stretch that starts about 2 miles east of town, properly known as the Langdon Cliffs and now managed by the National Trust.

From the White Cliffs of Dover Visitor Centre (01304-202756; www.nationaltrust.org.uk; Upper Rd; 10am-5pm Mar-Oct, 11am-4pm Nov-Feb), follow the stony path east along the clifftops for a bracing 2-mile walk to the stout Victorian South Foreland Lighthouse (NT; www.nationaltrust.org.uk; adult/child £6/3; guided tours 11am-5.30pm Fri-Mon mid-Mar–Oct). This was the first lighthouse to be powered by electricity, and was the site of the first international radio transmissions, in 1898.

A trail runs along the cliffs as far as St Margaret's Bay, a popular spot among locals. Bus 81 shuttles back to Dover or onto Deal every hour from St Margaret's Bay.

Dover

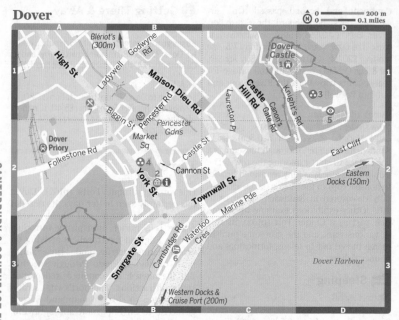

Dover

⊚ Top Sights
1	Dover Castle	C1

⊚ Sights
2	Dover Museum	B2
3	Roman Lighthouse	D1
4	Roman Painted House	B2
5	Secret Wartime Tunnels	D1

⊟ Sleeping
6	Dover Marina Hotel	B3

⊗ Eating
7	Allotment	A1

in Dover's townscape, this most impressive of castles was built to bolster the country's weakest point at the shortest sea crossing to mainland Europe. The highlights here are the unmissable secret wartime tunnels and the Great Tower, but the huge area across which it sprawls has a lot of other interesting sights, so allow at least three hours for your visit – more if you stand to admire the views across the Channel to France.

The site has been in use for as much as 2000 years. On the vast grounds are the remains of a **Roman lighthouse**, which

dates from AD 50 and may be the oldest standing building in Britain. Beside it is the restored Saxon **Church of St Mary in Castro**.

The robust 12th-century **Great Tower**, with walls up to 7m thick, is a medieval warren filled with interactive exhibits and light-and-sound shows that take visitors back to the times of Henry II.

The biggest draw of all, however, is the network of **secret wartime tunnels**. The claustrophobic chalk-hewn passageways were first excavated during the Napoleonic Wars and then expanded to house a command post and hospital in WWII. The highly enjoyable 50-minute guided tour (every 20 minutes, included in the ticket price) tells the story of one of Britain's most famous wartime operations, code-named Dynamo, which was directed from here in 1940 and saw hundreds of thousands of soldiers evacuated from the beaches at Dunkirk.

The story here is told in a very effective way, with video projected sharply onto the tunnel walls and sounds rumbling through the rock. At one point, the entire passageway is consumed in flames, and at others, visitors are plunged into complete darkness.

Roman Painted House RUINS
(https://karu.org.uk/roman_painted_house; 25 New St; adult/child £4/3; ⊙10am-5pm Tue-Sun Apr-Sep; P) A crumbling 1960s bunker is the unlikely setting for some of the most extensive, if stunted, Roman wall paintings north of the Alps. Several scenes depict Bacchus (Roman god of wine and revelry), which makes perfect sense as this large villa was built around AD 200 as a *mansio* (hotel) for travellers needing a little lubrication to unwind.

🛏 Sleeping & Eating

Blériot's GUESTHOUSE £
(☑01304-211394; www.bleriotsguesthouse.co.uk; 47 Park Ave; s/d/tr/f from £40/62/82/96; P🛜) This spacious eight-room guesthouse in a quiet residential location is within walking distance of all the sights. Some of the light-filled rooms have original Victorian fireplaces, there's a cosy lounge and the hosts are super friendly. Breakfast is £8 (£5 for kids) extra.

Dover Marina Hotel HOTEL ££
(☑01304-203633; www.dovermarinahotel.co.uk; Waterloo Cres; s/d from £59/69; 🛜) Just a few steps from Dover's beach, this seafront hotel crams 81 rooms of varying dimensions into a gently curving 1870s edifice. The undulating corridors show the building's age, but there's nothing wonky about the rooms with their colourful cushions, big-print wallpaper and contemporary artwork. Half the rooms have unrivalled sea views and 10 boast much-sought-after balconies.

⭐**Allotment** BRITISH ££
(☑01304-214467; www.theallotmentrestaurant. com; 9 High St; mains £13.50-18; ⊙noon-9pm Tue-Sat, 12.30-4pm Sun) Dover's best dining spot sources fish and meat from around Canterbury, to be seasoned with herbs from the tranquil garden out back. Cleanse your palate with a Kentish wine in a relaxed, understated setting as you admire the view of the Maison Dieu (13th-century pilgrims' hospital) directly opposite through the exquisite stained-glass frontage.

ℹ Information

Tourist Office (☑01304-201066; www.white cliffscountry.org.uk; Market Sq; ⊙9.30am-5pm Mon-Sat) Located in the **Dover Museum** (www. dovermuseum.co.uk).

ℹ Getting There & Away

BOAT

Ferries depart for France from the Eastern Docks below the castle. Fares vary according to season and advance purchase. Services seem to be in a constant state of flux, with companies rising and falling as often as the Channel's swell.

DFDS (☑0871-574 7235; www.dfdsseaways. co.uk) Services to Dunkirk (two hours, every two hours) and Calais (1½ hours, at least hourly).

P&O Ferries (☑01304-448888; www.po ferries.com) Runs to Calais (1½ hours, every 40 to 60 minutes).

BUS

Dover has bus connections to the following:
Canterbury (£5.70, 30 minutes, three hourly)
London Victoria (National Express 007; from £7.10, three to 3½ hours, every two hours)
Rye (bus 102; £6.70, 2¼ hours)
Sandwich (£4.20, 70 minutes, two hourly)

TRAIN

Dover is connected by train to Canterbury (£8.90, 28 minutes, two hourly), London St Pancras, Victoria and Charing Cross (£34.70, one to 2½ hours, up to five hourly), and Ramsgate (£10.60, 35 minutes, two hourly) via Sandwich.

EAST SUSSEX

Home to rolling countryside, medieval villages and a gorgeous coastline, this inspiring corner of England is besieged by weekending Londoners whenever the sun pops out. And it's not hard to see why as you explore the cobbled medieval streets of Rye, wander around historic Battle (where William the Conqueror first engaged the Saxons in 1066) and peer over the edge of Beachy Head or admire the sublimely undulating length of of the breathtaking Seven Sisters chalk cliffs near genteel Eastbourne. Brighton, a highlight of any visit, offers some kicking nightlife, offbeat shopping and British seaside fun. Off the beaten track, you can stretch your legs on the South Downs Way, which traverses England's newest national park, the South Downs National Park.

Rye

☑01797 / POP 9041
Possibly southeast England's quaintest town, Rye is a precious little nugget of the past, a medieval settlement that looks like

someone hit the temporal pause button. Even the most jaded sightseer can't fail to be wooed by Rye's cobbled lanes, mysterious passageways and crooked half-timbered Tudor buildings. Tales of resident smugglers, ghosts, writers and artists add to the mystique.

Rye was once one of the Cinque Ports (p162), occupying a high promontory above the sea. Today the town rises 2 miles from the briny depths and sheep graze where the Channel's strong tides once swelled (and could swell again: apocalyptic predictions see Rye under water again by the year 2050, due to rising sea levels).

⊙ Sights

Mermaid Street
AREA

Most start their exploration of Rye on famous Mermaid St, a short walk from the Rye Heritage Centre (p162). It bristles with 15th-century timber-framed houses with quirky names such as 'The House with Two Front Doors' and 'The House Opposite'.

Lamb House
MUSEUM

(NT; www.nationaltrust.org.uk; West St; adult/concession £7.90/3.95; ⊙11am-5pm Fri-Mon late Mar-Oct) This Georgian town house is a favourite stomping ground for local apparitions, but its most famous resident was American writer Henry James, who lived here from 1898 to 1916, during which time he wrote *The Wings of the Dove*. Until 2017 this was a private house, but with the tenants gone, the National Trust has opened up more rooms to the public and created a more hands-on experience. For budding writers there are writing spaces and courses on offer.

Ypres Tower
MUSEUM

(Rye Castle; www.ryemuseum.co.uk; Church Sq; adult/concession/child £4/3/free; ⊙10.30am-5pm Apr-Oct, to 3.30pm Nov-Mar) Just off Church Sq stands the sandcastle-esque Ypres Tower (pronounced 'wipers'). You can scramble through the 13th-century building to learn about its long history as a fort, prison, mortuary and museum (the last two at overlapping times), and an annexe contains one of the last surviving Victorian women's prisons in the country. From here, there are widescreen views of Rye Bay and even France on very clear days.

🏃 Driving Tour
Dover to Rye

START DOVER EASTERN DOCKS
END RYE
LENGTH 35.5 MILES; AT LEAST FOUR HOURS

If you've just rolled off a cross-Channel ferry or have a day away from a cruise ship docked in Dover, instead of heading north to London, why not explore this fascinating route along the white cliffs and across the flat marshes of the Kent–Sussex border to find some of the southeast's hidden corners? Buses 100, 101 and 102 (The Wave) follow this route between Dover, Lydd and Hastings.

Starting at the exit to Dover's frantic ❶**Eastern Docks**, where all cross-Channel ferries tie up, take the A20 along the seafront. After a few minutes, this dual carriageway begins to climb onto the famous white cliffs west of Dover. Your first stop is just outside town – take the turning for ❷**Samphire Hoe** country park, a ledge of parkland created between the white cliffs and the sea, using 5 million cu metres of chalk excavated during the construction of the Channel Tunnel. It's a fine spot for a picnic as you watch the 30 local species of butterfly flutter by.

On the A20 again, it's a mere 1.75 miles to the exit for the village of Capel-Le-Ferne (on the B2011). Well signposted at the end of the village is the ❸**Battle of Britain Memorial**, a striking monument to the pilots who took part in the decisive struggle with the Luftwaffe in the skies above Kent and Sussex. An airman seated at the centre of a huge Spitfire propeller looks out serenely across the Channel and there's a multimedia visitor centre and museum experience to enjoy. Returning to the B2011, a few gear changes will have you on the outskirts of ❹**Folkestone**. Take a left at the first roundabout then the sixth right onto Dover Rd. This will take you into the centre of this formerly grand old resort, once a favourite stomping ground of royal bon viveur King Edward VII and a forgotten piece of England's seaside past. Take a stroll through the seafront Leas Coastal Park with its subtropical flora, then halt

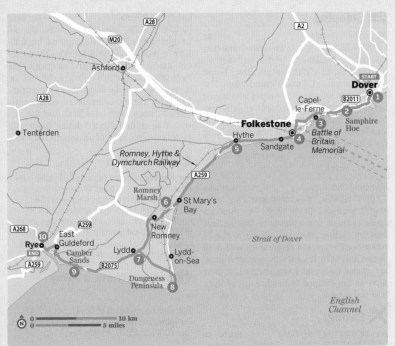

for fish and chips at the old fish market before ambling up through the Creative Quarter, Folkestone's old town, now occupied by artists' studios and craft shops.

Rolling out of Folkestone to the west on the A259 Sandgate Rd, you pass through Sandgate with its antique shops and shingle beach. From there it's another 2.5 miles to fascinating little ⑤ **Hythe**. You could spend a full day in this original Cinque Port (p162). Not only is it the eastern terminus of the fascinating narrow-gauge Romney, Hythe and Dymchurch Railway (RH&D Railway), but the Royal Military Canal also flows through the town and there's a quaint high street and beach to explore.

Heading further west, a series of not-so-attractive shingle resorts, including Dymchurch and St Mary's, are strung along the A259, cowering below their huge dykes, which keep the high tides from turning this stretch of coast into sea bottom. You've now left the white cliffs behind and are entering the ⑥ **Romney Marsh**, a flat, sparsely populated landscape of reed beds and sheep-dotted fields. There's a visitor centre (www.kentwildlifetrust.org.uk) between St Mary's Bay and New Romney (on the A259) for those with time.

Having negotiated New Romney, another of the original five Cinque Ports, take the turning to the left onto the B2075, which leads to ⑦ **Lydd**, a quaint former corporate member of the Cinque Ports. From here detour along the lonely Dungeness Rd, which heads across the flats of the eerie ⑧ **Dungeness Peninsula**, a low shingle spit dominated by its brooding nuclear power station. As well as boasting the southeast's largest seabird colony, it's also the western terminus of the RH&D Railway.

Back in Lydd, stick with the B2075 heading west for 6 miles until you reach Camber. Thought the entire south coast had just shingle beaches? Well, the main attraction here is ⑨ **Camber Sands**, a wide expanse of golden grains and dunes, ideal for picnicking and strolling.

The B2075 winds through shingly, scrubby wetlands until it rejoins the A259 at the hamlet of East Guldeford, where you should turn left towards Rye. Along the roads around here you will see the main source of revenue from the Romney Marsh – thousands of sheep grazing on the verdant flats. The A259 barrels across the marshes, eventually depositing you in ⑩ **Rye** (p159), one of the southeast's quaintest towns.

🛏 Sleeping

⭐ Jeake's House   HOTEL **££**

(☑ 01797-222828; www.jeakeshouse.com; Mermaid St; r £100-225; 🅿 🛜) Situated on Mermaid St, this 17th-century town house once belonged to US poet Conrad Aiken. The 11 rooms are named after writers who stayed here. The decor was probably slightly less bold then, missing the beeswaxed antiques and lavish drapery. Take a pew in the snug book-lined bar and, continuing the theme, enjoy breakfast in an 18th-century former Quaker chapel.

Mermaid Inn   HOTEL **£££**

(☑ 01797-223065; www.mermaidinn.com; Mermaid St; s/d from £90/140; 🅿 🛜) Few inns can claim to be as atmospheric as this ancient hostelry, dating from 1420. Each of the 31 rooms is different, but all are thick with dark beams and lit by leaded windows, and some are graced by secret passageways that now serve as fire escapes. It also has one of Rye's best restaurants.

🍴 Eating

Webbe's at the Fish Cafe   SEAFOOD **££**

(☑ 01797-222226; www.webbesrestaurants.co.uk; 17 Tower St; mains £13-18; ⊗ noon-2pm daily & 6-9.30pm Mon-Thu, 5.30-9.30pm Fri-Sun) Rye's best fish restaurant is a simple dining room flooded with natural light from large arched windows. The menu features local fish such as Rye Bay flounder in cider sauce and Rye cod in beer batter. The restaurant doubles as a cookery school and is the venue for the annual Scallop Week in March.

Landgate Bistro   BRITISH **££**

(☑ 01797-222829; www.landgatebistro.co.uk; 5-6 Landgate; mains £17-21; ⊗ 7-11pm Wed & Thu, 6.30-11pm Fri, noon-2.30pm Sat & Sat) Flee the medieval excesses of Rye's central eateries to the fresh inflections of this bistro, slightly off the tourist trail near the impressive 14th-century Landgate. The focus here is on competently crafted dishes using local lamb and fish, devoured in an understated dining space with tables gathered around an ancient fireplace.

ℹ Information

Rye Heritage Centre (☑ 01797-226696; www.ryeheritage.co.uk; Strand Quay; ⊗ 10am-5pm Apr-Oct, shorter hours Nov-Mar) See a town-model audiovisual history for £3.50 (kids £1.50) and, upstairs, a freaky collection of still-functional penny-in-the-slot novelty machines. Also runs themed walking tours of the town; see the website for details.

ℹ Getting There & Away

BUS

There are hourly buses to Dover (bus 102; £6.70, 2¼ hours) and twice-hourly services to Hastings (bus 100/101; £5.70, 40 minutes).

TRAIN

There are hourly trains to Hastings (£5.90, 19 minutes). For London St Pancras (£36.70, one hour, hourly), change in Ashford.

Hastings

☑ 01424 / POP 92,855

Forever associated with the Norman invasion of 1066 (even though the decisive events unfolded 6 miles away), Hastings prospered

---

CINQUE PORTS

Due to their proximity to Europe, southeast England's coastal towns were the frontline against raids and invasion during Anglo-Saxon times. In the absence of a professional army and navy, these ports were frequently called upon to defend themselves, and the kingdom, on land and at sea.

In 1278 King Edward I formalised this ancient arrangement by legally defining the Confederation of Cinque Ports (pronounced 'sink ports'). The five original ports – Sandwich, Dover, Hythe, Romney and Hastings – were awarded numerous perks and privileges in exchange for providing the king with ships and men. At their peak, the ports were considered England's most powerful institution after Crown and Church.

The importance of the ports eventually evaporated when the shifting coastlines silted up several Cinque Port harbours and a professional navy was based at Portsmouth. But still the pomp and ceremony remain. The Lord Warden of the Cinque Ports is a prestigious post now bestowed on faithful servants of the Crown. The Queen Mother was warden until she passed away, succeeded by Admiral Lord Boyce. Previous incumbents include the Duke of Wellington and Sir Winston Churchill.

BATTLE

'If there'd been no battle, there'd be no Battle', goes the saying in this unassuming village, which grew up around the hillside where invading French duke William of Normandy, aka William the Conqueror, scored a decisive victory over local king Harold in 1066. Visitors flock to this epicentre of 1066 country to see the spot where Harold got it in the eye, with the biggest crowd turning up mid-October to witness the annual re-enactment on the original battlefield.

The aptly named **Battle Abbey** (EH; www.english-heritage.org.uk; High St; adult/concession/child £13.60/12.20/8.20; ⊙10am-6pm Apr-Sep, to 4pm Sat & Sun Oct-Mar) marks the site of the pivotal event, which had an unparalleled impact on the country's subsequent social structure, language and, well, pretty much everything. Four years after, the Normans began constructing an abbey here, a penance ordered by the pope for the loss of life incurred. Only the foundations of the original church remain; the altar's position is supposedly the spot where Harold took an arrow in his eye.

There are train connections to Hastings (£4.50, 15 minutes, twice hourly) and London Charing Cross (£25.60, 80 minutes, twice hourly). Buses 304 and 305 (£3.40, 30 minutes) travel between Battle and Hastings.

as one of the Cinque Ports and, in its Victorian heyday, was one of Britain's most fashionable resorts. After a period of steady postwar decline, the town, with its restored **pier** (1-10 White Rock; ⊙10am-9pm) FREE and ruined **castle** (www.discoverhastings.co.uk; Castle Hill Rd; adult/concession/child £5.25/4.65/4.25; ⊙10.30am-3.30pm Thu-Sun), has enjoyed a mini-renaissance, and these days is an intriguing mix of family seaside resort, working fishing port and arty hang-out.

⊙ Sights

Stade   AREA
(Rock-A-Nore Rd) The seafront area called the Stade (below East Hill) is home to distinctive black clapboard structures known as Net Shops. These were built to store fishing gear back in the 17th century, but some now house fishmongers who sell off the catch of Europe's largest beach-launched fishing fleet, usually hauled up on the shingle behind. All these fishy goings-on keep the Stade very much a working place, with the combined pong of diesel and guts scenting the air.

Hastings Contemporary   GALLERY
(www.hastingscontemporary.org; Rock-A-Nore Rd; adult/concession £8/6; ⊙11am-4pm Fri-Sun) This large, purpose-built exhibition venue at the end of the Stade is used for temporary shows of contemporary British art as well as themed installations from the Jerwood collection. The building has a great cafe with sunny Channel views. The black-tiled

building was designed to blend in with the adjacent Net Shops.

Hastings Museum & Art Gallery   MUSEUM
(www.hmag.org.uk; Johns Pl, Bohemia Rd; ⊙10am-5pm Tue-Sat, noon-5pm Sun Apr-Oct, shorter hours Nov-Mar) FREE A short walk west of the train station, this marvellous little museum is housed in a red-brick mansion. Highlights include the intricately Moorish Durbar Hall and a section on John Logie Baird, who invented television while recuperating from an illness in Hastings between February 1923 and November 1924.

🛏 Sleeping

⭐ **Swan House**   B&B £££
(☎01424-430014; www.swanhousehastings.co.uk; 1 Hill St; s/d incl breakfast from £110/130; @🖧) Inside its 15th-century timbered shell, this four-room place blends contemporary and vintage chic to perfection. Rooms feature organic toiletries, fresh flowers, hand-painted walls and huge beds. The guest lounge, where pale sofas, painted floorboards and striking modern sculptures rub shoulders with beams and a huge stone fireplace, is a stunner. Minimum two-night stay at weekends.

✕ Eating & Drinking

St Mary in the Castle Cafe & Bar   CAFE £
(www.stmaryinthecastle.co.uk/cafe; Pelham Pl; mains £4.50-10; ⊙10am-6pm Sun-Thu, to 10pm Fri & Sat; 🖧✍) Amid the greasy cafes that line the seafront, it's a relief to find this laid-back oasis of decent food offering nutritious

DE LA WARR PAVILION

This restored Grade I–listed modernist marvel (www.dlwp.com) **FREE** on the seafront at Bexhill-on-Sea is a must for fans of art deco architecture. With its curvilinear and straight-edged, machine-age styling, the building, designed in 1935, today serves as a contemporary arts centre and hosts – in a quite intimate space – performances from such names as Goldfrapp, Saint Etienne and Jack Dee.

A cafe/bar serves cakes, pastries and drinks. Bexhill-on-Sea is 8km west of Hastings.

titbits such as tofu on toast, halloumi kebabs and a range of tempting specials. The cafe and bar is part of a larger arts centre and gallery; the latter is in the crypt of the church above and free to enter.

Hanushka Coffee House CAFE
(28 George St; ⏰9.30am-6pm) Hastings' best caffeine stop resembles a very well-stocked secondhand bookshop, with every inch of wall space packed with browsable titles. The low-lit and tightly packed space in between provokes inter-table interaction, or you can seek sanctuary on the sofas and perches in the window.

ℹ Information

Tourist Office (☎01424-451111; www.visit
1066country.com; Muriel Matters House, Pelham Pl; ⏰9am-5pm Mon-Fri, 10am-3pm Sat & Sun)

ℹ Getting There & Away

BUS

Hastings has the following bus connections:
Battle (£3.40, 28 minutes, hourly)
Eastbourne (bus 99; £5.20, 1¼ hours, three hourly)
Rye (bus 100/101; £5.70, 40 minutes, twice hourly)

TRAIN

Hastings has connections with Brighton (£14.70, one to 1¾ hours, two hourly), via Eastbourne, as well as London Charing Cross (£25.80, two hours, at least hourly), Battle (£4.50, 17 minutes, twice hourly) and Rye (£5.90, 20 minutes, hourly).

ℹ Getting Around

Hastings has two delightful old Victorian funiculars, the East Hill Cliff and West Hill Cliff Railways, useful if you need to get up onto the cliffs and don't fancy the walk. The **East Hill Cliff Railway** (Rock-A-Nore Rd; adult/child return £2.70/1.70; ⏰10am-5.30pm Apr-Sep, 11am-4pm Sat & Sun Oct-Mar) funicular ascends from the Stade to Hastings Country Park, while the **West Hill Cliff Railway** (George St; adult/child return £2.70/1.70; ⏰10am-5.30pm Mar-Sep, 11am-4pm Oct-Mar) funicular saves visitors' legs when climbing up to Hastings Castle. Otherwise the town can be easily tackled on foot.

Eastbourne

📋 01323 / POP 103,745

With its whitewashed late-Victorian hotels, Eastbourne's 3.5-mile sweeping, palm-tree-lined seafront is one of the UK's grandest, with one of the nation's finest Victorian piers (www.eastbournepier.com; ⏰24hr).

Holding the semi-official title as 'Britain's sunniest town', Eastbourne was also long known for its snoozing pensioners in deckchairs and fusty guesthouses. But while these perceptions endure, the town was long ago invigorated by an influx of students, the arrival of the southeast's largest Portuguese and Polish communities and the opening, over a decade ago, of the Towner Art Gallery, which energised Eastbourne's artistic persona.

Add to this the South Downs National Park that nudges its western suburbs, and the wind-lashed beauty of Beachy Head, and Eastbourne makes an enjoyable day trip from London or Brighton. It's also the start or end point for a hike along the 100-mile South Downs Way.

◉ Sights

★**Towner Art Gallery** GALLERY
(☎01323-434670; www.townereastbourne.org.uk; Devonshire Park, College Rd; ⏰10am-5pm Tue-Sun) **FREE** One of the southeast's most exciting exhibition spaces, this purpose-built structure has temporary shows of contemporary work on the ground and 2nd floors, while the 1st floor is given over to rotating themed shows created from the gallery's 5000-piece collection. Events take place in the auditorium, and the free tour focuses on the climate-controlled art store; see the website for details of both. At the time of writing, the gallery's exterior had been

transformed into a stunning maze of colours by German artist Lothar Götz.

🛏 Sleeping & Eating

Albert & Victoria   B&B ££
(📞 01323-730948; www.albertandvictoria.com; 19 St Aubyns Rd; s/d from £45/80; 🛜) Book ahead to stay at this delightful Victorian terraced house, whose fragrant rooms, canopied beds, crystal chandeliers and secluded walled garden for summer breakfasts are mere paces from the seafront promenade. The four rooms are named after four of Queen Victoria's offspring.

Lamb Inn   PUB FOOD ££
(📞 01323-720545; www.thelambeastbourne.co.uk; 36 High St; mains £7-20; ⊙noon-7pm Mon-Sat, to 5pm Sun) This ancient Eastbourne institution, less than a mile northwest of the train station in the under-visited Old Town, has been plonking Sussex ales on the bar for eight centuries, and now serves gourmet British pub grub and some token vegan platters. A holidaying Charles Dickens left a few smudged napkins here when he stayed across the road.

🛍 Shopping

★ Camilla's Bookshop   BOOKS
(📞 01323-736001; www.camillasbookshop.com; 57 Grove Rd; ⊙10am-5pm Mon-Sat) Literally packed to the rafters with over half a million musty volumes, this incredible second-hand-book repository, an interesting amble from the train station, fills three floors of a crumbling Victorian town house. It's the best place to source preloved reading matter on the south coast, if not the entire southeast.

ℹ Information

Tourist Office (📞 01323-415415; www.visit eastbourne.com; Compton St, Welcome Building; ⊙9.30am-5pm) Tourist information plus tickets to anything happening in Eastbourne.

ℹ Getting There & Away

BUS

There are buses to Brighton (bus 12; £4.80, 1¼ hours, up to every 10 minutes) and Hastings (bus 99; £5.20, 1¼ hours, three hourly).

TRAIN

Twice-hourly trains service Brighton (£11.60, 30 to 40 minutes) and London Victoria (£19.80, 1½ hours).

South Downs National Park

The South Downs National Park (www. southdowns.gov.uk), England's newest national park, is more than 600 sq miles of rolling chalk downs stretching west from Eastbourne to Winchester, a distance of about 100 miles. The South Downs Way extends its entire length. The park is all about rolling English countryside and views down to the coast. It's a delight at any time of year, though May to October is the best time for exploration.

⊙ Sights & Activities

Beachy Head   LANDMARK
(www.beachyhead.org.uk) The famous cliffs of Beachy Head are the highest point of the chalky rock faces that slice across the rugged coastline at the southern end of the South Downs. It's off the B2103, from the A259 between Eastbourne and Newhaven. From here the stunning Seven Sisters Cliffs undulate their way west. A clifftop path (a branch of the South Downs Way) rides the waves of chalk as far as picturesque Cuckmere Haven.

Beachy Head is a spot of thrilling beauty, the brilliant white chalk rising high into the blue Sussex sky. But on a darker note, it is also known as one of Europe's most frequented suicide spots.

Along the clifftop path, you'll stumble upon the tiny seaside hamlet of Birling Gap.

DON'T MISS

RHS GARDEN WISLEY

These fabulous horticultural gardens (📞 01483-224234; www.rhs.org.uk/ gardens/wisley; off the A3, Woking; adult/ child £14.95/7.45; ⊙9.30am-5pm Mon-Fri, 9am-5pm Sat & Sun; 🅿) are the UK's second-most-visited ticketed gardens after the Royal Botanic Gardens in Kew, London. Explore at your own leisure a wonderland of blooms, bushes and trees, admiring the Wisteria Walk, Oakwood, Orchard, Alpine Meadow, Bonsai Walk, Water Lily Pavilion, Exotic Garden and grass-verged Jellicoe Canal while keeping an eye out for riveting pieces of sculpture (including an astonishing metal head en route to the Pinetum) that pop out of the blue.

There is a handy National Trust cafe here and a lovely, secluded sun-trap of a beach that is popular with locals and walkers taking a breather.

Stupendous views of the Seven Sisters can be had from Hope Gap to the west, where parking is available.

Pevensey Castle   RUINS

(EH; www.english-heritage.org.uk; Castle Rd, Pevensey; adult/concession/child £6.90/6.20/4.10; ☉10am-5pm Apr-Oct, to 4pm Sat & Sun only Nov-Mar) The dramatic ruins of William the Conqueror's first stronghold sit 5 miles east of Eastbourne, just off the A259. Regular train services between London Victoria and Hastings via Eastbourne stop at Westham, half a mile from Pevensey. Picturesquely dissolving into its own moat, the castle marks the point where William the Conqueror landed in 1066, just two weeks before the Battle of Hastings. He wasted no time after his landing, building upon sturdy Roman walls to fashion this castle.

The castle was gainfully employed time and again through the centuries, right up to WWII, when it bristled with machine-gun nests while serving as a command and observation post in preparation for a Nazi invasion. You have to pay to enter the Inner Bailey of the castle itself, but not to wander around within the outer walls.

🛏 Sleeping

★**Belle Tout Lighthouse**   B&B £££

(☑01323-423185; www.belletout.co.uk; South Downs Way, Beachy Head; d from £175) Perched precariously close to the edge of the white cliffs, this early 18th-century decommissioned lighthouse somehow manages to contain six rooms, all imaginatively done out and all rather restricted space-wise. The highlight must be the Lantern Room, a circular guest seating area in the glass top of the building, the perfect place to enjoy a truly memorable Sussex sunset.

ℹ Getting There & Away

Bus 12 (up to every 10 minutes) heads through some of the South Downs National Park on the way to Brighton. A good place to alight is Cuckmere Haven, from where you can walk back to Eastbourne across the Seven Sisters. Bus 99 (every 20 minutes) runs from Eastbourne to Pevensey.

Lewes

☑01273 / POP 17,300

Strung out along an undulating high street flanked by elegant Georgian buildings, a part-ruined castle (www.sussexpast.co.uk; 169 High St; adult/concession/child £8.50/8/4.60; ☉10am-5.30pm Tue-Sat, 11am-5.30pm Sun & Mon Mar-Oct, to 3.45pm Nov-Feb; ℗) and a traditional brewery, Lewes (pronounced 'Lewis') is

---

THE CHANNEL ISLANDS

Just off the coast of France, Jersey, Guernsey, Sark, Herm and Alderney beckon with exquisite coastlines, shaded lanes and old-world charm. Not quite Britain and not quite France, the islands are proudly independent, self-governing British Crown dependencies that straddle the gap between the two. Their citizens owe their allegiance to Her Majesty and some still speak local dialects that stem from medieval Norman French, including Guernésiais (Dgèrnésiais) on Guernsey, Jèrriais on Jersey and Sercquiais on Sark. Other Norman languages, such as Auregnais (which was spoken on Alderney), are now extinct.

The warm Gulf of St Malo ensures subtropical plants and an incredible array of birdlife. The Channel Islands enjoy sunnier days and milder winters than the UK, attracting walkers and outdoorsy types for surfing, kayaking, coasteering and diving. Watch out for rip tides, especially around Jersey. Superb local seafood graces the tables of local restaurants in the culture hubs of St Helier (Guernsey) and St Peter Port (Jersey).

Numerous forts and castles dot the coastlines, while poignant museums – some housed in old war tunnels and bunkers – provide an insight into the islanders' fortitude during WWII.

There are daily flights to Guernsey from London Gatwick, as well as from Jersey, Manchester, Birmingham, Southampton and Bristol, and seasonal departures to other airports in the UK. Jersey receives daily flights from London Heathrow and London Gatwick, as well as from Liverpool, Manchester, Southampton, Bristol, Birmingham, Exeter and Guernsey, as well as several flights from Europe.

a charmingly affluent hillside town with a turbulent past and fiery traditions. Off the main drag, however, there's a more intimate atmosphere as you descend into twisting narrow streets called 'twittens' – the remainder of the town's original medieval street plan.

One of Lewes' claims to fame is that it straddles the 0 degrees line of longitude. An inconspicuous plaque on Western Rd marks the meridian, though modern measuring methods have actually placed the line around 100m to the east.

Lewes also holds what it claims is the biggest Bonfire Night bash in the world with tens of thousands of people descending on the town on 5 November to watch a carnival, fireworks display and effigies of villains of the day going up in flames.

🛏 Sleeping

Shelleys   HOTEL **£££**
(📞 01273-472361; www.the-shelleys.co.uk; 135-136 High St; r from £130; 🛜) Lewes' top address is this 16th-century manor house on the high street, brimful of grand old-fashioned charm and once home to the earl of Dorset and owned by the Shelley family (of Percy Bysshe fame). The stylish, country rooms are the best in Lewes, while an elegant restaurant overlooks the lovely walled garden.

ℹ Information

Tourist Office (📞 01273-483448; www.visit lewes.co.uk; 187 High St; ⊙ 9.30am-4.30pm Mon-Fri, to 2pm Sat, 10am-2pm Sun Apr-Sep, shorter hours Sat & closed Sun Oct-Mar)

ℹ Getting There & Away

Lewes has the following rail connections:
Brighton (£4.60, 15 minutes, four hourly)
Eastbourne (£8.40, 20 to 25 minutes, four hourly)
London Victoria (£19.80, 70 minutes, two hourly)

Brighton & Hove

📞 01273 / POP 290,000

Raves on the beach, Graham Greene novels, mods and rockers in bank-holiday fisticuffs, naughty weekends for Mr and Mrs Smith, and the UK's biggest gay scene – this coastal city evokes many images for the British. But one thing is certain: with its bohemian, hedonistic vibe, Brighton is where England's seaside experience goes from cold to cool.

Brighton is Britain's most colourful and outrageous city. Here burlesque meets contemporary design, microbrewed ales share bar space with 'sex on the beach' and stags watch drag.

The highlight for sightseers is the Royal Pavilion, a 19th-century party palace built by the Prince Regent, who kicked off Brighton's love of the outlandish.

The huge wind farm visible far off in the channel is the Rampion Offshore Wind Farm; learn all about it at the **Rampion Offshore Wind Farm Visitor Centre** (www.rampionoffshore.com/visitor-centre; 76-81 Kings Rd Arches; ⊙ 10am-6pm Tue-Sun May-Sep, to 4pm Oct-Apr) **FREE**.

◉ Sights

★ **Royal Pavilion**   PALACE
(📞 03000-290900; http://brightonmuseums.org. uk/royalpavilion; Royal Pavilion Gardens; adult/child £15.50/9.50; ⊙ 9.30am-5.45pm Apr-Sep, 10am-5.15pm Oct-Mar) The Royal Pavilion is the city's must-see attraction. The glittering party pad and palace of Prince George, later Prince Regent and then King George IV, it's one of the most opulent buildings in England, and certainly the finest example of early 19th-century chinoiserie anywhere in Europe. It's an apt symbol of Brighton's reputation for decadence. An unimpressed Queen Victoria called the Royal Pavilion 'a strange, odd Chinese place', but for visitors to Brighton it's an unmissable chunk of Sussex history.

The entire palace is an eye-popping spectacle, but some interiors stand out even amid the riot of decoration. The dragon-themed banqueting hall must be the most incredible in all of England. More dragons and snakes writhe in the music room, with its ceiling of 26,000 gold scales, and the then-state-of-the-art kitchen must have wowed Georgians with its automatic spits and hot tables. Prince Albert carted away all of the furniture, some of which has been loaned back by the present queen.

Brighton Museum & Art Gallery   MUSEUM
(www.brightonmuseums.org.uk; Royal Pavilion Gardens; adult/child £6.20/3.60; ⊙ 10am-5pm Tue-Sun) Set in the Royal Pavilion's renovated stable block, this museum and art gallery has a glittering collection of 20th-century art and design, including a crimson Salvador Dalí sofa modelled on Mae West's lips. There's also an enthralling gallery of world art, an impressive collection of Egyptian

Brighton & Hove

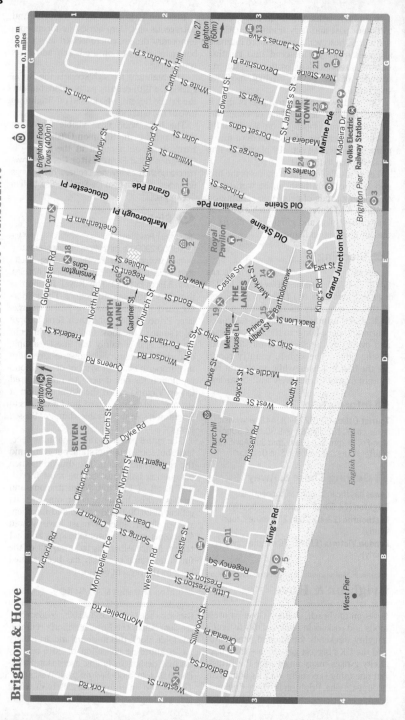

Brighton & Hove

◎ **Top Sights**
  1 Royal Pavilion E3

◎ **Sights**
  2 Brighton Museum & Art Gallery............ E2
  3 Brighton Pier... F4
  4 i360 Tower... B3
  5 Rampion Offshore Wind Farm
     Visitor Centre....................................... B3
  6 SEA LIFE Brighton................................ F4

⊜ **Sleeping**
  7 Artist Residence.................................... B2
  8 Baggies Backpackers A3
  9 Drakes..G4
 10 Hotel Pelirocco B3
 11 Hotel Una... B3
 12 Kipps Brighton....................................... F2
 13 No 27 Brighton.......................................G3

⊗ **Eating**
 14 English's of Brighton E3
 15 Food for Friends.................................... D3
 16 Gingerman.. A2
 17 Isaac At F1
 18 Iydea.. E1
 19 Riddle & Finns E3
 20 Terre à Terre E4

◎ **Drinking & Nightlife**
 21 Brighton Rocks......................................G4
 22 Concorde 2...G4
 23 Legends Club..G4
 24 Patterns F4

◎ **Entertainment**
 25 Brighton Dome....................................... E2
 26 Komedia Theatre.................................... E2

artefacts, and an 'Images of Brighton' multimedia exhibit containing a series of oral histories and a model of the defunct West Pier.

Brighton Pier   LANDMARK
(www.brightonpier.co.uk; Madeira Dr; ⊙11am-9pm Mon-Fri, 10am-10pm Sat, 10am-9pm Sun) Superb fun for the little people, this grand old Edwardian pier is the place to experience Brighton's full-on and shameless seaside kitsch. There are plenty of stomach-churning fairground rides and noisy amusement arcades to keep you entertained, and candyfloss and Brighton rock are on tap to ruin your teeth. Just west are the desolate remains of the West Pier (www.westpier.co.uk), a skeletal iron hulk that attracts flocks of starlings at sunset.

i360 Tower   TOWER
(☑03337-720360; www.britishairwaysi360. com; Lower King's Rd; adult/16-24 years/child £16.50/11.10/8.25; ⊙10am-7.30pm Sun-Thu, to 9.30pm Fri & Sat) This sci-fi column rises above the Brighton surf at the point where the now-defunct West Pier used to make landfall. The world's most slender tower is an uncompromising, 162m-tall column of reinforced steel and concrete, poking like a space-age cheese-stick from the seafront, with a huge, impaled, glass doughnut taking 'passengers' 138m above the city for gobsmacking views of the Sussex coast.

SEA LIFE Brighton   AQUARIUM
(☑01273-604234; www.visitsealife.com/brighton; Marine Pde; adult/child £21.50/13.50; ⊙9am-5.30pm, 10am-4pm in winter; ⊕) Not just for children, this aquarium is an underground exhibition of nature's fascinating water creatures. Walking around the church-like interior, visitors can get up close to eels, tropical fish and other sea life. For those who are keen, there are opportunities to feed the animals, touch starfish and ride a glass-bottomed boat over a pool of sharks, rays and turtles.

☞ Tours

**Brighton
Food Tours**   FOOD & DRINK
(☑07904 346603; www.brightonfoodtours.com; St Bartholomew's Church, Ann St; per person £55-70; ⊙Fri & Sat) Two enthusiastic local ladies show off the best of Brighton via a trail of tasters and tales. The walking-tours highlight culinary treats and street-food secrets, in keeping with the town's creative vibe. Options include the VIB (Very Independent Brighton) tour, Brighton Food & Beer tour, Brighton Wine Rebellion tour and Kemptown tour. Bring comfy shoes and an empty stomach.

Tours leave from several locations – at the time or writing, the main VIB tour left from St Bartholomew's Church on Ann St.

☆ Festivals & Events

Brighton Festival   PERFORMING ARTS
(www.brightonfestival.org; ⊙May) England's largest curated annual multi-arts festival, drawing star performers from around the globe for three weeks by the sea.

Brighton Fringe
PERFORMING ARTS

(www.brightonfringe.org; ⊙ May) As with the famous Edinburgh Festival, the Brighton Festival has its fringe – a month of irreverent comedy, art and theatre around the city.

Brighton Pride
LGBT+

(www.brighton-pride.org; ⊙ early Aug) The UK's biggest gay bash, with a rainbow-hued parade and concerts in Preston Park.

🛌 Sleeping

Kipps Brighton
HOSTEL £

(☑ 01273-604182; www.kipps-brighton.com; 76 Grand Pde; dm £18-35, s/d from £28/36; @ 🛜) These commendable budget digs have a real cafe vibe around reception, and facilities include a communal kitchen, while free movies plus pizza and pub nights aim to disconnect guests from their wi-fi-enabled devices.

Baggies Backpackers
HOSTEL £

(☑ 01273-733740; www.baggiesbackpackers.com; 33 Oriental Pl; dm/q from £16/60; 🛜) With a warm, familial atmosphere, worn-in charm, attentive service and clean, snug dorms, this long-established hostel is a Brighton institution. There's a cosy basement music and chill-out room, and a TV lounge. The hostel has a single four-person room.

★ No 27 Brighton
B&B ££

(☑ 01273-694951; www.brighton-bed-and-breakfast.co.uk; 27 Upper Rock Gardens; r £100-160; 🛜) Brighton's favourite B&B has five sumptuous rooms, perfectly presented with antique-style, but fresh, charm. All the fabrics, furniture and decoration have been painstakingly selected to fit a subtle and understated theme, based on people related to King George IV. Some rooms have sea views, but the superb decor is just as diverting. Breakfast (£7.50) is served on crisp linen and fine English china.

★ Hotel Pelirocco
HOTEL ££

(☑ 01273-327055; www.hotelpelirocco.co.uk; 10 Regency Sq; s/tw £59/84, d £99-155, tr/ste £165/249; 🛜) One of Brighton's sexiest and nuttiest places to stay, the Pelirocco is the ultimate venue for a flirty rock-and-roll weekend. Flamboyant rooms, some designed by artists, include the 'Lord Vader's Quarters', paying homage to *Star Wars;* the 'Do Knit Disturb' room, a knitted room with even a knitted telephone; the Rockabilly room, a shrine to 1950s nostalgia; a 'Modrophenia' room and a Bowie boudoir.

The room everyone wants, or wishes they could have, is the 'Lovers Lair' suite with 3m circular bed, mirrored ceiling and pole-dancing area.

Blanch House
BOUTIQUE HOTEL ££

(☑ 01273-603504; www.blanchhouse.co.uk; 17 Atlingworth St; s/d incl breakfast from £79/89; 🛜) Themed rooms are the name of the game at this boutique hotel, but there's nothing tacky about them – swish art deco styling rules in the Legacia Room, while the Snowstorm is a frosty vision in white and tinkling ice. The magnificently stylish fine-dining restaurant is all white leather banquettes and space-age swivel chairs, and there's a snazzy cocktail bar.

GAY & LESBIAN BRIGHTON

Brighton has the most vibrant LGBT+ community in the country outside London, with Brighton Pride the highlight of the annual calendar. Kemptown (aka Camptown) on and off St James's St is where it's all at. The old Brunswick Town area of Hove is a quieter alternative to the traditionally cruisy (and sometimes seedy) scene in Kemptown.

For up-to-date information on the LGBT+ scene in Brighton, check out www.realbrighton.com, or pick up the free monthly magazine *Gscene* (www.gscene.com) from LGBT venues.

Brighton Rocks (☑ 01273-600550; www.brightonrocksbar.co.uk; 6 Rock Pl; ⊙ 4-11pm Mon-Thu, noon-1am Fri & Sat, noon-9pm Sun; 🛜) Incongruously located in an alley of garages and used-car lots, this cocktail bar is firmly established on the Kemptown gay scene, but welcomes all comers with Sussex martinis and Bloody Marys, well-executed plates of food and theme parties.

Legends Club (www.legendsbrighton.com; 31-34 Marine Pde; ⊙ bar 11am-5am, club 10pm-5am Wed & Fri-Sun; 🛜) Located beneath the Legends Hotel, this is arguably the best gay bar and club in town.

★ **Hotel Una** BOUTIQUE HOTEL **£££**
(☏01273-820464; www.hotel-una.co.uk; 55-56
Regency Sq; d £155-210, ste from £165, spa room
from £295, all incl breakfast; ❄☎) All of the 19
generous rooms here wow guests with their
bold-patterned fabrics, supersized leather
sofas, free-standing baths and vegan, veggie
or carnivorous breakfast in bed. Some, such
as the two-level suite with its home cinema
and private bar, and the under-pavement
chambers with their own spa, are truly
showstopping and not as expensive as you
might expect.

All this plus a cool cocktail bar and lots
of time-warp period features make the Una
our *numero uno*. Most rooms are two-night
minimum stay at weekends.

★ **Artist Residence** BOUTIQUE HOTEL **£££**
(☏01273-324302; www.artistresidencebrighton.
co.uk; 34 Regency Sq; d £120-290; ☎) Eclectic doesn't quite describe the rooms at this
wonderful 24-room town-house hotel, set
amid the splendour of Regency Sq. As befits
the name, every bedroom is a hip blend of
bold wall murals, bespoke and vintage furniture, rough wood cladding and in-room roll-
top baths. The Set Restaurant downstairs
enjoys a glowing reputation.

Drakes BOUTIQUE HOTEL **£££**
(☏01273-696934; www.drakesofbrighton.com;
43-44 Marine Pde; r £110-300; ℙ❄@☎) This
stylishly minimalist boutique hotel oozes
understated class. So understated is the
entrance, in fact, you could easily miss it.
All rooms have similar decor in bold fabrics and European elm panelling, but it's
the feature rooms everyone wants – their
giant free-standing tubs are set in front of
full-length bay windows with widescreen
Channel views. The basement restaurant
is superb.

✗ Eating

★ **Iydea** VEGETARIAN **£**
(www.iydea.co.uk; 17 Kensington Gardens; mains
£5-8; ☺9.30am-5.30pm; ☎✎) Even by
Brighton's high standards, the food at this
multi-award-winning vegetarian cafe is a
treat. The daily-changing choices of curries,
lasagnes, felafel, enchiladas and quiches
are full of flavour and can be washed down
with a selection of vegan wines, organic
ales and homemade lemonades. If you're on
the hop, you can get any dish to take away
in plastic-free packaging.

★ **Terre à Terre** VEGETARIAN **££**
(☏01273-729051; www.terreaterre.co.uk; 71 East
St; mains from £16.95; ☺noon-10pm Tue-Sun;
✎❄) Take your taste buds around a meat-
free world in this vegetarian restaurant,
where inventive and flavourful dishes are
meticulously plated in a casual and friendly
ambience. The range is breathtaking, from
wasabi-crusted cashews to fondue soufflé and
steamed Szechuan buns, rounded off with
salt caramel truffles. A daily afternoon-tea
service includes a vegan option.

English's of Brighton SEAFOOD **££**
(☏01273-327980; www.englishs.co.uk; 29-31 East
St; mains £16-40; ☺noon-10pm) A 75-year-old
institution and celebrity haunt, this local
seafood paradise dishes up everything from
Essex oysters to locally caught lobster and
Dover sole. It's converted from fishers' cottages, with shades of the elegant style of the
Edwardian era inside, and has al fresco dining on the pedestrian square outside.

Riddle & Finns SEAFOOD **££**
(☏01273-721667; www.riddleandfinns.co.uk; 12b
Meeting House Lane; mains £14.50-22.50; ☺noon-
10pm Sun-Fri, 11.30am-11pm Sat) Regarded as
the town's most refined seafood spot, R&F
is light on gimmicky interiors (think white
butcher-shop tiles, marble tables and candles) but heavy on taste. With the kitchen
open to the street outside, chefs put on a
public cooking class with every dish as they
prepare your smoked haddock in champagne sauce or some wild sea bass.

WORTH A TRIP

THE DEVIL'S PUNCHBOWL

A delightfully scenic valley scooped out of the verdant Surrey hills, the Devil's Punchbowl (NT; www.nationaltrust.org. uk; London Rd, Hindhead; ⊙ dawn-dusk, cafe 10am-4pm; P) is a beautiful diversion that can swallow up an entire day of walking or cycling through heather-strewn landscape, dense woodland and across fields and crystal-clear streams. Five scenic hiking trails are marked out, from a 1.6km stroll to a more energetic 5km steeper-gradient walk. Legend attests that the depression was the result of Thor throwing a huge handful of earth into the Devil's face, leaving the hollow.

In geological terms, the Devil's Punchbowl is actually the result of a process called 'spring sapping', involving rainwater hitting an impermeable layer of clay and emerging as spring water, eroding the local sandstone and, over millennia, creating the vast bowl-like shape.

Food for Friends
VEGETARIAN ££

(☑ 01273-202310; www.foodforfriends.com; 17-18 Prince Albert St; mains £6-16; ⊙ 9am-10pm Sun-Thu, to 10.30pm Fri & Sat; 🖉) An ever-inventive choice of vegetarian and vegan food keeps loyal diners returning here to see and be seen – literally, by every passerby through the huge street-side windows. Kept fresh-looking, zestful and as popular as the day it opened in 1981, it also serves breakfast and brunch daily. Be prepared to wait for a table on busy shopping days.

Gingerman
MODERN EUROPEAN £££

(☑ 01273-326688; www.gingermanrestaurants. com; 21a Norfolk Sq; 2-/3-course menu £40/50, Sunday lunch 1/2/3 courses £23/30/35; ⊙ 12.30-2pm & 6-10pm Tue-Sun) Hastings seafood, Sussex beef, Romney Marsh lamb, local sparkling wines and countless other seasonal, local and British treats go into the adroitly flash-fried and slow-cooked dishes served at this snug 32-cover eatery. Reservations are advised. Norfolk Sq is a short walk west along Western Rd from the Churchill Sq shopping centre.

The tasting menu and vegetarian tasting menu are both £65.

Isaac At
BRITISH £££

(☑ 07765-934740; www.isaac-at.com; 2 Gloucester St; 3-course set menu £30, tasting menu £60; ⊙ 12.30-2.30pm Sat & 6-10.30pm Wed-Sat) 🖉 Tucked on a street corner, this intimate fine-dining restaurant is run by a small team of culinary talent, all aged under 30. Every ingredient is locally sourced, including the wines, with food miles for each ingredient noted on the menu. It's probably the homeliest high-end dining experience in the area. First-class, fresh and thoughtful food.

The three-course menu is available on Wednesday and Thursday evenings and Saturday lunch. Gluten-free and vegan menus are also provided.

🍷 Drinking & Nightlife

Concorde 2
CLUB

(☑ 01273-673311; www.concorde2.co.uk; Madeira Dr; ⊙ live shows 7.30-11pm Sun-Thu, 7-10pm Fri & Sat, club 11pm-4am Fri & Sat; 🖝) Brighton's best-known and best-loved club is a disarmingly unpretentious den. Each month there's a huge variety of club nights, live bands and emerging singers and concerts by international names.

Patterns
CLUB

(☑ 01273-894777; www.patternsbrighton.com; 10 Marine Pde; ⊙ Wed-Sat, hours vary; 🖝) Some of the city's top club nights are held downstairs at this ear-numbing venue in a former 1920s hotel. The music is top priority, attracting big-name acts and a young crowd. There's a fine terrace with superb views out to sea.

☆ Entertainment

Komedia Theatre
COMEDY

(☑ 01273-647100; www.komedia.co.uk; 44-47 Gardner St) The UK's top comedy venue attracts the best stand-up acts from the English-speaking world. Book well in advance.

Brighton Dome
THEATRE

(☑ 01273-709709; www.brightondome.org; Church St) Once the stables for King George IV's horses, this art deco complex within the Royal Pavilion estate houses three theatre venues. ABBA famously won the 1974 Eurovision Song Contest here. Restoration work was ongoing at the time of writing.

ℹ Information

Incredibly, Brighton closed its busy tourist office several years ago, replacing it with 13 visitor information points (VIPs) across the city – mostly racks of brochures in hotels, shops and museums; one is in Brighton train station.

Contact **Visit Brighton** (☑ 01273-290337; www.visitbrighton.com) for information.

❶ Getting There & Away

BUS

Services run between Brighton and London Victoria (from £11, 2½ hours) at least every two hours.

TRAIN

There are three trains hourly to London Victoria (£19.80, one hour), and half-hourly trains to London St Pancras (£19.10, 1¼ hours). London-bound services pass through Gatwick Airport (£9.30, 25 to 35 minutes, up to five hourly).

❶ Getting Around

Day citySaver bus tickets (£5) are available from the drivers of all Brighton and Hove buses. Alternatively, a £3.90 PlusBus ticket on top of your rail fare gives unlimited bus travel for the day.

The city operates a pricey pay-and-display parking scheme. In the town centre, it costs between £1 and £3.60 per hour for a maximum stay of two hours. Alternatively there's a Park & Ride 2.5 miles northwest of the centre at Withdean, from where bus 27 (return £5) zips into town.

Cab companies include **Brighton Streamline Taxis** (☑ 01273-202020; www.streamlinetaxis.org) and **Brighton & Hove Radio Cabs** (☑ 01273-204060; www.brightontaxis.com) and there's a taxi rank at the junction of East and Market Sts.

WEST SUSSEX

West Sussex offers pastoral escapes into a charming and historic corner of England. The serene hills and valleys of the South Downs ripple across this green county, fringed by a sheltered coastline. Time-warped Arundel and cultured, ancient Chichester make superb bases from which to explore the county's winding country lanes and remarkable Roman ruins.

Arundel

☑ 01903 / POP 3500

Arguably the prettiest town in West Sussex, Arundel is clustered around a vast fairy-tale castle, its hillside streets overflowing with antique emporiums, creaking bookshops, teashops, inviting eateries and intriguing art galleries. While much of the town appears medieval – the whimsical castle has been

home to the dukes of Norfolk for centuries – most of it dates back to Victorian times. The ostentatious 19th-century Catholic **cathedral** (www.arundelcathedral.org; London Rd; ⊙ 9am-6pm Apr-Oct, to dusk Nov-Mar) **FREE** is another of Arundel's dominating features.

◉ Sights

Arundel Castle   CASTLE
(www.arundelcastle.org;   adult/child/family £15/5/35; ⊙ 10am-5pm Tue-Sun Easter-Oct) An imposing bastion rising above Arundel, the castle was first built in the 11th century – the motte dates to 1068, the gatehouse dates from 1070 and the restored keep (which you can climb up to and explore) atop the motte was originally built of wood around the same time. Ransacked during the English Civil War, the rest of the castle is the result of reconstruction by the various dukes of Norfolk between 1718 and 1900. Don't miss the colossal Baron's Hall and the stunning library.

The current duke still lives in part of the castle, with eight bedrooms at his disposal, and only uses the halls and rooms that visitors can see for select functions. The formal gardens are also quite spectacular and worth exploration, while the magnificent tulip displays are a sight to behold in April. A recently opened feature is the water gardens – originally the 'stew ponds' where fish were kept – with its swans, ducks, round-house and charming thatched boathouse. Consult the website for information on family-friendly activities, such as jousting demonstrations in summer.

> **DON'T MISS**
>
> ### BOX HILL
>
> The famous setting of the picnic in Jane Austen's *Emma*, Box Hill (☑ 01306-885502; www.nationaltrust.org.uk/box-hill; Zig Zag Rd, Box Hill; ⊙ dawn-dusk; ℗) is pure bliss. A vast chunk of the chalk expanse of the North Downs, Box Hill offers some sublimely photogenic, entrancing and ranging views over the Surrey countryside. Popular with cyclists and family day trippers, Box Hill is home to almost infinite walking opportunities (check out the downloadable walks on the National Trust website) as well as a dense profusion of wildlife, trees and plants.

🛏 Sleeping & Eating

Arden Guest House
B&B ££

(📞 01903-884184; www.ardenhousearundel.com; 4 Queens Lane; d £99, without bathroom £89; P 🛜) For the classic British B&B experience, head to this seven-room guesthouse just over the river from the historical centre. Rooms are kept very pleasant, fresh and airy, the hosts are amiable and inviting, and breakfasts are cooked.

⭐ Motte & Bailey Cafe
CAFE £

(📞 01903-883813; www.motteandbaileycafe.com; 49 High St; mains £6.95-9.95; ⊙ 8.30am-4pm Mon & Tue, 8.30am-5pm & 6pm-late Wed-Sat, 8.30am-5pm Sun; 🖊) A modish interior of white, dark blue, varnished floorboards and glimpses of exposed brick, this airy and bright space is a welcome recuperation spot after castle explorations. There's ample vegetarian choice on the brief menu, which ranges from poached eggs and smashed avocado to delectable salmon, cod and prawn fishcakes, or just a bowl of its exceedingly tasty chips.

🔒 Shopping

⭐ Arundel Contemporary
ART

(www.arundelcontemporary.com; 53 High St; ⊙ 10am-4pm Sun-Tue & Thu, to 5pm Fri & Sat) This excellent art gallery eschews the mundane for some simply riveting pieces, carefully selected and curated. The ceramic works from South Korea–born Jin Eui Kim are exquisite in their patterns and fragile beauty, while a profusion of thought-provoking and engaging art hangs from the walls. The helpful owner is loquacious about each and every piece.

ℹ Getting There & Away

Arundel has the following train connections:

Brighton (£11.40, 1¼ hours, half-hourly) Change at Barnham or Ford.

Chichester (£4.90, 25 minutes, twice hourly) Change at Ford or Barnham.

London Victoria (£19.80, 1½ hours, twice hourly)

Chichester

📞 01243 / POP 26,795

A lively Georgian market town still almost encircled by its ancient Roman and medieval town walls, the administrative capital of West Sussex keeps watch over the plains between the South Downs and the sea. Visitors flock to Chichester's splendid cathedral, streets of handsome 18th-century town houses, its famous theatre and its pedestrianised shopping streets packed with big-name and independent shops. A Roman port garrison in its early days, the town is also a gateway to nearby Roman remains of immense archaeological value, as well as to Arundel and a popular stretch of attractive coast.

👁 Sights

Chichester Cathedral
CATHEDRAL

(www.chichestercathedral.org.uk; West St; ⊙ 7.15am-6.30pm, free tours 11.15am & 2.30pm Mon-Sat) This understated cathedral was begun in 1075 and largely rebuilt in the 13th century. The free-standing church tower went up in the 15th century – the spire dates from the 19th century, after its predecessor famously toppled over without warning in 1861. Inside, three storeys of beautiful arches sweep upwards and Romanesque carvings are dotted around. Interesting features to track down include a smudgy stained-glass window added by artist Marc Chagall in 1978 and a glassed-over section of Roman mosaic flooring.

Pallant House Gallery
GALLERY

(📞 01243-774557; www.pallant.org.uk; 9 North Pallant; adult/child £11/free; ⊙ 10am-4pm Tue-Sat, 11am-4pm Sun) A Queen Anne mansion, handsome Pallant House, and a 21st-century wing host this superb gallery. The focus is on mostly 20th-century British art. Show-stoppers Patrick Caulfield, Lucian Freud, Graham Sutherland, Frank Auerbach and Henry Moore are interspersed with international names such as Emil Filla, Le Corbusier and RB Kitaj. Most older works are in the mansion, while the newer wing is packed with pop art, contemporary work and a huge, colourful geometric mural from Lothar Götz on the staircase walls.

Chichester City Walls
ARCHITECTURE

(www.chichesterwalls.org/chichester-city-walls) Chichester's almost complete ring of Roman defensive walls are around 1.5 miles in length, and provide a pleasant escape from the retail bustle they now contain. Pick up a leaflet and booklet from the tourist office and head out along the route, much of which leads through parkland. Built to defend the town of Noviomagus Reginorum 1800 years ago, they are just about the most intact set of Roman city walls in Britain. Best accessed from West or East Sts.

Novium Museum　　　　　MUSEUM
(☑ 01243-775888; www.thenovium.org; Tower St;
⊙ 10am-3pm Tue-Fri, to 4pm Sat) FREE Chichester's purpose-built museum provides
a home for the eclectic collections of the
erstwhile District Museum, as well as some
artefacts from Fishbourne Palace and a
huge mosaic from Chilgrove Roman villa.
The highlight is the set of Roman *thermae*
(baths) discovered in the 1970s, around
which this £6-million wedge of architecture
was designed.

🛏 Sleeping & Eating

Trents　　　　　B&B ££
(☑ 01243-773714; 50 South St; d from £64; 🛜)
Neat and tidy Trents is one of very few places in which to hit the sack in the thick of the
city-centre action, with five snazzy rooms
above a trendy bar-restaurant. Guests heap
praise on the helpful staff and big breakfast.

Chichester Harbour Hotel　　BOUTIQUE HOTEL £££
(☑ 01243-778000; www.chichester-harbour-hotel.
co.uk; North St; s/d from £105/125; 🛜) An enticing option that boasts a stylish restaurant,
this Georgian hotel has comfortable, period
rooms spiced up with bold colours. Book
well ahead.

Purchases　　　　　BRITISH ££
(☑ 01243-771444; www.purchasesrestaurant.co.uk;
31 North St; mains £15-30, set menu 2/3 courses
£22.95/25.95; ⊙ 8am-10pm Mon-Sat, to 5pm Sun;
🛜) Aptly named for Chichester's shopping
streets, this crisply done-out, slightly upmarket restaurant plates up modern takes
on British classics such as beef Wellington,
beer-battered fish of the day and roast lamb
rump. The pre-theatre menu is much better
value than selecting from the main menu.
Very attractive and colourful accommodation is also provided.

ⓘ Information

Tourist Office (☑ 01243-775888; www.
visitchichester.org; Tower St; ⊙ 10am-5pm
Mon-Sat, to 4pm Sun summer, 10am-5pm Wed-

DON'T MISS

FISHBOURNE ROMAN PALACE

The largest-known Roman residence
in Britain, **Fishbourne Roman Palace** (☑ 01243-785859; www.sussexpast.
co.uk; Roman Way; adult/concession/child
£10/9.60/5.20; ⊙ 10.30am-4pm Mar-Oct,
reduced hours & days Nov-Feb) has an
area larger than Buckingham Palace.
Lying just off the A259 1.5 miles west
of Chichester, and chanced upon by
labourers laying a water main in the
1960s, this once-luxurious mansion
was probably built around AD 75 for a
Romanised local king, though debate
still swarms around the owner's identity.
Housed in a modern pavilion are its
foundations, hypocaust and painstakingly relaid mosaics. Take bus 700 from
outside Chichester Cathedral.

　　The centrepiece is a spectacular
mosaic floor depicting Cupid riding
a dolphin, flanked by sea horses and
panthers. There's also a fascinating little
museum and replanted Roman gardens.

Sat, to 4pm Sun winter) Located in the Novium
Museum.

ⓘ Getting There & Away

BUS
Chichester has bus connections to the following:
Brighton (bus 700; £5.20, three hours, twice
hourly)
Portsmouth (bus 700; £4.90, 70 minutes,
twice hourly)

TRAIN
Chichester has train connections to the
following:
Arundel (£4.90, 24 minutes, twice hourly)
Change at Ford or Barnham.
Brighton (£14.40, 50 minutes, half-hourly)
London Victoria (£19.80, 1½ hours,
half-hourly)
Portsmouth (£8.30, 30 to 40 minutes, three
hourly)

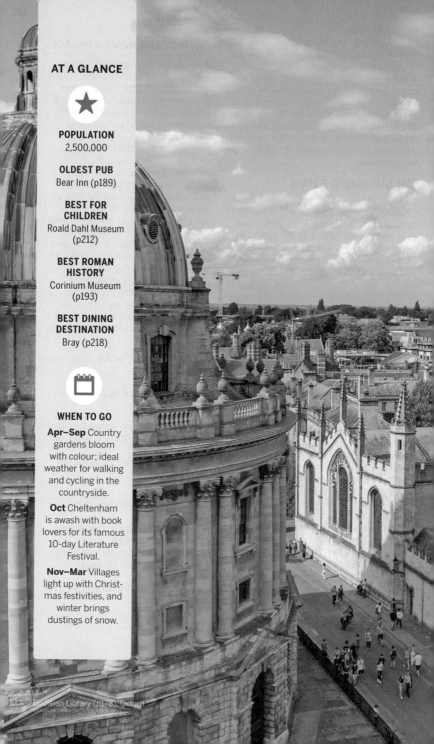

AT A GLANCE

⭐

POPULATION
2,500,000

OLDEST PUB
Bear Inn (p189)

**BEST FOR
CHILDREN**
Roald Dahl Museum
(p212)

**BEST ROMAN
HISTORY**
Corinium Museum
(p193)

**BEST DINING
DESTINATION**
Bray (p218)

📅

WHEN TO GO

Apr–Sep Country
gardens bloom
with colour; ideal
weather for walking
and cycling in the
countryside.

Oct Cheltenham
is awash with book
lovers for its famous
10-day Literature
Festival.

Nov–Mar Villages
light up with Christ-
mas festivities, and
winter brings
dustings of snow.

Bodleian Library (p178), Oxford
CHRISTIAN MUELLER/SHUTTERSTOCK ©

Oxford & the Cotswolds

S prinkled with picture-perfect villages and historic sites, this section of England that stretches westwards from London to the border with Wales comes as close to a fairytale version of England as you'll ever find. Green-cloaked hills, rose-clad stone cottages, graceful churches and thatched roofed houses abound. Add the university city of Oxford, with its majestic architecture, and you can see why the region draws visitors in droves.

The Cotswolds work their finest magic when you find your own romantic hideaway. Splendid country houses lie tucked away throughout Buckinghamshire, Bedfordshire and Hertfordshire. Further west, the Forest of Dean offers the promise of outdoorsy adventures.

This region deserves at least a week to be properly enjoyed.

INCLUDES

❶ Getting There & Around

A car will give you the greatest freedom, especially if you want to explore the scattered villages of the Cotswolds.

Local buses, run by various operators, link larger towns to each other and surrounding villages. For timetables, use the journey planner tool on Traveline (www.traveline.info).

Oxford, Moreton-in-Marsh, Stroud, Cheltenham, Gloucester, Bletchley, Hatfield, St Albans, Henley-on-Thames and Windsor are all serviced by trains, most with direct lines to London. Other direct trains go as far as Birmingham, Manchester and Newcastle (from Oxford), and Cardiff, Edinburgh and Exeter (from Cheltenham).

OXFORD

📞 01865 / POP 161,300

A glorious ensemble of golden-hued architecture and lush water meadows, Oxford ranks among England's most beautiful cities. In fact, as you stroll through its university college campuses, it can be hard to believe you're in modern England at all. Certain buildings stand out, like the domed and glowing Radcliffe Camera, or admire others built by famous English architects, Sir Christopher Wren and Nicholas Hawksmoor. One of the main joys of visiting Oxford lies in the sense of intellectual history being forged in the centuries-old colleges, each with its own permutations of Gothic chapels, secluded cloisters and tranquil quadrangles.

History

Strategically placed at the confluence of the Rivers Cherwell and Thames (called the Isis here, from the Latin Tamesis, because, well, this is Oxford after all), this was once a key Saxon town, heavily fortified by Alfred the Great during the war against the Danes. It continued to grow under the Normans, who founded its castle in 1071.

By the 11th century, the Augustinian abbey in Oxford had begun training clerics, and when Anglo-Norman clerical scholars were expelled from the Sorbonne in 1167, the abbey began to attract students in droves. The first three colleges – University, Balliol and Merton – were founded in the mid-13th century. Alongside Oxford's growing prosperity grew the enmity between local townspeople and new students ('town and gown'), culminating in the St Scholastica's Day Massacre in 1355, which started as an argument over beer but resulted in 90 deaths. Thereafter, the king ordered that the university be broken up into colleges, each of which developed its own traditions.

The university, largely a religious entity at the time, was rocked in the 16th century by the Reformation; the public trials and burning at the stake of Protestant heretics under Mary I; and by the subsequent hanging, drawing and quartering of Catholics under her successor Elizabeth I. As the Royalist headquarters, Oxford backed the losing side during the Civil War, but flourished after the restoration of the monarchy, with some of its most notable buildings constructed in the late 17th and early 18th centuries.

The arrival of the canal system in 1790 had a profound effect on Oxford. By creating a link with the Midlands' industrial centres, work and trade suddenly expanded beyond the academic core. This was further strengthened by the construction of the railways in the 19th century.

The city's real industrial boom came, however, when William Morris began producing cars here in 1913. With the success of his Bullnose Morris and Morris Minor, his Cowley factory went on to become one of the largest motor plants in the world. Although works have been scaled down since, Minis still run off BMW's Cowley production line today, although the Covid-19 pandemic had cast a shadow over its future.

◉ Sights

Oxford is a compact city, with its major sights largely congregated in the centre. Almost all, including the Bodleian Library and the Ashmolean Museum, are connected with the university, while several of the university colleges themselves are favourite visitor attractions. Plans to pedestrianise some city streets gained traction during the Covid-19 pandemic, promising to make outdoor dining and social distancing more achievable.

◉ City Centre

★ **Bodleian Library**   LIBRARY

(📞 01865-287400; www.bodleian.ox.ac.uk/bodley; Catte St; ⊙ 9am-5pm Mon-Sat, 11am-5pm Sun) At least five kings, dozens of prime ministers and Nobel laureates, and luminaries such as Oscar Wilde, CS Lewis and JRR Tolkien have studied in Oxford's Bodleian Library, a

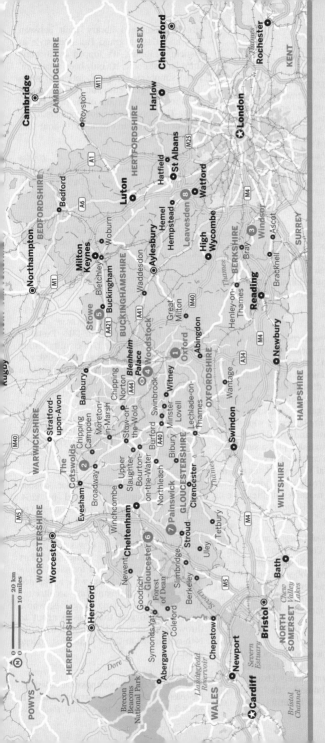

Oxford & the Cotswolds Highlights

1 Oxford (p178) Following in the inspirational footsteps of JRR Tolkien, CS Lewis and Lewis Carroll as you explore magical colleges.

2 The Cotswolds (p192) Strolling through gold-tinged Cotswolds villages, such as Chipping Campden or Broadway.

3 Windsor (p215) Catching a glimpse of how royalty relaxes at the Queen's weekend hideaway.

4 Blenheim Palace (p191) Lording it up at one of Britain's greatest stately homes, in Woodstock.

5 Stowe Gardens (p214) Getting lost in a serene world of spectacular 18th-century landscaped gardens.

6 Gloucester Cathedral (p211) Strolling the elegant cloisters of this exquisite Perpendicular Gothic creation.

7 Painswick (p206) Enjoying one of the most beautiful towns in the Cotswolds.

8 The Making of Harry Potter (p213) Unleashing your inner wizard at this working studio tour.

PORT MEADOW

Although archaeologists have identified traces of Bronze and Iron Age settlements bulging from this marshy Thames meadow, northwest of Jericho, it has remained untouched, never even ploughed, ever since. A treasure trove of rare plants, it's still grazed by cows and horses, and it's hugely popular with walkers (stopping off at riverside pub, the Trout) and runners. In winter it gets so waterlogged that hikers have to go round the edge rather than cutting straight across!

magnificent survivor from the Middle Ages. Wander into its central 17th-century quad, and you can admire its ancient buildings for free. Both Blackwell Hall and the exhibition rooms in the Weston Library can be visited free of charge. Audio and guided tours available.

★ Christ Church   COLLEGE
(☑ 01865-276492; www.chch.ox.ac.uk; St Aldate's; adult/child £15/14, pre-booking essential; ☉ 10am-5pm Mon-Sat, 2-5pm Sun) With its compelling combination of majestic architecture, literary heritage and double identity as (parts of) Harry Potter's Hogwarts, Christ Church attracts tourists galore. Among Oxford's largest colleges – *the* largest, if you include its bucolic meadow – and proud possessor of its most impressive quad, plus a superb art gallery and even a cathedral, it was founded in 1525 by Cardinal Wolsey. It later became home to Lewis Carroll, whose picnic excursions with the then-dean's daughter gave us *Alice's Adventures in Wonderland*.

Bridge of Sighs   BRIDGE
(Hertford Bridge; New College Lane) As you stroll along New College Lane, look up at the steeped Bridge of Sighs linking the two halves of Hertford College. Completed in 1914, it's sometimes erroneously described as a copy of the famous bridge in Venice, but it looks much more like that city's Rialto Bridge.

Radcliffe Camera   LIBRARY
(☑ 01865-287400; www.bodleian.ox.ac.uk; Radcliffe Sq; tours £15; ☉ tours 9.15am Wed & Sat, 11.15am & 1.15pm Sun) Surely Oxford's most photographed landmark, the sandy-gold Radcliffe Camera is a beautiful, light-filled,

circular, columned library. Built between 1737 and 1749 in grand Palladian style as 'Radcliffe Library', it's topped by Britain's third-largest dome. It's only been a 'camera', which simply means 'room', since 1860, when it lost its independence and became what it remains: a reading room of the Bodleian Library. The only way for nonmembers to see the interior is on an extended 1½-hour tour of the Bodleian.

Balliol College   COLLEGE
(☑ 01865-277777; www.balliol.ox.ac.uk; Broad St; ☉ 10am-5pm, to dusk in winter) Dating its foundation to 'about' 1263, Balliol College claims to be the oldest college in Oxford, though its current buildings are largely 19th-century. Scorch marks on the huge Gothic wooden doors between its inner and outer quadrangles, however, supposedly date from the public burning of three Protestant bishops, including Archbishop of Canterbury Thomas Cranmer, in 1556.

Exeter College   COLLEGE
(☑ 01865-279600; www.exeter.ox.ac.uk; Turl St; ☉ 2-5pm) FREE Founded in 1314, Exeter is known for its elaborate 17th-century dining hall, which celebrated its 400th birthday in 2018, and ornate Victorian Gothic chapel, a psychedelic blast of gold mosaic and stained glass that holds a tapestry created by former students William Morris and Edward Burne Jones, *The Adoration of the Magi*. Exeter also inspired former student Philip Pullman to create fictional Jordan College in *His Dark Materials*.

Merton College   COLLEGE
(☑ 01865-276310; www.merton.ox.ac.uk/visitor-information; Merton St) Founded in 1264, peaceful and elegant Merton is one of Oxford's three original colleges. Like the other two, Balliol and University, it considers itself the oldest, arguing that it was the first to adopt collegiate planning, bringing scholars and tutors together into a formal community and providing them with a planned residence. Its distinguishing architectural features include large gargoyles, whose expressions suggest that they're about to throw up, and the charming, diminutive 14th-century Mob Quad – the first college quad.

New College   COLLEGE
(☑ 01865-279500; www.new.ox.ac.uk/visiting-the-college; Holywell St; ☉ currently closed to visitors) New College isn't really *that* new.

Established in 1379 as Oxford's first undergraduate college, it's a glorious Perpendicular Gothic ensemble. Treasures in the chapel include superb medieval stained glass and Sir Jacob Epstein's disturbing 1951 statue of Lazarus, wrapped in his shroud; in term time, visitors can attend the beautiful choral Evensong service (6.15pm nightly). The 15th-century cloisters and evergreen oak featured in *Harry Potter and the Goblet of Fire*, while the dining hall is the oldest in Oxbridge.

Trinity College COLLEGE
(✆01865-279900; www.trinity.ox.ac.uk; Broad St; adult/child £3/2; ⊙9.30am-noon & 2pm-dusk) Founded in 1555, this small college boasts a lovely 17th-century garden quad, designed by Sir Christopher Wren. Its exquisite chapel, a masterpiece of English baroque, contains a limewood altar screen adorned with flowers and fruit carved by master craftsman Grinling Gibbons in 1694, and is looking fabulous after recent restoration work. Famous students have included Cardinal Newman, William Pitt the Elder, two British prime ministers, and the fictional Jay Gatsby, the Great Gatsby himself.

Museum of the History of Science MUSEUM
(✆01865-277293; www.mhs.ox.ac.uk; Broad St; ⊙noon-5pm Tue-Sun) FREE Students of science will swoon at this fascinating museum, stuffed to the ceilings with awesome astrolabes, astonishing orreries and early electrical apparatus. Housed in the lovely 17th-century building that held the original Ashmolean Museum, it displays everything from cameras that belonged to Lewis Carroll and Lawrence of Arabia, to a wireless receiver used by Marconi in 1896 and a blackboard that was covered with equations by Einstein in 1931, when he was invited to give three lectures on relativity.

University Church of St Mary the Virgin CHURCH
(✆01865-279111; www.university-church.ox.ac.uk; High St; church free, tower £5; ⊙10am-6pm Mon-Sat, noon-6pm Sun) The ornate 14th-century spire of Oxford's university church is arguably the dreamiest of the city's legendary 'dreaming spires'. The church is famous as the site where three Anglican bishops, including the first Protestant archbishop of Canterbury, Thomas Cranmer, were tried for heresy in 1556, during the reign of Mary I. All three were later burned at the stake

on Broad St. Visitors can climb the church's 1280 tower for excellent views of the adjacent Radcliffe Camera.

☉ Jericho & Science Area

★**Ashmolean Museum** MUSEUM
(✆01865-278000; www.ashmolean.org; Beaumont St; ⊙10am-5pm Tue-Sun, to 8pm last Fri of month; ♿) FREE Britain's oldest public museum, Oxford's wonderful Ashmolean Museum is surpassed only by the British Museum in London. It was established in 1683, when Elias Ashmole presented Oxford University with a collection of 'rarities' amassed by the well-travelled John Tradescant, gardener to Charles I. You could easily spend a day exploring this magnificent neoclassical building, and family-friendly pamphlets draw kids into select exhibits. Pre-booking required.

★**Pitt Rivers Museum** MUSEUM
(✆01865-270927; www.prm.ox.ac.uk; South Parks Rd; ⊙10am-5pm; ♿) FREE If exploring an enormous room full of eccentric and unexpected artefacts sounds like your idea of the perfect afternoon, welcome to the amulets-to-zithers extravaganza that is the Pitt Rivers museum. Tucked behind Oxford's natural history museum, and dimly lit to protect its myriad treasures, it's centred on an anthropological collection amassed by a Victorian general, and revels in exploring how differing cultures have tackled topics like 'Smoking and Stimulants' and 'Treatment of Dead Enemies'.

Oxford University Museum of Natural History MUSEUM
(✆01865-272950; www.oum.ox.ac.uk; Parks Rd; ⊙10am-5pm; ♿) FREE Housed in a glori-

> **TOLKIEN'S RESTING PLACE**
> ....
> *Lord of the Rings* author JRR Tolkien (1892–1973) is buried with his wife Edith at Wolvercote Cemetery (Banbury Rd, Wolvercote; ⊙7am-8pm Mon-Fri, 8am-8pm Sat & Sun Apr-Sep, to 5pm Oct-Mar), 2.5 miles north of Oxford city centre. Their gravestone bears the names Beren (for him) and Lúthien (for her), referencing the love between a mortal man and an elf maiden who gave up her immortality to be with him.

Oxford

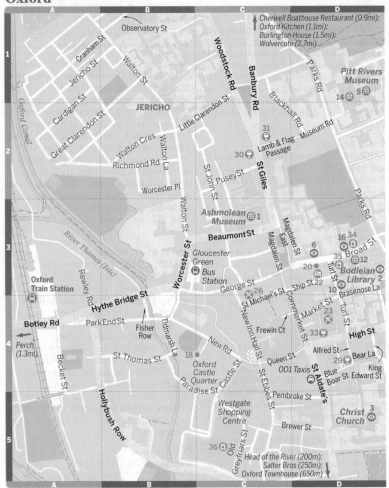

ous Victorian Gothic building, with cast-iron columns, flower-carved capitals and a soaring glass roof, this museum makes a superb showcase for some extraordinary exhibits. Specimens from all over the world include a 150-year-old Japanese spider crab, but it's the dinosaurs that really wow the crowds. As well as a towering T-rex skeleton – 'Stan', the second most complete ever found – you'll see pieces of Megalosaurus, which was in 1677 the first dinosaur ever mentioned in a written text.

⊙ Southeast Oxford

★ **Magdalen College** COLLEGE
(☏01865-276000; www.magd.ox.ac.uk; High St; adult/child £7/6, pre-booking required; ☺10am-7pm late Jun-late Sep, 1pm-dusk rest of year) Guarding access to a breathtaking expanse of private lawns, woodlands, river walks and even its own deer park, Magdalen ('mawd-lin'), founded in 1458, is one of Oxford's wealthiest and most beautiful colleges. Beyond its elegant Victorian gateway, you come to its medieval chapel and glorious 15th-century tower. From here,

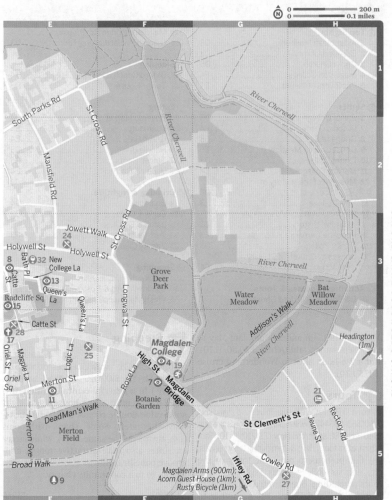

move on to the remarkable 15th-century cloisters, where the fantastic grotesques (carved figures) may have inspired CS Lewis' stone statues in *The Chronicles of Narnia*.

🏃 Activities

Magdalen Bridge Boathouse BOATING
(☎01865-202643; www.oxfordpunting.co.uk; High St; chauffeured 4-person punts per 30min £30, punt rental per hour £22; ⏰9.30am-dusk Feb-Nov) Right beside Magdalen Bridge, this boathouse is the most central location to hire a punt, chauffeured or otherwise. From here you can either head

downstream around the Botanic Garden and Christ Church Meadow, or upstream around Magdalen Deer Park. You can also hire rowboats and pedalos.

Salter Bros BOATING
(☎01865-243421; www.salterssteamers.co.uk; Folly Bridge; punt/rowboat/motorboat per hour £20/20/45; ⏰10am-6pm Easter-Oct) As well as renting out punts, rowing boats and motorboats for private hire, Salter Bros usually offers scenic cruises along the Thames, passing college boathouses and busy riverside pubs. Options include the 8-mile, two-hour trip to the historic market town of

Oxford

Abingdon (9.15am and 2.30pm, late May to early September, adult/child £20.80/11.70), and a 2½-hour Alice in Wonderland cruise (£17.50/10).

☞ Tours

Oxford Official Walking Tours   WALKING
(☑ 01865-686441; www.experienceoxfordshire.org; 15-16 Broad St; adult/child from £14/10; ☺ 10.45am & 1pm, extra tours 11am & 2pm during busy periods; ♿) Comprehensive two-hour tours of the city and its colleges, plus several themed tours, including one devoted to *Alice in Wonderland* and Harry Potter, another to CS Lewis and JRR Tolkien, and a third to Inspector Morse. Check online for details, or book at the tourist office.

**Bill Spectre's
Oxford Ghost Trail**   WALKING
(☑ 07941-041811; www.ghosttrail.org; Oxford Castle; adult/child £10/7; ☺ 6.30pm Fri & Sat; ♿) For a theatrical and entertaining voyage through Oxford's uncanny underbelly, plus the occasional magic trick, take a 1¾-hour tour with Victorian undertaker Bill Spectre. No bookings needed, audience participation more than likely.

🛏 Sleeping

Tower House   GUESTHOUSE ££
(☑ 01865-246828; www.towerhouseoxford.co.uk; 15 Ship St; s/d £100/125, d without bathroom £110; 🖭) In a peaceful central location, this listed 17th-century town house holds eight good-value double rooms, simple but tastefully decorated. Some share bathrooms (not always on the same floor), while larger en suites also have attractive tongue-and-groove panelling. Run as a social enterprise, profits go to a community charity.

Remont   B&B ££
(☑ 01865-311020; www.remont-oxford.co.uk; 367 Banbury Rd, Summertown; d/q £125/180; 🅿@🖭) All modern style, subtle lighting and ultracolourful furnishings, this boutique family-run guesthouse holds 25 varying rooms decked out in cool neutrals with silky bedspreads, abstract art, vibrant bedheads, writing desks and huge TVs. There's a sunny garden and roomy breakfast hall out back. It's 2.5 miles north of the centre, in an inconspicuous residential setting, but there's good public transport.

Acorn Guest House   B&B ££
(☑ 01865-247998; www.oxford-acorn.co.uk; 260 Iffley Rd; s/d £50/75; 🅿🖭🐾) Spread through

two adjoining houses, Acorn offers eight comfortable rooms at very reasonable prices, close to great pubs and restaurants and a short bus ride from the centre. Single rooms and 'budget' doubles share bathrooms; en suite facilities cost just £5 more. Everything has the feel of a family home, but key safes allow for a contactless check-in.

⭐**Oxford Coach & Horses** B&B **£££**
(☑ 01865-200017; www.oxfordcoachandhorses.co.uk; 62 St Clement's St; s/d £130/150; P 🛜) A former 18th-century coaching inn, this fabulous English-Mexican-owned boutique B&B hides behind a fresh powder-blue exterior, just a few metres from the Cowley Rd action. The eight light-filled rooms are cosy, spacious and individually styled in soothing pastels with exposed beams and splashes of turquoise and mauve. The converted ground floor houses an airy, attractive breakfast room.

⭐**Head of the River** HOTEL **£££**
(☑ 01865-721600; www.headoftheriveroxford.co.uk; Folly Bridge, St Aldate's; r incl breakfast £189; 🛜) One of the more central Oxford hotels, this large and characterful place at Folly Bridge, immediately south of Christ Church, was originally a Thames-side warehouse. Each of its 20 good-sized rooms is individually decorated with contemporary flair, featuring exposed brickwork and/or tongue-and-groove panelling plus modern fittings. Rates include breakfast cooked to order in the (excellent) pub (p188) downstairs.

Burlington House HOTEL **£££**
(☑ 01865-513513; www.burlington-hotel-oxford.co.uk; 374 Banbury Rd, Summertown; s/d incl breakfast £102/139; P 🛜) This small, well-managed hotel, in a beautifully refreshed Victorian home 2 miles north of central Oxford, offers 12 elegant contemporary rooms – some in a courtyard annex – with patterned wallpaper, immaculate bathrooms and luxury touches. Personal service is as sensational as the delicious breakfast, with organic eggs, homemade bread, yoghurt, granola and fresh juice. Public transport links are good.

Oxford Townhouse BOUTIQUE HOTEL **£££**
(☑ 01865-722500; www.theoxfordtownhouse.co.uk; 90 Abingdon Rd; s/d incl breakfast £136/166; P 🛜) Fifteen comfortable, subtly chic, minimalist-modern rooms, with white-and-navy striped blankets, varnished-wood desks and blue flourishes, in a gorgeously restyled pair of red-brick Victorian town houses, half a mile south of the centre. Some are quite small for the price, though. Colourful paintings of Oxford adorn the walls, and the breakfasts are classy.

🍴 Eating

⭐**Edamamé** JAPANESE **£**
(☑ 01865-246916; www.edamame.co.uk; 15 Holywell St; mains £7-10.50; ⊙ 11.30am-2.30pm Wed & Thu, 11.30am-2.30pm & 5-8.30pm Fri & Sat, noon-3.30pm Sun; 🍽) No wonder a constant stream of students squeeze in and out of this tiny diner – it's Oxford's top spot for delicious, gracefully simple Japanese cuisine. Changing noodle and curry specials include fragrant chicken miso ramen, tofu stir-fries, or mackerel with soba noodles; at the time of writing, it served sushi or sashimi on Thursday evenings only. No bookings; arrive early and be prepared to wait.

⭐**Vaults & Garden** CAFE **£**
(☑ 01865-279112; www.thevaultsandgarden.com; University Church of St Mary the Virgin, Radcliffe Sq; mains £9-10.50; ⊙ 9am-5pm; 🛜🍽) 🍃 This beautiful lunch venue spreads from the vaulted 14th-century Old Congregation House of the University Church into a garden facing the Radcliffe Camera. Come early and queue at the counter to choose from wholesome organic specials such as carrot and nutmeg soup, chicken panang

---

WORTH A TRIP

LE MANOIR AUX QUAT'SAISONS

Oxford food lovers make the 9-mile pilgrimage east to Le Manoir aux Quat'Saisons (☑ 01844-278881; www.belmond.com/le-manoir-aux-quat-saisons-oxfordshire; Church Rd, Great Milton; 5-course lunch/7-course dinner £105/190; ⊙ 6.30-9.30pm Mon, 11.45am-2.15pm & 6.30-9.30pm Tue-Sun), an impressive manor house that has enjoyed two Michelin stars since chef Raymond Blanc has been working his magic here for the past 35 years. Imaginative and complex dishes use ingredients from the amazing on-site kitchen garden. Book ahead and dress smartly.

It also has 32 hotel rooms, and a cookery school. It's truly a gastronomic destination hotel.

curry, or slow-roasted lamb shoulder with red currant. Breakfast and afternoon tea (those scones!) are equally good.

Covered Market

MARKET £

(www.oxford-coveredmarket.co.uk; Market St; prices vary; ⊙8am-5.30pm Mon-Sat, 10am-5pm Sun; 🛜🗾♿) A haven for impecunious students, this indoor marketplace holds 20 restaurants, cafes and takeaways. Let anyone loose here, and something's sure to catch their fancy. Brown's no-frills cafe, famous for its apple pies, is the longest-standing veteran. Look out too for Georgina's upstairs; two excellent pie shops; and good Thai and Chinese options. Traders keep their own varied hours.

Handle Bar

CAFE £

(🗾01865-251315; www.handlebaroxford.co.uk; Bike Zone, 28-31 St Michael's St; mains £8-13; ⊙8am-6pm Mon & Tue, 8am-11pm Wed-Fri, 9am-11pm Sat, 9am-5pm Sun; 🛜🗾) Upstairs above a bike shop, this chatty, friendly cafe has bikes galore, including penny-farthings, dangling from its ceiling and white-painted brick walls. It's usually packed with students, professionals and lucky tourists, all here for luscious, health-focused bites, like avocado and beetroot hummus toast, pan-fried tofu salad and granola breakfast 'pots', plus tasty cakes, smoothies, teas and coffees. Across from the bike shop downstairs is a coffee and cocktail bar serving the same menu.

Grand Café

TEAHOUSE £

(🗾01865-204463; www.thegrandcafe.co.uk; 84 High St; patisserie items £5-7, mains £9-13; ⊙9am-6.30pm Mon-Thu, to 7pm Fri-Sun; ♿) Boasting of being England's first-ever coffee house – though not, unlike its rival opposite, open ever since – the Grand looks very much the part, with its columns and gold leaf. While it serves sandwiches, bagels and a towering afternoon tea (from £18), it's the patisserie counter that's the real attraction: fresh, sweet pastry tarts and feather-light *mille-feuilles* pair brilliantly with tea.

Rusty Bicycle

GASTROPUB £

(🗾01865-435298; www.therustybicycle.com; 28 Magdalen Rd; mains £6.50-12; ⊙9am-11pm Sun-Thu, to midnight Fri & Sat; 🛜) This funky neighbourhood pub, tucked off Iffley Rd a mile out of town and brought to you by the people responsible for Jericho's Rickety Press, serves top-notch burgers and pizzas, along with excellent local beers in a popular beer garden.

🏃 Walking Tour
A Riverside Stroll in Central Oxford

START CHRIST CHURCH
END MAGDALEN COLLEGE
LENGTH 2.5 MILES; TWO HOURS

Few cities can match Oxford for retaining such glorious countryside so close to its centre. Oxford's secret lies in the fact that the riverside meadows just outside the medieval city walls belonged then, and still belong today, to hugely wealthy colleges that have never felt the urge to build on them, let alone sell them. Modern visitors can therefore simply step away from the busy city streets to enjoy an idyllic stroll along delightful rural footpaths.

Start by approaching ❶ **Christ Church** (p180) via the gates on St Aldate's. Follow Broad Walk straight ahead for 140m, until the college's visitor entrance is on your left, then turn right onto Poplar Walk. This broad avenue heads directly south, to reach the Thames after 410m. Turning right at the river would bring you to Folly Bridge, spanning the original 'oxen ford' for which Oxford is named, but turn left, downstream, and follow the waterfront footpath known as the Meadow Walk. You'll probably see rowing eights out on the Thames. Looking back the way you've come, you're now separated from Christ Church, a shimmering vision of splendour, by the broad expanse of ❷ **Christ Church Meadow** (www.chch.ox.ac.uk; St Aldate's; ⊙dawn-dusk; FREE), where you may see longhorn cattle grazing. After 180m, the path leaves the river, curving beside a cut-off channel that brings you in 360m to the River Cherwell. Once there, keep following the curve, and after another 450m you meet Broad Walk at its eastern end.

Across Merton Field, straight ahead, the long, high wall of ❸ **Merton College** (p180) traces the route of Oxford's medieval city wall. During the Middle Ages, the local Jewish community had to bury their dead outside the walls. Their funerals followed this footpath, which became known as Dead Man's Walk. The trees that tower over it stand within Merton's enclosed Fellows' Garden. JRR Tolkien's rooms overlooked this spot when he was writing *The Lord of the Rings*.

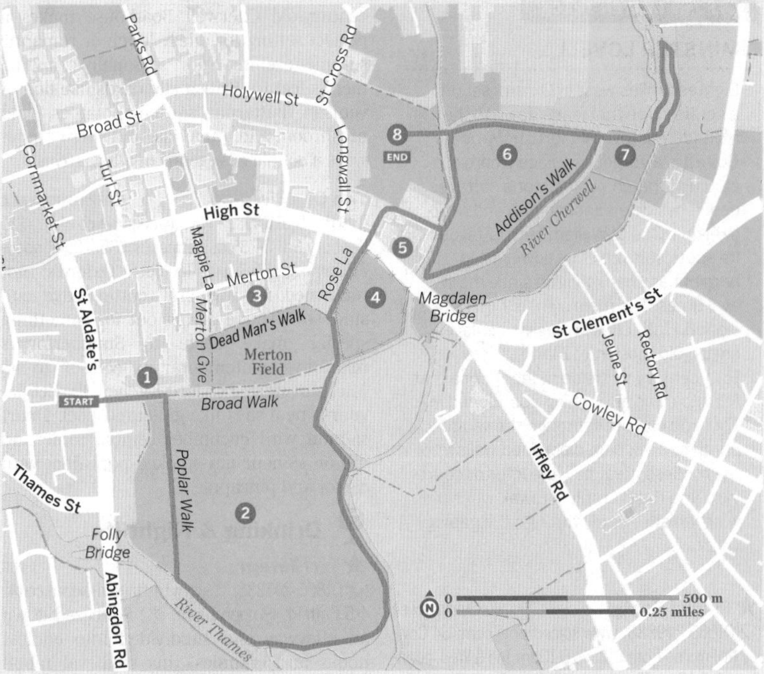

Ninety metres north of Broad Walk, fork right along Rose Lane, which leads up to High St along Merton's eastern boundary. The former Jewish cemetery now lies on your right, though for the past four centuries it's served instead as Oxford's 4 **Botanic Garden** (☎01865-610305; www.botanic-garden.ox.ac.uk; High St; adult/child £5.45/free; ⏲9am-5pm Mar-Oct, to 4pm Nov-Feb, last entry an hour before closing). If you've time, add an extra half-mile to this walk by dropping in to admire its greenhouses of rare plants, and relax in its tranquil spaces.

The visitors' entrance to 5 **Magdalen College** (p182) is directly across High St from the north end of Rose Lane. To continue your walk, pay for admission and head through the stunning 15th-century cloisters (during the university year, visitors can only enter in the afternoon). Tolkien's contemporary, CS Lewis, lived in Magdalen, and the grotesque carvings here reappeared in his *Chronicles of Narnia*.

Turn right beyond the cloisters, and you're swiftly back on the banks of the Cherwell. Get ready for the absolute highlight of the walk. Magdalen took over these riverside lands almost six centuries ago, and has left them to be enjoyed as open countryside ever since. Cross the footbridge straight ahead of you to reach the 6 **Water Meadow**, a triangular islet in the river. The gloriously bucolic footpath known as Addison's Walk takes just under a mile to loop around its perimeter. At its southern tip, you get a head-on view of punts and rowing boats setting off below Magdalen Bridge. The Water Meadow is one of just a half-dozen places where the snakeshead fritillary still grows; you may spot its purple or white flowers in late April.

Leave the Water Meadow by its northeastern end to enter smaller 7 **Bat Willow Meadow**, where Mark Wallinger's sculpture *Y*, resembling a two-dimensional tree, was installed amid genuine willows in 2008 to mark Magdalen's 550th anniversary. Immediately south, Angel and Greyhound Meadow was named for two long-vanished coaching inns that pastured their horses here. The secluded Fellows' Garden, across another bridge beyond, was laid out in 1866.

When you're ready to re-emerge into city life, retrace your footsteps back to the high street. Spare a glance, though, for the 8 **Grove Deer Park**, north of the college buildings. If you're here between July and early December, you may have encountered the college's own herd of deer browsing in the riverside meadows; before that, to spare the fritillaries, they're here in the Grove.

OFF THE BEATEN TRACK

MINSTER LOVELL

Eighteen miles west of Oxford, set on a gentle slope that leads down to the meandering River Windrush, Minster Lovell is a gorgeous village where a clutch of thatch-roofed stone cottages nestle beside an ancient pub and riverside mill. One of William Morris' favourite spots, this peaceful flower-filled hamlet has changed little since medieval times. The main sight is Minster Lovell Hall (EH; www.english-heritage.org.uk; Old Minster; ⊙24hr) FREE, a 15th-century riverside manor house that fell into ruins after being abandoned in 1747. You can pass through the vaulted porch to peek past blackened walls into the roofless great hall, the interior courtyard and the crumbling tower, while the wind whistles eerily through the gaping windows.

★ Spiced Roots   CARIBBEAN ££
(🖉 01865-249888; www.spicedroots.com; 64 Cowley Rd; mains from £12; ⊙6-10pm Tue & Wed, noon-3pm & 6-10pm Thu-Sat, noon-8pm Sun; 🖉) From black rice with pomegranates to oxtail with mac cheese and plantains – and, of course, spicy jerk chicken – everything is just perfection at this flawless Caribbean restaurant. There are plenty of vegetarian options, as well as curried fish or goat. And adding a cocktail or two from the thatched rum bar is pretty much irresistible. Look out for tasting classes.

★ Magdalen Arms   BRITISH ££
(🖉 01865-243159; www.magdalenarms.co.uk; 243 Iffley Rd; mains £14-26; ⊙11am-10pm Tue-Sat, to 9pm Sun; 🖉🖈) A mile beyond Magdalen Bridge, this extra-special neighbourhood gastropub has won plaudits from the national press. A friendly, informal spot, it offers indoor and outdoor space for drinkers, and dining tables further back. From vegetarian specials such as broad-bean tagliatelle to the fabulous sharing-size steak-and-ale pie (well, it's a stew with a suet-crust lid, really) everything is delicious, with gutsy flavours.

Cherwell Boathouse Restaurant   BRITISH ££
(🖉 01865-552746; www.cherwellboathouse.co.uk; Bardwell Rd; mains £18-22; ⊙noon-2.30pm & 6-9.30pm; 🖉) With its lovely riverside setting, 1.5 miles north of central Oxford, the century-old Cherwell Boathouse makes a perfect setting for a lazy lunch or romantic summer evening. Short seasonally changing menus feature British standards like lion of venison, butternut squash, potatoes, wild mushroom and game jus, and there are always a couple of vegetarian alternatives.

Two One Five   MODERN BRITISH £££
(🖉 01865-511149; www.twoonefive.co.uk; 215 Banbury Rd; 2-/3-course menus £35/40; ⊙noon-2.30pm & 6-9.30pm Tue-Sat) Oxford's not renowned for high-end, cutting-edge cuisine, so if you're crying out for something special, make haste to Summertown's relaxed-yet-contemporary successor to its Michelin-starred Oxford Kitchen. Expect flavoursome dishes like gin-cured Loch Duart salmon with cucumber, lemon, tonic and dill or 48-hour hay-smoked pork fillet with carrot and pineapple.

🍷 Drinking & Nightlife

★ Turf Tavern   PUB
(🖉 01865-243235; www.turftavern-oxford.co.uk; 4-5 Bath Pl; ⊙noon-10pm; 🛜) Squeezed down an alleyway and subdivided into endless nooks and crannies, this medieval rabbit warren dates from around 1381. The definitive Oxford pub, it's where Bill Clinton famously 'did not inhale'. Other patrons have included Oscar Wilde, Stephen Hawking and Margaret Thatcher. Home to a fabulous array of real ales and ciders, it's always pretty crowded, but there's outdoor seating, too.

★ Perch   PUB
(🖉 01865-728891; www.the-perch.co.uk; Binsey Lane, Binsey; ⊙10.30am-11pm Mon-Sat, to 10.30pm Sun; 🖈🛜) This thatched and wonderfully rural 800-year-old inn can be reached by road, but it's more enjoyable to walk half an hour upstream along the Thames Path, then follow an enchanting footpath punctuated by floral pergolas. Its huge willow-draped garden is an idyllic spot for a pint or two of Fullers, but summer crowds can mean a long wait for food.

Head of the River   PUB
(🖉 01865-721600; www.headoftheriveroxford.co.uk; Folly Bridge, St Aldate's; ⊙8am-10.30pm Sun-Thu, to 11.30pm Fri & Sat) For a summer-evening riverside drink, central Oxford holds no finer setting than the Thames-facing terrace of this imposing former warehouse – hence the hand-cranked crane, still outside – and later a boatyard. The beer's good, courtesy of

Fullers brewery. There's plenty of room indoors – as well as decent food, and a stylish hotel upstairs – but the lure of the river is irresistible.

Lamb & Flag   PUB

(12 St Giles; ⊘ noon-11pm Mon-Sat, to 10.30pm Sun; 🖥) This relaxed 17th-century tavern remains one of Oxford's nicest pubs for a sturdy pint or glass of wine. Thomas Hardy wrote (and set) parts of *Jude the Obscure* at these very tables, while CS Lewis and JRR Tolkien shifted their custom here in later years. The food's nothing special, but buying a pint helps fund scholarships at St John's College.

Bear Inn   PUB

(📋 01865-728164; www.bearoxford.co.uk; 6 Alfred St; ⊘ 11am-11pm Mon-Thu, 11am-midnight Fri & Sat, 11.30am-10.30pm Sun) Oxford's oldest pub – there's been a pub here since 1242 – the creaky old Bear requires almost everyone to stoop while passing from room to room. An ever-expanding collection of ties, framed and fading behind glass, covers walls and ceilings alike. Affiliated with Fuller's chain, it usually offers interesting guest ales, plus basic pub grub.

Eagle & Child   PUB

(📋 01865-302925; www.nicholsonspubs.co.uk/theeagleandchildoxford; 49 St Giles; ⊘ 11am-10pm Mon-Sat, noon-10pm Sun) Affectionately nicknamed the 'Bird & Baby', and a favourite haunt of JRR Tolkien, CS Lewis and their fellow Inklings, this quirky, rambling pub dates from 1650. Its narrow wood-panelled rooms still look great, and it's still serving decent real ales with a generic pub menu.

Varsity Club   COCKTAIL BAR

(📋 01865-248777; www.tvcoxford.co.uk; 9 High St; ⊘ noon-midnight; 🖥) At this sleekly minimalist rooftop cocktail bar, spectacularly located in the town centre, cocktails and small dishes are served with sensational views across Oxford's dreaming spires. Heaters, blankets and canopies keep things cosy in colder weather, while lounges and dance spaces sprawl across three floors below.

Trout   PUB

(📋 01865-510930; www.thetroutoxford.co.uk; 195 Godstow Rd, Wolvercote; ⊘ noon-10pm; 🖥) Three miles northwest along the Thames from Oxford – a wonderful walk– this old-world pub has been drawing drinkers for around four centuries, and was popularised by TV detective Inspector Morse. Its expansive riverside terrace is usually packed, and there are peckish ducks patrolling the parapet wall. If you fancy sampling its modern British cuisine, book a table in advance.

🛍 Shopping

★ Blackwell's   BOOKS

(📋 01865-792792; www.blackwells.co.uk; 48-51 Broad St; ⊘ 9am-6.30pm Mon & Wed-Sat, 9.30am-6.30pm Tue, 11am-5pm Sun) The most famous bookshop in the most studenty of cities, Blackwell's is, with its vast range of literature, treatises and guilty pleasures, a book-lover's dream. Be sure to visit the basement Norrington Room, an immense inverted step pyramid, lined with 3 miles of shelves and hailed in the Guinness Book of Records as the largest book-selling room in the world.

Blackwell's Art & Poster   ART

(📋 01865-333641; www.blackwell.co.uk; 27 Broad St; ⊘ 10am-6.30pm Mon-Sat, 11am-5pm Sun) Blackwell's split-level sibling store, all but opposite the main bookshop, specialises in reference books, coffee-table tomes, posters, cards and stationery, ranging across art forms from Expressionism to origami, and film stills to anime. Browsing is welcome, and leaving without a purchase near impossible.

Westgate Shopping Centre   MALL

(📋 01865-263600; www.westgateoxford.co.uk; Castle St; ⊘ shops 10am-8pm Mon-Fri, 9am-8pm Sat, 11am-5pm Sun, restaurants open longer hours;

WORTH A TRIP

THE REAL DOWNTON ABBEY

A 19th-century Victorian structure, **Highclere Castle** (📋 01635-253210; www.highclerecastle.co.uk; Newbury RG20 9RN; adult/child £24/14; ⊘ open on selected dates across the year) was used to film all six seasons of the hugely successful ITV/PBS TV series *Downtown Abbey*. Visitors can relive memories of the show (as if the Crawleys were once inhabitants) while gathering some insights into the private lives of the castle's real inhabitants, the Earl and Countess of Carnarvon. The castle itself covers 100,000 sq ft and has a total of 300 rooms, but only a limited number are open to the public.

WORTH A TRIP

VALE OF THE WHITE HORSE

Lying around 20 miles southwest of Oxford, this verdant valley is home to the historic market town of Wantage, birthplace of Alfred the Great (AD 849–899). Its most interesting attractions, however, are much older even than that. White Horse Hill, 7.5 miles west of Wantage, is decorated with Britain's most ancient chalk figure, the 3000-year-old Uffington White Horse, while the nearby hill fort known as Uffington Castle dates from 700 BC, and Wayland's Smithy is a neolithic long barrow.

The 10m-high, flat-topped mound known as Dragon Hill was believed by locals to be the site where St George slew the dragon. Archaeologists prefer to think that it's a natural formation, the summit of which was scraped level during the Iron Age and used for rituals.

☎) Originally built in 1972 on the site of Oxford's medieval West Gate, this enormous mall expanded in 2017. Like Alice it seems just to keep on growing, with around 100 big-name shops including a large John Lewis department store, plus indoor golf and a cinema. Several of the smart, contemporary chain restaurants on the top floor have outdoor roof-terrace seating with views over the city.

ℹ Information

The Oxford tourist office website (www.experienceoxfordshire.org) covers the whole of Oxfordshire and sells local Oxford guidebooks, makes reservations for local accommodation and walking tours, and sells tickets for events and attractions.

ℹ Getting There & Away

BUS

Oxford's chaotic outdoor **bus station** (Gloucester Green) is in the centre, on Gloucester Green near the corner of Worcester and George Sts. The main bus companies are **Oxford Bus Company** (☎ 01865-785400; www.oxfordbus.co.uk), **Stagecoach** (☎ 01865-772250; www.stagecoachbus.com) and **Swanbrook** (☎ 01452-712386; www.swanbrook.co.uk).

CAR & MOTORCYCLE

Driving and parking in central Oxford is a nightmare; consider booking accommodation that offers parking. There are five Park & Ride car parks along the major routes leading into town, all at least 2 miles out. Parking costs £2 to £4 per day, with a total charge of £6.80 if you use the buses that run to/from the centre every 15 to 30 minutes, and take 12 to 25 minutes for the journey.

TRAIN

Oxford's main train station is conveniently located just west of the city centre, roughly 10 minutes' walk from the main shopping area. Fares vary enormously according to what time you travel and how far in advance you book. Destinations include:

Birmingham (£20, 1¼ hours)
London Marylebone (£28, 1¼ hours)
London Paddington (£28, 1¼ hours)
Manchester (£40, 2¾ hours)
Moreton-in-Marsh (£12, 35 minutes)
Newcastle (£70, 4½ hours)
Winchester (£20, 1¼ hours)

ℹ Getting Around

BICYCLE

There's a real cycling culture in Oxford, and it's a popular way to get around the city for students and visitors alike. **Cyclo Analysts** (☎ 01865-424444; www.cycloanalysts.com; 150 Cowley Rd; per day/week from £10/36; ☺ 9am-6pm Mon-Sat) and **Summertown Cycles** (☎ 01865-316885; www.summertowncycles.co.uk; 200-202 Banbury Rd, Summertown; per day/week £18/35; ☺ 9am-5.30pm Mon-Sat, 10.30am-4pm Sun) sell, repair and rent out bikes, including hybrids.

BUS

Oxford Bus Company and Stagecoach serve an extensive local network with regular buses on major routes. Single journeys cost around £2.50 (return £4). Pay when you board the bus with a contactless card.

An unlimited bus travel ticket (per day) is available (adult/child £10/7). Buy tickets in advance on the Stagecoach Bus app.

TAXI

There are taxi ranks at the train and bus stations, as well as on St Giles and at Carfax. Alternatively, contact **001 Taxis** (☎ 01865-240000; www.001taxis.com) or **Oxford Cars** (☎ 01865-406070; www.oxfordcars.co.uk).

AROUND OXFORD

The Oxfordshire countryside abounds in rustic charm. To the northwest, Witney has a pretty town centre, but the major highlight is magnificent Blenheim Palace, birthplace of Sir Winston Churchill, adjoining attractive Woodstock. Southwest of Oxford, the Vale of the White Horse offers some intriguing prehistoric attractions.

Woodstock

📞 01993 / POP 2730

Woodstock, 8 miles northwest of Oxford, is a beautiful old town that has long had close links to royalty. Fine stone houses, venerable inns and pubs, and antique shops jostle shoulder to shoulder in its well-heeled centre, but what really draws the crowds here is Blenheim Palace, a majestic baroque extravaganza that was the birthplace of Sir Winston Churchill.

◉ Sights

★ Blenheim Palace   PALACE

(📞 01993-810530; www.blenheimpalace.com; Woodstock; adult/child £28.50/16.50, park & gardens only £18.50/8.60; ⊙ palace 10.30am-4.30pm, park & gardens 9.30am-6.30pm or dusk; 🅿) One of Britain's greatest stately homes, and a Unesco World Heritage Site, Blenheim Palace is a monumental baroque fantasy, designed by Sir John Vanbrugh and Nicholas Hawksmoor, and built between 1705 and 1722. Queen Anne gave the land, and the necessary funds, to John Churchill, Duke of Marlborough, as thanks for defeating the French at the 1704 Battle of Blenheim. Sir Winston Churchill was born here in 1874, and Blenheim (blen-num) remains home to the 12th duke.

Inside, beyond majestic oak doors, the palace is stuffed with statues, tapestries, sumptuous furniture, priceless china and giant oil paintings in elaborate gilt frames. Visits start in the Great Hall, a soaring space that's adorned with images of the first duke and topped by a 20m-high ceiling. From here, you can either wander through the various grand state rooms independently, or join one of the free 45-minute guided tours, which depart every 30 minutes (except on Sunday, when guides are stationed in all rooms). Highlights include the famous Blenheim Tapestries, a set of 10 large wall hangings commemorating the first duke's triumphs; the State Dining Room, with its painted walls and trompe l'Iœil ceilings; and the magnificent Long Library, overlooked by an elaborate 1738 statue of Queen Anne, where the 56m ceiling was decorated by Nicholas Hawksmoor.

Upstairs is the Untold Story tour, where a phantom chambermaid leads you on a half-hour audiovisual tour of tableaux that recreate important scenes from Blenheim's history. Between February and September you can also join additional tours (adult/child £5/4.50) of the duke's private apartments, the palace bedrooms or the household staff areas.

A separate sequence of rooms downstairs holds the Churchill Exhibition, included in the ticket price and dedicated to the life, work, paintings and writings of Winston Churchill. Official history has it that the future prime minister, grandson of the 7th duke and cousin of the 9th, was born by chance at the palace, after his mother went into premature labour. It's widely believed, however, that the tale was concocted to conceal that she was already pregnant when she married his father, seven months earlier. Winston Churchill is buried in the local parish church in Bladon, 1.5 miles south, just outside the grounds.

Ensure you have enough time to visit the vast, lavish gardens and parklands, parts of which were landscaped by the great

OXFORD & THE COTSWOLDS WOODSTOCK

DON'T MISS

KELMSCOTT MANOR

A gorgeous garden-fringed Tudor pile, Kelmscott Manor (📞 01367-252486; www.sal.org.uk/kelmscott-manor; Kelmscott; adult/child £10/5; ⊙ 11am-5pm Wed & Sat Apr-Oct), nestling near the Thames 20 miles west of Oxford (northwest of Faringdon), was bought in 1871 by a prestigious pair of artist-poets: Dante Gabriel Rossetti and William Morris, founder of the Arts and Crafts movement. The interior is true to Morris' philosophy that one should own nothing that is neither beautiful nor useful, and displays his personal effects along with fabrics and furniture designed by Morris and his associates. Closed for renovations, it will hopefully be ready for visitors again by the time you're reading this.

Lancelot 'Capability' Brown. Immediately outside, two large water terraces hold fountains and sphinxes, while a mini train (£1) takes visitors to the Pleasure Gardens, where features include a yew maze, adventure playground, lavender garden and butterfly house.

For quieter and longer strolls, there are glorious walks of up to 4.5 miles, leading past lakes to an arboretum, rose garden, cascade and Vanbrugh's Grand Bridge. Look out for the Temple of Diana, where Winston Churchill proposed to his future bride, Lady Clementine, on 10 August 1908.

🛏 Sleeping

Feathers HOTEL ££

(📞 01993-812291; www.feathers.co.uk; Market St; r incl breakfast from £109; 🛜) Oozing contemporary chic, this handsome 17th-century town house – previously a sanatorium, a draper's and a butcher's – offers stylish, comfortable rooms adorned with patterned wallpaper, modern art, fuzzy throws and rich-coloured fabrics. The smart bar downstairs stocks 401 types of gin.

★ Glove House B&B £££

(📞 01993-813475; www.theglovehouse.co.uk; 24 Oxford St; d/ste from £175/200; 🛜) Luxuriously renovated but proudly displaying evidence of its venerable age, this elegant 400-year-old town house conceals three sumptuous rooms, all with the added bonus of a glorious rear garden. The Charlbury suite has a freestanding copper bathtub in its wonderful lounge-equipped bathroom.

ℹ Getting There & Away

Stagecoach buses (p190) head to/from Oxford (30 minutes), Burford (45 minutes), Chipping Norton (20 minutes) and Witney (30 minutes). Buses S3 and 233 stop outside Blenheim Palace. See www.traveline.info for fares and timetables.

An unlimited bus travel ticket (per day) is available (adult/child £10/7). Buy tickets in advance on the Stagecoach Bus app.

THE COTSWOLDS

Undulating gracefully across six counties, the Cotswolds region is a delightful tangle of golden villages, thatched cottages, evocative churches and honey-coloured mansions. In 1966 it was designated an Area of Outstanding Natural Beauty, surpassed for size in England by the Lake District alone.

No one's sure what the name means, but 'wolds' are rolling hills, while 'cots' might be 'cotes', or sheep pens. Certainly the region owes its wealth, and exquisite architecture, to the medieval wool trade, when 'Cotswold Lion' sheep were prized across Europe. Attentions later turned towards textiles instead, but the Industrial Revolution passed the Cotswolds by. Hailed by William Morris in the 19th century as encapsulating a timeless English rural idyll, it remains both a moneyed residential area and a treasured tourist destination.

Criss-crossed by long-distance trails including the 102-mile Cotswold Way, these gentle yet dramatic hills are perfect for walking, cycling and horse riding.

🏃 Activities

Cycling

Gentle gradients and wonderfully scenic panoramas make the Cotswolds ideal for cycling. Quiet country lanes and byways crisscross the countryside, and only the steep western escarpment poses a significant challenge to the legs. You can also follow the signposted Thames Valley Cycle Way (NCN Routes 4 and 5) between Oxford and Windsor (and on to London).

Companies such as Cotswold Country Cycles (📞 01386-438706; www.cotswoldcountry cycles.com; Longlands Farm Cottage; 3-day/2-night tours from £285) organise maps, luggage transfers and B&B stays for a range of self-guided cycling tours.

Walking

The 102-mile Cotswold Way (www. nationaltrail.co.uk/cotswold-way) gives walkers a wonderful overview of the region. Meandering from Chipping Campden in the northeast to Bath in the southwest, it passes through some lovely countryside, linking ancient sites and tiny villages, with no major climbs or difficult stretches. It's also easily accessible from many points en route, if you fancy tackling a shorter section or a circular walk from your village of choice.

Other long-distance trails that pass through the Cotswolds include the 100-mile Gloucestershire Way, which runs from Chepstow to Tewkesbury via Stow-on-the-Wold; the 55-mile St Kenelm's Way into Worcestershire; and the 184-mile Thames Path (www.nationaltrail.co.uk/thames-path), which tracks from just southwest of Cirencester all the way to London.

Local tourist offices can advise on routes and usually sell walking maps.

Cirencester

🎵 01285 / POP 19,100

Charming Cirencester (siren-sester), the most significant town in the southern Cotswolds, is just 15 miles south of Cheltenham. Amazingly, under the Romans – who knew it as Corinium – Cirencester ranked second only to London in terms of size and importance, but little now survives from that era. The medieval wool trade brought further prosperity, with wealthy merchants funding the construction of a superb church.

Cirencester today is both elegant and affluent, but refreshingly unpretentious. Upmarket boutiques and fashionable delis now line its narrow streets, but its Monday and Friday markets remain at the core of its identity. Beautiful Victorian buildings flank the busy central square, while the surrounding streets showcase a harmonious medley of historic architecture.

◉ Sights

★ **Corinium Museum**   MUSEUM
(🎵 01285-655611; www.coriniummuseum.org; Park St; adult/child £5.60/2.70; ⏰10am-5pm Mon-Sat, 2-5pm Sun Apr-Oct, 10am-4pm Mon-Sat, 2-4pm Sun Nov-Mar; 🖽) Most of this wonderful modern museum is dedicated to Cirencester's Roman past; reconstructed rooms, videos and interactive displays bring the era to life. Among the highlights are some beautiful floor mosaics, unearthed locally and including a 4th-century mosaic depicting the mythical lyre-player Orpheus charming animals, and the 2nd-century 'Jupiter column', a carved capital depicting Bacchus and his drunken mates. There's also an excellent Stone Age room, an Anglo-Saxon section, and exhibits covering medieval Cirencester through to its prosperous wool trade.

St John the Baptist's Church   CHURCH
(🎵 01285-659317; www.cirenparish.co.uk; Market Sq; ⏰10am-4pm) One of England's largest parish churches, the cathedral-like St John's boasts an outstanding Perpendicular Gothic tower with flying buttresses (c 1400), plus a majestic three-storey south porch, built as an office in the late 15th century but

subsequently used as Cirencester's town hall. Soaring arches, magnificent fan vaulting and a Tudor nave adorn the light-filled interior, where a wall safe holds the Boleyn Cup, made for Anne Boleyn in 1535.

On some Wednesdays and summer Saturdays, it's possible to climb the tower (adult/child £3/1.50).

🛏 Sleeping

★ **No 12**   B&B ££
(🎵 01285-640232; www.no12cirencester.co.uk; 12 Park St; d/ste £130/150; 🅿🛜) This welcoming and very central Georgian town house offers four gloriously unfussy, very private rooms kitted out with a tasteful mix of antiques and modern furnishings. Romantic room 1 has an in-room bath, while the suite has two bathrooms and overlooks the lovely garden, with extra-long beds, piles of feather pillows and splashes of red throughout. The included breakfasts are superb.

Kings Head   LUXURY HOTEL ££
(🎵 01285-700900; www.kingshead-hotel.co.uk; 24 Market Pl; d/ste from £119/199; 🛜🏊) A coaching inn since the 14th century, this plush spot facing the church offers slick boudoirs and super-polished service. Exposed beams, red-brick walls and wood panelling pop up between Nespresso machines and Apple TVs. Enjoy the tucked-away spa, cosy bar and smart restaurant.

🍴 Eating

New Brewery Arts Cafe   CAFE £
(🎵 01285-657181; www.newbreweryarts.org.uk; Brewery Ct; mains £6-8.50; ⏰9am-5pm Mon-Sat; 🛜🍴🖽) Drop into this friendly daytime-only cafe, on the upper level of Cirencester's lively arts centre, for breakfast eggs, toast or pancakes, or for wholesome, good-value lunchtime sandwiches, salads and wraps. It also serves tasty cakes and fresh smoothies.

The Cotswolds

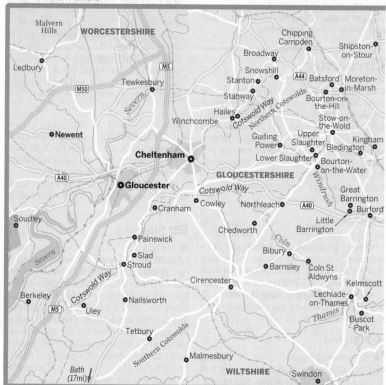

Made by Bob MODERN BRITISH **££**
(☑ 01285-641818; www.mbbbrasserie.co.uk; Corn Hall, 26 Market Pl; mains £8.50-22.50; ⊙8am-10pm Mon-Sat, noon-8.30pm Sun; ☑) Filling a substantial light-filled space inside a central mall, and focused around an enormous open-plan kitchen, Bob's is part deli, part brasserie, and popular for its casual atmosphere. The breakfast selection is excellent – granola, smashed avocado, full English – while lunch bites include salads, soups, pastas, risottos and charcuterie platters.

ⓘ Information

Tourist Office (☑ 01285-654180; www. cotswolds.com; Corinium Museum, Park St; ⊙10am-5pm Mon-Sat, 2-5pm Sun Apr-Oct, 10am-4pm Mon-Sat, 2-4pm Sun Nov-Mar) Doubling as the museum gift store, this helpful office can arrange accommodation and sells a leaflet detailing a self-guided walk around Cirencester.

ⓘ Getting There & Away

The closest station to Cirencester, at Kemble 4.5 miles south, is connected by train with London Paddington (£28, 1¼ hours).

Stagecoach (p190) serves Cirencester. Buses stop outside the Corn Hall on Market Pl. Buses run to/from Cheltenham (40 minutes), Gloucester (50 minutes), Northleach (20 minutes) and Tetbury (30 minutes). See www.traveline.info for fares and timetables.

An unlimited bus travel ticket (per day) is available (adult/child £10/7). Buy tickets in advance on the Stagecoach Bus app.

National Express (www.nationalexpress.com) coach destinations include Birmingham (£18, 2½ hours) and London Victoria (£25, 2½ hours).

Bibury

☑ 01285 / POP 630

Memorably described as 'England's most beautiful village' by no less an authority than William Morris, Bibury, 8 miles

Church of St Mary the Virgin   CHURCH
(Church Rd; ⊙10am-dusk) Bibury's Saxon-built church has been much altered since its original construction, but many 8th-century features are still visible among the 12th-, 13th- and 15th-century additions. It's just off the B4425 in the village centre.

🛌 Sleeping

New Inn   PUB ££
(☑01285-750651; www.new-inn.co.uk; Main St, Coln St Aldwyns; r incl breakfast £119-149; P🐾🖤) The jasmine-clad 16th-century New Inn, 2.5 miles southeast of Bibury, offers 14 spacious and atmospheric bedrooms divided between the main pub building and a neighbouring cottage. Idiosyncratic contemporary stylings include bold colours, fluffy throws, smart furnishings and the odd freestanding bathtub, while the pub itself, with its exposed beams, is the place for a burger and beer.

★Barnsley House   LUXURY HOTEL £££
(☑01285-740000; www.barnsleyhouse.com; B4425, Barnsley; r incl breakfast from £319; P🐾🖤) For pure indulgence and romance, this 1697 country house and its famously beautiful garden take some beating. Each of its 18 rooms is individually styled; some have lavish oriental touches or in-room baths, most are elegantly understated. Facilities include a spa, a pool, a private cinema, the Potager restaurant and the knowingly re-named Village Pub. Guests must be aged 14 or over.

❶ Getting There & Away
Most drivers approach Bibury along the B4425, which passes through the village centre halfway between Burford (9 miles northeast) and Cirencester (8 miles southwest).

Pulhams Coaches bus 855 heads to/from Cirencester (15 minutes) and Northleach (20 minutes); there's no Sunday service.

See www.traveline.info for fares and timetables.

northeast of Cirencester, epitomises the Cotswolds at its most picturesque. With a cluster of perfect cottages beside the River Coln, and a tangle of narrow streets flanked by attractive stone buildings, small wonder that it's a major halt on large-group Cotswold tours.

⊙ Sights

★Arlington Row   STREET
Bibury's most famous attraction, this ravishing row of rustic cottages – as seen in movies such as *Stardust* – was originally a 14th-century wool store, before being converted into workers' lodgings. They overlook Rack Isle, a low-lying, marshy area once used to dry cloth and graze cattle, and now a wildlife refuge. Visitors are reminded to admire the cottages but respect the residents' privacy as you stroll the flower-lined lane alongside.

Burford
☑01993 / POP 1410
Gliding down a steep hillside to an ancient (and still single-lane) crossing point on the River Windrush, 20 miles west of Oxford, Burford has hardly changed since its medieval glory days. Locals insist it's a town not a village, having received its charter in 1090, but it's a very small town, and a

very picturesque one too, home to an appealing mix of stone cottages, gold-tinged Cotswold town houses, and the odd Elizabethan or Georgian treasure.

Throw in a wonderfully preserved, centuries-old church and an array of delightful hotels and restaurants, and Burford makes an attractive stop. Antique shops, chintzy tearooms and specialist boutiques peddle nostalgia to the many summer visitors, but it's easy to escape the crowds and wander along quiet side streets, seemingly lost in time.

Sleeping & Eating

★ Star Cottage
B&B ££

(☑ 01993-822032; www.burfordbedandbreakfast. co.uk; Meadow Lane, Fulbrook; r £125, apt £150; ☎) A mile northeast of Burford, this wonderful old Cotswold cottage holds two comfortable and character-filled en-suite rooms done up in tastefully creative blues, whites and greys, with gorgeous quilted curtains. The smaller room holds a grand canopied bed; the larger has a beautiful bathroom; and the back barn hosts a separate four-person apartment. The home-cooked, locally sourced breakfasts are fantastic.

Lamb Inn
PUB £££

(☑ 01993-823155; www.cotswold-inns-hotels. co.uk/the-lamb-inn; Sheep St; s/d incl breakfast from £150/160; P🅿🛜🐾) A rambling 15th-century inn, off the main street, where the flagstone floors, exposed beams and creaking stairs are complemented by 17 opulent antique-furnished rooms. A few have four-poster beds, and one even has its own private garden, while modern touches include Nespresso machines and slick bathrooms.

Modern British cuisine is served in both the romantic restaurant and the bar.

Huffkins
CAFE £

(☑ 01993-824694; www.huffkins.com; 98 High St; mains £6-15; ⊙9am-4.30pm Mon-Fri, 9am-5pm Sat, 10am-5pm Sun; 🍴) The original outlet of a Cotswolds chain that's been baking and serving delicious scones, cakes and pies since 1890, this lively, friendly cafe is usually busy with locals enjoying quiches, soups, macaroni cheese or burgers. It also offers all-day cooked breakfasts and full-blown afternoon teas.

For a quick snack, pick up baked goods in its adjoining deli.

Swan Inn
MODERN BRITISH ££

(☑ 01993-823339; www.theswanswinbrook.co.uk; Swinbrook; mains £16-26; ⊙noon-2pm & 7-9pm; P) With a maze of lively rooms, roaring winter fires and bench tables overlooking a gorgeous orchard, this popular riverside gastropub, 3 miles east of Burford, oozes appeal. Its seasonal British menu mixes a pinch of creativity with quality, mostly local, ingredients, offering original starters (like Stilton soufflé) and sharing platters alongside succulent meaty mains. Bookings recommended.

Downton Abbey fans: this is the pub where Lady Sybil and Branson planned their elopement.

Shopping

Oxford Brush Company
HOMEWARES

(☑ 01993-824148; www.oxfordbrushcompany.com; 54 High St; ⊙9am-5pm Mon-Fri, 10am-4pm Sat & Sun) Yes, the only thing they sell here is brushes. But they are very nice brushes, the kind of brushes you might buy even if you didn't think you needed a brush. Perhaps a nailbrush? A clothes brush? Or just a brush to clean your other brushes?

Information

Tourist Office (☑ 01993-823558; www.oxford shirecotswolds.org; 33a High St; ⊙9.30am-5pm Mon-Sat, 10am-4pm Sun) Information on local walks.

Getting There & Away

Stagecoach and Swanbrook buses run to/from Burford. Local buses stop on High or Sheep Sts, but express services stop at the A40 roundabout, five minutes' walk south of the centre. Bus destinations include Cheltenham (45 minutes), Gloucester (1¼ hours), Oxford (45 minutes to 1¼ hours), Minster Lovell (15 minutes), Witney (20 minutes) and Woodstock (45 minutes).

See www.traveline.info for fares and timetables. An unlimited bus travel ticket (per day) is available (adult/child £10/7). Buy tickets in advance on the Stagecoach Bus app.

Northleach

☑ 01451 / POP 1840

Oddly under-visited, and refreshingly uncommercialised despite holding some interesting attractions, Northleach, 14 miles southeast of Cheltenham, has been a small market town since 1227. Late-medieval cottages, imposing merchants' stores and half-timbered Tudor houses jostle for position in a wonderful melange of styles around Market Sq and the narrow laneways that lead off it.

⊙ Sights

Chedworth
Roman Villa   ARCHAEOLOGICAL SITE
(NT; ☏01242-890256; www.nationaltrust.org.uk; Yanworth; adult/child £10.50/5.25; ⊙10am-5pm Apr-Oct, to 4pm mid-Feb–Mar & Nov; ℗) This large and luxurious Roman villa was rediscovered by a gamekeeper in 1864. Though the earliest section dates to around 175 CE, it was at its most magnificent around 362 CE, equipped with two sets of bathhouses, a water shrine and a dining room with underfloor heating. A fine modern gallery preserves several exquisite mosaics, though yet more, unearthed recently, had to be re-buried due to lack of resources.

It's at the far end of a dead-end rural road, 4.5 miles west of Northleach and signposted from the A429.

Church of St Peter & St Paul   CHURCH
(www.northleach.org; Church Walk) The grandeur and complexity of this masterpiece of the Cotswold Perpendicular style testifies to its wool-era wealth. Although the chancel and 30m tower date from the 14th century, it was extensively reworked during the 15th-century wool boom. A modern highlight is the 1964 stained-glass window depicting Christ in Glory, behind the altar, while earlier treasures include an unusual 14th-century font.

🍴 Sleeping & Eating

★**Wheatsheaf**   BOUTIQUE HOTEL £££
(☏01451-860244; www.cotswoldswheatsheaf.com; West End; r incl breakfast £123-255; ℗ 🛜 🐾) The 14 different rooms at this former coaching inn, very popular with an exclusive London set, blend atmospheric period touches, such as freestanding bathtubs, with modern comforts including power showers, organic toiletries and country-chic decor. Downstairs, an outrageously popular **restaurant** (☏01451-860244; www.cotswoldswheatsheaf.com; West End; mains £14.50-24; ⊙8-10am, noon-3pm & 6-9pm Mon-Thu & Sun, to 10pm Fri & Sat; ℗ 🛜 👶) adds a contemporary twist to delightful seasonal British dishes.

❶ Getting There & Away

Stagecoach buses head to/from Burford (15 minutes), Cheltenham (45 minutes), Cirencester (20 minutes), Gloucester (one hour) and Oxford (one hour). See www.traveline.info for fares and timetables.

An unlimited bus travel ticket (per day) is available (adult/child £10/7). Buy tickets in advance on the Stagecoach Bus app.

The Slaughters
☏ 01451 / POP 400

The picture-postcard villages of Upper and Lower Slaughter, roughly a mile apart and around 3.5 miles southwest of Stow-on-the-Wold, have somehow managed to maintain their unhurried medieval charm, despite receiving a multitude of visitors. Their names have nothing to do with abattoirs; they come from the Old English 'sloughtre', meaning slough or muddy place.

Meandering sleepily through the two villages, the River Eye passes a succession of classic gold-tinged Cotswolds houses. It's Lower Slaughter that's the real gem, with the river canalised between limestone banks to flow just a few inches below road level, and with flowery footpaths to either side. If you've time for a stroll, you can follow the Eye from one village to the other – the central stretch is away from the traffic – for a round trip that typically takes around two hours.

Old Mill   NOTABLE BUILDING
(☏01451-820052; www.oldmill-lowerslaughter.com; Lower Slaughter; ⊙10am-6pm Mar-Oct, to dusk Nov-Feb) Right on the River Eye, the Old Mill houses a cafe and crafts shop as well as a small museum, where you can find out all about the building's former life as a water-powered flour mill. A watermill is recorded as operating in this location as far back as the Domesday Book (1086).

Lords of the Manor   HISTORIC HOTEL £££
(☏01451-820243; www.lordsofthemanor.com; Upper Slaughter; r incl breakfast £240-465; ℗ 🛜 🐾) Although from the outside this 17th-century mansion appears to embody traditional rural splendour, its spacious, supremely tasteful rooms are surprisingly up to date. Expect

fresh, white styling, floral-print spreads and exposed beams, along with gorgeous countryside panoramas, superb service and a fantastic Michelin-starred restaurant (☑ 01451-820243; www.lordsofthemanor.com; Upper Slaughter; 3-/7-course dinner £72.50/£90; ☉ 6.45-9pm daily & noon-1.30pm Sat & Sun; P).

❶ Getting There & Away

Buses are not permitted in the Slaughters, so unless you're hiking or cycling, a car is your best option. To reach Lower Slaughter, detour half a mile west from the A429, 2.5 miles southwest of Stow-on-the-Wold or 6 miles northeast of Northleach. Upper Slaughter is another mile further west.

Stow-on-the-Wold

☑ 01451 / POP 2040

The highest town in the Cotswolds (244m), Stow-on-the-Wold centres on a large square surrounded by handsome buildings. The high-walled alleyways that lead into it originally served to funnel sheep into the fair, and it also witnessed a bloody massacre at the end of the English Civil War, when Roundhead soldiers dispatched defeated Royalists in 1646.

Standing on the Roman Fosse Way (now the A429), at the junction of six roads 4.5 miles south of Moreton-in-Marsh, Stow is still an important market town. It's also a major tourist destination, usually crowded with visitors in summer, and famous for hosting the twice-yearly (May and October) Stow Horse Fair.

◉ Sights

Cotswold Farm Park   ZOO
(☑ 01451-850307; www.cotswoldfarmpark. co.uk; Guiting Power; adult/child £10/9.50; ☉ 10.30am-5pm mid-Feb–late Dec; P 🚼) 🐾
Owned by TV presenter Adam Henson, Cotswold Farm Park sets out to introduce little ones to the world of farm animals, while also preserving rare breeds, such as Exmoor ponies and Cotswold Lion sheep. There are milking demonstrations, lamb-feeding sessions, an adventure playground, a 2-mile wildlife walk and pedal tractors to ride on. It's 6 miles west of Stow-on-the-Wold, signposted from the B4077 and B4068.

🏃 Driving Tour
Classic Cotswolds

START BURFORD
END WINCHCOMBE
LENGTH 54 MILES; ONE TO THREE DAYS

Given the Cotswolds' intricate spider's-web of winding country lanes that connect its market towns, villages and stately homes, it's impossible to cover every highlight in a single day. This tour, though, spans three counties and takes in some of the most picturesque spots in the northern half of the range. You could drive it in a day, but you'll enjoy it more if you stretch it into two or three, with plentiful stop-offs along the way.

Begin in Oxfordshire at the gorgeous hillside market town of ❶ **Burford** (p195), then head 10 miles west on the A40 into Gloucestershire, following signs to classic Cotswolds town ❷ **Northleach** (p196). The Cotswolds Discovery Centre here has excellent displays covering the history, geography, flora and fauna of the Cotswolds Area of Outstanding Natural Beauty (AONB). There's a fine church in town, and a fascinating Roman villa nearby.

From Northleach, spin 7 miles northeast on the A429 to ❸ **Lower Slaughter**, a serene riverside village lined with houses made of that irresistible Cotswolds golden stone. Spare the time if you can to stroll a mile northwest, along the river, to ❹ **Upper Slaughter**, less visited than its sibling but no less attractive. Book ahead, and you can have lunch in an exquisite Jacobean mansion, at Lords of the Manor.

Continue 3 miles north on the A429 to ❺ **Stow-on-the-Wold**, the highest Cotswold village at 244m. Explore the market square, then follow the A429 north, along the route of the ancient Roman Fosse Way. After 4.5 miles you'll reach ❻ **Moreton-in-Marsh** (p204), known for its weekly Tuesday market and great shops.

Next, zip 3 miles west on the A44 to tiny ❼ **Bourton-on-the-Hill**, filled with attractive 17th- and 18th-century cottages. It's famous for two things: the gibbeting cage in which the bodies of dead highwaymen were hung in the 19th century, and horse training – there are several stud farms in the vicinity. The Horse & Groom here is a good lunch option.

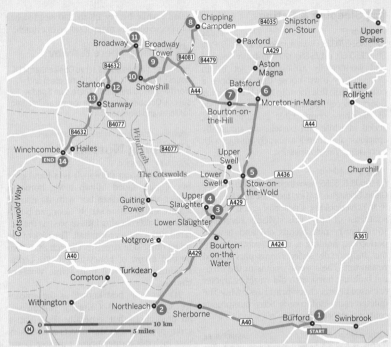

Head 3 miles west on the A44, then turn right (northeast) onto the B4081 to ⑧**Chipping Campden** (p201), one of the Cotswold's most bucolic towns. After admiring 15th-century St James' Church and the honey-toned buildings along High St, backtrack to the A44. Drive a mile northwest, crossing into the Worcestershire corner of the Cotswolds, and turn off at signposted ⑨**Broadway Tower** (p203), an 18th-century Gothic folly perched atop the escarpment.

Leaving Broadway Tower, continue 1 mile south and turn right (southwest) at the crossing. You'll soon see signs to pretty little ⑩**Snowshill**, a mile further on and one-time film set for *Bridget Jones's Diary*. If you're visiting in June or July, you'll swing by spectacularly purple fields of flowering lavender. From Snowshill, whizz 2.5 miles north to ⑪**Broadway** (p202), home to an excellent museum and gallery. After cruising along broad High St, hop on the B4632 southwest towards Cheltenham.

After 3 miles, take the left (east) turn-off to ⑫**Stanton**, a tiny stunner of a village. Its houses are crafted out of gold-tinged Cotswolds stone, with not a shop or quaint tearoom in sight. The buildings most likely to catch your eye are Jacobean Stanton Court and St Michael & All Angels' Church, the latter with its fine Perpendicular tower and beguiling medieval interior. Stanton Court once belonged to civil architect Sir Philip Stott (1858–1937), who restored many other Stanton houses.

You're sure to see walkers passing through Stanton, heading along the Cotswold Way to ⑬**Stanway**, a mile south; follow the narrow road that runs parallel to the trail. There's little more to idyllic Stanway than a few thatched-roofed cottages, a church and Stanway House, a magnificent Jacobean manor house concealed behind a triple-gabled gatehouse. Its beautiful baroque water gardens feature Britain's tallest fountain. The private home of the Earls of Wemyss for 500 years, the manor has a delightful, lived-in charm, with much of its original furniture and character intact.

Traverse Stanway, turn right (west) onto the B4077 and then left (southwest) back onto the B4632. After 3.5 miles, you'll reach ⑭**Winchcombe** (p205), an ancient Anglo-Saxon town and walkers' favourite with good sleeping and eating options, including 5 North St. You'll probably want to stay overnight to explore wonderful Sudeley Castle in the morning.

🛏 Sleeping & Eating

Number 9   B&B ££

(📞 01451-870333; www.number-nine.info; 9 Park St; s £50-60, d £75-85; 🛜) Centrally located and wonderfully atmospheric, set in an 18th-century town house that was once a coaching inn, this friendly B&B is all sloping floors, low ceilings and exposed beams. Two of the three comfortable en-suite rooms, styled in white and pastels, are unusually spacious, and there's a homely lounge with a crackling fire downstairs.

King's Head Inn   INN ££

(📞 01608-658365; www.thekingsheadinn.net; The Green, Bledington; s/d incl breakfast from £90/110; 🅿🛜) Overlooking a peaceful green 4 miles southeast of Stow, this stylishly revamped 16th-century pub blends old and new to perfection, holding a dozen subtly luxurious, individually styled rooms plus a good restaurant. The six cosy rooms in the original building burst with old-world character (exposed beams, check-print rugs), while the quieter courtyard rooms offer sumptuous contemporary design.

King's Head Inn   GASTROPUB ££

(📞 01608-658365; www.thekingsheadinn.net; The Green, Bledington; mains £14-26; ⊘ noon-2pm & 6.30-9pm Mon-Sat, noon-3pm & 6.30-9pm Sun; 🅿🍴) 'National Inn of the Year' in 2020, and set in a 16th-century cider house with a lovely garden 4 miles southeast of Stow, the King's Head is ideal for eating, drinking or both. Seasonal menus draw on local produce such as Cotswold lamb, adding Mediterranean flavours (mozzarella and pomegranate

DAYLESFORD ORGANIC

A country-chic temple to the Cotswolds' organic movement, 4 miles east of Stow, the sprawling **Daylesford Organic** (📞 01608-731700; www.daylesford.com; Daylesford; ⊘ 8am-8pm Mon-Sat, 10am-4pm Sun) operation was kickstarted 40 years ago when a family farm turned sustainable. Centred on a gleaming food hall, crammed with Daylesford-brand produce, it also holds an excellent cafe-restaurant serving organic-fuelled treats (£13 to £19), plus an upmarket boutique, rental cottages, and a luxury spa.

salad), while hearty £8 to £10 sandwiches or cheese platters make a satisfying lunch.

ℹ Getting There & Away

Pulhams Coaches buses serve Cheltenham (1¼ hours), Moreton-in-Marsh (10 minutes) and Northleach (30 minutes). There's no Sunday service October to April. See www.traveline.info for fares and timetables.

Chipping Norton

📞 01608 / POP 6300

Chipping Norton ('Chippy') is a handsome but slightly faded hilltop town, home to banks and businesses but with its market square still boasting stately Georgian buildings and old coaching inns as well as the pillared 19th-century town hall. The pick of the many quiet side streets is Church St, where beyond a row of honey-tinged 17th-century almshouses you'll find a fine wool-era church.

It's probably best known as the epicentre of the so-called 'Chipping Norton set', an amorphous but generally conservative group of political/media movers and shakers that includes former prime minister David Cameron, and Rebecca Brooks, former CEO of News International.

◉ Sights

Rollright Stones   ARCHAEOLOGICAL SITE

(www.rollrightstones.co.uk; off A3400, Great Rollright; suggested adult/child £1/50p; ⊘ 24hr) Linked by a footpath through open fields, the ancient Rollright Stones stand to either side of an unnamed road 4 miles north of Chipping Norton. The most remarkable, the King's Men, consist of the weathered remnants of a stone circle that surrounded a Neolithic ceremonial centre in around 2500 BC, while the taller King Stone probably marked a Bronze Age cemetery, a millennium later. Payment made online.

Cotswolds Distillery   DISTILLERY

(📞 01608-238533; www.cotswoldsdistillery.com; Phillip's Field, Whichford Rd, Stourton; tours £15; ⊘ tours 11am, 1pm & 3pm, shop & cafe 10am-5pm) 🍴 This ambitious, ecofriendly gin and whisky distillery sits tucked into the northern Cotswolds, 8 miles north of Chipping Norton. Join a tour of the facilities to learn how its delicious Cotswolds-flavoured liquors are produced, then wrap things up with a tasting session. Reservations essential.

🛏 Sleeping & Eating

⭐ **Falkland Arms**   PUB ££
(www.falklandarms.co.uk; 19-21 The Green, Great
Tew; s/d incl breakfast £85/90; ⊘ 3-9pm Mon & Tue,
noon-10pm Wed-Sat, noon-6pm Sun; P 🛜) For its
blissful bucolic setting and historic charm,
there's no beating the thatched, 16-century
Falkland Arms, in the picture-postcard village of Great Tew, 6 miles east of Chipping
Norton. The half-dozen freshly restored and
upgraded rooms are great value, the pub
downstairs serves fine ales and decent pub
grub (mains £13 to £20), and there's lovely
walking in every direction.

Wild Thyme   MODERN BRITISH ££
(⌖ 01608-645060;   www.wildthymerestaurant.
co.uk; 10 New St; ⊘ set menu supper clubs) This
little 'restaurant with rooms' thrills palates
with top-notch creative dishes packed with
flavour, such as asparagus and goat's cheese
risotto or steamed Cornish turbot with Japanese pickles. The desserts – from apple
crumble to chocolate fondant – are nothing
short of sublime.

Jaffé & Neale Bookshop Cafe   CAFE
(⌖ 01608-641033; www.jaffeandneale.co.uk; 1 Middle Row; ⊘ 9.30am-4pm Mon-Sat; 🛜) The cosy
little cafe in this busy independent bookshop
on the main square serves delicious cakes
and coffees at tables squeezed between the
bookshelves, or in the cosy upstairs reading
lounge with sofas.

❶ Getting There & Away

Stagecoach and/or Pulhams buses head to
Oxford (one hour), Witney (45 minutes), and
Woodstock (20 minutes). See www.traveline.info
for fares and timetables.

Chipping Campden

⌖ 01386 / POP 2310
A standout gem, even for an area of such
pretty towns, Chipping Campden is a glorious reminder of Cotswolds life in medieval
times. While 'Chipping' derives from the
Old English 'ceapen', meaning 'market', it
owes its conspicuous prosperity to its success in the wool trade. Its gracefully curving main street is flanked by a picturesque
array of stone cottages, fine terraced houses, ancient inns and historic homes, most
made of that beautiful honey-coloured
Cotswolds stone. Westington, southwest of

WORTH A TRIP

BATSFORD ARBORETUM

Created from 1880 onwards by Bertie
Mitford (Lord Redesdale), and later
briefly home to his famous granddaugh-
ters, the Mitford sisters, **Batsford
Arboretum** (⌖ 01386-701441; www.
batsarb.co.uk; Batsford Park; adult/child
£8.95/3.50; ⊘ 9am-4pm; P 🐕) is 1.5
miles west of Moreton. These exotic
22-hectare woodlands hold around
1600 species of labelled trees, bamboos
and shrubs. Drawn especially from Nepal, China and Japan, many are rare or
endangered, or were planted pre-WWI.
Highlights include flowering Japanese
cherries (at their best in spring), some
vast North American redwoods and an
enormous davidia, and the strangely
churchlike 'cathedral' lime.
   A 1.7-mile footpath from Moreton
leads direct to the arboretum itself;
motorists have to drive a mile north up
the approach road from the entrance
on the A44.

the centre, holds some especially striking
thatch-roofed cottages.
   As the northeastern end of the Cotswold
Way, which rambles 102 miles southwest
from here to Bath, Chipping Campden is a
popular way station for walkers and cyclists,
and welcomes crowds of visitors year-round.
Despite its obvious allure, though, it remains surprisingly unspoiled.

⊙ Sights

Hidcote   GARDENS
(NT; www.nationaltrust.org.uk; Hidcote Bartrim;
adult/child £8/4; ⊘ 10am-6pm Apr-Sep, to 5pm
Oct, shorter hours rest of year, closed Jan; P)
Hidcote, 4 miles northeast of Chipping
Campden, ranks among the finest Arts and
Crafts gardens in Britain. Laid out from
1907 onwards by American horticulturalist
Lawrence Johnston, and acquired by the National Trust in 1948, it consists of a series of
outdoor 'rooms' filled with flowers and rare
plants from across the globe. There's also a
cafe and garden centre.

Grevel House   HISTORIC BUILDING
(High St; ⊘ closed to the public) Built around
1380 for the supremely prosperous wool
merchant William Grevel, complete with
gargoyles and mullioned windows, Grevel

SHIN KICKING & CHEESE ROLLING

The medieval sport of shin kicking lives on in the extraordinary Cotswold Olimpicks (www.olimpickgames.co.uk; Dover's Hill, Chipping Campden; ☺late May/early Jun), first celebrated in 1612. One of England's most bizarre and entertaining traditional sports days, it still features many of the original events, such as tug o' war.

Equally odd is the age-old (and surprisingly hazardous) pastime of cheese rolling (Cooper's Hill; admission free; ☺last May bank holiday). Following a 200-year-old tradition, crowds run, tumble and slide down Cooper's Hill, 4.5 miles northeast of Painswick, pursuing an 8lb round of Double Gloucester cheese. The prize? The cheese itself – and the glory of catching it.

House is Chipping Campden's oldest building. It's still a private home, but you can admire its splendid Perpendicular Gothic-style gabled window and sundial from the street.

Court Barn Museum   MUSEUM
(☑ 01386-841951; www.courtbarn.org.uk; Church St; adult/child £5/free; ☺10am-5pm Wed-Sun Apr-Oct, to 4pm Nov-Mar) Ever since architect and designer Charles Robert Ashbee (1863–1942) moved his Guild of Handicraft here from East London in 1902, Chipping Campden has been linked with the Arts and Crafts movement. This small but interesting museum displays work by nine luminaries of the movement, which celebrated traditional artisans in an age of industrialisation. Sadly, robberies in 2011 and 2017 removed its prize jewellery collection, but surviving artefacts include sculpture, book-binding and ceramics. It also stages two selling exhibitions each year.

🛏 Sleeping & Eating

Eight Bells Inn   PUB ££
(☑ 01386-840371; www.eightbellsinn.co.uk; Church St; r incl breakfast £99-143; 🛜) This friendly and atmospheric 14th-century inn offers six bright, modern rooms with iron bedsteads, soothing neutral decor, flowery wallpaper and warm accents. Room 7 – there's no number 4 – with its chunky old-world beams, is

especially striking. The cosy pub downstairs serves contemporary country cooking.

★ **Badgers Hall**   BAKERY £
(☑ 01386-840839; www.badgershall.com; High St; afternoon tea per person £7.50-24.50; ☺8am-5.30pm Thu-Sat; 🍴) Set in a glorious old mansion facing the market hall, this definitive Cotswold tearoom is renowned for its no-holds-barred afternoon teas, served from 2.30pm onwards. Lunch is also a treat, starring the most wonderful cheese scones you've ever tasted. Guests staying in the cosy B&B rooms upstairs (£140) get to sample its baking all week; nonguests are welcome Thursday to Saturday only.

ℹ Information

Tourist Office (☑ 01386-841206; www.campdenonline.org; Old Police Station, High St; ☺9.30am-5pm mid-Mar–Oct, 9.30am-1pm Mon-Thu, to 4pm Fri-Sun Nov–mid-Mar) Pick up a town guide (£1.50) for a self-guided walk around Chipping Campden's most significant buildings. Between May and September, the Cotswold Voluntary Wardens run guided tours (suggested donation £3).

ℹ Getting There & Away

From Monday to Saturday, Johnsons Excelbus services head to/from Moreton-in-Marsh (50 minutes), Broadway (20 minutes) and Stratford-upon-Avon (50 minutes). See www.traveline.info for the latest fares and timetables.

Broadway
☑ 01386 / POP 2540

The graceful, golden-hued cottages of the quintessentially English village of Broadway, set at the foot of a steep escarpment, now hold antique shops, tearooms and art galleries, interspersed with luxurious hotels. One of the Cotswolds' most popular destinations, just 5 miles west of Chipping Campden, the village attracted the likes of writer-designer William Morris and artist John Singer Sargent during the Victorian era.

The village of Snowshill, 2.5 miles south, may look familiar; a local house starred in the hit film *Bridget Jones's Diary* as Bridget's parents' home.

◎ Sights

Snowshill Manor & Garden   HOUSE
(NT; www.nationaltrust.org.uk; Snowshill; adult/child £8/4; ☺noon-5pm daily mid-Mar–Oct, 11am-

2.30pm Sat & Sun Nov, closed Dec–mid-March) Once home to eccentric poet and architect Charles Paget Wade (1883–1956), this wonderful medieval mansion stands just over 2 miles south of Broadway. It now displays Wade's extraordinary collection of crafts and design, ranging from musical instruments to Southeast Asian masks and Japanese samurai armour.

Broadway Tower   TOWER

(📞01386-852390; www.broadwaytower.co.uk; Middle Hill; adult/child £8/4, with separate Nuclear Bunker tours; 🕙10am-5pm; 🅿) Built in 1798 to resemble an imaginary Saxon fort, this turreted Gothic folly looks down on Broadway from atop the escarpment, 1 mile southeast. William Morris spent a summer here, so exhibitions on its successive levels focus on the Arts and Crafts movement. The main reason to visit, though, is for the stunning all-round views from its rooftop platform.

Broadway Museum & Art Gallery   MUSEUM

(📞01386-859047; www.ashmoleanbroadway.org; Tudor House, 65 High St; adult/child £5/2; 🕙10am-5pm Tue-Sun Feb-Oct, to 4pm Tue-Sun Nov & Dec, closed Jan) Set in a magnificent 17th-century coaching inn, Broadway's town museum has close links with Oxford's prestigious Ashmolean Museum. Its fascinating displays of local crafts, art and antiques, and its stimulating temporary exhibitions draw exclusively on the Ashmolean collection, so the quality is consistently high. Paintings in the sumptuous upstairs galleries include 18th-century works by Joshua Reynolds and Thomas Gainsborough.

🛏️ Sleeping & Eating

Olive Branch   B&B ££

(📞01386-853440; www.theolivebranch-broadway.com; 78 High St; s/d from £95/120; 📶) At the quiet upper end of the high street, this snug B&B offers eight homey rooms cheerfully done up in pinks, creams and whites. Number 4 has its own four-poster bed, while the two top-floor rooms accommodate families. All hold umbrellas, tea and coffee, and walking information. The hospitable owners prepare good home-cooked breakfasts.

Foxhill Manor   DESIGN HOTEL £££

(📞01386-898164; www.foxhillmanor.com; Farncombe Estate; r incl breakfast from £439; 🅿🤶🍽️) Occupying a 1904 Arts and Crafts mansion on a sprawling hillside estate, 2.5 miles northeast of Broadway, this ultra-luxurious hideaway epitomises Cotswolds chic. From dazzlingly bold decor – rich oranges, grey metro tiles, twin window-facing baths – to period stucco-work, each of its five sleek rooms and three suites has an individual flair. An in-house chef prepares whatever you fancy eating.

Russell's   HOTEL £££

(📞01386-853555; www.russellsofbroadway.co.uk; The Green, 20 High St; r incl breakfast from £130; 🕙restaurant noon-2.15pm & 6-9.15pm Mon-Sat, noon-2.30pm Sun; 🅿🤶🍽️) Housed in the former workshop of furniture designer Gordon Russell, this Arts and Crafts–influenced hotel offers seven sizeable rooms, some with exposed beams, four-poster beds and armchairs, and all with contemporary bathrooms and fresh white styling. Choose from the á la carte or two-/three-course set menu (£30/£35) in the restaurant.

⭐ Mount Inn   PUB FOOD ££

(📞01386-584316; www.themountinn.co.uk; Stanton; mains £13-22; 🕙noon-2pm & 6-9pm Mon-Sat, to 8pm Sun; 🅿) Revelling in glorious hilltop views above pretty honey-washed Stanton, just off the Cotswolds Way 3.5 miles southwest of Broadway, this pub is not just idyllically located, it serves great food too: hearty country favourites, prepared with contemporary flair. Menus range over breaded local St Eadburgha cheese, beer-battered haddock, gammon steaks, mushroom-halloumi burgers and seasonal specials.

ℹ️ Getting There & Away

BUS

Marchants and Johnsons ExcelBus services head to Cheltenham (40 minutes), Chipping Campden (20 minutes), Moreton-in-Marsh (30 minutes), Stratford-upon-Avon (45 minutes) and Winchcombe (30 minutes). See www.traveline. info for the latest fares and timetables.

TRAIN

A limited rail service returned to Broadway in 2018 after a 58-year hiatus, with the reopening of the long-defunct Broadway Station. Most days in summer, following an intricate schedule, the volunteer-run Gloucestershire Warwickshire Railway (p206) runs excursion trains between Cheltenham racecourse and Broadway, via Winchcombe, for a return fare from £18.

OXFORD & THE COTSWOLDS BROADWAY

WORTH A TRIP

HIGHGROVE

The private residence of Prince Charles and the Duchess of Cornwall, a mile southwest of Tetbury, **Highgrove** (☑0303-123 7310; www.highgrovegardens.com; Doughton; tours £27.50; ☺Apr-Sep; P) is famous for its exquisite, sustainable, organic gardens, which include rows of shape-clipped yews and a 'carpet garden' modelled on an oriental rug. Two-hour garden tours run on select summer days, detailed on the website and varying from 17 days in a month to just one. They usually sell out far in advance, but last-minute tickets are sometimes available through **Highgrove Shop** (☑01666-505666; www.highgroveshop.com; 10 Long St; ☺9.30am-5pm Mon-Sat, 10.30am-4.30pm Sun).

Moreton-in-Marsh

☑ 01608 / POP 3820

Graced by an ultrabroad High St that follows the die-straight line of the Roman Fosse Way (now the A429) and is lined with beautiful 17th- and 18th-century buildings, Moreton-in-Marsh is a historic Cotswolds town that's sadly rather marred by the constant heavy traffic that hurtles right through the centre. Take the time to wander around, though – ideally on a Tuesday, when the weekly market bursts into life – and you'll find plenty of tearooms, cafes and pubs, along with intriguing shops. It's 4.5 miles north of Stow-on-the-Wold.

⊙ Sights

★**Cotswold Falconry Centre** BIRD SANCTUARY
(☑01386-701043; www.cotswold-falconry.co.uk; Batsford Park; adult/child £12/6; ☺10.30am-5pm mid-Feb–mid-Nov; P) Home to over 150 birds of prey (owl, vulture, eagle and, of course, falcon), this exciting spot stages displays of the ancient practice of falconry at 11.30am, 1.30pm and 3pm daily (plus 4.30pm April to October). The birds fly best on windy days. Hands-on experiences (from £40) include a one-hour 'Flying Start' during which visitors get to fly hawks.

Chastleton House HISTORIC BUILDING
(NT; ☑01608-674355; www.nationaltrust.org.uk; Chastleton; adult/child £10.50/6; ☺1-5pm Wed-Sun Mar-Oct; P) Four miles southeast of

Moreton-in-Marsh, signposted off the A44 halfway to Chipping Norton, Chastleton is one of England's finest and most complete Jacobean houses. Built between 1607 and 1612 and barely altered since, it's bursting with rare tapestries, family portraits and antique furniture; the Long Gallery is particularly resplendent. Outside, there's a wonderful topiary garden. Free garden tours run most afternoons.

🛏 Sleeping & Eating

White Hart Royal Hotel HOTEL ££
(☑01608-650731; www.whitehartroyal.co.uk; High St; s/d £100/110; P🐾) 'Royal' refers to the fact that Charles I stayed in this low-slung honey-coloured inn during the Civil War. He may not have used the iPod docks and flat-screen TVs, but he certainly walked down the atmospheric half-timbered corridors. Standard rooms these days are comfy and well-equipped, even if they lack character.

Martha's Coffee House CAFE £
(☑01608-651999; Gavel Cottage, High St; mains £7-9; ☺9am-5pm Mon-Sat, to 4pm Sun; 🐾🍴) In an appealing historic cottage on the main road, Martha's is a local mainstay, dependable from the moment it serves the first of its all-day pancake-and-eggs breakfasts to the last of its £7.50-per-person cream teas. Lunchtime sees good-value sandwiches and toasties, but the real highlights are the £4.50 savoury scones, featuring flavours like beetroot and basil.

Horse & Groom PUB FOOD ££
(☑01386-700413; www.horseandgroom.info; A44, Bourton-on-the-Hill; mains £12-23; ☺noon-3pm & 6.30-9.30pm Mon-Sat, to 8.30pm Sun; P🐾) 🍴 This laid-back but welcoming pub, in a tiny hamlet 2 miles west of Moreton-in-Marsh, is a firm favourite with well-heeled horsey types who appreciate its extravagant array of gins. As well as serving good food, with a menu that showcases local lamb, beef and fresh produce in general, it also has five swish rooms upstairs (£130 to £170).

ⓘ Getting There & Away

BUS

Pulhams, Stagecoach and/or Johnsons Excelbus buses head to/from Broadway (30 minutes), Cheltenham (1½ hours), Chipping Campden (50 minutes), Northleach (40 minutes) and Stow-on-the-Wold (10 minutes). See www.traveline.info for the latest fares and timetables.

TRAIN

The station is towards the northern end of town, just off High St. Trains head to/from Hereford (£20, 1¾ hours), Ledbury (£18, 1½ hours), London Paddington (£18, 1½ hours), Oxford (£12, 35 minutes) and Worcester (£14, 40 minutes). See www.thetrainline.com for the latest fares and timetables.

Winchcombe

☏ 01242 / POP 5020

Winchcombe, 8 miles northeast of Cheltenham, is very much a living, working town, where butchers, bakers and independent shops line the main streets. Capital of the Anglo-Saxon kingdom of Mercia, it remained a major trading town until the Middle Ages, and was a centre for (illegally) growing tobacco in the 17th century. Reminders of that illustrious past can still be seen in Winchcombe's dramatic stone and half-timbered buildings. Keep an eye out for the picturesque cottages on Vineyard St and Dents Tce. As Winchcombe is on the Cotswold Way and other trails, it's especially popular with walkers.

⊙ Sights

Sudeley Castle   CASTLE
(☏ 01242-604244;   www.sudeleycastle.co.uk; adult/child £12/5; ⊙ 10.45am-5pm mid-Mar–Oct; P♿) During its thousand-year history, this magnificent castle has welcomed many a monarch, including Richard III, Henry VIII and Charles I. Half a mile southeast of Winchcombe, it's most famous as the home and final resting place of Catherine Parr (Henry VIII's widow), who lived here with her fourth husband, Thomas Seymour. In fact it's the only private house in England where a queen is buried – Catherine lies in its Perpendicular Gothic St Mary's Church. It also boasts 10 splendid gardens.

Belas Knap Long Barrow   ARCHAEOLOGICAL SITE
(EH; www.english-heritage.org.uk; near Charlton Abbots; ⊙ dawn-dusk) FREE Dating from around 3000 BC, Belas Knap is one of the country's best-preserved neolithic burial chambers, complete with 'false' portal leading nowhere. The remains of 31 people were found when its four chambers were excavated. At 290m, views across Sudeley Castle and the surrounding countryside are breathtaking. The barrow can be accessed from Winchcombe by a 2½-mile hike south along the Cotswold Way. Alternatively, park on Corndean Lane and take a steep half-mile walk up across fields.

Hailes Abbey   RUINS
(EH; www.english-heritage.org.uk; Hailes; adult/child £6.90/4.10; ⊙ 10am-6pm Jul & Aug, to 5pm Easter-Jun, Sep & Oct; P) Now lying in ruins 3 miles northeast of Winchcombe, this 13th-century Cistercian abbey was once, thanks to a long-running medieval scam, one of England's main pilgrimage centres. The abbey was said – by Geoffrey Chaucer in *The Canterbury Tales*, among others – to possess a vial of Christ's blood. Until that was denounced during the Reformation as containing no more than coloured water, thousands of pilgrims contributed to the abbey's wealth. At the time of writing, the abbey was only open Friday to Sunday.

🍴 Sleeping & Eating

Wesley House   B&B ££
(☏ 01242-602366; www.wesleyhouse.co.uk; High St; s £75-85, d £95-110; ⊙ restaurant noon-2pm & 7-9pm Tue-Sat, noon-2pm Sun; 🛜🐾) Methodist founder John Wesley once stayed in this ravishing 15th-century half-timbered town house, which offers five pleasant rooms plus a warm welcome. 'Mumble Meadow', splashed with reds, overlooks the street, while 'Almsbury' has its own terrace gazing out across the countryside. Rates rise on Saturdays. Downstairs, the restaurant serves fabulous modern-British cuisine.

★5 North St   MODERN EUROPEAN £££
(☏ 01242-604566; www.5northstreetrestaurant. co.uk; 5 North St; 2-/3-course lunch £26/32, 3-/7-course dinner £54/74; ⊙ 12.30-1.30pm Tue-Sun & 7-9pm Wed-Sat; 🍴) This veteran gourmet restaurant is a treat from start to finish, from its splendid 400-year-old timbered exterior to the elegant, inventive creations you eventually find on your plate. Marcus Ashenford's cooking is rooted in traditional seasonal ingredients, but the odd playful experiment (think duck-egg pasta or malt ice cream) adds that extra magic. Vegetarians can enjoy a separate £45 menu.

ℹ Information

Tourist Office (☏ 01242-602925; www.winchcombe.co.uk; Town Hall, High St; ⊙ 10am-4pm daily Apr-Oct, to 3pm Sat & Sun Nov-Mar) Has maps of local walks and runs free guided town tours at 11am and 2.30pm on Sunday, from Easter to October.

ℹ Getting There & Away

BUS

Marchants buses travel to/from Broadway (30 minutes) and Cheltenham (20 minutes). See www.traveline.info for the latest fares and timetables.

TRAIN

Several days each week in summer, to a convoluted schedule, the **Gloucestershire Warwickshire Railway** (GWR; ☑ 01242-621405; www.gwsr.com; day pass adult/child £18/8; ☺ Mar-Dec; ♿) runs around five trains that stop at Winchcombe en route between Cheltenham (£5, 25 minutes) and Broadway (£9, 20 minutes).

Painswick

☑ 01452 / POP 1740

Among the Cotswolds' most beautiful and unspoiled villages, hilltop Painswick sits 10 miles southwest of Cheltenham. Cars stream through, along its single-lane main road, but other than walkers on the Cotswold Way, few visitors allow themselves the pleasure of wandering its narrow winding streets to admire picture-perfect cottages, handsome stone houses and medieval inns. Keep an eye out for Bisley St, the original main drag, which was superseded by the now ancient-looking New St in medieval times.

Bucolic little Slad, 2 miles south towards Stroud in the Slad Valley, was the much-loved home of writer Laurie Lee (1914–97), who immortalised its beauty in *Cider with Rosie*.

◉ Sights

Painswick Rococo Garden   GARDENS
(☑ 01452-813204; www.rococogarden.org.uk; off B4073; adult/child £10/4.90; ☺ 10.30am-5pm mid-Jan–Oct; ℗♿) England's only surviving rococo garden, half a mile north of Painswick, was laid out by Benjamin Hyett in the 1740s as a vast 'outdoor room'. Restored to its original glory thanks to a contemporary painting, it's absolutely stunning. Winding paths soften its geometrical precision, leading visitors to scattered Gothic follies that include the eccentric Red House, which has Latin quotes from the Song of Solomon etched into its stained-glass windows. There's also a children's nature trail and maze.

St Mary's Church   CHURCH
(www.beaconbenefice.org.uk/painswick; New St; ☺ 9.30am-dusk) Painswick centres on this fine 14th-century, Perpendicular Gothic wool church, surrounded by 18th-century tabletop tombs and clipped yew trees sculpted to resemble giant ice lollies. Legend has it that only 99 trees could ever grow here, as the devil would shrivel the 100th. To celebrate the millennium, they planted one anyway, and – lo and behold! – another one toppled. At the foot of the churchyard there's a rare set of iron stocks.

🛏 Sleeping & Eating

Troy House   B&B ££
(☑ 01452-812339; www.troyguesthouse.co.uk; Gloucester St; d/tr £85/115; ☎) This great little B&B sleeps guests in four sweet, spacious rooms, two of which occupy a separate rear cottage accessed across an attractive courtyard. They're prettily decked out with soothing cream decor, comfy beds and baskets of toiletries, and the freshly cooked breakfasts are excellent.

★ Painswick   LUXURY HOTEL £££
(☑ 01452-813688; www.thepainswick.co.uk; Kemps Lane; r/ste from £201/404; ☺ restaurant noon-2.30pm & 7-10pm; ℗☎) Focused on an imposing 18th-century house somehow squeezed into the heart of the village, and seriously chic within its stern stone walls, the Painswick offers 16 luxurious, individually decorated, pastel-painted rooms, some with four-poster beds, that spread through assorted outbuildings. As well as massage/treatment rooms, there's a futuristic bar, a colour-popping lounge and a good modern restaurant (mains £21 to £28).

Woolpack Inn   PUB FOOD ££
(☑ 01452-813429; www.thewoolpackslad.com; Slad; mains £19; ☺ noon-11pm Sun & Mon, to midnight Tue-Thu, to 1am Fri & Sat, food served 6-9pm Mon, noon-3pm & 6-9pm Tue-Sat, noon-4pm Sun; ☺) This lively little rural pub in Slad, 2 miles south of Painswick, was a favourite watering hole of local author Laurie Lee, whose portrait and books adorn its walls. Perfect for a pint, stocking excellent local beers including Uley Bitter, it also serves a daily-changing menu of classics such as gammon or fish and chips alongside pasta, burgers and curries.

ℹ Information

Tourist Office (☑ 01452-812278; www.painswicktouristinfo.co.uk; Gravedigger's Hut, St Mary's Church, New St; ☺ 10am-4pm Mon-Fri, to 1pm Sat Mar-Oct) Beside the main road, but accessed from within the church grounds.

ℹ️ Getting There & Away

Stagecoach bus 66 heads to/from Cheltenham (40 minutes) and Stroud (10 minutes). See www.traveline.info for the latest fares and timetables.

WESTERN GLOUCESTERSHIRE

West of the Cotswolds, Gloucestershire's greatest asset is the elegant Regency town of Cheltenham, home to tree-lined terraces, upmarket boutiques and a tempting assortment of hotels and restaurants. The county capital, Gloucester, is also worth visiting, to see its magnificent Perpendicular Gothic cathedral, while Berkeley, not far southwest, has a historic Norman castle. Further west, the Forest of Dean is a leafy backwater that's perfect for walking, cycling, kayaking and other adventurous activities.

Cheltenham

📞 01242 / POP 117,500

Cheltenham, on the western edge of the Cotswolds, owes its air of gracious refinement to its heyday as a spa resort during the 18th century. At that time, it rivalled Bath as *the* place for ailing aristocrats to recuperate, and it still boast many graceful Regency buildings and manicured squares. These days, however, it's better known for its racecourse, where the upper classes still arrive in droves for the mid-March Cheltenham Cup.

Cheltenham's excellent hotel and restaurant offerings make it a much more appealing base than Gloucester (12 miles west), but in the end this mid-tier town is unlikely to be the highlight of your trip.

Central Cheltenham extends around the grand tree-lined Promenade, with the fashionable Montpellier neighbourhood at its southern end.

👁️ Sights

The Promenade   STREET
Famed as one of the most beautiful streets in England, this broad, tree-lined boulevard leads down from the high street to Montpellier, and is flanked by imposing period buildings that are now filled with fancy shops. The striking Municipal Offices, behind the flower-filled Long Gardens on its western side, were built in 1825 as private

residences. A statue in front commemorates Cheltenham-born explorer Edward Wilson (1872–1912), who perished on Captain Scott's ill-fated second expedition to the Antarctic.

Montpellier   AREA
As well as plenty of handsome architecture, the village-y Montpellier district hosts a lively assortment of bars, restaurants, hotels, independent shops and boutiques. Along Montpellier Walk, 32 caryatids (draped female figures based on those of Athens' Acropolis), each balancing an elaborately carved cornice on her head, function as structural supports between the 1840s edifices that now serve as shops. The attractive Montpellier Gardens, directly opposite, were laid out in 1809, and are the focus of major local festivals.

Pittville Pump Room   NOTABLE BUILDING
(📞0844-576 2210; www.pittvillepumproom.org.uk; Pittville Park; ♿) **FREE** The Pittville Pump Room is Cheltenham's finest Regency building. Modelled on an ancient Athenian temple, it was built in 1830 as the centrepiece of a large new residential area a quarter of a mile north of the town centre. Admire its beautiful columned exterior, then wander into the main auditorium, where, if the pump is operating, you can sample the pungent spa waters from the ornate fountain. The lovely surrounding ornamental park is home to a lake, lawns and an aviary.

WORTH A TRIP

BERKELEY CASTLE

A superb red-stone structure, Berkeley Castle (📞01453-810303; www.berkeley-castle.com; adult/child £14/7; ⏰11am-5pm Sun-Wed Apr-Oct; 🅿️♿) has been home to the Berkeleys for nearly 900 years, and little has changed since it was built as a sturdy Norman fortress. Edward II was imprisoned here in 1327 and swiftly died, probably murdered on the orders of his wife and her lover. Highlights include its central 12th-century keep, the King's Gallery, complete with Edward's cell and dungeon, and the spectacular medieval Great Hall, lined with tapestries. Free 45-minute guided tours run every 30 minutes.

OXFORD & THE COTSWOLDS CHELTENHAM

Cheltenham

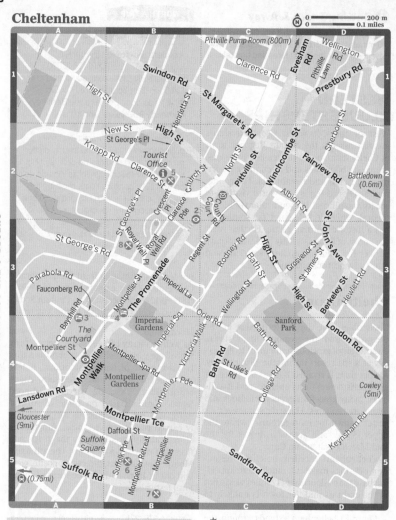

Cheltenham

◎ Sights

⌒ Sleeping

✕ Eating

✿ Festivals

Cheltenham
Literature Festival   LITERATURE
(☎01242-850270; www.cheltenhamfestivals.
com; ☉early Oct) One of the world's oldest
book-focused festivals kicks off over 10
days in autumn, hosting an astounding array of talks, workshops, interviews and debates by 600 top writers, actors, scholars
and other literary figures. Its headquarters is in Montpellier Gardens.

📖 Sleeping

⭐ Bradley   B&B ££

(📞 01242-519077; www.thebradleyhotel.co.uk; 19 Bayshill Rd; s/d from £115/120; 🅿🐾) This splendidly preserved Regency house in Montpellier has lost none of its original flair in its transition into a fabulous, wonderfully comfortable, luxury B&B. Each of the eight recently redecorated rooms has its own style, blending antique furniture, vintage trinkets and original artwork with modern amenities.

⭐ No 131   BOUTIQUE HOTEL £££

(📞 01242-822939; www.no131.com; 131 The Promenade; r incl breakfast from £199; 🅿) Set in a stunning Georgian town house, this exquisite luxury hotel holds 11 chic, supremely comfortable rooms that combine original artwork with antique touches such as 19th-century roll-top baths and contemporary comforts (Nespresso machines, iPod docks). Some have in-room baths, others step-down walk-in showers. Scented candles dot the corridors, the Crazy Eights bar buzzes (DJs Thursday to Saturday), and there's a luxe, laid-back vibe.

🍴 Eating

Boston Tea Party   CAFE £

(📞 01242-573935; www.bostonteaparty.co.uk; 45-49 Clarence St; mains £7.50-12; ⏱8am-5pm; 🅿🐾🎵) 🍴 A spacious, friendly, vintage-chic cafe chain, where relaxed decor – all blue faux-leather booths and rough wood tables, fresh flowers and colourful cans – makes the perfect setting for a contemporary British-international menu focused on ethically sourced ingredients. All-day breakfasts and brunches and tasty vegan and gluten-free choices keep it buzzing. Options include halloumi- or spiced-lamb-stuffed flatbreads, grain bowls and Vietnamese Banh-Mi sandwiches.

Tavern   GASTROPUB ££

(📞 01242-221212; www.thetaverncheltenham.com; 5 Royal Well Pl; mains £13-26; ⏱11.30am-10pm Mon-Fri, 10am-10pm Sat, to 5pm Sun; 🅿🎵) Behind its bare-bones exterior, this stylish gastropub serves Modern British food with a punch, amid exposed brick, bare wooden tables, blue-velvet booths and tile-covered floors. Classy mains – ricotta dumplings with chanterelle mushrooms, wild garlic and pine nuts; cod cheeks with Puy lentils and pancetta – plus steaks, and pub classics

from mac-cheese to burgers. The warm, welcoming service is spot on.

Daffodil   BRASSERIE ££

(📞 01242-700055; www.thedaffodil.com; 18-20 Suffolk Pde; mains £23-33; ⏱5-11pm Mon, Wed & Thu, noon-midnight Fri & Sat, noon-7pm Sun; 🅿🎵) This breathtaking brasserie conjures its retro setting, in a 1920s cinema, into fabulous art deco glamour, with a delightful daffodil theme from its tiled floor to the plaster cornices. Charcoal-grilled offerings range from halloumi or lobster to calves' liver and, especially, steaks, but it also has veggie options such as aubergine, coconut and lemongrass curry and open goat's-cheese ravioli.

⭐ Le Champignon Sauvage   FRENCH £££

(📞01242-573449; www.lechampignonsauvage. co.uk; 24-28 Suffolk Rd; set menus £33-90; ⏱12.30-1.30pm & 7.30-8.45pm Tue-Sat) For over 30 years, chef David Everitt-Matthias has been thrilling visitors and locals alike in this Michelin-starred Cheltenham favourite. Imaginative flavour combinations in his finely executed dishes include the likes of lamb loin with wild garlic pesto, sheep's curd and anchovy emulsion. We're not alone in thinking it's Gloucestershire's best restaurant. The set lunch and dinner menus are good value.

ℹ Information

Tourist Office (📞 01242-387492; www.visit-cheltenham.com; The Wilson, Clarence St; ⏱9.30am-5.15pm Mon-Wed, to 7.45pm Thu, to 5.30pm Fri & Sat, 10.30am-4pm Sun) A desk inside the Wilson Museum.

ℹ Getting There & Away

BUS

Stagecoach, Pulhams, Marchants and Swanbrook operate local buses from Cheltenham. Most buses depart from the bus station; some use stops along the Promenade.

Bus destinations include Broadway (40 minutes), Cirencester (40 minutes), Gloucester (45 minutes), Oxford (1½ hours), Stow-on-the-Wold (1¼ hours), Stratford-upon-Avon (1½ hours), Stroud (45 minutes) and Winchcombe (20 minutes). See www.traveline.info for the latest fares and timetables.

National Express coach destinations include Birmingham (£10, 1½ hours), Bristol (£9, 1½ hours), Leeds (£40, six hours), London Victoria (£23, three hours), Newcastle-upon-Tyne (£40, eight hours) and Nottingham (£28, 4¼ hours).

SLIMBRIDGE WETLAND CENTRE

A pioneer in wetlands conservation, **Slimbridge Wetland Centre** (WWT; ☑01453-891900; www.wwt.org.uk/slimbridge; Bowditch, Slimbridge; adult/child £14.50/8.40; ⊙9.30am-5.30pm Apr-Oct, to 5pm Nov-Mar; P), a 325-hectare reserve beside the River Severn 5 miles northeast of Berkeley, is a haven for migratory and resident birds. Hides are scattered throughout, and an observation tower affords spectacular 360-degree views for potential sightings of 200-plus feathered species, ranging from visiting swallows, peregrine falcons, white-fronted geese and Bewick's swans to hotpink resident flamingos. Migratory birds visit in winter, while spring brings plenty of chicks.

Activities include guided walks, otter talks, and self-guided 'canoe safaris' (£7).

TRAIN

Cheltenham Spa train station is a mile west of the centre. The pleasant 'Honeybourne Line' footpath leads through parkland to the heart of town in around 20 minutes, while buses (D/E; £2) run every 10 minutes. Train connections include:

Bath (£11.90, 1¼ hours)
Bristol (£9.10, 40 minutes)
Cardiff (£19.10, 1½ hours)
Edinburgh (£159.50, six hours)
Exeter (£31.30, 1¾ hours)
Gloucester (£4.80, 10 minutes)
London Paddington (£34.30, two hours)

Forest of Dean

POP 85,400

England's oldest oak forest is a wonderfully scenic place for outdoor adventures. Designated England's first National Forest Park in 1938, this 42-sq-mile woodland had previously been a royal hunting ground and a centre of iron and coal mining. Its mysterious depths supposedly inspired the forests of JRR Tolkien's Middle Earth, while key scenes in *Harry Potter & the Deathly Hallows* were filmed here.

There's no 'Dean' in the Forest of Dean – no one knows what it means – but it also gives its name to a Gloucestershire district that includes the towns of Newent and Coleford, north and west of the forest. To the northwest, the forest spills over into Herefordshire, while the River Wye skirts its western edge, offering glorious views to canoeists who paddle from the village of Symonds Yat.

The Dean Heritage Centre, outside Soudley within the forest's eastern fringe, is a good place to begin exploring.

◎ Sights & Activities

★ **International Centre for Birds of Prey**   BIRD SANCTUARY
(☑01531-820286; www.icbp.org; Boulsdon House, Newent; adult/child £12.50/7; ⊙10.30am-5.30pm Feb-Nov; P) Watch raptors swoop and dive at this large, long-standing countryside complex, 2 miles southwest of Newent (follow signs). There are three flyings per day (11.30am, 2pm and 4.15pm in summer; 11.30am, 1.30pm and 3.30pm in winter), along with aviaries housing 70 species of owls, falcons, kestrels, eagles, buzzards, hawks, kites and other birds of prey from all over the world. For the hands-on feel, choose from various 'experience days', devoted to specific birds (from £70).

Symonds Yat   VILLAGE
On the northwest edge of the Forest of Dean, squeezed between the River Wye and the towering limestone outcrop known as **Symonds Yat Rock** (Symonds Yat East; ⊙24hr; P), Symonds Yat is a tiny, endearing tangle of pubs, guesthouses and campsites, with great walks and a couple of canoeing centres. The river splits it into two halves, one in Gloucestershire and one in Herefordshire. They're connected by an ancient hand-hauled ferry (adult/child/bicycle £1.20/60p/60p; dawn to dusk).

Puzzlewood   FOREST
(☑01594-833187; www.puzzlewood.net; Perrygrove Rd, Coleford; adult/child £7/6; ⊙10am-5pm Apr-Oct, to 3.30pm Wed, Sat & Sun mid-Feb–Mar, Nov & Dec; P⊞) A pre-Roman open-cast iron mine, overgrown with eerie moss-covered trees, Puzzlewood is a 6-hectare woodland web of paths, weird rock formations, tangled vines, rickety bridges, uneven steps and dark passageways, all seemingly designed to disorientate. Parts of hit TV shows *Doctor Who* and *Merlin*, as well as *Star Wars The Force Awakens*, were shot here. There's a mile of pathways to explore and kids will love the farm animals.

Clearwell Caves   CAVE
(📞01594-832535;   www.clearwellcaves.com;
Clearwell; adult/child £8/6.50; ⊙10am-5pm Apr-
Aug, to 4pm mid-Feb–Mar & Sep-Dec; 🅿🚻) Descend into the damp subterranean world
of a 4500-year-old iron and ochre mine,
comprising a warren of dimly lit passageways, caverns and pools, and home to several species of bats. 'Deep Level Caving'
sessions (adult/child £25/18) take you even
further in. From November, the caves are
transformed into a hugely popular Christmas grotto.

Dean Forest Railway   RAIL
(📞01594-845840; www.deanforestrailway.co.uk;
Forest Rd, Lydney; day ticket adult/child £14/6;
⊙Wed, Sat & Sun mid-Mar–Oct; 🚻) Three days
a week for most of the year, classic steam
engines ply this 4.5-mile line between
Lydney and Parkend. Occasionally, though,
it operates diesel trains instead (check
online).

The standard ride is 30 minutes, but
special events range from Sunday lunch in
1st-class carriages to 'drive your own steam
engine' experiences. Thomas the Tank Engine makes the occasional appearance. Book
ahead.

**Wyedean Canoe
& Adventure Centre**   ADVENTURE SPORTS
(📞01600-890238;   www.wyedean.co.uk;
Symonds Yat East; half-day hire from £30) Hires
out canoes and kayaks, and organises
white-water trips, archery, high ropes, abseiling, caving, rock climbing and stand-up
paddle-boarding (SUP). Hours depend on
conditions.

> **DON'T MISS**
>
> ## GLOUCESTER CATHEDRAL
>
> Gloucester's spectacular **cathedral** (📞01452-528095; www.gloucestercathedral.org.uk; 12
> College Green; ⊙10am-5pm) is among the first and finest examples of the English Perpen-
> dicular Gothic style. Benedictine monks built a Norman church here in the 12th century,
> on the site of a Saxon abbey. After Edward II died mysteriously at nearby Berkeley Castle
> (p207) in 1327, he was buried here, and his tomb became a place of pilgrimage. Further
> elements, including the present-day tower, were added to the church during the 15th
> century.
>
> Inside, the finest features of Norman Romanesque and Gothic design are skilfully
> combined, with stout columns creating a sense of gracious solidity. The **Cloister**, which
> featured in the first, second and sixth Harry Potter films, is a real highlight. Completed
> in 1367, this airy space contains the earliest example of fan vaulting in England and is
> matched in beauty only by Henry VII's chapel at Westminster Abbey. When the sun
> shines through, the light-dappled Cotswold stone glows with a rosy light.
>
> From the breathtaking 14th-century wooden choir stalls, you'll get a good view of the
> imposing 22m-high **Great East Window**. The size of a tennis court, it was the largest in
> Europe when it was installed in the 1350s, and around 85% of the glass you see today is
> still original.
>
> Edward II's elaborate alabaster tomb, originally gilded and bejewelled, stands beneath
> the window in the northern ambulatory. Behind the altar, the glorious 15th-century **Lady
> Chapel** was largely destroyed during the Reformation, but following restoration work,
> completed in 2018, it's looking wonderful once more. In addition to its soaring vaulted
> roof and astonishingly delicate stone arches, its Arts and Crafts stained-glass windows
> rank among the cathedral's greatest treasures, featuring Adam and Eve, scenes from the
> life of Mary, and various English saints.
>
> Alongside the crypt, **St Andrew's Chapel** is emblazoned from floor to ceiling with
> colourful 19th-century frescoes that hint at how vibrant and dazzling the medieval Abbey
> must have been.
>
> **Tours** (from £3) give access to otherwise inaccessible areas including the 15th-
> century library and its illuminated manuscripts (weekly, 30 minutes); the 69m tower,
> with its amazing views (three weekly, one hour); and the Norman crypt (daily, 30 min-
> utes). Unexpected treasures in the five simple chapels in the crypt, the oldest part of
> the cathedral, range from a pillar carving of a mysterious moustachioed figure to a hefty
> granite font built by George Gilbert Scott in 1878.

OXFORD & THE COTSWOLDS FOREST OF DEAN

🛏 Sleeping

Garth Cottage
B&B ££

(📞 01600-890364; www.symondsyatbandb.co.uk; Symonds Yat East; per person £42.50; ⊘ mid-Mar–Oct; 🅿🛜) An exceedingly friendly and efficiently run family-owned B&B, right by the River Wye and alongside the ferry crossing. Comfy, chintzy, spotlessly maintained rooms have floral fabrics, tea and coffee kits, and gorgeous river views. Home-cooked breakfasts are excellent. Rates drop for longer stays.

Saracens Head Inn
INN ££

(📞 01600-890435; www.saracensheadinn.co.uk; Symonds Yat East; r incl breakfast from £129; 🅿🛜) Honey-toned woods, fresh cream decor and understated modern style make this revamped 16th-century riverside inn, overlooking Symond Yat's ferry crossing, a wonderful choice. Eight of its 10 bright, comfortable rooms have river views; the spacious lounge-equipped Upper Boathouse room is especially popular. The downstairs pub-restaurant is excellent.

★ Tudor Farmhouse
BOUTIQUE HOTEL £££

(📞 01594-833046; www.tudorfarmhousehotel. co.uk; High St, Clearwell; r incl breakfast from £189; 🅿🛜) Sleep in a chic, contemporary world of whites, creams and spiralling Tudor-era staircases, inside a beautifully updated farmhouse. Stylish rooms, most with exposed beams, check-print blankets and Nespresso machines, are scattered through the

---

WORTH A TRIP

THE ROALD DAHL STORY

Housed in an old coaching inn, in the village where children's and short story writer Roald Dahl lived until his death in 1990, this delightful small **museum** (www.roalddahl.com/museum; 81 High St, Great Missenden; adult/child £7.40/4.90; ⊘ 10am-4pm Thu-Sun, plus school holidays; 👶) is perfectly pitched to children and adults. A guided tour introduces you to Roald Dahl's favourite characters, the writer's original backyard shed where he did much of his writing, and other behind-the-scenes insights into the man via interactive displays. It's a 45-minute train ride from London.

---

main house. The spacious 'Roost' suite, with its claw-foot bath, is particularly romantic. More rooms sit in adjacent buildings. There's also an exceptional Modern British restaurant.

ℹ Information

Dean Heritage Centre (📞 01594-822170; www.deanheritagecentre.com; Camp Mill, Soudley; adult/child £8/6; ⊘ 10am-5pm Apr-Oct, to 4pm Nov-Mar; 🅿👶) The Forest's heritage museum doubles as its main information office.

ℹ Getting There & Away

BUS

Stagecoach is the main bus operator in the region, while National Express coaches run to Newent from cities further afield. See www. traveline.info for the latest fares and timetables.

TRAIN

Trains from Gloucester serve Lydney (£8.20, 20 minutes), on the southern side of the forest.

BUCKINGHAMSHIRE, BEDFORDSHIRE & HERTFORDSHIRE

Now poised at the edge of London's commuter belt, these three green-clad counties once served as rural boltholes for the city's rich and titled, especially when the stench and grime of the industrial age was at its peak. The sweeping valleys and forested hills remain scattered with majestic stately homes and splendid gardens, many of which are open to the public.

The 324-sq-mile Chilterns Area of Outstanding Natural Beauty (AONB; www. visitchilterns.co.uk) extends southwest from Hitchin (Hertfordshire), through Bedfordshire and Buckinghamshire, and into Oxfordshire.

St Albans

📞 01727 / POP 151,000

As Verulamium, encircled by a 2-mile wall and 26 miles from Londinium (London), St Albans was the third-biggest city in Roman Britain. Its current name derives from Alban, a Christian Roman soldier who was beheaded here around AD 250, becoming

THE HOME OF HARRY POTTER

Whether you're a fair-weather fan or a full-on Potterhead, the magical **Warner Bros Studio Tour: The Making of Harry Potter** (☑ 0345 084 0900; www.wbstudiotour.co.uk; Studio Tour Dr, WD25; adult/child £47/38; ⊙ 8.30am-10pm, hours vary Oct-May; P ♿) is well worth the admittedly hefty admission price. All visitors have to book tickets online, in advance, for a specific time slot, and arrive 20 minutes beforehand; allow three hours or more to do the complex full justice. Visits begin with a short film, before you're ushered through giant doors, though we won't say to where – it's just the first of many 'wow' moments.

You can then explore the rest of the complex at your own pace. One large hangar contains the most familiar interior sets – Dumbledore's office, the Gryffindor common room, Hagrid's hut – while another holds Platform 9¾, complete with the Hogwarts Express. An outdoor section features the exterior of Privet Drive, the purple triple-decker Knight Bus, Sirius Black's motorbike and a shop selling snacks and (sickly sweet) butterbeer. Video screens along the way burst into life to discuss elements of the production.

Other highlights include the animatronic workshop (say 'Hi' to the Hippogriff) and a stroll down Diagon Alley. All your favourite Harry Potter creatures are on display, from an enormous Aragog to Dobby the House-Elf, as well as props such as Harry's Invisibility Cloak. The most magical treat is saved for last – a shimmering, gasp-inducing 1:24 scale model of Hogwarts, used for exterior shots.

Then comes the biggest challenge for true fans and parents: a quite extraordinary gift shop stocked with all your wizardry accessories, including uniforms for each of the Hogwarts houses and replicas of the individually designed wands used by pretty much any character you can think of.

The Studio Tour is 20 miles northwest of London, not far off the M1 and M25 motorways. By rail, catch a train from London Euston to Watford Junction (approximately £10, 20 minutes), then a shuttle bus or taxi for the last 15-minute hop to the studios. There's also a Golden Tours tickets-and-transfer bus package direct from London and Birmingham.

the first English martyr. Now a bustling and prosperous market town, just beyond London's northwestern fringes, it's home to a huge and historic cathedral, amid a host of crooked Tudor buildings and elegant Georgian town houses.

◉ Sights

★ **St Albans Cathedral** CATHEDRAL
(☑ 01727-890210; www.stalbanscathedral.org; off High St & Holywell Hill; ⊙ 8.30am-5.45pm, free tours 11.30am & 2.30pm Mon-Fri, 11.30am & 2pm Sat, 2.30pm Sun) FREE Vast out of all proportion to the modern town, St Albans' majestic cathedral was founded as a Benedictine monastery by King Offa of Mercia in AD 793, around a shrine to St Alban, martyred five centuries earlier. It's now a glorious mash-up of Norman Romanesque and Gothic architecture, with rounded arches built using bricks salvaged from Roman Verulamium, and the country's longest medieval nave, adorned with 13th-century murals. A stone

reredos screens off the restored tomb of St Alban.

Verulamium Museum MUSEUM
(☑ 01727-751810; www.stalbansmuseums.org.uk; St Michael's St; adult/child £5/2.50, combined ticket with Roman Theatre £6.50/3.50; ⊙ 10am-5.30pm Mon-Sat, 2-5.30pm Sun) Based in what looks outside like a suburban house, this modern and highly engaging museum celebrates everyday life in Roman Verulamium. Assorted galleries cover themes like death, crafts and trade, with exhibits including farming utensils, armour, coins and pottery. Best of all are the five superb mosaic floors discovered locally, including a beautiful shell-shaped mosaic from AD 130.

⊫ Sleeping & Eating

St Michael's Manor Hotel HOTEL £££
(☑ 01727-864444; www.stmichaelsmanor.com; Fishpool St; d incl breakfast £155-200; P ☎) In a lovely location, with its own lake, this 500-year-old manor offers 30 opulent rooms

hidden down hushed carpeted corridors. Those in the manor itself are unshowy but comfortable, with historic charm, while the eight more contemporary 'luxury garden' rooms, named for plants and trees, are sumptuously sleek, with rich colours and patterned wallpaper; two have four-poster beds.

Lussmanns Fish & Grill　MODERN BRITISH ££
(☏01727-851941; www.lussmanns.com; Waxhouse Gate, off High St; mains £14-28; ☺noon-9pm Sun-Tue, to 9.30pm Wed & Thu, to 10.30pm Fri & Sat; ☏) ✐ This bright, modern restaurant, steps from the cathedral, serves a changing, season-focused, ethically sourced menu of creative British dishes with Mediterranean touches, such as pomegranate-infused salad or chicken with pancetta. The set lunches (two/three courses £15.50/18.50) offer great value.

ⓘ Information

Tourist Office (☏01727-864511; www.enjoy stalbans.com; St Peter's St; ☺10am-4pm Mon-Sat) In the St Albans Museum and Gallery.

ⓘ Getting There & Away

Regular trains connect St Albans City, a mile east of the centre, with London King's Cross/

WORTH A TRIP

HATFIELD HOUSE

For over 400 years, **Hatfield House** (☏01707-287010; www.hatfield-house.co.uk; Hatfield; adult/child £9/4, house & gardens £19/9; ☺garden 10am-5pm Thu-Sun Apr-Sep, house currently closed) has been home to the Cecils, one of England's most influential political families. This magnificent Jacobean mansion was built between 1607 and 1611 for Robert Cecil, first earl of Salisbury and secretary of state to both Elizabeth I and James I. Elizabeth spent much of her childhood in the 'Old Palace' here, and the house, which is awash with tapestries, furnishings and armour, proudly displays the Rainbow Portrait, depicting her holding a rainbow. Hatfield train station has trains to London King's Cross/St Pancras (20 minutes). Tickets must be pre-purchased.

St Pancras (£12.20, 20 minutes) and London Blackfriars (£12.20, 30 minutes).

Stowe

Located 3 miles northwest of the market town of Buckingham, and 14 miles west of Milton Keynes, Stowe has had a manor since before the Norman conquest. While the house itself is now a private school, the extraordinary Georgian gardens that surround it remain intact, and are definitely worth visiting. The most spectacular approach is via the 1.5-mile-long tree-lined Stowe Ave.

★**Stowe Gardens**　GARDENS
(NT; ☏01280-817156; www.nationaltrust.org.uk; New Inn Farm; adult/child £10/5; ☺10am-5pm mid-Feb–Oct, to 4pm Nov–mid-Feb; ☏) The glorious Stowe Gardens were shaped in the 18th century by Britain's greatest landscape gardeners. Among them was master landscape architect Lancelot 'Capability' Brown, who kick-started his career here as head gardener from 1741 until 1751. The gardens are famous for the temples and follies commissioned by the super-wealthy Richard Temple (1st Viscount Cobham), whose family motto was *Templa Quam Dilecta* (How Delightful are Your Temples). Paths meander past lakes, bridges, fountains and cascades, and through Capability Brown's Grecian Valley.

ⓘ Getting There & Away

You'll need a car to get to Stowe House and Gardens, which are well signposted 3 miles northwest of Buckingham.

Woburn

☏01525 / POP 930
The peaceful village of Woburn has been nestling blissfully in the Bedfordshire countryside since the 10th century. One of its best draws, Woburn Abbey, is closed for renovations until 2022, but the Woburn Safari Park is a popular destination for families.

Woburn Safari Park　ZOO
(www.woburnsafari.co.uk; Woburn Park; adult/child £24/19; ☺10am-6pm, check online for dates) Sprawling across 150 hectares, the country's largest drive-through animal reserve can only

BLETCHLEY PARK

During WWII, the very existence of Bletchley Park ([☎] 01908-640404; www.bletchleypark.org.uk; Bletchley; adult/12-17yr £18.25/10.75; ⊙ 9.30am-5pm Mar-Oct, to 4pm Nov-Feb; [P]) was England's best-kept secret. By breaking German and Japanese codes, as dramatised in the 2014 film *The Imitation Game*, Bletchley's team of almost 8500 scientists and technicians made a huge contribution to winning the war itself. Up to 20,000 enemy messages were intercepted each day, then decrypted, translated and interpreted. Inside Hut 11A, you can see the Bombe machine itself, crucial to cracking the famous Enigma code; volunteers explain its inner workings.

Entry includes an optional hour-long guided tour of the grounds – dress warm – and a multimedia guide. Both provide a real insight into the complex, frustrating and ultimately rewarding code-breaking process. The machines built here, by pioneers including Alan Turing, are now regarded as major steps in development of programmable computers. In fact, Facebook made a substantial donation to the site during the Covid-19 economic slowdown as homage.

Regular trains connect Bletchley station, close to the park, with London Euston (£16, 40 minutes).

be visited in your own car (so long as it's not a convertible!). Animals such as rhinos, tigers, lions, elephants and giraffes – grouped into separate enclosures, for obvious reasons – will approach your car, or, if they're monkeys, climb on top of it. The 'foot safari' area holds sea lions, penguins, meerkats and wallabies.

★**Paris House**   MODERN BRITISH £££
([☎] 01525-290692; www.parishouse.co.uk; Woburn Park, London Rd; tasting menu £75; ⊙ noon-1.30pm & 6.45-8.30pm Thu-Sun) On the Woburn Estate, Paris House is a handsome, black-and-white, half-timbered structure to which the 9th duke of Bedford took a shine while visiting the French capital. He shipped it back here, and it now holds Bedfordshire's top fine-dining restaurant, serving an exquisite tasting menu of beautifully presented contemporary cuisine. Phone bookings only.

❶ Getting There & Away

Woburn is 8 miles southeast of Milton Keynes, 7 miles southeast of Bletchley Park, and 22 miles northwest of St Albans. Woburn itself does not have a train station so a car is a must.

THE THAMES VALLEY

The prosperous valley of the River Thames, west of London, has long served as a country getaway for the English elite, from royalty on down. Within easy reach of the capital,

but utterly different in character, its pastoral landscape is peppered with handsome villages and historic houses.

It's Windsor Castle, favoured residence of the Queen, that really draws the crowds here, but Ascot, with its royal race-meet in June, and Henley-on-Thames, with its rowing regatta a month later, both boast their days in the sun. Meanwhile, the riverside village Bray has a genuine claim to be the country's gastronomic capital.

Windsor & Eton

[☎] 01753 / POP 32,200

Facing each other across the Thames, with the massive bulk of Windsor Castle looming above, the twin riverside towns of Windsor and Eton have a rather surreal atmosphere. Windsor on the south bank sees the daily pomp and ritual of the changing of the guards, while schoolboys dressed in formal tailcoats wander the streets of tiny Eton to the north.

Thanks to its tourist trade, Windsor is filled with expensive boutiques, grand cafes and buzzing restaurants. Eton is far quieter, its single commercial street flanked by antique shops and art galleries. Both are easily accessible on a day trip from London.

Windsor & Eton

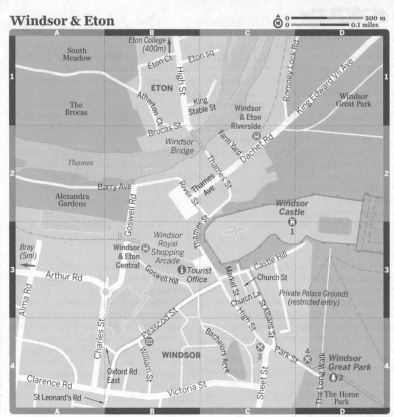

Windsor & Eton

◎ Top Sights
1 Windsor Castle	C3
2 Windsor Great Park	D4

✖ Eating
3 A la Russe	C4
4 Two Brewers	D4

◎ Sights

★ **Windsor Castle** CASTLE
(☎03031-237304; www.royalcollection.org.uk;
Castle Hill; adult/child £23.50/13.50; ☺10am-
5.15pm Mar-Oct, to 4.15pm Nov-Feb; ♿; ☒702
from London Victoria, ☒London Waterloo-Windsor
& Eton Riverside, ☒London Paddington-Windsor
& Eton Central via Slough) The world's largest
and oldest continuously occupied fortress,
Windsor Castle is a majestic vision of battlements and towers. Used for state occasions,

it's one of the Queen's principal residences –
when she's at home, the Royal Standard flies
from the Round Tower.

Frequent, free guided tours introduce visitors to the castle precincts, divided into the
Lower, Middle and Upper Wards. Free audio
tours guide everyone through its lavish State
Apartments and beautiful chapels; certain
areas may be off limits if in use.

★ **Windsor Great Park** PARK
(☎01753-860222; www.windsorgreatpark.co.uk;
Windsor; ☺dawn-dusk) FREE Windsor Great
Park stretches south from Windsor Castle almost all the way to Ascot, 7 miles southwest.
Accessed via Park St, it covers just under 8
sq miles and holds a lake, walking tracks,
woods, gardens and a deer park where red
deer roam free. Its 2.7-mile Long Walk leads
from King George IV Gate to the 1831 Copper Horse statue (of George III) on Snow

Hill, the park's highest point. Paid parking by card only.

Runnymede
HISTORIC SITE

(NT; 01784-432891; www.nationaltrust.org.uk; Windsor Rd, Old Windsor; ⊙site dawn-dusk, car park 8.30am-7pm Apr-Sep, to 5pm Feb, Mar, Oct & Nov, to 4pm Dec & Jan; P) FREE Over 800 years ago, in June 1215, King John met his barons in this unassuming field, 3 miles southeast of Windsor. Together they hammered out an agreement on a basic charter of rights that guaranteed the liberties of the king's subjects, and restricted the monarch's absolute power. The document they signed, the Magna Carta, was the world's first constitution. The field remains much as it was, plus a few modern memorials and two 1929 lodges, designed by Edwin Lutyens.

Eton College
NOTABLE BUILDING

(01753-370600; www.etoncollege.com; High St, Eton; adult/child £10/free; ⊙tours 2pm & 4pm Fri Apr-Aug) Eton College is England's most famous public – as in, private and fee-paying – boys' school, and arguably the most enduring symbol of the British class system. High-profile alumni include 20 British prime ministers, countless princes, kings and maharajas, Princes William and Harry, George Orwell, John Maynard Keynes, Bear Grylls and Eddie Redmayne. It can only be visited on guided tours, on summer Fridays, which take in the school yard, chapel and the Museum of Eton Life. To visit, book online.

Activities

Legoland Windsor
AMUSEMENT PARK

(www.legoland.co.uk; Winkfield Rd, Windsor; £47-60; ⊙10am-6pm Jul & Aug, reduced hours rest of year) The child-oriented Legoland theme park, 3 miles southwest of Windsor, is more about white-knuckle thrills than building Lego-brick castles, though its many rides, from submarines to roller coasters, do zoom past vast Lego-built models. Adults and children pay the same prices, while 'Q-Bots', enabling you to avoid long queues for popular rides, cost up to £80 extra per person.

Shuttle buses connect Legoland with Windsor's Theatre Royal (return adult/child £5/2.50, 20 minutes; www.courtneybuses. com), from around 9.30am until 30 minutes after park closure.

Eating

Two Brewers
PUB FOOD ££

(01753-855426; www.twobrewerswindsor. co.uk; 34 Park St, Windsor; mains £15-26; ⊙11.30am-10pm Mon-Sat, noon-10pm Sun) This atmospheric 18th-century inn, at the gateway to Windsor Great Park, serves tasty, well-prepped food ranging from soups, salads and fishcakes to steak, cod loin and cheeseboards.

Sunny benches front the flower-covered exterior; inside are low-beamed ceilings, dim lighting and a roaring winter fire.

A la Russe
FRENCH, MEDITERRANEAN ££

(01753-833009; www.alarusse.co.uk; 6 High St, Windsor; mains £13-23, 2-/3-course lunch menus £12.50/16.50; ⊙6-9.30pm Mon, noon-2.30pm & 6-9.30pm Tue-Sat) A fine array of set-price lunch and dinner menus and warm, friendly service make this Continental-style bistro excellent value. As well as French classics such as rabbit with mustard and chicken supreme, it also serves pasta dishes, chilli pork and assorted steaks. It's a quick walk down High St from the castle, towards the Great Park.

Information

Tourist Office (01753-743900; www. windsor.gov.uk; Old Booking Hall, Windsor Royal Shopping Arcade, Thames St, Windsor; ⊙10am-5pm Apr-Sep, to 4pm Oct-Mar) Tickets for attractions and events, plus guidebooks and walking maps.

ROYAL ASCOT

Don your finest duds and join the glitterati at Royal Ascot (08443-463000; www.ascot.co.uk; Ascot; Windsor Enclosure per day from £37, Queen Anne Enclosure per day from £75; ⊙mid-Jun), the biggest racing meet of the year, going strong since 1711. The royal family, A-list celebrities and other rich and famous folk gather for this five-day festival, 7 miles southwest of Windsor, to show off their Jimmy Choos and place the odd bet. It's essential to book tickets well in advance.

OXFORD & THE COTSWOLDS WINDSOR & ETON

ROCK AND MORE AT READING FESTIVAL

Each August Bank Holiday weekend since 1989 (well except in 2020 when it was cancelled due to Covid-19), around 80,000 revellers descend on the industrial town of Reading for the Reading Festival (☎02070-093001; www.readingfestival.com; tickets day/weekend £80/250; ☉ late Aug), one of the UK's biggest and most accessible music festivals. The three-day extravaganza draws headliners across genres, although rock dominates. One-day tickets are available as well as multi-day camping.

Reading has regular trains to/from London Paddington (£20.20, 25 minutes to one hour).

❶ Getting There & Away

BUS

Green Line buses (www.greenline.co.uk) connect Windsor and Eton with London Victoria (1½ hours) and Heathrow terminal 5 (40 minutes). Courtney Buses (www.courtneybuses.com) offers services between Windsor and Bray (30 minutes). See www.traveline.info for the latest fares and timetables.

TRAIN

The quickest rail route from London connects London Paddington with Windsor & Eton Central, opposite the castle, but you have to change at Slough (£10.50, 30 to 45 minutes). London Waterloo has slower but direct services to Windsor & Eton Riverside, on Dachet Rd (£10.50, 45 minutes to one hour).

Bray

☎ 01628 / POP 4650

This tiny village of flint, brick and half-timbered cottages, strung along the Thames between Windsor and Maidenhead, is also considered by many to be the gastronomic capital of Britain. Bray is home to two of the four UK restaurants to be awarded the highest possible rating of three stars by foodie bible, the Michelin guide. There's little more to do here than to dine fabulously, the river is tucked away behind the mansions.

Eating

⭐ Fat Duck   MODERN BRITISH £££

(☎01628-580333; www.thefatduck.co.uk; High St; degustation menu per person £250-325; ☉noon-1.15pm & 7-8.15pm Tue-Sat) Arguably Britain's most famous restaurant, the Fat Duck is the flagship property of Heston Blumenthal. A pioneer of 'molecular' cuisine, he transformed the place from a rundown pub into a three-starred restaurant that was once voted the world's best. Reserve your 'ticket' in advance and enjoy a journey-themed, seasonally changing set menu. Drinks and service are charged in addition to the dining price.

⭐ Waterside Inn   FRENCH £££

(☎01628-620691; www.waterside-inn.co.uk; Ferry Rd; mains £55-68, 2-/3-course lunch Wed-Fri £52/63.50; ☉noon-2pm & 7-10pm Wed-Sun, closed late Dec-end Jan) From the moment the uniformed valet greets you until the last tray of petit fours is served, this three-Michelin-starred riverfront restaurant is something special. For more than 40 years, chef Alain Roux has worked his magic, constructing exceptional dishes for a small army of staff to serve, in a room overlooking the Thames. It also has rooms (from £275).

Hind's Head   GASTROPUB £££

(☎01628-626151; www.hindsheadbray.com; High St; mains £20-40, 5-course tasting menu £62; ☉noon-2pm & 6-9pm Mon-Sat, noon-3.30pm Sun; ℗) Oozing atmosphere, this sumptuous 15th-century pub offers diners the chance to experience Heston Blumenthal's highly creative cuisine in a relatively affordable, and more informal setting. The dishes are less adventurous than you might expect, but still have plenty of whimsical touches.

❶ Getting There & Away

Bray is a short drive from Windsor but there are limited parking options in town. Courtney Buses (www.courtneybuses.com) offers a service between Windsor and Bray (30 minutes).

Henley-on-Thames

☎ 01491 / POP 11,494

The attractive commuter town of Henley, 15 miles northwest of Windsor, is synonymous with its annual rowing tournament, the Henley Royal Regatta (www.hrr.co.uk; tickets

£25-32, on-site parking £34; ⊘ early Jul). For the rest of the year, it remains a pretty riverside town that's a delight to stroll around, particularly along the Thames.

★ **River & Rowing Museum** MUSEUM
(☑ 01491-415600; www.rrm.co.uk; Mill Meadows; adult/child £12.50/10; ⊘ 10am-4pm Thu-Mon; P ♿) This excellent modern museum examines why Henley is so crazy for rowing. The airy 1st-floor galleries tell the story of rowing as an Olympic sport, with striking displays that include the early-19th-century Royal Oak, Britain's oldest racing boat. Downstairs, a sweet 3D exhibition pays homage to Kenneth Grahame's *The Wind in the Willows*. The romanticised river that book so lovingly depicts was inspired by the Thames around Henley.

ⓘ Getting There & Away

Trains run to/from London Paddington (£16.70, one hour), but you have to change at Slough and/or Twyford.

AT A GLANCE

★

POPULATION
1.1 million

BIGGEST CITY
Bristol: 428,234

BEST BUILDING
Royal Crescent
(p236)

BEST BRIDGE
Clifton Suspension
Bridge (p227)

BEST HARBOUR
Porlock Weir
(p252)

📅

WHEN TO GO
May & Jun Upfest
celebrates street
art in Bristol; music-
festival fever takes
hold at Glastonbury.

Sep Warm weather,
with seasonal at-
tractions still open.
Bath's accommoda-
tion prices begin to
descend from August
highs.

Oct Exmoor's deer
rut sees huge stags
battle for supremacy.

Clifton Suspension Bridge (p227), Bristol
JOANNE JEAN/SHUTTERSTOCK ©

Bristol, Bath & Somerset

H istoric city, edgy urban hub, jagged coasts and forgotten moors – this region is as richly rewarding as it is diverse. Bath delivers dazzling Georgian architecture; some of the gems in England's crown. In dynamic Bristol creative types hang out in cool cafes surrounded by famous street art. Nearby sit hippy haven Glastonbury, and Wells, a delightful, diminutive cathedral city. In beguiling Exmoor wild ponies roam, russet moors surge towards sheer cliffs, and red deer hide in densely wooded coombes. Add empty beaches, geothermal pools, snazzy spas, stately homes, rural backroads and plenty of rustic pubs and you're faced with the best kind of travelling dilemma: what to do first?

INCLUDES

Activities

Cycling

Routes here range from disused railway lines to rural lanes. The 14-mile Bristol and Bath Railway Path (www.bristolbathrail waypath.org.uk) is a flat, largely traffic-free trail that's dotted with public art.

Exmoor's rollercoaster roads see you powering up 500m at Dunkery, while the National Park's bridleways offer superb, challenging off-road mountain biking.

Sweeping from Bristol to the west of Cornwall, the National Cycle Network (NCN Route 3) is a 328-mile trail that takes in Wells, Glastonbury and the southern edge of Exmoor.

Sustrans (www.sustrans.org.uk) and local tourist offices can advise further.

Walking

Sometimes called the 630-mile adventure, the South West Coast Path (www.south westcoastpath.org.uk) stretches from Minehead in Somerset via Land's End to Poole in Dorset. You can pick it up along the coast for short and spectacular day hikes or tackle longer stretches.

Exmoor National Park offers a tempting blend of open moorland and 34 miles of precipitous cliffs, while the 51-mile Coleridge Way (www.coleridgeway.co.uk) cuts from Nether Stowey in the Quantock Hills to Lynmouth, in the footsteps of the eponymous Romantic poet.

Other Activities

Local firms offer guided caving, coasteering, and climbing sessions. In Bristol you can take kayaking and stand-up paddleboarding lessons in the central harbour (🕿 0117-422 5858; www.supbristol.com; Baltic Wharf, Cumberland Rd; 1½hr £25, 2½hr £40).

Climbers enjoy higher-grade sport and trad routes at limestone Cheddar Gorge (p245). The Avon Gorge also offers memorable climbs. Check with the BMC (www.thebmc.co.uk) for updates on local restrictions.

ⓘ Getting Around

BUS

Bus provision in Bristol and Bath is good; inevitably services become more patchy the further into the countryside you go. National Express (www.nationalexpress.com) can provide the quickest bus link between cities and larger towns.

PlusBus (www.plusbus.info) adds local bus travel to your train ticket (£2 to £4 per day). Participating cities include Bath and Bristol. Buy tickets at train stations.

First (www.firstgroup.com) runs buses in and around Bath, Bristol, Glastonbury and Wells. Smaller operators provide services around Exmoor National Park.

First offers subregional tickets, such as the Freedom Travelpass (one day/week £13.50/59). This gives unlimited bus and train travel in Bath, Bristol and northeast Somerset, although it doesn't cover Glastonbury, Wells or Exmoor. Day Rover and Ranger tickets are available for specific areas.

CAR & MOTORCYCLE

The main car-hire firms have offices at Bristol Airport, and in and around Bath and Bristol; rates reflect those elsewhere in the UK.

Bath and Bristol have efficient Park & Ride services, helping avoid traffic congestion and pricy parking. Having your own wheels gives you more freedom as you head into rural areas.

TRAIN

Bristol is a main train hub with links including those to Bath, London Paddington, Scotland and Birmingham, plus services to Exeter, Swindon, Weymouth and Portsmouth.

Key regional rail firms are GWR (www.gwr. com), CrossCountry (www.crosscountrytrains. co.uk) and South Western Railway (www.south westernrailway.com). For timetables and fares see National Rail (www.nationalrail.co.uk).

The Freedom of the South West Rover offers either three days' train travel in seven days (adult/child £106/53) or eight days' travel in 15 days (£148/74). Journeys are unlimited in an area west of, and including, Bath, Bristol, Salisbury, Portsmouth and Weymouth.

BRISTOL

🕿 0117 / POP 428,234

Bristol is a city that's on the rise. Derelict docks are becoming leisure venues, heritage attractions ooze imagination and a world-class street-art scene adds colour and spice.

History

Bristol began as a Saxon village and developed into the medieval river port of Brigstow, an important trading centre for cloth and wine. In 1497 'local hero' John Cabot (actually a Genoese sailor called Giovanni Caboto) sailed from Bristol to discover Newfoundland. By the 18th century Bristol's docks were the second largest in the country.

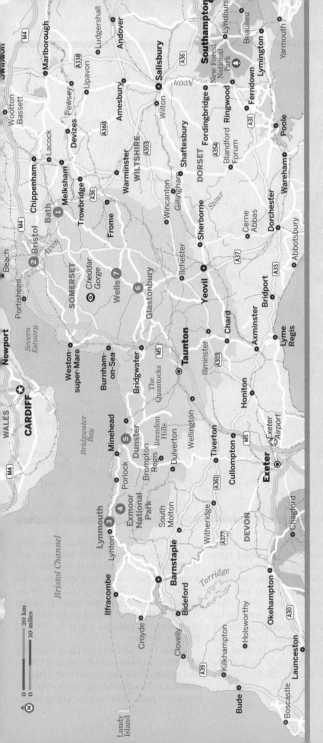

Bristol, Bath & Somerset Highlights

1 Bath (p233) Exploring atmospheric Roman baths then swimming in a stylish modern-day spa.

2 Bristol (p225) Striding around the deck of Brunel's groundbreaking steamship, the SS Great Britain.

3 Lynmouth (p253) Rattling up steep-sided cliffs in a water-powered, Victorian railway.

4 Exmoor National Park (p249) Watching out for red deer amid deep valleys and open moors.

5 Dunster (p252) Discovering a charismatic russet castle set high on a wooded hill.

6 Glastonbury (p246) Touching base with your inner hippy in the UK's counter-culture hub.

7 Wells (p244) Marvelling at exquisite architecture in a pocket-sized cathedral city.

Bristol

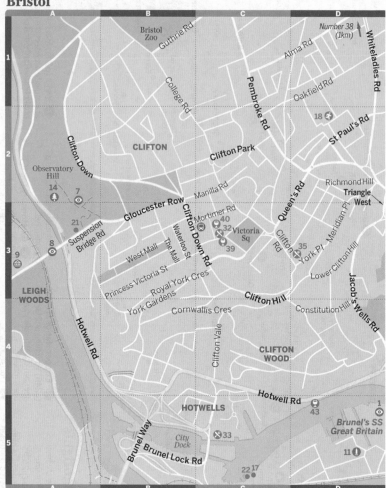

They enabled the city to play a major part in the so-called Triangular Slave Trade, in which Africans were enslaved, shipped to New World colonies and bartered for sugar, tobacco, cotton and rum. Bristol traders transported more than 500,000 enslaved people and much of the city's 18th-century splendour – including Clifton's grand terraces – were partly financed on the profits. The M Shed Museum (p226) takes an honest look at the story, referencing also the local campaigners who fought for abolition.

After being usurped by rival ports, Bristol repositioned itself as an industrial and shipbuilding centre, and in 1840 became the western terminus for the newly built Great Western Railway line from London. Its audacious chief engineer was Isambard Kingdom Brunel, whose Bristol legacy includes the Clifton Suspension Bridge (p227) and SS Great Britain.

Bristol's industrial importance made it a target for German bombing during WWII, and much of the city centre and harbourside was reduced to rubble. Fast-forward 40 years and parts of Bristol, including Stokes

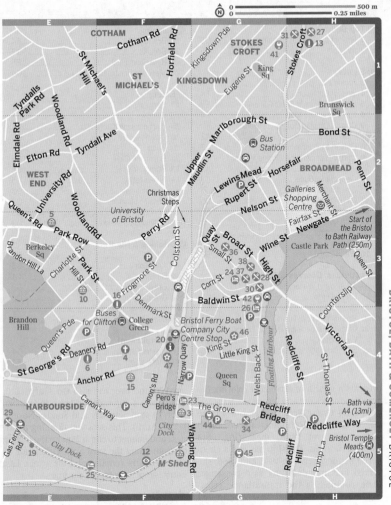

Croft, became known for a counterculture tradition, occasional neighbourhood riots and a burgeoning street-art scene. One of those leaving his creative mark on city walls was Banksy – an anonymous artist whose works sell for millions of pounds. The city is also home to Oscar-winning Aardman Animations, creators of *Wallace and Gromit*.

In July 2020, Bristol's historic links with slavery made the national headlines when, during the Black Lives Matter protests, a crowd toppled a statue of 17th-century slave-trader Edward Colston and threw it in the harbour.

◉ Sights

★ **Brunel's SS Great Britain**   HISTORIC SHIP
(☑ 0117-926 0680; www.ssgreatbritain.org; Great Western Dock, Gas Ferry Rd; adult/child/family £18/10/48; ⏰ 10am-6pm Apr-Oct, to 4.30pm Nov-Mar) This mighty, innovative steamship was designed by engineering genius Isambard Kingdom Brunel in 1843. You get to wander the galley, surgeon's quarters and dining saloon and see a massive replica steam engine at work. Highlights are going below the 'glass sea' on which the ship sits to view the screw propeller and climbing up the rigging in Go Aloft!. The **Being Brunel** exhibit

Bristol

presents a wealth of artefacts exploring the great engineer's life and legacy.

The SS *Great Britain* was one of the largest and most technologically advanced steamships ever built, measuring 98m from stern to tip. The ship has had a chequered history. Between 1843 and 1886, she served her intended duty as a passenger liner, completing the transatlantic crossing between Bristol and New York in just 14 days. Unfortunately, enormous running costs and mounting debts led her towards an ignominious fate: she was eventually sold off and subsequently served as a troop vessel, quarantine ship, emigration transport and coal hulk, before finally being scuttled near Port Stanley in the Falklands in the 1930s.

Happily, that wasn't the end. The ship was towed back to Bristol in 1970, and has since undergone an impressive 30-year restoration. It's resulted in a multisensory experience: prepare to stroll the deck, peep into luxury cabins, listen to passengers' stories and catch a whiff of life on board. Those

aged 10 and over can also Go Aloft! (£10; 11.30am to 4.30pm daily March to October, noon to 4pm Saturday and Sunday November to April). This sees you donning a harness and helmet to climb 25m up the rigging and out along the yard arm. Tickets for SS *Great Britain* remain valid for a year. Last entry is one hour before closing.

★ **M Shed**   MUSEUM
(☏0117-352 6600; www.bristolmuseums.org.uk; Princes Wharf; ◎10am-5pm Tue-Sun; ☏) **FREE** Set amid the iconic cranes of Bristol's dockside, this impressive museum is a treasure trove of memorabilia. It's divided into four main sections: People, Place, Life and the vast Working Exhibits outside. They provide an absorbing overview of Bristol's history – from slaves' possessions and *Wallace and Gromit* figurines to a Banksy artwork. There are regular guided walks and trips on the museum's boats, trains and cranes (free to £6); see the website for details.

It's all highly interactive and child-friendly, especially the rides on the steam and electric cranes (tickets £3), steam trains (single/return £2.50/3.50) and tug and fire boats (adult/child £6/4). Another highlight is Banksy's unsettling *Grim Reaper* stencil, which used to sit on the waterline of the nightclub boat *Thekla*. It was removed amid much controversy and can now be found on the 1st floor.

The museum's imaginatively themed guided tours help bring the city's past to life.

Clifton Suspension Bridge   BRIDGE
(📞0117-974 4664; www.cliftonbridge.org.uk; Suspension Bridge Rd) The 76m-high Clifton Suspension Bridge that spans the Avon Gorge was designed by master engineer Isambard Kingdom Brunel, with construction beginning in 1836. It's free to walk or cycle across; car drivers pay a £1 toll. The **visitor centre** (⊙10am-5pm; 📶) **FREE** at the bridge's western end is worth exploring.

The free **bridge tours** (⊙3pm Sat & Sun Easter-Oct) are excellent, as are the two-hour **Hard Hat Tours**, which go inside one of the massive supporting towers (£14; book ahead).

We the Curious   MUSEUM
(📞 0117-915 1000; www.wethecurious.org; Anchor Rd; adult/child £15/10; ⊙10am-5pm Mon-Fri, to 6pm Sat & Sun) Bristol's interactive science museum is a playful, hands-on space where 300 'exhibits' fly the flag for curiosity, scientific collaboration and creativity. Meet Aardman characters, become an animator, discover cosmic rays, walk through a tornado and explore subjects ranging from anatomy to flight. There are also performances from the Live Science Team, immersive **planetarium shows** (£2.50 to £3.50) and weekly stargazing sessions (£10) for those aged over 15.

Matthew   HISTORIC SHIP
(📞0117-927 6868; www.matthew.co.uk; Princes Wharf; ⊙10am-4pm Tue-Sun Mar-Oct, Sat & Sun Nov-Feb) **FREE** The most striking thing about this replica of the vessel in which John Cabot made his landmark voyage from Bristol to Newfoundland in 1497 is its size. At 24m it looks tiny but it would have carried an 18-strong crew. Step aboard to climb below into their quarters, walk the deck and gaze up at the rigging.

Bristol Museum & Art Gallery   MUSEUM
(📞0117-922 3571; www.bristolmuseums.org.uk; Queen's Rd; ⊙10am-5pm Tue-Sun; 📶) **FREE** This classic Edwardian museum delivers some surprises. Look out for the *Paint-Pot Angel* by street artist Banksy in the entrance hall. A funerary statue with an upturned pot of pink paint on her head, she's designed to challenge our expectations of museum exhibits and the value of art. Just above sits the Bristol Boxkite, a prototype propeller-powered biplane, which dangles from the ceiling.

Georgian House   HISTORIC BUILDING
(📞0117-921 1362; www.bristolmuseums.org.uk; 7 Great George St; ⊙11am-4pm Sat-Tue Apr-Dec) **FREE** You'll find insights into two sides of the Georgian trade in enslaved Africans in this ornate 18th century house. It was the home of both the wealthy slave plantation owner and sugar merchant John Pinney, and his enslaved valet Pedro Jones. A small display outlines their stories, alongside a huge kitchen, book-lined library and basement plunge-pool.

The Downs   PARK
The grassy parks of Clifton Down and Durdham Down (often called just the Downs) fan out from the Clifton Suspension Bridge, making a fine picnic spot. Nearby, the **Clifton Observatory** (📞0117-974 1242; www.cliftonobservatory.com; Litfield Rd, Clifton Down; adult/child £5/2.50; ⊙10am-5pm Mar-Sep, to 4pm Oct-Feb) houses a **camera obscura** and a tunnel leading down to the **Giant's Cave**, a natural cavern that emerges halfway down the cliff with dizzying views across the Avon Gorge.

🏃 Activities

⭐ Bristol Street Art Tours   WALKING
(Where the Wall; 📞07748 632663; www.wherethewall.com; adult/child £11/6; ⊙2-6 per week) Some serious spray-paint skills (including Banksy's) are on show in two-hour tours starting in the city centre and ending in counter-culture Stokes Croft. Or join an hour-long **Stencil Art Spray Session** (£15, Saturday, 2pm) to 'get your hands on the cans'.

⭐ Bristol Lido   BATHHOUSE
(📞0117-933 9530; www.lidobristol.com; Oakfield Pl; nonmembers £25; ⊙nonmembers 1-4pm Mon-Fri)

BRISTOL, BATH & SOMERSET BRISTOL

BANKSY – STREET ARTIST

If there's one Bristolian nearly everyone has heard of, it's Banksy (www.banksy.co.uk) – the guerrilla street artist whose distinctive stencilled style and provocative artworks have earned him worldwide notoriety.

It's thought Banksy was born in 1974 in the Bristol area and honed his skills in a local graffiti outfit. His works take a wry view of 21st-century culture – especially capitalism, consumerism and the cult of celebrity. Among his best-known pieces are the production of spoof banknotes (featuring Princess Diana's head instead of the Queen's), a series of murals on Israel's West Bank barrier (depicting people digging holes under and climbing ladders over the wall) and a painting of a caveman pushing a shopping trolley at the British Museum (which the museum promptly claimed for its permanent collection). His documentary *Exit Through the Gift Shop*, about an LA street artist, was nominated for an Oscar in 2011.

Once despised by the authorities, Banksy's artworks have become a tourist magnet. Highlights include those in our Art & History Waking Tour (p231). It's also worth hunting out these pieces:

Paint-Pot Angel (Bristol Museum & Art Gallery, p227) Pink paint meets funerary monument.

Mild Mild West (Canteen Bar, Stokes Croft) A Molotov cocktail–wielding teddy bear facing three riot police.

Valentine's Day mural (Barton Hill) A girl catapulting red flowers onto the side of a house.

The tourist office (p232) can advise on locations, while the Bristol Street Art Tours (p227) take in the main Banksy sites.

Bristol's public hot tub dates back to 1849 – a naturally heated, 24m pool with a water temperature of a balmy 24°C. Admission includes three hours' use of the pool, sauna, steam room and outdoor hot tub.

If you want to visit outside the times listed, consider one of their Spa packages (from £95).

Cycle the City CYCLING
(☏ 07873 387167; www.cyclethecity.org; 1 Harbourside) These guided bike tours are an ideal way to discover off-the-beaten track Bristol. Opt for a two-hour highlights trip (£18), a Food Tour (£40) or a tour focused around cheese and wine. You can pre-book bike hire too (per day £18).

Bristol Walks & Tours WALKING
(☏ 0333-321 0101; www.bristolwalks.co.uk; adult/child £8/3; ⊗Mar-Nov) The Highlights tour takes in the old town, city centre and Harbourside and runs on Saturday at 11am. A walk looking at Bristol's links with the Slave Trade and its abolition starts at noon on Sunday. Both leave from the tourist office (p232), there's no need to book.

⚜ Festivals & Events

★**Upfest** ART
(www.upfest.co.uk; ⊗May/Jun) **FREE** Where better for a street-art festival than the city that brought us Banksy? Upfest sees 250 artists descending on the city to paint live, in front of audiences, at scores of venues. There are music gigs and affordable art sales too.

International Balloon Fiesta AIR SHOW
(www.bristolballoonfiesta.co.uk; ⊗Aug) More than 100 brightly coloured hot-air balloons, often of mind-boggling shapes, fill the skies at Ashton Court in what is the largest event of its type in Europe. The highlights are the fireworks and Nightglow flights.

🛏 Sleeping

★**Kyle Blue** HOSTEL £
(☏ 0117-929 0609; www.kylebluebristol.co.uk; Wapping Wharf; dm/s/d £29/60/70; ☐) What a boon for budget travellers: a boutique hostel set on a boat that's moored in easy reach of the central sights. Cabins are compact but supremely comfy, the showers and kitchen gleam and the smart lounge is the ideal spot to watch the river traffic float by.

Bristol YHA
HOSTEL £

(☑0345 371 9726; www.yha.org.uk; 14 Narrow Quay; dm £18-35, s/d/tr 59/69/79; @🛜) Few hostels can boast a position as good as this one, right beside the river in the centre of town. Facilities in the converted red-brick warehouse include kitchens, a cycle store, a games room and the excellent Grainshed cafe-bar.

★Brooks
B&B ££

(☑0117-930 0066; www.brooksguesthousebristol. com; Exchange Ave; d £93-120, tr £99-133, trailers £111-129; 🛜) Welcome to urban glamping – four vintage Airstream trailers sit in a bijou AstroTurf roof garden slap bang in the heart of Bristol. They're predictably tiny (ranging from 16ft to 20ft) but still have sleek seating areas, pocket-sized bathrooms and rooftop views. Guesthouse bedrooms are compact but smart, featuring subtle tones and checked throws.

Mercure Bristol Brigstow
HOTEL ££

(☑0117-929 1030; www.mercure.com; 5 Welsh Back; r £85-133; ✳🛜) A harbourside location and attractive modern design make the Mercure a sound, central option. Bedrooms are made less corporate by hardwood floors, big circular rugs and gently curving walls.

★Number 38
B&B £££

(☑0117-946 6905; www.number38clifton.com; 38 Upper Belgrave Rd; s £115, d £125-180, ste £220; P🛜) Set on the edge of the Downs, this upmarket B&B is *the* choice for style-conscious travellers. Rooms are huge and contemporary in soft grey and blue tones. Waffle bathrobes and designer bath goodies ramp up the luxury, while sweeping city views unfold from most bedrooms and the roof terrace.

🍴 Eating

★Primrose Cafe
CAFE £

(☑0117-946 6577; www.primrosecafe.co.uk; 1 Boyce's Ave; dishes £7-12; ⊙9am-5pm Mon-Sat Apr-Oct, 9am-5pm Mon-Sat Nov-Mar, 9.30am-4pm Sun year-round; 🥗) 🍴 The Primrose richly deserves its status as a Clifton institution, thanks to decades of serving towering homemade cakes and imaginative lunches, such as halloumi and courgette burgers, and slow-cooked pheasant. Pavement tables and a secluded roof garden add to the appeal, as do belt-busting brunches that are served impressively late (to 3.30pm); the eggs Benedict and Belgian waffles are legendary.

★Canteen
CAFE £

(☑0117-923 2017; www.canteenbristol.co.uk; 80 Stokes Croft; mains £5-10; ⊙noon-3pm & 5-9pm Mon-Sat, noon-4pm Sun; 🛜) 🍴 Occupying the ground floor of an old office block, this community-run cafe-bar sums up Bristol's alternative character: it's all about slow food, local suppliers and fair prices, whether you pop in for breakfast, veggie chilli, sit-down supper or nightly live music. The bar stays open until 11pm (1am Friday and Saturday).

The Banksy mural Mild Mild West is on the wall outside.

Ooweevegan
VEGAN £

(☑0117-280 0152; www.ooweevegan.com; 65 Baldwin St; mains £8; ⊙11.30am-10.30pm Sun-Thu, to 11pm Fri & Sat; 🥗) Looking every inch a fast-food outlet, Oowee turns that meat-heavy genre on its head. Here plant-based versions include crispy, fried not-chicken burgers, beyond meat quarter pounders and dirty fries.

Source
CAFE £

(☑0117-927 2998; www.source-food.co.uk; 1 Exchange Ave; mains £7-15; ⊙8am-4pm Mon & Sat,

---

EXPLORING BRISTOL'S WATERWAYS

Bristol has grown up around its harbour and docks. Exploring by water takes you to the heart of the city.

Bristol Ferry Boat Company (p233) A 16-stop waterbus linking Bristol Temple Meads train station, the city centre and the SS *Great Britain*.

SUP Bristol (p222) Discover the city's waterways while mastering stand-up paddleboard techniques.

All Aboard Watersports (☑0117-929 0801; www.allaboardwatersports.co.uk; Underfall Yard, Cumberland Rd; per 2½hr £15) Kayak activity sessions in the city's iconic harbour.

Matthew (p227) Set sail aboard a replica of a 15th-century transatlantic explorer's ship.

Bristol Packet (☑0117-926 8157; www. bristolpacket.co.uk; Wapping Wharf, Gas Ferry Rd; cruises from adult/child £7/5) Classic boat trips ranging from 45-minute harbour tours to cruises up the Avon Gorge.

to 4.30pm Tue-Fri) Local, seasonal produce is piled high at the deli counters of this market cafe, from sourdough bread and artisan cheese to charcuterie and smoked salmon and eels. Breakfast (8am to 11.45am) includes pancakes and kippers with capers; lunch might feature shellfish bisque or lamb sausage and chickpea stew.

Small St Espresso
CAFE £

(www.smallstreetespresso.co.uk; 23 Small St; snacks £4-6; ⊙7.30am-4.30pm Mon-Fri, 9.30am-4.30pm Sat) A gleaming pale-blue espresso machine sits at the heart of this artisan coffee house where caffeine connoisseurs sit at tiny clumps of tables munching on banana bread and sourdough toast. Opt for a house blend or the guest single origin; for cold-brewed or Aeropressed – this is coffee as craft.

St Nicholas Market
MARKET £

(St Nicks Market; ☑0117-922 4014; www.bristol. gov.uk/web/st-nicholas-markets; Corn St; ⊙9.30am-6pm Mon-Sat, 10am-5pm Sun) The city's lively covered market includes a bevy of food stalls selling everything from local gourmet Pieminister pies and mezze platters to cuts from the Low & Slow Smokehouse. Lines can be long at lunchtime, but it's worth the wait. Look out, too, for the Wednesday Farmers Market (9.30am to 2.30pm).

★Poco
TAPAS ££

(☑0117-923 2233; www.pocotapasbar.com; 45 Jamaica St; tapas £5-9; ⊙9am-midnight Mon-Fri, 10am-midnight Sat, 10am-11pm Sun; ☑) ✔ Having started life as a food truck touring the UK's festivals, Poco has now set up shop in a chilled-out Stokes Croft tapas bar. Vast jars of candied lemons and chilli oil line the shelves, while the open-plan kitchen creates generously sized dishes such as spicy charred broccoli, crunchy potatoes and soft wood pigeon with lentils and pear.

★Rosemarino
ITALIAN ££

(☑0117-973 6677; www.rosemarino.co.uk; 1 York Pl; mains £8-16; ⊙9am-3pm & 6-10pm Tue-Sat, 9am-3pm Sun; ☑) A firm favourite among Bristol's cognoscenti, Rosemarino brings a warm, home-cooked Italian foodie hug to Clifton's streets. Pesto, anchovies, taleggio and sage infuse dishes with Mediterranean flavours; the truffle-laced slow-cooked ox-cheek lasagna is a delight.

Chomp
BURGERS ££

(☑07872 354375; www.chompgrill.co.uk; 10 St Nicholas St; mains £11-35; ⊙6-10pm Mon-Fri, 5-10pm Sat, 6-9pm Sun) In this dimly lit shrine to the three Bs (beef, burgers and bourbon), specials might see succulent patties slathered with Gorgonzola, while steaks are West Country raised and aged for around 25 days. Wine is on offer, but the smart money is on a pint of the punchy Chomp House Brew.

Riverstation
BRITISH ££

(☑0117-914 4434; www.riverstation.co.uk; The Grove; bar/restaurant mains £14/17; ⊙10am-10pm Mon-Sat, to 6pm Sun) Riverstation's waterfront views are hard to beat, but it's the food that truly shines. Rich, classical flavours define dishes served up in the restaurant and less-formal bar. Expect truffle-fragranced wild mushrooms for breakfast, seasonal risotto for lunch, and stone bass and samphire for dinner.

Pump House
GASTROPUB ££

(☑0117-927 2229; www.the-pumphouse.com; Merchants Rd; mains £17-22; ⊙noon-3pm & 6-9pm Mon-Sat, noon-5pm Sun; ☑☑) A big, mirror-backed bar, red tile floors, retro signage and tall ceilings complete the transformation of this Victorian pumping station into warmly welcoming waterside gastropub. Innovative takes on pub grub classics dot the menu: truffle cauliflower cheese, beef with black garlic butter, and salt-baked veg. Or just sip a Butcombe beer on the harbourside terrace.

🍷 Drinking & Nightlife

★Grain Barge
PUB

(☑0117-929 9347; www.grainbarge.com; Mardyke Wharf, Hotwell Rd; ⊙noon-11pm Sun-Wed, to 11.30pm Thu-Sat) Even in a city awash with harbourside bars this former 1930s cargo vessel is a special spot. Bristol Beer Factory ales grace the pumps, floor to ceiling windows frame wide water views and the top deck terrace allows you to watch the boats drift by.

Bell
PUB

(☑0117-909 6612; www.butcombe.com; 18 Hillgrove St; ⊙4pm-midnight Mon, 2pm-midnight Tue-Thu, 3pm-1am Fri & Sat, 3pm-midnight Sun) Tucked away in a side road lined with street art, the Bell is a mellow favourite meeting point for Stokes Croft locals, with scuffed floorboards, well-worn tables, newspapers on the bar and Bristol's Butcombe brews on tap.

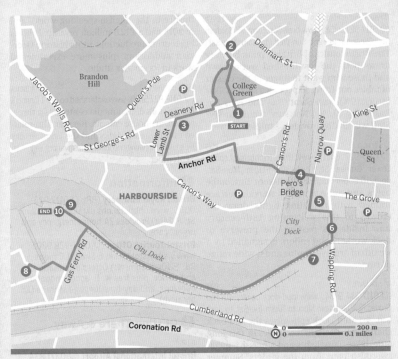

🏃 Walking Tour
Bristol: Art & History

START BRISTOL CATHEDRAL
END SS GREAT BRITAIN
LENGTH 1.7 MILES; THREE HOURS

Hunt out the medieval choir and Saxon carvings in **1 Bristol Cathedral** (☎0117-926 4879; www.bristol-cathedral.co.uk; College Green; ⏱8am-5pm Mon-Fri, to 3.15pm Sat & Sun) **FREE** then cross College Green to find the **2 Well Hung Lover** (Frogmore St), a saucy Banksy depicting a cheating spouse. Re-cross College Green to the right, passing Bristol Library. Go down the steps immediately after it to see your second Banksy – the **3 Castles Stencil** (Lower Lamb St) beside the delivery dock proclaims 'you don't need planning permission to build castles in the sky'. Continue on Lower Lamb St, then turn left along busy Anchor Rd, turning right at We the Curious. Edge the square to emerge onto the harbour side. Cross padlock-studded **4 Pero's Bridge** and turn right to feel cobbles under your feet and see crane arms ahead. Drop by the **5 Arnolfini** (☎0117-917 2300; www.arnolfini.

org.uk; 16 Narrow Quay; ⏱11am-6pm Tue-Sun; ☎) **FREE** to check out its exhibitions, art bookshop and cafe. Then cross the **6 Prince Street Swing Bridge** to pass under four mighty cranes. Head into the **7 M Shed** (p226) museum and upstairs to see slavery and *Wallace and Gromit* exhibits and your third Banksy: the *Grim Reaper*, which the artist originally painted on the side of a nightclub boat. Then continue along the waterside path, coveting houseboats and reading plaques until you see the masts of Brunel's mighty SS *Great Britain*. Go left up Gas Ferry Rd, then right through an alleyway (signed Harbourside Walk). Duck around the front of the clock tower of the white building to see your fourth Banksy: **8 Girl With A Pierced Eardrum**, a street-art twist on that famous Vermeer portrait. Retrace your steps – the water-view **9 Harbourside Kitchen** (☎0117-926 0680; www.ssgreatbritain.org; Great Western Dockyard; mains £6-10; ⏱9am-6pm Easter-Oct, to 4.30pm Nov-Easter; ☎), right outside the **10 SS Great Britain** (p225), is a prime place to refuel.

BrewDog Bristol
CRAFT BEER

(☑0117-927 9258; www.brewdog.com; 58 Baldwin St; ⊙noon-midnight Sun-Wed, to 1am Thu-Sat) The Bristol outlet of Britain's punk brewery draws both the just-finished work crowd and those who want to linger at the cluster of tables out front. Expect ales such as Tsar Struck (9%), 5am Saint (5%) and Faux Fox Raspberry (0.5%). Not sure which to try? Staff will gladly provide a sampler or two.

Ostrich
PUB

(☑0117-927 6411; www.theostrichbristol.co.uk; Lower Guinea St; ⊙11.30am-11pm Mon-Sat, noon-10.30pm Sun; 🐾) Well-kept Butcombe beers and an extensive waterside terrace framed with twinkling lights draw the crowds to this welcoming 18th-century inn. Inside, its past as the preserve of dock workers and sailors is signalled by a wealth of archive photos and a wide range of rums.

Mud Dock
PUB

(☑0117-934 9734; www.mud-dock.co.uk; 40 The Grove; ⊙10am-4pm Mon, to 10pm Tue-Sat, to 5pm Sun; 🐾) Mud Dock epitomises the laid-back charm of Bristol's harbourside. In this long attic, bikes, fairy lights and a massive metal swordfish hang from the girders. Summer sees people packing the mellow waterside terrace, enjoying craft ales and cracking views.

Amoeba
CRAFT BEER

(☑0117-946 6461; www.amoebaclifton.co.uk; 10 Kings Rd; ⊙4pm-midnight Mon-Thu, 1pm-1am Fri & Sat, 1pm-midnight Sun) Some 70 craft beers, 60 cocktails (£9 to £14) and a hundred-and-something (who's counting?) spirits draw style-conscious drinkers to this chilled-out wine bar, where patrons sit on bench seats smothered in cushions and nibble on platters of charcoal crackers and artisan cheese (£8).

Albion
PUB

(☑0117-973 3522; www.thealbionclifton.co.uk; Boyce's Ave; ⊙noon-11pm Sun-Wed, to midnight Thu-Sat) Cliftonites make a beeline for this village local for a post-work pint, drawn by the sofas, log burner, a beer terrace framed by fairy lights and Bath Ales on tap.

☆ Entertainment

★ Bristol Old Vic
THEATRE

(☑0117-987 7877; www.bristololdvic.org.uk; 16 King St) Established in 1766, the much-respected Old Vic is the longest continuously running theatre in the English-speaking world, and in 2018 had a £12.5-million revamp. It hosts big touring productions in its historic Georgian auditorium, plus more experimental work in its smaller studio.

Watershed
CINEMA

(☑0117-927 5100; www.watershed.co.uk; 1 Canon's Rd) Bristol's digital-media centre has a three-screen, art-house cinema. Regular film-related events include talks and the Encounters Festival (www.encounters-festival.org.uk) in September.

❶ Information

Bristol Royal Infirmary (BRI; ☑0117-923 0000; www.uhbristol.nhs.uk; Upper Maudlin St; ⊙24hr) Provides 24-hour emergency and urgent care.

Bristol Tourist Office (☑0117-929 9205; www.visitbristol.co.uk; E-Shed, 1 Canons Rd; ⊙10am-5pm; 🐾) Offers information and advice, plus free wi-fi, accommodation bookings, and day-time luggage storage (£5 per item).

❶ Getting There & Away

AIR

Bristol International Airport (☑0371 334 4444; www.bristolairport.co.uk) Bristol's airport is 8 miles southwest of the city. Destinations in the UK and Ireland include Aberdeen, Belfast, Edinburgh, Cork, Glasgow and Newcastle (mainly handled by easyJet). Direct links with cities in mainland Europe include those to Barcelona, Berlin, Milan and Paris.

Bristol Airport Flyer (http://flyer.bristolairport.co.uk) Runs shuttle buses (one way/return £8/13, 30 minutes, every 10 minutes at peak times) from the bus station and Bristol Temple Meads train station.

Arrow (☑01275-475000; www.arrowprivatehire.co.uk) Bristol Airport's official taxi service. Prices start from £33 (one way) from the city centre.

BUS

Bristol's **bus station** (Marlborough St; ⊙ticket office 8am-6pm) is 500m north of the city centre. From there buses shuttle into central areas and fan out around the city. There's a taxi rank nearby.

National Express (www.nationalexpress.com) coaches include those running direct to the following:

Bath (£5, 50 minutes, one a day).

Exeter (£6, two hours, five daily).

London Victoria (£11, three hours, hourly).

TRAIN

Bristol's main train station, Bristol Temple Meads, is just over a mile east of the city centre.

Direct services include the following:

TO	COST (£)	TIME (HR)	FREQUENCY
Bath Spa	8	15min	4 per hour
Birmingham	35	2	hourly
Edinburgh	95	7	hourly
Exeter	19	1½	half-hourly
Glasgow	96	8½	2 daily
London Paddington	36	2	half-hourly

Getting Around

BICYCLE

Bristol Cycle Shack (☑ 0117-955 1017; www.bristolcycleshack.co.uk; 25 Oxford St; per 24hr from £15; ☺11am-6pm Mon, 9am-6pm Tue-Fri, 10am-5pm Sat) Hires out bikes from its base just east of Bristol Temple Meads train station.

Cycle the City (p228) Rents out bikes (if pre-booked) and runs cycling tours from the central harbour area.

BOAT

Bristol Ferry Boat Company (☑ 0117-927 3416; www.bristolferry.com; 4 stops adult/child £2/1/50) boats leave roughly hourly from the dock at Cannon's Rd near the tourist office. Its Hotwells service runs west, with stops including the SS *Great Britain,* while the Temple Meads service runs east, with stops including Welsh Back, Castle Park (for Cabot Circus) and Temple Meads (for the train station). Fares depend on distance travelled; an all-day pass is adult/child £7/6.

BUS

Bus journeys in Bristol's city centre cost £1.20 for up to three stops; longer trips cost £2.50. A day pass (£5) provides unlimited travel.

Bus 8 Runs every 15 minutes from Bristol Temple Meads train station, via College Green in the city centre, to Clifton and on to Bristol Zoo Gardens.

MetroBus The M2 service (www.metrobusbristol.co.uk; single £2.25) links Bristol Temple Meads train station with Long Ashton Park & Ride via the city centre and SS *Great Britain.* Buy tickets (no cash) before boarding.

CAR & MOTORCYCLE

Heavy traffic and pricey parking make driving in Bristol a headache.

Park & Ride Buses (☑ 0345-602 0121; www.travelwest.info/park-ride/bristol; peak/off-peak return £5/3.50; ☺6am-9pm Mon-Sat, 9.30am-6pm Sun; ☎) include those running into central Bristol from Portway to the north-west (off Junction 18 of the M5) daily, and Brislington to the southeast (from near the A4), Monday to Saturday only.

TAXI

You can usually find a cab at the taxi ranks at the train and bus stations and on **St Augustine's Pde** (Narrow Quay).

To phone for a cab, try **V Cars** (☑ 0117-925 2626; www.v-cars.com) or **Bristol Taxis** (☑ 0117-944 4666; www.bristol-taxis.com; ☺24hr). If you're taking a nonmetered cab, agree on the fare in advance.

BATH

☑ 01225 / POP 88,850

Bath is one of Britain's most appealing cities. Exquisite Roman and Georgian architecture, counter-culture hang-outs and swish spas make it hard to resist.

History

Legend has it King Bladud, a Trojan refugee and father of King Lear, founded Bath some 2800 years ago when his pigs were cured of leprosy by a dip in the muddy swamps. The Romans established the town of Aquae Sulis in 44 CE and built the extensive baths complex and a temple to the goddess Sulis-Minerva.

In 944 a monastery was founded on the site of the present abbey, helping Bath's development as an ecclesiastical centre and wool-trading town. But it wasn't until the early 18th century that Ralph Allen and the celebrated dandy Richard 'Beau' Nash made Bath the centre of fashionable society. Allen developed the quarries at Coombe Down, constructed Prior Park and employed the two John Woods (father and son) to create Bath's signature buildings.

During WWII, Bath was hit by the Luftwaffe during the so-called Baedeker raids, which targeted historic cities in an effort to sap British morale. In 1987 Bath became the only city in Britain to be declared a Unesco World Heritage Site in its entirety.

Sights

★**Roman Baths**   HISTORIC BUILDING
(☑ 01225-477785; www.romanbaths.co.uk; Abbey Church Yard; adult £16-23, child £8.50-15.50; ☺9am-9pm mid-Jun–Aug, to 5pm Mar–mid-Jun,

Bath

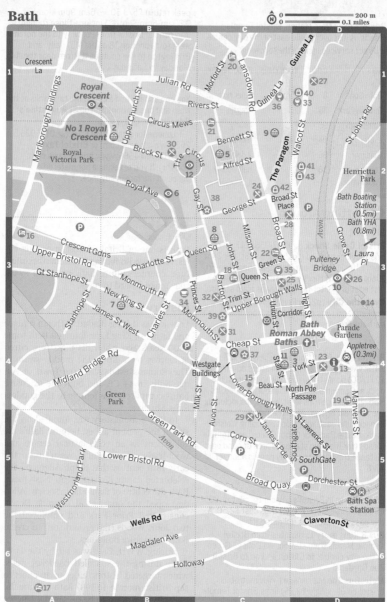

Sep & Oct, 9.30am-5pm Nov-Feb) In typically ostentatious style, the Romans built a bathhouse complex above Bath's 46°C (115°F) hot springs. Set alongside a temple dedicated to the healing goddess Sulis-Minerva, the baths now form one of the world's best-preserved ancient Roman spas, and are encircled by 18th- and 19th-century buildings. To dodge the worst of the crowds and the more expensive tickets, avoid weekends and July and August. Fast-track online tickets bypass the queues.

The heart of the complex is the **Great Bath**, a lead-lined pool filled with steam-

Bath

BRISTOL, BATH & SOMERSET BATH

ing, geothermally heated water from the so-called 'Sacred Spring' to a depth of 1.6m. Though now open-air, the bath would originally have been covered by a 45m-high barrel-vaulted roof.

More bathing pools and changing rooms are to the east and west, with excavated sections revealing the hypocaust system that heated the bathing rooms. After luxuriating in the baths, Romans would have reinvigorated themselves with a dip in the circular cold-water pool.

The King's Bath was added sometime during the 12th century around the site of the original Sacred Spring. Every day, 1.5 million litres of hot water still pour into the pool. Beneath the Pump Room are the remains of the Temple of Sulis-Minerva.

Digital reconstructions pop up in some sections of the complex, especially in the Temple Courtyard and the West and East Baths, which feature projections of bathers. There is also a museum displaying artefacts discovered on the site. Look out for the famous gilded bronze head of Minerva and a striking carved gorgon's head, as well as some of the 12,000-odd Roman coins

thrown into the spring as votive offerings to the goddess.

The complex of buildings around the baths was built in stages during the 18th and 19th centuries. John Wood the Elder and his son, John Wood the Younger, designed the buildings around the Sacred Spring, while the famous Pump Room (Stall St; ⊙ 9.30am-5pm) FREE was built by their contemporaries, Thomas Baldwin and John Palmer, in neoclassical style, complete with soaring Ionic and Corinthian columns. The building now houses a restaurant (snacks £5-9, 1/2/3 courses £16/22/28; ⊙ 9.30am-4pm), where offerings include magnificent afternoon teas (from £20, or £36 with champagne). You can also taste samples of the spring waters (50p), which were believed in Victorian times to have curative properties. If you're lucky, you might even have music provided by the Pump Room's string trio.

Admission to the Roman Baths includes an audio guide, featuring commentary in 12 languages – there's also one especially for children and a guide in sign language. One of the English guides is read by bestselling author Bill Bryson. Free hourly guided

LOCAL KNOWLEDGE

ORIENTATION

Bath's blockbuster sights are concentrated in two key, fairly small areas: in the city centre around the Roman Baths where you'll also find Bath Abbey and the Victoria Art Gallery, and in northern Bath around the Royal Crescent – the Circus, Jane Austen Centre and Fashion Museum are nearby.

The two neighbourhoods are around half a mile apart and walking between the two is a pleasant way to soak up the city's atmosphere and see the architecture. Many people spend the first day sightseeing in the city centre, and the second in northern Bath.

tours start at the Great Bath on the hour. The last entry to the complex is an hour before closing.

★ **Bath Abbey** CHURCH
(☑01225-422462; www.bathabbey.org; Abbey Church Yard; suggested donation adult/child £5/2.50; ⊙9.30am-5.30pm Mon, 9am-5.30pm Tue-Fri, to 6pm Sat, 12.15-1.45pm & 4-6.30pm Sun) Looming above the city centre, Bath's huge abbey church was built between 1499 and 1616, making it the last great medieval church raised in England. Its most striking feature is the west facade, where angels climb up and down stone ladders, commemorating a dream of the founder, Bishop Oliver King.

★ **Royal Crescent** ARCHITECTURE
Bath is famous for its glorious Georgian architecture, and it doesn't get any grander than this semicircular terrace of majestic town houses overlooking the green sweep of Royal Victoria Park. Designed by John Wood the Younger (1728–82) and built between 1767 and 1775, the houses appear perfectly symmetrical from the outside, but the owners were allowed to tweak the interiors, so no two houses are quite the same. No 1 Royal Crescent (☑01225-428126; www.no1royal crescent.org.uk; 1 Royal Cres; adult/child/family £11/5.40/27; ⊙10am-5pm) offers an intriguing insight into life inside.

A walk east along Brock St from the Royal Crescent leads to the Circus, a ring of 33 houses divided into three semicircular terraces. Plaques on the houses commemorate famous residents such as Thomas

Gainsborough, Clive of India and David Livingstone. The terrace was designed by John Wood the Elder, but he died in 1754, and it was completed by his son in 1768.

To the south along Gravel Walk is the **Georgian Garden** (☑01225-394041; off Royal Ave; ⊙9am-7pm) **FREE**, restored to resemble a typical 18th-century town-house garden.

Jane Austen Centre MUSEUM
(☑01225-443000; www.janeausten.co.uk; 40 Gay St; adult/child £12/6.20; ⊙9.45am-5.30pm Apr-Oct, 10am-4pm Sun-Fri, 9.45am-5.30pm Sat Nov-Mar) Bath is known to many as a location in Jane Austen's novels, including *Persuasion* and *Northanger Abbey*. Although Austen lived in Bath for only five years, from 1801 to 1806, she remained a regular visitor and a keen student of the city's social scene. Here, guides in Regency costumes regale you with Austen-esque tales as you tour memorabilia relating to the writer's life in Bath.

Pulteney Bridge BRIDGE
Elegant Pulteney Bridge has spanned the River Avon since the late 18th century and is a much-loved, much-photographed landmark (the view from Grand Parade, southwest of the bridge, is the best). It's also one of only four bridges in the world with shops lining both sides.

Museum of Bath Architecture MUSEUM
(☑01225-333895; www.museumofbatharchitec ture.org.uk; The Countess of Huntingdon's Chapel, off the Paragon; adult/child £7/3.50; ⊙1-5pm Mon-Fri, 10am-5pm Sat & Sun mid-Feb–Nov) The intriguing stories behind the building of Bath's most striking structures are explored here, using maps, drawings, antique tools, displays on Georgian construction methods and a 1:500 scale model of the city. On weekdays in July and August, it opens at 11am.

A joint ticket covering the Museum of Bath Architecture, No 1 Royal Crescent, the **Herschel Museum of Astronomy** (☑01225-446865; www.herschelmuseum.org.uk; 19 New King St; adult/child £7/3.50; ⊙1-5pm Mon-Fri, 10am-5pm Sat & Sun) and Beckford's Tower costs adult/child/family £16/8/40.

🏃 Activities

★ **Thermae Bath Spa** SPA
(☑01225-331234; www.thermaebathspa.com; Hot Bath St; spa £37-42; treatments from £72; ⊙9am-9.30pm, last entry 7pm) Taking a dip in

the Roman Baths might be off limits, but you can still sample the city's curative waters at this fantastic modern spa complex, housed in a shell of local stone and plate glass. The showpiece is the open-air rooftop pool, where you can bathe in naturally heated, mineral-rich waters with a backdrop of Bath's cityscape – a don't-miss experience, best enjoyed at dusk.

Bath Boating Station BOATING
(☑ 01225-312900; www.bathboating.co.uk; Forester Rd; adult/child per hour £8/4, per day £20/10; ☺ 10am-5.30pm Wed-Sun Easter-Sep) You can pilot your own vessel down the Avon from this Victorian-era boathouse, which rents out traditional rowing boats, punts, kayaks and Canadian canoes. It's in the suburb of Bathwick, a 20-minute walk northeast from the city centre.

Pulteney Cruisers BOATING
(☑ 01225-863600; www.bathboating.com; Pulteney Bridge; adult/child £10/5; ☺ mid-Mar–Oct) Pulteney Cruisers offers frequent, hour-long cruises up and down the River Avon from the Pulteney Bridge area.

☞ Tours

★ **Bizarre Bath Comedy Walk** WALKING
(www.bizarrebath.co.uk; adult/student £10/7; ☺ 8pm Apr-Oct) A multi-award-winning stroll that's billed as 'hysterical rather than historical'. That it actually has little to do with Bath doesn't matter a bit. Leaves nightly from outside the Huntsman Inn. There's no need to book.

Mayor's Guide Tours WALKING
(www.bathguides.org.uk; ☺ 10.30am & 2pm Sun-Fri, 10.30am Sat) FREE The excellent historical two-hour tours provided free by the Mayor's Corp of Honorary Guides leave from within the Abbey Churchyard, outside the Pump Room. There are extra tours at 6pm on Tuesdays and Thursdays May to August. Booking isn't required.

✲ Festivals & Events

Bath Festival CULTURAL
(☑ 01225-614180; www.bathfestivals.org.uk; ☺ May) A multi-arts festival that features classical, jazz, world and folk music with fiction, debate, science, history, politics and poetry.

Bath Fringe Festival THEATRE
(www.bathfringe.co.uk; ☺ mid-May–early Jun) Theatre-focused festival that also includes folk and world music gigs, dance and performance walks.

🛏 Sleeping

Bath YHA HOSTEL £
(☑ 0345 371 9303; www.yha.org.uk; Bathwick Hill; dm £21-30, d/q from £69/99; P @ 🖣) Split across an Italianate mansion and modern annexes, this impressive hostel is a steep climb (or a short hop on bus U1/U18) from the city. The listed building means the rooms are huge, and some have period features such as cornicing and bay windows.

St Christopher's Inn HOSTEL £
(☑ 01225-481444; www.st-christophers.co.uk; 9 Green St; dm £26-30, d £59; 🖣) The Bath outpost of this European hostel chain has cheerful staff, clean if small rooms, a central location and a party vibe, thanks to the drinks and food deals in the popular in-house bar. If you're not a night owl you might like to look elsewhere.

Haringtons HOTEL ££
(☑ 01225-461728; www.haringtonshotel.co.uk; 8 Queen St; r £120-200; P 🖣 🐾) If Bath's classical trappings aren't to your taste, head for this strictly modern city-centre crash pad, with vivid colour schemes, clashing wallpapers and a fun, young vibe. The location is fantastic, with the central sights just a few minutes' walk away.

Hill House Bath B&B ££
(☑ 01225-920520; www.hillhousebath.co.uk; 25 Belvedere; r £95-135; P 🖣) When you walk through the door of this four-storey Georgian townhouse it almost feels like you're staying with friends. The decor is quietly quirky: moustache-themed cushions, retro pictures and objets d'art abound.

ⓘ MUSEUM DISCOUNTS

Saver tickets covering the Roman Baths and the Fashion Museum cost adult/child/family £26/16/70.

There is also a joint ticket (adult/child/family £16/8/40) that includes entry into No 1 Royal Crescent, the Museum of Bath Architecture and the Herschel Museum of Astronomy.

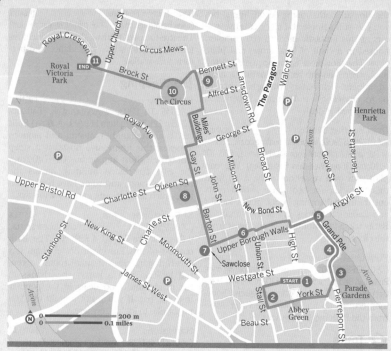

Walking Tour
Historic Bath

START BATH ABBEY
END ROYAL CRESCENT
LENGTH 1.5 MILES; TWO HOURS

Explore ❶ **Bath Abbey** (p236), an iconic edifice built on the site of an 8th-century chapel. Next, head south along Stall St for views of the 19th-century ❷ **Pump Room** (p235). Turn left onto York St, following it east to ❸ **Parade Gardens**, a landscaped Victorian park beside the River Avon.

Grand Parade leads north. Look out for the ❹ **Empire**, built as a luxurious hotel in 1901, on the corner. Next comes ❺ **Pulteney Bridge**, designed by Robert Adams in 1773, one of only a handful in the world to be lined with shops (the most famous other example is Florence's Ponte Vecchio). West of the bridge, ❻ **Upper Borough Walls** marks the northern extent of medieval Bath; look out for sections of the medieval wall that remain.

At Sawclose spot the elaborate facade of Bath's ❼ **Theatre Royal** (p243); it's been staging productions since 1805. Then follow Barton St on to ❽ **Queen Sq**. The oldest of Bath's Georgian squares, it was built to demonstrate the talents of its architect, John Wood the Elder.

Head north on to Gay St, and right on to George St. Next to Clayton's Kitchen restaurant, Miles' Buildings (an alley) leads north, emerging at the ❾ **Assembly Rooms** (NT; ☎ 01225-477789; www.nationaltrust.org.uk; 19 Bennett St; ☺10.30am-6pm Mar-Oct, to 5pm Nov-Feb) **FREE**, the heart of Georgian Bath's social life. After Bennett St turn left to reach the ❿ **Circus** (p236), designed to echo the Colosseum in Rome. The three-tiered pillars feature classical architectural styles (Doric, Ionic and Corinthian), while the facades are studded with masonic symbols.

Brock St leads west to Bath's Georgian glory, the Royal Crescent. Constructed by John Wood the Younger in 1774, the terrace is now Grade I listed, making it as architecturally significant as Buckingham Palace. ⓫ **No 1 Royal Crescent** (p236) is open to the public.

Appletree
B&B ££

(☑ 01225-337642; www.appletreebath.com; 7 Pulteney Gardens; r £95-160; 🅿🛜) Owner, Ling, ran a city-centre hotel for 15 years, and those skills shine throughout this classy B&B. Bedrooms are named after the eponymous fruit. The best is Royal Gala, which features a sleigh bed and sofa, but even the cheaper rooms are bright and fresh and dotted with Asian art.

Brooks
B&B ££

(☑ 01225-425543; www.brooksguesthouse.com; 1 Crescent Gardens, Upper Bristol Rd; s from £62, d £85-125; 🛜) In the smoothly comfy rooms at Brooks, a scattering of antiques meet plush modern furnishings, smart bathrooms and top-notch toiletries. Add eggs Benedict for breakfast, and an honesty bar and you have a stylish, fairly central bolthole.

Henry
B&B ££

(☑ 01225-424052; www.thehenry.com; 6 Henry St; s £85-105, d £105-150, f £150-210; 🛜) This tall terrace is just a few steps from the centre of Bath. The seven simple, small rooms are jazzed up with striped cushions and mints on the pillows.

★Queensberry
HOTEL £££

(☑ 01225-985086; www.thequeensberry.co.uk; 4 Russell St; r £235-323, ste £460-510; 🅿🛜) Stylish but unstuffy Queensberry is Bath's best luxury spoil. In these Georgian town houses heritage roots meet snazzy gingham checks, bright upholstery, original fireplaces and free-standing tubs. It's witty (see The Rules on the website), independent (and proud of it), and service is first-rate.

★Grays Bath
B&B £££

(☑ 01225-403020; www.graysbath.co.uk; 9 Upper Oldfield Park; r £125-185; 🅿🛜) Boutique treat Grays is a beautiful blend of modern, pared-down design and family treasures, many picked up from the owners' travels. All the rooms are individual: choose from floral, polka dot or maritime stripes. Perhaps the pick is the curving, six-sided room in the attic, with partial city views.

✗ Eating

★Thoughtful Bread Company
BAKERY £

(☑ 01225-471747; www.thethoughtfulbreadcompany.com; 19 Barton St; baked goods £2-5;

⊗ 8am-5pm Tue-Sat, 9am-4pm Sun) 🌿 Come lunchtime they could well be queuing out the door of this snug artisan bakery, where chunky loaves sit alongside delicate macaroons and salted-caramel bombs. Its vegan donuts are fruit-dotted, multi-coloured works of art.

Bertinet Bakery
BAKERY £

(☑ 01225-313296; www.bertinetbakery.com; 1 New Bond St Pl; baked goods £2.50-5; ⊗ 8am-5pm Mon-Fri, 8.30am-5.30pm Sat, 10am-4pm Sun) Temptation is all around at Richard Bertinet's take-out bakery, be it in the shape of rich quiches, cheese-studded croissants, *viennoiserie*, fresh-baked bread or irresistible pistachio swirls.

Adventure
CAFE £

(☑ 01225-462038; www.adventurecafebar.co.uk; 5 Princes Bldgs, George St; mains £6-11; ⊗ 8am-1am Mon-Fri, 9am-1am Sat & Sun; 🛜☑) 🌿 This cool cafe-bar offers something for everyone at most times of the day: breakfast bagels, lunchtime burgers and late-night pizza, cocktails and beer. There's great outdoor seating at the back.

Sally Lunn's
CAFE £

(☑ 01225-461634; www.sallylunns.co.uk; 4 North Pde Passage; mains £7-13, afternoon tea £8-40; ⊗ 10am-8pm) Eating a Bath Bunn (a bit like brioche) at Sally Lunn's is a Bath tradition. It's all about proper English tea here, brewed in bone-china teapots, with finger sandwiches and dainty cakes.

Noya's Kitchen
VIETNAMESE £

(☑ 01225-684439; www.noyaskitchen.co.uk; 7 St James's Pde; mains £7-12; ⊗ 11.45am-3pm Tue-Sat, plus 6-9pm Wed & Thu, 7-10pm Fri & Sat) Let the fragrances wafting from this intimate Vietnamese restaurant draw you in for fresh, aromatic, delicately flavoured dishes. Lunch menus are admirably short, evenings bring *pho* (noodle soup) on Wednesday, zingy curries on Thursday and the immensely popular, five-course Supper Club (£45) on Friday and Saturday – book well in advance.

The Oven
PIZZA ££

(☑ 01225-311181; www.theovenpizzeria.co.uk; 3 Sawclose; pizzas £9-15; ⊗ noon-10.30pm Sun-Thu, to 11pm Fri & Sat; ☑🧒) Bath's best pizzeria is a little slice of Italy with a warm atmosphere, cool tunes and basil-scented air. The wood-fired pizzas are authentic; thin, crisp and piled with prime ingredients such

240

BILLY STOCK/SHUTTERSTOCK ©

JEREMY RICHARDS/SHUTTERSTOCK ©

PHILIP BIRD LRPS CPAGB/SHUTTERSTOCK ©

PHIL WOOLLEY/SHUTTERSTOCK ©

1. Dunster (p252)
One of the oldest villages in Exmoor features a castle on a wooded hill.

2. Royal Crescent (p236), Bath
The semicircular terrace of town houses is a stunning example of Georgian architecture.

3. Red deer (p251), Exmoor National Park
Autumn rutting season is a popular time to visit this large wild red deer population.

4. Brunel's SS Great Britain (p225), Bristol
You can explore this groundbreaking steamship designed in 1843.

as smoked mozzarella, grilled asparagus and toasted hazelnuts. The tiramisu is gorgeous and vast.

The Circus
MODERN BRITISH ££

(☑ 01225-466020; www.thecircusrestaurant.co.uk; 34 Brock St; mains lunch £14-20, dinner £18-25; ☺ 10am-11pm Mon-Sat; ☑) Chef Ali Golden has turned this bistro into one of Bath's destination addresses. The menu mixes traditional British fare with global influences – here slow-cooked lamb and caramelised cauliflower meet harissa-infused aubergine, and rabbit in velouté cream sauce.

Acorn
VEGETARIAN ££

(☑ 01225-446059; www.acornvegetariankitchen.co.uk; 2 North Pde Passage; lunch 2/3 courses £20/25, dinner 2/3 courses £30/39; ☺ noon-3pm & 5.30-9.30pm; ☑) ☑ Revelling in an ethical and eco ethos, Bath's premier vegetarian restaurant brings vegetables and grains to a whole new level of deliciousness. Contemporary fine dining using imaginative cookery methods and global flavours result in beautiful plates of food. The six-course taster menu (£50) is worth the outlay – it's a true celebration of plant-based food.

Chez Dominique
FRENCH ££

(☑ 01225-463482; www.chezdominique.co.uk; 15 Argyle St; mains £18-24; ☺ 11.30am-3pm & 5-11pm Mon-Sat, 11.30am-3.30pm & 6-9pm Sun) The unfussy decor here prepares you for classic French bistro cooking, with time-honoured methods and ingredients delivering punchy flavours. From the chalked-up *soupe du jour* and steak with *pommes frites* to the salted-caramel ice cream, it's a gorgeous dollop of France.

Corkage
BISTRO ££

(☑ 01225-422577; www.corkagebath.com; 132a Walcot St; ☺ 5-11pm Tue, 5-11.30pm Wed & Thu, noon-11.30pm Fri & Sat) At this intimate, friendly neighbourhood bistro the aromas of imaginative dishes fill the air and regiments of bottles fill the shelves. It offers scaled-down versions of main courses (£6 to £13) and an extensive international wine list.

★ Menu Gordon Jones
MODERN BRITISH £££

(☑ 01225-480871; www.menugordonjones.co.uk; 2 Wellsway; 7 courses £65, with wines £120; ☺ 12.30-2pm & 7-9pm Tue-Sat; ☑) Gordon Jones delights in delivering dining laced with surprise. Menus are dreamt up daily and showcase the chef's taste for experimental ingredients such as wild New Forest mushrooms and Dorset snails. The presentation is eye-catching (perhaps featuring test tubes or paper bags) and Gordon himself often pops out to explain the dishes. Reservations essential.

🍷 Drinking & Nightlife

★ Bell
PUB

(www.thebellinnbath.co.uk; 103 Walcot St; ☺ 11.30am-11pm Mon-Thu, to midnight Fri & Sat, noon-10.30pm Sun; ☎) ☑ The locals loved

---

BATH'S ARTISAN QUARTER

Bath is rightly famous for its rich past. But hidden among the heritage is a cool, contemporary city. It's in evidence in the self-styled Artisan Quarter around Walcot St. You won't be knee-deep in craftspeople, but independent shops, bistros and a classic live-music pub make it worth a visit.

Fine Cheese Co (☑ 01225-448748; www.finecheese.co.uk; 31 Walcot St; dishes £7-16; ☺ 9am-5pm Mon-Sat) Exquisite pastries, punchy coffee, a vast cheese selection and creative specials.

Yellowshop (www.yellowshop.co.uk; 72 Walcot St; ☺ 10.30am-5.30pm Mon-Sat, noon-4pm Sun) Pre-loved clothing heaven crammed with cowboy boots, chunky sweaters and faded jeans.

Katherine Fraser (☑ 01225-461341; www.katherinefraser.co.uk; 74 Walcot St; ☺ 10am-5pm Mon-Sat) An artisan weaver works amid beautiful, bold designs.

Bath Aqua Glass Workshop (☑ 01225-428146; www.bathaquaglass.com; 105 Walcot St; ☺ 9.30am-4pm Mon-Fri, 11.15am-2.15pm Sat) Look through the open doors to see craftspeople at work, or head inside for a demo.

Topping & Company (☑ 01225-428111; www.toppingbooks.co.uk; The Paragon; ☺ 8.30am-8pm) Some 50,000 books, rolling library ladders, free tea and proper coffee.

the Bell so much they bought it; the pub is a co-operative, owned by more than 500 customers and staff. Get chatting to some of them over table football, bar billiards, backgammon and chess, while sipping one of nine real ales. Or enjoy the DJ sets and live music spanning folk and jazz to the blues.

★Colonna & Smalls   CAFE
(☑07766 808067; www.colonnaandsmalls.co.uk; 6 Chapel Row; ☺8am-5.30pm Mon-Fri, 8.30am-5.30pm Sat, 10am-4pm Sun; ☏) If you're keen on caffeinated beans, this is a cafe not to miss. A mission to explore coffee means there are three guest espresso varieties, and smiling staff are on hand to share their expertise. They'll even tell you that black filter coffee – yes, filter coffee – is actually the best way to judge high-grade beans.

Star   PUB
(☑01225-425072; www.abbeyales.co.uk; 23 The Vineyards, The Paragon; ☺noon-midnight Sun-Wed, to 12.30am Thu, to 1am Fri & Sat) Few pubs are registered relics, but the Star is just that. First licensed in 1760, historic features include 19th-century bar fittings, wooden benches and four drinking snugs. It's the brewery tap for Bath-based Abbey Ales; some beers are served in traditional jugs, and you can even ask for a pinch of snuff in the 'smaller bar'.

Old Green Tree   PUB
(☑01225-448259; 12 Green St; ☺11am-11pm Mon-Sat, noon-6.30pm Sun) In this tiny, traditional, entirely wood-panelled pub you'll be welcomed warmly to a fuss-free atmosphere, a minuscule lounge bar and a good range of real ales.

☆ Entertainment

Moles   LIVE MUSIC
(☑01225-437537; www.moles.co.uk; 14 George St; ☺5pm-3am Mon-Thu, to 4am Fri & Sat) Bath's main music venue keeps the crowds happy with indie, alternative, house and hip-hop, club classics, DJ sets and cheesy pop hits (Tuesdays) spanning five decades.

Little Theatre Cinema   CINEMA
(☑0871 9025735; www.picturehouses.com; St Michael's Pl) An excellent art-house cinema screening fringe films and foreign-language flicks in art-deco surrounds.

SHOPPING IN BATH

Bath's shops are some of the best in the west. The city's main shopping centre is **SouthGate** (www.southgatebath.com; ☺shops 9am-6pm Mon-Wed, Fri & Sat, 9am-7pm Thu, 11am-5pm Sun), where you'll find all the major chain stores.

High-quality, independent shops line the narrow lanes just north of Bath Abbey and Pulteney Bridge. Milsom St is good for upmarket fashion, while Walcot St has food shops, design stores, vintage-clothing retailers and artisans' workshops.

Theatre Royal   THEATRE
(☑01225-448844; www.theatreroyal.org.uk; Sawclose) Bath's historic theatre dates back more than 200 years. Major touring productions appear in the main auditorium and smaller shows take place in the Ustinov Studio.

ℹ Information

Bath Tourist Office (☑01225-614420; www.visitbath.co.uk; 2 Terrace Walk; ☺9.30am-5.30pm Mon-Sat, 10am-4pm Sun, closed Sun Nov-Jan) Offers advice and information. Also runs an accommodation booking service and sells a wide range of local books and maps.
Royal United Hospital (☑01225-428331; www.ruh.nhs.uk; Combe Park; ☺24hr) Offers 24-hour emergency and urgent care.

ℹ Getting There & Away

BUS
Bath's **bus and coach station** (Dorchester St) is near the train station.

National Express (www.nationalexpress.com) coaches include those running direct to:
Bristol (£5, 50 minutes, daily)
London Heathrow (£27, 2½ hours, two-hourly)
London Victoria (£15, three hours, hourly)

Services to many other destinations change at Bristol.

First Bus (www.firstgroup.com) is the biggest local bus company. Services to:
Bristol (bus 38/39/X39; £6.60, one hour, four per hour Monday to Saturday, half-hourly on Sunday)
Wells (bus 172/173/174; £6.60, 1½ hours, two per hour Monday to Saturday, hourly Sunday)

BRISTOL, BATH & SOMERSET BATH

TRAIN

Bath's train station, Bath Spa, is at the south end of Manvers St. Some services connect through Bristol, including many to the southwest and north of England. Direct services include the following:

TO	COST (£)	TIME (HR)	FREQUENCY
Bristol	8	15min	4 per hour
Cardiff Central	12	1¼	hourly
London Paddington	35	1½	hourly
Salisbury	12	1	half-hourly

❶ Getting Around

BICYCLE

Bath is hilly. The canal paths along the Kennet and Avon Canal and the 13-mile **Bristol & Bath Railway Path** (www.bristolbathrailwaypath.org.uk) are great to explore by bike.

Bath Bike Hire (☑ 01225-447276; www.bath-narrowboats.co.uk; Sydney Wharf, Bathwick Hill; adult/child per day £18/15; ⊗9am-5pm) A 10-minute walk from the centre. Handy for the canal and railway paths.

BUS

BathRider (adult/child £4.50/3.50) A multi-operator, all-day ticket covering a 3-mile radius of central Bath. It's valid until 3am the next day. A seven-day ticket costs adult/child £20/15.

Bus U1 Runs from the bus station, via High St and Great Pulteney St, up Bathwick Hill, past the YHA to the university every 20 minutes (£2.50).

Bus 11 Goes to Bathampton (£2.50, 10 minutes, hourly) from the bus station.

CAR & MOTORCYCLE

Bath has serious traffic problems, especially at rush hour. **Park & Ride services** (☑0871 200 22 33; www.firstgroup.com; return Mon-Fri £3.60, Sat & Sun £3.10; ⊗6.15am-8.30pm Mon-Sat, 9.30am-6pm Sun) operate from Lansdown to the north, Newbridge to the west and Odd Down to the south. It takes about 10 minutes to the centre; buses leave every 10 to 15 minutes.

There's a central car park underneath the SouthGate shopping centre (two/eight hours £3.50/11).

TAXI

There's a taxi rank at Bath Spa train station, or call **V Cars Bath** (☑ 01225-464646; www.v-cars.com; ⊗24hr).

SOMERSET

With its pastoral landscape of hedgerows, fields and hummocked hills, sleepy Somerset is the very picture of the rural English countryside, and makes the perfect escape from the bustle of Bath and the hustle of Bristol. Things certainly move at a drowsier pace around these parts – it's a place to drink in the sights at your own pace.

The cathedral city of Wells is an atmospheric base for exploring the limestone caves and gorges around Cheddar, while the hippie haven of Glastonbury is handy for venturing on to the high hills of the Quantocks. To the west sits Exmoor National Park, where sheer cliffs meet open moors roamed by red deer.

❶ Information

The Taunton **tourist office** (☑ 01823-340470; www.visitsomerset.co.uk/taunton; Market House, Fore St; ⊗9.30am-4.30pm Mon-Sat) has info about Somerset as a whole.

The website www.visitsomerset.co.uk is a useful source of information.

❶ Getting There & Around

The M5 heads south past Bristol to Bridgwater and Taunton, while the A39 leads west across the Quantocks to Exmoor.

Key train services link Bath, Bristol, Bridgwater, Taunton and Weston-super-Mare.

First (www.firstgroup.com) is a key local bus operator.

For timetables and general information, contact **Traveline South West** (www.travelinesw.com).

Wells & Around

☑ 01749 / POP 10,530

In Wells, small is beautiful. This is England's smallest city, and only qualifies for the title thanks to a magnificent medieval cathedral, which sits beside the grand Bishop's Palace – the official residence of the Bishop of Bath and Wells since the 12th century. Medieval buildings and cobbled streets radiate out from the cathedral green to a marketplace that has been the bustling heart of Wells for nine centuries (Wednesday and Saturday are market days).

CHEDDAR GORGE

Carved out by glacial meltwater during the last ice age, **Cheddar Gorge** (☎01934-742343; www.cheddargorge.co.uk; adult/child £20/15; ⊙10am-5pm, to 5.30pm late July-Aug) is England's deepest natural canyon, in places towering 138m above the twisting B3135. The gorge is riddled with subterranean caverns with impressive displays of stalactites and stalagmites. Highlights are Gough's Cave and the multimedia Dreamhunters exhibit in Cox's Cave; deeper caves can be explored on caving trips with **Rocksport** (☎01934-742343; www.cheddargorge.co.uk/rocksport; Cheddar Gorge; adult/child £25/19).

Cheddar is also famous as the home of one of the nation's favourite cheeses, produced here since the 12th century. At the **Cheddar Gorge Cheese Company** (☎01934-742810; www.cheddargorgecheeseco.co.uk; The Cliffs, Cheddar; adult/child £2/free; ⊙10am-5pm Easter-Oct, winter hours vary), you can watch the cheesemaking process, sample the produce, then buy some whiffy souvenirs.

Cheddar Gorge is 10 miles northwest of Wells on the A371.

◉ Sights

★ **Wells Cathedral**　　　　CATHEDRAL
(Cathedral Church of St Andrew; ☎01749-674483; www.wellscathedral.org.uk; Cathedral Green; requested donation adult/child £6/5; ⊙7am-7pm Apr-Sep, to 6pm Oct-Mar) Wells' gargantuan Gothic cathedral sits plumb in the centre of the city, surrounded by one of the largest cathedral closes in England. It was built in stages between 1180 and 1508, and showcases several Gothic styles. Among its notable features are the **West Front**, decorated with more than 300 carved figures, and the famous **scissor arches**, an ingenious architectural solution to counter the subsidence of the central tower. Don't miss the **High Parts Tour** (adult/child £13/10; ⊙Mon-Sat May-Oct) that heads up into the roof.

Bishop's Palace　　　　HISTORIC BUILDING
(☎01749-988111; www.bishopspalace.org.uk; Market Pl; adult/child £9/4.50; ⊙10am-6pm Apr-Oct, to 4pm Nov-Mar) Built for the bishop in the 13th century, this moat-ringed palace is purportedly the oldest inhabited building in England. Inside, the palace's state rooms and ruined great hall are worth a look, especially on one of the free tours, but it's the shady gardens that are the real draw. The natural springs after which Wells is named bubble up in the palace's grounds.

Wookey Hole　　　　CAVE
(☎01749-672243; www.wookey.co.uk; Wookey Hole; adult/child £20/16; ⊙10am-5pm Apr-Oct, to 4pm Nov-Mar, closed Mon-Fri Dec–mid-Feb; ℗) The River Axe has gouged out this network of deep limestone caverns, which are famous for striking stalagmites and stalactites, one of which is the legendary Witch of Wookey Hole who, it's said, was turned to stone by a local priest. Admission to the caves is by guided tour. Up on top you'll find 20 beyond-kitsch attractions ranging from animatronic dinosaurs to pirate adventure golf. Wookey Hole is 2 miles northwest of Wells; look out for brown tourist signs on the A371.

🛏 Sleeping

Ancient Gate House Hotel　　　　HOTEL **££**
(☎01749-672029; www.ancientgatehouse.co.uk; 20 Sadler St; s £80-113, d £88-166; ☎) This old hostelry is built right into the cathedral's west gate. Rooms are decorated in regal reds and duck-egg blues. The best have four-poster beds and knockout cathedral views through latticed windows; they're £15 extra, and worth it. Prices rise significantly at weekends.

No 23　　　　B&B **££**
(☎01749-677648; www.bedandbreakfastinwells. co.uk; 23 Glastonbury Rd; s/d £103/110; ℗☎) It's a 15-minute walk from the centre of Wells to this sweet, redbrick B&B. Inside, smart, contemporary rooms have all the home comforts, your breakfast has quality ingredients and owner Liz has a dry sense of humour.

Beryl　　　　B&B **£££**
(☎01749-678738; www.beryl-wells.co.uk; Hawkers Lane; s £75-100, d £120-170, tr from £165; ℗☎☎) This grand gabled mansion offers a beautiful blast of English eccentricity. Every inch of the house is crammed with antique atmosphere, and the rooms boast grandfather

clocks, chaise longues and four-posters galore. It's about a mile from Wells.

Eating

Strangers with Coffee CAFE £
(☎07729 226200; www.facebook.com/StrangersWithCoffee; 31 St Cuthbert St; cakes from £2.50, mains from £6; ⊙7.30am-4pm Tue-Sat) The motto 'life is too short to drink bad coffee' is something they've taken to heart here as staff work caffeinated magic with the best beans in town. There's a tempting selection of multi-storey cakes to match.

Good Earth CAFE £
(☎01749-678600; www.thegoodearthwells.co.uk; 4 Priory Rd; mains £7-11; ⊙9am-4.30pm Mon-Sat; ☑) ✐ They've been running this cafe, wholefood store and homeware shop for 40 years now. Plenty of time to perfect serving up towering quiches, colourful salads and filling-packed jacket potatoes in a light-filled, cheerful, relaxed space.

Goodfellows EUROPEAN ££
(☎01749-673866; www.goodfellowswells.co.uk; 5 Sadler St; dinner mains £14-24; ⊙noon-3pm Sun & Mon, 10am-3pm Tue-Sat & 6-9pm Wed-Sat) There's a choice of eating options in Goodfellows' three vibrant rooms: the continental cafe menu offers cakes, pastries and light lunches (from £6), or book for an evening fine-dining experience – £33 gets you three classy courses, while the five-course seafood tasting menu (£50) is an absolute treat.

❶ Information

Tourist Office (☎01749-671770; www.wellssomerset.com; Town Hall, Market Pl; ⊙10am-4pm)

❶ Getting There & Away

The bus station is south of Cuthbert St, on Princes St. Useful services include:

Bath (bus 172/173/174; £6.60, 1½ hours, two per hour Monday to Saturday, hourly Sunday)

Bristol (bus 376; £6.60, 1¼ hours, half-hourly)

Cheddar (bus 126; £3.85, 25 minutes, hourly Monday to Saturday) Continues to Weston-super-Mare (£4, 1½ hours)

Glastonbury (bus 376; £2.40, 15 minutes, half-hourly)

Glastonbury
☎01458 / POP 8930

Ley lines converge, white witches convene and shops are filled with the aroma of smouldering joss sticks in good old Glastonbury, the southwest's undisputed capital of alternative culture. Now famous for the musical mudfest of a festival, held on Michael Eavis' farm in nearby Pilton, Glastonbury has a much more ancient past: the town's iconic tor was an important pagan site and is often linked to King Arthur. Some also believe the area is a hub of positive otherworldly energy. Whatever the truth of the legends swirling round Glastonbury, one thing's for certain – watching the sunrise from the top of the tor is an experience you won't forget in a hurry.

◉ Sights

★ **Glastonbury Tor** LANDMARK
(NT; ☎01278-751874; www.nationaltrust.org.uk; ⊙24hr) FREE Topped by the ruined, 15th-century Chapel of St Michael, the iconic hump of Glastonbury Tor is visible for miles around, and provides Somerset with one of its most unmistakable landmarks. It takes half an hour to walk up from the start of the trail on Wellhouse Lane; the steepest sections are stepped. Between April and September the Tor Bus (adult/child return £3.30/1.50) runs every half-hour from St Dunstan's car park near Glastonbury Abbey to the trailhead.

The tor is the focal point for a wealth of local lore. According to Celtic legend, the tor is the home of Arawn or Gwyn ap Nudd, king of the underworld and lord of the faeries. A more famous legend identifies the tor as the mythic Isle of Avalon, where King Arthur was taken after being mortally wounded in battle, and where Britain's 'once and future king' sleeps until his country calls again. Others believe that the tor marks an ancient mystical node where invisible lines of energy, known as ley lines, converge.

It's easy to see why the tor has inspired so many myths. It's a strange presence in an otherwise pan-flat landscape, and in ancient times (when the area around Glastonbury was covered by water for much of the year) the tor would indeed have appeared as an island, wreathed in mist and cut off by rivers, marshes and bogs.

Glastonbury

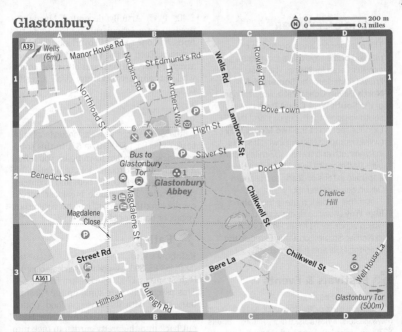

★ **Glastonbury Abbey** RUINS
(☎ 01458-832267; www.glastonburyabbey.com; Magdalene St; adult/child £8.60/4.70; ☺ 9am-8pm Jun-Aug, to 6pm Mar-May, Sep & Oct, to 4pm Nov-Feb) The scattered ruins of Glastonbury Abbey give little hint that this was once one of England's great seats of ecclesiastical power. It was torn down following Henry VIII's dissolution of the monasteries in 1539, and the last abbot, Richard Whiting, was hung, drawn and quartered on the tor. Today's striking ruins include some of the nave walls, the remains of St Mary's chapel, and the crossing arches, which may have been scissor-shaped like those in Wells Cathedral.

The grounds also contain a museum, a cider orchard and a herb garden. According to legend, the abbey's famous holy thorn tree sprang from the staff of Joseph of Arimathea, Jesus' great-uncle, who is said to have visited the abbey following Christ's death. It blooms at Christmas and Easter.

The abbey even has an Arthurian connection. In the 12th century, monks supposedly uncovered a tomb in the abbey grounds inscribed *Hic iacet sepultus inclitus rex arturius in insula avalonia,* or 'Here lies buried the renowned King Arthur in the Isle of Avalon'. Inside the tomb were two entwined skeletons, purportedly those of Arthur and his wife Guinevere. The bones were reburied beneath the altar in 1278, but were lost following the abbey's destruction.

Chalice Well & Gardens GARDENS
(☎ 01458-831154; www.chalicewell.org.uk; Chilkwell St; adult/child £4.60/2.30; ☺ 10am-6pm Apr-Oct, to 4.30pm Nov-Mar) Shaded by yew trees and criss-crossed by quiet paths, the Chalice Well and Gardens have been sites of pilgrimage since the days of the Celts. The iron-red waters from the 800-year-old well are rumoured to have healing properties, good for everything from eczema to smelly feet. Some legends also identify the well as the hiding place of the Holy Grail.

HIKING ON EXMOOR

The open moors and a profusion of marked bridleways make Exmoor an excellent area for hiking. The best-known routes are the **Somerset & North Devon Coast Path**, which is part of the **South West Coast Path** (www.southwestcoastpath.org.uk), and the Exmoor section of the **Two Moors Way** (www.twomoorsway.org), which starts in Lynmouth and travels 102 miles south over Dartmoor to Ivybridge. From there a 15-mile extension leads to the south Devon coast at Wembury.

Another superb route is the **Coleridge Way** (www.coleridgeway.co.uk), which winds for 51 miles from Lynmouth to Nether Stowey, crossing Exmoor, the Brendon Hills and the Quantocks.

Festivals & Events

Glastonbury Festival of Contemporary Performing Arts MUSIC
(www.glastonburyfestivals.co.uk; Pilton; tickets £270; ⊙ Jun or Jul) A majestic (and frequently mud-soaked) extravaganza of music, theatre, dance, cabaret, carnival, spirituality and general all-round weirdness that's been held on farmland in Pilton, just outside Glastonbury, since 1970 (bar periodic 'fallow' years to let the farm recover). Tickets usually go on sale in the autumn, and always sell out within a matter of minutes.

Sleeping

Check whether nearby **Street YHA** (☎0345 371 9143; www.yha.org.uk; Ivythorn Hill, Street; P), which switched to exclusive hire in 2020, has resumed taking individual bookings.

★ **Covenstead** B&B ££
(☎01458-830278; www.covenstead.co.uk; Magdalene St; s £75, d £80-120; P⊗) It's as if they've distilled the wacky essence of Glastonbury and poured it all over this weirdly wonderful B&B. The downstairs is a riot of oddities: mock skeletons, witches hats, upcycled antlers and draped python skins. Bedroom themes range from fairy via green man and Gothic to Halloween honeymoon. A tad crazy, yes, but also delightfully done.

Magdalene House B&B ££
(☎01458-830202; www.magdalenehouseglastonbury.co.uk; Magdalene St; s £80-110, d £95-110, tr £140; P⊗) Artfully decorated Magdalene used to be a school run by Glastonbury's nuns, and one room still overlooks the abbey grounds. Each of the tall, light rooms is an array of olive, oatmeal and other soft tones, while tasteful artworks give it all a restful feel.

Glastonbury Townhouse B&B ££
(☎01458-831040; www.glastonburytownhouse.co.uk; Street Rd; r £80-120; P⊗) In this solid, red-brick, Edwardian town house you'll find a clutch of quiet rooms, lots of painted furniture, supremely comfy beds and a contemporary vibe. The organic breakfast, served overlooking the garden, can be vegetarian, vegan, or dairy- or gluten-free.

Eating

Rainbow's End VEGETARIAN £
(☎01458-833896; www.rainbowsendcafe.com; 17b High St; mains £7-10; ⊙noon-4pm Fri-Mon; ☑) This psychedelic cafe sums up the Glastonbury spirit, with its all-veggie food, potted plants and mix-and-match furniture. Head out back into the pretty garden to tuck into homity pie, a hot quiche, and scrumptious homemade cake.

George & Pilgrim PUB FOOD ££
(☎01458-831146; www.historicinnz.co.uk; 1 High St; mains £7-22; ⊙food noon-3pm & 6-9pm) In hippy-chic Glastonbury a rarity: an ancient inn with one of the town's most authentically historic interiors – timbers, flagstones and all. Tuck into everything from homemade scotch eggs with dill mayonnaise to its signature slow-braised Somerset lamb.

Information

Tourist Office (☎01458-832954; www.glastonburytic.co.uk; Magdalene St; ⊙10am-4pm Mon-Sat, 11am-3pm Sun) In the town hall.

Getting There & Away

There is no train station in Glastonbury. Useful bus routes include:

Taunton (bus 29; £5, 1¼ hours, four to seven daily Monday to Saturday)

Wells (bus 376; £2.40, 15 minutes, every half hour)

EXMOOR NATIONAL PARK

Exmoor is more than a little addictive, and chances are you won't want to leave its broad, russet views. In the middle sits the higher moor, an empty, expansive, other-worldly landscape of tawny grasses and huge skies. In the north, sheer, rock-strewn river valleys cut into the plateau and coal-black cliffs lurch towards the sea.

Amid these towering headlands, charismatic Porlock and the twin villages of Lynton and Lynmouth are atmospheric places to stay. Relaxed Dulverton delivers a country-town vibe, while appealing Dunster has cobbled streets and a russet-red castle. Everywhere on Exmoor life is attuned to the rhythms and colours of the seasons – new-born livestock in spring, purple heather in late summer, gold-bronze leaves in autumn, and crisp days and log fires in winter. It all ensures Exmoor delivers insights into an elemental and traditional world.

 Activities

★ **Exmoor Adventures**   OUTDOORS
(☑ 07976 208279; www.exmooradventures.co.uk; Old Bus Garage, Porlock Weir) Sessions covering all skill levels for couples, families and small groups in kayaking, canoeing and SUP (per person £35/65 per half-/full day), mountain biking (from £30 per half day), coasteering (£30) and rock climbing (£65).

Cycling

Cycling is hugely popular on Exmoor's formidable hills. The 328-mile **West Country Way** (NCN Route 3) from Bristol to Padstow crosses the park, as does the **Devon Coast to Coast** (NCN Route 27), between Ilfracombe and Plymouth.

Exmoor is also an exhilarating off-road cycling destination, with a wealth of accessible bridleways and tracks. National Park visitor centres can advise.

The mountain bike sessions run by Exmoor Adventures include day-long trips down red and black trails (£80) and night rides (£40). It also rents mountain bikes (£25 per day).

Pompys   CYCLING
(☑ 01643-704077; www.pompyscycles.co.uk; Mart Rd, Minehead; per day £18; ⊙ 9am-4pm Mon-Sat) Bike sales and hire.

Walking

Open moors and a profusion of marked bridleways make Exmoor an excellent hiking area. Good routes include:

Somerset & North Devon Coast Path Part of the **South West Coast Path** (www.southwestcoastpath.org.uk).

Two Moors Way (www.twomoorsway.org) Tracking 117 miles south from Lynmouth, over Dartmoor and onto the south Devon coast at Wembury.

Coleridge Way (www.coleridgeway.co.uk) Winds for 51 miles from Lynmouth to Nether Stowey, crossing Exmoor, the Brendon Hills and the Quantocks.

Tarka Trail (www.tarkatrail.org.uk) A coastal section sweeps from Lynton to Bideford, before heading down into north Devon.

Exmoor National Park

STARGAZING ON EXMOOR

Exmoor holds the distinction of being named Europe's first International Dark Sky Reserve, in recognition of the night-time inky blackness overhead. But what does that mean in practice? Namely, a whole host of local organisations striving to limit light pollution, plus, for visitors, some simply spectacular star displays.

The Exmoor National Park Authority (ENPA; www.exmoor-nationalpark.gov.uk) has produced the excellent, free *Dark Skies Guide*, which includes star charts, tips and maps pinpointing the best local light-free spots. Download it from the website, or pick one up at visitor centres.

It's worth seeing if the ENPA is staging any guided moonlit strolls, and whether the Exmoor Dark Skies Festival is running – it tends to be held over two weeks from late October.

Or just look upwards on your own. For optimum stargazing, central, higher Exmoor is best – try Brendon Two Gates (on the B3223) or Webber's Post (just north of Dunkery Beacon).

See if walks run by the Exmoor National Park Authority are running. Past events include deer safaris, nightjar birdwatching walks and dark-sky strolls.

Exmoor National Park Authority (ENPA) tourist offices also sell a great range of day walk leaflets (£1).

Pony Trekking & Horse Riding

Exmoor is prime riding country, with stables offering pony and horse treks from around £50 for a two-hour ride.

Check if local stables Outovercott Stables (www.outovercott.co.uk) and Burrowhayes Farm (www.burrowhayes.co.uk) have resumed riding sessions:

Brendon Manor   HORSE RIDING
(☑ 01598-741246; www.brendonmanor.com; Brendon Manor; per 1hr/2hr £30/50) Runs a full range of horse-riding trips, from one to three hours, that head onto the open moor and down into the valleys. Depending on distancing regulations, groups may be capped at four and beginners may be limited to one-hour rides. Based 4 miles southeast of Lynton.

ℹ️ Information

Active Exmoor (www.visit-exmoor.co.uk/active-exmoor)

Exmoor National Park Authority (ENPA; www.exmoor-nationalpark.gov.uk) Website of the authority that runs the moor.

Lonely Planet (www.lonelyplanet.com/england/southwest-england/exmoor-national-park) Destination information, hotel bookings and more.

Visit Exmoor (www.visit-exmoor.co.uk) The official visitor website.

The Exmoor National Park Authority runs three tourist offices:

Dulverton (☑ 01398-323841; www.visit-exmoor.co.uk; 7 Fore St; ☉10am-4pm Apr-Oct, reduced hours Nov-Mar)

Dunster (☑ 01643-821835; www.visit-exmoor.co.uk; Dunster Steep; ☉10am-4pm Apr-Oct, reduced hours Nov-Mar)

Lynmouth (☑ 01598-752509; www.visit-exmoor.co.uk; The Esplanade, Lynmouth; ☉10am-4pm)

There's also a council-run tourist office in **Porlock** (☑ 01643-863150; www.porlock.co.uk; West End, Porlock; ☉10am-2pm Mon-Sat Easter-Oct, to 12.30pm Mon-Sat Nov-Easter).

ℹ️ Getting Around

BUS

Exmoor isn't that easy to navigate without your own vehicle, but if you plan ahead you can get around by bus. Key routes include:

Bus 198 Links Dulverton with Dunster (£4.20, 1¼ hours) two to three times daily, Monday to Saturday, before going onto Minehead.

Bus 309/310 Runs from Barnstaple to Lynton and Lynmouth (£3.60, one hour, hourly Monday to Saturday).

Bus 398 Links Dulverton with Tiverton (£5.50, 45 minutes, three daily Monday to Saturday).

Check whether bus 300 is running. In recent years this vintage (1950s) vehicle has shuttled between Minehead and Lynmouth via Porlock twice each weekday from mid-July to early September.

TRAIN

The nearest mainline train station is Tiverton Parkway, on the London Paddington to Penzance line.

Bus 1 (£2.40, 25 minutes, hourly Monday to Saturday, five on Sunday) links the station with Tiverton town, 13 miles away.

Dulverton

☎ 01398 / POP 2490

The southern gateway to Exmoor National Park, Dulverton sits at the base of the Barle Valley near the confluence of two key rivers: the Exe and Barle. A traditional country town, it's home to a collection of gun sellers, fishing-tackle stores and gift shops, and makes an attractive edge-of-moor base.

◉ Sights

★ Tarr Steps   LANDMARK
(P) Exmoor's most famous landmark is an ancient stone clapper bridge shaded by gnarled old trees. Its huge slabs are propped up on stone columns embedded in the River Barle. Local folklore aside (which declares it was used by the Devil for sunbathing), it first pops into the historical record in the 1600s, and has had to be rebuilt after 21st-century floods. The steps are signed off the B3223 Dulverton–Simonsbath road, 5 miles northwest of Dulverton.

It's a 450m walk from the car park to the bridge itself. You can also hike there from Dulverton along the banks of the River Barle (12 miles return).

Exmoor Pony Centre   WILDLIFE RESERVE
(☎ 01398-323093; www.exmoorponycentre.org. uk; Ashwick, near Dulverton; donations requested; ⊙ 10am-4pm Mon, Wed-Fri & Sun early Feb-Oct; P) You'll see them cantering across the open moor, but this is a great way to get up close to Exmoor's stubby ponies. Originally bred as beasts of burden, they're famously hardy despite their diminutive size.

🛏 Sleeping & Eating

Town Mills   B&B ££
(☎ 01398-323124; www.townmillsdulverton.co.uk; 1 High St; s/d/ste £95/105/125; P🖨) The top choice in Dulverton town itself is a thoroughly contemporary riverside mill with creamy carpets, magnolia-coloured walls and bursts of floral art.

Tarr Farm   HOTEL £££
(☎ 01643-851507; www.tarrfarm.co.uk; Tarr Steps, TA22 9QA; s/d £90/160; P🖨🐾) This is the place to really lose yourself: a charming farmhouse nestled among the woods near the Tarr Steps bridge, 7 miles from Dulverton. The

nine contemporary bedrooms are spacious and luxurious, with spoil-yourself extras such as organic bath goodies and homemade biscuits. The farm is also renowned for its food.

Exclusive Cake Co   BAKERY £
(☎ 01398-324131; www.exclusivecakecompany. co.uk; Northmoor Rd; snacks from £3; ⊙ 7am-2pm Mon-Fri, 9am-2pm Sat) Real rarities stack the shelves here: bread made with Exmoor ale, cheese and wholegrain mustard; Somerset cider cake; venison and port pie. Note the typically Exmoor warning: 'Game pies may contain lead shot'.

Tantivy   DELI £
(☎ 01398-323465; www.tantivyexmoor.co.uk; 12 Fore St; snacks from £3; ⊙ 9am-5pm; 🖨) Alongside maps, books and gift shop trinkets you'll also find a good little deli, packed with cured meats, cheese, locally smoked fish, ice cream, wine and beer. Or be tempted by the punchy takeaway espressos and gorgeous, gooey cakes.

★ Woods   BISTRO ££
(☎ 01398-324007; www.woodsdulverton.co.uk; 4 Bank Sq; mains £13-19; ⊙ bar noon-3pm & 7-11pm, food noon-2pm & 7-9.30pm) With its deer antlers, hunting prints and big wood-burning stove, multi-award-winning Woods is Exmoor to its core. No surprise then to find menus with full-bodied ingredients: expect confit leg of guinea fowl, slow-roast lamb

---

LOCAL KNOWLEDGE

EXMOOR RED DEER

Exmoor supports one of England's largest wild red deer populations, best experienced in autumn when the annual 'rutting' season sees stags bellowing, charging at each other and clashing antlers in an attempt to impress prospective mates.

Check the Exmoor National Park Authority (ENPA) website to see if their deer-spotting hikes are running. Also check whether the following firms have resumed off-road jeep safaris (per half-day £25).

Red Stag Safari (www.redstagsafari. co.uk)

Barle Valley Safaris (www.exmoorwild-lifesafaris.co.uk)

Discovery Safaris (www.discoverysafaris.com)

shoulder, and asparagus and wild garlic risotto. The clutch of tables outside and in the flower-framed courtyard garden are first-come, first-served.

Dunster

📞 01643 / POP 1220

Centred on a scarlet-walled castle and a medieval yarn market, Dunster is one of Exmoor's oldest villages, a tempting tangle of cobbled streets, bubbling brooks and pack-horse bridges.

◉ Sights

★ **Dunster Castle**   CASTLE
(NT; 📞 01643-821314; www.nationaltrust.org. uk; Castle Hill; gardens adult/child £8/4; ⊙ 11am-5pm Mar-Oct; 🅿) Rosy-hued Dunster Castle crowns a densely wooded hill. Built by the Luttrell family, which once owned much of northern Exmoor, the oldest sections are 13th century, while the turrets and exterior walls are 19th-century additions. The parkland and colourful terraced gardens feature riverside walks, a working watermill, a pop-up cafe and views across Exmoor's shores.

🛏 Sleeping & Eating

Dunster Castle Hotel   HOTEL ££
(📞 01643-823030; www.thedunstercastlehotel. co.uk; 5 High St; d £110-195; 🛜) Everything feels rich in this former coaching inn, from the ruby-red furnishings and puffed-up quilts, to the burnished trunks and gilt-framed mirrors. The best rooms overlook Dunster's cobbled High St.

Millstream Cottage   B&B ££
(📞 01643-822413; www.millstreamcottagedunster. co.uk; 2 Mill Lane; s £65, d £80-90) In the 1600s this was Dunster's workhouse. Now it's a sweet-as-pie guesthouse with country-cottage-style rooms with beams, pine doors and stone fireplaces. Breakfast treats include porridge, toast with Exmoor jams and smoked haddock and poached eggs.

Luttrell Arms   HISTORIC HOTEL £££
(📞 01643-821555; www.luttrellarms.co.uk; High St; r £210-260; 🅿🛜🐾) In medieval times, the baronial Luttrell Arms was the guesthouse of the Abbots of Cleeve. The grander rooms have private terraces and garden access. But even the standard digs are gorgeous; expect a plethora of four-poster beds, brass plates, beams and a plaster fireplace or two.

The acclaimed food (noon to 3pm and 6.30pm to 9.30pm; mains £12 to £29) ranges from sumptuous cream teas to classic, locally sourced à la carte.

★ **Reeve's**   BRITISH £££
(📞 01643-821414; www.reevesrestaurantdunster. co.uk; 20 High St; mains £16-28; ⊙ 6-9pm Tue-Sat, noon-2pm Sun) The leafy, parasol-dotted garden at Reeve's sets the scene for some seriously stylish, award-winning cuisine. The complex creations showcase Exmoor produce. Opt for venison wellington steeped in red wine sauce, or meltingly tender lamb roasted with rosemary and garlic. To finish? Some toasted walnut bread with local hard and soft cheeses.

Porlock & Porlock Weir

📞 01643

The coastal village of Porlock is one of the prettiest on the Exmoor coast; the huddle of thatched cottages lining its main street is framed on one side by the sea and on the other by steeply sloping hills. Winding lanes lead to the charismatic breakwater of Porlock Weir, 2 miles to the west, with an arching pebble beach and striking coastal views.

◉ Sights & Activities

★ **Porlock Weir**   HARBOUR
(🅿) Porlock Weir's stout granite quay curves around a shingly beach, which is backed by pubs, fisherfolks' storehouses and a scattering of seasonal shops. The weir has been around for almost a thousand years (it's named in the Domesday Book as 'Portloc'). It makes a glorious place for a picnic lunch and a stroll, with stirring views across the Vale of Porlock and easy access to the South West Coast Path.

The shingle beach to the west of the weir forms part of the Porlock Ridge and Saltmarsh SSSI (Site of Special Scientific Interest), a popular spot for local birdwatchers.

Holnicote Estate   ARCHITECTURE
(NT; 📞 01643-862452; www.nationaltrust.org.uk; near Porlock; 🅿) **FREE** The 50-sq-km Holnicote Estate sweeps southeast out of Porlock, taking in a string of impossibly pretty villages. Picturesque Bossington leads to charming Allerford and its 15th-century packhorse bridge. The biggest village, Selworthy, offers eye-catching Exmoor views

and cob-and-thatch cottages clustering around the village green.

Porlock's Hills
SCENIC DRIVE

If you're driving (or cycling) into Porlock, choose from several picturesque routes. On the main road (the A39) Porlock Hill is a snaking, brake-burning 25% gradient descent. The New Rd toll road (cars £3) peels off the A39 some 3 miles west of Porlock to sweep into the village through pine forests and around U-bends. Another toll road, the Porlock Scenic (Worthy) Toll Rd (cars £2), provides an alternative, bouncing, route in and out of Porlock Weir.

🛏 Sleeping

Burrowhayes Farm
CAMPGROUND £

(☑ 01643-862463; www.burrowhayes.co.uk; West Luccombe; sites per 2 adults £17-19; ☺ mid-Mar–Oct; 🅿) The large sweep of grass at the centre of this peaceful, well-run site is reserved for tents. Pitches are spacious, but arrive early to avoid the slopes. It's 1 mile east of Porlock.

Sea View
B&B ££

(☑ 01643-863456; www.seaviewporlock.co.uk; High Bank, Porlock; s from £40, d £75-78; 🅿🛜) Value-for-money Sea View has tiny rooms that are pleasantly packed with painted furniture, trinkets and oil paintings. Thoughtful extras include blister plasters and muscle soak for hikers tackling Porlock's precipitous hills.

Cottage
B&B ££

(☑ 01643-862996; www.cottageporlock.co.uk; High St, Porlock; s/d/tr £50/75/90; 🅿🛜) Evidence of the Cottage's 18th-century origins remains – a big fireplace in the guest lounge, duck-your-head lintels and quirkily shaped bedrooms. The decor though is stylishly modern, with light-coloured furniture in rooms of earthy or aquamarine tones.

🍴 Eating & Drinking

Porlock Weir Hotel
PIZZA ££

(☑ 01643-800400; www.porlockweirhotel.co.uk; Porlock Weir; pizzas £10-13; ☺ pizzas noon-9pm) Grandstand views of Porlock's sweeping pebble beach, a sea-view terrace bar and crispy wood-fired pizzas (eat there or takeaway). Bliss.

Ship Inn
PUB FOOD ££

(Top Ship; ☑ 01643-862507; www.shipinnporlock.co.uk; High St, Porlock; snacks £6, mains £11-17; ☺ noon-2.30pm & 6-8.30pm; 🅿🐕) Romantic poet Samuel Taylor Coleridge and pal Robert Southey both downed pints in this 13th-century thatched Porlock inn – there's even a snug still dubbed 'Southey's Corner'. Substantial pub food – mainly steaks, local fish, roasts and stews – is served in the beer gardens or the roomy restaurant.

Locanda On The Weir
ITALIAN £££

(☑ 01643-863300; www.locandaontheweir.co.uk; Porlock Weir; mains £20-26; ☺ 7-9pm Wed-Sun, longer summer hours; 🅿🛜🍴) The chef-proprietor hails from Italy so the dishes at this smart inn are a happy fusion of Exmoor produce and flavours of the Med. Your gnocchi could come with gorgonzola and truffle, the local lamb might be roasted in fragrant spices, while the fish might be *baccala' alla Livornese* (cod with capers, potatoes and olives).

Ship Inn
PUB

(Bottom Ship; ☑ 01643-863288; www.shipinnporlockweir.co.uk; Porlock Weir; ☺ 11am-11pm, winter hours vary) The Bottom Ship (so called because – yep – it's at the bottom of the hill onto Porlock Weir) is loved by locals for its huge terrace, flagstone floors, wood burner, real ales (including Exmoor Stag) and ciders (including Cheddar Valley).

Lynton & Lynmouth
☑ 01598

Tucked in amid precipitous cliffs and steep, tree-lined slopes, these twin coastal towns are a landscape-painter's dream. Bustling Lynmouth sits beside the shore, a busy harbour lined with pubs and souvenir shops. On the clifftop, Lynton feels much more genteel and well-to-do. A cliffside railway links the two: it's powered by the rushing West Lyn River, which feeds numerous cascades and waterfalls nearby.

👁 Sights

⭐ Cliff Railway
HERITAGE RAILWAY

(☑ 01598-753486; www.cliffrailwaylynton.co.uk; The Esplanade, Lynmouth; one way adult/child £3/2; ☺ 11am-4pm) This extraordinary piece of Victorian engineering involves two cars with tiny balconies, that are linked by a steel cable, descending and ascending the steeply sloping cliff face according to the weight of water in the cars' tanks. All burnished wood and polished brass, it's been running since 1890 and makes for an unmissable ride.

HIKES AROUND LYNTON & LYNMOUTH

The plunging cliffs and densely wooded valleys around Lynton and Lynmouth make for memorable day hikes. Some paths are particularly popular so ask at local tourist offices about the less-trod trails. A good map helps, such as Ordnance Survey's *Explorer OL9*.

Valley of the Rocks Spot formations dubbed the Devil's Cheesewring and Ragged Jack, and feral goats wandering cliff-side paths. Quieter routes to the valley are the inland ones snaking south and west from Lynton.

Countisbury Common Open, hilly terrain, leading north to the lighthouse at Foreland Point.

Watersmeet A quieter route into this popular, waterfall-dotted valley is to hike in from Leeford village to the east, or Coombe Park Wood to the south.

Lyn Cleave After the Glen Lyn Gorge, head up to a ridge-top hike across fields towards Higher and Lower East Lyn.

Trentishoe Down Some 8 miles west of Lynmouth, four separate car parks are gateways to the coast path and the wooded Heddon Valley far below.

Flood Memorial   MUSEUM
(The Esplanade, Lynmouth; ⊙10am-5pm Easter-Oct) FREE On 16 August 1952 a huge wave of water swept through Lynmouth following torrential rain. The devastation was immense: 34 people lost their lives, and four bridges and countless houses were washed away. This exhibition features photos of the aftermath and personal testimonies of those involved. It's volunteer run – hours may vary.

🛏 Sleeping

Heddon Valley   CAMPGROUND £
(☑01643-863905; www.nationaltrust.org.uk; Heddon Valley, near Parracombe; sites per 2 adults £20; ⊙mid-Jul–Aug; P) It's kept deliberately bare-bones in this unmanicured, pop-up campsite, so prepare to collect your own water and sit on a compost toilet while you listen to the surf hitting the shore far below.

⭐ Bath Hotel   HOTEL ££
(☑01598-752238; www.bathhotellynmouth.co.uk; The Harbour, Lynmouth; d £90-145, ste £155; P🐾🏠) The Bath Hotel has been a feature of the town since Victorian times. These days it's a swish affair with premium rooms featuring gorgeously nautical styling, Victorian curios, supremely comfortable beds and expansive harbour and headland views. The 'Austerity' rooms are much less snazzy – but they're also £50 cheaper.

Lynn Valley   B&B ££
(☑01598-753300; www.lynvalleyguesthouse.com; Riverside Rd, Lynmouth; s from £60, d £80-110, q £150; P🏠) Walkers love this smart little guesthouse thanks to baths to soak in and a setting right on the coast path. Even if you're not hiking you'll like the crisp, bright decor, harbour views and mini-decanters of sherry in the rooms.

North Walk House   B&B £££
(☑01598-753372; www.northwalkhouse.co.uk; North Walk, Lynton; s from £93, d £150-190; P🏠) Polished wooden floors, colourful rugs, sparkling bathrooms and a cliff-side terrace give North Walk House a boutique, hideaway feel. The sweeping views over the sea and rugged headlands are fantastic, while the all-organic breakfasts feature Exmoor bacon and sausages, and Aga-baked eggs.

Rising Sun   INN £££
(☑01598-753223; www.risingsunlynmouth.co.uk; Harbourside, Lynmouth; d £145-170) A former 14th-century smugglers' haunt has been transformed into an intimate hideaway with a sleek designer feel. Elegant flourishes are all around, from the subtle lighting to the local art. Ask for a sea-view room to watch the tide rise and fall in the harbour just outside.

🍴 Eating

Esplanade Fish Bar   FISH & CHIPS £
(☑01598-753798; 2 The Esplanade, Lynmouth; mains from £8; ⊙noon-8pm) An award-winning chippy set a few steps from the rough-sand beach.

★ **Ancient Mariner** PUB FOOD ££
(📞 01598-752238; www.bathhotellynmouth.co.uk; The Harbour, Lynmouth; mains £12-19; ⏱ 10-11.30am, noon-4pm & 5.30-9pm; 📶) The Mariner brings a burst of shipwreck chic to Lynmouth, thanks to a copper bar top, curved ship's decking, covered outdoor seating and a figurehead that isn't entirely clothed. Drink it all in while tucking into a stacked-high Mariner Burger, complete with Exmoor ale and black-treacle-braised brisket, onion jam and blue-cheese mousse.

Vanilla Pod BISTRO ££
(📞 01598-753706; www.thevanillapodlynton.co.uk; 10 Queen St, Lynton; snacks from £5, mains £13-18; ⏱ 10am-4pm & 6-9pm, closed Feb; 📶 🖊) They've got all meal times covered here: it might be bacon butties for breakfast, mezze for lunch or grilled sea bass for supper. Plus afternoon cream teas.

❶ Getting There & Away

Bus 309/310 Runs year-round from Barnstaple via Parracombe to Lynton and Lynmouth (£3.60, one hour, hourly Monday to Saturday).

Bus 300 A seasonal, vintage (1950s) bus that shuttles between Minehead and Lynmouth (£10, 55 minutes), via Porlock (£6, 15 minutes). Services run twice daily Monday to Friday, from mid-July to early September only.

AT A GLANCE

POPULATION
3 million

BIGGEST CITY
Southampton:
236,882

BEST BEACH
Chesil Beach (p279)

**BEST CHALK
FIGURE**
Cerne Giant (p275)

BEST HILL FORT
Maiden Castle (p276)

WHEN TO GO
Apr & May Camp-
sites, B&Bs and
beachside cafes
reopen ahead of
summer crowds.

Jun–Aug School
holidays bring busier
beaches and attrac-
tions – and higher
accommodation
costs.

Sep & Oct Quieter
and still warm – an
ideal time to hike
in Dorset, the New
Forest and the Isle of
Wight.

Beach near Durdle Door (p274)
ICTUS PHOTOGRAPHY/SHUTTERSTOCK

Hampshire, Wiltshire & Dorset

For holidays amid the best of ancient England, head to three counties with a checklist of charms. Wiltshire offers mighty, mysterious Stonehenge, plus – in lesser-known Avebury – the largest stone circle in the world. Dorset tempts you to swim in picturesque coves before sipping cider beside thatched pubs. The Jurassic Coast sees you foraging for fossils and discovering wave-carved sea stacks and bays. On the Isle of Wight, chalky white cliffs frame campsites dotted with vintage camper vans. Portsmouth excels at maritime history, the New Forest delivers tranquil woods, and everywhere hilltop castles litter landscapes studded with stately homes. Bewitching and engaging, these three counties offer endless delights to explore.

INCLUDES

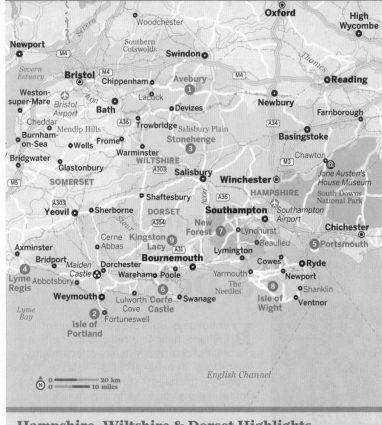

Hampshire, Wiltshire & Dorset Highlights

1 Avebury (p289) Wandering around the largest stone circle in the world.

2 Isle of Portland (p279) Discovering world-class statues carved into the rock at Tout Quarry.

3 Stonehenge (p288) Embarking on a magical dawn walk inside the massive sarsen ring.

4 Lyme Regis (p280) Foraging for fossils that pop out from crumbling cliffs.

5 Portsmouth Historic Dockyard (p262) Staring at the ancient timbers of Henry VIII's salvaged warship.

6 Corfe Castle (p273) Roaming the towering, shattered ruins of a mighty fortress.

7 New Forest (p263) Spotting deer and wild ponies as you cycle amid woods.

8 Isle of Wight (p270) Exploring a fortress set on the chalk cliffs of a holiday isle.

9 Kingston Lacy (p274) Revelling in the ornate interiors of Dorset's finest stately home.

🏃 Activities

Walking

Connecting Poole in Dorset with Minehead in Somerset, the legendary South West Coast Path (www.southwestcoastpath.org. uk) stretches for 630 miles around the end of England. The Dorset section includes the World Heritage Site Jurassic Coast – a 95-mile strip of shore where rock formations, beaches and cliffs span 185 million years of geology.

On the Isle of Wight, a testing 67-mile coast path encircles a network of rural and family-friendly trails. The New Forest

National Park offers gentle, picturesque walking along hundreds of miles of paths through heathland and ancient woods.

Other hiking highlights are Wiltshire's 87-mile Ridgeway National Trail (www.nationaltrail.co.uk/ridgeway), which starts near Avebury and winds through chalk downland and the wooded Chiltern hills.

Cycling

The New Forest has more than 140 miles of car-free trails that snake through wildlife-rich heaths and woods. Routes range from short, family-friendly rides to 20-mile jaunts.

Just offshore, the Isle of Wight boasts 200 miles of bike-friendly trails and a hilly, but hugely popular 65-mile Round the Island Cycle Route.

Launched in 2020, the 220-mile, circular King Alfred's Way connects four national trails. It starts in Winchester and takes in Salisbury, Stonehenge and Avebury.

Mountain-biking highlights include the largely off-road South Downs Way, which traces a chalk ridge for 100 miles from Winchester to Eastbourne on the coast.

Good information sources are Sustrans (www.sustrans.org.uk) and local tourist offices.

Watersports

World-class sailing hubs include the vast, 890-hectare Portland Harbour near Weymouth, and the yachting havens of the Isle of Wight and Poole. Stand-up paddleboarding (SUP) and sit-on-top kayaks can be hired out by the hour in sheltered coastal spots. Firms offering windsurfing lessons, coasteering and guided sea-kayaking tours pepper the coasts.

Weymouth and Portland offer top-class diving, with a wide range of depths, environments and wrecks. Local firms hire out gear and run dive trips.

Climbing

Dorset draws climbers with its creamy white coastal crags. The Isle of Portland has a wealth of prime limestone sport routes for all grades, plus some bouldering and deep-water solo options.

 **Getting There & Around**

BUS

The region's bus links are good. As ever in England, connections reduce and service frequency falls the further you go from main urban areas.

National Express (www.nationalexpress.com) Often provides the quickest bus link between cities and larger towns.

First (www.firstgroup.com) Key provider in Dorset and Portsmouth.

More (www.wdbus.co.uk) Useful service across Wiltshire and Dorset and into the New Forest. Day tickets (adult/child £9/6) for the biggest zone (ABC) are good value. An unlimited weekend ticket costs £16.

Stagecoach (www.stagecoachbus.com) Key bus provider in Hampshire.

PlusBus (www.plusbus.info) Adds local bus travel to your train ticket (£2 to £4 per day) in towns including Portsmouth, Salisbury and Weymouth. Buy tickets at train stations.

CAR & MOTORCYCLE

Routes range from motorways in the east, via A roads and busy streets, to winding country lanes. In the New Forest some are unfenced – prepare for animals on the roads.

Some of the coastal routes, especially in Dorset and on the isles of Wight and Portland, offer spectacular views.

TRAIN

South Western Railway (www.southwesternrailway.com) is the main operator. It runs trains from London and the southeast to destinations including Winchester, Portsmouth, Southampton, Salisbury and Weymouth. It also provides services to the New Forest, and links the region with Exeter and Bristol.

The Freedom of the South West Rover pass takes in much of the region. It offers three days of train travel in seven days (adult/child £106/53) or eight days travel in 15 days (£148/74). Journeys are unlimited in an area west of, and including, Portsmouth, Salisbury, Bath and Bristol.

HAMPSHIRE

Hampshire's history is regal and rich. Kings Alfred the Great, Knut and William the Conqueror all based their reigns in its ancient cathedral city of Winchester, whose jumble of historic buildings sits in the centre of undulating chalk downs. The county's coast is awash with heritage, too – in rejuvenated Portsmouth you can clamber aboard the pride of Nelson's navy, HMS *Victory*, and wonder at the *Mary Rose* (Henry VIII's flagship), before wandering wharfs buzzing with restaurants, shops and bars. Hampshire's southwestern corner claims the open heath and woods of the New Forest National Park.

Winchester

☎ 01962 / POP 116,600

Calm, collegiate Winchester is a mellow must-see. The past still echoes strongly around the flint-flecked walls of this ancient cathedral city. It was the capital of Saxon kings and a power base of bishops, and its statues and sights evoke two of England's mightiest myth makers: Alfred the Great and King Arthur (he of the round table). Winchester's architecture is exquisite, from the handsome Elizabethan and Regency buildings in the narrow streets to the wondrous cathedral at its core, while its river valley location means there are charming waterside trails to explore.

◉ Sights

Check whether tours of prestigious **Winchester College** (☎ 01962-621209; www.winchestercollege.org; College St), suspended in 2020, have resumed.

★ Winchester Cathedral   CATHEDRAL

(☎ 01962-857200; www.winchester-cathedral.org.uk; The Close; adult/child £10/free; ⊙ 10am-4pm) One of southern England's most awe-inspiring buildings, 11th-century Winchester Cathedral boasts a fine Gothic facade, one of the longest medieval naves in Europe (164m) and a fascinating jumble of features from all eras. Other highlights include the intricately carved medieval choir stalls, which sport everything from mythical beasts to a mischievous green man. Look out too for Jane Austen's grave (near the entrance) – there's a brass plaque and a window commemorating the celebrated writer alongside.

Today's cathedral sits beside foundations that mark Winchester's original 7th-century minster church. The cathedral was begun in 1070 and completed in 1093, and was subsequently entrusted with the bones of its patron saint, St Swithin (Bishop of Winchester from 852 to 862). He is best known for the proverb stating that if it rains on St Swithin's Day (15 July), it will rain for a further 40 days and 40 nights.

Soggy ground and poor construction spelled disaster for the early church. The original tower collapsed in 1107 and major restructuring continued until the mid-15th century. Look out for the monument at the far end of the building to diver William Walker, who saved the cathedral from collapse by delving repeatedly into its waterlogged underbelly from 1906 to 1912 to bolster rotting wooden foundations with vast quantities of concrete and brick.

Distancing regulations at the time of research may affect what you can see and do. Check the cathedral website for details of whether the **Winchester Bible** is on display. As the biggest, brightest and best-surviving 12th-century English Bible, the dazzling, four-volume tome has vivid illuminated pages. It was commissioned in 1160, possibly by the grandson of William the Conqueror. If the crypt is open it offers views of *Sound II*, an enigmatic life-size depiction of a contemplative man by Anthony Gormley.

If the Tower and Roof Tours (£6.50) are running they'll lead through narrow stairwells, up 213 steps, across an interior gallery high above the nave, through the bell chamber and out onto the roof. When operating, the highly informative, one-hour Cathedral Body Tours and the atmospheric Crypt Tours are included in the admission price.

Regular services include those on Sunday at 10am and Wednesday at noon.

The cathedral's tree-fringed lawns make for tranquil spots to take time out, especially on the quieter south side beyond the cloisters.

★ Wolvesey Castle   CASTLE

(EH; ☎ 0370 333 1181; www.english-heritage.org.uk; College St; ⊙ 10am-5pm Apr-Oct, to 4pm Sat & Sun Nov-Mar) **FREE** The fantastical, crumbling remains of early-12th-century Wolvesey Castle huddle in the protective embrace of the city's walls. Completed by Henry de Blois, it served as the Bishop of Winchester's residence throughout the medieval era, with Queen Mary I and Philip II of Spain celebrating their wedding feast here in 1554.

Round Table & Great Hall   HISTORIC BUILDING

(☎ 01962-846476; www.hants.gov.uk/greathall; Castle Ave; adult/child £3/free; ⊙ 10am-5pm) Winchester's cavernous Great Hall is the only part of 11th-century Winchester Castle that Oliver Cromwell spared from destruction. Crowning the wall like a giant-sized dartboard of green and cream spokes is what centuries of mythology have dubbed King Arthur's Round Table. It's actually a 700-year-old copy, but is fascinating nonetheless. It's thought to have been constructed in the late 13th century and then painted in the reign of Henry VIII (King Arthur's image is unsurprisingly reminiscent of Henry's youthful face).

Winchester

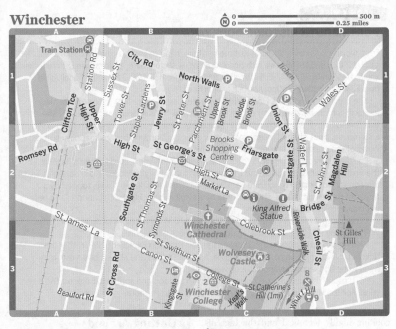

Winchester

🏃 Activities

Winchester's tempting walks include the 1-mile **Keats' Walk** through the water meadows to the Hospital of St Cross. Its beauty is said to have prompted the poet to pen the ode *To Autumn;* pick up the trail near Wolvesey Castle. Alternatively, head down Wharf Hill, through the water meadows to St Catherine's Hill (1 mile), or take the tranquil **Riverside Walk** from Wolvesey Castle along the River Itchen's banks to High St.

🛏 Sleeping

⭐ 16a   B&B £££
(📞 07730 510663; www.16a-winchester.co.uk; 16a Parchment St; r £145-185; 🛜) The word 'boutique' gets bandied around freely, but here it fits. The sumptuous conversion of this old dance hall sees an antique piano and honesty bar frame a wood-burning stove. Gorgeous bedrooms feature exposed brick, lofty ceilings, vast beds and baths on the mezzanines with views of the stars.

⭐ Wykeham Arms   INN £££
(📞 01962-853834; www.wykehamarmswinchester. co.uk; 75 Kingsgate St; s £84, d £144-194; 🅿🛜) At 250-odd years of age, the Wykeham bursts with history – it used to be a brothel and also put Nelson up for a night (some say the events coincided). Creaking stairs lead to plush bedrooms that manage to be both deeply established and on-trend – sleigh beds meet jazzy fabrics, oak dressers sport stylish lights. Simply smashing.

🍴 Eating & Drinking

⭐ Black Rat   MODERN BRITISH £££
(📞 01962-844465; www.theblackrat.co.uk; 88 Chesil St; mains £18-29; ⊙ 6-9.15pm Wed-Sun, noon-2.15pm Sat & Sun) The aromas are irresistible, the food frankly fabulous, the

PORTSMOUTH HISTORIC DOCKYARD

For a world-class collection of maritime heritage, head to **Portsmouth Historic Dockyard** (☑023-9283 9766; www.historicdockyard.co.uk; Victory Gate; all-attraction Explorer ticket adult/child/family £44/34/95, 1 attraction adult/child from £24/19, 3 attractions adult/child from £34/24; ⊙10am-5.30pm Apr-Oct, to 5pm Nov-Mar).

The blockbuster draw is Henry VIII's favourite flagship, the **Mary Rose** (www.maryrose.org), which sank suddenly off Portsmouth while fighting the French in 1545. She was raised from the bottom in 1982 in an extraordinary feat of marine archaeology. A £35-million, boat-shaped museum has now been built around her, giving uninterrupted views of the preserved timbers of her massive hull.

Equally impressive is **HMS Victory** (www.hms-victory.com), Lord Nelson's flagship at the Battle of Trafalgar (1805) and the site of his famous dying words 'Kiss me, Hardy', after victory over the French had been secured. This remarkable ship is topped by a forest of ropes and masts, and weighted by a swollen belly filled with cannons and paraphernalia for an 850-strong crew.

Other nautical sights include the Victorian **HMS Warrior** (www.hmswarrior.org), the WWI warship **HMS M.33** and a wealth of imaginative museums.

Visiting more than one exhibit makes the all-attraction Explorer ticker, rather than tickets to visit single ships, the best value. As for all sights and attractions, visits may need to be booked in advance; check well ahead.

Portsmouth has regular rail connections with London and southern England and beyond. For the Historic Dockyard, get off at Portsmouth Harbour.

cooking highly technical and the ingredients dare to surprise – expect chalk stream trout to be joined by wasabi and beetroot ice cream, and meats to be smoked with hay. That'll be why the Black Rat deserves its Michelin star.

The decor is vaguely bohemian, the garden features heated huts and the extensive drinks menu lists 45 gins.

Black Boy PUB
(☑01962-861754; www.theblackboypub.com; 1 Wharf Hill; ⊙noon-2.30pm & 5-11pm Mon-Fri, noon-midnight Sat, noon-10.30pm Sun) Two open fires, a random array of dented antiques, a clutch of draught ciders and five real ales make this a legendary local. There's also a spacious, heated, sheltered garden out back.

❶ Information

Tourist Office (☑01962-840500; www.visitwinchester.co.uk; Guildhall, High St) Set in Winchester's Victorian Guildhall – check it's reopened to visitors.

❶ Getting There & Away

Winchester is 65 miles west of London. Trains leave half-hourly to hourly for London Waterloo (£19, 1¼ hours) and hourly for Portsmouth (£13, one hour).

❶ Getting Around

Bicycle Bikes can be hired from **Bespoke Biking** (www.bespokebiking.com; 4 Middle Brook St; per half-/full day £15/25; ⊙9am-5pm Mon-Sat, 10am-4pm Sun). It's best to book.

Car Park & Ride car parks (per day £3) are signed off junctions 10 and 11 of the M3. Services run roughly from 6.30am to 6.30pm, Monday to Saturday.

Taxi There are taxi ranks on the High St, and outside the train station and tourist office, or call **Wintax** (☑01962-250250; www.wintaxcars.com).

New Forest

With typical, accidental, English irony the New Forest is anything but new – it was first proclaimed a royal hunting preserve in 1079. It's also not much of a forest, being mostly heathland ('forest' is from the Old French for 'hunting ground'). Designated a national park in 2005, the forest's combined charms make it a joy to explore. Wild ponies mooch around pretty scrubland, deer flicker in the distance and rare birds flit among the foliage. Genteel villages dot the landscape, connected by a web of walking and cycling trails.

🏃 Activities

⭐ **New Forest Activities**   ADVENTURE SPORTS
(📞 01590-612377; www.newforestactivities.co.uk;
High St, Beaulieu) Runs a wide range of sessions including canoeing (adult/child per 90 minutes from £29/16), kayaking (per two hours from £40/37) and archery (adult/child per 90 minutes £24/13).

Walking

The forest is gentle, largely level hiking territory. Ordnance Survey (OS) produces a detailed 1:25,000 Explorer map (New Forest; *OL22*, £9); *Pathfinder New Forest Short Walks* (£8) features 20 circular day hikes of 2 to 6 miles.

The New Forest Centre (p264) in Lyndhurst stocks maps and guides.

Check whether Forestry England's programme of guided walks (📞 0300 068 0400; www.forestry.gov.uk/newforestevents), suspended in 2020, have resumed.

Cycling

The New Forest makes for superb cycling, with 100 miles of routes linking the main villages and the key railway station at Brockenhurst. *The New Forest By Bike* map (£4.50) features 12 routes ranging from 8 to 32 miles. The *New Forest Cycling Guide* (£4) features six day-cycle routes of between 4 and 22 miles on a 1:25,000 OS map. Maps and guides can be bought from an information point in Lyndhurst's New Forest Centre.

To rent bikes, you'll need to pay a deposit (usually £20 to £25) and provide identification.

AA Bike Hire   CYCLING
(📞 02380-283349; www.aabikehirenewforest.co.uk; Fernglen, Gosport Lane, Lyndhurst; per day adult/child £10/5; ⊘9am-5.30pm Apr-Oct) Based in Lyndhurst's main car park.

Woods Cyclery   CYCLING
(New Forest Cycle Hire; 📞 02380-282028; www.thewoodscyclery.co.uk; 56 High St, Lyndhurst; per day adult/child £20/10; ⊘9am-5pm Tue-Sun) Also rents out electric bikes and kids' bike seats.

Cyclexperience   CYCLING
(New Forest Cyclehire; 📞 01590-624808; www.cyclex.co.uk; Train Station, Brockenhurst; per day adult/child from £18.50/9; ⊘10am-5pm) Based in a vintage railway carriage. They also deliver bikes across the national park and rent out electric bikes (per half-day £30 to £35).

Horse Riding

Social distancing measures at the time of research may mean stables can only take experienced riders, and that you need to bring your own riding hat. Expect to pay from £33 per hour. Check online for updates.

Local stables include **Arniss Equestrian Centre** (📞 01425-654114; www.arnissequestrian.co.uk; Godshill, Fordingbridge) and **Burley Villa** (Western Riding; 📞 01425-610278; www.burleyvilla.co.uk; Bashley Common Rd, near New Milton).

🛏 Sleeping

Campers can ask whether **Forestry England** (www.campingintheforest.co.uk) has reopened its 10 or so relatively rural New Forest sites.

ℹ Information

New Forest (www.thenewforest.co.uk) The area's official visitor website.

New Forest Centre (📞 01425-880020; www.thenewforest.co.uk; main car park, Lyndhurst; ⊘10.30am-4.30pm) Has a Visitor Information Point stocked with maps, leaflets and books.

ℹ Getting There & Around

BUS

National Express (www.nationalexpress.com) Buses stop at Ringwood and Southampton.

Bus 6 (hourly Monday to Saturday, five on Sunday) Runs from Southampton to Lyndhurst (£5, 40 minutes), Brockenhurst (£6.70, 50 minutes) and Lymington (£6.70, 1¼ hours).

Bus X1/X2 Links Bournemouth with Lymington (£6.50, 1½ hours, half-hourly Monday to Saturday, four on Sunday).

New Forest Tour (📞 01202-338420; www.thenewforesttour.info; per 1/2/5 days adult £17/23/34, child £9/11/16; ⊘9am-6pm early Jul-Aug) Three connecting routes of hop-on, hop-off buses, stopping at Lyndhurst's main car park, Brockenhurst train station, Lymington, Ringwood, Beaulieu and Exbury.

TRAIN

Two trains an hour run to Brockenhurst from London Waterloo (£26, two hours) via Winchester (£16, 30 minutes) and on to Bournemouth (£8, 20 minutes).

Local trains shuttle twice an hour between Brockenhurst and Lymington (£4, 11 minutes).

Lyndhurst & Brockenhurst

The quaint country villages of Lyndhurst and Brockenhurst are separated by just 4 miles. Their picturesque accommodation and superb eating options ensure they're atmospheric bases from which to explore the New Forest.

Sights

New Forest Centre   MUSEUM

(☑ 02380-283444; www.newforestcentre.org.uk; main car park, Lyndhurst; ⏱ 10.30am-4.30pm; 🔊) **FREE** Features a local labourer's cottage (complete with socks drying beside the fire), potato dibbles and a cider press. The mini-film makes for an accessible introduction to the park – listen, too, for recordings of the autumn pony sales, which take place after the annual drifts (round-ups).

The centre also houses a Visitor Information Point, with leaflets, maps and books.

Beaulieu   HISTORIC BUILDING

(☑ 01590-612345; www.beaulieu.co.uk; adult/child £25/10; ⏱ 10am-5pm) Petrolheads, historians and ghost-hunters gravitate to Beaulieu (*bew*-lee) – a vintage car museum, stately home and tourist complex centred on a 13th-century Cistercian monastery. Motor-maniacs will be in raptures at Lord Montague's **National Motor Museum**. Tickets are valid for a year; Beaulieu is served by the New Forest Tour (p263).

Sleeping & Eating

⭐ **Pig**   BOUTIQUE HOTEL £££

(☑ 01590-622354; www.thepighotel.com/brockenhurst; Beaulieu Rd, Brockenhurst; r £189-350; 🅿🔊) One of the New Forest's classiest hotels remains an utter delight: log baskets, croquet mallets and ranks of guest gumboots give things a country-house air; espresso machines and mini-larders lend bedrooms a luxury touch. The effortless elegance makes it feel like you've just dropped by a friend's (very stylish) rural retreat.

The Pig's 25-mile-radius menus change hourly depending on what's been found foraging or in the hotel's kitchen garden. Look out for lovage and potato soup, chalk stream trout and Beaulieu venison. Or plump for veg- and meat-topped flat breads (£13) from the wood-fired oven. Food (mains £15 to £21) is served between noon and 9.30pm.

Daisybank Cottage   B&B £££

(☑ 01590-622086; www.bedandbreakfast-newforest.co.uk; Sway Rd, Brockenhurst; s £130-140, d £140-150; 🅿🔊) The seven gorgeous themed bedrooms here are mini pamper palaces. Enjoy aromatic smellies in gleaming bathrooms, stylish luxurious furnishings and lots of little extras: handmade chocolates, smartphone docks, digital radios, and breakfasts, packed with New Forest produce, delivered to your room.

Snakecatcher   PUB ££

(☑ 01590-622348; www.thesnakecatcher.co.uk; Lyndhurst Rd, Brockenhurst; mains £9-15; ⏱ noon-11pm Mon-Wed, to 11.30pm Thu-Sat, to 10.30pm Sun; 🍴) In this handsome red-brick pub near Brockenhurst station you'll find local real ales, craft beers, ciders and a wide range of tasty burgers. Eat inside or go alfresco in the vast astro-turfed garden beside the pop-up bar.

ℹ Getting There & Away

Bus 6 Shuttles between Lyndhurst and Lymington (£4.40, hourly Monday to Saturday, five on Sunday), via Brockenhurst; as does the New Forest Tour (p263).

Trains Run twice an hour between Brockenhurst and Lymington (£4, 11 minutes).

Buckler's Hard

For such a tiny place, this picturesque huddle of 18th-century cottages, near the mouth of the River Beaulieu, has a big history. It started in 1722, when a duke of Montague built a port to finance a Caribbean expedition. His dream faltered, but when war with France came, this embryonic village and sheltered gravel waterfront became a secret boatyard where several of Nelson's triumphant Battle of Trafalgar warships were built. In the 20th century it played its part in the preparations for the D-Day landings.

Sights

Buckler's Hard Story   MUSEUM

(☑ 01590-616203; www.bucklershard.co.uk; adult/child £7.50/5.20; ⏱ 10am-5pm Apr-Sep, to 4pm Oct-Mar) The hamlet's fascinating Maritime Museum and heritage centre chart the inlet's shipbuilding history and role in WWII, and feature immaculately preserved 18th-century workshops and labourers' cottages.

Sleeping & Eating

⭐ **Master Builder's House**   HOTEL £££

(☑ 01590-616253; www.hillbrookehotels.co.uk; d £135-180; 🅿) In this beautifully restored 18th-century hotel, room styles range from stately to crisp. Soft lighting, burnished trunks and plush fabrics abound.

HAMPSHIRE, WILTSHIRE & DORSET NEW FOREST

Your dining options range from classy restaurant fare to family-friendly grub in the cool hotel **bar** (mains £14-27; ⊙ noon-9pm).

Lymington

🎣 01590 / POP 15,400

Yachting haven, New Forest base and jumping-off point to the Isle of Wight – the appealing Georgian harbour town of Lymington has several strings to its tourism bow. This former smuggler's port offers nautical shops, prime eating and sleeping spots and, in **Quay St**, an utterly quaint cobbled lane.

Activities

Puffin Cruises   BOATING
(🎣 07850 947618; www.puffincruiseslymington.com; Lymington Quay; adult/child from £8.50/4.50; ⊙ 10am-4pm Apr-Oct) Runs 30-minute cruises on the *Puffin Billi* that meander down the winding Lymington River to saltmarshes packed with birds. Smaller swashbucklers love the half-hour pirate-themed *Black Puffin* trips that set off to search for lost treasure.

🛏 Sleeping

★ Teddy's Farm   CAMPGROUND £
(Battramsley Farm; 🎣 07815 189767; www.teddysfarm.co.uk; Shirley Holms Rd, Boldre; campsite per pitch £24, bell tent per 2 nights £350; ⊙ mid-Jul–early Sep) The affable Teddy presides over a chilled-out site where undulating fields are home to firepits for hire, compost loos and alfresco showers. The glamping field has four-person, pre-pitched bell tents, complete with bunting and tealight chandeliers. It's 2 miles north of Lymington.

Mill at Gordleton   HOTEL ££
(🎣 01590-682219; www.themillatgordleton.co.uk; Silver St, Hordle; d £105-150, ste £180-299; 🅿 🛜) Step inside here and know, instantly, you're going to be looked after beautifully. Velvet and gingham dot the gorgeous rooms (each one comes with a sweet soft toy duck), while the garden is a magical mix of rushing water, fairy lights and modern sculpture. The Mill is 4 miles west of Lymington.

Stanwell House   BOUTIQUE HOTEL £££
(🎣 01590-677123; www.stanwellhouse.com; 14 High St; d £145, ste £255-295; @ 🛜 🐾) There are boutique tweaks everywhere at Stanwell. Swish Georgian rooms manage to be both period and modern: the four-poster ones sport reproduction furniture and subtle colours, while the suites are simply irresistible

– two even have their own roof terrace for sunny days and moonlit nights.

Eating

Deep Blue   FISH & CHIPS £
(🎣 01590-679491; www.deepbluerestaurants.com; 130 High St; fish & chips £10; ⊙ 11.30am-3pm daily, plus 5-7.30pm Sun-Thu, 5-8pm Fri & Sat) 🌿 They're often queuing out the door at this classic British chippy, which dishes up sustainable fish, freshly cut chips, mushy peas and pickled eggs. Eat in or take away.

Ship   PUB FOOD ££
(🎣 01590-676903; www.theshiplymington.co.uk; The Quay; mains £12-26; ⊙ kitchen noon-10pm Mon-Sat, to 9pm Sun; 🐾) A pub for all seasons: knock back summertime drinks on the waterside terrace; in winter, a toasty log burner gets you warm. Well-judged food ranges from plant-based dirty burgers and crispy pizzas to juicy fillet steaks.

★ Elderflower   MODERN BRITISH £££
(🎣 01590-676908; www.elderflowerrestaurant.co.uk; 5 Quay St; mains £17-37, 4/5/7 courses £50/60/70; ⊙ noon-2.30pm & 6.30-9.30pm Wed-Fri, 9.30am-2.30pm & 6.30-10pm Sat, 9.30am-4pm Sun) An Anglo-French feel infuses Elderflower – from the garlic-laced snails to the black treacle cured bacon. Innovative puddings are a real treat – where else can you get a squid-ink doughnut with blackcurrant gel? Ask if the classy takeaway menu, which features oysters, lobster and chateaubriand, is still running.

ⓘ Getting There & Away

Lymington has two train stations: Lymington Town and Lymington Pier. Isle of Wight ferries connect with Lymington Pier. Trains run to Southampton (£11, 50 minutes), with a change at Brockenhurst, twice an hour.

Wightlink Ferries (🎣 0333 999 7333; www.wightlink.co.uk) has car and passenger ferries that run hourly to Yarmouth on the Isle of Wight (40 minutes). An adult/child foot-passenger single costs £13.60/6.80; day returns cost £17.60/8.80. Summer-time fares for a car and two passengers start at around £67 for a short-break return.

ISLE OF WIGHT

These days the Isle of Wight has the air of a holiday destination busy reinventing itself. For decades this slab of rock anchored off

Isle of Wight

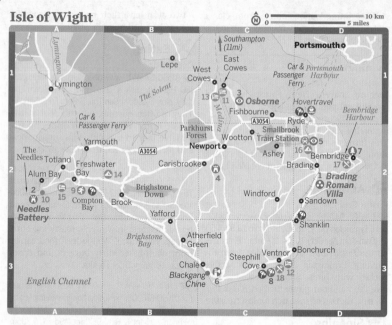

Isle of Wight

Portsmouth was a magnet for vacationing families, and it still has seaside kitsch by the bucket and spade. But now the proms and amusement arcades are framed by pockets of cool. Just-caught seafood is served in kooky fishers' cafes, and glamorous camping rules – here sites are dotted with yurts and vintage camper vans. Yet still the isle's principal appeal remains: a mild climate, myriad outdoorsy activities and a 67-mile shore lined with beaches, dramatic white cliffs and tranquil sand dunes.

🏃 Activities

Cycling

With 200 miles of cycle routes, the Isle of Wight makes pedal pushers smile. The island's official visitor website (www.visit isleofwight.co.uk) lists suggested trips (complete with maps), ranging from family-friendly tootles along former railway lines to the 65-mile Round the Island Cycle Route.

Bike rentals start at around £18/65 per day/week. Many firms deliver and collect on orders over £30.

The IW Cycle Festival is usually held in late August; see online for updates.

Walking

This is one of the best spots in southern England for rambling, with 500 miles of well-marked walking paths, including 67 miles of coastal routes.

Look on the isle's visitor website to see if the walking festival, held over two weeks in May or October, is running.

Watersports

Watersports are serious business on the Isle of Wight. Cowes is the sailing centre; surfers, windsurfers and kitesurfers flock to the southwest, especially around Compton Bay, while powerboats run trips out to the Needles rocks.

Isle of Wight
Adventure Activities   ADVENTURE SPORTS
(www.adventureactivitiesisleofwight.co.uk; Gate La, Freshwater) Delivers two-hour activity sessions, including kayaking (adult/child £40/25) and coasteering (adult/child £45/30).

 Festivals

Isle of Wight Festival   MUSIC
(www.isleofwightfestival.com; ☉mid-Jun) The isle's festival tradition kicked off in 1968, when an estimated 200,000 hippies came to see The Doors, The Who, Joni Mitchell and rock icon Jimi Hendrix's last performance. Generations on, its gatherings are still some of England's top musical events. The festival was cancelled in 2020 because of Covid-19, but will hopefully be back in 2021.

Cowes Week   SAILING
(www.aamcowesweek.co.uk; ☉early Aug) Cowes Week, first held in 1826, is one of the biggest and longest-running sailing regattas in the world. It's due to resume in 2021.

❶ Information

www.visitisleofwight.co.uk The island's official visitor website.
Information Points Collections of leaflets and maps include those at Yarmouth Harbour Office, Newport bus station and the bus staton on Ryde Esplanade.

❶ Getting There & Away

Hovertravel (☑ 01983-717717; www.hover-travel.co.uk; Quay Rd, Ryde; day-return adult/ child £24/12) Shuttles foot passengers be-tween Southsea (a Portsmouth suburb) and Ryde, half-hourly to hourly.

Red Funnel (☑ 02380-248500; www.redfunnel. co.uk) Runs car-and-passenger ferries between Southampton and East Cowes (same-day return adult/child £19/9.50, from £60 with car, 60 minutes, hourly), and high-speed passenger ferries between Southampton and West Cowes (same-day return adult/child £27.20/13.60, 25 minutes, one to two per hour).

Wightlink Ferries (☑ 0333 999 7333; www. wightlink.co.uk) Operates passenger ferries at least every hour from Portsmouth to Ryde (day-return adult/child £20.60/10.30, single adult/child £16.10/8.05, 22 minutes). It also runs hourly car-and-passenger ferries from Ports-mouth to Fishbourne (45 minutes) and from Lym-ington to Yarmouth (40 minutes). For both, an adult/child foot-passenger single is £13.60/6.80; day returns cost £17.60/8.80. Car fares start at around £67 for a short-break return.

❶ Getting Around

BUS

Southern Vectis (www.islandbuses.info) runs buses between the eastern towns roughly every 30 minutes. Regular services to the remoter southwest, especially between Blackgang Chine and Brook, are less frequent.

Check whether the **Island Coaster** service, suspended in 2020, has resumed. Between April and September it normally runs along the south-ern shore from Ryde in the east to Yarmouth in the west.

CAR

Enterprise (☑ 01983-559357; www.enterprise. co.uk; 50 Crocker St, Newport; per day from £25) Hires out cars from its offices in the island's capital, Newport.

TRAIN

South Western Railway (www.southwestern railway.com) runs Island Line trains twice hourly from Ryde to Shanklin (same-day return £4.80, 25 minutes), via Smallbrook Junction, Brading and Sandown.

Cowes

☑ 01983 / POP 14,200

Pack your yachting cap – the hilly Georgian harbour town of Cowes is famous for the Cowes Week annual yachting regatta. Fibre-glass playthings and vintage sailing boats line Cowes' waterfronts, which are lopped into East and West Cowes by the pictur-esque River Medina.

The island's capital, Newport, is 5 miles south.

> **ⓘ CAR FERRY COSTS**
>
> The cost of car ferries to the Isle of Wight can vary enormously. Save by booking ahead, asking about special offers and travelling off-peak (midweek and later in the day). Long stays tend to be cheaper and some deals include admission to island attractions. Booking online can mean paying around £20 less.

⊙ Sights

★ Osborne HISTORIC SITE
(EH; ☑ 0370 333 1181; www.english-heritage.org. uk; York Ave, East Cowes; adult/child £19/11.40; ⊙ 10am-5pm Apr-Oct, to 4pm Sat & Sun Nov-Mar; ℗) Lemon-frosted and Italianate, Osborne House is pure Victorian pomp. Built in the 1840s at the behest of Queen Victoria, the monarch grieved here for many years after her husband's death. Extravagant rooms include the opulent Royal Apartments and Durbar Room; other highlights are horse and carriage rides, the Swiss Cottage – where the royal ankle-biters would play – and the stroll down Rhododendron Walk to Her Majesty's private beach.

Carisbrooke Castle CASTLE
(EH; ☑ 01983-522107; www.english-heritage.org. uk; Castle Hill, Newport; adult/child £11.30/6.80; ⊙ 10am-5pm Apr-Oct, 10am-4pm Sat & Sun Nov-Mar; ℗) Charles I was imprisoned here before his execution in 1649. Today you can clamber the sturdy ramparts and stroll around the bowling green the doomed monarch used.

⊨ Sleeping

★ onefiftycowes B&B ££
(☑ 07795 296399; www.onefiftycowes.co.uk; 150 Park Rd, West Cowes; s £70-75, d £90-110; ℗ 🛜) All the trappings of a luxury hotel, all the individuality of a B&B – at onefiftycowes, wicker chairs sit beside stand-alone sinks; feature fireplaces are stacked with sea-smoothed pebbles. The best room is Solent, where a pair of binoculars is waiting to help you gaze at the partial sea views.

Fountain HOTEL ££
(☑ 01983-292397; www.oldenglishinns.co.uk; High St, West Cowes; s £55-80, d 77-115; 🛜) Georgian-repro style rules at this appealing harbourside inn, where mock-flock wallpaper and old, wooden furniture define comfy rooms; number 21 has slanting ceilings and prime views of the ferry quay. The snug bar and sunny terrace are good places to sample pints and pub-grub classics (mains from £12; food served 11am to 10pm).

Ryde to Bembridge

The nippiest foot-passenger ferries between Wight and Portsmouth alight in Ryde, a workaday but appealing Victorian town rich in the trappings of the British seaside. Next come the cutesy village of Brading, with its fine Roman villa, and photogenic Bembridge Harbour, which is fringed by sandy beaches.

Further south lie the twin resort towns of Sandown and Shanklin, with promenades and hordes of families wielding buckets and spades.

⊙ Sights

★ Brading Roman Villa RUINS
(☑ 01983-406223; www.bradingromanvilla.org. uk; Morton Old Rd, Brading; adult/child £9.50/4.75; ⊙ hours vary) The exquisitely preserved mosaics here (including a famous cockerel-headed man) make this one of the finest Romano-British sites in the UK. Wooden walkways lead over rubble walls and brightly painted tiles, allowing you to gaze right down onto the ruins below.

St Helens Duver NATURE RESERVE
(NT; ☑ 01983-741020; www.nationaltrust.org.uk; near St Helens; ⊙ 24hr; ℗) At this idyllic sand-and-shingle spit bordering the mouth of the River Yar, trails snake past swathes of sea pink, marram grass and rare clovers. It's signed from the village of St Helens, near Bembridge Harbour.

Isle of Wight Steam Railway HERITAGE RAILWAY
(☑ 01983-882204; www.iwsteamrailway.co.uk; Smallbrook Junction; adult/child return from £13/6.50; ⊙ 4-9 trains daily mid-Apr–Sep) Chugs along for the one-hour return journey from Smallbrook Junction to Wootton.

⊨ Sleeping & Eating

★ Vintage Vacations CAMPSITE ££
(☑ 07802 758113; www.vintagevacations.co.uk; Hazelgrove Farm, Ashey Rd; 2-/4-/6-person caravans per week £630/720/780; ⊙ Apr-Oct; ℗) The bevy of 1960s Airstream trailers on this farm

is vintage chic personified. The gleaming aluminium shells shelter retro radios and lovingly selected mismatched crockery. Alternatively, opt for a beach-shack retreat, a 1930s scout hut, or the Mission: a late-Victorian tin chapel.

Best Dressed Crab   SEAFOOD **££**
(✆01983-874758; www.thebestdressedcrabin town.co.uk; Fisherman's Wharf, Bembridge Harbour; mains £9-28; ⊙10am-4pm daily Mar-Dec, Sat & Sun Jan & Feb) Welcome to an idyllic spot to munch your lunch. At this bijou cafe tacked on to a pontoon, the day's crab and lobster harvest is turned into supremely tasty sandwiches, salads and soups. Best eaten at one of the tables perched beside the water as local fishing boats unload their catch.

Ventnor & Steephill Cove

The Victorian town of Ventnor slaloms so steeply down the island's southern coast that it feels more like the south of France. The shops in the town's winding streets are worth browsing, the seafront is worth a stroll, and nearby atmospheric Steephill Cove is well worth a detour.

◉ Sights

Steephill Cove   BEACH
(www.steephillcove-isleofwight.co.uk) A 1-mile walk west along the coast path from Ventnor leads to Steephill Cove – a tiny, sandy bay fringed by stone cottages and rickety-looking shacks. Beach finds festoon porches dotted with driftwood furniture and draped with fishing nets; a tiny clapboard lighthouse presides over the scene. It's all studiedly nautical, but still very nice.

Steephill Cove is off-limits to cars but you can park at the nearby Botanical Gardens (£5) and walk down.

St Catherine's Oratory   LIGHTHOUSE
(near Niton) FREE Known locally as the Pepperpot, this 34ft, octagonal, 14th-century tower constitutes England's only surviving medieval lighthouse.

🛏 Sleeping & Eating

Harbour View   GUESTHOUSE **££**
(St Augustine Villa; ✆01983-852285; www.harbour viewhotel.co.uk; The Esplanade, Ventnor; s £77-93, d £86-102; P🛜) Country-house collectables dot this Italianate Victorian villa, where wing-

backed chairs sit in stately bedrooms and rich red fabrics frame superb sea views. They'll have you watching the sun set from your sofa or the waves roll from your four-poster bed. The window-seated Tower Room has light pouring in from three sides. At the time of research the rates didn't include breakfast; look for updates online.

Hambrough   B&B **£££**
(✆01983-856333; www.thehambrough.com; Hambrough Rd, Ventnor; d £140-230; 🛜) What you see from the pick of the rooms at the Hambrough is truly fabulous – the suites have balconies with wrap-around sea views, while you can watch the waves from the bathtub in room 4. The furnishings are smooth and smart, rather than stunning; comfort comes courtesy of mini-fridges, underfloor heating and espresso machines.

Crab Shed   CAFE **£**
(✆01983-855819; www.steephillcove-isleofwight. co.uk; Steephill Cove; snacks from £5; ⊙noon-3pm Apr-Sep) Lobster pots and fishing boats line the slipway outside a shack that's a riot of sea-smoothed spars, cork floats and faded buoys. Irresistible takeaway treats include meaty crab salads, mackerel ciabatta and crumbly crab pasties.

Spyglass Inn   PUB FOOD **££**
(✆01983-855338; www.thespyglass.com; The Esplanade, Ventnor; mains £10-27; ⊙noon-9pm) When a beachfront pub is this bedecked with pirate paraphernalia, ships' lanterns and lifebelts, you tend to be wary of the meals. No need. The seafood platters and salads here are renowned, especially the grilled, garlic-butter-laced lobster – book these, they tend to sell out. There are lots of wave-side tables at which to down a pint.

West Wight

Rural and remote, Wight's westerly corner is where the island really comes into its own. Sheer white cliffs rear from a surging sea as the stunning coastline peels west to Alum Bay and the most famous chunks of chalk in the region: the **Needles**. These jagged rocks rise, shardlike, out of the sea, like the backbone of a prehistoric sea monster. West Wight is also home to arguably the isle's best beach: sandy, windswept **Compton Bay**.

⊙ Sights & Activities

★ **Needles Battery** FORT
(NT; ☑ 01983-754772; www.nationaltrust.org.uk; The Needles; adult/child £5/2.50; ⊙ 10am-5.30 mid-Mar–Oct) The Victorian fort complex at Wight's western tip was built in 1862 to prepare for a French invasion that never came. The site went on to serve in two world wars and then became a secret Cold War rocket-testing base. Walk to the battery along the cliffs from Alum Bay (1 mile) or hop on the summer-only, open-top **Needles Breezer tourist bus** (www.islandbuses. info; per 24hr adult/child £10/5; ⊙ 10am-5pm mid-Mar–Oct) that runs regularly between battery and bay.

Needles Pleasure Cruises BOATING
(☑ 01983-761587; www.needlespleasurecruises. co.uk; Alum Bay; adult/child £7/4; ⊙ 10.30am-4.30pm Apr-Oct) Twenty-minute voyages run half-hourly from Alum Bay beach to the towering Needles chalk stacks, providing cracking views of those soaring white cliffs.

🛏 Sleeping

Ask if **Totland Bay YHA** (☑ 03452 602912; www.yha.org.uk; Hirst Hill, Totland Bay; P@🛜) has reopened for individual bookings.

★ **Tom's Eco Lodge** CAMPSITE ££
(☑ 01983-758729; www.tomsecolodge.com; Tapnell Farm, Yarmouth; 2-person pod per night from £155, 4-person log cabin per 4 nights from £665; P🛜) ✎ Eco pods, log cabins, safari tents – the full gamut of comfy camping options sit happily on this spacious, sea-view site. They're beautifully decked out with their own showers and loos; some even have log-burning stoves.

DORSET

Holiday hotspot Dorset has one of Britain's best shorelines. It boasts the Jurassic Coast – a World Heritage Site flecked with sea-carved bays, crumbly cliffs and beaches loaded with fossilised souvenirs. Swimming, kayaking and hiking here are memorable. Inland, Thomas Hardy's lyrical landscape serves up vast Iron Age hill forts, rude chalk figures, fairy-tale castles and must-see stately homes. Then there's the Isle of Portland's rugged, bleak appeal and sailing waters that have hosted Olympic events. It's true the county's charms can make some places over-busy in peak season, but if you avoid the honeypots in the height of summer, and seek out the lesser-trod trails, Dorset still delights.

ⓘ Information

Visit Dorset (www.visit-dorset.com) The county's official tourism website.

Lonely Planet (www.lonelyplanet.com) Destination information, hotel bookings, traveller forum and more.

ⓘ Getting There & Around

BUS

First (www.firstgroup.com/wessex-dorset-south-somerset) Runs services linking the main towns. A useful route is bus X53, which links Weymouth with Axminster, running along the shore.

More (www.morebus.co.uk) Key bus operator in Bournemouth, Poole and surrounding rural areas.

TRAIN

Cross Country (www.crosscountrytrains. co.uk) Runs regular direct trains from Manchester to Bournemouth (£96, five hours) via Birmingham.

GWR (www.gwr.com) Provides direct services from Bristol, via Bath and Dorchester West, to Weymouth (£21, 2½ hours, at least two daily).

South Western Railway (www.southwestern railway.com) Links London Waterloo with Weymouth (£35, three hours), via Southampton, Bournemouth, Poole and Dorchester South. Also runs services between Waterloo and Exeter St David's, which call at Sherborne and Gillingham.

Bournemouth

☑ 01202 / POP 183,490
If one thing has shaped Bournemouth, it's the beach. This glorious, 7-mile strip of soft sand first drew holidaymakers in the Victorian days. More than 150 years later, it's still drawing sun-loving crowds. Sometimes a few too many – when restrictions were first eased immediately after England's 2020 Covid-19 lockdown, the resort became a byword for temporarily overcrowded beaches and gridlocked roads.

But Bournemouth is more than just a full-on party town. If you're savvy about avoiding the crowds, you'll find some hip hideaways, fine restaurants and colourful gardens.

Sights

Bournemouth Beach
BEACH

Bournemouth's long sandy shore regularly clocks up seaside awards. It stretches from Southbourne in the far east to Alum Chine in the west – an immense promenade backed by some 3000 deckchairs, ornamental gardens, kids' playgrounds, cafes and 200 beach huts. The resort also has two piers: Bournemouth Pier and Boscombe Pier.

Conscious that in 2020 Bournemouth's beaches were at times too crowded, the local council produced the BCP Beach Check app. It allows you to spot and avoid congested areas.

Russell-Cotes
MUSEUM

(📱01202-451858; www.russellcotes.com; East Cliff Promenade; adult/child £7.50/4; ⊙10am-5pm Tue, Wed, Sat & Sun) Ostentation oozes from almost every inch of this arresting structure – a mash-up of Italianate villa and Scottish baronial pile. It was built at the end of the 1800s for Merton and Annie Russell-Cotes as somewhere to showcase the remarkable range of souvenirs gathered on their world travels.

Alum Chine
GARDENS

(Mountbatten Rd; ⊙24hr) FREE Bournemouth's 1920s heyday is beautifully evoked at a subtropical enclave containing plants from the Canary Islands, New Zealand, Mexico and the Himalaya; their bright-red bracts, silver thistles and purple flowers are set against the glittering sea. It's 1.5 miles west of Bournemouth Pier.

Sleeping

★ Mory House
B&B ££

(📱01202-433553; www.moryhouse.co.uk; 31 Grand Ave, Southbourne; s/d/f £105/125/175; P🐾) In this serene, pristine B&B, stained glass and an elegant stairwell hint at the house's Edwardian age. Contemporary bedrooms are styled in muted colours; the pick is number 3, where the pint-sized balcony is an ideal spot to nibble on a home-baked cookie. Mory House is in the beach-backed suburb of Southbourne, 3 miles east of central Bournemouth.

Amarillo
B&B ££

(📱01202-553884; www.amarillohotel.co.uk; 52 Frances Rd; s £50, d £80-115; P🐾) At great-value Amarillo smart bedrooms feature jazzy wallpaper, white wooden furniture and subtle lighting. The two single loft rooms have shared bathrooms.

Urban Beach
HOTEL £££

(📱01202-301509; www.urbanbeach.co.uk; 23 Argyll Rd; s £72, d £130-145; P@🐾) Stylish Urban Beach revels in a 'no worries' air that sees free loans of wellingtons, umbrellas and DVDs. Soft brown, dark grey and flashes of terracotta define bedrooms – some have bay windows, others sport velvet chairs and there's even a chandelier or two.

Eating & Drinking

★ Urban Reef
BISTRO ££

(📱01202-443960; www.urbanreef.com; Undercliff Dr, Boscombe; snacks from £6, mains £10-25; ⊙8am-10pm, winter times vary; 🐾) 🍴 On sunny weekends a cool crowd queues out the door at Urban Reef. They're drawn by a waterfront deck and balcony, punchy coffee, top-notch snacks and quality, sustainable, imaginative fare. On stormy days head for the spacious, 1st-floor à la carte bistro for sweeping sea views. On fine days their takeaway menu appeals.

James & White
BISTRO ££

(📱01202-280656; www.jamesandwhitebarandkitchen.com; 42 Sea Rd, Boscombe; mains £9-21; ⊙11am-11pm Mon-Fri, 9am-11pm Sat & Sun; 🐾) A mellow soundtrack and a sea-view terrace give this chilled-out grill a surf-bar vibe. Brunch ranges from healthy vegan cooked breakfasts to French toast laced with maple syrup and topped with berries. The grill menu takes in vodka-spiked cheese fondue, hot-stone-cooked steaks and spiced lamb skewers – best enjoyed while sipping a craft beer, watching the waves.

> **WORTH A TRIP**
>
> ## MONKEY SANCTUARY
>
> Monkey World (📱01929-462537; www.monkeyworld.co.uk; Longthorns, BH20 6HH; adult/child/family £16/11/32; ⊙10am-5pm; P) overflows with the 'aah' factor. The sanctuary's 26 hectares are home to bounding, noisy colonies of chimpanzees, orangutans, gibbons, marmosets and some ridiculously cute ring-tailed lemurs. Most have been rescued from primate smuggling rings, circuses, laboratories, working on beaches or being mistreated as pets. Monkey World is near Wool, 5 miles west of Wareham.

West Beach
SEAFOOD ££

(☎ 01202-587785; https://west-beach.co.uk; Pier Approach; mains £15-30; ⊙ 9-11am & noon-9.30pm) The seafood and setting are hard to beat – book a table on the decking beside the sand, watch the waves lap Bournemouth Pier and tuck into perfectly cooked, perfectly fresh fish: perhaps turbot with chorizo and capers, or a full-flavoured lobster thermidor.

★ Sixty Million Postcards
PUB

(www.sixtymillionpostcards.com; 19 Exeter Rd; ⊙ noon-11pm Mon-Sat, to 10.30pm Sun) An oasis of hipster grunginess amid pound-a-pint Bournemouth, Sixty Million draws a decidedly beatnik crowd. Worn wooden floors, fringed lampshades and a sun terrace dotted with brightly coloured chairs set the scene for craft beers, unusual ciders, classic nachos and towering burgers (mains £6 to £11).

ⓘ Information

Tourist Office (☎ 01202-451781; www.bournemouth.co.uk; Pier Approach; ⊙ 9.30am-5pm) Set right beside Bournemouth Pier.

ⓘ Getting There & Around

BUS

Direct National Express (www.nationalexpress.com) buses departing from Bournemouth's coach station, which is near the train station, include:

Bristol (£18, three hours, daily)
London Victoria (£15, 2½ hours, hourly)
Southampton (£7, 50 minutes, four per day)

Useful local buses include:

Poole (M1/M2, £2.80, 35 minutes, every 5 minutes)
Salisbury (X3, £7, 1¼ hours, at least hourly)

Morebus Zone A Dayrider (adult/child £4.30/2.80) gives a day's unlimited travel in much of Poole, Bournemouth and neighbouring Christchurch.

TRAIN

Direct services include those to:
Dorchester South (£12, 45 minutes, half-hourly to hourly)
London Waterloo (£25, 2½ hours, half-hourly)
Poole (£4, 10 minutes, half-hourly)
Weymouth (£14, one hour, hourly)

Poole

☎ 01202 / POP 147,640

In the quaint old port of Poole there's a whiff of money in the air: the town borders Sandbanks, a sandy beach backed by some of the world's most expensive chunks of real estate. Big bucks aside, Poole also boasts excellent restaurants and is the springboard for a raft of watersports and some irresistible boat trips.

◉ Sights & Activities

Brownsea Island
ISLAND

(NT; ☎ 01202-707744; www.nationaltrust.org.uk; Poole Harbour; ferry & admission adult/child £17.50/9.50; ⊙ 9am-5.30pm late Mar-Oct) On this small, wooded island in the middle of Poole Harbour, trails weave through heath and woods, past peacocks, red squirrels, red deer and a wealth of birdlife – the water-framed views to the Isle of Purbeck are stunning. Free guided walks focus on the wartime island, birdlife, smugglers and pirates. Ferries to the island leave from Poole Quay at least hourly.

Poole Museum
MUSEUM

(☎ 01202-262600; www.boroughofpoole.com/museums; 4 High St; ⊙ 10am-1pm & 2-5pm Apr-Oct) FREE The building alone is worth seeing – a beautifully restored 15th-century warehouse. The star exhibit is a 2300-year-old Iron Age logboat dredged up from Poole Harbour. At almost 10m long and weighing some 14 tonnes, it's the largest to be found in southern Britain and probably carried 18 people.

Sandbanks
BEACH

A 2-mile, wafer-thin peninsula of land that curls around the expanse of Poole Harbour, Sandbanks is studded with some of the most expensive houses in the world. But the white-sand beaches that border them are free, have some of the best UK water-quality standards and are home to a host of watersports operators.

Poole Harbour Watersports
WATER SPORTS

(☎ 01202-700503; www.pooleharbour.co.uk; 284 Sandbanks Rd) Delivers lessons for small groups in stand-up paddleboarding (SUP; per 1½ hours £25), windsurfing (per six hours £78) and kitesurfing (per day £99), plus memorable kayak and SUP tours (per three hours £45).

CORFE CASTLE

The startling, fractured battlements of **Corfe Castle** (NT; ☎ 01929-481294; www.national trust.org.uk; The Square; adult/child £10/5; ⊙10am-6pm Apr-Sep, to 5pm Mar & Oct, to 4pm Nov-Feb) were once home to Sir John Bankes, Charles I's right-hand man. The Civil War saw the castle besieged by Cromwellian forces; in 1646 the plucky Lady Bankes directed a six-week defence and the castle fell only after being betrayed from within. The Round-heads then gunpowdered Corfe Castle apart; turrets and soaring walls still sheer off at precarious angles – the splayed-out gatehouse looks like it's just been blown up.

The **Swanage Steam Railway** (☎ 01929-425800; www.swanagerailway.co.uk; per person single/return £8/12.50; ⊙daily Apr-Oct, Sat & Sun Nov, Dec & Mar) stops at Corfe Castle as it shuttles between Swanage and Norden. You may have to pre-book a table to board the train; look online for updates.

🛏 Sleeping

Loch Fyne   HOTEL ££
(☎ 01202-609000; www.greenekinginns.co.uk; 47 Haven Rd, Canford Cliffs; s/d from £75/90; P⊛) There's a touch of the colonial tea planta-tion about the exterior of this smart hotel, set above the eponymous seafood restau-rant. Small but cheerful bedrooms feature bursts of tartan in earthy or maritime tones. It's also just a 1.5-mile stroll to Sandbanks beach.

Blue Shutters   B&B ££
(☎ 01202-748129; www.blueshutters.co.uk; 109 North Rd; s/d from £80/103; P⊛) It's a lit-tle way out (2 miles from Poole Quay and 4 miles from Sandbanks) but bay windows and neutral colour schemes here keep the bedrooms light and bright. Other pluses include a quiet garden, a sunny patio and parking (at a real premium in Poole town).

Merchant House   B&B £££
(☎ 01202-661474; www.themerchanthouse.org. uk; 10 Strand St; s £110, d £140-160) Tucked one street back from Poole Quay, tall, red-brick Merchant House is boutiquery at its best. Hefty wooden sculptures, wicker rocking chairs and crisp linen ensure it's stylish; the odd teddy bear keeps it cheery, too.

🍴 Eating

Rockfish   SEAFOOD ££
(☎ 01202-836255; www.therockfish.co.uk; 9 The Quay; mains £10-18; ⊙noon-3.30pm & 4-9pm) 🍷 Restaurateur Mitch Tonks has bagged a prime spot on the quay for the Poole outpost of his eight-strong West Country restaurant chain. Set in a high-ceilinged converted pottery, it delivers his trademark sustainable, beautifully cooked,

super-fresh local fish with the usual friend-ly flair and panache.

Storm   SEAFOOD ££
(☎ 01202-674970; www.stormfish.co.uk; 16 High St; mains £14-19; ⊙noon-8pm Mon-Wed) How rare is this? The dish you're eating could well have been caught by the chef. At chilled-out Storm, fisher Pete also rattles the pots 'n' pans, delighting in dishing up intense Goan fish curry, seafood ramen, and a classic Poole Bay Dover sole *à la meuniére*.

Check the website to see if longer opening hours have resumed.

Poole Arms   PUB FOOD ££
(☎ 01202-673450; www.poolearms.co.uk; 19 Poole Quay; mains £8-19; ⊙11am-11pm Mon-Sat, noon-11pm Sun) The grub at this ancient, green-tiled pub is strong on locally landed seafood – try the homemade fish pie, local crab or Poole rock oysters (£2.25 each). Order some New Forest beer, then settle down on the terrace overlooking the quay.

★ Guildhall Tavern   FRENCH £££
(☎ 01202-671717; www.guildhalltavern.co.uk; 15 Market St; mains £18-23; ⊙11.30am-3.30pm & 6-9.30pm Tue-Sat) Poole's top table consist-ently delights, combining local ingredients with lashings of French elan. Fish features strongly – the rope-grown mussels poached in Muscadet are superb as is the sea bass flambéed with Pernod – but the boeuf bour-guignon also makes carnivores smile.

ℹ Information

Tourist Office (☎ 01202-262600.; www.poole tourism.com; 4 High St; ⊙10am-1pm & 2-5pm Apr-Oct) Set inside Poole Museum.

WORTH A TRIP

KINGSTON LACY

Set some 2 miles west of Wimborne, Dorset's must-see stately home (NT; ☑ 01202-883402; www.nationaltrust.org. uk; Wimborne Minster; adult/child £10/5; ⊙ house hours vary, grounds 9am-6pm Mar-Oct, 10am-4pm Nov-Feb; P) looks every inch the setting for a period drama. Highlights include the gold- and gilt-smothered Spanish Room, the hieroglyphics in the Egyptian Room and the elegant marble staircase and loggia. The opening hours and days for the house vary – see the website for updates. In the extensive landscaped grounds, hunt out the restored Japanese Tea Garden and the Iron Age hill fort of Badbury Rings.

ⓘ Getting There & Around

BOAT

Brittany Ferries (☑ 0330 159 7000; www.brittany-ferries.com) Services between Poole and Cherbourg in France were suspended in 2020; check the website to see if they've resumed.

Sandbanks Ferry (☑ 01929-450203; www.sandbanksferry.co.uk; per pedestrian/car £1/4.50; ⊙ 7am-11pm) Makes the four-minute trip from Sandbanks to Studland every 20 minutes. It's a shortcut from Poole to Swanage, Wareham and the Isle of Purbeck, but the summer queues can be a pain.

BUS

A Morebus Zone A Dayrider (adult/child £4.30/2.80) gives a day's unlimited travel in much of Poole and Bournemouth.

Bournemouth Bus M1/M2, £2.80, 35 minutes, every 5 minutes

London Victoria National Express, £18, 3½ hours, every two hours

Sandbanks Bus 60, £3.80, 25 minutes, half-hourly or hourly, from mid-July to early September

TAXI

Dial-a-Cab (☑ 01202-666822; www.pooletaxis.co.uk)

TRAIN

Direct services include:

Bournemouth £4, 10 minutes, half-hourly

Dorchester South £10, 30 minutes, hourly

London Waterloo £30, 2¼ hours, half-hourly to hourly

Weymouth £13, 45 minutes, hourly

Lulworth Cove

POP 740

In this stretch of southeast Dorset the coast steals the show. For millions of years the elements have been creating an intricate shoreline of curved bays, caves, stacks and weirdly wonderful rock formations – most notably the massive natural arch at Durdle Door.

The charismatic hamlet of Lulworth Cove is a pleasing jumble of thatched cottages and fishing gear, which winds down to a perfect crescent of white cliffs. Inevitably it all gets very busy in summer; avoid peak season if you can.

◉ Sights & Activities

Check whether **Jurassic Coast Activities** (☑ 01305-835301; www.jurassiccoastactivities.co.uk), which suspended kayaking tours in 2020, is up and running again.

★ **Durdle Door** LANDMARK
(www.lulworth.com; near Lulworth Cove, BH20 5PU; parking half-/full day £5/10) The poster child of Dorset's Jurassic Coast, this immense, 150-million-year-old Portland stone arch was created by a combination of massive earth movements and erosion. Today it's framed by shimmering bays; bring a swimsuit and head down the hundreds of steps for an unforgettable dip.

The beach and car park can get very busy in summer. You can pre-book a parking space, or join the throngs hiking the coast path from Lulworth Cove (2.5 miles return). A quieter and much more rewarding (if testing) walk is east along the coast from Ringstead, or from the car park 0.5 miles northeast of that village (7.4 miles return).

Lulworth Cove Visitor Centre MUSEUM
(☑ 01929-400587; www.lulworth.com; main car park; ⊙ 10am-5pm Easter-Sep, to 4pm Oct-Easter) FREE Excellent displays outline how geology and erosion have combined to shape the area's remarkable shoreline. Staff can advise about walks, too.

A money-saving tip: if you're heading onto Durdle Door, your Lulworth Cove parking ticket (per half-/full day £5/10) is also valid at the two, non-premium-rate Durdle Door car parks.

Stair Hole Bay BAY
Stair Hole Bay sits just a few hundred metres west of Lulworth Cove. This diminutive semicircle is almost enclosed by cliffs that

feature tiny rock arches – a route in that's popular with kayakers. On the landward side is the delightfully named Lulworth Crumple, where layers of rock form dramatically zigzagging folds.

Lulworth Castle CASTLE
(EH; ☏ 01929-400352; www.lulworth.com; adult/child £6/4, parking £3; ⏲ 10.30am-5pm Sun-Fri Apr-Dec) A confection in creamy, dreamy white, this baronial pile looks more like a French chateau than a traditional English castle. Built in 1608 as a hunting lodge, it's survived extravagant owners, extensive remodelling and a disastrous fire in 1929. It has been extensively restored, especially the kitchen and cellars. Ask whether the tower has reopened – it offers sweeping coastal views.

🛏 Sleeping

Check whether Lulworth YHA (☏ 0345 371 9331; www.yha.org.uk; School Lane, West Lulworth; ℗), which switched to exclusive hire for 2020, has reopened to individual bookings.

Durdle Door Holiday Park CAMPSITE £
(☏ 01929-400200; www.lulworth.com; West Lulworth, BH20 5PU; sites £28-44; ⏲ Mar-Oct; ℗ 🛜) An attractive, spacious site, just minutes from the creamy cliffs, and 1.5 miles west of the hamlet of Lulworth Cove. Opt for a good old tent, or a four-person wooden pod (£85).

⭐ **Lulworth Cove Inn** INN £££
(☏ 01929-400333; www.lulworth-coveinn.co.uk; Main Rd; d £135-150; ℗ 🛜) One to delight your inner beachcomber. In this veritable vision of driftwood-chic, whitewashed floorboards and aquamarine panels frame painted wicker chairs and roll-top baths. Add cracking sea views, a mini roof terrace and top-quality gastropub grub (mains £13 to £17, food served from noon to 9pm) and you have an irresistible inn.

Rudds of Lulworth B&B £££
(☏ 01929-400552; www.ruddslulworth.co.uk; Main Rd; d £85-185, ste £160-200; 🛜🐾) An idyllic setting, pared-down designs, top-notch linen and pamper-yourself toiletries combine to make this a memorable place to stay, especially if you opt for a room with Lulworth Cove views. Or just lounge beside the pool, which also overlooks that circle of bay.

🍴 Eating & Drinking

Boat Shed CAFE ££
(☏ 01929-400810; www.lulworth.com; Main Rd; snacks from £3, mains £7-17; ⏲ 9.30am-5pm Apr-Sep, to 4pm Oct-Mar) Views don't come much better than from the terrace of this converted fishers' storage shack set right beside Lulworth's glittering circular cove. The food spans fine brunches, Dorset cream teas, meze platters and – of course – fish.

Castle PUB
(☏ 01929-400311; www.butcombe.com/the-castle-inn-dorset; 8 Main Rd, West Lulworth; ⏲ noon-9pm; 🛜🐾) A picture-perfect, rambling thatched inn with a swish new interior, large terrace and regularly changing selection of prime Dorset ciders.

HAMPSHIRE, WILTSHIRE & DORSET LULWORTH COVE

WORTH A TRIP

THE CERNE GIANT

Nude, full frontal and notoriously well endowed, the Cerne Giant (NT; ☏ 01297-489481; www.nationaltrust.org.uk; Cerne Abbas; ⏲ 24hr; ℗) FREE chalk figure, on the hillside above the village of Cerne Abbas, is revealed in all his glory – and he's in a state of excitement that wouldn't be allowed in most magazines. The giant is around 60m high and 51m wide and his age remains a mystery; some claim he's Roman, but the first historical reference comes in 1694, when three shillings were set aside for his repair. These days a car park provides grandstand views.

The Victorians found it all deeply embarrassing and allowed grass to grow over his most outstanding feature. Today the hill is grazed by sheep and cattle, though only the sheep are allowed to do their nibbling over the giant – the cows would do too much damage to his lines.

Down in the village, the New Inn (☏ 01300-341274; www.thenewinncerneabbas.co.uk; 14 Long St; d £100-140, ste £160-190; ℗ 🛜) – which is more than 400 years old – makes a quaint place to stay.

The village is eight miles north of Dorchester.

JURASSIC COAST

The kind of massive, hands-on geology lesson you wish you'd had at school, the Jurassic Coast is England's first natural World Heritage Site, putting it on a par with the Great Barrier Reef and the Grand Canyon. This striking shoreline stretches from Exmouth in East Devon to Swanage in Dorset, encompassing 185 million years of the earth's history in just 95 miles. It means you can walk, in just a few hours, many millions of years in geological time.

It began when layers of rocks formed, their varying compositions determined by different climates: desertlike conditions gave way to higher, then lower, sea levels. Massive earth movements then tilted all the rock layers, forcing most of the oldest formations to the west, and the youngest to the east. Next, erosion exposed the different strata.

The differences are very tangible. Devon's rusty-red Triassic rocks are 200–250 million years old. Lyme Regis' fossil-rich, dark-clay Jurassic cliffs are 190 million years old. Pockets of much younger, creamy-coloured Cretaceous rocks (a mere 65–140 million years old) pop up, notably around Lulworth Cove, where erosion has sculpted a stunning display of bays, stacks and rock arches.

The coast's website (www.jurassiccoast.org) is a great information source; also look out locally for the highly readable *Official Guide to the Jurassic Coast* (£4.95).

Upstairs sit 12 cosy bedrooms (doubles £155 to £175), which team mod cons (such as digital radios) with modern, country-cottage styling.

ℹ Getting There & Away

Bus X54 (two to five daily, Monday to Saturday) stops at Lulworth Cove en route between Weymouth and Wareham and Poole.

Dorchester

📞 01305 / POP 19,060

With Dorchester you get two towns in one: a real-life, bustling county town and Thomas Hardy's fictional Casterbridge. The Victorian writer was born nearby and his literary locations can still be found among Dorchester's Georgian terraces. Add cracking archaeological sites and attractive places to eat and sleep and you have an appealing base for a night or two.

◉ Sights

After a multi-million-pound refurbishment, **Dorset County Museum** (📞 01305-262735; www.dorsetcountymuseum.org; High West St) is due to open in 2021; see the website for updates.

Access to the two main Thomas Hardy sites near Dorchester was suspended in 2020. Check online to see if you can now visit his thatched birthplace, **Hardy's Cottage** (NT; 📞 01305-262366; www.nationaltrust.org.uk; Higher Bockhampton), and his home in later life, **Max Gate** (NT; 📞 01305-262538; www.nationaltrust.org.uk; Alington Ave).

Hardy fans can also hunt down the Casterbridge literary locations tucked away in modern Dorchester's streets. They include **Lucetta's House** (Trinity St), a grand Georgian affair with ornate doorposts, while a nearby red-brick, mid-18th-century building (now a bank) is named as the inspiration for the **House of the Mayor of Casterbridge** (South St). Check whether the **tourist office** (📞 01305-267992; www.visit-dorset.com; Dorchester Library, Charles St) has reopened; it sells book location guides.

⭐ **Maiden Castle**　ARCHAEOLOGICAL SITE
(EH; www.english-heritage.org.uk; Winterborne Monkton; ◷ dawn-dusk; 🅿) **FREE** Occupying a massive slab of horizon on the southern fringes of Dorchester, imposing Maiden Castle is the largest and most complex Iron Age hill fort in Britain. The first defences were built on the site around 500 BCE – in its heyday it was densely populated with clusters of roundhouses and a network of roads. The Romans besieged and captured Maiden Castle in 43 CE – an ancient Briton skeleton with a Roman crossbow bolt in the spine was found at the fort.

Roman Town House　HISTORIC BUILDING
(www.dorsetcouncil.gov.uk; Northern Hay; ◷24hr) **FREE** The knee-high flint walls and beautifully preserved mosaics here powerfully conjure up the Roman occupation of Dorchester (then Durnovaria). Peek into the summer dining room to see the under-

floor heating system (hypocaust), where charcoal-warmed air circulated around pillars to produce a toasty room temperature of 18°C (64°F). Search for 'Roman Town House' on the Dorset Council website for more information.

Sleeping

★ Beggars Knap   B&B **££**

(☑07768 690691; www.beggarsknap.co.uk; 2 Weymouth Ave; s £80-90, d £100-115, f from £125; P✿) Despite the name, this altogether fabulous, vaguely decadent guesthouse is far from impoverished. Opulent rooms drip with chandeliers and gold brocades; beds draped in fine cottons range from French sleigh to four-poster. You could pay much, much more and get something half as nice.

Westwood   B&B **££**

(☑01305-268018; www.westwoodhouse.co.uk; 29 High West St; s/d/f from £90/107/127; ✿♿) A skilled designer's been at work in this 18th-century town house, producing a contemporary-meets-Georgian style: muted greens, brass lamps, subtle checks and mini-sofas. The modern bathrooms glint, while tiny fridges harbour fresh milk for your tea.

Yalbury Cottage   HOTEL **££**

(☑01305-262382; www.yalburycottage.com; Lower Bockhampton; s/d £85/125; P✿) Yalbury is almost your archetypal English cottage, framed by flowers and crowned by moss-studded thatch. Inside fresh, simple, gently rustic bedrooms overlook the garden or fields. It's in Lower Bockhampton, 3 miles east of Dorchester.

Eating

★ Taste   BRASSERIE **££**

(☑01305-257776; www.facebook.com/pg/taste restaurant; Trinity St; mains £10-18; ⊘9am-2pm Mon-Wed, Fri & Sat) 🥦 One of Dorchester's best, buzziest brunch and lunch spots has fleets of fans thanks to a buy-local ethos and emphasis on super-fresh sustainable ingredients. They crop up in everything from platters, tapas and melts to classy bistro dishes: grilled steak, confit duck and garlicky linguine.

Cow & Apple   BURGERS **££**

(☑01305-266286; www.cowandapple.co.uk; 30 Trinity St; burgers £9-16; ⊘5-9pm Tue-Fri, noon-5pm Sat) Piled high and oozing all the trim-

mings, the dirty burgers here are decidedly good – spice things up with jalapeños, brie or a seriously sticky BBQ sauce. The cider list – more than 50 types – could take a while to work through.

Brewers Arms   PUB FOOD **££**

(☑01305-889361; www.thebrewersarms.com; Burnside, Martinstown; mains £10-14; ⊘noon-3pm & 6-11pm Tue-Sat, noon-3pm Sun) Dorset produce and homemade dishes pack the menu of this charming village pub – from the steak and Stilton pie to the homemade rhubarb crumble. Or just head to the sunny beer garden and chill out with a pint of golden ale.

It's set in the pretty village of Martinstown, 3 miles west of Dorchester.

ℹ Getting There & Away

BUS

London Victoria (National Express, £18, 3¾ hours, one daily)

Lyme Regis (Bus X51, £5, 1¼ hours, hourly Monday to Saturday, three on Sunday)

Sherborne (Bus X11, £4.90, 1¼ hours, four daily Monday to Friday)

Weymouth (Bus 10, £2.20, 20 minutes, half-hourly)

TRAIN

Dorchester has two train stations.

Trains leave Dorchester West for Bath and Bristol (£21, two to 2½ hours, at least two daily).

Services from Dorchester South, running at least hourly, include:

Bournemouth (£12, 45 minutes)

London Waterloo (£30, three hours)

Southampton (£26, 1¾ hours)

Weymouth (£5, 10 minutes)

Weymouth

☑01305../ POP 52,200

At just over 225 years old, Weymouth is a weather-worn resort with a couple of tricks up its faded sleeve. Candy-striped kiosks and deckchairs line a golden, 3-mile beach; chuck in cockles and chippies and prepare to promenade down seaside memory lane. But Weymouth is about more than just that sandy shore; the town boasts a historic harbour, some fine seafood restaurants and easy access to the watersports centres of the neighbouring Isle of Portland.

⊙ Sights & Activities

Check whether Coastline Cruises (☎ 01305-785000; www.coastlinecruises.com; Trinity Rd) has resumed its 90-minute sailings, suspended in 2020, to Portland.

Sandworld   SCULPTURE
(☎ 07411 387529; www.sandworld.co.uk; Lodmoor Country Park, Preston Beach Rd; adult/child £7.75/5.75; ⊙ 10am-3.30pm) Set up by a third-generation Weymouth sand sculptor, the intricate creations here include lifelike representations of fairy-tale castles, sly dragons and scenes from films spanning *Finding Nemo* and *Star Wars* to Disney favourites.

Nothe Fort   FORT
(☎ 01305-766626; www.nothefort.org.uk; Barrack Rd; adult/child £8/2; ⊙ 11am-4pm Apr-Oct) Weymouth's photogenic 19th-century defences are studded with cannons, searchlights and 30cm coastal guns. Exhibits detail Dorset's Roman invasion, a Victorian soldier's drill and Weymouth in WWII.

🛏 Sleeping & Eating

★ Roundhouse   B&B ££
(☎ 01305-761010; www.roundhouse-weymouth.com; 1 The Esplanade; d £105-125; 🛜) The decor here is as gently eccentric as the owner – interiors combine snazzy modern art with comfy sofas and bursts of purple and bright blue. But the big draw is the view – you can see both the beach out front and the harbour behind from all bedrooms.

Old Harbour View   B&B £££
(☎ 01305-774633; www.oldharbourviewweymouth.co.uk; 12 Trinity Rd; s/d £90/130; P 🛜) In this pristine Georgian terrace you get boating themes in the fresh, white bedrooms, and boats right outside the front door. One room overlooks the busy quay, the other faces the back.

Marlboro   FISH & CHIPS £
(☎ 01305-785700; www.marlbororestaurant.co.uk; 46 St Thomas St; mains £9-14; ⊙ 11.30am-9.45pm) 🌱 A sustainable slant and a 40-year history help lift this traditional chippy, just metres from Weymouth's quay, above its rivals. Mackerel features among the long list of super-fresh fish. Take it away and duck the seagulls or get munching in the bay-windowed, licensed cafe (open till 8pm).

★ Crustacean   SEAFOOD ££
(☎ 01305-777222; www.crustaceanrestaurant.co.uk; 59 St Mary St; mains £15-37; ⊙ noon-9pm Mon-Thu, to 9.30pm Fri & Sat) At Crustacean you'll find an imaginative chef with a passion for the finest, freshest fish and seafood. Get cracking on a whole lobster, slurp some oysters, lunch on a robust chowder or dine on pan-fried sea bass with a creamy saffron sauce.

ⓘ Getting There & Away

BUS

Dorchester Bus 10 (£2.20, 20 minutes, half-hourly)

Fortuneswell Bus 1 (£2.20, 20 minutes, four per hour to hourly)

London Victoria National Express (£12, four hours, one direct daily)

Portland Bill Bus 501 (£2.60, 50 minutes, seven daily, runs from late July to August)

The Jurassic Coaster/Bus X53 (four to five daily, no service winter Sundays) travels west from Weymouth to Axminster (2½ hours), via Abbotsbury (20 minutes) and Lyme Regis (1¼ hours).

TRAIN

Trains running at least hourly include the following direct services:

Bournemouth (£14, one hour)

Dorchester South (£5, 10 minutes)

London Waterloo (£29, 3½ hours)

Direct services every two hours:

Bath (£20, two hours)

Bristol (£20, 2¾ hours)

Isle of Portland

The 'Isle' of Portland is a hard, high comma of rock fused to the rest of Dorset by the ridge of Chesil Beach. On its 150m central plateau, a quarrying past still holds sway, evidenced by huge craters and large slabs of limestone. Portland offers jaw-dropping views down on to 18-mile Chesil Beach and the neighbouring Fleet – Britain's biggest tidal lagoon.

Proud, and at times bleak and rough around the edges, Portland is decidedly different from the rest of Dorset, and is all the more compelling because of it. The Isle's industrial heritage, watersport facilities, rich birdlife and starkly beautiful cliffs make it worth at least a day trip.

The isle's biggest settlement is Fortuneswell, at the northern end; beachside Chiswell sits alongside.

Sights

★ Tout Quarry
SCULPTURE

(near Fortuneswell; ⊙dawn-dusk; P) FREE Portland's white limestone has been quarried for centuries and has been used in some of the world's finest buildings, such as the British Museum and St Paul's Cathedral. Tout Quarry's disused workings now house more than 50 sculptures that have been carved into the rock in situ, resulting in a fascinating combination of the raw material, the detritus of the quarrying process and the beauty of chiselled works.

Tout Quarry is signed off the main road, just south of Fortuneswell.

★ Portland Lighthouse
LIGHTHOUSE

(☑01305-821050; www.trinityhouse.co.uk; Portland Bill; adult/child £7.50/5.50; ⊙hours vary; P) For a real sense of Portland's remote nature, head to its southern tip, Portland Bill, to climb the 41m-high, candy-striped lighthouse. It offers breathtaking views of rugged cliffs and the Race, a surging vortex of conflicting tides. The interactive displays in the former lighthouse-keepers' cottages include *Into the Dark*, a recreation of sailing into stormy seas.

Tours run on varying days (often Sunday, Tuesday and Thursday); see the website for dates and pre-booking requirements.

Portland Castle
CASTLE

(EH; ☑01305-820539; www.english-heritage.org. uk; Liberty Rd, Castletown; adult/child £6.90/4.10; ⊙10am-4pm Apr-Oct) A particularly fine product of Henry VIII's castle-building spree, with expansive views over Portland Harbour.

Activities

Andrew Simpson Centre
BOATING

(☑01305-457400; www.aswc.co.uk; Osprey Quay, Portland Harbour) Activities include Royal Yachting Association (RYA) sailing lessons (adult/child per two days £199/180). Look out for their £20 taster sessions.

OTC
WATER SPORTS

(Official Test Centre; ☑01305-230296; www. otc-windsurf.com; Osprey Quay, Portland Harbour) Offers lessons in stand-up paddleboarding (SUP; one/two hours £25/40) and windsurfing (two hours/one day/two days

£59/139/225). It also rents out SUP boards (per hour £10).

Sleeping & Eating

Portland YHA (☑03453 719339; www.yha.org. uk; Castle Rd, Castletown; P ⊚) suspended individual bookings in 2020; see the website for updates.

★ Queen Anne House
B&B ££

(☑01305-820028; www.queenannehouse.co.uk; 2 Fortuneswell; s/d £70/95; ⊚) It's impossible to know which room to pick: White, with skylight, beams and a hobbit-esque door; Lotus, with its grand furniture; ornate Oyster with its half-tester bed; or Garden, a suite with a French bath and mini-conservatory. It doesn't matter, though – they're all great value and gorgeous.

★ Crab House Cafe
SEAFOOD ££

(☑01305-788867; www.crabhousecafe.co.uk; Ferrymans Way, Wyke Regis; mains £14-30; ⊙noon-2.30pm & 6-9pm Wed-Sat, noon-3.30pm Sun) This is where the locals head on hot summer days, to sit beside Fleet Lagoon in beach-shack-chic, tucking into fresh-as-it-gets seafood. Fish is enlivened by chilli, curry, lemon and herbs, crab comes spicy Chinese-style or whole for you to crack, and the oysters are served with either pesto and parmesan or bacon and cream. Opening hours can vary.

Cove House
PUB

(☑01305-820895; www.thecovehouseinn.co.uk; 91 Chiswell Seafront; ⊙11.30am-9pm) Head to this history-rich fishers' inn for a Chesil Beach–side beer terrace with expansive views, memorable sunsets and great pub grub (mains £9 to £12).

❶ Getting There & Away

Bus 1 runs from Weymouth to Fortuneswell (£2.20, 20 minutes, four per hour to hourly).

Bus 501 operates between Weymouth and Portland Bill from late July to August (£2.60, 50 minutes, seven daily).

Chesil Beach

One of the most breathtaking beaches in Britain, Chesil is 18 miles long, 15m high and moving inland at the rate of 5m a century. This mind-boggling, 100-million-tonne pebble ridge is the baby of the Jurassic Coast. A mere 6000 years old, its stones range from pea-sized in the west to hand-sized in the east.

◉ Sights

Chesil Beach Centre NATURE CENTRE
(Fine Foundation; ☏ 01305-206191; www.dorset
wildlifetrust.org.uk; Ferrybridge; parking per hour £1;
⊙ 10am-5pm Easter-Sep, to 4pm Oct-Easter; 🅿)
FREE This centre at the start of the bridge to
Portland is a great gateway to Chesil Beach.
The pebble ridge is at its highest here – 15m
compared to 7m at Abbotsbury. From the
car park an energy-sapping hike up sliding
pebbles leads to the constant surge and rattle of waves on stones and dazzling views of
the sea, with the thin pebble line and the expanse of the Fleet Lagoon behind.

★ Abbotsbury Swannery WILDLIFE RESERVE
(☏ 01305-871858; www.abbotsbury-tourism.co
.uk; New Barn Rd, Abbotsbury; adult/child £10/5;
⊙ 10am-5pm late Mar-Oct) Every May some
600 free-flying swans choose to nest at
this swannery, which shelters in the Fleet
Lagoon, protected by the ridge of Chesil
Beach. Wandering the network of trails that
wind between the swans' nests is an awe-
inspiring experience that's punctuated by
occasional territorial displays (snuffling
coughs and stand-up flapping), ensuring that
even the liveliest children are stilled.

The swannery is near the picturesque
village of Abbotsbury, 10 miles from Weymouth, off the B3157.

Lyme Regis

☏ 01297 / POP 3670
Fantastically fossil-packed Lyme Regis packs
a heavyweight historical punch. Rock-hard
relics of the past pop out repeatedly from
the surrounding cliffs – exposed by the
landslides of a retreating shoreline. Lyme is
now a pivot point of the Unesco-listed Jurassic Coast: fossil fever is definitely in the
air and everyone, from proper palaeontolo-
gists to those out for a bit of fun, can engage
in a spot of coastal rummaging. Add sandy
beaches and some delightful places to sleep
and eat, and you get a charming base for
explorations.

◉ Sights & Activities

Lyme Regis Museum MUSEUM
(☏ 01297-443370; www.lymeregismuseum.co.uk;
Bridge St; up to 2 people £12, family £15; ⊙ 10am-
4pm Wed-Sat) In 1814 local teenager Mary
Anning found the first full ichthyosaur
skeleton near Lyme Regis, propelling the
town onto the world stage. An incredibly

famous fossilist in her day, Miss Anning did
much to pioneer the science of modern-day
palaeontology. This museum, on the site of
her former home, tells her story and exhibits its spectacular fossils and other prehistoric
finds.

Cobb LANDMARK
First built in the 13th century, Lyme's iconic, curling sea defences have been strengthened and extended over the years, and hence
don't present the elegant line they once did,
but it's still hard to resist wandering their
length to the tip.

Dinosaurland MUSEUM
(☏ 01297-443541; www.dinosaurland.co.uk;
Coombe St; adult/child £5/4; ⊙ 10am-5pm mid-
Feb–mid-Oct, winter hours vary; ♿) This joyful,
mini, indoor Jurassic Park overflows with
fossilised remains; look out for belemnites,
a plesiosaurus and an impressive locally
found ichthyosaur. Lifelike dinosaur models
will thrill youngsters – the rock-hard tyran-
nosaur eggs and 73kg dinosaur dung will
have them in raptures.

★ Undercliff WALKING
This wildly undulating, 304-hectare nature reserve just west of Lyme was formed
by massive landslides. They've left a challenging hiking landscape of slipped cliffs,
fissures and ridges, where paths snake between dense vegetation, exposed tree roots
and tangles of brambles. The Undercliff
starts a mile west of central Lyme Regis; follow footpath signs from Holmbush Car Park.

🛏 Sleeping & Eating

Lyme Townhouse B&B ££
(☏ 01929-400252; www.lyme-townhouse.co.uk; 8
Pound St; d £105-135; 🛜) With stylish decor
and luxury flourishes this good-value guesthouse is hard to resist. Most of the seven
rooms are on the small size (as signalled by
the categories Super-Snug and Snug), but
the central location, sea glimpses and views
onto the town make it hard to beat.

Alexandra HERITAGE HOTEL £££
(☏ 01297-442010; www.hotelalexandra.co.uk;
Pound St; d £180-£285; 🅿 🛜) It's like the setting
for an Agatha Christie mystery, minus the
murder. Wicker chairs dot manicured lawns,
glittering Lyme Bay sweeps out behind. The
best bedrooms boast bay windows and sea
views; the (much cheaper) back-facing ones
are charming too.

FOSSIL HUNTING

On Dorset's Jurassic Coast, fossil fever is catching. Lyme Regis sits in one of the most unstable sections of Britain's shore, and regular landslips mean nuggets of prehistory keep tumbling from the cliffs.

Joining a guided walk aids explorations. Three miles east of Lyme, the **Charmouth Heritage Coast Centre** (☑ 01297-560772; www.charmouth.org; Lower Sea Lane, Charmouth; ☺ 11am-4pm daily Easter-Oct, Fri-Mon Nov-Easter) **FREE** runs between one and 10 small-group fossil-hunting walks (adult/child £8/4) per week in the summer and school holidays.

Or, in Lyme itself, Lyme Regis Museum runs three to seven small-group fossil-hunting walks per week (up to six people £125), with times dictated by the tides. Also in Lyme, check whether local expert **Brandon Lennon** (☑ 07854 377519; www.lymeregisfossilwalks.com) has resumed his walks. All fossil-hunting trips are popular – book well ahead.

For the best chances of a find, visit within two hours of low water. If you do hunt by yourself, official advice is to check tide times and collect on a falling tide, observe warning signs, keep away from cliffs, only pick up from the beach and always leave some behind for others. Oh, and tell the experts if you find a stunner.

It's also the perfect spot for a proper English **afternoon tea** (£10 to £31), complete with scones, jam and dainty sandwiches.

★ **Oyster & Fish House** SEAFOOD ££
(☑ 01297-446910; www.theoysterandfishhouse.co.uk; Cobb Rd; mains £16-26; ☺ noon-10pm; 🅿) Expect sweeping views of the Cobb and dazzling food at this super-stylish, open-plan cabin. Dishes depend on the day's catch, but the crab might be wok-fried, the lobster soup might be laced with Somerset cider and the bacon chops might come with cockles.

Harbour Inn PUB FOOD ££
(☑ 01297-442299; www.harbourinnlymeregis.co.uk; 23 Marine Pde; mains £13-19; ☺ noon-2.30pm & 5-9pm, closed Sun eve Oct-Mar) A flower-framed, beachside veranda, smart but snug interior and some of the best bistro/pub grub in town – the bouillabaisse is suitably intense.

ℹ Information

At the time of research Lyme's tourist office had closed. Check for updates at www.visit-dorset.com/visitor-information.

ℹ Getting There & Away

Bus X51 (£5, 1¼ hours, hourly Monday to Saturday, three on Sunday) Shuttles to Dorchester.
Jurassic Coaster/Bus X53 (four to five daily, no service winter Sunday) Goes east to Weymouth (£7.80) via Chesil Beach, and west to Axminster (£6.20), with regular connections on to Exeter from there.

Sherborne

☑ 01935 / POP 9520

Sherborne gleams with a mellow, orangey-yellow stone – it's been used to build a cluster of 15th-century buildings and the impressive abbey church. This serene town exudes wealth, thanks partly to a batch of exclusive private schools.

◉ Sights

Sherborne Abbey CHURCH
(☑ 01935-812452; www.sherborneabbey.com; Abbey Cl; suggested donation £4; ☺ check website for hours) At the height of its influence, the magnificent Abbey Church of St Mary the Virgin was the central cathedral of 26 succeeding Saxon bishops. Established early in the 8th century, it became a Benedictine abbey in 998 and functioned as a cathedral until 1075. The church has mesmerising fan vaulting that's the oldest in the country, a central tower supported by Saxon Norman piers and an 1180 Norman porch.

Sherborne Old Castle CASTLE
(EH; ☑ 01935-812730; www.english-heritage.org.uk; Castleton; adult/child £5.90/3.50; ☺ 10am-5pm Wed-Sun Apr-Oct; 🅿) These days the epitome of a picturesque ruin, Sherborne's Old Castle was built by Roger, Bishop of Salisbury, in 1120 – Elizabeth I gave it to her one-time favourite Sir Walter Raleigh in the late 16th century. It became a Royalist stronghold during the English Civil War, but Cromwell reduced it to rubble after a 16-day siege in 1645, leaving just the fractured southwest gatehouse, great tower and north range.

Sherborne New Castle GARDENS
(☑ 01935-812072; www.sherbornecastle.com; New Rd; adult/child £9/free; ☺ 10am-5pm Apr-Sep; P) Sir Walter Raleigh began building the impressive Sherborne New Castle in 1594, but only got as far as the central block before being imprisoned by James I. James promptly sold the castle to Sir John Digby, who added the splendid wings you see today. In 1753 the grounds received a mega-makeover at the hands of landscape-gardener extraordinaire Capability Brown, who added a massive lake and the 12-hectare waterside gardens.

🛏 Sleeping & Eating

★ **Cumberland House** B&B ££
(☑ 01935-817554; www.bandbdorset.co.uk; Greenhill; d £80-85; P 🛜) Artistry emanates from these history-rich rooms – bright scatter rugs sit on flagstone floors, and lemon and oatmeal walls undulate between wonderfully wonky beams. Gourmet breakfasts include freshly squeezed orange juice, fresh-fruit compote and homemade granola.

Stoneleigh Barn B&B ££
(☑ 01935-817258; www.stoneleighbarn.co.uk; North Wootton; d/f £100/120; P 🛜) Warm, weathered stone and extensive gardens ensure this 18th-century barn delights on the outside. Inside, exposed trusses frame spacious rooms named after their attractive colour schemes – choose from Red or Blue.

George PUB £
(☑ 01925-812785; www.thegeorgesherborne.co.uk; 4 Higher Cheap St; mains £8-11; ☺ noon-5pm daily, plus 6-9pm Mon & Tue; 🛜) It's five centuries since Sherborne's oldest, cosiest inn pulled its first pint; today it signals its age with wooden settles polished smooth by countless behinds. Pub-grub fare includes ham and egg and a 'roast of the day'.

★ **Green** MODERN BRITISH ££
(☑ 01935-813821; www.greenrestaurant.co.uk; 3 The Green; mains £13-22; ☺ noon-2.30pm & 6.30-9.30pm Tue-Sat) In this affable, elegant spot, the food is pure West Country elan. Goodies might include Dorset crab with chargrilled hake, or a confit Devon duck terrine. For a great-value feed, plump for the cracking *menu du jour* (three-course lunch £23; dinner £27).

❶ Information

Sherborne's **tourist office** (☑ 01935-815341; www.visit-dorset.com; Digby Rd) suspended in-person visits in 2020. Call for updates.

❶ Getting There & Away

BUS

Dorchester, via Cerne Abbas (Bus X11, £4.90, 1¼ hours, four daily Monday to Friday)
Yeovil (Bus 58, £2.70, 30 minutes, every one to two hours)

TRAIN

Exeter (£20, 1¼ hours, every one to two hours)
London Waterloo (£44, 2¼ hours, hourly)
Salisbury (£14, 45 minutes, hourly)

WILTSHIRE

Wiltshire is rich in the reminders of ritual and packed with not-to-be-missed sights. Its verdant landscape is littered with more mysterious stone circles, processional avenues and ancient barrows than anywhere else in Britain. It's a place that teases and tantalises the imagination – here you'll experience the prehistoric majesty of Stonehenge and the atmospheric stone ring at Avebury. Add the serene 800-year-old cathedral at Salisbury, the supremely stately homes at Stourhead and Longleat and the impossibly pretty village of Lacock, and you have a county crammed full of English charm waiting to be explored.

❶ Getting There & Around

BUS

Wiltshire's bus coverage can be patchy, especially in the northwest.

First (www.firstgroup.com) Runs services to Weymouth, Portland, Dorchester and the X53 Jurassic Coaster between Weymouth and Axminster.

Salisbury Reds (www.salisburyreds.co.uk) Covers Salisbury and many rural areas; offers network-wide, one-day Rover Tickets (adult/child £9.20/6) and seven-day passes (Salisbury area £15, network-wide £26).

TRAIN

Trains run at least hourly east from Salisbury to London Waterloo (£25, 1½ hours) and west to Exeter (£21, 2¾ hours). Another line runs north to Bath (£11, one hour, hourly) and Bristol (£13, 1¼ hours, hourly).

Salisbury

☑ 01722 / POP 40,300

Centred on a majestic cathedral that's topped by the tallest spire in England, Salisbury has been an important provincial city

Salisbury

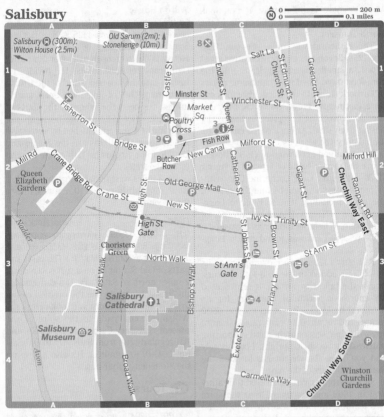

for more than a thousand years. Its streets form an architectural timeline ranging from medieval walls and half-timbered Tudor town houses to Georgian mansions and Victorian villas.

◎ Sights

★ **Salisbury Cathedral**　　　　CATHEDRAL
(☎01722-555150; www.salisburycathedral.org.uk; The Close; requested donation adult/child £7.50/3; ⊘9am-4pm Mon-Sat) Few of England's stunning churches can hold a candle to the grandeur and sheer spectacle of 13th-century Salisbury Cathedral. This elaborate, early English Gothic–style structure has pointed arches, flying buttresses, a sombre, austere interior and outstanding statuary and tombs. Check the website to see if the daily tower tours have resumed and if the cathedral's 13th-century copy of the

Magna Carta is on display. If not, look out for the high-resolution facsimile in the North Transept.

The cathedral was built between 1220 and 1258. Beyond its highly decorative West Front, a small passageway leads into the 70m-long nave, lined with handsome pillars of Purbeck stone. In the north aisle look out for a fascinating medieval clock, probably the oldest working timepiece in the world, dating from 1386. At the eastern end of the ambulatory, the glorious Prisoners of Conscience stained-glass window (1980) hovers above the ornate tomb of Edward Seymour (1539–1621) and Lady Catherine Grey. Other monuments and tombs line the sides of the nave, including that of William Longespée, son of Henry II and half-brother of King John. When the tomb was excavated a well-preserved rat was found inside Longespée's skull.

Salisbury's 123m-high crowning glory, its spire, was added in the mid-14th century, and is the tallest in Britain. It represented an enormous technical challenge for its medieval builders – it weighs around 6500 tonnes and required an elaborate system of cross-bracing, scissor arches and supporting buttresses to keep it upright. Look closely and you'll see the weight has buckled the four central piers of the nave.

Sir Christopher Wren surveyed the cathedral in 1668 and calculated that the spire was leaning by 75cm. A brass plate in the floor of the nave is used to measure any shift, but no further lean was recorded in 1951 or 1970. Despite this, reinforcement of the notoriously 'wonky spire' continues to this day.

If distancing regulations mean the one-way system is still in operation, you may be lucky enough to be routed through the normally out-of-bounds stonemasonry yard, one of only nine in the country.

★ Salisbury Museum   MUSEUM
(☑ 01722-332151; www.salisburymuseum.org.uk; 65 The Close; adult/child £8/4; ☺ 11am-4pm Thu-Sun) The hugely important archaeological finds in the Wessex Gallery include the Stonehenge Archer, the bones of a man found in the ditch near the stone circle – one of the arrows found alongside probably killed him. With gold coins dating from 100 BCE and a Bronze Age gold necklace, it's a powerful introduction to Wiltshire's prehistory.

Wilton House   HISTORIC BUILDING
(☑ 01722-746700; www.wiltonhouse.co.uk; Wilton; house & grounds adult/child £15.50/8; ☺ 11.30am-5pm Sun-Thu May-Aug; 🅿) Stately Wilton House is due to reopen at Easter 2021 after significant refurbishments. It provides an insight into the rarefied world of the British aristocracy. One of England's finest stately homes, it's been the house of the Earls of Pembroke since 1542, and has been expanded, improved and embellished by successive generations. Highlights are the Single and Double Cube Rooms by 17th-century architect Inigo Jones.

It's 3 miles west of Salisbury; bus PR/R 3 runs from Salisbury (£3, 10 minutes, one to three hourly).

Old Sarum   ARCHAEOLOGICAL SITE
(EH; ☑ 01722-335398; www.english-heritage.org.uk; Castle Rd; adult/child £5.90/3.50; ☺ 10am-5pm Apr-Oct, to 4pm Nov-Mar; 🅿) The vast ramparts of Old Sarum sit on a turf-covered hill 2 miles north of Salisbury. You can wander the grassy ramparts, see the original cathedral's stone foundations and look across the Wiltshire countryside to the spire of the present Salisbury Cathedral. Buses X4 and R11 regularly run from Salisbury to Old Sarum (£4.40, 10 minutes). It's also a stop on the Stonehenge Tour bus.

 Tours

Salisbury Guides   WALKING
(☑ 07873-212941; www.salisburycityguides.co.uk; adult/child £7/4; ☺ 11am daily Apr-Oct, 11am Sat & Sun Nov-Mar) These 90-minute trips leave from the tourist office.

🛏 Sleeping

St Ann's House   B&B ££
(☑ 01722-335657; www.stannshouse.co.uk; 32 St Ann St; d £65-90; 🛜) Utter elegance reigns at 18th-century St Ann's, where cast-iron fireplaces, mini-chandeliers and sash windows cosy up to warm colours and well-chosen antiques. Breakfast goodies include locally baked bread and homemade orange and star anise marmalade.

Cathedral View   B&B ££
(☑ 01722-502254; www.cathedral-viewbandb.co.uk; 83 Exeter St; s £90, d £100-140; 🅿🛜) Admirable attention to detail defines this Georgian town house, where miniature flower displays and home-baked biscuits sit in quietly elegant rooms. Breakfasts include prime Wiltshire sausages and the B&B's own bread and

SHAFTESBURY: HISTORIC HILLTOP TOWN

Crowning a ridge of hogbacked hills and overlooking pastoral meadows, the agreeable market town of Shaftesbury circles around its medieval **abbey ruins** (☑ 01747-852910; www.shaftesburyabbey.org.uk; Park Walk; donation requested; ⊙ 10am-4pm Sat & Sun Apr-Oct). Once England's largest and richest nunnery, it was founded in 888 by King Alfred the Great; his daughter, Aethelgifu, was its first abbess. St Edward is thought to have been buried here, and King Knut died at the abbey in 1035. Most of the buildings were dismantled by Henry VIII, but you can still spot the foundations amid swathes of grass and wildflowers, and hunt out the medieval-inspired herb and fruit-tree collections. A few minutes' walk away you'll find **Gold Hill** – an often-photographed, painfully steep, cobbled slope lined with chocolate-box cottages.

The imposing ruins of **Old Wardour Castle** (EH; ☑ 01747-870487; www.english-heritage.org.uk; near Tisbury; adult/child £5.90/3.50; ⊙ 10am-5pm Wed-Sun; Ⓟ) sit some 4 miles east of Shaftesbury. Built around 1393, it suffered severe damage during the English Civil War. The views from the upper levels are fabulous, while its grassy lawns make a fine spot for a picnic.

Bus 29 links Shaftesbury with Salisbury (£5.20, one hour) every one to two hours, Monday to Saturday.

---

jam, while homemade lemon drizzle cake will be waiting for your afternoon tea.

★ Chapter House INN £££
(☑ 01722-341277; www.thechapterhouseuk.com; 9 St Johns St; s £95-145, d £115-155; 🛜) In this 800-year-old boutique beauty, wood panels and wildly wonky stairs sit beside duck-your-head beams. The cheaper bedrooms are swish but the posher ones are stunning, starring slipper baths and the odd heraldic crest. The pick is room 6, where King Charles is reputed to have stayed. Lucky him.

They're also renowned for perfectly cooked, top-quality steaks, ribs and roasts (mains £13 to £23).

🍴 Eating & Drinking

Craft Bar BURGERS £
(Salisbury Arms; ☑ 01722-41170; www.thecraftbar.wordpress.com; 31 Endless St; meals £11; ⊙ 6-9.30pm Wed-Sat) It's a winning combo: towering burgers, hand-cut fries, creative cocktails and craft beer and cider. All set in a pub with a relaxed vibe.

★ Anokaa INDIAN ££
(☑ 01722-414142; www.anokaa.com; 60 Fisherton St; mains £16-19; ⊙ 5-9pm Sun-Fri, noon-9pm Sat; 🍴) The neon and ultra-modern decor signals what's in store here: a contemporary, multilayered take on high-class Indian cuisine. The spice and flavour combos make the ingredients sing, the meat-free menu makes vegetarians gleeful, and the early evening

deal (two courses with wine for £16) makes everyone smile.

Haunch of Venison PUB
(☑ 01722-411313; www.haunchpub.co.uk; 1 Minster St; ⊙ 11am-11pm Mon-Sat, to 6pm Sun) Featuring wood-panelled snugs, spiral staircases and crooked ceilings, this 14th-century drinking den is packed with atmosphere – and ghosts. One is a cheating whist player whose hand was severed in a game – look out for his mummified bones on display inside.

☆ Entertainment

Live performances at the renowned **Salisbury Playhouse** and **Salisbury Arts Centre** were suspended in 2020. Check **Wiltshire Creative** (www.wiltshirecreative.co.uk) for updates on all cultural events.

ℹ Information

Tourist Office (☑ 01722-342860; www.visitwiltshire.co.uk/salisbury; Fish Row; ⊙ 9am-5pm Mon-Fri, 10am-4pm Sat; 🛜)

ℹ Getting There & Away

BUS
National Express (www.nationalexpress.com) services stop at Millstream Approach, near the train station. Direct services include:

Bath (£11, 1½ hours, one daily)
Bristol (£6, two hours, one daily)
**London Victoria via Heathrow (£12, three hours, two daily)

Local services leave from stops around the town; they include:

Devizes (bus 2, £5.70, 1¼ hours, hourly Monday to Saturday)

Shaftesbury (bus 29, £5.20, one hour, every one to two hours Monday to Saturday)

Stonehenge (☑ 01202-338420; www.thestonehengetour.info; incl admissions adult/child/ £32/21, bus-only adult/child £16/10) Tour buses leave Salisbury train station regularly.

TRAIN

Salisbury's train station is half a mile northwest of the cathedral. Half-hourly connections include:

Bath (£12, one hour)
Bristol (£20, 1¼ hours)
London Waterloo (£25, 1½ hours)
Southampton (£10, 40 minutes)

Hourly connections:
Exeter (£20, two hours)
Portsmouth (£20, 1¼ hours)

Stonehenge

Welcome to Britain's most iconic archaeological site. This compelling ring of monolithic stones has been attracting a steady stream of pilgrims, poets and philosophers for the last 5000 years and is still a mystical, ethereal place – a haunting echo from Britain's forgotten past, and a reminder of those who once walked the ceremonial avenues across Salisbury Plain.

◉ Sights

★ Stonehenge   ARCHAEOLOGICAL SITE
(EH; ☑ 0370 333 1181; www.english-heritage.org.uk; near Amesbury; adult/child £21/13; ⊙ 9.30am-5pm, hours may vary; 🅿) An ultramodern makeover at ancient Stonehenge has brought an impressive visitor centre and the closure of an intrusive road (now restored to grassland). The result is a strong sense of historical context, with dignity and mystery returned to an archaeological gem.

Stonehenge operates by pre-booked, timed tickets – secure yours well in advance. At the time of research, opening hours were reduced; check whether summertime early evening visits have resumed. The VIP Stone Circle Experience (p288), where you walk within the stone circle itself, is highly recommended.

Stonehenge is one of Britain's great archaeological mysteries: despite countless theories about the site's purpose, from a sacrificial centre to a celestial timepiece, no one knows for sure what drove prehistoric Britons to expend so much time and effort on its construction, although recent archaeological findings show the surrounding area was sacred for hundreds of years before work began.

The first phase of building started around 3000 BCE, when the outer circular bank and ditch were erected. Within these were 56 pits called **Aubrey Holes**, named after John Aubrey, who discovered them in the 1600s. Cremations were buried around these pits; it's thought they may also have held timber posts or stones.

About 500 years later, Stonehenge's main stones were dragged to the site, erected in a circle and crowned by massive lintels to make the trilithons (two vertical stones topped by a horizontal one). The 30 huge slabs of stone were worked carefully to ensure they locked together. The sarsen stones were cut from an extremely hard rock found on the Marlborough Downs, 20 miles from the site. It's estimated that dragging one of the 50-tonne stones across the countryside would have required about 600 people.

Two curving rows of smaller 'bluestones' were also added. The four Station stones were probably set up at around the same time. Then in around 2300 BCE the central bluestones were rearranged forming inner circles and ovals, which were later rearranged to form a **bluestone horseshoe**.

It's thought some of the mammoth 4-tonne bluestone blocks were hauled from the Preseli Mountains in South Wales, some 250 miles away – an extraordinary feat for Stone Age people equipped with only the simplest of tools. Although no one is entirely sure how the builders transported the stones so far, it's thought they probably used a system of ropes, sledges and rollers fashioned from tree trunks – Salisbury Plain was still covered by forest during Stonehenge's construction.

Today, three of the five sets of stones in the **trilithon horseshoe** are intact; the other two have just a single upright. Of the major **sarsen circle** of 30 massive vertical stones, 17 uprights and six lintels remain.

Stonehenge

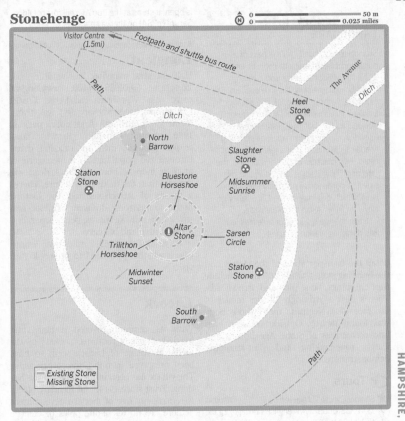

Just inside this circle are the South and North Barrows, each originally topped by a stone. Like many stone circles in Britain (including Avebury, 22 miles away), the stones are aligned to coincide with sunrise at the midsummer solstice, which some claim supports the theory that the site was some kind of astronomical calendar.

Prehistoric pilgrims would have entered the site via the Avenue, whose entrance to the circle is marked by the Slaughter Stone and the Heel Stone, located slightly further out on one side.

A decision on long-standing plans to turn parts of the main A303 road, which runs close to the site, into a tunnel has been repeatedly delayed. The proposed tunnel aims to reduce traffic around Stonehenge, although opponents fear it could damage other monuments in the area.

Stonehenge's visitor centre (p288) is some 1.5 miles from the stones. A fleet of trolley buses makes the 10-minute trip, although it's more atmospheric to walk, via a 2.6-mile circular trail through the ancient landscape.

Visiting the site is free for English Heritage and National Trust members, but they still have to secure a timed ticket. If social-distancing measures are in place, visitor numbers and hours will be reduced, making it harder to secure a time slot – book well ahead.

Trains run from London Waterloo to Salisbury station (£27, 1½ hours, every half hour), nine miles from Stonehenge. Stonehenge Tour (p286) buses depart from Salisbury station frequently when Stonehenge is open.

★ **Visitor Centre** MUSEUM
(EH; ☑0370 333 1181; www.english-heritage.org.uk; incl access to Stonehenge adult/child £21/13; ☉9.30am-5pm, hours may vary) The highlight here is a 360-degree projection of Stonehenge through the ages and seasons – complete with midsummer sunrise and swirling starscape. Engaging audiovisual displays

STONEHENGE'S RITUAL LANDSCAPE

Stonehenge actually forms part of a huge complex of ancient monuments.

North of Stonehenge and running roughly east–west is the **Cursus**, an elongated embanked oval; the smaller **Lesser Cursus** is nearby. Theories abound as to what these sites were used for, ranging from ancient sporting arenas to processional avenues for the dead. Two clusters of burial mounds, the **Old** and **New Kings Barrows**, sit beside the ceremonial pathway the **Avenue**, which originally linked Stonehenge with the River Avon, 2 miles away.

Stonehenge's visitor centre has leaflets detailing walking routes.

detail the transportation of the stones and the building stages, while 300 finds include flint chippings, bone pins and arrowheads. There's also a strikingly lifelike model of the face of a Neolithic man whose body was found nearby. Outside you can step into recreations of Stone Age houses and watch rope-making and flint-knapping demonstrations.

 Tours

★ **Stone Circle Experience**   WALKING
(☎ 0370 333 0605; www.english-heritage.org.uk; adult/child £47/28) Visitors normally have to stay outside the stone circle, but on these hour-long, self-guided walks, you get to wander around the heart of the archaeological site, getting up-close views of the iconic bluestones and trilithons. Tours occur in the evening or early morning, when the quieter atmosphere and slanting sunlight add to the effect. Each visit only takes 15 people; book at least three months in advance.

Salisbury Guided Tours   HISTORY
(☎ 07775 674816; www.salisburyguidedtours.com; per person from £59) Runs a wide range of expert-led trips to Stonehenge, the wider ritual landscape and Salisbury.

🛈 **Getting There & Away**

No regular buses go to the site.

The Stonehenge Tour (p286) leaves Salisbury's train station frequently when Stonehenge is open. It stops at the Iron Age hill fort of Old Sarum (p284) on the way back.

Longleat

Half ancestral mansion, half wildlife park, **Longleat** (☎ 01985-844400; www.longleat. co.uk; near Warminster; adult/child £26/19; ⏰ 10am-5pm, hours may vary; P) was transformed into Britain's first safari park in 1966, turning Capability Brown's landscaped grounds into an amazing drive-through zoo populated by a menagerie of animals more at home in the African wilderness than the fields of Wiltshire. There's a throng of attractions, too: the historic house, animatronic dinosaur exhibits, narrow-gauge railway, mazes, pets' corner, butterfly garden and bat cave.

It's just off the A362, 3 miles from Frome. Check whether you need to pre-book your visit.

Lacock

POP 1160

With its geranium-covered cottages and higgledy-piggledy rooftops, pockets of the medieval village of Lacock seem to have been preserved in mid-19th-century aspic. The village has been in the hands of the National Trust since 1944, and in many places is remarkably free of modern development – there are no telephone poles or electric street lights and the main car park on the outskirts keeps visitors' cars away. Unsurprisingly, it's a popular location for costume dramas and feature films – the village and its abbey pop up in the *Harry Potter* films, *Downton Abbey*, *The Other Boleyn Girl* and BBC adaptations of *Wolf Hall*, *Moll Flanders* and *Pride and Prejudice*.

◉ **Sights**

Lacock Abbey   ABBEY
(NT; ☎ 01249-730459; www.nationaltrust.org.uk; Hither Way; adult/child £10/5; ⏰ 10.30am-5pm Mar-Oct, 11am-4pm Nov-Feb) Lacock Abbey is a window into a medieval world. It was founded in 1232 by Ela, Countess of Salisbury, and some of the original structure is evident in the cloisters; there are traces of medieval wall paintings, too. Check whether the abbey's deeply atmospheric rooms, temporarily closed in 2020, have reopened. Highlights include the stunning Gothic entrance hall and the bizarre terracotta figures; hunt out

the scapegoat with a lump of sugar on its nose.

Admission to the abbey includes entry into the **Fox Talbot Museum**. It profiles William Henry Fox Talbot (1800–77), who pioneered the photographic negative. A prolific inventor, he began developing the system in 1834 while working at Lacock Abbey. The museum details his groundbreaking processes and displays a superb collection of his images.

🛏 Sleeping & Eating

★ Sign of the Angel INN ££
(📞 01249-730230; www.signoftheangel.co.uk; 6 Church St; s £85-115, d £115-145; 🅿 🤟 🐕) Every inch of this gorgeous, 15th-century restaurant-with-rooms is rich in heritage pizzazz. Burnished beams, slanting floors and open fires meet duck-down duvets, upcycled furniture and neutral tones, delivering a fresh provincial rustic feel. Treats include luxury toiletries and chef-baked cookies.

Pear Tree INN ££
(📞 01225-704966; www.peartreewhitley.co.uk; Top Lane, Whitley; d £95-135, q £150; 🅿 🤟) It takes a lot of skill to make rooms look so beautifully casual and yet so smart – the bedrooms here are a mash-up of mullioned windows, worn wooden chairs, waterfall showers and framed cartoons. Rooms in the ancient inn have more heritage features; those in the converted barn have a sleeker feel. It's 4 miles southwest of Lacock.

The **restaurant** (mains £16 to £20) is famous for its terrace, beamed sunroom and inventive dishes crammed with kitchen garden produce. Food is served from noon to 2.30pm and 6pm to 9pm.

Red Lion INN ££
(📞 01249-730456; www.redlionlacock.co.uk; 1 High St; d £99-130; 🅿 🤟) In historic Lacock, where better to sleep than a Georgian coaching inn that oozes ambience. Step on flagstone floors past open fires, up a grand staircase to sweet rooms where padded cushions line stone window frames with picture-postcard views. The kitchen does the pub classics well (mains £13, served 11.30am to 8.30pm).

Avebury

POP 530

While the tour buses head straight for Stonehenge, prehistoric purists make for the massive stone circle at Avebury. Though it lacks the dramatic trilithons of its sister site across Salisbury Plain, Avebury is just as rewarding to visit. It's bigger and older, and a large section of the village is actually inside the stones – footpaths wind around them, allowing you to really soak up the extraordinary atmosphere. Avebury also boasts an encircling landscape that's rich in prehistoric sites.

◉ Sights

Visits to the National Trust's imaginatively restored **Avebury Manor** were suspended in 2020; it's worth checking to see whether they've resumed.

★ Avebury Stone Circle ARCHAEOLOGICAL SITE
(NT; 📞 01672-539250; www.nationaltrust.org.uk; parking per day £7; ⊙ dawn-dusk; 🅿) **FREE** With a diameter of 348m, Avebury is the largest stone circle in the world. It's also one of the oldest, dating from 2500 to 2200 BCE. Today, more than 30 stones are in place; pillars show where missing stones would have been. Wandering between them emphasises the site's sheer scale, evidenced also by the massive bank and ditch that line the circle; the quieter northwest sector is particularly atmospheric.

Avebury henge originally consisted of an outer circle of 98 standing stones of up to 6m in length, many weighing 20 tonnes. The stones were surrounded by another circle delineated by a 5m-high earth bank and a ditch up to 9m deep. Inside were smaller stone circles to the north (27 stones) and south (29 stones).

DON'T MISS

STOUREAD

Overflowing with vistas, temples and exotic trees, **Stourhead** (NT; 📞 01747-841152; www.nationaltrust.org.uk; Mere; gardens adult/child £13/6.50; ⊙ gardens 9am-5pm; 🅿) is landscape gardening at its finest. The magnificent 18th-century gardens spread across the valley, with a picturesque 2-mile garden circuit taking you past ornate follies, around a centrepiece lake and to the Georgian Temple of Apollo. A 3.5-mile side trip can be made from near the Pantheon to a 50m-high folly called King Alfred's Tower. Stourhead is off the B3092, 10 miles south of Frome.

Avebury

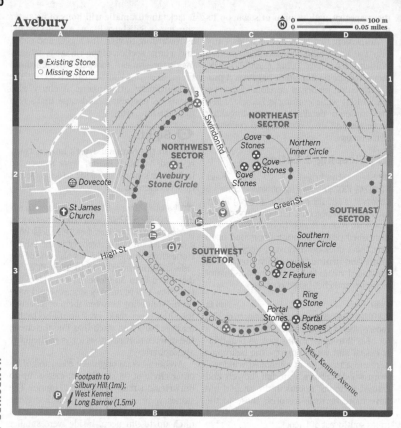

In the Middle Ages, when Britain's pagan past was an embarrassment to the Church, many of the stones were buried, removed or broken up. In 1934 wealthy businessman and archaeologist Alexander Keiller supervised the re-erection of the stones; he later bought the site for posterity using funds from his family's marmalade fortune.

Modern roads into Avebury neatly dissect the circle into four sectors. Starting at High St near the **Henge Shop** (☎ 01672-539229; www.hengeshop.com; High St; ⊙ 9.30am-5pm) and walking round the circle in an anticlockwise direction, you'll encounter 11 standing stones in the southwest sector. They include the **Barber Surgeon Stone**, named after the skeleton of a man found under it – the equipment buried with him suggests he was a barber and surgeon.

The southeast sector starts with huge **portal stones** marking the entry to the circle from **West Kennet Avenue**. The **southern inner circle** stood in this sector and within this ring was the **obelisk** and a group of stones known as the **Z Feature**. Just outside this smaller circle, only the base of the **Ring Stone** survives.

In the **northern inner circle** in the northeast sector, three sarsens remain of what would have been a rectangular cove. The northwest sector has the most complete collection of standing stones, including the massive 65-tonne Swindon Stone, one of the few never to have been toppled.

Check whether the National Trust–run guided walks of the site (£3), which were suspended in 2020, have resumed.

Silbury Hill ARCHAEOLOGICAL SITE
(EH; www.english-heritage.org.uk; near Avebury; P) FREE Rising abruptly from the fields just south of Avebury, 40m-high Silbury Hill is the largest artificial earthwork in Europe, comparable in height and volume to the Egyptian pyramids. It was built in stages from around 2500 BCE, but the precise reason for its construction remains unclear. Direct access to the hill isn't allowed, but you can view it from footpaths on the north side and a lay-by on the A4.

For the most atmospheric views, walk from Avebury village – head through the main National Trust car park, cross the main road, then pick up the footpath just to the west that cuts south across the fields (2 miles return) to the hill's north side.

West Kennet
Long Barrow ARCHAEOLOGICAL SITE
(EH; www.english-heritage.org.uk; near Marlborough; ☉dawn-dusk) FREE England's finest burial mound dates from around 3500 BCE. Its entrance is guarded by huge sarsens and its roof is made out of gigantic overlapping capstones. About 50 skeletons were found when it was excavated. The barrow is a half-mile walk across fields from a parking lay-by beside the A4.

A footpath leads from Avebury Stone Circle to West Kennet (3 miles return), passing the vast earthwork of Silbury Hill en route.

🛏 Sleeping

Avebury Lodge B&B £££
(☑01672-539023; www.aveburylodge.co.uk; High St; s/d/tr £155/200/255; P🐾) It's as if gentlemanly archaeologists are still in situ: antiquarian prints of stone circles smother the walls, pelmets and chandeliers are dotted around, and whenever you glance from a window, a bit of Avebury henge appears. It's lovely, but arguably not good value for money – it's the location that pushes the room rates up here.

🍷 Drinking & Nightlife

Red Lion PUB
(☑01672-539266; www.oldenglishinns.co.uk; High St; ☉11am-10pm Sun-Thu, to 11pm Fri & Sat) Having a pint here means downing a drink at the only pub in the world inside a stone circle. The best table is the Well Seat, where the glass tabletop covers a 26m-deep, 17th-century well – believed to be the last resting place of at least one unfortunate villager.

The kitchen rustles up hearty pub-food standards (mains £8 to £12, served 11am to 9pm).

ℹ Getting There & Away

Bus 49 runs hourly to Swindon (£3.20, 30 minutes) and Devizes (£3.20, 20 minutes), Monday to Saturday. There are six services on Sunday.

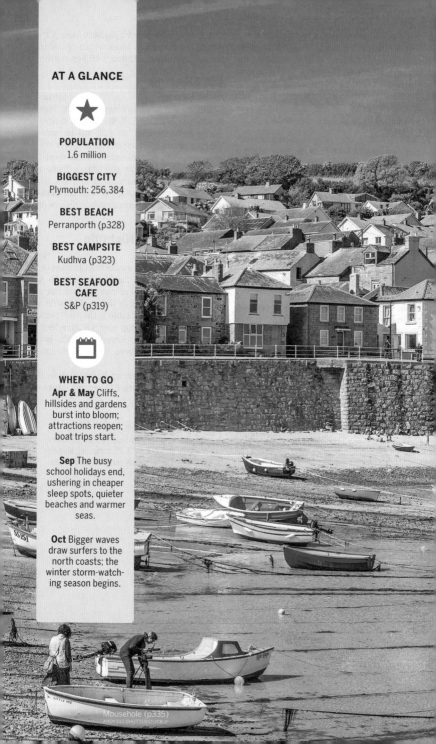

AT A GLANCE

★

POPULATION
1.6 million

BIGGEST CITY
Plymouth: 256,384

BEST BEACH
Perranporth (p328)

BEST CAMPSITE
Kudhva (p323)

**BEST SEAFOOD
CAFE**
S&P (p319)

📅

WHEN TO GO
Apr & May Cliffs,
hillsides and gardens
burst into bloom;
attractions reopen;
boat trips start.

Sep The busy
school holidays end,
ushering in cheaper
sleep spots, quieter
beaches and warmer
seas.

Oct Bigger waves
draw surfers to the
north coasts; the
winter storm-watch-
ing season begins.

Mousehole (p335)
ANDY333/SHUTTERSTOCK ©

Devon, Cornwall & the Isles of Scilly

Welcome to England's wild, wild west – a land of gorse-clad cliffs, booming surf, white sand and widescreen skies. Flung out on a finger of land, Devon and Cornwall are packed with potential and made for making memories. Here you can hike roller-coaster clifftop trails, kayak sleepy creeks and go wild swimming on deserted moors. Foodie fans delight in cracking fresh crab, sampling just-caught fish and sipping wines in vineyard cafes. The past is ever present in neolithic monuments, medieval castles and ruined mine stacks clinging to cliffs. Hang out on surfer beaches or stargaze under inky skies – whatever you do, Devon and Cornwall help you breathe deeply, rediscover, reinvent and revive.

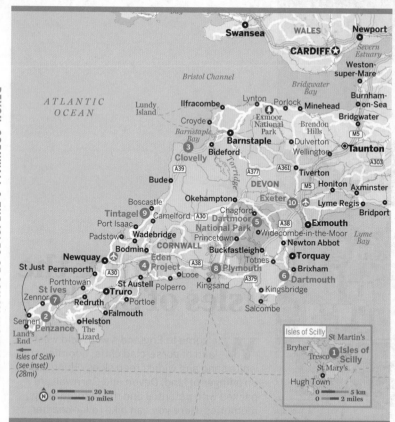

Devon, Cornwall & the Isles of Scilly Highlights

1 Isles of Scilly (p347)
Ferry-hopping around an idyllic archipelago.

2 Penzance (p336)
Discovering a geothermally heated lido and a medieval island abbey.

3 Clovelly (p318) Strolling the cobbled streets of a pretty fishing village.

4 Eden Project (p342)
Marvelling at space-age biomes in a disused Cornish claypit.

5 Dartmoor National Park (p311) Wild swimming in streams and moorland pools.

6 Dartmouth (p303)
Touring the pretty grounds of Agatha Christie's home.

7 Tate St Ives (p329)
Getting inspired by art in this Cornish port.

8 Plymouth (p307)
Exploring colonial history then sampling gin on a distillery tour.

9 Tintagel (p322)
Pondering Arthurian legends at a fairytale clifftop fortress.

10 Exeter (p296)
Clambering up to the roof of a gloriously gothic cathedral.

🏃 Activities

Walking

The sheer diversity of landscapes in Devon and Cornwall gives walkers itchy feet. Some of the most dramatic sections of the South West Coast Path are to be found here.

The epic route sweeps for 630 miles from Minehead in Somerset via Land's End in Cornwall to Poole in Dorset. Along the way are countless memorable day hikes, which can often be teamed with inland sections to make circular trails. The South West Coast Path Association (www.southwestcoastpath.

org.uk) has a detailed website and publishes an annual guide.

For wilderness hikes, Dartmoor National Park has 368 sq miles to explore. Longer self-guided hikes include the 117-mile, coast-to-coast Two Moors Way (www.twomoorsway.org) and the 18-mile Templer Way.

On Bodmin Moor the 60-mile Copper Trail starts in the village of Minions and takes in a wealth of photogenic ruined mines. In both moors, rounded hills, or tors, pepper a rolling, primitive landscape studded with stone rows and prehistoric remains.

Cycling

The cycling in Devon and Cornwall is superb, if strenuous. The 328-mile West Country Way (NCN Route 3) connects the far west of Cornwall with Bristol, taking in Mevagissey, the Eden Project, Bude, north Devon and the fringes of Exmoor en route.

The 99-mile Devon Coast to Coast powers from North Devon's beaches, alongside the Taw and Torridge estuaries, around the western edge of Dartmoor to Plymouth's seafront.

Dartmoor National Park's unfenced, undulating roads offer steep hill climbs and are popular for touring. The moor's picturesque mountain-bike routes include those ranging from 6 to 18 miles along disused granite quarry tramways around Princetown.

Many cycle trails trace the routes of former railway lines, including Cornwall's popular 18-mile Camel Trail linking Padstow with Bodmin Moor, and Devon's 11-mile Granite Way between Okehampton and Lydford.

Sustrans (www.sustrans.org.uk) and local tourist offices can provide more information.

Surfing & Boating

North Cornwall, and to a slightly lesser extent north Devon, have the best surf in England. Party-town Newquay is the epicentre; other top spots are Bude in Cornwall and Croyde in Devon. Region-wide surf conditions can be found at www.magicseaweed.com.

For sailing, key ports include Falmouth, Fowey, Plymouth and Dartmouth.

Other Activities

Devon and Cornwall are prime places for lessons in kitesurfing, windsurfing, diving, sea kayaking, white-water kayaking, wakeboarding and climbing. Stand-up paddleboarding (SUP) continues to grow in popularity, as does wild swimming – in everything from moorland pools to secret coves.

Climbers of all abilities head to Dartmoor's granite crags and bouldering spots. In Torquay, Anstey's Cove has limestone sport and trad routes, while in north Cornwall Bosigran offers legendary granite, single- and multi-pitch sea-cliff routes.

Check out www.visitsouthwest.co.uk for links to activity operators.

❶ Getting Around

BUS

The region's bus services are generally reliable, providing a safe, cost-effective way to travel. Services are better in urban areas, but can dwindle to one a day, a week or even none, in rural areas.

National Express (www.nationalexpress.com) runs frequent services between the region's cities, major towns and resorts. Example direct services include Penzance to Torquay (£21, four hours, one daily) and Plymouth to Torquay (£10, one hour, two daily).

The following are key local bus firms.

First Kernow (www.firstgroup.com/cornwall) Major operator in Cornwall.

Stagecoach (www.stagecoachbus.com) Devon's main cross-county operator.

Stagecoach offers a range of weekly Megarider passes covering individual towns (eg Exeter, adult £15) and wider areas (eg North Devon £16; the South West £30).

PlusBus (www.plusbus.info) adds local bus travel to your train ticket (£2 to £4 per day). Participating towns and cities include Exeter, Torquay, Plymouth, Totnes, Truro, Newquay, Penzance and Falmouth. Buy tickets at train stations.

CAR & MOTORCYCLE

National car-hire firms have offices at Exeter and Newquay airports and the region's cities and bigger towns.

There are no motorways west of Exeter and while many stretches of key A roads are dual carriageway, some aren't; the lesser A roads are rarely so. They can become severely congested at peak holiday times.

Petrol stations are fairly plentiful, but it's still worth filling up before heading into rural areas and onto the moors.

TRAIN

Major companies operating in Devon and Cornwall include **GWR** (www.gwr.com),

CrossCountry (www.crosscountrytrains.co.uk) and **South Western Railway** (www.southwesternrailway.com).

Stops on GWR's London Paddington–Penzance service include Exeter, Plymouth, Liskeard, St Austell and Truro. Spur lines run to Barnstaple, Paignton, Gunnislake, Looe, Falmouth, St Ives and Newquay.

CrossCountry trains run from Penzance to Scotland, via Exeter, Bristol, the Midlands and the North.

South Western Railway provides links between Exeter and London and the southeast. Other destinations include Bournemouth, Portsmouth, Salisbury and Bristol.

The Freedom of Devon and Cornwall Rover pass offers three days train travel in seven days (adult/child £53/26) or eight days travel in 15 days (£85/42). It allows unlimited travel across the two counties.

DEVON

Devon's rippling, beach-fringed landscape is studded with historic homes, vibrant cities and wild, wild moors. Here you can hike rugged coast paths, take scenic boat trips, or get lost in hedge-lined lanes that aren't even on your map. Discover collegiate Exeter, touristy Torquay, yachting-haven Dartmouth, bewitching Salcombe and alternative Totnes. Or escape to wilderness Dartmoor and the remote, surf-dashed north coast. In Devon you can sample wines made from the vines beside you and food that's fresh from field, furrow or sea. However you decide to explore – surfing, cycling, kayaking, horse riding, sea swimming or barefoot beachcombing – visiting Devon might feel like coming home.

ℹ Information

Visit Devon (www.visitdevon.co.uk) The official tourism website.

ℹ Getting Around

BUS

Most bus services between larger towns and villages are run by Stagecoach (www.stagecoachbus.com), with a number of smaller coach companies offering buses to other areas. Inevitably Dartmoor has fewer services.

Bus passes include the Devon Day Ticket (adult/child/family £9.60/6.40/19.20) which covers all companies. The Stagecoach South West Explorer (adult/child/family

£8.30/5.50/16.60) and South West Megarider Gold tickets (one week £30) only cover Stagecoach buses. Day Rider tickets, covering different parts of Devon, may be cheaper than standard return fares. Check the Stagecoach website for details.

Travel Devon (www.traveldevon.info) features a useful interactive bus-route map.

TRAIN

Devon's main line links Exeter with Plymouth and Cornwall. Branch lines include the 39-mile Exeter–Barnstaple Tarka Line, the 15-mile Plymouth–Gunnislake Tamar Valley Line and the scenic Exeter–Torquay Paignton line. The Dartmouth Steam Railway (p304) provides views of the lush River Dart.

The Freedom of Devon & Cornwall Rover ticket (three days off-peak travel in seven days adult/child £52/26, eight days travel in 15 days £85/43) is good value if you're using the train extensively.

Exeter

☎ 01392 / POP 117,770

Well-heeled and comfortable, Exeter exudes evidence of its centuries-old role as the spiritual and administrative heart of Devon. The city's Gothic cathedral presides over pockets of cobbled streets; medieval and Georgian buildings and fragments of the Roman city wall stretch out all around. A snazzy contemporary shopping centre brings bursts of the modern, thousands of university students ensure a buzzing nightlife, and the vibrant quayside acts as a launch pad for cycling or kayaking trips. Throw in some stylish places to stay and eat, and you have a relaxed but lively base for explorations.

History

Exeter's past can be read in its buildings. The Romans marched in around AD 55; their 17-hectare fortress included a 2-mile defensive wall, crumbling sections of which remain, especially in Rougemont and Northernhay Gardens. Saxon and Norman times saw growth: a castle went up in 1068, the cathedral 40 years later. The Tudor wool boom brought Exeter an export trade, riches and half-timbered houses. Prosperity continued into the Georgian era, when hundreds of merchants built genteel homes. The Blitz of WWII brought devastation; in just one night in 1942, 156 people died and 12 hectares of the city were

Exeter

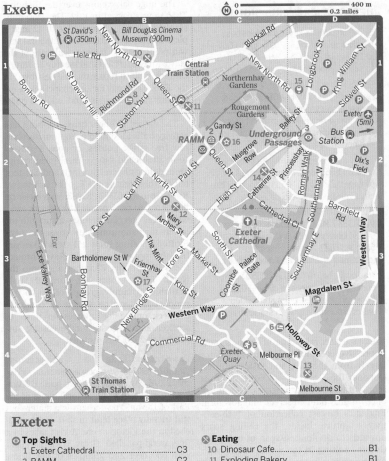

Exeter

⊙ Top Sights
1 Exeter Cathedral	C3
2 RAMM	C2
3 Underground Passages	D2

⊕ Activities, Courses & Tours
Exeter Cathedral Roof Tours	(see 1)
4 Redcoat Tours	C2
5 Saddles & Paddles	C4

🛏 Sleeping
6 Globe Backpackers	C4
7 Hotel du Vin Exeter	D3
8 Silversprings	B1
9 Telstar	A1

✹ Eating
10 Dinosaur Cafe	B1
11 Exploding Bakery	B1
12 Herbies	B2
13 Hourglass	D4
14 Lloyd's Kitchen	C2

❂ Drinking & Nightlife
15 Old Firehouse	D1

✦ Entertainment
16 Exeter Phoenix	C2
17 Exeter Picturehouse	B3

flattened. In the 21st century, the £220 million Princesshay Shopping Centre added shimmering glass and steel lines. But 2016 saw a serious fire at the Royal Clarence Hotel, a much-loved 18th-century building in the heart of Cathedral Yard.

⊙ Sights & Activities

★ **Exeter Cathedral**   CATHEDRAL
(Cathedral Church of St Peter; ☎ 01392-285983; www.exeter-cathedral.org.uk; The Close; adult/child £5/free; ⊙ 10am-4pm Mon-Sat) Magnificent in warm, honey-coloured stone,

UPDATES: EXETER'S SIGHTS

Some of Exeter's key attractions suspended operations in 2020 due to Covid-19 regulations. Check their websites to see whether they've opened up again.

Royal Albert Memorial Museum & Art Gallery (RAMM; ☑01392-265858; www.rammuseum.org.uk; Queen St; ☎) FREE Imaginative, insightful displays on the city's Roman history, world cultures, echinoderms and fine art.

Exeter's Underground Passages (☑01392-665887; www.exeter.gov.uk/passages; 2 Paris St) Hard hat tours of the city's medieval vaulted passages.

Bill Douglas Cinema Museum (☑01392-724321; www.bdcmuseum.org.uk; Old Library, Prince of Wales Rd; ⊙10am-5pm; P) FREE Superb collection of movie-themed artefacts and memorabilia.

Redcoat Tours (☑01392-265203; www.exeter.gov.uk/leisure-and-culture) FREE Wide range of free, engaging guided walks around the city's historic streets.

Exeter's cathedral is one of Devon's most impressive ecclesiastical sights and dates largely from the 12th and 13th centuries. Outside, the **Great West Front** features scores of weather-worn figures. They line a once brightly painted screen and now form England's largest collection of 14th-century sculpture. Inside, the ceiling soars upwards to the longest span of unbroken Gothic vaulting in the world, dotted with ornate ceiling bosses in gilt and vibrant colours.

The site has been a religious one since at least the 5th century, but the Normans started the current building in 1114; the towers of today's cathedral date from that period. In 1270, a 90-year remodelling process began, introducing a mix of Early English and Decorated Gothic styles.

The cathedral's exquisitely symmetrical ceiling soars up and along, towards the north transept and the 15th-century **Exeter Clock**: in keeping with medieval astronomy, the clock shows Earth as a golden ball at the centre of the universe with the sun, a fleur-de-lis, travelling around it. Still ticking and whirring, it chimes on the hour.

The huge oak canopy over the **Bishop's Throne** was carved in 1312. The 1350 **minstrels' gallery** is decorated with 12 angels playing musical instruments. Cathedral staff will point out the famous sculpture of the lady with two left feet and the tiny **St James Chapel**, built to repair the one destroyed in the Blitz. Look out for the chapel's unusual carvings: a cat, a mouse and, oddly, a rugby player.

The cathedral offers **brass rubbing** and activity trails for children. You can also borrow free **audio guides**, or book a **guided tour** (adult/child £10/5). These include trips around the cathedral precincts and cloisters, but the highlight is the **Exeter Cathedral Roof Tour** (☑01392-285983; www.exeter-cathedral.org.uk; per 5 people £40; ⊙times vary), which sees you clambering way up into the towers for panoramic views over the city's rooftops. Scaling some 251 steps takes you into the roof void above the Nave, through the bell's Ringing Chamber and onto the North Tower. Tours are currently only available to family groups of up to five people but check the website for changes.

Check online for updates on times of services, and to see if choral evensong, suspended in 2020, has resumed.

Powderham Castle HISTORIC BUILDING
(☑01626-890243; www.powderham.co.uk; adult/child £10/8; ⊙gardens 10am-5pm, house 11.30am-3.30pm Fri-Sun; P) The historic home of the Earl of Devon, Powderham is a stately but still friendly place built in 1391 and remodelled in the Victorian era. A visit takes in a fine wood-panelled Great Hall, parkland with 650 deer and glimpses of life 'below stairs' in the kitchen. Powderham is on the River Exe near Kenton, 8 miles south of Exeter.

Saddles & Paddles OUTDOORS
(☑01392-424241; www.sadpad.com; Exeter Quay; ⊙9am-6pm Thu-Tue) This hire shop beside the quay rents out bikes (adult per hour/day £7/18), SUP boards (£15/45), single and double kayaks (£12/45) and Canadian canoes (£18/60). It also offers advice on suggested routes featuring the canal and River Exe (p300).

🛏 Sleeping

Globe Backpackers HOSTEL £
(☑01392-215521; www.exeterbackpackers.co.uk; 71 Holloway St; dm/d £18.50/45; P☎) A firm favourite among budget travellers, this spot-

lessly clean, rambling former town house boasts three doubles and roomy dorms. Current measures include limited numbers, reduced occupancy of dorms and allocated showers but this may change in future.

★ Telstar
B&B ££

(☑ 01392-272466; www.telstar-hotel.co.uk; 77 St David's Hill; s £40-50, d £60-85, f £85-105; P 🛜) 'Victoriana with a twist' best defines this excellent B&B, where stately fireplaces meet mock-flock wallpaper and stag heads wear aviator goggles. Rooms team a heritage feel with modern comforts; bathrooms feature 19th-century-style tiles. If you like outdoors space, request the double with its own roomy deck.

Silversprings
APARTMENT ££

(☑ 01392-494040; www.silversprings.co.uk; 12 Richmond Rd; 1 bedroom apt £85-99, 2 bedroom apt £110-140; P 🛜) There are so many reasons to make these sleek, serviced apartments your Exeter pied-à-terre. Tucked away off a square a short walk from the city centre, each has a lounge and mini-kitchen, plus home comforts such as a DVD player and satellite TV.

★ Hotel du Vin Exeter
BOUTIQUE HOTEL £££

(☑ 01392-790120; www.hotelduvin.com/locations/exeter; Magdalen St; s from £112, d £136-171; @🛜🏊) This grand red-brick edifice (once Exeter's eye hospital) is now part of the plush Hotel du Vin chain. Quietly stylish rooms combine Victorian architecture (bay windows, cornicing, wood floors) with bold colours, offbeat wallpapers and Scandi-style sofas. There's a smart octagon-shaped restaurant, an excellent bar and a swish spa.

🍴 Eating

★ Exploding Bakery
CAFE £

(☑ 01392-427900; www.explodingbakery.com; 1 The Crescent, Queen St; snacks from £3; ⊙ 8am-4pm Mon-Fri, 9am-4pm Sat; 🛜) 🖋 One of Exeter's hippest little bakeries flies the flag for ethical ingredients, delivers superb flat whites and makes gorgeous cakes with imaginative flavours – the lemon, polenta and pistachio is a hit.

Dinosaur Cafe
MIDDLE EASTERN £

(☑ 01392-490951; 5 New North Rd; mains £8-10; ⊙ noon-9pm Mon-Sat) At this cheery mezze bar a clutch of pavement tables and chunky wooden furniture set the scene for tasty couscous, kofta and spicy *mücver* fritters. The Turkish breakfasts (eggs, pepperoni and feta) are a welcome change from the norm.

Herbies
VEGETARIAN £

(☑ 01392-258473; www.herbiesrestaurant.co.uk; 15 North St; mains £8-14; ⊙ 11am-2.30pm & 6-9pm Tue-Fri, 11.30am-3.30pm & 6-9.30pm Sat; 🖋) Herbies has been cheerfully feeding Exeter's plant-based food aficionados since 1990. Expect classics such as pea and courgette risotto, in various vegetarian, vegan and gluten-free versions.

Hourglass
PUB FOOD ££

(☑ 01392-258722; www.hourglassexeter.co.uk; 21 Melbourne St; dishes £7-15, roasts £16; ⊙ 5-9.30pm Wed-Sat, noon-2.30pm Sun) Exeter's foodies love the Hourglass thanks to a convivial atmosphere, historic feel (they pulled the first pint in 1848), small plates such as homemade pappardelle with rabbit ragu, and legendary Sunday roasts.

Lloyd's Kitchen
BISTRO ££

(☑ 01392-499333; www.lloydskitchen.co.uk; 16 Catherine St; mains £9-24; ⊙ noon-3pm Mon-Thu, 9am-3pm & 6-10pm Fri & Sat, 10am-3pm Sun) White-tiled walls and bare lightbulbs welcome you to a bistro where Devon ingredients – from honey to chicken and beef – pepper the menu. Dishes range from Thai cod and prawn fishcakes for lunch, to pan-fried scallops and steak for dinner.

Or opt for a great-value three-course evening meal (£25).

WORTH A TRIP

RIVER COTTAGE RESTAURANTS

Known for his media campaigns on sustainability and organic food, TV chef Hugh Fearnley-Whittingstall launched his culinary career back in 1999 as he learned how to run a smallholding. These days his idyllic farm and kitchen garden host dining events ranging from pizza lunches (per person £15) and picnics (£25) to slap-up multi-course feasts (£80). They're very popular, so book well ahead. The farm runs cooking and foraging courses, and you can also eat at his canteen (☑ 01297-631715; www.rivercottage.net; Trinity Sq, Axminster; mains £8-16; ⊙ 10am-4pm Tue-Sat; 🖋) in nearby Axminster.

LOCAL KNOWLEDGE

EXETER'S FOOT & CYCLE PATHS

Foot and cycle paths head southeast from Exeter Quay to join the Exe Valley Way, a trail shadowing both the Exeter Canal and the ever-broadening River Exe, which meets the sea around 10 miles away. The paths and waterways make for good biking, hiking and kayaking trips: the first 3 miles are a blend of heritage city, countryside and light industrial landscape; the later sections are more rural.

About 1.5 miles downstream from Exeter Quay the route reaches the laid-back Double Locks pub, which features real ale and a waterside terrace. The Exminster Marshes Nature Reserve starts about 2 miles further on. Around 2 miles inside the reserve, the waterside Turf pub clings to a slither of land – an idyllic setting for good grub and summer barbecues. You can also navigate this route on the canal by kayak, making for an enjoyable, non-tidal paddle past pubs.

After the Turf pub, a rougher trail connects with a path to appealing Powderham Castle (p298).

Hire bikes, kayaks, SUPs and canoes from Exeter's Saddles & Paddles (p298).

Drinking & Nightlife

Old Firehouse   PUB
(☑ 01392-277279; www.oldfirehouseexeter.co.uk; 50 New North Rd; ⊙ 4-11pm Sun, Wed & Thu, to 1am Fri & Sat) Step into the snug, candlelit interior of this Exeter institution and instantly feel at home. Dried hops hang from rafters above flagstone floors and walls of exposed stone. The range of draught ciders and cask ales is truly impressive, while the pizzas (served from 4pm) have kept countless students fed.

Turf   PUB
(☑ 01392-833128; www.turfpub.net; near Exminster; ⊙ 10am-9pm Easter-Oct, hours vary Nov-Easter) The location of this former lock-keeper's house is simply superb: bookending a slither of land snaking between mudflats and the Exeter Canal. The views are expansive, the welcome is warm, and the BBQs (mains £8 to £14) and alfresco bar add a holiday vibe. Walk from the Exminster Marshes Nature Reserve (1 mile), or cycle from Exeter Quay (allow 2½ hours each way).

☆ Entertainment

Exeter Phoenix   ARTS CENTRE
(☑ 01392-667080; www.exeterphoenix.org.uk; Gandy St; ⊙ 10am-11pm Tue-Sat; ☎) The Phoenix Arts Centre has a cool cafe-bar. Check online for the latest on its indie cinema, galleries and performance space.

Exeter Picturehouse   CINEMA
(☑ 0871 902 5730; www.picturehouses.co.uk; 51 Bartholomew St W) An independent cinema, screening mainstream and art-house movies.

ℹ Information

Ask if **Exeter Tourist Office** (☑ 01392-665700; www.visitexeter.com; Dix's Field), closed due to distancing measures in 2020, has reopened.

ℹ Getting There & Away

AIR

Exeter International Airport (☑ 01392-367433; www.exeter-airport.co.uk) is 6 miles east of the city. Flights connect with UK cities including Manchester, Newcastle, Edinburgh and Glasgow, and with the Isles of Scilly and the Channel Islands.

Bus 56 links the airport with Exeter St David's train station (£4, 30 minutes) hourly between 6am and 11pm Monday to Saturday, and between 8am and 7pm on Sunday.

BUS

Exeter's **bus station** (Paris St) is at the heart of a multimillion-pound revamp; services may be relocated to other city centre stops.

Lyme Regis Bus 9A (£7.70, at least hourly, six on Sunday). No Sunday service in winter.

Plymouth Bus X38 (£7.70, 1¼ hours, six daily Monday to Saturday, two on Sunday).

TRAIN

Main-line services stopping at St David's train station include:

Bristol £30, 1¼ hours, half-hourly

London Paddington £60, 2½ hours, half-hourly to hourly

Penzance £30, three hours, half-hourly to hourly

Plymouth £10, one hour, half-hourly to hourly

Torquay £8, 45 minutes, half-hourly to hourly

Totnes £8, 45 minutes, half-hourly

ℹ Getting Around

BICYCLE

Saddles & Paddles (p298) Rents out bikes.

BUS

Bus H (two to four per hour) links Exeter St David's train station with Exeter Central train station (£1) and the High St, passing near the bus station.

TAXI

There are taxi ranks at Exeter St David's and **Exeter Central** (Queen St) train stations.
Apple Central Taxis (☎ 01392-666666; www.appletaxisexeter.co.uk)
Z Cars (☎ 01392-595959)

Torquay

☎ 01803 / POP 65,245

A seaside resort since Victorian times Torquay remains a classic destination for the good, old-fashioned British summer getaway. It bills itself as the heart of the 'English Riviera' thanks to a palm-lined seafront and russet-red cliffs. Its visitors are a curious mix of elderly tourists, sun-seeking families and stag and hen parties. But with a smattering of fine-dining restaurants and boutique B&Bs, Torquay also has something a bit more classy. The closure in 2020 of one of the resort's key attractions – the Living Coasts zoo – has been a blow, but Torquay's unique model village, a cliff railway, Agatha Christie connections and a bevy of fine beaches still have plenty of appeal.

◉ Sights & Activities

Torquay boasts no fewer than 20 beaches and an impressive 22 miles of coast. Tidal **Torre Abbey Sands** (Torbay Rd) is central, locals head for the sand-and-shingle beaches beside the 73m red-clay cliffs at **Oddicombe Beach**, and sea swimmers love picturesque **Anstey's Cove**.

⭐**Babbacombe Model Village**   MUSEUM
(☎ 01803-315315; www.model-village.co.uk; Hampton Ave, Babbacombe; adult/child £12.50/10.50; ⊙ 10am-6pm Fri-Mon, to 6.30pm Tue-Thu Apr-Aug, to 5.30pm Sep, to 5pm Oct, to 4pm Nov-Mar; ℗) There are 425 tiny buildings, inhabited by 13,160 even tinier people, on display at this Lilliputian attraction. The epitome of English eccentricity, settings include a small-scale Stonehenge, a football stadium, a beach (complete with nude sunbathers), an animated circus, a castle (under attack from a fire-breathing dragon) and a thatched village where firefighters are tackling a blaze. It's bizarre but brilliant.

⭐**Paignton Zoo**   ZOO
(☎ 01803-697500; www.paigntonzoo.org.uk; Totnes Rd, Paignton; adult/child £18.55/15.30; ⊙ 10am-5pm Apr-Oct, to 4.30pm Nov-Mar; ℗) In this innovative, 32-hectare zoo spacious enclosures recreate habitats from savannah and wetland to tropical forest and desert. Highlights include the orangutan island, a glass-walled big-cat enclosure and a lemur wood. Then there's the crocodile swamp with pathways winding over and beside Nile, Cuban and saltwater crocs.

DEVON, CORNWALL & THE ISLES OF SCILLY TORQUAY

WORTH A TRIP

BRIXHAM

An appealing, pastel-painted tumbling of fisher cottages leads down to Brixham's horseshoe harbour, where arcades and gift shops coexist with winding streets, brightly coloured boats and one of England's busiest fishing ports.

Life in Brixham revolves around the fish market. It sells more than £40 million worth of fish a year, making it England's biggest by value of fish sold. Check with the tourist office (p303) to see whether early-morning tours have resumed. At the harbour look out for a replica of the **Golden Hind** (☎ 01803-856223; www.goldenhind.co.uk; The Quay; adult/child £7/5; ⊙ 10am-4.30pm Mar-Oct), Francis Drake's famous globetrotting ship. Don't miss gorgeous art-deco, open-air **Shoalstone Pool** (☎ 07799 414702; www.shoalstonepool.com; Berry Head Rd; requested donation adult/family £2/5; ⊙ 10am-6pm May-Sep), built into natural rock to the east of the breakwater.

The most enjoyable way to arrive in Brixham is aboard the venerable Western Lady (p303), which runs along the coast between Brixham Harbour and Torquay.

AGATHA CHRISTIE

Torquay is the birthplace of one-woman publishing phenomenon Dame Agatha Mary Clarissa Christie (1890–1976), a writer of murder mysteries who is beaten only by the Bible and William Shakespeare in terms of sales. Her characters are world famous: Hercule Poirot, the moustachioed, conceited Belgian detective; and Miss Marple, a surprisingly perceptive busybody.

Born Agatha Miller in Torquay's Barton Rd, the young writer had her first piece published by the age of 11. By WWI she'd married Lieutenant Archie Christie and was working at the Red Cross Hospital in Torquay Town Hall, acquiring a knowledge of poisons that would lace countless plot lines, including that of her first novel, *The Mysterious Affair at Styles* (1920). Christie made her name with *The Murder of Roger Ackroyd* six years later with the use of what was then an innovative and cunning plot twist.

Then came 1926: in one year her mother died, Archie asked for a divorce and the writer mysteriously disappeared for 10 days, her abandoned car prompting a massive search. She was eventually discovered in a hotel in Harrogate, where she'd checked in under the name of the woman her husband wanted to marry. Christie always maintained she'd suffered amnesia; some critics saw it as a publicity stunt.

Christie later married archaeologist Sir Max Mallowan, and their trips to the Middle East provided masses of material for her work. By the time she died in 1976, Christie had written 75 novels and 33 plays.

Torquay's harbourside tourist office stocks the free *Agatha Christie Literary Trail* leaflet, which guides you around significant local sites. **Torquay Museum** (☑01803-293975; www.torquaymuseum.org; 529 Babbacombe Rd; adult/child £7.10/4.40; ☉10am-4pm Mon-Sat) has a fine collection of photos and handwritten notes relating to Christie's famous detectives, as well as a recreation of Hercule Poirot's art-deco study, featuring furniture and props from the ITV adaptation *Agatha Christie's Poirot*.

The highlight, though, is Greenway, the author's bewitching summer home and gardens near Dartmouth. To get there, take the ferry from Dartmouth, hike from Kingswear (4 miles) or check whether the steam train from Paignton (p304) is once again stopping at nearby Greenway Halt.

Babbacombe Cliff Railway RAIL
(☑01803-328750; www.babbacombecliffrailway.co.uk; Babbacombe Downs Rd; adult/child return £2.90/2.10; ☉9.30am-4.30pm Feb-Oct, hours may vary) A marvel of engineering, Babbacombe's glorious 1920s funicular railway sees you climbing into a tiny carriage and rattling up and down rails set into the cliff on a journey down to picturesque Oddicombe Beach. At the very least, it saves you the steep walk back up.

🛏 Sleeping

⭐ **The 25** B&B ££
(☑01803-297517; www.the25.uk; 25 Avenue Rd; r £119-225; P🛜) 'We banished magnolia,' says the owner proudly. And how: the playful bedrooms here team zebra print with acid yellow, or burgundy with peacock blue. Pop-art flourishes, and great gadgets abound; play with the mood lighting via the iPad or watch TV in the shower. Great value, great fun.

Hillcroft B&B ££
(☑01803-297247; www.thehillcroft.co.uk; 9 St Lukes Rd; d £75-95 ste £120-130; P🛜) One of the better B&B options in Torquay town, with bedrooms styled after Morocco, Bali, Lombok and Tuscany. The spacious suites include Provençal, with an ormolu bed and sitting room, and India, with Indian art and a four-poster bed.

⭐ **Cary Arms** BOUTIQUE HOTEL £££
(☑01803-327110; www.caryarms.co.uk; Babbacombe Beach; d £125-365, ste £355-470; P🛜🐕) In a dreamy spot beside Babbacombe's sands, this heritage hotel has more than a hint of a New England beach retreat. Bright, light-filled rooms with white furniture shimmer with style, but for the best view book a stylish beach 'hut', complete with Smeg fridge, mezzanine bedroom and knockout beach-view patio.

Eating

Number 7
SEAFOOD ££

(☑ 01803-295055; www.no7-fish.com; 7 Beacon Tce; mains £14-22; ⊙ noon-1.45pm Wed-Sat & 7-9pm Mon-Sat) Excellent, no-fuss fish is the order of the day at this small family-run bistro. Super-fresh crab, lobster, scallops and cod steaks can be seared, grilled or roasted, and laced with garlic butter or dusted with Moroccan spices.

On the Rocks
BISTRO ££

(☑ 01803-203666; www.ontherocks-torquay.co.uk; 1 Abbey Cres; mains lunch £20/25, dinner 2/3 courses £25/30; ⊙ 1-3pm & 6-9pm) Sliding doors and pavement tables make the most of the seaside view at this relaxed, informal cafe-bistro – it's just a shame the main beach road gets in the way. Still, it's a pleasant spot to tuck into Brixham scallops, juicy West Country steaks or spicy bean burgers.

★ Elephant
MODERN BRITISH £££

(☑ 01803-200044; www.elephantrestaurant.co.uk; 3 Beacon Tce; mains £15-27, 8-course tasting menu £80; ⊙ noon-2pm & 6-10pm Tue-Sat; ⚑) The jumbo on Torquay's fine-dining scene: Michelin-starred and critically lauded, Elephant belongs to chef Simon Hulstone, whose taste for seasonal food (much of it grown on his own farm) and delicate presentation takes centre stage. The food is modern with classical underpinnings – though expect surprising flavour combos – and every plate looks as pretty as a painting.

The set lunch (two/three courses £25/28) is a steal.

ℹ Information

Torquay Tourist Office (☑ 01803-211211; www.theenglishriviera.co.uk; 5 Vaughan Pde; ⊙ 9.30am-1pm, hours may vary) By the central harbour.

ℹ Getting There & Away

BUS
Brixham Stagecoach Bus 12 (£4.50, 30 minutes, half-hourly) runs via Paignton.
Totnes Stagecoach Gold (£3.50, 35 minutes, half-hourly to hourly). From Totnes bus 92 goes on to Dartmouth.

FERRY
Between April and September the **Western Lady** (☑ 01803-293797; www.westernladyferry.com; single/return £2/3) shuttles between Torquay and Brixham – a 30-minute ride. Buy tickets at the **kiosk** (6 Vaughn Pde) before boarding.

TRAIN
Trains run directly from Exeter Central to Torquay (£8, 45 minutes, half-hourly to hourly) and on to Paignton (52 minutes), for the same fare.

Dartmouth
☑ 01803/ POP 5,060

Home to the nation's most prestigious naval college, the riverside town of Dartmouth is one of Devon's prettiest. It's awash with pastel-coloured 17th- and 18th-century buildings that lean at all angles, and is edged by yachts and clanking boat masts. It may be distinctly chic, but it's still a working port, and the triple draw of riverboat cruises, the art-deco estate of Coleton Fishacre and Greenway, the former home of Agatha Christie, make Dartmouth all but irresistible.

Dartmouth is on the west side of the Dart estuary. It's linked to the village of Kingswear on the east bank by fleets of car and foot ferries, also providing key transport links to Torquay. It makes a picturesque base for exploring Devon's south coast.

◉ Sights & Activities

★ Greenway
HISTORIC BUILDING

(NT; ☑ 01803-842382; www.nationaltrust.org.uk; Greenway Rd, Galmpton; gardens adult/child £8/4; ⊙ 10.30am-5pm mid-Feb–Oct, 11am-4pm Sat & Sun Nov & Dec) High on Devon's must-see list, the captivating summer home of crime-writer Agatha Christie sits beside the placid River Dart. Here the bewitching waterside gardens include features that pop up in Christie's mysteries. If distancing measures mean you can go inside, you'll see a series of rooms where the furnishings and knick-knacks are much as the author left them. The most atmospheric way to arrive is by **Greenway Ferry** (☑ 01803-882811; www.greenwayferry.co.uk; adult/child return £9.50/7; ⊙ 5-8 ferries daily mid-Mar–Oct).

The gardens feature woods speckled with magnolias, while daffodils and hydrangeas frame the water. The planting creates intimate, secret spaces – the boathouse and the views over the river are sublime. In Christie's book *Dead Man's Folly*, Greenway doubles as Nasse House, with the boathouse making an appearance as a murder scene.

Christie owned Greenway between 1938 and 1959, and the house feels frozen in time – if it's reopened (extra charges will apply) you'll see piles of hats in the lobby, her books in the library and her clothes in the wardrobe.

Check whether the Dartmouth Steam Railway, which runs from Paignton, is once again stopping at nearby Greenway Halt. You can also hike to Greenway along the picturesque **Dart Valley Trail** from Kingswear (4 miles).

★ **Coleton Fishacre** HISTORIC BUILDING
(NT; ☑ 01803-842382; www.nationaltrust.org.uk; Brownstone Rd, near Kingswear; adult/child £8/4; ☉ 10.30am-5pm mid-Feb–Oct, 11am-4pm Sat & Sun Nov & Dec; ℗) For an evocative glimpse of Jazz Age glamour, visit the former seaside retreat of the D'Oyly Carte family of theatre impresarios. Built in the Arts and Crafts style in the 1920s, the house has a croquet terrace that leads to deeply shelved subtropical gardens and suddenly revealed vistas of the sea. Check whether the house's interior has reopened. Its faultless art-deco embellishments include original Lalique tulip uplighters, comic bathroom tiles and a stunning saloon.

You can get here by car, but the most dramatic way to arrive is to hike 4 miles along the cliffs from Kingswear.

Dartmouth Castle CASTLE
(EH; ☑ 01803-833588; www.english-heritage.org. uk; Castle Rd; adult/child £8/4.70; ☉ 10am-6pm Wed-Sun Apr-Sep, to 5pm Oct, to 4pm Sat & Sun Nov-Mar; ℗) Discover maze-like passages, atmospheric guardrooms and great views from the battlements of this picturesque castle. The best way to arrive is via the tiny, open-top **Castle Ferry** (www.dartmouthcastleferry.co.uk; adult/child single £2.50/1.50; ☉ 10am-4.45pm Easter-Sep, to 3.45pm Oct), or walk or drive along the coast road from Dartmouth (1.5 miles).

★ **Dartmouth Steam Railway** RAIL
(☑ 01803-555872; www.dartmouthrailriver.co.uk; Torbay Rd, Paignton; adult/child return £19/11.50; ☉ 4-9 trains daily mid-Feb–Oct) Chugging from seaside Paignton to the beautiful banks of the River Dart, these vintage trains roll back the years to the age of steam. The 7-mile, 30-minute journey puffs past Goodrington Sands to the village of Kingswear, where ferries shuttle across to picturesque Dartmouth.

The service is run by the **Dartmouth Steam Railway & Riverboat Company**. It operates a wealth of other trips, including coastal cruises and excursions on a paddle steamer; see the website for a full round-up.

🛌 Sleeping

Alf Resco B&B ££
(☑ 01803-835880; www.cafealfresco.co.uk; Lower St; d from £99-115, apt £135; 📶) Not content with providing some of the town's yummiest food, Alf's also offers a batch of characterful rooms, including bunk beds in the 'Crew's Quarters' and the self-contained 'Captain's Cabin', squeezed in under the rafters with plenty of nautical trappings (lanterns, panelled walls and watery views).

★ **Bayard's Cove** B&B £££
(☑ 01803-839278; www.bayardscoveinn.co.uk; 27 Lower St; d £114-190, f £165-320; 📶) Crammed with character and bursting with beams, Bayard's Cove's seven rooms have you sleeping within whitewashed stone walls and beside huge church candles. The lavish family suites feature grand double beds and kids' cabins, complete with bunk beds and tiny TVs. There are even estuary glimpses from the rooms.

🍴 Eating

★ **Alf Resco** CAFE £
(☑ 01803-835880; www.cafealfresco.co.uk; Lower St; dishes from £7; ☉ 7am-2pm; 📶) This indie cafe is the preferred hang-out for a variety of discerning Dartmouthians, from yachties and families to riverboat crews, all tucking into cracking coffee, copious all-day breakfasts, granola pots, smoked fish platters, healthy salads and gooey cakes.

Crab Shell SANDWICHES £
(☑ 01803-839036; 1 Raleigh St; sandwiches £5.50; ☉ 10.30am-2.30pm, winter hours vary) Sometimes all you want is a classic crab sarnie, and this little kiosk will happily oblige: the shellfish is landed on the quay a few steps away. Salmon, lobster and mackerel butties are also available.

Rockfish SEAFOOD ££
(☑ 01803-832800; www.therockfish.co.uk; 8 South Embankment; mains £9-17; ☉ noon-3.30pm & 4-9pm) At the Dartmouth outpost of award-winning chef Mitch Tonks' eight-strong West Country bistro chain, seafood is firmly the speciality, and the weathered boarding and maritime decor fit right in

along Dartmouth's streets. The fish and chips are delicious.

★ **Seahorse** SEAFOOD **£££**
(☑ 01803-835147; www.seahorserestaurant.co.uk; 5 South Embankment; mains £23-34; ☺ noon-2.30pm & 6-9.30pm Tue-Sat) What celebrity chef Rick Stein is to Cornwall, Mitch Tonks is to Devon – a seafood supremo with a clutch of restaurants. The Seahorse is the original and the best: a classic fish restaurant where the just-landed produce is roasted over open charcoals.

Check whether the seasonal pop-up Seahorse al Mare, in a nearby quayside marquee with adjustable sides, has opened up again.

ⓘ Information

Dartmouth Tourist Office (☑ 01803-834224; www.discoverdartmouth.com; Mayor's Ave; ☺ 10.30am-12.30pm & 1.30-4pm Mon-Sat)

ⓘ Getting There & Away

BUS

Plymouth Bus 3 (£7.60, 2¼ hours, hourly Monday to Saturday) travels via Kingsbridge. On Sunday two buses travel only as far as Kingsbridge (£7, one hour).
Totnes Bus 92 (£3.90, 45 minutes, every two hours Monday to Saturday, two Sunday).

FERRY

Two appealing car and foot-passenger ferries regularly shuttle across the River Dart, providing shortcuts to Torquay.
Dartmouth–Kingswear Higher Ferry (☑ 07866 531687; www.dartmouthhigherferry. com; per car/pedestrian one-way £6.70/70p; ☺ 6.30am-10.50pm Mon-Sat, from 8am Sun) Avoids narrow streets.
Dartmouth–Kingswear Lower Ferry (www. southhams.gov.uk; per car/pedestrian £6/1.50; ☺ 7.10am-10.45pm)

TRAIN

The Dartmouth Steam Railway links Kingswear and Paignton. The nearest mainline connections are from Totnes.

Totnes

☑ 01803/ POP 8070

Totnes has such a reputation for being alternative that local jokers wrote 'twinned with Narnia' under the town sign. For decades famous as Devon's hippie haven, ecoconscious Totnes also became Britain's first 'transition town' in 2005, when it began to reduce its dependence on oil. Sustainability aside, Totnes boasts a sturdy Norman castle and a mass of fine Tudor buildings, and is the springboard for a range of outdoor activities.

◉ Sights & Activities

Totnes Castle CASTLE
(EH; ☑ 01803-864406; www.english-heritage.org. uk; Castle St; adult/child £6/3.50; ☺ 10am-4pm daily Apr-Oct, to 3pm Sat & Sun Nov-Mar) High on a hilltop above town, Totnes' castle is a fine example of a Norman 'motte and bailey' castle (a round keep sitting on a raised earthwork). Although the interior is largely empty, the views over Totnes' rooftops are captivating.

Dartington Estate HISTORIC SITE
(☑ 01803-847000; www.dartington.org; ☺ dawn-dusk; Ⓟ) **FREE** Henry VIII gave this pastoral 324-hectare estate to two of his wives (Catherines Howard and Parr). The 14th-century manor house is surrounded by a deer park, walking trails and riverbanks from which you can kayak and swim. There's also a heritage B&B (p306), cool campsite and good cafe (p306). It's about 2 miles northwest of Totnes, a peaceful riverside walk from the town.

★ **Dynamic Adventures** ADVENTURE SPORTS
(☑ 01803-862725; www.dynamicadventurescic. co.uk; Park Rd, Dartington Estate) On summer weekends this superb activity centre offers kayak and SUP hire on a tranquil stretch of the River Dart (10am to 5pm, per hour £10). There are also plenty of wild swimming spots nearby.

Check to see whether it has resumed lessons in sea kayaking, caving, rock climbing and archery.

Totnes Kayaks KAYAKING
(☑ 07799 403788; www.totneskayaks.co.uk; The Quay, Stoke Gabriel; single kayak half/full day £33/40; ☺ 10am-5pm Jul & Aug, 10am-5pm Fri-Sun Apr-Jun, Sep & Oct) Five miles southeast of Totnes in Stoke Gabriel, this friendly outdoors company rents out single and double sit-on-top kayaks.

🛏 Sleeping

Camp Dartington CAMPGROUND **£**
(☑ 01803-847077; www.dartington.org; Upper Dr, Dartington Estate; adult/child £12/8) Hip tent-only campsite with ancient woods to walk

in, a river to swim in and views onto Dartmoor. Bring your own off-ground firepit.

★ **Dartington Hall**   B&B ££
(☑01803-847150; www.dartington.org; Dartington Estate; s/d from £55/90; P 🛜) 🍴 The wings of this idyllic ancient manor house have been carefully converted into rooms that range from heritage themed to deluxe modern. Ask for one overlooking the grassy, cobble-fringed courtyard, and settle back for a truly tranquil night's sleep.

★ **Cott Inn**   PUB ££
(☑01803-863777; www.cottinn.co.uk; Cott Lane, Dartington; s/d £110/135; P) The 14th-century Cott is pretty much the perfect English inn: rambling, thatched and lined with beams. Rooms blend undulating walls with artfully distressed furniture and crisp eco-linens. Ingredients for the classy gastro pub fare are sourced locally – lamb from Dartington, potatoes from Kingsbridge and crab from Salcombe.

🍴 Eating & Drinking

Green Table   BISTRO £
(www.dartington.org; Dartington Estate; dishes £5-9; ☺10am-4pm; 🛜 🍴) 🍴 It's the ethos and ingredients that make this stylish, light-filled bistro stand out – dishes brim with locally sourced, seasonal, often organic food. Check whether it's still operating as takeaway only. If it is, the wide terrace provides plenty of outdoor seating.

Rumour   PUB FOOD ££
(☑01803-864682; www.rumourtotnes.com; 30 High St; mains £7-20; ☺noon-9.30pm; 🍴) 🍴 Rumour is a local institution – a narrow, cosy pub-restaurant with low lighting and local art. It's famous for its pizzas (£9 to £14), but you'll also find risottos, steaks, stews and fish of the day. The bar is open from 11am to 11pm.

★ **Riverford**
Field Kitchen   MODERN BRITISH £££
(☑01803-227391; https://fieldkitchen.riverford.co .uk; Wash Farm; 3-course brunch/lunch/dinner £20/28/32; ☺sittings 12.30pm & 7pm Wed-Fri, 10am, 12.30pm & 7pm Sat, noon & 3.30pm Sun; 🍴) 🍴 This ecofriendly, organic, plough-to-plate farm is where everyone wants to eat. What began as a food-box scheme has now branched out into a delightful barn bistro serving mammoth set-course meals. Dishes are packed with rustic flavours: expect delicious salads, roast meats, imaginative veggie options and irresistible desserts.

★ **Totnes Brewing Co**   MICROBREWERY
(☑01803-849290; www.thetotnesbrewingco.co .uk; 59 High St; ☺5pm-midnight Mon-Thu, from noon Fri-Sun) There are scores of craft beers to choose from at this trendy town hangout, from its own brews to Trappist-style wheat beers and imperial stouts. It's no dark old dive – expect stripped wood and big glass windows looking out on to the high street.

ℹ Getting There & Away

BUS

Dartmouth Bus 92 (£3.90, 45 minutes, every two hours Monday to Saturday, two Sunday).
Exeter Bus 7 (£6.30, 1¼ hours, two to seven daily).
Plymouth Stagecoach Gold (£3.70, one hour, half-hourly Monday to Saturday, hourly Sunday).
Torquay Stagecoach Gold (£3.50, 35 minutes, half-hourly Monday to Saturday, hourly Sunday).

TRAIN

Trains run at least hourly to Exeter (£8, 45 minutes) and Plymouth (£8, 30 minutes).

Salcombe

☑01548 / POP 3350

Oh-so-chic Salcombe sits charmingly at the mouth of the Kingsbridge estuary, its network of ancient, winding streets bordered by sparkling waters and sandy coves. Its beauty has pushed many properties here above the £1 million mark, and a significant number of houses are second homes. Out of season, Salcombe can have a ghost-town feel, but the pretty port's undoubted appeal remains, offering tempting opportunities to catch a ferry to a beach, head out kayaking and savour local seafood.

◉ Sights & Activities

Check whether the excellent **Sea Kayak Salcombe** (☑01548-843451; www.southsands-sailing.co.uk; South Sands), which suspended guided trips in 2020, is up and running again.

★ **South Sands** BEACH

(P) Although it gets busy in the summer holidays, South Sands has immense charm. It's something to do with the broad beach (at low tide), the cool cafe and the impossibly cute **South Sands Ferry** (☑07831 568684; www.southsandsferry.co.uk; Whitestrand Quay; adult/child one-way £4.50/3.50; ⊙9.45am-5.30pm Apr-Oct), which delivers you onto an improbable motorised platform.

To avoid the ferry queues, head up Fore St then continue south for around 2 miles on Cliff Rd, sticking to the waterfront.

★ **Mill Bay** BEACH

(P) Salcombe's best high-tide beach, sand-filled Mill Bay sits across the water on the east side of the estuary. Get there by taking the East Portlemouth passenger **ferry** (Salcombe Ferry; ☑01548-842061; return adult/child £3/2; ⊙9am-6pm). You can then either walk the lane south from East Portlemouth's ferry dock, or – at low tide – stroll along the sandy shore.

Between April and October the East Portlemouth Ferry departs from Jubilee Pier (off Fore St); from November to March it leaves from Whitestrand Quay.

Salcombe Kayaks KAYAKING

(☑07834 893191; www.salcombekayaks.co.uk; per week from £90) Rents out sit-on-top kayaks by the week and will deliver to your accommodation. It may have resumed daily hire; check online for updates.

Whitestrand BOATING

(☑01548-843818; www.whitestrandboathire.co.uk; Whitestrand Quay; per half/full day from £100/135; ⊙9am-5pm) Will hire you a motorboat so you can explore the Salcombe estuary at your own pace. Fuel is extra.

🛏 **Sleeping**

Waverley B&B ££

(☑01548-842633; www.waverleybandb.co.uk; Devon Rd; s/d £60/95; P🛜) Opt for a top-floor room at this sweet edge-of-town B&B where you'll sleep among candy stripes and sea hues. Window seats give glimpses of the estuary. It's great value for Salcombe.

Fortescue PUB £££

(☑01548-842868; www.thefortsalcombe.co.uk; Union St; d incl breakfast £135-160; P🛜) The bedrooms may be above a busy town-centre locals' pub, but they're a treat. The exposed

stone speaks of the building's 300-year history; chunky wooden headboards and pristine bathrooms bring things bang up to date.

✖ **Eating & Drinking**

Salcombe Yawl DELI £

(☑01548-288380; 10 Clifton Pl; snacks from £3; ⊙9am-5pm) The wide-ranging goodies on offer here span sourdough toasties, Scotch eggs and huge Cornish pasties.

★ **Crab Shed** SEAFOOD ££

(☑01548-844280; www.crabshed.com; Fish Quay, Gould Rd; mains £11-21; ⊙noon-2.30pm & 6-9pm) With a terrace set plumb on the water's edge, this smart shack has you eating fish and shellfish just metres from its landing spot. Homemade stock ensures bisques and bouillabaisse are intensely flavoured, the pan-seared scallops melt in your mouth and the sweet Salcombe crab is superb.

Ferry Inn PUB

(☑01548-844000; www.theferryinnsalcombe.com; Fore St; ⊙11am-11pm Sun-Thu, to midnight Fri & Sat; 🛜) If the sun is shining, this is an unbeatable location: the big beer terrace clings to the waterfront, providing cracking harbour views.

Bo's Beach Cafe CAFE

(☑01548-843451; www.southsandssailing.co.uk; South Sands; ⊙9am-5pm Apr-Oct) Espressos laden with caffeine, tempting cakes, tasty pizzas, a chilled vibe, a waterside terrace and sandy feet. Perfect.

🛈 **Getting There & Away**

Bus 606 runs to Kingsbridge (£4, 30 minutes, hourly Monday to Saturday).

Plymouth

☑01752 / POP 256,380

For decades, some have dismissed Plymouth as sprawling and ugly, pointing to its architectural eyesores and sometimes palpable poverty. But the arrival of a multimillion-pound museum and ongoing waterfront regeneration beg a rethink. Yes the city, an important Royal Naval port, suffered heavy WWII bomb damage, and even today it can appear more gritty than pretty, but Plymouth is also packed with possibilities: swim in an art-deco lido, tour a gin distillery, learn to SUP, kayak and sail, roam an aquarium, then take a harbour boat trip. And the aces

Plymouth

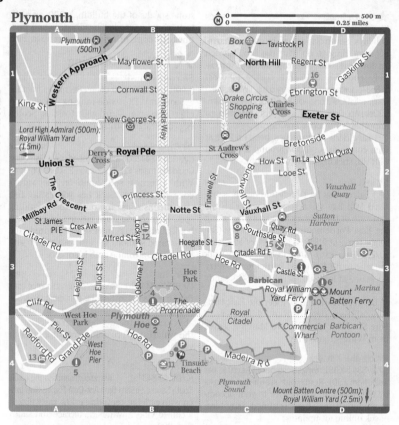

Plymouth

◎ **Top Sights**

◎ **Sights**

◈ **Activities, Courses & Tours**

◉ **Sleeping**

◈ **Eating**

◉ **Drinking & Nightlife**

in the pack? The history-rich Barbican district and Plymouth Hoe – a cafe-dotted, wide, grassy headland offering captivating views of a boat-studded bay.

History

Plymouth's history is dominated by the sea. The first recorded cargo left in 1211 and by the late 16th century it was the port of choice for explorers and adventurers. It has waved off Sir Francis Drake, Sir Walter Raleigh, the fleet that defeated the Spanish Armada, the pilgrims who founded America, Charles Darwin, Captain Cook and countless boats carrying emigrants to Australia and New Zealand.

During WWII Plymouth suffered horrendously at the hands of the German Luftwaffe; more than 1000 civilians died in the Blitz, which reduced the city centre to rubble. The 21st century has brought both regeneration to waterfront areas, and the Box – a museum that is a significant heritage draw.

◉ Sights

★ Box MUSEUM

(📞01752-304774; www.theboxplymouth.com; Tavistock Pl; ⊙10am-5pm Tue-Sun) FREE Looking as if it's been deposited by a giant hand, the shimmering, £46 million block that is the Box is impossible to ignore. Inside the museum and archive hub, galleries feature 14 massive, suspended ships' figureheads, a full-sized woolly mammoth, artfully arranged natural-history specimens and the kind of map, film and photography archives that'll keep you absorbed for hours.

The *Mayflower 400 Legend & Legacy* exhibition (non-residents £5, due to finish in September 2021) marks the Pilgrim Fathers' 1620 voyage from Plymouth, England to what is now Plymouth, Massachusetts. It's been created in partnership with the indigenous Wampanoag community and uses objects and images to explore the impact and legacy of colonialism and of the *Mayflower*'s voyage.

★ Plymouth Hoe LANDMARK

Francis Drake supposedly spied the Spanish fleet from this memorial-backed grassy headland overlooking Plymouth Sound (the city's wide bay); the bowling green on which he continued to finish his game after the sighting is reputed to have been where his statue now stands.

Barbican AREA

(www.barbicanwaterfront.com) Plymouth's historic harbour features part-cobbled streets lined with Tudor and Jacobean buildings, and old dockside warehouses that have been turned into bars and restaurants. It's also famous as the point from which the Pilgrim Fathers set sail for the New World in 1620: the Mayflower Steps (Sutton Harbour) mark the approximate spot.

Plymouth Gin Distillery DISTILLERY

(📞01752-665292; www.plymouthdistillery.com; 60 Southside St; tours £11; ⊙tour times vary) This heavily beamed distillery has been concocting gin since 1793, making it the oldest working producer of the spirit in England. Regular tours thread past the stills and take in a tutored tasting before retiring to the beautiful Grade II–listed cocktail bar for a complimentary G&T.

National Marine Aquarium AQUARIUM

(📞0844 893 7938; www.national-aquarium.co.uk; Rope Walk; adult/child £19.50/14.40; ⊙10am-5pm) The UK's biggest aquarium boasts an impressive Atlantic Ocean tank where 2.5 million litres of water are home to sand tiger sharks, lemon sharks, barracuda, rays and Friday, a green turtle. Other highlights are the vibrant fish of the Great Barrier Reef tank.

LOOK II STATUE

(West Hoe Pier) When seen from certain angles Antony Gormley's twice-life-size figure made out of 22 hollow iron blocks takes on a human form. Gazing out to sea, it invites us to consider the yearning to set sail.

🚶 Activities

★ Tinside Lido SWIMMING

(📞01752-261915; www.everyoneactive.com/centre/tinside-lido; Hoe Rd; adult/child £5/4; ⊙noon-5.30pm Mon-Fri, 10am-5.30pm Sat, Sun & school holidays late May-early Sep) This glorious open-air, unheated, saltwater swimming pool is one of Plymouth's best-loved sights. Nestled beneath the Hoe with views onto Plymouth Sound, it's a gem of the Jazz Age, built in 1935 with gracious white curves and strips of light- and dark-blue tiles. Like something straight out of an F Scott Fitzgerald novel, it makes for a gorgeous dip.

★ Ocean City Kayaking KAYAKING

(📞07376 954991; www.oceancityseakayaking.com; Tinside Beach; half/full day from £60/110) Be guided by the effortlessly cool Tom (who has been known to transport his sea kayak by skateboard) on trips heading along Plymouth's striking shoreline, around Drake's Island, or out to the breakwater more than 2 miles away.

Mount Batten Centre WATER SPORTS
(☑01752-404567; www.mount-batten-centre.com; 70 Lawrence Rd) An excellent centre where watersports tuition includes two-hour taster sessions on sit-on-top kayaks and stand-up paddleboarding (£27).

It's on the Mount Batten peninsula and is linked to Plymouth's Barbican by a **passenger ferry** (☑07930 838614; www.mountbattenferry .co.uk; Barbican Pontoon; adult/child single £2/1).

Plymouth Boat Trips BOATING
(☑01752-253153; www.plymouthboattrips.co.uk; Barbican Pontoon) The pick of this firm's trips is the **Cawsand Ferry**, a 30-minute blast across the bay to the quaint, pub-packed Cornish fishing villages of Kingsand and Cawsand (adult/child single £5/2.50, six daily, Easter to October). Year-round, one-hour excursions head around Plymouth's dockyard and naval base (adult/child £8.50/5).

🛏 Sleeping

Residence One B&B ££
(☑01752-262318; www.bistrotpierre.co.uk; 7 Royal William Yard; d £105-140, ste £165) Your chance to sleep in the former digs of an admiral. The exquisite rooms in this listed building team fluffy duvets and sea-chic styling with original shutters and cast-iron radiators. And all just a few steps from the shore.

Sea Breezes B&B ££
(☑01752-667205; www.plymouth-bedandbreak-fast.co.uk; 28 Grand Pde; s £55-75, d £74-95, f £95-125; 🛜) With its sea-themed colours and pristine rooms Sea Breezes is a supremely comfortable place to stay. Add a charming owner, cast-iron bedsteads, old-fashioned alarm clocks and sea views, and you have a winner.

Imperial HOTEL ££
(☑01752-227311; www.imperialplymouth.co.uk; Lockyer St; s £61-91, d £82-125, f £112-141, incl breakfast; P 🛜) The pick of the small hotels on Plymouth Hoe is this 1840s town house. A few heritage features remain but its revamp has made it quite modern, with beige carpets, wooden furniture and the odd bit of candy-striped wallpaper.

⭐**St Elizabeth's House** BOUTIQUE HOTEL £££
(☑01752-344840; www.stelizabeths.co.uk; Longbrook St, Plympton St Maurice; d £140-160; P 🛜) In this 17th-century manor house turned boutique bolthole, free-standing slipper baths, oak furniture and Egyptian cotton grace the rooms; the suites feature palatial bathrooms and private terraces. It's in the suburb-village of Plympton St Maurice, 5 miles east of Plymouth.

🍴 Eating & Drinking

⭐**Jacka Bakery** BAKERY £
(☑01752-262187; 38 Southside St; snacks £4-9; ⊘9am-2.30pm Wed-Mon) Quietly groovy, fantastically friendly and extremely good at baking things, Jacka is much loved by locals. It excels at vast sausage rolls, immense croissants, cinnamon swirls, and irresistible sourdough loaves.

Lord High Admiral PUB FOOD £
(The LHA; ☑01752-256881; www.the-lha.co.uk; 33 Stonehouse St; dishes £4-7, pizza £5-10) The 2020 COVID lockdown saw this old drinking den morph into a community lifeline, sporting the tagline 'it's now a hub, not a pub'. Its cosy rooms and bijou beer garden are home to the **Hutong Cafe** (8am to 2pm), a collection point for **Tilt** burgers (Thursday, Friday and Saturday nights), a craft beer **bar** (4pm to 9pm) and **Kneed Pizza** (4pm to 9pm). They're all excellent.

Harbour SEAFOOD ££
(☑01752-228556; www.harbourbarbican.co.uk; 21 Sutton Harbour; mains £12-22; ⊘11am-9pm) With harbour-view picture windows in an airy, open-plan dining room, and a takeaway hatch, Harbour is a sound seafood choice whatever the weather. And it's not just fish and chips – expect monkfish curry, clam chowder and scallop burgers.

⭐**Dolphin** PUB
(☑01752-660876; 14 The Barbican; ⊘10am-10pm) This gloriously unreconstructed Barbican boozer is all scuffed tables, padded bench seats and an authentic, no-nonsense atmosphere. Feeling peckish? Get a fish-and-

---

SHOPPING IN PLYMOUTH

The £200m **Drake Circus** centre (www.drakecircus.com; 1 Charles St; ⊘9am-6pm Mon-Wed, Fri & Sat, to 8pm Thu, 10.30am-4.30pm Sun) draws shoppers to the city centre; other well-known names line the nearby pedestrianised streets.

The independent stores of the Barbican cater to a less mainstream market, featuring galleries, gift shops and antiques markets.

ROYAL WILLIAM YARD

In the 1840s this stately complex of waterfront warehouses supplied stores for countless Royal Navy vessels. Roaming past a former slaughterhouse, bakery, brewery and cooperage underlines just how big the supplies operation was. Today it's home to sleek apartments and a cluster of B&Bs, restaurants, galleries, cafes and pubs, including the **Vignoble** (📞01752-222892; www.levignoble.co.uk; Royal William Yard; ⏱noon-9pm Sun-Thu, to 10pm Fri & Sat) wine bar.

The yard is 2 miles west of the city centre. Hop on bus 34 (£1.40, nine minutes, half-hourly) or, better still, catch the hourly **ferry** (📞07979 152008; www.royalwilliamyard. com/getting-here/by-waterbus; Barbican Pontoon; one-way adult/child £3.50/2.50; ⏱10am-5pm May-Sep).

chip takeaway from Harbour, just over the road, then settle in with your pint.

Bread & Roses PUB
(📞01752-659861; www.breadandrosesplymouth. co.uk; 62 Ebrington St; ⏱4-10pm Mon-Fri, noon-10pm Sat & Sun; 🛜) Plymouth's arty crowd loves this characterful combo of hip boozer and social-enterprise cultural hub. Amid its Edwardian-meets-modern decor you'll find a good pint, occasional appearances by cool local bands and lots of people hatching creative plans.

ℹ️ Information

Tourist Office (📞01752-306330; www.visit plymouth.co.uk; 3 The Barbican; ⏱9am-5pm Mon-Sat, 10am-4pm Sun Apr-Oct, 10am-4pm Mon-Sat Nov-Mar)

ℹ️ Getting There & Away

BUS

National Express services call at Plymouth's **bus station** (Mayflower St).

Bristol £23, three hours, four to six daily
London Victoria £28, 5½ hours, six daily
Penzance £7, 2¾ hours, five daily

Local services include the following.

Exeter Bus X38 (£7.70, 1¼ hours, six daily Monday to Saturday, two on Sunday).
Totnes Stagecoach Gold (£3.70, one hour, half-hourly Monday to Saturday, hourly Sunday).

TRAIN

Direct services include the following.

Bristol Temple Meads £37, two hours, hourly
Exeter £10, one hour, half-hourly to hourly
London Paddington £60, 3¼ hours, hourly
Penzance £11, two hours, half-hourly
Totnes £8, 30 minutes, half-hourly to hourly

Dartmoor National Park

Dartmoor (📞01822-890414; www.visitdart-moor.co.uk) is Devon's wild heart. Covering 368 sq miles, the national park feels like it has tumbled out of a Tolkien tome, with its honey-coloured heaths, moss-smothered boulders, tinkling streams and eerie granite hills (known locally as tors).

On sunny days, Dartmoor is idyllic: ponies wander at will and sheep graze beside the road. It makes for a cinematic location, used to memorable effect in Steven Spielberg's WWI epic *War Horse*. But when sleeting rain and swirling mists arrive, you'll understand why Dartmoor is also the setting for Sir Arthur Conan Doyle's *The Hound of the Baskervilles*: the moor morphs into a bleak wilderness where tales of a phantom hound can seem very real indeed.

Dartmoor is an outdoor activities hotspot for hiking, cycling, riding, climbing and white-water kayaking, and has plenty of rustic pubs and country-house hotels where you can hunker down when the fog rolls in.

🏃 Activities

Dartmoor is a fantastic place to get out and be active, whether that means an afternoon hike or a horseback hack. For a broad-based overview, multiactivity providers such as **Adventure Okehampton** (📞01837-53916; www.adventureokehampton.com; YHA Bracken Tor, Klondyke Rd; per half/full day £25/50; ⏱school holidays only) and **CRS Adventures** (📞01364-653444; www.crsadventures.co.uk; Holne Park; per person per day from £35) offer a range of ways to get your pulse racing.

Walking

Some 730 miles of public footpaths snake across Dartmoor's open heaths and rocky

Dartmoor National Park

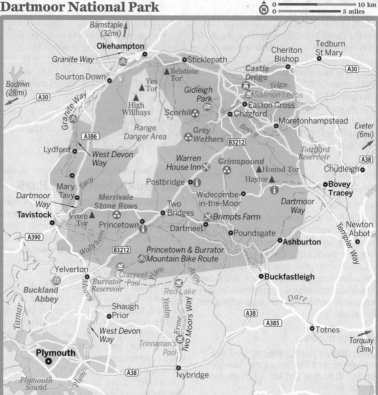

tors. The Ordnance Survey (OS) Pathfinder *Dartmoor Walks* (£13) guide includes 28 hikes of 4 to 11 miles, while its *Dartmoor Short Walks* (£8) features 20 family-friendly treks of up to 5.5 miles.

Templer Way An 18-mile two- to three-day stretch from Haytor to Teignmouth.

West Devon Way A 37-mile trek linking Okehampton and Plymouth.

Dartmoor Way (www.dartmoorway.co.uk) A 100-mile loop circling from Buckfastleigh in the south, through Moretonhampstead, northwest to Okehampton and south through Lydford to Tavistock.

Two Moors Way (www.twomoorsway.org) An epic, 117-mile trek from Wembury on the south Devon coast, across Dartmoor and Exmoor to Lynmouth, on the north coast.

Be prepared for Dartmoor's notoriously fickle weather and carry a map and a compass – many trails are not waymarked. The

Ordnance Survey (OS) Explorer 1:25,000 map *Dartmoor, OL28* (£9), is the most comprehensive and shows park boundaries and Ministry of Defence firing-range areas.

★**Moorland Guides** HIKING
(www.moorlandguides.co.uk; adult/child from £5/ free) A superb range of walks, from one-hour rambles to strenuous all-day hikes, on themes spanning heritage, geology, wildlife, myths and navigation. The hikes leave from various locations – you'll be told where at the time of booking.

Cycling

Visits from the Tour of Britain have helped ensure powering up Dartmoor's hill climbs is increasingly popular. Good off road routes include:

Granite Way Part of NCN Route 27, running for 11 miles off-road along a former railway line between Okehampton and Lydford.

Princetown Railway Opt for 6-mile or 18-mile loops from Princetown along disused tramways to Burrator Reservoir.

Princetown to Burrator A 12-mile trail taking in permitted bridleways and open moorland.

Tourist offices sell the *Dartmoor for Cyclists* map (£15).

Devon Cycle Hire   CYCLING
(🖉 01837-861141; www.devoncyclehire.co.uk; Sourton Down, near Okehampton; per day adult/child £17/11; ⊘9am-5pm Thu-Tue Apr-Sep, plus Wed school holidays) Located right on the Granite Way (part of NCN Route 27). Will deliver bikes for a small charge.

Fox Tor Cafe Cycle Hire   CYCLING
(🖉 01822-890238; www.foxtorcafe.com/cycles; Fox Tor Cafe, Two Bridges Rd; per day adult/child £18.50/10; ⊘9am-5pm) Handy for the Princetown and Burrator mountain-bike routes.

Outdoor Swimming

Wild swimmers love Dartmoor's rivers, natural pools and cascades.

Trinnaman's Pool A deep pool with tumbling cascades. A 20-minute riverside walk north from Ivybridge.

Salmon Leaps Cascades and a decent pool. Near Chagford; hike there from the Castle Drogo (p317) car park.

Crazywell Pool A large pool in open moorland, 1 mile northeast of Burrator Reservoir.

Red Lake A remote, former china clay pit. An 8-mile hike north from Ivybridge up the Two Moors Way.

The book *Wild Swimming Walks; Dartmoor and South Devon* (£15) by Sophie Pierce and Matt Newbury features 28 hikes and dips.

Be aware the water can be fast flowing and dangerously cold; seek safety advice from tourist offices and www.devonandcornwallwildswimming.co.uk – the website also has a wild swimming map.

Moretonhampstead, Chagford, Bovey Tracey, Buckfastleigh and Ashburton also have small, elegant, seasonal, unheated outdoor pools. Times vary; local tourist offices can advise.

Horse Riding

Cholwell   HORSE RIDING
(🖉 01822-810526; www.cholwellridingstables.co.uk; near Mary Tavy; 1/2hr rides £25/46) A family-run stables that leads small groups of novices and experts. It's near an old silver mine on the edge of the moor near the village of Mary Tavy, about halfway between Okehampton and Tavistock.

ⓘ Information

Dartmoor National Park Authority (DNPA; www.dartmoor.gov.uk) The DNPA is the main administrative body for Dartmoor. It runs a number of visitor centres.

DNPA Haytor (🖉 01364-661520; TQ13 9XT, off B3387; ⊘10am-4pm Apr-Oct) Four miles west of Bovey Tracey.

DNPA Postbridge (🖉 01822-880272; PL20 6TH, beside B3212; ⊘10am-4pm Apr-Oct) New, state-of-the-art visitor centre and displays.

DNPA Princetown (🖉 01822-890414; Tavistock Rd; ⊘10am-4pm Apr-Oct, winter hours vary) Also home to the National Park Tourist Office, Princetown (p314).

Visit Dartmoor (www.visitdartmoor.co.uk) Official tourism site, has information on accommodation, activities, sights and events.

ⓘ Getting There & Around

Key Dartmoor bus services reach in from Tavistock and Yelverton in the south west, Newton Abbot in the south and Exeter in the east. DNPA tourist offices can advise.

Bus 1 (four per hour Monday to Saturday, hourly Sunday) Shuttles from Plymouth to Tavistock

> **ⓘ WARNING**
>
> The military uses three adjoining areas of Dartmoor as training ranges where live ammunition is used. Tourist offices can outline these locations; they're also marked on Ordnance Survey (OS) maps. You're advised to check if the hiking route you're planning falls within a range; if it does, find out if firing is taking place when you're planning to walk via the **Firing Information Service** (🖉 0800 458 4868; www.mod.uk/access). During the day, red flags fly at the edges of in-use ranges; red flares burn at night. Even when there's no firing, beware of unidentified metal objects lying in the grass. Don't touch anything you find: note its position and report it to the **authorities** (🖉 01837-657210).

(£5.20, one hour) via Yelverton (£4.70, 30 minutes).

Bus 98 (one daily Monday to Saturday) Runs from Tavistock to Princetown, Two Bridges and Postbridge, then circles back to Yelverton.

Bus 173 (two daily Monday to Saturday) Links Exeter with Chagford and Moretonhampstead.

Bus 672 Runs once a week (Wednesday) between Widecombe-in-the-Moor, Buckfastleigh, Ashburton and Newton Abbot.

Check whether the summer-only Haytor Hoppa Bus 271 (suspended in 2020) has resumed services linking Newton Abbot, Haytor and Widecombe-in-the-Moor.

Princetown

📱 01822/ POP 1366

Set in the heart of the remote higher moor, Princetown is dominated by the grey, foreboding bulk of Dartmoor Prison, and on bad-weather days the town can have a remote, even bleak, feel. But it's also an evocative reminder of the harsh realities of moorland life and, thanks to some good places to eat and stay, makes an atmospheric base for archaeological explorations, walks and bike rides.

◉ Sights

Check whether the absorbing **Dartmoor Prison Museum** (📱 01822-322130; www.dartmoor-prison.co.uk; 🅿), which suspended visits in 2020, has reopened.

National Park Tourist Office, Princetown   MUSEUM

(DNPA; 📱 01822-890414; www.dartmoor.gov.uk; Tavistock Rd; ⊙ 10am-4pm Apr-Oct, winter hours vary) FREE At the tourist office–visitor centre, displays include those on the moor's archaeology and wildlife, as well as a children's discovery zone.

The building used to be the Duchy Hotel; one former guest was Sir Arthur Conan Doyle, who went on to write *The Hound of the Baskervilles*. Dartmoor lore recounts that local man Henry Baskerville took the novelist on a carriage tour, and the brooding landscape he encountered, coupled with legends of huge phantom dogs, inspired the thriller.

Merrivale Stone Rows   ARCHAEOLOGICAL SITE

FREE These two parallel stone rows are up to 260m long, with large stone slabs, or 'terminal stones' at the eastern end. In the centre, hunt out the circular remains of a tiny stone burial chamber. Some 100m south of the rows' west end you'll find a stone circle of 11 small stones; 40m southwest again is a slanting, 3m standing stone or menhir.

The site is beside the B3357, 3 miles west of Princetown, near the Eversfield Organic cafe.

🛌 Sleeping & Eating

Tor Royal Farm   B&B **££**

(📱 01822-890189; www.torroyal.co.uk; Tor Royal Lane, near Princetown; s £70, d £85-115, tr £130; 🅿 🛜) An easygoing, country-cottage-styled farmhouse packed with lived-in charm. Heritage-style rooms feature cream-and-white furniture, puffy bedspreads and easy chairs. They'll even rustle up an evening meal, probably featuring the farm's own reared beef or lamb.

Two Bridges   HOTEL **£££**

(📱 01822-892300; www.twobridges.co.uk; Two Bridges; r incl breakfast £99-200; 🅿 🛜) The definitive Dartmoor heritage hotel rejoices in polished wood panels, huge inglenook fireplaces, and a guest list that includes Wallis Simpson, Winston Churchill and Vivien Leigh. The Premier and Historic rooms have massive wooden four-poster beds and antique furniture aplenty; cheaper rooms are heavy on the florals. It's 1.5 miles northeast of Princetown.

★ Fox Tor Cafe   CAFE **£**

(📱 01822-890238; www.foxtorcafe.com; Two Bridges Rd; mains £6-13; ⊙ 9am-4pm Mon-Fri, to 5pm Sat & Sun; 🛜 🐾) Known as FTC to locals, this friendly little cafe is a favourite for hearty breakfasts, doorstep sandwiches and massive chunks of cake, but it does more filling fare, too, such as spicy chilli and mushroom stroganoff. On cold, wet Dartmoor days the two wood-burning stoves are particularly welcoming.

Fox Tor also hires out bikes (p313).

Eversfield Organic   CAFE **£**

(Dartmoor Inn; 📱 01837-871400; www.eversfieldorganic.co.uk; Merrivale; snacks £3-6; ⊙ 10am-6pm; 🐾) An organic Dartmoor farm has set up shop in this old moorland pub, offering torview alfresco tables, covered seating and an all-organic menu of homemade pasties, barbecued burgers, ice cream, lager and wine.

It's just over the road from the Merrivale Stone Rows (p314), 3 miles west of Princetown.

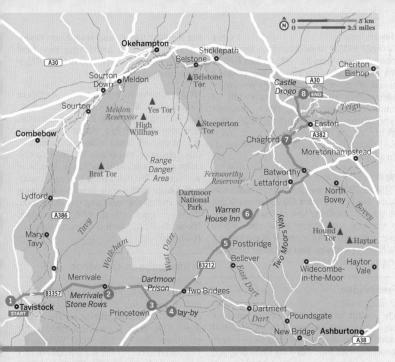

Driving Tour
A Dartmoor Road Trip

START TAVISTOCK
ND CASTLE DROGO
ENGTH 20 MILES; ONE DAY

Driving on Dartmoor is like being inside a feature film: compelling 360-degree views are screened all around. This scenic, west-to-east trans-moor traverse sweeps up and through this wilderness, taking in a bleak prison, prehistoric remains, a rustic pub and unique castle.

Start by strolling among the fine 19th-century architecture of ① **Tavistock**, perhaps dropping by its Pannier Market to rummage for antiques. Next take the B3357 towards Princetown. It climbs steeply (expect ears to pop), crosses a cattle grid (a sign you're on the unfenced moor) and crests a hill to reveal swaths of honey-coloured tors.

Just after the Eversfield Organic Cafe at the Dartmoor Inn, park on the right and stroll over the rise (due south) to explore the ② **Merrivale Stone Rows**. Back in the car, after a short climb, turn right towards Princetown, glimpsing the brooding bulk of Dartmoor Prison (signs warn you can't stop here; there's a better vantage point later). In the heart of rugged ③ **Princetown**, turn left onto the B3212 towards Two Bridges; the ④ **lay-by** immediately after you leave Princetown provides prime Dartmoor Prison views.

Follow signs for Moretonhampstead; soon an expansive landscape unfurls. At ⑤ **Postbridge**, stroll over the 700-year-old bridge, then dangle hot feet in the cold River Dart. Next, the ⑥ **Warren House Inn** (p316) makes an atmospheric spot for lunch. After the sign to Manaton, at Batworthy, take the easy-to-miss lane left, signed ⑦ **Chagford**, to visit its thatch-dotted square and time-warp shops. Finally head to ⑧ **Castle Drogo** (p317) to explore the gardens of a unique modern castle, and maybe have a bracing dip in the nearby River Teign.

Dewerstone CAFE £

(☑01822-890037; www.dewerstone.com; Tavistock Rd; snacks from £3; ⊙10am-5pm Fri-Sun; 🛜) At the cafe-shop run by the clothing brand of choice for Dartmoor's eco-aware adventurers you'll find a rack full of muddy mountain bikes, Dawn Roasters espresso and energy-boosting cakes. Plus plenty of its trademark hoodies, recycled-plastic-bottle board shorts and wooden sunglasses.

★ **Prince of Wales** PUB FOOD ££

(☑01822-890219; www.princeofwalesbunkhouse. co.uk; Tavistock Rd; mains £10-20; ⊙noon-10pm; P🛜) Roaring fires, low ceilings, a friendly landlord – the Prince is the place where everyone pops in for a pint of home-brewed Jail Ale, a Dartmoor beef burger or beer-battered cod and chips.

Postbridge

☑01822/ POP 170

The quaint hamlet of Postbridge owes its popularity, and its name, to its medieval stone slab or clapper bridge: a 13th-century structure with four, 3m-long slabs propped up on sturdy columns of stacked stones. Walking the bridge takes you across the rushing East Dart; it's a picturesque spot to whip off your boots and plunge your feet into the icy stream.

Check whether **Dartmoor YHA** (Bellever; ☑0845 371 9622; www.yha.org.uk; P🛜), which switched to exclusive hire in 2020, has resumed individual bookings.

Brimpts Farm CAMPGROUND £

(☑0845 034 5968; www.brimptsfarm.co.uk; Dartmeet; sites per tent £8, 4-person pods from £40; P) A beauty of a Dartmoor farm, as traditional as afternoon tea, and all the better for it. Choose from the basic camp-

> ### ⓘ DRIVING ON DARTMOOR
>
> Dartmoor's roads are gorgeous to drive, but large stretches have unfenced grazing, so you'll come across Dartmoor ponies, sheep and even cows in the middle of the road. Many sections have a 40mph speed limit. Car parks on the moor can be little more than lay-bys; their surface can be rough to very rough. Break-ins at isolated car parks are not unknown – keep valuables stashed out of sight.

ing fields or timber-and-aluminium camping pods, all with bewitching moorland views. It's on the B3357, Two Bridges–Dartmeet road.

★ **Warren House Inn** PUB FOOD ££

(☑01822-880208; www.warrenhouseinn.co.uk; near Postbridge; mains £10-16; ⊙bar 11am-9pm, food noon-3pm & 6-8pm, shorter winter hours; P) Marooned amid miles of moorland, this Dartmoor institution exudes a hospitality only found in pubs in the middle of nowhere. A fire that's been burning (apparently) since 1845 warms stone floors, trestle tables and hikers munching on robust food; the Warreners Pie (local rabbit) is legendary. It's on the B3212, some 2 miles northeast of Postbridge.

Widecombe-in-the-Moor

☑01364/ POP 570

With its honey-grey buildings and imposing church tower, this is archetypal Dartmoor, down to the ponies grazing on the village green. The village is commemorated in the traditional English folk song 'Widecombe Fair', a reference to the traditional country pageant that takes place on the second Tuesday of September.

St Pancras Church CHURCH

(☑01364-621334; The Green) St Pancras' immense 40m tower has seen it dubbed the Cathedral of the Moor. In 1638 a violent storm knocked a pinnacle from the roof, killing several parishioners. As ever on Dartmoor, the Devil was blamed, said to be in search of souls.

★ **Rugglestone Inn** PUB FOOD £

(☑01364-621327; www.rugglestoneinn.co.uk; mains £11; ⊙food noon-2pm & 6-8pm) Just one pint at this wisteria-clad pub is enough to make you want to drop everything and move to Dartmoor. It's a classic wood-beamed, low-ceilinged, old-fashioned history-packed village boozer. There's a picturesque beer garden, a strong range of real ales on tap, and a menu featuring lasagne, curries, quiches and homemade pies.

Chagford & Moretonhampstead

☑01647 / POP 3150

One of the prettiest of Dartmoor's villages, Chagford's stone-walled cottages, white-washed buildings and thatched roofs are backed by views of tors and set around a quintessential village square. The market town of Moretonhampstead sits 5 miles to the southeast.

◎ Sights

★ Castle Drogo HISTORIC BUILDING
(NT; ☑ 01647-433306; www.nationaltrust.org.uk; near Drewsteignton; gardens adult/child £5/2.50; ◎ 11am-5pm mid-Mar–Oct; P) Three miles northeast of Chagford sits an outlandish architectural flight of fancy. Designed by Sir Edwin Lutyens for self-made food-millionaire Julius Drewe, it was built between 1911 and 1931 and was intended to be a medieval-style castle but with modern comforts. Although currently the focus of a massive six-year restoration project, the gardens remain open.

The castle car park is also a starting point for spectacular hikes in the plunging, densely wooded Teign Gorge. Bring your swimsuit for a bracing dip at Salmon Leaps (p313).

⌂ Sleeping & Eating

Moretonhampstead's backpacker hostel, **Sparrowhawk** (☑ 01647-440318; www.sparrowhawkbackpackers.co.uk; 45 Ford St; dm/d/f £19/45/55; ☞) ✦ suspended individual bookings in 2020; ask if they've reopened the dorms.

★ Gidleigh Park HOTEL £££
(☑ 01647-432367; www.gidleigh.co.uk; Gidleigh, near Chagford; r £240-500, ste from £750, mains £14-32, 3-course dinner £115; ◎ restaurant 12.30-9pm Tue-Sat; P ☞) Without doubt Devon's grandest, fanciest and priciest hotel. At the end of a long private drive, the mock-Tudor house is an unashamedly opulent pamper pad: vast suites with wet-room showers, luxurious lounges with crackling fires and a restaurant overseen by multiple-award-winning Chris Eden. It's 2 miles west of Chagford.

★ Horse PIZZA £
(☑ 01647-440242; www.thehorsedartmoor.co.uk; 7 George St, Moretonhampstead; pizza £7-14; ◎ 12.30-2.30pm Tue-Sat & 6.30-8.30pm Wed-Sat) One of Dartmoor's coolest gastropubs dishes up simple but superb pizzas (made from twice-risen, focaccia dough, no less), plus platters of fennel salami, buffalo mozzarella and memorable Dartmoor beef bresaola.

WORTH A TRIP

COOL CAMPING

There's every chance you'll fall utterly in love with **Vintage Vardos** (☑ 07977 535233; www.fishertonfarm.com; Higher Fisherton Farm, near Atherington; campsite per night £260-330; ◎ Easter-Oct; P), an enchanting encampment of restored Romany caravans 15 miles southeast of Croyde. The three brightly painted, two-person wagons boast log burners, funky fabrics and snug sleeping platforms. Night lights in jam jars lead to a firepit fringed by log benches, a hamper full of crockery and ranks of cast-iron pans.

There's even a bailer-twine-sprung outdoor bed, so you can slumber under the stars. It's all done with love and humour, and is impossible to resist.

Blacks DELI £
(☑ 01647-433545; www.blacks-deli.com; 28 The Sq, Chagford; snacks £4-7; ◎ 7.30am-2pm Mon-Sat) Tempting breads, cheeses, olives, pies and pasties are stacked high. Homemade quiches might include leek and Stilton or spicy pepper with chorizo.

Croyde & Braunton
☑ 01271 / POP 8911

Croyde has the kind of cheerful, chilled vibe you'd expect from its role as North Devon's surf central. The old world meets a new surfing wave here: thatched roofs peep out over racks of wetsuits; crowds of hip wave-riders sip beers outside 17th-century inns; and powerful waves line up to roll in towards acres of sand. The traffic-thronged village of Braunton sits 2 miles inland.

◎ Sights & Activities

The water's hard to resist in Croyde. **Ralph's** (☑ 01271-890147; Hobb's Hill; surfboard & wetsuit hire per 4/24hr £12/18, bodyboard & wetsuit £10/15; ◎ 9am-dusk mid-Mar–Dec) is among those hiring out wetsuits and surfboards. Lessons are provided by **Surf South West** (☑ 01271-890400; www.surfsouthwest.com; Croyde Burrows car park; half/full day £35/65; ◎ mid-Mar–mid-Nov) and **Surfing Croyde Bay** (☑ 0800 188 4860; www.surfingcroydebay.co.uk; Freshwell Camping; half/full day £35/70). They also run coasteering and SUP lessons (per day £40 to £60).

★ **Museum of British Surfing** MUSEUM
(📞 01271-815155; www.museumofbritishsurfing.org.uk; Caen St, Braunton; adult/child £2/free; ⊙ 11am-3pm Fri-Sun Easter-Dec) Few museums are this cool. Vibrant surfboards and vintage wetsuits line the walls; sepia images catch your eye. The stories are compelling: 18th-century British sailors riding Hawaiian waves – England's 1920s homegrown surf pioneers. Here, heritage meets hanging ten.

Braunton Burrows WILDLIFE RESERVE
(www.explorebraunton.org; near Braunton; 🅿) **FREE** The vast network of dunes here is the UK's largest. Paths wind past sandy hummocks, salt marshes, purple thyme, yellow hawkweed and pyramidal orchids. The burrows fringe an immense sweep of sandy beach, and were the main training area for American troops before D-Day. Mock landing craft are still hidden in the tufted dunes near the car park at its southern tip.

🛏 Sleeping & Eating

Cherry Tree Farm CAMPGROUND £
(📞 01271-890495; www.cherrytreecampingcroyde.co.uk; off Moor Lane, Croyde; sites per 2 adults £26; 🅿) ✎ Large grassy pitches, a no-caravans policy and broad ocean views make this chilled-out campsite a sought-after choice. You can also often put up a tent in unpitched fields. The 10-minute walk into the village means it's away from Croyde's crowds.

Ocean Pitch CAMPSITE £
(📞 07581 024348; www.oceanpitch.co.uk; Moor Lane, Croyde; sites per 2 adults £30; ⊙ mid-Jun–early Sep; 🅿 📶) A surfers' favourite, with brilliant views of the breakers, luxury sleeping pods (£99 per night) and classic VW campers (£99 per night).

★ **Baggy's** HOSTEL, B&B ££
(📞 01271-890078; www.baggys.co.uk; Baggy Point, Croyde; dm/d from £33/110; 🅿 📶) Baggy's is light, bright and inviting with lots of wood, minimal clutter and stylish double rooms. The surfy cafe has an outside deck where you can eat breakfast while watching the waves.

Dorms may be limited to three guests from the same household.

★ **Biffen's Kitchen** STREET FOOD £
(www.biffenskitchen.com; Ocean Pitch Campsite, Moor Lane; dishes £4.50-7; ⊙ 8.30-10.30am Tue-Sun & 5-8pm Wed-Sat mid-Apr–Sep; ✎) Inspired by surf-themed street food, the eponymous Biff set up this snack shack in 2019 after ditching a London marketing job to ride north Devon's waves. Expect chipotle jackfruit tacos, jerk chicken curry and plenty of beach-bum flair.

ℹ Information

Braunton Tourist Office (📞 01271-816688; www.visitbraunton.co.uk; Caen St, Braunton; ⊙ 10am-3pm Mon-Fri year-round, plus to 1pm Sat Jun-Dec) Inside the town's (free) museum. It's volunteer run, so hours may vary.

ℹ Getting There & Away

Bus 21/21A links Braunton with Croyde (£2, 15 minutes, hourly Monday to Saturday), Ilfracombe (£2.10, 30 minutes, half-hourly daily) and Barnstaple (£2.90, 20 minutes, half-hourly daily).

DON'T MISS

CLOVELLY

The quintessential picture-postcard Devon village, Clovelly (📞 01237-431781; www.clovelly.co.uk; adult/child £8/4.60; ⊙ 9am-5pm, book visits in advance; 🅿) has cottages that cascade down cliffs to meet a curving crab claw of a harbour that's lined with lobster pots and backed by a deep-blue sea.

Clovelly is privately owned, and admission is charged at the hilltop visitor centre. The village's cobbled streets are so steep that cars can't cope, so supplies are brought in by sledge; you'll see these big bread baskets on runners leaning outside homes. Charles Kingsley, author of the children's classic *The Water Babies*, spent much of his early life in Clovelly – don't miss his former house, or the highly atmospheric fishers' cottage and the village's twin chapels.

The village website outlines places to stay, including the smart harbourside hotel and local B&Bs.

Ilfracombe

📞 01271/ POP 11,180

If there's anywhere that sums up the faded grandeur of the British seaside, it's surely Ilfracombe. Parts look decidedly tired, but it's also framed by precipitous cliffs, golf greens and a promenade strung with twinkling lights. The resort also springs a mighty surprise in the form of *Verity*; a towering, startling statue by the provocative artist Damien Hirst.

◉ Sights & Activities

Check whether **Tunnelsbeaches** (www. tunnelsbeaches.co.uk), Ilfracombe's atmospheric, tidal, Victorian bathing pools have reopened.

★ Verity   LANDMARK
(The Pier) Pregnant, naked and holding aloft a huge spear, Damien Hirst's 20m-high statue *Verity* towers above Ilfracombe's harbour mouth. On the seaward side her skin is peeled back, revealing sinew, fat and foetus. Critics say she detracts from the scenery; the artist says she's an allegory for truth and justice. Either way, she's drawing the crowds.

Ilfracombe Aquarium   AQUARIUM
(📞 01271-864533; www.ilfracombeaquarium.co.uk; The Pier; adult/child £6.25/5.25; ⊙10am-4pm or 5pm late May–Sep, to 3pm early Feb–late May & Oct) Recreates aquatic environments from Exmoor to the Atlantic, via estuary, rock pool and harbour.

Ilfracombe Princess   BOATING
(📞 01271-879727; www.ilfracombeprincess.co.uk; The Pier; adult/child £12/6; ⊙1-4 trips daily Easter-Oct) Hop aboard this cute little yellow boat for a one-hour cruise along a dramatic shore to see seals and smuggler's caves.

🛏 Sleeping & Eating

Ocean Backpackers   HOSTEL £
(📞 01271-867835; www.oceanbackpackers.co.uk; 29 St James Pl; s/d/tr/q £38/50/66/80; P@🛜) Brightly painted en-suite rooms, low prices and a cheerful, backpacker vibe make this convivial hostel an appealing option.

At the time of writing, dorms (beds from £20) and bedrooms were only available to household groups.

★ Norbury House   B&B ££
(📞 01271-863888; www.norburyhouse.co.uk; Torrs Park; d £110-130, tr £135; P🛜) Each of the

A REMOTE SLEEP SPOT

For a tucked-away North Devon hideaway, try **Peppercombe Bothy** (NT; 📞 0344-335 1296; www.nationaltrust.org. uk; Peppercombe; hut per night £28; P), a four-person stone hut 7 miles east along the coast from Clovelly. The definition of bare-bones, it has two sleeping platforms, a sink with running water and a terrace with its own firepit. Arguably the best bit is the outdoor loo with unforgettable sea views.

rooms in this gorgeous guesthouse is done up in a different style: choose from pop art, art deco or contemporary chic. Fabulous furnishings, light-filled interiors, charming hosts and cracking sea-and-town views seal the deal.

★ S&P   SEAFOOD ££
(📞 01271-865923; www.sandpfish.co.uk; 1 The Cove; dishes £6-15, seafood platters £64; ⊙10am-4pm Mon-Sat, 11am-4pm Sun) Seafood doesn't get much fresher than S&P's cafe and fishmongers – its trawlers land catches just metres away. The covered outdoor tables on the harbourside are prime places to tuck into lobster sandwiches, Devon oysters and shellfish platters crammed with cockles, mussels, lobster and crab. And perhaps sip a Prosecco or chilled white wine.

ℹ Information

Tourist Office (📞 01271-863001; www.visit-ilfracombe.co.uk; The Seafront; ⊙11am-3pm Mon-Sat) Inside the seafront Landmark Theatre building.

ℹ Getting There & Away

Bus 21/21A Runs to Barnstaple (£2.90, one hour, half-hourly) via Braunton (£2.10, 30 minutes).

CORNWALL

You can't get further west than the ancient Celtic kingdom of Cornwall (or Kernow, as it's known to Cornish speakers). Blessed with the southwest's wildest coastline and most breathtakingly beautiful beaches, this proudly independent peninsula has always marched to its own tune.

While the staple industries of old – mining, fishing and farming – have all but disappeared, Cornwall has since reinvented itself as one of the nation's creative corners. Whether it's exploring the space-age domes of the Eden Project, sampling the culinary creations of a celebrity chef or basking on a deserted beach, you're guaranteed to feel the itch of inspiration. Time to let a little Kernow into your soul.

❶ Getting There & Away

The county's main airport (p328) is just outside Newquay, with regular links to London Heathrow, Leeds Bradford, Dublin and Cork. **First Kernow** (www.firstgroup.com/cornwall) bus 56 (£4, 30 minutes) shuttles to the airport from Newquay every one or two hours.

The main train line from London Paddington runs through the centre of the county before ending at Penzance, stopping at major towns in between. Trains also link Cornwall with the Midlands, the north of England and Scotland.

The major road into Cornwall, the A30, is prone to summer traffic jams. The A38 from Plymouth over the Tamar Bridge into Cornwall is an alternative, but can be a more circuitous route. You only pay the Tamar Bridge toll (cars £2) when leaving Cornwall.

❶ Getting Around

Bus, train and ferry timetables can be found on the Traveline South West (www.travelinesw.com) website.

Great Scenic Railways (www.greatscenicrailways.com) links to timetables for Cornwall's picturesque railway branch lines.

BUS

Cornwall's main provider, **First Kernow** (📞 0345 646 0707; www.firstgroup.com/cornwall), runs most buses between major towns. Around 20 smaller companies also provide services.

A one-day ticket covering all First Kernow buses costs adult/child/family £15/7/30. The Ride Cornwall Ranger covers both bus and train travel.

You can buy a series of day and multi-day tickets through the First app; prices can be several pounds cheaper than buying on board.

TRAIN

Cornwall's main railway line follows the coast as far as Penzance, with branch lines to Gunnislake, Looe, Newquay, Falmouth and St Ives.

Most trains are provided by **GWR** (Great Western Railway; 📞 0345 7000 125; www.gwr.com), although **CrossCountry Trains** (📞 03447 369 123; www.crosscountrytrains.co.uk) also run through major stations.

Both companies have useful apps featuring timetable queries and e-ticket purchases.

TRANSPORT PASSES

Several passes cover public transport in Cornwall.

Ride Cornwall Ranger (adult/child/family £18/9/36) is the best all-round value covering a day's bus and train travel across Cornwall, and between Cornwall and Plymouth. The ticket can be purchased from train and bus stations, and from bus drivers, and is valid after 9am Monday to Friday and weekends.

The **Freedom of Devon & Cornwall Rover** (three days off-peak travel in seven days adult/child £52/26, eight days travel in 15 days £85/43) is good value if you're using the train extensively through Devon and Cornwall.

Off-peak day-return tickets offer good value on Cornwall's branch railway lines; Truro to Falmouth costs £4.80.

If you have a permanent address in Cornwall (eg a holiday home), you can also buy a **Devon & Cornwall Railcard** (£12), which gives a 30% discount on off-peak train travel within Devon and Cornwall, including all the branch lines.

Bude

📞 01288 / POP 9220

A scant few miles from the Devon border, Bude is a breezy seaside town with a batch of impressive beaches and a 1930s seawater lido that seems to sprout from the rock. The town is also a springboard for hikes on the stunning coastline that stretches out to either side.

◉ Sights & Activities

Bude's beaches include popular, sandy **Summerleaze**, just off the town centre. Three miles south of town is **Widemouth Bay** (pronounced *wid*-muth), a broad, sandy beach great for both families and surfers. Two miles further is the shingly beach of **Millook**, followed by the dramatic cliffs around **Crackington Haven**, 10 miles south of Bude.

Three miles north of town are the National Trust–owned **Northcott Mouth** and **Sandymouth**.

A mile further on is pebbly **Duckpool**, often quiet even in summer.

★ Bude Castle   MUSEUM

(📞 01288-357300; www.thecastlebude.org.uk; The Wharf; ◷10am-4pm; 🚸) 🆓 Housed in a striking folly behind Summerleaze beach, the modern, bright, engaging displays here take in shipwrecks, life-saving and Bude's story as a holiday resort.

Bude Sea Pool SWIMMING
(www.budeseapool.org; Summerleaze Beach; ⊘24hr) **FREE** The walls of Bude's handsome saltwater lido were integrated into an existing rock bowl, creating a sheltered pool were you can swim in the sea but are protected from its force. Built in the 1930s and measuring an impressive 90m by 45m, it's perfect for kids – it also warms up fast on sunny days.

Big Blue Surf School SURFING
(☑01288-331764; www.bigbluesurfschool.co.uk; Summerleaze Beach; per lesson £30) A well-established school offering lessons mainly to beginner and intermediate surfers. Also runs women-only sessions and those for surfers with disabilities.

🍴 Sleeping & Eating

Elements HOTEL ££
(☑01288-352386; www.elements-life.co.uk; Marine Dr; incl breakfast s £65, d £100-160, f £160; P🕲🐾🌊) Despite a boxy exterior, this clifftop hotel sports soothing sea colours, bold fabrics, big coastal views and thoughtful mod cons including DVD library, Bluetooth speakers and Playstation 2 in the family rooms.

Edgcumbe B&B ££
(☑01288-353846; www.edgcumbe-hotel.co.uk; Summerleaze Cres; s/d/f from £65/130/135; P🕲🐾) There's a friendly, laid-back feel to this bright, modern B&B – helped by a location just a few minutes' walk from Summerleaze Beach. Some bedrooms offer lounge area, luxury bathroom and sea views. Its Deck bistro (4pm to 8pm, mains from £9) rustles up tasty surf 'n' turf focused food.

★ Beach at Bude HOTEL £££
(☑01288-389800; www.thebeachatbude.co.uk; Summerleaze Cres; incl breakfast d £125-215, ste £195-355; P🕲🐾) Space, style and broad views steal the show at the Beach at Bude. Pale wood furniture, Lloyd Loom chairs and peach-and-taupe colours conjure the feel of a New England beach cabin. The suites sleep four.

Life's a Beach CAFE £
(☑01288-355222; www.lifesabeach.info; 16 Summerleaze Cres; mains £7-12; ⊘food 10am-7pm, bar to 9pm) Beloved of locals, Life's a Beach (or LAB as it's known) is a top spot for a baguette, burger, salt and pepper squid or some grilled fish. It's at its best as the sun goes down over the best view in town.

ℹ️ Information

Bude Tourist Office (☑01288-354240; www.visitbude.info; The Crescent; ⊘10am-5pm Mon-Sat, plus to 4pm Sun summer) Beside the main long-stay car park.

ℹ️ Getting There & Away

First Kernow bus 95 (£4 to £6.50, one to four daily) runs between Bude and Boscastle (30 minutes), Tintagel (one hour) and Camelford (1½ hours).

Bus 10 (two to three daily) connects Camelford with Port Isaac (£3.50, 30 minutes) and Polzeath (£6, one hour).

Boscastle

☑01840 / POP 640

Tucked into the crook of a steep coombe (valley) at the confluence of three rivers, Boscastle's seafaring heritage stretches back to Elizabethan times. With its quaint cottages, flower-clad cliffs, tinkling streams and a sturdy quay, it's almost impossibly photogenic. But the peaceful setting belies a stormy incident: in 2004 Boscastle was hit by one of Britain's largest-ever flash floods, which carried away cars, bridges and buildings. Happily, the village has been rebuilt to its picturesque best.

👁 Sights

Boscastle Harbour HARBOUR
(NT; ☑01840-250010; www.nationaltrust.org.uk) Dramatic to hike, Cornwall's north shore is highly hazardous for ships. Boscastle sprung up because it was the only spot for 40 miles where a harbour could be built. Strolling from the village beside the narrow channel towards the sea reveals a compact, curving harbour wall, a sharply curling promontory and the Meachard, a tiny island. Look out for the blowhole at Penally Point. If conditions are right, it spouts water across the harbour entrance an hour either side of low tide.

🍴 Sleeping & Eating

Pint-sized **Boscastle YHA** (☑0345 371 9006; www.yha.org.uk; Palace Stables, The Harbour) suspended bookings from individual travellers in 2020 – ask if they've resumed.

Pencuke Farm
CAMPING £

(☑ 01840-230360; www.pencukefarm.co.uk; Pencuke La, St Gennys; sites per 4 adults £18, hut £150; P @ ⊛) This organic farm, roughly halfway between Boscastle and Bude, is a great place to pitch a tent. They've limited camping to just nine pitches in the spacious sea-view meadow; campfires seal the deal. Or opt for an Atlantic-view shepherd's hut (sleeps four), with hot tub, wood burner and sea views.

Boscastle House
B&B ££

(☑ 01840-250654; www.boscastlehouse.co.uk; Doctors Hill; d £128; P ⊛) The best of Boscastle's B&Bs occupies a Victorian house overlooking the valley. Five classy rooms have a bright, contemporary feel that mixes neutral colours with bold print wallpapers. Charlotte has bay-window views; Nine Maidens has twin sinks and a free-standing bath; and Trelawney has its own sofa.

★ Boscastle Farm Shop
CAFE £

(☑ 01840-250827; www.boscastlefarmshop. co.uk; Hillsborough Farm, near Boscastle; dishes £6-11; ⊙ 9am-5pm; P) In the spacious cafe of this excellent farm shop, tall windows look out onto green fields and the coast. It's the perfect setting for breakfasts of dry-cured local bacon, sandwiches packed with Tregida smoked salmon, or Ruby Red burgers with Cornish blue cheese. The drinks menu features prime Cornish lager, cider and wine.

❶ Information

Boscastle Tourist Office (☑ 01840-250010; www.visitboscastleandtintagel.com; The Harbour; ⊙ 10am-5pm Mar-Oct, 10.30am-4pm Nov-Feb) Near the quay.

❶ Getting There & Away

Coastal bus 95 (£4 to £6.50, one to four daily) stops in Boscastle on its way from Bude (30 minutes), then continues on to Tintagel (25 minutes) and Camelford (45 minutes).

From Camelford, catch connecting bus 10 to Port Isaac (£3.50, 30 minutes, two to three daily).

Tintagel

☑ 01840 / POP 1720

The spectre of legendary King Arthur looms large over Tintagel and its dramatic clifftop castle. Though the present-day ruins mostly date from the 13th century, archaeological digs have revealed the foundations of a much earlier fortress, fuelling speculation that Arthur may indeed have been born at the castle, as locals like to claim. It's a stunningly romantic sight, with crumbling walls teetering precariously above the sheer cliffs, and is well worth exploring for half a day.

⦿ Sights

★ Tintagel Castle
CASTLE

(EH; ☑ 01840-770328; www.english-heritage.org. uk; Castle Rd; adult/child £14.50/8.70; ⊙ 10am-5pm) Famous as the supposed birthplace of King Arthur, Tintagel's epic clifftop castle has been occupied since Roman times and once served as a residence for Cornwall's Celtic kings. The present castle is largely the work of Richard, Earl of Cornwall, who built a base here during the 1230s. An elegant new footbridge now spans a plunging 60m gully, linking the two sides of the medieval castle and recreating a land bridge that existed 500 years ago.

Although the Arthurian links might be tenuous, it's hard to think of a more soul-stirring spot for a stronghold. Though much of the castle has long since crumbled, it's still possible to make out the footprint of the Great Hall and several other rooms. There's also a curious tunnel that's still puzzling archaeologists; it may have been used as a larder or cold store.

Trails lead along the headland to the atmospheric medieval chapel of St Materiana, and on the beach below the castle the rocky mouth of Merlin's Cave is exposed at low tide – local legend claims it's where the wizard once cast his spells.

★ St Nectan's Glen
WATERFALL

(☑ 01840-779538; www.st-nectansglen.co.uk; near Trethevy; adult/child £6/4.70; ⊙ 10am-4pm) Hidden away in a secret valley a mile east of Tintagel, this little glen feels like something from a fairy tale. Fringed by climbing ivy and shrubs, a 60ft waterfall tumbles across the slate into a kieve (plunge pool). It's a mystical spot, supposedly frequented by Cornish *piskies* (pixies), and legendarily associated with King Arthur – you'll see ribbons and offerings dangling from the trees around the pool. It's also a bracing spot for a dip, although the water's icy-cold.

ℹ️ Getting There & Away

First Kernow bus 95/96 (£4 to £6.50, one to four daily) stops in Tintagel en route from Camelford (15 minutes) to Bude (50 minutes).

Port Isaac

🎵 01208 / POP 720

Port Isaac is a classic Cornish fishing town, where cobbled alleyways, slender *opes* (lanes) and cob-walled cottages collect around a medieval harbour and slipway. The picturesque setting draws the cameras – the hit TV series *Doc Martin* is filmed here – and some top restaurants.

A short walk east along the coast leads to the harbour of Port Gaverne. Hiking 2.5 miles west along the shore leads to the sheltered inlet of Port Quin, now owned by the National Trust.

🛏️ Sleeping & Eating

Old School Hotel HOTEL **££**

(📞01208-880721; www.theoldschoolhotel.co.uk; Fore St; incl breakfast s £67-101, d £119-185, tr from £200; 🅿️🛜) A small hotel that was originally Port Isaac's schoolhouse. Eagle-eyed fans of the *Doc Martin* TV series might recognise it as the show's village school. Appropriately, rooms are named after school subjects: the best are Latin, with its sleigh bed and cupboard bathroom; Biology, with its sofa and church-style windows; and split-level Mathematics, with bunk beds and a shared terrace.

★ Fresh from the Sea SEAFOOD **££**

(📞01208-880849; www.freshfromthesea.co.uk; 18 New Rd; sandwiches £6.50-12, mains £8.50-30; ⊙9am-4pm Mon-Sat) Local man Callum Greenhalgh takes his boat *Mary D* out daily in search of crab and lobster, then sells the catch at his tiny Port Isaac shop. Seafood doesn't get any fresher; a crab salad costs £15 and a whole lobster is £30. If in season, oysters from nearby Porthilly cost £2.25 each.

★ Outlaw's New Road SEAFOOD **£££**

(📞01208-880896; www.nathan-outlaw.com; 6 New Rd; mains £22-60; ⊙noon-2pm & 6-9pm Tue-Sat; 🍴) Top chef Nathan Outlaw reimagined his double-Michelin-starred Restaurant Nathan Outlaw into a more accessible, fun-loving place. Dishes are pared down and cheaper, but the winning emphasis on fresh ingredients and the skill and simplicity of the cooking remains.

TREEHOUSE HIDEOUT

Meaning hideout in Cornish, **Kudhva** (www.kudhva.com; Sanding Rd, Trebarwith Strand; 2-person tent/pod £58/120, 6-person cabin £360; ⊙Apr-Oct) combines a cluster of ubermodern sleeping pods on stilts with a wooden cabin, and tents suspended in trees. It's an irresistible, off-grid retreat and a magical reimagining of a former slate quarry, complete with firepits, wild swimming spots, a wood-fired hot tub and corking coastal views.

It's tucked away 2 miles southeast of Tintagel, near the gorgeous low-tide beach of Trebarwith Strand.

Outlaw's Fish Kitchen SEAFOOD **£££**

(📞01208-881183; www.nathan-outlaw.com; 1 Middle St; per person £80; ⊙noon-3pm & 6-9pm Tue-Sat; 🍴) Nathan Outlaw's tiny, Michelin-starred, harbourside restaurant has only three tables and specialises in a set, seven-dish seafood menu for the whole table to share. It's dictated by whatever's landed on the day by local fishers; it might feature raw scallops, cured brill and Dover sole.

ℹ️ Getting There & Away

First Kernow bus 96/55 stops in Port Isaac two to five times daily en route between Camelford (£4.50, 30 minutes) and Wadebridge (£3.50, 50 minutes).

Padstow & Rock

🎵 01841 / POP 4196

If anywhere symbolises Cornwall's increasingly chic credentials, it's Padstow. This old fishing port has become the county's most cosmopolitan corner thanks to the arrival of a bevy of celebrity chefs, and restaurants and boutiques now sit alongside pubs and pasty shops. Whether the town's held onto its soul in the gentrification process is debatable, but it's hard not to be charmed by the seaside setting.

Across the Camel Estuary from Padstow lies Rock, a small village turned uberexclusive getaway. Nearby, the sandy sweep of Daymer Bay unfurls along the estuary, a lifelong favourite of poet John Betjeman.

WORTH A TRIP

CORNISH VINEYARDS

Cornwall might not seem an obvious place for winemaking, but they've been producing award-winning vintages at the **Camel Valley Vineyard** (☑ 01208-77959; www.camelvalley.com; Nanstallon; tours £5-12; ☺ shop 10am-5pm Mon-Fri, tours 2.30pm Mon-Fri Apr-Sep; ℗), on the north side of Bodmin Moor, since 1989. The range includes award-winning whites and rosés, and a bubbly that's Champagne in all but name. The wines have a fresh, light quality that comes from the mild climate and pure sea air. Book for a tour and to sip wines by the glass on the sun terrace, or just drop by the shop.

Around 5 miles south of Padstow, Trevibban Mill offers pre-booked tours, tastings and classy bar snacks best enjoyed on a picture-perfect, flower-framed patio.

◉ Sights & Activities

Padstow is surrounded by fine beaches, including the so-called Seven Bays: Trevone, Harlyn, Mother Ivey's, Booby's, Constantine, Treyarnon and Porthcothan.

In the middle of the Camel estuary runs a treacherous sandbank known as the Doom Bar, which has claimed many ships over the years, and also gave its name to a popular local ale.

★ **Trevibban Mill**   VINEYARD
(☑ 01841-541413; www.trevibbanmill.com; Dark Lane, St Issey; ☺ noon-5pm Wed-Sun, tours Wed, Thu & Sat) Trevibban is a fine place to sample vintages in a dreamy Cornish setting. Book for a tour (£15), which leads you around the vineyard and winery before finishing with a tutored tasting of five wines. Or just turn up for a tasting of seven wines (£15). Allow time to sit on the bewitching patio framed by wildflower meadows and sip a crisp, chilled white wine.

Trevibban's **Winery Bar** (snacks £1.50 to £3, platters £11 to £19) offers elegant nibbles and light meals. Here hummus might come with beetroot and pomegranate, the charcuterie plate includes English salami, and platters feature irresistible Cornish cheeses.

National Lobster Hatchery   HATCHERY
(☑ 01841-533877; www.nationallobsterhatchery.co.uk; South Quay; adult/child £4/2; ☺ hours vary) ✐ In an effort to combat falling lobster stocks, this harbourside hatchery rears baby lobsters in tanks before returning them to the wild. Displays detail the crustaceans' life cycle, and there are tanks where you can watch the residents in action. Check the website for updates on opening hours.

★ **Camel Trail**   CYCLING
(☑ 0300 1234 202; www.cornwall.gov.uk/camel-trail) The old Padstow–Bodmin railway was closed in the 1950s, but reemerged decades later as the Camel Trail, now Cornwall's most popular cycle route. The main section starts in Padstow and heads east through Wadebridge (5.75 miles). The trail then runs on all the way to Poley Bridge on Bodmin Moor (18 miles).

Bikes can be hired from **Trail Bike Hire** (☑ 01841-532594; www.trailbikehire.co.uk; unit 6, South Quay; per day adult/child from £15/10; ☺ 9am-5pm) in Padstow, or from **Bridge Bike Hire** (☑ 01208-813050; www.bridgebikehire.co.uk; off Commissioners Rd; per day adult/child from £14/10; ☺ 10am-5pm) in Wadebridge. Most people do the route from Padstow and back, so it's quieter (and much, much easier to find parking) if you start from the Wadebridge side.

Padstow Sealife Safaris   BOATING
(☑ 07754 822404; www.padstowsealifesafaris.co.uk; North Quay; 2hr cruises adult/child £39/25) Scenic trips to see the local seabird colonies and offshore islands around Padstow. A shorter one-hour tour (adult/child £22.50/15) heads to a seal cave.

✵ Festivals & Events

May Day   CULTURAL
(☺ 1 May) Also known as Obby Oss Day, Padstow's biggest party is said to have its roots in an ancient pagan fertility rite, and sees two coloured 'osses (red and blue) twirl through the streets before meeting up beneath the maypole. It attracts thousands of visitors, so plan well ahead.

⊨ Sleeping

Treyarnon Bay YHA   HOSTEL £
(☑ 0845 371 9664; www.yha.org.uk; Treyarnon Bay; sites £15, d £29, 4-person bell tent £99; ☺ reception 7-10am & 5-10pm; ℗ 🛜) Set in a super 1930s beach hostel on the bluffs above Treyarnon Bay, the sleeping options here range from

bring-your-own tents to camping pods, bell tents and private rooms. The sunsets are spectacular. It's 4.5 miles east of Padstow.

Dorm beds were made temporarily unavailable in 2020; see online for updates.

Woodlands
B&B **£££**

(☑ 01841-532426; www.woodlands-padstow.co.uk; Treator; s/d £126/146; P ⑦ ⑧) Offering green fields and distant flashes of sea, this is a great B&B base for Padstow. Cosy rooms feature creams and frills, and the breakfasts are prodigious. It's a mile or so from Padstow's harbourside, beside the A389.

Althea House
APARTMENT **£££**

(☑ 07980 017113; www.altheahouse-padstow.co.uk; 64 Church St; per night/week from £300/750; P ⑦) If you want to stay in Padstow proper, this charming ivy-clad house is hard to beat. There are two stylish self-catering suites: Rafters is accessed via a private staircase, while Driftwood has a pine four-poster bed. Both suites have sofas, Nespresso coffee machine, bath and small studio kitchen.

Treverbyn House
B&B **£££**

(☑ 07534 095961; www.treverbynhouse.com; Station Rd; d £135-140; P ⑦) The sweeping views of Padstow's sandy estuary from this gorgeous guesthouse linger long in the memory. Choose from yellow- or green-themed rooms or a romantic turret hideaway. Either way you get oriental rugs, brass bedsteads and a table on the terrace at which to enjoy breakfasts of homemade jams and smoked kippers.

✕ Eating

Check whether the popular seafood bar **Prawn on the Lawn** (☑ 01841-532223; www.prawnonthelawn.com; 11 Duke St; mains £7.50-45), which relocated to a farm a mile outside Padstow for the summer of 2020, has moved back to town.

★ Chough Bakery
BAKERY **£**

(☑ 01841-533361; www.thechoughbakery.co.uk; 1-3 The Strand; pasties £3-5; ⊙ 9am-5pm Mon-Sat) A family-run bakery right in the heart of town, renowned for traditionally made pasties – it regularly scoops top honours in the World Pasty Championships.

Rojano's in the Square
ITALIAN **££**

(☑ 01841-532796; www.paul-ainsworth.co.uk; 9 Mill Sq; pizza & pasta £8.50-20; ⊙ 8.30am-10pm) Under the stewardship of Michelin-starred chef Paul Ainsworth, this excellent little Italian bistro turns out fantastic wood-fired pizza, spicy pasta and antipasti. It's a fun and laid-back place to dine, and prices are very reasonable.

Cornish Arms
GASTROPUB **££**

(☑ 01841-532700; www.rickstein.com; St Merryn; mains £13-23; ⊙ noon-10pm) This country pub near the village of St Merryn is owned by Rick Stein's foodie empire, and offers everything from scampi in a basket to 10oz rump steak – all with creative twists and firm local provenance, naturally. It's a 3-mile drive from Padstow.

Look online to see if they're still rustling up takeaway wood-fired pizzas (£10 to £14, served 4pm to 9pm).

★ Paul Ainsworth at No 6
BRITISH **£££**

(☑ 01841-532093; www.paul-ainsworth.co.uk; 6 Middle St; 4-course lunch/dinner £75/85; ⊙ noon-2.30pm & 6-9.30pm Tue-Sat) Rick Stein might be the household name, but Paul Ainsworth is often touted as Padstow's pretender to the throne. His food combines surprising flavours and impeccable presentation with a refreshingly unpretentious approach, and the town-house setting is a relaxed, unfussy place to dine. Now Michelin-starred, this is Padstow's most sought-after table and gets booked up months in advance.

★ Seafood Restaurant
SEAFOOD **£££**

(☑ 01841-532700; www.rickstein.com; Riverside; 3-course lunch £40, mains £20-58; ⊙ noon-10pm) The restaurant that started the Stein dynasty, and still one of Cornwall's top places to eat. Stein senior rarely puts in any hours these days – Rick's son Jack runs the show. As ever, fish is the raison d'être: from fresh lobster to turbot, John Dory and *fruits de mer,* all served in an elegant, light-filled dining room.

❶ Information

Padstow Tourist Office (☑ 01841-533449; www.padstowlive.com; South Quay; ⊙ 10am-2pm Mon, Tue, Thu & Fri, hours may vary) At the Padstow Harbour Commissioners.

❶ Getting There & Away

BOAT

Black Tor Ferry (☑ 01841-532239; www.padstow-harbour.co.uk; adult/child single £3/1.50, bikes £4) Departure points for the

LOCAL KNOWLEDGE

CARNEWAS AT BEDRUTHAN

The stately rock stacks of **Carnewas at Bedruthan** (Bedruthan Steps; NT; www.nationaltrust.org.uk) loom from the landscape roughly halfway between Newquay and Padstow. These mighty granite pillars have been carved out by relentless wind and waves. Those same natural forces caused a rockfall in early 2020, prompting the closure of the steps onto the beach (check the website for updates). The clifftop footpaths remain open and deliver dramatic views; walking options include a 4.5-mile loop.

ferry that links Padstow with Rock vary; look for notices at the harbour. The first ferry from Padstow is at 8am year-round. The last ferry back from Padstow is at 7pm from June to mid-September, at 6pm from April to May and from mid-September to mid-October, and at 5pm from mid-October to March.

The last ferry leaves Rock 15 minutes before the final Padstow ferry.

CAR

There are a couple of car parks beside the harbour in Padstow, but they fill up quickly, so it's usually better to park at one of the large car parks at the top of town and walk down.

BUS

First Kernow bus A5 runs along the coast to Newquay (£5.40, one hour, four to five times daily) taking in Harlyn Bay, Porthcothan Bay, Carnewas at Bedruthan (Bedruthan Steps), Mawgan Porth and Watergate Bay.

Newquay

📞 01637 / POP 20,340

Despite a genuinely gorgeous coast, for many years surf-central Newquay has been better known for its boisterous nightlife, trashy clubs, rowdy pubs and blinking amusement arcades. But if you know where to look, the town also has trendy bistros, clifftop cafes, gourmet bakeries and health-food shops. And along the coast, a bevy of boutique hotels are attracting a more discerning clientele. Yes, Newquay's bargain-basement vibe is still there, but it's not the whole story.

Sights

Newquay has a truly knockout location among some of North Cornwall's finest beaches. The trio close to town – **Towan**, **Great Western** and **Tolcarne** – are guaranteed to be packed in the middle of summer. Most surfers head for **Fistral**, on Newquay's western edge, but the very best beaches such as **Crantock**, **Holywell Bay** and **Watergate Bay** lie a couple of miles out of town.

Trerice   HISTORIC BUILDING

(NT; 📞 01637-875404; www.nationaltrust.org.uk; Kestle Mill; gardens adult/child £5/2.50; ⊗ gardens 10am-5pm) Built in 1751, the grounds of this Elizabethan manor are home to an allium-filled knot garden, bright borders and a turf maze. Visits inside the house were suspended in 2020. It features an elaborate barrel-roofed ceiling in the Great Chamber, and 576 panes of 16th-century stained glass in the great window. It's around 3 miles southeast of Newquay.

Blue Reef Aquarium   AQUARIUM

(📞 01637-878134; www.bluereefaquarium.co.uk/newquay; Towan Promenade; adult/child £11.80/9; ⊗ 10am-6pm; 🚼) The deep-sea denizens at this small aquarium include reef sharks, loggerhead turtles and a giant Pacific octopus. If they're operating limited visitor numbers, prepare for long queues. There's a discount for online bookings.

Newquay Zoo   ZOO

(📞 01637-873342; www.newquayzoo.org.uk; Trenance Gardens; adult/child £14.85/11.15; ⊗ 10am-5pm; 🚼) Pint-sized Newquay Zoo's population of penguins, lemurs, meerkats and zebras will keep the kids happy.

Check to see whether set feeding times have resumed.

🏃 Activities

Newquay is brimming with surf schools, but quality is variable. Choose one that offers small-group sessions with a no-stag-party policy. Ask about teachers' accreditation and experience, and whether they travel to beaches other than Fistral – good schools follow the best waves.

Extreme Academy   WATER SPORTS

(📞 01637-860840; www.extremeacademy.co.uk; Watergate Bay) Owned by the nearby Watergate Bay Hotel, this watersports provider offers lessons in surfing, stand-up paddleboarding (SUP) and hand-planing (which involves catching a wave with a miniature surfboard attached to your wrist). A 2½-hour beginners' surf lesson costs £35, bodyboarding £25 and SUP £40. Or opt for a three-hour SUP tour (£45), where you snorkel, stop for a cup of tea and look out for spider crabs.

The Academy also hires out wetsuits (per three hours £8) and boards (per three hours from £8).

Rip Curl English
Surf School   SURFING
(Newquay Activity Centre; ☑ 01637-879571; www.englishsurfschool.com; Towan Promenade; lessons from £35) Based on Towan Beach, this is one of the most experienced and efficient large schools, linked with Rip Curl and staffed by English Surfing Federation–approved instructors (including the British team coach). Taster lessons cost £35; a set of four lessons is £150.

The surf school is part of the Newquay Activity Centre (www.newquayactivitycentre.co.uk). It offers bodyboarding lessons (two hours £38), as well as coasteering sessions (two hours £45) and kayak and SUP tours (two hours £45). Or just hire kit including wetsuits (two hours/day £10/14), surfboards (£12/15), SUP boards (£15/25) and kayaks (£15/25).

EboAdventure   OUTDOORS
(Newquay Water Sports Centre; ☑ 01637-498200; www.eboadventure.co.uk; South Quay Hill; per 3hr session/tour from £35/45) As well as surfing, Ebo offers kayak tours, stand-up paddleboarding and coasteering from its base at Newquay Harbour.

🛌 Sleeping

St Bernard's   B&B ££
(☑ 01637-872932; www.stbernardsguesthouse.com; 9 Berry Rd; d from £75; P 🛜 🐾) Bright, modern bedrooms, a central location, off-site parking (£2.50) and accommodating hosts make this family-run B&B a good-value choice. They'll even offer you breakfast in bed.

★ Scarlet   HOTEL £££
(☑ 01637-861800; www.scarlethotel.co.uk; Tredragon Rd, Mawgan Porth; r £250-370; P 🛜 🐾) 🌊 For out-and-out luxury, Cornwall's fabulously chic adults-only eco-hotel takes the crown. In a regal location above Mawgan Porth, 5 miles from Newquay, it screams designer style, from the huge sea-view rooms with their sleek furniture and minimalist decor to the outdoor pool and cliffside alfresco hot tubs. The restaurant's a beauty, too.

★ Watergate Bay Hotel   HOTEL £££
(☑ 01637-860543; www.watergatebay.co.uk; Watergate Bay; d incl breakfast from £330; P 🛜 🐾) At beach-side Watergate Bay you can watch the surfers from your bath. Rooms are decked out in coastal colours and slatted wood, and the glorious indoor pool overlooks the bay. It's posh but reassuringly unpretentious: wet feet and sandy footprints are not a problem here. Prices plummet off-peak.

🍴 Eating

The summer of 2020 saw Emily Scott, of the remowned St Tudy Inn (p347), set up a pop-up bistro at Watergate Bay; see if she's returned.

★ Pavilion Bakery   BAKERY £
(www.pavilionbakery.com; 37 Fore St; breads £3.50, pizza £8-10; ⊗8am-8pm Tue-Sat, to 4pm Sun, to 3pm Mon) To hip Pavilion's stunning sourdoughs, artisan breads and melt-in-your-mouth croissants you can now add irresistible takeaway wood-fired pizzas topped with seasonal ingredients (served noon to 8pm Tuesday to Saturday). Also look out for culinary collaborations that turn the place into a pop-up bistro.

Sprout   VEGETARIAN £
(☑01637-875845; www.sprouthealth.co.uk; Crescent Lane; mains £4-6; ⊗10am-4.30pm Mon-Sat; 🍴) At this excellent wholefood shop the one-pot veggie meals (such as vegan African peanut stew) are delicious and sell out fast – almost as fast as the delectable gluten-free cakes.

Fern Pit   CAFE ££
(☑ 01637-873181; www.fernpit.co.uk; Riverside Cres, Pentire; mains £5-17; ⊗10am-6pm; P) Locals love this legendary clifftop hang-out because of the breathtaking views, terraced garden and sandwiches crammed with crab that's been caught by the cafe's own boat. You can walk or drive here from Fistral Beach's southern end. Or check if the ferry and footbridge access from the Crantock Beach side of the Gannel estuary, suspended in 2020, has resumed.

You can even pre-order cooked lobster (per pound £11) to take away.

★ Fish House Fistral   SEAFOOD ££
(☑ 01637-872085; www.thefishhousefistral.com; Fistral Beach; mains lunch £9-20, dinner £19-25; ⊗noon-9.30pm) This beachside seafooderie has become a firm favourite for local diners

and Fistral visitors alike, and it's thoroughly deserved. Filling fishy dishes are the catch of the day, underscored by French, Italian and Asian flavours, and the beach-shack vibe is bang-on.

Beach Hut BISTRO ££
(📞 01637-860543; www.watergatebay.co.uk; Watergate Bay; mains £12-23; ⊙ 9am-9pm) After a beach walk or a quick surf at Watergate, this is where everyone heads for a coffee, cake or something more filling. With big picture windows filled with wide sea views, it's a lovely spot to eat easygoing dishes such as burgers, meze, mussels, pad Thai and seafood curry.

Lewinnick Lodge BISTRO ££
(📞 01637-878117; www.lewinnicklodge.co.uk; Pentire Head; mains £8-18; ⊙ 8am-10pm) There's a knock-out perspective of Newquay's coastline from the long terrace of this restaurant, perched on the cliffs of Pentire Head. The decor is modern – lots of wood and plate glass – and the food is decent: steamed Cornish mussels, slow-cooked pork burgers and seaweed- and sesame-crusted tofu.

🍸 Drinking & Nightlife

Brash bars abound and the town centre gets notoriously rowdy on Friday and Saturday nights, especially in summer.

Tom Thumb BAR
(📞 01637-498180; www.tom-thumb.co.uk; 27a East St; ⊙ 3-11.30pm) Newquay's classiest cocktail bar has reclaimed wood furniture, a cool spiral staircase and a fine selection of home-mixed drinks, ranging from originals and classics to Driving Juice (aka alcohol free).

ℹ Information

Newquay Tourist Office (📞 01637-838516; www.visitnewquay.org; Marcus Hill; ⊙ 9am-5pm Mon-Fri, 10am-4pm Sat & Sun Apr-Sep, 10am-4pm Mon-Fri, to 3pm Sat & Sun Oct-Mar) Distancing measures may mean you can't go in, but you'll be able to talk to staff by phone, or through a hatch.

ℹ Getting There & Away

AIR

Cornwall Airport Newquay (NQY; 📞 01637-860600; www.cornwallairportnewquay.com; St Mawgan) Cornwall's main airport is 5 miles northeast of Newquay. It has regular connections to London Heathrow with British Airways

(www.britishairways.com); Leeds Bradford with Eastern Airways (www.easternairways.com); Dublin and Cork with Aer Lingus (www.aerlingus.com) and the Isles of Scilly with IoS Skybus.

First Kernow (www.firstgroup.com/cornwall) bus 56 (£4, 30 minutes) runs to the airport from Newquay every one or two hours.

Taxis cost around £18 from the town centre.

BUS

Newquay's bus station is on Manor Rd. The following services are operated by First Kernow.

Padstow Bus A5 (£5.40, one hour, four to five times daily) heads up the coast via Watergate Bay, Mawgan Porth, Carnewas at Bedruthan (Bedruthan Steps), Porthcothan and Harlyn Bay.

St Agnes Bus 87 (£5.40, 50 minutes, hourly in summer) stops at Perranporth en route to St Agnes and continues to Truro.

Truro Bus 91 (£5.40, one hour, hourly Monday to Saturday, five on Sunday).

TRAIN

Newquay is at the end of a branch line that runs to Par (£5.20, 50 minutes, five to seven daily) on the main London Paddington–Penzance line.

Perranporth to Porthtowan

Southwest of Newquay, Cornwall's craggy northern coastline dips and curves through a stunning panorama of wild, sea-smacked cliffs and golden bays. Tempting stops include the family-friendly beach of Perranporth, the old mining town of St Agnes and the surfy hang-out of Porthtowan.

◎ Sights & Activities

★ **Perranporth Beach** BEACH
(🅿 🚻) Perranporth's huge, flat, sandy beach is a favourite for everyone: dog-walkers, families, kite-buggiers and surfers alike. Its main draw is its sheer size – more than a mile long, backed by dunes and rocky cliffs – meaning there's usually space even on the busiest days.

★ **Chapel Porth** BAY
(NT; 📞 01872-552412; www.nationaltrust.org.uk; parking per day £4; 🅿) Two miles southwest of St Agnes sits one of Cornwall's most beautiful coves. Chapel Porth is a wild, rocky beach framed by steep, gorse-covered cliffs. Above the cove is the ruined engine stack of Wheal Coates, and from here the coast

path winds all the way to the blustery outcrop of **St Agnes Head**. It's a panorama that graces many a postcard – don't forget your camera.

Blue Hills Tin Streams WORKSHOP
(✆01872-553341; www.cornishtin.com; Trevellas Coombe; adult/child £7/3; ⊙10am-2pm Tue-Sat mid-Apr–mid-Oct) A mile east of St Agnes (signed to Wheal Kitty) is the rocky valley of **Trevellas Porth**, home to one of Cornwall's last tin manufacturers. You can watch the whole tinning process, from mining and smelting through to casting and finishing. It sells handmade jewellery too.

✖ Eating & Drinking

Chapel Porth Cafe CAFE £
(✆01872-552487; Chapel Porth; sandwiches & cakes £3-6; ⊙10am-5pm, shorter winter hours) This cafe down on the edge of Chapel Porth beach is a local institution, serving hot chocolate, cheesy baguettes, sausage butties, flapjacks and the house speciality: hedgehog ice cream (vanilla ice cream topped with clotted cream and hazelnuts).

★ Blue Bar BAR
(✆01209-890329; www.bluebarporthtowan.com; Beach Rd, Porthtowan; mains £8-18; ⊙10am-11pm; 🛜) For a seaside sundowner the Blue Bar, with its casual surf vibe, is hard to beat. If the tables overlooking the sand are full, you can take away everything from draught Korev lager to plant-based burgers, stone-baked pizzas and dirty chips. Brunch (served 10am to 11.45am) brings maple-syrup-laced waffles with bacon and toasted banana bread.

Watering Hole BAR
(✆01872-572888; www.the-wateringhole.co.uk; 19 St Pirans Rd, Perranporth Beach; ⊙10am-11pm) Generations of Cornish youth have passed through this venerable beach bar, which is set right on Perranporth's expanse of golden sand. With a sweep of outdoor tables it's a prime spot for a post-surf coffee or a beer as the sun goes down. It also has regular alfresco live music ranging from Ibiza classics to funk and soul.

ⓘ Getting There & Away

Bus 87 (hourly in summer) runs between Newquay and Truro, taking in Perranporth and St Agnes en route.

St Ives

✆01736 / POP 9960

If there was a prize for the prettiest of Cornish ports, St Ives would be a clear contender. A tightly packed cluster of slate roofs, fishers' cottages and church towers spread out around turquoise bays – it's an unfailingly dazzling sight. Once a busy pilchard harbour, St Ives later became the centre of Cornwall's arts scene in the 1920s and '30s, when luminary figures such as Barbara Hepworth, Terry Frost, Ben Nicholson and Naum Gabo migrated here in search of artistic freedom.

St Ives remains an artistic centre, with numerous galleries lining its cobbled streets, as well as the renowned Tate St Ives. The town is also one of Cornwall's holiday home hot spots, and is packed with tourists in summer - visit in spring or autumn if you can.

⊙ Sights

Ask if **Leach Pottery** (✆01736-799703; www.leachpottery.com; Higher Stennack), a museum in the studio of ground-breaking potter Bernard Leach, has reopened. At the time of writing, only the shop was open. It sells works by contemporary potters, but by appointment only.

★ Tate St Ives GALLERY
(✆01736-796226; www.tate.org.uk/stives; Porthmeor Beach; adult/child £9.50/free, joint ticket with Barbara Hepworth Museum £12/free; ⊙10am-5.20pm, last admission 4pm) St Ives' most illustrious gallery boasts a new monumental exhibition space that's been added to the museum's original, spiral-shaped core. Focusing on the

ⓘ PARKING IN ST IVES

Parking is one of the main headaches for anyone planning on visiting St Ives: traffic can be very bad in summer, and attempting to drive through the town centre is a recipe for holiday nightmares.

The largest car park by far is Trenwith, a brisk uphill walk from town; it's usually the likeliest to have spaces in summer.

Another useful alternative worth considering is to use the park-and-ride system by leaving your car at St Erth or Lelant stations, and then catching the scenic St Ives train line into town.

West Cornwall

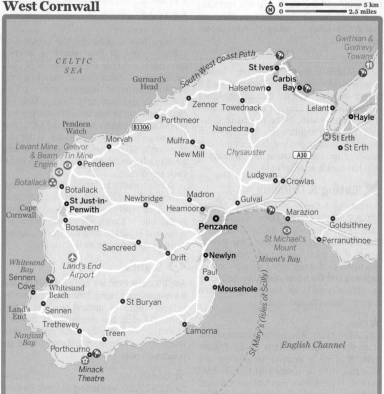

coterie of experimental artists who congregated at St Ives after WWII and turned the little seaside town into a magnet for modern artists, the museum showcases the work of Barbara Hepworth, Terry Frost, Peter Lanyon and Patrick Heron in luminous, white-walled surroundings.

Barbara Hepworth Museum MUSEUM
(☑ 01736-796226; www.tate.org.uk/stives; Barnoon Hill; joint ticket with Tate St Ives adult/child £12/free; ⊘ 10am-5.20pm Mar-Oct, to 4pm Nov-Feb) Barbara Hepworth (1903–75) was one of the leading abstract sculptors of the 20th century and a key figure in the St Ives art scene. Her studio on Barnoon Hill has remained almost untouched since her death and the adjoining garden contains several of her most notable sculptures, many of which were inspired by the elemental forces she discovered in her adopted Cornish home: rock, sea, sand, wind, sky.

Hepworth's work is scattered throughout St Ives; look for works outside the Guildhall and inside the 15th-century St Ia parish church.

🏃 Activities

The largest town beaches are **Porthmeor** and **Porthminster**, both of which have sand and space aplenty. Between them juts the grassy promontory known as the Island, topped by the tiny pre-14th-century **Chapel of St Nicholas**. On the peninsula's east side is the little cove of **Porthgwidden**, a smaller beach that can be a good place to escape the crowds.

St Ives Boats BOATING
(☑ 0777 300 8000; www.stivesboats.co.uk; The Wharf; adult/child from £20/10; 🐾) 🦭 St Ives Boats runs daily, one-hour trips along the scenic shore, including seal-spotting cruises and trips out to the stubby Godrevy Lighthouse.

It's an accredited wildlife-safe operator, and the crew features a marine mammal medic, specialising in the rescue of dolphins and seals.

Sleeping

Parking in summer is scarce; check if your accommodation has its own or a deal with a car park.

Saltwater B&B ££
(☑ 07391 086299; www.saltwaterstivesbb.co.uk; 3 Belmont Tce; d £110-150, tr £130-180; ☜) It's driftwood-chic all the way at Saltwater, where bright blue and yellow bedrooms have USB charging points; most also have sea views. It's a few minutes' walk from Porthmeor, and offers surfboard hire and breakfast in bed.

Mustard Tree B&B ££
(☑ 01736-795677; www.mustard-tree.co.uk; St Ives Rd, Carbis Bay; s/d/t £100/124/170; ⓟ) If bagging a bedroom amid St Ives' picture-postcard-pretty streets is proving a problem, try this friendly B&B in nearby Carbis Bay. The contemporary rooms may be simple, but there's free parking and St Ives is just a three-minute train ride away.

★ Primrose House B&B £££
(☑ 01736-794939; www.primroseonline.co.uk; Primrose Valley; s/d from £165/185; ⓟ ☎ ⓦ) Chic Primrose Valley has one massive selling point – it's a one-minute walk from Porthminster's sands. Other pluses include light rooms, wicker lamps, Scandi-style dressers, wooden cladding and model ships. Some rooms also boast balconies with sea views.

Trevose Harbour House B&B £££
(☑ 01736-793267; www.trevosehouse.co.uk; 22 The Warren; d £210-295; ☜) In this stylish six-room town house you'll find a sea-themed combo of fresh whites and stripy blues. It's been beautifully finished, with Neal's Yard bath goods, iPod docks and retro design pieces in the rooms; there's also a book-lined lounge and minimalist courtyard patio.

Channings APARTMENT £££
(☑ 01736-799500; www.channingsstives.co.uk; 3 Talland Rd; 10 people per week from £1100; ⓟ ☎ ⓦ) The panoramic sea views from the slanting windows of this five-bedroom Victorian terrace are hard to leave – unless perhaps you're heading to its patio overlooking St Ives Bay. Decor is modern and there's parking for three cars.

Eating

Moomaid of Zennor ICE CREAM £
(www.moomaidofzennor.com; The Wharf; ice cream from £2.50; ⏱ 9.30am-10pm Apr-Sep, to 5pm Oct-Mar) Moomaid's ice cream is legendary locally. It makes its many flavours on the home farm just outside Zennor, using only its own milk and Rodda's clotted cream. Exotic concoctions include Prosecco sorbet and salted almond.

Searoom BISTRO £
(☑ 01736-794325; www.stivesliquor.co/searoom; 1 Wharf House, The Wharf; dishes £3.50-10; ⏱ noon-9pm Mon-Sat) Run by the St Ives Liquor Company (makers of the town's premium craft gin), this wharf-side restaurant specialises in Cornish-tinged small plates ranging from sushi to chips with crab meat, and glazed mackerel rolls. It's great for cocktails and has a cracking harbour view.

★ Porthminster Beach Café BISTRO ££
(☑ 01736-795352; www.porthminstercafe.co.uk; Porthminster Beach; mains £15-22; ⏱ 9am-10pm) Less a beach cafe, more a full-blown bistro with a gorgeous sun-trap terrace and superb Mediterranean-influenced menu, specialising in seafood. Tuck into rich bouillabaisse, seafood curry or Provençal fish soup, and settle back to enjoy the breezy beach vistas.

Porthminster Kitchen BISTRO ££
(☑ 01736-799874; www.porthminster.kitchen; The Wharf; mains £15-19; ⏱ 9am-10pm) This relaxed place rustles up beachy dishes like seafood linguine, Goan fish curry and pan-fried scallops. The most sought-after seats are on the 1st-floor harbour-front terrace.

Porthgwidden Beach Cafe CAFE ££
(☑ 01736-796791; www.porthgwiddencafe.co.uk; Porthgwidden; mains £10-16; ⏱ 9am-10pm) Head to the dreamy terrace beside Porthgwidden's beach huts to savour classy dishes like smoked-haddock chowder or spicy dressed crab.

Blas Burgerworks BURGERS ££
(☑ 01736-797272; www.blasburgerworks.co.uk; The Warren; meals £13-15; ⏱ 5-9.30pm; ☑) ✿ Check whether St Ives' boutique burger joint has reopened its dining room after closing it due to distancing measures. If it hasn't you can still pre-order its succulent patties to take away. For full-blooded flavour try a beef or bean burger topped with Cornish Blue cheese, with a side of chips and truffle aioli.

St Ives

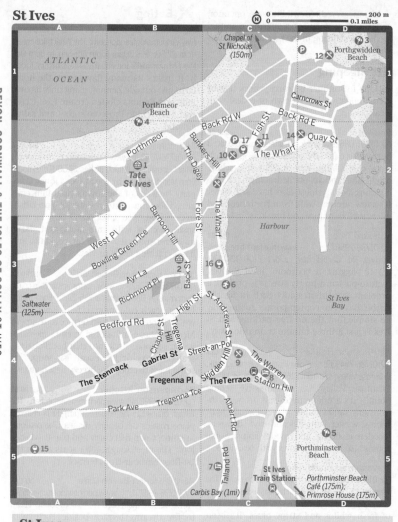

St Ives

One Fish Street   SEAFOOD **£££**
(📞07521 295047; www.onefishstreet.co.uk; 1 Fish St; 3/6 courses £30/45; ⏰5-9.30pm Tue-Sat) The six-course tasting menu here depends on what's been landed just yards away on the day. It might include white crab with heritage-tomato gazpacho, oysters with wasabi and seaweed, and Thai cod and coconut curry. Or opt for the early-evening three-course menu to get a sense of the chef's skills.

🍷 Drinking & Nightlife

Brewhouse   CAFE-BAR
(📞01736-793467; www.stives-brewery.co.uk; Trewidden Rd; cakes from £3; ⏰9am-5pm Mon-Sat) A terrace with superb views down onto the bay and an awesome array of cakes make this cafe-bar a memorable spot to tuck into vegan banana loaf, freshly baked doughnuts and punchy coffee. It's run by St Ives Brewery so you can also sample its flagship brews – Boilers, a golden session ale, and the hoppy IPA-style Knill By Mouth.

Hub   BAR
(📞01736-799099; www.hub-stives.co.uk; The Wharf; ⏰11.30am-9pm, to 10pm Fri & Sat) The open-plan Hub is the heart of St Ives' (admittedly limited) nightlife: coffee and burgers by day, cocktails after dark, and a harbour-front balcony and terrace.

Sloop Inn   PUB
(📞01736-796584; www.sloop-inn.co.uk; The Wharf; ⏰11am-11pm) On sunny days, the picnic tables of this whitewashed, beam-lined boozer are one of the most popular spots for a harbourside pint in town.

ℹ️ Information

Check whether the **Tourist Office** (www.stives-cornwall.co.uk; 01736-796297), in the town's Library in Gabriel St, has reopened.

ℹ️ Getting There & Away

BUS

Bus 17 (£5.40, 30 minutes, half-hourly Monday to Saturday, hourly Sunday) Runs to Penzance, via Lelant.

Bus A3 (four daily) Heads along the north coast via Zennor, the Gurnard's Head pub, Geevor Tin Mine and St Just to Land's End (£5.40, 1¼ hours). At Land's End the bus becomes the A1 and continues onto Porthcurno and Penzance.

Bus A2 (6 daily) Goes via St Erth train station to Penzance (£5.40, one hour) via Marazion (for St Michael's Mount).

TRAIN

The branch train line from St Ives is worth taking just for the coastal views. Trains shuttle between St Ives train station via Carbis Bay to St Erth (£3, 11 minutes, half-hourly) where you can catch connections along the Penzance–London Paddington main line.

Zennor & St Just-in-Penwith

📞01736 / POP: 5000

The superbly scenic B3306 coast road between St Ives and Zennor ventures into a wild, remote landscape of ancient farmland, windswept moors and ruined mine stacks. The industrial heritage here makes it well worth a visit, and it feels a far cry from Cornwall's over-touristed harbour towns.

Tiny Zennor is set around the medieval Church of St Senara, while 9 miles further west, sits the old granite village of St Just-in-Penwith. It's been linked with mining and quarrying for centuries, but these days is mainly known as a hub for artists, sculptors and creative types.

👁️ Sights

Church of St Senara   CHURCH
This little church in the hamlet of Zennor dates from at least 1150. Inside, a famous carved chair depicts the legendary Mermaid of Zennor, who is said to have fallen in love with the singing voice of local lad Matthew Trewhella. Locals say you can still sometimes hear them singing down at nearby Pendour Cove – and even if you don't, the views along the coast path are reward enough.

★ Geevor Tin Mine   MINE
(📞01736-788662; www.geevor.com; Pendeen; adult/child £16.10/9; ⏰9am-5pm Sun-Thu, hours may vary) Just north of St Just near Pendeen, this historic mine closed in 1990 and now provides a powerful insight into the dark, dingy and dangerous conditions in which Cornwall's miners worked. Above ground, you can view the dressing floors and the original machinery used to sort the minerals and ores, before taking a guided tour into some of the underground shafts.

WORTH A TRIP

MINACK THEATRE & PORTHCURNO

Teetering right out on Cornwall's far-western tip, the sandy wedge of Porthcurno is one of the best beaches in west Cornwall for swimming and sunbathing. Around the headland, the lesser-known beach of **Pednvounder** is good if you like to sunbathe *au naturel* – it's one of Cornwall's few naturist beaches.

But the area is best known for its spectacular clifftop theatre, the **Minack** (☑ 01736-810181; www.minack.com; performance tickets £10-40, admission adult/child £6/3), carved out of the granite rock with sweeping views of the Atlantic waves below. Created between the 1930s and 1970s by theatre-lover Rowena Cade, there are few finer places to watch a play than this. You can also book daytime visits to explore the terraces and subtropical gardens and take in the ocean views.

Porthcurno was also once a crucial hub for transatlantic telecommunications; it's well worth seeing if the **Porthcurno Telegraph Museum** (☑ 01736-810966; www.telegraphmuseum.org), which tells the compelling story, has reopened.

★ **Botallack**   RUINS
(NT; Crowns Engine House; ☑ 01736-786934; www.nationaltrust.org.uk) Clinging to the cliffs near Levant, this dramatic complex of mine workings is one of the most atmospheric sights from Cornwall's industrial past. The main mine stack, properly known as the Crowns, teeters picturesquely on the cliff edge above a cauldron of boiling surf. It's famously photogenic and a frequent filming location, most recently used by the BBC in *Poldark*. The National Trust website has a 1-mile looped walking trail taking in Botallack.

During its 19th-century heyday, the mine was one of the county's richest and deepest, producing 14,500 tonnes of tin and 20,000 tonnes of copper ore from shafts that snaked nearly half a mile out to sea. Look out for the Count House, which was once home to the captain of the mine.

Levant Mine & Beam Engine   HISTORIC SITE
(NT; ☑ 01736-786156; www.nationaltrust.org.uk; Trewellard, Pendeen) It's worth checking if visits to this clifftop site have resumed after being suspended in 2020. Levant is one of the world's only working beam engines. Built in 1840, these great machines were the driving forces behind the Cornish mining boom, powering mineral trains, running lifts down into mine shafts and pumping water from underground tunnels. Closed in 1930, it's since been lovingly restored by a team of enthusiasts, and is a sight to behold when it's in full steam.

Levant was also the site of one of Cornwall's worst mining disasters: in 1919 a link between the rod and engine broke, sending 31 men to their deaths. More recently it was also used as a location in the BBC's recent *Poldark* adaptation.

Cape Cornwall   LANDMARK
(ℙ) Jutting out from the cliffs near St Just is Cornwall's only cape, a craggy outcrop of land topped by an abandoned mine stack. Below the cape is the rocky beach of **Priest's Cove**, while nearby are the ruins of **St Helen's Oratory**, supposedly one of the first Christian chapels built in West Cornwall.

🛏 Sleeping & Eating

See if the **Zennor Chapel Guesthouse** (☑ 01736-798307; www.zennorchapelguesthouse.com; Wayside St; ℙ), which suspended bookings in the summer of 2020, has reopened.

★ **Gurnard's Head**   BRITISH ££
(☑ 01736-796928; www.gurnardshead.co.uk; B3306, near Zennor; mains £11.50-24, d £135-200; ℙ 🛜 🐕) On the rolling coast road between Zennor and St Just, you can't miss the Gurnard's – its name is emblazoned on the roof. It's earned a reputation as one of west Cornwall's top dining pubs, known for classic, traditionally inspired British dishes, and a top Sunday roast. Wooden furniture, book-lined shelves and sepia prints conjure a cosy, lived-in feel.

The bedrooms are delightful, with their warm colours, country-cottage styling, Roberts radios and fresh flowers.

Land's End & Sennen

Beyond St Ives, the coastline gets wilder and emptier as you near Cornwall's tip at Land's End, the westernmost point of mainland England, where the coal-black cliffs plunge into the pounding surf, and the views can stretch all the way to the Isles of Scilly.

You don't have to head into the Legendary Land's End (☑ 01736-871501; www.landsend-landmark.co.uk; day ticket adult/child £12.60/9; ⊙ 10am-5pm Mar-Oct; ⛴) theme park itself, instead you can just pay for parking (£6) and go for an exhilarating clifftop stroll, looking out for the historic Longships Lighthouse on a reef 1.25 miles out to sea. Consider booking parking to guarantee a space.

From Land's End, follow the coast path west to the secluded cove of Nanjizal Bay, or east to the old harbour of Sennen, which overlooks the glorious beach of Whitesand Bay, the area's most impressive stretch of sand.

Mousehole

☑ 01736 / POP 697

With a tight tangle of cottages and alleyways gathered behind the granite breakwater, Mousehole (pronounced *mowzle*) looks like something from a children's storybook (a fact not unnoticed by author Antonia Barber, who set her much-loved fairy tale *The Mousehole Cat* here). In centuries past this was Cornwall's busiest pilchard port, but the fish dried up in the late 19th century, and the village now survives mostly on tourist traffic. Packed in summer and deserted in winter (Mousehole is renowned for its high proportion of second homes), it's ripe for a wander, with a maze of slips, net lofts and courtyards.

🛏 Sleeping & Eating

★ **Old Coastguard** HOTEL £££
(☑ 01736-731222; www.oldcoastguardhotel.co.uk; The Parade; d incl breakfast £135-200; ⊙ food noon-3pm & 5.30-9.30pm; P ⊛ ☎ 🐾) Run by the owners of the Gurnard's Head, this coastal beauty ranks as one of Cornwall's top shoreside hotels. Stylish rooms team gingham with painted wood; the best have sea views. The day's catch takes prominence in the excellent **restaurant** (mains £15 to £25) and sunny days bring meals on the gently sloping lawns.

2 Fore St FRENCH ££
(☑ 01736-731164; www.2forestreet.co.uk; Fore St; mains £8-17; ⊙ noon-9pm) This laid-back harbour-side bistro majors in French-inspired classics – unsurprising, given the head chef trained under Raymond Blanc. There's a small dining room, a sweet garden and a locally focused menu strong on the very freshest seafood.

❶ Getting There & Away

Bus M6 makes the 20-minute journey along the seafront to Penzance (£3.40, half-hourly to hourly), stopping in Newlyn en route.

ST MICHAEL'S MOUNT

Looming up in the middle of Mount's Bay and connected to the mainland at Marazion via a cobbled causeway, St Michael's Mount (NT; ☑ 01736-710507; www.stmichaelsmount. co.uk; Marazion; castle adult/child £11.50/5.50, gardens adult/child £8.50/4; ⊙ hours vary) is an unforgettable sight, and one of Cornwall's most iconic images.

There's been a monastery here since at least the 5th century, but the present abbey was mostly built by Benedictine monks during the 12th century (the same religious order also constructed the island's sister abbey at Mont St-Michel in France). Highlights of the main house include the rococo drawing room, the armoury and the 14th-century church, but it's the amazing clifftop gardens that really steal the show. Thanks to the local subclimate, many exotic flowers and shrubs flourish here, and it's all a riot of colour in summer.

Recent excavations found an axe head, a dagger and a metal clasp, proving the island has been inhabited since at least the Bronze Age, but it was almost certainly used by prehistoric people long before. According to some scholars, the island may have been a trading post for locally mined copper and tin for several thousand years.

Distancing regulations could mean you have to book a timed slot in which to start your visit to the island. If restrictions are in force you might have to walk to the island at low tide via the causeway from Marazion. If no restrictions are in place you can probably either stroll along the causeway (the most atmospheric way to arrive) or, in summer, hop on a boat (adult/child £2/1). Check online to see whether cheaper joint tickets to the castle and gardens have been reinstated.

Penzance

☑ 01736 / POP 21,040

Overlooking the majestic sweep of Mount's Bay, the old harbour of Penzance has a salty, sea-blown charm that feels altogether more authentic than many of Cornwall's polished-up ports. Its streets and shopping arcades still feel real and a touch ramshackle, and there's nowhere better for a windy-day walk than the seafront Victorian promenade. The town also has a superb array of places to eat, and a significant tourist draw in the now geothermally heated 1930s Jubilee Pool.

◉ Sights & Activities

★ Tremenheere
Sculpture Garden   GARDENS
(☑ 01736-448089; www.tremenheere.co.uk; near Gulval; adult/child £9/4.50; ⊙ 10.30am-5.30pm; ⊞) In this magical, tropical-plant-filled valley you get to hunt out site-specific works of art. Highlights include *Black Mound*, a pile of tree stumps by David Nash; *Camera Obscura* by Billy Wynter, which offers a unique panorama of the gardens and Mount's Bay; Amy Cooper's *Se Bryck*, a sea-view brick armchair; and, in a dig at Cornwall's tricky second homes issue, Richard Wood's *Holiday Homes*. The gardens are just over 2 miles northeast of Penzance.

The garden's super takeaway cafe, **TK Hut** (10am to 3pm, snacks from £4) rustles up brunches, salad boxes, coffee and homemade cakes to eat on the sloping lawns.

Penlee House Gallery & Museum   GALLERY
(☑ 01736-363625; www.penleehouse.org.uk; Morrab Rd; adult/child £6/3; ⊙ 10am-5pm Mon-Sat Apr-Oct, to 4pm Nov-Mar) This small museum is ideal for a primer on the artistic heritage of West Cornwall. It showcases a fine collection of paintings by artists of the Newlyn School (including Stanhope and Elizabeth Forbes, Walter Langley and Lamorna Birch) inside a handsome 19th-century building.

★ Jubilee Pool   SWIMMING
(☑ 01736-369224; www.jubileepool.co.uk; Western Promenade Rd; main pool adult/child £4.25/3, geothermal pool £11.75/8; ⊙ 10am-5pm Tue-Sun early Jun-Nov, winter hours vary) In a triumph of engineering and imagination, a £1.8-million upgrade has turned Penzance's art-deco seawater pool into the UK's first geothermally heated lido. Sections of the gorgeous 1930s open-air pool are now heated to a toasty

35°C. The rest – sleek, sharp and whitewashed – is still beautiful but the water undeniably more bracing.

As elsewhere, distancing measures may mean pool sessions have to be booked. Demand for the geothermal section is very high, so reserve well in advance.

The project has also brought new changing rooms and a cafe. The aim is to be able to open year-round; check online for updates.

🛏 Sleeping

Check to see if individual bookings at **Penzance YHA** (☑ 0345 371 9653; www.yha.org.uk; Castle Horneck, Alverton; ℗ 🛜) have resumed.

★ Venton Vean   B&B ££
(☑ 01736-351294; www.ventonvean.co.uk; Trewithen Rd; d £98-105, tr £142; 🛜) The picture of a modern B&B, finished in stylish greys and blues, with stripped wood floors, bay windows and a keen eye for design. The sumptuous breakfast choice includes pancakes, smoked Newlyn fish and avocado on sourdough toast.

Boswarthen Farm   CAMPSITE ££
(☑ 07731 776767; www.boswarthenfarm.co.uk; near Madron; 3 nights glamping tent £390, lodge/caravan £405/235) There are three glamping choices at this rustic dairy farm near Madron: safari-style tents, a two-storey lodge-tent and a vintage caravan. The safari tents are spacious, with kitchen units and dining areas, a wood-burning stove and two bedroom areas, while the lodge adds a mezzanine floor.

★ Artist Residence Penzance   B&B £££
(☑ 01736-365664; www.artistresidence.co.uk; 20 Chapel St; d £95-250, tr/ste from £135/209; 🛜⛶🐾) Hands down Penzance's most entertaining hotel, this converted town house on Chapel St has been impeccably renovated to team period architecture with modern style. Details abound: Robert's radios, roll-top baths, antique furniture, old tea chests and the odd wall mural or two.

🍴 Eating & Drinking

★ Tolcarne Inn   PUB FOOD ££
(☑ 01736-363074; www.tolcarneinn.co.uk; Tolcarne Pl; mains lunch £6.50-12, dinner £19-24; ⊙ noon-2.30pm & 6.30-9.30pm) The ethos at this Newlyn inn is refreshingly honest – top-quality fish, seafood and locally sourced meat, served with minimal fuss. It's a snug

Penzance

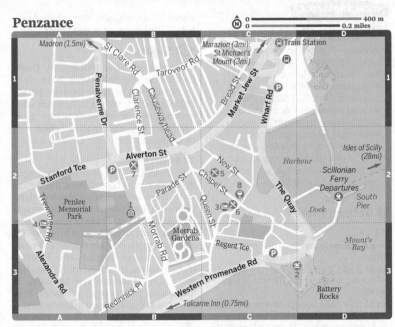

space, full of smuggler's pub charm, with blackboard menus, whitewashed walls and a cluster of outdoor tables tucked in beside the harbour wall.

Clubhouse   BISTRO **££**
(☑01736-365664; www.artistresidence.co.uk; 20 Chapel St; mains £12-21; ◎8-10.30am & 6-9pm daily, plus noon-2.30pm Fri-Sun) With its exposed brick, scuffed timber, bare bulbs and blazing wood-burner, the bistro on the ground floor of the Artist Residence Penzance nails the gourmet hipster vibe. Tuck into everything from garlicky squid and charred seabass to beer-can smoked chicken with house slaw.

Bakehouse   MEDITERRANEAN **££**
(☑01736-331331; www.bakehouserestaurant.co.uk; Chapel St; mains £14-20, steaks £11-25; ◎noon-2pm & 6-9pm Tue-Sat) Laid-back double-floored diner down an alley off Chapel St with it's own palm-fringed, fairy-light-festooned dining courtyard. Steaks take the honours here: choose your cut and match it with your choice of sauce or spicy rub. You'll also find a couple of seafood and veggie options.

★Shore   MODERN BRITISH **£££**
(☑01736-362444; www.theshorerestaurant.uk; 14 Alverton St; 5 courses £60; ◎1 sitting at 7pm Tue-Sat) ✐ This brilliant seafood bistro is

all about precisely cooked, classic fish and shellfish, sourced from the Newlyn day boats and served with a strong French-Italian influence and lashing of creative flair.

Admiral Benbow   PUB
(☑01736-363448; 46 Chapel St; ◎4-11pm) On historic Chapel St, the salty old Benbow looks as if it's dropped from the pages of *Treasure Island,* with nautical decor mostly reclaimed from shipwrecks: anchors, lanterns, figureheads and all.

LOCAL KNOWLEDGE

FORAGING COURSES

If lockdown's piqued an interest in micro-explorations, then Rachel Lambert is the woman to help you zoom in on plants with her **Wild Walks Southwest** (☑07903 412014; www.wildwalks-southwest.co.uk; adult/child £45/20). An expert in nutrition and wild food, she leads small groups on three-hour foraging expeditions around west Cornwall. As well as species identification and cooking tips, you also get tasters of the finished foods.

ⓘ Getting There & Away

BUS

The **bus station** (Wharf Rd) is next to the train station.

Bus 17 (£5.40, 30 minutes, half-hourly Monday to Saturday, hourly Sunday) Runs to St Ives, via Lelant.

Bus A1 (four daily) Goes via Newlyn and Porthcurno to Land's End (£5.40), where it becomes the A3 and continues along the north coast to St Ives via St Just, Geevor Tin Mine, the Gurnard's Head pub and Zennor.

Bus A2 Shuttles to St Ives (£5.40, one hour, six daily) via Marazion (for St Michael's Mount).

Bus U4 Runs to Falmouth (£7.40, 1½ hours, hourly Monday to Saturday, six on Sunday) via Marazion and Helston.

TRAIN

Penzance is the last stop on the line from London Paddington. Regular daily services include the following.

Exeter £30, three hours

London Paddington £63, five hours

St Ives £4.70, 50 minutes, change at St Erth

Truro £7.40, 40 minutes

The Lizard

Cornwall's coast takes a wild turn around the Lizard Peninsula, where fields and heaths plunge into a melee of black cliffs, churning surf and sawtooth rocks. Bordered by the River Helford and framed by treacherous seas, the Lizard was once an ill-famed graveyard for ships, and the peninsula still has a raw, untamed edge. Wind-lashed in winter, in summer its clifftops blaze with wildflowers, and its beaches and coves are perfect for a bracing wild swim. Remote Lizard village and the increasingly foodie port of Porthleven, make good bases.

◉ Sights

The white towers of 18th-century **Lizard Lighthouse** rise from Lizard Point. Visits to the excellent **heritage centre** (☑01326-290202; www.trinityhouse.co.uk/lighthouse-visitor-centres/lizard-lighthouse-visitor-centre; Lizard Point) were suspended in 2020 – check if it's reopened and has resumed guided tours.

★**Kynance Cove**   BEACH
(NT; ☑01326-222170; www.nationaltrust.org.uk; ℗) A mile north of Lizard Point, this National Trust–owned inlet is an absolute showstopper at low tide, studded with craggy offshore islands rising out of searingly blue seas that seem almost tropical in colour. The cliffs around the cove are rich in serpentine, a red-green rock popular with Victorian trinket makers. It's an impossibly beautiful spot and, when the seas aren't too rough, an exhilarating place to swim. It gets very busy in summer; if you can, arrive before 11am.

★**Cornish Seal Sanctuary**   ANIMAL SANCTUARY
(☑01326-221361; www.visitsealife.com/gweek; Gweek; adult/child £15.50/12.50; ⊙10am-5pm) The 'ah' factor goes into overdrive at this sea-life centre some 5 miles east of Helston. It cares for sick and orphaned seals washed up along the Cornish coastline before returning them to the wild. The website outlines whether talks and feeding sessions have resumed.

🛏 Sleeping & Eating

Check whether **Lizard YHA** (☑0845 371 9550; www.yha.org.uk; Lizard Point), which is set right beside the lighthouse, has resumed individual bookings.

★**Henry's Campsite**   CAMPSITE £
(☑01326-290596; www.henryscampsite.co.uk; Caerthillian Farm, Lizard village; adult/child £12/6; 🐾) In this endearingly eccentric campsite, sites are private and the garden is dotted with flotsam and jetsam – hand-painted signs, old buoys and fishing tackle. It's a prime place to rent a firepit and settle back to gaze at sunsets and sea views.

Kynance Cove Cafe   CAFE £
(☑01326-290436; www.kynancecovecafe.co.uk; Kynance Cove; mains £5-14; ⊙9am-5.30pm) There can be few beachside cafes in Cornwall with a finer location than this, huddled

among the rocks on the edge of Kynance Cove. Sample pasties, crab sandwiches and burgers, chased down with classic cream teas and yummy cakes, all best savoured at one of the picnic tables.

★ Kota
INTERNATIONAL ££

(☑ 01326-562407; www.kotarestaurant.co.uk; Harbour Head; 2/3 courses £25/30, mains £16-28; ⊙ 6-9.30pm Mon-Sat) Porthleven's top restaurant is run by half Maori, half Chinese-Malay chef Jude Kereama. Set in an old harbourside mill, the menu is spiced with Far Eastern and fusion flavours, underpinned by classic French credentials. The dishes look beautiful, with edible flowers and other flourishes.

Kota also offers three smart double **bedrooms** (from £80).

Halzephron Inn
PUB FOOD ££

(☑ 01326-240406; www.halzephron-inn.co.uk; mains £10-15; ⊙ bar 11am-11pm; food noon-2pm & 6-9pm) The Halzephron sits high on the hills above the cove of Gunwalloe. It's a classic Cornish local – whitewashed and slate-topped, with brassy trinkets and stout beams. Picnic tables either overlook rolling fields or a sweep of Mounts Bay, making it just the spot to tuck into seabass with samphire, moules marinière or steak and ale pie.

Falmouth

☑ 01326 / POP 21,790

Few seaside towns in Cornwall boast such an arresting location as Falmouth, overlooking the broad Fal River as it empties into the English Channel. Surrounded by green hills and blue sea, Falmouth is an appealing jumble of lanes, old pubs, slate roofs and trendy cafes. With its wealth of bars and bistros, trio of beaches and excellent maritime museum, it's an ideal base for exploring Cornwall's fine gardens and south coast.

Though it now derives much of its revenue from nearby Falmouth University, the town made its fortune during the 18th and 19th centuries thanks to lucrative maritime trade. Falmouth has the world's third-deepest natural harbour, and the town grew rich when tea clippers, trading vessels and mail packets stopped here to unload their cargoes. The port is still an important centre for ship repairs – spot the dockyard cranes as you head to Pendennis Point.

◉ Sights

Falmouth's trio of beaches – Gyllyngvase, Swanpool and Maenporth – aren't quite up to north-coast standards, but they're nice enough. The beaches have car parks, but they fill up quickly in summer.

★ National Maritime Museum
MUSEUM

(☑ 01326-313388; www.nmmc.co.uk; Discovery Quay; adult/child £14/7; ⊙ 10am-5pm) Falmouth's big museum is the sister outpost of the National Maritime Museum in Greenwich, London. Imaginative displays focus on Falmouth's history as a port, and on the broader impact of the sea on history and culture. The centrepiece is the five-storey **Flotilla Gallery**, where an array of small vessels, ranging from rowboats to rescue craft, are suspended from the ceiling.

From the top floor of the Lookout tower, there's a 360-degree panorama across Falmouth Bay. Regular nautically themed exhibitions cover subjects ranging from the Titanic and Captain Bligh to the tradition of tattooing. Check to see whether the hour-long heritage boat tours have resumed. Admission tickets are valid for one year.

★ Potager Garden
GARDENS

(☑ 01326-341258; www.potagergarden.org; High Cross, Constantine; suggested donation £3; ⊙ 10am-5pm Thu-Sun) Rescued from dilapidation by its current owners, this gorgeous garden has been renovated by volunteers into a delightful working garden modelled on the French 'potager'. Highlights include the 30m greenhouse, and the super veggie **cafe** (mains £6 to £10), popular with lunching locals at weekends. The garden is 6 miles southwest of Falmouth.

Glendurgan
GARDENS

(NT; ☑ 01326-250906; www.nationaltrust.org.uk; Mawnan Smith; adult/child £5/2.50; ⊙ 10.30am-5pm Tue-Sun) Glendurgan was established by Alfred Fox in the 1820s to show off the weird and wonderful plants brought back from the far corners of the empire, from Himalayan rhododendrons to Canadian maples and New Zealand tree ferns. Tumbling down a stunning subtropical valley, the garden offers breathtaking views of the Helford and leads to a secluded beach near Durgan village. Glendurgan is 7 miles southwest of Falmouth.

Trebah Garden GARDENS

(☑ 01326-252200; www.trebahgarden.co.uk; Mawnan Smith; adult/child £11/5.50; ⊘ 10.30am-4.30pm, last entry 2.30pm) Trebah Garden was planted in 1840 by Charles Fox, younger brother of Alfred, who established neighbouring Glendurgan Garden. It's less formal, with gigantic rhododendrons, gunnera and jungle ferns lining the sides of a steep ravine leading down to the quay and shingle beach. There's also a great takeaway cafe.

Pendennis Castle CASTLE

(EH; ☑ 01326-316594; www.english-heritage.org. uk; Castle Dr; adult/child £12/7.30; ⊘ 10am-5pm; ℗) Designed in tandem with its sister castle in St Mawes across the estuary, this Tudor castle sits proudly on Pendennis Point, and was built as part of Henry VIII's massive coastal castle-building program. You can wander around the central keep and the Tudor gun deck, as well as the governor's bedroom, a WWI guardhouse and the WWII-era Half-Moon Battery.

🏃 Activities

★ AK Wildlife Cruises WILDLIFE WATCHING

(☑ 01326-753389; www.akwildlifecruises.co.uk; Premier Marina; adult/child from £50/40) 🏆 Run by the amiable and unfailingly enthusiastic 'Captain Keith', this specialist wildlife cruise sets out from Falmouth Harbour in search of local marine life. Depending on the season, there's a good chance of spotting dolphins, porpoises, basking sharks, puffins and seals – it's not unheard of to spy minke whales.

Fal River Boat Trips BOATING

(Enterprise Boats; ☑ 01326-741194; www.falriver. co.uk/ferries/enterprise-boats; Prince of Wales Pier; return adult/child £14/7; ⊘ 2 sailings daily, Sun-Fri Apr-Sep) Falmouth's main pier is the departure point for a range of boat trips. One of the best is the regular two-hour round trip from Falmouth to Trelissick Gardens (p342), via St Mawes.

Gylly Adventures KAYAKING

(☑ 07341 890495; www.gyllyadventures.co.uk; Gyllyngvase Beach, Cliff Rd; tours per person £45) 'Gylly' Beach's watersports company hires the usual kit: stand-up paddleboards (per hour £15), kayaks (per hour £12), wetsuits (per hour £6) and bodyboards (per hour £5). It also offers great, small-group guided kayaking trips. Options include a tour of

Falmouth harbour, a paddle into local caves, and (best of all) a night kayak trip illuminated by LED head torches.

🛏 Sleeping

★ Highcliffe B&B ££

(☑ 01326-314466; www.highcliffefalmouth.com; 22 Melvill Rd; s £65, d £105-150, ste £145-160; ℗ 🛜) Vintage furniture and upcycled design pieces give each of the soothing rooms here an individual feel. The pick of the bunch is the light-filled Attic Penthouse, with skylight windows overlooking Falmouth Bay. Room-service breakfasts in picnic baskets might feature toasted muffins, pancakes with bacon, or homemade granola with compote.

Bosanneth B&B ££

(☑ 01326-314649; www.bosanneth.co.uk; 1 Stracey Rd; d £90-130; ℗ 🛜) There's a mix-and-match decorative vibe running through this eight-room B&B. Some of the rooms feel vintage, with old mirrors, reclaimed furniture and classic colours, while others go for a more up-to-date look. The 'oasis' garden, with a sea-view sun deck, is a particular delight.

★ Greenbank HOTEL £££

(☑ 01326-312440; www.greenbank-hotel.co.uk; harbourside; s/d/tr incl breakfast from £160/220/250; ℗ 🛜) 🏆 Greenbank is the queen of Falmouth's hotels, with a knockout position right beside the boat-filled estuary. It feels like the setting for an Agatha Christie novel – nautical knick-knacks and ships in cabinets dot public areas, while tall windows look out on to the water. Modern rooms are done out in cream with bursts of aquamarine; the best boast edge-of-the-water views.

🍽 Eating

★ Espressini CAFE £

(39 Killigrew St; snacks from £4; ⊘ 9am-3pm Thu-Sat; 🛜) Cornwall's best coffee house, bar none, is run by committed coffee aficionado Rupert Ellis. The choice of blends, roasts and coffees fills a 2m blackboard. Exquisitely crafted edibles might encompass beetroot and goats-cheese tart, towering breakfast baps and squidgy dark-chocolate brownies.

★ Stone's Bakery BAKERY £

(☑ 07791 003183; www.stonesbakery.co.uk; 35 High St; breads £2-3.50; ⊘ 8.30am-1.30pm

Wed-Sat; 🛜) Freshly baked loaves line the window like pieces of art at this gorgeous bakery, which focuses on traditional hand-shaped rustic loaves – the tangy maltster and the organic sourdough are as delicious as you'll taste.

Harbour Lights FISH & CHIPS £
(📞 01326-316934; www.harbourlights.co.uk; Arwenack St; fish & chips from £8; ⏰noon-9pm Sun-Thu, to 9.30pm Fri & Sat) 🍴 Falmouth's classic – and best – chippy keeps notching up awards (it was voted one of Britain's top 10 in 2019). All the fish is responsibly sourced; the day's catch might mean you tuck into lemon sole, pollock or hake. Check online to see if the restaurant, with Fal River views, has reopened.

Meat Counter BURGERS £
(📞 01326-312220; www.facebook.com/themeat counterfalmouth; 25 Arwenack St; burgers £7-13; ⏰noon-9pm; 🛜🌱) Perennially popular with Falmouth's hungry students, this specialist burger joint turns out the best patties in town. The teetering stacks feature beef, chicken or falafel topped by garlic mayo, wild rocket and dirty American cheese. The side order might be Cornish sea-salt skin-on fries. If distancing is in force, it's likely to be takeaway and delivery only.

Ferryboat Inn GASTROPUB ££
(📞 01326-250625; www.ferryboatcornwall.co.uk; Helford Passage; mains £8-14; ⏰food noon-3pm & 4.30-8pm) This age-old riverside pub is a Cornish classic. The picnic tables have dreamy views over the Helford River; inside, it's all wood, slate and open plan. Dishes might include seafood chowder, Thai fish curry, brioche lobster rolls and truffle fries. Visit the website to see if you need to order food online in advance.

🍸 Drinking & Nightlife

A tip for ale-loving bookworms: check whether the fabulous combo of bookshop and pub that is **Beerwolf Books** (📞 01326-618474; www.beerwolfbooks.com; 3 Bells Ct) has reopened.

Chintz Symposium BAR
(📞 07538 006495; www.thechintzbar.com; Old Brewery Yard; ⏰3-11.30pm Mon-Fri, 1-11.30pm Sat & Sun; 🛜) Wine, charcuterie, cheese and cocktails take centre stage at this uber-trendy, slightly surreal hang-out. Junk-shop furniture, wooden toys, no parking signs and glowing lanterns fill the sunny courtyard and A-framed attic space. The wine list is copious.

Chain Locker PUB
(📞 01326-311085; www.chainlockerfalmouth.co.uk; Quay St; ⏰10am-11pm) One of Falmouth's oldest pubs, and also one of the town's best-loved waterside drinking dens. Old signs, ships' ephemera and black-and-white photos dot the bar; the dockside tables are perfect on a sunny day.

Working Boat PUB
(📞 01326-314283; www.theworkingboat.co.uk; Greenbank Quay; ⏰11am-midnight) With its quayside tables, alfresco pop-up bar, sea-themed styling and wide harbour views, you can't get much more nautical than the Working Boat. Rustic pizzas and beer-battered fish and chips (mains from £10) seal the deal.

ℹ Information

The **Fal River Information Centre** (📞 01326-741194; www.falriver.co.uk; 11 Market Strand, Prince of Wales Pier; ⏰10am-5pm Mon-Sat, hours may vary) advises on ferries and books accommodation.

ℹ Getting There & Away

Falmouth is at the end of the railway branch line from Truro (£4.70, 30 minutes, one to two per hour). Truro is on the main Penzance to London Paddington line.

Bus coverage is also fairly good, with regular links between the big towns in the area, and at least one bus service serving most of the local villages. Falmouth has several services that head to the Lizard and Helston.

Falmouth's Moor Bus Station is central. First Kernow (www.firstgroup.com/cornwall) routes include the following.

Helston (£5.80, one hour, hourly Monday to Saturday) Bus 35/35A, stops at Glendurgan and Trebah gardens en route.

Penzance (£7.40, 1½ hours, hourly Monday to Saturday, six on Sunday) Bus U4, via Helston and Marazion.

Redruth (£5.80, 40 minutes, hourly Monday to Friday, every two hours Sunday) Bus U2, via Penryn.

Truro (£5.80, 1¼ hours, half-hourly Monday to Saturday, hourly Sunday) Bus U1, via Penryn.

Buses 65 and 67 regularly shuttle from Falmouth to Gyllyngvase and Swanpool beaches.

Truro

📞 01872 / POP 18,700

Dominated by the three mighty spires of its 19th-century cathedral, which rises above town like a neo-Gothic supertanker, Truro is

THE EDEN PROJECT & THE LOST GARDENS OF HELIGAN

Five miles from St Austell, at the bottom of a china clay pit, the giant biomes of the **Eden Project** (☑01726-811911; www.edenproject.com; Bodelva; adult/child £28.50/15; ⊙9.30am-6pm; P) – the world's largest greenhouses – have become Cornwall's most famous landmark, and an absolutely essential visit. Looking rather like a lunar landing station, Eden's bubble-shaped biomes maintain miniature ecosystems that enable all kinds of weird and wonderful plants to flourish – from stinky rafflesia flowers and banana trees in the Rainforest Biome to cacti and soaring palms in the Mediterranean Biome. The Eden site is 3 miles northeast of St Austell.

The Eden Project is the brainchild of former record producer turned entrepreneur Tim Smit, who also rescued the **Lost Gardens of Heligan** (☑01726-845100; www.heligan.com; Pentewan; adult/child £16/8; ⊙10am-6pm Mar-Oct, to 5pm Nov-Feb; P) from ruin. Formerly the family estate of the Tremaynes, Heligan's magnificent 19th-century gardens fell into disrepair following WWI, but have been splendidly restored by an army of gardeners and volunteers. In this horticultural wonderland you'll encounter formal lawns, working kitchen gardens, fruit-filled greenhouses, a secret grotto and 25m-high rhododendron, plus a lost-world Jungle Valley of ferns, palms and tropical blooms. Heligan is 10 miles southwest of the Eden Project.

Cornwall's capital and its only city. It's the county's main centre for shopping and commerce: the streets here are lined with high-street chains and independent shops, while the twice-weekly farmers market brings field-fresh produce to town.

◎ Sights

★ Trelissick GARDENS

(NT; ☑01872-862090; www.nationaltrust.org.uk; grounds £4; ⊙grounds 10.30am-5pm) Grandly located at the head of the Fal estuary, 4 miles south of Truro, Trelissick is one of Cornwall's most beautiful aristocratic estates. Its formal garden, which is filled with magnolias and hydrangeas, is surrounded by fields and parkland that is criss-crossed by walking trails. The prettiest route is to head to the estate's pebble beach and then wander upriver along the Fal's wooded banks.

Truro Cathedral CATHEDRAL

(☑01872-276782; www.trurocathedral.org.uk; High Cross; suggested donation £5; ⊙10am-3pm Mon-Sat, 1-3pm Sun) Built on the site of a 16th-century parish church in soaring Gothic Revival style, Truro Cathedral was completed in 1910, making it the first cathedral built in England since St Paul's. Inside, the vast nave contains some fine Victorian stained glass and the impressive Father Willis Organ.

Royal Cornwall Museum MUSEUM

(☑01872-272205; www.royalcornwallmuseum.org.uk; River St; ⊙10am-3pm Tue-Thu & Sat, noon-6pm Fri) FREE Collections at the county's main museum encompass everything from geological specimens to a ceremonial carriage and Bronze Age lunalae (ornate collars shaped like crescent moons). Upstairs the ancient civilisations section features Egyptian, Greek and Roman artefacts. Artworks change frequently and might include pieces by Turner, van Dyck and the Newlyn artist Stanhope Forbes.

☐ Sleeping

Mannings Hotel HOTEL ££

(☑01872-270345; www.manningshotels.co.uk; Lemon St; r £95-125, apt £135-145; P ☎) At the best place to stay in the city centre, a part-Georgian building has been tastefully modernised, with bright colours and functional furniture. The nine self-contained apartments come with small kitchen and spiral staircase. Its Secret Garden pop-up cafe-bistro is a fun spot for an alfresco drink.

Merchant House HOTEL ££

(☑01872-272450; www.merchant-house.co.uk; 49 Falmouth Rd; s/d/f incl breakfast from £75/110/150; P ☎ ♨ ☎) This Victorian house with a cheery sea-blue colour scheme is handy for town. Some bedrooms have skylights, others overlook the garden.

✕ Eating & Drinking

Farmers Market MARKET £

(www.trurofarmers.co.uk; Lemon Quay; snacks from £3; ⊙9am-3pm Wed & Sat) The green and white stalls that pop up twice a week here are piled high with locally produced bread, cheese, fruit, veg, eggs, smoked fish, cakes and preserves. You'll also find street food that might span curries, slow-smoked brisket and churros.

Bustopher Jones   BISTRO ££

(☑ 01872-430000; www.bustopher-jones.co.uk; 62 Lemon St; mains £13-21; ⊗ 5-10pm Mon-Wed, to 3am Fri, to 2am Sat, noon-4pm Sun) Head to the covered, heated garden lounge at impeccably designed Bustopher Jones to indulge in a little downtown dining on burgers, steaks and grilled fish. Or sip on something from their extensive drinks list – the cocktails are mini works of art.

★ 108 Coffee   CAFE

(☑ 07582 339636; 109 Kenwyn St; ⊗ 8am-2pm Mon-Sat) Set up by unapologetic coffee nuts Paul and Michelle, this is Truro's premier place for a caffeine fix. The beans come courtesy of Cornish coffee roasters Origin, and the flat whites and espressos are among the county's best.

Old Ale House   PUB

(☑ 01872-271122; www.old-ale-house.co.uk; 7 Quay St; ⊗ noon-11pm) A proper ale-drinker's pub, with sawdust on the floor, beer mats on the ceiling and a menu of guest ales. Most of the beers come from Skinner's Brewery, rejoicing under names like Betty Stogs (4%, bitter), Penny Come Quick (4.5%, milk stout) and the fabled Cornish Knocker (4%, golden ale).

❶ Information

Truro Tourist Office (☑ 01872-274555; www.visittruro.org.uk; 30 Boscawen St; ⊗ 9am-5.30pm Mon-Fri, to 5pm Sat)

❶ Getting There & Away

BUS

Truro's bus station is beside Lemon Quay.

Falmouth (£5.80, 1¼ hours, half-hourly Monday to Saturday, hourly Sunday) Bus U1, via Penryn.

Penzance (£5.80, 1½ hours, hourly) Bus T1.

St Ives (£5.80, 1½ hours, hourly) Bus T2.

TRAIN

Truro is on the main London Paddington–Penzance line and the branch line to Falmouth. Frequent connections include the following.

Bristol £51, 3½ hours

Exeter £19.60, 2¼ hours

Falmouth £45, 30 minutes

London Paddington £70, 4½ hours

Penzance £8, 40 minutes

Fowey

☑ 01726 / POP 2130

Fowey makes a bewitching south-coast base. In this working port turned well-heeled holiday town, pastel-coloured houses, portside pubs and tiered terraces overlook the wooded banks of the River Fowey. The town has been an important port since Elizabethan times, and later became the adopted home of the writer Daphne du Maurier, who used the nearby house at Menabilly Barton as the inspiration for *Rebecca*.

A passenger ferry (p345) shuttles to the impossibly pretty village of **Polruan**, on the east side of Fowey harbour. A few miles north along the creek, the riverside hamlet of **Golant** is also well worth a detour, with a waterfront pub for lunch and excellent kayaking opportunities.

◉ Sights & Activities

Polkerris Beach   BEACH

(☑ 01726-813306; www.polkerrisbeach.com) Some 3 miles west of Fowey, this is the area's largest and busiest beach. Sailing lessons, windsurfing and stand-up paddleboarding are all available.

Fowey River Expeditions   KAYAKING

(☑ 01726-833627; www.foweyexpeditions.co.uk; Albert Quay; adult/child £30/15; ⊗ Apr-Oct) On these guided, two-hour, entry-level tours in single and double open cockpit canoes you'll either head up river towards Golant or explore Fowey harbour.

More experienced kayakers can also hire boats for self-guided trips (single/double kayak per day £30/45).

★ Encounter Cornwall   KAYAKING

(☑ 07976 466123; www.encountercornwall.com; The Boatshed, Golant; adult/child £30/20) These three-hour guided kayaking trips might form some of the most memorable moments of your Cornish stay. Setting off from Golant, just north of Fowey, tours see you gliding up creeks and backwaters, spotting egrets, kingfishers and seals. Encounter also offers two-hour early-morning and 'sundowner' expeditions (adult/child £25/15).

WORTH A TRIP

POLPERRO & MEVAGISSEY

Even in a county where picturesque fishing harbours seem to fill every cove, it's hard not to fall for Polperro – a warren of cottages, boat stores and alleyways, all set around a stout granite harbour. Unsurprisingly, this was once a smugglers' hideout, and it's still a place with a salty, sea-dog atmosphere, despite the inevitable summer crowds. The coast path between Polperro and Looe is particularly scenic. The main car park is 750m uphill from the village, from there it's a 15-minute stroll down to the quayside.

Just along the coast, the little village of Mevagissey hasn't been gentrified to quite the same degree as other ports along the coast, and feels all the better for it. There are alleys to wander, great pubs, secondhand bookshops and galleries to browse, and the harbour is one of the best places on the south coast for crabbing. In summer, ferries run along the coast from Mevagissey Harbour to Fowey.

⏚ Sleeping

Old Embassy House   B&B ££
(☑ 01726-834939;   www.oldembassyhouse.co.uk;
Lostwithiel St; s £95-125, d £105-125; 🅿🛜) At
friendly Old Embassy House design themes
range from four poster, via geometric to seaside. The best bedroom is nautically themed,
1st-floor Lantic, which has a window seat
with views down onto the tree-framed,
boat-dotted river below.

★ Coriander Cottages   APARTMENT £££
(☑ 01726-834998;   www.foweyaccommodation.
co.uk; Penventinue Lane; 1-bed cottages £130-
150; 🅿🛜♿) 🌿 A delightfully rural cottage
complex on the outskirts of Fowey, with
ecofriendly accommodation in open-plan,
self-catering barns, all with quiet country
views. The stone barns have been beautifully modernised, and use a combination
of solar panels, ground-source heating and
rainwater harvesting to reduce environmental impact. Handily, cottages are available
per night, so you're not restricted to weekly
stays.

Old Quay House   HOTEL £££
(☑ 01726-833302; www.theoldquayhouse.com; 28
Fore St; incl breakfast d £250-360, ste from £400;
🛜) The epitome of Fowey's upmarket trend,
this exclusive quayside hotel is all natural
fabrics, rattan chairs and tasteful mono-
chrome tones, and the rooms are a mix of
estuary-view suites and attic penthouses. It's
right in the centre of town, in a handsome
riverside building. The restaurant specialises in upmarket seafood.

✕ Eating & Drinking

Kittows   DELI £
(☑ 01726-832639;   www.kittowsfowey.co.uk;   3
South St; ⊙8.30am-5.30pm Mon-Sat, 9am-4pm

Sun) The deli at Fowey's fifth-generation
butcher sells perfect picnic goodies: fish
and meat kebabs, cooked crab and lobster, Fowey Valley Cider and Cornish Blue
cheese.

Sam's   BISTRO ££
(☑ 01726-832273; www.samscornwall.co.uk; 20
Fore St; mains £12-18; ⊙noon-9.30pm) Sam's has
been a stalwart in Fowey for years. Alfresco, river-view tables, booth seats, Day-Glo
menus and a lively local vibe keep the feel
laid-back, and the menu of flash-cooked fish,
salads, steaks and gourmet burgers proves
perennially popular.

Sam's on the Beach   BISTRO ££
(☑ 01726-812255; www.samscornwall.co.uk; Polkerris; mains £15-24, pizza £8-16; ⊙noon-10pm Sun-
Fri, 9am-10pm Sat) Lodged in the old lifeboat
house on Polkerris, this beachside outpost of
the mini Sam's empire dishes up pan-seared
sardines, mussels cooked in Cornish cider
and sourdough pizza fresh from the wood-
fired oven. All made memorable thanks to
tables beside the sands and cracking bay
views.

King of Prussia   PUB
(☑ 01726-833694; www.kingofprussiafowey.co.uk;
3 Town Quay; ⊙11am-11pm) Fowey has lots of
pubs, but you might as well go for the one
with the best harbour view, named after
notorious 'free trader' (aka smuggler) John
Carter – the eponymous Prussia refers to
Cornwall's Prussia Cove.

Pub-grub meals (mains £13 to £20) include mussels steamed with chorizo, coq au
vin and blue-cheese gnocchi.

❶ Information

Fowey's Website (www.fowey.co.uk) has tourist
information.

ℹ Getting There & Away

Bus 24 (hourly Monday to Saturday, six on Sunday) runs to St Austell, Heligan and Mevagissey. It also stops at Par train station, where you can catch trains on the main London–Penzance line.

Polruan Ferry (www.ctomsandson.co.uk/polruan-ferry; Whitehouse Pier; adult/child £2.30/1, bicycle £1.70, dog 40p; ⊙7am-11pm Mon-Sat, 10am-11pm Sun mid-Jul–Sep, 8am-9pm Mon-Sat, 10am-5pm Sun Oct–mid-Jul) Passenger ferry to Polruan. In winter and on summer evenings, it runs from Town Quay; in summer during the day, it runs from Whitehouse Pier on the Esplanade.

Bodinnick Ferry (Fowey slipway; www.ctomsandson.co.uk/bodinnick-ferry; car & 2 passengers £5, pedestrian/bicycle £2/free; ⊙7am-8pm Mon-Fri, 9am-8pm Sat & Sun May-Sep, last ferry 7pm Oct-Apr) Car ferry crossing the river to Bodinnick.

Looe

🕽 01503 / POP 5110

Nestled in the crook of a steep-sided valley, the twin settlements of East and West Looe stand on either side of a broad river estuary, connected by an arched Victorian bridge built in 1853. There's been a settlement here since the days of the Domesday Book, and the town thrived as a medieval port before reinventing itself as a holiday resort for well-to-do Victorians – famously, the town installed one of the county's first 'bathing machines' beside **Banjo Pier** (named for its circular shape) in around 1800, and it's been a popular beach retreat ever since.

In contrast to Fowey, Looe feels a little behind-the-times – chip shops, souvenir sellers and chintzy B&Bs still very much rule the roost here – but if it's a classic seaside town you're looking for, you've definitely found it in Looe.

◉ Sights

Looe Island   ISLAND
(www.cornwallwildlifetrust.org.uk/looeisland; guided walks £25) A mile offshore from Hannafore Point is densely wooded Looe Island (officially known as St George's Island), a 9-hectare nature reserve and haven for marine wildlife. You can explore on foot, or take a guided walk with the island ranger, who can help spot local wildlife including grey seals, cormorants, shags and oystercatchers. Book well in advance.

Between April and September, the **Moonraker** (🕽 07814 264514; Buller Quay; return adult/child £10/5, plus landing fee £4/1) putters over from Looe's Buller Quay. Trips are dependent on weather and tides; booking essential.

🛏 Sleeping

Penvith Barns   B&B **££**
(🕽 01503-240772; www.penvithbarns.co.uk; St-Martin-by-Looe; r £95-119; 🅿 🛜 🐾) Escape the Looe crowds at this rural barn conversion in the nearby hamlet of St-Martin-by-Looe. Rooms range from small to spacious: the Piggery is tiny and tucked under the eaves, while the Dairy has enough space for a spare bed and sofa. Each room has its own private entrance. Two-night minimum in summer.

Commonwood Manor   B&B **££**
(🕽 01503-262929; www.commonwoodmanor.com; St Martins Rd; d £90-130; 🅿 🛜 🐾) In a prime position on the East Looe hillside, this elegant villa with a long river-view terrace is a cut above your average B&B. Room design spans cream to floral, and if you bag one of the bay-window bedrooms, you'll have the

---

DON'T MISS

COTEHELE

At the head of the Tamar Valley sits the Tudor manor of **Cotehele** (NT; 🕽 01579-351346; www.nationaltrust.org.uk; St Dominick; gardens adult/child £8/4; ⊙gardens 10am-5pm), one of the Edgcumbe dynasty's modest country retreats. The gardens sweep down past the 18th-century Prospect Folly to Cotehele Quay, where there's a discovery centre exploring the history of the Tamar Valley and a vintage sailing barge, the **Shamrock**.

If the interior has reopened you'll see a cavernous great hall and an unparalleled collection of Tudor tapestries, armour and furniture.

A short walk inland leads to the restored **Cotehele Mill**. If it's operating, you'll be able to watch the original waterwheel grinding corn several days a week, and see a miller and baker at work. The house is famous for its Christmas wreath, a massive ornamental ring of foliage made from materials gathered on the estate.

best views in town. There's usually a two-night minimum.

ℹ Information

Check to see whether the **Looe Tourist Office** (☑ 01503-262072; www.looeguide.co.uk; Guildhall, Fore St) is back up and running.

ℹ Getting There & Away

Looe sits at the end of a railway branch line that links to the main London Paddington to Penzance service at Liskeard. The journey (adult/child return £4.60/3.30, 30 minutes, hourly) tracks through wooded valleys out to the seaside; a day out in itself.

Bodmin Moor

It can't quite boast the wild majesty of Dartmoor, but Bodmin Moor has a bleak beauty all of its own. With its heaths and granite hills, including Rough Tor ('rowtor', 400m) and Cornwall's highest point, Brown Willy (420m), it's a desolate place that works on the imagination, with prehistoric remains and legends of mysterious beasts.

The northern and central parts of the Moor are largely barren and treeless, while the southern section is greener. Apart from the hills, the moor's main landmark is Jamaica Inn, made famous by Daphne du Maurier's novel of the same name.

⊙ Sights & Activities

For an intriguing insight into life for the British aristocracy, check whether the interior of the magnificent manor house of **Lanhydrock** (NT; ☑ 01208-265950; www.nationaltrust.org.uk) has reopened.

It's also worth seeing whether the **Bodmin & Wenford Railway** (☑ 01208-73555; www.bodminrailway.co.uk) is up and running again.

★ **Golitha Falls**   WATERFALL
(near Redgate) **FREE** With water cascading down a 90m drop, these crashing falls are one of the most renowned beauty spots on the moor. The site is surrounded by the remains of an ancient oak wood that once covered much of the moor. The falls are just over a mile west of St Cleer. There's a car park half a mile's walk from the reserve, near Draynes Bridge.

Carnglaze Caverns   CAVE
(☑ 01579-320251; www.carnglaze.com; near St Neot; adult/child £8/5; ⊙ 10am-5pm, to 8pm Aug; 🚗 👶) Slate was once an important local export on Bodmin Moor, and these deep caverns were cut out by hand by miners, leaving behind an atmospheric network of caves and a glittering underground pool. The site is just outside St Neot and well-signed.

Cheesewring   ARCHAEOLOGICAL SITE
(near Minions) Looking like a gigantic game of granite Jenga, this stack of rocks on the edge of the small village of Minions is said to have been the work of giants – but the truth is even stranger. A combination of wind, rain and natural erosion has carved out the outcrop's peculiar disc-like shapes. The name refers to the formation's similarity to the bags of apple pulp (or cheeses) that are used in cider presses.

PREHISTORIC SITES OF BODMIN MOOR

The highest concentration of prehistoric sites is found in the southern moor. Near the small village of Minions, about 2 miles east of Siblyback Lake, the curious triple stone circles known as the **Hurlers** are said to be the remains of men turned to stone for daring to play the Cornish sport of hurling on a Sunday. Nearby is the **Cheesewring**, a weird stack of granite stones that's said to be the work of local giants, but is actually the result of natural erosion. Three miles south near Darite is **Trethevy Quoit** – sometimes known as King Arthur's Quoit or the Giant's House – another example of Cornwall's distinctive Neolithic burial chambers, standing almost 4.5m high.

But the most impressive monument is the structure known as **King Arthur's Hall**, a huge rectangle of standing stones measuring 20m across and 50m long. It's an archaeological conundrum; nothing of its size exists anywhere else in Cornwall, and so far experts are stumped as to what it was used for. The current explanation is that it may have been a ceremonial pool, but it's really anyone's guess. It's reached via a muddy trail from St Breward.

Eating

★ **Woods Cafe** CAFE £
(☑01208-78111; www.woodscafe.co.uk; Cardinham Woods; mains £6-12; ◷10.30am-3pm Mon-Fri, to 4pm Sat & Sun) In an old forester's cottage lost among the trees of Cardinham, this cracking cafe has become a locals' favourite thanks to home-baked cakes, cockle-warming soups and sausage sandwiches. Perfect for post-walk sustenance.

★ **St Tudy Inn** MODERN BRITISH ££
(☑01208-850656; www.sttudyinn.com; St Tudy; mains £14-25; ◷hours vary) Locally lauded chef Emily Scott temporarily relocated to a pop-up cafe at Watergate Bay for the summer of 2020. Check whether she's back at this smart moorland village pub, to deliver imaginative food combining traditional British flavours with a modern, season-driven style.

There is also a selection of elegant **rooms** (doubles from £140) in attached barns.

ISLES OF SCILLY

While only 28 miles west of the mainland, in many ways the Isles of Scilly feels like a different world. Life on this archipelago of around 140 tiny islands seems hardly to have changed in decades: there are no traffic jams, no supermarkets, no multinational hotels, and the only noise pollution comes from breaking waves and cawing gulls. That's not to say that Scilly is behind the times – you'll find a mobile-phone signal and broadband internet on the main islands – but life ticks along at its own island pace. Renowned for glorious beaches, there are few places better to escape.

Only five islands are inhabited: St Mary's is the largest, followed by Tresco, while only a few hardy souls live on Bryher, St Martin's and St Agnes. Regular ferry boats run between all five islands.

Unsurprisingly, summer is by far the busiest time. Many businesses shut down completely in winter.

❶ Information

Isles of Scilly Tourist Information Centre
(☑01720-620600; www.visitislesofscilly.com; Porthcressa Beach; ◷9am-1pm & 4-5pm) The islands' only tourist office.

Simply Scilly (www.simplyscilly.co.uk) Unofficial tourist site.

❶ Getting There & Away

Isles of Scilly Travel (☑01736-334220; www.islesofscilly-travel.co.uk) There are frequent flights year-round from Land's End Airport, near St Just (adult/child £90/71, 20 minutes) and from Newquay Airport (£115/88, 30 minutes). Between mid-March and October flights also run from Exeter (£169/124, one hour). Planes only fly Monday to Saturday.

Scillonian III (☑01736-334220; www.islesofscilly-travel.co.uk; ◷mid Mar–Oct) Scilly's ferry plies the notoriously choppy waters between Penzance and St Mary's (one-way adult/child £55/29). There's at least one daily crossing in summer, but there are no ferries in winter. It sails in most weathers, but seasickness is a distinct possibility: be prepared.

Penzance Helicopters (☑01736-780828; www.penzancehelicopters.co.uk; Penzance Heliport, Jelbert Way; single £130; ◷Mon-Sat) These 15-minute flights link Penzance Heliport with St Mary's and Tresco.

❶ Getting Around

Inter-island ferries between St Mary's and the other islands are provided by the **St Mary's Boatmen's Association** (☑01720-423999; www.scillyboating.co.uk; adult/child return to any island £10/5). If you're staying at one of the hotels on Tresco, there's also a separate transfer service.

The only bus and taxi services are on St Mary's.

St Mary's

☑01720 / POP 1650

First stop for every visitor to Scilly (unless you're arriving aboard your own private yacht) is St Mary's, the largest and busiest of the islands, and home to the vast majority of hotels, shops, restaurants and B&Bs. Just over 3 miles at its widest point, St Mary's is shaped like a crooked circle, with a claw-shaped peninsula at its southwestern edge – home to the island's capital, Hugh Town, and the docking point for the Scillonian ferry. The main airport is a mile east near Old Town.

◉ Sights & Activities

Isles of Scilly Museum MUSEUM
(☑01720-422337; www.iosmuseum.org; Church St, Hugh Town; adult/child £3.50/1) Check whether the excellent Isles of Scilly Museum, which suspended visits in 2020, has reopened. It provides an evocative introduction to the islands' history, with an eclectic mix of archaeological finds and

artefacts from shipwrecks. Among the collection are Neolithic remains such as tools and jewellery, clay pipes left behind by generations of sailors, a couple of sailing boats and a small exhibition on Edward Heath, the British prime minister who loved Scilly so much he was buried here.

St Mary's Bike Hire   CYCLING
(📞 07552 994709; www.stmarysbikehire.co.uk; The Strand; half/full day £8.50/13.50, week £65; ⊙9am-5pm Mon-Sat Mar-Oct, plus 9am-noon Sun Jun-Aug) Rents out bikes from a base in Hugh Town, but can also deliver island-wide (£2.50 per bike). It also hires out electric bikes (half/full day £16.50/25) and a tandem (£17.50/27).

🕜 Tours

Scilly Walks   WALKING
(📞 01720-423326; www.scillywalks.co.uk; adult/ child £7/3.50) Three-hour archaeological and historical tours of St Mary's, plus regular guided walking trips to other islands, conducted by local historian and archaeologist Katherine Sawyer.

Island Wildlife Tours   WALKING
(📞 01720-422212; www.islandwildlifetours.co.uk; half/full day £7/14) Regular birdwatching and wildlife walks with local character and resident ornithologist Will Wagstaff, the undisputed authority on Scilly's natural history. Most tours start in the morning on St Mary's, but there are regular walks on other islands too. You need to add on the cost of the boat transfer.

Island Sea Safaris   BOATING
(📞 01720-422732; www.islandseasafaris.co.uk) Trips to see local seabird and seal colonies (adult/child £38/29), plus one-hour 'island taster' tours (£26 per person).

🛏 Sleeping

Garrison Campsite   CAMPSITE £
(📞 01720-422670; www.garrisonholidaysscilly. co.uk; Tower Cottage, Garrison; adult/child £14/7; 🛜🐾) St Mary's main campsite sits in a lofty spot above Hugh Town, beside the Garrison fort. It's a big site, covering 3.5 hectares, with plenty of pitches (some with electrical hook-ups), plus wi-fi, a small shop and a laundry-shower block. It also offers pre-erected tents (two/four people per three nights £175/315).

Mincarlo   B&B ££
(📞 01720-422513; www.mincarloscilly.com; s £45-55, d £83-120; 🛜🐾) There's no better location on St Mary's than this little guesthouse in a prime spot with views all the way to Hugh Town from the western end of Town Beach. Rooms are plain and cosy (the attic's a bargain), breakfast is great, and owners Nick and Bryony are full of local info.

Star Castle   HOTEL £££
(📞 01720-422317; www.star-castle.co.uk; Garrison; s/d from £130/145; 🛜🐾🐾) Shaped like an eight-pointed star, this former fort on Garrison Point is one of Scilly's top hotels, with heritage-style castle rooms and more-modern garden suites. It's fairly formal but the views are some of the best on the island, and the grassy gardens – set right into the ramparts – are a delight.

Atlantic   INN £££
(📞 01720-422417; www.atlanticinnscilly.co.uk; Hugh St; r £140-195; 🛜🐾🐾) The fresh, summery rooms in this age-old inn come complete with colourful prints, pastel colours and plush fabrics – the best have captivating edge-of-the-water views. The food (mains £13 to £18) takes in fish and chips, burgers and Thai curries, best enjoyed on the glass-framed, harbour-side terrace.

✗ Eating

Dibble & Grub   CAFE £
(📞 01720-423719; www.dibbleandgrub.co.uk; Porthcressa; lights meals £6-9; ⊙10am-10pm Apr-Sep; 🍴) At the terrace of Dibble & Grub you're just paces from the sands of Porthcressa beach. The menu gives island ingredients a Mediterranean twist; choose from Cornish pork souvlaki or breakfast ciabatta with Scilly free-range eggs, chased by a zingy raspberry smoothie.

Juliet's Garden   BISTRO ££
(📞 01720-422228; www.julietsgardenrestaurant. co.uk; Seaways/Porthlow; lunch mains £7-15; ⊙10am-5pm; 🍴) St Mary's bistro has been in business for over three decades and is still the best place to eat. Set in a converted barn 15 minutes' walk from town, it's fringed by a glorious, sea-view garden. Gourmet sandwiches feature treacle-glazed salmon and hand-picked local crab, or opt for smoked cheese and spinach on toasted flatbread. They might open early evening too – check the website.

ⓘ Getting Around

Public transport on the island might be affected by distancing regulations. Check with the tourist office (p347) whether the airport bus is running to Hugh Town, and whether the **Island Rover** (☑01720-422131; www.islandrover.co.uk) vintage bus tours are operating.

For taxis on St Mary's, try **Toots** (☑01720-422142; www.tootstaxi.co.uk). Or rent a bike from St Mary's Bike Hire.

Tresco

☑01720 / POP 167

A short boat hop across the channel from St Mary's brings you to Tresco, the second-largest island, once owned by the monks of Tavistock Abbey, and now privately leased by the Dorrien-Smith family from the Duchy of Cornwall.

The main attraction here is the fabulous subtropical garden, but the rest of the island is a lovely place just to explore by bike. The whole place is privately leased, so it feels a little more manicured than the other, more community-driven islands, especially since the focus here is very much on high-end visitors.

◉ Sights

★**Tresco Abbey Garden**   GARDENS
(☑01720-424108; www.tresco.co.uk/enjoying/abbey-garden; adult/child £15/5; ⊙10am-4pm) Tresco's key attraction – and one of Scilly's must-see gems – is this subtropical estate, laid out in 1834 on the site of a 12th-century Benedictine priory by the horticultural visionary Augustus Smith. The 7-hectare gardens are now home to more than 20,000 exotic species, from towering palms to desert cacti and crimson flame trees, all nurtured by the temperate Gulf Stream. Admission also covers the **Valhalla collection**, made up of figureheads and nameplates salvaged from ships wrecked off Tresco.

🛏 Sleeping & Eating

★**New Inn**   PUB, HOTEL **£££**
(☑01720-423006; www.tresco.co.uk; r £175-300; ⊙food noon-2.30pm & 6.30-9pm; 🛜🐾) By Tresco standards, the New Inn is a bargain. The rooms are soothingly finished in buttery yellows and pale blues, although inevitably you'll have to fork out for a view. The inn itself serves tasty food (mains £10 to £18),

with dishes such as mackerel burgers, baked Tresco duck eggs and Bryher-crab mac and cheese.

Ruin Beach   CAFE **££**
(☑01720-424849; www.tresco.co.uk; mains £12-21, pizzas £13-16; ⊙noon-3pm & 6-9pm) With a beach-side terrace, a relaxed vibe and flavoursome food, the Ruin makes for a memorable place to feast on dishes fresh from the wood-fired oven. It's as equally adept at producing beetroot, scallops and peppers as it is crispy pizzas.

Bryher

Only around 80 people live on Bryher, Scilly's smallest and wildest inhabited island. Covered by rough bracken and heather, and fringed by white sand, this slender chunk of rock takes a fearsome battering from the Atlantic – Hell Bay hasn't earned its name for nothing. But on a bright sunny day, it's an island idyll par excellence, ideal for exploring on foot.

The island has a strong sense of community; you'll see little stalls selling freshly cut flowers, homegrown veg, jams and packets of fudge.

🛏 Sleeping & Eating

Bryher Campsite   CAMPSITE **£**
(☑01720-422068; www.bryhercampsite.co.uk; per person £11.50; 🛜) Bare-bones but beautiful, the island's campsite sits in a secluded spot surrounded by drystone walls and is just steps from the sea. Hot showers and tractor transport from the quay are included in the nightly rates. Its four-person bell tents (per week £500 to £565) come complete with kitted-out kitchen, picnic benches and deck chairs.

★**Hell Bay**   HOTEL **£££**
(☑01720-422947; www.hellbay.co.uk; d incl breakfast £360-640; 🅿🛜🐾) Pretty much the poshest place to stay in Scilly, and a true island getaway, Hell Bay blends New England–style furnishings with sunny golds, sea blues and pale wood beams. It has the feel of a luxurious beach villa, with lovingly tended gardens and an excellent restaurant (mains £14 to £25).

The prices here roughly halve in spring and autumn.

Bryher Shop DELI £
(📞01720-423601; www.bryhershop.co.uk; ⊙9am-2pm Mon-Sat) Pick up all your essential supplies at the island's charming general store, which also has a post office. Opening hours may have increased – check the website.

Fraggle Rock CAFE £ £
(📞01720-422222; www.bryher.co; mains £9-16; ⊙9am-9pm; 🎅) This relaxed cafe also doubles as Bryher's pub. The menu is mainly quiches, salads and burgers, ideally served in the front garden, where chickens scratch around and there are views out to Hangman's Rock. It's a lively evening hang-out in season.

St Martin's

📞 01720 / POP 113

The third-largest and furthest north of the islands, St Martin's (www.stmartinsscilly.co.uk) is the main centre for Scilly's flower-growing industry, and the island's fields are a riot of colourful blooms in season. It's also blessed with gin-clear waters and the kind of untouched sands you'd more usually associate with St Lucia than Cornwall.

◉ Sights & Activities

Check whether **Scilly Seal Snorkelling** (📞01720-422848; www.scillysealsnorkelling.com) has resumed its guided swims.

St Martin's Vineyard WINERY
(📞01720-423418; www.stmartinsvineyard.co.uk; Higher Town) The UK's smallest and most southwesterly vineyard produces its own range of organic white, rosé and red wines. If guided tours aren't being held because of distancing measures, self-guided tours (adult/child £7.50/1) and tastings of four wines are available instead. See the website for the latest opening hours.

🛏 Sleeping

Accommodation here is limited apart from a super-expensive hotel and a handful of B&Bs.

St Martin's Campsite CAMPSITE £
(📞01720-422888; www.stmartinscampsite.co.uk; Oaklands Farm, Middletown; per person £11.50-12.50, dogs £3; ⊙Apr-Sep; 🐕) The second-largest campsite in Scilly, at the western end of Lawrence's Bay, has 50 pitches (maximum 100 people) spread across three fields. You'll find showers, stunning sunsets and views of a glittering Milky Way. Book well ahead.

Polreath B&B £ £ £
(📞01720-422046; www.polreath.com; Higher Town; d £140-150; 🎅) This friendly granite cottage has small rooms and a sunny conservatory serving cream teas, homemade lemonade and evening meals. Weekly stays required May to October.

🍴 Eating & Drinking

Island Bakery BAKERY £
(📞01720-42211; www.theislandbakery-stmartins.com; Higher Town; bread & cakes £2-5, pizza £9-12.50; ⊙9am-5pm Mon-Sat Easter-Oct) Gorgeous organic breads, Cornish pasties, pies and takeaway pizzas. Best followed up by homemade cakes.

Adam's Fish & Chips FISH & CHIPS £
(📞01720-423082; www.adamsfishandchips.co.uk; Higher Town; fish & chips takeaway adult/child £10/7; ⊙hours vary) The fish here is about as fresh as it gets – whatever's caught on the day is what ends up in your batter. At the time of writing opening hours and days varied, but orders had to be placed by 5pm. Check for updates at the village shop or call ahead.

Seven Stones PUB
(📞01720-423777; www.sevenstonesinn.com; Lower Town; ⊙11am-3pm & 5-11pm Wed-Mon) St Martin's only boozer is a lively, welcoming place with cracking views over the islands from the terrace and a menu featuring gourmet Stones Burgers, Scilly produce and net-fresh seafood. Food (mains £8 to £14) is served from noon to 2pm and 6pm to 8pm.

St Agnes

📞 01720 / POP 83

Scilly's southernmost island feels really remote, with a string of empty coves and a scattering of prehistoric sites. Visitors disembark at Porth Conger, near the old lighthouse, from where you wander along the coast path around the whole island.

At low tide, a narrow sandbar appears and provides a bridge to the neighbouring island of Gugh, where many ancient burial sites and a few chamber tombs can be found.

🛏 Sleeping & Eating

★ **Troytown Farm** CAMPSITE £

(☎ 01720-422360; www.troytown.co.uk; adult/child £10.25/5.75, tents £2-8) The journey to St Agnes' beach-side campsite is quite an event – you're met at the quay and your luggage is trundled to the campsite by tractor trailer while you make the 15-minute walk. The camping field is small, but wonderfully located on the island's sunset coast, surrounded by drystone walls and a sea-blue, big-sky horizon.

Luggage transfer costs £4 per person. The campsite also rents pre-pitched, four-person bell tents (from £480 to £515 per week) and three two- to four-person self-catering cottages (£385 to £1045 per week). Bring a torch, as the island gets very, very dark.

★ **Turk's Head** PUB FOOD ££

(☎ 01720-422434; The Quay; mains £14-16; ⊙ 10.30am-9pm) You can almost smell the history at Britain's most southerly alehouse. It's covered in maritime memorabilia – model ships in glass cabinets, vintage maps of the islands, black-and-white photos of seafarers. There are few finer places than the cove-side terrace in which to sup a pint.

Hearty food takes in everything from imaginative burgers and curries to mackerel caught on the pub's own boat.

AT A GLANCE

POPULATION
4.3 million

**MILES OF
COASTLINE**
490

BEST VILLAGE
Cley-next-the-Sea
(p383)

BEST BEACH
Holkham National
Nature Reserve
(p386)

**BEST FIVE-STAR
DINNER**
Midsummer House
(p366)

WHEN TO GO

**Apr, May, Sep &
Oct** Mild weather
and fewer crowds;
Cambridge colleges
close April to June
for exams.

Jun–Aug Warm
weather and
festivals, but prices
peak and things get
busy on the coast.

Nov & Dec Music
fills Cambridge's
King's College
Chapel in Decem-
ber; Christmas
services at
medieval churches
everywhere.

Ely Cathedral (p368)
NASTYA ARSENTYEVA/SHUTTERSTOCK ©

Cambridge & East Anglia

Bulging gently eastwards towards the sea, the vast flatlands of East Anglia were once one of the wealthiest parts of the country, before reverting to backwater status during the Industrial Revolution. Farmers relied on working horses here as recently as the 1960s, and tales of witchcraft still permeate the folklore of this agreeably traditional corner of the country.

For visitors, East Anglia is best known for its rich Roman, Saxon, Viking and medieval history, its sweeping sandy beaches and bucolic rural landscapes that once inspired Constable and Gainsborough. Against this rustic backdrop, the dynamic university city of Cambridge rises out of the Fens like a beacon.

Cambridge & East Anglia Highlights

1 **Cambridge** (p357) Punting along the Granta before poking a nose into the historic colleges of Cambridge University.

2 **Sandringham** (p387) Pulling back the curtain on royal life in the Queen's country estate.

3 **Norfolk Broads** (p384) Canoeing or boating through tranquil waterways with swans and windmills for company.

4 **Holkham** (p386) Admiring the lavish excess of the grand Palladian home, before tottering over to the endless sands of Holkham Beach.

5 **Lavenham** (p374) Weaving between the leaning timbered houses of this museum-piece medieval market town.

6 **Norwich** (p379) Mixing history and culture in this elegant, historic wool city, home to one of England's grandest cathedrals.

7 **Aldeburgh** (p376) Dining on spray-fresh seafood and walking the prom in this agreeably gentle seaside town.

8 **Imperial War Museum** (p366) Unleashing your inner plane-spotter in the aircraft-filled hangers of this remarkable military museum.

History

Stone Age peoples, Romans, Vikings and Saxons laid the foundations for what would later become East Anglia, but the region's heyday came with the wool boom of the Middle Ages when Flemish weavers settled in the area. Wealth from the wool trade paid for the construction of grand churches, guildhalls and cathedrals, and the foundation of the first colleges of Cambridge University.

By the 17th century, large parts of the Fens had been drained and converted into arable land, and locals turned their attention to revolution. Oliver Cromwell, the uncrowned king of the Parliamentarians, was a small-time merchant residing in Ely when he answered God's call to take up arms and remove Charles I from the throne.

East Anglia's fortunes waned in the 18th century, as the money shifted north to Industrial Revolution towns in northern England. The region reverted to a quiet backwater, but experienced a minor revival during WWII as new British and American airbases were founded to aid the fight against Nazi Germany.

Activities

With its flat terrain and waterways, East Anglia is a magnet for walkers, cyclists, boaters and kayakers.

Walking

Linking Knettishall Heath, near Thetford, to Cromer, the **Peddars Way and Norfolk Coast Path** (www.nationaltrail.co.uk) is a seven-day, 93-mile national trail that meanders between the fishing villages of the North Norfolk coast.

Curving further south, the 50-mile **Suffolk Coast Path** (www.ldwa.org.uk) links Felixstowe and Lowestoft, via Snape Maltings, Orford, Aldeburgh, Dunwich and Southwold.

Cycling

Mountain bikers head for Norfolk's **Thetford Forest** (www.forestryengland.uk/thetford-forest) `FREE`, while much of the popular on- and off-road **Peddars Way** path is also open to cyclists.

Boating & Canoeing

East Anglia's coast and the Norfolk Broads are a playground for boating enthusiasts – those without their own craft can easily hire boats and canoes and arrange lessons at inland hubs such as Wroxham or along the coast.

ℹ️ Information

Visit East of England (www.visiteastofengland.com) provides regionwide info, or contact the individual county tourist boards.

ℹ️ Getting There & Around

Trains and buses provide easy links into and around East Anglia, though many bus services stop on Sundays.

AIR

London Stansted Airport (www.stanstedairport.com; Stansted Mountfichet, Essex) (actually closer to Cambridge) and **Norwich International Airport** (☑ 01603-411923; www.norwichairport.co.uk; Holt Rd) are the main air hubs. Stansted has connections worldwide, while Norwich mainly serves domestic destinations.

BUS

First (www.firstgroup.com) and **Stagecoach** (www.stagecoachbus.com) run the bulk of the region's bus networks, with local companies connecting smaller towns and villages.

TRAIN

Greater Anglia (www.greateranglia.co.uk) runs most services into and around East Anglia; the **Anglia Plus Pass** is valid for a week; you can pay to use it for one day (£24.70) or three days (£49.40) within that time.

CAMBRIDGESHIRE

Many visitors to Cambridgeshire never make it outside the handsome university city of Cambridge, sucked in by the gravitational pull of its history, culture and architecture. But beyond this breathtaking seat of learning lie the flat Fens, offering fine walking and cycling, the extraordinary cathedral at Ely and the rip-roaring Imperial War Museum at Duxford.

Cambridge

 01223 / POP 136,800

England's second great university was founded just a few decades after Oxford, its arch-rival at the top of the national university tables, and the city that surrounds it swims with medieval magnificence. Like Oxford, Cambridge is a sophisticated seat of learning, and a hotbed of archaic academic traditions. Also like Oxford, the old centre is peppered with handsome historic buildings, and the streets are friendly to cyclists and pedestrians and unfriendly to cars – wise travellers come by bus or train.

Perhaps the most striking thing about Cambridge, once you get over the initial wow-factor of the colleges and historic buildings, is the way the countryside seems to spill into the city centre. The looping River Cam – known in the centre as the Granta – is lined with green parks and patches of common land, some still used for grazing livestock, lending the city a surprisingly rural mood.

History

Cambridge has been inhabited since at least the Iron Age, but its fortunes soared in the 11th century, when an Augustinian order of monks set up shop here, creating religious seats of learning that later morphed into the colleges of Cambridge University.

When the rival university town of Oxford exploded in a riot between town and gown in 1209, many scholars upped sticks to Cambridge, cementing the city's reputation and prestige. The first proper Cambridge college, Peterhouse (never Peterhouse *College*), was founded in 1284, and in 1318 Pope John XXII declared Cambridge to be an official university by papal bull.

By the 14th century, colleges had proliferated across the city, and the colleges continued to be a powerful patriarchy right up until 1869, when the first women-only college was established. By 1948, Cambridge minds had broadened sufficiently to allow women to actually graduate!

⊙ Sights

As well as the famous colleges and museums, look out for the golden **Corpus Clock** (Bene't St) just south of King's College, which displays the time through a series of concentric LED lights, while a hideous-looking insect 'time-eater' inches across the top of the dial.

If you need to catch your breath, take a picnic to **Jesus Green** (Park Parade), a lovely stretch of parkland tucked into a curve of the Granta.

★**King's College Chapel**   CHURCH
(☏01223-331100; www.kings.cam.ac.uk; King's Pde; adult/child £10/8; ⊙9.30am-3.15pm Mon-Sat, 1.15-2.30pm Sun term time, 9.30am-4.30pm rest of year) This grandiose, limestone-faced, 16th-century chapel is one of England's most extraordinary Gothic monuments. During services, the sound of the chapel's famous choir reverberates off the walls and rises to an almost impossibly intricate fan-vaulted ceiling – the world's largest. Think of it as a firework display, expressed as architecture. At the time of writing, the chapel was only open at set times – check ahead for the latest opening times.

Founded in 1446 as an act of piety by Henry VI, the chapel was only finished by Henry VIII around 1516, and lofty **stained-glass windows** flank the chapel's sides, filling the interior with light. The glass is original, reputedly spared from the excesses of England's 17th-century Civil War thanks to a personal order from Oliver Cromwell, himself a Cambridge graduate.

The antechapel and the choir are divided by a superbly carved **wooden screen**, designed and executed by Peter Stockton for Henry VIII. Look for the king's initials entwined with those of Anne Boleyn on the screen. Beyond, the high **altar** is framed by Rubens' masterpiece *Adoration of the Magi* (1634). To the left of the altar in the side chapels, an **exhibition** charts the construction of this landmark monument.

Under normal circumstances, visitors congregate here for **Evensong** (5.30pm Monday to Saturday, 10.30am and 3.30pm Sunday). Each Christmas Eve, King's College Chapel stages the **Festival of Nine Lessons & Carols**, broadcast globally by the BBC.

★**Trinity College**   COLLEGE
(☏01223-338400; www.trin.cam.ac.uk; Trinity St) The largest of Cambridge's colleges, Trinity grabs attention with an extraordinary

A VERY LEARNED BOOKSTORE

Facing the grand chapel of King's College, the **Cambridge University Press** (www.cambridge.org; 1-2 Trinity St; ⊙10am-5.30pm Mon Sat, 11am-5pm Sun) is the oldest university press in the world – founded by royal charter from Henry VIII in 1534. It's also the official printer of the British monarchy. With Cambridge being at the frontline of academic thinking and research, it's always worth popping in to read the latest on everything from gender rights to quantum field theory.

Cambridge

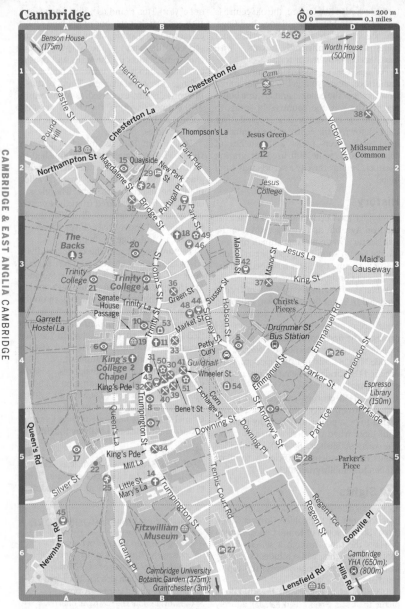

Tudor gateway, capped by a stern-looking statue of the college founder, Henry VIII. Beyond lies the vast Great Court flanked by cloisters and Gothic halls and spires. The famous, musty **Wren Library** contains more than 55,000 books published before 1820, including works by Shakespeare, St Jerome, Newton and Swift and an original *Winnie the Pooh* (both AA Milne and his son, Christopher Robin, were graduates).

Cambridge

CAMBRIDGE & EAST ANGLIA CAMBRIDGE

As you enter Trinity through the part-gilded gate, take a closer look at the **statue** of the college's founder. The king holds a golden orb in his left hand, while his right grips not the original sceptre but a table leg, put there by student pranksters and never replaced.

The expansive **Great Court** is ringed by grand architecture. To the right of the entrance is a small tree, said to be a descendant of the apple tree made famous by Trinity alumnus Sir Isaac Newton. Other alumni include Francis Bacon, Lord Byron, Tennyson and HRH Prince Charles.

Across from the main gate is the college's Hogwarts-like **hall**, with its dramatic hammerbeam roof and lantern. Behind are the dignified cloisters of **Nevile's Court**, while to the right is the college's imposing 16th-century **chapel**.

★**Fitzwilliam Museum**   MUSEUM
(www.fitzmuseum.cam.ac.uk; Trumpington St; by donation; ⊙10am-5pm Tue-Sat, from noon Sun) Fondly dubbed 'the Fitz' by locals, this colossal neoclassical treasure house was one of the first public art museums in Britain, built to house the fabulous collection that the seventh Viscount Fitzwilliam bequeathed to his old university. There are obvious parallels to the British Museum, and highlights include Roman, Egyptian and Cypriot grave goods, artworks by great masters and one of the country's finest collections of ancient, medieval and modern pottery.

The **lower galleries** are filled with priceless treasures spanning the ancient world; look for the Roman-era 'Swiss army knife', intricate suits of armour, and Roman coffins intricately carved with scenes of bacchanalian excess.

The upper galleries showcase works by Leonardo da Vinci, Titian, Rubens, the impressionists, Gainsborough, Constable, Rembrandt and Picasso.

Guided tours of the museum were suspended at the time of research – check ahead to see if they have resumed.

★ The Backs   PARK
The rear ends of the grand colleges along King's Pde spill onto the banks of the river in a long sweep of parks, gardens and even grazing pastures for livestock. Collectively known as the Backs, these genteel spaces are abuzz with student activity. While the colleges are closed, the Backs are best glimpsed from the pathways and bridges along the Granta or from the comfort of a rented or chauffeured punt. When the colleges reopen, visitors should be free to explore these spaces more fully.

If you're exploring from the water, check out the famous, fanciful Bridge of Sighs in the grounds of St John's College (p362), and the nearby Kitchen Bridge, designed by Christopher Wren. The oldest river crossing is at Clare College (☑01223-333200; www.clare.cam.ac.uk; Trinity Lane), built in 1639 and ornamented with decorative balls (one allegedly vandalised by its architect in protest at the measly fee he was paid).

Most curious of all is the flimsy-looking wooden Mathematical Bridge (visible from Silver St) that joins the two halves of Queens' College (p362). It was first built in 1749 using what were then world-leading engineering principles.

Gonville & Caius College   COLLEGE
(☑01223-332400; www.cai.cam.ac.uk; Trinity St) Known locally as Caius (pronounced 'keys'), Gonville and Caius boasts three fascinating gates – known as Virtue, Humility and Honour – symbolising the progress of the good student. Down the alley beside the college, the Porta Honoris (an occult-looking, sundial-topped confection that pays a nod to the Treasury at Petra in Jordan) leads to the Senate House (Senate House Passage) and thus graduation.

The college was actually founded twice, first by a priest called Gonville, in 1348, and then again in 1557 by Dr Caius (a Latin-version of the name Keys), a brilliant physician who undermined his legacy by insisting in the statutes that the college admit no 'deaf, dumb, deformed, lame, chronic invalids, or Welshmen'.

Former students include Francis Crick (of DNA-discoverers Crick and Watson) and the late, great Stephen Hawking, who was a fellow here for more than 50 years.

Christ's College   COLLEGE
(☑01223-334900; www.christs.cam.ac.uk; St Andrew's St) Christ's College has been educating the great and the good for 500 years and the gleaming Great Gate is emblazoned with heraldic carvings of Tudor roses, a portcullis and spotted Beaufort yale (mythical antelope-like creatures). Its founder, Lady Margaret Beaufort, mother of Henry VII, hovers above like a guiding spirit. A stout oak door leads into picturesque First Court, Cambridge's only circular front court.

Dedicated to alumnus Charles Darwin, the college gardens feature plant species brought back from his famous Galapagos voyage. The Second Court has a gate to the Fellows' Garden (open Monday to Friday only), which contains a mulberry tree under which 17th-century poet John Milton reputedly wrote Lycidas.

Magdalene College   COLLEGE
(☑01223-332100; www.magd.cam.ac.uk; Magdalene St) A former Benedictine hostel, riverside Magdalene – properly pronounced 'Maud-lyn' – is home to the famous Pepys Library (☑01223-332115) FREE, housing 3000 books bequeathed by the mid-17th-century diarist to his old college. This idiosyncratic library covers everything from illuminated medieval manuscripts to the Anthony Roll, a 1540s depiction of the Royal Navy's ships.

Emmanuel College   COLLEGE
(☑01223-334200; www.emma.cam.ac.uk; St Andrew's St) Looking rather unadorned from the outside, the 16th-century Emmanuel College ('Emma' to students) is famous for its exquisite chapel designed by Sir Christopher Wren. Seek out the plaque commemorating John Harvard, a scholar here in the 1630s, who later settled in New England and left his money to a certain Cambridge College in Massachusetts – now Harvard University.

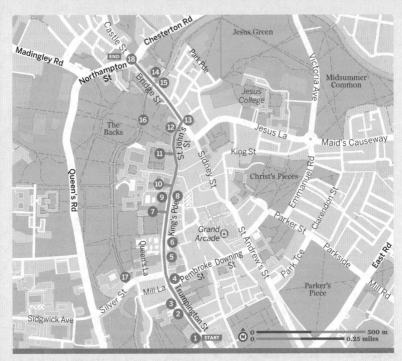

City Walk
The Colleges and the Backs

START FITZWILLIAM MUSEUM
END KETTLE'S YARD
LENGTH 3 MILES; FOUR HOURS

To start your exploration of this most learned of cities, brush up your knowledge at the **1 Fitzwilliam Museum** (p359) amid mummies and old masters. Follow Trumpington St north past **2 Peterhouse**, Cambridge's oldest college, and **3 Little St Mary's** (p363), one of the city's oldest churches. Pause for a Chelsea bun break at **4 Fitzbillies** (p365), the city's favourite bakery, then continue north past **5 Corpus Christi College** (p362), former stomping ground of Christopher Marlowe, and note the Harry Potter-esque **6 Corpus Clock** (p357) on the corner. Just beyond lies **7 King's College Chapel** (p357), arguably the crown and sceptre in Cambridge's architectural crown jewels.

Cross the road to **8 Great St Mary's Church** (p363), where a steep climb up the tower will deliver Cambridge's most spectacular views. Continue past the neo-classical **9 Senate House** and nip right into Senate House Passage to view the occult-looking Porta Honoris, the most impressive of the three gateways to **10 Gonville & Caius College**. Next comes **11 Trinity College** (p357); if it's open, duck through the Tudor gateway to view the extraordinary collection of tomes in the Wren Library. Continue along St John's St past the arms-topped gatehouse of **12 St John's College** (p362) to reach the **13 Round Church** (p362), an enigmatic, Templar relic.

Follow Bridge St and Magdalene St towards **14 Magdalene College** and rent a punt from **15 Scudamore's** (p363) at Quayside for a behind-the-scenes tour of the college Backs (look out for the ecclesiastical-looking **16 Bridge of Sighs** and the skeletal timbers of the **17 Mathematical Bridge**). Return your punt to Quayside and end as you started, surrounded by artworks, in the light-filled spaces of **18 Kettle's Yard** (p362).

❶ VISITING CAMBRIDGE'S COLLEGES

Cambridge University comprises 31 colleges, and under normal circumstances, most welcome visitors. However, all the colleges closed temporarily to outsiders during the pandemic.

The colleges are expected to reopen as the situation improves, and assuming this happens, visitors should once again be allowed to explore the college compounds and gardens and specific buildings. However, every year, the colleges close to visitors over the two-week Christmas break, and also while students are preparing for and sitting exams, between early April and mid-June.

Visits are at the discretion of the college porters (gatekeepers who look after the day-to-day running of the colleges), so contact colleges in advance to check current opening times and admission fees.

Queens' College COLLEGE

(☑01223-335511; www.queens.cam.ac.uk; Silver St) Genteel 15th-century Queens' College sits elegantly astride the river; the two halves of the college are connected by the precarious-looking **Mathematical Bridge**, best viewed from the Backs (p360). Highlights include two elegant medieval courtyards and the beautiful half-timbered **President's Lodge**. Dutch scholar and reformer Desiderius Erasmus, whose name was later taken for the European student exchange program, studied here from 1510 to 1514.

Corpus Christi College COLLEGE

(☑01223-338000; www.corpus.cam.ac.uk; King's Pde) Graceful Corpus Christi was founded in 1352, a heritage reflected in its venerable buildings and monastic atmosphere. Within the medieval **Old Court**, note the fascinating sundial and plaque to past student Christopher Marlowe (1564–93), author of *Doctor Faustus* and *Tamburlaine*. The less dramatic **New Court** (a mere 200 years old) leads to the **Parker Library**, which holds the world's finest collection of Anglo-Saxon manuscripts (open only to visitors on guided city tours).

St John's College COLLEGE

(☑01223-33860; www.joh.cam.ac.uk; St John's St) Alma mater of six prime ministers (including India's Manmohan Singh), poet William Wordsworth, anti-slavery campaigner William Wilberforce and Douglas Adams (author of *The Hitchhiker's Guide to the Galaxy*), St John's is highly photogenic. Founded in 1511 by Henry VII's mother, Margaret Beaufort, it sprawls along both riverbanks, connected by the ecclesiastical-looking **Bridge of Sighs**, a masterpiece of stone tracery and a common focus for student pranks.

Cambridge University Botanic Garden GARDENS

(☑01223-336265; www.botanic.cam.ac.uk; 1 Brookside; adult/child £6.60/free; ◷10am-6pm Apr-Sep, to 5pm Feb, Mar & Oct, to 4pm Nov-Jan; ♿) ☙ Founded by Charles Darwin's mentor, Professor John Henslow, the beautiful Botanic Garden is a gorgeous green expanse, full of hidden corners, tiny paths and secret spaces. There are more than 8000 plant species here, from mature trees in the arboretum to an army of carnivorous pitcher plants in Victorian-era greenhouses. Under normal circumstances, hour-long guided tours (free) run from May through to September; check to see if they've resumed.

The gardens are 1200m south of the city centre, accessible from either Trumpington Rd or Hills Rd.

Kettle's Yard GALLERY

(☑01223-748100; www.kettlesyard.co.uk; Castle St; ◷11am-5pm Wed-Sun) FREE If you've ever wondered what art gallery curators do at home, pop into Kettle's Yard, a living art gallery created by HS 'Jim' Ede, a former curator at the Tate Gallery in London. A lifetime's collection of artworks and found objects is displayed inside a line of elegantly converted cottages, including works by Miró, Henry Moore and lesser-known artists such as WWI-era sculptor Henri Gaudier-Brzeska and primitive nautical artist Alfred Wallis.

A modern annexe showcases some quirky contemporary exhibitions.

Round Church CHURCH

(☑01223-311602; www.roundchurchcambridge.org; Bridge St; £3.50; ◷10am-4.30pm Fri & Sat, from 12.30pm Sun) Looking like a prime setting for a Dan Brown novel, Cambridge's atmospheric Round Church is one of only four round medieval churches in England. It was built by the mysterious Knights Templar in 1130, making it older than the university, and the unusual circular knave is ringed by chunky Norman pillars. Guided walks explore the church and local area, leaving on Saturday and Sunday at 2.15pm.

Great St Mary's Church   CHURCH
(☑ 01223-747273; www.gsm.cam.ac.uk; Senate House Hill; tower per person/family £6/16; ⊗ 11am-5pm Tue-Sun) **FREE** The foundations of Cambridge's sublime university church date from 1010, but it burnt to the ground in the 1290s, so most of what you can see today comes from a 1351 reconstruction and a grand Gothic remodelling from 1478 to 1519. The melody of its chiming clock was copied for the chimes of Big Ben in London.

The tower was added in 1690; buy a ticket to climb it for truly awe-inspiring views over Cambridge's dreaming spires. Check out the 3D model outside before you head up so you know what you're looking at.

Little St Mary's Church   CHURCH
(☑ 01223-366202; www.lsm.org.uk; Trumpington St; ⊗ 8am-6pm) **FREE** This small, modest-looking church was formerly St Peter's-without-Trumpington-Gate, giving nearby Peterhouse its name. Inside is a memorial to student Godfrey Washington, great-uncle of George. His family coat of arms was the stars and stripes, reputedly the inspiration for the US flag. Check ahead to see if it is admitting visitors.

Polar Museum   MUSEUM
(☑ 01223-336540; www.spri.cam.ac.uk/museum; Lensfield Rd) **FREE** In this compelling university museum, the trials, victories and tragic mistakes of such great Polar explorers as Roald Amundsen, Ernest Shackleton and Captain Scott are powerfully evoked, using paintings, photographs, equipment, maps, journals and even last messages left for loved ones. The museum was temporarily closed in 2020 – check ahead for the latest opening times.

 Activities

Scudamore's Punting   BOATING
(☑ 01223-359750; www.scudamores.com; Mill Lane; chauffeured punt trips per bench/boat from £70/120, 6-person punt hire from £51; ⊗ 10am-7pm Mon-Fri, to 8pm Sat & Sun) At this long-established operator, you can hire punts to pole

yourself along the Granta, or take chauffeured trips to Granchester and the Backs. Prices are flexible and staff cruise the jetty offering discounts. Note that you can hire just a row of seats to reduce rates.

It has a second hire station north of the centre at Quayside.

Cambridge Chauffeur Punts   BOATING
(☑ 01223-354164; www.punting-in-cambridge. co.uk; Silver St Bridge; chauffeured punts from adult/child £20/12 per hour, 6-person self-punt per hour £30; ⊗ 9am-8pm Jun & Aug, 10am-dusk Apr, May, Sep & Oct) Runs regular chauffeured punting tours of the Backs and to Granchester; also offers self-hire.

Jesus Green Lido   SWIMMING
(☑ 01223-302579; www.better.org.uk; Jesus Green; adult/child £5/2.50; ⊗ 7am-7pm Mon-Fri, 10am-6pm Sat & Sun May-Sep) This slender, 1920s open-air swimming pool near the river in Jesus Green is unheated, but hugely popular, with sunbathers as well as swimmers.

 Tours

With the (hopefully temporary) closure of the tourist office, **walking tours** run by official Blue Badge and Green Badge guides run from beside the Guildhall on Peas Hill at 11am and 1.30pm (one hour tour adult/child £10/5), taking in the main sights.

GREAT GRADUATES

The honour roll of famous Cambridge students and academics is an international who's who of high achievers. This is the town where Newton refined his theory of gravity, where Whipple invented the jet engine, where Stephen Hawking wrote *A Brief History of Time*, where Crick and Watson (relying heavily on the work of Rosalind Franklin, also a scientist at Cambridge) discovered DNA.

Alongside Britain's favourite comedians – everyone from Rowan Atkinson to the Monty Python team found an audience thanks to the university's Footlights Dramatic Club – you'll find 98 Nobel Prize winners (more than any other institution in the world), 13 British prime ministers, nine archbishops of Canterbury, plus an immense number of scientists, poets and authors.

PRANKSTERS & NIGHT CLIMBERS

In a city of intellectual high achievement, it shouldn't be entirely surprising to find students turning their great minds to pranks and mischief. The most impressive prank ever to take place in Cambridge – lifting an Austin Seven van on to the roof of the landmark Senate House (p360) in 1958 – involved a great deal of planning from four Mechanical Sciences students; copycats later suspended another Austin Seven from the ornate Bridge of Sighs (p362).

King's College has long been a target of 'night climbers'. A Trinity College student, Geoffrey Winthrop Young, wrote the definitive *Roof Climber's Guide to Trinity* back in 1900. Cast an eye upwards towards the nearby pinnacles of King's College Chapel (p357) and you'll often spot out-of-place objects – anything from traffic cones to Santa hats.

Finally, there's the Cubes (Cambridge University Breaking and Entering Society): its objective is to access places members shouldn't be and leave distinctive calling cards – the most famous being the wooden mallard in the rafters of Trinity's Great Hall.

★ Festivals & Events

Bumps
SPORTS
(www.cucbc.org/bumps; ☉ Feb & Jun) Traditional rowing races along the Cam (or the Granta, as the Cambridge stretch is called), in which college boat clubs compete to 'bump' the crew in front.

Beer Festival
BEER
(www.cambridgebeerfestival.com; ☉ May) Hugely popular five-day beer and cider extravaganza on Jesus Green, featuring brews from all over the country.

Folk Festival
MUSIC
(www.cambridgefolkfestival.co.uk; ☉ late Jul-early Aug) This acclaimed four-day festival pushes the envelope of what is usually classified as folk music. It's hosted by Cherry Hinton Hall, 4 miles southeast of the city centre.

⊨ Sleeping

Cambridge YHA
HOSTEL £
(☎ 0345-371 9728; www.yha.org.uk; 97 Tenison Rd; r £35-49; @ ☜) A smart, friendly and deservedly popular hostel with compact rooms (and dorms, but these were closed during the pandemic) and good facilities. Handily, it's very near the train station.

Rosa's
B&B £
(☎ 01223-512596; www.rosasbedandbreakfast. co.uk; 53 Roseford Rd; s £65; P ☜; ☐ 8) Handy for solo travellers: a friendly, family-run B&B with three bright, snug singles, decorated in calming tones. It's 2 miles north of the city centre; bus 8 runs nearby.

Worth House
B&B ££
(☎ 01223-316074; www.worth-house.co.uk; 152 Chesterton Rd; s/d/tr from £100/110/150; P ☜) The welcome is warm and the rooms are delightful at this friendly, upbeat B&B. In the rooms, cool greys and whites meet flashes of colour, bathrooms have a hint of glam and the breakfast is a feast.

Benson House
B&B ££
(☎ 01223-311594; www.bensonhouse.co.uk; 24 Huntingdon Rd; s/d from £80/125; P ☜) Little things lift Benson a cut above the average B&B – think real feather pillows, tasteful textiles, tea served from Royal Doulton china and award-winning breakfasts.

★ University Arms Hotel
LUXURY HOTEL £££
(☎ 01223-606066; www.universityarms.com; Regent St; r from £240) This extravagant but refined hotel looks as old as the Cambridge colleges, but the grand frontage is actually a skilful reconstruction of a historic wing that was demolished to build a modern eyesore in the 1960s. Inside, the hotel oozes class, and the best rooms have fabulous bathrooms with free-standing bathtubs and views over Parker's Piece common.

★ Varsity Hotel
BOUTIQUE HOTEL £££
(☎ 01223-306030; www.thevarsityhotel.co.uk; Thompson's Lane; d £190-325; ✳ @ ☜) Modernist Varsity soars above the old part of Cambridge, topped by a terrace (p366) with eye-popping views. The 44 sleek rooms come with designer flourishes such as parquet floors, roll-top baths and floor-to-ceiling windows, plus espresso machines, smartphone docks and other hip tech – an elegant experience all round.

★**Duke House**   B&B **£££**

(📞01223-314773; www.dukehousecambridge.co.uk; 1 Victoria St; apt from £110, r from £140; 🅿🛜) Set in the house owned by the Duke of Gloucester when he was a student at Magdalene College, this beautifully styled B&B has gleaming white rooms with elegant armchairs and floral chandeliers, a gorgeous pale blue lounge and a roof terrace. It's just outside the hubbub near Christ's Pieces.

Hotel du Vin   BOUTIQUE HOTEL **£££**

(📞01223-928991; www.hotelduvin.com; 15-19 Trumpington St; d/ste from £150/240; @🛜) This maze-like luxe hotel near the 'Fitz' oozes history, as well it should – it's spread over five Georgian mansions formerly owned by the University of Cambridge. Reached via narrow corridors, the atmospheric rooms have free-standing roll-top baths, monsoon showers and floating-on-air beds. Other perks include a cosy cellar bar and a cool bistro (mains £16 to £23).

Eating

For cheap eats, join the students cruising the line of Asian and Middle Eastern restaurants east of the centre on **Mill Road**, or try the street food in the central **market** (Market Hill; ⏱10am-4pm Mon-Sat).

Fitzbillies   CAFE **£**

(www.fitzbillies.com; 52 Trumpington St; mains £5-15; ⏱8.30am-5pm Mon-Fri, 9am-5.30pm Sat & Sun) Cambridge's oldest bakery has a soft, doughy place in the hearts of generations of students. Its stock-in-trade is sticky Chelsea buns and cream teas (available to eat in or beautifully boxed to take away), but it also serves upmarket sandwiches, bacon rolls, English breakfasts and salads.

There's a smaller **branch** (www.fitzbillies.com; 36 Bridge St; light mains £5-15; ⏱8.30am-5pm Mon-Fri, 9am-6pm Sat & Sun) on Bridge St.

Aromi   ITALIAN **£**

(📞01223-300117; www.aromi.co.uk; 1 Bene't St; mains from £5; ⏱9am-7pm Sun-Thu, to 9pm Fri & Sat; 🍴) A pocket-sized bakery cafe with downstairs seating and a ground-floor counter stacked with delectable sourdough sandwiches and Sicilian pizzas, topped with parma ham, rucola and the like, and sold by the slice.

Aromi has another **cafe** (www.aromi.co.uk; Peas Hill; snacks from £5; ⏱11am-9pm) and gelateria (with great ice cream) just a few doors down on Peas Hill.

Espresso Library   CAFE **£**

(📞01223-367333; www.espressolibrary.com; 210 East Rd; mains £6-15; ⏱8am-4pm; 🛜🍴) Customers with laptops at almost every table send a signal that this industrial-chic cafe is a student favourite. Thank the coffee, the cyclist-friendly attitude, and the wholesome food – sourdough sandwiches, soups, frittata and shaksuka.

Locker   CAFE **£**

(www.thelockercafe.co.uk; 54 King St; snacks £3.50-7.50; ⏱8.30am-5.30pm Mon-Fri, from 9.30am Sat, 10am-4pm Sun; 🛜🍴) 🌱 Fair-trade coffee, salmon bagels, and avocados (and other things) smashed on sourdough toast lift this artsy, wholesome cafe above the herd. Its toasties have a faithful student following.

It's also home to occasional gigs and photography displays.

Pint Shop   MODERN BRITISH **££**

(📞01223-981070; www.pintshop.co.uk; 10 Peas Hill; 2/3 courses £22/26; ⏱noon-9pm Mon-Wed, to 10pm Thu-Sat, to 6pm Sun) Popular Pint Shop is part craft-beer sampling house, part hearty kitchen. Wash down tasty pub grub (charred salmon, burgers, flatbread kebabs) with artisan ciders, ales and fruit beers (including coconut, passionfruit and mango).

Smokeworks   BARBECUE **££**

(📞01223-365385; www.smokeworks.co.uk; 2 Free School Lane; mains £7.50-19.50; ⏱noon-8pm Mon & Tue, to 9pm Wed-Sat, to 5pm Sun; 🛜) This dark, industrial-looking dining room draws a young, hip crowd of carnivores with melt-in-your-mouth rib racks, wings and wonderfully smoky pulled pork. For drinks, try the house beers or salted-caramel milkshakes in glasses the size of your head.

TIME FOR TEA

Packed afternoon teas – sandwiches, scones, pastries, buns, and a hint of the 1920s – are all the rage in Cambridge. Pick your park and grab a gorgeously boxed afternoon tea to go from **Harriet's Cafe Tearooms** (www.harrietscafetearooms.co.uk; 16-17 Green St; cakes & sandwiches from £3, afternoon tea from £12.95; ⏱10am-3.30pm Mon-Fri, 9.30am-4.30pm Sat, 10.30am-3.30pm Sun) or Fitzbillies, who also serve similarly packaged Chelsea buns.

IMPERIAL WAR MUSEUM

Plane-spotters will be in aviation heaven at the **Imperial War Museum** (☑ 01223-835000; www.iwm. org.uk; Duxford; adult/child including donation £19.80/9.90; ☉ 10am-6pm; [P] [★]). Europe's biggest aircraft museum, with around 200 vintage aircraft – many veterans of WWI and WWII – spread across a series of enormous hangars. You'll see everything from dive bombers to biplanes, Hurricanes and the Concorde, which was moved here after ending service in 2003. The awe-inspiring **American Air Museum** hangar pays homage to US WWII servicemen and planes.

Cambridge Chop House   BRITISH ££
(☑ 01223-359506; www.cambscuisine.com/cambridge-chop-house; 1 King's Pde; mains £17-27; ☉ 11.30am-8.30pm Mon-Fri, to 9pm Fri & Sat, to 5pm Sun) The window seats here look right onto King's College and the food is pure English establishment: hearty steaks, grilled chops, breaded coley, roast meats and grilled lobster. Schedule a long walk afterwards to burn off the calories.

Sticks'n'Sushi   SUSHI ££
(☑ 01223-907900; www.sticksnsushi.com; 2 Wheeler St; mains £10-25; ☉ noon-9pm Mon-Thu, to 10pm Fri & Sat) Lovely soy-saucy smells linger around the entrance to this Asian restaurant. Although part of a Danish-Japanese chain, it's chic and vaguely New York-ey; the menu runs from sushi and sashimi bites to meaty skewers.

★ Midsummer House   MODERN BRITISH £££
(☑ 01223-369299; www.midsummerhouse.co.uk; Midsummer Common; set lunch/tasting menu £115/230; ☉ 10am-5pm Wed-Sat) A lone house in parkland beside the Granta, the region's top table shows off the culinary creativity of chef Daniel Clifford, recipient of two Michelin stars. Set menus, which include champagne and hot infusions or coffee, might include such delights as salted beetroot with venison tartare and buttermilk poached Cornish cod with champagne beurre blanc.

🍷 Drinking & Nightlife

★ Roof Terrace   BAR
(☑ 01223-306030; www.thevarsityhotel.co.uk; Varsity Hotel, Thompson's Lane; ☉ 2pm-10pm Mon-Thu, from noon Fri & Sat) The rooftop terrace at the Varsity Hotel (p364) is an achingly cool eyrie perched high above the old town, and people flood here every afternoon for sundowners looking out over the rooftops. Smart dress recommended.

★ Cambridge Brew House   MICROBREWERY
(☑ 01223-855185; www.thecambridgebrewhouse. com; 1 King St; ☉ 4-10pm Mon-Fri, noon-11pm Sat, noon-10pm Sun) Order a pint here and there's a good chance it'll have been brewed in the gleaming vats beside the bar. Add a buzzy vibe, eclectic upcycled decor, dirty burgers and British tapas (mains from £10) and you have the kind of pub you wish was just down your road.

Eagle   PUB
(☑ 01223-505020; www.eagle-cambridge.co.uk; Bene't St; ☉ 11am-11pm Mon-Thu, to midnight Fri & Sat, to 10.30pm Sun; 🔊 ★) Cambridge's most famous pub has loosened the tongues of many an illustrious academic, among them Nobel Prize–winning scientists Crick and Watson, who discussed their research into DNA here. The interior is 15th-century, wood-panelled and rambling; note the WWII airmen's signatures on the ceiling.

Hidden Rooms   COCKTAIL BAR
(☑ 01223-514777; www.hiddenrooms.co.uk; 7b Jesus Lane; ☉ 6.30-10pm Fri & Sat) Hard to find – the name is no accident – this is a cocktail bar for aficionados of the craft. It's under Pizza Express, but the moody leather booths feel like stepping into a David Lynch movie. Reserve ahead.

Ta Bouche   COCKTAIL BAR
(www.tabouche.co.uk; 10-15 Market Passage; ☉ 9.30am-1am Mon-Thu, to 2am Fri & Sat, 10am-midnight Sun) A carnival-coloured, fun-filled cocktail bar that pulls in a crowd on any going-out night, with good-value specials that appeal to student pocketbooks. It serves globe-trotting street food by day, cocktails by night.

Maypole   PUB
(☑ 01223-352999; www.maypolefreehouse.co.uk; 20a Portugal Pl; ☉ noon-2pm & 5-11pm Tue-Thu, noon-11pm Fri & Sat, noon-3pm Sun) A dozen pumps dispensing real ale, artisan gin, a roomy beer garden and a friendly, unreconstructed vibe make this red-brick pub a student favourite. There's hearty, homemade Italian food.

Granta

PUB

(01223-505016; 14 Newnham Rd; ⏰11am-11pm Sun-Thu, to 11.30pm Fri & Sat) The exterior of this picturesque waterside pub, overhanging a pretty mill pond, may look familiar from its cameos in TV dramas. With its snug deck, riverside terrace and punts moored up alongside, it's an atmospheric spot to sit and watch the world drift by.

Fez

CLUB

(0203-475 2176; www.cambridgefez.com; 15 Market Passage; ⏰from 10pm Tue-Sun) Moroccan-themed Fez serves up an international menu of hip hop, dancehall, R&B, techno, funk, indie, house and garage; in normal circumstances, it hosts regular slots from top-name DJs.

⭐ Entertainment

Live entertainment ground to a halt during the pandemic, but the following venues are expected to reopen in 2021.

ADC

THEATRE

(01223-300085; www.adctheatre.com; Park St) This famous student-run theatre is home to the university's Footlights comedy troupe, whose past members include Emma Thompson, Rowan Atkinson and Stephen Fry.

Cambridge Arts Theatre

THEATRE

(01223-503333; www.cambridgeartstheatre. com; 6 St Edward's Passage) Cambridge's biggest bona-fide theatre hosts everything from highbrow drama and dance, to panto and shows fresh from London's West End.

Corn Exchange

PERFORMING ARTS

(01223-357851; www.cornex.co.uk; Wheeler St) Venue attracting the top names, from pop and rock to comedy.

Junction

PERFORMING ARTS

(01223-511511; www.junction.co.uk; Clifton Way) Theatre, dance, comedy, club nights and an eclectic line-up of live bands; close to the railway station.

Portland Arms

LIVE MUSIC

(01223-357268; www.theportlandarms.co.uk; 129 Chesterton Rd; ⏰noon-3pm & 4.30-10pm Tue-Thu, to 11pm Fri & Sat, noon-5pm Sun) A popular student haunt, the 200-capacity Portland is the best spot in town to catch a gig from up-and-coming Cambridge bands.

ℹ Information

Visit Cambridge (www.visitcambridge.org) closed during the pandemic, along with the tourist office in the Guildhall on Peas Hill. It's likely to reopen, in the meantime, brochures on local attractions can be picked up at cafes, tourist sights and the train station.

If you need to leave a bag for the day, try **Campkins Cameras** (01223-368087; www. campkinscameras.com; 12a King's Parade; per bag £5; ⏰9am-5pm Mon-Sat, 11am-4pm Sun) opposite King's College.

ℹ Getting There & Away

BUS

National Express buses run from London Victoria (from £19, 12 daily, 2½ hours), dropping you at Parkside just east of Cambridge's city centre.

Take bus 9/9X from the Drummer St bus station for Ely (£5, hourly, one hour). All-day Dayrider tickets (£7) cover trips as far afield as Ely, King's Lynn and Bury St Edmunds.

CAR

Cambridge's centre is largely pedestrianised and savvy travellers park and walk (or cycle). All the car parks tend to fill up fast in the morning; the underground parking under the **Grand Arcade** (www.grandarcade.co.uk; Downing St;

OFF THE BEATEN TRACK

GRANTCHESTER

With its thatched cottages, flower-filled gardens, breezy meadows and classic cream teas, Grantchester is the picture-postcard image of England. Walk, punt or cycle here from central Cambridge, then flop into a deckchair under a leafy apple tree and wolf down cakes or light lunches at the lovely Orchard Tea Garden (01223-840230; www. theorchardteagarden.co.uk; 47 Mill Way; lunch mains £6-10; ⏰9am-6pm Apr-Oct, to 4pm Wed-Sun Nov-Mar), a favourite haunt of the Bloomsbury Group who came to camp, picnic, swim and push back social boundaries. If you don't feel up to the walk or punt, bus 18 runs here from Cambridge's Drummer St bus station (£2.80, 15 minutes, hourly Monday to Saturday).

9am-7pm Mon-Sat, 10am-5pm Sun) mall is conveniently central.

Circling the city on major road routes are five **Park & Ride car parks** (www.cambridgepark andride.info). Parking is currently free for up to 18 hours but you'll pay £3 return for a bus to the centre (services run every 10 to 15 minutes – check the schedule on arrival).

TRAIN
The train station is 1.5 miles southeast of the centre (easily accessible by bus). Trains zip very regularly to London (from £19.90, one hour), Ely (£4.70, 15 minutes, half-hourly), King's Lynn (£10.70, one hour, hourly), Stansted Airport (£11.40, 30 minutes to one hour, every 20 minutes) and other local hubs.

ⓘ Getting Around

BICYCLE
Cambridge is incredibly bike-friendly; recommended bicycle-hire outfits include:

S&G Cycles (☑ 01223-311134; 15 Laundress Lane; per hour/day from £7/18; ⓢ 9am-4pm Mon-Sat, from 11am Sun) A simple operation near the Silver St bridge.

Rutland Cycling (☑ 0330-555 0080; www. rutlandcycling.com; Corn Exchange St; per half-day/day from £12/18; ⓢ 8am-5pm Mon-Fri, 9am-5pm Sat, 10am-4pm Sun) In the heart of town at the Grand Arcade shopping centre. There's a branch (☑ 01223-352728; www. rutlandcycling.com; 156 Great Northern Rd) just off Station Rd by the train station.

BUS
Local buses zip around town from the main Drummer St bus station (or nearby roads). Most services operate from around 6am until around 11pm, but there are few buses on Sundays.

All-day Dayrider bus tickets (£4.50) cover 24 hours of unlimited bus travel around Cambridge. Take bus 18 for Granchester (£2.80, hourly, 15 minutes). Buses C1, C3 and C7 stop at the train station (£1 to £2.20, 30 minutes).

TAXI
If you don't Uber, call local firm **Panther Taxi** (☑ 01223-715715; www.panthertaxis.co.uk).

Ely

☑ 01353 / POP 20,100

Sleepy Ely (*ee-lee*) feels like a gentle backwater, but the city gave English history one of its greatest heroes – or villains, depending on who you speak to – Oliver Cromwell. Ely's once-powerful status is obvious from its imposing Georgian town houses and the soaring cathedral that dominates the city centre.

The name Ely comes from the eels that once inhabited the surrounding Fens, but the city built its fortunes on the production of opium, with high-class ladies holding 'poppy parties' and families calming their children with highly effective 'poppy tea'.

◉ Sights

The engaging **Ely Museum** (www.elymuseum.org.uk), in the old town jail on Market St, is closed for renovations until 2021.

★ **Ely Cathedral**　　　　CATHEDRAL
(☑ 01353-667735; www.elycathedral.org; The Gallery; adult/child £8/free; ⓢ 10am-4pm Mon-Sat, 1-3.30pm Sun) Ely's soaring Gothic Cathedral's was dubbed the 'Ship of the Fens' because its towering spire was visible for miles across the vast, flat sweep of Cambridgeshire. It's an eye-catching structure, best known for the fascinating 14th-century **Lady Chapel**, which has been preserved much as it was at the end of the English Civil War, after iconoclasts had hacked and defiled most of its delicate statues.

Inside, cast your eyes upwards to admire the striking **Octagon**, which transfers the weight of the tower onto eight monumental columns. There's some stunning stained glass (look out for the masons hard at work raising the Tower of Babel), and the attached **Stained Glass Museum** (☑ 01353-660347; www.stainedglassmuseum.com; adult/child £4.50/free; ⓢ 10.30am-5pm Mon-Sat, 12.30-4.30pm Sun) has panels collected from across Europe.

Tours of the cathedral and tower were suspended at the time of writing, but should resume, so check ahead. Evensong shows off the building's impressive acoustics; check to see if visitors are able to attend.

Oliver Cromwell's House　　MUSEUM
(☑ 01353-662062; www.olivercromwellshouse. co.uk; 29 St Mary's St; adult/child £5.20/3.50; ⓢ 10am-5pm Apr-Oct, 11am-4pm Nov-Mar) England's premier Puritan lived in this attractive, half-timbered house with his family from 1636 to 1647, when he was the local tithe collector, before embarking on his momentous campaign to separate the king from his throne (and head) and institute a parliamentary republic. Inside are thought-provoking audiovisual displays on Cromwell's life and times (pick up a handset as you enter).

🛏 Sleeping

⭐ Peacocks   B&B ££

(📞07900 666161; www.peacockstearoom.co.uk;
65 Waterside; s/d from £110/135; 📶) Walk into
the roomy suites in this wisteria-covered
house near the quay and you'll feel instantly
at home. In the Cottage Suite, floral Laura
Ashley wallpaper sets a late Victorian mood;
in the Brewery Suite, vintage books, gilt mirrors and antiques conjure up a Victorian
gentlemen's club.

Its award-winning **cafe** (📞01353-661100;
snacks from £8, cream teas £9-19; ⊙10.30am-5pm
Wed-Sun, plus Tue Jul-Aug) serves cream teas,
soups, salads, sandwiches and more substantial mains.

Riverside   B&B ££

(📞01353-661677; www.riversideinn-ely.co.uk; 8
Annesdale; s £59-79, d £80-169; 🅿📶) This Georgian guesthouse on Ely's quay looks out-
wardly traditional, but inside, rooms are full
of rich reds and golds and Regency stripes.
It's all very grand, and the glam finish extends to the bathrooms. Rooms at the front
look towards the houseboats bobbing about
on the River Great Ouse.

🍴 Eating

⭐ The Almonry   CAFE £

(📞01353-666360; off High St; cream tea £6, light
meals from £7; ⊙9am-4pm Mon-Sat, from 11am
Sun) This elegant tearoom and restaurant
sits in neatly pruned gardens at the back
of the cathedral compound, serving cream
teas, sandwiches and a few more ambitious
mains – chicken breast stuffed with brie and
asparagus, squash and chickpea burgers and
the like. The cathedral views are sublime.

Old Fire Engine House   BRITISH ££

(📞01353-662582; www.theoldfireenginehouse.
co.uk; 25 St Mary's St; lunch 2/3 courses £18/24,
mains £17; ⊙10.30am-8.30pm Mon-Sat, 12.15-2pm
Sun; 🍴) 🌿 Eating in this elegant town house
restaurant is like stepping into an East Anglian farmhouse kitchen. It's all about seasonal and local produce, so dishes might
include local lamb shoulder with mint and
lemon, plum crumble and mitoon of pork (a
coarse local pâté).

ℹ Information

Tourist Office (📞01353-662062; www.visitely.
org.uk; 29 St Mary's St; ⊙10am-5pm Apr-
Oct, 11am-4pm Nov-Mar) In Oliver Cromwell's
House; ask about local walks.

ℹ Getting There & Away

You can walk to Ely from Cambridge along the 17-
mile riverside Fen Rivers Way. The 9/9X bus runs
here from Cambridge (£5, hourly, one hour). Rail
connections include:

Cambridge (£4.70, 20 minutes, up to four per
hour)

King's Lynn (£7.50, 30 minutes, one or two
per hour)

Norwich (£18.50, one hour, every 30 minutes)

ESSEX

The inhabitants of Essex have put up with
years of jokes from the rest of England, but
you'll see through the reality show stereo-
types if you venture up here in person. The
south of the county may feel like an extension of London's East End, but head into the
countryside and you'll find charming villages, dripping with history, and landscapes
that have changed little since Constable
painted them in the early 19th century.

Colchester

📞01206 / POP 194,706

Dominated by a sturdy Norman castle and
extensive Roman walls, Colchester is Britain's oldest recorded town, dating from
the 5th century BCE. In 43 CE the Romans
came, saw and conquered, and constructed
Camulodunum, which was razed by Boudica just 17 years later. The thriving market
town that emerged from the ruins later saw
extensive action in the Norman Conquest,
the Reformation and the English Civil War.

⊙ Sights

The best of the city's half-timbered houses are clustered together in the Tudor-era
Dutch Quarter, just north of High St, founded by Flemish weavers in the 16th century. Along gorgeous **Maidenburgh Street**,
you can see glimpses of a Roman theatre
through the windows of houses built over
the ruins.

⭐ Colchester Castle   CASTLE

(📞01206-282939; https://colchester.cimuseums.
org.uk; Castle Park; adult/child £10/5.95; ⊙10am-
5pm Mon-Sat, from 11am Sun) Built in 1076 on
the foundations of the Roman Temple of
Claudius, England's largest surviving Norman keep is bigger than the White Tower in
London. Over the centuries it's been a royal

residence, a prison and home to the Witch-finder General. Among the treasures inside, look out for the Roman-era Colchester Vase, decorated with scenes of hunting and gladiatorial combat, and the Fenwick Treasure, a horde of Roman jewels hidden during Boudica's siege.

firstsite   ARTS CENTRE
(☑01206-713700; https://firstsite.uk; Lewis Gardens; ⊙10am-5pm; ♿) FREE This shiny, curved, glass-and-copper arts centre rises above a section of the Roman Walls; inside are art spaces hosting cutting-edge shows by visiting big names, plus a cinema, a calm cafe, and a restored Roman mosaic visible through a glass floor.

Hollytrees Museum   MUSEUM
(☑01206-282920; https://colchester.cimuseums.org.uk; Castle Park; ⊙10am-5pm Mon-Sat) FREE In this Georgian town house by the park, toys, costumes, ornaments and clocks conjure up the domestic life of the wealthy original owners and their servants. Look for the shipwright's baby carriage in the shape of a boat, and the intricate, envy-inducing doll's house.

🛏 Sleeping & Eating

For a gourmet picnic in Castle Park, pick up ingredients at H Gunton Ltd (www.guntons.co.uk; 81-83 Crouch St; ⊙9am-2pm Mon-Fri, to 4pm Sat), a gorgeous deli that has hardly changed since it opened in 1936.

Four Sevens   B&B ££
(☑01206-546093; www.foursevens.co.uk; 28 Inglis Rd; r with/without bathroom from £75/65; P🛜) This far-from-frilly B&B is housed in a graceful Victorian house, a mile southwest of the centre (just off the B1022 to Maldon). It's set on a genteel residential street and the spacious, modern rooms get plenty of light.

North Hill   HOTEL ££
(☑01206-574001; www.northhillhotel.com; 51 North Hill; s/d from £85/95; 🛜) A sleek contemporary hotel with loads of calm common spaces, spread across three historic buildings on the hill leading down to North Station. Ask for a room in the cottage-style back building for wonky beams and exposed red brick alongside modern creature comforts.

The hotel's excellent Green Room restaurant (open noon to 2pm and 6pm to 9pm Monday to Saturday and noon to 5pm Sunday) serves tasty comfort-food with a

contemporary twist – so treats such as confit duck leg with radish and kohlrabi (mains £11 to £21).

🛈 Information

Tourist Office (☑01206-282920; www.visitcolchester.com; Castle Park; ⊙10am-5pm Mon-Sat) Inside the Hollytrees Museum.

🛈 Getting There & Away

Trains run to London Liverpool St (£25, one hour, every 15 minutes); the station is a 20-minute walk north of the centre, or take bus 62 (£1.90, 10 minutes, every 15 minutes).

Direct National Express buses go to and from London Victoria (from £6.60, three hours, four daily). Regional buses leave from the stand on Osborne St.

Dedham Vale

John Constable's romantic visions of meandering hedgerows and babbling brooks were inspired by and painted in this serene corner of the country. The artist was born in East Bergholt in 1776 and painted his most famous work, *The Hay Wain,* nearby at Flatford Mill in 1821. Today, the pretty village of Dedham is the best base for exploring Constable Country – on foot, by bike, or by rowboat along the River Stour.

👁 Sights & Activities

The best way to get from Dedham to Flatford is to follow the river through pretty water meadows fringed by weeping willows. It's a 1½-mile walk, or you can rent rowboats in Dedham at the Boathouse Restaurant (☑01206-323153; www.dedhamboathouse.com; Mill Lane; boats per hour £16; ⊙9.30am-4pm Tue-Sun).

Flatford   HISTORIC SITE
(NT; ☑01206-298260; www.nationaltrust.org.uk; Bridge Cottage, near East Bergholt; parking £5; ⊙10am-6pm Apr-Oct, to 3.30pm Sat & Sun Nov-Mar; P) FREE Preserved immaculately by the National Trust, the cluster of 16th- and 17th-century buildings at Flatford has changed little since Constable's time. At least five of the painter's greatest works were created here, and the view across the millpond from Flatford Mill (now an education centre) towards Willy Lott's House is like stepping into *The Hay Wain* in real life. There's an exhibition on the painter near the car park, and tiny Bridge Cottage, with its

knee-high windows, has been restored as it was in Constable's day.

🛏 Sleeping & Eating

★ Dedham Hall   B&B ££
(📞 01206-323027; www.dedhamhall.co.uk; Brook St, Dedham; s/d £75/120; 🅿) An air of old England infuses Dedham Hall, a delightfully relaxed 15th-century farmhouse set in a gorgeous garden. Inside, candlesticks perch above red-brick fireplaces, beams poke through walls and ceilings and sunlight spills through windows over soft sofas and freshly made beds.

Sun Inn   INN ££
(📞 01206-323351; www.thesuninndedham.com; High St, Dedham; s/d £90/145; 🅿🛜) This mustard-yellow inn is the epitome of heritage-chic: the 15th-century atmosphere of the pub downstairs gives way to cool modern design when you get into the bedrooms. Each room is different, but all have have been designed with taste and sensitivity.

Milsoms   HOTEL £££
(📞 01206-322795; www.milsomhotels.com; Stratford Rd, Dedham; r £155-230; 🅿❄🛜) Vine-cloaked, yellow-brick Milsoms is where those who can come to stay, lured here by great food and cool design with a sense of fun – think zebra stripes, riveted tin and black leather upholstery. Bicycle and canoe hire means easy access to all of Dedham Vale.

★ Le Talbooth   BRITISH £££
(📞 01206-323150; www.milsomhotels.com; Gunn Hill; mains £21-42; ⊙ noon-2.15pm & 6-8pm Mon-Sat) Most of the menu at this swish restaurant overlooking the River Stour has been produced in the local area, from Dedham beef fillet to Thetford forest venison. Chefs elevate traditional British food into the realms of gastronomy; desserts are simply divine.

ⓘ Getting There & Away

Manningtree train station, on the Colchester–Ipswich line, is a lovely 2-mile walk from Flatford Mill.

Bus links from Colchester:

Dedham Panther Travel (www.panther-travel.co.uk) Bus 81 (£4.60, 30 minutes, every two hours. Monday to Saturday)

East Bergholt Ipswich Bus (www.ipswichbuses.co.uk) Buses 93 and 94 (£8.50, 40 minutes, every two hours Monday to Saturday)

Saffron Walden
📋 01799 / POP 15,504

The dainty 12th-century market town of Saffron Walden is a delightful knot of half-timbered houses, narrow lanes and ancient churches. It gets its name from the purple saffron crocus (the source of the world's most expensive spice), which was cultivated in the surrounding fields between the 15th and 18th centuries. Oliver Cromwell used the timbered Old Sun Inn on Church St as his HQ during the Civil War.

◎ Sights

★ Audley End
House & Gardens   HISTORIC BUILDING
(EH; 📞 01799-522842; www.english-heritage.org.uk; off London Rd; adult/child £19/11.40; ⊙ timed visits 10am-3pm; 🅿👪) Palatial in scale, the fabulous early Jacobean Audley End House was clearly designed to place its creator, the first Earl of Suffolk, at the top table of the English gentry. The house eventually did become a royal palace when it was purchased by Charles II in 1668. The rooms inside are lavishly decorated with priceless furniture, oil paintings, woodcarvings and taxidermy. The elegant gardens, designed by Lancelot 'Capability' Brown, include a walled kitchen garden full of traditional varieties.

Saffron Walden Museum   MUSEUM
(📞 01799-510333; www.saffronwaldenmuseum.org; Museum St; adult/child £2.50/free; ⊙ 10am-5pm Tue-Sat, from 2pm Sun; 👪) In this excellent museum dating back to 1835, you'll find eclectic collections covering everything from Essex history and 18th-century costumes to geology, Victorian toys and ancient Egyptian artefacts.

Bridge End Gardens   GARDENS
(Bridge End; ⊙ 8am-4pm Mon-Thu, to noon Fri) FREE Careful restoration has returned these seven interlinked gardens to their former Victorian glory. An elegant sprawl of water features, gazebos and manicured hedges, it's a great place to play hide and seek; check to see if the maze has reopened.

🍴 Eating

Eight Bells   PUB FOOD ££
(📞 01799-522790; www.theeightbellssaffronwalden.com; 18 Bridge St; mains £15-26; ⊙ noon-3pm & 6-10pm Mon-Sat, noon-6pm Sun; 🍴) Medieval meets design mag at this historic 16th-century pub, where ancient timbers

collide above walls crammed with mismatched paintings. The menu is more traditional, with steaks, roasts (including nut) and posh burgers.

ℹ Information

Tourist Office (☑ 01799-524002; www.visitsaffronwalden.gov.uk; 1 Market Pl; ⊙ 9.30am-5pm Mon-Sat) Has a good leaflet on the town's historic buildings.

ℹ Getting There & Away

Bus 7 runs between Saffron Walden and Cambridge (£5, 1¼ hours), hourly between Monday and Saturday. Bus 132 makes the same journey every two hours on Sunday, passing the Duxford air museum.

The nearest train station is 2 miles west of Saffron Walden at Audley End, served by trains from Cambridge every 20 minutes (£8.20, 20 minutes). Bus 59 is one of several buses from Saffron Walden that pass close to the entrance to Audley End (£2.40, 15 minutes, every two hours Monday to Saturday).

Southend-on-Sea

☑ 01702 / POP 174,300

London's closest beach, Southend is the English seaside at its most uninhibited. Gambling machines beep and jangle, fairground rides gallop and nightlife bubbles out onto the seafront. But there's also another, gentler Southend, best experienced in the old fishing village of Leigh-on-Sea, a short train-ride west of the hubbub.

◉ Sights

The seaside fun is centred on the pier and the flanking **Adventure Island** (☑ 01702-443400; www.adventureisland.co.uk; Western Esplanade; day passes £20-32; ⊙ 11am-8pm, but hours vary) theme park, but the best stretch of beach is east of the centre towards Shoeburyness.

For a more interesting take on the English seaside, take the local train west to **Leigh-on-Sea**, a pocket of cobbled lanes, historic seafront pubs and gelato stands, flanking a busy line of working cockle sheds.

Southend Pier　　　　　LANDMARK
(www.southend.gov.uk/pier; Western Esplanade; adult/child £2/1; ⊙ 10.15am-8pm Jul-Sep, to 6pm Mar-Jun & Oct-Nov, to 6pm Wed-Sun Dec-Mar) Welcome to the world's longest pier – a staggering 1.341 miles long, to be precise – built in 1830 and still standing despite numerous

mishaps, from boat crashes to fires. It's a long, windy stroll to the restored Pier Head, with its cafe and quirky **museum** (☑ 01702-611214; www.southendpiermuseum.co.uk; Western Esplanade; adult/child £1.50/50p; ⊙ 11am-5pm Sat, Sun, Tue & Wed May-Oct); hopping on the **Pier Railway** (one way adult/child £5/2.50) saves the long slog back.

🛏 Sleeping & Eating

The area around the pier is crammed with places serving so-so fish and chips. For more exciting food, head to Leigh-on-Sea.

★ **Roslin Beach**　　　　　HOTEL £££
(☑ 01702-586375; www.roslinhotel.com; Thorpe Esplanade; r from £179; ⊙ food noon-9pm; 🅿 ❀ 🛜 🐾) Seafront Roslin takes the classic seaside hotel and sprinkles some design-magazine stardust. Facing the best part of Southend beach, the interior is full of designer flourishes – candlelit lanterns, flower bouquets, palm-tree wallpaper – and rooms manage to feel both nostalgic and modern, thanks to an art-deco-green colour scheme and masses of soft upholstery.

Osborne Bros　　　　　SEAFOOD £
(☑ 01702-477233; High St, Leigh-on-Sea; snacks/mains from £3/9; ⊙ 9am-4pm Mon-Fri, 8am-5pm Sat & Sun) Part fish stall, part bare-bones cafe, Osborne's is set right on Old Leigh's waterfront, so you can enjoy views of the boats on the Thames Estuary while tucking into cockles, crabs, smoked haddock, jellied eels and seafood platters, washed down with a pint from the pub next door.

Boatyard　　　　　SEAFOOD ££
(☑ 01702-475588; www.theboatyardrestaurant.co.uk; 8/13 High St; mains £14-23; ⊙ noon-8pm Thu-Sat, to 5pm Sun) A swanky alternative to the terrace restaurants along the waterfront, with its own wooden deck overlooking the water, a cruise-ship-like interior, and a quality menu of ale-battered cod, peppercorn steaks, antipasti, prawn and crayfish cocktails and the like.

ℹ Information

Tourist Office (☑ 01702-215620; www.visitsouthend.co.uk; Southend Pier, Western Esplanade; ⊙ 10.15am-8pm) At the pier.

ℹ Getting There & Away

Trains from London Liverpool St and Fenchurch St (£13, 1¼ hours, every 15 minutes) run to both Southend Victoria station and nearby Southend

Central, also the departure point for trains to Leigh-on-Sea (£3.10, 10 minutes, every 15 minutes).

SUFFOLK

While Essex is influenced by London's gravitational pull, sleepy Suffolk moves to its own rhythms. The county made its money on the back of the medieval wool trade, and magnificent churches and lavish timbered houses attest to this prosperous past. Then there's the coast, with lovely seaside resorts such as Aldeburgh and Southwold offering fresh seafood and gentle promenades in place of fairground rides and amusement arcades.

Long Melford

📞 01787 / POP 3918

A thin strip of a village, pretty Long Melford sprawls south from a village green flanked by not one but two medieval mansions and a medieval church and hospital. Fine restaurants, tearooms and antique shops provide more reasons to meander through.

👁 Sights

Kentwell Hall   HISTORIC BUILDING
(📞 01787-310207; www.kentwell.co.uk; adult/child £10.75/7.50; ⊙ hours vary; 🅿) Gorgeous, turreted, Tudor-era Kentwell Hall may date from the 1500s, but it's still used as a private home, lending it a wonderfully lived-in feel. The mansion is framed by a rectangular moat, lush gardens and a rare-breeds farm, and during Tudor re-enactment events, the whole estate bristles with bodices, codpieces and hose. Opening hours are erratic; call for the latest information.

Melford Hall   HISTORIC BUILDING
(NT; 📞 01787-379228; www.nationaltrust.org.uk; Hall St; 🅿) From outside, the romantic Elizabethan mansion of Melford Hall has changed little since the days when Queen Elizabeth I was an honoured guest. Inside, there's a panelled banqueting hall, masses of Regency and Victorian finery, and a display on Beatrix Potter, a cousin of the Hyde Parkers, who owned the house from 1786 to 1960. Melford Hall is usually open Wednesday to Sunday in summer, but this may change – call for the latest hours and fees.

WORTH A TRIP

IPSWICH

You may find yourself passing through Suffolk's county capital en route to the coast or countryside. If you have a few hours to kill, the Tudor-era **Christchurch Mansion** (📞 01473-433554; https://ipswich.cimuseums.org.uk; Soane St, Ipswich; ⊙10am-5pm Mon-Sat, 11am-5pm Sun, to 4pm Nov-Feb) **FREE** displays an impressive collection of paintings by Thomas Gainsborough and John Constable. The train station is a 15-minute walk south of the centre; county buses leave from the Old Cattle Market bus station on Turret Lane.

Holy Trinity   CHURCH
(📞 01787-310845; www.longmelfordchurch.com; Church Walk; donation requested; ⊙10am-6pm) Surrounded by jellybean-shaped hedges, magnificent Holy Trinity looks more like a cathedral than a church. Inside, you can see a series of 15th-century stained glass panels that survived both the Reformation and the English Civil War. The red-brick mansion in front of the churchyard once served as a medieval hospital.

🛏 Sleeping & Eating

Black Lion   HOTEL ££
(📞 01787-312356; www.theblacklionlongmelford.com; The Green; r/ste from £90/130; 🅿 🕸) At the Black Lion, you'll find a heritage-meets-design mag mash-up of old paintings, cast-iron fireplaces, luxe upholstery and fine fabrics. Colour schemes range from calm off-whites to vivid greens and the restaurant downstairs serves good steaks, fish and upmarket takes on pub classics (mains £15 to £23, served noon to 2.30pm and 6pm to around 9pm Wednesday to Sunday).

★ Scutcher's   MODERN BRITISH £££
(📞 01787-310200; www.scutchers.com; Westgate St; mains £24-29; ⊙noon-2pm & 7-9.30pm Thu-Sat) Beautiful reinventions of traditional recipes have made this unpretentious place renowned throughout the Stour Valley. Expect interesting riffs on classic dishes made with turbot, sea bass, lamb loin, calves' liver and farm-fresh local produce.

DON'T MISS

SUTTON HOO

Located 11 miles northeast of Ipswich off the B1083, the green hummocks of **Sutton Hoo** (NT; ☑ 01394-389700; www.nationaltrust.org.uk; near Woodbridge; adult/child £8/4; ☺ 10.30am-3.30pm Sat-Wed; P ♿) were just a topographical oddity until the local land-owner, Edith Pretty, paid for one of the mounds to be excavated, uncovering the boat burial of an Anglo Saxon king and a hoard of exquisite gold and silver grave goods.

The king in question is believed to be Raedwald, who ruled from around 600 CE; his intricate, jewelled helmet, shield and sword are among the finest treasures housed in the British Museum in London (replicas of his boat and treasures are displayed at Sutton Hoo).

Paths encircle 18 unexcavated burial mounds surrounding the king's burial site, and a viewing tower offers dramatic views over the 'royal cemetery'. Check to see if access to the tower and tours of the site have resumed.

There's no public transport, but the site is a 1¼-mile walk from Melton station, on the Ipswich–Lowestoft line.

❶ Getting There & Away

Chambers (www.chambersbus.co.uk) bus 753 runs to Bury St Edmunds (£4.60, one hour, hourly Monday to Saturday), Sudbury (£1.70, 10 minutes) and Lavenham (£4.10, 25 minutes).

Lavenham

☑ 01787 / POP 1722

One of England's most immaculately preserved medieval towns, tiny Lavenham built its fortunes on the wood trade, which paid for this atmospheric sprawl of wonky, leaning, timbered houses and pubs. Many buildings here feature original pargeting (ornamental plasterwork) from the 15th century. It's all very lovely and heavily touristed; come early in the morning if you want uninterrupted photographs.

◉ Sights

Lavenham Guildhall   HISTORIC BUILDING
(NT; ☑ 01787-247646; www.nationaltrust.org.uk; Market Pl; adult/child £9.30/4.65; ☺ 10.30am-4pm Wed-Sun) Lavenham's triangular marketplace is dominated by the whitewashed guildhall, a superb example of close-studded, timber-framed, early-16th-century architecture. It's now a museum with displays on the wool trade and medieval guilds; in its tranquil garden you can see plants that produced typical medieval dyes.

Little Hall   HISTORIC BUILDING
(☑ 01787-247019; www.littlehall.org.uk; Market Pl; adult/child £4/free; ☺ 2-4pm Sat & Sun) The caramel-coloured, 14th-century Little Hall was once home to a successful wool merchant, and the interiors have been restored to their medieval splendour through the efforts of the Gayer-Anderson twins, who made it their home in the 1920s and 1930s.

St Peter & St Paul   CHURCH
(www.lavenhamchurch.onesuffolk.net; Church St; ☺ 10am-4pm) Built between 1485 and 1530, this soaring late-Perpendicular church was one of Suffolk's last great wool churches, with fine woodwork and stained glass, and a churchyard full of gravestones carved with skulls and cherubs.

☷ Sleeping & Eating

Angel   HOTEL ££
(☑ 01787-247388;   www.theangellavenham. co.uk; Market Pl; r from £79; ☺ food noon-3pm & 6-9pm Mon-Fri, noon-9pm Sat, 6-8pm Sun; P ☎) In Lavenham's oldest building, narrow corridors lead to gorgeously renovated, large, bright rooms with exposed timbers. Downstairs, it's English pub all the way, with Suffolk ales and good-quality pub grub, from pizzas and burgers to steaks, salads and sandwiches (mains £9 to £15), which you can eat at outdoor tables facing the square.

★ **Swan at Lavenham**   HOTEL £££
(☑ 01787-247477; www.theswanatlavenham.co.uk; High St; r £110-180, ste from £210; P ☎) Marvellously medieval, the stylish Swan is Lavenham's signature place to stay – a bent and leaning timbered coaching inn, with flawless service, fine modern British cuisine and rooms decorated in soothing colours and bound by a latticework of ancient beams.

The house spa offers a full range of relaxing treatments in rooms lit by candles and sunlight.

★ **Great House**   MODERN BRITISH £££
(📞01787-247431; www.greathouse.co.uk; Market Pl; 3-course lunch/dinner from £23/28; ⊗noon-2.30pm Wed-Sun, 7-9.30pm Tue-Sat) Contrasting cultures combine at this elegant restaurant, so expect East Anglian ingredients and French and Italian gastronomy. Dining here could see you eating *pâté en croûte,* Gravlax salmon, roast Suffolk pork or handmade gnocchi.

🛈 Getting There & Away

Chambers bus 753 connects Lavenham to Bury St Edmunds (£4.50, 30 minutes, hourly Monday to Saturday), continuing to Long Melford (£4.10, 25 minutes) and Sudbury (£4.30, 35 minutes).

Bury St Edmunds

📞 01284 / POP 41,113

A centre of pilgrimage for centuries, Suffolk's second city is rich in history and attractively decked out with handsome Georgian architecture. Named for the Anglo-Saxon king Edmund the Martyr, it rewards those who step off the tourist trail with fine food, and a pleasing fragrance of yeast and malt thanks to the enormous Greene King brewery.

👁 Sights

Abbey Gardens   RUINS
(Mustow St; ⊗dawn-dusk) FREE Now a picturesque, skeletal ruin, Bury's once-mighty abbey is still impressive, despite being plundered for building stone after the dissolution of the monasteries. Dotted around a pretty park behind the cathedral (once part of the abbey itself), sections of eroded masonry form fantastical shapes against the greenery, marking out an immense complex that was once one of Britain's largest religious buildings.

St Edmundsbury Cathedral   CATHEDRAL
(📞01284-748720; www.stedscathedral.org; Angel Hill; by donation; ⊗10am-4pm Mon-Sat) Bury's cathedral was once a minor part of the abbey, but after the Reformation it became the focus of attention. Most of the building is early 16th century, but the 45m-high tower was only completed in 2005, using traditional stone-working techniques. Ask if tours of the tower have resumed. Next to the cathedral is the appealingly ancient Norman Tower, the original entrance to the great abbey church.

Moyse's Hall   MUSEUM
(📞01284-706183; www.moyseshall.org; Cornhill; adult/child £5/3; ⊗10am-5pm Mon-Sat, noon-4pm Sun; 🐾) Set in an impressive 12th-century undercroft, Moyse's Hall museum displays a curious collection of artefacts, from a locket of Mary Tudor's hair to the death mask of 19th-century murderer William Corder (and, contentiously, a book bound in his skin!). Check out the fascinating displays on the town's ruined abbey and the chilling Bury witch trials.

Theatre Royal   HISTORIC BUILDING
(NT; 📞01284-769505; www.theatreroyal.org; Westgate St; tours £7.50; ⊗tours 11am Wed, Thu & Sat) Britain's only working Regency playhouse features ornate gilding, an elegant round of boxes and a *trompe l'oeil* ceiling painted to resemble the open sky. Its secrets are revealed on fascinating guided front-of-house and backstage tours – call to check things are running as normal.

St Mary's Church   CHURCH
(📞01284-754680; www.wearechurch.net; Honey Hill; donation requested; ⊗10am-4pm Mon-Sat, to 3pm Oct-Easter) Once part of the abbey, St Mary's is one of the largest parish churches in England, and it contains the tomb of Mary Tudor – Henry VIII's sister and a onetime queen of France. Built around 1430, it's famous for its hammer-beam roof, with a host of vampire-like angels swooping from the ceiling.

🛏 Sleeping

Fox Inn   INN ££
(📞0845 6086040; www.greenekinginns.co.uk; 1 Eastgate St; r from £115; P🐾) Tied to the Greene King brewery, this historic pub offers rooms in converted animal barns, with bleached beams, weathered brick walls and even some of the old livestock tethering

---

🛈 **THE APEX**

Bury's cutting-edge arts' centre and music venue, the Apex (📞01284-758000; www.theapex.co.uk; 1 Charter Sq), boasts a lively program of live music, theatre, art shows and more.

rings. Posh wallpaper, leather sofas and the odd chandelier add extra class.

★ **Chantry** HOTEL **£££**
(☑01284-767427; www.chantryhotel.com; 8 Sparhawk St; r £120-175; 🅿@🛜) This family-run town house B&B has the feel of a country hotel, with a gorgeous collection of four-poster, metal-framed and antique timber beds, set in inviting rooms with the odd original Georgian feature. There's a convivial lounge and tiny bar to help guests feel right at home.

Angel HOTEL **£££**
(☑01284-714000; www.theangel.co.uk; 3 Angel Hill; r from £135; 🅿🛜) Almost hidden behind a cloak of vines and climbers, Bury's grand dame hotel faces the abbey gates across Angel Hill, flanked by a string of stately Georgian mansions. Rooms feature designer fabrics and wallpapers and quirky design details (brass tubs, cowskin armchairs, antique beds), and higher categories come with ecclesiastical views.

🍴 Eating & Drinking

★ **Pea Porridge** MODERN BRITISH **££**
(☑01284-700200; www.peaporridge.co.uk; 29 Cannon St; mains £12-22; ⊙6.30-8.30pm Thu, noon-1.30pm & 6.30-9.30pm Fri & Sat) Happy chatter and enticing aromas greet you at this intimate neighbourhood restaurant where local, seasonal produce is cooked up together with ingredients from the Med. Tickle your tastebuds with Moorish fish soup, rabbit *kibbeh* (Levantine meatballs) and grilled Galician octopus.

Maison Bleue FRENCH **£££**
(☑01284-760623; www.maisonbleue.co.uk; 31 Churchgate St; 3-course meals £32-55; ⊙noon-2pm & 7-9.30pm, closed Mon) You may want to dress up to eat in this elegant restaurant, serving modern French cuisine with real flair. Fabulous set meals take in such flavour sensations as halibut with chorizo butter, Aylesbury duck with beetroot and plum sauce, and sea trout with coconut and lime.

★ **Old Cannon** PUB
(☑01284-768769; www.oldcannonbrewery.co.uk; 86 Cannon St; ⊙11am-11pm; 🛜) 🍺 In this microbrewery, gleaming mash tuns (malt mashing vats) sit alongside the bar, where you can quaff the end results – try the feisty Gunner's Daughter (ABV 5.5%) or Powder Monkey (4.75%), named in homage to naval gun traditions. Ask about brewery tours.

Nutshell PUB
(☑01284-764867; www.thenutshellpub.co.uk; The Traverse; ⊙11am-11pm, to 10.30pm Sun) Beer tables, a handful of chairs, a ceiling smothered in international banknotes, a suspended pufferfish: it's amazing what they've squeezed into this thimble-sized, timber-framed pub, recognised by the *Guinness Book of Records* as Britain's smallest.

ℹ️ Information

Tourist Office (☑01284-764667; www.visit-burystedmunds.co.uk; The Apex, Charter Sq; ⊙10.30am-4pm Mon-Sat) In the Arc Shopping Centre; ask about city tours.

ℹ️ Getting There & Away

BUS
The main bus station is on St Andrew's St North. Direct services include:

Cambridge Stagecoach bus 11 (£5, one hour, hourly Monday to Saturday)

Lavenham Chambers bus 753 (£4.50, 30 minutes, hourly Monday to Saturday)

TRAIN
The train station is a 10-minute walk north of the centre of town. Services include:

Cambridge (£11.40, 40 minutes, hourly)

Ipswich (£10, 40 minutes, two per hour)

Aldeburgh

☑01728 / POP 3225

The coastal town of Aldeburgh (pronounced *orld*-bruh) floats in a charming time warp. Along the pebble shore, wooden sheds sell ocean-fresh seafood hauled in by the boats perched on the beach, while sightseers stroll along the prom, with nary a slot machine in sight. The town follows the shoreline in a thin strip, dotted with interesting shops, galleries and cafes. Aldeburgh's two festivals and connections with composer Benjamin Britten are also a big draw.

👁 Sights

The pebble beach runs north to **Thorpeness**, with its pretty windmill; it's a pleasant walk and on the way you'll pass Maggi Hambling's sculpture **Scallop**, a giant metal shell incised with quotes from the opera *Peter Grimes* by composer Benjamin Britten, who spent much of his life in Aldeburgh. In

ORFORD NESS

Formerly owned by the Ministry of Defence, wind-whipped, remote **Orford Ness** (NT; ☑ 01394-450900; www.nationaltrust.org.uk) is the largest vegetated shingle spit in Europe. The lonely shoreline is dominated by a line of forbidding-looking **pagodas** that were used to test the explosive triggers for nuclear weapons (fortunately, without the radioactive parts). Today, you're more likely to spot wading birds, madcap hares and rare coastal plants. Ferries operate from Orford Quay.

The adjacent village of Orford is a gorgeous spot, full of historic houses and cute pubs and dominated by a striking 12th-century **castle** (EH; www.english-heritage.org.uk; adult/child £7.90/4.70; ☺ tours hourly 10am-noon, 2pm & 3pm Fri-Sun; P) formed from three conjoined towers. While you're here, don't miss the fresh Butley oysters, fish pie, potted crab and grilled lobster at the **Butley Orford Oysterage** (☑ 01394-450277; www.pinneysoforford.co.uk; Market Hill; mains £14-28; ☺ noon-2.15pm daily, plus 6.30-9pm Wed-Fri, 6-9pm Sat) on the market square; it also runs a **deli** (☑ 01394-459183; www.pinneysoforford.co.uk; Quay St; from £4; ☺ 10am-4.30pm, to 4pm Sun) near the quay.

the distance, you'll spot the looming mass of Sizewell nuclear power station.

Moot Hall   MUSEUM
(www.aldeburghmuseum.org.uk; Market Cross Pl; adult/child £3/1; ☺ 1-4pm Apr-Oct, 1-4pm Sat & Sun Nov-Mar) The town museum is worth a visit as much for the gorgeous building – a 16th-century merchant's house constructed from oak timbers and herringbone brick – as for the displays inside, which cover fishing, shipbuilding, coastal defences and Regency-era tourism.

RSPB Minsmere   NATURE RESERVE
(RSPB; www.rspb.org.uk; near Westleton; adult/child £9/5; ☺ reserve dawn-dusk, visitor centre 10am-4pm; P) About 8 miles north of Aldeburgh, the nature reserve at RSPB Minsmere is home to one of England's rarest birds, the bittern, along with dozens of other migratory bird species, best spotted in the autumn. Trails run across the marshes that line the foreshore to hides that offer prime spotting opportunities. The reserve borders the National Trust–administered **Dunwich Heath** (NT; www.nationaltrust.org.uk; Dunwich; parking £6; ☺ 10am-5pm), another fine spot for coastal birdwatching.

★ Festivals & Events

Aldeburgh Festival   MUSIC
(www.snapemaltings.co.uk/season/aldeburgh-festival; ☺ Jun) Founded by Benjamin Britten in 1948, this exploration of classical music takes in new and reinterpreted pieces, as well as the classics.

⌂ Sleeping & Eating

Wentworth Hotel   HOTEL £££
(☑ 01728-452312; www.wentworth-aldeburgh.com; s/d from £127/230; P ☎) Aldeburgh's grandest hotel is an elegant old dame at the end of the promenade, with a lavish, Regency-style dining room, tasteful bedrooms with fine fabrics and little dabs of colour, and a healthy dose of nostalgia. Seaview rooms come at a premium, but you can watch the shore from the terrace.

Fish & Chip Shop   FISH & CHIPS £
(☑ 01728-452250; www.aldeburghfishandchips.co.uk; 226 High St; mains £5-8; ☺ noon-2pm daily, plus 5-8pm Thu-Sat) Aldeburgh has a reputation for the finest fish and chips in the area, and this cheerful takeaway is the place to find out why. The same owners operate two sit-down restaurants along the strip, but it's more fun to perch on the seawall.

★ Lighthouse   MODERN BRITISH ££
(☑ 01728-453377; www.lighthouserestaurant.co.uk; 77 High St; mains £12-22.50; ☺ noon-3pm & 5-9.30pm; ♪) The owner of this interesting, unpretentious eatery was formerly a waiter here, and he's taken the place to new heights with a fine menu of modern British dishes, many featuring cod, sole and other seafood bought fresh from the boats on the beach.

❶ Getting There & Away

Bus 64/65 links Aldeburgh with Ipswich (return £6.80, 1½ hours, hourly Monday to Saturday). From there you can connect to the rest of the region.

WORTH A TRIP

THOMAS GAINSBOROUGH'S HOUSE

The great English painter Thomas Gainsborough (1727–1788) made his fortune from portraits of the gentry and Suffolk landscapes, and many of his works are displayed in his atmospheric **birthplace** (📞01787-372958; www.gainsborough.org; 46 Gainsborough St) in the village of Sudbury. The museum closed for renovations in 2020; when it reopens look out for the exquisite *Portrait of Harriett, Viscountess Tracy*, celebrated for its delicate portrayal of drapery. Call for the latest opening hours and prices.

Buses run at least hourly (not Sundays) from Sudbury to Ipswich (£5.50, one hour) and Colchester (£4.70, 50 minutes). Bus 753 (hourly Monday to Saturday) runs through Long Melford (£1.70, 10 minutes) and Lavenham (£4.30, 25 minutes) to Bury St Edmunds (£4.70, one hour).

Southwold

📞01502 / POP 1098

Southwold's reputation as a holiday getaway for well-heeled Londoners earned it the nickname 'Kensington-on-Sea' – indeed, city-slickers have been escaping here since at least the Regency period. With its fine sand beach, beachfront bathing huts, and general absence of seaside kitsch, the resort has long been a favourite hangout for artists, including JMW Turner, Charles Rennie Mackintosh, Lucian Freud and Damien Hirst.

◉ Sights

Southwold's shorefront promenade is its main attraction, but amble inland and you'll find pretty streets of Regency houses and a squat 19th-century **lighthouse**.

Southwold Pier AREA
(📞01502-722105; www.southwoldpier.co.uk; North Pde; ⊙pier 10am-7pm, to 5pm winter) **FREE** At the north end of the strip, the 190m-long pier, first built in 1899, is worth a visit for its eccentric **Under the Pier Show**, a kooky collection of handmade coin-operated amusement machines combining daft fun with political satire. The same maker built the Heath Robinson–esque water clock further along the pier.

Adnams BREWERY
(📞01502-727225; www.adnams.co.uk; Adnams Pl; tours £20; ⊙tours daily Mar-Sep) Southwold's huge brewery fills the streets with pleasant smells, and with advance booking you can tour the premises and be amazed at the high-tech kit inside these venerable Victorian buildings. Hour-long tours (for over-18s only) also include a tutored tasting of the house beers, including the ever-popular Ghost Ship (4.5%). Call for timings.

✸ Festivals & Events

Latitude Festival ART
(www.latitudefestival.co.uk; Henham Park; ⊙Jul) An eclectic mix of music, literature, dance, drama and comedy set in a country estate.

⊨ Sleeping & Eating

★**Sutherland House** HOTEL £££
(📞01502-724544; www.sutherlandhouse.co.uk; 56 High St; r from £175; P🛜) Past guests at this former mayor's residence include the prince who later became James II, and the Earl of Sandwich. Modern-day travellers can enjoy a hint of the same extravagant lifestyle in sumptuous rooms with pargeted ceilings, exposed beams and free-standing baths.

Classy meals (mains £17 to £32, noon to 2pm and 6.30pm to 9pm, closed Monday) range from aged sirloin steaks to pan-seared halibut and whole lobster.

Swan HOTEL £££
(📞01502-722186; www.theswansouthwold.co.uk; Market Sq; s/d £155/200; P🛜🐾) A super-stylish pub-hotel owned by the Adnams brewery, so you can be sure the beer in the bar has been expertly stored. The building is 17th-century, but rooms are anything but traditional – think four-poster beds with neon-pink posts, turquoise wine-bottle carpets and designer lamps.

Two Magpies BAKERY £
(www.twomagpiesbakery.co.uk; 88 High St; snacks from £3, pizzas from £8; ⊙8am-5pm Sun-Fri, to 8.30pm Sat) This enterprising bakery produces all manner of tasty buns, breads, pastries and savoury treats, including delicious sourdough pizzas on Saturday evenings. Ask about its speciality baking courses.

ⓘ Getting There & Away

Bus 146 links Southwold with Norwich (£4.70, 1½ hours, hourly Monday to Saturday).

For services south, including those to and from Aldeburgh, catch bus 99A to Halesworth (£2.50, 30 minutes, every two hours Monday to Saturday) and continue on the 521 (£4.80, one hour, three daily).

NORFOLK

At the risk of sounding like Alan Partridge, there's more to Norfolk than Norwich and the Broads (though the historic county capital and the meandering waterways that surround it are both wonderful places to spend time). Continue north, and you'll hit some lavish stately homes and some of England's loveliest coastal resorts – all brick-edged, flint-stone houses, windswept, bird-filled marshes and endless strips of sand.

Norwich

☑ 01603 / POP 132,512

Norwich (norr-ich) – the affluent and easy-going home of TV's Alan Partridge – is one of East Anglia's most historic cities, and its winding, part-pedestrianised streets are crammed with ancient flint churches and venerable timbered buildings that speak volumes about the wealth that the wool trade brought to Norfolk in the medieval period. The castle and cathedral are obvious drawcards, but it's worth staying on to haggle for antiques in eclectic emporiums and feast at some of the county's finest restaurants.

◉ Sights

The area known as **Tombland**, opposite Norwich Cathedral, is where the city's market was originally located ('tomb' is an old Norse word for empty, relating to the open market place). Enter through the archway of the precariously leaning **Augustine Steward House**, duck behind the church, and follow Princes St to cobbled **Elm Hill**, Norwich's most perfect medieval street, curving downhill towards the river. The thatched, timbered house containing the **Britons Arms** (www.britonsarms.co.uk; 9 Elm Hill; light mains from £5.50; ⊙10am-4pm Mon-Sat) coffee house has been here since 1347.

★**Norwich Cathedral**   CATHEDRAL
(☑ 01603-218300; www.cathedral.org.uk; 65 The Close; donations requested; ⊙10am-4pm Mon-Fri, 10am-3pm Sat, 1-3pm Sun) Norwich's most impressive landmark is its magnificent,

medieval Anglican cathedral (not to be confused with the Catholic cathedral, a Victorian copy on the north side of town). Its needle spire soars higher than any other church in England, apart from Salisbury, and its fan-vaulted ceiling is a masterpiece of medieval engineering. Be sure to check out the collection of ornate ceiling bosses in the medieval cloisters, featuring everything from pagan-inspired green men to devouring dragons.

★**Norwich Castle**   MUSEUM
(☑ 01603-495897; www.museums.norfolk.gov.uk; Castle Hill) An imposing cube of masonry crowning a hilltop overlooking central Norwich, this massive 12th-century castle is one of England's best-preserved examples of Anglo-Norman military architecture. Inside, a superb **interactive museum** crams in lively exhibits on Boudica and the Iceni, the Anglo-Saxons, the Vikings and the gruesome medieval punishments once carried out here. Call ahead to check the latest opening times and prices.

★**Museum of Norwich**   MUSEUM
(☑ 01603-629127; www.museums.norfolk.gov.uk; Bridewell Alley; adult/child £6.20/5.30; ⊙10am-4.30pm Tue-Sat) Be on your best behaviour: this engaging little museum is set in a 14th-century house of correction. Displays here explore Norwich's prominence as England's second city in the Middle Ages and its 19th-century industrial heritage.

★**Blickling Hall**   HISTORIC BUILDING
(NT; ☑ 01263-738030; www.nationaltrust.org.uk; Blickling; adult/child £10/5; ⊙house noon-4pm, grounds 10am-4pm; P ♿) Gorgeous Blickling was remodelled in the 17th century for Sir Henry Hobart, James I's chief justice, but the house is best known for its previous owners, the Boleyn family, though the jury is out on whether Anne Boleyn actually lived here before her unfortunate marriage to Henry VIII. Impressive enough from the outside, Blickling is something else on the inside – many of the extravagant interiors date to the early 17th century, including some of the finest Jacobean moulded plaster ceilings still in existence.

Sainsbury Centre for Visual Arts   GALLERY
(☑ 01603-593199; www.scva.ac.uk; University of East Anglia (UEA); ⊙9am-6pm Tue-Fri, 10am-5pm Sat & Sun; ☐22, 25, 26) FREE The eclectic art collection of Sir Robert Sainsbury (of

Norwich

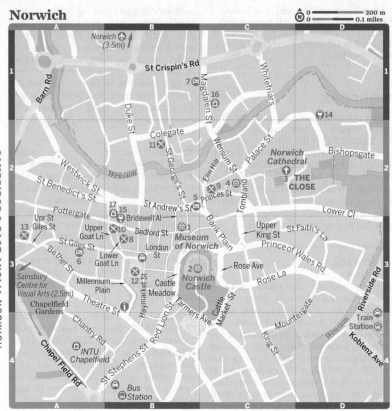

Norwich

◉ Top Sights
1 Museum of Norwich	B3
2 Norwich Castle	B3
3 Norwich Cathedral	C2

◉ Sights
4 Augustine Steward's House	C2

🛏 Sleeping
5 3 Princes	B2
6 38 St Giles	A3
7 Gothic House	B1

✖ Eating
8 Biddy's Tearoom	B3

9 Britons Arms	C2
10 Grosvenor Fish Bar	B3
11 Last Wine Bar & Restaurant	B2
12 Norwich Market	B3
13 Roger Hickman's	A3

🍷 Drinking & Nightlife
14 Adam & Eve	D1
15 Birdcage	B3

🛍 Shopping
16 Looses Emporium	C1
17 St Gregory's Antiques Collectables	B2

supermarket fame) is displayed in the first major public building by renowned architect Norman Foster. Displayed around the hangar-like space are striking sculptures and paintings (including many works by Francis Bacon, David Hockney, Henry Moore, Degas and Giacometti) mixed in with ethnological curiosities from dozens of tribal cultures.

The gallery is in the University of East Anglia's grounds, 2 miles west of the city centre. To get there take bus 22, 25 or 26 (£2.80, 15 minutes).

🛏 Sleeping

Gothic House   B&B **££**
(📞 01603-631879; www.gothic-house-norwich.
com; King's Head Yard, Magdalen St; s/d £75/105;
🅿 🛜) Tucked into a courtyard at the quiet
end of town, this handsome town-house
B&B will whisk you back to the Regency era.
Wood panelling, columns and cornices border the swirling stairs that lead to striking
floral rooms with intricate timber windows.

⭐ 3 Princes   B&B **£££**
(📞 01603-622699; www.3princes-norwich.co.uk; 3
Princes St; s/d from £89/185; 🛜) A handsome
old town house with a walled, tree-shaded
courtyard garden, 3 Princes puts you in the
medieval heart of the city, yards from lovely
Elm Hill. Behind the historic exterior, the
wood-floored rooms come in a modernist
colour scheme of greys and whites, with
small swatches of blue from cushions and
bedspreads.

38 St Giles   B&B **£££**
(📞 01603-662944; www.38stgiles.co.uk; 38 St
Giles St; s/d from £125/150; 🅿 🛜) Boutique 38
St Giles reinvents the English B&B with period glamour. The lavish rooms are all vintage
furniture, fine fabrics, damask blinds, and
floor rugs laid over polished floorboards.
The excellent breakfasts feature all sorts of
local and organic ingredients, and you can
swap a full English for crème fraiche pancakes with bacon and fresh berries.

🍴 Eating

For cheap eats, try the globe-trotting food
stands inside the town's partly covered
market (Market Pl; snacks from £3; 🕙 9am-3pm
Mon-Sat).

⭐ Grosvenor Fish Bar   FISH & CHIPS **£**
(www.fshshop.com; 28 Lower Goat Lane; mains
from £5; 🕙 10.45am-7.30pm Mon-Sat) At this hip
chippy, fish and chips comes as fresh cod
goujons and chips fried in vegan-friendly
oil, a 'Big Mack' is a crispy mackerel fillet in
a roll, and the 'Six Quid Squid' (squid rings
with garlic aioli) really is £6. Either eat in
the basement, take away, or they'll deliver to
the Birdcage pub opposite.

Biddy's Tearoom   CAFE **£**
(www.biddystearoom.com; 15 Lower Goat Lane;
cakes from £3; 🕙 10.30am-4pm) Biddy's
takes the traditional tearoom into design-
magazine territory, with reclaimed furniture, leather armchairs, vintage sweet jars,
premium teas and giant, rich sticky buns
stuffed with cinnamon, raspberries and
chocolate that could feed a family. The baking is top class; it also does breakfasts, finger
sandwiches and afternoon teas.

⭐ Roger Hickman's   MODERN BRITISH **£££**
(📞 01603-633522; www.rogerhickmansrestaurant.
com; 79 Upper St Giles St; 2/3 courses lunch
£22/27, dinner £40/50; 🕙 noon-2.30pm & 7-10pm
Wed-Sat) Understated elegance is the name
of the game in this prestigious modern British establishment. The dining room is elegant and intimate, and the creations of chef
Roger Hickman feature imaginative preparations of pigeon, lamb loin, halibut, cep
mushrooms, parsnip gnocchi and fermented
beetroot among other top-tier ingredients.

Last Wine Bar & Restaurant   BRITISH **£££**
(📞 01603-626626; www.lastwinebar.co.uk; 70
St George's St; mains £18-29; 🕙 noon-2.30pm &
6-9.30pm Mon-Sat) The decor in this stylish
bar and eatery reflects the building's past
life as a shoe factory, with lasts (wooden
shoe moulds) as light fittings and Singer sewing machine tables. Impressively,
the food lives up to the setting – venison,
duck, hake, steaks, posh burgers, and some
above-average options for vegetarians.

🍷 Drinking & Nightlife

⭐ Birdcage   PUB
(www.thebirdcagenorwich.co.uk; 23 Pottergate;
🕙 noon-9pm Fri & Sat; 🛜) Footloose and fancy
free, this beatnik public house is currently
open just at weekends, but as things normal-
ise, expect a revival of its regular program
of poetry, cabaret, life-drawing and music
events throughout the week. The ales are
real, the cocktails cool, and you can ferry in
fish and chips from the Grosvenor Fish Bar
over the road.

Adam & Eve   PUB
(📞 01603-667423; Bishopsgate; 🕙 11am-11pm
Mon-Sat, noon-10.30pm Sun) Charming, Dutch-
eaved Adam & Eve is Norwich's oldest surviving pub, founded way back in 1249, when
medieval masons used to drop by while
constructing Norwich cathedral. Tiny, with
a sunken floor and part-panelled walls, it
attracts a mixed band of regulars, choristers
and ghost hunters. Check opening hours in
advance.

ANTIQUE NORWICH

In Norwich's emporiums, you can find everything from bone china and Ormolu clocks to military uniforms, tin toys, salvaged shop signs and fibreglass Daleks from *Dr Who*. Start the rummaging in the sprawling **St Gregory's Antiques & Collectable** (01603-305372; www.facebook.com/stgregorysantiques; St Gregory's Church, Pottergate; 10am-5pm Mon-Fri, to 6pm Sat, 11am-4pm Sun), set inside the historic St Gregory's Church, or browse finds from more than 60 dealers in the Aladdin's Cave–like **Looses Emporium** (01603-665600; www.loosesemporium.co.uk; 23-35 Magdalen St; 10am-5pm Mon-Fri, 9am-6pm Sat, 10am-4pm Sun).

Information

Tourist Office (01603-989500; www.visitnorwich.co.uk; Millennium Plain; 10am-5.30pm Mon-Sat) Inside the Forum complex; ask about local walking tours.

Getting There & Around

AIR

Norwich International Airport (01603-411923; www.norwichairport.co.uk; Holt Rd) is 4 miles north of town. Get here on bus 501 from the centre (adult/child £3.80/1.10, every 10 to 15 minutes).

BUS

The **bus station** (Queen's Rd) is 400m south of the castle on Queens Rd. **National Express** (www.nationalexpress.com) covers longer routes; **First** (www.firstgroup.com), **Konect** (www.konectbus.co.uk) and others operate in and around the city:

Cromer Bus X44 (£4.20, one hour, hourly Monday to Saturday)

Wroxham Konect 5B (£3, one hour, hourly)

King's Lynn First Excel (£6.40, 1½ hours, hourly Monday to Saturday)

London Victoria (£13.30, three hours, every two hours)

TRAIN

The train station is off Thorpe Rd, 600m east of Norwich Castle. Destinations include:

Cambridge (£19.50, 1¼ hours, hourly)

Colchester (£13.50, one hour, every 30 minutes)

London Liverpool St (£10, two hours, every 30 minutes)

Cromer

 01263 / POP 7683

The once-fashionable Victorian resort of Cromer still flourishes as a busy fishing port, famous for the sweet-tasting brown crabs which are hauled in daily during the March to October crabbing season. The long, cliff-edged seafront is lined with fishing boats and the tractors that pull them onto the pebbles, and the beach sees some impressive swell for surfers.

Sights & Activities

Cromer's historic **pier** (01263-512495; www.cromerpier.co.uk; Esplanade; 10am-dusk) **FREE** has existed in one shape or another since around 1391, and it hosts one of the country's last end-of-pier shows (think dancers, sing-alongs and nostalgia).

Surfers can rent boards and take lessons at **Glide Surf School** (01263-805005; www.glidesurfschool.co.uk; lessons adult/child £27/32, board hire per day from £17; 9.30am-5.30pm Mon-Sat, to 4pm Sun Apr-Oct, 10am-4pm Sat & Sun Nov-Mar), just east of the pier.

Felbrigg Hall   HISTORIC BUILDING
(NT; 01263-837444; www.nationaltrust.org.uk; Felbrigg; adult/child £8/4; house noon-3pm, garden 10am-4pm; P) An elegant Jacobean mansion boasting a fine, painting-filled Georgian interior, Felbrigg is 2 miles southwest of Cromer, off the B1436. Topped by a curious parapet spelling out the family motto, the house sits amid attractive gardens that include a walled-kitchen garden and an 18th-century orangery. Call ahead to see if longer opening hours have resumed.

Henry Blogg Museum   MUSEUM
(RNLI Lifeboat Museum; 01263-511294; www.rnli.org; The Gangway; 10am-5pm Tue-Sun Apr-Sep, to 4pm Oct, Nov, Feb & Mar) **FREE** Hands-on gizmos add to the appeal of this excellent museum housed in the local lifeboat station and named after highly decorated local coxswain Henry Blogg. Inside, you can learn to tap out a message in Morse and spell your name in semaphore flags, while learning tales of the brave sea rescues carried out by the station.

Sleeping & Eating

★ **Red Lion**   INN ££
(01263-514964; www.redlioncromer.co.uk; Brook St; s/d/ste from £68/125/145; P) Coloured floor tiles, wooden banisters

and stained glass signal this seafront inn's 18th-century heritage, but stylish, sea-themed rooms bring the package bang up to date. All bedrooms come with bathtubs. You can see the sea from the dreamy deluxe suite (room 7), which also has its own sea-facing balcony.

★ **Davies** SEAFOOD £

(📞01263-512727; 7 Garden St; crab £3.50-6; ⊙8.30am-5pm Mon-Sat, 10am-4pm Sun) At this Cromer institution, the crabs on sale were caught on the owner's boat, the *Richard William*, and boiled, cracked and dressed on the premises. Other treats include cockles, mussels and homemade fish pâté. Hours are often reduced in winter.

Rocket House CAFE £

(📞01263-519126; www.rockethousecafe.co.uk; The Gangway; mains £6.50-11; ⊙9am-4pm Mon-Fri, 10am-5pm Sat & Sun; 🔲) Upstairs in the same art-deco building as the lifeboat station and Henry Blogg Museum, this much-loved cafe has a balcony that almost perches you over the waves. The menu jumps from sandwiches, burgers and salads to fish and chips and dressed Cromer crab.

❶ Getting There & Away

Trains link Cromer with Norwich (£8.20, 45 minutes, hourly). Bus X44 also runs to Norwich (£4.20, one hour, hourly Monday to Saturday), while the daily **Coasthopper CH1** (www.sanders coaches.com) runs west along the coast as far as Wells-next-the-Sea (£4.40, one hour, hourly), where there are frequent connections on to King's Lynn.

Cley-next-the-Sea

📌 01263 / POP 437

A strong contender for the title of prettiest Norfolk village, sleepy Cley (pronounced 'cly' to rhyme with 'tie') is a dainty huddle of brick-edged flint houses spilling onto bird-filled marshes, centred on an *extremely* photogenic windmill.

◉ Sights

Cley Marshes NATURE RESERVE

(📞01263-740008; www.norfolkwildlifetrust.org.uk; near Cley-next-the-Sea; adult/child £4.50/free; ⊙reserve dawn-dusk, visitor centre 10am-5pm Mar-Oct, to 4pm Nov-Feb; 🅿) 🐾 One of England's premier birdwatching sites, Cley Marshes hosts more than 300 resident bird species and numerous migratory visitors – all easily spotted from the visitor centre and a network of walking trails and bird hides tucked among the golden reeds. Marsh harriers, bitterns and bearded reedlings are top spots here.

🛏 Sleeping & Eating

★ **Cley Windmill** B&B £££

(📞01263-740209; www.cleywindmill.co.uk; High St; d £159-295, apt per week from £495; 🅿) If you've ever fancied staying in a windmill, you won't find one much lovelier than this fully intact, 19th-century gem. The curiously shaped but cosy rooms are named after their former working lives, and many look directly over reed-filled salt marshes. A cute four-person self-catering cottage sits just next door.

The windmill has a great kitchen too – satisfying Norfolk-themed taster menus cost £32.50 (6.30pm to 8pm, bookings required).

★ **Picnic Fayre** DELI £

(📞01263-740587; www.picnic-fayre.co.uk; High St; snacks from £3; ⊙9am-4pm Mon-Sat, from 10am Sun) A deli to ditch the diet for, fully stocked with imaginative variations on English picnic classics – pork pies with chorizo, sausages smothered with sweet-chilli sauce, and home-baked lavender bread.

Blakeney

📌 01263 / POP 801

The pretty village of Blakeney was once a busy fishing and trading port before its harbour silted up. It's since become a popular spot for day-trippers, who sit and admire the yachts on the creek, take seal-spotting boat

---

❶ BUSING THE NORTH NORFOLK COAST

Though the villages on the north Norfolk coast feel agreeably isolated, it's easy to get between them thanks to excellent bus links. The daily **Coasthopper CH1** (www.sanderscoaches.com) runs from Cromer to Wells-next-the-Sea (£4.40, one hour, hourly), via Cley-next-the-Sea and Blakeney. At Wells, you can hop onto the **Coastliner 36** (www.lynxbus.co.uk) to King's Lynn (£5.80, 1¾ hours, hourly), via Holkham and Burnham Deepdale. A special all-day £10 ticket allows unlimited travel on both routes.

THE NORFOLK BROADS

Why Should I Visit a Swamp?

These vast wetlands were formed when the rivers Wensum, Bure, Waveney and Yare flooded gaping holes created by 12th-century crofters digging for peat. In the process, a vast and valuable wetland ecosystem was created – as well as a playground for leisure boating. Today, there are 125 miles of winding waterways to explore; pop into the **visitor centre** (📞 01603-782281; www.visitthebroads.co.uk; Station Rd, Hoveton; ☉ 9am-5pm Easter-Nov) in Hoveton for local information.

If you prefer not to sleep on the water, **St Gregory's B&B** (📞 01603-784319; www.stgregoryswroxham.co.uk; 11 Stalham Rd, Hoveton; s/d from £60/80; 🅿 🛜) in Hoveton is a fine spot to regain your land legs, and there are plenty of cafes nearby and over the bridge in Wroxham.

Exploring by Boat

The main hubs for renting boats are Wroxham and Hoveton, just northeast of Norwich, and the villages along the A149 between Potter Heigham and Stalham, on the edge of Hickling Broad. Launches range from basic day-boats with outboard motors to comfortable live-aboard cruisers with cabins, kitchens and bathrooms; most operators rent by the half-day, day or week, and renters receive an introduction to inland navigation before setting off.

Broads Tours (📞 01603-782207; www.broadstours.co.uk; The Bridge, Wroxham; boat hire per hour/day from £21/130, tours adult/child from £9.50/6; ☉ 8am-5.30pm Mar-Oct) Lets out boats by the day, as well as running popular one- to two-hour riverboat tours.

Barnes Brinkcraft (📞 01603-782625; www.barnesbrinkcraft.co.uk; Riverside Rd, Wroxham; canoe hire per half-/full day £30/45, boat hire per hour/day £20/121, 4-berth boat per week from £600; ☉ Apr-Oct) Has day-boats, canoes and live-aboard cruisers.

Sutton Staithe Boatyard (📞 01692-581653; www.dayboathire.com; Sutton Staithe; boat hire per half-/full day £80/120, canoe hire per half-/full day £25/40) Rents out boats and canoes at the quieter end of the Broads near Sutton.

For longer boating holidays, try **Blakes** (📞 0345 498 6184; www.blakes.co.uk; 4-berth boat per week from £600) or **Richardson's** (📞 01692-668981; www.richardsonsboatingholidays.co.uk; The Staithe, Stalham; boats per week from £550).

Exploring by Canoe

Canoes and kayaks can be rented for £35 to £40 per day at most of the big boating hubs. Hickling Broad offers lovely paddling, with fewer day boats competing for space.

Whispering Reeds (📞 01692-598314; www.whisperingreeds.net; Staithe Rd, Hickling; canoe hire per 3/6hr £25/40; ☉ Easter-Oct) On the edge of Hickling Broad.

Waveney River Centre (📞 01502-677343; www.waveneyrivercentre.co.uk; Burgh St Peter; kayak & canoe hire per day £35; ☉ Easter-Oct) On the River Waveney near Lowestoft.

---

trips from the quay, or walk into the **Blakeney National Nature Reserve** (NT; 📞 01263-740241; www.nationaltrust.org.uk; ☉ dawn-dusk) FREE with long camera lenses in search of migratory birds. The spit on the far side of the reeds serves up a stunning, lonely sweep of sand.

👉 Tours

At the end of the nature reserve, **Blakeney Point** is home to thousands of grey and common seals. who come to this secluded spot to pup, in winter and summer respectively. **Bishop's Boats** (📞 01263-740753; www.bishops

boats.com; Blakeney Quay; adult/child £13/7; ☉ 1-4 boats daily Mar-Oct) runs here daily from Blakeney quay; **Beans Seal Trips** (📞 01263-740505; www.beansboattrips.co.uk; Morston Quay; adult/child £13/7; ☉ 1-3 daily) runs from nearby Morston Quay, 1.5 miles east.

🛏 Sleeping & Eating

Kings Arms　　　　　　　　　　　　INN ££
(📞 01263-740341; www.blakeneykingsarms.co.uk; Westgate St; r from £100; 🅿 🛜 🐾) Simple, old-fashioned rooms (colourful carpets, bedspreads, pine furniture) in a pub that's been welcoming fishermen for centuries. Order

Mark the Canoe Man (☑ 07873-748408; www.thecanoeman.com; canoe hire 3/6hr £45/55, guided trips from £40; ☉ Apr-Oct) Arranges guided trips to areas the cruisers can't reach, as well as renting canoes and kayaks for self-paddling; you can put in at Wroxham, Horning, Beccles and other locations.

Exploring on Foot & by Bike

Despite its waterlogged reputation, the Broads are criss-crossed by a web of walking trails, including the 61-mile **Weavers' Way**, which links Cromer to Great Yarmouth.

The 15-mile section between Aylsham and Stalham is open to bicycles, and you can pick up wheels at **Broadland Cycle Hire** (☑ 07887 480331; www.norfolkbroadscycling.co.uk; Bewilderwood, Hoveton; bike hire adult/child per day £18/7, per week £70/30; ☉ 10am-5pm Easter-Oct), based at the Bewilderwood adventure park near Hoveton.

Sights & Activities that Don't Involve Water?

Whether on foot, in a car, or in a boat, the following sights are well worth visiting.

Museum of the Broads (☑ 01692-581681; www.museumofthebroads.org.uk; The Staithe, Stalham; adult/child £6/2, boat trips £5/3; ☉ 10am-4.30pm Sun-Fri Easter-Oct) Just off the A149 in Stalham, this folky museum features fine boats and some interesting displays on the life and history of the local marshmen. You can ride on a steam launch too.

Toad Hole Cottage (☑ 01692-678763; www.howhilltrust.org.uk; How Hill; ☉ 10am-5pm Easter-Oct) **FREE** The life of Fen dwellers is revealed at this tiny cottage, a restored eel-catcher's home. You can also explore the gardens of attractive How Hill House, and follow a picturesque nature trail (adult/child £2.50/150) past some of the 'skeleton' windmills that were used to drain sections of the marshes.

Bewilderwood (☑ 01692-633033; www.bewilderwood.co.uk; Horning Rd, Hoveton; adult/child £17.50/15.50; ☉ 10am-5.30pm Easter-Oct; ⛟; ☐ 5B) A forest fantasy playground for children and families, with zip wires, rope bridges, treehouses, boat trips, marsh walks, aerial mazes and more, to trigger young imaginations.

St Helen's Church (☑ 01603-270340; Ranworth; ☉ 10.30am-5pm) The 'Cathedral of the Broads' is a handsome 14th-century structure, and inside you can see a magnificent painted medieval rood screen and a 15th-century *antiphoner* (illustrated book of prayers).

Bure Valley Steam Railway (☑ 01263-733858; www.bvrw.co.uk; Aylsham; adult/child return £14.50/7; ☉ 2-7 trains daily Apr-Oct; ℗) Steam buffs will love this miniature loco, which puffs along 9 miles of narrow-gauge tracks between Aylsham and Wroxham.

Getting Around

Wroxham is the easiest place to reach by public transport; Konect bus 5B runs from Norwich (£3, 45 minutes, hourly Monday to Saturday), continuing to Stalham (£3.20, 35 minutes).

---

some substantial pub grub (mains from £10 to £15; meals served noon to 9pm), then, for great theatre gossip, ask landlady Marjorie about her career on the stage.

Moorings   MODERN BRITISH **££**
(☑ 01263-740054; www.blakeney-moorings.co.uk; High St; mains £17-27; ☉ 11am-2.30pm & 6pm-9pm Tue-Sat) Perfectly pitched fish dishes have won this bright, friendly bistro a loyal following – try the spicy Norfolk crab cakes or about the most East Anglian dish you could imagine: sea trout, clams and samphire, with saffron jus.

Wells-next-the-Sea

☑ 01328 / POP 2165

After the marsh-fringed villages of Cley and Blakeney, Wells feels like a return to the classic English seaside. From the busy fishing quay a mile-long road runs out over former marshland to the vast, sandy Wells Beach, backed by a pastel sweep of elevated beach huts and a long bank of dunes. It's extremely family-friendly and gets very busy on sunny days – come early to bag a parking space.

◉ Sights & Activities

Lovely **Wells Beach** is the main focus of attention. There's a good beach cafe, and a miniature train (per person £1.50) connects town and beach during the tourist season.

Wells Maltings ART CENTRE
(☑01328-710885; www.wellsmaltings.org.uk; Staithe St; ⊙exhibitions 10am-4pm) **FREE** Part music venue, part theatre, part cinema, part museum and part exhibition space, Wells Maltings is the town's cultural hub. Check the website to see what's happening.

Wells & Walsingham Railway RAIL
(☑01328-711630; www.wwlr.co.uk; Stiffkey Rd; adult/child return £9.50/7.50; ⊙4-5 trains daily Mar-Nov) The longest 10.25in narrow-gauge railway in the world puffs for five picturesque miles from Wells to the village of Little Walsingham, a Catholic pilgrimage site since medieval times, centred on the ruins of Reformation-ravaged Walsingham Priory.

🛏 Sleeping & Eating

Check to see if the **Wells YHA hostel** (www.yha.org.uk) on Church Plain has reopened to guests.

★**Old Custom House** B&B ££
(☑01328-711463; www.eastquay.co.uk; East Quay; s/d from £100/120, ste s/d £110/130; Ⓟ🖤) This stately but comfortable white house by the quay has worn timbers, alcoves full of books and gorgeous creek views. Choose from snug 'Captain's Quarters' rooms or the grand four-poster suite. It also has two cute self-catering cottages for longer stays.

Wells Beach Cafe CAFE £
(www.holkham.co.uk; Wells Beach; mains from £5; ⊙10am-5pm Mon-Fri, from 9am Sat & Sun; 🖤🖤) This pastel-blue weatherboard cafe keeps beachgoers stocked up with bacon baps, chips, homemade chilli and takeaway hot chocolates. Outside there's a corral of picnic tables; inside there's a wood-burning stove for when the wind whips round.

Wells Crab House SEAFOOD £££
(☑01328-710456; www.wellscrabhouse.co.uk; 38 Freeman St; mains £18-30; ⊙noon-2.30pm & 6-9pm Tue-Sat, noon-3pm Sun) This temple to seafood can be booked out weeks in advance, so plan ahead if you want to feast on Wells crab, buttered lobster, crayfish tails, smoked salmon, cockles and more. Look out for more ambitious seafood dishes such as plaice fillets stuffed with chorizo, peppers and preserved lemons.

❶ Information

Tourist Office (☑01328-710885; www.north-norfolk.org; Wells Maltings, Staithe St; ⊙10am-3pm Wed-Mon) Lots of local leaflets and maps.

❶ Getting There & Away

Wells is a pivot point for coastal bus services. The daily Coasthopper CH1 runs east to Cromer (£4.40, one hour, hourly); the Coastliner 36 runs west to King's Lynn (£5.80, 1¾ hours, hourly).

Holkham

☑01328 / POP 220

The village of Holkham was the pet project of a single family. The Cokes, hereditary Earls of Leicester, constructed both lavish Holkham Hall, and the immaculate village of brick and flint houses that surrounds it.

◉ Sights

★**Holkham National Nature Reserve** NATURE RESERVE
(www.holkham.co.uk; parking per hour/day £2/9; ⊙car park 6am-6pm; ♿) 🅟 The shoreline in front of Holkham is a stunning sweep of dune-backed sand, divided from the village by a wide buffer of salt marshes, meadows and pine forest. It's arguably Norfolk's prettiest beach, but it's no secret, and visitors come in droves to paddle, sunbathe, picnic and scan the dunes for rare birds from hides on the edge of the woods. Access to the 14-sq-mile reserve is from the car park opposite Holkham village, but be ready for a 1-mile walk to the sand.

★**Holkham Hall & Estate** HISTORIC BUILDING
(☑01328-713111; www.holkham.co.uk; adult/child £17/8.50, parking £4; ⊙noon-4pm Sun, Mon & Thu Mar-Oct, grounds daily 9am-5pm, till 4pm Nov-Mar; Ⓟ♿) 🅟 Holkham Hall was the ancestral seat of the Earls of Leicester and the present earl still lives in the palatial 18th-century Palladian mansion constructed by Earl Thomas Coke. The perfectly symmetrical, Italianate house was essentially constructed as a display case for the earl's astonishing collection of classical sculpture and painting, assembled during a grand tour of Europe from 1712 to 1718. Guided visits explore the guest rooms, with their original tapestry and *cafoy* (fabric) wall coverings, and

THE QUEEN'S COUNTRY ESTATE

Both monarchists and republicans will find fuel for their respective positions at **Sandringham** (01485-545400; www.sandringhamestate.co.uk; adult/child £15.30/7.50 plus booking fee; 10am-4pm selected dates Apr-Oct; P; 35), the Queen's extravagant country estate.

No luxury was spared when this elegant stately home was built in 1870 by the then Prince and Princess of Wales (who later became King Edward VII and Queen Alexandra). Appropriately, the house is still decorated as it was in Edwardian times, and an army of gardeners still tends to the vast sea of gardens and grounds.

It's surreal to imagine generations of royals treating this grand house as just a family home. The stables today house a flag-waving museum filled with royal memorabilia. The superb vintage-car collection includes the very first royal motor from 1900.

Sandringham is 6 miles northeast of King's Lynn off the A149. Bus 35 runs from King's Lynn (£2.80, 20 minutes, every two hours).

the warren of hidden passageways used by servants.

Sleeping

★ Victoria   INN £££

(01328-711008; www.holkham.co.uk; Park Rd; s/d from £125/150; P🛜🐾) In the village of staff houses constructed to service Holkham Hall, the graceful, flint-fronted Victoria is an elegant place to stay or dine after exploring the hall and beach. Spread over several buildings, rooms pay a subtle nod to Edwardian design, with gleaming bathrooms and soft upholstery. The kitchen cooks up a storm (mains £7 to £27), using produce sourced from Holkham Estate; check if it has reopened to nonguests.

Burnham Deepdale & Around

01485 / POP 877

The stretch of coast spanning the tiny villages of Burnham Deepdale, Brancaster Staithe, Titchwell and Thornham is a lovely span of marshes, creeks and distant dune-backed beaches. Just inland, the hamlet of **Burnham Thorpe** was the childhood home of Admiral Lord Nelson. A side lane from Brancaster provides the easiest access to the sand. Contact the **tourist office** (01485-210256; www.deepdalebackpackers.co.uk; Burnham Deepdale; 9am-5pm Mon-Sat, 10am-4pm Sun) at Deepdale Farm for information on kitesurfing or windsurfing.

Sights

RSPB Titchwell Marsh   NATURE RESERVE

(RSPB; 01485-210779; www.rspb.org.uk; Titchwell; adult/child £5/2.50; 9.30am-5pm Mar-Oct, to 4pm Nov-Feb; P) About 3 miles west of Burnham Deepdale, the marshland, sandbars and lagoons of Titchwell Marsh nature reserve attract vast numbers of birds, and similar numbers of birders. In spring, listen out for the booming call of the bittern; summer brings marsh harriers, avocets, terns and nesting bearded tits. In winter you'll see more than 20 species of wading birds and countless ducks and geese.

Sleeping & Eating

★ Deepdale

Backpackers & Camping   HOSTEL £

(01485-210256; www.deepdalebackpackers.co.uk; Burnham Deepdale; dm £13-21, r £40-110, sites £9-59; P@🛜) For backpackers it doesn't get much better than this: you can camp in the grounds (in your own tent or motor home), stay in private rooms, or – in normal times – sleep in spick-and-span ensuite dorms in converted stables. There's a capacious and well-equipped kitchen, a barbecue area, hot showers, and a colourful lounge warmed by a wood-burning stove. Check to see if dorm beds are available again.

★ Titchwell Manor   HOTEL £££

(01485-210221; www.titchwellmanor.com; Titchwell, near Brancaster; r £150-290; P@🛜) Dreamy Titchwell Manor is a swish, contemporary reinvention of a grand Victorian house. Inside, you'll find a modern-meets-mid-century theme, with bold designer wallpaper, Regency curtains and eclectic furniture; rooms at the front gaze across the marshes to the sea.

HOUGHTON HALL

Built for Britain's first de-facto prime minister, Sir Robert Walpole, in 1730, Palladian-style Houghton Hall (☑01485-528569; www.houghtonhall. com; near King's Lynn; adult/child £16/ free; ☺11am-5pm Wed, Thu & Sun May-late Sep; P) is famed for its lavish interiors, overflowing with gilt, tapestries, murals, woodcarving, statuary and heirloom furniture. The surrounding park and the 2-hectare walled garden are dotted with contemporary sculptures by Rachel Whiteread, Henry Moore and others. Houghton Hall is just off the A148, 13 miles east of King's Lynn. Hours vary; call for the latest information.

★White Horse   MODERN BRITISH ££
(☑01485-210262; www.whitehorsebrancaster. co.uk; Main Rd, Brancaster Staithe; mains £14-26; ☺noon-9pm; P🐾) Backing onto a sweep of marshland, the White Horse celebrates Norfolk seafood in all its myriad forms: locally smoked salmon and prawns, saffron-pickled cockles, Brancaster oysters, dressed Cromer crab. It also serves plenty of local meats and poultry. Dine inside or under a marquee in the garden; the sharing seafood platter (£62) is a veritable feast.

King's Lynn

☑01553 / POP 42,800

Historically one of England's most important ports, King's Lynn was long known as 'the Warehouse on the Wash' after the nearby bay at the mouth of the River Great Ouse. In its heyday, it was said you could cross from one side of the river to the other by simply stepping from boat to boat. A certain nautical tang still remains, but most visitors come to admire the magnificent town houses built by medieval merchants along the cobbled streets, and enjoy the relaxed, unfussed pace of life.

◉ Sights

Start your explorations at the 15th-century town hall, then follow a genteel row of town houses along Queen St to Purfleet Quay, where a statue of Charles II crowns the Custom House, built in 1683. Along the riverbank, note the sturdy flood defences, built to end centuries of inundation from the Great Ouse. Continue along King St past the 15th-century St George's Guildhall (www.shakespearesguildhalltrust.org.uk; 29 King St; ☺10am-2pm Mon-Sat), where Shakespeare reputedly performed, and a succession of courtyards crowded with medieval merchants' warehouses.

Stories of Lynn   MUSEUM
(☑01553-774297; www.storiesoflynn.co.uk; Saturday Market Pl; adult/child £3.95/1.95; ☺10am-4.30pm) The lower levels of King's Lynn's town hall – a magnificent chequerboard flint structure that started life in 1421 as a guildhall – are given over to a highly entertaining interactive museum telling the stories of local seafarers, explorers, mayors and ne'er-do-wells. Don't miss local murderer Eugene Aram relating his sorry tale in the Georgian-era jail.

Lynn Museum   MUSEUM
(☑01553-775001; www.museums.norfolk.gov. uk; Market St; adult/child £4.70/4, Oct-Mar free; ☺10am-5pm Tue-Sat) The town museum is worth a nosey for its fairground relics, gold Iceni coins and the Seahenge Gallery, which tells the fascinating story of the early Bronze Age timber circle that lay submerged off Holme-next-the-Sea for 4000 years, before being rediscovered in 1998.

True's Yard   MUSEUM
(☑01553-770479; www.truesyard.co.uk; North St; adult/child £3/1.50; ☺10am-4pm Tue-Sat) Few of the fishermen's cottages that once sprawled inland from the quayside survived the decline of fishing at King's Lynn, but you can see two 18th-century homes restored to their lived-in state at this intriguing museum, alongside displays on shipbuilding and fishing culture. Spare a thought for the families who once lived squeezed like sardines into these tiny dwellings.

King's Lynn Minster   CHURCH
(St Margaret's Church; ☑01553-772858; www. stmargaretskingslynn.org.uk; St Margaret's Pl; ☺noon-2pm Tue & Thu) Built in a patchwork of styles, this great church includes Flemish brasses and a remarkable 17th-century moon dial, which informed residents of the tide, not the time. You'll find historic flood-level markings by the west door. Hours vary; call for the latest information.

 Festivals & Events

King's Lynn Festival CULTURAL
(www.kingslynnfestival.org.uk; ☺ Jul) East Anglia's most important cultural gathering, with a diverse mix of music, from medieval ballads to opera, as well as literary talks.

Sleeping & Eating

★ **Bank House** BOUTIQUE HOTEL ££
(☎ 01553-660492; www.thebankhouse.co.uk; King's Staithe Sq; s £85-120, d £115-220; ⓟ 🛜)
A statue of Charles I casts an eye over arrivals to this handsome Georgian town house near the quay, but inside the rooms are modern and fun-filled, with lots of soft upholstery and eye-pleasing splashes of colour.

Set behind arched windows in a wood-floored annexe, the house brasserie (dishes £14 to £25, open noon to 8pm) serves seriously good modern British food.

Marriott's Warehouse BRITISH ££
(☎ 01583-818500; www.marriottswarehouse.co.uk; South Quay; mains £13-18; ☺ 10am-2.30pm & 5-9pm Mon-Sat, 10am-3pm Sun) This restored 16th-century warehouse is a great place for a pint or a bite overlooking the River Great Ouse. Enjoy steaks, smoked salmon, mushroom burgers, fish and chips and more, either inside or outdoors next to a sculpture of drying fish fillets.

ℹ️ Information

Tourist Office (☎ 01553-763044; www.visit westnorfolk.com; Town Hall, Saturday Market Pl; ☺ 10am-5pm Mon-Sat, from noon Sun Apr-Sep, to 4pm Oct-Mar) At the town hall.

ℹ️ Getting There & Away

Bus From Monday to Saturday, the **Coastliner 36** (www.lynxbus.co.uk) bus runs from King's Lynn along the north Norfolk coast to Wells-next-the-Sea (£5.80, 1¾ hours), where you can swap to the **Coasthopper CH1** (www.sanderscoaches.com) to Cromer (£4.40, one hour, hourly). A special all-day £10 ticket allows unlimited travel on both routes.

Train There are hourly trains from Cambridge (£10.70, one hour) via Ely, and from London King's Cross (£38.60, 1¾ hours).

AT A GLANCE

POPULATION
7.7 million

LARGEST CITY
Birmingham

BEST HISTORIC PUB
Ye Olde Trip to Jerusalem (p436)

BEST GASTROPUB
Hammer & Pincers (p449)

BEST FARM SHOP
Ludlow Food Centre (p432)

WHEN TO GO
Jun–Sep Typically warm and sunny; the best season for walking and cycling.

Oct–Feb Chilly, often damp weather; some sights closed; festive lights, fairs and celebratory menus in the lead-up to Christmas.

Mar–May Lengthening days; spring blossoms; flourishing cultural activities.

ye olde trip to jerusalem
1189AD

the oldest inn in England

GHOST WALK
EVERY SATURDAY

Great range of Local Beers on sale here supported by NOTTINGHAM BREWERY

Birmingham & the Midlands

I f you're searching for quintessentially English countryside – green valleys, chocolate-box villages of wonky black-and-white houses, woodlands steeped in legend and magnificent stately homes – you'll find it here in the country's heart.

You'll also find the relics of centuries of industrial history, exemplified by the World Heritage–listed mills of Ironbridge and the Derwent Valley, and today's dynamic cities, including Britain's second-largest, Birmingham: a canal-woven industrial crucible reinvented as a cultural and creative hub. Beyond are tumbling hills where the air is so clean you can taste it and walkers and cyclists head to vanish into the vastness of the landscape.

Birmingham & the Midlands Highlights

1 Library of Birmingham (p394) Surveying the buzzing city of Birmingham from its library's rooftop 'secret garden'.

2 Peak District (p457) Hiking, cycling or driving through England's first national park.

3 Lincoln (p441) Strolling the William the Conqueror–built castle walls overlooking the soaring cathedral in this historic city.

4 Ironbridge Gorge (p425) Museum-hopping in the birthplace of the Industrial Revolution.

5 King Richard III: Dynasty, Death & Discovery (p447) Learning about King Richard III's life and death and the discovery of his remains in Leicester.

6 Stratford-upon-Avon (p407) Visiting the Bard's schoolroom and reimagined town house before catching an RSC performance in his Tudor hometown.

7 Morgan Motor Company (p417) Touring Great Malvern's venerable car factory and taking a car for a spin through the surrounding hills.

8 Burghley House (p445) Wandering the halls and gardens of this stately Stamford home.

Activities

Famous walking trails such as the **Pennine Way** and **Limestone Way** wind across the Peak District's hills, while challenging cycling routes include the **Pennine Cycleway**. The Marches, tracing the English–Welsh border, are also wonderful walking territory.

Watersports abound at Rutland Water; Hereford and Ironbridge Gorge offer canoeing and kayaking.

Getting There & Around

Birmingham Airport (p401) and East Midlands Airport (p454), near Derby, are the main air hubs.

There are excellent rail connections to towns across the Midlands. **National Express** (☑08717 818181; www.nationalexpress.com), at Birmingham Coach Station, and local bus companies connect larger towns and villages to each other and to destinations further afield, though services are reduced in the low season. For general route information, consult Traveline for the **East Midlands** (☑0871 200 2233; www.travelineeastmidlands.co.uk) or the **West Midlands** (☑0871 200 2233; www.travelinemidlands.co.uk). Ask locally about discounted all-day tickets.

BIRMINGHAM

☑0121 / POP 1,128,100

Regeneration, renewal and grand-scale construction continue apace in Britain's second-largest city. A state-of-the-art library, a gleaming shopping centre atop revitalised New St station and beautifully restored Victorian buildings are just some of the successful initiatives of its Big City Plan, following the striking Mailbox and Bullring shopping malls and the iconic Selfridges building's 'bubble-wrapped' facade. Work is underway on extensions to the Metro (light rail/tram) network, and on the centrepiece Paradise development's new hotels, public spaces, and glitzy residential and commercial buildings, with final completion due in 2025.

Alongside Birmingham's picturesque canals, waterside attractions, outstanding museums and galleries is an explosion of gastronomic restaurants, cool and/or secret cocktail bars and craft breweries. Thriving legacies of the city's industrial heritage include its Jewellery Quarter, Cadbury manufacturing plant and former custard factory turned cutting-edge creative hub.

And in 2022 – all things going well – Birmingham will host the Commonwealth Games. 'Brum', as it's locally dubbed, is buzzing.

◉ Sights

◉ City Centre

Birmingham's grandest civic buildings are clustered around pedestrianised **Victoria Square**, at the western end of New St, dominated by the stately facade of **Council House**, built between 1874 and 1879, and the 1834 **Town Hall** (☑0121-780 4949; www.thsh.co.uk/town-hall), styled after the Temple of Castor and Pollux in Rome. Public art here includes modernist sphinxes and a **fountain** topped by a naked female figure, dubbed 'the floozy in the Jacuzzi', overlooked by a disapproving **statue of Queen Victoria**.

To the west, **Centenary Square** is bookended by the art-deco Hall of Memory War Memorial, the **International Convention Centre** (ICC; ☑0121-200 2000; www.theicc.co.uk; 8 Centenary Sq) and the **Symphony Hall** (☑0121-289 6333; www.thsh.co.uk; 8 Centenary Sq). There's a gleaming golden **statue** of the leading lights from Birmingham's Industrial Revolution: Matthew Boulton, James Watt and William Murdoch. Centenary Sq's showpiece is the spiffing Library of Birmingham.

★ **Library of Birmingham**   LIBRARY
(☑0121-242 4242; www.birmingham.gov.uk/libraries; Centenary Sq; ⊙ground fl 9am-9pm Mon & Tue, 11am-9pm Wed-Fri, to 5pm Sat, rest of bldg 11am-7pm Mon & Tue, to 5pm Wed-Sat) Resembling a glittering stack of gift-wrapped presents, the Francine Houben–designed Library of Birmingham is an architectural triumph. The 2013-opened building features a subterranean amphitheatre, spiralling interior, viewing decks and glass elevator to the 7th-floor 'secret garden' with panoramic views over the city. In addition to its archives, and photography and rare-book collections (including Britain's most important Shakespeare collection), there are gallery spaces, 160-plus computers and a cafe. The British Film Institute Mediatheque provides free access to the National Film Archive.

Birmingham Back to Backs   HISTORIC BUILDING
(NT; ☑0121-666 7671; www.nationaltrust.org.uk; 55-63 Hurst St; 75min tour adult/child £8.65/5.25; ⊙tours by reservation Tue-Sun) Quirky tours of

this cluster of restored back-to-back terraced houses take you through four working-class homes, telling the stories of those who lived here between the 1840s and the 1970s. Book ahead by phone for the compulsory guided tour. For an even more vivid impression of what life was like here, you can book to stay in basic three-storey period cottages at 52 and 54 Inge St (doubles with wi-fi from £130). Guests receive a free Back to Backs tour.

Birmingham Museum
& Art Gallery   MUSEUM, GALLERY
(📞 0121-348 8000; www.birminghammuseums. org.uk; Chamberlain Sq; ⏰10am-5pm Sat-Thu, 10.30am-5pm Fri) FREE Major Pre-Raphaelite works by Rossetti, Edward Burne-Jones and others are among the highlights of the delightful Birmingham Museum & Art Gallery's impressive collection of ancient treasures and Victorian art. Excellent temporary exhibitions range from historical collections to emerging contemporary artists.

Its **Edwardian Tearooms** are an elegant spot for tea and have 'champagne buzzers' installed in its booths to order bubbles at the touch of a button. There's also a casual cafe.

Birmingham Cathedral   CATHEDRAL
(📞 0121-262 1840; www.birminghamcathedral. com; Colmore Row; by donation; ⏰7.30am-6.30pm Mon-Fri, to 5pm Sat & Sun) Dedicated to St Philip, this small but perfectly formed cathedral was constructed in a neoclassical style between 1709 and 1715. Pre-Raphaelite artist Edward Burne-Jones was responsible for the magnificent stained-glass windows.

Times for free guided tours and concerts are posted on its website's What's On page.

Thinktank   MUSEUM
(📞 0121-348 8000; www.birminghammuseums. org.uk; Millennium Point, Curzon St; adult/child £14/10.25, planetarium show £2.50; ⏰10am-5pm) Surrounded by the footprints of vanished factories, the Millennium Point development incorporates this entertaining and ambitious attempt to make science accessible to children. Highlights include galleries on the past (Birmingham's industrial breakthroughs), present (how stuff works) and future, as well as an outdoor science garden and a planetarium.

St Martin's Church   CHURCH
(📞 0121-600 6020; www.bullring.org; Egbaston St; ⏰10am-4pm Mon-Sat, 9am-7pm Sun) Birmingham architect Alfred Chatwin designed this Victorian Gothic church in the Bullring. The 1873-completed structure occupies a site where a church has stood since 1290 and is thought to have been a place of worship as far back as Saxon times.

👁 Birmingham Canals

During the industrial age, Birmingham was a major hub on the English canal network and today the city has more miles of canals than Venice. Narrow boats still float through the heart of the city, passing a string of glitzy wharf-side developments.

Ikon Gallery   GALLERY
(📞 0121-248 0708; www.ikon-gallery.org; 1 Oozells Sq; ⏰11am-4pm Tue-Sun) FREE Within the glitzy Brindley Pl development of banking offices and designer restaurants, a converted Gothic schoolhouse contains the cutting-edge Ikon Gallery. Prepare to be thrilled, bemused or outraged, depending on your take on conceptual art.

National Sea Life Centre   AQUARIUM
(📞 0121-643 6777; www.visitsealife.com; 3a Brindley Pl; £18.30; ⏰10am-5pm Mon-Fri, to 6pm Sat & Sun) Exotic marine creatures including otters, jellyfish, piranhas and razor-jawed hammerhead sharks swim in the Sir Norman Foster–designed National Sea Life Centre. Tickets must be pre-purchased online. Check for information about various talks, feeding times, tours and activities.

👁 Jewellery Quarter

Birmingham has been a major jewellery player since Charles II acquired a taste for it in 17th-century France. The gentrifying Jewellery Quarter, three-quarters of a mile northwest of the city centre, still produces 40% of UK-manufactured jewellery. Dozens of workshops open to the public are listed online at www.jewelleryquarter.net.

Take the Metro from Snow Hill or the train from Moor St to the Jewellery Quarter station.

Museum of the Jewellery Quarter   MUSEUM
(📞 0121-348 8140; www.birminghammuseums.org. uk; 75 Vyse St; adult/child £7/3; ⏰10.30am-4pm Tue-Sat) The Smith & Pepper jewellery factory is preserved as it was on its closing day in 1981 after 80 years of operation. Guided tours lasting around one hour explain the long history of the trade in Birmingham and let you watch master jewellers at work. Entry to the temporary exhibition space and shop is free.

Birmingham

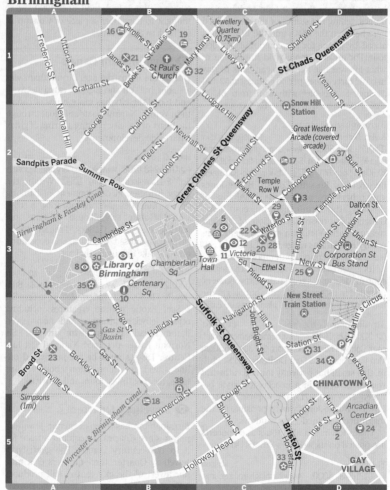

⊙ Outlying Areas

★ **Barber Institute of Fine Arts**   GALLERY
(☎0121-414 7333; www.barber.org.uk; University of Birmingham, Edgbaston; ⊙10am-5pm Mon-Fri, 11am-5pm Sat & Sun) **FREE** At the University of Birmingham, 3 miles south of the city centre, the Barber Institute of Fine Arts has an astonishing collection of Renaissance masterpieces; European masters, such as Rubens and Van Dyck; British greats, including Gainsborough, Reynolds and Turner; and classics from modern titans Picasso, Magritte and others. Trains run from Birmingham New St to University station (£2.80, seven minutes, every 10 minutes), from where it's a 10-minute walk.

Custard Factory   ARTS CENTRE
(☎0121-224 7777; www.digbeth.com/spaces/custardfactory; Gibb St; ⊙shops 10am-6pm Tue-Sat, event times vary) Just over a mile southeast of the city centre, Digbeth's creative quarter centres on the Custard Factory, a hip art-and-design enclave set in the converted buildings of the factory that once churned out British favourite Bird's Custard. The open-plan space is now full of artists' galleries, quirky design boutiques,

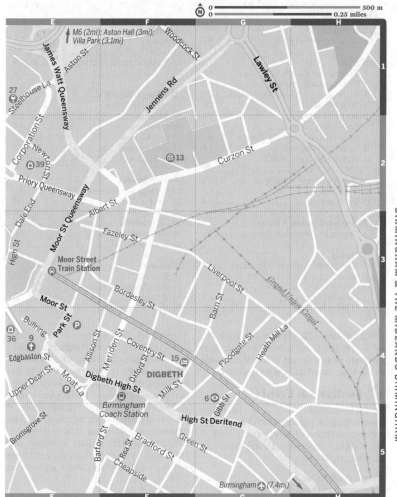

vintage-clothing outlets, one-off shops such as a skateboard specialist, and affordable, offbeat cafes and pop-up street-food stalls.

Cadbury World   MUSEUM
(🖉 0121-393 6004; www.cadburyworld.co.uk; Linden Rd, Bournville; adult/child £18/13.25; ⊙9am-4.30pm, hours vary) The next best thing to Willy Wonka's chocolate factory is Cadbury World, 4 miles south of Birmingham. It educates visitors about the history of cocoa and the Cadbury family, sweetening the deal with free samples, displays of chocolate-making machines and chocolate-themed attractions, including a 4D cinema with motion-sensor

seats. Opening hours vary substantially; bookings are essential. Trains run from Birmingham New St to Bournville (£2.90, seven minutes, every 10 minutes), from where it's a signposted 10-minute walk.

Surrounding the aromatic chocolate works, pretty Bournville Village was built by the philanthropic Cadbury family to accommodate early-20th-century factory workers.

👉 Tours

Sherborne Wharf Boat Trips   CRUISE
(🖉 0121-455 6163; www.sherbornewharf.co.uk; Sherborne St; 65min cruise adult/child £8/6;

Birmingham

⊙11.30am, 1pm, 2.30pm & 4pm daily Easter-Oct, Sat & Sun Nov & Jan-Easter) Nostalgic narrow-boat cruises depart from the quay-side by the International Convention Centre.

 Festivals & Events

Crufts Dog Show   ANIMAL SHOW
(www.crufts.org.uk; ⊙early Mar) The world's greatest collection of pooches on parade at the National Exhibition Centre over four days in early March.

Birmingham Pride   LGBT
(www.birminghampride.com; ⊙late May) One of the biggest and most colourful celebrations of LGBT+ culture in the country takes place over a weekend in late May.

⎰ Sleeping

Chains dominate Birmingham's hotel scene, which is aimed at business travellers, ensuring high weekday prices. Look out for cheap deals at weekends. Accommodation is often limited but several new hotels are set to open over the coming years.

B&Bs are concentrated outside the city centre in Acocks Green (to the southeast) or Edgbaston and Selly Oak (to the southwest).

Birmingham Central Backpackers   HOSTEL £
(☑0121-643 0033; www.birminghambackpackers. com; 58 Coventry St; dm/d incl breakfast from £12.35/38; @🛜) Despite the railway-bridge-right-next-door setting, Birmingham's purple-and-turquoise backpacker hostel is recommended for its convenience to the bus station and for its choice of clean, multicoloured dorms or capsule-style pods. Excellent facilities include a lounge with DVDs and regular movie nights, a bar (note you can't BYO alcohol) and a self-catering kitchen.

★ **St Pauls House**   BOUTIQUE HOTEL ££
(☑0121-272 0999; www.saintpaulshouse.com; 15-20 St Paul's Sq; d from £99; P❄🛜) Overlooking a park in the Jewellery Quarter, this independent hotel has 34 fresh, contemporary rooms with welcoming touches, such as hot-water bottles in woollen covers. Upcycled decor in its hip bar (with live music Saturday nights and Sunday afternoons) and restaurant includes industrial-style ropes (as wall hangings and in furnishings) referencing the building's original use as a rope factory.

Bloc   HOTEL ££
(☑0121-212 1223; www.blochotels.com; 77 Caroline St; d/apt from £79/114; ❄🛜) Located in

the Jewellery Quarter, Bloc excels in sharp, contemporary pod design. Rooms are tiny but space is cleverly stretched: flatscreen TVs are built into walls; there's under-bed storage; and bathrooms are compact but with luxe shower heads. Apartments have a kitchenette. Book carefully: rooms come with window or without.

Hotel du Vin BOUTIQUE HOTEL **£££**
(☑ 0121-794 3005; www.hotelduvin.com; 25 Church St; d/ste from £179/249; ✳ @ 🕏) Housed in the Victorian red-brick former Birmingham Eye Hospital, this branch of the upmarket Hotel du Vin chain has real class, with wrought-iron balustrades and classical murals. Its 66 rooms have spectacular bathrooms; there's a spa and a gym, a bistro with worn floorboards and a stellar wine list, plus a pub and lounge bar with comfy leather furniture.

Hotel Indigo BOUTIQUE HOTEL **£££**
(☑ 0121-643 2010; www.ihg.com; The Cube, Wharfside St; d from £174; 🕏) A stylish operation on the 23rd and 24th floors of the Mailbox's annexe, the Cube, Birmingham's branch of the high-end Hotel Indigo chain marries a handy location with snazzy amenities and great views from its 52 rooms (some with balcony). There's a spa and small pool in the same building.

 Eating

Pushkar INDIAN **££**
(☑ 0121-643 7978; www.pushkardining.com; 245 Broad St; mains £8.25-19, 5-course vegetarian/meat tasting menu £30/41; ⊙ 5-11pm Mon-Sat) Classy north Indian and Punjabi cuisine takes centre stage in this glass-fronted, white table-clothed, gold-trimmed dining room. The elegant presentation extends to boxed menus and serviette-wrapped naan bread as well as stunning cocktails. Its swanky spin-off, **Praza** (☑ 0121-456 4500; www.praza.co.uk; 94-96 Hagley Rd, Edgbaston; mains £8-19, Sun Indian afternoon tea £20; ⊙ 5-11pm Mon-Sat, 1-9pm Sun), in Edgbaston, is also superb.

Purecraft Bar & Kitchen GASTROPUB **££**
(☑ 0121-237 5666; www.purecraftbars.com; 30 Waterloo St; mains £9-18.50; ⊙ noon-10pm Tue-Sat) Fabulous dishes created in Purecraft's open kitchen come with suggested beer pairings. The regularly changing menu might include Lawless Lager–battered fish and chips (with Veltins Pilsener); Brewer's Grain asparagus and broad-bean risotto (with Odell St Lupulin American Pale Ale); or grilled plaice with

beer-and-parsley butter and Jersey Royal new potatoes (with Purity Mad Goose). Cards only (no cash).

Lasan INDIAN **££**
(☑ 0121-212 3664; www.lasan.co.uk; 3-4 Dakota Bldgs, James St; mains £14-25; ⊙ noon-2.30pm & 5-10pm Tue-Fri, noon-11pm Sat, to 9pm Sun) Expletive-loving chef Gordon Ramsay famously proclaimed elegant, upmarket Lasan, in Birmingham's Jewellery Quarter, Britain's 'Best Local Restaurant'. Its changing menu of elevated Indian dishes are served in an intimate dining room, accompanied by cocktails (and mocktails).

★ **Simpsons** BRITISH **£££**
(☑ 0121-454 3434; www.simpsonsrestaurant.co.uk; 20 Highfield Rd, Edgbaston; 2-/3-course lunch menu £40/50, 3-course dinner menu £75; ⊙ 12.30-2.30pm & 6-10pm Wed-Fri, 12.30-3.30pm & 6.30-9pm Sat, 1-5pm Sun; 🚗 🛏) It's worth the 2.5-mile journey southwest of the centre to this gorgeous Georgian mansion in leafy Edgbaston for sensational Michelin-starred menus (kids and vegetarians catered for) in its contemporary dining rooms. You can also stay in one of three luxurious bedrooms upstairs (from £150) or take an all-day cookery class (Wednesday and Saturday, £150) at its Eureka Kitchen. Book ahead.

Adam's BRITISH **£££**
(☑ 0121-643 3745; www.adamsrestaurant.co.uk; New Oxford House, 16 Waterloo St; 3-course mid-week lunch menu £45, 3-course/tasting dinner menu £75/97; ⊙ noon-2pm & 7-9pm Tue-Sat) Michelin-starred Adam's wows with intricately prepared and presented flavour combinations, such as lamb sweetbreads with goats curd, mint and radish, monkfish with wild mussels, champagne and caviar, and pear, toasted hay, caramel and praline. English vintages are represented on its excellent wine list, which has extensive by-the-glass options. Book well ahead.

 Drinking & Nightlife

Independent pubs and bars proliferate throughout the city.

Nightlife hubs in Birmingham include Broad St (aka the 'golden mile' – some say for the prevalence of fake tan here) and Chinatown's **Arcadian Centre** (www.thearcadian.co.uk; Hurst St; ⊙ individual venue hours vary).

Postindustrial Digbeth has alternative clubs and club events in and around the Custard Factory (p396).

★ **Jekyll & Hyde**   PUB
(☑ 0121-236 0345; www.thejekyllandhyde.co.uk; 28 Steelhouse Lane; ⊘ noon-11pm Mon-Thu, to midnight Fri, to 1am Sat; 🐾) Potent cocktails (or rather 'elixirs, concoctions and potions') at this trippy spot are served in sweets jars, watering cans, teapots and miniature bathtubs – even a top hat. Downstairs, Mr Hyde's emporium has a cosy drawing room and an *Alice in Wonderland*–themed courtyard; upstairs is Dr Jekyll's Gin Parlour with over 100 different gins.

Lost & Found   BAR
(www.the-lostandfound.co.uk; 8 Bennett's Hill; ⊘ 11am-10pm Mon-Sat, noon-10pm Sun; 🐾) Fictitious Victorian-era explorer/professor Hettie G Watson is the inspiration for the botanical-library theme of this bar in an 1869-built former bank. Inside the domed entrance, amid soaring columns and timber panelling, its elevated seating is surrounded by plants, books, globes and maps. Hettie's 'secret emporium' bar-within-a-bar has antique mirrors, brass and steel fixtures, and more plants.

Wellington   PUB
(www.thewellingtonrealale.co.uk; 37 Bennett's Hill; ⊘ 10am-midnight) The pastel wallpaper, timber bar and polished brass give the impression the Welly is frozen in time, but this spruced-up pub sheltering a timber-decked roof terrace is the best in the city for real ale. Its 27 hand-pulled beers and ciders include favourites from Black Country and Wye Valley as well as rare brews.

Snacks are limited to pork scratchings, pretzels et al, but you can BYO food or have takeaway delivered.

Bacchus   BAR
(☑ 0121-632 5445; www.nicholsonspubs.co.uk; Burlington Arcade, New St; ⊘ noon-10pm Mon-Fri, 11am-10pm Sat & Sun; 🐾) Buried beneath the Burlington Arcade, this darkened drinking den has the ambience of a decadent underworld. Down a faux-marble-encased staircase, crumbling pillars and giant Grecian murals give way to soaring medieval-style stone arches, swords, suits of armour and candelabras. There's a great range of cask ales, gins and whiskies.

Canalside Cafe   CAFE
(☑ 0121-643 3170; 35 Worcester Bar, Gas St; ⊘ 9am-11pm Mon-Sat, to 10.30pm Sun) Narrow boats glide past the terrace of this 18th-century lock-keeper's cottage, where the low-ceilinged interior is strung with nautical paraphernalia and warmed by an open fire. Drop by for a cuppa, a real ale, or a steaming mulled cider in winter.

☆ **Entertainment**

Sunflower Lounge   LIVE MUSIC
(☑ 0121-632 6756; www.thesunflowerlounge. com; 76 Smallbrook Queensway; ⊘ bar noon-1am Mon-Thu, noon-2am Fri & Sat, 2pm-1am Sun) This quirky little indie bar pairs a magnificent alternative soundtrack with a packed program of live gigs and DJ nights.

Electric Cinema   CINEMA
(☑ 0121-643 7879; www.theelectric.co.uk; 47-49 Station St; standard/sofa seats £11.50/12.80, sofa seats with waiter service £16.80) Topped by its art-deco sign, this is the UK's oldest working cinema, operating since 1909. It screens mainly art-house films. Be waited upon in plush two-seater sofas, or have a drink in the small bar, which has a traditional absinthe fountain, cocktails themed around films currently showing and 'poptails' (popcorn-flavoured cocktails, in lieu of popcorn being available).

Birmingham Repertory Theatre   THEATRE
(The Rep; ☑ 0121-236 4455; www.birmingham-rep. co.uk; Centenary Sq) Founded in 1913, today theatre production company 'the Rep' has three performance spaces: the Main House; the more experimental Door; and a 300-seat studio theatre presenting edgy drama and musicals, with an emphasis on contemporary work.

Jam House   LIVE MUSIC
(☑ 0121-200 3030; www.thejamhouse.com; 3-5 St Paul's Sq; ⊘ 6pm-midnight Tue & Wed, to 1am Thu, to 2am Fri & Sat) Pianist Jools Holland was the brains behind this moody, smart-casual music venue (dress accordingly). Acts range from jazz big bands to famous soul crooners. Over 21s only.

O2 Academy   LIVE MUSIC
(☑ 07704 001028; www.academymusicgroup.com/ o2academybirmingham; 16-18 Horsefair, Bristol St; ⊘ box office noon-4pm Mon-Sat) Birmingham's leading venue for big-name rockers and tribute bands as well as up-and-coming talent.

🛍 **Shopping**

Great Western Arcade   SHOPPING CENTRE
(www.greatwesternarcade.co.uk; btwn Colmore & Temple Rows; ⊘ individual shop hours vary) Topped with a glass roof, this tile-floored

Victorian-era arcade is a jewel filled with mostly independent shops.

Swordfish Records MUSIC
(www.swordfishrecords.co.uk; 66 Dalton St; ⏲10am-5.30pm Mon-Sat) A Birmingham institution, this independent record shop down a tiny backstreet brims with new and secondhand vinyl (and some CDs), including its own label releases. Robert Plant, Duran Duran's John Taylor, Dave Grohl and Neil Diamond are among its past customers. It's a great place to find out about under-the-radar gigs and festivals.

Mailbox MALL
(www.mailboxlife.com; 7 Commercial St; ⏲mall 10am-7pm Mon-Sat, 11am-5pm Sun, individual shop hours vary) Birmingham's stylish canal-side shopping experience, the redevelopment of the former Royal Mail sorting office, comes complete with designer hotels, a fleet of up-market restaurants, the luxury department store Harvey Nichols and designer boutiques. Its super-snazzy metallic extension, the Cube (www.thecube.co.uk), houses Marco Pierre White's panoramic Steakhouse Bar & Grill on the 25th floor.

Bullring MALL
(www.bullring.co.uk; St Martin's Circus; ⏲10am-8pm Mon-Fri, 9am-8pm Sat, 11am-5pm Sun, individual shop hours vary) Split into two vast retail spaces – the East Mall and West Mall – the Bullring has all the international brands and chain cafes you could ask for, plus the standout architectural wonder of Selfridges, which looks out over the city like the compound eye of a giant robot insect.

ℹ Information

Comprehensive tourist information is available at www.visitbirmingham.com.

The ground-floor reception of the Library of Birmingham (p394) can also provide information for tourists.

➡ The city centre, especially south of the Bullring and on and around Broad St, can get very rowdy with revellers on weekend nights.

➡ Digbeth bus station and its surrounds can be quite rough after dark.

ℹ Getting There & Away

AIR
Birmingham Airport (BHX; ☎0871 222 0072; www.birminghamairport.co.uk), 8 miles east of the city centre, has direct flights to destinations around the UK and Europe, as well as direct long-haul routes to Dubai, India and the USA.

Fast and convenient trains run regularly between Birmingham New St and Birmingham International stations (£3.90, 15 minutes, every 10 minutes). Birmingham International is linked to the terminal by the Air-Rail Link monorail (free, two minutes, frequent), which runs from 3.30am to 12.30am.

Alternatively, take bus X1 (£2.50, 35 minutes, up to two hourly) from Moor St Queensway, which run 24 hours.

A taxi from the airport to the city centre typically costs £30 to £45.

BUS
Most intercity buses run from **Birmingham Coach Station** (☎0871 781 8181; Mill Lane, Digbeth).

National Express (www.nationalexpress. com) coaches link Birmingham with major cities across the country, including the following.
London Victoria £3 to £14.40, 3¼ hours, hourly or better
Manchester £3 to £24, 2½ hours, every 90 minutes
Oxford £8 to £25, 1¾ hours, six daily

TRAIN
Most long-distance trains leave from Birmingham New St station, but Chiltern Railways runs to London Marylebone (£25, two hours, two per hour) from Birmingham Snow Hill, and West Midlands Railway runs to Stratford-upon-Avon (£8.60, 40 minutes, half-hourly) from Birmingham Moor St stations.

Construction on the High Speed Rail (HS2) line – connecting London with Birmingham in just 40 minutes – is set to commence in 2029 and to be completed by 2033.

Useful services from New St include the following.
Derby £20.40, 40 minutes, two per hour
Leicester £15.40, one hour, hourly
Lichfield £5.70, 30 minutes, up to three per hour
London Euston £92, 1½ hours, up to four per hour
Manchester £39.60, 1½ hours, three per hour
Nottingham £35.20, 1¼ hours, up to three per hour
Shrewsbury £16.20, one hour, two per hour

ℹ Getting Around

CAR
During central Birmingham's ongoing construction, traffic into and around the city is severely disrupted and parking is limited. Check with your accommodation about access (don't rely

on your satnav, or assume hotels' car parks are operational). Updated details of road closures are posted at www.birmingham.gov.uk/roadworks.

A 'Clean Air Zone' levying fees on older vehicles to reduce pollution in Birmingham is set to come into effect in 2021; visit www.brum breathes.co.uk for information.

PUBLIC TRANSPORT

Local buses run from a convenient hub located on Corporation St, just north of where it connects with New St. For routes, download a copy of the *Network Birmingham Map and Guide* from www.nxbus.co.uk. Single-trip tickets start from £1.50.

Be aware that bus stops may change during construction works in the city centre and journey times may be extended.

Birmingham's single tram line, the Metro (www.westmidlandsmetro.com), links Centenary Sq with Wolverhampton via Victoria Sq, New St station, the Jewellery Quarter, West Bromwich and Dudley.

An extension from Centenary Sq to Edgbaston is due to open in 2021.

Tickets start from £1.50.

Various saver tickets covering buses and trains are available from the **Network West Midlands Travel Centre** (www.networkwest-midlands.com; ⊗ 8.30am-5.30pm Mon-Sat) at New St station.

WARWICKSHIRE

Warwickshire could have been just another picturesque county of rolling hills and market towns were it not for the English language's most famous wordsmith. William Shakespeare was born and died in Stratford-upon-Avon, and the sights linked to his life draw tourists from around the globe. Famous Warwick Castle attracts similar crowds. Elsewhere visitor numbers dwindle but Kenilworth has atmospheric castle ruins, Rugby celebrates the sport that takes its name at its World Rugby Hall of Fame, and Coventry, the UK City of Culture from mid-2021 to mid-2022, claims two extraordinary cathedrals and an unmissable motoring museum.

ℹ Getting There & Around

Coventry is the main transport hub, with frequent rail connections to London Euston and Birmingham New St.

Coventry

☏ 024 / POP 352,900

Coventry was once a bustling hub for the production of cloth, clocks, bicycles, automobiles and munitions. It was this last industry that drew the German Luftwaffe in WWII: on the night of 14 November 1940, the city was so badly blitzed that the Nazis coined a new verb, *coventrieren,* meaning 'to flatten'. A handful of medieval streets that escaped the bombers offer a glimpse of old Coventry.

The city faced a further setback with the collapse of the British motor industry in the 1980s, but is undergoing a resurgence today thanks to its redeveloped and expanded university, and its vibrant cultural scene, which saw it awarded the UK City of Culture 2021, bringing renewed investment and new openings.

◉ Sights

★ **Coventry Transport Museum** MUSEUM
(☏ 024-7623 4270; www.transport-museum.com; Hales St; adult/child £14/7, speed simulator adult/child £5/3.50; ⊗ 10am-5pm, last admission 3pm) This stupendous museum has hundreds of vehicles, from horseless carriages to jet-powered, land-speed-record breakers. There's a brushed-stainless-steel DeLorean DMC-12 (of *Back to the Future* fame) with gull-wing doors, alongside a gorgeous Jaguar E-type, a Daimler armoured car and, for 1970s British-design-oddity enthusiasts, a Triumph TR7 and an Austin Allegro 'Special'. View the Thrust SCC, the current holder of the World Land Speed Record and the Thrust 2, the previous record holder. Kids will love the 4D Thrust speed simulator.

Also on display are 300 bicycles and 120 motorcycles. Tickets are valid for multiple entries over one year.

★ **Coventry Cathedral** CATHEDRAL
(☏ 024-7652 1210; www.coventrycathedral.org.uk; Priory Row; cathedral & ruins by donation, tower climb adult/child £5/2.50, Blitz Experience Museum £1; ⊗ cathedral & tower 10.30am-3pm Mon-Sat, to 2.30pm Sun, ruins 9am-5pm daily, museum closed Nov–mid-Feb, hours can vary) The evocative ruins of St Michael's Cathedral, built around 1300 but destroyed by Nazi incendiary bombs in the Blitz, stand as a memorial to Coventry's darkest hour and as a symbol of peace and reconciliation. Climb the 180 steps of the **Gothic spire** for panoramic views.

RUGBY

Warwickshire's second-largest hub, Rugby is an attractive market town whose history dates to the Iron Age. But it's most famous for the sport that was invented here and now takes its name, and is a place of pilgrimage for fans.

The game was invented at a prestigious Rugby School in 1823 when William Webb Ellis is said to have caught the ball during a football match and broken the rules by running with it. Situated just across from the **Webb Ellis Rugby Football Museum** (☑01788-567777; 5-6 Matthews St; ⊙9.30am-5pm Mon-Sat) FREE, the school itself is closed to the public, but you can peek at the hallowed ground through the gates on Barby Rd. A **statue of William Webb Ellis** (cnr Lawrence Sheriff St & Dunchurch Rd) stands outside the main Rugby School gates.

The whizz-bang interactive **World Rugby Hall of Fame** is inside the **Rugby Art Gallery & Museum** (☑01788-533217; www.ragm.co.uk; Little Elborow St; ⊙gallery & museum 10am-4pm Tue-Fri, to 3pm Sat, World Rugby Hall of Fame 10.15am-4.15pm Tue-Fri, to 3.15pm Sat) FREE complex. You'll need to book separate timeslots for the Hall of Fame and for the Art Gallery & Museum.

The top place to stay is **Brownsover Hall** (☑01788-546100; www.brownsoverhall.co.uk; Brownsover Lane, Old Brownsover; d from £112; P ⊛), a Grade II–listed Gothic Revival manor (where Frank Whittle designed the turbo jet engine) with 47 rooms split between the creaking old house with a monumental central timber staircase and the more modern converted stables (dinner, bed and breakfast packages available). Set in 2.8 hectares of woodland and manicured gardens, it's 2.7 miles north of Rugby.

Rugby is 13 miles east of Coventry, served by regular trains (£6.30, 10 minutes, up to four per hour). Trains also link Rugby with Birmingham (£10.50, 40 minutes, up to four per hour).

Symbolically adjoining St Michael's Cathedral's sandstone walls is the Sir Basil Spence–designed modernist architectural masterpiece Coventry Cathedral, with a futuristic organ, stained glass, and Jacob Epstein statue of the devil and St Michael.

Volunteers at the **Blitz Experience Museum** provide a vivid overview of Coventry before the Blitz and in its aftermath. Children must be aged over eight to climb the tower.

Fargo Village   CULTURAL CENTRE
(www.fargovillage.co.uk; Far Gosford St; ⊙hours vary) Markets, live-music gigs, moonlight cinema screenings and workshops (eg gardening or blacksmithing) are just some of the events that take place at this post-industrial cultural hub spread over a former car-radiator plant. Shops here sell everything from secondhand books to upcycled furniture; there are also art-and-craft studios, a barber shop and a brilliant microbrewery, the Twisted Barrel, along with cafes, bakeries and street-food stalls.

St Mary's Guildhall   HISTORIC BUILDING
(☑024-7683 3328; www.stmarysguildhall.co.uk; Bayley Lane; ⊙10am-4pm Sun-Thu mid-Mar–Sep) FREE One of the most evocative insights into pre-WWII Coventry is this half-timbered and brick hall where the town's trades came together in the Middle Ages to discuss town affairs. As one of England's finest guildhalls, it was chosen to be a jail for Mary Queen of Scots. Stained-glass windows glorify the kings of England; further down the hall stands WC Marshall's statue of Lady Godiva. Look out for the Coventry Tapestry, dating from 1500, depicting the Virgin Mary's assumption. The vaulted stone undercroft houses an atmospheric cafe.

**Herbert Art Gallery
& Museum**   GALLERY, MUSEUM
(☑024-7623 7521; www.theherbert.org; Jordan Well; ⊙10am-4pm Mon-Sat, noon-4pm Sun) FREE Behind Coventry's twin cathedrals, the Herbert has an eclectic collection of paintings and sculptures (including work by TS Lowry, Stanley Spencer and David Hockney), and thought-provoking history galleries spanning natural history and archaeology to Coventry's social and industrial history. Poignant and uplifting exhibits focus on conflict, peace and reconciliation. There are lots of activities aimed at kids, creative workshops for adults (calligraphy, silversmithing etc) and a light-filled cafe.

BIRMINGHAM & THE MIDLANDS COVENTRY

🛌 Sleeping & Eating

★ **Coombe Abbey Hotel** HISTORIC HOTEL **££**
(📞024-7645 0450; www.coombeabbey.com; Brinklow Rd, Binley; d incl breakfast from £129; 🅿🛜) Queen Elizabeth I lived as a child at this 200-hectare estate, 5.5 miles east of Coventry. The 12th-century abbey was converted into a stately manor in 1581, with parkland, formal gardens and a lake. Many of its 121 uniquely decorated rooms have ornate four-poster beds; some have bathrooms hidden behind bookcases. There's a glass-paned conservatory restaurant and regular themed banquets.

Golden Cross PUB FOOD **££**
(📞024-7655 1855; www.thegoldencrosscoventry.co.uk; 8 Hay Lane; mains £9.50-15; ⏱11.30am-9.30pm Mon-Thu, to 10.30pm Fri & Sat, to 6pm Sun; 🛜) Constructed in 1583, this beautiful Tudor building with beamed ceilings, original stained glass and a toasty wood-burning stove is an inviting place for a pint, but the food – entirely gluten-free – such as ale-battered cod with mushy peas, bavette with tarragon butter or jerk-spiced sweetcorn with lime mayo, merits a visit in its own right. Live music plays on Saturdays.

ℹ Information

Tourist Office (📞024-7623 4284; www.visitcoventryandwarwickshire.co.uk; Herbert Art Gallery & Museum, Jordan Well; ⏱10am-4pm Mon-Sat, noon-4pm Sun) Located in the reception area of the Herbert Art Gallery & Museum (p403).

ℹ Getting There & Away

BUS

Buses X17 and X18 go to Kenilworth (£3.10, 40 minutes) and Warwick (£3.40, 45 minutes) five times daily Monday to Saturday.

TRAIN

Regular services include the following.
Birmingham (£4.90, 30 minutes, every 10 minutes)
London Euston (£56, 1¼ hours, every 10 to 20 minutes)
Rugby (£6.30, 10 minutes, up to four per hour)

Kenilworth

📞01926 / POP 22,413

An easy deviation off the A46 between Warwick and Coventry, the atmospheric ruin of Kenilworth Castle was the inspiration for Walter Scott's 1821 novel *Kenilworth*, and it still feels pretty inspiring today. The town is essentially split into two by Finham Brook: the historic village-like area, of most interest to visitors, is on the northern side, while the southern side is the commercial centre.

⦿ Sights

Kenilworth Castle CASTLE, RUINS
(EH; 📞01926-852078; www.english-heritage.org.uk; Castle Green; adult/child £12.60/7.60; ⏱10am-6pm Apr-Sep, to 5pm Oct, to 4pm Sat & Sun Nov-mid-Feb, to 4pm Wed-Sun mid-Feb-Mar) This spine-tingling ruin sprawls among fields and hedges on Kenilworth's outskirts. Built in the 1120s, the castle survived the longest siege in English history in 1266, when the forces of Lord Edward (later Edward I) threw themselves at the moat and battlements for six solid months. The fortress was dramatically extended in Tudor times, but it fell in the English Civil War and its walls were breached and water defences drained. Don't miss the magnificent restored Elizabethan gardens.

Download a free audio guide to your phone from the website.

Stoneleigh Abbey HISTORIC BUILDING
(📞01926-858535; www.stoneleighabbey.org; B4115; adult/child grounds & tour £14/5, grounds only £7/1.50; ⏱tours hourly 10am-3pm, grounds to 5pm Sun-Thu Easter-Oct; 🅿) The kind of stately home that makes film directors go weak at the knees, Stoneleigh name-drops Charles I and Jane Austen among its past visitors. Completed in 1726 and only viewable on tours (included in admission), the splendid Palladian west wing contains richly detailed plasterwork ceilings and wood-panelled rooms. A 'reflecting lake' effect is created by the widened stretch of the River Avon, which runs through the grounds. It's 2 miles east of Kenilworth.

The original abbey was founded by Cistercian monks in 1154, though little remains except the 14th-century gatehouse; the house was built on the site of the monastery by the wealthy Leigh family (distant cousins of the Austens) in the 16th century.

🛌 Sleeping & Eating

Old Bakery B&B **££**
(📞01926-864111; www.theoldbakery.eu; 12 High St; s/d/tr from £75/80/90; ⏱bar 5.30-11pm Mon-Thu, 5-11pm Fri & Sat, 5-10.30pm Sun; 🅿🛜) East of the castle, with restaurants nearby, this appealing 14-room B&B has attractively attired modern

rooms and a cosy, welcoming bar serving well-kept real ales on the ground floor.

★ **Cross** GASTROPUB £££
(☏ 01926-853840; www.thecrosskenilworth.co.uk; 16 New St; 2-/3-course menus lunch £29/35, dinner £55/65; ⊗ noon-2pm & 6.30-9.30pm Tue-Thu, noon-2pm & 6-9.30pm Fri, noon-2.30pm & 6-9.30pm Sat, noon-3.30pm Sun; ☏ ⊛) One of England's culinary jewels, this Michelin-starred gastropub occupies a romantic 19th-century inn. Prepare to be dazzled by exquisite creations like seared scallops with seaweed butter, duck breast with smoked beetroot and raspberry vinegar, and brioche pudding with apple-and-blackberry compote and bay-leaf ice cream.

Vegetarian menus are available; junior gourmands have their own three-course children's menu (£17).

❶ Getting There & Away

From Monday to Saturday, buses X17 and X18 run five times daily between Coventry (£3.10, 40 minutes) and Kenilworth and on to Warwick (£4.40, 30 minutes). There are no buses on Sunday.

Warwick

☏ 01926 / POP 31,345
Regularly name-checked by Shakespeare, Warwick was the ancestral seat of the earls of Warwick, who played a pivotal role in the Wars of the Roses. Despite a devastating fire in 1694, Warwick remains a treasure house of medieval architecture, with rich veins of history and charming streets, dominated by the soaring turrets of Warwick Castle.

◉ Sights

★ **Warwick Castle** CASTLE
(☏ 01926-495421; www.warwick-castle.com; Castle Lane; castle adult/child £20/17, castle & dungeon £30/17; ⊗ 10am-5pm Apr-Sep, to 4pm Oct-Mar; ℙ) Founded in 1068 by William the Conqueror, stunningly preserved Warwick Castle is the biggest show in town. The ancestral home of the earls of Warwick remains impressively intact, and the Tussauds Group has filled the interior with flamboyant, family-friendly attractions that bring the castle's rich history to life. Waxworks populate the private apartments; there are also jousting tournaments, daily trebuchet firings, themed evenings and a dungeon. Discounted online tickets provide fast-track entry. Great accommodation options are available on-site.

Collegiate Church of St Mary CHURCH
(☏ 01926-403940; www.stmaryswarwick.org.uk; Old Sq; church by donation, tower adult/child £3/1.50; ⊗ 10am-4.30pm Mon-Sat, 12.30-4.30pm Sun) This magnificent 1123-founded Norman church was badly damaged in the Great Fire of Warwick in 1694, but is packed with 16th- and 17th-century tombs. Highlights include the Norman crypt with a 14th-century extension; the impressive Beauchamp Chapel, built between 1442 and 1464 to enshrine the mortal remains of the earls of Warwick; and, up 134 steps, the tower, which provides supreme views over town (kids must be aged over eight).

Lord Leycester Hospital HISTORIC BUILDING
(☏ 01926-491422; www.lordleycester.com; 60 High St; adult/child £8.50/5, garden only £2; ⊗ 10am-5pm Tue-Sun Apr-Sep, to 4pm Oct-Mar) A survivor of the 1694 fire, the wonderfully wonky Lord Leycester Hospital has been used as a retirement home for soldiers (but never as a hospital) since 1571. Visitors can wander around the chapel, guildhall, regimental museum and restored walled garden, which includes a knot garden and a Norman arch.

🛏 Sleeping & Eating

Tilted Wig PUB ££
(☏ 01926-400110; www.tiltedwigwarwick.co.uk; 11 Market Pl; d £85; ☏) Bang on the central Market Pl, this brilliantly named 17th-century Georgian inn has four snug but comfortable rooms overlooking the square and some of the better pub food in town, such as Warwickshire rare-breed sausages with creamy garlic mash or pork belly with apple and black-pudding croquettes (mains £10.50 to £20).

Rose & Crown PUB ££
(☏ 01926-411117; www.roseandcrownwarwick.co.uk; 30 Market Pl; d/f incl breakfast from £92/102; ☏) Dating from the 17th century, this family-run inn on the town square has five lovely, spacious and tastefully decorated rooms upstairs from the pub and another eight in the building across the lane, as well as great ales and bottled beers, and an excellent Modern British menu (mains £13 to £20). Four of its rooms are set up for families.

★ **Warwick Castle Accommodation** RESORT £££
(☏ 0871 097 1228; www.warwick-castle.com; Warwick Castle; glamping/lodge/tower ste per night from £145/172/588; ⊗ tower ste & lodge year-round, glamping Easter-Sep; ℙ ☏) Atmospheric

Warwick

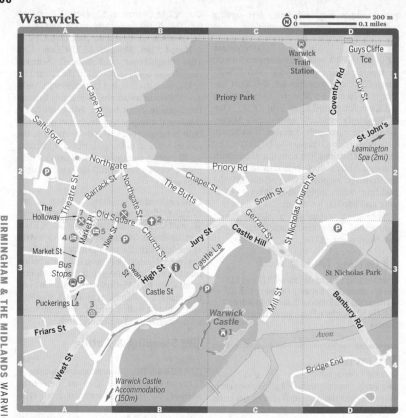

N 0 ——————— 200 m
0 ——————— 0.1 miles

Warwick

◎ Top Sights
1 Warwick Castle.....................................C4

◎ Sights
2 Collegiate Church of St Mary............B3
3 Lord Leycester Hospital.....................A3

⊜ Sleeping
4 Rose & Crown.......................................A3
5 Tilted Wig...A3

⊗ Eating
6 Old Coffee Tavern...............................B2
7 Tailors...A3

accommodation at Warwick Castle (p405) includes two days' castle admission. The castle itself contains two four-poster-bed Tower Suites (including a private tour, champagne and breakfast). The riverside Knight's Village has woodland and knight-themed lodges (all with terrace and some with kitchenette) and

medieval entertainment. Themed tents (with shared bathrooms) make up the 'glamping' ground. All sleep up to five people.

Old Coffee Tavern BRITISH ££
(☑ 01926-679737; www.theoldcoffeetavern.co.uk; 16 Old Sq; mains £10.50-15.50; ⊗ kitchen 7am-10pm Mon-Fri, noon-10pm Sat, to 8pm Sun, bar 7am-11pm Mon-Thu, to 12.30am Fri, 8am-12.30am Sat, to 10pm Sun; ☎) An 1880-built beauty with many of its Victorian features intact, this tavern was originally established as a teetotal alternative to Warwick's pubs. Today you can order real ales, craft ciders, wines and cocktails, along with elevated versions of British classics like toad-in-the-hole and chicken-and-ham-hock pie. Upstairs are 10 stylish oyster-toned guest rooms (doubles including breakfast from £125).

Tailors BRITISH £££
(☑ 01926-410590; www.tailorsrestaurant.co.uk; 22 Market Pl; 2-/3-course lunch menus £20/25,

3-/6-course dinner menus £35/59; ⊙ 6.30-8.30pm Tue, noon-1.30pm & 6.30-8.30pm Wed-Sat) Set in a former tailor's shop, this elegant restaurant, owned and run by two hotshot chefs, serves prime ingredients – guinea fowl, pork belly and lamb from named farms – complemented by intricate creations like brown-butter crumb and black truffle and fennel candy.

ℹ Information

Tourist Office (☑ 01926-492212; www. visitwarwick.co.uk; Court House, Jury St; ⊙ 9.30am-4.30pm Mon-Fri, 10am-4.30pm Sat year-round, plus 10am-4pm Sun Apr–mid-Dec) Within the flagstone-floored Court House (1725). A Heritage Walk map costs £1.

ℹ Getting There & Away

BUS

Buses depart from outside **Westgate House** (Market St).

Stagecoach X17 and X18 run to Coventry (£4.40, 40 minutes, five daily Monday to Saturday) via Kenilworth (£4.10, 30 minutes). Bus X18 also runs to Stratford-upon-Avon (£5.50, 40 minutes, two per hour Monday to Saturday, hourly Sunday).

TRAIN

The train station is half a mile northeast of the town centre on Station Rd.

Trains run to Birmingham (£7.50, 30 minutes, two per hour), Stratford-upon-Avon (£7.30, 25 minutes, every two hours) and London Marylebone (£48, 1½ hours, up to four per hour; some require a change in Leamington Spa).

Stratford-upon-Avon

☑ 01789 / POP 27,455

The author of some of the most quoted lines ever written in the English language, William Shakespeare was born in Stratford in 1564 and died here in 1616. Experiences linked to his life in this unmistakably Tudor town range from the touristy (medieval recreations and Bard-themed tearooms) to the humbling (Shakespeare's modest grave in Holy Trinity Church) and the sublime (taking in a play by the world-famous Royal Shakespeare Company).

◉ Sights

★**Shakespeare's Birthplace**   HISTORIC BUILDING
(☑ 01789-204016; www.shakespeare.org.uk; Henley St; adult/child £15/11; ⊙ 10am-4pm Mon-Fri, to

5pm Sat & Sun) Start your Shakespeare quest at the house where the renowned playwright was born in 1564 and spent his childhood days. John Shakespeare owned the house for a period of 50 years. William, as the eldest surviving son, inherited it upon his father's death in 1601 and spent his first five years of marriage here. Behind a modern facade, the house has restored Tudor rooms, live presentations from famous Shakespearean characters and an engaging exhibition on Stratford's favourite son.

★**Shakespeare's New Place**   HISTORIC SITE
(☑ 01789-338536; www.shakespeare.org.uk; cnr Chapel St & Chapel Lane; adult/child £12.50/8; ⊙ 10am-5pm Apr-Aug, to 4.30pm Sep & Oct, to 3.30pm Nov-Mar) When Shakespeare retired, he swapped the bright lights of London for a comfortable town house at New Place, where he died of unknown causes in April 1616. The house was demolished in 1759, but an attractive Elizabethan knot garden occupies part of the grounds. A major restoration project has uncovered Shakespeare's kitchen and incorporated new exhibits in a reimagining of the house as it would have been. You can also explore the adjacent Nash's House, where Shakespeare's granddaughter Elizabeth lived.

Holy Trinity Church   CHURCH
(☑ 01789-266316; www.stratford-upon-avon.org; Old Town; Shakespeare's grave adult/child £3/2; ⊙ noon-2pm Mon-Thu, to 4pm Fri, 11am-4pm Sat) The final resting place of the Bard, where he was also baptised and where he worshipped, is said to be the most visited parish church in England. Inside are handsome 16th- and 17th-century tombs (particularly in the Clopton Chapel), some fabulous carvings on the choir stalls and, of course, the grave of William Shakespeare, with its ominous epitaph: 'cvrst be he yt moves my bones'.

MAD Museum   MUSEUM
(☑ 01789-269356; www.themadmuseum.co.uk; 4-5 Henley St; adult/child £7.80/5.20, combination ticket with Shakespeare's School Room £13.10/8.60; ⊙ 10am-5.30pm) Fun, hands-on exhibits at Stratford's Mechanical Art & Design Museum (aka MAD) make physics accessible for kids, who can build their own gravity-propelled marble run, use their energy to light up electric panels, and pull levers and turn cranks to animate displays. Tickets are valid all day, so you can come and go as you please.

BIRMINGHAM & THE MIDLANDS STRATFORD-UPON-AVON

Stratford-upon-Avon

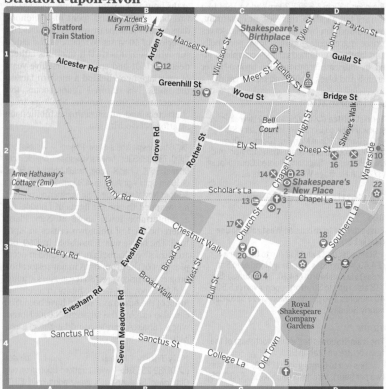

Mary Arden's Farm HISTORIC SITE, FARM
(☑ 01789-338535; www.shakespeare.org.uk; Station Rd, Wilmcote; adult/child £15/10; ⊗ 10am-5pm Apr-Aug, to 4.30pm Sep & Oct; 🅿) Shakespeare genealogists can trace the family tree to the childhood home of the Bard's mother at Wilmcote, 3 miles west of Stratford. Aimed squarely at families, the working farm traces country life over the centuries, with nature trails, falconry displays and a collection of rare-breed farm animals. You can get here on the **City Sightseeing bus** (☑ 01789-299123; www.city-sightseeing.com; adult/child 24hr £15/7.50, 48hr £23/11.50; ⊗ 9.30am-5pm Apr-Oct), or cycle via Anne Hathaway's Cottage, following the Stratford-upon-Avon Canal towpath. Note that, unlike the other Shakespeare properties, it's closed from November to March.

Shakespeare's School Room HISTORIC SITE
(☑ 01789-203170; www.shakespearesschoolroom.
org; King Edward VI School, Church St; adult/child £8.50/5.50, combination ticket with MAD Museum £13.10/8.60; ⊗ 11am-5pm) Shakespeare's alma mater, King Edward VI School (still a prestigious grammar school today), incorporates a vast black-and-white timbered building, dating from 1420, that was once the town's guildhall, where Shakespeare's father John served as bailiff (mayor). In the Bard's former classroom, you can sit in on mock-Tudor lessons, watch a short film and test yourself on Tudor-style homework.

It's adjacent to the 1269-built **Guild Chapel** (www.guildchapel.org.uk; cnr Chapel Lane & Church St; by donation; ⊗ 10am-4pm).

Anne Hathaway's Cottage HISTORIC BUILDING
(☑ 01789-338532; www.shakespeare.org.uk; Cottage Lane, Shottery; adult/child £12.50/8; ⊗ 9am-5pm Apr-Aug, to 4.30pm Sep & Oct, 10am-3.30pm Nov-Mar) Before tying the knot with Shakespeare, Anne Hathaway lived in Shottery, 1 mile west of the centre of Stratford, in this delightful thatched farmhouse. As well

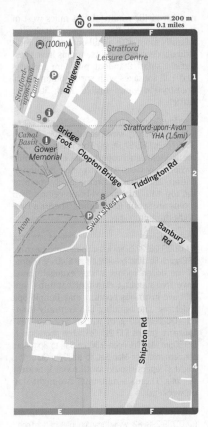

Stratford-upon-Avon

◎ Top Sights
1 Shakespeare's Birthplace	C1
2 Shakespeare's New Place	C2

◎ Sights
3 Guild Chapel	C2
4 Hall's Croft	C3
5 Holy Trinity Church	C4
6 MAD Museum	D1
7 Shakespeare's School Room	C3

☺ Activities, Courses & Tours
8 Avon Boating	E2
9 City Sightseeing	E1
10 Stratford Town Walk	D2

🛏 Sleeping
11 Arden Hotel	D3
12 Emsley Guesthouse	B1
13 Townhouse	C3

✴ Eating
14 Edward Moon's	C2
15 Fourteas	D2
16 Lambs	D2
Rooftop Restaurant	(see 22)
17 Salt	C3
Townhouse	(see 13)

⬤ Drinking & Nightlife
18 Dirty Duck	D3
19 Old Thatch Tavern	C1
20 Windmill Inn	C3

✦ Entertainment
21 Other Place	D3
22 Royal Shakespeare Company	D2
Swan Theatre	(see 22)

⬤ Shopping
23 Chaucer Head	D2

as period furniture, it has gorgeous gardens and an orchard and arboretum, with examples of all the trees mentioned in Shakespeare's plays. A footpath (no bikes allowed) leads to Shottery from Evesham Pl.

Hall's Croft   HISTORIC BUILDING
(☎01789-338533; www.shakespeare.org.uk; Old Town; adult/child £8.50/5.50; ⊙10am-5pm Apr-Aug, to 4.30pm Sep & Oct, 11am-3.30pm Nov-Mar) The handsome Jacobean town house belonging to Shakespeare's daughter Susanna and her husband, respected doctor John Hall, stands south of Stratford's centre. The exhibition offers fascinating insights into medicine in the 16th and 17th centuries, and the lovely walled garden sprouts with aromatic herbs employed in medicinal preparations.

☞ Tours

Avon Boating   BOATING
(☎01789-267073; www.avon-boating.co.uk; The Boathouse, Swan's Nest Lane; river cruises adult/

child £7/5; ⊙9am-dusk Easter-Oct) Avon Boating runs 40-minute river cruises that depart every 20 minutes from either side of the main bridge. It also hires rowboats, canoes and punts (per hour £7, minimum charge £12) and motorboats (per hour £50).

Stratford Town Walk   WALKING
(☎07855 760377; www.stratfordtownwalk.co.uk; town walk adult/child £7/3, ghost walk £8/5; ⊙town walk 11am Sun-Fri, 11am & 2pm Sat, ghost walk by reservation 7.30pm Sat) Popular two-hour guided town walks depart from Waterside, opposite Sheep St (prebooking not necessary).

Chilling ghost walks lasting 90 minutes leave from the same location but must be booked ahead.

WORTH A TRIP

CHARLECOTE PARK

A youthful Shakespeare allegedly poached deer in the grounds of **Charlecote Park** (NT; ☏ 01789-470277; www.nationaltrust.org.uk; Loxley Lane, Charlecote; house & garden adult/child £11.45/5.70, garden only £8/4; ☉ house 11am-4.30pm Thu-Tue mid-Mar–Oct, noon-3.30pm Thu-Tue mid-Feb–mid-Mar, noon-3.30pm Sat & Sun Nov & Dec, garden 9am-5pm Mar-Oct, to 4.30pm Nov-Feb), a lavish Elizabethan pile on the River Avon, 5 miles east of Stratford-upon-Avon. Fallow deer still roam the grounds today. The interiors were restored from Georgian chintz to Tudor splendour in 1823. Highlights include Victorian kitchens, filled with culinary moulds, and an original 1551 Tudor gatehouse.

Bus X17 runs to Charlecote hourly from Stratford (£5.50, 30 minutes, two per hour Monday to Friday, hourly Saturday and Sunday).

Festivals & Events

Stratford Literary Festival LITERATURE
(☏ 01789-470185; www.stratfordliteraryfestival. co.uk; ☉ late Apr/early May) A highlight of Stratford's cultural calendar is the week-long annual Stratford Literary Festival, which has attracted literary big-hitters of the calibre of Robert Harris, PD James and Simon Armitage.

Sleeping

Stratford-upon-Avon YHA HOSTEL £
(☏ 0345 371 9661; www.yha.org.uk; Wellesbourne Rd, Alveston; dm/d/glamping from £18/49/59; P☎) Set in a large 200-year-old mansion 1.5 miles east of the town centre, this superior 134-bed hostel attracts travellers of all ages. Of its 32 rooms and dorms, 16 are en suite. There's a canteen, bar and kitchen. Buses 6 and 15 (£3.60, 12 minutes, up to two per hour) run here from Bridge St. Wi-fi is in common areas only.

Tepee-style glamping tents and hut-like camping pods with kitchenette are available from April to September.

Stag at Red Hill INN ££
(☏ 01789-764634; www.stagredhill.co.uk; Alcester Rd, Alcester; d/f incl breakfast from £78/128; P☎) Stratford's formidable one-time courthouse and prison, dating back over 500 years, is now an idyllic country inn 4 miles west of the town centre. Its nine rooms (including a family room with a pull-out sofa) are individually decorated; deluxe rooms have chesterfield sofas. Standout pub fare includes Red Hill sausages with spring-onion mash. Countryside views unfold from its beer garden.

Emsley Guesthouse B&B ££
(☏ 01789-299557; www.theemsley.co.uk; 4 Arden St; d/f from £82/97; P☎) This lovely five-bedroom Victorian property has a personable owner, very clean and attractive accommodation, and a large, pretty family room at the top with an exposed-beam ceiling. Two rooms are set up for families. There's a two-night minimum stay.

Townhouse BOUTIQUE HOTEL £££
(☏ 01789-262222; www.stratfordtownhouse.co.uk; 16 Church St; d incl breakfast from £140; ☎) Some of the dozen rooms at this exquisite hotel have free-standing claw-foot bathtubs, and all have luxurious bedding and Temple Spa toiletries. The building is a centrally located 400-year-old gem with a first-rate **restaurant** (mains £13-21; ☉ kitchen noon-3pm & 5-9.30pm Mon-Fri, noon-9.30pm Sat, to 8pm Sun, bar 8am-midnight Mon-Sat, to 10.30pm Sun; ☎). Light sleepers should avoid room 1, nearest the bar. There's a minimum two-night stay on weekends.

Arden Hotel HOTEL £££
(☏ 01789-298682; www.theardenhotelstratford.com; Waterside; s/d incl breakfast from £134/169; P☎) Facing the Swan Theatre, this elegant property has a sleek brasserie and champagne bar. Its 45 rooms feature designer fabrics and its bathrooms are full of polished marble. Interconnecting rooms are ideal for families. Kids receive welcome bags with games.

Eating

Fourteas CAFE £
(☏ 01789-293908; www.thefourteas.co.uk; 24 Sheep St; dishes £4.50-9.50, afternoon tea with/ without Prosecco £20/15; ☉ 9.30am-5.30pm Mon-Sat, 10.30am-5.30pm Sun) Breaking with Stratford's Shakespearean theme, this tearoom takes the 1940s as its inspiration with beautiful old teapots, framed posters and staff in period costume. As well as premium loose-leaf teas and homemade cakes, there are all-day breakfasts, soups, sandwiches (including a chicken and bacon 'Churchill

club') and lavish afternoon teas. Gluten-free scones, cakes and sandwiches are available.

Lambs
MODERN EUROPEAN ££

(☑01789-292554; www.lambsrestaurant.co.uk; 12 Sheep St; mains £13-25; ⊙5-9pm Mon, noon-2pm & 5-9pm Tue-Sat, noon-2pm & 6-9pm Sun) Lambs swaps Shakespeare chintz in favour of modern elegance but throws in authentic 16th-century ceiling beams for good measure. The menu embraces Gressingham duck, Hereford steaks and, yes, lamb (a herb-crusted rack with dauphinoise potatoes, mustard green beans and rosemary jus), backed by a strong wine list.

Edward Moon's
BRITISH ££

(☑01789-267069; www.edwardmoon.com; 9 Chapel St; mains £12-20; ⊙noon-2.30pm & 5-9pm Tue-Thu, noon-2.30pm & 5-9.30pm Fri & Sat, noon-3pm Sun; 🖭) Named after a famous travelling chef who cooked up the flavours of home for the British colonial service, this snug independent restaurant serves hearty English dishes, such as steak-and-ale pie and meltingly tender lamb shank with redcurrant gravy. Kids get a two-course menu for £7.95.

Rooftop Restaurant
INTERNATIONAL ££

(☑01789-403449; www.rsc.org.uk; 3rd fl, Royal Shakespeare Theatre, Waterside; mains £14-26; ⊙10.30am-9.30pm Mon-Thu, to 9.45pm Fri & Sat, to 3.30pm Sun; 🖝🖭) Glorious views of the River Avon extend from the dining room and outdoor terrace of this restaurant atop the Royal Shakespeare Theatre (p414). Global flavours range from crab linguine to Sri Lankan cauliflower, squash and cashew curry; there are various set menus, including for vegans and gluten-free diners, and for kids. Its bar mixes the best cocktails in town.

★Salt
BRITISH £££

(☑01789-263566; www.salt-restaurant.co.uk; 8 Church St; 4-/6-course lunch menu £45/55, 8-course dinner menu £78; ⊙noon-2pm & 6.30-10pm Wed-Sat, noon-2pm Sun) Stratford's gastronomic (and Michelin) star is this intimate, beam-ceilinged bistro. In the semi-open kitchen, owner-chef Paul Foster produces stunning creations influenced by the seasons: spring might see glazed parsley root with chicory and black-truffle shavings, onglet of beef with malted artichoke, cured halibut with oyster and apple emulsion, and sea-buckthorn mille-feuille with fig and goat's-milk ice cream.

Recreate its magic at its cookery school (half-day courses from £95).

🍷 Drinking & Nightlife

★Old Thatch Tavern
PUB

(www.oldthatchtavernstratford.co.uk; Greenhill St; ⊙11.30am-11pm Mon-Sat, noon-11pm Sun; 🖭) To truly appreciate Stratford's olde-worlde atmosphere, join the locals for a pint at the town's oldest pub. Built in 1470, this thatch-roofed treasure has great real ales and a gorgeous summertime courtyard.

Dirty Duck
PUB

(www.greeneking-pubs.co.uk; Waterside; ⊙noon-11.30pm Mon-Thu, to midnight Fri & Sat, to 11pm Sun; 🖭) Also called the 'Black Swan', this enchanting riverside alehouse is the only pub in England to be licensed under two names. It's a favourite thespian watering hole, with a roll call of former regulars (Olivier, Attenborough et al) that reads like a who's who of actors.

Windmill Inn
PUB

(www.greeneking-pubs.co.uk; Church St; ⊙11am-11pm Sun-Thu, to midnight Fri & Sat; 🖭) Ale was already flowing at this low-ceilinged pub when rhyming couplets gushed from Shakespeare's quill. Flowers frame the white-washed facade; there's a shaded rear beer garden.

☆ Entertainment

★Royal Shakespeare Company
THEATRE

(RSC; ☑box office 01789-331111; www.rsc.org.uk; Waterside; ⊙tour times vary, tower 10am-5pm Sun-Fri, 10am-12.15pm & 2-5pm Sat mid-Mar–mid-Oct, 10am-4.30pm Sun-Fri, to 12.15pm Sat

> ### ⓘ SHAKESPEARE HISTORIC HOMES
>
> Five of the most important buildings associated with Shakespeare – Shakespeare's Birthplace (p407), Shakespeare's New Place (p407), Hall's Croft (p409), Anne Hathaway's Cottage (p408) and Mary Arden's Farm (p408) – contain museums that form the core of the visitor experience at Stratford. All are run by the Shakespeare Birthplace Trust (www.shakespeare.org.uk).
>
> A Full Story ticket (adult/child £22/14.50) covering all five properties is available online or at the sites, and provides up to a 60% discount off individual admission prices.

mid-Oct–mid-Mar) Stratford has two grand stages run by the world-renowned Royal Shakespeare Company – the **Royal Shakespeare Theatre** and the Swan Theatre on Waterside – as well as the smaller Other Place. The theatres have witnessed performances by such legends as Lawrence Olivier, Richard Burton, Judi Dench, Helen Mirren, Ian McKellan and Patrick Stewart. One-hour guided tours (on hold at the time of research) take you behind the scenes.

Zipping up the lift/elevator of the Royal Shakespeare Theatre's **tower** rewards with panoramic views over the town and River Avon. Spectacular views also unfold from its 3rd-floor Rooftop Restaurant (p411), which opens to a terrace.

Contact the RSC for performance times, and book well ahead as capacity is limited (though there are plans to stream performances as well).

There are often special deals for under-25-year-olds, students and seniors. A few tickets are held back for sale on the day of performances but get snapped up fast.

Other Place   THEATRE
(📌 box office 01789-331111; www.rsc.org.uk; 22 Southern Lane) The smallest stage of the Royal Shakespeare Company (p411) has 200 seats.

ALTON TOWERS

Phenomenally popular **Alton Towers** (📌 0871 222 3330; www.altontowers.com; Farley Lane, Alton; adult/child amusement park £53/44, water park £16.50/12.50; ☺ hours vary), 4 miles east of Cheadle off the B5032, offers maximum G-force for your buck. Wild rides include the Th13teen, Nemesis, Oblivion, Galactica and Wickerman coasters. Gentler thrills span carousels and stage shows to a pirate-themed aquarium and splashtastic water park.

Check seasonal schedules online and pre-purchase tickets to skip ticket queues and take advantage of discounted entry deals. Five on-site hotels with themed rooms offer perks such as an hour's early park entry.

Your own transport is best (a monorail loops between the car park and the main entrance). In summer, one daily bus links Alton Towers with Stoke-on-Trent, Nottingham and Derby; schedules are available from Traveline (p394).

New work is presented here; it also hosts regular free live music and spoken word nights.

Swan Theatre   THEATRE
(📌 01789-331111; www.rsc.org.uk; Waterside) Hosting productions by the Royal Shakespeare Company (p411), this grand stage has a capacity of 426 people.

🛍 Shopping

Chaucer Head   BOOKS
(www.chaucerhead.com; 21 Chapel St; ☺ 11am-5.30pm Mon-Fri, 10am-5pm Sat) Bargain-priced paperbacks through to rare antiquarian books worth thousands of pounds are stocked at the Chaucer Head, which was originally founded in Birmingham in 1830 and relocated to literary-famed Stratford in 1960.

ℹ Information

Tourist Office (📌 01789-264293; www.shakespeares-england.co.uk; Bridge Foot; ☺ 9am-5.30pm Mon-Sat, 10am-4pm Sun) Just west of Clopton Bridge.

ℹ Getting There & Away

BUS

Buses run from Stratford's Riverside bus station (behind the Stratford Leisure Centre on Bridgeway).

National Express services run to London Victoria (£10.50, three hours, four direct services per day).

CAR

If you're driving, be warned that town car parks charge high fees, 24 hours a day.

TRAIN

From Stratford-upon-Avon train station, West Midlands Railway runs to Birmingham (£8.60, 40 minutes, half-hourly); Chiltern Railways serves London Marylebone (£38.20, 2¼ hours, up to two per hour), some with a change in Leamington Spa; and East Midlands runs to Warwick (£7.30, 25 minutes, every two hours).

The nostalgic **Shakespeare Express Steam Train** (📌 0121-708 4960; www.vintagetrains.co.uk; return 1st/2nd class £45/35; ☺ Sun Jul–mid-Sep) chugs twice every Sunday in summer between Stratford and Birmingham Moor St; the one-way journey time is one hour.

ℹ Getting Around

From 10am to 6pm April to October, a 1937-built, hand-wound chain ferry yo-yos across the Avon between the west bank and the east bank (one-way 20p).

A bicycle is handy for getting out to the outlying Shakespeare properties. **Stratford Bike Hire** (📞 07711-776340; www.stratford bikehire.com; The Stratford Greenway, Seven Meadows Rd; bike hire per half/full day from £10/15; ⊗ 9.30am-5pm) will deliver to your accommodation for free within a 6-mile radius of Stratford.

STAFFORDSHIRE

Wedged between the ever-expanding conurbations of Birmingham and Manchester, Staffordshire is surprisingly green, with the northern half of the county rising to meet the rugged hills of the Peak District.

Regular trains and buses serve Lichfield, Stafford and other major towns.

Lichfield

📞 01543 / POP 32,219

Even without its magnificent Gothic cathedral – one of the most spectacular in the country – this charming cobbled market town would be worth a visit to tread in the footsteps of lexicographer and wit Samuel Johnson, and natural philosopher Erasmus Darwin, grandfather of Charles. Johnson once described Lichfield folk as 'the most sober, decent people in England', which was rather generous considering that this was the last place in the country to stop burning people at the stake.

◉ Sights

★**Lichfield Cathedral**　　　CATHEDRAL
(📞 01543-306150; www.lichfield-cathedral.org; 19 Cathedral Close; adult/child £2/free; ⊗ 9.30am-4pm Mon-Sat, 12.30-4pm Sun) Crowned by three dramatic towers, Lichfield Cathedral is a Gothic fantasy, constructed in stages from 1200 to 1350. The enormous vaulted nave is set slightly off line from the choir, creating a bizarre perspective when viewed from the west door, and carvings inside the cathedral still bear signs of damage caused by Civil War soldiers sharpening their swords.

In the octagonal Chapter House, you can view the illuminated *Chad Gospels,* created around AD 730; an ornate Anglo-Saxon bas-relief known as the *Lichfield Angel;* and

WORTH A TRIP

LORD LICHFIELD'S SHUGBOROUGH

A regal, neoclassical mansion, **Shugborough** (NT; 📞 01889-880166; www.nationaltrust.org.uk; Great Haywood; adult/child house & grounds £13/6.50, grounds only £8/4; ⊗ house 11am-4.30pm Mar-Oct, 10am-3pm Dec, grounds 9am-5pm Mar-Oct, to 4pm Nov & Dec) is the ancestral home of royal photographer Lord Lichfield. A good proportion of the wall space is devoted to his work; the highlight is the staterooms' collection of exquisite Louis XV and XVI furniture. One-hour guided tours (included in admission) run between 11am and 1pm. Shugborough is 6 miles east of Stafford on the A513; bus 825 linking Stafford and Lichfield stops 1 mile from the manor (£4.40, 30 minutes, hourly Monday to Saturday).

a faded but glorious medieval wall painting above the door.

The grand west facade positively bows under the weight of 113 statues of bishops, saints and kings of England. Be sure to stroll the delightful, once-fortified Cathedral Close, ringed with imposing 17th- and 18th-century houses.

Erasmus Darwin House　　HISTORIC BUILDING
(📞 01543-306260; www.erasmusdarwin.org; Beacon St; house £5, garden free; ⊗ house 10am-3.30pm Thu-Sun, garden 10am-3.30pm daily) After turning down the job of royal physician to King George III, Erasmus Darwin became a leading light in the Lunar Society, debating the origins of life with luminaries including Wedgwood, Boulton and Watt decades before his grandson Charles came up with the theory of evolution. The former house of the 'Grandfather of Evolution' contains intriguing exhibits, including his notebook containing drawings of his inventions. At the back, a fragrant culinary and medicinal herb garden leads to Cathedral Close.

Samuel Johnson Birthplace Museum　　MUSEUM
(📞 01543-264972; www.samueljohnsonbirthplace. org.uk; Breadmarket St; ⊗ 10.30am-4.30pm Mar-Oct, 11am-3.30pm Nov-Feb) FREE This absorbing museum charts the life of the pioneering lexicographer, wit, poet and critic Samuel

THE POTTERIES – STOKE-ON-TRENT

Situated at the heart of the Potteries (the famous pottery-producing region of Stafford-shire), Stoke-on-Trent is famed for its ceramics. Don't expect cute little artisanal producers: this was where pottery shifted to mass production during the Industrial Revolution, and Stoke today is a sprawl of industrial townships tied together by flyovers and bypasses. There are dozens of active potteries that you can visit in the greater area, including the famous Wedgwood factory.

The **tourist office** (☑01782-236000; www.visitstoke.co.uk; Bethesda St, Hanley; ◷10am-5pm Mon-Sat, 11am-4pm Sun) has information on all the potteries that are open to the public.

Potteries Museum & Art Gallery (☑01782-236000; www.stokemuseums.org.uk; Bethesda St, Hanley; ◷10am-5pm Mon-Sat, 11am-4pm Sun) Providing a thorough overview of the Potteries area's history, this museum and gallery houses an extensive ceramics display, from Toby jugs and jasperware to outrageous ornamental pieces. Other highlights include treasures from the 2009-discovered Staffordshire Hoard (the largest hoard of Anglo-Saxon gold and silver metalwork ever found, incorporating 5.1kg of gold, 1.4kg of silver and some 3500 pieces of jewellery); displays on the WWII Spitfire, created by the Stoke-born aviator Reginald Mitchell; and artworks by TS Lowry and Sir Henry Moore.

Some temporary exhibitions incur an extra charge.

World of Wedgwood (☑01782-282986; www.worldofwedgwood.com; Wedgwood Dr, Barlaston; factory tour & museum adult/child £10/8, museum only free; ◷factory 10am-4pm Mon-Fri, museum to 5pm daily) Set in attractive parkland 8 miles south of Hanley, the modern production centre for Josiah Wedgwood's porcelain empire displays an extensive collection of historic pieces, including plenty of Wedgwood's delicate, neoclassical blue-and-white jasperware at its museum. On weekdays there are guided factory tours lasting 45 minutes (reserve in advance). Pot throwing (over-12s only) and design workshops take place at its Master Craft and Decorating studios.

Johnson, who moved to London from his native Lichfield and devoted nine years to producing the first major dictionary of the English language. Johnson's dictionary helped define the word 'dull' with this example: 'to make dictionaries is dull work'. On the 1st floor, a short dramatised film narrates Johnson's life story. It's a lovely property to explore.

Hub at St Mary's MUSEUM
(☑01543-414749; www.thehubstmarys.co.uk; Market Sq; ◷9.30am-1pm Tue-Thu, to 8pm Fri & Sat, 11am-3pm Sun) Dating from 1870, the revamped St Mary's Church contains the town's library and art gallery, along with a performance space for theatre, live music and events, and a cafe. Climb the tower's 120 steps for sweeping city views.

🛏 Sleeping & Eating

George Hotel HOTEL ££
(☑01543-414822; www.thegeorgelichfield.co.uk; 12-14 Bird St; s/d from £90/109; ⓟ🛜) An old Georgian pub has been upgraded into a comfortable, midrange hotel with 45 rooms

that scores points for location rather than atmosphere.

Swinfen Hall Hotel HISTORIC HOTEL £££
(☑01543-481494; www.swinfenhallhotel.co.uk; Swinfen; s/d/ste incl breakfast from £140/150/315; ⓟ🛜) Georgian manor house Swinfen Hall, built in 1757, sits 3 miles southeast of Lichfield amid 40 wooded hectares with formal gardens, wild hay meadows and a deer park. Parkland views extend from its 17 rooms, which have either traditional or contemporary styling. Its fine-dining restaurant has multicourse tasting menus accompanied by wine flights.

Damn Fine Cafe CAFE £
(www.facebook.com/damnfinecafe; 16 Bird St; dishes £2.50-6.50; ◷9am-2pm Tue-Fri, to 3pm Sat & Sun) Teeming with locals, this cafe is a handy spot for all-day bacon-and-sausage or vegetarian toad-in-the-hole breakfasts, soup, mozzarella melts and sandwiches on a variety of breads.

Trooper GASTROPUB ££
(☑01543-480413; www.thetrooperwall.co.uk; Watling St, Wall; mains £13.50-28, steaks £18-45;

kitchen noon-9.15pm Mon-Wed, to 9.45pm Thu-Sat, to 8pm Sun, bar noon-midnight Mon-Sat, to 10pm Sun; 🖶) 🍴 Idyllically situated 3 miles southwest of Lichfield in the tiny village of Wall, this gastropub prides itself on ingredients sourced from local suppliers and herbs from its gardens. Chargrilled wagyu steaks are the house speciality, alongside contemporary twists on pub classics, such as ham-and-cider pie. In fine weather, enjoy its fabulous real ales in the sunny beer garden.

Its three-course kids' menu (£10) has the option of a mini 4oz steak with fries.

Wine House   BRITISH **££**

(📳01543-419999;   www.thewinehouselichfield.co.uk; 27 Bird St; mains £12.50-28; ⊘noon-10pm Mon-Sat, to 6pm Sun) Well-chosen wines complement the upmarket pub fare at these smart, red-brick premises. Choices range from slow-cooked pork belly with apple sauce to steaks and seafood, such as line-caught sea bass with white wine, shallots and clams.

🍷 Drinking & Nightlife

Beerbohm   BAR

(http://beerbohm.co.uk; 19 Tamworth St; ⊘11am-11pm Tue-Sat; 📶) Behind a peppermint-painted traditional shopfront, Beerbohm's richly coloured lounge-style interior is filled with handmade furniture. Its discerning drinks list includes local ales and small-batch gins, English wines and artisan malt whiskies plus imported craft beers (some gluten-free). It doesn't serve food but provides plates and cutlery for you to bring your own.

Whippet Inn   PUB

(21 Tamworth St; ⊘noon-2.30pm & 4.30-10pm Wed & Thu, noon-10pm Fri & Sat, to 5pm Sun) Ales and craft keg beers from independent British breweries are the hallmark of this adorable little one-room micropub, along with a wonderful selection of ciders and wines, but it resolutely doesn't serve lager or spirits. Artisan bar snacks include pork pies, Scotch eggs and sausage rolls.

ℹ Information

Tourist Office (📳01543-308924; www.visitlichfield.co.uk; Market Sq; ⊘9.30am-4pm Mon-Sat) In the Hub at St Mary's.

ℹ Getting There & Away

The bus station is opposite the main Lichfield City train station on Birmingham Rd. Bus 825 serves Stafford (£4.60, 1¼ hours, hourly Monday to Saturday).

Lichfield has two train stations.

Lichfield City Trains to Birmingham (£5.70, 30 minutes, up to three per hour) leave from Lichfield City station in the town centre.

Lichfield Trent Valley Trains to London Euston (£56, 1¾ hours, up to two per hour) run from Lichfield Trent Valley station on the eastern side of town, 1.5 miles east of the centre, with a change in Birmingham.

WORCESTERSHIRE

Famed for its eponymous condiment, invented by two Worcester chemists in 1837, Worcestershire marks the transition from the industrial heart of the Midlands to the peaceful countryside of the Marches along

---

NATIONAL BREWERY CENTRE

Burton-upon-Trent grew up around its 7th-century abbey, which was famed for its healing spring waters. Brewing began here around 1700 and in the early 18th century, the River Trent was opened for navigation, allowing Burton to become a major brewing centre. Its fascinating history is brought to life through two-hour guided tours of the **National Brewery Centre** (📳01283-532880; www.nationalbrewerycentre.co.uk; Horninglow St, Burton-upon-Trent; adult/child £11.95/6.95; ⊘centre 10am-5pm, guided tours 11am & 2pm Thu-Sun), a vast complex that contains a museum and still has a microbrewery today. Staff can point you to Burton's other breweries and traditional ale houses.

During tours, you'll learn, for example, that Burton developed pale ale to export to colonial-era India: the origins of IPA (Indian Pale Ale) today; and also taste samples (there are soft drinks for kids).

Trains run from Derby (£8, 15 minutes, up to three per hour) and Birmingham (£17.80, 30 minutes, up to three per hour) to Burton's train station; a half-mile walk southwest of the National Brewery Centre.

the English–Welsh border. The southern and western fringes of the county burst with lush countryside and sleepy market towns, while the capital is a classic English county town, whose magnificent cathedral inspired the composer Edward Elgar to write some of his greatest works.

Activities

The 210-mile riverside Severn Way winds through Worcestershire en route from Plynlimon in Wales to the sea at Bristol. A shorter challenge is the 100-mile Three Choirs Way, linking Worcester to Hereford and Gloucester. The Malvern Hills are also prime country for walking and cycling; information is available at www.malvernhillsaonb.org.uk.

❶ Getting There & Around

Worcester is a convenient rail hub. Kidderminster is the southern railhead of the quaint Severn Valley Railway (p428).

Buses and trains connect larger towns, but bus services to rural areas can be frustratingly infrequent. Search the transport pages at www.worcestershire.gov.uk or Traveline (p394) for bus companies and timetables.

Worcester

☎01905 / POP 101,328

Worcester (*woos*-ter) has enough historic treasures to forgive the architectural eyesores from the postwar love affair with all things concrete. The home of the famous Worcestershire sauce (an unlikely combination of fermented tamarinds and anchovies), this ancient cathedral city was the site of the last battle of the Civil War, the Battle of Worcester, which took place on 3 September 1651. The defeated Charles II only narrowly escaped the pursuing Roundheads by hiding in an oak tree, an event still celebrated in Worcester every 29 May, when government buildings are decked out with oak sprigs.

◎ Sights

★ Worcester Cathedral   CATHEDRAL
(☎01905-732900; www.worcestercathedral.co.uk; 8 College Yard; cathedral by donation, tower adult/child £5/free, tours £7/free; ◎cathedral 11am-3pm Mon-Sat, 1-3pm Sun, tower hours vary, tours 11am & 2.30pm Mon-Sat Mar-Nov, Sat Dec-Feb) Rising above the River Severn, Worcester's majestic cathedral is the final resting place of Magna Carta signatory King John. The strong-legged can scale 235 steps to the top

of the tower (confirm times ahead), from where Charles II surveyed his troops during the disastrous Battle of Worcester. Hour-long tours run from the gift shop. Several works by local composer Edward Elgar had their first public outings here – to appreciate the acoustics, come for evensong (5.30pm Monday to Saturday, 4pm Sunday).

Royal Worcester Porcelain Works   MUSEUM
(☎01905-21247; www.museumofroyalworcester.org; Severn St; adult/child incl audio guide £6.50/free; ◎10am-5pm Thu-Sat, to 4pm Sun) Up there with the country's most famous potteries, the Royal Worcester porcelain factory gained an edge over its rivals by picking up the contract to provide fine crockery to the British monarchy. An entertaining audio tour reveals some quirkier sides to the Royal Worcester story, including its brief foray into porcelain dentures and 'portable fonts' designed for use during cholera outbreaks. The shop has some splendid pieces, from monk-shaped candle snuffers to decorated thimbles and pill boxes.

Greyfriars   HISTORIC BUILDING
(NT; ☎01905-23571; www.nationaltrust.org.uk; Friar St; adult/child £5.45/2.70; ◎11am-5pm Tue-Sat Mar-Oct, to 4pm Nov–mid-Dec) Friar St was largely chock-a-block with historic architecture until the iconoclastic 1960s when much was demolished, including the lovely medieval Lich Gate. Some creaky old almshouses survive and Greyfriars was saved in the nick of time by the National Trust, offering the chance to poke around a timber-framed merchant's house from 1480. It's full of atmospheric wood-panelled rooms and is backed by a pretty walled garden.

🛏 Sleeping

Diglis House Hotel   HOTEL ££
(☎01905-353518; www.diglishousehotel.co.uk; Severn St; s/d/ste incl breakfast from £90/115/145; 🅿🛜) Next to the boathouse in a gorgeous waterside setting, this rambling yet cosy 28-room Georgian house is a short stroll from the cathedral. The best rooms have four-poster beds, luxe bathrooms and river views. Its elegant restaurant (mains £12 to £18) opens to a terrace overlooking the river. Guests can work out at the nearby gym for free.

🍴 Eating & Drinking

★ Old Rectifying House   BRITISH ££
(☎01905-619622; www.theoldrec.co.uk; North Pde; mains £12-29; ◎kitchen 6-9pm Tue-Thu, to 9.30pm

Fri & Sat, bar noon–11pm Tue–Thu & Sun, to midnight Fri & Sat; 🅿️ 🛗) Worcester's hippest dining space has a candlelit, painted-brick interior and umbrella-shaded terrace tables. Its switched-on menu features dishes such as braised pork cheek with a crispy ham bonbon. DJs often hit the decks in the lounge bar, which mixes craft cocktails including a 'Hedgerow Shire' with local gin and birch liqueur.

Kids, vegetarians and vegans are catered for; vegan dishes include a Sunday nut roast (advance orders essential).

★ **Cardinal's Hat**   PUB
(📞 01905-724006; www.the-cardinals-hat.co.uk; 31 Friar St; ⊙ 4-10pm Mon, noon-10pm Tue-Sun; 🛜) Dating from the 14th century, and claiming a resident ghost, Worcester's oldest and grandest pub retains original features, including timber panelling and log-burning stoves. English craft beers and ciders dominate the taps, while the kitchen specialises in pies (eg steak, red wine and Stilton, £11). Upstairs are six Georgian-style boutique guest rooms (doubles £82.50 to £125).

ℹ️ Information

Tourist Office (📞 01905-726311; www.visitworcestershire.org; Guildhall, High St; ⊙ 9.30am-5pm Mon-Fri, 10am-4pm Sat) Inside the Grade I–listed Guildhall, dating from 1721.

ℹ️ Getting There & Away

BUS
The **bus station** (Crowngate Centre, Friary Walk) is inside the Crowngate Centre on Friary Walk. National Express has services to London Victoria (£18.50, 3¾ hours, two daily Monday to Friday, one Saturday and Sunday).

TRAIN
Worcester Foregate is the main rail hub, but services also run from Worcester Shrub Hill.
Birmingham £9, one hour, up to three per hour
Great Malvern £5.90, 15 minutes, up to two per hour
Hereford £10.60, 50 minutes, hourly
Ledbury £7.70, 25 minutes, hourly
London Paddington £44.60, 2½ hours, up to three per hour

Great Malvern

📞 01684 / POP 29,626
Tumbling down the side of a forested ridge about 7 miles southwest of Worcester, the picturesque spa town of Great Malvern is the

---

THE FIRS – ELGAR'S BIRTHPLACE
....
England's most popular classical composer is celebrated at the humble country **cottage** (NT; www.nationaltrust.org.uk/the-firs; Crown East Lane, Lower Broadheath; adult/child £8/5.10) where Edward Elgar was born in 1857. A sculpture of Elgar, sitting on a bench looking out over the Malvern Hills, created by artist Jemma Pearson, is in the flower-filled garden.

The property is run by the National Trust; check the website for opening times as well as details of concerts here. It's 4 miles west of Worcester; you'll need your own transport.

---

gateway to the Malverns, a soaring 9-mile-long range of volcanic hills that rise unexpectedly from the surrounding meadows. In Victorian times, the medicinal waters were prescribed as a panacea for everything from gout to sore eyes – you can test the theory by sampling Malvern water straight from the ground at public wells dotted around the town.

⊙ Sights

★ **Morgan Motor Company**   FACTORY, MUSEUM
(📞 01684-573104; www.morgan-motor.com; Pickersleigh Rd; museum free, tours adult/child £24/12; ⊙ museum 8.30am-5pm Mon-Thu, to 2pm Fri, tours by reservation) Morgan has been hand-crafting elegant sports cars since 1909. You can see the mechanics at work on two-hour guided tours of the unassuming shed-like buildings comprising the factory (pre-bookings essential), and view a fleet of vintage classics adjacent to the museum. If buying one of these beautiful machines is beyond your budget, it's possible to hire one (per day/weekend/week from £235/635/1095, including insurance) for a spin through the Malvern Hills.

Great Malvern Priory   MONASTERY
(📞 01684-561020; www.greatmalvernpriory.org.uk; Church St; ⊙ 9am-5pm) 𝗙𝗥𝗘𝗘 The 11th-century Great Malvern Priory is packed with remarkable features, from original Norman pillars to surreal modernist stained glass. The choir is enclosed by a screen of 15th-century tiles and the monks' stalls are decorated with delightfully irreverent 14th-century

LOCAL KNOWLEDGE

WALKING IN THE MALVERN HILLS

The jack-in-the-box Malvern Hills, which dramatically pop up out of the Severn plains on the boundary between Worcestershire and Herefordshire, rise to the lofty peak of the Worcester Beacon (419m), reached by a steep 3-mile climb above Great Malvern. More than 100 miles of trails traipse over the various summits, which are mostly capped by exposed grassland, offering the kind of views that inspire orchestral movements.

Great Malvern's tourist office has racks of pamphlets covering popular hikes, including a map of the mineral-water springs, wells and fountains of the town and surrounding hills. The enthusiast-run website www.malverntrail.co.uk is also a goldmine of useful walking information.

A single £4.40 parking ticket per day is valid at locations throughout the hills.

misericords, depicting everything from three rats hanging a cat to the mythological reptile, the basilisk. Charles Darwin's daughter Annie is buried here.

Sleeping & Eating

Abbey Hotel HOTEL £££
(01684-892332; www.sarova-abbeyhotel.com; Abbey Rd; d/f from £139/179; P 🛜 🐾) Tangled in vines like a Brothers Grimm fairy-tale castle, this stately property has 103 elegant rooms in a prime location by the local-history museum and priory.

Mac & Jac's CAFE £
(www.macandjacs.co.uk; 23 Abbey Rd; dishes £4-13; 9am-4pm Wed-Fri, to 5pm Sat, 10am-4pm Sun) Creative salads, flatbreads, sharing plates, spelt risotto and a savoury tart of the day are served at this light, bright cafe set in a chic white-painted shopfront near the priory.

St Ann's Well Cafe CAFE, VEGETARIAN £
(01684-560285; www.stannswell.co.uk; St Ann's Rd; mains £5.50, cakes £2.90; 11.30am-3.30pm Tue-Fri, 10am-4pm Sat & Sun;) A s-t-e-e-p climb above St Ann's Rd (so best to check opening times beforehand), this quaint cafe is set in an early-19th-century villa, with mountain-fresh spring water bubbling into

a carved basin by the door. All-vegetarian food (including vegan options) spans soups to pies, filled baguettes, cakes, pastries and puddings.

Fig Tree MEDITERRANEAN ££
(01684-569909; www.thefigmalvern.co.uk; 99b Church St; breakfast dishes £6.50-9.50, mains lunch £8.50-13, dinner £16.50-24; 10am-2pm & 5.30-9.30pm Tue-Sat;) Tucked down an alleyway off Church St, this 19th-century former stable serves hearty breakfasts (including vegan options), and Mediterranean-inspired fare at lunch (focaccia, pastas and salads) and dinner (chorizo-stuffed squid, lamb souvlaki with tzatziki and saffron rice). Don't miss its signature almond-and-lemon polenta cake with fig ice cream.

🛈 Information

Tourist Office (01684-892289; www.visitthemalverns.org; 6 Church St; 10am-5pm Apr-Oct, 10am-5pm Mon-Sat, to 4pm Sun Nov-Mar) The tourist office is a mine of walking and cycling information.

🛈 Getting There & Away

Buses are limited, making trains your best bet. The train station is east of the town centre, off Avenue Rd.

Rail services include the following.

Hereford £9.70, 30 minutes, hourly
Ledbury £5.50, 10 minutes, up to two per hour
Worcester £5.90, 15 minutes, up to two per hour

HEREFORDSHIRE

Adjoining the Welsh border, Herefordshire is a patchwork of fields, hills and cute little black-and-white villages, many dating back to the Tudor era and beyond.

🏃 Activities

As well as the famous **Offa's Dyke Path**, which follows the English–Welsh border for 177 miles alongside the 8th-century Offa's Dyke, walkers can follow the **Herefordshire Trail** (www.herefordshiretrail.com) on a 150-mile circular loop through Leominster, Ledbury, Ross-on-Wye and Kington.

Only slightly less ambitious is the 136-mile **Wye Valley Walk** (www.wyevalleywalk.org), which runs from Chepstow in Wales through Herefordshire and back out again to Plynlimon.

The **Three Choirs Way** is a 100-mile route connecting the cathedrals of Hereford, Worcester and Gloucester.

Cyclists can trace the **Six Castles Cycleway** (NCN Route 44) from Hereford to Leominster and Shrewsbury, or NCN Route 68 to Great Malvern and Worcester.

❶ Getting Around

Trains run frequently to destinations including Hereford and Ledbury, with bus connections on to the rest of the county. For bus timetables, contact Traveline (p394).

Hereford

♪ 01432 / POP 58,896

Surrounded by apple orchards and rolling pastures at the heart of the Marches, Hereford straddles the River Wye. This lively city's key draw for visitors is its magnificent cathedral.

◉ Sights

★**Hereford Cathedral**　　　　CATHEDRAL
(*♪* 01432-374200; www.herefordcathedral.org; 5 College Cloisters, Cathedral Close; cathedral entry by donation, Mappa Mundi £6; ⊙ cathedral 10am-3pm Mon-Sat, noon-3pm Sun, Mappa Mundi 10am-3pm Mon-Sat) After Welsh marauders torched the original Saxon cathedral, the Norman rulers of Hereford erected a larger, grander cathedral on the same site. The building was subsequently remodelled in a succession of medieval architectural styles.

The signature highlight is the magnificent **Mappa Mundi**, a single piece of calfskin vellum intricately painted with some rather fantastical assumptions about the layout of the globe in around 1290. The same wing contains the world's largest surviving **chained library** of rare manuscripts manacled to the shelves.

Cider Museum Hereford　　　　MUSEUM
(*♪* 01432-354207; www.cidermuseum.co.uk; Pomona Pl) Mills and presses, glassware, watercolours, photographs and films are among the displays at this former cider-making factory (Bulmer's original premises), along with costrels (minibarrels) used by agricultural workers to carry their wages, which were partially paid in cider. Download brochures outlining walks through Herefordshire's orchards from its website. It's half a mile west of the city centre; follow Eign St and turn south along Ryelands St.

The museum was closed at the time of research – check the website for updates.

🛏 Sleeping

Charades　　　　B&B **££**
(*♪* 01432-269444; www.charadeshereford.co.uk; 32 Southbank Rd; s/d from £75/85; [P][@][🛜]) Handy for the bus station, this imposing Victorian house dating from 1877 has six inviting rooms with high ceilings, big and bright windows, and some with soothing countryside views. The house itself has character in spades – look for old service bells in the hall and the plentiful *Titanic* memorabilia. Traditional or vegetarian breakfasts are available.

★**Castle House**　　BOUTIQUE HOTEL **£££**
(*♪* 01432-356321; www.castlehse.co.uk; Castle St; s/d/ste from £140/175/200; [P][🛜]) In a regal Georgian town house where the Bishop of Hereford once resided, this tranquil 16-room hotel has two sophisticated restaurants using ingredients sourced from its own nearby farm, a sunny garden spilling down to Hereford's former castle moat, and magnificent rooms and suites. Another eight newer rooms (some wheelchair accessible) are a short walk away at 25 Castle St.

🍴 Eating & Drinking

★**Burger Shop**　　　　BURGERS **£**
(*♪* 01432-351764; www.aruleoftum.com; 32 Aubrey St; burgers £7.50-11.50; ⊙ noon-9pm Sun-Wed, to 10pm Thu-Sat; [🛜][♿]) Exposed brick, elongated wooden benches and a courtyard garden are the backdrop for brilliant brioche-bun burgers such as the Hereford Hop (pulled beef shin, Hereford Hop cheese, dill pickles and mustard mayo). Vegan burgers are cooked on a separate grill; you can order gluten-free buns made from quinoa flour. Alongside local ciders, kickin' cocktails include a vodka-fuelled Marmalade Mule.

Hereford Deli　　　　DELI **£**
(*♪* 01432-341283; www.thehereforddeli.com; 4 The Mews, St Owen St; sandwiches £2-3; ⊙ 8am-6pm Mon-Fri, 9am-4pm Sat) At this gourmet emporium with a clutch of tables, fantastic sandwiches are a steal. Combinations include curried free-range chicken with mango chutney, Scottish smoked salmon with lemon-and-dill butter, or local roast beef with Cropwell Bishop Stilton and rosehip jelly. It's hidden down a narrow laneway near a large public car park.

HEREFORDSHIRE CIDER

The **Herefordshire Cider Route** (www.ciderroute.co.uk) drops in on numerous local cider producers, where you can try before you buy, and then totter off to the next cidery. Mindful of road safety, tourist offices have maps and guide booklets to help you explore by bus or bicycle.

If you only have time to visit one Herefordshire cider-maker, make it **Westons Cider Mills** (☑01531-660108; www.westons-cider.co.uk; The Bounds, Much Marcle; tours adult/child £12.50/5; ⊙9am-5pm Mon-Fri, 10am-5pm Sat & Sun), whose house brew is even served in the Houses of Parliament. Informative tours (1½ hours) start at 11am, 12.30pm, 2pm and 3.30pm from Monday to Friday, with free cider and perry tastings for the grown-ups. There's also a fascinating bottle museum, and a restaurant that incorporates cider in its dishes. It's just under a mile west of the tiny village of Much Marcle.

★ **Beer in Hand** PUB
(https://beer-in-hand.square.site; 136 Eign St; ⊙5-10pm Thu-Sat) Ciders at this independent pub are sublime and most are locally sourced. It's also the tap room for its own Odyssey beers (such as Black Out, a dark-malt, full-bodied American black ale brewed with fresh oranges, which it brews on the nearby National Trust Brockhampton Estate). There are board games but no TVs.

ⓘ Information

Tourist Office (☑01432-383837; www.facebook.com/tichereford; 8 St Owen's St; ⊙10am-4pm Tue-Sat) Located inside Hereford's town hall.

ⓘ Getting There & Away

BUS

The bus station is on Commercial Rd, 500m northeast of the city centre.

Bus 33 runs to Gloucester (£4.50, 1¾ hours, hourly Monday to Saturday) via Ross-on-Wye (£4, one hour).

TRAIN

The train station is 950m northeast of the city centre.

Regular services include the following:
Birmingham £18.90, 1½ hours, hourly
Ledbury £6.90, 15 minutes, hourly
London Paddington £61.20, three hours, up to two per hour – either direct or with a change in Newport, South Wales
Ludlow £10.90, 25 minutes, up to two per hour
Worcester £10.60, 50 minutes, hourly

Ledbury

☑01531 / POP 9290

Creaking with history and dotted with antique shops, Ledbury's crooked black-and-white streets zero in on a delightfully leggy medieval **Market House**. The timber-framed structure is precariously balanced atop a series of wooden posts supposedly taken from the wrecked ships of the Spanish Armada.

Almost impossibly cute Church Lane, crowded with tilting timber-framed buildings, runs its cobbled way from High St to the town church.

⌂ Sleeping & Eating

Feathers Hotel HOTEL ££
(☑01531-635266; www.feathersledbury.co.uk; 25 High St; d incl breakfast from £115; P🐾🤍) A Ledbury landmark, this black-and-white Tudor hotel built in 1564 looms over the main street. Of its 22 rooms, those in the oldest part of the building come with sloping floorboards, painted beams and much more character than rooms in the modern extension. There's an atmospheric wood-panelled restaurant (mains £14 to £29), and an indoor swimming pool.

Verzon House Hotel HOTEL ££
(☑01531-670381; www.verzonhouse.com; Hereford Rd, Trumpet; s/d/ste from £80/100/180; P🤍) 🍃 The ultimate country-chic retreat, this lovely Georgian farmhouse 3.8 miles northwest of Ledbury on the A438 has nine luxuriously appointed rooms with free-standing baths, goose-down pillows and deep-pile carpets. Locally sourced produce underpins the Modern British menu at its restaurant (mains £17 to £32).

Malthouse Cafe & Gallery CAFE ££
(☑01531-634443; Church Lane; mains lunch £5-7.50, dinner £14-19; ⊙9am-5pm Tue-Thu, 9am-5pm & 6-11pm Fri & Sat, 10am-4pm Sun & Mon; 🖋) Set back from the street in a cobbled courtyard, this ivy-draped building is a delightful spot for breakfast (such as poached eggs with a thyme, leek and parsnip cake) or lunch

(black-pudding sausage rolls, goats cheese and rosemary filo parcels). On Friday and Saturday evenings, mains might include mustard-glazed pork belly or slow-cooked Herefordshire beef ribs.

Shopping

★ Malvern Hills Vintage
ANTIQUES

(☑ 01531-633608; www.malvernhillsvintage.com; Lower Mitchell Barns, Eastnor; ☺ shop & cafe 10am-5pm Wed-Sat, 11am-5pm Sun) A vast timber barn 1.5 miles northeast of Ledbury is packed to the rafters with retro, antique and industrial treasures – everything from Victorian lamps and brass cash registers to mahogany dressers, oak-framed mirrors, leather Chesterfields and even classic cars, such as a 1974 MG Midget RWA 1275 convertible. On the mezzanine, its tearoom serves scones, cakes and slices.

❶ Getting There & Away

Buses are limited, but regular train services include the following.

Great Malvern £5.50, 10 minutes, up to two per hour

Hereford £6.90, 15 minutes, hourly

Worcester £7.70, 25 minutes, up to two per hour

Ross-on-Wye

☑ 01989 / POP 10,582

Set on a red sandstone bluff over a kink in the River Wye, hilly Ross-on-Wye was propelled to fame in the 18th century by Alexander Pope and Samuel Taylor Coleridge, who penned tributes to philanthropist John Kyrle, 'Man of Ross', who dedicated his life and fortune to the poor of the parish.

◎ Sights

Market House
GALLERY

(☑ 01989-769398; www.madeinross.co.uk; Market Pl; ☺ 11am-3pm) 🆓 The 17th-century Market House sits atop weathered sandstone columns in Market Pl. The salmon-pink building is now home to artist collective Made in Ross, whose members live and work in a 20-mile radius, and exhibit and sell their arts and crafts here. Regular markets take place on the square at the front.

⊫ Sleeping & Eating

King's Head
INN ££

(☑ 01989-763174; www.kingshead.co.uk; 8 High St; d/f from £77/95; ⓟ 🛜 🐾) Dating from the 14th century, this half-timbered inn is a charmer. Some of its 15 sage- and oyster-toned rooms have four-poster beds, and there's a timber bar serving local ales and ciders, and a candlelit, book-lined library, as well as a conservatory restaurant. There is limited parking available for guests.

Pots & Pieces
CAFE £

(www.potsandpieces.com; 40 High St; dishes £3-8.50; ☺ 9am-3pm Mon-Fri, 10am-4.45pm Sat, 11am-2.45pm Sun) Browse ceramics and crafts at this tearoom by the marketplace, and choose from cakes such as lemon drizzle, coffee, and walnut and carrot. Savoury options include quiches, sandwiches and a soup of the day.

Truffles Delicatessen
DELI £

(www.trufflesdeli.co.uk; 46 High St; dishes £3.50-7.50; ☺ 10am-4pm Mon-Fri, 9am-5pm Sat) Packed to the rafters with local artisan products (cheeses, breads, chutneys et al), Truffles also has stellar sandwiches, soups and salad boxes to take away for a riverside picnic.

❶ Getting There & Away

The bus stand is on Cantilupe Rd. Bus 33 runs to Hereford (£4, 50 minutes, hourly Monday to Saturday). In the opposite direction, it serves Gloucester (£4.50, 45 minutes, hourly Monday to Saturday).

BLACK & WHITE VILLAGES

A triangle of Tudor England survives almost untouched in northwest Herefordshire, where higgledy-piggledy black-and-white houses cluster around idyllic village greens, seemingly oblivious to the modern world. A delightful 40-mile circular drive follows the **Black and White Village Trail** (www.blackandwhitetrail.org), meandering past the most handsome timber-framed buildings. It starts at Leominster and loops round through Eardisland and Kington, the southern terminus of the 30-mile waymarked Mortimer Trail footpath from Ludlow.

Pick up guides to exploring the villages by car, bus or bicycle at tourist offices.

SHROPSHIRE

Sleepy Shropshire is a glorious scattering of hills, castles and timber-framed villages tucked against the Welsh border. Highlights include castle-crowned Ludlow, industrial Ironbridge and the beautiful Shropshire Hills, which offer the best walking and cycling in the Marches.

Activities

The rolling Shropshire Hills call out to walkers like a siren. Between Shrewsbury and Ludlow, the landscape rucks up into dramatic folds, with spectacular trails climbing the flanks of Wenlock Edge and the Long Mynd near Church Stretton. The county is also crossed by long-distance trails, including the famous Offa's Dyke Path and the popular Shropshire Way, which meanders around Ludlow and Church Stretton.

Mountain bikers head for the muddy tracks that scramble over the Long Mynd near Church Stretton, while road riders aim for the Six Castles Cycleway (NCN 44), which runs for 58 miles from Shrewsbury to Leominster.

Tourist offices sell copies of *Cycling for Pleasure in the Marches,* a pack of five maps and guides covering the entire county.

ⓘ Getting There & Away

Shrewsbury is the local transport hub, with good bus and rail connections. Church Stretton and Ludlow also have handy rail services.

From May to September, **Shropshire Hills Shuttles** (www.shropshirehillsaonb.co.uk; single ticket £3, Day Rover ticket adult/child £10/4) runs an hourly bus service along popular hiking routes on weekends and bank holidays.

Shrewsbury

 01743 / POP 71,715

A delightful jumble of winding medieval streets and timbered Tudor houses leaning at precarious angles, Shrewsbury was a crucial front in the conflict between the English and the Welsh in medieval days. Even today, the road bridge running east towards London is known as the English Bridge to mark it out from the Welsh Bridge leading northwest towards Holyhead. Shrewsbury is also the birthplace of Charles Darwin (1809–82).

The pronunciation of the town's name has long been a hot topic. A charity debate hosted by University Centre Shrewsbury in 2015 declared '*shroos*-bree' (rhyming with 'grew') the winner over the posher '*shrows*-bree' (rhyming with 'grow'), as did a survey by the *Shropshire Star,* though you'll still hear both pronunciations in the town and across British media.

Sights

Shrewsbury Castle   CASTLE, MUSEUM
(📞01743-358516; www.soldiersofshropshire.co.uk; Castle St; castle adult/child £4.50/2, grounds free; ⊙10.30am-5pm Mon-Wed, Fri & Sat, to 4pm Sun Apr–mid-Sep, to 4pm Mon-Wed, Fri & Sat mid-Feb–Mar & mid-Sep–mid-Dec) Hewn from flaking red Shropshire sandstone, the town castle contains the Shropshire Regimental Museum. There are fine views from Laura's Tower and the battlements. The lower level of the Great Hall dates from 1150.

Shrewsbury Abbey   CHURCH
(📞01743-232723; www.shrewsburyabbey.com; Abbey Foregate; by donation; ⊙10am-4pm Apr-Oct, 10.30am-3pm Nov-Mar) All that remains of a vast, cruciform Benedictine monastery founded in 1083 is the lovely red-sandstone Shrewsbury Abbey. Twice used for meetings of the English Parliament, the abbey church lost its spire and two wings when the monastery was dissolved in 1540. It sustained further damage in 1826 when engineer Thomas Telford ran the London–Holyhead road right through the grounds. Nevertheless, you can still see some impressive Norman, Early English and Victorian features, including an exceptional 14th-century west window.

St Mary's Church   CHURCH
(www.visitchurches.org.uk; St Mary's St; by donation; ⊙11am-3pm Mon-Fri) The fabulous interior of this tall-spired medieval church contains an impressive collection of stained glass, including a 1340 window depicting the Tree of Jesse (a biblical representation of the lineage of Jesus) and a magnificent oak ceiling in the nave, which largely collapsed in a huge gale in 1894 when the top of the spire blew off. Much of the glass in the church is sourced from Europe, including some outstanding Dutch glass from 1500.

Shrewsbury Prison   HISTORIC BUILDING
(📞01743-343100; www.shrewsburyprison.com; The Dana; prison adult/child £15/9.50, ghost tour £20/15; ⊙prison tours 10am-5pm, ghost tours 7.30pm & 9.30pm) Built in 1793, this was a working prison as recently as 2013. Today

Shrewsbury

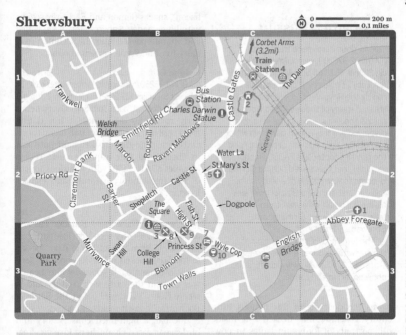

Shrewsbury

◎ Sights
1 Shrewsbury Abbey	D2
2 Shrewsbury Castle	C1
3 Shrewsbury Museum & Art Gallery	B3
4 Shrewsbury Prison	C1
5 St Mary's Church	C2

🛏 Sleeping
6 Lion & Pheasant	C3
7 Lion Hotel	C3

✕ Eating
8 Ginger & Co	B3
9 Golden Cross	B3

🍸 Drinking & Nightlife
10 Henry Tudor House	C3

tours are led by former prison guards: when you arrive, you're 'processed' as a prisoner and escorted into the general population wing, before having the opportunity to enter a cell, which is ominously locked behind you. Alternatively, you can take a self-guided tour. Chilling evening ghost tours (minimum age 12 years) include the prison's execution room where 11 inmates were hanged.

Shrewsbury Museum & Art Gallery MUSEUM
(☑ 01743-258885; www.shrewsburymuseum.org.uk; The Square; adult/child £5/3; ⊙ 10am-5pm Mon-Sat, 11am-4pm Sun) Diverse exhibits at Shrewsbury's town museum cover everything from Roman treasures to Shropshire gold, including the Bronze Age Perry Bracelet. Its Prehistory and Roman Gallery is free of charge.

🛏 Sleeping

Corbet Arms PUB ££
(☑ 01743-709232; www.thecorbetarms.com; Church Rd, Uffington; d/f incl breakfast from £80/105; P 🖨) Peacefully situated 4 miles east of Shrewsbury in the pint-sized village of Uffington on the banks of the River Severn, this family-friendly pub has nine stylish en-suite rooms reached by a staircase. Try for top-floor room 10, which has exposed beams, a spacious sitting area and panoramic views of the surrounding countryside. High-quality pub food includes outstanding Sunday roasts.

Lion Hotel HOTEL ££
(☑ 01743-353107; www.thelionhotelshrewsbury. com; Wyle Cop; s/d/ste incl breakfast from £74/109/135; P 🖨) A gilded wooden lion

COSFORD RAF MUSEUM

This famous aerospace **museum** (☎01902-376200; www.rafmuseum.org. uk; Shifnal; ☺10am-5pm Mar-Oct, to 4pm Nov-Feb) 13 miles east of Ironbridge is run by the Royal Air Force, whose pilots steered many of these winged wonders across the skies. Among the 70 aircraft displayed are the Vulcan bomber (which carried Britain's nuclear deterrent) and the tiny helicopter-like FA330 Bachstelze glider that was towed behind German U-boats to warn them of enemy ships. You can also try out a Black Hawk simulator. It's a half-mile walk from Cosford train station, on the Birmingham–Shrewsbury line.

The Red Arrows stunt team paint the sky with coloured smoke during the **Cosford Air Show** (www.cosfordair show.co.uk) in early June.

crowns the doorway of this famous 16th-century coaching inn, decked out inside with portraits of lords and ladies in powdered wigs. Charles Dickens was a former guest, and the lounge is warmed by a grand stone fireplace. Its 59 rooms are lovely, right down to the period-pattern fabrics and ceramic water jugs.

Lion & Pheasant   BOUTIQUE HOTEL **£££**
(☎01743-770345; www.lionandpheasant.co.uk; 50 Wyle Cop; s/d incl breakfast from £99/130; [P][?]) This former coaching inn is now a stylish town house offering 22 individually styled rooms with comfy goose- and duck-down pillows, and some with Severn views. Original features throughout the property include magnificent exposed timber beams. Classy Modern British fare is served in the whitewashed restaurant (mains £16 to £27). Parking for overnight guests is first come, first served.

✗ Eating & Drinking

Ginger & Co   CAFE **£**
(www.gingerandcocoffee.com; 30-31 Princess St; dishes £3.50-11.50; ☺8.30am-3pm Mon-Thu, to 4pm Fri & Sat, 10am-3pm Sun; 🖉) A successful crowd-funding campaign propelled the opening of this airy, L-shaped cafe filled with upcycled furniture. It's a great option for a light brunch or lunch (avocado on artisan toast with oak-smoked streaky

bacon), snacks (lemon and Earl Grey scones with homemade raspberry jam), good coffee and vitamin-packed smoothies. Gluten-free, dairy-free and vegan options abound.

Golden Cross   BRITISH **££**
(☎01743-362507; www.goldencrosshotel.co.uk; 14 Princess St; mains £12.50-21.50; ☺noon-2.30pm & 6-9.30pm Wed-Sat, noon-3pm Sun) Overwhelmingly romantic, this candlelit inn dating from 1428 has an upmarket pub menu (port- and clementine-glazed baked ham, pot-roast ox cheek) and four exquisite guest rooms (doubles £75 to £150) with luxurious touches like freestanding bathtubs and chaises longues.

Henry Tudor House   PUB
(www.henrytudorhouse.com; Barracks Passage; mains £13.50-25; ☺bar noon-11pm Tue-Thu, to 1am Fri & Sat, to 10pm Sun, kitchen to 10pm Tue-Sat, to 9pm Sun) Tucked off Wyle Cop, this seriously overhanging black-and-white beauty was built in the early 15th century and is where Henry VII stayed before the Battle of Bosworth. Today it melds old and new with a zinc bar, a light-filled conservatory and birdcage-encased chandeliers. Live gigs regularly take to the stage.

Food (mackerel with cucumber puree, Shropshire beef Wellington) is superb, too.

❶ Information

The **tourist office** (☎01743-258888; www. originalshrewsbury.co.uk; The Square; ☺10am-5pm Mon-Sat, 11am-4pm Sun) shares space with the Shrewsbury Museum & Art Gallery.

❶ Getting There & Away

BUS

The **bus station** (Smithfield Rd) is beside the river.

Direct services include the following.
Church Stretton Bus 435, £3.90, 40 minutes, hourly Monday to Friday, every two hours Saturday
Ironbridge Bus 96, £4.90, 50 minutes, four daily
Ludlow Bus 435, £4.50, 1¼ hours, hourly Monday to Friday, every two hours Saturday

TRAIN

The train station is on the northeastern edge of the town centre at the bottom of Castle Foregate.

Destinations include the following.
Birmingham £16.20, one hour, two per hour
Holyhead £46.40, 2½ hours, hourly

London Euston £106.50, 2¾ hours, every 20 minutes, change in Crewe or Birmingham
Ludlow £14.20, 30 minutes, hourly

Ironbridge Gorge

🎯 01952 / POP 2582

Strolling or cycling through the woods, hills and villages of this leafy river gorge, it's hard to believe such a peaceful enclave could really have been the birthplace of the Industrial Revolution. Nevertheless, it was here that Abraham Darby perfected the art of smelting iron ore with coke in 1709, making it possible to mass-produce cast iron for the first time.

Abraham Darby's son, Abraham Darby II, invented a new forging process for producing single beams of iron, allowing Abraham Darby III to astound the world with the first-ever iron bridge, constructed in 1779. The bridge remains the focal point of this World Heritage Site, and 10 very different museums tell the story of the Industrial Revolution in the buildings where it took place.

🔵 Sights

★ **Iron Bridge**   BRIDGE
(www.ironbridge.org.uk; ⊘ bridge 24hr, tollhouse 10am-5pm) FREE The arching Iron Bridge, which gives the area its name, was built to flaunt the new technology invented by the pioneering Darby family. At the time of its construction in 1779, nobody could believe that anything so large – it weighs 384 tonnes – could be built from cast iron without collapsing under its own weight. There's a small exhibition on the bridge's history at the former **toll house**. The bridge is dramatically illuminated at night.

★ **Museum of the Gorge**   MUSEUM
(www.ironbridge.org.uk; The Wharfage; ⊘ 10am-5pm) FREE An ideal place to kick off your Ironbridge Gorge visit is at the Museum of the Gorge. Occupying a Gothic riverside warehouse, it offers an overview of the World Heritage Sites using film, photos and exhibits, including a 12m-long 3D model of the town in 1796.

Enginuity   MUSEUM
(www.ironbridge.org.uk; Wellington Rd; adult/child £9.95/6.95; ⊘ 10am-4pm mid-Mar–Sep, closed Mon Oct–mid-Mar) Kids will love this levers-and-pulleys science centre where they can control robots, move a steam locomotive with their bare hands (and a little engineering know-

how) and power up a vacuum cleaner with self-generated electricity.

Blists Hill Victorian Town   MUSEUM
(🎯 01952-433424; www.ironbridge.org.uk; Legges Way; adult/child £20/12; ⊘ 10am-5pm Wed-Sun) Set at the top of the Hay Inclined Plane (a cable lift that once transported coal barges uphill from the Shropshire Canal), Blists Hill is a lovingly restored Victorian village repopulated with townsfolk in period costume, busy with day-to-day chores. There's even a bank, where you can exchange your modern pounds for shillings to use at the village shops. In summer, a Victorian fair is an added attraction for young ones, as is the ice rink in November and December.

Darby Houses   MUSEUM
(🎯 01952-433424; www.ironbridge.org.uk; Darby Rd; adult/child £6.50/4.50, incl Museum of Iron £11.95/7.95; ⊘ 11am-3pm mid-Mar–Sep) Just uphill from the Museum of Iron (p427), these beautifully restored 18th-century homes housed generations of the Darby family in gracious but modest Quaker comfort. In the Rosehill house, kids and adults can try on Victorian dress and view china displays. The highlight of the Darby family house is the study where Abraham Darby III designed the Iron Bridge.

Coalport China Museum   MUSEUM
(www.ironbridge.org.uk; Coalport High St; adult/child £9.95/6.95; ⊘ 10am-4pm daily mid-Mar–Sep, closed Mon Oct–mid-Mar) As ironmaking fell into decline, Ironbridge diversified into manufacturing china pots, using the fine clay mined around Blists Hill. Dominated by a pair of towering bottle kilns, the atmospheric old china-works now contains an absorbing museum tracing the history of the industry, with demonstrations of traditional pottery techniques.

> ℹ️ **IRONBRIDGE GORGE PASSPORT**
>
> The 10 Ironbridge museums are administered by the Ironbridge Gorge Museum Trust (www.ironbridge.org.uk). You'll save considerably by buying a Passport ticket (adult/child £27.50/17.50) at any of the museums or from the tourist office (p428). Valid for 12 months, it allows unlimited entry to all of Ironbridge Gorge's sites.

Ironbridge Gorge

500 m
0.25 miles

100 m
0.05 miles

High St
Waterloo St
12

Severn

Ironbridge Rd

Iron
1 Bridge
8 13

Ironbridge Rd
11

Severn Bank

The Wharfage
10

Ladywood

Telford Golf Club

3

Legges Way

Coalport High St
5

Woodside Roundabout

Woodside Rd

Lees Farm Roundabout

The Lloyds

Church Rd
7

Telford (5mi)

Madeley Rd

9

Calcutts Rd

Bedlam
Furnaces
Waterloo St

High St

Severn

Woodside Ave

See Enlargement

Darby Rd

Wellington Rd

Beech Rd

Buildwas Rd

Dale End
Paradise Rd

The Wharfage
14

Museum of
the Gorge

2

Dale End
Park

4

6

Ironbridge Gorge

On Wednesdays during summer, you can also view the **Tar Tunnel** (Coalport High St) accompanied by a guide.

Jackfield Tile Museum   MUSEUM
(www.ironbridge.org.uk; Salthouse Rd; adult/child £9.95/6.95; ⊙10am-5pm) Once the largest tile factory in the world, Jackfield was famous for its encaustic tiles, with ornate designs produced using layers of different coloured clay. Tiles are still produced here today for period restorations. Gas-lit galleries recreate ornately tiled rooms from past centuries, including Victorian public conveniences. The museum is on the south bank of the Severn – cross the footbridge at the bottom of the Hay Inclined Plane.

Coalbrookdale Museum of Iron   MUSEUM
(www.ironbridge.org.uk; Wellington Rd; adult/child £9.95/6.95, incl Darby Houses £11.95/7.95; ⊙10am-4pm Wed-Sun) Set in the brooding buildings of Abraham Darby's original iron foundry, the Coalbrookdale Museum of Iron contains some excellent interactive exhibits. As well as producing the girders for the Iron Bridge, the factory became famous for heavy machinery and extravagant ornamental castings, including the gates for London's Hyde Park.

🏃 Activities

**Ironbridge Canoe
& Kayak Hire**   CANOEING, KAYAKING
(☑07594 486356; www.ironbridgecanoeandkayakhire.co.uk; 31 High St; canoe/kayak rental per half/full day from £45/85; ⊙by appointment Mon-Fri, 9am-8pm Sat & Sun Easter-Oct) In summer, when the river is at a safe level, you can rent canoes and kayaks to explore the gorge and surrounding areas.

Shropshire Raft Tours   RAFTING
(☑01952-427150; www.shropshirerafttours.co.uk; The Wharfage; rafting trips adult/child £14.95/6.95, canoe & kayak hire per hour/day £15/40, bike hire per half/full day from £19/29; ⊙equipment hire 9am-5pm Easter-Oct, tours by reservation 11.30am, 2pm & 4.30pm Easter-Oct, plus 7pm Jul & Aug) 🚣 Ironbridge Gorge might not have any rapids but you can take a gentle, highly enjoyable 90-minute trip along a 1.2-mile stretch of the River Severn floating past stunning gorge scenery with this eco-conscious outfit. Life jackets are provided. It also hires canoes, kayaks and bikes, including electric bikes.

🛏 Sleeping

⭐ **Library House**   B&B ££
(☑01952-432299; www.libraryhouse.com; 11 Severn Bank; s/d from £75/100; 🅿🤶) Up an alley off the main street, this lovingly restored Georgian library building built in 1730 is hugged by vines, backed by a beautiful garden and decked out with stacks of vintage books, curios, prints and lithographs. There are three charmingly well-preserved, individually decorated rooms, named Milton, Chaucer and Eliot. The affable dog dashing around is Millie.

Calcutts House   B&B ££
(☑01952-882631; www.calcuttshouse.co.uk; Calcutts Rd; d from £80; 🅿🤶) This former ironmaster's pad dates from the 18th century. Traditionally decorated rooms have heaps of character, and one is furnished with an outsized 200-year-old four-poster bed. It's tucked away on the south bank around the corner from the Jackfield Tile Museum, a mile east of the bridge.

SEVERN VALLEY RAILWAY

The historic steam or diesel locomotives of the **Severn Valley Railway** (☑ 01299-403816; www.svr.co.uk; Hollybush Rd, Bridgnorth; adult/child one-way £14.50/9.50, day ticket £21/14; ☺daily May-Sep, Sat & Sun Oct-Apr) chug between Bridgnorth, 9 miles southwest of Ironbridge Gorge, and Kidderminster (one hour), starting from Bridgnorth's station on Hollybush Rd. Check the calendar for additional event dates, such as afternoon teas, gin and whisky tastings, 1940s re-enactments and evening ghost trains.

Cyclists can follow a beautiful 20-mile section of the Mercian Way (NCN Route 45) beside the railway line towards the Wyre Forest; bikes are free to bring on board the trains.

'Driving experiences', during which you can learn how to drive the steam or diesel trains, start from £160.

✖ Eating & Drinking

Pondicherry   INDIAN ££
(☑01952-433055; www.pondicherryrestaurant.co.uk; 57 Waterloo St; mains £11-17; ☺5-10pm Wed-Sun) Original features of this 1862-built former police station and courtroom include four lock-up cells (one's now the takeaway waiting area), the magistrate's bench and blue-painted bars on the windows. Above-average contemporary Indian cuisine includes crowd-pleasers like tandoori platters and chicken tikka masala along with chef specialities, such as lamb *saag mamyam* (braised Staffordshire lamb with spinach and spices).

D'arcys at the Station   MEDITERRANEAN ££
(☑01952-884499; www.darcysironbridge.co.uk; Ladywood; mains £11.50-15; ☺6-9.30pm Wed-Sat) Just over the bridge by the river, the handsome old station building is the backdrop for flavoursome Mediterranean dishes, from Moroccan chicken to Cypriot kebabs and Tuscan bean casserole. Kids aged over 10 are welcome.

Restaurant Severn   EUROPEAN £££
(☑01952-432233; www.restaurantsevern.co.uk; 33 High St; 2-/3-course menus £29/36; ☺6-11pm Thu-Sat) The menu at this highly praised fine-dining restaurant changes frequently but might feature dishes such as Shropshire venison medallions with cognac and sundried-cranberry sauce. The setting is intimate, food is artistically presented and the riverside location beautiful.

Malthouse   PUB
(☑01952-433712; www.themalthouseironbridge.co.uk; The Wharfage; ☺bar 11.30am-11pm Sun-Thu, to 12.30am Fri & Sat, kitchen to 9.30pm) This renovated inn on the Severn's riverbanks makes a great place to drink, eat and/or sleep. Local ales, craft gins and cocktails feature on the drinks list, the street-food-inspired menu spans fish tacos to southern fried chicken (mains £10 to £19) and ultra-contemporary rooms (doubles including breakfast from £75) are splashed with vibrant colours. Live music plays on weekends.

ℹ Information

Tourist Office (☑01952-433424; www.discovertelford.co.uk/visitironbridge; The Wharfage; ☺10am-5pm) Located at the Museum of the Gorge (p425).

ℹ Getting There & Away

The nearest train station is 6 miles away at Telford, from where you can travel to Ironbridge by bus (£4.80, 15 minutes, four daily Monday to Friday, three Saturday). The same bus continues to Much Wenlock (£4.90, 30 minutes).

Buses also link Ironbridge with Shrewsbury (£4.90, 50 minutes, four daily Monday to Saturday).

Much Wenlock

☑01952 / POP 2877

With one of those quirky names that abound in the English countryside, Much Wenlock is as charming as it sounds. Surrounding the time-worn ruins of Wenlock Priory, the streets are studded with Tudor, Jacobean and Georgian houses, and locals say hello to everyone. This storybook English village also claims to have jump-started the modern Olympics.

◉ Sights

Wenlock Priory   RUINS
(EH; ☑01952-727466; www.english-heritage.org.uk; 5 Sheinton St; adult/child incl audio guide £6.90/4.10; ☺10am-5pm) The maudlin Cluniac ruins of Wenlock Priory rise up from vivid green lawns, sprinkled with animal-shaped topiary. The priory was raised by Norman monks over the ruins of a Saxon monastery from AD 680, and its hallowed remains

include a finely decorated chapterhouse and an unusual carved lavabo, where monks came to ceremonially wash before eating.

Guildhall HISTORIC BUILDING
(📞 01952-727509; www.muchwenlock-tc.gov.uk; Wilmore St; ⏰ 11am-4pm Fri-Mon Apr-Oct) FREE Built in classic Tudor style in 1540, the wonky Guildhall features some splendidly ornate woodcarving. One of the pillars supporting it was used for public floggings in medieval times.

🛏 Sleeping & Eating

Wilderhope Manor YHA HOSTEL £
(📞 0845 371 9149; www.yha.org.uk; Longville-in-the-Dale; dm/d/f from £13/39/69, camping per person £12; ⏰ hostel year-round, camping Apr-Oct; 🅿 @ 🛜) A gloriously atmospheric gabled greystone Elizabethan manor, with spiral staircases, wood-panelled walls, an impressive stone-floored dining hall and spacious, oak-beamed rooms – this is hostelling for royalty. Wi-fi is available in public areas. In the warmer months, the camping field has space for a handful of tents. It's 7.5 miles southwest of Much Wenlock, best reached by your own wheels.

Raven Hotel INN ££
(📞 01952-727251; www.ravenhotel.com; 30 Barrow St; d/ste incl breakfast from £120/150; 🅿 🛜) Much Wenlock's finest place to stay is this 17th-century coaching inn and converted stables with oodles of charm and country-chic styling in its spacious guest rooms. Overlooking a flower-filled courtyard, the excellent restaurant (lunch mains £13 to £22, two-/three-course dinner menus £29/39) serves Mediterranean and British fare.

Fox PUB FOOD ££
(📞 01952-727292; www.foxinnmuchwenlock.co.uk; 46 High St; mains £9-22; ⏰ kitchen 5-9pm Mon-Fri, noon-9pm Sat, to 8pm Sun, bar to 11pm; 🛜) Warm yourself by the massive fireplace, then settle down in the dining room to savour locally sourced venison, pheasant and beef, swished down with a pint of Shropshire ale, in this 16th-century inn. Candlelit dinners here are lovely. It also has five contemporary rooms (single/double/family from £65/85/100).

ℹ Information

Tourist Office (📞 01952-727679; www.visit muchwenlock.co.uk; The Square; ⏰ 10.30am-1pm & 1.30-4pm daily Apr-Oct, Fri-Sun Nov-Mar) Has a modest museum of local history (adult/child £2.50/1).

ℹ Getting There & Away

Buses link Shrewsbury with Much Wenlock (£4.80, 35 minutes, hourly Monday to Saturday) and continue on to Bridgnorth (£4.50, 15 minutes).

Buses also serve Ironbridge (£4.90, 30 minutes, four daily Monday to Friday, three Saturday).

Church Stretton & Around

📞 01694 / POP 2789

Tucked in a deep valley formed by the Long Mynd and the Caradoc Hills, Church Stretton is an ideal base for walks or cycling trips through the Shropshire Hills. Although black-and-white timbers are heavily in evidence, most of the buildings in town are 19th-century fakes, built by the Victorians who flocked here to take the country air.

◉ Sights & Activities

Walking is the big draw here. The tourist office has maps and details of local mountain-biking circuits and horse-riding stables. Information on activities is also available at www.shropshiresgreatoutdoors.co.uk.

Acton Scott Estate FARM
(📞 01694-781307; www.shropshire.gov.uk/acton -scott; Marshbrook; adult/child £9/5; ⏰ farm 10am-4pm Fri-Sun, courses Apr-Dec) On the sprawling Acton Scott Estate, 4 miles south of Church Stretton, this historic working farm has traditional breeds of poultry and livestock, and daily demonstrations of Victorian farming techniques, such as barrel making, horseshoeing and cartwheel construction. Book ahead for courses including blacksmithing, beekeeping, plant identification and 19th-century cookery.

Snailbeach MINE
(📞 07716 116732; www.shropshiremines.org. uk; Shop Lane, Snailbeach; site free, mine tours adult/child £15/5; ⏰ site 24hr, tours by reservation Thu & Sun Apr-Oct) The former lead- and silver-mining village of Snailbeach, 11 miles northwest of Church Stretton, is littered with intriguing, rusting machinery relics. You can download a self-guided trail from the website of the **Bog Centre tourist office** (📞 01743-792484; www.bogcentre.co.uk; The Bog, Stiperstones; ⏰ noon-5pm Mon, 10am-5pm Tue-Sun Easter-Sep, noon-4pm Mon, 10am-4pm Tue-Sun Oct; 🛜) to explore the site, or reserve ahead for guided tours (waterproof footwear required) that take you into the mine.

★ **Kerry Vale Vineyard** WINERY
(☑ 01588-620627; www.kerryvalevineyard.co.uk; Pentreheyling; tours £20-40; ⊙ tours by appointment Thu, Sat & Sun mid-Mar–Nov, shop & cafe 10am-4pm Tue-Sun mid-Mar–Oct, to 3pm Nov & Dec) More than 6000 vines are now planted over 2.4 hectares of the former Pentreheyling Roman Fort, where pottery and metalwork have been uncovered and are displayed at the winery shop. Tours range from an hour-long guided walk through the vines, with a talk on the site's Roman history and tastings, to two-hour guided visits with tastings, a tutorial and an afternoon tea including the vineyard's own sparkling wine. Or pop by the cafe for a wine tasting flight.

It's 19 miles southwest of Church Stretton.

🛏 Sleeping

Bridges Long Mynd YHA HOSTEL £
(☑ 03452-602569; www.yha.org.uk; Bridges; dm from £22, camping per person from £10; P) ⏵ On the Long Mynd's western side, this wonderfully isolated hiker favourite, with 38 beds (plus garden tent sites), is housed in a former school in the tiny hamlet of Bridges. No wi-fi, no mobile-phone reception, no credit cards. Cross the Mynd to Ratlinghope, from where it's 1.1 miles southwest, or take buses run by Shropshire Hills Shuttles (p422) in season.

The Bridges pub is nearby, but the hostel also provides breakfast (£6), packed lunches (£5) and three-course evening meals (£12.50) incorporating ingredients from its own vegetable garden.

Mynd House B&B B&B ££
(☑ 01694-722212; www.myndhouse.co.uk; Ludlow Rd, Little Stretton; s/d from £62/87; P �) Just under 2 miles south of Church Stretton, this inviting guesthouse has splendid views across the valley and backs directly onto the Mynd. Its eight rooms are named after local landmarks. There's a small bar and lounge stocked with local books, as well as bike storage and a room for drying your boots.

✗ Eating & Drinking

Van Doesburg's DELI £
(☑ 01694-722867; www.thegourmetfoodshop.com; 3 High St; dishes £1.85-5; ⊙ 9am-4pm Tue-Sat; ⏵) A fantastic place to pick up picnic ingredients, Van Doesburg's has over 80 British cheeses and other deli items, such as chutneys. Ready-to-eat dishes to take away

include chicken-and-mushroom pies, salads, quiches, soups and outstanding sandwiches (eg roast beef with pickles and mustard or farmhouse cheddar with plum-and-apple relish). Phone ahead to order customised hampers.

Bridges PUB FOOD ££
(☑ 01588-650260; www.thebridgespub.co.uk; Ratlinghope; mains £8-15.50; ⊙ kitchen 12.30-8.30pm, bar noon-11pm; �Ⓦ⚘) Some 5 miles northeast of Church Stretton, at the base of Long Mynd by the river, this is one of those secret country pubs revered for its Three Tuns ale, live music, riverside terrace, relaxed accommodation (dorm/double/family from £30/60/140) and impressive food (lamb shank and mint sauce, beef lasagne...). Mini burgers are among the choices on the kids' menu.

Three Tuns PUB
(www.thethreetunsinn.co.uk; Salop St, Bishop's Castle; ⊙ noon-11pm Mon-Sat, to 10.30pm Sun; �) In the pretty village of Bishop's Castle, 13 miles southwest of Church Stretton, the tiny Three Tuns Brewery has been rolling barrels of nut-brown ale across the courtyard since 1642. It's a lively local, and the ales are delicious. Jazz, blues and brass bands perform regularly in summer.

ⓘ Information

Tourist Office (☑ 01694-723133; www.churchstretton.co.uk; Church St; ⊙ 9.30am-1pm & 1.30-5pm Mon-Sat Apr-Sep, 9.30am-1pm & 1.30-3pm Mon-Sat Oct-Mar) Adjoining the library, Church Stretton's tourist office has abundant walking information.

ⓘ Getting There & Away

BUS

Bus 435 runs from Church Stretton north to Shrewsbury (£4, 40 minutes, hourly Monday to Friday, every two hours Saturday) and south to Ludlow (£4, 30 minutes, hourly Monday to Friday, every two hours Saturday).

On summer weekends, Shropshire Hills Shuttles (p422) runs an hourly service from the Carding Mill Valley near Church Stretton to the villages atop the Long Mynd, passing the YHA at Bridges, and Stiperstones near the Snailbeach mine.

TRAIN

Trains between Ludlow (£8) and Shrewsbury (£6.90) stop in Church Stretton hourly, taking 15 minutes from either end.

Ludlow

☑ 01584 / POP 11,003

On the northern bank of the swirling River Teme, this genteel market town fans out from the rambling ruins of its fine Norman castle, with some magnificent black-and-white Tudor buildings lining its cobbled streets. Premium produce from the lush surrounding countryside has helped the town become a gastronomic beacon, with superb markets, delis, restaurants and food festivals.

⊙ Sights

Ludlow Castle   CASTLE

(☑ 01584-873355; www.ludlowcastle.com; Castle Sq; adult/child £8/3.50; ⊙ 10am-5pm mid-Mar-Oct, to 4pm Nov–early Jan & early Feb–mid-Mar, to 4pm Sat & Sun early Jan–early Feb) Perched in an ideal defensive location atop a cliff above a crook in the river, the town castle was built to ward off the marauding Welsh – or to enforce the English expansion into Wales, perspective depending. Founded after the Norman conquest, the castle was dramatically expanded in the 14th century.

The Norman chapel in the inner bailey is one of the few surviving round chapels in England, and the sturdy keep (built around 1090) offers wonderful views over the hills.

Ludlow Brewing Company   BREWERY

(☑ 01584-873291; www.theludlowbrewingcompany.co.uk; The Railway Shed, Station Dr; tours £8; ⊙ tours by reservation 3pm Mon-Fri, 2pm Sat, visitor centre & taproom 11am-5pm Sun-Thu, 10am-7pm Fri & Sat) 🍴 Up an inconspicuous laneway, the Ludlow Brewing Company produces award-winning all-natural brews and sells directly from the brewery and its airy, post-industrial-style bar. Tours include six samples.

Church of St Laurence   CHURCH

(www.stlaurences.org.uk; 2 College St; admission by donation; ⊙ 10am-5pm) One of Britain's largest parish churches, the church of St Laurence contains grand Elizabethan alabaster tombs and delightfully cheeky medieval misericords carved into its medieval choir stalls, including a beer-swilling chap raiding his barrel. The Lady Chapel contains a marvellous Jesse Window, originally dating from 1330 (although the glass is mostly Victorian). Four windows in St John's Chapel date from the mid-15th century, including the honey-coloured Golden Window. Climb 200 steps up the tower (included in donation) for stunning views.

🎎 Festivals & Events

Ludlow Spring Festival   CULTURAL

(www.ludlowspringfestival.co.uk; ⊙ mid-May) The two-day Ludlow Spring Festival uses the castle as its dramatic backdrop for beer, cider and food stalls, a vintage car show and live concerts.

Ludlow Food Festival   FOOD & DRINK

(www.ludlowfoodfestival.co.uk; ⊙ early Sep) At Ludlow Castle, the Ludlow Food Festival spans three days in early September, with over 180 exhibitors from the town and the Welsh Marches.

🛏 Sleeping

Feathers Hotel   HISTORIC HOTEL ££

(☑ 01584-875261; www.feathersatludlow.co.uk; 21 Bull Ring; d from £109; ℗ 🕾) Behind its impossibly ornate timbered Jacobean facade, this 1619-built treasure is all tapestries, creaky furniture, timber beams and stained glass: you can almost hear the cavaliers toasting the health of King Charles. The best rooms are in the old building; rooms in the newer wing lack character and romance. Dinner, bed and breakfast packages are available at its restaurant.

Clive Arms   BOUTIQUE HOTEL ££

(☑ 01584-856565; www.theclive.co.uk; Bromfield Rd, Bromfield; d/f incl breakfast from £114/150; ℗ ❋ 🕾) For foodies, this is Ludlow's ultimate place to stay. Located 4 miles northwest of town adjoining the Ludlow Food Centre (p432), it has its own top-end restaurant; breakfast is served at the Ludlow Kitchen. Many of its 18 spacious rooms are on ground level; family rooms have two sleeping areas separated by a bathroom, giving parents and kids their own space.

Charlton Arms   INN ££

(☑ 01584-872813; www.thecharltonarms.co.uk; Ludford Bridge; d incl breakfast £100-195; ℗ 🕾) The pick of the rooms at this landmark inn overlook the River Teme, and the pick of those have terraces (one with an outdoor hot tub as well as a four-poster bed). Its pub, also opening to a terrace, serves top-quality Modern British cuisine. Service is superb. There's a large free car park on-site.

🍴 Eating

Ludlow Kitchen   CAFE £

(☑ 01584-856000; www.ludlowfarmshop.co.uk; Bromfield Rd, Bromfield; breakfast £3.50-9, lunch mains £6-13; ⊙ 8am-4pm Mon-Sat, to 3.30pm

Sun; ⏱) 🍴 Produce from the Ludlow Food Centre artisanal farm shop is served at its sunlit cafe. Fantastic breakfasts (granola with homemade yoghurt; full English fry-ups with farmhouse eggs, artisan bacon and black pudding; eggs royale) are the precursor to lunch dishes such as Ludlow Brewing Company beer-battered fish with zingy tartare.

Fish House   SEAFOOD ££
(📞01584-879790; www.thefishhouseludlow.co.uk; 51 Bull Ring; dishes £8-12, sharing platters £25-60; ⏱kitchen noon-3pm Wed-Sat, shop to 4pm Wed-Sat) Except on Saturdays when it's first come, first served, bookings are recommended for the barrel tables at this stylish fish and oyster bar. It sources Britain's best seafood – Whitby crab and lobster, Arbroath smokies, Bigbury Bay oysters – and serves it with organic bread, lemon and mayo, along with wines, local ales, ciders and champagne.

Bistro 7   BISTRO ££
(📞01584-877412; www.bistro7ofludlow.co.uk; 7 Corve St; mains £16-26; ⏱noon-3pm & 6-10pm Tue-Sat) Ludlow's red-brick former post office is the setting for creative bistro cooking. Knowledgeable staff can guide you through the regularly changing menu, which might feature dishes like wood-pigeon salad, black-pudding-stuffed pork loin and red-wine-poached plums with rosemary meringue. Or finish with a platter of local cheeses served with nettle and spiced-apple chutney.

Mortimers   BRITISH £££
(📞01584-872325; www.mortimersludlow.co.uk; 17 Corve St; 2-/3-course lunch menu £26.50/29.50, 3-course dinner menu £55, 7-course tasting menu £65, with paired wines £105; ⏱6.30-8.30pm Wed, noon-2pm & 6.30-8.30pm Thu-Sat, noon-2pm Sun; ⏱) For fine dining, this is Ludlow's top table. Dark timber panelling and cosy nooks create a romantic backdrop for intricate dishes such as scallops with truffled pumpkin puree or lacquered Ludlow duck with pastrami-wrapped celeriac. Vegetarians can pre-book a meat-free version of Saturday evening's seven-course tasting menu, featuring creations like asparagus with roast baby beetroot and sorrel panna cotta.

🛍 Shopping

★Ludlow Food Centre   FOOD & DRINKS
(📞01584-856000; www.ludlowfarmshop.co.uk; Bromfield Rd, Bromfield; ⏱8.30am-5pm Mon-Sat, 9am-4pm Sun) 🍴 More than 80% of the cheeses, meats, breads, fruit and vegetables are sourced from the surrounding region and tantalisingly displayed at this enormous farm shop, including many produced on the estate. Watch through viewing windows to see traditional preserves, pies, ice cream and more being made. It's signposted 2.8 miles northwest of Ludlow off Bromfield Rd (the A49).

Look out for regular events including tastings. There's a kids' playground and a picnic area. Produce is used by the adjoining cafe-restaurant, the Ludlow Kitchen (p431).

Ludlow Market   MARKET
(www.ludlowmarket.co.uk; Castle Sq; ⏱9.30am-2pm Mon, Wed, Fri & Sat) Ludlow Market's stalls sell fresh produce, artisan food and drink, flowers, books, gifts and more. Various spin-off markets (farmers markets, flea markets, book markets and craft markets) take place on Thursdays and Sundays.

ℹ Information

Tourist Office (📞01584-875053; www.ludlow.org.uk/ludlowvisitorcentre.html; 1 Mill St; ⏱10am-4pm Mon-Sat Mar-Dec, to 2pm Mon-Sat Jan & Feb) On the 3rd floor of the Ludlow Assembly Rooms (📞01584-878141; www.ludlowassemblyrooms.co.uk; 1 Mill St; adult/child standard £8/6, balcony £9/7), which contains the town cinema and hosts live entertainment.

ℹ Getting There & Away

BUS
Bus 435 runs to Shrewsbury (£4.80, 1¼ hours, hourly Monday to Saturday) via Church Stretton (£4, 30 minutes).

TRAIN
Trains run frequently from the station located on the north edge of town to Hereford (£10.90, 25 minutes, hourly) and Shrewsbury (£14.20, 30 minutes, hourly), via Church Stretton (£8, 15 minutes).

NOTTINGHAMSHIRE

Say Nottinghamshire and people think of one thing – Robin Hood. Whether the hero woodsman existed is hotly debated, but the county plays up its connections to the outlaw. Storytelling seems to be in Nottinghamshire's blood – local wordsmiths include provocative writer DH Lawrence, of *Lady Chatterley's Lover* fame, and hedonistic poet Lord Byron. Designated a Unesco City of Literature in 2015, the city of Nottingham is the bustling hub; venture into the surrounding countryside and you'll discover historic towns and stately homes surrounding the green bower of Sherwood Forest.

Getting There & Away

National Express and **Trent Barton** (01773-712265; www.trentbarton.co.uk) buses provide the majority of bus services. See Traveline (p394) for timetables. Trains run frequently to most large towns, and to many smaller villages in the Peak District.

Nottingham

0115 / POP 321,550

Forever associated with men in tights and a sheriff with anger-management issues (aka the Robin Hood legend), Nottingham is a dynamic county capital with big-city aspirations, evocative historical sights, and a buzzing music and club scene thanks to its spirited student population.

Sights

Nottingham Castle CASTLE, GALLERY

(www.nottinghamcastle.org.uk; Lenton Rd) Nottingham's castle crowns a sandstone outcrop worm-holed with caves and tunnels. Founded by William the Conqueror, the original castle was held by a succession of English kings before falling in the English Civil War.

Its 17th-century manor-house-like replacement is undergoing major renovations, and is closed until spring 2021. When it reopens, it will feature a new Robin Hood Gallery, a Rebellion Gallery, covering social unrest from medieval times, and displays on art and manufacturing, including salt-glazed stoneware and lacemaking.

Access to the cave system will be extended, parts of the castle grounds will be remodelled to reveal more of the medieval site, and a new visitor centre and cafe will open here. The 17th-century cottages comprising the **Museum of Nottingham Life at Brewhouse Yard** (www.nottinghamcity.gov.uk; Castle Blvd) will also reopen in mid-2021.

The much-snapped **statue of Robin Hood** (Castle Rd) stands in the former moat and remains accessible while works take place.

Wollaton Hall HISTORIC BUILDING

(0115-876 3100; www.wollatonhall.org.uk; Wollaton Park, Derby Rd; tours adult/child £10/free, grounds free; tours noon & 2pm, grounds 8am-dusk Mon-Fri, from 9am Sat & Sun) Built in 1588 for coal mogul Sir Francis Willoughby by avant-garde architect Robert Smythson, Wollaton Hall sits within 200 hectares of grounds roamed by fallow and red deer. Tours lasting one hour lead you through extravagant rooms from the Tudor, Regency and Victorian periods. There's also a natural-history museum here.

Wollaton Hall is 2.5 miles west of Nottingham city centre; take bus L2 or 30 from Victoria bus station (£4.20, 15 minutes, every 15 minutes Monday to Saturday, half-hourly Sunday).

The hall starred as Wayne Manor in 2012's Batman film *The Dark Knight Rises*.

City of Caves CAVE

(0115-952 0555; www.nationaljusticemuseum.org.uk/venue/city-of-caves; Garner's Hill; adult/child £8.75/7.65, incl National Justice Museum £17.60/15.10; tours 10am-4pm) Over the centuries, the sandstone underneath Nottingham has been carved into a honeycomb of caverns and passageways. Tours lead you through a WWII air-raid shelter, a medieval underground tannery, several pub cellars and a mock-up of a Victorian slum dwelling. Book ahead.

BYRON'S NEWSTEAD ABBEY

Founded as an Augustinian priory in around 1170, **Newstead Abbey** (01623-455900; www.newsteadabbey.org.uk; Newstead; house & gardens adult/child £10/6, park free; house & gardens noon-4pm Sat & Sun, park 10am-5pm daily) was converted into a residence in 1539. This evocative lakeside property inextricably associated with the original tortured romantic, Lord Byron (1788–1824), who inherited the house in 1798, selling it in 1818.

Newstead Abbey is 12 miles north of Nottingham, off the A60. Pronto buses (£3.80, 25 minutes, every 10 minutes Monday to Saturday, half-hourly Sunday) from Victoria bus station stop at the gates, a mile from the house and gardens.

Byron's old living quarters are full of suitably eccentric memorabilia, and the landscaped grounds include a monument to his yappy dog, Boatswain.

Nottingham

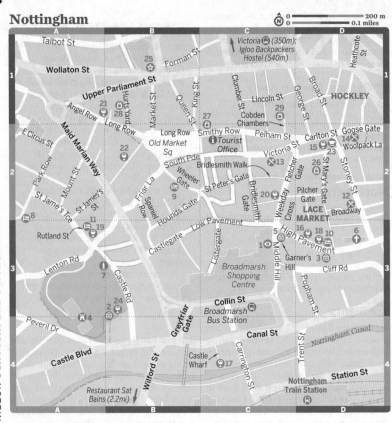

Nottingham

The entrance is adjacent to the Nottingham Contemporary gallery.

National Justice Museum
MUSEUM

(☏0115-952 0555; www.nationaljusticemuseum.org.uk; High Pavement; adult/child £12.05/8.75, incl City of Caves £17.60/15.10; ⊙9.30am-5pm Thu-Mon) In the grand Georgian Shire Hall, the National Justice Museum offers a ghoulish stroll through centuries of British justice, including medieval trials by fire and water. There are costumed characters representing historical figures, and activities, exhibitions and re-enacted courtroom performances regularly take place. Tickets are valid all day.

Nottingham Contemporary
GALLERY

(☏0115-948 9750; www.nottinghamcontemporary.org; Weekday Cross; ⊙10am-6pm Tue-Sat, 11am-5pm Sun) FREE Behind its lace-patterned concrete facade, Nottingham Contemporary holds edgy, design-driven exhibitions of paintings, prints, photography and sculpture.

Its shop sells works by Nottingham and UK-based artists, designers and crafts people, and its cafe specialises in locally sourced food.

St Mary's Church
CHURCH

(www.stmarysnottingham.org; 40 High Pavement; ⊙10am-3pm Mon-Sat, 9.30am-8pm Sun) The most atmospheric time to visit this beautiful stone church with a history stretching back to Saxon times is during evensong (6.15pm Wednesday during term time, 6.30pm Sunday year-round).

⚐ Tours

★ Ezekial Bone Tours
WALKING

(☏07941 210986; www.ezekialbone.com; Robin Hood Town Tour adult/child £14.50/8; ⊙Robin Hood Town Tour 2pm Sat Mar-Oct) Hugely entertaining, history-focused tours led by multi-award-winning 'modern-day Robin Hood' Ezekial Bone (aka historian/actor/writer/local legend Ade Andrews) are a highlight of visiting Nottingham. Robin Hood Town Tours lasting 2½ hours depart from the Cross Keys pub (www.crosskeysnottingham.co.uk; 15 Byard Lane; ⊙9am-11pm Sun-Thu, to midnight Fri, to 1am Sat).

Various other tours, including Lace Market tours, Magic Lantern backstage tours of the Theatre Royal and Robin Hood Sherwood Forest tours are also available by request.

✲ Festivals & Events

Goose Fair
FAIR

(⊙early Oct) The five-day Goose Fair has evolved from a medieval travelling market to a modern funfair with over 500 attractions and rides.

Robin Hood Beer & Cider Festival
DRINK

(www.beerfestival.nottinghamcamra.org; ⊙mid-Oct) This four-day tasting festival features more than 1000 beers and 250 ciders and perries.

Robin Hood Live
CULTURAL

(www.visit-nottinghamshire.co.uk/whats-on/robin hood-live-p454861; ⊙varies) The family-friendly Robin Hood Live – a medieval celebration featuring costumed performances and activities – takes place over two days each year. Check with the tourist office (p439) for location information and dates.

⌦ Sleeping

Igloo Hybrid Hostel
HOSTEL £

(☏0115-948 3822; www.igloohostel.co.uk; 4-6 Eldon Chambers, Wheeler Gate; dm from £20, s/d sleep box from £32/64, s with/without en suite from £39/34, d with/without en suite £84/72; ☏) The sister property of the much-loved Igloo Backpackers Hostel (☏0115-947 5250; 100 Mansfield Rd; dm/s/d/tr from £20/40/80/84; ☏) has a central location footsteps from the Old Market Sq. Cabin-style 'sleep boxes' incorporate USB ports and reading lights; there's a well-equipped self-catering kitchen and a sociable courtyard garden.

St James Hotel
BOUTIQUE HOTEL ££

(☏0115-941 1114; www.stjames-hotel.com; 1 Rutland St; s/d/ste from £65/80/185; ☏) Patterned wallpaper, richly coloured textured fabrics and designer elements, such as stag heads made from stainless steel, set the striking St James apart. More than 500 books line its library shelves; there's a public car park next door.

★ Lace Market Hotel
BOUTIQUE HOTEL £££

(☏0115-948 4414; www.lacemarkethotel.co.uk; 29-31 High Pavement; s/d/ste incl breakfast from £76/140/194; P✻☏) In the heart of the gentrified Lace Market, this elegant Georgian town house has 42 sleek rooms with state-of-the-art furnishings and amenities, some with air-conditioning. Its adjoining pub, the Cock & Hoop (25 High Pavement; ⊙noon-11pm Sun-Thu, to midnight Fri & Sat), serves real ales and traditional pub food all day.

Hart's
BOUTIQUE HOTEL **£££**

(☑0115-988 1900; www.hartsnottingham.co.uk; Standard Hill, Park Row; d/ste incl breakfast from £169/309; P☎) Within the former Nottingham General Hospital compound, this swish hotel has ultra-contemporary rooms (some with small terrace) in a striking modernist building. Its renowned **restaurant** (mains £16.50-25.50, 2-/3-course menus £22/28; ☻7am-2.30pm & 6-10pm Mon-Sat, 7.30am-2.30pm & 6-9pm Sun; ☑) is housed in a historic red-brick wing. Work out in the small gym or unwind in the private garden.

✖ Eating

★Delilah Fine Foods
DELI, CAFE **£**

(☑0115-948 4461; www.delilahfinefoods.co.uk; 12 Victoria St; dishes £4-15, platters £19-26; ☻9am-5pm Wed-Mon; ☑) ✐ Impeccably selected cheeses (more than 150 varieties), pâtés, meats and more from artisan producers are available to take away or eat on-site at this foodie's fantasy land, housed in a grand former bank with mezzanine seating. It doesn't take reservations but you can pre-order customised hampers for a gourmet picnic.

Annie's Burger Shack
BURGERS, AMERICAN **£**

(☑0115-684 9920; www.anniesburgershack. com; 5 Broadway; burgers £9-13, breakfast £6-10; ☻8-10.30am daily plus noon-9.30pm Sun-Wed, 4-9.30pm Thu, noon-10pm Fri & Sat; ☎☑) More than 30 different burgers (available in vegan, veggie or meat versions) are on the menu at Annie's, a wildly popular joint in the Lace Market that stays true to its owner's US roots (and adds real ales to its offerings). Midweek breakfast menus feature American classics (blueberry pancakes with maple syrup and bacon, Boston franks 'n' beans). Book ahead.

Larder on Goosegate
BRITISH **££**

(☑0115-950 0111; www.thelarderongoosegate.co.uk; 16-22 Goosegate; mains £15-24, afternoon tea from £16.50; ☻5.30-10pm Tue-Thu, noon-2.30pm & 5.30-11pm Fri & Sat) Floor-to-ceiling windows fill this 1st-floor restaurant with light and provide bird's-eye views of busy Goosegate below. Blue-goats-cheese and beetroot cheesecake, Shetland Queen scallops with wild-garlic butter and roast spring lamb with smoked aubergine are among its superbly executed British dishes. On Fridays and Saturdays, afternoon tea is served on antique bone china. Book ahead.

Restaurant Sat Bains
GASTRONOMY **£££**

(☑0115-986 6566; www.restaurantsatbains.com; Lenton Lane; 7-/10-course tasting menus £125/155; ☻6-9pm Wed & Thu, to 9.45pm Fri & Sat; ☑) ✐ Boundary-pushing chef Sat Bains has been awarded two Michelin stars for his wildly inventive tasting menus (no à la carte; dietary restrictions can be catered for with advance notice). Book *well* ahead and beware of hefty cancellation charges. It also has chic guest rooms (double £180 to £260, suite £375). It's 2 miles southwest of the city centre off the A52.

☐ Drinking & Nightlife

★Ye Olde Trip to Jerusalem
PUB

(☑0115-947 3171; www.triptojerusalem.com; Brewhouse Yard, Castle Rd; ☻11am-11pm Sun-Thu, to midnight Fri & Sat; ☎) Carved into the cliff below the castle, this atmospheric alehouse claims to be England's oldest pub. Founded in 1189, it supposedly slaked the thirst of departing crusaders, and its warren of rooms and cobbled courtyards make it the most ambient place in Nottingham for a pint.

Call ahead to ask about tours of its cellars and caves.

★Crafty Crow
PUB

(www.magpiebrewery.com/craftycrow; 102 Friar Lane; ☻noon-11pm Sun-Thu, 11am-midnight Fri & Sat; ☎) ✐ Rotating brews at this beer specialist include several from its own Nottingham-based Magpie Brewery, made from British hops and malts, plus hand-pulls from local microbreweries and craft beers and ciders on tap. Timber-planked walls line the TV-free split-level space; don't miss the bathrooms with sinks and taps made out of kegs. Gastropub food is locally sourced.

Outpost Coffee Roasters
COFFEE

(www.outpost.coffee; 2 Stoney St; ☻8am-5pm Mon-Fri, 9am-5pm Sat, 10am-4pm Sun; ☎) ✐ Outpost roasts sustainably sourced beans on the city-centre's northwestern edge and brews them up here at its espresso bar. Oat, almond and soy milk is available; you can also order turmeric lattes.

Dragon
PUB

(☑0115-941 7080; www.the-dragon.co.uk; 67 Long Row; ☻noon-11.30pm Sun-Wed, to midnight Thu, to 1am Fri & Sat; ☎) The Dragon has a fabulous atmosphere any time, thanks to homemade food, a beer garden and DJs Thursday to

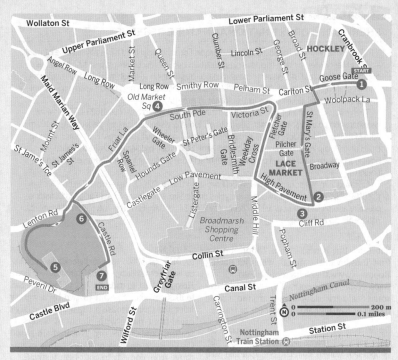

🏃 Walking Tour
On the Trail of Robin Hood

START GOOSE GATE
END YE OLDE TRIP TO JERUSALEM
LENGTH 1.2 MILES; TWO HOURS

While the origins of the Robin Hood legend are shrouded in mystery, on this walk you can discover more about the famous outlaw's connections to Nottingham as you take in some of the city's most historic sights.

Begin as Robin Hood likely did on arriving from Sherwood Forest at **1 Goose Gate**, once one of the entrances to the city (today no remains of the medieval walls are visible). Head southwest on St Mary's Gate to reach **2 St Mary's Church** (p435), mentioned in the 1450 *Ballad of Robin Hood and the Monk*. Robin Hood was allegedly recognised here by a monk he had previously robbed. The monk reported him to the Sherriff of Nottingham, who arrested him.

Just west of the church on High Pavement is the former Shire Hall and County Gaol, where the sheriff held office. There was a court on this site since 1375 or earlier, and a jail from 1449; today the **3 National Justice Museum** (p435) is located here.

Walk north along Weekday Cross and west on Victoria St to **4 Old Market Sq**. The square is mentioned in *Robin Hood and the Potter* (c 1500), in which Robin Hood disguises himself as a pot pedlar, and goes on to demonstrate his archery prowess.

Take Friar Lane southwest and cross Maid Marian Way to reach **5 Nottingham Castle** (p433). A Robin Hood gallery is the centrepiece of the castle's multimillion-pound renovations unveiled in 2021.

Just below the castle gates, on Castle Rd, you'll see Nottingham's iconic **6 statue of Robin Hood** (p433), along with smaller statues and bas-relief plaques depicting his Merry Men.

Continue downhill along Castle Rd to what's believed to be England's oldest pub, the 1189 **7 Ye Olde Trip to Jerusalem**, for a post-walk pint. Robin Hood is said to have escaped from the castle via underground caves and tunnels to the cliff-carved pub.

SHERWOOD FOREST NATIONAL NATURE RESERVE

If Robin Hood wanted to hide out in Sherwood Forest today, he'd have to disguise himself and his Merry Men as day trippers on mountain bikes. Now covering just 182 hectares of old-growth forest, it's nevertheless a major destination for Nottingham city dwellers. The week-long **Robin Hood Festival** (www.robinhoodfestival.org) is a massive medieval re-enactment that takes place in the forest in August.

The reserve's state-of-the-art, curved-timber **tourist office** (☑01623-677321; www.visitsherwood.co.uk; Forest Corner, Edwinstowe; forest & visitor centre free, parking £4; ⊙10am-6pm Mar-Sep, to 4pm Oct-Feb) 🖉 provides information about the forest's wildlife, walking trails and Robin Hood legends – including the 800-year-old **Major Oak**, a broad-boughed oak tree (propped up by supporting rods) alleged to have sheltered Robin of Locksley.

Located 2 miles south of Sherwood Forest on the B6030, **Sherwood Pines Cycles** (☑01623-822855; www.sherwoodpinescycles.co.uk; Sherwood Pines Forest Park, Old Clipstone; bike hire adult/child per hour £9.50/8, per day £35/24; ⊙9am-5pm Thu-Tue, to 7pm Wed) rents mountain bikes for exploring the area's trails.

Saturday. But it peaks from 7.30pm on the first Tuesday of the month when its Racing Room (www.theracingroom.co.uk) hosts Race Night (race entry £5), with an awesome Scalextric slot-car race around a scale model of Nottingham along 180ft of track.

Boilermaker
COCKTAIL BAR
(www.boilermakerbar.co.uk; 36b Carlton St; ⊙5pm-1am Mon-Fri, 2pm-1am Sat, 7pm-1am Sun) Entering what appears to be an industrial boilermaker's shop and navigating your way through two secret doors brings you into this cavernous, low-lit speakeasy spinning chilled lounge music. Out-there cocktail combinations (eg Figgy Stardust, with tequila, artichoke-based Cynar liqueur, figs, pomegranate shrub and black walnuts) add to the unique-and-then-some experience.

Malt Cross
PUB
(www.maltcross.com; 16 St James's St; ⊙4-10pm Tue-Thu, 2-10pm Fri, 11am-10pm Sat, noon-10pm Sun) A fine place for a pint, the Malt Cross occupies a stately old Victorian music hall, where past performers included Charlie Chaplin. It's now a community space run by the Christian Charity Trust hosting art exhibitions and live music. Top-notch bar food includes towering burgers.

Brass Monkey
COCKTAIL BAR
(www.brassmonkeybar.co.uk; 11 High Pavement; ⊙8pm-4am Mon-Sat) Nottingham's original cocktail bar rocks the Lace Market with DJ sets and quirky takes on favourites such as elderflower mojitos. The roof terrace gets packed on summer evenings. Happy hour runs to midnight.

Canal House
PUB
(☑0115-955 5060; www.castlerockbrewery.co.uk/pubs/the-canalhouse; 48-52 Canal St; ⊙11am-11pm Mon-Wed, to midnight Thu, to 1am Fri & Sat, to 10.30pm Sun; 🖥) Split in two by a watery inlet, the Canal House is the best of the city's canal-front pubs, with plenty of waterside seating and beers by Nottingham-based Castle Rock Brewery on tap. Regular events range from comedy to craft-beer festivals.

☆ Entertainment

Theatre Royal & Royal Concert Hall
PERFORMING ARTS
(☑0115-989 5555; www.trch.co.uk; Theatre Sq, Upper Parliament St) Nottingham's 19th-century Theatre Royal and adjoining 20th-century Royal Concert Hall host musicals, touring theatre shows and veteran music acts.

🛍 Shopping

Five Leaves Bookshop
BOOKS
(☑0115-837 3097; www.fiveleavesbookshop.co.uk; Swann's Yard, 14a Long Row; ⊙10am-5pm Mon-Sat) Opened as an extension of its own publishing imprint in 2013, this splendid independent bookshop is hidden down a passageway off Low Row. In addition to its own titles, it stocks fiction, poetry and non-fiction works (politics, poetry, counterculture, LGBT, cityscapes and landscapes) by other independent and commercial publishers. Readings, book launches and talks regularly take place.

Debbie Bryan
FASHION & ACCESSORIES
(☑0115-950 7776; www.debbiebryan.co.uk; 18 St Mary's Gate; ⊙noon-4pm Fri & Sun, to 5pm

Sat) In Nottingham's historic Lace Market quarter, Debbie Bryan revives its traditions, designing and making lace creations spanning jewellery to clothing and homewares, such as lampshades and framed lace artworks. Scones, cakes and slices are served at the on-site tearoom. Ask about design workshops.

Updated details of opening times are posted online.

Studio Chocolate   CHOCOLATE
(📞0115-947 4903; www.studio-chocolate.co.uk; 3 Cobden Chambers; ⊙10am-4pm Wed-Sun) Nottingham chocolatier Ellie Wharrad works with premium-grade chocolate to handcraft and hand paint pralines. Unique flavour combinations at her shop include gin and tonic, beer caramel and pear cider; ask about regular chocolate-making classes. Enter via Pelham St.

Rob's Records   MUSIC
(www.facebook.com/robsrecordsnottingham; 3 Hurts Yard; ⊙11am-5.30pm Mon-Sat) Vinyl records, along with CDs, DVDs, videos and cassettes cram every conceivable floor, wall and ceiling space at this music lover's nirvana.

ℹ️ Information

Nottingham's **tourist office** (📞0844 477 5678; www.visit-nottinghamshire.co.uk; The Exchange, 1-4 Smithy Row; ⊙10am-3pm Wed-Sat) has racks of information along with Robin Hood merchandise.

ℹ️ Getting There & Away

AIR
East Midlands Airport (p454) is 13.5 miles southwest of central Nottingham; Skylink buses pass the airport (one-way/return £5.40/10.80, one hour, at least hourly, 24 hours).

BUS
Local services run from the Victoria bus station, behind the Victoria shopping centre on Milton St. Bus 26 runs to Southwell (£4.50, one hour, every 30 minutes) and bus 90 to Newark (£5.60, 55 minutes, five daily Monday to Saturday, every two hours Sunday).

Long-distance buses operate from the **Broadmarsh bus station** (Collin St).

Frequent National Express services:
Birmingham £12, 1½ hours, four daily
Leicester £5, 45 minutes, three daily
London Victoria £28, 3½ hours, hourly

TRAIN
The train station is on the southern edge of the city centre.
Derby £8, 30 minutes, three hourly
Grantham £11.60, 35 minutes, up to two per hour
Lincoln £12.60, 55 minutes, hourly
London King's Cross/St Pancras £61, 1¾ hours, up to three per hour
Manchester £29.20, 1¾ hours, hourly

Newark-on-Trent
📞 01636 / POP 27,700
Newark-on-Trent paid the price for backing the wrong side in the English Civil War. After surviving four sieges by Oliver Cromwell's men, the town was ransacked by Roundheads when Charles I surrendered in 1646. Today, the riverside town is a peaceful place worth a stop to wander its castle ruins.

👁️ Sights

Newark Castle   CASTLE
(www.newark-sherwooddc.gov.uk/newarkcastle; Castle Gate; grounds free, tours adult/child £5.50/2.75; ⊙grounds dawn-dusk, tours by reservation Wed & Fri-Sun) In a pretty park overlooking the River Trent, the ruins of Newark Castle include an impressive Norman gate and a series of underground passages and chambers. The real King John, portrayed as a villain in the Robin Hood legend, died here in 1216. Book tour tickets online at www.palacenewarktickets.com. Concerts, festivals and various cultural events regularly take place in the grounds.

Newark Air Museum   MUSEUM
(📞01636-707170; www.newarkairmuseum.org; Drove Lane, Winthorpe; adult/child £9.50/5; ⊙10am-5pm Mar-Oct, to 4pm Nov-Feb) Situated 2 miles east of Newark by the Winthorpe Showground, this aviation museum has over 100 aircraft, including a fearsome Vulcan bomber, a Vampire T11, a Gloster Meteor and a de Havilland Tiger Moth, along with a small exhibition on the Royal Air Force.

🍴 Eating & Drinking

Old Bakery Tea Rooms   CAFE £
(📞01636-611501; www.oldbakerytearooms.co.uk; 4 Queens Head Ct; pastries £2-5, mains £6-12; ⊙9.30am-5pm Mon-Sat; 📶) Everything, including heavenly sweet and savoury scones, is baked fresh on the premises at the Old Bakery Tea Rooms, housed in an enchanting

15th-century Tudor building. Lunch specials include soups, frittata, bruschetta and smoked-salmon brioche. Cash only.

Castle Barge BAR
(☎01636-677320; www.castlebarge.com; The Wharf; ⊙10.30am-midnight) Moored on the River Trent overlooking Newark Castle, this former grain barge, which once plied the waters between Hull and Gainsborough, is an idyllic spot for a local ale inside or up on deck, with additional picnic seating on the riverbanks. Its menu includes stone-baked pizzas.

❶ Information

Tourist Office (☎01636-655765; www.newark-sherwooddc.gov.uk; 14 Appleton Gate; ⊙10am-4pm) On the northeastern edge of the historic centre.

❶ Getting There & Away

Buses 28 and 29 serve Southwell (£4.70, 35 minutes, two per hour).

Newark has two train stations.

Newark Castle East Midlands trains serve Nottingham (£6.80, 30 minutes, up to two per hour) and Lincoln (£5.80, 30 minutes, up to two per hour).

Newark North Gate Trains on the East Coast Main Line serve London King's Cross (£46.80, 1½ hours, up to four per hour); destinations to the north require a change in Doncaster (£25.50, 30 minutes, hourly).

Southwell

☑ 01636 / POP 7297

A graceful scattering of grand, wisteria-draped country houses, pretty little Southwell is straight out of the pages of a novel from the English Romantic period.

◉ Sights

★ **Southwell Minster** CHURCH
(www.southwellminster.org; Church St; suggested donation £5; ⊙8am-7pm Mar-Oct, to 6.30pm Nov-Feb) Rising from the village centre, the awe-inspiring Southwell Minster, built over Saxon and Roman foundations, blends 12th- and 13th-century features, including zigzag door frames and curved arches. Its chapterhouse features some unusual stained glass and detailed carvings of faces, animals and leaves of forest trees.

Southwell Workhouse MUSEUM
(NT; ☎01636-817260; www.nationaltrust.org.uk; Upton Rd; adult/child £8/4; ⊙noon-5pm Wed-Sun Marearly Nov) On the road to Newark, 1 mile east of the village centre, the Southwell Workhouse is a sobering reminder of the tough life faced by paupers in the 19th century. You can explore the factory floors and workers' chambers accompanied by an audio guide narrated by 'inmates' and 'officials'. One-hour guided tours of the exteriors take place at 11am.

🛏 Sleeping & Eating

Saracen's Head Hotel HISTORIC HOTEL ££
(☎01636-812701; www.saracensheadhotel.com; Market Pl; s/d/f/ste incl breakfast from £90/100/130/150; ▣❄🐾) Set around a flower-filled courtyard in the village heart, this rambling, black-and-white timbered coaching inn has 27 beautifully refurbished rooms (some with four-poster beds and claw-foot baths) across its old and new wings. Illustrious past guests included Charles I, Lord Byron and Dickens. Its oak-panelled restaurant serves traditional British fare (mains £10 to £21.50).

Family rooms sleep up to four; baby cots are available.

Old Theatre Deli CAFE, DELI £
(☎01636-815340; www.theoldtheatredeli.co.uk; 4 Market Pl; dishes £5.50-11.50; ⊙8.30am-4pm Mon-Fri, to 5pm Sat) Artisan breads from the Midlands' renowned Hambleton Bakery, gourmet sandwiches, quiches, pies, salads and hot specials, such as corn-and-bacon fritters, are among the treats to take away or eat inside or out on the pavement terrace. You can also order picnic hampers complete with blankets. It's housed inside a Georgian former theatre.

❶ Getting There & Away

Bus 26 runs from Nottingham (£4.50, one hour, every 30 minutes). For Newark-on-Trent, take bus 28 or 29 (£4.70, 35 minutes, two per hour).

LINCOLNSHIRE

Lincolnshire unfolds over low hills and the sparsely populated, pancake-flat Fens where the farmland is strewn with windmills and, more recently, wind turbines. Surrounding the history-steeped county town of Lincoln you'll find seaside resorts, scenic waterways, serene nature reserves and stone-built towns tailor-made for English period dramas.

Two of the county's most famous 'yellow-bellies' (as Lincolnshire locals call themselves) were Sir Isaac Newton, whose home, Woolsthorpe Manor, can be visited, and the late former prime minister Margaret Thatcher, the daughter of a humble green-grocer from the market town of Grantham.

Activities

Traversing the area occupied by Norse invaders in the 9th century, the 147-mile **Viking Way** walking trail snakes across the gentle hills of the Lincolnshire Wolds from the banks of the River Humber to Oakham in Rutland.

Cyclists can find information on routes across the county in any of the local tourist offices. The 33-mile **Water Rail Way** is a flat, sculpture-lined on-road cycling route that follows the River Witham through classic Fens countryside along the former railway line between Lincoln and Boston.

ⓘ Getting There & Around

East Midlands trains connect Lincoln, Newark Castle and Nottingham. Newark North Gate and Grantham lie on the East Coast Main Line between London King's Cross and Edinburgh.

Local buses link Lincolnshire's towns, but services are slow and infrequent. Check the transport pages at www.lincolnshire.gov.uk.

Comprehensive transport information is available from Traveline (p394).

Lincoln

 01522 / POP 97,541

Ringed by historic city gates – including the Newport Arch on Bailgate, a relic from the original Roman settlement – this beautiful city's old centre is a tangle of cobbled medieval streets surrounding its 11th-century castle and colossal 12th-century cathedral. The lanes that topple over the edge of Lincoln Cliff are lined with Tudor town houses, ancient pubs and independent shops.

Flanking the River Witham at the base of the hill, the new town is less absorbing, but the revitalised Brayford Waterfront development by the university is a popular spot to watch the boats go by.

◉ Sights

★ Lincoln Cathedral   CATHEDRAL
(☑01522-561600; www.lincolncathedral.com; Minster Yard; cathedral adult/child £8/4.80 Mon-Sat; ☺10am-4pm Mon-Sat, 11am-3.30pm Sun)

Towering over the city like a medieval sky-scraper, Lincoln's magnificent cathedral is a breathtaking representation of divine power on earth. The great tower rising above the crossing is the third-highest in England at 83m, but in medieval times, a lead-encased wooden spire added a further 79m, topping even the great pyramids of Giza. One-hour **guided tours** (included in admission) take place at least twice daily Monday to Saturday; there are also tours of the roof and tower (£5, book in advance).

The vast interior of the church is too large for modern congregations – services take place instead in **St Hugh's Choir**, a church within a church running east from the crossing. The choir stalls are accessed through a magnificent carved stone screen; look north to see the stunning rose window known as the Dean's Eye (c 1192), mirrored to the south by the floral flourishes of the Bishop's Eye (1330). There's more stained glass in the three Services Chapels in the north transept.

Beyond St Hugh's Choir, the **Angel Choir** is supported by 28 columns topped by carvings of angels and foliate scrollwork. Other interesting details include the 10-sided **chapterhouse** – where Edward I held his parliament and where the climax of *The Da Vinci Code* was filmed in 2005.

The best time to hear the organ resounding through the cathedral is during **evensong**; check times online.

★ Lincoln Castle   CASTLE
(☑01522-554559; www.lincolncastle.com; Castle Hill; castle day ticket adult/child £14/7.50, walls only £10/5.50, grounds free; ☺10am-5pm Apr-Sep, to 4pm Oct-Mar) One of the first castles erected by the victorious William the Conqueror, in 1068, to keep his new kingdom in line, Lincoln Castle offers awesome views over the city and miles of surrounding countryside. A major 2015-completed restoration program opened up the entire castle walls and gave the 1215 **Magna Carta** (one of only four copies) a swanky, subterranean new home. One-hour guided tours, included in the castle admission, depart from the eastern gate; check the blackboard for times.

Bishops' Palace   RUINS
(EH; ☑01522-527468; www.english-heritage.org.uk; Minster Yard; adult/child £6.90/4.10; ☺10am-6pm Wed-Sun Apr-Sep, to 5pm Wed-Sun Oct, to 4pm Sat & Sun Nov-Mar) Beside Lincoln Cathedral lie the time-ravaged but still imposing

Lincoln

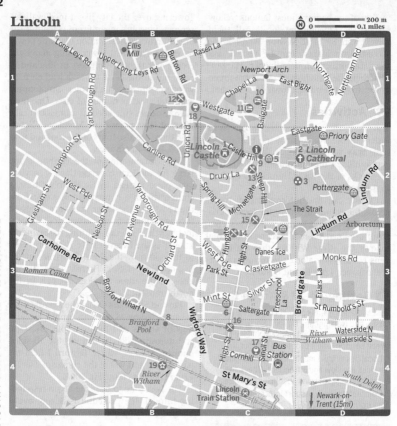

Lincoln

ruins of the 12th-century Bishops' Palace, gutted by parliamentary forces during the Civil War. From here, the local bishops once controlled a diocese stretching from the Humber to the Thames. Grapevines are planted in its hillside terraced garden.

Museum of Lincolnshire Life   MUSEUM

(☎01522-782040; www.lincolnshire.gov.uk; Old Barracks, Burton Rd; ☺10am-4pm) FREE Displays at this charming community museum housed in an old Victorian barracks span everything from Victorian farm implements to the tin-can tank built in Lincoln for WWI.

Collection   MUSEUM

(☎01522-782040; www.thecollectionmuseum.com; Danes Tce; ☺10am-4pm Wed-Mon) FREE Archaeology bursts into life at this museum, with loads of hands-on displays. Kids can handle artefacts and dress up in period costume. Check out the crushed skull of a 4000-year-old 'yellowbelly' (as locals are dubbed), pulled from a Neolithic burial site near Sleaford. Free one-hour tours run at 2pm on Saturdays. Look out for various evening events.

Exchequergate   HISTORIC BUILDING

Located between the castle and the cathedral, the triple-arched, battlement-topped Exchequergate, where the church's tenants paid their rent, dates from the 14th century. A black-and-white chequered cloth was used to help count the payments, giving rise to the term exchequer.

Lincoln Guildhall   HISTORIC BUILDING

(☎01522-873303; www.lincoln.gov.uk; Saltergate; tour free; ☺by 90min guided tour 10am, noon & 2pm Mon, Wed & Fri) Arcing over Lincoln's High St, the guildhall has been home to the city council since its completion in 1520. Regalia here includes the sword of Richard II.

☞ Tours

Ghost Walks   WALKING

(☎01673-857574; www.lincolnghostwalks.co.uk; adult/child £6/4; ☺7pm Wed-Sat) Genuinely spooky 75-minute ghost walks depart adjacent to the tourist office year-round. Bookings aren't required; turn up 10 minutes before tours begin.

Brayford Belle   CRUISE

(☎01522-708508; www.lincolnboattrips.co.uk; Brayford Wharf North; adult/child £7/4; ☺tours 11am, 12.15pm, 1.30pm & 2.45pm Tue-Sun Easter-Sep, hours vary Oct) Boat trips lasting around 50 minutes aboard the *Brayford Belle* travel along the River Witham and Fossdyke Navigation, a canal system dating to Roman times. No credit cards.

🛏 Sleeping

Castle Hotel   BOUTIQUE HOTEL ££

(☎01522-538801; www.castlehotel.net; Westgate; s/d/coach house incl breakfast from £90/120/220; P🛜) Each of the Castle Hotel's 18 rooms have been exquisitely refurbished in olive, truffle and oyster tones, as has its family-friendly four-person coach house. It was built on the site of Lincoln's Roman forum in 1852; the red-brick building's incarnations variously included a school and a WWII lookout station. Take advantage of great-value dinner, bed and breakfast deals with its award-winning restaurant **Reform** (☎01522-538801; www. reformrestaurant.co.uk; mains £15-25; ☺noon-2.30pm & 7-9pm Wed-Sat, noon-3pm Sun).

Bail House   B&B ££

(☎01522-541000; www.bailhouse.co.uk; 34 Bailgate; d/f from £65/125; P🛜❄) Stone walls, worn flagstones, secluded gardens and one room with an extraordinary timber-vaulted ceiling are just some of the charms of this lovingly restored Georgian town house in central Lincoln. There's limited on-site parking, a garden and a children's playground, and even a seasonal heated outdoor swimming pool. Family rooms sleep four.

✕ Eating

Stokes High Bridge Café   CAFE £

(☎01522-513825; www.stokescoffee.com; 207 High St; dishes £5.50-10.50; ☺8am-4pm Mon-Sat, 10am-4pm Sun; 🛜) A Lincoln landmark, this soaring 1540-built black-and-white Tudor building is England's only one atop a medieval bridge (1160). Within its preserved half-timbered interior, 1892-established, family-run roastery Stokes brews superb coffees made from speciality beans. Classic fare includes English breakfasts (served all day), traditional roasts and afternoon teas.

Cheese Society   CHEESE £

(www.thecheesesociety.co.uk; 1 St Martin's Lane; dishes £5-10.50, cheese boards £10-22; ☺kitchen 11am-3.30pm Mon-Fri, to 4pm Sat, shop 10am-4.30pm Mon-Fri, to 5pm Sat) Not only does this light, bright place stock over 90 mostly British cheeses, it also serves them at its 12-seat cafe. Try its elaborate cheese boards or dishes such as twice-baked Dorset Blue Vinney soufflé or Wensleydale and herb scones with smoked salmon.

BIRMINGHAM & THE MIDLANDS LINCOLN

THE HOME OF SIR ISAAC NEWTON

Sir Isaac Newton fans may feel the gravitational pull of **Woolsthorpe Manor** (NT; ☎01476-862823; www.nationaltrust.org.uk; Water Lane; house & grounds adult/child £9.20/4.60, grounds only £4.10/2.90; ⊙11am-5pm Wed-Mon mid-Mar–Oct, Fri-Sun Nov–mid-Mar), the great man's birthplace, about 8 miles south of Grantham. The humble 17th-century house contains reconstructions of Newton's rooms; the apple that inspired his theory of gravity allegedly fell from the tree in the garden. There's a nifty kids' science room and a cafe. Take Centrebus 9 from Grantham (£3.80, 20 minutes, four per day Monday to Saturday).

Brown's Pie Shop
PIES ££

(☎01522-527330; www.brownspieshop.co.uk; 33 Steep Hill; mains £9.75-26.50; ⊙noon-2.30pm & 5-9.30pm Mon-Fri, noon-9.30pm Sat, to 8pm Sun) Hearty 'pot pies' (no pastry bottoms) at this long-established, quintessentially British restaurant are stuffed with locally sourced beef, rabbit and game. Pies aside, traditional dishes include Lincolnshire sausages with caramelised onion gravy and slow-roasted pork belly.

★ Bronze Pig
BRITISH £££

(☎01522-524817; www.thebronzepig.co.uk; 4 Burton Rd; mains £18-27, 2-/3-course lunch menus £25/29; ⊙by reservation 6-9pm Tue, noon-1.30pm & 6-9pm Wed-Sat, noon-2pm Sun) BBC *MasterChef* finalist Irishman Eamonn Hunt and Sicilian chef Pompeo Siracusa have taken Lincoln's dining scene by storm since opening the Bronze Pig. Their exceptional Modern British cooking has an Italian accent and ingredients are locally sourced. Reserve well ahead and prepare to be wowed. It also has four deluxe guest rooms (doubles from £105).

Jews House
EUROPEAN £££

(☎01522-524851; www.jewshouserestaurant.co.uk; 15 The Strait, Steep Hill; mains £16.50-27; ⊙6-9.30pm Thu-Sat, 1-4pm Sun) This local favourite serves gourmet fare (roast wood pigeon, truffle custard and bacon foam; baked lemon sole with scallop mousse) in one of England's oldest houses, the 1160-built Romanesque Jews House.

 Drinking & Entertainment

Cosy Club
BAR

(www.cosyclub.co.uk; Sincil St; ⊙9am-11pm Sun-Wed, to midnight Thu, to 1am Fri & Sat; ☎) Spectacularly converted with soaring skylit ceilings, this 1848-built corn exchange now contains one of Lincoln's liveliest bars. Along with cocktails like English Rose (gin, rosewater, strawberries and sparkling wine) and the Earl's Breakfast (vodka, Earl Grey tea and lime juice), it serves breakfast, brunch, tapas and international dishes.

Strugglers Inn
PUB

(www.facebook.com/thestrugglersinn; 83 Westgate; ⊙noon-midnight Tue-Sat, to 11pm Sun & Mon) A sunny walled-courtyard beer garden out the back, an interior warmed by an open fire and a superb selection of real ales on tap make this the pick of Lincoln's independent pubs.

Engine Shed
LIVE MUSIC

(☎0871 220 0260; www.engineshed.co.uk; Brayford Pool) Lincoln's largest live-music venue occupies a former railway-container storage facility. Past acts have included Kings of Leon, Fat Boy Slim and Manic Street Preachers. Music aside, it also hosts sports events, comedy and pop-up markets.

ⓘ Information

Tourist Office (☎01522-545458; www.visitlincoln.com; 9 Castle Hill; ⊙10am-5pm Mon-Sat, 10.30am-4pm Sun) In a half-timbered, 16th-century building.

ⓘ Getting There & Away

BUS
The **bus station** (Melville St) is just northeast of the train station in the new town.

Stagecoach buses include bus 1 to Grantham (£6.10, 1½ hours, hourly Monday to Saturday, five on Sunday).

TRAIN
The train station is 250m east of the Brayford Waterfront development in the new town.

Boston £15.30, 1¼ hours, hourly, change at Sleaford

London King's Cross £88.50, 2¼ hours, up to three per hour, some require a change in Newark or Peterborough

Newark-on-Trent Newark Castle, £5.80, 30 minutes, two per hour

Nottingham £12.60, one hour, hourly

Sheffield £21.60, 1¼ hours, hourly

Stamford

📞 01780 / POP 19,704

One of England's prettiest towns, Stamford seems frozen in time, with elegant streets lined with honey-coloured limestone buildings and hidden alleyways dotted with alehouses, interesting restaurants and small independent boutiques. A forest of historic church spires rises overhead and the gently gurgling River Welland meanders through the town centre. It's a favourite with filmmakers seeking the postcard vision of England, and has appeared in everything from *Pride and Prejudice* to the *Da Vinci Code*.

◉ Sights

★ Burghley House   HISTORIC BUILDING
(📞 01780-752451; www.burghley.co.uk; Barnack Rd; house & garden adult/child £17/9, garden only £9.50/5.50, park free; ⊙ house 10.30am-5pm Wed-Sun Apr-early Oct, garden 10.30am-1pm & 2-4.30pm daily Apr-Oct, park 7am-6pm daily year-round) Set in more than 810 hectares of grounds, landscaped by Lancelot 'Capability' Brown, opulent Burghley House (bur-lee) was built by Queen Elizabeth's chief adviser William Cecil, whose descendants still live here. It bristles with cupolas, pavilions, belvederes and chimneys; the lavish staterooms are a particular highlight. In early September the renowned Burghley Horse Trials take place here. The estate is 1.3 miles southeast of Stamford; follow the marked path for 15 minutes through the park by Stamford's train station.

St Mary's Church   CHURCH
(www.stamfordbenefice.com; St Mary's St; ⊙ 8am-6pm, hours can vary) An endearingly wonky 13th-century broach spire tops the 12th-century St Mary's Church. Classical concerts are held here in summer; tickets (from £14) are sold at Stamford's tourist office.

🛏 Sleeping & Eating

William Cecil at Stamford   HISTORIC HOTEL ££
(📞 01780-750070; www.hillbrookehotels.co.uk; High St, St Martin's; d/f incl breakfast from £110/160, lunch mains £10.50-14.95, 2-/3-course dinner menus £29.50/35; 🅿🛜) Within the Burghley Estate, this stunningly renovated hotel has 27 rooms inspired by Burghley House, with period furnishings and luxuries such as Egyptian cotton linens and complimentary organic vodka. The smart **restaurant** turns out stylish British classics and opens to a wicker-chair-furnished patio.

Family rooms sleep four; interconnecting rooms are also available.

★ George Hotel   HISTORIC HOTEL £££
(📞 01780-750750; www.georgehotelofstamford.com; 71 High St, St Martin's; s/d/ste/4-poster incl breakfast from £145/250/270/310, mains £24-42; 🅿🛜🍽) Stamford's luxurious landmark inn opened its doors in 1597. Today its 45 individually sized and decorated rooms impeccably blend period charm and modern elegance. Superior Modern British cuisine is served at its oak-panelled **restaurant**, while its more informal garden-room restaurant hosts afternoon tea in its courtyard. Its two bars include a champagne bar.

🍺 Drinking & Nightlife

Tobie Norris   PUB
(www.kneadpubs.co.uk; 12 St Paul's St; ⊙ noon-11pm Mon-Thu, to midnight Fri & Sat, to 10.30pm Sun; 🛜) A wonderful stone-walled, flagstone-floored pub dating from 1280, the Tobie Norris has a warren of rooms with open fireplaces, a sunny, flower-filled courtyard and local ales. Wood-fired pizzas are a highlight of its wide-ranging menu (mains £14 to £18).

BELTON HOUSE

Amid 14.2 hectares of elegant formal gardens, **Belton House** (NT; 📞 01476-566116; www.nationaltrust.org.uk; Belton; house & grounds adult/child £15.70/10, grounds only £8/4; ⊙ house 12.30-5pm Wed-Sun Mar-Oct, grounds 10am-5pm Mar-Oct, to 4pm Nov-Feb) is a dream filming location for English period dramas, *Jane Eyre, Tom Jones* and the Colin Firth version of *Pride and Prejudice* among them. Built in 1688 in classic Restoration style, the house retains stunning original features, including ornate woodcarvings by master Dutch carver Grinling Gibbons. It's off the A607 2.5 miles northeast of Grantham, served by Stagecoach bus 1 (£2, 15 minutes, hourly Monday to Saturday, every two hours Sunday).

The surrounding 526-hectare grounds have been home to a fallow deer herd for more than 300 years. Also on the site are a farm shop, a restaurant, a cafe and an adventure playground.

LINCOLNSHIRE: BOMBER COUNTY

The Royal Air Force (RAF) was formed in 1918 following WWI and two years later its college was established in Lincolnshire. During WWII, England's 'Bomber County' was home to numerous squadrons and by 1945 had more airfields (49) than any other in the country. US Navy flying boats flew antisubmarine patrols from here and B-29 bombers were also based here.

Just south of Lincoln, the International Bomber Command Centre has a moving memorial and an attached museum. Lincoln's tourist office (p444) has details of other aviation legacies throughout the county.

International Bomber Command Centre (☑ 01778-421420; www.internationalbcc. co.uk; Kanwick Hill, LN4 2HQ; memorial free, museum adult/child £8.70/5.50; ⊙ memorial 24hr, museum 9.30am-5pm Tue-Sun) This 4.5-hectare site 1.5 miles south of Lincoln centres on a 31m-high metallic spire (at 102ft, the exact length of the wingspan of a Lancaster Bomber) surrounded by rusted-metal walls inscribed with the names of the 57,861 men and women who served and supported Britain's Bomber Command. Next to the memorial, a state-of-the-art museum has high-tech interactive displays covering the history of Bomber Command, including poignant stories from those who witnessed WWII's bombings first-hand.

Battle of Britain Memorial Flight Visitor Centre (☑ 01522-782040; www.lincolnshire. gov.uk; Dogdyke Rd, Coningsby; museum free, hangar tours adult/child £9/5; ⊙ hangar tours by reservation 10am-4pm Mon-Fri) See Spitfires and the four-engined *Lancaster City of Lincoln* on 90-minute hangar tours. Bus IC5 (£4.80, one hour, hourly Monday to Saturday) runs here from Lincoln.

Lincolnshire Aviation Heritage Centre (☑ 01790-763207; www.lincsaviation.co.uk; East Kirkby, near Spilsby PE23 4DE; adult/child £9/3; ⊙ 9.30am-5pm Tue, Thu & Sat Easter-Oct, 10am-4pm Tue, Thu & Sat Nov-Easter) An original WWII Bomber Command airfield complete with its original wartime control tower is now home to the Lincolnshire Aviation Heritage Centre, with wartime planes and automobiles on display. It's 30 miles southeast of Lincoln via the A153; there's no public transport.

The star attraction is an Avro Lancaster Bomber from 1941, one of only three still working (for £350, you can ride in it around the airfield, though not in the air, on Saturdays by reservation).

Paten & Co PUB

(www.kneadpubs.co.uk; 7 All Saints' Pl; ⊙ noon-midnight Mon-Sat, to 6pm Sun; 🐾) When the current owners stripped back this 18th-century building during renovations, they uncovered Paten & Co wine and spirits merchants' painted sign and got permission to use the original name. Twists on old-fashioned cocktails (eg raspberry and thyme Collins) are its speciality, along with charcoal-smoked street food. The top floor has breathtaking views of All Saints' church spires.

All Saints Brewery BREWERY

(www.allsaintsbrewery.co.uk; 22 All Saints' St; ⊙ noon-11pm Mon-Sat, to 10.30pm Sun; 🐾) 🍺 Victorian-era steam-brewing equipment is used to make organic fruit beers at this operation, which has revived the site's original 1825 brewery after it was shuttered for several decades. Try its cherry, strawberry,

raspberry and apricot brews at the attached pub or in the umbrella-shaded courtyard. Bar staff can advise on informal brewery tours.

❶ Information

Tourist Office (☑ 01780-755611; www. stamfordartscentre.com; 27 St Mary's St; ⊙ 9.30am-5pm Mon-Sat; 🐾) Inside the Stamford Arts Centre.

❶ Getting There & Away

BUS

Centrebus 4 runs to Grantham (£4.70, 1¼ hours, three per day Monday to Saturday) and Centrebus 9 serves Oakham (£3.60, 30 minutes, five daily Monday to Friday, four Saturday).

TRAIN

Trains run to Birmingham (£41.50, 1¾ hours, hourly), Cambridge (£27.20, 1¼ hours, hourly),

Nottingham (£26.80, 1¾ hours, hourly) with a change in Leicester (£21.50, 40 minutes) and Stansted Airport (£43.50, 2½ hours, every two hours).

LEICESTERSHIRE

Leicestershire was a vital creative hub during the Industrial Revolution, but its factories were a major target for German air raids in WWII and most towns in the county still bear the scars of wartime bombing. Nevertheless, there are some impressive remains, from Roman ruins to Elizabethan castles and King Richard III's resting place at Leicester Cathedral following the 21st-century discovery of his unmarked grave in a car park in the busy, multicultural capital Leicester.

ℹ️ Getting There & Around

Leicester is well served by buses and trains. For bus routes and timetables, visit the 'Roads and Transport' pages at www.leicestershire.gov.uk.

Regular buses connect Rutland to Leicester, Stamford and other surrounding towns.

Leicester

📞 0116 / POP 348,300

Built over the buried ruins of two millennia of history, Leicester (les-ter) suffered at the hands of the Luftwaffe and postwar planners but an influx of textile workers from India and Pakistan from the 1960s transformed the city into a bustling multicultural hub.

The astonishing 2012 discovery and 2013 identification of the remains of King Richard III in a Leicester car park sparked a flurry of developments, including a spiffing visitor centre on the site, and the restoration of the cathedral, where the king was reburied in 2015.

◉ Sights

★ **King Richard III: Dynasty, Death & Discovery**   MUSEUM
(www.kriii.com; 4a St Martin's Pl; adult/child £9.25/4.75; ☉ 10am-4pm Sun-Fri, to 5pm Sat) Built following the incredible 2012 discovery and 2013 DNA testing of King Richard III's remains, Leicester's high-tech King Richard III visitor centre encompasses three fascinating sections. Dynasty explores his rise to become the final Plantagenet king. Death

delves into the Battle of Bosworth, when Richard became the last English king to be killed in battle. Discovery details the University of Leicester's archaeological dig and identification, and lets you view the site of the grave in which he was found.

Its Murder, Mystery and Mayhem exhibition covers the key players, battles and milestones of the Wars of the Roses between the House of York (symbolised by a white rose) and the House of Lancaster (red rose).

★ **Leicester Cathedral**   CATHEDRAL
(📞 0116-261 5357; www.leicestercathedral.org; Peacock Lane; by donation; ☉ 11am-3pm Wed-Sat, noon-3pm Sun) Pride of place at this substantial medieval cathedral goes to the contemporary limestone tomb atop the vault where the remains of King Richard III were reburied in 2015, following the discovery of his skeleton nearby. Look too for the striking carvings on the cathedral's roof supports.

Every day except Sunday, 30-minute King Richard III tours (adult/child £3.50/free) depart at 11am, noon, 2pm and 3pm. One-hour guided tours (adult/child £5/free) are available on request.

National Space Centre   MUSEUM
(📞 0116-261 0261; www.spacecentre.co.uk; Exploration Dr; adult/child £15.50/12.50; ☉ 10am-4pm Mon-Fri, to 5pm Sat & Sun) Although British space missions usually launch from French Guiana or Kazakhstan, Leicester's space museum is a fascinating introduction to the mysteries of the spheres. The ill-fated 2003 Beagle 2 mission to Mars was controlled from here. Fun, kid-friendly displays cover

---

WORTH A TRIP

ALTHORP HOUSE

The ancestral home of the Spencer family, **Althorp House** (📞 01604-770107; www.spencerofalthorp.com; A428, Althorp; adult/child £14/7; ☉ 11am-4pm Aug) – pronounced 'altrup' – is the final resting place of Diana, Princess of Wales, commemorated by a memorial. The outstanding art collection features works by Rubens, Gainsborough and van Dyck. Profits go to charities supported by the Princess Diana Memorial Fund.

Althorp is off the A428, 5.5 miles northwest of Northampton, and is not served by public transport.

Leicester

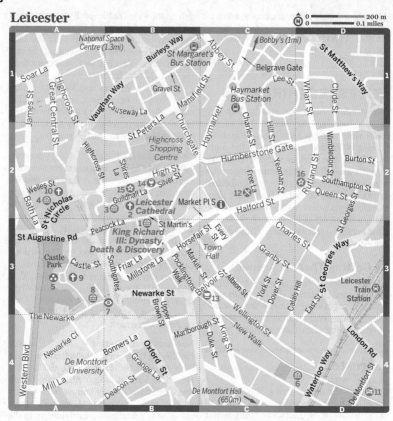

Leicester

◎ Top Sights

◎ Sights

⬤ Sleeping

⊗ Eating

◯ Drinking & Nightlife

⊕ Entertainment

everything from astronomy to the status of current space missions. It's 1.5 miles north of the city centre. Take bus 54 (£1.60, 15 minutes, every 10 minutes Monday to Saturday, every 20 minutes Sunday) from **Haymarket bus station** (Charles St).

Leicester Castle   RUINS
(www.leicestercastle.co.uk; Castle View) Scattered around the **Newarke Houses Museum** (☑ 0116-225 4980; www.leicestermuseums.org; The Newarke; ⊙ noon-4.30pm Thu-Sun) FREE are the ruins of Leicester's medieval castle,

where Richard III spent his final days before the Battle of Bosworth. The monumental gateway known as the Magazine (Newarke St) was once a storehouse for cannonballs and gunpowder. Dating from the 12th century and clad in Georgian brickwork, the Great Hall (Castle Yard) stands behind a 15th-century gate near the church of St Mary de Castro (www.facebook.com/pg/mdcleicester; 15 Castle View; ⊙ noon-2pm, hours can vary), where Geoffrey Chaucer was married in 1366.

Leicester Museum & Art Gallery
MUSEUM, GALLERY
(☑ 0116-225 4900; www.leicestermuseums.org; 53 New Walk; ⊙ 11am-4.30pm Mon-Fri, to 5pm Sat & Sun; 🖐) FREE Highlights of this grand Victorian museum include the dinosaur galleries (a reliable favourite with kids), the painting collection (with works by Turner and Degas), ceramics by Picasso, and the Egyptian gallery, where real mummies rub shoulders with displays on Boris Karloff's 1932 film *The Mummy*. Reserve a timeslot in advance.

Guildhall
HISTORIC BUILDING
(☑ 0116-253 2569; www.leicestermuseums.org; Guildhall Lane; ⊙ noon-4.30pm Thu-Sun) FREE Leicester's perfectly preserved 14th-century guildhall, one of England's finest, is reputed to be the city's most haunted building.

Jewry Wall Museum
MUSEUM
(EH; www.english-heritage.co.uk; St Nicholas Circle; ⊙ 11am-4.30pm Feb-Oct) FREE This museum exploring the history of Leicester from Roman times to the modern day was undergoing renovations at the time of writing, and is expected to reopen to the public in spring 2021. In front of the museum is the Jewry Wall, part of Leicester's Roman baths. Tiles and masonry from the baths were incorporated in the walls of neighbouring St Nicholas Church (www.stnicholasleicester.com; St Nicholas Circle; by donation; ⊙ 2-4pm Sat, 6.30-8.30pm Sun, hours can vary).

Activities

Great Central Railway
RAIL
(☑ 01509-632323; www.gcrailway.co.uk; return adult/child £18/9) Steam locomotives chug from Leicester North station on Redhill Circle to Loughborough Central, following the 8-mile route along which Thomas Cook ran the original package tour in 1841. The locos operate most weekends year-round and some summer weekdays; check timetables online.

For Leicester North station, take bus 25 (£1.60, 20 minutes, every 10 minutes) from Haymarket bus station.

Sleeping

Businesslike chain hotels are plentiful in Leicester's centre, with more bucolic options in the surrounding areas including Rutland.

Belmont Hotel
HOTEL ££
(☑ 0116-254 4773; www.belmonthotel.co.uk; 20 De Montfort St; s/d/f/ste from £71/90/115/125; P🅿❄@🛜) Owned and run by the same family for four generations, the 19th-century Belmont has 74 stylish, contemporary, individually designed rooms and a fantastic location overlooking leafy New Walk. Family rooms have a double bed and bunks. Its restaurant is highly regarded; the two bars, Jamie's and Bowie's, open to a terrace and a conservatory respectively.

Eating

Bobby's
INDIAN £
(☑ 0116-266 0106; www.bobbys-restaurant.co.uk; 154-156 Belgrave Rd; dishes £5-7.50; ⊙ 11am-9pm Mon, Wed & Thu, to 10pm Fri, 10am-10pm Sat & Sun; ☑) The top pick along Leicester's Golden Mile – lined with sari stores, jewellery emporiums and curry houses – is Bobby's, a 1970s-established institution serving all-vegetarian classics.

HAMMER & PINCERS

For a mind-blowing meal, head to Hammer & Pincers (☑ 01509-880735; www.hammerandpincers.co.uk; 5 East Rd, Wymeswold; mains £20-35, 3-course dinner menu £55, with wine £90; ⊙ noon-2pm & 6-9.30pm Tue-Sat, to 4pm Sun; ☑), an idyllic gastropub at the edge of the cute village of Wymeswold. Everything is homemade, down to the breads and condiments; seasonal specialities might include cider-cured sea trout, gin-marinated pheasant and rosemary rhubarb sorbet. Don't miss its signature twice-baked cheese soufflé. It's 16 miles north of Leicester via the A46.

Check the website for rates and availability of three luxury en-suite guest rooms built in 2020.

Belgrave Rd is about 1 mile northeast of Leicester's city centre. Follow Belgrave Gate and cross Burleys Flyover; alternatively, numerous buses (£1.60, seven minutes, every five minutes) run from St Margaret's bus station.

Good Earth
VEGETARIAN £

(☎ 0116-262 6260; www.facebook.com/veggiegood earth; 19 Free Lane; mains £3.50-7.50; ⊗ noon-3pm Mon-Fri, to 4pm Sat; 🖉) This venerable vegetarian cafe has a daily changing menu of wholesome veggie bakes, huge salads and homemade cakes, and hosts occasional evening events such as live-music gigs. Cash only.

★ John's House
BRITISH £££

(☎ 01509-415569; www.johnshouse.co.uk; Stonehurst Farm, 139-141 Loughborough Rd, Mountsorrel; 2-/3-course lunch menus £26/30, 2-/3-/7-course dinner menus £48/55/79; ⊗ noon-2pm & 7-9pm Tue-Sat) Chef John Duffin was born here on 16th-century Stonehurst Farm, 8 miles north of Leicester. After working in Michelin-starred restaurants, he returned in 2014 to open his restaurant, and has since gained a Michelin star of his own. Multicourse menus (no à la carte) showcase his imagination in dishes like creamed Porthilly oysters with smoked Mountsorrel eels and foraged lovage.

Still a working farm today, Stonehurst (www.stonehurstfarm.co.uk) also has a fabulous farm shop, a tearoom, a petting farm and a motor museum housing vintage vehicles.

Drinking & Nightlife

Bread & Honey
COFFEE

(www.breadnhoneycoffee.com; 15 King St; ⊗ 7.45am-3pm Mon-Fri; 🖧) Beans from single farm estates and co-ops sourced and roasted by London-based Monmouth are brewed at this little bare-boards hole in the wall; the flat whites are the best for miles around. Steaming soups, preservative-free bread, made-from-scratch hot dishes and fantastic cakes (chocolate fudge cake with white-chocolate icing, honey-glazed banana loaf...) are all available, too.

Globe
PUB

(www.theglobeleicester.com; 43 Silver St; ⊗ 11am-10pm Mon-Thu, to 11pm Fri & Sat, to 8pm Sun) In the atmospheric Lanes – a tangle of alleys south of the High St – this old-fashioned pub has fine draught ales and a crowd that rates its drinks by quality rather than quantity.

Entertainment

Cookie
LIVE MUSIC

(☎ 0116-253 1212; www.thecookieleicester.co.uk; 68 High St; ⊗ bar 3-11pm Tue & Wed, noon-11pm Thu, to 1am Fri & Sat, to 5pm Sun, concert hours vary) With a capacity of 350 in its brick cellar, this indie venue is a brilliant place to catch live bands and comedy nights in an intimate setting.

Curve Theatre
THEATRE

(☎ 0116-242 3595; www.curveonline.co.uk; 60 Rutland St; backstage tours adult/child £5/4) This sleek artistic space hosts big-name shows and some innovative modern

---

THE BATTLE OF BOSWORTH

Given a few hundred years, every battlefield ends up simply a field, but the site of the **Battle of Bosworth** (☎ 01455-290429; www.bosworthbattlefield.org.uk; Ambion Lane, Sutton Cheney; adult/child £8.95/5.75, guided walk £4.50/3; ⊗ heritage centre 10.30am-4pm Sat-Wed, grounds dawn-dusk) – where Richard III met his maker in 1485 – is enlivened by an entertaining heritage centre full of skeletons and musket balls; guided walks around the site last 90 minutes. Enthusiasts in period costume re-enact the battle each August.

Although it lasted just a few hours, the Battle of Bosworth marked the end of the Plantagenet dynasty and the start of the Tudor era. This was where the mortally wounded Richard III famously proclaimed: 'A horse, a horse, my kingdom for a horse'. (Actually, he didn't: the quote was invented by that great Tudor propagandist William Shakespeare.)

After visiting the battlefield, head for lunch at the 17th-century coaching inn, **Hercules Revived** (☎ 01455-699336; www.herculesrevived.co.uk; Sutton Cheney; mains £11-23; ⊗ kitchen noon-2.30pm & 6-9pm Mon-Sat, noon-4pm Sun, bar to 11.30pm daily), which serves top-tier gastropub food.

The battlefield is 16 miles southwest of Leicester at Sutton Cheney, off the A447; there's no public transport.

theatre, and has good accessibility for theatregoers who are aurally or visually impaired. Call the ticket office to book backstage tours.

De Montfort Hall   LIVE MUSIC
(☑ 0116-233 3111; www.demontforthall.co.uk; Granville Rd) Orchestras, ballets, musicals and other big song-and-dance performances are all featured on the bill at this huge venue.

ℹ Information

Tourist Office (☑ 0116-299 4444; www. visitleicester.info; 51 Gallowtree Gate; ☺10am-4pm) Helpful office with reams of city and county info.

ℹ Getting There & Away

BUS

Intercity buses operate from **St Margaret's bus station** (Gravel St), north of the city centre. The useful Skylink bus runs to East Midlands Airport (£7.40, 50 minutes, at least hourly, 24 hours) and continues on to Derby (£7.40, 1¼ hours).

National Express services:

Coventry £10, 45 minutes, three daily

London Victoria £18.90, 2¾ hours, every two hours

Nottingham £5, 45 minutes, three daily

TRAIN

East Midlands trains:

Birmingham £26.60, one hour, up to two per hour, some with a change in Derby

Derby £14.30, 20 minutes, three daily

London St Pancras £92, 1¼ hours, up to four per hour

Rutland

Tiny Rutland was merged with Leicestershire in 1974, but in 1997 regained its 'independence' as England's smallest county.

Rutland centres on Rutland Water, a vast artificial reservoir created by the damming of the Gwash Valley in 1976. Covering 4.19 sq miles, the reservoir attracts some 20,000 birds, including ospreys.

◉ Sights & Activities

**Rutland Water
Nature Reserve**   NATURE RESERVE
(☑ 01572-770651; www.lrwt.org.uk/rutland-water; Egleton; adult/child incl parking £6/3.50; ☺9am-5pm Mar-Oct, to 4pm Nov-Feb) Near Oakham,

GEORGE WASHINGTON'S ANCESTRAL HOME

An impressively preserved Tudor mansion, **Sulgrave Manor** (☑ 01295-760205; www.sulgravemanor.org.uk; Manor Rd, Sulgrave; adult/child £7.20/3.60; ☺11am-5pm Thu, Fri & Sun Apr-Sep) was built by Lawrence Washington in 1539. The Washington family lived here for almost 120 years before Colonel John Washington, the great-grandfather of America's first president, George Washington, sailed to Virginia in 1656.

Sulgrave Manor is 20 miles southwest of Northampton, just off the B4525 near Banbury; you'll need your own wheels to get here.

the Rutland Water Nature Reserve has 31 hides throughout the reserve and a viewing section upstairs in the **Anglian Water Birdwatching Centre**, which has an exhibition on the area's abundant birdlife, including ospreys, long-tailed tits, lesser whitethroats, bullfinches, garden warblers and jays. Look out too for water voles, which thrive here. The reserve's **Lyndon Visitor Centre** (☑ 01572-737378; Manton; adult/child incl parking £6/3.50; ☺9am-5pm mid-Mar–early Sep), for which tickets are valid, opens in warmer months.

Rutland Watersports   WATER SPORTS
(☑ 01780-460154; www.anglianwater.co.uk; Whitwell Leisure Park, Bull Brigg Lane, Whitwell; windsurf/kayak/SUP rental per hour from £26/10/12.50; ☺9am-8pm Wed & Thu, to 7pm Fri-Tue Apr-Oct, shorter hours Nov-Mar) Aquatic activities offered by Rutland Watersports include windsurfing, kayaking and stand-up paddleboarding (SUP). You can hire gear or take lessons.

Rutland Belle   CRUISE
(☑ 01572-787630; www.rutlandwatercruises. com; Bull Brigg Lane, Whitwell; adult/child £10/7; ☺hourly noon-3pm Mon-Sat, 11am-3pm Sun mid-Jul–Aug, shorter hours Apr–mid-Jul, Sep & Oct) Take a 45-minute round-trip cruise from Whitwell to Normanton on the southern shore of the Rutland reservoir. On some afternoons, it also runs later birdwatching cruises lasting 90 minutes (adult/child £15/10).

STOKE BRUERNE & THE GRAND UNION CANAL

Brightly painted barges frequent this charming little village 8.2 miles south of Northampton on the Grand Union Canal, the main thoroughfare of England's canal network. From here, you can follow the waterways all the way to Leicester, Birmingham or London.

A converted corn mill houses the entertaining **Canal Museum** (☑ 01604-862229; www.canalrivertrust.org.uk; 3 Bridge Rd; adult/child £4.75/3.10; ⊙ 10am-5pm Apr-Oct, shorter hours Nov-Mar), which charts the history of the canal network and its barge workers, lock-keepers and pit workers. Scale models abound; outside you can see the historic narrowboat *Sculptor*, listed on the National Historic Boat Register.

The **Boat Inn** (☑ 01604-862428; www.boatinn.co.uk; Bridge Rd; mains restaurant £19-26, bistro £8.50-11.50; ⊙ restaurant noon-2pm & 7-9pm Tue-Sat, noon-2.30pm Sun, bar 9am-11pm Mon-Sat, to 10.30pm Sun) is a canal-side landmark. With picnic tables on the quay, this sociable local pub has a relaxed bistro serving pub classics until 9pm, a more formal restaurant with refined dishes such as steaks, and a great range of ales.

🛏 Sleeping & Eating

Hambleton Hall　　　HISTORIC HOTEL £££
(☑ 01572-756991; www.hambletonhall.com; Ketton Rd, Hambleton; s/d/ste incl breakfast from £225/325/650; 🅿 🛜 🏊 🐾) One of England's finest country hotels, rambling former hunting lodge Hambleton Hall, built in 1881, sits on a peninsula jutting out into Rutland Water, 3 miles east of Oakham. Its luxurious floral rooms and Michelin-starred restaurant (two-course lunch menu £34.50, three-/four-course dinner menus £83/103) are surrounded by gorgeous gardens, which also shelter an outdoor heated swimming pool (May to September).

Otters Fine Foods　　　DELI, CAFE £
(☑ 01572-756481; www.ottersfinefoods.co.uk; 44 High St, Oakham; dishes £6.50-11; ⊙ 9am-5.30pm Mon-Sat) A pretty brick terrace with a slate roof houses this Oakham deli. Pick up sandwiches, quiches, soups, salads, cheeses, meats, charcuterie and more for a lakeside picnic, or preorder a hamper. If it's not picnic weather, dine at its in-store cafe.

❶ Getting There & Away

Bus 9 links Oakham with Stamford (£3.60, 30 minutes, hourly Monday to Friday, four services Saturday) via Rutland Water's north shore.

Trains link Oakham with Leicester (£16.20, 30 minutes, every two hours).

DERBYSHIRE

The Derbyshire countryside is painted in two distinct tones: the lush green of rolling valleys criss-crossed by dry-stone walls, and the barren mottled-brown hilltops of the high, wild moorlands. The biggest draw here is the Peak District National Park, which preserves some of England's most evocative scenery, attracting legions of hikers, climbers, cyclists and cave enthusiasts.

❶ Getting There & Around

East Midlands Airport (p454) is the nearest air hub, and Derby is well served by trains, but connecting services to smaller towns are few. In the Peak District, the Derwent Valley Line runs from Derby to Matlock. Edale and Hope lie on the Hope Valley Line from Sheffield to Manchester.

For a comprehensive list of Derbyshire bus routes, visit the 'Transport and Roads' pages at www.derbyshire.gov.uk.

Derby

☑ 01332 / POP 248,752
Gloriously sited at the southeastern edge of the Derbyshire hills that roll towards the Peak District, Derby is one of the Midlands' most energetic, creative cities. This was one of the crucibles of the Industrial Revolution: almost overnight, a sleepy market town was transformed into a major manufacturing centre, producing everything from silk to bone china and, later, locomotives and Rolls-Royce aircraft engines. The city suffered the ravages of industrial decline in the 1980s, but bounced back with impressive cultural developments and a rejuvenated riverfront.

⊙ Sights

Royal Crown Derby Factory　　MUSEUM, FACTORY
(☑ 01332-712800; www.royalcrownderby.co.uk; 194 Osmaston Rd; museum & factory tour adult/

child £5/2.50, museum only £2/1; ☉museum 10am-4pm Mon-Sat, factory tours 11am & 1.30pm Mon-Thu, 11am Fri) Derby's historic potteries still turn out some of the finest bone china in England, from edgy Asian-inspired designs to the kind of stuff your grandma collects. Reservations are essential for factory tours, which last 90 minutes and include a visit to the museum. Royal Crown Derby's china (including seconds and discontinued items) is sold at its on-site shop, and is used as tableware at its elegant tearoom.

Derby Cathedral   CATHEDRAL
(☑ 01332-341201; www.derbycathedral.org; 18 Irongate; cathedral by donation, tower tours adult/child £8/4; ☉cathedral 8.30am-5.30pm, tower tours vary) Founded in AD 943 and reconstructed in the 18th century, Derby Cathedral's vaulted ceiling towers above a fine collection of medieval tombs, including the opulent grave of the oft-married Bess of Hardwick, who at various times held court at Hardwick Hall, Chatsworth House and Bolsover Castle. Check the website for dates when historians lead tours up 189 steps into the Tudor tower, the second-highest bell tower in the UK.

Peregrine falcons nest in the tower; follow their progress at www.derbyperegrines.blogspot.com.

Derby Museum & Art Gallery   MUSEUM
(☑ 01332-641901; www.derbymuseums.org; The Strand; ☉10.30am-4.30pm Tue-Sat, noon-4pm Sun) FREE Local history and industry displays include fine ceramics produced by Royal Crown Derby and an archaeology gallery, along with paintings by renowned artist Joseph Wright of Derby (1734–97).

Quad   GALLERY, CINEMA
(☑ 01332-290606; www.derbyquad.co.uk; Market Pl; gallery free, cinema tickets adult/child £9/7; ☉gallery 11am-5pm Mon-Sat, noon-5pm Sun) A striking modernist cube on Market Pl, Quad contains a futuristic art gallery and an arthouse cinema.

🛏 Sleeping

Coach House   B&B ££
(☑ 01332-554423; www.coachhousederby.com; 185a Duffield Rd; s/d from £90/105; P🛜🐕) Surrounded by a rambling cottage garden, this red-brick 1860-built property 1.7 miles north of Derby has four countrified rooms with richly patterned wallpapers in the main house, and three contemporary loft-style rooms in the superbly converted

stables. Personalised touches include free homemade brownies. Vegan and gluten-free breakfasts are possible (reserve ahead). Off-street parking is first come, first served.

Farmhouse at Mackworth   INN ££
(☑ 01332-824324; www.thefarmhouseatmackworth.com; 60 Ashbourne Rd; d/f incl breakfast from £90/110; P🛜) The Farmhouse at Mackworth is just 2.5 miles northwest of Derby in undulating countryside, with the bonus of plentiful free parking. The designer inn's 10 boutique rooms have checked fabrics, rustic timber cladding and chrome fittings, plus amenities including Nespresso machines and fluffy robes. There's a fabulous bar and a restaurant with a Josper charcoal oven (mains £12 to £32).

Cathedral Quarter Hotel   HOTEL ££
(☑ 07710 982690; www.cathedralquarterhotel.com; 16 St Mary's Gate; d/ste incl breakfast from £95/145; ❄🛜) A bell's peal from the cathedral, this grand Georgian edifice houses a 38-room hotel. The service is as polished as the grand marble staircase, and there's an on-site spa and a fine-dining restaurant (2-/3-course dinner menu £23/26).

★Cow   INN £££
(☑ 01332-824297; www.cowdalbury.com; The Green, Dalbury Lees; d incl breakfast from £135; P🛜🐕) This whitewashed 19th-century inn 6.5 miles west of Derby has solid oak floors, stone walls and timber-lined ceilings. Its 12 individually styled rooms range from Victorian and art deco to retro vintage, and feature locally handcrafted mattresses and Egyptian cotton sheets. The bar-restaurant's stools are fashioned from milk cans; food is sourced within a 30-mile radius (mains £10.50 to £17.50).

Dishes might include ham hock Scotch egg, pulled barbecue chicken with chestnut pesto, and rhubarb and custard fool with pink-peppercorn shortbread.

🍴 Eating

Wonky Table   BISTRO ££
(☑ 01332-295000; www.wonkytable.co.uk; 32 Sadler Gate; small plates £4.50-9, mains £10-18; ☉5-11pm Fri, noon-4pm & 5-11pm Sat, noon-6pm Sun; 🍴) Inside an inviting retro-vintage dining room with exposed-brick walls, Wonky Table has a variety of small tapas-style sharing dishes such as heritage beetroot, orange and goats-cheese terrine or black-pudding-stuffed chicken wings, along with mains like

CONKERS & THE NATIONAL FOREST

The National Forest (www.nationalforest.org) is an ambitious project to generate new areas of sustainable woodland by planting 30 million trees in Leicestershire, Derbyshire and Staffordshire, covering a total area of 51,800 hectares or 200 sq miles. More than 9 million saplings have already taken root. Visitor attractions here include the kid-friendly nature centre, **Conkers** (☑ 01283-216633; www.visitconkers.com; Rawdon Rd, Moira; adult/child £7.30/6.30; ⊙ 10am-6pm Easter-Sep, to 5pm Oct-Easter). There are also several bike trails; bikes can be hired from **Hicks Lodge** (☑ 01530-274533; Willesley Wood Side, Moira; bike hire per 3hr adult/child £17.50/15; ⊙ trails 8am-dusk, bike hire & cafe 9am-5pm Fri-Wed, to 9pm Thu mid-Feb–Oct, 10am-4pm Mon-Wed & Fri, 9am-9pm Thu, to 5pm Sat & Sun Nov–mid-Feb).

If you fancy overnighting, the **National Forest YHA** (☑ 0845 371 9672; www.yha.org.uk; 48 Bath Lane, Moira; dm/d/f from £16/58/77; P 🛜) ✎ has impressive eco features (such as rainwater harvesting and solar biomass boiler usage), 23 spotless en-suite rooms, bike storage, and a restaurant serving local produce and organic wines. It's 300m west of Conkers along Bath Lane.

halloumi, lentil and green-bean curry or pork loin with pickled plums.

Darleys
BRITISH £££

(☑ 01332-364987; www.darleys.com; Waterfront, Darley Abbey Mill; 2-/3-course menus lunch £25/29.50, dinner £36/40; ⊙ noon-2pm & 6-8.30pm Tue-Fri, 12.30-2.30pm & 7-9pm Sat, noon-4pm Sun; ✎) Two miles north of the city centre, this upmarket restaurant has a gorgeous setting in a bright converted mill overlooking the river, with a beautiful waterside terrace. It serves classy fare such as sea trout with cockle cream, curry oil and a samphire pakora. Vegetarian and vegan menus are available at all times.

Drinking & Nightlife

★ Old Bell Hotel
PUB

(www.bellhotelderby.co.uk; 51 Sadler Gate; ⊙ noon-11pm Sun-Thu, to 1.30am Fri & Sat) Dating from 1650 and hosting Bonnie Prince Charlie's soldiers in 1745, this history-steeped black-and-white inn was restored by local entrepreneur Paul Hurst, retaining original features, antiques and photographs. There's a central courtyard and, allegedly, several ghosts. Real-ale tasting flights, snacks and lunches are served in its Tavern and Tudor bars; the Belfry Bar has an upmarket steakhouse.

Tap
PUB

(www.brewerytap-dbc.co.uk; 1 Derwent St; ⊙ 5-11pm Tue & Wed, noon-11pm Thu & Sun, to midnight Fri & Sat) The Tap serves its own brews, guest ales and over 80 craft beers from around the world in elegant Victorian surrounds.

Shopping

Bennetts
DEPARTMENT STORE

(www.bennettsofderby.co.uk; 8 Irongate) Founded as an ironmongers in 1734, Bennetts is the world's oldest department store. It was closed at the time of research while major renovations were carried out under new owners, and will showcase new brands, along with premium food and drinks at its two restaurants and bar – check the website for reopening details.

❶ Information

Tourist Office (☑ 01332-643411; www.visit derby.co.uk; Market Pl; ⊙ 9.30am-8pm Mon-Sat) Under the Assembly Rooms in the main square.

❶ Getting There & Away

AIR

East Midlands Airport (EMA; ☑ 0808 169 7032; www.eastmidlandsairport.com), 11.5 miles southeast of Derby, is served by regular Skylink buses (£4.70, 40 minutes, at least hourly). Buses operate 24 hours.

BUS

Local and long-distance buses run from Derby's bus station, immediately east of the Westfield shopping mall. High Peak has buses every two hours between Derby and Buxton (£6.60, 1¾ hours), via Matlock (£4.60, 45 minutes) and Bakewell (£5.20, 1¼ hours). One bus continues to Manchester (£8, 2¼ hours).

Other services:

Leicester Skylink; £7.40, 1¼ hours, one to two hourly

Nottingham Red Arrow; £5.40, 35 minutes, at least three per hour

TRAIN
The train station is about half a mile southeast of the city centre on Railway Tce.

Birmingham £20.40, 40 minutes, two per hour

Leeds £42.70, 1½ hours, hourly

London St Pancras £68, 1½ hours, up to two hourly

Nottingham £8, 30 minutes, two per hour

Ashbourne

📞 01335 / POP 8377

Perched at the southern edge of the Peak District National Park, Ashbourne is a pretty patchwork of steeply slanting stone streets lined with cafes, pubs and antique shops.

🏃 Activities

Ashbourne Cycle Hire Centre   CYCLING
(📞 01335-343156; www.peakdistrict.gov.uk; Mapleton Rd; per half/full day standard bike from £14/17, electric bike £32/36; ⊙ 9.30am-5pm Mar-Oct, shorter hours Nov-Feb) Situated 1km northwest of town, the Cycle Hire Centre is right on the Tissington Trail, at the end of a huge and atmospheric old railway tunnel leading under Ashbourne. Helmets, puncture-repair kits and maps are included. You can also rent mountain bikes, children's bikes, bikes with baby seats, trailers for buggies and tandems.

🛌 Sleeping & Eating

Compton House   B&B ££
(📞 01335-343100; www.comptonhouse.co.uk; 27-31 Compton St; s/d from £55/75; 🅿🛜) Fresh, clean, frilly rooms, a warm welcome and a central location make this the pick of Ashbourne's B&Bs. There's a minimum two-night stay on weekends.

Flower Cafe   CAFE £
(www.facebook.com/theflowercafeashbourne; 5 Market Pl; mains £5-12.50; ⊙ 8.30am-4pm Tue-Sun; 🖉) Soups such as parsnip, chorizo and chestnut, broccoli and Stilton, and spicy bean and lentil are a year-round speciality at this cute-as-a-button cafe where everything is homemade. In summer it also cooks delicious quiches (cheesy leek and mushroom; bacon, brie and cranberry...). Gluten-free and dairy-free dishes are plentiful.

ℹ Information

Tourist Office (📞 01335-343666; www.visitpeakdistrict.com; Market Pl; ⊙10am-2pm Mon, Tue, Thu & Fri, 9am-1pm Wed) Inside the town hall.

ℹ Getting There & Away

Bus services include the following.

Buxton High Peak routes 441 and 442; £4.50, 1¼ hours, hourly Monday to Saturday

Derby Trent Barton Swift; £4.50, 40 minutes, hourly Monday to Saturday, five Sunday

Matlock Bath

📞 01629 / POP 753

Matlock Bath (not to be confused with the larger, workaday town of Matlock, 2 miles north) looks like a British seaside resort that somehow lost its way and ended up at the foot of the Peak District National Park. Following the River Derwent through a sheer-walled gorge, the main promenade is lined with amusement arcades, tearooms, fish-and-chip shops, pubs and shops catering to the motorcyclists who congregate here on summer weekends. Outside summer, the town is considerably quieter. The area's industrial history is evident in the many surrounding mills, which can be visited.

⊙ Sights

Peak District Lead Mining Museum   MUSEUM
(📞 01629-583834; www.peakdistrictleadmining-museum.co.uk; The Grand Pavilion, South Pde; museum adult/child £5.50/3.50, mine £6.50/4, combined ticket £10/6; ⊙11am-3.45pm Wed, Sat & Sun Apr-Oct, Sat & Sun Nov-Mar; ♿) An educational introduction to the mining history of Matlock is provided by this enthusiast-run museum set in an old Victorian dance hall. Kids can wriggle through its maze of tunnels and shafts while adults browse historical displays. After the mine tour, you can go into the workings of the **Temple Mine** and pan for 'gold' (well, shiny minerals). Reservations for mine tours are recommended, as are sturdy shoes, as the mine can be muddy.

Cromford Mill   MUSEUM
(📞 01629-823256; www.cromfordmills.org.uk; Mill Lane, Cromford; adult/child £10/free; ⊙10am-5pm) Founded in the 1770s by Richard Arkwright, the Cromford Mill was the first modern factory, producing cotton on automated machines powered by a series of waterwheels along the River Derwent. This prototype inspired a succession of mills, ushering in the industrial age. It's 1 mile south of Matlock Bath (a 20-minute walk), or you can take the train one stop to Cromford (£2.60, five minutes, hourly).

Caudwell's Mill   MUSEUM

(☑ 01629-734374; www.caudwellsmill.co.uk; Rowsley; ⊙ 9am-5pm Mon-Sat, 10am-4pm Sun) FREE This chugging, grinding, water-powered mill still produces flour the old-fashioned way – 20 different types are for sale, along with six different oat products, and yeast and biscuits. Also here is a tearoom. You can get to Rowsley directly from Matlock Bath by bus (£3.60, 20 minutes, hourly) on the route to Bakewell.

At the time of research the upper floors were being restored, but it's free to walk around the lower levels.

Masson Mills   MUSEUM

(☑ 01629-581001; www.massonmills.co.uk; Derby Rd; adult/child £5/free; ⊙ 10am-5.30pm Mon-Sat, to 5pm Sun Jan-Nov) A museum tells the story of the valley's textile mills at this large complex 1 mile south of Matlock Bath. The attached shopping village is full of outlet stores for big clothing brands.

🏃 Activities

Heights of Abraham   AMUSEMENT PARK

(☑ 01629-582365; www.heightsofabraham.com; Dale Rd; adult/child £19/13; ⊙ 10am-5pm mid-Mar–early Nov; ♿) A spectacular cable-car ride (accessible with admission ticket only) from the bottom of the gorge brings you to this hilltop leisure park – its cave and mine tours and fossil exhibitions are a winner with kids. The cave is a constant 10°C, so bring a jacket.

🛌 Sleeping

Grouse & Claret   INN ££

(☑ 01629-733233; www.grouseclaretpub.co.uk; Station Rd, Rowsley; d incl breakfast from £92; P 🛜) Located in the village of Rowsley, 6.2 miles northwest of Matlock Bath, this 18th-century stone inn has eight comfy, country-style wallpapered rooms, a restaurant specialising in spit-roasted chicken, and a huge, sunny beer garden with umbrella-shaded tables.

Hodgkinson's Hotel & Restaurant   HOTEL ££

(☑ 01629-582170; www.hodgkinsons-hotel.co.uk; 150 South Pde; s/d/f incl breakfast from £60/110/155; P 🛜) The eight rooms at this central Grade II–listed Victorian beauty conjure up Matlock's golden age with antique furnishings, cast-iron fireplaces, flowery wallpaper, handmade soaps and goose-down duvets. The restaurant (open Tuesday to Saturday evenings; two-/three-course menus £28/32) has just 18 seats, so bookings are advised. From April to September there's a minimum two-night stay on weekends.

🛍 Shopping

Scarthin Books   BOOKS

(www.scarthinbooks.com; The Promenade, Cromford; ⊙ 9am-6pm Mon-Sat, 10am-6pm Sun) More than 100,000 new and secondhand books cram into 12 rooms in this biblio-paradise, which hosts regular literary events and has a vegetarian cafe (dishes £3 to £6.50) serving organic pizza, soups, wraps, pies and burritos.

ℹ Information

Tourist Office (☑ 01629-583834; www.visitpeakdistrict.com; The Grand Pavilion, South Pde; ⊙ 10am-5pm Apr-Sep, 11am-3pm Oct-Mar) At the Peak District Lead Mining Museum (p455).

ℹ Getting There & Away

Matlock is a hub for buses around the Peak District.

Bakewell High Peak; £3.50, 35 minutes, every two hours

Derby High Peak; £4.60, 40 minutes, every two hours

Trains run hourly between Matlock Bath and Derby (£6.70, 35 minutes, every two hours).

Chesterfield

☑ 01246 / POP 103,800

The eastern gateway to the Peaks, Chesterfield is a busy service centre that's famed for the twisted spire atop its church.

Nearby is the magnificent Elizabethan mansion Hardwick Hall.

◉ Sights

Hardwick Hall   HISTORIC BUILDING

(NT; ☑ 01246-850430; www.nationaltrust.org.uk; Doe Lea; house & garden adult/child £13.95/7, garden only £8/4, incl Hardwick Old Hall £20.75/11.10; ⊙ house 11am-5pm Wed-Sun mid-Feb–Oct, to 3pm Wed-Sun Nov–mid-Feb, garden 10am-5pm daily year-round) One of the most complete Elizabethan mansions in the country, Hardwick Hall was designed by eminent architect Robert Smythson. The building featured all the latest mod-cons of the time, including fully glazed windows. The atmospheric interiors are decked out with magnificent

DON'T MISS

KEDLESTON HALL

Sitting pretty in vast landscaped grounds, neoclassical **Kedleston Hall** (NT; 📞 01332-842191; www.nationaltrust.org.uk; Kedleston Rd, Quarndon; house & gardens adult/child £13.60/6.80, garden only £10/5; ⏰ house noon-5pm Sat-Thu Feb-Oct, garden 10am-5pm Feb-Oct, to 4pm Nov-Jan) is a must for fans of stately homes. Entering the house through a grand portico, you'll reach the breathtaking Marble Hall with massive alabaster columns and statues of Greek deities.

Kedleston Hall is 5 miles northwest of Derby, off the A52. Bus 114 between Derby and Ashbourne (£3.60, 25 minutes, six daily Monday to Saturday) stops at the gates when the hall is open.

The Curzon family has lived here since the 12th century, but the current wonder was built by Sir Nathaniel Curzon in 1758. Meanwhile, the poor old peasants in Kedleston village had their humble dwellings moved a mile down the road, as they interfered with the view. Ah, the good old days...

Highlights include Indian treasures amassed by Viceroy George Curzon, and a domed, circular saloon modelled on the Pantheon in Rome, as well as 18th-century-style pleasure gardens.

tapestries and oil paintings of forgotten dignitaries.

Hardwick Hall is 10 miles southeast of Chesterfield, just off the M1; it's best reached by your own wheels.

The hall was home to the 16th-century's second-most powerful woman, Elizabeth, Countess of Shrewsbury (known to all as Bess of Hardwick), who amassed a staggering fortune by marrying wealthy noblemen with one foot in the grave. Hardwick Hall was constructed using her inheritance from husband number four, who shuffled off this mortal coil in 1590.

Set aside time to explore the formal gardens or the longer walking trails of Hardwick Park.

Next door to the manor are the ruins of Bess' first house, **Hardwick Old Hall**, which is undergoing renovations until 2022.

St Mary & All Saints Church   CHURCH
(📞 01246-206506; www.crookedspire.org; Church Way; spire tours adult/child £6/4; ⏰ church 9am-4pm Mon-Sat) Chesterfield is worth a visit to see the astonishing crooked spire that rises atop St Mary & All Saints Church. Dating from 1360, the 68m-high spire is twisted in a right-handed corkscrew that leans several metres southwest. It's the result of the lead casing on the south-facing side having buckled in the sun. Spire tours lasting 45 minutes take you up into the tower. Tours typically take place at 2.30pm on Saturdays; call to confirm.

ℹ Information

Tourist Office (📞 01246-345777; www.visit peakdistrict.com; Ryknell Sq; ⏰ 9.30am-5pm Mon-Fri) Directly opposite St Mary & All Saints Church.

ℹ Getting There & Away

BUS
From Chesterfield coach station on Beetwell St, buses 170 and X70 serve Bakewell (£3.60, 45 minutes, hourly Monday to Saturday).

TRAIN
Chesterfield lies on the main rail line between Nottingham (£11.70, 35 minutes, up to three hourly) and Derby (£12.70, 20 minutes, up to three hourly), which continues to Sheffield (£4.60, 20 minutes). The station is just east of the centre.

PEAK DISTRICT

Rolling across the Pennines' southernmost hills is the glorious Peak District National Park. Ancient stone villages are folded into creases in the landscape, and the hillsides are littered with stately homes and rocky outcrops. The Dark Peak is dominated by exposed moorland and gritstone 'edges', while to the south, the White Peak is made up of the limestone dales.

No one knows how the Peak District got its name – certainly not from the landscape, which has hills and valleys, gorges and lakes, wild moorland and gritstone escarpments,

Peak District National Park

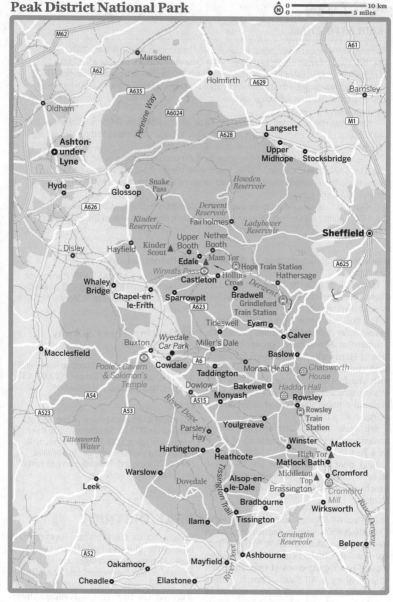

but no peaks. The most popular theory is that the region was named for the Pecsaetan, the Anglo-Saxon tribe who once populated this part of England.

Founded in 1951, the Peak District was England's first national park and is Europe's busiest. But even at peak times, there are 555 sq miles of open English countryside in which to find solitude.

🏃 Activities

Walking

The Peak District is one of the most popular walking areas in England, with numerous awe-inspiring vistas of hills, dales and sky that attract legions of hikers in summer. The White Peak is perfect for leisurely strolls, which can start from pretty much anywhere. Be sure to close gates behind you as you go. When exploring the rugged territory of the Dark Peak, make sure your boots are waterproof and beware of slipping into rivulets and marshes.

The Peak's most famous walking trail is the Pennine Way, which runs north from Edale for 268 miles, finishing in the Scottish Borders. If you don't have three weeks to spare, you can reach the pretty town of Hebden Bridge in Yorkshire comfortably in three days.

The 46-mile Limestone Way winds through the Derbyshire countryside from Castleton to Rocester in Staffordshire, following footpaths, tracks and quiet lanes. Many people walk the 26-mile section between Castleton and Matlock in one long, tiring day, but two days is better. Tourist offices have a detailed leaflet.

Other popular routes include the High Peak Trail, the Tissington Trail and the Monsal Trail & Tunnels. Numerous short walks are available.

Cycling

Plunging dales and soaring scarps provide a perfect testing ground for cyclists, and local tourist offices are piled high with cycling maps and trail guides. For easy traffic-free riding, head for the 17-mile High Peak Trail, which follows the old railway line from Cromford, near Matlock Bath, to Dowlow near Buxton. The trail winds through beautiful hills and farmland to Parsley Hay, where the Tissington Trail, part of NCN Route 68, heads south for 13 miles to Ashbourne. Trails are off-road on dedicated cycle paths, suitable for road bikes.

Mirroring the Pennine Way, the Pennine Bridleway is another top spot to put your calves through their paces. Around 120 miles of trails have been created between Middleton Top and the South Pennines, and the route is suitable for horse riders, cyclists and walkers. You could also follow the Pennine Cycleway (NCN Route 68) from Derby to Buxton and beyond. Other popular routes include the Limestone Way, running south from Castleton to Staffordshire, and the Monsal Trail & Tunnels between Bakewell and Wyedale, near Buxton.

The Peak District National Park Authority (☑ 01629-816200; www.peakdistrict.

gov.uk) operates cycle-hire centres at Ashbourne (p455), Derwent Reservoirs (p464) and Parsley Hay (☑ 01298-84493; www.peakdistrict.gov.uk; Parsley Hay; per half/full day standard bike £14/17, electric bike £32/36; ☻ 10am-4.30pm mid-Feb–early Nov). You can hire a bike from one location and drop it off at another for no extra charge.

Caving & Climbing

The limestone sections of the Peak District are riddled with caves and caverns, including a series of 'showcaves' in Castleton, Buxton and Matlock Bath. The website www.peakdistrictcaving.info, run by the Derbyshire Caving Association, has comprehensive information. Peaks & Paddles (☑ 07896 912871; www.peaksandpaddles.org; canoeing & caving from £55, abseiling from £25; ☻ by reservation) runs caving trips, along with canoeing and abseiling expeditions.

England's top mountaineers train in this area, which offers rigorous technical climbing on a series of limestone gorges, exposed tors (crags) and gritstone 'edges' that extend south into the Staffordshire Moorlands. Gritstone climbing in the Peak District is predominantly on old-school trad routes, requiring a decent rack of friends, nuts and hexes. Bolted sport routes are found on several limestone crags in the Peak District, but many use ancient pieces of gear and most require additional protection. Contact the British Mountaineering Council (www.thebmc.co.uk) for advice and details of local resources.

ⓘ Getting There & Away

Buses run from regional centres such as Sheffield and Derby to destinations across the Peak District. Be aware that many services close down completely in winter. Bakewell and Matlock (not Matlock Bath) are the two main hubs – from these you can get anywhere in the Peak District. Timetables are available from all tourist offices as well as Traveline (p394). Trains run to Matlock Bath, Buxton, Edale and several other towns and villages.

Bakewell

☑ 01629 / POP 3950

The second-largest town in the Peak District, charming Bakewell is a great base for exploring the limestone dales of the White Peak. Filled with storybook stone buildings, the town is ringed by famous walking trails and stately homes, but it's probably best known for its famous Bakewell pudding, a pastry shell filled with jam and a custard-like mixture of eggs, butter, sugar and almonds, invented here in 1820.

◉ Sights

★ Chatsworth House   HISTORIC BUILDING

(☑01246-565300; www.chatsworth.org; house & gardens adult/child £23/12.50, gardens only £14/7.50, playground £7, park free; ⊙9.30am-5.30pm late May-early Sep, shorter hours mid-Mar–late May & early Sep-early Jan) Known as the 'Palace of the Peak', this vast edifice 3 miles northeast of Bakewell has been occupied by the earls and dukes of Devonshire for centuries. Inside, the lavish apartments and mural-painted staterooms are packed with priceless paintings and period furniture. The house sits in 25 sq miles of grounds and ornamental gardens, some landscaped by Lancelot 'Capability' Brown. Kids will love the farmyard adventure playground.

From Bakewell, take bus 218 (£2.70, 15 minutes, half-hourly).

The manor was founded in 1552 by the formidable Bess of Hardwick and her second husband, William Cavendish, who earned grace and favour by helping Henry VIII dissolve the English monasteries. Mary, Queen of Scots was imprisoned at Chatsworth on the orders of Elizabeth I in 1569.

Look out for the portraits of the current generation of Devonshires by Lucian Freud.

Also on the estate is one of the country's premier farm shops (p462) and an attached cafe.

Walkers can take footpaths through Chatsworth park via the mock-Venetian village of Edensor (en-sor), while cyclists can pedal via Pilsley.

Haddon Hall   HISTORIC BUILDING

(☑01629-812855; www.haddonhall.co.uk; Haddon Rd; adult/child £18.50/free; ⊙10.30am-5pm daily late Mar-Sep, Fri-Mon Oct, to 4pm daily Dec) With stone turrets, time-worn timbers and walled gardens, Haddon Hall, 2 miles southeast of Bakewell on the A6, looks exactly like a medieval manor house should. Founded in the 12th century, it was expanded and remodelled throughout medieval times but lay dormant from 1700 until its restoration in the 1920s. Take the High Peak bus from Bakewell (£2.50, 10 minutes, every two hours) or walk along the footpath through the fields, mostly on the east side of the river.

Spared from the more florid excesses of the Victorian period, Haddon Hall has been used as the location for numerous period blockbusters (such as 2005's *Pride and Prejudice* and 1998's *Elizabeth*).

Thornbridge Brewery   BREWERY

(☑01629-815994; www.thornbridgebrewery.com; Buxton Rd; tours £12.50; ⊙tours by reservation 3pm Wed, Thu & Fri, shop 9am-4.30pm Mon-Fri) Brews by this riverside brewery include bottled varieties (such as a fruity strawberry-blonde ale, I Love You Will You Marry Me), keg beers (Vienna-style lager Kill Your Darlings) and cask ales (including its hoppy Brother Rabbit). Tours lasting 1½ hours take you behind the scenes and include tastings in Thornbridge glasses, which you get to keep afterwards. Under-five-year-olds aren't permitted on tours. It's half a mile from the centre of Bakewell on the northwestern edge of town.

Old House Museum   MUSEUM

(☑01629-813642; www.oldhousemuseum.org.uk; Cunningham Pl; adult/child £5/2.50; ⊙10.30am-4pm Wed-Sat late Mar-early Nov) Bakewell's local-history museum occupies a time-worn stone house that was built as a tax collector's premises during Henry VIII's rule and was expanded in the Elizabethan era, before being split into tiny mill workers' cottages during the Industrial Revolution. Check out the Tudor toilet and the displays on wattle and daub, a traditional technique for building walls using woven twigs and cow dung.

🏃 Activities

The scenic Monsal Trail follows the path of a disused railway line from Combs Viaduct on the outskirts of Bakewell to Topley Pike in Wye Dale (3 miles east of Buxton), including a number of reopened old railway tunnels, covering 8.5 miles in all.

For a rewarding shorter walk, follow the Monsal Trail for 3 miles to the dramatic viewpoint at Monsal Head, where you can pause for refreshment at the Monsal Head Hotel (p462), which serves real ales and excellent Modern British cuisine. With more time, continue to Miller's Dale, where viaducts give a spectacular vista across the steep-sided valley. The tourist offices at Bakewell and Buxton have full details.

Other walking routes go to the stately homes of Haddon Hall and Chatsworth House.

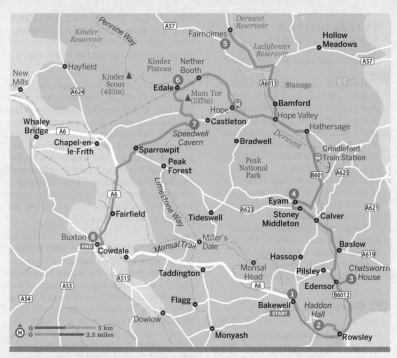

Driving Tour
Peak District

START BAKEWELL
END BUXTON
LENGTH 52 MILES; ONE TO TWO DAYS

Although you can drive this route in just a few hours, there's a lot to see and even more to do, so pack your hiking boots and consider breaking your journey overnight.

Fuel up at pretty ① **Bakewell** (p459), famed for its distinctive pudding. Head south on the A6 for 3.5 miles to Rowsley. Turn left on winding Church Lane for 2 miles to visit medieval manor ② **Haddon Hall**.

Return to Rowsley, turn left on the A6 and left on the B6012 – follow it for 2.9 miles before turning right to reach the 'Palace of the Peak', ③ **Chatsworth House**.

Back on the B6012, turn right to join the A619. At Baslow, home to the country hotel and Michelin-starred restaurant Fischer's Baslow Hall, turn left at the roundabout and travel along the A623 for 3.4 miles to the turn-off for ④ **Eyam** (p463). Drive up the hill to its quaint museum, where you can learn

about the town's plague history. There's fantastic walking here.

Continue up the hill. Turn right on Edge Rd, then right on Sir William Hill Rd and left on the B601 at Grindleford. Continue to Hathersage and turn left on the A6187 to Hope Valley. Turn right on the A6013, passing Ladybower Reservoir, to reach the ⑤ **Derwent Dam Museum** (p464). Learn about the Dambusters squadron's 'bouncing bombs' tests during WWII.

It's 5.8 miles back to the Hope Valley turn-off. Turn right onto Hathersage Rd, then right on Edale Rd. Follow the valley to stretch your legs at prime walking spot ⑥ **Edale** (p464). Scenery peaks as you climb the steep hill near 517m-high Mam Tor to Winnats Rd. Follow the spectacular former coral-reef canyon Winnats Pass to ⑦ **Speedwell Cavern** (p466), half a mile west of charming Castleton.

From Speedwell Cavern, head west along Arthurs Way onto Winnats Rd. Turning right on the A623 brings you to the riot of Victoriana in former spa town ⑧ **Buxton** (p466).

ℹ PEAK DISTRICT TRANSPORT PASSES

Handy bus passes cover travel in the Peak District.

The Peaks Plus ticket (adult/child £7.50/5) offers all-day travel on High Peak buses, including the Transpeak between Ashbourne, Matlock Bath and Buxton. The Peaks Plus Xtra ticket (£12.50/8) includes all transport on Transpeak and TM buses between Derby, Sheffield and Buxton.

The Derbyshire Wayfarer ticket (adult/child £13.40/6.70) covers buses and trains throughout the county and as far afield as Sheffield.

The Greater Manchester Wayfarer ticket (adult/child £14.40/7.20) covers trains and buses in the Peak District, along with Greater Manchester and parts of Cheshire and Staffordshire.

🛏 Sleeping & Eating

Rutland Arms Hotel   HOTEL £££
(📞01629-812812; www.rutlandarmsbakewell.co.uk; The Square; d incl breakfast from £168; 🅿🐕📶😺) Jane Austen is said to have stayed in room 2 of this aristocratic, 1804-built stone coaching inn while working on *Pride and Prejudice*. Its 33 rooms are in the main house and adjacent courtyard building; higher-priced rooms have lots of Victorian flourishes. Upmarket British classics (£14 to £23) such as pheasant and parsnip pie are served at its restaurant.

★Chatsworth Estate
Farm Shop Cafe   CAFE, DELI £
(www.chatsworth.org; Pilsley; dishes £6.50-15.50; ⊙cafe 9am-5pm Mon-Sat, 10am-5pm Sun, shop 9am-6pm Mon-Sat, 11am-5pm Sun; 🐕) 🍴 One of the finest places to eat in the Peak District, this bucolic cafe serves hearty breakfasts (eggs Benedict with Chatsworth-cured bacon or salmon, strawberry-and-honey Chatsworth yoghurt with muesli) until 11.30am, segueing to lunches (steak-and-kidney suet pudding, traditional roasts) until 3pm, and an afternoon menu. Over half the products at its adjacent farm shop are produced on the estate.

Old Original
Bakewell Pudding Shop   BAKERY, CAFE £
(www.bakewellpuddingshop.co.uk; The Square; dishes £8-13; ⊙9am-5pm) One of those that claims to have invented the Bakewell Pudding, this place has a lovely 1st-floor tearoom with exposed beams. It serves light meals and afternoon teas on tiered trays.

Monsal Head Hotel   BRITISH ££
(📞01629-640250; www.monsalhead.com; Monsal Trail; mains £10.50-20; ⊙kitchen noon-9pm, bar 11am-11pm; 🅿📶😺) At the dramatic viewpoint of Monsal Head, its namesake hotel serves real ales and brilliant British cuisine, such as Cheshire cheese and horseradish soufflé, braised Derbyshire beef with smoked-garlic mash, and blackberry crumble with spiced vanilla custard and crystallised stinging-nettle leaves. Book ahead to stay in its seven simple but comfortable rooms (doubles including breakfast from £130).

Piedaniel's   FRENCH ££
(📞01629-812687; www.piedaniels-restaurant.com; Bath St; mains £14-28; ⊙noon-2pm & 7-9pm Tue-Sat) Chefs Eric and Christiana Piedaniel's Modern French cuisine is the toast of the in-town restaurants. A whitewashed dining room is the exquisite setting for the likes of Normandy onion soup with cider and Gruyère cheese, followed by pork roulade with braised red cabbage and grain-mustard sauce, and flaming crêpes Suzette.

★Fischer's Baslow Hall   GASTRONOMY £££
(📞01246-583259;   www.fischers-baslowhall. co.uk; 259 Calver Rd, Baslow; 2-/3-course lunch menus £38/46.50, 3-course/tasting dinner menus £79.50/90; ⊙noon-1.30pm & 7-9pm; 📶🐕) This 1907-built manor house, 4 miles northeast of Bakewell, has a magnificent dining room showcasing British produce (Derbyshire lamb, Yorkshire game, Cornish crab...) along with vegetables from its kitchen garden. Six sumptuous floral bedrooms are in the main house, with another five in the adjacent garden house (doubles including breakfast from £287, including a three-course dinner menu from £444).

🛍 Shopping

Lambton Larder   FOOD & DRINKS
(www.thelambtonlarder.com; Rutland Sq; ⊙9am-2pm Mon-Thu, to 4pm Fri & Sat) Peak District–roasted Full Moon coffee, Matlock Bath honey, Bakewell puddings, and locally cured meats, chutneys, jams and pies fill the shelves of this enticing deli, along with over 50 British cheeses, including artisan varieties made nearby at the Hope Valley's Cow Close Farm. You can also pick up sandwiches,

wraps and soups for a riverside picnic (hampers available too).

Bakewell Market
MARKET

(Granby Rd; ⊙9am-2.30pm Mon) Local producers including Hope Valley Ice Cream, Peak Ales, Bittersweet Chocolates, Brock & Morten (cold-pressed oils) and Caudwell Mill (flour) are among the 160-plus regular stalls at Bakewell's lively Monday market.

ℹ Information

Tourist Office (☑01629-816558; www.visit-peakdistrict.com; Bridge St; ⊙10.30am-4pm) In the old Market Hall, with a photography gallery on the mezzanine.

ℹ Getting There & Away

Bakewell lies on the High Peak bus route. Buses run every two hours to Buxton (£5.10, 30 minutes), Derby (£6.60, 1¼ hours) and Matlock Bath (£3.50, 35 minutes). One service a day continues to Manchester (£8, 1¾ hours).

Other services:

Castleton Bus 173; £3.40, 50 minutes, four per day Monday to Saturday, via Tideswell (£3.10, 30 minutes)

Chesterfield Buses 170 and X70; £3.60, 45 minutes, hourly Monday to Saturday

Eyam

☑01433 / POP 969

Quaint little Eyam (ee-em), a former lead-mining village, has a poignant history that's all the more resonant in light of the global Covid-19 pandemic. In 1665 the town was infected by the dreaded Black Death plague, carried here by fleas on a consignment of cloth from London, and the village rector, William Mompesson, convinced villagers to quarantine themselves. Some 270 of Eyam's 800 inhabitants succumbed, while surrounding villages remained relatively unscathed. The village's heartbreaking yet uplifting story is beautifully told in the 2001 novel *Year of Wonders: A Novel of the Plague* by Geraldine Brooks.

Today, Eyam's sloping streets of old cottages backed by rows of green hills are delightful to wander.

◉ Sights

Eyam Parish Church
CHURCH

(St Lawrence's Church; www.eyamchurch.org; Church St; by donation; ⊙9am-6pm Easter-Sep, to

4pm Oct-Easter) Many victims of the village's 1665 Black Death plague outbreak were buried at Eyam's church, whose history dates back to Saxon times. You can view stained-glass panels and moving displays telling the story of the outbreak. The churchyard contains a cross carved in the 8th century.

Eyam Museum
MUSEUM

(☑01433-631371; www.eyam-museum.org.uk; Hawkhill Rd; adult/child £3/2.50; ⊙10am-4pm Tue-Sun Easter-Oct) Vivid displays on the Eyam plague are the centrepiece of the engaging town museum, alongside exhibits on the village's history of lead mining and silk weaving.

Eyam Hall
HISTORIC BUILDING

(☑01433-630080; www.eyamhall.net; Main Rd; craft centre free, house & garden adult/child £12/6; ⊙craft centre 10am-4.30pm Wed-Sun year-round, house & garden 11am-3pm Wed, Thu & Sun mid-Feb–late Apr) Surrounded by a traditional English walled garden, this solid-looking 17th-century manor house with stone windows and door frames has a craft centre, a bookshop, a craft-beer shop and a superb bistro (mains £12.50 to £18) in its grounds.

🛏 Sleeping & Eating

Miner's Arms
PUB ££

(☑01433-630853; www.theminersarmseyam.co.uk; Water Lane; s/d from £45/70; 🖧) Although

---

THE CATHEDRAL OF THE PEAK

Dominating the former lead-mining village of Tideswell, the massive parish church of St John the Baptist – aka the **Cathedral of the Peak** (☑01298-871317; www.tideswellchurch.org; Commercial Rd, Tideswell; ⊙8.30am-5.30pm) – has stood here virtually unchanged since the 14th century. Look out for the wooden panels inscribed with the Ten Commandments and the grand 14th-century tomb of local landowner Thurston de Bower, depicted in full medieval armour. It's 8 miles east of Buxton, linked by bus 65 (£4.10, 30 minutes, every two hours Monday to Saturday).

Bus 173 links Tideswell with Bakewell (£3.10, 20 minutes, seven per day Monday to Saturday). Four services a day Monday to Saturday continue from Tideswell to Castleton (£3, 20 minutes).

its age isn't immediately obvious, this traditional village inn was built shortly before the Black Death hit Eyam in 1665. Inside you'll find beamed ceilings, affable staff, a blazing open fire, comfy en-suite rooms and good-value pub food (mains £11 to £15.50).

Village Green CAFE £
(📞 01433-631293; www.cafevillagegreen.com; The Square; dishes £3-8; ⊙ 9am-4pm Thu-Mon; 🛜) On the village square, with tables on the cobblestones outside, this sweet cafe has homemade soups, a mouthwatering array of cakes and slices (some gluten-free), and decent coffee.

ℹ Getting There & Away

Bus services include the following.
Bakewell Bus 275; £3.90, 25 minutes, five per day Monday to Saturday
Buxton Bus 65; £4.70, 40 minutes, every two hours Monday to Saturday, three Sunday
Sheffield Bus 65; £6.10, one hour, every two hours Monday to Saturday, three Sunday

Derwent Reservoirs

North of the Hope Valley, the upper reaches of the Derwent Valley were flooded between 1916 and 1935 to create three huge reservoirs – the Ladybower, Derwent and Howden Reservoirs – to supply Sheffield, Leicester, Nottingham and Derby with water. These constructed lakes soon proved their worth – the Dambusters (Royal Air Force Squadron No 617) carried out practice runs over Derwent Reservoir before unleashing their 'bouncing bombs' on the Ruhr Valley in Germany in WWII.

These days, the reservoirs are popular destinations for walkers, cyclists and mountain bikers – and lots of ducks, so drive slowly!

⊙ Sights & Activities

Derwent Dam Museum MUSEUM
(📞 01433-650953; www.dambusters.org.uk; Fairholmes; ⊙ 10am-4.30pm Mon-Fri, 9.30am-5.30pm Sat & Sun Apr-Oct, shorter hours Nov-Mar) FREE The exploits of the Royal Air Force Squadron No 617, aka the Dambusters, are the focus of the Derwent Dam Museum in the lower car park just south of the dam where they tested their 'bouncing bombs'. The relocated museum, adjacent to the tourist office, is due to open sometime in 2021.

Derwent Cycle Hire Centre CYCLING
(📞 01433-651261; www.peakdistrict.gov.uk; Fairholmes; per half/full day standard bike £14/17, electric bike £32/36; ⊙ 9.30am-4.30pm early Feb–early Nov) Fairholmes' cycle-hire centre rents wheels including mountain bikes, kids' bikes and electric bikes.

ℹ Information

Tourist Office (📞 01433-650953; www.visit peakdistrict.com; Fairholmes; ⊙ 10am-4.30pm Mon-Fri, 9.30am-5.30pm Sat & Sun Apr-Oct, shorter hours Nov-Mar) Provides walking and cycling advice.

Edale

📞 01433 / POP 353

Surrounded by majestic Peak District countryside, this cluster of stone houses centred on a pretty parish church is an enchanting place to pass the time. Edale lies between the White and Dark Peak areas, and is the southern terminus of the Pennine Way. Despite the remote location, the Manchester–Sheffield train line passes through the village, bringing throngs of weekend visitors.

🛏 Sleeping & Eating

Fieldhead Campsite CAMPSITE £
(📞 01433-670386; www.fieldhead-campsite.co.uk; Fieldhead; site per person/car £7/3.50; ⊙ Feb-Dec; 🅿🛜) Next to the Moorland Tourist Office, this pretty and well-equipped campsite spreads over six fields, with some pitches right by the river. Showers cost 20p. No campervans are allowed; fires and barbecues are not permitted.

Edale YHA HOSTEL £
(📞 0845 371 9514; www.yha.org.uk; Rowland Cote, Nether Booth; dm/d/f from £16/68/102; 🅿🛜) Spectacular views across to Back Tor unfold from this country-house hostel 1.5 miles east of Edale, signposted from the Hope road. All 157 beds are bunks; wi-fi in public areas only. Check availability ahead as it's often busy with school groups.

Stonecroft B&B ££
(📞 01433-670262; www.stonecroftguesthouse. co.uk; Grindsbrook; s/d from £65/110; 🅿🛜) 🍴 This handsomely fitted-out 1900s stone house has three comfortable guest rooms (two doubles, one single). Host Julia's organic breakfasts are gluten-free, with vegetarian and vegan options; packed lunches (£7.50) and Friday- and Saturday-evening meals

(£35) available by request when booking. Bike rental costs £25 per half-day. Pick-up from the train station can be arranged. Kids aren't permitted.

Newfold Farm Cafe CAFE **£**

(🖉 01433-670401; www.facebook.com/newfold farmcafe; Grindsbrook; dishes £2-9.50; ⊗ 8am-5pm daily Apr-Sep, Sat & Sun only Oct-Mar; 🖼) Fuel up on soups, jacket potatoes and pizzas, and choose from a tempting selection of cakes (gluten-free and vegan options available) at this cheerful cafe close to the village school.

Rambler Inn PUB FOOD **££**

(🖉 01433-670268; www.theramblerinn.co.uk; Grindsbrook; mains £9-14; ⊗ kitchen noon-9pm Mon-Sat, to 8pm Sun, bar to 11pm daily; 🖼🖉🖼) Opposite the train station, this stone pub warmed by open fires serves real ales and pub standards, such as stews and sausages and mash, plus veggie options like spiced lentil and coconut soup. There's a kids' menu, nine basic B&B rooms (double/triple from £100/120) and occasional live music.

❶ Information

Moorland Tourist Office (🖉 01433-670207; www.peakdistrict.gov.uk; Fieldhead; ⊗ 9.30am-5pm Apr-Sep, reduced hours Oct-Dec & Feb-Mar) Topped by a sedum-turf 'living roof', with a waterfall splashing across its glass panels, this eco-conscious visitor centre has maps, displays on the moors and an adjacent campsite.

❶ Getting There & Away

Trains run from Edale to Manchester (£12.20, 45 minutes, hourly) and Sheffield (£7.80, 40 minutes, hourly).

Castleton

🖉 01433 / POP 742

Guarding the entrance to the forbidding Winnats Pass gorge, charming Castleton is a magnet for Midlands visitors on summer weekends – come midweek if you want to enjoy the sights in relative peace and quiet. Castleton village's streets are lined with leaning stone houses, with walking trails criss-crossing the surrounding hills. The atmospheric ruins of Peveril Castle crown the ridge above, while the bedrock below is riddled with fascinating caves.

⊙ Sights & Activities

Situated at the base of 517m-high Mam Tor, Castleton is the northern terminus of the Limestone Way, which follows narrow, rocky Cave Dale, far below the east wall of the castle. The tourist office (p466) has maps and leaflets, including details of numerous easier walks.

Peveril Castle CASTLE, RUINS

(EH; 🖉 01433-620613; www.english-heritage.org. uk; adult/child £7.60/4.60; ⊗ 10am-5pm Wed-Sun Easter-Oct, to 4pm Sat & Sun Nov-Easter) Topping the ridge to the south of Castleton, a 350m walk from the town centre, this evocative castle has been so ravaged by the centuries that it almost looks like a crag itself. Constructed by William Peveril, William the Conqueror's son, the castle was used as a hunting lodge by Henry II, King John and Henry III, and the crumbling ruins offer swooping views over the Hope Valley. Before heading up here, check ahead to avoid closures for maintenance.

Castleton Museum MUSEUM

(🖉 01629-816572; www.peakdistrict.gov.uk; Buxton Rd; ⊗ 9.30am-5pm Apr-Sep, 10am-5pm Mon-Fri, 9.30am-5pm Sat & Sun Oct-Mar) FREE Attached to the tourist office (p466), the cute town museum has displays on everything from mining and geology to rock climbing, hang-gliding and the curious Garland Festival (p466).

Treak Cliff Cavern CAVE

(🖉 01433-620571; www.bluejohnstone.com; Buxton Rd; adult/child £12.50/6; ⊗ 9am-4.30pm Mar-Oct, to 3.30pm Nov-Feb) Captivating Treak Cliff has a forest of stalactites and exposed seams of colourful Blue John Stone, which is still mined to supply the jewellery trade. Audio tours (downloadable from the website) focus on the history of mining – prebook a timeslot online. Check too for details of workshops where you can polish your own Blue John Stone. It's just under a mile west of Castleton's village centre.

Blue John Cavern CAVE

(🖉 01433-620638; www.bluejohn-cavern.co.uk; Old Mam Tor Rd; adult/child £14/7; ⊗ 9.30am-4pm Mon-Fri, to 5pm Sat & Sun Apr-Oct, to dusk Nov-Mar) Up the southeastern side of Mam Tor, 2 miles west of Castleton, Blue John is a maze of natural caverns with rich seams of Blue John Stone that are still mined every winter. Access is via a one-hour guided tour that departs every 20 minutes, and involves a climb of 245 steps. A walking trail leads here from Winnats Pass, just west of Castleton; the tourist office has maps.

Speedwell Cavern
CAVE

(📞 01433-623018; www.speedwellcavern.co.uk; Winnats Pass; tour £17; ⏰ 10am-5pm daily Apr-Oct, Sat & Sun Nov-Mar) Just over half a mile west of Castleton at the mouth of Winnats Pass, this claustrophobe's nightmare is reached by descending 106 steps for an eerie boat ride through flooded tunnels, emerging by a huge subterranean lake called the Bottomless Pit. Tours last 45 minutes; tickets must be pre-purchased online. New chambers are discovered here all the time by potholing expeditions.

Peak Cavern
CAVE

(📞 01433-620285; www.peakcavern.co.uk; Peak Cavern Rd; adult/child £15/8; ⏰ 10am-5pm daily Apr-Oct, Sat & Sun Nov-Mar) Castleton's most convenient cave is easily reached by a pretty 250m streamside walk south of the village centre. It has the largest natural cave entrance in England, known (not so prettily) as the Devil's Arse.

Dramatic limestone formations are lit with fibre-optic cables. Buy tickets ahead online.

★ Festivals & Events

Garland Festival
CULTURAL

(www.castleton-garland.com; ⏰ 29 May) Castleton celebrates Oak Apple Day on 29 May (28 May if the 29th is a Sunday) as it has for centuries, with the Garland King (buried under an enormous floral headdress) and Queen parading through the village on horseback.

🛏️ Sleeping & Eating

Ye Olde Nag's Head Hotel
PUB ££

(📞 01433-620248; www.yeoldenagshead.co.uk; Cross St; d £65-95; 🛜🐾) The cosiest of the 'residential' pubs along the main road has nine comfortable, well-appointed rooms; top-category rooms have four-poster beds and spas. Ale tasting trays are available in its bar, which has regular live music and a popular restaurant serving pub classics (mains £9 to £19).

Three Roofs Cafe
CAFE £

(www.threeroofscafe.com; The Island; dishes £6-11; ⏰ 10am-4pm Mon-Fri, to 5pm Sat & Sun; 🛜) Castleton's most popular purveyor of cream teas also has filling sandwiches, pies, fish and chips, burgers and jacket potatoes. Opposite the turn-off to the tourist office.

★ Samuel Fox
BRITISH £££

(📞 01433-621562; www.samuelfox.co.uk; Stretfield Rd, Bradwell; 2-/3-/7-course menus £34/44/54; ⏰ 6-9pm Wed-Sat Feb-Dec; 🅿🛜) In the Hope Valley village of Bradwell, 2.5 miles southeast of Castleton, this enchanting inn owned by pedigreed chef James Duckett serves exceptional British cuisine: venison with pickled red cabbage; roast pheasant with braised sprouts, bacon and parsnips. Guests staying in its four pastel-shaded guest rooms upstairs (doubles including breakfast from £130) can dine on Monday and Tuesday evenings.

Vegetarian menus are available. Look out for dinner, bed and breakfast deals.

ℹ️ Information

Tourist Office (📞 01629-816572; www.visit peakdistrict.com; Buxton Rd; ⏰ 9.30am-5pm Apr-Sep, 10am-5pm Mon-Fri, 9.30am-5pm Sat & Sun Oct-Mar) In the Castleton Museum (p465).

ℹ️ Getting There & Away

BUS

Bus 173 serves Bakewell (£3.40, 50 minutes, four daily Monday to Saturday), via Hope (£2, five minutes), and in the opposite direction from Castleton, Tideswell (£3.30, 30 minutes).

Buses 271 and 272 run to Sheffield (£4.20, one hour, four per day Monday to Friday, three Saturday).

TRAIN

The nearest train station is at Hope, an easy 2-mile walk east of Castleton, on the line between Sheffield (£6.20, 30 minutes, hourly) and Manchester (£12.50, 55 minutes, hourly).

Buxton

📞 01298 / POP 22,115

The 'capital' of the Peak District National Park, albeit just outside the park boundary, Buxton is a confection of Georgian terraces, Victorian amusements and parks in the rolling hills of the Derbyshire dales. The town built its fortunes on its natural warm-water springs, which attracted health tourists in Buxton's turn-of-the-century heyday.

Today, visitors are drawn here by the flamboyant Regency architecture and the natural wonders of the surrounding countryside. Tuesdays and Saturdays are market days, bringing colour to the grey limestone marketplace.

Buxton

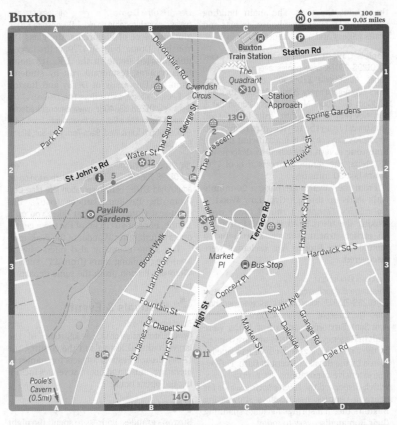

N 0 ————— 100 m
0 ————— 0.05 miles

Buxton

◎ Top Sights
1 Pavilion Gardens A2

◎ Sights
2 Buxton Crescent Heritage
   Experience C2
3 Buxton Museum & Art Gallery..............C3
4 Devonshire Dome....................................B1

⦿ Activities, Courses & Tours
5 Buxton Tram...B2
Devonshire Spa ....(see 4)

⊟ Sleeping
6 Grosvenor House B2
7 Old Hall Hotel...B2
8 Roseleigh Hotel B4

⊗ Eating
9 Columbine Restaurant............................C3
10 La Capri's C1

◉ Drinking & Nightlife
11 Old Sun Inn B4

✪ Entertainment
12 Opera House B2

⊟ Shopping
13 Cavendish Arcade....................................C1
14 Scrivener's Books & Bookbinding........B4

◉ Sights & Activities

★ **Pavilion Gardens**   GARDENS
(www.paviliongardens.co.uk; St John's Rd; ⊙9am-
6pm Jul & Aug, shorter hours Sep-Jun) FREE Adjoining Buxton's opulent opera house are the
equally flamboyant Pavilion Gardens. These
9.3 hectares are dotted with domed pavilions; concerts take place in the bandstand

throughout the year. The main building contains a tropical greenhouse, an arts and crafts gallery and a nostalgic cafe.

Poole's Cavern   CAVE
(☑01298-26978; www.poolescavern.co.uk; Green Lane; adult/child £11/5.50; ☉10am-4.30pm, tours 10am-4pm every 20min Mar-Oct, 10.30am, 12.30pm & 2.30pm Mon-Fri, every 20min Sat & Sun Nov-Feb) A pleasant mile-long stroll southwest from the town centre brings you to Poole's Cavern. This magnificent natural limestone cavern is reached by descending 28 steps; the temperature is a cool 7°C. Tours last 50 minutes.

From the cavern's car park, a 20-minute walk leads up through Grin Low Wood to **Solomon's Temple**, a ruined tower overlooking the town. Built in 1896 to replace an earlier structure, it sits atop a burial mound where Bronze Age skeletons were discovered.

Buxton Crescent
Heritage Experience   MUSEUM
(☑01298-213577; www.buxtoncrescentexperience. com; The Crescent; ☉10am-4.30pm Mon-Sat, to 4pm Sun) Buxton's extravagant baths were built in Regency style in 1854 and are fronted by the **Crescent**, a grand, curving facade inspired by the Royal Crescent in Bath. Following extensive renovations, its **pump room**, which dispensed the town's spring water for nearly a century, has displays showcasing Buxton's thermal springs heritage spanning their Roman discovery to today.

Within the complex is a **five-star hotel** (double/suite from £155/195) and lavish **spa** including the original Victorian baths with naturally heated 28°C water.

The tourist office is located here.

Adjacent to the complex is **St Anne's Well**, where Buxton's restorative waters still flow freely; bring a bottle to fill up.

Buxton Museum
& Art Gallery   MUSEUM, GALLERY
(☑01629-533540; www.derbyshire.gov.uk/leisure/ buxton-museum/buxton-museum-and-art-gallery. aspx; Terrace Rd; ☉10am-5pm Tue-Sat year-round, plus noon-4pm Sun Easter-Sep) `FREE` In a handsome Victorian building, the town museum has records of fossils found in the Peak District, photographs, fine arts, bric-a-brac covering the town's social history and curiosities from Castleton's Victorian-era 'House of Wonders', including Harry Houdini's handcuffs.

Devonshire Dome   HISTORIC BUILDING
(www.devonshiredome.co.uk; 1 Devonshire Rd) A glorious piece of Victoriana, the glass Devonshire Dome, built in 1779, is the largest unsupported dome in the UK. It's home to a training restaurant run by students from the University of Derby and Buxton & Leek College, as well as the **Devonshire Spa** (☑01298-338408; www.devonshiredome. co.uk; 1 Devonshire Rd; spa treatments from £40; ☉10am-6pm Tue & Wed, 9am-7pm Thu-Sat, 10am-5pm Sun).

★ Buxton Tram   BUS
(☑01298-79648; www.discoverbuxton.co.uk; adult/child £8/5; ☉by reservation late Mar–Oct) From the Pavilion Gardens (p467), this eight-seat vintage milk float takes you on a 12mph, hour-or-so circuit of the town centre on its entertaining 'Wonder of the Peak' tour.

The same company also offers several hour-long walking tours (from £7), such as Victorian Buxton, from the same departure point.

☆ Festivals & Events

Buxton Festival   ARTS
(www.buxtonfestival.co.uk; ☉Jul) One of the largest cultural festivals in the country, the 17-day Buxton Festival attracts top names in literature, music and opera at venues including the opera house.

🛏 Sleeping

Buxton's grandest address to spend the night is the 2020-opened Buxton Crescent Hotel.

Old Hall Hotel   HISTORIC HOTEL **££**
(☑01298-22841; www.oldhallhotelbuxton.co.uk; The Square; s/d incl breakfast from £69/89; 🛜🐾) There's a tale to go with every creak of the floorboards at this history-soaked establishment, supposedly the oldest hotel in England. Among other esteemed residents, Mary, Queen of Scots stayed here from 1576 to 1578, albeit against her will. The rooms still retain their grandeur (some have four-poster beds), and there are several bars, lounges and dining options.

Roseleigh Hotel   B&B **££**
(☑01298-24904; www.roseleighhotel.co.uk; 19 Broad Walk; d from £94; P🛜) This gorgeous family-run B&B in a roomy old Victorian house has lovingly decorated rooms, many with fine views over the Pavilion Gardens. The owners are a welcoming couple, both seasoned travellers, with plenty of interesting

stories. There's a minimum three-night stay on summer weekends.

Grosvenor House
B&B **££**

(☑01298-72439; www.grosvenorbuxton.co.uk; 1 Broad Walk; s/d/f from £55/77/100; P🛇) Overlooking the Pavilion Gardens, the Grosvenor is an old-school Victorian guesthouse with a huge parlour overlooking the park. Its eight rooms (including one family room sleeping three people plus space for a cot) have antique furniture and patterned wallpaper and drapes. At peak times, there's a minimum two-night stay and singles aren't available.

✗ Eating & Drinking

La Capri's
MEDITERRANEAN **££**

(☑01298-71392; www.lacapris.co.uk; 7 The Quadrant; tapas £4-6, mains £9-16; ☺4-10.30pm Tue-Thu, noon-11pm Fri & Sat, to 10.30pm Sun; 🛇) Small tapas and *cicchetti* (Venetian small dishes), such as rosemary- and garlic-marinated prawns, grilled pork belly with balsamic fig glaze, and chorizo-stuffed mushrooms, are the speciality of this snazzy shop on the Quadrant (count on around three dishes per person). Larger mains include paella, pasta and stone-baked pizzas.

Columbine Restaurant
MODERN BRITISH **££**

(☑01298-78752; www.columbinerestaurant.co.uk; 7 Hall Bank; mains £14.50-24; ☺7-10pm Mon & Wed-Sat) ⊘ On the lane leading down beside the town hall, this understated restaurant is the top choice among discerning Buxtonites. The chef conjures up imaginative dishes primarily made from local produce, such as High Peak lamb with mint butter. Two of its three dining areas are in the atmospheric stone cellar. Bookings are recommended.

Old Sun Inn
PUB

(www.facebook.com/oldsuninnbuxton; 33 High St; ☺4-10pm Mon & Wed, noon-10pm Thu-Sun; 🛇) The cosiest of Buxton's pubs, this 17th-century coaching inn has a warren of rooms full of original features, proper cask ales and a lively crowd that spans the generations.

☆ Entertainment

Opera House
OPERA

(☑01298-72190; www.buxtonoperahouse.org.uk; Water St; tours £10; ☺tours by reservation) Designed by theatre architect Frank Matcham in 1903 and restored in 2001, Buxton's gorgeous opera house hosts a full program of drama, dance, concerts and comedy. Guided backstage tours lasting 90 minutes can be booked via the website. Its neighbouring **Pavilion Arts Centre** also hosts performances and has a 360-seat cinema.

🛍 Shopping

Scrivener's Books & Bookbinding
BOOKS

(☑01298-73100; www.scrivenersbooks.co.uk; 42 High St; ☺10am-4pm Tue-Sat, noon-4pm Sun) At this delightfully chaotic bookshop, sprawling over five floors, books are filed in piles and the Dewey system has yet to be discovered.

Cavendish Arcade
SHOPPING CENTRE

(www.cavendisharcade.co.uk; Cavendish Circus; ☺9am-6pm Mon-Sat, 10am-5pm Sun, individual shop hours vary) Covered by a barrel-vaulted, stained-glass canopy, Cavendish Arcade houses boutiques selling upmarket gifts.

Glass floor panels reveal the thermal baths (on the site of earlier Roman baths) that were once here.

ℹ Information

Tourist Office (☑01298-214577; www.visit peakdistrict.com; Pump House, The Crescent; ☺9.30am-4pm Apr-Oct, 10am-4pm Fri-Sun Nov-Mar; 🛇) At the Buxton Crescent Heritage Experience; can provide details of walks and activities in the area.

ℹ Getting There & Away

Buses stop on both sides of the road at Market Pl. A High Peak service runs to Derby (£6.60, 1¾ hours, every two hours), via Bakewell (£5.10, 30 minutes) and Matlock Bath (£6.60, one hour); five services daily continue to Manchester (£8, 1¼ hours). Buses also run to Ashbourne (£4.50, 1¼ hours, 10 daily Monday to Friday, eight Saturday).

Northern Rail has trains to/from Manchester (£12.50, one hour, hourly).

Flavours of England

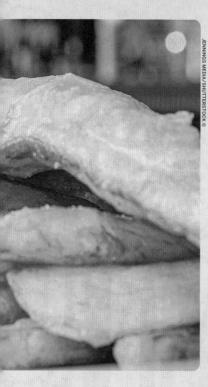

JENNINGS MEDIA/SHUTTERSTOCK ©

England shook off its reputation for bland food this century. Now it's possible to find good-quality meals that focus on locally sourced or seasonally grown ingredients anywhere in the country. There's still no English equivalent of *bon appetit*, but at least the term can be used genuinely these days – without a lashing of irony!

Breakfast

For many visitors to England, the culinary day begins in a hotel or B&B with the phenomenon known as the 'Full English' – a large plateful of mainly fried food that may be a shock if you usually have just a bowl of cereal. But perseverance is recommended, as there's enough fuel here to see you through hours of sightseeing.

Lunch & Dinner

For lunch or an evening meal, England has a good range of local and international options at any budget, but you should definitely sample two quintessentially English eateries: the cafe and the pub. In cities, cafes are a good cheaper option, while in country areas they're often called teashops – perfect for a traditional afternoon tea. Pubs are the obvious place to sample traditional English beer, as well as being a reliable option for good-value meals. The most food-focused establishments are now called 'gastropubs'.

Fish and chips **2.** Cornish pasty shop, St Ives (p329) Afternoon tea with cucumber sandwiches

ENGLISH CLASSICS

Fish & chips Long-standing favourite, best sampled in coastal towns.

Sandwich Global snack today, but an English 'invention' from the 18th century.

Ploughman's lunch Bread and cheese, a pub menu regular, perfect with a pint.

Roast beef & Yorkshire pudding Traditional English Sunday lunch.

Cumberland sausage Northern speciality, so big it's coiled to fit on your plate.

Cornish pasty Once restricted to the southwest, now available country-wide.

AT A GLANCE

POPULATION
5,288,200

HIGHEST LAKE
Malham Tarn
(377m; p508)

**BEST
MICROBREWERY**
Brass Castle (p487)

BEST FESTIVAL
Whitby Goth
Weekends (p499)

BEST MEAL
Cochon Aveugle
(p484)

WHEN TO GO
Apr–Jul Daffodils
bloom in Dales and
North York Moors;
Malton Food Lovers
Festival; Great
Yorkshire Show in
Harrogate.

Aug & Sep Perfect
hiking weather
in Dales; Walking
Festival in Richmond;
Harrogate Autumn
Flower Show.

Oct–Mar Goth
Weekends in Whitby;
week-long Jorvik
Viking Festival in
York.

York Minster (p477)
DAVID KORNSLAPA/SHUTTERSTOCK ©

Yorkshire

With a population as big as Scotland's and an area half the size of Belgium, Yorkshire – made up of four separate counties – is almost a country in itself. It has its own flag, dialect and celebration – Yorkshire Day. People have long been drawn here for walking and cycling, framed by some of Britain's finest scenery – brooding moors and green dales rolling down to a dramatic coast. Medieval York is the heart-throb, but there are countless other atmospheric towns and villages, abbey ruins, castles and gardens. But Yorkshire refuses to fade into the past – once-derelict urban areas are regenerating and modern Britishness is fusing with Yorkshire heritage.

Yorkshire Highlights

1 **York** (p477) Exploring the medieval streets of the city and its awe-inspiring cathedral.

2 **Yorkshire Dales National Park** (p501) Getting off the beaten track and exploring lesser-known corners, like Swaledale.

3 **Fountains Abbey** (p488) Wandering among the atmospheric medieval ruins.

4 **North Yorkshire Moors Railway** (p496) Riding on one of England's most scenic train lines.

5 **Whitby** (p496) Sitting on the pier and munching the world's best fish and chips.

6 **Castle Howard** (p485) Reliving the story of *Brideshead Revisited*.

7 **Malham Cove** (p504) Pulling on your hiking boots and tackling the steep paths around this scenic cove.

8 **Leeds** (p509) Getting stuck into Yorkshire's craft-beer scene, hopping around innovative brewery taprooms.

9 **Hull** (p522) Exploring maritime heritage and the regenerated marina area of Yorkshire's biggest east-coast town.

10 **Malton** (p486) Touring artisan food and drink producers in a revitalised Georgian market town.

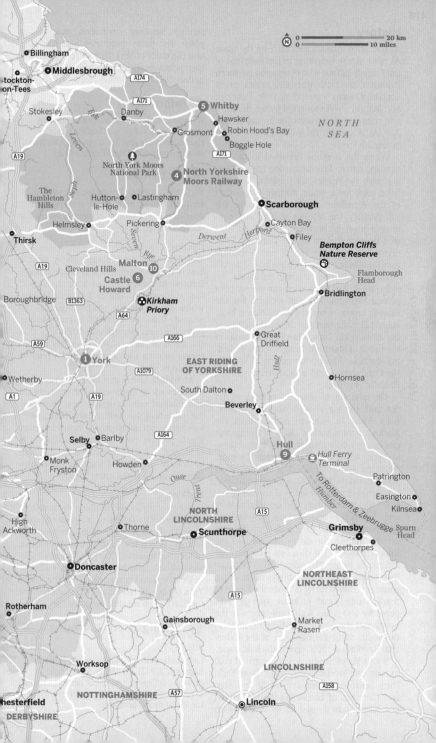

History

As you drive through Yorkshire on the main A1 road, you're following in the footsteps of the Roman legions who conquered northern Britain in the 1st century CE. In fact, many Yorkshire towns – including York, Catterick and Malton – were founded by the Romans, and many modern roads (including the A1, A59, A166 and A1079) follow the alignment of Roman roads.

When the Romans departed in the 5th century, native Britons battled for supremacy with the Angles, an invading Teutonic tribe, and, for a while, Yorkshire was part of the Kingdom of Northumbria. In the 9th century, the Vikings arrived and conquered most of northern Britain, an area that became known as the Danelaw. They divided the territory that is now Yorkshire into *thridings* (thirds), which met at Jorvik (York), their thriving commercial capital.

In 1066 Yorkshire was the scene of a pivotal showdown in the struggle for the English crown, when the Anglo-Saxon king, Harold II, rode north to defeat the forces of the Norwegian king, Harold Hardrada, in the Battle of Stamford Bridge, before returning south for his appointment with William the Conqueror – and a fatal arrow – in the Battle of Hastings.

The inhabitants of northern England did not take the subsequent Norman invasion lying down. In order to subdue them, the Norman nobles built a chain of formidable castles throughout Yorkshire, including those at York, Richmond, Scarborough, Skipton, Pickering and Helmsley. The Norman land grab formed the basis of the great estates that supported England's medieval aristocrats.

By the 15th century, the duchies of York and Lancaster had become so wealthy and powerful that they ended up battling for the English throne in the Wars of the Roses (1455–87). The dissolution of the monasteries by Henry VIII from 1536 to 1540 saw the wealth of the great abbeys of Rievaulx, Fountains and Whitby fall into the hands of noble families, and Yorkshire quietly prospered for 200 years, with fertile farms in the north and the Sheffield cutlery business in the south, until the big bang of the Industrial Revolution transformed the landscape.

South Yorkshire became a centre of coal mining and steel-making, while West Yorkshire nurtured a massive textile industry, and the cities of Leeds, Bradford, Sheffield and Rotherham flourished. By the late 20th century, another revolution was taking place. The heavy industries had died out, and the cities of Yorkshire were reinventing themselves as shiny, high-tech centres of finance, digital innovation and tourism.

ℹ Information

The Yorkshire Tourist Board (www.yorkshire.com) has plenty of general leaflets and brochures. For more specific information, try the excellent network of local tourist offices.

🏃 Activities

Yorkshire's varied landscape of wild hills, tranquil valleys, high moors and spectacular coastline offers plenty of opportunities for outdoor activities.

Cycling

Yorkshire is prime cycling country, with a vast network of cycle-friendly country lanes. Interest in cycling surged after the region hosted the start of the 2014 Tour de France, which also led to the establishment of the annual **Tour de Yorkshire** (www.letour.yorkshire.com) cycle race in 2015. Note that the national parks also attract lots of motorists so even minor roads can be busy at weekends.

Mountain bikers can avail themselves of the network of bridleways, former railways and disused mining tracks now converted for two-wheel use. **Dalby Forest** (Map p495; www.forestry.gov.uk/dalbyforest), near Pickering, sports purpose-built mountain-biking trails of all grades from green to black, and there are newly waymarked trails at the Sutton Bank National Park Centre (p493).

Walking

For shorter walks and rambles, the best area is the **Yorkshire Dales**, with a great selection of walks through scenic valleys or over wild hilltops, plus a few higher summits thrown in for good measure. The East Riding's **Yorkshire Wolds** hold hidden delights, while the quiet valleys and dramatic coast of the **North York Moors** are also home to some excellent trails. For longer walks, see p484.

ℹ Getting There & Around

BUS

Long-distance coaches operated by **National Express** (☑ 0871 781 8181; www.nationalexpress.com) serve most cities and large towns in Yorkshire from London, the south of England, the Midlands and Scotland.

Bus transport around Yorkshire is frequent and efficient, especially between major towns. Services are more sporadic in the national parks, but are still adequate for reaching most places if you're not in a rush, particularly in summer (June to September).

CAR

The major north–south road transport routes – the M1 and A1 motorways – run through the middle of Yorkshire, serving the key cities of Sheffield, Leeds and York. If you're arriving by sea from northern Europe, Hull in the East Riding district is the region's main port.

Traveline Yorkshire (☑ 0871 200 2233; www.traveline.info) Provides public-transport information for all of Yorkshire.

TRAIN

The main rail line between London and Edinburgh runs through Yorkshire, with at least 10 trains calling each day at York and Doncaster, where you can change trains for other Yorkshire destinations. There are also direct links to northern cities such as Manchester and Newcastle. For timetable information, contact **National Rail Enquiries** (☑ 03457 48 49 50; www.nationalrail.co.uk).

NORTH YORKSHIRE

History has been kind to the rolling hills of England's largest county. Unlike the rest of northern England, North Yorkshire was left untouched by the dirty paw of the Industrial Revolution, leaving it alone to do what it's being doing since the Middle Ages – living off the sheep's back.

Rather than closed-down factories, mills and mines, the manmade monuments dotting the landscape in these parts are of the stately variety – the great houses and wealthy abbeys that sit, ruined or restored, as a reminder that sheep's woolly wealth went a long way.

All the same, North Yorkshire's biggest attraction is an urban one. While the genteel spa town of Harrogate and the storied seaside resort of Whitby have many fans, nothing compares to the unparalleled splendour of medieval York, England's most-visited city outside London.

York

☑ 01904 / POP 153,717

No other city in northern England says 'medieval' quite like York – minus the smells, open slaughterhouses and ridiculously low life expectancy. Instead, what you get is an

ⓘ YORK PASS

If you plan on visiting a number of sights, the **YorkPass** (www.yorkpass.com) will save you some money. The one-day city pass (adult/child £48/30) gives you free access to city centre attractions including York Minster and Jorvik, while the multi-day York & Beyond pass (two/three/six days adult £65/80/130, child £35/40/70) also includes attractions throughout the North York Moors. You can buy it at the York Tourist Office (p487) or online.

enchanting spider's web of narrow streets and alleyways enclosed within a magnificent circuit of 13th-century walls. At its heart is the immense, awe-inspiring York Minster, one of the most beautiful Gothic cathedrals in the world. York's long history and rich heritage is woven into virtually every brick and beam, and the modern, tourist-oriented city – with its myriad museums, restaurants, cafes and traditional pubs – is a carefully maintained heir to that heritage.

Try to avoid the inevitable confusion by remembering that around these parts, *gate* means street and *bar* means gate.

⊙ Sights

★ **York Minster**   CATHEDRAL
(☑ 01904-557200; www.yorkminster.org; Deangate; adult/child £11.50/free; ⊙ 11am-4.30pm Mon-Thu, from 10am Fri & Sat, 12.30-2.30pm Sun) York Minster is the largest medieval cathedral in northern Europe, and one of the world's most beautiful Gothic buildings. Seat of the archbishop of York, primate of England, it is second in importance only to Canterbury, seat of the primate of *all* England – the separate titles were created to settle a debate over the true centre of the English Church. Note that the quire, east end and undercroft close in preparation for evening service around the time of last admission.

The first church on this site was a wooden chapel built for the baptism of King Edwin of Northumbria on Easter Day 627; its location is marked in the crypt. This was replaced with a stone church built on the site of a Roman basilica, parts of which can be seen in the foundations. The first Norman minster was built in the 11th century and, again, you can see surviving fragments in the foundations and crypt.

York

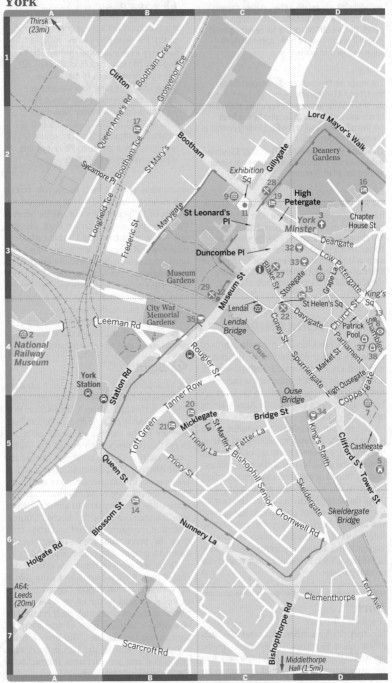

A
B
C
D

Thirsk (23mi)

Clifton

Bootham Cres

Grosvenor Tce

Queen Anne's Rd

Bootham Tce

17

St Mary's

Bootham

Lord Mayor's Walk

Gillygate

Deanery Gardens

16

Sycamore Pl

Longfield Tce

Frederic St

Marygate

Exhibition Sq

28

9

19

High Petergate

11

St Leonard's Pl

York Minster

3

Chapter House St

Deangate

Museum Gardens

Duncombe Pl

32

Low Petergate

33

4

Grape La

King's Sq

29

12

Museum St

Blake St

27

Stonegate

15

St Helen's Sq

Church St

13

8

Shambles

City War Memorial Gardens

Lendal

Coney St

22

Davygate

Patrick Pool

37

35

Lendal Bridge

Ouse

Spurriergate

Market St

Parliament

38

National Railway Museum

2

Leeman Rd

Rougier St

Ouse Bridge

High Ousegate

Coppergate

7

York Station

Station Rd

Tanner Row

20

Micklegate

St Martin's La

Fetter La

Bridge St

34

King's Staith

Castlegate

5

Clifford St

Tower St

21

Trinity La

Bishophill Senior

Skeldergate

Skeldergate Bridge

14

Queen St

Priory St

Cromwell Rd

Blossom St

Nunnery La

Holgate Rd

A64; Leeds (20mi)

Scarcroft Rd

Bishopthorpe Rd

Clementhorpe

Terry Ave

Middlethorpe Hall (1.5mi)

A
B
C
D

1
2
3
4
5
6
7

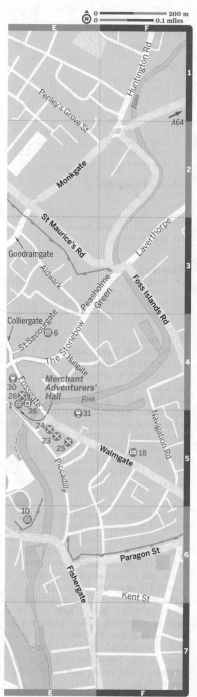

The present minster, built mainly between 1220 and 1480, manages to encompass all the major stages of Gothic architectural development. The transepts (1220–55) were built in Early English style; the octagonal chapter house (1260–90) and nave (1291–1340) in the Decorated style; and the west towers, west front and central (or lantern) tower (1470–72) in Perpendicular style.

Closed for the duration of the pandemic emergency are the massive tower – reached via a fairly claustrophobic climb of 275 steps – and the undercroft. When it reopens you can explore its excellent interactive exhibition, York Minster Revealed.

The cathedral is open longer hours for worshippers.

★ **National Railway Museum**   MUSEUM
(www.railwaymuseum.org.uk; Leeman Rd; ⊙10am-5pm Wed-Sun; P 🚻) FREE York's National Railway Museum – the biggest in the world, with more than 100 locomotives – is well presented and crammed with fascinating stuff. It is laid out on a vast scale and housed in a series of giant railway sheds – allow at least two hours to do it justice. The museum also now includes a high-tech simulator experience of riding on the Mallard (£3), which set the world speed record for a steam locomotive in 1938 (126mph). Pre-booking only.

Highlights for trainspotters include a replica of George Stephenson's Rocket (1829), the world's first 'modern' steam locomotive; a 1960s Japanese Shinkansen bullet train; and an exhibition dedicated to the world-famous Flying Scotsman, the first steam engine to break the 100mph barrier (now restored to full working order and touring the UK). There's also a massive 4-6-2 loco from 1949, which has been cut in half to demonstrate how it works (daily talk at 4pm).

Even if you're not a rail nerd, you'll enjoy looking through the gleaming, silk-lined carriages of the royal trains used by Queens Mary, Adelaide and Victoria, and King Edward VII.

The museum is about 400m west of the train station. A road train (adult/child £3/2) runs between the minster and museum every 30 minutes from 11am to 4pm, weather permitting.

★ **Merchant Adventurers' Hall**   HISTORIC BUILDING
(📞01904-654818; www.merchantshallyork.org; Fossgate; adult/child £6.50/free; ⊙10am-4.30pm

YORKSHIRE YORK

York

Sun-Fri, to 1.30pm Sat) York's most impressive semi-timbered building is still owned by the fraternity that built it almost 650 years ago and it is the oldest surviving guildhall of its kind in Britain. The owner was originally a religious fraternity and one of the hall's chambers is still a chapel, but the building's name refers to the pioneering business exploits that made the fraternity's fortunes while 'adventuring' their money in overseas markets at a time when York was an important international port.

Jorvik Viking Centre MUSEUM
(✉ticket reservations 01904-615505; www.jorvikvikingcentre.co.uk; Coppergate; adult/child £12.50/8.50, with Barley Hall £15/10, with Dig £15.75/12, 3-site ticket £18/12.50; ⊙10am-5pm Apr-Oct, to 4pm Nov-Mar) Interactive multimedia exhibits aimed at bringing history to life often achieve exactly the opposite, but the much-hyped Jorvik manages to pull it off with aplomb. It's a smells-and-all reconstruction of the Viking settlement unearthed here during excavations in the late 1970s, experienced via a 'time-car' monorail that transports you through 9th-century Jorvik (the Viking name for York). Book your timed-entry tickets online.

Barley Hall HISTORIC BUILDING
(✉01904-615505; www.barleyhall.co.uk; 2 Coffee Yard; adult/child £6.50/3.50, with Jorvik £15/10, with Dig £10/7.75, 3-site ticket £18/12.50; ⊙10am-5pm Apr-Oct, to 4pm Nov-Mar) This restored medieval townhouse, tucked down an alleyway, includes a permanent exhibition of life in the times of Henry VIII. It was once the home of York's Lord Mayor. The centrepiece is a double-height banquet hall decorated with the Yorkshire rose – peek at it through a window in the alleyway if you don't want to pay to enter.

Dig MUSEUM
(✉01904-615505; www.digyork.com; St Saviour's Church, St Saviourgate; adult/child £7/6.50, with Jorvik £15.50/12, with Barley Hall £10/7.75, 3-site ticket £18/12.50; ⊙10am-5pm, last admission 4pm; ♿) Under the same management as Jorvik and housed in an atmospheric old church, Dig gives you the chance to be an 'archaeological detective', unearthing the secrets of York's distant past as well as learning something of the archaeologist's world – what they do, how they do it and so on. Aimed mainly at kids, it's much more hands-on than Jorvik and a lot of its merit depends on how good – and entertaining – your guide is.

The Shambles
STREET

The Shambles takes its name from the Saxon word *shamel,* meaning 'slaughterhouse' – in 1862 there were 26 butcher shops on this street. Today the butchers are long gone, but this narrow cobbled lane, lined with 15th-century Tudor buildings that overhang so much they seem to meet above your head, is the most picturesque in Britain, and one of the most visited in Europe, often filled with visitors wielding cameras.

York Castle Museum
MUSEUM

(www.yorkcastlemuseum.org.uk; Tower St; adult/child £10/free; ⊗ guided tour only, 10am-4pm Thu-Sun) This excellent museum has displays of everyday life through the centuries, with reconstructed domestic interiors, a Victorian street and a prison cell where you can try out a condemned man's bed – and it could be that of highwayman Dick Turpin (imprisoned here before being hanged in 1739). For the time being all visits are by pre-booked guided tour only.

York Art Gallery
GALLERY

(☑01904-687687; www.yorkartgallery.org.uk; Exhibition Sq; adult/child £8/free; ⊗11am-4pm Wed-Sun; ♿) As well as an impressive collection of Old Masters, York Art Gallery possesses works by LS Lowry, Pablo Picasso, Grayson Perry, David Hockney, and the controversial York artist William Etty who, in the 1820s, was the first major British painter to specialise in nudes. A unique feature is the gallery's hands-on sculpture sessions (where you can handle the works), and its brilliant interactive ceramics centre (www.centreofceramicart.org.uk), housing more than 1000 pieces dating from Roman times to the present day.

Clifford's Tower
CASTLE

(EH; www.english-heritage.org.uk; Tower St; adult/child £5.90/3.50; ⊗10am-6pm Apr-Sep, to 5pm Oct, to 4pm Nov-Mar) There's precious little left of York Castle except for this evocative stone tower, a highly unusual four-lobed design built into the castle's keep after the original one was destroyed in 1190 during anti-Jewish riots. An angry mob forced 150 Jews to be locked inside the tower and the hapless victims took their own lives rather than be killed. There's not much to see inside, but the views over the city are excellent. Pre-booked tickets only.

Tours

Association of Voluntary Guides
WALKING

(www.avgyork.co.uk; ⊗tours 10.15am & 1.15pm year-round, 6.15pm Jun-Aug) **FREE** Two-hour city walking tours, setting out from Exhibition Sq in front of York Art Gallery.

★ Brewtown
BREWERY

(☑01904-636666; www.brewtowntours.co.uk; £70; ⊗11.30am-5pm) These craft-brewery minivan tours are a fuss-free way to get behind the scenes at Yorkshire's smaller breweries, some of which only open to the public for these tours. Owner Mark runs different routes (around York, Malton or Leeds) depending on the day of the week; each tour visits three breweries with tastings along the way, and sometimes even beer-pairing nibbles.

City Cruises York
BOATING

(www.citycruisesyork.com; Lendal Bridge; adult/child from £10.50/6; ⊗tours 10.30am, noon, 1.30pm & 3pm; ♿) These hour-long cruises on the River Ouse depart from King's Staith and, 10 minutes later, Lendal Bridge. Special lunch, afternoon-tea and evening cruises are also offered. You can buy tickets on board or book at the office by Lendal Bridge.

Ghost Hunt of York
WALKING

(☑01904-608700; www.ghosthunt.co.uk; adult/child £10/6.66; ⊗tours 6pm & 7.30pm) Kids will love this award-winning and highly entertaining 75-minute tour laced with authentic ghost stories. It begins on the Shambles, whatever the weather (it's never cancelled), and there's no need to book – just turn up and wait till you hear the handbell ringing...

Festivals & Events

Jorvik Viking Festival
CULTURAL

(www.jorvik-viking-festival.co.uk; ⊗mid-Feb) For a week in mid-February, York is invaded by Vikings as part of this festival, which features battle re-enactments, themed walks, markets and other bits of Viking-related fun.

York Food Festival
FOOD & DRINK

(www.yorkfoodfestival.com; ⊗late Sep) A 10-day celebration of all that's good to eat and drink in Yorkshire, with food stalls, tastings, a beer tent, cookery demonstrations and more. The main event is in late September, but there's a small taster festival in June and a chocolate festival on Easter weekend.

Cleveland Way (www.nationaltrail.co.uk/clevelandway) A venerable moor-and-coast classic that circles the North York Moors National Park on its 109-mile, nine-day route from Helmsley to Filey.

Coast to Coast Walk (www.wainwright.org.uk/coasttocoast.html) One of England's most popular walks: 190 miles across northern England from the Lake District through the Yorkshire Dales and North York Moors National Parks. The Yorkshire section takes a week to 10 days and offers some of the finest walking of its kind in England.

Dales Way (www.dalesway.org.uk) A charming and not-too-strenuous 80-mile amble from the Yorkshire Dales to the Lake District. It starts at Ilkley in West Yorkshire, follows the River Wharfe through the heart of the Dales and finishes at Bowness-on-Windermere.

Pennine Way (www.nationaltrail.co.uk/pennineway) The Yorkshire section of England's most famous walk runs for more than 100 miles via Hebden Bridge, Malham, Horton-in-Ribblesdale and Hawes, passing near Haworth and Skipton.

White Rose Way (www.nationaltrail.co.uk/yorkshirewoldsway) A beautiful but oft-overlooked 79-mile walk that winds through the most scenic part of Yorkshire's East Riding district. It starts at Hessle near the Humber Bridge and ends at the tip of Filey Brigg, a peninsula on the east coast just north of the town of Filey. Billed as 'Yorkshire's best-kept secret', it takes five days and is an excellent beginners' walk.

🛌 Sleeping

Safestay York
HOSTEL £

(📞01904-627720; www.safestay.com; 88-90 Micklegate, YO1 6JX; dm/tw/f from £14/65/80; @ 🛜) Housed in a Grade I Georgian town house, this is a large boutique hostel with contemporary, colourful decor and good facilities including a bar with pool table. Rooms are mostly en suite and have a bit more character than you'd usually find in hostels, with the added intrigue of plaques outside doors describing the history of different rooms in the house.

It's popular with school groups and stag and hen parties – don't come here looking for peace and quiet. Family rooms are strategically positioned right at the top of the house.

York YHA
HOSTEL £

(📞0345 371 9051; www.yha.org.uk; 42 Water End, Clifton; s/d/tr from £39/49/69; 🅿️🛜) Originally the Rowntree (Quaker confectioners) mansion, this handsome Victorian house makes a spacious and child-friendly youth hostel, with more than 250 beds, a broad garden and onsite restaurant. It's often busy, so book early. It's about a mile northwest of the city centre; there's a riverside footpath from Lendal Bridge (poorly lit, so avoid after dark).

Alternatively, take bus 2 from the train station or Museum St, though be aware it doesn't run in the evenings.

Fort
HOSTEL £

(📞01904-620222; www.thefortyork.co.uk; 1 Little Stonegate; dm/d from £10/50; 🛜) This boutique hostel showcases the interior design of young British talents, creating affordable accommodation with a dash of character and flair. There are six- and eight-bed dorms, along with five doubles, but don't expect a peaceful retreat – it's central and there's a lively club downstairs (earplugs are provided!). Towels are included, as well as free tea, coffee and laundry.

⭐ Lawrance
APARTMENT ££

(📞01904-239988; www.thelawrance.com/york; 74 Micklegate; 1-/2-bed apt from £90/190; ❄️🛜) Set back from the road in a huddle of old red-brick buildings that once formed a factory, the Lawrance is an excellent find: super-swish serviced apartments with all mod cons on the inside and heritage character on the outside. Some apartments are split-level and all are comfy and spacious, with leather sofas, flatscreen TV and luxurious fixtures and fittings.

Hotel Indigo
BOUTIQUE HOTEL ££

(📞01904-231333; www.hotelindigoyork.co.uk; 88-96 Walmgate; r from £60) One of the best midrange options in town is this hotel on Walmgate, which opened in 2019 and manages to be ignored by most visitors despite being inside the city walls and a short walk from the Shambles. The colourful rooms are well appointed and comfortable.

Lamb & Lion Inn
INN **££**

(☑ 01904-612078; www.lambandlioninnyork.com; 2-4 High Petergate; d from £70; 🛜) Occupying a perfect spot in the shadow of Bootham Bar, the Lamb & Lion is a quaint 1756 Georgian pub with 12 simple period rooms, an AA Rosette gastropub, and possibly York's best beer garden out back. Even if you don't stay, it's a good place for a drink around the old city walls.

Bar Convent
B&B **££**

(☑ 01904-643238; www.bar-convent.org.uk; 17 Blossom St; s/d from £60/100; 🛜) This mansion just outside Micklegate Bar is less than 10 minutes' walk from the train station. It houses England's oldest working convent, a cafe, meeting rooms and also offers good B&B accommodation. Open to visitors of all faiths and none. Charming bedrooms are modern and well-equipped, breakfasts are superb, and there's a garden and hidden chapel to enjoy.

Hedley House Hotel
HOTEL **££**

(☑ 01904-637404; www.hedleyhouse.com; 3 Bootham Tce; d/f from £75/100; 🅿🛜) 🐾 This large red-brick terrace-house hotel sports a variety of options including family-friendly rooms sleeping up to five and self-catering apartments. The designer lounge has the feel of a much bigger hotel, plus there's a yoga studio and Jacuzzi on the outdoor terrace at the back. It's five minutes' walk from the city centre through the Museum Gardens.

★ Grays Court
HISTORIC HOTEL **£££**

(☑ 01904-612613; www.grayscourtyork.com; Chapter House St; d £180-240, ste £265-300; 🅿🛜) This medieval mansion with just 11 rooms feels like a country-house hotel. It's set in lovely gardens with direct access to the city walls, and bedrooms combine antique furniture with modern comfort and design. The oldest part of the building was built in the 11th century, and King James I once dined in the Long Gallery.

✗ Eating

★ Mannion & Co
CAFE, BISTRO **£**

(☑ 01904-631030; www.mannionandco.co.uk; 1 Blake St; mains £7-14; ⊙10am-4pm Sun-Mon & Wed-Thu, 9am-4pm Fri-Sat) Expect to queue for a table at this busy bistro (no reservations), with its convivial atmosphere and selection of delicious daily specials. Regulars on the menu include eggs Benedict for breakfast, a chunky Yorkshire rarebit (cheese on toast) made with home-baked bread, and lunch platters of cheese and charcuterie. Oh, and pavlova for pudding.

Cave du Cochon
PIZZA **£**

(☑ 01904-633669; www.caveducochon.uk; 19 Walmgate; mains £7-10; ⊙5-10pm Wed-Fri, noon-10pm Sat-Sun) New York–style sourdough pizza is the mainstay at this elegant wine bar – the sister business to the Cochon Aveugle (p484). It also serves some locally sourced charcuterie (£22) and cheese (£15) from one of the UK's very best producers, the Courtyard Dairy near Settle.

★ Hairy Fig
CAFE **£**

(☑ 01904-677074; www.thehairyfig.co.uk; 39 Fossgate; mains £6-12; ⊙9am-4.30pm Mon-Sat) This cafe-deli is a standout in York. On the one side you have the best of Yorkshire tripping over the best of Europe, with Italian white anchovies and truffle-infused olive oil stacked alongside York honey mead and baked pies; on the other you have a Dickensian-style sweet shop and backroom cafe serving dishes crafted from the deli.

Star Inn the City
BRITISH **££**

(☑ 01904-619208; www.starinnthecity.co.uk; Lendal Engine House, Museum St; mains £16-25; ⊙9.30-11.30am, noon-9.30pm Mon-Sat, to 7.30pm Sun; 👶) Its riverside setting in a Grade II–listed engine house and quirky British menu make Andrew Pern's York outpost of the Star Inn (p495) an exceedingly pleasant place to while away the hours. Expect country-themed cosiness in winter, and dining out on the broad terrace in summer.

Chopping Block at Walmgate Ale House
BRITISH **££**

(www.thechoppingblock.co.uk; 25 Walmgate; mains £14-18; ⊙5-10pm Tue-Fri, noon-10pm Sat, to 9pm Sun; 🍴) This restaurant above a pub wears its Yorkshire credentials with pride. Local produce underpins the menu, which turns out mainly meat dishes (lamb shoulder, confit of duck leg, pork belly), given a French-flavoured gourmet twist, that are fine examples of contemporary British cuisine. Vegetarian options include tasty dishes like pea pancakes with spiced cauliflower.

No 8 Bistro
BISTRO **££**

(☑ 01904-653074; www.cafeno8.co.uk; 8 Gillygate; dinner mains £17; ⊙noon-10pm Mon-Fri,

9am-10pm Sat & Sun; 🛜 📶) 🥢 A cool little place with modern artwork mimicking the Edwardian stained glass at the front, No 8 offers a day-long menu of top-notch bistro dishes using fresh local produce, such as Jerusalem artichoke risotto with fresh herbs, and Yorkshire lamb slow-cooked in hay and lavender. Booking recommended.

Bettys   CAFE ££

(📞 01904-659142; www.bettys.co.uk; 6-8 St Helen's Sq; mains £6-14, afternoon tea £18.50; ⊙ 9am-7pm; 📶) Old-school afternoon tea, with white-aproned waiters, linen tablecloths and a teapot collection ranged along the walls. The house speciality is the Yorkshire Fat Rascal, a huge fruit scone smothered in melted butter, while breakfast and lunch dishes, like bacon and raclette rösti, and Yorkshire rarebit, show off Betty's Swiss-Yorkshire heritage. Book ahead, or be prepared to queue.

★ Cochon Aveugle   FRENCH £££

(📞 01904-640222; www.lecochonaveugle.uk; 37 Walmgate; 4-course lunch £75, 8-course tasting menu £95; ⊙ 6-9pm Wed-Sat, noon-1.30pm Sat) 🥢 Black-pudding macaroon? Salt-baked gurnard with lardo? Warm hen's yolk with smoked taramasalata? Fussy eaters beware – this small restaurant with huge ambition serves an ever-changing tasting menu (no à la carte) of infinite imagination and invention. You never know what will come next, except that it will be delicious. Bookings are essential. Its wine bar, Cave du Cochon (p483), is a few doors away.

🍷 Drinking & Nightlife

★ Blue Bell   PUB

(📞 01904-654904; 53 Fossgate; ⊙ 11am-11pm Mon-Thu, to midnight Fri & Sat, noon-10.30pm Sun; 🛜) This is what a proper English pub looks like – a tiny, 200-year-old wood-panelled room with a smouldering fireplace, decor untouched since 1903, a pile of ancient board games in the corner, friendly and efficient bar staff, and weekly cask-ale specials chalked on a board. Bliss, with froth on top – if you can get in (it's often full).

House of Trembling Madness   BAR

(📞 01904-640009; www.tremblingmadness.co.uk; 48 Stonegate; ⊙ 10am-midnight Mon-Sat, from 11am Sun) When a place describes itself as a 'medieval drinking hall', it clearly deserves investigation. The ground floor and basement host an impressive shop stacked with craft beers, gins, vodkas and even absinthes;

but head upstairs to the 1st floor and you'll find the secret drinking den – an ancient timber-framed room with high ceilings, a bar and happy drinkers.

Guy Fawkes Inn   PUB

(📞 01904-466674; www.guyfawkesinnyork.com; 25 High Petergate; ⊙ 11am-11pm Mon-Thu & Sun, to midnight Fri & Sat) The man who famously plotted to blow up the Houses of Parliament and inspired Bonfire Night in the UK was born on this site in 1570. Walk through the lovely Georgian wood-panelled pub to find Guy Fawkes' grandmother's cottage at the far end of the back patio, watched over by a giant wall mural.

Brew York   MICROBREWERY

(📞 01904-848448; www.brewyork.co.uk; Enterprise Complex, Walmgate; ⊙ noon-11pm Tue-Sat, to 9pm Sun) Housed in a cavernous old warehouse, half the floor space in this craft brewery is occupied by giant brewing tanks while the rest is given over to simple wooden drinking benches and a bar with rotating keg and cask beers. At the far end of the brewery there's a small riverside terrace overlooking Rowntree Wharf.

Perky Peacock   CAFE

(Lendal Bridge; ⊙ 7am-5pm Mon-Fri, 9am-5pm Sat, to 4pm Sun) One of York's charms is finding teeny places like this cafe, shoe-horned into historic buildings. In this case the host is a 14th-century, rotund watchtower crouched by the riverbank. Sup an excellent coffee under the ancient wood beams, or grab a street-side table for a tasty pastry.

King's Arms   PUB

(📞 01904-659435; King's Staith; ⊙ noon-11pm Mon-Sat, to 10.30pm Sun) York's best-known pub enjoys a fabulous riverside location, with tables spilling out onto the quayside. It's the perfect spot on a summer evening, but be prepared to share it with a few hundred other people.

🛍 Shopping

Fossgate Books   BOOKS

(📞 01904-641389; fossgatebooks@hotmail. co.uk; 36 Fossgate; ⊙ 10am-5.30pm Mon-Sat) A classic, old-school secondhand bookshop, with towers of books on the floor and a maze of floor-to-ceiling shelves crammed with titles covering every subject under the sun, from crime fiction and popular paperbacks to arcane academic tomes and 1st editions.

The Shop That Must Not Be Named
GIFTS & SOUVENIRS

(30 The Shambles; ⊙10am-6pm) This shop on the Shambles – the street said to be the inspiration for Diagon Alley – has everything to cast a spell over Harry Potter fans. Wands? Tick. Quidditch fan gear? Tick. Potions? Tick. Pure magic for muggles. There's now no less than three Potter shops on the Shambles, but this is the original and still the most convincing.

Shambles Market
FOOD

(www.shamblesmarket.com; The Shambles; ⊙9am-5pm) Yorkshire cheeses, Whitby fish and local meat make good fodder for self-caterers at this anything-goes market behind the Shambles, which also touts arts, crafts and Yorkshire flat caps. The food-court section near where the Shambles joins Pavement is a good spot for cheap eats, coffee and ice-cream at picnic tables.

ℹ️ Information

York Tourist Office (📞01904-550099; www.visityork.org; 1 Museum St, YO1 7DT; ⊙9am-5pm Mon-Sat, 10am-4pm Sun) Visitor and transport info for all of Yorkshire, plus accommodation bookings (for a small fee) and ticket sales.

ℹ️ Getting There & Away

BUS

York does not have a bus station; intercity buses stop outside the train station, while local and regional buses stop here and also on **Rougier St** (Rougier St), about 200m northeast of the train station.

For timetable info call **Traveline Yorkshire** (📞0871 200 2233; www.yorkshiretravel.net) or check the computerised 24-hour information points at the train station and Rougier St. There's a bus information point (8am to 4pm Monday to Saturday) in the train station's Travel Centre.
Birmingham £34, four hours, three daily
Edinburgh £28, 5½ hours, three daily
London from £30, 5½ hours, three daily
Newcastle £10, 2¼ hours, two daily

CAR

A car is more hindrance than help in the city centre, so use one of the six Park & Ride (www.itravelyork.info/park-and-ride) car parks at the edge of the city. If you want to explore the surrounding area, rental options include **Europcar** (📞0371 384 3458; www.europcar.co.uk; Queen St; ⊙8am-6pm Mon-Fri, to 4pm Sat), located next to the long-stay car park at the train station.

TRAIN

York is a major railway hub, with frequent direct services to many British cities.
Birmingham £74, 2¼ hours, two per hour
Edinburgh £59, 2½ hours, two to three per hour
Leeds £7.70, 25 minutes, at least every 15 minutes
London King's Cross £57.50, two hours, every 30 minutes
Manchester £30.40, 1½ hours, four per hour
Newcastle £22.50, one hour, four to five per hour
Scarborough £9.20, 50 minutes, hourly

ℹ️ Getting Around

Central York is easy to get around on foot – you're never more than 20 minutes' walk from any of the major sights.

BICYCLE

The tourist office has a useful free map showing York's cycle routes, or visit iTravel-York (www.itravelyork.info/cycling). Castle Howard (15 miles northeast of York via Haxby and Strensall) is an interesting destination, and there's also a section of the **Trans-Pennine Trail cycle path** (www.transpenninetrail.org.uk) from Bishopthorpe in York to Selby (15 miles) along the old railway line.

BUS

Local bus services are operated by First York (www.firstgroup.com/york). Single fares range from £1.60 to £4, and a day pass valid for all local buses is £4.50 (available on the bus or at Park & Ride car parks).

Castle Howard

Stately homes may be two a penny in England, but you'll have to try pretty damn hard to find one as breathtakingly stately as **Castle Howard** (📞01653-648333; www.castlehoward.co.uk; YO60 7DA; adult/child house & grounds £22/12, grounds only £12.95/8.50; ⊙house 10am-2pm Wed, Fri & Sat, grounds to 5.30pm daily, pre-booked tickets only; 🅿️), a work of theatrical grandeur and audacity set in the rolling Howardian Hills. This is one of the world's most beautiful buildings, instantly recognisable from its starring role as Sebastian Flyte's home in both screen versions of Evelyn Waugh's 1945 paean to the English aristocracy, *Brideshead Revisited*.

When the Earl of Carlisle hired his pal Sir John Vanbrugh to design his new home in 1699, he was hiring a man who had no formal training and was best known as a playwright. Luckily, Vanbrugh hired Nicholas Hawksmoor, who had worked as Christopher Wren's clerk of works on St Paul's Cathedral. Not only did Hawksmoor have a big part to play in the design, bestowing on the house a baroque cupola modelled after St Paul's – the first on a domestic building in England – but he and Vanbrugh would later work wonders with Blenheim Palace. Today the house is still home to the Hon Nicholas Howard and his family and he can often be seen around the place.

As you wander about the peacock-haunted grounds, views open up over Vanbrugh's playful Temple of the Four Winds, Hawksmoor's stately mausoleum and the distant hills. Inside, you'll find the house split into two distinct styles; the east wing, which includes the Great Hall, was built in the 1700s and is extravagantly baroque in style, whereas the west wing wasn't completed until the 1800s, by which time the fashion was for much more classical Palladian. The house is full of treasures – the breathtaking Great Hall with its soaring Corinthian pilasters, Pre-Raphaelite stained glass in the chapel, and corridors lined with classical antiquities.

The pandemic forced the estate to move to an exclusively online booking system so as to control the flow of visitors. The advantage of limited numbers is that you'll have plenty of space to appreciate this hedonistic marriage of art, architecture, landscaping and natural beauty, but the downside is that the talk and tours of the house and gardens were suspended for the duration of the crisis. There are also boat tours down at the lake, and the entrance courtyard has a good cafe, a gift shop and a farm shop filled with foodie delights from local producers – you could quite easily spend an entire day at the site.

Castle Howard is 15 miles northeast of York, off the A64. Bus 181 from York goes to Malton via Castle Howard (£11 return, one hour, four times daily Monday to Saturday year-round).

Malton

📞 01653 / POP 4888

It was the legendary late Italian chef Antonio Carluccio who first gave Malton the moniker of 'Yorkshire's food capital', and this sweet market town has worked hard to make the title stick. With good reason,

too – the food scene is fabulous for a town of its size, with overflowing delis championing produce from the moors, wolds and dales, pint-sized artisan food and drink businesses, food-focused tours and a monthly food market.

Although there are no specific sights to speak of, the town does have some lovely Georgian architecture and independent shops. And like York, Malton has a crooked Shambles, now crammed with vintage shops, where butchers would have once slaughtered the lambs brought in for the town's sheep markets.

The town also has connections to Charles Dickens, who regularly visited a friend here. He wrote *A Christmas Carol* here on one of his trips.

⭐ Festivals & Events

Malton Food Lovers Festival FOOD & DRINK
(www.visitmalton.com/food-festival-yorkshire; ⊙ end May) The biggest event on the calendar is Malton's annual three-day Food Lovers Festival with cooking demos, street food and music, attracting celebrity chefs and more than 30,000 visitors each May.

✕ Eating & Drinking

⭐**Talbot Yard** FOOD HALL **£**
(www.visitmalton.com/talbot-yard-food-court; Yorkersgate; dishes £4-7; ⊙ hours vary) Across the road from the Talbot Hotel, this huddle of converted stables has been reimagined as an extraordinary food court housing the stuff of gourmands' dreams. Here you'll find the only UK shop from award-winning macaron master Florian Poirot, and the home base of artisan Yorkshire bakery Blue Bird, among others. Come for gelato, posh pork pies, freshly ground coffee, Chelsea buns and macarons.

Talbot Yard is the main focus of the **Malton Artisan Food Tour**, but it's also easy to browse independently, and is perfect for picnic fodder.

La Pizzeria PIZZA **£**
(📞 01653-690768; www.fatchefcompany.co.uk; 51 Wheelgate; mains £7-10; ⊙ 11.30am-3pm & 5-9pm Tue-Fri, 11.30am-9pm Sat & Sun) Delicious wood-fired pizza in a modern, casual setting with blackboard specials and cocktails. A simple, winning concept and welcome change from pies, roasts and fish and chips.

Malton Relish DELI £

(✆01653-699389; www.maltonrelish.co.uk; 58 Market Pl; dishes £4-9; ⏰9am-5.30pm Mon-Sat, 10am-4pm Sun) This lovely deli overlooking Malton's market square is a good place to shop for local produce or sit down and taste it. The menu includes sandwiches, cheese boards and light lunches such as broccoli, pancetta and Yorkshire blue-cheese quiche with salad. Its monthly supper-club evening is worth looking into (book ahead), and there's a cute antiques store upstairs.

⭐**Brass Castle** MICROBREWERY

(✆01653-698683; www.brasscastle.co.uk; 10 Yorkersgate; ⏰noon-7pm Fri-Sun) This microbrewery began life in a garage in 2011 and surprised even itself when its beer won a prestigious CAMRA Beer Festival award within the first two months of production. Fast forward six years and it finally opened this taproom in central Malton. Its beers are unfiltered, vegan and gluten-free, and the taproom always has experimental brews on rotation.

ⓘ Getting There & Away

Malton is easily accessible by train from York (£11.70, 25 minutes, hourly), and the train station is less than a 10-minute walk south from Market Pl.

The town is also a stop on the Coastliner 840 bus route that runs from Leeds to Whitby via York and Pickering. Departures from/to Leeds and York are hourly; Whitby and Pickering buses are less frequent.

Harrogate

📞 01423 / POP 75,070

Queen Victoria's favourite spot for a spa break, prim and pretty Harrogate has long been associated with a certain kind of old-fashioned Englishness – the kind that seems the preserve of retired army majors and formidable dowagers who always vote Tory and get all their news from the *Daily Telegraph*. They come to Harrogate to enjoy the flower shows and gardens that fill the town with magnificent displays of colour, especially in spring and autumn. It is here that Agatha Christie fled to, incognito, in 1926 to escape her broken marriage.

And yet, this picture of Victoriana redux is not quite complete. While it's undoubtedly true that Harrogate remains a firm favourite of visitors in their golden years, the town has plenty of smart hotels and trendy dining spots catering to the boom in Harrogate's latest trade – conferences. All those dynamic young sales-and-marketing guns have to eat and sleep somewhere.

◉ Sights & Activities

Royal Pump Room Museum MUSEUM

(www.harrogate.gov.uk; Crown Pl; adult/child £3/1; ⏰10.30am-5pm Mon-Sat, 2-5pm Sun Apr-Oct, to 4pm Nov-Mar) You can learn all about Harrogate's history as a spa town in the ornate Royal Pump Room, built in 1842 over the most famous of the town's sulphurous springs. It gives an insight into how the phenomenon of visiting spas to 'take the waters' shaped the town, and records the illustrious visitors it attracted. Beside the stained-glass counter where tonics would have once been dispensed, you can sit down and watch old black-and-white film of patients taking treatments such as peat baths.

The ritual of visiting spa towns as a health cure became fashionable in the 19th century and peaked during the Edwardian era in the years before WWI.

Montpellier Quarter AREA

(www.montpellierharrogate.com) The most attractive part of town is the Montpellier Quarter, overlooking Prospect Gardens between Crescent Rd and Montpellier Hill. It's an area of pedestrianised streets lined with restored 19th-century buildings that are now home to art galleries, antique shops, fashion boutiques, cafes and restaurants – an upmarket annex to the main shopping area around Oxford and Cambridge Sts.

⭐**Turkish Baths** SPA

(✆01423-556746; www.turkishbathsharrogate. co.uk; Parliament St; Mon from 6pm & Tue-Thu £19, Mon & Fri £23, Sat & Sun £32, guided tour per person £5; ⏰guided tours 9-10am Wed) Plunge into Harrogate's past at the town's fabulously tiled Turkish Baths. This mock-Moorish facility is gloriously Victorian and offers a range of watery delights: hot rooms, steam rooms, a plunge pool and so on, plus use of the original wooden changing cubicles and historic Crapper toilets. There's a complicated schedule of opening hours that are by turns single sex or mixed, so call or check online for details. The weekly guided tour of the building is fascinating and cheap – book ahead.

DON'T MISS

FOUNTAINS ABBEY

The alluring and strangely obsessive water gardens of the Studley Royal estate were built in the 18th century to enhance the picturesque ruins of 12th-century **Fountains Abbey** (NT; www.fountainsabbey.org.uk; adult/child £13/6.50; ⊙10am-5pm Mar-Oct, to 4pm Sat-Thu Nov-Jan, 10am-4pm Feb; ℙ). Together, they present a breathtaking picture of pastoral elegance and tranquillity that have made them a Unesco World Heritage site and the most visited of all the National Trust's pay-to-enter properties.

After falling out with the Benedictines of York in 1132, a band of rebel monks came here to establish their own monastery. Struggling to make it alone, they were formally adopted by the Cistercians in 1135. By the middle of the 13th century, the new abbey had grown wealthy from trading wool and had become the most successful Cistercian venture in the country. After the Dissolution, when Henry VIII confiscated Church property, the abbey's estate was sold into private hands, and between 1598 and 1611 Fountains Hall was partly built using stone from the abbey ruins. The hall and ruins were united with the Studley Royal estate in 1768.

Studley Royal was owned by John Aislabie, once Chancellor of the Exchequer, who dedicated his life to creating the park after a financial scandal saw him expelled from Parliament. The main house of Studley Royal burnt down in 1946, but the superb landscaping, with its serene artificial lakes, survives almost unchanged from the 18th century.

The remains of the abbey are impressively grandiose, gathered around the sunny Romanesque cloister, with a huge vaulted cellarium leading off the west end of the church. Here, the abbey's 200 lay brothers lived, and food and wool from the abbey's farms were stored. At the east end is the soaring Chapel of Nine Altars, and on the outside of its northeast window is a green man carving (a pre-Christian fertility symbol).

A choice of scenic walking trails leads for a mile from the abbey ruins to the famous water gardens, designed to enhance the romantic views of the ruined abbey. Don't miss **St Mary's Church** (⊙noon-4pm Easter-Sep) FREE above the gardens.

Fountains Abbey is 4 miles west of Ripon off the B6265. Bus 139 travels from Ripon to Fountains Abbey visitor centre year-round (£4.40 return, 15 minutes, four times daily on Monday, Thursday and Saturday).

✦ Festivals & Events

Spring Flower Show   FAIR
(www.flowershow.org.uk; £17.50; ⊙late Apr) The year's main event, held at the Great Yorkshire Show Ground. A colourful three-day extravaganza of blooms and blossoms, flower competitions, gardening demonstrations, market stalls, crafts and gardening shops.

Great Yorkshire Show   FAIR
(www.greatyorkshireshow.co.uk; adult/child £25/12.50; ⊙mid-Jul) Staged over three days by the Yorkshire Agricultural Society. Expect all manner of primped and prettified farm animals competing for prizes, and entertainment ranging from showjumping and falconry to cookery demonstrations and hot-air-balloon rides.

Autumn Flower Show   FAIR
(www.flowershow.org.uk; £17.50; ⊙late Sep) Fruit- and veg-growing championships, cookery demonstrations and kid's events.

🛏 Sleeping

Hotel du Vin   BOUTIQUE HOTEL ££
(☎01423-856800;   www.hotelduvin.com/locations/harrogate; Prospect Pl; r/ste from £140/250; ℙ⊚) An extremely stylish boutique hotel with dapper lounge – the loft suites with exposed oak beams, hardwood floors and extravagant bathrooms featuring two claw-footed baths and dual showers are among the nicest rooms in town, but even the standard bedrooms are spacious and very comfortable (though they can be noisy). Rates can plummet at quiet times, so keep an eye online.

Ascot House Hotel   BOUTIQUE HOTEL ££
(☎01423-531005; 53 King's Rd, HG1 5HJ; r from £50; 🚍2A & 2B from city centre) This traditional Victorian house is now a 19-room boutique hotel with comfy, modern rooms. Nothing too fancy, but the service is friendly, the wi-fi is strong and the breakfast (£12) is sensational.

Unbeatable at this price. It's less than a mile north of the centre.

Acorn Lodge
B&B **££**

(☏ 01423-525630; www.acornlodgeharrogate. co.uk; 1 Studley Rd; s/d from £48/69; P 🛜) Attention to detail is spot on at Acorn Lodge: stylish decor, crisp cotton sheets, powerful showers and perfect poached eggs for breakfast. Rooms 5, 6 and 7 in the eaves at the top of the house are particularly lovely. The location is good too, just a 10-minute walk from the town centre.

★ Inn at Cheltenham Parade
BOUTIQUE HOTEL **£££**

(☏ 01423-505041; www.harrogatebrasserie.co.uk; 26-30 Cheltenham Pde; s/d £80/90, apt from £99; P 🛜) The incredibly central location makes this one of Harrogate's most appealing places to stay. Rooms are all individual, with subtle colour combinations and the occasional leather armchair; number 5 has a huge bathroom, and there's a pair of sweet studios with little balconies tucked at the top of the house. Behind the main building, there are also two larger apartments that would suit families.

Eating

Baltzersen's
CAFE **£**

(☏ 01423-202363; www.baltzersens.co.uk; 22 Oxford St; mains £8.95-11; ⏲ 8am-5pm Mon-Sat, 10am-4pm Sun; 🛜👶) This simple Scandi-style cafe serves Nordic waffles and pastries, plus Norwegian stew and open-sided sandwiches such as curried herring with potato salad. It also has great coffee, courtesy of North Star in Leeds and Falcon in nearby Pannal.

Bettys
CAFE **£**

(☏ 01423-814070; www.bettys.co.uk; 1 Parliament St; mains £5-13, afternoon tea £18.50; ⏲ 9am-9pm; 👶) Arguably the most famous tearoom in Britain, Bettys is a Yorkshire institution. It was established in 1919 by a Swiss immigrant confectioner who took the wrong train, ended up in Yorkshire and decided to stay. Everything's made in-house, and there is almost always a queue for a table for speciality tea and cake; book your table online.

Tannin Level
BISTRO **££**

(☏ 01423-560595; www.tanninlevel.co.uk; 5 Raglan St; mains £15.95-28.95; ⏲ noon-2pm & 5.30-9pm Tue-Fri, to 9.30pm Sat, noon-5pm Sun) 🍴 Old terracotta floor tiles, polished mahogany tables and gilt-framed mirrors and paintings create a relaxed yet elegant atmosphere at this

popular bistro. A competitively priced menu based on seasonal British produce – think Yorkshire lamb rump or heirloom courgette and Yorkshire Fettle cheese tart – makes this a popular choice. Book ahead.

🍸 Drinking & Nightlife

★ Bean & Bud
COFFEE

(☏ 01423-508200; www.beanandbud.co.uk; 14 Commercial St; ⏲ 8am-3pm Mon-Tue & Thu-Fri, to 4pm Sat, 10am-4pm Sun; 🛜) Small and bohemian, this cafe takes its drinks seriously, with names of coffee growers and altitudes of their plantations displayed proudly on the walls. It's also the sort of place that serves single-origin hot chocolates and puts fairtrade unrefined sugar on the tables. There's a choice of two or three freshly ground blends every day, plus top-quality white, green, oolong and black teas.

★ Major Tom's Social
CRAFT BEER

(☏ 01423-566984; www.majortomssocial.co.uk; The Ginnel, off Montpellier Gardens; ⏲ noon-11.30pm Sun-Thu, to 1am Fri & Sat) Grungy and effortlessly cool, this 1st-floor drinking den is the type of place where locals cram onto sociable wooden bench tables and talk rubbish all night, sampling far more of the interesting draught beers than they meant to. Mismatched retro sofas and walls lined with vintage film and music posters complete the picture. There's also a cheap pizza menu (£7.50 to £9.50).

Harrogate Tap
CRAFT BEER

(☏ 01423-501644; www.harrogatetap.co.uk; Station Pde; ⏲ 11am-11pm Sun-Thu, to midnight Fri, from 10am Sat; 🛜) Set in a restored red-brick railway-station building dating from 1862, the Tap does a grand job of conjuring up the ambience of a bustling Victorian pub, but with the added attractions of a dozen rotating hand-pulled cask ales, another dozen keg taps and a menu of around 120 bottled craft beers from all over the world.

Hales Bar
PUB

(☏ 01423-725570; www.halesbar.co.uk; Crescent Rd; ⏲ noon-11pm Sun-Thu, to 1am Fri & Sat) There's a touch of the gothic about this candlelit coaching house, which claims to be the oldest pub in Harrogate (c 1766). It is still partially illuminated by its original gas lighting (look behind the bar – apparently this is the place to come in a blackout), but far more impressive are the theatrical Victorian open-flame cigarette lighters that still line the bar.

🛍 Shopping

Spirit of Harrogate   DRINKS
(www.wslingsby.co.uk/experience; 5-7 Montpellier Pde; ⊙11am-5.30pm Mon-Sat) Craft gin is the raison d'être of this quaint shop, which local gin brand Slingsby runs as a bottle shop by day and as a convivial setting for gin-tasting sessions by night. On alternate Friday evenings and Saturday afternoons it holds a 'Spirit of Gin' experience, which includes a talk on the history of gin, tasters and nibbles for £30; book ahead.

ℹ️ Information

Harrogate Tourist Office (☑01423-537300; www.visitharrogate.co.uk; Crescent Rd; ⊙10am-5pm Mon-Sat Aug-Oct, 9.30am-5pm Nov-Mar)

ℹ️ Getting There & Away

Bus Harrogate & District (www.harrogatebus. co.uk) bus 36 connects Harrogate with Leeds (£6.70, 45 minutes, two to four hourly) and Ripon (£6.70, 30 minutes).

Train There are trains to Harrogate from Leeds (£9.10, 35 minutes, every 30 minutes) and York (£9.40, 35 minutes, hourly).

Scarborough

☑01723 / POP 61,749

A redeveloped Victorian spa, grand water park and Edwardian gardens are the remaining vestiges of Scarborough's 18th- and 19th-century heyday, when its natural spa waters made it a popular seaside holiday town. Its two large beaches are still a draw, but the downbeat city centre feels like it's stuck in the past, and not in a fashionably retro sort of way.

Cliff-scaling tramways ferry visitors down to the South Bay promenade, lined with arcades and fish-and-chip shops, while sitting on the headland are the toothsome ruins of its medieval castle.

🔴 Sights & Activities

Scarborough Castle   CASTLE
(EH; www.english-heritage.org.uk; Castle Rd; adult/child £7.90/4.70; ⊙10am-6pm Apr-Sep, to 5pm Oct-Mar) The massive medieval keep of Scarborough Castle occupies a commanding position atop its headland. Legend has it that Richard I loved the views from here so much that his ghost just keeps coming back. Take a walk out to the edge of the cliffs, where

you can see the 2000-year-old remains of a **Roman signal station**. There's also a cafe and picnic tables. Visits are by pre-booked time slots only.

Peasholm Park   PARK
(www.peasholmpark.com; Columbus Ravine; ⊙24hr) 🆓 Set back from North Bay, Scarborough's beautiful Edwardian pleasure gardens, complete with hilltop pagoda, are famous for their summer sessions of **Naval Warfare** (adult/child £4.50/2.50; ⊙3pm Mon, Thu & Sat Jul & Aug), when large model ships re-enact famous naval battles on the boating lake (check the website for dates).

Rotunda Museum   MUSEUM
(☑01723-353665; www.scarboroughmuseums trust.com; Vernon Rd; adult/child £3/free; ⊙10am-5pm Tue-Sun; ♿) The Rotunda Museum is dedicated to the coastal geology of northeast Yorkshire, which has yielded many of Britain's most important dinosaur fossils. The strata in the local cliffs were also important in deciphering England's geological history. Founded by William Smith, 'the father of English geology', who lived in Scarborough in the 1820s, the museum has original Georgian exhibits as well as a hands-on gallery for kids. Admission by pre-booked time slot only.

Sea Life   AQUARIUM
(www.sealife.co.uk; Scalby Mills; adult/child under 3 £15.60/free; ⊙10am-4pm Mon-Fri, to 5pm Sat & Sun, last admission 1hr before closing; 🅿♿) At this family-oriented attraction you can see coral reefs, turtles, octopuses, seahorses, otters and many other fascinating creatures. The biggest draws are the talks and feeding times at the seal pool and penguin enclosure. The centre is at the far north end of North Beach; the miniature North Bay Railway (p492) runs the 0.75-mile route. You need to pre-book your ticket online. A lot of the attractions are outdoors, so it's not an ideal rainy-day refuge.

🛏 Sleeping & Eating

⭐ **Windmill**   B&B **££**
(☑01723-372735; www.scarborough-windmill. co.uk; Mill St; d/f from £85/120, apt £100-130; 🅿🛜) Quirky doesn't begin to describe this place, a beautifully converted 18th-century windmill in the middle of town. There are two self-catering apartments in the windmill itself, along with cottages, a family room and four-poster doubles around a

Scarborough

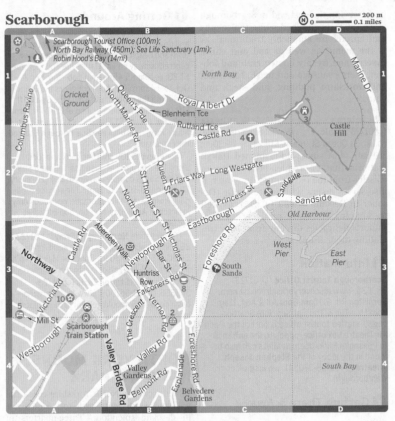

Scarborough

⊙ Sights
1 Peasholm Park	A1
2 Rotunda Museum	B4
3 Scarborough Castle	D1
4 St Mary's Church	C2

🛏 Sleeping
5 Windmill	A3

🍴 Eating
6 Golden Grid	C2
7 Lanterna	B2

🍷 Drinking & Nightlife
8 Cat's Pyjamas	B3

✪ Entertainment
9 Naval Warfare	A1
10 Stephen Joseph Theatre	A3

cobbled courtyard. Try to secure the upper apartment (from £100 a night) in the windmill, which has great views from its wraparound balcony.

Cat's Pyjamas CAFE **£**
(📞 01723-331721; www.thecatspyjamascafebars. co.uk; 2 St Nicholas Cliff; dishes £6-10; ⊙ 8am-5pm Sun-Thu, 9am-10pm Fri & Sat; 🛜) Tucked inside the heritage Central Tramway shed and with sea views from its upstairs seating area, this 1920s-themed cafe and gin bar is a breath of fresh air in staid Scarborough. It serves simple brunches and lunches such as posh fish butties, plus coffee, cakes and G&Ts accompanied by jazz and swing music.

Golden Grid FISH & CHIPS **££**
(📞 01723-360922; www.goldengrid.co.uk; 4 Sandside; mains £10-20; ⊙ 11am-8.45pm Mon-Thu, 10.30am-9.30pm Fri-Sun; 👶) The Golden Grid is a sit-down fish restaurant that has

been serving the best cod in Scarborough since 1883. Its starched white tablecloths and aprons are staunchly traditional, as is the menu: as well as cod and chips, oysters, and freshly landed crab and lobster, there's sausage and mash, roast beef and Yorkshire pudding, and steak and chips.

★ Lanterna   ITALIAN £££
(☑ 01723-363616;   www.lanterna-ristorante. co.uk; 33 Queen St; mains £19-24; ⊙ 7-9.30pm Tue-Sat) 🍴 A snug, old-fashioned Italian trattoria that does splendid versions of classics from the old country. In winter, it also serves dishes with white truffle (October to December, £30 to £45). As well as sourcing Yorkshire produce, the chef imports delicacies directly from Italy (including the truffles).

🛈 Information

Scarborough Tourist Office (☑ 01723-383636; www.discoveryorkshirecoast.com; Burniston Rd; ⊙ 10am-6pm Jul & Aug, 11am-5pm Mon-Tue & Thu-Sat Sep-Jun) Scarborough's staffed tourist office is part of the Open Air Theatre box office, opposite the entrance to Peasholm Park. Useful leaflets can also be found in the lobby of the **Stephen Joseph Theatre** (☑ 01723-370541; www.sjt.uk.com; Westborough).

🛈 Getting There & Away

BUS

Bus 128 (www.eyms.co.uk) travels along the A170 from Helmsley to Scarborough via Pickering, while Arriva (www.arrivabus.co.uk) buses 93 and X93 come from Middlesborough and Whitby via Robin Hood's Bay. Coastliner (www. coastliner.co.uk) bus 843 runs to Scarborough from Leeds and York.

Helmsley £9.20, 1¾ hours, hourly Monday to Saturday, at least four daily on Sunday

Leeds £13.70, 2¾ hours, hourly

Whitby £7, one hour, once or twice hourly

York £14, 1¾ hours, hourly

TRAIN

Book in advance for cheaper tickets to York and Leeds.

Hull £16, 1½ hours, nine daily Monday to Saturday, six on Sunday

Leeds £33.60, 1¼ hours, hourly

Malton £9.60, 25 minutes, hourly

York £19.20, 45 minutes, hourly

🛈 Getting Around

Tiny Victorian-era funicular railways rattle up and down Scarborough's steep cliffs between town and beach. The **Central Tramway** (www.centraltramway.co.uk; Marine Pde; per person £1.20; ⊙ 10am-5.45pm mid-Feb–Jun, Sep & Oct, to 9.45pm Jul & Aug) connects the Grand Hotel with the promenade, while the **Spa Cliff Lift** (www.scarboroughspa.co.uk/cliff-lift; Esplanade; per person £1.50; ⊙ at least 10am-5pm, hours vary) runs between Scarborough Spa and the Esplanade.

Open-top bus 109 shuttles back and forth along the seafront between Scarborough Spa and the Sands complex on North Bay (£2, every 20 minutes 9.30am to 3pm). The service runs daily from Easter to September, weekends only in October. An all-day, hop-on, hop-off ticket costs £3.

The miniature **North Bay Railway** (☑ 01723-368791; www.nbr.org.uk; return adult/child £4.50/3.50; ⊙ 10.30am-3pm Apr-May & Sep, to 5.30pm Jul & Aug) also runs to North Beach.

For a taxi, call **Station Taxis** (☑ 01723-366366, 01723-361009; www.taxisinscarborough.co.uk); £6 should get you to most places in town.

NORTH YORK MOORS NATIONAL PARK

Inland from the North Yorkshire coast, the wild and windswept North York Moors rise in desolate splendour. Three-quarters of all the world's heather moorland is found in Britain, and this is the largest expanse in England. Ridgetop roads climb up from lush green valleys to the bleak open moors, where weather-beaten stone crosses mark the lines of ancient roadways. In summer, heather blooms in billowing drifts of purple haze.

This is classic walking country. The moors are criss-crossed with footpaths old and new, and dotted with pretty, flower-bedecked villages. The national park is also home to one of England's most picturesque steam railways, and at its eastern edge lies historic Whitby – one of England's dreamiest and most haunting coastal towns.

The park produces the useful *Out & About* visitor guide, available from tourist offices and hotels, with information on things to see and do as well as a monthly events calendar. See also www.northyorkmoors.org.uk.

North York Moors National Park

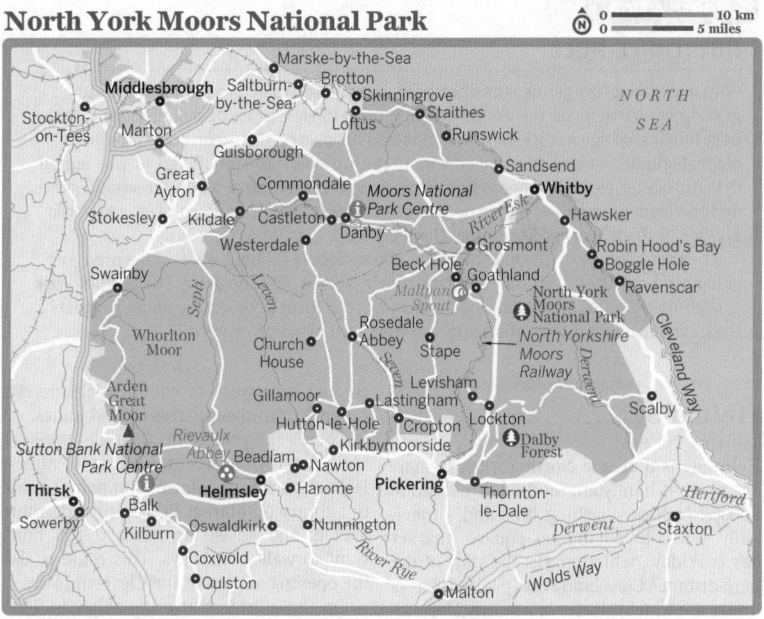

Activities

Yorkshire Cycle Hub CYCLING
(☎01287-669098; www.yorkshirecyclehub.co.uk; Fryup; ⏱9.30am-4.30pm Mon-Tue & Thu-Sun; 👪) Wedged in the middle of the North York Moors National Park, this centre is a great aid for local and visiting cycling enthusiasts. There's cycle hire (mountain bikes and e-bikes), a repairs shop, a simple bunkhouse (£35 per night; there are plans to add camping pods), bike wash and storage, and an excellent cafe with a log-burner and fabulous rural views.

North York Moors Guided Walks WALKING
(☎01439-772738; www.northyorkmoors.org.uk) FREE Each year the national park publishes a schedule of mostly free guided walks led by volunteers and specialists. Some skirt high moors along ancient paths to seek out medieval sites or ruined castles; others pass through bluebell woods, track birds, or delve into the myths and mysteries of the coastal villages. Places must be booked online or by phone.

Information

There are two national park visitor centres, providing information on walking, cycling, wildlife and public transport.

Moors National Park Centre (☎01439-772737; www.northyorkmoors.org.uk; Lodge Lane, Danby; parking 2/24hr £3/5.50; ⏱10am-5pm; 👪)

Sutton Bank National Park Centre (☎01845-597426; www.northyorkmoors.org.uk; Sutton Bank, by Thirsk; ⏱10am-5pm Apr-Oct, to 4pm Nov-Mar; 📶)

Getting Around

On Sundays and bank holiday Mondays from late May to September, a number of minibus services aimed at hikers shuttle around various locations within the national park; all are detailed on the Moorsbus (www.moorsbus.org) website.

For example, the **Moors Explorer** (☎01482-592929; www.eastyorkshirebuses.co.uk; all-day hop-on, hop-off ticket £12.50) service runs from Hull to the Moors National Park Centre in Danby with stops along the way, but only runs six or so times a year. An all-day hop-on, hop-off ticket costs £12.50. Download the EYMS app with timetables and track bus arrival times live.

The North Yorkshire Moors Railway (p496), running between Pickering and Whitby, is an excellent way of exploring the central moors in summer.

If you're planning to drive on the minor roads over the moors, beware of wandering sheep and lambs – hundreds are killed by careless drivers every year.

WORTH A TRIP

HUTTON-LE-HOLE

With a scatter of gorgeous stone cottages, a gurgling brook and a flock of sheep grazing contentedly on the village green, Hutton-le-Hole must be a contender for the best-looking village in Yorkshire. The dips and hollows on the green may have given the place its name – it was once called simply Hutton Hole; the Frenchified 'le' was added in Victorian times. The village is home to a couple of tearooms, a pub, ice-cream shops and the fascinating **Ryedale Folk Museum** (www.ryedalefolkmuseum.co.uk; adult/child £8.75/7; ⊙10am-5pm Apr-Sep, to 4pm Mar & Oct-Nov).

The tourist office (in the folk museum) has leaflets (£1) about walks in the area, including a 4-mile (2½-hour) circuit to the nearby village of Lastingham. The Daffodil Walk is a 3.5-mile circular walk following the banks of the River Dove. As the name suggests, the main drawcard is the daffs, usually at their best in March or April.

Helmsley

☑ 01439 / POP 1515

Helmsley is a classic North Yorkshire market town, a handsome huddle of old stone houses, historic coaching inns and – inevitably – a cobbled market square (market day is Friday), which marks the start of the long-distance Cleveland Way (p482). It basks under the watchful gaze of a sturdy Norman castle ruin and stately home surrounded by rolling fields. Nearby are the romantic ruins of Rievaulx Abbey, several excellent restaurants and a fistful of country walks.

◉ Sights

★ **Rievaulx Abbey**   RUINS
(EH; www.english-heritage.org.uk; adult/child £11/6.60; ⊙10am-6pm Apr-Sep, to 5pm Oct, to 4pm Sat & Sun Nov–mid-Feb, daily Mar; **P**) In the secluded valley of the River Rye about 3 miles west of Helmsley, amid fields and woods loud with birdsong, stand the magnificent ruins of Rievaulx Abbey (*ree*-voh). The extensive remains give a wonderful sense of the size and complexity of the community that once lived here, and their story is fleshed out in a series of fascinating exhibits in the attached museum. There's also a cafe with floor-to-ceiling windows and an outdoor terrace from which to gawp at the ruins.

This idyllic spot was chosen by Cistercian monks in 1132 as a base for their missionary activity in northern Britain. St Aelred, the third abbot, famously described the abbey's setting as 'everywhere peace, everywhere serenity, and a marvellous freedom from the tumult of the world'. But the monks of Rievaulx were far from unworldly and soon created a network of commercial interests ranging from sheep farms to lead mines.

There's an excellent 3.5-mile **walking trail** from Helmsley to Rievaulx Abbey; Helmsley's tourist information point (inside the library on Market Pl) can provide route leaflets and advise on buses if you don't want to walk both ways. This route is also the opening section of the Cleveland Way.

On the hillside above the abbey is **Rievaulx Terrace**, built in the 18th century by Thomas Duncombe II as a place to admire views of the abbey. Note that there's no direct access between the abbey and the terrace, and the two sites have separate admission fees. Their entrance gates are about a mile apart along a narrow road (a 20-minute walk steeply uphill if you're heading from the abbey to the terrace).

Helmsley Castle   CASTLE
(EH; www.english-heritage.org.uk; Castlegate; adult/child £7.90/4.70; ⊙10am-6pm Apr-Sep, to 5pm Oct, to 4pm Fri-Sun Nov-Mar; **P**) The impressive ruins of 12th-century Helmsley Castle are defended by a striking series of deep ditches and banks, to which later rulers added the thick stone walls and defensive towers. Only one tooth-shaped tower survives, following the dismantling of the fortress after the Civil War. The castle's tumultuous history is well explained in the 14-century West Range at the back of the site.

**National Centre
for Birds of Prey**   ANIMAL SANCTUARY
(☑ 01439-772080; www.ncbp.co.uk; Duncombe Park; adult/child £9/6.50; ⊙10am-5.30pm) Set in 300 acres of parkland that make up the Duncombe estate, this relatively new conservation centre has the north's largest collection of vultures, eagles, owls, hawks, falcons

and other birds of prey. The aviaries are huge and the visitor interaction is terrific. The signposting is engaging – 'I'm a turkey vulture...to keep cool, I poo on my legs and feet' – and you can try your hand (literally) at falconry in the Raptor Experience (£65, over 10s only). There's also a good on-site cafe.

Duncombe Park GARDENS
(www.duncombepark.com; adult/child £5/3; ⊙10.30am-5pm Sun-Fri Apr-Aug; P🅿️) On the outskirts of Helmsley lies the superb ornamental landscape of Duncombe Park estate, laid out in 1718 for Thomas Duncombe (whose son would later build Rievaulx Terrace), with the stately Georgian mansion of Duncombe Park House at its heart. From the house (not open to the public) and formal gardens, wide grassy walkways and terraces lead through woodland to mock-classical temples, while longer walking trails are set out in the landscaped parkland, now protected as a nature reserve.

🛏 Sleeping

Feathers Hotel INN ££
(📞01439-770275; www.feathershotelhelmsley. co.uk; Market Pl; s/d from £80/120; P🛜🐾) One of a number of old coaching inns on the market square that offer B&B, decent grub and a pint of hand-pumped real ale. The rooms have a contemporary touch, but there are historical trimmings throughout.

Canadian Fields CAMPGROUND ££
(📞01439-772409; www.canadianfields.co.uk; Gale Lane; safari tents £80-100; ⊙Feb–mid-Nov; P🐾) This luxury campsite 3 miles east of Helmsley offers comfortable and unusual accommodation in spacious 'safari tent' cabins with kitchens, electricity and wood-burning stoves under canvas, alongside private outdoor showers. There are also sites where you can pitch your own tent (from £15 a night), and a bar-restaurant housed in a giant tepee provides a convivial social hub.

Feversham Arms HOTEL £££
(📞01439-772935; www.fevershamarmshotel.com; High St; d/ste from £160/230; P🛜🏊) Just behind Helmsley's church, the Feversham Arms has a snug and sophisticated atmosphere where country charm meets boutique chic. Service is excellent and rooms are comfy (the luxury pool suites with balcony are especially light and spacious), but it's the spa and lovely heated outdoor pool that brings guests from far and wide; the on-site restaurant is not worth the money.

🍴 Eating

Vine Cafe CAFE £
(📞01439-771194; www.vinehousecafehelmsley. co.uk; Helmsley Walled Garden, Cleveland Way; mains £7-11; ⊙10am-5pm Apr-Oct; 🅿️🖐) Goodies plucked from the gardens take centre stage at this whimsical cafe housed in vine-draped Victorian greenhouses within creepers distance of Helmsley Walled Garden. Everything on the menu is fresh and simple, like the homemade hummus and chickpea curry, organic frittata and Helmsley butcher's ham sandwich. It's licensed, too, so you can take a Yorkshire G&T with lunch in the sun.

★ **Star Inn** MODERN BRITISH £££
(📞01439-770397; www.thestaratharome.co.uk; Harome, YO62 5JE; mains £18-34; ⊙noon-2pm Tue-Sat, 4.30-8.30pm Mon-Sat, noon-6.30pm Sun; P🖐) This thatch-roofed country pub is home to a Michelin-starred restaurant, with a menu specialising in top-quality produce from the surrounding countryside: Whitby crab with pickled cockles and avocado 'ice', or roast English quail with braised salsify and bergamot preserve. The tasting menu (£85, £175 with matching wines) is magnificent. Harome is about 2 miles southeast of Helmsley off the A170.

The Star is the sort of place you won't want to leave, and the good news is you don't have to – the adjacent lodge has nine magnificent bedrooms (£150 to £240), each decorated in classic but luxurious country style.

★ **Hare Inn** MODERN BRITISH £££
(📞01845-597769; www.thehare-inn.com; Scawton; tasting menu £85, half-board package from £167; ⊙noon-2.30pm & 6-9pm Wed-Sat; P) 🍃 Drowsing in a secluded hamlet 4 miles west of Helmsley, the Hare is a 21st-century restaurant in a 13th-century inn, where gourmet dining is relaxed, informal and even fun. There's no à la carte, just a seasonal tasting menu, and only seven tables; bookings must be made in advance. In 2019 they added a couple of guest rooms.

ℹ Getting There & Away

Buses stop in the main square. From Scarborough, bus 128 (£9.20, 1¾ hours, hourly Monday to Saturday) runs to Helmsley via Pickering, with an additional Sunday service April to October (six daily).

YORKSHIRE HELMSLEY

Pickering

☎ 01751 / POP 6830

Pickering is a lively market town with an imposing Norman castle that advertises itself as the 'gateway to the North York Moors'. That gateway is also the terminus of the wonderful North Yorkshire Moors Railway, a picturesque survivor from the great days of steam.

Two scenic drives head north across the moors: the A169 to Whitby leads past the **Hole of Horcum** beauty spot and the hiking trails of Goathland (p499); and the Blakey Ridge road (beginning 6 miles west of town) passes the pretty village of Hutton-le-Hole (p494) and the famous **Lion Inn** on the way to Danby.

◉ Sights

★ North Yorkshire Moors Railway   HERITAGE RAILWAY

(NYMR; www.nymr.co.uk; Park St; Pickering–Whitby day-rover ticket adult/child £35/20; ☺ Easter-Oct, reduced service Nov-Easter) This privately owned railway runs for 18 miles through beautiful countryside from Pickering to Whitby. Lovingly restored steam locos pull period carriages with wooden booths, appealing to railway buffs and day trippers alike. For visitors without wheels, it's excellent for reaching out-of-the-way spots and devising walks between stations. You must book online.

Pickering Castle   CASTLE

(EH; www.english-heritage.org.uk; Castlegate; adult/child £5.90/3.70; ☺ 10am-6pm Apr-Sep, to 5pm Oct) Pickering Castle is a lot like the castles we drew as kids: thick stone outer walls circle the keep, and the whole lot is perched atop a high motte (mound) with great views of the surrounding countryside. Founded by William the Conqueror around 1070, it was added to and altered by later kings, but there's not much of it left.

⌨ Sleeping

★ White Swan Hotel   HOTEL £££

(☎ 01751-472288; www.white-swan.co.uk; Market Pl; incl breakfast s from £140, d £170-220; ℗ 🛜) The top spot in town successfully combines a smart pub, a superb restaurant serving a daily changing menu of local produce (mains £14 to £22) and a luxurious boutique hotel. Nine rooms lie within the converted coach house itself, but the best are in a

quiet, hidden block out back, where guests get the added perks of underfloor heating and free robes.

✖ Eating & Drinking

Black Swan   PUB

(☎ 01751-798209; www.blackswan-pickering.co.uk; 18 Birdgate; mains £14-20; ☺ 11.30am-11pm Mon-Thu, to 11.30pm Fri & Sat, to 10.30pm Sun; 🛜) This 18th-century coaching inn has had an ambitious makeover to return it to its former glory. The food is recommended, the beers are brewed in-house (ask behind the bar and you might get a mini guided tour of the microbrewery), and there's also a 1920s-themed cocktail den that you enter around the back of the pub. Fresh, modern B&B rooms upstairs cost from £95.

ⓘ Getting There & Away

Bus 128 between Helmsley (£5.70, 40 minutes) and Scarborough (£7, one hour) runs hourly via Pickering. Bus 840 between Leeds and Whitby also travels via Pickering (hourly).

Whitby

☎ 01947 / POP 13,213

Wonderful, a little weird and occasionally weather-beaten Whitby is a town with three distinct personalities. The huddle of 18th-century fisher's cottages along the East Cliff are testament to its longtime role as a busy commercial and fishing port – it was here that 18th-century explorer Captain James Cook earned his sea legs. The genteel Victorian suburb atop the West Cliff is a clue to Whitby's place as a traditional seaside resort complete with sandy beach, amusement arcades and promenading holidaymakers.

Keeping a watchful eye over the town and the River Esk that divides it is an atmospheric ruined abbey, the inspiration and setting for part of Bram Stoker's Gothic horror story *Dracula*. But tales of witchery and ghostly legends have haunted Whitby ever since Anglo-Saxon St Hilda landed here to found a monastic community in 657 CE. The town embraces its pseudo-sinister reputation, which culminates in two hugely successful Goth Weekends each year.

◉ Sights

★ Whitby Abbey   RUINS

(EH; www.english-heritage.org.uk; East Cliff; adult/child £10/6; ☺ 10am-6pm Apr-Sep, to 5pm Oct, to 4pm Nov-Mar; ℗) There are ruined abbeys,

Whitby

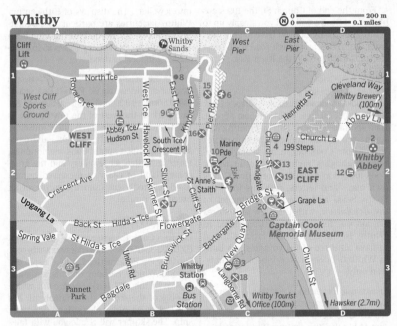

Whitby

and there are picturesque ruined abbeys. And then there's Whitby Abbey, dominating the skyline above the East Cliff like a great Gothic tombstone silhouetted against the sky. Looking as though it was built as an atmospheric film set rather than a monastic establishment, it is hardly surprising that this medieval hulk inspired the Victorian novelist Bram Stoker (who holidayed in Whitby) to make it the setting for Count Dracula's dramatic landfall.

The stately mansion beside the abbey ruins was built by the Cholmley family, who leased the Whitby estate from Henry VIII after the dissolution of England's monasteries in the 1530s. Following a £1.5 million revamp in 2019, the abbey has dramatically improved its museum, added a small coffee shop with outdoor seating in the abbey grounds, and replaced its free audio guide with a more family-friendly 'ammonite quest' to explore the site with.

From the end of Church St, the 199 steps of Church Stairs will lead you steeply up to Whitby Abbey. By car, you have to approach from the A171 Scarborough road to the east side of the bridge over the River Esk.

★ Captain Cook Memorial Museum
MUSEUM

(www.cookmuseumwhitby.co.uk; Grape Lane; adult/child £6.50/free; ⊙9.45am-5pm Apr-Oct, 11am-4pm mid-Feb–Mar) This fascinating museum occupies the house of the ship owner with whom Cook began his seafaring career. Highlights include the attic where Cook lodged as a young apprentice, Cook's own maps and letters, etchings from the South Seas, and a wonderful model of the *Resolution,* with the crew and stores all laid out for inspection. Cook lived in Whitby for nine years and later returned to have all three of his voyage ships built in Whitby's dockyards. Pre-booked admission only.

Endeavour Experience Whitby
MUSEUM

(www.hmbarkendeavour.co.uk; Endeavour Wharf; adult/child £5/1.50; ⊙10am-5pm, last admission 4pm; ♠) In the 18th century, Whitby was one of Britain's greatest shipbuilding centres, James Cook was apprenticed here and the original HM Bark *Endeavour* was built in the town. It was aboard this ship that Cook charted New Zealand and the east coast of Australia for the first time.

In 2018, a full-size replica of the *Endeavour* became a permanent fixture in Whitby harbour and opened to the public as a visitor attraction. On board, 11 cabins have been transformed into a cafe, mini galleries and interactive exhibits about life at sea and Cook's 1768 voyage of discovery aboard *Endeavour*. Highlights include the 'Sea Shanty' karaoke room, animated film projections in the Great Cabin and a display of Southern Hemisphere constellations the crew would have used for navigation.

Museum of Whitby Jet
MUSEUM

(☑01947-667453; www.museumofwhitbyjet.com; Wesley Hall, Church St; ⊙9.30am-5.30pm) **FREE** Housed inside a 1901 chapel, this small museum has created a temple to Whitby jet – one of the town's most prized exports, a gothic icon, and a favourite gem of Queen Victoria. The exhibition explores how jet is formed over millions of years on the Yorkshire coast and has historically been turned into jewellery. The displays of 19th-century Whitby jet curios are particularly fascinating if you're a fan. Beyond the museum lies a shop and Albert's Eatery (mains £5-16), specialising in local seafood.

Whitby Museum
MUSEUM

(www.whitbymuseum.org.uk; Pannett Park; adult/child £5/free; ⊙9.30am-4.30pm Tue-Sun; ♠) Set in a park to the west of the town centre is the wonderfully eclectic Whitby Museum, with displays of fossil plesiosaurs and dinosaur footprints, Captain Cook memorabilia, ships in bottles, jet jewellery and the gruesome 'Hand of Glory', a preserved human hand reputedly cut from the corpse of an executed criminal.

🏃 Activities

Captain Cook Experience
BOATING

(☑01723-364100; www.endeavourwhitby.com; Fish Quay, Pier Rd; 25min trip £5) Take a spin out beyond Whitby harbour on this authentic replica of the HM Bark *Endeavour,* which at 40% of the size of the original still has the feel of an atmospheric large voyaging ship. The skipper will regale you with tales of Captain Cook's ordeals at sea and his long-standing associations with Whitby. Good fun for young and old.

Whitby Coastal Cruises
BOATING

(☑07981 712419; www.whitbywhalewatching. net; Brewery Steps; 3½hr trip £15) Spot birds, seals, dolphins or even steam trains on a coastal or River Esk boat trip with this long-running family business. September is whale-watching season, during which time you can join its sister business Whitby Whale Watching on a trip (£40) where the chances of seeing minke whales (and more rarely humpbacks) are high.

Tours

★ Whitby Ghost Walks
WALKING

(☑01947-880485; www.whitbywalks.com; Whale Bone Arch, West Cliff; adult/child £5/3; ⊙7.30pm) Whitby wouldn't be Whitby without ghoulish tales and strange happenings, and nobody knows them better than Dr Crank, who manages to confidently keep to the right side of naff with his fascinating 75-minute tour around West Cliff's most haunted and storied alleyways. You'll learn of legends like the screaming tunnel, the hand of glory and the headless horseman, plus tidbits of local history.

Hidden Horizons   OUTDOORS

(☑ 01723-817017; www.hiddenhorizons.co.uk; adult/child from £9/6) You can get down on the beaches around Whitby to hunt for fossils (and there's plenty to find), take a dinosaur-footprint walk, go rock-pooling, or join a star-gazing session with this local tour company. Sessions are entertaining but also educational. Check the online calendar for upcoming events, and book ahead.

🎆 Festivals & Events

Whitby Goth Weekends   CULTURAL

(www.whitbygothweekend.co.uk; tickets 1/2 days £40/70; ⊙ late Apr/early May & late Oct/early Nov) Goth heaven attracting more than 8000 visitors biannually, with live-music gigs, events and the Bizarre Bazaar – dozens of traders selling Goth gear, jewellery, art and music. Held twice yearly in late April or early May and late October or early November (around Halloween).

Whitby Steampunk Weekend   CULTURAL

(www.wsofficial.com; Whitby Pavilion; ⊙ late Jul) Science fiction meets Victoriana fantasy in Whitby on the last weekend in July, when fans of the steampunk genre descend for balls, costumed promenading, entertainment and shopping at the Steampunk Emporium. A little bit Gothic, a little bit geeky – very Whitby. Events are anchored on the Whitby Pavilion on West Cliff.

🛏 Sleeping

Whitby YHA   HOSTEL £

(☑ 0845 371 9049; www.yha.org.uk; Church Lane; tw/f from £35/30; ⓟ🛜) With an unbeatable setting in an old mansion next to the abbey, this hostel is incredibly popular – you'll have to book well in advance to get your body into one of the bunks here. Hike up the 199 steps from the town, or take bus 97 from the train station to Whitby Abbey (twice hourly Monday to Saturday).

★ La Rosa Hotel   HOTEL ££

(☑ 01947-606981; www.larosa.co.uk/hotel; 5 East Tce; d incl breakfast £90-145; ⓟ🛜) Weird, but wonderful. Lewis Carroll, author of *Alice in Wonderland,* once stayed in this house while holidaying in Whitby. Entering today is like stepping through the looking glass into a world of love-it-or-hate-it Victorian bric-a-brac and kitsch, peppered with vintage film props. Eight quirky and atmospheric bedrooms, great sea views, no TV,

GOATHLAND

This picture-postcard halt on the North Yorkshire Moors Railway stars as Hogsmeade train station in the Harry Potter films, while the village appeared as Aidensfield in the British TV series *Heartbeat*. It's also the starting point for lots of easy and enjoyable walks, often with the chuff-chuff-chuff of passing steam engines in the background.

The hamlet of Beck Hole is home to the wonderfully atmospheric **Birch Hall Inn** (www.beckhole.info; Beck Hole; ⊙ 11am-11pm May-Sep, 11am-3pm & 7.30-11pm Wed-Mon Oct-Apr; 👶🍺), which is less 'hall' and more like two 18th-century cottages where you drink in a tiny sitting room (or outside by the beck). Drinks are served through a hole in the wall: order a pork pie and pint of ale brewed in the village. Cash only.

an in-house bar, and breakfast served in a basket in your room.

Rosslyn House   B&B ££

(☑ 01947-604086; www.rosslynhousewhitby.co.uk; 11 Abbey Tce; s/d/f from £65/85/105; 🛜) Lovely Victorian terrace house that stands out amid the sea of B&Bs on West Cliff, with a friendly welcome and bright, modern decor. The single room is snug; the family room large (though the hotel does not admit children under 12). There's a convenient drying room for walkers.

★ Marine Hotel   INN £££

(☑ 01947-605022; www.the-marine-hotel.co.uk; 13 Marine Pde; r from £150; 🛜) Feeling more like mini-suites than ordinary hotel accommodation, the four bedrooms at the Marine are quirky, stylish and comfortable; it's the sort of place that makes you want to stay in rather than go out. Ask for one of the two rooms with a balcony – they have great views across the harbour.

🍴 Eating

★ Rusty Shears   BRITISH £

(☑ 01947-605383; 3 Silver St; brunch £4-8; ⊙ 9.30am-5pm; 🛜) This vintage cafe covers many bases. There's an astounding drinks menu with more than 100 gins and gin flights (despite the fact it's closed evenings), a walled courtyard for alfresco light

ROBIN HOOD'S BAY

Picturesque Robin Hood's Bay has nothing to do with the hero of Sherwood Forest – the origin of its name is a mystery, and the locals call it Bay Town or just Bay – but it was once a major centre for smuggling. All that is in the past – well explored in the volunteer-led **Bay Museum** (http://museum.rhbay.co.uk; Fisherhead; ☉ hours vary, school holidays only) – and the fishing village is now just one of the prettiest spots on the Yorkshire coast.

Leave your car at the parking area in the upper village (£4.40 for four hours), where 19th-century ships' captains built comfortable Victorian villas, and walk downhill to Old Bay, the oldest part of the village (don't even think about driving down). This maze of narrow lanes and passages is dotted with tearooms, pubs, craft shops and artists' studios (there's even a tiny cinema), and at low tide you can go down onto the beach and fossick around in the rock pools.

Robin Hood's Bay is 6 miles southeast of Whitby. Bus 93 runs hourly between Whitby and Scarborough via Robin Hood's Bay.

lunches, and a cluster of retro-styled rooms for cosy chats over excellent coffee and cakes like treacle tart or Yorkshire tea loaf. The brunches with Fortune's smoked bacon and creamy scrambled eggs deserve a medal.

Cornish Bakery BAKERY £
(92 Church St, YO22 4BH; mains £3.60-4.30; ☉8am-5pm) It might be far from Cornwall, but this superb bakery serves freshly made Cornish pasties as well as delicious pastries including *pain au raisin* and Portuguese-style *pastel de nata*. Rinse them down with an expertly brewed coffee and you've fuelled up for the walk up the 199 steps to the abbey.

Humble Pie 'n' Mash BRITISH £
(☑01947-606444; www.humblepie.tccdev.com; 163 Church St; pie meal £9.99; ☉noon-8pm) Superb homemade gravy-laden pies with fillings ranging from haggis and neeps (turnips) to roast veg and goats cheese, served in a cosy timber-framed cottage with a 1940s nostalgia vibe. No bookings, cash only.

★**Magpie Cafe** SEAFOOD ££
(☑01947-602058; www.magpiecafe.co.uk; 14 Pier Rd; mains £13-28; ☉11.30am-9pm; 🛜🚼) 🌣 The Magpie flaunts its reputation for serving the 'World's Best Fish and Chips'. Damn fine they are too, but the world and his dog knows about it and summertime queues can stretch along the street. Takeaway fish and chips cost £7.95; the sit-down restaurant is more expensive, but offers a wide range of seafood dishes, from grilled sea bass to paella.

★**White Horse & Griffin** BRITISH ££
(☑01947-604857; www.whitehorseandgriffin.com; 87 Church St; mains £14-24; ☉8-9.30am, noon-

3pm & 5-9pm Mon-Sat, 12.30-4pm & 5.30-9pm Sun; 🛜🚼) This splendid old coaching inn is as old as Captain Cook, and indeed the man himself used it as a meeting place to fix his crews in the 17th century. Squeeze into the narrow bar and the restaurant behind it is barely noticeable, but what a find: expect elegantly presented, top-quality British cooking that celebrates both local seafood and meat.

Quayside FISH & CHIPS ££
(☑01947-825346; www.quaysidewhitby.co.uk; 7 Pier Rd; mains £10-16; ☉11am-8pm Mon-Sat, to 7pm Sun; 🚼) 🌣 Top-notch, award-winning fish and chips. The queues aren't nearly as long as at nearby competitor the Magpie Cafe, but that might be because they don't have 'world's best' on their tagline. Oh, the power of advertising.

Star Inn the Harbour BRITISH ££
(☑01947-821900; www.starinntheharbour.co.uk; Langborne Rd; mains £12-28; ☉11.30am-9pm Mon-Fri, noon-9pm Sat, to 7pm Sun) Yorkshire food hero Andrew Pern, of Michelin-starred Star Inn (p495) fame, gutted the former tourist office to create this spin-off restaurant on the harbour front in his home town of Whitby. It's no surprise that the theme is nautical and the menu leans heavily on its fishy environs, though there are also playful dishes such as Yorkshire pudding and foie gras.

🍷 Drinking & Nightlife

★**Whitby Brewery** MICROBREWERY
(☑01947-228871; www.whitby-brewery.com; Abbey Lane, East Cliff; ☉11am-5pm; 🚼) Walkers are pleased as punch when they find this

place on the clifftop behind Whitby Abbey. There's just enough room inside the modern brew plant for three tables – half the space is taken up by a gloriously incongruous Edwardian bar counter, behind which the bartender is well and truly trapped. There's a short selection of craft ales, and extra seating out front.

Green Dragon CRAFT BEER
(www.thegreendragonwhitby.co.uk; Grape Lane; ⊘noon-7.30pm Mon-Sat, to 6pm Sun) In a quaint old house on Whitby's most crooked lane, Green Dragon has grabbed the bull by the horns and dragged Britain's progressive craft-beer scene into this traditional real-ale town. It's part bottle shop, part teeny-weeny beer bar with five rotating taps running Yorkshire breweries like Northern Monk, Abbeydale and Vocation. It also sells mead and absinthe.

☆ Entertainment

Dracula Experience THEATRE
(✒ 01947-601923; 9 Marine Pde; adult/child £3/2.50; ⊘9.45am-5pm Easter-Oct, Sat & Sun Nov-Easter) There's definitely an element of Gothic geekdom about this theatrical walk-through of *Dracula*'s tale, with special effects, an occasional live actor appearing out of thin air and many a thing that goes bump in the night designed to spook you in the darkness. Wonderfully weird and very Whitby; not suitable for under eights.

ⓘ Information

Whitby Tourist Office (✒ 01723-383636; www.visitwhitby.com; Harbour Master's Office, Langborne Rd; ⊘9am-5pm May-Oct, to 4pm Thu-Sun Nov-Apr)

ⓘ Getting There & Away

BUS
Two buses, 93 and X93, run south to Scarborough (£6.20, one hour, every 30 minutes), with every second bus going via Robin Hood's Bay (£5.20, 15 minutes, hourly); and north to Middlesborough (£7, one hour, hourly), with fewer services on Sunday. The **bus station** is next to Whitby's train station.

The Coastliner service 840 runs from Leeds to Whitby (£15.70, 3¼ hours, four times daily Monday to Saturday, twice on Sundays, though you'll need to change at Malton) via York and Pickering.

Coming from the north, you can get to Whitby by train along the Esk Valley Railway from Middlesbrough (£7.50, 1½ hours, four daily), with connections from Durham and Newcastle. From the south, it's easier to get a train from York to Scarborough, and then a bus from Scarborough to Whitby.

YORKSHIRE DALES NATIONAL PARK

The Yorkshire Dales – named from the old Norse word *dalr*, meaning 'valleys', and protected as a national park since the 1950s – are beloved as one of England's best hiking and cycling areas. The park's glacial valleys are characterised by a distinctive landscape of high heather moorland, stepped skylines and flat-topped hills, punctuated by delightful country pubs and windswept trails.

Down in the green valleys, patchworked with drystone dykes and little barns, are picture-postcard villages where sheep still graze on village greens. And in the limestone country of the southern Dales you'll find England's best examples of karst scenery (created by rainwater dissolving the underlying limestone bedrock).

The whole area is seriously scenic and easy to explore. Consequently it's popular with holidaying Britons – book accommodation ahead as there are no big hotels here. Beds get particularly scarce on public holiday weekends and during events such as the annual Tour de Yorkshire.

ⓘ Getting There & Away

About 90% of visitors to the park arrive by car, and the narrow roads can become extremely crowded in summer. Parking can also be a serious problem.

We recommend that you use public transport where possible, but bus services are limited and many run in summer only – some on Sundays and bank holidays only. Pick up a DalesBus timetable from tourist offices, or consult the DalesBus (www.dalesbus.org) website.

By train, the best and most interesting access to the Dales is via the famous **Settle–Carlisle Line** (SCL; ✒ 01768-353200; www.settle-carlisle.co.uk). Trains run between Leeds and Carlisle, stopping at Skipton, Settle and numerous small villages, offering unrivalled access to the hills straight from the station platform.

Yorkshire Dales National Park

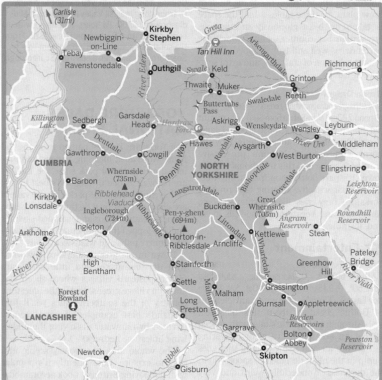

Skipton

☏ 01756 / POP 14,623

Home to one of England's best-preserved medieval castles and gateway to the southern Dales, this busy market town takes its name from the Anglo-Saxon *sceape ton* (sheep town). There are no prizes for guessing how it made its money. Monday, Wednesday, Friday and Saturday are market days, bringing crowds from all over and giving the town something of a festive atmosphere.

The Leeds–Liverpool Canal carves right through central Skipton, making the town a good jumping-off point for canal-boat trips.

◉ Sights & Activities

★ **Skipton Castle** CASTLE
(www.skiptoncastle.co.uk; High St; adult/child £8.70/5.50; ⏱10am-4pm) What makes Skipton Castle so fascinating is its splendid state of preservation, providing a striking contrast to the ruins you'll see elsewhere. Although it is lauded as one of the best-preserved medieval castles in England, many of its most memorable features date to Tudor times. Entrance is through the original Norman archway, which leads to a Tudor courtyard with a yew tree planted by Lady Anne Clifford in 1659, and beyond that is a warren of rooms to explore. Grab the informative free illustrated guide to the castle from the ticket office, available in several languages.

Pennine Cruisers BOATING
(☏01756-795478; www.penninecruisers.com; The Wharf, Coach St; per person £4; ⏱10.30am-dusk Mar-Oct) No trip to Skipton is complete without a cruise along the Leeds–Liverpool Canal, which runs through the middle of town. Pennine Cruisers runs half-hour trips along the canal and back, as well as canal-boat day hire, skippered trips and longer holiday rentals. Pre-booking essential.

🛏 Sleeping

★ Pinfold
GUESTHOUSE **££**
(✆ 07510-175270; www.thepinfoldskipton.co.uk; Chapel Hill; r £60-80; P 🛜) This petite, room-only guesthouse has three light and airy, oak-beamed rooms with a lovely fresh country feel. Forgive the tiny shower rooms, because the excellent location around the corner from Skipton Castle more than compensates. The Littondale room has its own entrance, parking and small grassy patio. The Little Pinfold Cottage, a one-room self-catering cottage across the street, has been added more recently.

Park Hill
B&B **££**
(✆ 01756-792772; www.parkhillskipton.co.uk; 17 Grassington Rd; d £95; P 🛜) From the complimentary glass of sherry on arrival to the hearty breakfasts based on local produce, such as farm-fresh eggs and home-grown tomatoes, this B&B provides a real Yorkshire welcome. It enjoys an attractive semi-rural location half a mile north of the town centre, on the B6265 road towards Grassington. No children under 12.

🍴 Eating & Drinking

Bizzie Lizzies
FISH & CHIPS **£**
(✆ 01756-701131; www.bizzielizzies.co.uk; 36 Swadford St; mains £10-13; ⏱ 11am-9pm; 🖶) An award-winning, old-fashioned fish-and-chip restaurant overlooking the canal, with a busy takeaway counter offering fish and chips for £6.65 (counter open to 11.30pm). Gluten-intolerant? No problem – Bizzie Lizzies also dishes up gluten-free chips accredited by Coeliac UK.

★ Le Caveau
BRITISH **£££**
(✆ 01756-794274; www.lecaveau.co.uk; 86 High St; 2/3-course menu £22.50/28.50; ⏱ noon-2.30pm & 7-9pm Tue-Fri, 5-9pm Sat) 🍴 Thanks to the stylish decoration there's no hint that this 16th-century cellar was once a prison for sheep rustlers. It's now one of Skipton's best bistros, offering a seasonal menu built lovingly around fresh local produce, with tempting dishes such as twice-baked smoked Ribblesdale goats-cheese soufflé and slow-roasted Nidderdale lamb shoulder.

Narrow Boat
PUB
(www.markettowntaverns.co.uk; 38 Victoria St; ⏱ noon-11pm; 🛜🖶🐾) Down a back alley beside Skipton's canal basin, this friendly pub is essentially a modern craft-beer bar but still manages to cultivate a traditional feel with wooden beams and old bar furniture. The beer selection is great; soak it up with interesting bar food such as halloumi chips, southern fried chicken burgers and a rotating range of flatbread pizzas.

ℹ Information

Tourist Office (✆ 01756-792809; www.welcometoskipton.com; Town Hall, High St; ⏱ 9.30am-4pm Mon-Sat)

ℹ Getting There & Away

Skipton is the last stop on the Metro rail network from Leeds (from £5.80, 45 minutes, frequent departures). Buses 580 to 582 link Skipton with Settle Monday to Saturday (£6.20, 40 minutes, hourly during the day), with many departures continuing on to Ingleton. There are also twice daily buses from Skipton to Malham (£4.70, 40 minutes) Monday to Saturday, and frequent departures from Skipton to Grassington.

Grassington

✆ 01756 / POP 1611

A good base for jaunts around the south Dales, Grassington's handsome Georgian centre teems with walkers and visitors throughout summer, soaking up an atmosphere that – despite the odd touch of faux rusticity – is as attractive and traditional as you'll find in these parts.

OFF THE BEATEN TRACK

FORBIDDEN CORNER

There can surely be no other place like **Forbidden Corner** (✆ 01969-640638; www.theforbiddencorner.co.uk; Tupgill Park Estate, near Leyburn; adult/child £13/11; ⏱ noon-dusk Mon-Sat Easter-Oct, Sun only Nov & Dec; P 🖶) in the world: a modern walled garden furnished with Victorian-style follies, some veering into Gothic horror, others merely surreal fantasy. There's no map, so it's a case of diving in to explore the many tunnels, twisted turns and dead-ends – an experience that may make you feel like you've fallen into David Bowie's *Labyrinth*. Small children are guaranteed to feel scared witless at some turns; adults may leave feeling a little rattled, too. Tickets must be pre-booked.

WORTH A TRIP

BRITAIN'S HIGHEST PUB

At an elevation of 528m (1732ft) **Tan Hill Inn** (☑ 01833-628246; www.tanhillinn. com; Tan Hill, Swaledale; ⊙ 8am-11.30pm Jul & Aug, 9am-9.30pm Sep-Jun; ⚇ ⚇ ⚇) is Britain's highest pub. Built to cater for 19th-century miners, it perches in the middle of nowhere about 11 miles northwest of Reeth. At times the howling wind can make it feel a bit wild up here, but inside it's unexpectedly comfortable and welcoming, with an ancient fireplace in the atmospheric, stone-flagged public bar and leather sofas in the lounge.

 Festivals & Events

Grassington Festival   ART
(www.grassington-festival.org.uk; ⊙ mid-Jun–early Jul) Highlight of the cultural year in the Yorkshire Dales is the Grassington Festival, a two-week arts extravaganza that attracts many big names in music, theatre and comedy, and also includes offbeat events like drystone-walling workshops.

Grassington 1940s Weekend   FAIR
(www.grassington1940sweekend.co.uk; ⊙ Sep) This vintage celebration brings classic cars, planes and army vehicles to town, as well as WWII military re-enactment encampments, for a weekend in mid-September.

🛏 Sleeping & Eating

Ashfield House   B&B ££
(☑ 01756-752584; www.ashfieldhouse.co.uk; Summers Fold; d/ste from £89/155; P ⚇) A secluded 17th-century country house with a walled garden, open fireplaces, honesty bar and all-round cosy feel. It's just off the main square.

★Devonshire Fell   HOTEL ££
(☑ 01756-718111; www.devonshirefell.co.uk; Burnsall; r from £95; P ⚇ ⚇) This former gentleman's club for mill owners in the scenic village of Burnsall has a very contemporary feel and spacious rooms, many with beautiful valley views. The conservatory (used as a restaurant, breakfast room and for afternoon tea) has a stunning outlook. It's 3 miles southeast of Grassington, which can be reached via a walking path by the river.

Corner House Cafe   CAFE £
(☑ 01756-752414; www.cornerhousegrassington. co.uk; 1 Garr's Lane; mains £7-10; ⊙ 10am-4pm; ⚇ ⚇ ⚇) This cute little white cottage, just uphill from the village square, serves good coffee and unusual homemade cakes (citrus and lavender-syrup sponge is unexpectedly delicious), as well as tasty made-to-order sandwiches and lunch specials such as Dales lamb hotpot or chicken and chorizo gratin. Breakfast, served till 11.30am, ranges from cinnamon toast to the full-English fry-up.

ⓘ Information

Grassington National Park Centre (☑ 01756-751690; Hebden Rd; 2/24hr parking £3/6; ⊙ 10am-5pm Apr-Oct, to 3pm Sat & Sun Nov, Dec, Feb & Mar)

ⓘ Getting There & Away

Grassington is 6 miles north of Skipton; take bus 72 from Skipton bus or train station (£5, 30 minutes, hourly Monday to Saturday), or X43 (hourly, Sunday and public holidays) from the bus station only. For onward travel, bus 72 continues up the valley to the villages of Kettlewell and Buckden.

Malham

POP 238

Even in the Dales, where competition is fierce, Malham is quite the looker. Stone cottages and inns huddle around a river that meanders through the village centre – which is always busy with walkers drawn to its world-famous hiking paths. If you're only visiting one village in the Dales, make it this one.

The village is set within the largest area of limestone country in England, stretching west from Grassington to Ingleton – a distinctive landscape pockmarked with potholes, dry valleys, limestone pavements and gorges. Two of the most spectacular features – Malham Cove and Gordale Scar – are within walking distance of Malham's centre.

◉ Sights & Activities

★Malham Cove   NATURAL FEATURE
North of Malham village, a 0.75-mile field walk beside a lovely babbling stream leads to Malham Cove, a huge rock amphitheatre lined with 80m-high vertical cliffs. A large

glacial waterfall once tumbled over this cliff, but it dried up hundreds of years ago. You can hike up the steep steps on the left-hand side of the cove (follow Pennine Way signs) to see the extensive limestone pavement above the cliffs – a filming location in *Harry Potter and the Deathly Hallows*.

Peregrine falcons nest at the top in spring, when the Royal Society for the Protection of Birds (RSPB) sets up a birdwatching lookout with telescopes near the base of the cliff – call the national park centre (p506) for the schedule as it changes every year.

Malham Tarn   LAKE

A glacial lake and nature reserve 3.5 miles north of Malham village, accessible via a 1.5-mile walk north from Malham Cove, or by car. There are two car parks: the one at the southern edge is bigger and picks up a trail that skirts the eastern side of the lake; the one to the north (follow signs to Arncliffe/Grassington) allows easy access to an extensive bog-skimming boardwalk that wends through fen and woodland scrub. Roe deer, heron and water voles can sometimes be spotted here.

Malham Landscape Trail   WALKING

(www.malhamdale.com) This 5-mile circular trail is one of the best day hikes in Yorkshire, linking three impressive natural features: Malham Cove; spectacular **Gordale Scar**, a deep limestone canyon with scenic cascades; and the remains of an Iron Age settlement, and **Janet's Foss** waterfall. A leaflet describing the trail in detail can be downloaded from the website or picked up at pubs and hotels in the village.

🛏 Sleeping & Eating

⭐**Lister Barn**   B&B **£££**

(📞01729-830444; www.listerarms.co.uk; Cove Rd; d £120-165; P🛜🐕🅿) The Lister Arms pub runs this chic barn conversion on the main road through the village, with eight modern rooms centred on a lovely open-plan communal area with free herbal teas and a log burner to huddle around after long walks. One room is suitable for wheelchair users and there are two family rooms with bunks and a separate bedroom.

Lister Arms   PUB FOOD **££**

(📞01729-830444; www.thwaites.co.uk; Cove Rd; mains £10-17; ⊙8am-11pm Mon-Sat, to 10.30pm Sun; P🛜🐕🅿) This comfy coaching inn is the best spot in Malham to kick back after a walk, with open fires for chilly days, a beer garden out back and classic pub meals, plus chalkboard specials. In the busy summer months drinkers lounge out on the grass in front of the pub.

YORKSHIRE MALHAM

RIBBLESDALE & THE THREE PEAKS

Scenic Ribblesdale cuts through the southwestern corner of the Yorkshire Dales National Park, where the skyline is dominated by a trio of distinctive hills known as the Three Peaks: Whernside (735m), Ingleborough (724m) and Pen-y-ghent (694m). Easily accessible via the Settle–Carlisle railway line (p501), this is one of England's most popular areas for outdoor activities, attracting thousands of hikers, cyclists and cavers each weekend.

At the head of the valley, 5 miles north of Horton, is the spectacular 30m-high Ribblehead Viaduct, built in 1874 and, at 400m, the longest on the Settle–Carlisle Line. You can hike there along the Pennine Way and travel back by train from Ribblehead station.

In a huddle of old stone barns is the simply marvellous **Courtyard Dairy** (📞01729-823291; www.thecourtyarddairy.co.uk; Crows Nest Barn, Austwick, near Settle; ⊙9.30am-5.30pm Mon-Sat, 10am-5pm Sun), a cheesemongers and cafe that has arguably the best farmhouse cheeses in the Yorkshire Dales. Owners Andy and Kathy Swinscoe are passionate supporters of small-scale producers, and deli staff are eager to hand out tasters. The cafe upstairs in the eaves of the barn slathers the cheese all over its menu. Come here to try 'Raclette Anglaise' and inventive grilled-cheese-sandwich wedges such as Wensleydale and caramelised-carrot chutney. Don't miss the delicious rich fruit cake with a slab of local Dales cheese: a Yorkshire tradition. There's also a small, hugely informative museum about cheesemaking in Yorkshire, maturing rooms you can peer into, and Andy runs one-day cheesemaking courses (£120) on-site; check the website for dates.

GRANTLEY HALL

Just outside the boundary of the national park is the Palladian pile of **Grantley Hall** (☑01765-667970; www.grantleyhall.co.uk; B6265, Ripon; r from £385, with dinner from £485), built in the 17th century for Thomas Norton and now Yorkshire's most luxurious hotel.

Opulence and the highest aesthetic considerations permeate the 47 rooms (huge beds and Tielle linen, gorgeous Italian marble bathrooms) and sweeping public spaces, including the Michelin-starred restaurant, **Shaun Rankin at Grantley Hall**. It's a classic country-house hotel, but the overall look is enhanced by some graceful modern notes. The enormous **Three Graces Spa** has an 18-metre pool, two gyms and a snow room, as well as altitude training facilities, making this the kind of destination that would suit an Olympic athlete in training as it would Lord Grantham in repose. In a separate building, the pan-Asian restaurant **EightyEight** (mains £25) is also superb.

It's 4 miles west of Ripon, off the B6265.

❶ Information

Malham National Park Centre (☑01729-833200; www.yorkshiredales.org.uk; parking 2/24hr £3.50/6; ☺10am-5pm Apr-Oct, to 4pm Sat & Sun Nov, Dec, Feb & Mar) In the car park at the southern edge of Malham village; the walking leaflets it sells (£1.50) include more detail than the free leaflet given out around the village.

❶ Getting There & Away

There are at least two buses a day Monday to Saturday year-round from Skipton to Malham (£4.70, 35 minutes). The scenic Malham Tarn Shuttle bus route links Settle with Malham (£4.30, 30 minutes), Malham Tarn and Ingleton six times daily on Sundays and bank holidays only, Easter to October. Check the DalesBus website (www.dalesbus.org) or ask at Malham National Park Centre for details.

Note that Malham is reached via narrow roads that can get very congested in summer, so leave your car at the national park centre and walk into the village.

Hawes

POP 1137

Right at the heart of Wensleydale, Hawes is a thriving, pretty market town (Tuesday is market day) surrounded by rolling hills and drystone walls that will be familiar to fans of the 1970s TV series, *All Creatures Great and Small,* based on James Herriot's books. It has several antique, art and craft shops, and the added attraction of its own waterfall in the village centre. The village can get pretty busy in summer, so leave the car in the parking area beside the national park centre at the eastern entrance to the village.

A mile northwest of Hawes, the pretty village of Hardraw has an even more impressive waterfall, a country church and an excellent old pub offering accommodation for those who prefer a quieter rural base. The whole area is also full of hiking trails.

◉ Sights

Hardraw Force WATERFALL
(www.hardrawforce.com; Hardraw; adult/child £4/2; ℗) About 1.5 miles north of Hawes is 30m-high Hardraw Force, the highest unbroken waterfall in England, but by international standards not that impressive (except after heavy rain). Access is via a lovely landscaped walk (400m) from the car park behind the Green Dragon Inn. There's an admission fee (coins only) to access the walk, and a cafe selling local ice cream.

Wensleydale Creamery MUSEUM
(www.wensleydale.co.uk; Gayle Lane; adult/child £1.95/free; ☺10am-4pm; ℗🚻) Wensleydale Creamery is devoted to the production of a crumbly white cheese that's the favourite of animation characters Wallace and Gromit. You can visit the cheese museum, watch cheesemakers in action in the viewing gallery (Monday to Friday), and then try-before-you-buy in the shop (which is free to enter). An interactive exhibit for kids explains the process from grass to cow to cheese.

Dales Countryside Museum MUSEUM
(☑01969-666210; www.dalescountrysidemuseum.org.uk; Station Yard; adult/child £4.80/free; ☺10am-5pm Feb-Dec; ℗🚻) Sharing a building with the national park centre, the Dales Countryside Museum is a beautifully presented social history of the area that explains the forces shaping the landscape,

from geology to lead mining to land enclosure and the railways.

🛌 Sleeping & Eating

★ Green Dragon Inn   INN ££
(☑ 01969-667392; www.thegreendragoninn-hardraw.com; Hardraw; d/ste £90/110; P🛜🐾) A lovely old pub with flagstone floors, low timber beams, ancient oak furniture and Theakston on draught, the Dragon serves up a tasty steak-and-ale pie and offers B&B in pleasant, simple rooms behind the pub, as well as a pair of fancy suites above the bar. It's 1 mile northwest of Hawes.

ℹ️ Information

Hawes National Park Centre (☑ 01969-666210; Station Yard; parking 2/24hr £2.50/5; ⊙10am-5pm Apr-Oct, closes early Nov, Dec, Feb & Mar, closed Jan)

Richmond

☑ 01748 / POP 8415

The handsome market town of Richmond perches on a rocky outcrop overlooking the River Swale and is guarded by the ruins of a massive castle, beneath which a small, frothy waterfall flows. It has been a garrison town for centuries and home to one of England's most decorated regiments, which now resides nearby at modern-day Catterick Garrison.

Elegant Georgian buildings and photogenic stone cottages line the streets that radiate from the broad cobbled market square (market day is Saturday), with glimpses of the surrounding hills and dales peeking through the gaps. There are plenty of local walks, and the town makes a pleasant base for exploring the northern Dales.

For themed walks, alongside talks, films and other events, visit the town during the **Richmond Walking & Book Festival** (☑ 01748-824243; www.booksandboots.org; ⊙Sep/Oct).

◉ Sights

★ Georgian Theatre Royal   HISTORIC BUILDING
(www.georgiantheatreroyal.co.uk; Victoria Rd; adult/child £5/2; ⊙tours hourly 10am-4pm Mon-Sat mid-Feb–mid-Nov) Built in 1788, this is the most complete Georgian playhouse in Britain. It closed in 1848 and was used as an auction house into the early 20th century, reopening as a working theatre again

in 1963 after a period of restoration. Fascinating tours (starting on the hour) include a look at the country's oldest surviving stage scenery, painted between 1818 and 1836.

Richmond Castle   CASTLE
(EH; www.english-heritage.org.uk; Tower St; adult/child £6.90/4.10; ⊙10am-5pm Wed-Sun) The impressive heap that is Richmond Castle, founded in 1070, has had many uses through the years, including a stint as a prison for conscientious objectors during WWI (there's a small and fascinating exhibition about their part in the castle's history – enter through the shop). The best part of a visit is the view from the top of the remarkably well-preserved 30m-high keep, which dates to the late 12th century and towers over the town.

🛌 Sleeping & Eating

Frenchgate Hotel   BOUTIQUE HOTEL ££
(☑ 01748-822087; www.thefrenchgate.co.uk; 59-61 Frenchgate; s/d incl breakfast from £98/148; P🛜) Nine elegant bedrooms occupy the upper floors of this converted Georgian town house, with flash touches such as memory-foam mattresses and heated marble floors in luxurious bathrooms. Parts of the house date to 1650, so we can forgive a crack here or peeling paint there. Downstairs there's an excellent restaurant (three-course dinner £39), an oasis of a garden and a private rear car park.

★ George & Dragon   PUB FOOD £
(☑ 01748-518373; www.georgeanddragonhudswell.co.uk; Hudswell; mains £9-11; ⊙food served noon-2pm & 5-8pm Mon-Sat, noon-4pm Sun; 🛜🐾) A mile and a half west of Richmond, the George & Dragon is a genuine local pub,

YORKSHIRE RICHMOND

> **BIKING IN THE DALES**
>
> The centre of mountain biking in the Yorkshire Dales, the **Dales Bike Centre** (☑ 01748-884908; www.dalesbikecentre.co.uk; Fremington; mountain bike/e-bike per day from £40/50; ⊙9am-5pm), 12 miles west of Richmond, provides quality bike rentals (mountain and road bikes, as well as e-bikes), a bike shop and repair service, advice and trail maps, guided rides (£199 per day for up to seven people), a cosy cafe with decent coffee and comfortable bunkhouse accommodation (two-bunk room £58 a night).

MASHAM BREWERIES

Located 9 miles northwest of Ripon, the little village of Masham is famous for producing some of Yorkshire's best beers. Yorkshire's best-known brewery, **Theakston's** (☑01765-680000; www.theakstons.co.uk; The Brewery, Masham; tour adult/child £8.50/4.95; ☺10.30am-4.30pm Sep-Jul, to 5pm Aug), was founded way back in 1827, then taken over by global brewer Scottish & Newcastle in 1987, but since 2004 has been back in family hands. Old Peculier, its most famous ale, takes its name from the Peculier of Masham, a medieval parish court established to deal with offences such as drunkenness and brawling. There's a visitor centre that doubles as a bar, and four tours a day (five in August).

Across the village, **Black Sheep Brewery** (☑01765-680101; www.blacksheepbrewery.com; Wellgarth, Masham; tours adult/child £9.50/4.95; ☺10am-5pm Sun-Wed, to 11pm Thu-Sat; P 🚼) was founded in 1992 by the 'black sheep' of the Theakston family, Paul Theakston, who left to start his own brewery after the controversial Scottish & Newcastle takeover. It's now almost as famous as its near neighbour, with four entertaining tours a day, an excellent casual bistro, and a bar where you can sample most of the Black Sheep brews.

owned and managed by the community. It serves a small menu of freshly prepared pub grub, including roast beef and Yorkshire pudding on Sundays, and has won awards for its excellent rotating beer selection. The backyard terrace has gorgeous Dales views.

The Station BRITISH £
(☑01748-850123; www.thestation.co.uk; Station Yard; mains £7-11; ☺10am-4pm Mon-Tue, to 7pm Thu-Sat, 9am-4pm Sun) Richmond's defunct Victorian railway station has been converted into a bold multipurpose space housing exhibition galleries, an independent cinema, craft brewery (offering tastings and sales) and ice-cream parlour. Locals come for takeaway lunch at Angel's Share Bakery, which bakes fresh breads, quiches and local specialities such as Yorkshire curd tart on-site. Take your goodies to the grassy picnic area outside.

ℹ Information

Richmond Tourist Office (☑01609-532980; www.richmond.org; Richmond Library, Queens Rd; ☺10am-5pm Mon-Fri, to 1pm Sat) A tiny tourist office with less information than can be found at other outlets across Yorkshire.

ℹ Getting There & Away

From Darlington (on the railway between London and Edinburgh) it's easy to reach Richmond on bus X26 or X27 (£6.20, 30 minutes, every half-hour, hourly on Sunday). All buses stop in Trinity Church Sq.

On Sundays and bank-holiday Mondays only, from May to September, the Northern Dalesman bus 830 runs from Richmond to Hawes (£4.70, 1½ hours, twice daily) via Reeth, and the afternoon bus continues to Ribblehead.

WEST YORKSHIRE

It was the tough and unforgiving textile industry that drove West Yorkshire's economy from the 18th century onward. The woollen mills, factories and canals built to transport raw materials and finished products defined much of the county's landscape. The mills have long since closed, and recent decades have seen the hard-bitten landscape soften once more.

Leeds and Bradford, two adjoining cities so big they've virtually become one, are undergoing radical redevelopment and reinvention, prettifying their centres and tempting more adventurous tourists with new museums, galleries and restaurants. Beyond the cities lies a landscape of wild moorland dissected by deep valleys dotted with old mill towns and villages, scenes that were so vividly described by the Brontë sisters, West Yorkshire's most renowned literary export and biggest tourist draw.

ℹ Getting There & Around

The Metro is West Yorkshire's highly efficient train and bus network, centred on Leeds and Bradford, which are also the main gateways to the county. For transport information, contact **West Yorkshire Metro** (☑0113-245 7676; www.wymetro.com).

Day Saver tickets (£9) are good for one day's unlimited travel on Metro buses and trains from 9.30am to 4pm and after 6.30pm on weekdays, and all day at weekends. A range of additional Rover tickets covering buses and/or trains, plus heaps of useful Metro maps and timetables, are available from bus and train stations and most tourist offices in West Yorkshire.

Leeds

0113 / POP 474,632

Just an hour south of the southern Dales and one of the fastest-growing cities in the UK, Leeds is the glitzy embodiment of rediscovered northern self-confidence. A decade and a half of redevelopment has transformed the city centre from a near-derelict mill town into a vision of 21st-century urban chic, with architecturally eye-catching malls woven into the fabric of the city centre, a revitalised Victorian mill district and an innovative independent dining and drinking scene. The decision by national broadcaster Channel 4 to move its HQ north from London just adds an extra feather to Leeds' cap.

People come from all over the north to indulge in shopping weekends, concert trips and the lively nightlife, giving the town a decidedly confident Yorkshire swagger. Excellent transport links to the Dales, York, Harrogate, Manchester and Haworth (of Brontë literary fame) can make it a good base, without the touristy veneer of neighbouring York.

Sights

★ Royal Armouries   MUSEUM

(www.royalarmouries.org; Armouries Dr; 10am-5pm Wed-Sun, last admission 3.30pm; P) FREE Leeds' most interesting museum was originally built in 1996 to house armour and weapons from the Tower of London, but subsequently expanded to cover 3000 years of combat and self-defence, becoming home to the national collections. The exhibits are as varied as they are fascinating, covering subjects such as jousting, fencing and Indian elephant armour. Walk east along the river from Centenary Footbridge (approx 10 minutes), or take the water taxi (p516) from Granary Wharf outside the train station's southern entrance.

Leeds Art Gallery   GALLERY

(www.leeds.gov.uk/artgallery; The Headrow; 10am-4pm Tue-Sat) FREE This major gallery is packed with 19th- and 20th-century British heavyweights – Turner, Constable, Stanley Spencer, Wyndham Lewis et al – along with contemporary pieces by more recent arrivals such as Damien Hirst and Antony Gormley, sculptor of the *Angel of the North*. The stunning Tiled Hall Cafe – formerly a reading room and then a sculpture court – is the city's most elegant spot for a break.

Leeds Industrial Museum   MUSEUM

(Armley Mills; 0113-378 3173; www.leeds.gov.uk/museumsandgalleries/armleymills; Canal Rd, Armley; adult/child £4.50/2.50; 10am-5pm Tue-Fri, 1-5pm Sat-Sun; P; 15 from city centre) One of the world's largest textile mills has been transformed into a museum telling the story of Leeds' industrial past, both glorious and ignominious. The city grew rich from the textile industry, but at some cost in human terms – working conditions were Dickensian. As well as a selection of mill machinery, there's an informative display about how cloth is made. The museum is 2 miles west of the city centre; take the bus from Vicar Lane near Kirkgate Market.

Kirkstall Abbey   CHURCH

(www.leeds.gov.uk/kirkstallabbey; Abbey Rd, Kirkstall; 10am-4.30pm Tue-Sun Apr-Sep, to 4pm Oct-Mar; 33, 33A or 757 from city centre) FREE Leeds' most impressive medieval structure is beautiful Kirkstall Abbey, founded in 1152 by Cistercian monks from Fountains Abbey in North Yorkshire. These days the city makes good use of it as an atmospheric backdrop for pop-up events and a monthly weekend food market (April to November; check online for dates). It's 3 miles northwest of the centre.

Across the road is the **Abbey House Museum** (www.leeds.gov.uk/museumsandgalleries; Abbey Walk, Kirkstall; adult/child £5.45/2.80; 10am-noon & 1-4pm Wed-Fri & Sun, noon-5pm Sat; P), which was once the Great Gate House to the abbey. It contains meticulously reconstructed shops and houses that evoke Victorian Leeds, plus rotating exhibitions mostly aimed at kids.

Tetley   GALLERY

(0113-320 2423; www.thetetley.org; Hunslet Rd; 11am-4pm Wed-Sun) Tetley Brewery's defunct 1930s offices have been converted into a contemporary-arts venue with a restaurant and pub on the ground floor, spilling out onto an outdoor terrace. Upstairs the old meeting rooms have been put to good use as quirky gallery spaces, housing rotating exhibitions from international and local artists and photographers. An immaculately preserved 1930s lift dominates the central stairwell shaft.

Henry Moore Institute   GALLERY

(www.henry-moore.org/hmi; The Headrow; 10am-5pm Tue-Sun) FREE Housed in a converted Victorian warehouse in the city

Leeds

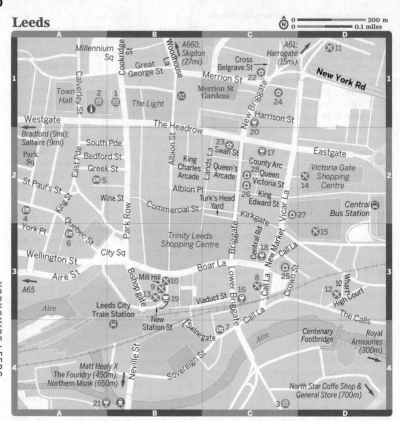

centre, this gallery showcases the work of 20th-century sculptors, but not, despite the name, anything by Henry Moore (1898–1986), who graduated from the Leeds School of Art. To see works by Moore, head to the Yorkshire Sculpture Park (p514) and Hepworth Wakefield (p514).

✨ Festivals & Events

Leeds Indie Food   FOOD & DRINK
(www.leedsindiefood.co.uk; ☉ mid-May; 🐾) This home-grown festival takes over Leeds' food scene for two weeks each May and has become one of the UK's most inventive celebrations of independent local producers, restaurants, cafes and boozers. There are dozens of quirky events around town, such as kitchen takeovers, wine- and beer-pairing dinners, film nights, food-photography workshops, foraging walks and brewery crawls.

Leeds Beer Week   BEER
(www.leedsbeerweek.co.uk; ☉ late Aug) Tap takeovers, food- and beer-pairing evenings, new beer launches, beer cocktail menus – expect Leeds' city bars to be raining craft beer during this annual week of events, spread across independent venues all over town. Some events are drop-in but some need to be booked ahead (check online); it takes place the week running up to the August bank holiday.

Leeds Festival   MUSIC
(www.leedsfestival.com; ☉ end Aug) The August bank holiday weekend sees 50,000-plus music fans converge on Bramham Park, 10 miles outside the city centre, for the Leeds Festival. Spread across several stages, it's one of England's biggest rock-music extravaganzas. There are various camping/glamping options on site, or you can buy day tickets.

Leeds

YORKSHIRE LEEDS

🛏 Sleeping

Roomzzz Leeds City APARTMENT ££
(📞0203-504 5555; www.roomzzz.com/aparthotels/leeds-city; 10 Swinegate; studio from £74, 2-person apt from £95; @🛜) This outfit offers bright and modern luxury apartments complete with fitted kitchen, with the added advantage of 24-hour hotel reception and a great city-centre location. There are two other branches, both on Burley Rd, but this is by far the most central.

Quebecs BOUTIQUE HOTEL ££
(📞0113-244 8989; www.quebecshotel.co.uk; 9 Quebec St; d/ste from £89/189; 🅿🛜) Victorian grace at its opulent best is the theme of Quebecs, a conversion of the former Leeds & County Liberal Club. The elaborate wood panelling and heraldic stained-glass windows in the public areas are mirrored by the grand design flourishes in the bedrooms, but it's a listed building (which means no double glazing) so expect some street noise.

⭐ **Chambers** APARTMENT £££
(📞0113-386 3300; www.morethanjustabed.com; 30 Park Pl; 2-person apt £120-190, parking per night £14; 🅿🛜) This grand Edwardian office building has been converted into 63 luxury serviced apartments, ranging from two-person studios to a two-bedroom penthouse (£350 a night) that will sleep up to four adults. Simple, fresh and spotlessly clean, there's also a 24-hour reception with great service, a gym, honesty bar and pretty little patio for aperitifs or night caps.

⭐ **Dakota** HOTEL £££
(📞0113-322 6261; http://leeds.dakotahotels.co.uk; 8 Russell St; d/ste from £136/270; ✳🛜) Raising the bar for luxury sleeps in Leeds, this gleaming hotel has quickly become popular thanks to its central location close to shops and bars, swanky yet muted designer interior and five-star service. Rooms are plush, modern and classic, and the suites are like mini-apartments, with open-plan lounge area and dressing room with robes.

🍴 Eating

Belgrave Music Hall & Canteen STREET FOOD £
(www.belgravemusichall.com; 1 Cross Belgrave St; mains £6.95-12.95; ⦿food served 11am-10pm; 🛜🍽) This bar and music venue has two great kitchens. Dough Boys serves artisan pizza (watch out for the napalm chilli sauce); Patty Smiths offers brunch and probably the best burgers in Yorkshire, all at great-value prices. Every second Saturday of the month the place hosts the **Belgrave Feast** (11am to 8pm), an art market and street-food festival.

Bundobust INDIAN £
(📞0113-243 1248; www.bundobust.com; 6 Mill Hill; dishes £4-6.75; ⦿kitchen noon-9.30pm Mon-Thu, to 10pm Fri & Sat, to 8pm Sun; 🥂) What could be more Yorkshire than craft beer and Indian street food rolled into one no-frills, brick-walled bar? The beers come from both local and international breweries, and food inspiration comes from vegetarian street-hawker

ART IN YORKSHIRE

Yorkshire Sculpture Park (☑ 01924-832631; www.ysp.co.uk; Bretton Park, near Wakefield; £6; ◷ 10am-6pm; P 🚻 🐾) One of England's most impressive collections of national and international sculpture is scattered across the formidable 18th-century estate of Bretton Park, 200-odd hectares of lawns, fields and trees. The park is partly a homage to local heroes Barbara Hepworth (1903–75), who was born in Wakefield, and Henry Moore (1898–1986), though more of their works are on display at the Hepworth Wakefield. Advance booking is required.

The rural setting is especially fitting for Moore's work, as the artist was hugely influenced by the outdoors and preferred his art to be sited in the landscape rather than indoors. Other highlights include pieces by Andy Goldsworthy and Eduardo Paolozzi, and Roger Hiorns' famous work *Seizure 2008/2013*, an apartment coated in blue copper sulphate crystals (open weekends only). There's also a program of temporary exhibitions and installations by visiting artists, plus a bookshop and cafe.

The park is 12 miles south of Leeds and 18 miles north of Sheffield, just off Junction 38 on the M1 motorway. If you're on public transport, take a train from Leeds to Wakefield (£4.70, 15 to 30 minutes, frequent departures), or from Sheffield to Barnsley (£5.20, 25 minutes, four hourly), and then take bus 96, which runs between Wakefield and Barnsley via Bretton Park (£3.40 to £4, 30 minutes, hourly Monday to Saturday).

Hepworth Wakefield (☑ 01924-247360; www.hepworthwakefield.org; Gallery Walk, Wakefield; parking £5; ◷ 10am-5pm Wed-Sun; P) West Yorkshire's standing in the international arts scene got a boost in 2011 when the Yorkshire Sculpture Park was joined by this award-winning gallery of modern art, housed in a stunningly angular building on the banks of the River Calder. The gallery has been built around the works of Wakefield-born sculptor Barbara Hepworth, perhaps best known for her work *Single Form*, which graces the UN Headquarters in New York.

The gallery is smaller than it looks from the outside, but showcases more than a dozen Hepworth originals, as well as works by other 20th-century British artists including Ivon Hitchens, Paul Nash, Victor Pasmore, John Piper and Henry Moore.

The gallery is near the centre of Wakefield, a 10-minute walk south of Wakefield Kirkgate train station, easily reached from Leeds by train (£3.90, 15 to 30 minutes, three to four hourly).

Salts Mill (☑ 01274-531163; www.saltsmill.org.uk; Victoria Rd, Saltaire; ◷ 9am-4pm Fri, to 5pm Sat-Sun; P) Saltaire, a Victorian-era landmark and Unesco World Heritage Site, was an industrial village purpose-built in 1851 by philanthropic wool baron and teetotaller Titus Salt. The village's huge factory was once the largest in the world. It is now Salts Mill, a splendidly bright and airy cathedral-like building where the main draw is a permanent exhibition of works by Bradford-born artist David Hockney.

offerings across India. The okra fries are a favourite with drinkers; more substantial bites include paneer and mushroom tikka, and biryani bhaji balls.

Friends of Ham DELI ££
(☑ 0113-242 0275; www.friendsofham.co.uk; 4-8 New Station St; dishes £6-19; ◷ 11am-11pm Mon-Wed, to midnight Thu-Sat, to 10pm Sun; 🤵) This stylish bar serves the finest charcuterie and cheeses – Spanish, French, British – accompanied by fine wines and craft beers. The food is carefully selected and prepared, and utterly delicious; you can order individual tapas-like portions, or huge sharing platters with olive-oil-drizzled bread. Brunch served 11am till 2pm.

Reliance BRITISH ££
(☑ 0113-295 6060; www.the-reliance.co.uk; 76-78 North St; mains £12.50-18; ◷ noon-10pm Mon-Wed, to 10.30pm Thu-Sat, to 8.30pm Sun; 🤵) ⌀ The Reliance is a comfortable-as-old-slippers bar where you can happily while away an afternoon reading or chatting with a Yorkshire beer or good glass of natural wine in hand. Yet it's also one of Leeds' best gastropubs, serving Sunday roasts, seasonal Modern British dishes like pig cheeks with beetroot and smoked apple, and platters of home-made charcuterie.

Tharavadu
SOUTH INDIAN ££

(☑0113-244 0500; www.tharavadurestaurants.
com; 7-8 Mill Hill; mains £13-18; ☻noon-2pm &
6-9.30pm Mon-Thu, noon-2pm & 5-10pm Fri & Sat)
This Michelin-guide-recommended restaurant is the go-to for a classy South Indian meal in Leeds city centre, with a Keralan menu that's heavy on fish curries and regional specialities such as whole crab and spiced king prawns. The restaurant is snug and packs diners in like sardines, which guarantees a lively atmosphere. Book in advance, especially on weekends.

Matt Healy X The Foundry
EUROPEAN ££

(☑0113-245 0390; www.mhfoundry.co.uk; 1 Saw
Mill St; mains £13-27; ☻5-9.30pm Thu, noon-
9.30pm Fri-Sat, to 7pm Sun) Matt Healy, in case you're wondering, was a 2016 *MasterChef: The Professionals* finalist. In 2018 he took over The Foundry, a red-brick warehouse restaurant, and breathed new life into it with creative, high-end sharing plates such as harissa-spiced lamb with giant couscous and sous vide duck breast with baby beets. It's good but pricey; there's a two-course lunch deal with wine for £22.50.

Shears Yard
MODERN BRITISH ££

(☑0113-244 4144; www.shearsyard.com; 11-15
Wharf St; mains £14-16; ☻5.30-10pm Tue-Sat,
11am-3pm Sat, noon-4pm Sun; ☑) ✎ Acres of exposed brick, concrete floors and a soaring roof provide an industrial-chic setting (it's a former rope-making yard) for painterly presentations of imaginative dishes such as ox-cheek fritter with roast-onion consommé, or squid with puffed potato and coriander emulsion. An eight-course tasting menu is available at lunch on Saturdays (£30) and dinner on Fridays and Saturdays (£40).

★ The Man Behind the Curtain
BRITISH £££

(☑0113-243 2376; www.themanbehindthecurtain.
co.uk; 68-78 Vicar Lane; lunch/dinner tasting menu
£85/120; ☻6.30-8.15pm Tue-Thu, 12.15-2pm &
6-9.15pm Fri-Sun) You'll have to book a couple of months in advance to stick your cutlery into Michael O'Hare's Michelin-starred tasting menu. His inventive reinterpretations of classic British dishes are as masterful as they are whimsical (yellow-fin tuna flavoured with a Fisherman's Friend lozenge?), while the presentation is brilliantly theatrical.

★ Ox Club
GRILL £££

(☑07470 359961; www.oxclub.co.uk; Bramleys
Yard, The Headrow; mains £22-32; ☻5-10pm Tue-
Sat, brunch 11am-3pm Sat & Sun) Arguably the best restaurant in Leeds (or at least, the best without a Michelin star), Ox Club occupies an intimate, minimalist space and champions local produce with a deceptively simple menu. Though it bills itself as a grill restaurant, the Modern British dishes are far more inventive than what you'll find in your average barbecue joint – venison tartare with smoked fat, for example.

★ The Owl
BRITISH £££

(www.theowlleeds.co.uk; Kirkgate Market;
2-/3-course lunch £24/27, 4-/5-course dinner
£40/47; ☻8.30am-5.30pm Mon-Thu, to 10pm Fri-
Sat) Kirkgate Market's first new pub for 150 years is home to an exquisite dining experience. The menu – staunchly British, locally sourced and wonderfully inventive – is pub grub transformed by a gourmet wand. How about north sea trout with caviar sauce? The Tap Room menu is perfect if you just want to graze over a pint.

🍷 Drinking & Nightlife

★ Laynes Espresso
COFFEE

(☑07828 823189; www.laynesespresso.co.uk;
16 New Station St; ☻7am-7pm Mon-Fri, 9am-
6pm Sat & Sun; ☎) ✎ Locals have Laynes to thank for the complete reinvention of the Leeds coffee scene; when it opened in 2011 there was nothing else like it in the city. Now expanded and serving excellent all-day brunch – buckwheat pancakes and smashed avocado on toast, naturally – and Yorkshire rarebit alongside strong coffee, it's still the best indie cafe in town for an espresso or flat white.

★ Northern Monk
BREWERY

(☑0113-243 0003; www.northernmonk.com; The
Old Flax Store, Marshall St; ☻3-8pm Wed, 3-10pm
Thu, noon-10pm Fri-Sat, to 8pm Sun) So successful has this craft brewery become that its beers are now stocked in UK supermarkets. But it's best drunk at the source, in the brewery's Grade II–listed taproom just south of Leeds city centre in the regeneration 'hood of Holbeck. Draft options run the gamut from hoppy IPAs or rich porters to small-batch collaborations and guest beers; brewery tours also available.

North Star Coffee Shop & General Store
COFFEE

(www.northstarroast.com; Unit 33, The Boulevard,
Leeds Dock; ☻7.30am-5.30pm Mon-Fri, 9am-
5pm Sat, 10am-4pm Sun) This minimalist cafe and coffee emporium is attached to the

production facility of Leeds' first independent roastery, near the Royal Armouries. Watch the daily grind through giant glass doors and inhale the aromas while sampling a flat white and cake (baked fresh on-site each day), or indulge in brunch – the slow-cooked scrambled eggs on a buttery four-cheese rye scone is small yet deliciously decadent.

Headrow House BAR
(☎0113-245 9370; www.headrowhouse.com; Bramleys Yard, The Headrow; ⏰noon-10pm) A former textile mill and one-time grotty dive pub, the historic building that now houses Headrow House was given a hefty makeover to transform it into the four-floor nightlife venue it is today. The ground-floor beer hall sells its own pilsner straight from tanks lining one wall. Upstairs there's a cocktail bar and Leeds' best roof-terrace drinking spot. It's also home to Ox Club (p513) restaurant.

North Bar CRAFT BEER
(www.northbar.com; 24 New Briggate; ⏰11am-1am Mon & Tue, to 2am Wed-Sat, noon-midnight Sun; 📶) This narrow bar has long been an institution in Leeds as a haven of international craft beers. It now brews its own under the banner North Brewing Co, and they're rather good. Drink them here, or visit the brewery taproom (Sheepscar Grove), which is BYO food and open Fridays 4pm to 10pm and Saturdays noon to 10pm, a 10-minute walk north of North Bar.

Water Lane Boathouse CRAFT BEER
(☎0113-246 0985; www.waterlaneboathouse.com; Water Lane; ⏰11am-11pm Sun-Thu, to 12.30am Fri & Sat) Watch canal boats chug into Granary Wharf from the floor-to-ceiling windows or generous outside seating area at this beer bar, occupying a prime historic spot on the water close enough to clink glasses with boaters. The top-quality global craft beers are pricey, but the setting is hard to beat. There's also tasty pizza available from £6.

Bar Fibre CLUB
(www.barfibre.com; 168 Lower Briggate; ⏰noon-1am Sun-Thu, to 3am Fri, to 4am Sat) In the heart of Leeds' LGBT+ area, spilling out onto the cheekily named Queen's Court, this is the city's most popular gay bar, although it's not just the gay crowd that loves its party atmosphere. This is where the beautiful people congregate; the dress code is...dressy, so look your best or you won't get in. Download the bar's app for deals such as buy one, get one free.

HiFi Club CLUB
(☎0113-242 7353; www.thehificlub.co.uk; 2 Central Rd; ⏰11pm-4am Tue-Sun) If it's Tamla Motown or the percussive beats of dance-floor jazz that shake your booty, this is the spot for you. Also has stand-up comedy sessions (£14) on Saturdays from 7pm, which can be combined with dinner at **Art's Cafe** (☎0113-243 8243; www.artscafebar.com; 42 Call Lane; mains £13-18; ⏰noon-11pm Mon-Sat, to 9pm Sun; 📶🍷) for £26.95 (book online).

☆ Entertainment

★ Belgrave Music Hall & Canteen LIVE MUSIC
(☎0113-234 6160; www.belgravemusichall.com; 1 Cross Belgrave St; ⏰11am-midnight Sun-Thu, to 3am Fri & Sat) Belgrave is the city's best live-music venue, with a diverse roll call of acts from burlesque to comedy and folk to hip-hop. Its three floors also encompass a huge bar bristling with craft-beer taps, two kitchens (p511), loads of shared tables and sofa space, and a fantastic roof terrace with views across the city. Why would you ever leave?

Domino JAZZ
(www.thedomino.co.uk; 7 Grand Arcade; Fri & Sat night admission £5; ⏰6pm-3am Mon-Sun) A wooden door at the back of Lords' barbershop takes you down to this broody basement cocktail bar and live-jazz club. Shows are free and start around 9pm most nights. Grab a booth and enjoy the table service.

City Varieties LIVE MUSIC, COMEDY
(☎0113-243 0808; www.leedsheritagetheatres.com; Swan St) Founded in 1865, City Varieties is the world's longest-running music hall, where the likes of Harry Houdini, Charlie Chaplin and Lily Langtry once trod the boards. Its program features stand-up comedy, live music, pantomime and old-fashioned variety shows.

🛍 Shopping

Corn Exchange SHOPPING CENTRE
(www.leedscornexchange.co.uk; Call Lane; ⏰10am-6pm Mon-Wed, Fri & Sat, to 9pm Thu, 10.30am-4.30pm Sun; 📶) The dramatic Corn Exchange, built in 1863 to house grain-trade merchants, has a wonderful wrought-iron roof that today shelters a fine collection of independent shops and boutiques. It sells everything from vinyl and craft beer to fashion, jewellery and Yorkshire design.

YORKSHIRE'S BLACK GOLD

For close to three centuries, West and South Yorkshire were synonymous with coal production. The collieries shaped and scarred the landscape, and entire villages grew up around the pits. The industry came to a shuddering halt in the 1980s, but the imprint of coal is still very much in evidence, even if there's only a handful of collieries left. One of these, the former Caphouse Colliery, is now the National Coal Mining Museum for England (www.ncm.org.uk; Overton, near Wakefield; parking £2, tour £4, miniature train return £1.50; ☺10am-5pm Wed-Sun, last tour 3.15pm; P ♿) FREE.

The highlight of a visit is the underground tour (departing every 10 to 15 minutes): equipped with helmet and head-torch, you descend almost 140m in the 'cage', then follow subterranean passages to the coal seam, where massive drilling machines now stand idle. Former miners work as guides and explain the detail – sometimes with a suitably authentic and almost impenetrable mix of local dialect and technical terminology.

The museum is 10 miles south of Leeds on the A642 between Wakefield and Huddersfield, reached via Junction 40 on the M1. By public transport, take a train from Leeds to Wakefield (£3.90, 15 to 30 minutes, three to four hourly), and then bus 232 or 128 towards Huddersfield (£3.10, 25 minutes, hourly).

Kirkgate Market   MARKET
(www.leeds.gov.uk/leedsmarkets; Kirkgate; ☺8am-5.30pm Mon-Sat) Britain's largest covered market sells fresh meat, fish, and fruit and vegetables, as well as household goods, and also has a popular street-food hall and the fabulous Owl (p513) pub. The best section is at the top near Vicar Lane, where the original Victorian stalls are still inhabited by traders – this was where UK retailing giant Marks & Spencer started out in 1884.

Victoria Quarter   SHOPPING CENTRE
(www.victorialeeds.co.uk; Vicar Lane; ☎) The mosaic-paved, stained-glass-roofed Victoria Quarter shopping arcade, between Briggate and Vicar Lane, is well worth visiting for aesthetic reasons alone, as is County Arcade, which runs parallel. Dedicated shoppers can join the footballers' wives browsing boutiques such as Louis Vuitton and Vivienne Westwood. The flagship store here is Harvey Nichols (www.harveynichols.com; 107-111 Briggate; ☺10am-7pm Mon-Sat, 11am-5pm Sun).

ℹ Information

Leeds Tourist Office (☏0113-378 6977; www.visitleeds.co.uk; Leeds Art Gallery, Headrow; ☺10am-5pm Mon-Sat, 11am-3pm Sun; ☎) In the basement of the city art gallery.

ℹ Getting There & Away

AIR
Leeds Bradford International Airport (www.leedsbradfordairport.co.uk) is 11 miles northwest of the city via the A65, and has flights to a range of domestic and international destinations. The Flying Tiger 757 bus (£4, 40 minutes, every 20 to 30 minutes) runs between Leeds bus and train stations and the airport. A taxi costs about £22.

BUS
National Express (www.nationalexpress.com) serves most major cities, while Yorkshire Coastliner (www.coastliner.co.uk) buses run to York, Pickering, Malton, Scarborough and Whitby. A Daytripper Plus ticket (£16) gives unlimited travel on all Coastliner buses for a day. The **Central Bus Station** is near Victoria Gate Shopping Centre.

London £11.60 to £33, 4½ hours, hourly

Manchester £6, 1¼ hours, at least hourly

Scarborough £13.50, three hours, hourly

Whitby £19.30, 3½ hours, four daily Monday to Saturday, twice daily Sundays

York £7, 1¼ hours, at least hourly

TRAIN
Leeds train station has good rail connections with the rest of the country and Manchester's international airport. It's also the starting point for trains on the scenic Settle–Carlisle line (p501). Tickets for Manchester and York can be had for a song if you book ahead and can be flexible on times.

London King's Cross £59, 2¼ hours, at least hourly

Manchester £10.30, one to 1½ hours, every 10 to 20 minutes

Manchester Airport £24, 1½ hours, three hourly

Sheffield £9.40, one hour, six hourly

York £8.30, 25 minutes, at least every 15 minutes

❶ Getting Around

Leeds has a compact city centre and it's quicker to walk everywhere than attempt to take a bus. CityBus 70 South Bank (£1 flat fare) links the train station with Leeds Dock (for the Royal Armouries), but a nicer way to travel between the two is the **water taxi** (www.leedsdock.com/whos-here/watertaxis; £1; ⊘ every 15min 7am-7pm Mon-Fri, 10am-6pm Sat-Sun) that runs from Granary Wharf, at the train station's southern entrance.

Various WY Metro (www.wymetro.com) Day Rover passes covering trains and/or buses are good for reaching Bradford, Haworth and Hebden Bridge.

Bradford

🖊 01274 / POP 349,561

Their suburbs may have merged into one sprawling urban conurbation, but Bradford remains far removed from its much more glamorous neighbour, Leeds.

Thanks to its role as a major player in the wool trade, Bradford attracted large numbers of immigrants from Bangladesh and Pakistan during the 20th century. Despite occasional racial tensions, these new arrivals have helped reinvigorate the city and give it new energy, plus a reputation for superb curry restaurants – Bradford has been crowned Curry Capital of Britain six times in recent years. But the main reason to visit is still the National Science & Media Museum.

◉ Sights

National Science & Media Museum MUSEUM
(www.scienceandmediamuseum.org.uk; off Little Horton Lane; ⊘10am-6pm Wed-Sun) FREE Bradford's top attraction is housed in an impressive glass-fronted building and chronicles the story of photography, film, TV, radio and the web from 19th-century cameras and early animation to digital technology and the psychology of advertising. International visitors may find themselves a little lost with the British-focused TV exhibits, but there is lots of other hands-on stuff, including a trippy interactive image-and-sound tech gallery and a room crammed with 1980s video games (Pacman! Street Fighter!).

The museum looks out over City Park, Bradford's award-winning central square, which is home to the Mirror Pool, the country's largest urban water feature.

✕ Eating

Bradford is famous for its curries, so don't miss out on trying one of the city's hundred or so restaurants. A great help is the Bradford Curry Guide (www.visitbradford.com/explore/bradford_curry_guide.aspx), which helps sort the rogan josh from the rubbish nosh.

Kashmir INDIAN £
(🖊01274-726513; 27 Morley St; mains £5-8; ⊘11am-1am Sun-Thu, to 4am Fri & Sat; 🖊) Don't be put off by the dodgy-looking facade: Bradford's oldest curry house has top tucker, served with no frills and no booze (although it is BYO). At quieter times you'll be seated in the windowless basement, with all the character of a 1950s factory canteen, but the food is still excellent. It's just around the corner from the National Science & Media Museum.

Zouk Tea Bar INDIAN, PAKISTANI £
(🖊01274-258025; www.zoukteabar.co.uk; 1312 Leeds Rd; mains £9-13; ⊘noon-midnight; 🖊🖊🖊) This modern and stylish cafe-restaurant staffed by chefs from Lahore offers an up-market menu and some unusual twists on traditional Indian and Pakistani food, such as delicious shawarma wraps and curried lamb shank slow-cooked in aromatic spices. It's in a Bradford suburb; the 72 bus that runs between Bradford Interchange and Leeds bus station will drop you outside.

❶ Getting There & Away

Bradford is on the Metro train line from Leeds (£4.60, 20 minutes, three to five per hour) and also a stop on the line that links Leeds with Hebden Bridge.

Hebden Bridge

🖊 01422 / POP 4235

Tucked tightly into a fold of a steep-sided valley, Yorkshire's funkiest small town is a former mill centre that refused to go gently with the dying of industry's light. Instead, it raged a bit and then morphed into an attractive outdoorsy tourist trap with a distinctly bohemian atmosphere. The town is home to university academics, artists, diehard hippies and a substantial gay community. All of this explains the abundance of vintage shops, organic and vegan cafes, and second-hand bookstores. Walking trails leading from the centre of town and up into the hills are another attraction.

⊙ Sights & Activities

Gibson Mill   HISTORIC BUILDING
(NT; ☑ 01422-846236; www.nationaltrust.org.uk; parking £5; ⊙ 11am-4pm mid-Mar–Oct, to 3pm Sat & Sun Nov–mid-Mar; ℗) ∕ This renovated, sustainably powered 19th-century cotton mill is home to a visitor centre covering the industrial and social history of the mill and its workers. Although it is currently closed, you can visit the cafe (11am to 4pm) or wander amid the woods and waterfalls of local beauty spot **Hardcastle Crags** (open dawn to dusk, admission free), 1.5 miles north of town, reachable via a 45-minute walk from St George's Sq, partly following the river. Go to www.hbwalkersaction.org.uk for directions.

Hebden Bridge Mill   HISTORIC BUILDING
(www.innovationhebdenbridge.co.uk; St George's Sq; ⊙ hours vary) The spindly chimney of Hebden Bridge's old red-brick mill is a central landmark that predates the town itself, and was saved from demolition in 1974. It is now a home for vintage stores and small studios, anchored by the Innovation Shop & Cafe-Bar on the ground floor, where the mill's working water wheel and Archimedes' screw (water pump) are located. Heritage panels explain the history of the site, which is now run on sustainable water power. Shop opening hours vary; weekends are most reliable.

Heptonstall   VILLAGE
(www.heptonstall.org) Above Hebden Bridge lies the much older village of Heptonstall, its narrow cobbled street lined with 500-year-old cottages and the ruins of a beautiful **13th-century church**. But it's the churchyard of the newer **St Thomas' Church** (1854) that draws literary pilgrims, for here is buried the poet Sylvia Plath (1932–63), whose husband, poet Ted Hughes (1930–98), was born in nearby Mytholmroyd. You'll have to hunt hard to find her grave, in the new cemetery beyond the church's far wall.

Hebden Bridge Cruises   CRUISE
(☑ 07966 808717; www.hebdenbridgecruises.com; Stubbing Wharf, King St; adult/child from £10/7; ⊙ 1pm & 2.15pm Sat) Join a colourful canal boat for a 40-minute guided cruise along the Rochdale Canal. There's also an afternoon-tea cruise (adult/child £18/12), a 50-minute fish-and-chip cruise (adult/child £23/15) where you feast on bat-tered haddock and chips or a 90-minute Sunday-lunch cruise (adult/child £33/20). Departs from the Stubbing Wharf Pub, half a mile west of the town centre.

🛏 Sleeping

Hebden Bridge Hostel   HOSTEL **£**
(☑ 01422-843183, 07786 987376; www.hebdenbridgehostel.co.uk; Birchcliffe Centre, Birchcliffe Rd; s/tw/q from £35/55/75; ⊙ Easter–early Nov; ℗ 🛜) ∕ Just a 10-minute walk uphill from the town centre, this eco-hostel is set in a peaceful stone building, complete with sunny patio, tucked behind a former Baptist chapel. There's a cosy library, comfy and clean en-suite rooms, and a vegetarian-food-only kitchen. An inconvenience is that the hostel locks guests out of their rooms from 10am to 5pm daily.

★**Thorncliffe B&B**   B&B **££**
(☑ 01422-842163, 07949 729433; www.thorncliffe.uk.net; Alexandra Rd; s/d £55/75; 🛜) This delightful Victorian house is perched on the hill above town, and the guest accommodation is right at the top of the house – a spacious and peaceful attic double with private bathroom and lovely views across the valley, and a 1st-floor en-suite double room, but without the views. A healthy vegetarian continental breakfast is served in your room.

🍴 Eating & Drinking

Mooch   CAFE **£**
(☑ 01422-846954; www.moochcafebar.wordpress.com; 24 Market St; mains £4-10; ⊙ 9am-8pm Mon-Thu, to 10pm Fri-Sat, 10am-8pm Sun; 🛜 ∕ ♿) This chilled-out little cafe-bar exemplifies Hebden's alternative atmosphere, with a menu that includes a full-vegan breakfast, brie-and-grape ciabatta, and Mediterranean lunch platters of olives, hummus, stuffed vine leaves, tabbouleh and more. There are also bottled beers, wine, excellent espresso, and a petite enclosed outdoor terrace through the back.

Leila's Kitchen   VEGETARIAN **£**
(☑ 01422-843587; www.leilaskitchen.co.uk; Old Oxford House, Albert St; mains £5-8; ⊙ 9am-4pm Mon & Wed-Fri, to 9pm Sat, 10am-4pm Sun; ∕) ∕ A lovely vegetarian cafe that serves primarily Persian-style cuisine, but also has a fine selection of vegan dishes and other veggie bits like Welsh rarebit and a particularly tasty chickpea burger.

YORKSHIRE HEBDEN BRIDGE

★ **Vocation & Co**   CRAFT BEER
(☑ 01422-844838; www.vocationbrewery.com; 10 New Rd; ☺ noon-11pm; ☎) A goldmine for hopheads, the first taproom from local craft brewer Vocation Brewery is housed in an imposing Victorian building overlooking Hebden Bridge's marina. Inside it's quite a contrast: an ultramodern, minimalist set-up with 20 draught lines including beers from other top northern breweries such as Magic Rock and Cloudwater, plus a delicious taco menu (Tuesday to Sunday).

☆ Entertainment

Trades Club   LIVE MUSIC
(☑ 01422-845265; www.thetradesclub.com; Holme St) Built in 1923 as a social club by the local trade unions, this place was revived in the 1980s and has since gone on to become one of the UK's coolest live-music venues, hosting names as big and diverse as the Buzzcocks, Patti Smith, the Fall and George Ezra in recent years, as well as a host of up-and-coming indie talent.

ⓘ Information

Hebden Bridge Visitor Centre (☑ 01422-843831; www.hebdenbridge.co.uk; Butlers Wharf, New Rd; ☺ 10am-5pm) Has a good stock of maps and leaflets on local walks and bicycle routes.

ⓘ Getting There & Away

There's only one main road through town and it can become horribly congested on sunny days, so try to arrive by train. Hebden Bridge is on the line from Leeds (£6.20, 50 minutes, every 20 minutes Monday to Saturday, twice hourly on Sunday) to Manchester (£10.50, 35 minutes, three or four per hour).

Haworth

☑ 01535 / POP 6380

It seems that only Shakespeare himself is held in higher esteem than the Brontë sisters – Emily, Anne and Charlotte – judging by the thousands of visitors a year who come to pay their respects at Haworth's handsome parsonage where the literary classics *Jane Eyre* and *Wuthering Heights* were penned.

Not surprisingly, the village is the beating heart of a cottage industry that has grown up around Brontë-linked tourism, but even without the literary associations Haworth – the upper village rather than the workaday town below – is worth a visit. Its cobbled

heritage high street has become a home for interesting independent vintage, craft and art shops selling work by local Yorkshire artisans, and it's possible to strike out onto the famed Brontë moors right from the parsonage's back door.

◉ Sights

Haworth Parish Church   CHURCH
(www.haworthchurch.co.uk; Church St; ☺ 12.30-3.30pm Sun & Wed) The Brontë family vault lies beneath a pillar in the southeast corner of this handsome parish church, which was built on the site of an older church where Patrick Brontë served as vicar between 1820 and 1861; it was demolished in 1879. A polished brass plaque on the floor commemorates Charlotte and Emily; Anne is buried at St Mary's Church (Castle Rd; ☺ 10am-4pm Mon-Fri, 1-4pm Sun May-Sep) FREE in Scarborough.

Brontë Parsonage Museum   MUSEUM
(☑ 01535-642323; www.bronte.org.uk; Church St; adult/child £9.50/4; ☺ 10am-5pm Wed-Sun) Set in a pretty garden overlooking Haworth parish church and graveyard, the house where the Brontë family lived from 1820 to 1861 is now a museum. The rooms are meticulously furnished and decorated exactly as they were in the Brontë era, including Charlotte's bedroom, her clothes and her writing paraphernalia. There's also an informative exhibition, which includes the fascinating miniature books the Brontës wrote as children.

Keighley & Worth Valley Railway   HERITAGE RAILWAY
(www.kwvr.co.uk; Station Rd; adult/child return £15/7) This vintage railway runs steam and classic diesel engines between Keighley and Oxenhope via Haworth. The classic 1970 movie *The Railway Children* was shot along this line: Mr Perks was stationmaster at Oakworth, where the Edwardian look has been meticulously maintained. Trains operate about hourly every day June to August but the timetable is sporadic in other months; check the website. Tickets to view the Haworth platform and incoming trains cost 50p, but you can get a good look from the nearby pedestrian bridge.

🛏 Sleeping

Apothecary Guest House   B&B £
(☑ 01535-643642; www.theapothecaryguesthouse. co.uk; 86 Main St; s/d £40/60; ☎) A quaint and ancient building at the top end of Main St,

with narrow, slanted passageways that lead to simple rooms with cheerful modern decor; excellent value.

★ **Old Registry**   B&B **££**
(✆ 01535-646503;   www.theoldregistryhaworth. co.uk; 2-4 Main St; d £80-135; 🅿 🛜) This place is a bit special. It's an elegantly rustic guesthouse where each of the carefully themed rooms has either a four-poster bed, whirlpool bath or valley views. The Secret Garden room has a glorious view across parkland to the lower village with, if you're lucky, a steam train chuffing sedately by. Parking is £3 per night, at nearby Haworth Old Hall.

🍴 Eating & Drinking

Cobbles & Clay   CAFE **£**
(www.cobblesandclay.co.uk;   60 Main St;   mains £6-9;   ⊙ 9am-5pm;   🛜 ⊘ 👫) This buzzy, child-friendly cafe not only offers fair-trade coffee and healthy salads and snacks – Tuscan bean stew, or hummus with pita bread and raw veggie sticks – but also provides the opportunity to indulge in a bit of pottery painting. Its ploughman's lunch comes with local Haworth cheese.

Hawthorn   BRITISH **££**
(✆ 01535-644477;   www.thehawthornhaworth. co.uk; 103-109 Main St; mains £12-28; ⊙ 5-11pm Wed-Fri, noon-11pm Sat-Sun) The former home of a well-known Georgian clockmaker is now a classy, candlelit restaurant-bar serving Modern British dishes such as pea-and-ham soup with quails egg, Yorkshire Dales lamb and North Sea hake with foraged garlic. There's also a Josper grill for making delicious steaks.

Haworth Steam Brewery   MICROBREWERY
(✆ 01535-646059;   www.haworthsteambrewery. co.uk; 98 Main St; ⊙ 11am-11pm Thu-Sat, to 6pm Sun-Wed) This cosy bar must surely be one of Britain's smallest microbreweries, serving its own award-winning real ales and Haworth's Lamplighter gin, plus specials such as an IPA and gin created for Haworth's annual steampunk weekend in November. There's also a good pub-grub menu (mains £10 to £14) with brewhouse lamb shank, Whitby scampi and beef-brisket sandwiches.

🛍 Shopping

Cabinet of Curiosities   GIFTS & SOUVENIRS
(www.the-curiosity-society.myshopify.com;   84 Main St; ⊙ 10am-5.30pm) It was to this apothecary that Branwell Brontë staggered for his laudanum drug hits in the 1840s, contributing to his untimely death in September 1848. The current owners have restored it to its Victorian glory and it's now a fancy shop selling Gothic curios and beautiful bath products. Well worth a look inside.

ⓘ Information

The Brontë Parsonage Museum has information about the town.

ⓘ Getting There & Away

From Leeds, the easiest approach is via Keighley, which is on the Metro rail network. The B1, B2 and B3 buses (www.keighleybus.co.uk) run from Keighley bus station to Haworth (£3.20, 20 minutes, every 20 minutes) and the hourly B3 continues to Hebden Bridge. However, the most interesting way to get from Keighley to Haworth is via the Keighley & Worth Valley Railway.

SOUTH YORKSHIRE

What wool was to West Yorkshire, so steel was to South Yorkshire. A confluence of natural resources – coal, iron ore and ample water – made this part of the country a crucible of the British iron and steel industries. From the 18th to the 20th centuries, the region was the industrial powerhouse of northern England.

Sheffield's and Rotherham's blast furnaces and the coal pits of Barnsley and Doncaster may have closed long ago, but the hulking reminders of that irrepressible Victorian dynamism remain, not only in the old steelworks and pit heads (some of which have been converted into museums and exhibition spaces), but also in the grand civic buildings that grace Sheffield's city centre, fitting testaments to the untrammelled ambitions of their 19th-century patrons.

Sheffield

🎵 0114 / POP 518,090
The steel industry that made Sheffield famous is long gone, but after many years of decline this industrious city is on the up again – like many of northern England's cities, it has grabbed the opportunities presented by urban renewal with both hands and, shored up by a thriving student population, is working hard to reinvent itself.

Some of its old foundries, mills and forges are now interesting museums celebrating

South Yorkshire's industrial heyday, and Kelham Island in particular is in the throes of a fascinating redevelopment. Sheffield isn't likely to win any prizes for its looks anytime soon, but its history is interesting enough to warrant a day's exploration.

◎ Sights

★ Kelham Island Museum   MUSEUM

(www.simt.co.uk; Alma St; adult/child £7/free; ⊙ 11am-3pm Mon-Wed, to 4pm Sat-Sun; P) Sheffield's prodigious industrial heritage is the subject of this excellent museum, set on a human-made island in the city's oldest industrial district. Exhibits cover all aspects of industry, from steel-making to knife-sharpening. The most impressive display is the thundering 12,000-horsepower River Don steam engine (the size of a house), which gets powered up twice a day, at noon and 2pm. The museum is 800m north of the city centre; take the tram (£1.70) from Sheffield train station to the Shalesmoor stop.

Winter Gardens   GARDENS

(Surrey St; ⊙ 8am-8pm Mon-Sat, to 5pm Sun) Pride of place in Sheffield's city centre goes to this wonderfully ambitious public space with a soaring glass roof supported by graceful arches of laminated timber. The 21st-century architecture contrasts sharply with the nearby Victorian town hall and the Peace Gardens – complete with fountains, sculptures, and lawns full of lunching office workers.

Millennium Gallery   GALLERY

(www.museums-sheffield.org.uk; Arundel Gate; ⊙ 10am-4pm) FREE Sheffield's cultural revival is embodied in this collection of four galleries under one roof. Inside, the Ruskin Collection houses an eclectic display of paintings, manuscripts and interesting objects established and inspired by Victorian artist, writer, critic and philosopher John Ruskin, who saw Sheffield as the embodiment of Britain's industrial age. The Sykes Gallery Metalwork Collection charts the transformation of Sheffield's steel industry into craft and design, with 13,000 glinting objects – the 'Sheffield steel' stamp now has the cachet of designer chic.

Graves Gallery   GALLERY

(www.museums-sheffield.org.uk; Surrey St; ⊙ 11am-4pm Tue-Sat) FREE This gallery has a neat and accessible display of British and European art from the 16th century to the present day, plus touring exhibitions; the big names represented include Turner, Sisley, Cézanne, Gauguin, Miró, Klee, LS Lowry and Damien Hirst.

Abbeydale Industrial Hamlet   MUSEUM

(www.simt.co.uk; Abbeydale Rd S; adult/child £4/free; ⊙ 10am-4pm Mon-Thu & Sat, 11am-4.45pm Sun; P) In the days before steel mills, metalworking was carried out in hamlet communities like Abbeydale, situated by rivers and dams that were harnessed for water power. This industrial museum, now swallowed up by Sheffield's suburban sprawl, gives an excellent run-down of that innocent era, with restored 18th-century forges, workshops and machinery including the original, working waterwheel. It's 4 miles southwest of the centre on the A621 (towards the Peak District).

🛏 Sleeping

Leopold Hotel   BOUTIQUE HOTEL ££

(✆ 0114-252 4000; www.leopoldhotels.com; 2 Leopold St; r/ste from £60/100; ☎) Housed in a Grade II–listed former grammar-school building, Sheffield's first boutique hotel offers style and sophistication at a reasonable rate. Rooms can suffer late-night noise from the bars on Leopold Sq – ask for a quiet room at the back.

Houseboat Hotels   HOUSEBOAT ££

(✆ 07776 144693; www.houseboathotels.com; Victoria Quays, Wharfe St; r from £95; P) Here's something a bit different: kick off your shoes and relax on board your very own permanently moored houseboat, complete with self-catering kitchen and patio area. You can choose between the Laila Mai or Millie Grace, each a double bedroom (with flatscreen TV), decent-sized bathroom, a kitchenette and a dining area (where the bench folds out into another bed).

✕ Eating

Street Food Chef   MEXICAN £

(✆ 0114-275 2390; www.streetfoodchef.co.uk; 90 Arundel St; mains £3-6; ⊙ 5-9pm Wed-Thu, to 10pm Fri, noon-9pm Sat, to 7pm Sun) Local students flock to this down-to-earth, healthy Mexican canteen, which started life as a street-food truck and now has several outlets in Sheffield. It focuses on freshly prepared, great-value burritos, tacos and quesadillas, available to eat in or take away. Look for its brekky and lunch deals, and gluten- or dairy-free options.

THE AGE OF STEEL

At its peak, the Templeborough steelworks was the world's most productive steel smelter, with a 10,000-strong workforce manning six 3000°C furnaces that produced 1.8 million tonnes of metal a year. It has now been reborn as **Magna** (☑01709-720002; www.visitmagna.co.uk; Sheffield Rd, Templeborough, Rotherham; adult/child £12.95/10.95; ⊙10am-5pm, last entry 4pm; ℗♿), an unashamed celebration of heavy industry, and a hands-on paradise for kids of all ages. Displays are based on the themes of earth, air, water and fire. The latter section is especially impressive, with a towering tornado of flame as a centrepiece and the chance to use a real electric arc to create your own tiny puddle of molten steel (if only for a moment or two). The hourly 'Big Melt' – a massive sound, light and fireworks show – memorably re-enacts the firing up of one of the original arc furnaces.

Magna is 4 miles northeast of Sheffield, just off the M1 near Rotherham; phone before visiting as it closes at 2pm some days.

Blue Moon Cafe VEGETARIAN £
(www.bluemooncafesheffield.com; 2 St James St; mains £8; ⊙8.30am-4pm Mon-Sat; ☑) A Sheffield institution offering tasty veggie and vegan creations, breakfasts till 11am and a rotation of single-price mains with a side of rice. It's famed for the magnificent heritage room within which it sits, with high blue ceilings and an atrium glass roof – perfect for a spot of Saturday afternoon lounging.

Marmaduke's CAFE £
(www.marmadukes.co; 22a Norfolk Row; mains £6-12; ⊙9am-5pm Mon-Sat, 10am-4pm Sun; ☎☑) ⚑ This appealingly cramped and chaotic cafe, crammed with recycled furniture and fittings, and run by a young and enthusiastic crew, serves an all-day breakfast menu that highlights local and organic produce, and lunch dishes that range from deli sandwiches and quiches to vegetarian specials such as the halloumi and herb burger. They've opened a second cafe on **Cambridge St** (42 Cambridge St; mains £6-9.50; ⊙8.30am-5pm Mon-Fri, 9am-5pm Sat, to 4pm Sun).

Vero Gusto ITALIAN ££
(☑0114-276 0004; www.verogusto.com; 12 Norfolk Row; mains £15-31; ⊙5-11pm Tue-Sat; ☎) Gusto is a *real* Italian restaurant, from the Italian waistcoated servers dishing out homemade Italian food to the genuine Italian coffee enjoyed by Italian customers reading Italian newspapers...you get the idea. Bookings essential.

Drinking & Nightlife

Fat Cat PUB
(☑0114-249 4801; www.thefatcat.co.uk; 23 Alma St; ⊙noon-11pm Sun-Thu, to midnight Fri & Sat)

The 'Cat' is an old-fashioned independent boozer in a handy spot around the corner from Kelham Island Museum. It serves Kelham Island Brewery beers and ales made in the building next door, along with pork pies and pub grub. Its fans are an eclectic mix of students and local fixtures.

Sheffield Tap CRAFT BEER
(☑0114-273 7558; www.sheffieldtap.com; Sheffield Train Station; ⊙11am-11pm Sun-Thu, 10am-midnight Fri & Sat; ☎) This lovingly restored Edwardian railway bar is a reliable stalwart for Sheffield beer drinkers. It has several bar areas, and the aroma of hops and malts gets stronger as you approach the far room where the bar produces its own Two Tapped Brew Co beers, with working brewery kit towering above drinking tables. Dozens of other local and international beers are sold here, too.

⭐ Entertainment

Showroom CINEMA
(☑0114-275 7727; www.showroomworkstation.org.uk; 15 Paternoster Row) This is the largest independent cinema in England, set in a grand art-deco complex and screening a great mix of art-house, offbeat and not-quite-mainstream films.

Leadmill LIVE MUSIC
(☑0114-272 7040; www.leadmill.co.uk; 6 Leadmill Rd) Every touring band has played the dark and dingy Leadmill on the way up (or on the way down), and it remains the best place in town to hear live rock and alternative music. There are club nights too, but they tend to play cheesy 1970s and '80s disco classics.

ℹ Information

There's no tourist office, but www.welcome toshelffield.co.uk is a good source of information.

ℹ Getting There & Away

For all travel-related info for Sheffield and South Yorkshire, contact **Travel South Yorkshire** (☑ 01709-515151; www.travelsouthyorkshire. com).

BUS

The bus station, called the Interchange, is just east of the centre, about 250m north of the train station. National Express coaches run from here to London (from £6, 4½ hours, eight daily).

TRAIN

Prices can double on the day of travel; book ahead.
Leeds £11.90, one hour, two to five hourly
London St Pancras £79, 2¼ hours, at least hourly
Manchester £9.40, one hour, twice hourly
York £6.70, 1¼ hours, twice hourly

EAST RIDING OF YORKSHIRE

The rolling farmland of the East Riding of Yorkshire meets the sea at Hull, a no-nonsense port that looks to the broad horizons of the Humber estuary and the North Sea for its livelihood. Just to its north, and in complete contrast to Hull's salt and grit, is Beverley, the East Riding's most attractive town, with lots of Georgian character and one of England's finest churches.

Hull

☑ 01482 / POP 284,321

The principal port town of England's east coast, Hull (properly known but rarely referred to as Kingston-upon-Hull) grew up around an economy focused on wool, wine trading, whaling and fishing.

A major program of refurbishment on the back of the city's title as UK City of Culture in 2017 improved the old waterfront but more importantly sparked a cultural flowering – especially in the Fruit Market district around Humber St, where derelict buildings have been reclaimed as artists' studios, and cool cafes and bars have flourished. Hard-bitten Hullensians may smirk, but their city has developed serious cool kudos.

The city centre isn't exactly pretty, but the old cobbled Georgian enclave is an under-the-radar delight. Other attractions include fascinating museums, Philip Larkin heritage (the poet lived here) and an excellent aquarium.

◉ Sights

★ The Deep   AQUARIUM
(☑ 01482-381000; www.thedeep.co.uk; Tower St; adult/child £13.50/11.50; ◷ 10am-6pm, last entry 5pm; P ♿) Hull's biggest tourist attraction is The Deep, Britain's most spectacular aquarium, housed in a colossal angular building that appears to lunge above the muddy waters of the Humber like a giant shark's head. Inside, it's just as dramatic, with echoing commentaries and computer-generated interactive displays that guide you through the formation of the oceans, the evolution of sea life and global conservation issues.

The largest aquarium tank is 10m deep, filled with sharks, stingrays, moray eels and colourful coral fishes. A glass elevator plies up and down inside the tank, though you'll get a better view by taking the stairs. Don't miss the cafe on the top floor, which has a great view of the Humber estuary.

★ Old Town   AREA
Hull's Old Town is where a grand minster and cobbled streets flush with Georgian town houses give a flashback to the prosperity the town once knew. It occupies the thumb of land between the River Hull to the east and Princes Quay to the west. Recent regeneration efforts have brought back to life the dockside **Fruit Market**, where vintage shops, art studios and independent bars and cafes are flourishing along Humber St; and the indoor **Trinity Market**, now housing street-food vendors.

★ Wilberforce House   MUSEUM
(www.hullcc.gov.uk/museums; High St; ◷ 10am-4.30pm Mon-Sat, to 4pm Sun) FREE The wealth that Britain amassed as the world's first industrial nation was directly aided by the transatlantic slave trade, and this important museum ensures that the facts are told, detailing the part that Britain played in bringing millions of Africans to Europe between the 17th and 19th centuries. Wilberforce House (1639) was the birthplace in 1759 of politician and antislavery crusader William Wilberforce, whose campaigning efforts eventually led to the abolition of slavery in England in 1833.

Humber St Gallery GALLERY

(www.humberstreetgallery.co.uk; 64 Humber St; ⊙ 11am-3pm Thu-Sun, cafe to 4pm Thu-Fri, to 6pm Sat-Sun) FREE This slick three-storey contemporary gallery in a former banana-ripening warehouse anchors Hull's revamped Fruit Market. Rotating exhibitions celebrate international and local visual art, design, photography and film, but a permanent feature is a beloved piece of 1960s graffiti by Len 'Pongo' Rood saved from demolition by local campaigners. Behold *Dead Bod* – a rusty shed wall from Hull's docks that would have once signified home for returning sailors. The site was demolished in 2015, but *Dead Bod* lives on in Humber St Gallery's cafe.

Ferens Art Gallery GALLERY

(☑ 01482-300300; www.hullcc.gov.uk/ferens; Queen Victoria Sq; ⊙ 10am-4.30pm Mon-Sat, to 4pm Sun; ▥) FREE The permanent art collection at this fine gallery ranges from old masters like Frans Hals and Antonio Canaletto to modern works by Lucian Freud, Peter Nash, Peter Blake, David Hockney and Gillian Wearing.

Humber Bridge BRIDGE

(www.humberbridge.co.uk; ℗) Opened in 1981, the Humber Bridge swoops gracefully across the broad estuary of the River Humber. Its 1410m span made it the world's longest single-span suspension bridge – until 1998 when it lost the title to Japan's Akashi Kaikyo bridge, but it is still a Grade I–listed structure. The best way to appreciate the scale of the bridge, and the vastness of the estuary, is to walk or cycle out along the footway from the Humber Bridge tourist office at its north end on Ferriby Rd.

The bridge is a mile west of the small riverside town of Hessle, about 4 miles west of Hull. It links Yorkshire to Lincolnshire along the A15, opening up what was once an often-overlooked corner of the country.

Bus 350 runs from Hull Paragon Interchange to Ferriby Rd in Hessle (25 minutes, every 30 minutes), from where it's a 300m walk to the tourist office.

Hull Pier Toilets HISTORIC BUILDING

(Nelson St) There are not too many places where a public toilet counts as a tourist attraction, but coach parties regularly stop to take photos of these Edwardian lavatories. The building is interesting but inside they're not very special. Serviceable, but no tourist attraction, that's for sure.

🛏 Sleeping

Hull Trinity Backpackers HOSTEL £

(☑ 01482-223229; www.hulltrinitybackpackers.com; 51-52 Market Pl; s/tw from £32/45; 🛜) This centrally located hostel with simple rooms is just the ticket for a cheap sleep in Hull. It's clean and friendly, and the owner is passionate about showing off the city's best sides. There's a lovingly designed common area, free laundry, fluffy bedding and bike storage. Plus handy USB and plug sockets by each bed.

★ Hideout APARTMENT ££

(☑ 01482-212222; www.hideouthotel.co.uk; North Church Side; d from £90, 1-bed apt £110-130, 2-bed apt from £130; ℗🛜) These luxury serviced apartments show just how far Hull has come since its City of Culture year. Slick and contemporary, it's the type of place where staff put retro radio on for you before check-in, and leave an easel in the living room for spontaneous creative scribbles. It's also incredibly central, in the shadow of the Old Town's minster.

🍴 Eating

★ Thieving Harry's CAFE £

(www.thievingharrys.co.uk; 73 Humber St; mains £5-9; ⊙ kitchen 10am-4pm Mon-Fri, 9am-4pm Sat, to 6pm Sun; 🖉) Thieving Harry's has all the trappings of a favourite local cafe: friendly faces, a breezy casual vibe, strong coffee and generous brunches, all wrapped up in a comfy warehouse conversion with mismatched retro furniture and lovely marina views of bobbing boats. The menu is interesting, with excellent dishes like fried eggs with chorizo, sourdough and coriander sour cream, plus good veggie options.

★ The Old House BRITISH ££

(☑ 01482-210253; www.shootthebull.co.uk/the-old-house; 5 Scale Lane; mains £15-29; ⊙ 4-9.30pm Wed-Thu, from noon Fri-Sat, to 6pm Sun) Once an old pub, now the base of Hull street-food brand Shoot the Bull, this lovely restaurant does refined comfort food exceptionally well. Locally sourced meat and fish might translate into blow-torched mackerel followed by a rare-breed beef pie with smoked eel mash and parsley sauce. Its signature dish is on the street-food menu: a butter-lathered, rare-breed flat-iron steak sandwich in a posh bun.

A second outlet focusing solely on street food is inside Trinity Market in the Old Town.

Tapasya Marina INDIAN ££

(📞01482-242607; www.tapasyarestaurants.co.uk; 2-3 Humber Dock St; mains £14-20) Marrying old and new in a converted warehouse with giant windows onto Hull's marina and a projector showing old black-and-white films, this sharp modern restaurant specialises in fine-dining Indian fusion cuisine using the best seasonal, local produce. Savour dishes like roe deer biryani with Himalayan basmati rice, or Yorkshire lamb drenched in fragrant masala sauce with a side of indulgently buttery nan.

Hitchcock's Vegetarian Restaurant VEGETARIAN ££

(📞01482-320233; www.hitchcocksrestaurant.co.uk; 1 Bishop Lane, High St; per person £22; ⏱8-10.30pm Tue-Sat; 🖊🦽) The word 'quirky' could have been invented to describe this place. It's an atmospheric maze of small rooms, with an all-you-can-eat vegetarian buffet whose theme – Mexican, Indian, Caribbean, whatever – is chosen by the first person to book that evening. But the food is excellent and the welcome is warm. Bookings necessary..

 Drinking & Entertainment

★Olde Black Boy PUB

(📞01482-215040; 150 High St; ⏱5-11.30pm Mon & Tue, from noon Wed-Sun) A favourite watering hole of poet Philip Larkin, Hull's oldest pub has been serving ale since 1729. Oak floors and roof beams, dark-wood panelling and a snug log fire in winter make for a great atmosphere. There's live folk music on Wednesday afternoons.

Humber St Distillery COCKTAIL BAR

(📞01482-219886; www.hsdc.co.uk; 18 Humber St; ⏱noon-11pm Tue-Sun) This ambitious, gin-obsessed cocktail bar in the heart of Hull's Fruit Market area has dark-wood bar panelling offset by exposed-brick walls. The gin menu is a tome of around 150 world gins, including many local and limited-edition releases; you can take a gin flight (weeknights only); and the bar has even started producing its own gin.

Two Gingers COFFEE

(www.twogingerscoffee.co.uk; Paragon Arcade, Paragon St; ⏱8am-4pm Mon-Fri, 10am-4pm Sat & Sun) Inside pretty Paragon Arcade, this Australian-style speciality coffee house is bright, minimalist and focused firmly on the main event: excellent coffee.

Minerva PUB

(www.minerva-hull.co.uk; Nelson St; ⏱11.30am-11pm Mon-Sat, noon-11pm Sun; 🦽) Try a pint of Black Sheep at this lovely 200-year-old pub down by the waterfront. On a sunny day you can sit outdoors and watch the ships go by, while tucking into a plate of fish and chips (£9.50). A unique feature is its real-ale and gin flights.

🛈 Information

Hull Tourist Office (📞01482-300306; www.visithullandeastyorkshire.com; Paragon Interchange, Ferensway; ⏱8am-6.30pm Mon-Fri, from 9am Sat, 10am-5pm Sun) Inside Hull's Paragon Interchange, at the train station.

🛈 Getting There & Away

BOAT
The ferry port is 3 miles east of the centre at King George Dock; a bus connects the train station with the ferries. There are ferry services to Zeebrugge (Belgium) and Rotterdam (Netherlands).

BUS
Intercity buses depart from Hull Paragon Interchange. Mega Bus (https://uk.megabus.com) runs cheap buses to London. The X62 is a direct link to Leeds. During summer the X21 runs directly to Scarborough, but at other times of year you'll need to change at Bridlington. The X46/47 to York runs via Beverley.

London £20, 4½ hours, four daily
Leeds £6, two hours, three daily
York £13, 1¾ hours, hourly

TRAIN
The train station is part of Hull Paragon Interchange, an integrated rail and bus station.

Leeds £6.70, one hour, hourly
London King's Cross £47, 2¾ hours, every two hours
York £32, 1¼ hours, hourly

Beverley

📞01482 / POP 10,109

Handsome Beverley is one of the most attractive towns in Yorkshire, largely due to its magnificent minster – a rival to any cathedral in England – and the tangle of streets that lie beneath it, each brimming with Georgian and Victorian buildings.

All the sights are a short walk from either the train or bus station. There's a large market on Saturdays in the square called Saturday

Market, and a smaller one on Wednesdays in the square called...Wednesday Market.

🅞 Sights

Beverley Minster
CHURCH

(www.beverleyminster.org; St John St; ⊗11am-3pm Wed-Sat, noon-3pm Sun) FREE One of the great glories of English religious architecture, Beverley Minster is the most impressive church in the country that is not a cathedral. The soaring lines of the exterior are imposing, but it is inside that the charm and beauty lie. The 14th-century north aisle is lined with original stone carvings, mostly of musicians; much of our knowledge of early musical instruments comes from these images. Look out for the bagpipe player. You'll also see goblins, devils and grotesque figures.

Construction began in 1220 – this was the third church to be built on this site, with the first dating from the 7th century – and continued for two centuries, spanning the Early English, Decorated and Perpendicular periods of the Gothic style.

Close to the altar, the elaborate and intricate Percy Canopy (1340), a decorative frill above the tomb of local aristocrat Lady Eleanor Percy, is a testament to the skill of the sculptor and the finest example of Gothic stone carving in England. In complete contrast, in the nearby chancel is the 10th-century Saxon frith stool, a plain and polished stone chair that once gave sanctuary to anyone escaping the law.

In the roof of the tower is a restored treadwheel crane, where workers ground around like hapless hamsters to lift the huge loads necessary to build a medieval church.

Beverley Westwood
PARK

(Walkington Rd) The western edge of Beverley is bounded by this large area of common pasture studded with mature trees, which has been used as grazing for local livestock for centuries. The land, owned 'in common' by the community since 1380, is overseen by the Pasture Masters, a group of men elected from the Freemen of Beverley each March. Contented cows amble across the unfenced road, while walkers stroll and enjoy the gorgeous views of Beverley Minster.

🛏 Sleeping & Eating

Kings Head
INN ££

(☑01482-868103; www.kingsheadpubbeverley. com; 38 Saturday Market; r/ste from £90/150; P🖻) A Georgian coaching inn given a modern makeover, the Kings Head is a lively pub with 10 bright and stylish rooms above the bar. The pub opens late on weekend nights, but earplugs are supplied for those who don't want to join the revelry.

Vanessa Delicafe
CAFE £

(☑01482-868190; www.vanessadelicafe. co.uk; 21-22 Saturday Market; mains £4.50-10; ⊗9.30am-5pm Mon-Thu, 9am-5pm Fri-Sat; 🖻📶) This popular cafe sits above a delicatessen, with sofas and bookshelves scattered among the tables, and window seats overlooking the market square. Settle down for cappuccino and cake with the Sunday papers, or tuck into hearty lunch specials such as venison burger or a Yorkshire platter of pork pie, roast ham, cheese and chutney.

⭐ Pipe & Glass Inn
GASTROPUB £££

(☑01430-810246; www.pipeandglass.co.uk; West End, South Dalton; mains £16-35; ⊗noon-2pm & 6-9.30pm Tue-Sat, noon-4pm Sun; P🅿🖻📶) 🍃 Set in a picturesque hamlet 4 miles northwest of Beverley, this charming Michelin-starred country pub has a delightfully informal setting, with weathered timber tables, stone hearths and leather sofas. Yet a great deal of care is lavished on the food – even seemingly simple dishes such as fish pie are unforgettable. After your meal, you can tour its herb gardens.

If you want to stay the night, there are five luxurious bedrooms to choose from (£200 to £245 per night, including breakfast), but the waiting list for a weekend night is several months long; weeknights can be booked about two months in advance.

🅘 Information

Beverley Tourist Office (☑01482-391672; www.visithullandeastyorkshire.com/beverley; Treasure House, Champney Rd; ⊗9.30am-5pm Mon, Wed & Fri, to 8pm Tue & Thu, 9am-4pm Sat) Beverley Tourist Office lives inside Treasure House, also home to the town's art gallery, next to the library.

🅘 Getting There & Away

There are frequent bus services from Hull, including numbers 121, 122, 246 and X46/X47 (£5.20, 30 minutes, hourly). Bus X46/X47 links Beverley with York (£7.90, 1¼ hours, hourly).

Trains run regularly to Scarborough (£14.90, 1¼ hours, every one to two hours) and Hull (£7.30, 15 minutes, twice hourly).

AT A GLANCE

POPULATION
6.6 million

TALLEST BUILDING
Deansgate Square
– South Tower,
Manchester
(201m/659ft)

**BEST
FOOTBALL TOUR**
Anfield Stadium Tour
(p549)

**BEST
ARTS CENTRE**
HOME (p540)

**BEST
GASTROPUB**
Freemasons at
Wiswell (p556)

WHEN TO GO
Apr–Jul Aintree
Grand National; Isle
of Man's TT Trophy;
biennial Manchester
International
Festival.

Aug & Sep Driest
weather; start of
the football season;
Manchester Pride.

Oct–Mar Isle of Man
food and walking
festivals; Manches-
ter Food & Drink
Festival.

Manchester, Liverpool & Northwest England

Revolution, music and football: if you were to limit the story of the northwest to these three alone, it would still be a page-turner. Forged on the anvil of the Industrial Revolution, the region fomented social change, organised the first league of the world's most popular sport and produced some of the most enduring popular music. At the heart of it all is mighty Manchester, a city built on innovation and bursting with creativity. Nearby is its perennial rival Liverpool, fiercely proud of its ability to hold its own in most matters, from food to football. Between them is Chester, a Tudor gift enveloped by Roman walls. The bucolic charms of the Lancashire countryside lie to the north, while offshore is the Isle of Man, so pretty that Unesco gave it Biosphere Reserve status.

Manchester, Liverpool & Northwest England Highlights

1 Liverpool Cathedral (p545)
Being overwhelmed by Sir Giles Gilbert Scott's awesome neo-Gothic masterpiece.

2 Beatles' Childhood Homes (p550) Visiting the Liverpool houses where John and Paul grew up – and wrote their earliest hits.

3 Rows (p544) Exploring Chester's Tudor-era shopping district.

4 Football (p540) Taking a tour of your favourite team's ground or – better still – going to a match.

ℹ️ Information

Visit North West (www.visitnorthwest.com) is the centralised tourist authority, but all cities and most towns have their own dedicated tourist authorities; for the Isle of Man check out **Isle of Man** (www.visitisleofman.com).

ℹ️ Getting There & Away

Both Manchester and Liverpool have international airports and are well served by trains from all over the UK, including London, only two hours away. The West Coast Line serves Preston, Lancaster and Blackpool. For Lancashire's smaller towns, there's an extensive bus service. The Isle of Man is accessible by ferry from Liverpool and Heysham, and there are regular flights from throughout the UK.

ℹ️ Getting Around

The towns and cities covered are all within easy reach of each other, and are well linked by public transport. The two main cities, Manchester and Liverpool, are only 34 miles apart and are linked by hourly bus and train services. Chester is 18 miles south of Liverpool, but is also easily accessible from Manchester by train or via the M56. Blackpool is 50 miles to the north of Manchester and Liverpool, and is also well connected on the M6.

MANCHESTER

📞 0161 / POP 510,746

Manchester is a city on the move. Upwards and outwards, mostly: the skyline is getting taller and old neighbourhoods are getting a new lease of life. The one-time engine room of the Industrial Revolution is now spearheading a digital upheaval, with four universities feeding a tech cluster that is Britain's largest outside London.

The result – besides lots of construction and rising property prices – is a steady uptick in the city's choice of bars, hotels and restaurants, including Manchester's first Michelin star for four decades.

And while many locals aren't all that enthused about what they consider the gentrification of their beloved city – this is, after all, a radical burgh that incubated communism, suffragism, vegetarianism and a bunch of other 'isms' aimed at improving humanity's lot – Manchester doesn't look like it's slowing down any time soon.

History

Canals and steam-powered cotton mills were what transformed Manchester from a small, disease-infested provincial town into a big, disease-infested industrial city. It all happened in the 1760s, with the opening of the Bridgewater Canal between Manchester and the coal mines at Worsley in 1763, and with Richard Arkwright patenting his super cotton mill in 1769. Thereafter Manchester and the world would never be the same again. When the canal was extended to Liverpool and the open sea in 1776, Manchester – dubbed 'Cottonopolis' – kicked into high gear and took off on the coal-fuelled, steam-powered gravy train.

There was plenty of gravy to go around, but the good burghers of 19th-century Manchester made sure that the vast majority of the city's swollen citizenry (with a population of 90,000 in 1801, and two million 100 years later) never got their hands on any of it despite producing most of it. Their reward was life in a new kind of urban settlement: the industrial slum. Working conditions were dire, with impossibly long hours, child labour, work-related accidents and fatalities all commonplace. Mark Twain commented that he would like to live here because the 'transition between Manchester and Death would be unnoticeable'. So much for Victorian values.

The wheels started to come off towards the end of the 19th century. The USA had begun to flex its own industrial muscles and was taking over a sizeable chunk of the textile trade; production in Manchester's mills began to slow, and then it stopped altogether. By WWII there was hardly enough cotton produced in the city to make a tablecloth. The postwar years weren't much better: 150,000 manufacturing jobs were lost between 1961 and 1983, and the port – still the UK's third largest in 1963 – finally closed in 1982 due to declining traffic.

The 21st century has been much kinder to Manchester, with ongoing developments continuing to transform the city and its outlying suburbs into a powerhouse of development and innovation.

👁️ Sights

👁️ City Centre

⭐ **People's History Museum**   MUSEUM
(📞 0161-838 9190; www.phm.org.uk; Left Bank, Bridge St, Spinningfields, M3 3ER; ⏰ 10am-5pm Tue-Sun) **FREE** The story of Britain's 200-year march to democracy is told in all its pain and pathos at this superb museum, housed in a

MANCHESTER IN ONE DAY

Start your exploration in the light-filled galleries of the Manchester Art Gallery, home to one of the most important collections in the north. The Science & Industry Museum will take up at least a couple of hours – more if you've got kids or you're a science geek. Alternatively, the People's History Museum is a fascinating exploration of social history. Lunch at Rudy's (p537) or take your pick at Mackie Mayor (p538).

Hop on the tram to Salford Quays, where you can explore the Imperial War Museum North (p534) or take a guided tour of the BBC's northern headquarters at MediaCity-UK (p534); fans of Manchester United should take the tour of Old Trafford (p540), where you'll get to stand in the tunnel and pretend you're a player. Make dinner reservations (well in advance) for Mana (p538).

After dinner, there's drinks at the Refuge (p539) or at a choice of bars in the Northern Quarter. Alternatively, you can always head south towards Castlefield and take in a film or a play at the superb HOME (p540) arts centre.

refurbished Edwardian pumping station. You clock in on the 1st floor (literally: punch your card in an old mill clock, which managers would infamously fiddle with so as to make employees work longer) and plunge into the heart of Britain's struggle for basic democratic rights, labour reform and fair pay.

Amid artifacts like the (tiny) desk at which Thomas Paine (1737–1809) wrote *Rights of Man* (1791), and an array of beautifully made and colourful union banners, are compelling interactive displays, including a screen where you can trace the effects of all the events covered in the museum on five generations of the same family. The 2nd floor takes up the struggle for equal rights from WWII to the current day, touching on civil rights for gay people, anti-racism initiatives and the defining British sociopolitical landmarks of the last half-century, including the founding of the National Health Service (NHS), the Miners' Strike and the widespread protests against the Poll Tax.

⭐ **Science & Industry Museum** MUSEUM
(MOSI; ☑ 0161-832 2244; www.scienceandindustrymuseum.org.uk; Liverpool Rd, M3 4FP; suggested donation £4, special exhibits £6-10; ⊙ 10am-5pm Wed-Sun; 🚸; 🚎 1 or 3, 🚊 Deansgate-Castlefield) Manchester's rich industrial legacy is explored in this excellent museum set within the enormous grounds of the old Liverpool St station, the oldest rail terminus in the world. The large collection of steam engines, locomotives and original factory machinery tells the story of the city from the sewers up, while a host of new technology looks to the future.

It's an all-ages kind of museum, but the emphasis is on making sure the young 'uns don't get bored – they could easily spend

a whole day poking about, testing an early electric-shock machine here and trying out a printing press there. You can get up close and personal with fighter jets and get to grips with all kinds of space-age technology; the museum also includes an astronaut virtual-reality experience called Space Descent VR with Tim Peake (£6). A unifying theme is that Manchester and Mancunians had a key role to play: this is the place to discover that Manchester was home to the world's first stored-program computer (a giant contraption nicknamed 'baby') in 1948 and that the world's first steam-powered submarine was built to the designs of local curate Reverend George Garrett in 1879.

Admission by pre-booked ticket only. A new exhibition space will open in spring 2021.

⭐ **Manchester Art Gallery** GALLERY
(☑ 0161-235 8888; www.manchesterartgallery.org; Mosley St, M2 3JL; ⊙ 11am-4pm Thu-Sun; 🚊 St Peter's Square) **FREE** A superb collection of British art and a hefty number of European masters are the highlights at the city's top art gallery. It's home to the best assemblage of Pre-Raphaelite art as well as a permanent collection of pre-17th-century art, mostly by Dutch and early Renaissance masters. It also hosts exciting exhibitions of contemporary art and the newish *What is Manchester Art Gallery?*, which tells the story of the gallery and its city connections. Tickets must be pre-booked online.

⭐ **Chetham's Library
& School of Music** LIBRARY
(☑ 0161-834 7861; www.chethamsschoolofmusic.com; Long Millgate; donation suggested £3; ⊙ timed entry hourly 10am-noon &

MANCHESTER, LIVERPOOL & NORTHWEST ENGLAND MANCHESTER

Manchester

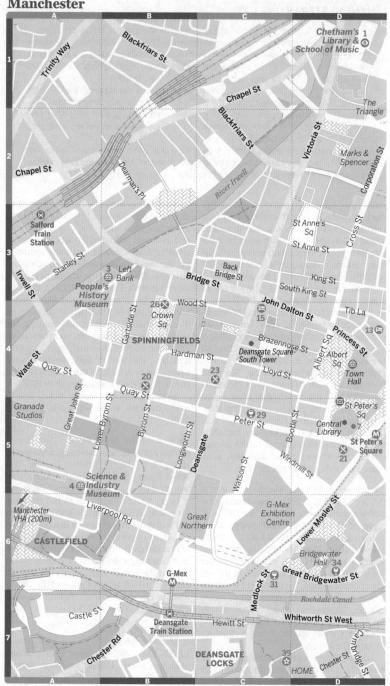

Chetham's Library & School of Music 1

The Triangle

Chapel St

Blackfriars St

Blackfriars St

Trinity Way

Chapel St

Dearman's Pl

River Irwell

Victoria St

Marks & Spencer

Corporation St

Salford Train Station

Stanley St

St Anne's Sq

St Anne St

Cross St

Irwell St

3 Left Bank

People's History Museum

Bridge St

Back Bridge St

King St

South King St

Gartside St

Wood St

John Dalton St

15

Tib La

13

26 Crown Sq

SPINNINGFIELDS

Hardman St

Brazennose St

Deansgate Square South Tower

Lloyd St

Albert Sq

Princess St

Water St

Quay St

Great John St

20 Quay St

Lower Byrom St

Byrom St

23

Albert Sq

Town Hall

Granada Studios

Longworth St

Deansgate

Peter St

29

Watson St

Bootle St

Windmill St

Central Library

St Peter's Sq

7

St Peter's Square

21

Science & Industry Museum 4

Manchester YHA (200m)

Liverpool Rd

Great Northern

G-Mex Exhibition Centre

Lower Mosley St

CASTLEFIELD

Bridgewater Hall 34

G-Mex

Great Bridgewater St

Medlock St 31

Castle St

Deansgate Train Station

Hewitt St

Rochdale Canal

Whitworth St West

Cambridge St

Chester Rd

DEANSGATE LOCKS

39

HOME

Chester St

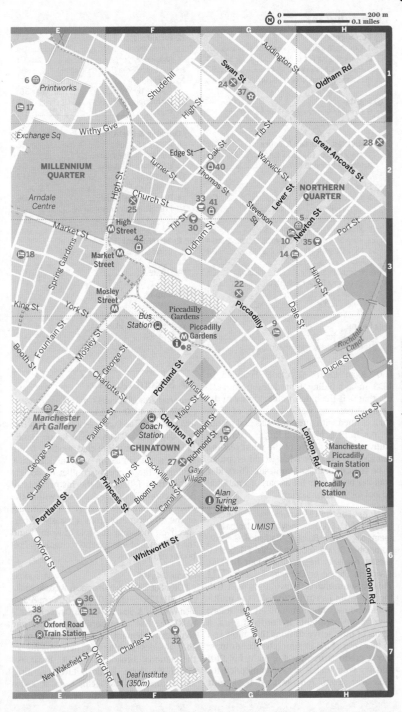

0   200 m
0   0.1 miles

Addington St

Oldham Rd

Swan St
24   37

6   Printworks

17

Shudehill

High St

Tib St

Great Ancoats St

28

Exchange Sq

Withy Gve

MILLENNIUM
QUARTER

Arndale
Centre

Edge St

Oak St

Warwick St

Turner St

Thomas St

40

Church St
25

33   41

High St

Tib St

30

Oldham St

Lever St

NORTHERN
QUARTER

Stevenson
Sq

5
Newton St

10   35

14

Port St

Market St

High
Street

42

Spring Gardens

18

Market
Street

Mosley
Street

22

Piccadilly

Hilton St

Dale St

Rochdale Canal

King St

York St

Fountain St

Booth St

Mosley St

George St

Charlotte St

Piccadilly
Gardens

Bus
Station

Piccadilly
Gardens

8

9

Ducie St

Store St

Manchester
Art Gallery

2

Faulkner St

Portland St

Minshull St

Major St

Choriton St

Bloom St

Coach
Station

CHINATOWN

16

1

Major St

Sackville St

Richmond St

27

Bloom St

19

Gay
Village

Alan
Turing
Statue

London Rd

Manchester
Piccadilly
Train Station

Piccadilly
Station

George St

St James St

Portland St

Princess St

Canal St

UMIST

Whitworth St

Oxford St

36

38   12

Oxford Road
Train Station

Charles St

32

Sackville St

London Rd

New Wakefield St

Oxford Rd

Deaf Institute
(350m)

Manchester

1.30-3.30pm Mon-Fri; ⊞ Victoria) Founded in 1653 in a building that dates from 1421, Chetham's is the oldest public library in the English-speaking world, a trove of dark shelves lined with ancient books and manuscripts. In 1845, Marx and Engels spent time studying in the alcove of the main reading room, prep work for what would eventually be the Communist Manifesto. The wider complex has its own life as part of a national school for young musicians.

National Football Museum   MUSEUM
(☎0161-605 8200; www.nationalfootballmuseum.com; Urbis Building, Cathedral Gardens, Corporation St, M4 3BG; adult/child £11/6, Manchester residents free; ⊙10am-4pm Thu-Sun; ⊞Victoria Station or Exchange Square) FREE This museum charts the evolution of British football from its earliest days to the multibillion-pound phenomenon it is today. One of the highlights is **Football Plus**, a series of interactive stations that allow you to test your skills in simulated conditions; buy a credit (three for £6, eight for £10) and try your luck – it's recommended for kids over seven. You must pre-book your tickets online.

⊙ Salford Quays

Imperial War Museum North   MUSEUM
(☎0161-836 4000; www.iwm.org.uk/north; Trafford Wharf Rd, The Quays; ⊙10am-5pm; ⊞Harbour City or MediaCityUK) FREE Inside Daniel Libeskind's aluminium-clad modern building is a war museum with a difference, exploring the effects of conflict on society rather than fetishising the instruments of destruction. Six mini exhibitions within the main hall examine war since the beginning of the 20th century from a variety of perspectives, including the role of women and the influence of science and technology. Pre-book online.

MediaCityUK   ARTS CENTRE
(☎0161-886 5300; www.mediacityuk.co.uk; adult/child £11/7.25; ⊙tours 10.30am, 12.30pm & 3pm Mon-Wed, Sat & Sun; ⊞Harbour City or MediaCityUK) The BBC's northern home is but one significant element of this vast 81-hectare site. Besides hosting six departments of the national broadcaster (BBC Breakfast, Children's, Sport, Radio 5 Live, Learning, and Future Media & Technology), it is also home to the set of the world's longest-

running soap opera, ITV's perennially popular *Coronation Street,* which you can visit on a **tour** (www.itv.com/coronationstreettour; The Studios at dock10; adult/child £35/17.50; ⊙10am-4pm selected weekend days; 🚇MediaCityUK).

You can visit the BBC's set-up and see the sets of some of TV's most iconic programmes on a guided 90-minute tour that also includes a chance for kids to 'make' a programme in an interactive studio; see www.bbc.co.uk/showsandtours. There are plenty of cafes and restaurants in the area.

Lowry ARTS CENTRE
(🎫 box office 0843-208 6000; www.thelowry.com; Pier 8, Salford Quays; ⊙10am-6pm, later during performances; 🚇Harbour City or MediaCityUK) With multiple performance spaces, bars, restaurants and shops, this contemporary arts centre attracts more than a million visitors a year to its myriad functions, which include everything from big-name theatrical productions to comedy, kids' theatre and even weddings. The centre is also home to 300 beautifully humanistic depictions of urban landscapes by LS Lowry (1887–1976), who was born in nearby Stretford, and after whom the complex is named.

Activities

Three Rivers Gin GUIDED TOUR
(🎫0161-839 2667; www.manchesterthreerivers.com; 21 Red Bank Parade, M4 4HF; £95; ⊙7.30pm Thu-Sat, plus 1pm Sat & Sun) This award-winning Manchester micro-distillery cranks back the shutters a few times a week to let visitors behind the scenes with the master distiller. Its three-hour 'Gin Experience' starts with a potted history of Manchester and the city's relationship with gin, throws in several gin cocktails and culminates in mixing botanicals to cook up your own 1L batch to take home.

Tours

Manchester Guided Tours WALKING
(🎫07505 685942; www.manchesterguidedtours.com; £12; ⊙11am) A daily walking tour of the city's highlights (departing from the Central Library at 11am), including Manchester Cathedral and the Royal Exchange. There's also a huge range of other themed tours including music, Victorian heritage and a tasty food and drink tour.

New Manchester Walks WALKING
(🎫07769 298068; www.newmanchesterwalks.com; £10-12) The complete menu of tours includes explorations of every aspect of Manchester's personality, from music to history and politics to pubs. There are a handful of football-related walks and an extensive list of 'weird and wonderful' walks, from Victorian eating habits to the history of Strangeways prison. Starting points differ.

Festivals & Events

Manchester Day PARADE
(www.manchesterday.co.uk; ⊙mid-Jun) A day to celebrate all things Manchester, inspired by New York's Thanksgiving Day parade: 50 performances across three city centre squares culminate in a colourful parade.

Manchester International Festival ART
(🎫0161-238 7300; www.mif.co.uk; ⊙Jul) A three-week-long biennial arts festival of artist-led new work across visual arts, performance and popular culture. Recent performers included Damon Albarn, Marina Abramović, Björk and the Steve McQueen Band. 2022 will see the opening of the Factory, a new multimedia arts venue that will be a flagship host of the festival.

★Manchester Pride Festival LGBT
(🎫0161-831 7700; www.manchesterpride.com; ⊙late Aug; 🚇Piccadilly Gardens) One of England's biggest celebrations of LGBT+ life, held over three days of the August bank holiday weekend at the end of the month. There's a big party in the Gay Village (£10 to £15), live gigs at nearby Mayfield (one

MANCHESTER POLICE MUSEUM

One of the city's best-kept secrets is this superb **museum** (🎫0161-856 4500; www.gmpmuseum.co.uk; 57a Newton St; ⊙10.30am-3.30pm Tue) FREE housed within a former Victorian police station. The original building has been magnificently – if a little creepily – brought back to life, and you can wander in and out of 19th-century cells where prisoners rested their heads on wooden pillows, visit a restored magistrates' court from 1895 and examine the case histories (complete with mugshots and photos of weapons) of some of the more notorious names to have passed through its doors.

WHITWORTH ART GALLERY

Manchester's second-most important **art gallery** (☑ 0161-275 7450; www.whitworth.manchester.ac.uk; University of Manchester, Oxford Rd, M15 6ER; ⏲ 10am-5pm Fri-Wed, to 9pm Thu; ☑ 15, 41, 42, 43, 140, 143 or 147 from Piccadilly Gardens) **FREE** is arguably its most beautiful, following a restoration that saw the doubling of its exhibition space through the opening of its sides and back, and the construction of glass-screened promenades. Inside is a fine collection of British watercolours, the best selection of historic textiles outside London and galleries devoted to the work of artists from Dürer and Rembrandt to Lucian Freud and David Hockney.

All this high art aside, you may find that the most interesting part of the gallery is the group of rooms dedicated to wallpaper – proof that bland pastels and horrible flowery patterns are not the final word in home decoration. There's also a lovely cafe on the grounds.

night/weekend £35/65), debates, films, lectures and community projects (the Superbia Weekend), and a huge parade.

Manchester Food & Drink Festival
FOOD & DRINK

(www.foodanddrinkfestival.com; Albert Sq; ⏲ late Sep-early Oct) Manchester's superb foodie scene shows off its wares over 10 days between the end of September and the beginning of October. Farmers markets, pop-up restaurants and gourmet events are just part of the UK's biggest urban food fest. Much of the action takes place on Albert Sq, in front of the town hall.

🛏 Sleeping

★ Qbic
HOTEL £

(www.qbichotels.com/manchester; John Dalton House, Deansgate, M2 6JR; r from £60; 🛜🖳) 🚲 Qbic's eco-friendly hotel philosophy arrives in Manchester with aplomb in this brilliant budget option. The rooms are compact but cleverly designed, while the recycled furniture, refillable toiletries and glass carafes are just the most visible examples of its commitment to sustainability (there are also solar panels on the roof). Comfortable, convenient and eco-conscious – it's how all hotels should be.

NQ1 Manchester
HOSTEL £

(☑ 0161-236 4414; www.selina.com; 50 Newton St; s/d from £48/54; ℗ @ 🛜; ☑ all city centre) Newly refurbished and part of the Selina hostel group, at this former millinery the selection of rooms and co-working spaces make it one of the best budget options in town. The location is a boon: smack in the heart of the Northern Quarter, you won't have to go far to get the best of alternative Manchester.

Manchester YHA
HOSTEL £

(☑ 0345 371 9647; www.yha.org.uk; Potato Wharf; d from £29; ℗ @ 🛜; ☑ Deansgate-Castlefield) This purpose-built canalside hostel in the Castlefield area is one of the best in the country. It's a top-class option, with four- and six-bed dorms, all with bathroom, as well as three doubles and a host of good facilities. Potato Wharf is just left off Liverpool Rd.

Roomzzz
APARTMENT ££

(☑ 0161-236 2121; www.roomzzz.com; 36 Princess St; r from £70; ❄ @ 🛜; ☑ all city centre) The inelegant name belies the designer digs inside this beautifully restored Grade II–listed building, which features serviced apartments equipped with a kitchen and the latest connectivity gadgetry, including sleek iMac computers and free wi-fi throughout. There's a small pantry, with food for sale downstairs. Highly recommended if you're planning a longer stay. There's also a **branch** (www.roomzzz.com; Corn Exchange, Exchange Sq; r from £100; ☑ Exchange Square) in the Corn Exchange, with rooms ranging in size from snug to spacious.

Hotel Brooklyn
HOTEL ££

(☑ 0161-518 2936; www.bespokehotels.com/hotelbrooklyn; 59 Portland St; r/ste from £60/120; ❄ @ 🛜) This New York City–themed hotel has 189 comfortable rooms kitted out in nu-retro style (Smeg fridges, rotary dial phones, old-style sound systems) spread across 10 floors of a new building. There's a bar on the 9th floor and Runyon's Restaurant on the ground floor, which serves upscale New York diner fare. A little gimmicky, sure, but it's a very good hotel nonetheless.

ABode
HOTEL **££**

(📞 0161-247 7744; www.abodemanchester.co.uk; 107 Piccadilly; r from £90; ❄ @ 🤏; 🚇 all city centre, 🚇 Piccadilly Gardens) The original fittings at this converted textile factory have been combined successfully with 61 bedrooms divided into four categories of ever-increasing luxury: Comfortable, Desirable, Enviable and Fabulous on Fifth, the last being five seriously swanky top-floor suites.

Kimpton Clocktower Hotel
HOTEL **££**

(📞 0161-288 2222; www.kimptonclocktowerhotel.com; Oxford St, M60 7HA; r from £90; @ 🤏 ❄; 🚇 St Peter's Square) Beyond the triple-height lobby of this 19th-century beaut are 270 newly refurbished loft-style rooms that are incredibly popular with both leisure and business visitors alike. From the lobby you can access the wonderful Refuge (p539).

Cow Hollow
BOUTIQUE HOTEL **££**

(📞 07727 159727; www.cowhollow.co.uk; 57 Newton St; r/ste from £90/120; 🤏; 🚇 all city centre) Set in a stick-thin 19th-century weavers' mill, Cow Hollow has 16 snug rooms graced with original beams, brick walls and flashy bathrooms; some have original machinery incorporated into the decor. Little luxury touches include Hypnos beds, goose-down duvets, and free Prosecco and tapas each evening. Reception is in the ground-floor bar.

Velvet Hotel
BOUTIQUE HOTEL **££**

(📞 0161-236 9003; www.velvetmanchester.com; 2 Canal St; r from £80; 🤏 ❄; 🚇 all city centre) Nineteen beautiful bespoke rooms here each ooze style: there's the sleigh bed in room 24, the double bath of room 34, and the saucy framed photographs of a stripped-down David Beckham (this is Gay Village, after all!). Despite the tantalising decor and location, this is not an exclusive hotel and is as popular with straight visitors as it is with the same-sex crowd.

⭐ King Street
Townhouse
BOUTIQUE HOTEL **£££**

(📞 0161-667 0707; www.eclectichotels.co.uk; 10 Booth St; r/ste from £180/£280; ❄ @ 🤏 ❄; 🚇 all city centre) This beautiful 1872 Italian Renaissance–style former bank is now an exquisite boutique hotel with 40 bedrooms ranging from snug to suite. Furnishings are the perfect combination of period elegance and contemporary style. On the top floor is a small spa with an infinity pool overlooking the town hall; downstairs is a nice bar and restaurant. Online rates are cheaper.

Stock Exchange Hotel
HOTEL **£££**

(📞 0161-470 3901; www.stockexchangehotel.co.uk; 4 Norfolk St, M21DW; d from £200; ❄ @ 🤏) The 1906 Stock Exchange building is now a modish 40-room hotel in the heart of the city. It's modern and luxurious, but you're never too far from the purpose of the Edwardian original: the Bull & Bear restaurant is where the trading floor used to be, while check-in (including tea and biscuits) is in the trader's lounge.

🍴 Eating

Rudy's
PIZZA **£**

(📞 0161-820 8292; www.rudyspizza.co.uk; 9 Cotton St, Ancoats, M4 5BF; pizzas £4.90-8.40; ⊘ noon-10pm Mon-Sat, to 9pm Sun; 🚇 Piccadilly Gardens, bua 42, 42B, 142 from city centre) Makers of the best pizza in town, Rudy's can be a tough table to get (put your name down and wait), but it is oh, so worth it. It makes its own dough, and uses proper San Marzano tomatoes and *fior di latte* mozzarella to create pies that a Neapolitan would approve of. There's another branch on Peter St.

Grub
STREET FOOD **£**

(www.grubmcr.com; 50 Redbank, M4 4HF; ⊘ 4-10pm Wed-Fri, from noon Sat, noon-6pm Sun) 🌱 A mix of ever-changing traders make this street-food collective one of the most exciting places in town to get a bite. There's a global slant and a heavy focus on plant-based cuisine (including vegan wine and spirits); there's even a dog bar that gives out free (vegan) doggie biscuits. On Sundays, everything is vegan.

Northern Soul Grilled Cheese
SANDWICHES **£**

(www.northernsoulmcr.com; 10 Church St; mains £4.90-7.50; ⊘ 8.30am-3pm Mon-Fri, to 5.30pm Sat)

ℹ NEW IN 2021

After a major renovation, 2021 will see the long-awaited reopening of the excellent **Manchester Jewish Museum** (📞 0161-834 9879; www.manchester-jewishmuseum.com; 190 Cheetham Hill Rd, M8 8LW). Across the Irwell in Salford, the historic grounds of Worsley New Hall – a Gothic-style mansion built in the 19th century for the Duke of Bridgewater – will be transformed into **RHS Garden Bridgewater**, a 62-hectare landscaped garden managed by the Royal Horticultural Society.

Carving out a niche for artery-clogging, gooey grilled-cheese delights in Manchester's grungy Northern Quarter, Northern Soul bills itself as 'gourmet' but there's nothing fancy about the makeshift shack it occupies, or its prices. The menu features cheese sandwiches in various guises, plus deliciously tangy mac 'n' cheese, and milkshakes. There's another branch on Tib St.

Richmond Tea Rooms CAFE **£**
(☑ 0161-237 9667; www.richmondtearooms.com; Richmond St; mains £5-11, afternoon teas £8.25-26.95; ⬜ all city centre) If the Mad Hatter were to have a tea party in Manchester, it would be in this haphazard tearoom with a potpourri of period furniture and a counter painted to look like the icing on a cake. Sandwiches and light meals are the mainstay, but the real treat is the selection of afternoon teas, complete with finger sandwiches, scones and cakes.

Bundobust INDIAN **£**
(☑ 0161-359 6757; www.bundobust.com; 61 Piccadilly; dishes £3.75-6.75; ⊘ noon-9.30pm Mon-Thu, to 10pm Fri & Sat, to 8pm Sun; 🖋; ⬜ all city centre, 🚇 Piccadilly Gardens) Enjoy Indian veggie street food and craft beer at this export from Leeds. The format's the same in Manchester, right down to the pallet wall-panelling at the entrance, but this basement venue is much bigger than the original. Bookings only.

★ **Refuge by Volta** INTERNATIONAL **££**
(☑ 0161-233 5151; www.refugemcr.co.uk; Oxford St; small plates £5.50-11; ⊘ noon-2.45pm & 5-9pm Mon-Thu, to 9.30pm Fri, noon-9.30pm Sat, noon-9pm Sun; ⬜ all city centre) Manchester's snazziest dining room occupies one half of the Refuge, one of the city's best bars. The menu is made up of *voltini,* sharing plates with global influences from the Middle East to Korea (think lamb shawarma and kimchi), inspired by the travels of restaurateurs and DJs Luke Cowdrey and Justin Crawford (aka the Unabombers). Superb.

★ **Mackie Mayor** FOOD HALL **££**
(www.mackiemayor.co.uk; 1 Eagle St; mains £9-15; ⊘ 10am-10pm Tue-Thu, to 11pm Fri, 9am-11pm Sat, 9am-8pm Sun; ⬜ all city centre) This restored former meat market is now home to a superb food hall with a fine selection of 10 individual traders. The pizzas from Honest Crust are divine; the pork-belly bao from Baohouse is done just right; Nationale 7 does wonders with a basic sandwich; and Tender Cow serves really tasty steaks. Dining is communal, across two floors.

Oast House INTERNATIONAL **££**
(☑ 0161-829 3830; www.theoasthouse.uk.com; The Avenue Courtyard, M3 3AY; mains £11.50-19.50; ⊘ noon-midnight Mon-Wed & Sun, to 1am Thu-Sat; ⬜ all city centre) Modelled on a Kentish oast house (a medieval kiln used to dry out hops), this is one of the most popular spots in Spinningfields. The broad-ranging menu has burgers, kebabs, steaks and rotisserie chickens cooked in the BBQ oven, but you can also get a delicious fondue and a fine selection of homemade pies.

★ **Mana** BRITISH **£££**
(www.manarestaurant.co.uk; 42 Blossom St, M4 6BF; set lunch/dinner £65/140; ⊘ noon-1.30pm & 7pm-late Thu-Sat, 7pm-late Wed; ⬜ 74, 76, 216, 217, 230, 231 from city centre) Manchester's first Michelin star since 1977 has come courtesy of ex-Noma chef Simon Martin, who takes dishes recognisable from a classic British menu (roast chicken, poached turbot, scallops) and delivers them with a host of new flavours (Daurenki caviar, grand fir and – for the chicken – sage tea). This is edible art.

20 Stories BRITISH **£££**
(☑ 0161-204 3333; www.20stories.co.uk; 1 Spinningfields, Hardman Sq; mains £19-35; ⊘ noon-2.45pm & 5.30-10.15pm Mon-Thu, noon-3.45pm & 5.30-10.30pm Fri & Sat, noon-3.15pm & 5.30-8.45pm Sun; ⬜ all city centre) The most anticipated opening of 2018 was this rooftop restaurant atop a 20-storey tower, marshalled by local star Aiden Byrne (formerly of Manchester House). Great views and great food, courtesy of Byrne's signature style of supremely elegant, unpretentious cuisine. There's an outdoor terrace with a firepit and a grill that serves good burgers and fish and chips.

Adam Reid at the French MODERN BRITISH **£££**
(☑ 0161-932 4198; http://the-french-manchester. co.uk; Midland Hotel, 16 Peter St; lunch/dinner tasting menu £75/99; ⊘ 6.30-8.30pm Tue-Thu, 5.30-9.30pm Fri, noon-1pm & 5.30-9.30pm Sat; ⬜ St Peter's Square) 🖋 Adam Reid's exquisite Modern British cuisine is considered one of Manchester's culinary highlights, with each dish of the seven-course tasting menu exquisitely prepared and presented. The room is dark and moody, the soundtrack indie rock – an interesting counterpoint to the subtlety of the food. Reservations are very much recommended.

Hawksmoor STEAK **£££**
(☑ 0161-836 6980; www.thehawksmoor.com; 184-186 Deansgate, M3 2EQ; steaks £21-36; ⊘ 5-10pm

Mon-Fri, noon-3pm & 5-10pm Sat, noon-9pm Sun;
⊠ St Peter's Square) Hawksmoor is the place
to go for steak. Everything inside this Grade
II–listed former courthouse is carefully put
together to create a 1930s-style atmosphere,
which is the perfect setting to indulge your
most carnivorous instincts. The steaks – also
available by weight – are prepared perfectly
and the sides – including dripping fries, tri-
ple-cooked chips, mac 'n' cheese – are just
divine.

Drinking & Nightlife

★ Refuge   BAR
(☎ 0161-233 5151; www.refugemcr.co.uk; Oxford St;
⊗ 8am-midnight Mon-Wed, to 1am Thu, to 2am Fri &
Sat, to 11.30pm Sun; ⊠ all city centre) Occupying
what was once the Victorian Gothic ground
floor of the Refuge Assurance Building, this
is not just Manchester's most beautiful bar,
but arguably its coolest too – all thanks to
the rep and aesthetic sensibilities of its creative director duo, DJs and restaurateurs
Luke Cowdrey and Justin Crawford, aka the
Unabombers, who run Homoelectric, the
best club nights in the northwest.

Fac251   CLUB
(☎ 0161-272 7251; www.factorymanchester.com;
112-118 Princess St; £1-6; ⊗ 11pm-4am Thu-Mon;
⊠ all city centre) Located in Tony Wilson's former Factory Records HQ, Fac251 is one of
the most popular venues in town. There are
three rooms, all with a broad musical appeal,
from drum and bass to Motown and indie
rock. There's something for everybody, from
Monday's Quids In (for students) to the Big
Weekender on Saturday (commercial R & B).

Peveril of the Peak   PUB
(☎ 0161-236 6364; 127 Great Bridgewater St;
⊗ 11am-11pm; ⊠ Deansgate-Castlefield) The best
of Manchester's collection of beautiful Victorian pubs. Check out the gorgeous glazed
tilework outside.

Britons Protection   PUB
(☎ 0161-236 5895; 50 Great Bridgewater St;
⊗ noon-midnight Mon-Thu, to 1am Fri & Sat, to 11pm
Sun; ⊠ Castlefield-Deansgate) Whisky – over
300 different kinds of it (the Cu Dhub 'black
whisky' is a particular treat with its touch of
coffee and honey) – is the beverage of choice
at this liver-threatening, proper English pub
that also does home-style meals (gammon,
pies etc). An old-fashioned boozer with open
fires in the back rooms and a cosy atmosphere, it's perfect on a cold evening.

Albert's Schloss   BEER HALL
(www.albertsschloss.co.uk; 27 Peter St; ⊗ 8am-
2am Mon-Fri, 9.30am-2am Sat & Sun; ⊠ St Peter's
Square) The strapline says 'Cook Haus and
Bier Palace', and this big version of a night
out in Central Europe is just that. The *bier*
is unpasteurised Pilsner Urquell, shipped
directly from the brewery near Prague. The
food is more local, but still true to theme –
you can get all kinds of wursts, sauerbraten
and 'schweins in blankets'. *Wunderbar!*

North Tea Power   CAFE
(☎ 0161-833 3073; www.northteapower.co.uk; 36
Tib St; ⊗ 8am-7pm Mon-Fri, from 9am Sat, 10am-
6pm Sun; 🛜) The name may say tea but the
interior of this cafe screams coffee shop.
North Tea Power is one of Manchester's
early adopters of the artisanal coffee scene,
with the requisite communal tables, industrial pillars and Macbook-wielding tribe.
As well as flat whites, AeroPress and pour-
overs, the menu features a load of loose-leaf
teas, cakes and all-day breakfast options.

Port Street Beer House   CRAFT BEER
(www.portstreetbeerhouse.co.uk; 39-41 Port St;
⊗ noon-midnight Sun-Fri, to 1am Sat; ⊠ Piccadilly
Gardens) Fans of real ale love this Northern
Quarter boozer, with its seven hand pulls, 18
draught lines and more than 100 beers from
around the world, including gluten-free ales
and some heavy hitters: Brewdog's Tactical
Nuclear Penguin is a £45 stout, but at 32%
alcohol you won't need more than one. It
hosts regular tastings and tap takeovers.

Black Dog Ballroom   BAR
(☎ 0161-839 0664; www.blackdogballroom.co.uk;
52 Church St; ⊗ 4-10pm Mon-Fri, from noon Sat &
Sun; 🛜; ⊠ all city centre) A basement bar with
a speakeasy vibe, but there's nothing illicit

FOOTBALL TOURS

Manchester United Museum & Tour (📞0161-826 1326; www.manutd.com; Sir Matt Busby Way; tours adult/child £18/12; ⊙museum 9.30am-5pm Mon-Sat, 10am-4pm Sun, tours every 10 min 9.40am-4.30pm Mon-Sat, to 3.30pm Sun, closed match days; 🚇Old Trafford or Exchange Quay) You don't have to be a fan of the world's most famous football club to enjoy a visit to its impressive 75,000-plus-capacity Old Trafford stadium, but it helps. The museum tour includes a walk down the tunnel onto the edge of the playing surface, where Manchester United's superstar footballers ply their lucrative trade.

Other highlights of the excellent tour include a seat in the stands, a stop in the changing rooms and a peek at the players' lounge (from which the manager is banned unless invited by the players) – all ecstatic experiences for a Man United devotee. The museum has a comprehensive history of the club and a state-of-the-art call-up system that means you can view your favourite goals.

Manchester City Stadium Tour (📞0161-444 1894; www.mancity.com; Etihad Campus; tours adult/child £25/15; ⊙9am-5pm Mon-Sat, 10am-4pm Sun except match days; 🚇Etihad Campus) On this 90-minute tour of Manchester City's stadium you'll visit both the home and away dressing rooms (note the huge difference between the two), the pitchside dugouts, the press room and the Tunnel Club, where VIP guests get to see the players walk through on match days. The tour also includes a visit to the trophy room, now full of trophies won under the tutelage of superstar manager Josep 'Pep' Guardiola.

Other tours combine the stadium with the nearby academy. Online bookings are cheaper.

---

about drinking here: the cocktails are terrific (it runs occasional mixology sessions), the atmosphere is always buzzing and the music always good and loud – the resident DJs spin some great tunes Thursday through Saturday nights.

☆ Entertainment

★ HOME ARTS CENTRE
(📞0161-200 1500; www.homemcr.org; 2 Tony Wilson Pl, First St; tickets £5-25; ⊙box office noon-8pm, bar 10am-11pm Mon-Thu, to midnight Fri & Sat, 11am-10.30pm Sun; 🚇all city centre) One of Britain's best arts centres, HOME has two theatre spaces that host provocative new work in a variety of contexts, from proscenium sets to promenade pieces. The five cinema screens show the latest indie releases as well as classics. There's also a ground-floor bar and a cafe that serves good food on the 1st floor.

Band on the Wall LIVE MUSIC
(📞0161-834 1786; www.bandonthewall.org; 25 Swan St; ⊙5pm-late; 🚇all city centre) A top-notch venue that hosts everything from rock to world music, with splashes of jazz, blues and folk thrown in.

Gorilla LIVE MUSIC
(📞0161-826 2998; www.thisisgorilla.com; 54-56 Whitworth St, M1 5WW; ⊙11pm-late; 🚇all city centre) Brilliant mid-sized venue to see up-and-comers, alternative artists and big stars looking to enhance their alternative credentials. There's a bar and a restaurant too.

Deaf Institute LIVE MUSIC
(www.thedeafinstitute.co.uk; 135 Grosvenor St; ⊙10am-midnight; 🚇all city centre) This is an excellent venue in a former institute for deaf people; it also includes a smaller venue in the basement and a cafe on the ground floor. It's where you'll hear alt rock and pop by dozens of local bands we guarantee you've never heard of (as well as some visiting bands you may have).

🛍 Shopping

Oi Polloi CLOTHING
(www.oipolloi.com; 63 Thomas St; ⊙10am-6pm Mon-Sat; 🚇all city centre) Besides the impressive range of casual footwear, this hip boutique also stocks a huge range of designers including A Kind of Guise, LA Panoplie, Nudie Jeans Co and Maison Kitsuné.

Tib Street Market MARKET
(📞0161-234 7357; Tib St; ⊙10am-5pm Sat; 🚇all city centre) Local designers get a chance to display their wares at this weekly market, where you can pick up everything from purses to lingerie and hats to jewellery.

Oxfam Originals VINTAGE
(Unit 8, Smithfield Bldg, Oldham St; ⊙10am-6pm Mon-Sat, noon-5pm Sun; 🚇all city centre) If you're

into retro, this terrific store has high-quality gear from the 1960s and '70s. Shop in the knowledge that it's for a good cause.

❶ Information

Tourist Office (www.visitmanchester.com; 1 Piccadilly Gardens; ⊙ 9.30am-5pm Mon-Sat, 10.30am-4.30pm Sun; ⊠ Piccadilly Gardens) This is mostly a self-service tourist office, with brochures and interactive maps to help guide visitors.

❶ Getting There & Away

AIR

Manchester Airport (☑ 0808-169 7030; www.manchesterairport.co.uk) The airport is 12 miles south of the city.

Bus £4.20, 30 minutes, every 20 minutes to Piccadilly Gardens

Metrolink £4.20, 40 minutes, every 12 minutes; change at Cornbrook or Firswood for city centre

Taxi £20 to £30, 25 to 40 minutes

Train £5, 20 minutes, every 10 minutes to Piccadilly Station

BUS

National Express (☑ 08717 81 81 81; www.nationalexpress.com) serves most major cities from the **coach station** (Chorlton St), including the following:

Leeds £6, one hour, hourly

Liverpool £4, 1½ hours, hourly

London £8.40, 4¼ hours, hourly

TRAIN

Manchester Piccadilly (east of Piccadilly Gardens) is the main station for most mainline train services across Britain; Victoria Station (north of the National Football Museum) serves destinations in the northwest including Blackburn, Halifax and Huddersfield but also Leeds and Liverpool. The two stations are linked by Metrolink. Off-peak fares are considerably cheaper. Destinations include the following:

Blackpool £9.50, 1¼ hours, half-hourly

Liverpool Lime St £15.30, 45 minutes, half-hourly

London Euston £64, three hours, seven daily

Newcastle £76, three hours, six daily

❶ Getting Around

BUS

The Metroshuttle is a free service with three separate routes around the heart of Manchester every 10 minutes. Pick up a map from the tourist office. Most local buses start from Piccadilly Gardens.

METROLINK

The **Metrolink** (www.metrolink.co.uk) light-rail network is the best way to get between Victoria and Piccadilly train stations, and further afield to Salford Quays, Didsbury and other suburbs, as well as the Trafford Centre. It also serves the airport, but you need to change at either Cornbrook or Firswood. Trams run every few minutes throughout the day from 6am to 11pm. Buy your tickets from the platform machine.

TRAIN

Castlefield is served by Deansgate station with suburban rail links to Piccadilly, Oxford Rd and Salford stations.

CHESTER

☑ 01244 / POP 118,200

Chester's Tudor-and-Victorian heart is justifiably famous as one of Britain's prettiest town centres. This collection of black-and-white timber-framed beauties and red-sandstone buildings surrounded by an original set of Roman-era walls is one of the northwest's biggest tourist attractions.

Beyond the cruciform-shaped historic centre, Chester is an ordinary, residential town; it's hard to believe today, but throughout the Middle Ages Chester made its money as the most important port in the northwest. However, the River Dee silted up over time and Chester fell behind Liverpool in importance.

◉ Sights & Activities

★ **City Walls**   LANDMARK
A good way to get a sense of Chester's unique character is to walk the 2-mile circuit along the walls that surround the historic centre. Originally built by the Romans around 70 CE, the walls were altered substantially over the following centuries, but have retained their current position since around 1200. The tourist office's *Walk Around Chester Walls* leaflet is an excellent guide and you can also take a 90-minute guided walk.

Of the many features along the walls, the most eye-catching is the prominent Eastgate, where you can see the most famous clock in England after London's Big Ben, built for Queen Victoria's Diamond Jubilee in 1897.

At the southeastern corner of the walls are the wishing steps, added in 1785. Local legend claims that if you can run up and down these uneven steps while holding your breath your wish will come true.

Chester

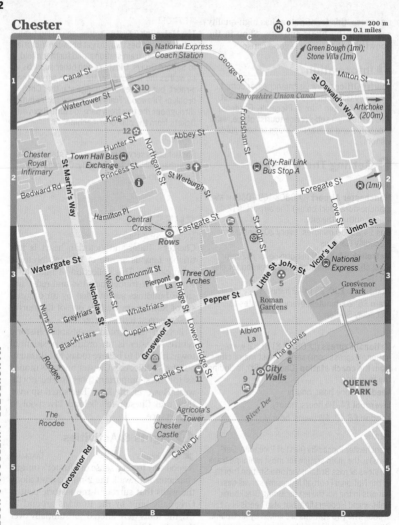

Just inside Southgate, known here as **Bridgegate** (as it's located at the northern end of the Old Dee Bridge), is the **Bear & Billet** pub, Chester's oldest timber-framed building, built in 1664, and once a toll gate into the city.

Chester Cathedral
CATHEDRAL
(☎ 01244-324756; www.chestercathedral.com; 12 Abbey Sq; ⊙ 10am-4pm Mon-Sat, noon-4pm Sun) **FREE** Chester Cathedral was originally a Benedictine abbey built on the remains of an earlier Saxon church dedicated to St Werburgh (the city's patron saint); it was shut down in 1540 as part of Henry VIII's Disso-

lution frenzy, but reconsecrated as a cathedral the following year. Despite a substantial Victorian facelift, the cathedral retains much of its original 12th-century structure. You can amble about freely, but the **tours** (www. chestercathedral.com; adult/child 1hr tour £8/6, 30min tour £6; ⊙ full tour 11am & 3pm daily, short tour 12.30pm & 1.15pm Mon & Tue, 2pm & 4pm Wed-Sat) are excellent, as they take you up to the top of the panoramic bell tower.

Roman Amphitheatre
ARCHAEOLOGICAL SITE
(Little St John St) **FREE** Just outside the city walls is what was once an arena that seated 7000 spectators (making it the country's

Chester

largest); some historians have suggested that it may have also been the site of King Arthur's Camelot and that his knights' 'round table' was really just this circular construction. Excavations continue; during summer months there are occasional shows held here.

Blue Planet Aquarium   AQUARIUM
(www.blueplanetaquarium.com; Cheshire Oaks, CH65 9LF; adult/child £18/13; ☉10am-5pm; ☐1 or X1 from Bus Exchange) Things aren't done by halves around Chester, where you'll find Blue Planet, which was the country's largest aquarium when it opened in 1998. It's home to 10 different kinds of shark, which can be viewed from a 70m-long moving walkway that lets you eye them up close. The aquarium is at the Cheshire Oaks Outlet Centre (p544), 7 miles north of Chester at Junction 10 of the M53 to Liverpool. Pre-booking essential.

Grosvenor Museum   MUSEUM
(☑01244-972197; www.grosvenormuseum. westcheshiremuseums.co.uk; 27 Grosvenor St; ☉10.30am-1pm & 2-4.30pm Tue-Sat, last admission 3.45pm) FREE This excellent museum has the country's most comprehensive collection of Roman tombstones. At the back of the museum is a preserved Georgian house, complete with kitchen, drawing room, bedroom and bathroom. Pre-booking only.

Chester Boat   BOATING
(☑01244-325394; www.chesterboat.co.uk; Boating Station, Souters La, The Groves; 30min/2hr cruise £7/15; ☉11am-5pm) Runs hourly 30-minute and two-hour cruises (the latter at noon and 2.30pm Saturday and Sunday) up and down the Dee, including a foray into the gorgeous Eaton Estate, home of the Duke and Duchess

of Westminster. All departures are from the riverside along the promenade known as the Groves.

🛏 Sleeping

Stone Villa   B&B ££
(☑01244-345014; www.stonevillachester.co.uk; 3 Stone Pl, Hoole Rd; s/d from £65/95; 🅿🐾; ☐9 from city centre) This award-winning, beautiful 1850 villa has everything you need for a memorable stay. Elegant bedrooms, a fabulous breakfast and welcoming, friendly owners all add up to excellent lodgings. The property is about a mile from the city centre. You can even rent the whole house – which sleeps 22 – for £900 a night.

ABode Chester   HOTEL ££
(☑01244-347000; www.abodechester.co.uk; Grosvenor Rd; r/ste from £74/249; 🅿🌺🐾) Contemporary hotel with 84 rooms all equipped with handcrafted Vispring beds and handsome bathrooms complete with monsoon showers. Good toiletries, flat-screen TVs and cashmere throws on the beds give it a touch of elegance. Rooms come in categories: Comfortable, Desirable, Enviable, Most Enviable and Fabulous suites. South-facing rooms have great views of the Roodee racecourse.

★ **Edgar House**   BOUTIQUE HOTEL £££
(☑01244-347007; www.edgarhouse.co.uk; 22 City Walls; ☉r from £199) These award-winning digs are the ultimate in boutique luxury: a Georgian house with seven rooms, each decorated in its own individual style – some have free-standing claw-foot tubs and French doors that lead onto an elegant terrace. There's beautiful art on the walls and fabulous touches of the owners' gorgeous aesthetic throughout.

DON'T MISS

THE ROWS

Besides the City Walls, Chester's other great draw is the Rows, a series of two-level, half-timbered galleried arcades along the four streets that fan out in each direction from the Central Cross. Aside from the 13th-century **Three Old Arches** building, the architecture is a handsome mix of Victorian and Tudor (original and mock) buildings that house a fantastic collection of independently owned shops.

The origin of the Rows is a little unclear, but it is believed that as the Roman walls slowly crumbled, medieval traders built their shops against the resulting rubble banks, while later arrivals built theirs on top.

Chester Grosvenor Hotel & Spa   HOTEL **£££**
(☎ 01244-324024; www.chestergrosvenor.com; 58 Eastgate St; r from £160; P @ ✿) The black-and-white timbered Grosvenor is the city's top hotel by location (right next to the Eastgate Clock) and quality, offering a five-star experience throughout. The lobby's main feature is the chandelier, with 28,000 pieces of crystal; move on from there to the huge rooms with exquisite period furniture. There's also a top spa (open to nonguests) and a Michelin-starred restaurant.

✗ Eating

★ **The Kitchen**   LEBANESE **£**
(www.thekitchenstoryhouse.co.uk; Storyhouse, Hunter St; mains £7-10; ✿ 8am-9.30pm Mon-Sat, 9.30am-9pm Sun) Delicious meze and other small plates from the Levant are the mainstay at the ground-floor restaurant in Storyhouse, Chester's exciting award-winning arts centre. The brunch menu (available from 10am) is a treat – how about harissa sausage and streaky bacon roll or cumin-spiced rice with smoked haddock and kedgeree?

Joseph Benjamin   MODERN BRITISH **££**
(☎ 01244-344295; www.josephbenjamin.co.uk; 134-140 Northgate St; mains £14-17; ✿ noon-2.30pm & 5-10pm Wed-Sun) A bright star in Chester's culinary firmament is this combo restaurant, bar and deli that delivers carefully prepared local produce to take away or eat in. Excellent sandwiches and gorgeous salads are the mainstay of the takeaway menu,

while the more formal dinner menu features fine examples of Modern British cuisine.

Artichoke   MODERN BRITISH **££**
(www.artichokechester.co.uk; The Steam Mill, Steam Mill St; mains £7-13; ✿ 3.30-9pm Mon-Fri, from 12.30pm Sat, 12.30-7pm Sun) One of a number of warehouse conversions along the Shropshire Union Canal (now known as the Canal Quarter), this cafe-bar serves sandwiches and smaller bites as well as tasty main courses, such as sea trout in a sweet pea wasabi velvet cream, and confit of duck legs with Jersey potatoes, pancetta and red cabbage. It's a popular drinking spot too.

Simon Radley at the Grosvenor   MODERN BRITISH **£££**
(☎ 01244-324024; www.chestergrosvenor.com; 58 Eastgate St, Chester Grosvenor Hotel; tasting menu Tue-Thu £79, Fri & Sat £99; ✿ 6.30-7.30pm Tue-Sat) Simon Radley's formal restaurant has served near-perfect Modern British cuisine since 1990, when it was first awarded the Michelin star that it has kept ever since. The food is divine and the wine list extensive. It's one of Britain's best, but a little stuffy: smart attire only and no children under 12 allowed. Oh, and switch your mobile phone to silent.

🍷 Drinking & Entertainment

Brewery Tap   PUB
(www.the-tap.co.uk; 52-54 Lower Bridge St; ✿ noon-11pm Mon-Sat, to 10.30pm Sun) If you're looking for the best pint in the city, the aficionados at the Campaign for Real Ale (Camra) reckon you'll get it at this boozer in a Grade II–listed Jacobean banqueting hall; its seven taps offer a rotating range of quality brews from all over England.

★ **Storyhouse**   ARTS CENTRE
(☎ 01244-409113; www.storyhouse.com; Hunter St) The 1930s art deco Odeon has been converted into an award-winning modern arts centre with two theatre spaces – a larger 800-seat arena and a 150-seat studio theatre – plus a cinema that screens indie and art movies. The Lebanese-inspired Kitchen restaurant on the ground floor is excellent.

🔒 Shopping

Cheshire Oaks Outlet Centre   SHOPPING CENTRE
(www.mcarthurglen.com; Ellesmere Port; ✿ 10am-8pm Mon-Fri, 9am-8pm Sat, 10am-6pm Sun; 🚌 1 or X1 from Bus Exchange) Britain's largest shopping outlet, Cheshire Oaks has 145 stores

offering discounts of up to 60% on goods from previous seasons. The village layout means the shops are divided into helpful districts, dotted with restaurants and cafes along the way. It's 7 miles north of Chester.

ℹ Information

Tourist Office (📞 01244-402111; www. visitchester.com; Town Hall, Northgate St; ⊗10am-5pm Mon-Sat, to 4pm Sun) Tourist information, accommodation-booking service and brochures.

ℹ Getting There & Away

BUS

Local buses leave from the **Town Hall Bus Exchange** (Princess St). **National Express** (📞 08717 81 81 81; www.nationalexpress.com) coaches stop on Vicar's Lane, just opposite the tourist office by the Roman amphitheatre. Destinations include the following:
Birmingham £18.30, two hours, four daily
Liverpool £7, 45 minutes, four daily
London £34.60, 5½ hours, three daily
Manchester £6.50, 1¼ hours, three daily

TRAIN

The train station is about a mile from the city centre via Foregate St and City Rd, or Brook St. City-Rail Link buses are free for people with rail tickets, and operate between the station and **Bus Stop A** (Frodsham St). Destinations include the following:
Liverpool £7.70, 45 minutes, hourly
London Euston £64.40, 2½ hours, hourly
Manchester £18.60, one hour, hourly

ℹ Getting Around

A car's not much use in town, as much of the centre is closed to traffic from 10.30am to 4.30pm. The city is easy to walk around anyway, and most places of interest are close to the wall. There are regular buses to the aquarium.

LIVERPOOL

📞 0151 / POP 552,267

It's hard not to be infected by a Liverpudlian's love for their own city. For decades this was a hardscrabble town beset by all manner of social ills, but still the love endured, finding its expression in a renowned gallows wit and an obsession with football.

With the worst of times now firmly behind them, it's much easier to feel the love. The city's impressive cultural heritage,

dating back to when Liverpool was Britain's second-most important city, is a source of justifiable pride to Scousers – as the locals are named, after Scouse, a fish-and-biscuit stew popular with sailors – but what really excites them is the ongoing programme of urban regeneration that is transforming a once dilapidated city centre into one of the most pleasant cities in northern England.

History

Liverpool grew wealthy on the back of the triangular trading of slaves, raw materials and finished goods (the horrors of which are documented at the International Slavery Museum, p550). From 1700 ships carried cotton goods and hardware from Liverpool to West Africa, where they were exchanged for slaves, who in turn were carried to the West Indies and Virginia, where they were exchanged for sugar, rum, tobacco and raw cotton.

As a great port, the city drew thousands of Irish and Scottish immigrants, and its Celtic influences are still apparent. Between 1830 and 1930, however, nine million emigrants – mainly English, Scots and Irish, but also Swedes, Norwegians and Russian Jews – sailed from here to the New World.

The start of WWII led to a resurgence of Liverpool's importance. More than one million American GIs disembarked here before D-Day and the port was, once again, hugely important as the western gateway for transatlantic supplies. The GIs brought with them the latest American records, and Liverpool was thus the first European port of call for the new rhythm and blues that would eventually become rock and roll. Within 20 years, the Mersey Beat was *the* sound of British pop, and four mop-topped Scousers had formed a skiffle band...

◉ Sights

The main attractions are Albert Dock (west of the city centre) and the trendy Ropewalks area (south of Hanover St and west of the two cathedrals). Lime St station, the bus station and the Cavern Quarter – a mecca for Beatles fans – lie just to the north.

◉ City Centre

★**Liverpool Cathedral** CHURCH
(📞 0151-709 6271; www.liverpoolcathedral.org.uk; Upper Duke St; Tower Experience adult/student £5.50/4.50; ⊗11am-2.45pm Mon-Fri, to 2.30pm Sat, 12.30-2.30pm Sun; 🚌82 & 86 from city

Liverpool

N

200 m
0.1 miles

Dalby St

Pembroke Pl

London Rd

Hotham St

Lord Nelson St

William Brown St

St George's Hall

Lime St

Train Station

Lime St

Queen Sq

Victoria St

Hatton Gdn

Dale St

Cavern Quarter

Williamson Sq

Temple La

Tithebarn St

Moorfields

Old Hall St

Mersey Tunnel

Chapel St

Rumford St

Cook St

Castle St

Mathew St

Harrington St

Lord St

James St

Water St

Goree Piazza

New Quay

King Edward St

Bath St

William Jessop Way

Princes Dock

Cunard Building

Mersey Ferry

Port of Mann

Liverpool Building

PIER HEAD

Canning Half Tide Basin

International Slavery Museum

ALBERT DOCK

The Beatles Story

Canning Dock

Salthouse Dock

Strand St

Liverpool ONE Bus Station

Liver St

Wapping Basin

Wapping

Wapping Dock

King's Pde

Monarch's Quay

BALTIC TRIANGLE

Tabley St

Park La

Nelson St

CHINATOWN

Great George St

Berry St

Roscoe St

Leece St

Upper Duke St

Liverpool Cathedral

ROPEWALKS

Duke St

Slater St

Wood St

Seel St

Par St

Campbell St

Concert Sq

Colquitt St

Bold St

Hanover St

School La

Paradise St

Church St

Clayton Sq

Ranelagh St

Renshaw St

Central

Mt Pleasant

Brownlow Hill

Mt Pleasant

Russell St

Copperas Hill

Brownlow Hill

Clarence St

Rodney St

Hardman St

Hope St

Hope Pl

Rice St

Myrtle St

Falkner St

Catherine St

Blackburne Pl

Canning St

Blackburne Tce

Oxford St

Metropolitan Cathedral of Christ the King

Walker Art Gallery

World Museum

District (200m), Botanical Garden (300m); Constellations (350m)

Mersey

The Wirral (2mi)

Mersey Tunnel

Liverpool

centre) Britain's largest church, this magnificent neo-Gothic building is also the world's largest Anglican cathedral. It was designed by Sir Giles Gilbert Scott (creator of the red telephone box) and is a stunning bit of architecture, managing at once to provoke awe at its size as well as a profound feeling of intimacy. Pre-booking is essential to climb the tower, which affords views as far as Blackpool (on a clear day).

The Tower Experience was closed at the time of writing, but once it reopens you can enjoy *Great Space,* a 10-minute, panoramic high-definition movie about the history of the cathedral, which was begun in 1904 but not completed until 1978; and a view of Great George, the world's heaviest set of bells. The vast interior is marked by a studied emptiness, but worth noting is the organ, split between two chambers on opposite sides of the Choir and comprising 10,268 pipes and 200 stops, making it most likely the world's largest operational model. The cathedral is also home to a collection of artworks, including a piece over the West Doors called *For You* by Tracey Emin: a pink neon sign that says 'I felt you and I knew you loved me'. Guides are on hand to offer tours; a donation of £3 is suggested.

★ **Walker Art Gallery**   GALLERY
(📞0151-478 4199; www.liverpoolmuseums.org.uk/walker; William Brown St; ⊙10am-5pm Wed-Sun;

🚇all city centre) FREE The city's foremost art gallery is the national gallery for northern England, housing an outstanding collection of art from the 14th to the 21st centuries. Its strong suits are Pre-Raphaelite art, modern British art and sculpture – not to mention the rotating exhibits of contemporary expression. It's a family-friendly place too: the ground-floor Big Art for Little Artists gallery is designed for under-eights and features interactive exhibits and games that will (hopefully) result in a lifelong love affair with art.

★ **World Museum**   MUSEUM
(📞0151-478 4399; www.liverpoolmuseums.org.uk/wml; William Brown St; ⊙10am-5pm Wed-Sun; 🚇all city centre) FREE Natural history, science and technology are the themes of the oldest museum in town, which opened in 1853. Its exhibits range from live bugs to human anthropology. This vastly entertaining and educational museum is spread across five themed floors, from the aquarium on the 1st floor to the planetarium on the 5th, where you'll also find exhibits dedicated to space (moon rocks, telescopes etc) and time (clocks and timepieces from the 1500s to 1960). Highly recommended.

Western Approaches Museum   MUSEUM
(www.liverpoolwarmuseum.co.uk; 1-3 Rumford St; adult/child £13.50/8; ⊙10am-4.15pm Wed-Sun; 🚇all city centre) Between 7 February 1941 and 15 August 1945 the secret command

LIVERPOOL IN ONE DAY

Start your day at the Beatles Story (p550) on the Albert Dock: it's an excellent intro to the Fab Four, but fans should make sure they've booked a morning tour (p550) to Mendips and 20 Forthlin Rd, the childhood homes of John Lennon and Paul McCartney respectively; the tour leaves from Albert Dock. If you're not a die-hard Beatles fan, then visit the International Slavery Museum and then head into town for a visit to the stunning cathedral (p545). For lunch, try the Salt House (p552).

If you've still got a cultural hunger, you can explore the Walker Art Gallery (p547) or the wonderful natural science exhibits of the World Museum (p547). Football fans should make the trip to Anfield and take the tour of Liverpool Football Club (p553). For dinner, go to Wreckfish (p551) or Art School (p552).

After dinner, be sure to get a drink at the Philharmonic Dining Rooms (p553), after which you can take in a gig across the street at the Philharmonic Hall (p554). If you're into something a little more adrenalised, the clubs of the Baltic Triangle are worth a punt: our favourite is Constellations (p554), which always has something interesting going on.

centre for the Battle of the Atlantic was in the basement rooms of Derby House. Known as Western Approaches because its main task was to monitor enemy approaches in the Atlantic west of the British Isles, the labyrinthine nerve centre of Allied operations is pretty much as it was at war's end. Highlights include the all-important map room, where you can imagine playing a real-life, full-scale version of Risk.

⊙ Albert Dock

Liverpool's biggest tourist attraction is Albert Dock, 2.75 hectares of water ringed by enormous cast-iron columns and impressive five-storey warehouses that make up the country's largest collection of protected buildings and are a World Heritage Site. A fabulous redevelopment programme has really brought the dock to life – here you'll find several outstanding museums and an extension of the Tate Gallery, as well as some good restaurants and bars.

★ **International Slavery Museum** MUSEUM
(☑0151-478 4499; www.liverpoolmuseums.org.uk/ism; Albert Dock; ⊙10am-5pm Wed-Sun) FREE
Museums are, by their very nature, a document of the past, but the extraordinary International Slavery Museum resonates very much in the present. It reveals slavery's unimaginable horrors – and Liverpool's own role in the triangular slave trade – in a clear and uncompromising manner. It does this through a remarkable series of multimedia and other displays, and it doesn't baulk at confronting racism, slavery's shadowy ideological justification for this inhumane practice.

The history of slavery is made real through a series of personal experiences, including a carefully kept ship's log and captain's diary. These tell the story of one slaver's experience on a typical trip, departing Liverpool for West Africa. The ship then purchased or captured as many slaves as it could carry before embarking on the gruesome 'middle passage' across the Atlantic to the West Indies. The slaves that survived the torturous journey were sold for sugar, rum, tobacco and raw cotton, which were then brought back to England for profit. Exhibits include original shackles, chains and instruments used to punish rebellious slaves – each piece of metal is more horrendous than the next.

Royal Liver Building 360 MUSEUM
(☑0151-559 1950; www.rlb360.com; Pier Head; adult/child £15/10; ⊙9am-6.30pm Mar-Sep, to 5.30pm Oct-Feb) One of Pier Head's trio of Edwardian buildings known as the 'Three Graces', the Royal Liver Building (pronounced lie-ver) opened to the public for the first time in 2019. The 70-minute tour takes you through the history of the building and some of its beautiful rooms right to the clock tower at the top, crowned by the famous 5.5m copper Liver Bird that is the city's symbol.

Merseyside Maritime Museum MUSEUM
(☑0151-478 4499; www.liverpoolmuseums.org.uk/maritime; Albert Dock; ⊙10am-5pm Wed-Sun; 🚌all city centre) FREE The story of one of the world's great ports is the theme of this excellent museum and, believe us, it's a graphic and compelling page-turner. One of the many great exhibits is Emigration to

a New World (in the basement), which tells the story of nine million emigrants and their efforts to get to North America and Australia; the walk-through model of a typical ship shows just how tough conditions on board really were.

Museum of Liverpool
MUSEUM

(☏ 0151-478 4545; www.liverpoolmuseums.org.uk/mol; Pier Head; ⏰ 10am-5pm Wed-Sun; 🚇 all city centre) FREE Liverpool's storied past is explored through an interactive exploration of the city's cultural and historical milestones: the railroad, poverty, wealth, *Brookside* (a popular '80s and '90s TV soap opera set in the city), the Beatles and football (the film on what the game means to the city is worth the 15 minutes). The desire to tell all of the city's rich story means there isn't a huge amount of depth, but the kids will love it.

The museum is constantly introducing new elements and temporary exhibitions, with a view towards ensuring that all visits are connected with a contemporary experience of the city. Recent exhibits include a retrospective of Linda McCartney's photographs, German expressionist prints and a show on artificial intelligence.

Tate Liverpool
GALLERY

(☏ 0151-702 7400; www.tate.org.uk/liverpool; Albert Dock; special exhibitions adult/child from £6/5; ⏰ 10am-5.50pm; 🚇 all city centre) FREE Touted as the home of modern art in the north, this gallery features a substantial checklist of 20th-century artists across its four floors, as well as touring exhibitions from the mother ship on London's Bankside. But it's all a little sparse, with none of the energy we'd expect from the world-famous Tate.

👣 Tours

⭐ Anfield Stadium Tour
TOUR

(www.liverpoolfc.com; Anfield Stadium; stadium tour adult/child £20/15; ⏰ 9am-5pm except match days; 🚌 26 & 27 from Liverpool ONE Bus Station, 17 from Queens St Bus Station) For fans of Liverpool FC, Anfield is a special place, and this is reflected in the reverential tone of the hour-long self-guided audio tour that starts at the top of the new Main Stand (with a video greeting from manager Jürgen Klopp) and continues down to pitchside. Stops along the way include the home and away dressing rooms and the luxurious players' lounge.

You'll also see the press room and the home dugout, accessed via the 'walk of champions' tunnel, where you can touch the iconic 'This is Anfield' sign. Also included is the new 'Boom Room' exhibition, which tells the story of how Klopp and his charges won the league title in 2020 – after a 30-year wait. Staff positioned at various points throughout the tour are on hand to answer questions, generally with a touch of humour that makes the whole experience a memorable one for fans and especially kids. The ground is 2.5 miles northeast of the city centre.

Old Docks Tour
TOURS

(☏ 0151-478 4499; www.liverpoolmuseums.org.uk/maritime; Merseyside Maritime Museum, Albert Dock; ⏰ 10.30am, noon & 2.30pm Mon-Wed; 🚇 all city centre) Free and a lot of fun, the guided tours of the Old Dock – the world's first commercial enclosed wet dock – offer an insight into the history of Liverpool as a powerful port city (and the source of all its wealth). You'll also get to see the bed of the Pool, the creek that gave the city its name.

Magical Mystery Tour
CULTURAL

(☏ 0151-703 9100; www.cavernclub.org; per person £19.95; ⏰ tours hourly 11am-4pm; 🚇 all city centre) This two-hour tour takes in all the Beatles-related landmarks – their birthplaces, childhood homes, schools and places such as Penny Lane and Strawberry Field – before finishing up in the Cavern Club (which isn't the original). It departs from opposite the tourist office on Albert Dock.

THE THREE GRACES

The area to the north of Albert Dock is known as Pier Head, after a stone pier built in the 1760s. This is still the departure point for ferries across the River Mersey, and was for millions of migrants their final contact with European soil.

The Museum of Liverpool is an impressive architectural interloper, but pride of place in this part of the dock still goes to the trio of Edwardian buildings known as the 'Three Graces', dating from the days when Liverpool's star was still ascending: the Port of Liverpool Building, the Cunard Building and the Royal Liver Building, which is topped by Liverpool's symbol, the famous 5.5m copper Liver Bird, and recently opened as a museum.

DON'T MISS

BEATLEMANIA LIVES

They broke up more than 50 years ago and two of their members are dead, but the Beatles are bigger business than ever in Liverpool.

Most of it centres around tiny Mathew St, site of the original Cavern Club, which is now the main thoroughfare of the 'Cavern Quarter', an unashamedly commercial effort to cash in on the legacy of the Fab Four. Here you can shuck oysters in the Rubber Soul Oyster Bar, buy a George pillowcase in the From Me to You shop and put it on the pillows of the Hard Days Night Hotel. The **Beatles Story** (☎ 0151-709 1963; www.beatlesstory. com; Albert Dock; adult/child/student £16/9/12.50; ☷ 10am-4.30pm; ⬚ all city centre) in Albert Dock is the city's most visited museum, but if you really want to dig deep into Beatles lore, we strongly recommend a visit to the National Trust–owned **Mendips**, the home where John lived with his aunt from 1945 to 1963, and **20 Forthlin Rd**, the plain terraced home where Paul grew up, available only by prebooking a place on the **Beatles' Childhood Homes Tour** (☎ 0151-427 7231; www.nationaltrust.org.uk; Jury's Inn, 31 Keel Wharf, Wapping Dock; adult/child £23/7.25; ☷ 10am, 11am, 2.10pm & 3pm Wed-Sun Mar-Nov). Just around the corner from Mendips is **Strawberry Field Forever** (☎ 0151-252 6130; www.strawberryfieldliverpool.com; Beaconsfield Rd, Woolton; £8.95; ☷ 10am-5pm Tue-Sun; ⬚ 75 from Liverpool ONE Bus Station), a wonderful new museum on the grounds of the old Salvation Army home where John used to play as a child.

If you'd rather do it yourself, the tourist offices stock the *Discover Lennon's Liverpool* guide and map, and Ron Jones' *The Beatles' Liverpool*.

✦ Festivals & Events

★ Grand National   SPORTS
(☎ 0151-523 2600; http://aintree.thejockeyclub. co.uk; Aintree Racecourse, Ormskirk Rd; ☷ Apr; ⬚ 300, 311, 345, 350 & 351 from Liverpool ONE Bus Station, ⬚ Aintree from Liverpool Central) The world's most famous steeplechase takes place on the first Saturday in April and is run across 4.5 miles and over the most difficult fences in world racing. Book tickets well in advance. Aintree is 6 miles north of the city centre.

Liverpool Sound City   MUSIC
(www.soundcity.uk.com; Baltic Triangle; ☷ May; ⬚ all cross-city buses) The first weekend in May sees one of the biggest alternative-music festivals in town take over the Baltic Triangle and Cains Brewery.

Liverpool International
Music Festival   MUSIC
(☎ 0151-239 9091; www.limfestival.com; Sefton Park; ☷ late Jul; ⬚ 75 from Lime St Station) A festival showcasing local bands and international acts during the last weekend of July. There's even a VIP experience that gives you access to private bars.

International Beatleweek   MUSIC
(www.internationalbeatleweek.com; ☷ late Aug; ⬚ all main bus station services) Sing along to your favourite Beatles song with 70 tribute acts from 20 countries during the last week in August. Organised by the Cavern Club, there are some serious and talented acts on display; some are so good you'll wonder if they're even better than the real thing. They're not.

🛏 Sleeping

Tune Hotel   HOTEL £
(☎ 0151-239 5070; www.tunehotels.com; 3-19 Queen Bldgs, Castle St; r from £25; ❄ @ 🛜; ⬚ all city centre) A slightly upscale version of a pod hotel, Tune offers a comfortable night's sleep (courtesy of a superb mattress and good-quality linen) in a range of en-suite rooms. The cheapest of them have no windows and are quite small, but at this price and in this location, it's an easy sacrifice to make. Bathrooms have power showers.

★ Hope Street Hotel   BOUTIQUE HOTEL ££
(☎ 0151-709 3000; www.hopestreethotel.co.uk; 40 Hope St; r/ste from £110/175; @ 🛜; ⬚ all city centre) One of the best digs in town is this Scandi-chic hotel on the city's most elegant street. King-sized beds draped in Egyptian cotton, oak floors with underfloor heating and sleek modern bathrooms are the norm in the original hotel as well as its new extension, where there's also a huge spa. Breakfast, taken in the marvellous London Carriage Works (p552), is £18.50.

Titanic Liverpool
HOTEL **££**

(📞 0151-559 1444; www.titanichotelliverpool.com; Stanley Dock, Regent Rd; r/ste from £100/200; 🅿️❄️@🛜; 🚌 135 & 235 from Liverpool ONE Bus Station) The preferred choice of visiting football teams is this fabulous warehouse conversion on Stanley Dock, now a huge hotel with massive rooms decorated in Scandi-minimalist style – lots of space, leather and earth-tones. Downstairs is the Rum Bar – a tribute to the primary stock of the 19th-century warehouse – and the basement is home to a nice spa.

Hard Days Night Hotel
HOTEL **££**

(📞 0151-236 1964; www.harddaysnighthotel.com; Central Bldgs, North John St; r £70-140, ste from £250; @🛜; 🚌 all city centre) You don't have to be a fan to stay here, but it helps: unquestionably luxurious, the 110 ultramodern rooms are decorated with specially commissioned drawings of the Beatles. And if you opt for one of the suites, named after Lennon and McCartney, you'll get a white baby grand piano in the style of 'Imagine' and a bottle of fancy bubbly.

Hotel Pullman
HOTEL **££**

(📞 0151-945 1000; www.all.accor.com; King's Pde, L3 4FP; r/ste from £90/110; 🅿️❄️@🛜) Part of the French Accor group, the new Pullman is a contemporary, business-friendly hotel in the heart of the Liverpool docks. The 219 rooms are designed for maximum comfort but lack any real character, which may be irrelevant to its core demographic – business travellers and visitors on a weekend break.

Malmaison
HOTEL **££**

(📞 0151-229 5000; www.malmaison.com; 7 William Jessop Way, Princes Dock; r/ste from £70/130; 🅿️@🛜; 🚌 135 or 235 from Liverpool ONE Bus Station) Malmaison's preferred colour scheme of plum and black is everywhere in this purpose-built hotel, which gives it an air of contemporary sophistication. Everything about the Liverpool Mal is plush, from the huge beds and the deep baths to the heavy velvet curtains and the excellent buffet breakfast. After a while you'll ignore the constantly piped music of the Beatles.

★ 2 Blackburne Terrace
B&B **£££**

(www.2blackburneterrace.com; 2 Blackburne Tce; r £160-180; ❄️@🛜; 🚌 all city centre) This exquisite B&B, in a converted Grade II–listed Georgian town house from 1826, might just be the most elegant option in town. It only has four rooms, but each is impeccably appointed with a mix of period furniture and modern touches. Breakfast is fabulous and the lounge an absolute delight. Only Room 1 has a shower; all have free-standing baths.

🍴 Eating

Mowgli Street Food
INDIAN **£**

(www.mowglistreetfood.com; 69 Bold St; mains £3.95-8.95; ⏱ noon-9.30pm Mon-Sat, to 9pm Sun; 🚌 all city centre) Nisha Katona's ambition to serve authentic Indian street food has been so successful that this is just the first of a handful of restaurants spread throughout the northwest and south as far as Oxford. You'll find no stodgy curries or bland kormas here, just flavoursome dishes that would pass muster with a resident of Delhi.

★ Wreckfish
MODERN BRITISH **££**

(www.wreckfish.co; 60 Seel St; 2-/3-course menu £34/39; 🚌 all city centre) Restaurateur Gary Usher's crowd-funded restaurant is a marvellous example of Modern British cuisine at its best: nothing overly fussy, but everything done just right. From the open kitchen come fine dishes such as a roast wing of skate in a brown butter dressing and a near-perfect ribeye with truffle and parmesan chips.

Duke Street Market
FOOD HALL **££**

(www.dukestreetmarket.com; 46 Duke St; mains £8-15; ⏱ noon-10pm Wed, Thu & Sun, to 11pm Fri & Sat) 🍴 This food hall has become a huge hit in town, its six vendors – ranging from meaty Bone & Block to healthy Indigo Greens – granting a range of equally tasty options under one roof. Last orders are at 9pm (8pm on Sunday).

Monro
GASTROPUB **££**

(📞 0151-707 9933; www.themonro.com; 92 Duke St; 2-/3-course lunch £19.95/24.95, mains £12-17; ⏱ 10am-10pm Thu-Sat, from 11am Sun; 🚌 all city centre) 🍴 The Monro is one of the city's favourite spots for lunch, dinner and, especially, weekend brunch. The constantly changing menu of classic British dishes made with ingredients sourced as locally as possible has transformed this handsome old pub into a superb dining experience. It's tough to find pub grub this good elsewhere.

Belzan
DELI **££**

(📞 0151-733 8595; www.belzan.co.uk; 371 Smithdown Rd, Toxteth; mains £10-12; ⏱ 11am-6.30pm Mon-Wed, to 11pm Thu-Sat; 🚌 86 from Liverpool ONE Bus Station) By day, this is one of the city's best spots to pick up charcuterie, cheeses and other deli delicacies as well as lunch

SPEKE HALL

A marvellous example of an Elizabethan half-timbered hall, Speke Hall (NT; www.national trust.org.uk; adult/child £12/6; ⊘12.30am-5pm Wed-Sun, also Tue Aug; ⊒500 from Liverpool ONE Bus Station) is filled with gorgeously timbered and plastered rooms. The house contains several 'priest's holes', where the hall's sympathetic owners hid Roman Catholic priests during the anti-Catholic 16th and 17th centuries.

This diagonally patterned Tudor house dates from 1490 to 1612 and was once surrounded by thousands of acres of land, but these days all that remains is the drive and an oasis of meticulously maintained gardens; the hall's Chapel Farm became the nucleus of nearby Liverpool Airport.

The afternoon tours to Paul McCartney's and John Lennon's childhood homes (p550) leave from Speke Hall.

Call ahead to check opening and tour times; pre-booking is recommended. Speke Hall is about 7.5 miles from central Liverpool; the bus will drop you about 0.6 miles from the entrance.

options like confit rabbit leg or celeriac *boulangère*. From Thursday through Saturday, the five-course evening tasting menu (£40) elevates things even further. Menus change monthly, but be ready for food that is both relaxed and occasionally challenging. Book ahead.

Etsu
JAPANESE ££

(☑0151-236 7530; www.etsu-restaurant.co.uk; 25 The Strand, off Brunswick St; mains £13-17, 15-piece sashimi £15.50; ⊘noon-2.30pm & 5-9pm Tue, Thu & Fri, 5-9pm Wed & Sat, 4-9pm Sun; ⊒all city centre) The best Japanese food in town is in this contemporary spot on the ground floor of an office building. The speciality of the house is its fresh sushi and sashimi, but you'll find the usual selection of Japanese classics, from chicken *kara-age* (crispy fried chicken pieces marinated in soy, ginger and garlic) to *unagi don* (grilled eel over rice).

Salt House
SPANISH ££

(www.salthousetapas.co.uk; Hanover Sq; tapas £6-9; ⊘noon-10.30pm; ⊒all city centre) Liverpool has grown fond of its Spanish tapas bars, and this gorgeous spot – half deli, half restaurant – is the best of them. The cooking is authentic, varied and delicious, from the choice of charcuterie to the wonderful fish dishes. The takeaway counter at the deli does fab sandwiches too.

Art School
MODERN BRITISH ££

(☑0151-230 8600; www.theartschoolrestaurant. co.uk; 1 Sugnall St; 3-course prix fixe £34, tasting menu £95; ⊘noon-2pm & 6-9.15pm Thu-Sat, noon-4pm Sun; ☑; ⊒all city centre) The old lantern room of a Victorian 'home for destitute

children' is now one of the top spots in town for contemporary British cuisine, courtesy of chef Paul Askew (ex–London Carriage Works). Take your pick of expertly presented British classics from a series of menus, including two vegetarian and one vegan. The wine list is superb.

London Carriage Works
MODERN BRITISH £££

(☑0151-705 2222; www.thelondoncarriageworks. co.uk; 40 Hope St; 2-/3-course meal £24.50/30, mains £12-30; ⊘7-10am, noon-3pm & 5-10pm Mon-Fri, 8-11am & noon-10pm Sat, to 9pm Sun; ⊒all city centre) This award-winning restaurant successfully blends ethnic influences from around the globe with staunch British favourites and serves up the result in a beautiful dining room – actually more of a bright glass box divided only by a series of sculpted glass shards. Reservations are recommended.

🍷 Drinking & Nightlife

Ropewalks is Liverpool's busiest bar district – with a lot of late-night spots that keep them drinking and dancing until the wee hours – but there's a fine selection of great bars spread throughout the city. If you're looking to hang with the city's creative crowd, you'll most likely find them in the Baltic Triangle.

★ Botanical Garden
BAR

(www.baltictriangle.co.uk/botanical-garden; 49 New Bird St; ⊘noon-11pm Mar-Sep; ⊒all city centre) A seasonal pop-up that specialises in gin cocktails, this is one of the city's coolest summer bars. There's a fine selection of beers if you prefer, and a kitchen that serves excellent Mexican food; in rainy weather you can retreat to the indoor greenhouse, which has a bar made from a converted VW camper van. Weekends feature top-class DJs.

⭐ **Grapes** PUB
(www.thegrapesliverpool.co.uk; 60 Roscoe St; ☺3.30pm-1am Sun-Wed, to 2am Thu-Sat; 🚇all city centre) One of the friendliest boozers in town is this superb old pub that serves a fine range of local ales (Bier Head, from the Liverpool Organic Brewery, is our favourite). The Beatles would stop in here during their Cavern days, but that's well down the list of reasons to stop by this wonderful, higgledy-piggledy classic.

Roscoe Head PUB
(📞0151-709 4365; www.roscoehead.co.uk; 24 Roscoe St; ☺11.30am-midnight Tue-Sat, noon-midnight Sun, 11.30am-11pm Mon; 🚇all city centre) This venerable old pub, which serves a good selection of ales to its ever-loyal clientele, is an institution among Liverpool boozers. It gets pretty crowded at weekends, but that just makes for an even better atmosphere.

24 Kitchen Street CLUB
(📞0780 1982583; www.facebook.com/24kitchenstreet; 24 Kitchen St; ☺9pm-4am Fri & Sat; 🚇all city centre) This venue splits its focus between the arts and electronic music (tickets £8 to £12). The converted Victorian building is one of the best places in town to dance.

Philharmonic Dining Rooms PUB
(36 Hope St; ☺10am-midnight; 🚇all city centre) This extraordinary bar, designed by the shipwrights who built the *Lusitania,* is one of the most beautiful in all of England. The interior is resplendent with etched and stained glass, wrought iron, mosaics and ceramic tiling – and if you think that's good, just wait until you see inside the marble men's toilets, the only heritage-listed lav' in the country.

As per the name, they also serve food (mains £10 to £15), such as fish and chips and a fine selection of pie dishes.

Arts Club CLUB
(📞0151-707 6171; www.academymusicgroup.com/artsclubliverpool; 90 Seel St; ☺7pm-3am Mon-Sat; 🚇all city centre) This converted theatre is home to one of Liverpool's most beloved clubs, despite going through several name and management changes. It still hosts some fabulous nights (£5 to £13), with a

mix of live music and DJs keeping everyone entertained with some of the best music in town.

Merchant BAR
(www.themerchantliverpool.co.uk; 40 Slater St; ☺noon-midnight Mon-Thu & Sun, to 2am Fri, to 3am Sat; 🚇all city centre) In a converted merchant's house, Merchant has something of a Scandi feel to it (stripped-back walls, wooden bar tables), making it one of the coolest spots in town. The bar serves 50 different craft beers, gin by the goblet and – wait for it – Prosecco on tap. Good DJs provide the soundtrack.

☆ Entertainment

⭐ **Liverpool Football Club** FOOTBALL
(📞0151-263 9199, ticket office 0151-220 2345; www.liverpoolfc.com; Anfield Rd; 🚌26 from Liverpool ONE Bus Station, 17 from Queen Square Bus Station or 917 from St Johns La) Led by their magnetic manager Jürgen Klopp, Liverpool FC won the domestic league in 2020 for the first time in 30 years, reaffirming their status as one of Britain's most successful teams. With a huge global following, Liverpool are also one of the world's most famous football clubs. They play their home games at the wonderful Anfield stadium, north of the city centre.

The experience of a live match – and especially the sound of the fans singing the club's anthem, 'You'll Never Walk Alone', is one of England's sporting highlights. If you can't get a ticket for a game, you can still visit the stadium as part of the Anfield Stadium Tour (p549), which brings fans to the home dressing room and down the tunnel into the pitchside dugout. On match days, the **Soccerbus** (www.merseyrail.org; Sandhills

---

THE BALTIC TRIANGLE

Forget Ropewalks – most of Liverpool's best nightlife is in the Baltic Triangle (www.baltictriangle.co.uk), a once-run-down area of warehouses, roughly between the city centre and the docks just north of Toxteth, that is now the city's self-styled creative hub. The best spots to check out include 24 Kitchen Street, pop-up gin bar Botanical Garden, the-recycling-yard-turned-multipurpose-venue Constellations (p554) and District (p554), the first venue to open in the area.

Station; single/return adult £2/3.50, child £1/1.50; ☉from 2hr before kick-off) runs from Sandhills Station on the Merseyrail Northern Line.

★ **Constellations**   LIVE PERFORMANCE
(☑0151-345 6302; www.constellations-liv.com; 35-39 Greenland St; ☉9am-midnight Mon-Thu, to 2am Fri & Sat, 10am-midnight Sun; ☐all city centre) Whether you're looking to join a drumming circle, take part in a martial-arts workshop or lose yourself at a rave, this terrific venue in a former recycling yard will have something worth checking out. In good weather DJs play in the garden – one of the best spots in town. It does Sunday meals in summer.

Philharmonic Hall   CLASSICAL MUSIC
(☑0151-709 3789; www.liverpoolphil.com; Hope St; ☐75, 80, 86 from city centre) One of Liverpool's most beautiful buildings, the art deco Phil is home to the city's main orchestras and is the place to go for classical concerts and opera – as well as a broad range of other genres, from synth pop to avant-garde.

District   LIVE MUSIC
(☑07812 141936; 61 Jordan St; ☉7pm-4am Fri & Sat) The first venue to open in the Baltic Triangle, District is an old-school club in a warehouse, hosting live music and cinema screenings as well as fabulous dance-floor nights. The sound system is reputed to be the best in Liverpool.

Cavern Club   LIVE MUSIC
(☑0151-236 1965; www.cavernclub.org; 8-10 Mathew St; entry before/after 2pm free/£5; ☉10am-midnight Mon-Wed & Sun, to 1.30am Thu, to 2am Fri & Sat; ☐all city centre) The Cavern Club was where the Beatles played their early gigs. This is a reconstruction (albeit a faithful one), and not in the exact same location (the original was a few doors away), but the 'world's most famous club' is still a great spot to see local bands, including (invariably) Beatles cover bands.

ℹ Information

Tourist Office (www.visitliverpool.com; Liverpool Central Library, William Brown St; ☉9.30am-5pm; ☐all city centre) Leaflets, maps and information are provided in the small tourist office.

ℹ Getting There & Away

AIR

Liverpool John Lennon Airport (☑0870 750 8484; www.liverpoolairport.com; Speke Hall Ave; ☐86 or 500 from city centre) serves 70 destinations across the UK, Europe and Africa.

The airport is 8 miles south of the centre.
Arriva 500 (www.arriva.co.uk; adult/child £4.50/2.50; ☉4.30am-7pm) runs every 30 minutes to Liverpool ONE bus station and takes about 30 minutes. A taxi to the city centre should cost no more than £20.

BUS

All coaches arrive and depart from **Liverpool ONE Bus Station** (www.merseytravel.gov.uk; Canning Pl). There are services to/from most major towns, including the following:
Birmingham £5.90, 2½ hours, five daily
London £12.90, five to six hours, six daily
Manchester £4, one hour, hourly
Newcastle £26, 5½ hours, three daily

TRAIN

Liverpool's main station is Lime St. It has hourly services to almost everywhere, including the following:
Chester £7.70, 45 minutes
London Euston £37, 3¼ hours
Manchester £6.30, 45 minutes

ℹ Getting Around

If you plan on using a lot of public transport you should invest in a MetroCard, a contactless fare card available throughout the city for an initial cost of £1. You can then load up the following fare-saver passes on it:
Saveaway (adult/child £5.55/2.85) A single-day pass valid for off-peak travel on buses, trains and Mersey ferries.
Solo Ticket (1/3/5 days £4.90/13.80/21.50) For unlimited bus travel throughout Merseyside.

BOAT

The famous **Mersey ferry** (www.merseyferries.co.uk; one-way/return £2.80/3.70) crossing for Woodside and Seacombe departs from Pier Head Ferry Terminal, next to the Royal Liver Building (to the north of Albert Dock).

BUS

Liverpool ONE Bus Station is in the city centre. Local public transport is coordinated by **Merseytravel** (www.merseytravel.gov.uk).

CAR

You won't really have much use for a car in Liverpool, but there's plenty of car-parking space, either in sheltered or open monitored car parks. Costs range from around £5 to £13 per day, with the exception being the huge car park at Liverpool ONE, which costs £2.70 an hour and £17 for a day. Car break-ins are a significant problem, so leave absolutely nothing of value in your vehicle.

MANCHESTER, LIVERPOOL & NORTHWEST ENGLAND LIVERPOOL

TRAIN

Merseyrail (www.merseyrail.org) is an extensive suburban rail service linking Liverpool with the Greater Merseyside area. There are four stops in the city centre: Lime St, Central (handy for Ropewalks), James St (close to Albert Dock) and Moorfields (for the Liverpool War Museum).

LANCASHIRE

As you travel north, past the concrete blanket that covers much of the southern half of the county, Lancashire's undulating landscape begins to reveal itself in all its bucolic glory. East of Blackpool – the faded queen of beachside holidays – the Ribble Valley is a gentle and beautiful appetiser for the Lake District that lies beyond the county's northern border. Lancaster is the county's handsome Georgian capital.

Blackpool

☑ 01253 / POP 150,331

Blackpool's enduring appeal – in the face of low-cost airlines transporting its natural constituents to sunnier coasts – is down to its defiant embrace of a more traditional kind of holiday, coupled with the high-tech adrenaline hit of its famed Pleasure Beach amusement park.

The town is also famous for its tower and its three piers. A successful ploy to extend the brief summer holiday season is the Illuminations, when – from early September to early November – 5 miles of the Promenade are illuminated with thousands of electric and neon lights.

⊙ Sights

★ Blackpool Tower   AMUSEMENT PARK
(☑0844 856 1000; www.theblackpooltower.com; 1/2/3 attractions adult £13.95/21.60/29.60, child £11.25/17.20/24.40; ⊙from 10am, closing hours vary) Built in 1894, this 154m-high tower is Blackpool's most recognisable landmark. Watch a 4D film on the town's history in the Blackpool Tower Eye before taking the lift up to the observation deck, which has great views and only a (thick) glass floor between you and the ant-sized people below.

Down at ground level, the dungeon exhibit sits alongside the old Moorish circus and the magnificent rococo ballroom, with its extraordinary sculptured and gilded plasterwork, murals, chandeliers and couples gliding across the beautifully polished wooden floor to the melodramatic tones of a huge Wurlitzer organ. There's also Jungle Jim's adventure playground for kids and Dino Golf on level 7 – a nine-hole mini-golf course.

You need to book online; you can buy tickets that include one, two or three attractions in the tower.

Blackpool Pleasure Beach   AMUSEMENT PARK
(☑box office 0871 222 9090, enquiries 0871 222 1234; www.blackpoolpleasurebeach.com; Ocean Beach; 1-day Unlimited Ride e-ticket adult/child from £39/33; ⊙hours vary, usually 10am-8pm in summer) The lifeblood of Blackpool's commercial life is the Pleasure Beach, a 16-hectare collection of more than 145 rides that attracts some seven million visitors annually. As amusement parks go, it's Britain's most popular by far. You buy an e-ticket online that is downloaded to your phone.

North Pier   LANDMARK
(Promenade) FREE Built in 1862 and opening a year later, the most famous of Blackpool's three Victorian piers once charged a penny for admission; its plethora of unexciting rides are now free.

🛏 Sleeping

Number One   BOUTIQUE HOTEL ££
(☑01253-343901;   www.numberoneblackpool. com; 1 St Lukes Rd; r from £135; 🅿🛜) Far fancier than anything else around, this stunning boutique guesthouse is all luxury and contemporary style. Everything exudes a discreet elegance, from the dark-wood furniture and high-end mod cons to the topnotch breakfast. It's on a quiet road just set back from the South Promenade near the Pleasure Beach amusement park.

Big Blue Hotel   HOTEL ££
(☑01253-400045;   www.bigbluehotel.com; Blackpool Pleasure Beach; r from £105; 🅿@🛜) A handsome family hotel with smartly kitted-out rooms. Kids are looked after with DVD players and computer games, while its location at the southern entrance to Blackpool Pleasure Beach should ensure that everyone has something to do.

ℹ Information

Tourist Office (☑01253-478222; www.visit blackpool.com; Festival House, Promenade; ⊙9am-5pm Mon-Sat, 10am-4pm Sun) The

GREAT LANCASHIRE GASTROPUBS

Freemasons at Wiswell (☑01254-822218; www.freemasonsatwiswell.com; 8 Vicarage Fold, Wiswell; mains £27-40, 5-course tasting menu £60; ☺noon-2.30pm & 6-9pm Wed-Sat, noon-6pm Sun) Steven Smith's multi-award-winning restaurant in the lovely village of Wiswell serves a proper feast of the best of New British cuisine. The room is classic English pub, with plain wooden tables and a roaring fire, in contrast to the sophisticated menu. We recommend the suckling pig, slow cooked and served with black pudding, baked sweet potato and fermented-rhubarb sauce.

White Swan (www.whiteswanatfence.co.uk; 300 Wheatley Ln Rd, Fence, Burnley; 4-course tasting menu £45; ☺noon-2pm & 5.30-8.30pm Tue-Thu, to 9.30pm Fri & Sat, noon-4pm Sun) It mightn't look like much from the outside, but this pub in the working village of Fence serves simply outstanding Modern British cuisine. It's all courtesy of chef Tom Parker, who cut his chops in the kitchen of Michelin-starred Northcote Hotel (p558). The tasting menu is divine; the award-winning Taylors ales heavenly.

Cartford Inn (☑01995-670166; www.thecartfordinn.co.uk; Cartford La, Little Eccleston; mains £18-28; ☺5.30-9pm Mon, noon-2pm & 5.30-9pm Tue-Thu, to 10pm Fri & Sat, noon-8.30pm Sun) The decor at this higgledy-piggledy pub might be a touch eccentric, but the menu is anything but – with classic British pub grub exalted by classic French cooking techniques. You won't eat a nicer oxtail, beef skirt and real ale suet pudding, while the desserts are so good you won't feel bad for ordering two. You can also **stay** (☑01995-670166; www.thecartfordinn.co.uk; Cartford La, Little Eccleston; r £150, cabins £250) here.

tourist office is just south of the North Pier on the Promenade.

❶ Getting There & Away

BUS

The central coach station is on Talbot Rd, near the town centre. Services include the following:

London £23.40, seven hours, four daily

Manchester £9.10, 1¾ hours, four daily

TRAIN

The main train station is Blackpool North, about five blocks east of the North Pier on Talbot Rd. Most arrivals change in Preston, but there's a direct service from the following:

Liverpool £9.20, 1½ hours, seven daily

Manchester £9.50, 1¼ hours, half-hourly

Preston £7.20, 30 minutes, half-hourly

❶ Getting Around

With more than 14,000 car-parking spaces in Blackpool, you'll have no problem finding a spot. A host of travel-card options for trams and buses ranging from one day to a week are available at the tourist office and most newsagents. The **tramway** (1 stop £1.90, up to 16 stops £2.10; ☺from 10.30am Apr-Oct) shuttles funsters for 11 miles, including along the pier and as far as the Fylde Coast (also serving the central-corridor car parks), every eight minutes or so throughout the day.

Lancaster

☑01524 / POP 143,500

Lancashire's handsome Georgian county town is a quiet enough burg these days, but its imposing castle and beautiful, honey-coloured architecture are evidence of its former power and wealth accrued in its 18th-century heyday, when it was an important trading port and a key player in the slave trade.

◎ Sights

★**Lancaster Castle**   CASTLE
(☑01524-64998; www.lancastercastle.com; Castle Park; adult/child £8.50/7; ☺9.30am-5pm, guided tours hourly 10am-3pm Mon-Fri, every 30min Sat & Sun) Lancaster's most imposing building is its castle, built in 1150 but added to over the centuries: the **Well Tower** dates from 1325 and is also known as the Witches' Tower because its basement dungeon was used to imprison the accused in the infamous Pendle Witches Trial of 1612. Also dating from the early 14th century is the impressive twin-towered **gatehouse**. Also imprisoned here was George Fox (1624–91), founder of the Quaker movement. The castle was heavily restored in the 18th and 19th centuries to suit a new function as a prison, and it continued to house Category C prisoners until 2011 – the A wing of the prison is part of the guided tour.

Visits are by guided tour only as the castle is used as a Crown Court.

Williamson Park & Tropical Butterfly House
GARDENS

(Tropical Butterfly House adult/child £4/3; ⊙9am-5pm Apr-Sep, to 4pm Oct-Mar; 🚌18 from bus station) Lancaster's highest point is the 22-hectare spread of this gorgeous park, the highlights of which (besides the views) are the Tropical Butterfly House, full of exotic and stunning species, and the Ashton Memorial, a 67m-high baroque folly built by Lord Ashton (the son of the park's founder, James Williamson) for his wife. The memorial stands on what was once Lancaster Moor, the spot where until 1800 those sentenced to death at the castle were brought to meet the hangman. Take the bus from the station, or else it's a steep, short walk up Moor Lane.

Lancaster Priory
CHURCH

(☑01524-65338; www.lancasterpriory.org; Priory Cl; ⊙9.30am-5pm) Immediately next to Lancaster Castle is the equally fine priory church, founded in 1094 but extensively remodelled in the Middle Ages.

🛏 Sleeping

Sun Hotel & Bar
HOTEL ££

(☑01524-66006; www.thesunhotelandbar.co.uk; 63-65 Church St; r from £75; P🐾) A fine hotel in a 300-year-old building with a rustic, old-world look that stops at the bedroom doors – beyond them are 16 stylish and contemporary rooms. The pub downstairs is one of the best in town and a top spot for a bit of grub; mains cost between £10 and £12.

The Borough
BOUTIQUE HOTEL ££

(☑01524-64170; www.theboroughlancaster.co.uk; 3 Dalton Sq; r from £60; P@🐾) The Borough has nine beautifully appointed rooms – each with an Italian-marble wet-room bathroom for added luxury – spread over two floors of this elegant Georgian building. The downstairs bar has a microbrewery attached, so you don't have to go far to get your fill of locally made cask ales.

🍴 Eating & Drinking

★ Bay Horse Inn
GASTROPUB ££

(☑01524-791204; www.bayhorseinn.com; Bay Horse La, Ellel; mains £14-32; ⊙5.30-8pm Wed-Sun; 🚌40, 41 & 42 from Lancaster Bus Station) One of Lancashire's best spots for exquisite local dishes is this handsome pub 6 miles south of town. Chef Craig Wilkinson displays his locavore

links with a sign outside showing distances to the farms that supply his produce, which he then transforms into fabulous dishes such as slow-cooked, maize-fed duck legs with grilled figs or a perfectly grilled hake fillet.

★ The Hall
CAFE

(☑01524-65470; www.thecoffeehopper.com; 10 China St; ⊙10am-4pm Mon-Fri & Sun, to 5pm Sat) Nitro, Chemex, batch brew, siphon...whichever way you want it, this superb cafe in the old parish hall can satisfy even the most demanding coffee connoisseur with the perfect brew. It's part of Atkinsons Coffee Roasters, which has been roasting beans since 1840. It also does excellent sandwiches and cakes.

🔒 Shopping

★ Charter Market
MARKET

(www.lancaster.gov.uk; Market Sq; ⊙9am-4.30pm Wed & Sat Apr-Oct, to 4pm Nov-Mar) Lancaster's historic market is one of the best in the northwest, a gathering place for local producers. You'll find potted shrimp from Morecambe Bay, locally made hotpots and pies, as well as a range of more exotic dishes from around the world. It extends from Market Sq onto Market St and Cheapside.

★ Atkinsons Coffee Roasters
COFFEE

(☑01524-65470; www.thecoffeehopper.com; 12 China St; ⊙9am-5pm Mon-Sat, 11am-4pm Sun) Atkinsons is one of Britain's most prestigious coffee merchants, serving up all kinds of exotic beans and loose-leaf teas since 1840. It has been at this location since 1901: inside, the walls are covered in original tea and coffee urns, while original direct flame roasters from the 1930s give off a fabulous aroma. It's worth popping in just for the scent.

ℹ Information

Tourist Office (☑01524-582394; www.visit lancaster.org.uk; The Storey, Meeting House Lane; ⊙10am-4pm Mon-Sat) Books, maps, brochures and tickets for a variety of events and tours.

ℹ Getting There & Away

Lancaster Bus Station is the main hub for transport throughout Lancashire, with regular buses to all the main towns and villages.

Lancaster is on the main west-coast railway line and on the Cumbrian coast line. Destinations include the following:

Carlisle £22.80, one hour, hourly
Manchester £19.20, one hour, hourly

Ribble Valley

Known locally as 'Little Switzerland', Lancashire's most attractive landscapes lie east of brash Blackpool and north of the sprawling urban areas of Preston and Blackburn.

Clitheroe, the Ribble Valley's largest market town, is best known for its impressive Norman keep, built in the 12th century and now, sadly, standing empty; it offers great views of the river valley below.

The northern half of the valley is dominated by the sparsely populated moorland of the Forest of Bowland, an Area of Outstanding Natural Beauty since 1964 and a fantastic place for walks. The southern half features rolling hills, attractive market towns and ruins, with the River Ribble flowing between them.

Sights & Activities

Norman Keep &
Castle Museum   HISTORIC BUILDING
(www.lancashire.gov.uk; Castle Hill; museum adult/child £4.40/3.30; ⊙ keep dawn-dusk, museum 11am-4pm Mar-Oct, noon-4pm Mon, Tue & Fri-Sun Nov-Feb) Dominating the skyline for the last 800 years, this Norman keep is England's smallest and the only remaining castle in the country to have kept a royal garrison during the Civil War. It was built in 1186 and captured by Royalist troops in 1644, but managed to avoid destruction afterwards. The extensive grounds are home to a museum that explores 350 million years of local history.

★ Cycle Adventure   CYCLING
(☑ 07518 373007; www.cycle-adventure.co.uk) A bike-hire service that will deliver and collect a bike almost anywhere in the northwest of England. Day rates range from £25 for a mountain bike to £34 for a road bike. A child's mountain bike costs from £19 a day. Helmets and other gear are also available, and it has lots of information, trail maps and other guides.

Ribble Way   WALKING
One of the most popular long-distance paths in northern England is the Ribble Way, a 70-mile footpath that follows the River Ribble from its source at Ribblehead (in the Yorkshire Dales), passing through Clitheroe to the estuary at Preston.

Lancashire Cycle Way   CYCLING
(www.visitlancashire.com) The Ribble Valley is well covered by the northern loop of the Lancashire Cycle Way; for more information about routes, safety and more, check out Cycle Adventure.

Sleeping & Eating

★ Inn at Whitewell   INN £££
(☑ 01200-448222; www.innatwhitewell.com; Forest of Bowland; r from £140) Once the home of Bowland's forest keeper, this superb guesthouse with antique furniture, peat fires and Victorian claw-foot baths is one of the finest accommodations in northern England. Everything is top-notch, including the views: it's like being in the French countryside. Its restaurant is excellent too.

Parkers Arms   GASTROPUB ££
(☑ 01200-446236; www.parkersarms.co.uk; Newton-in-Bowland; mains £19-28; ⊙ noon-2pm & 6-8pm Thu-Sat, 12.30-5pm Sun) This unspoilt village pub is where you'll find the simply exceptional cooking of terroir chef Stosie Madi. She's best known for her superb pies, but her menus – which change up to twice daily depending on what's available – explore the very best of Lancashire cuisine, from Newton venison with local bramble and unpasteurised cheese to a superb Lancashire hotpot.

★ Northcote Hotel   MODERN BRITISH £££
(☑ 01254-240555; www.northcote.com; Northcote Rd, Langho; tasting menu £85; ⊙ noon-2.30pm & 6-9.30pm Wed-Sun) One of the finest restaurants in northern England, Northcote's Michelin-starred menu is the unpretentious, delicious creation of chef Lisa Goodwin-Allen and sommelier Craig Bancroft. Duck, lamb, beef and chicken are given Modern British treatment and the result is fantastic. Upstairs are 26 beautifully styled bedrooms (£180 to £330), making this one of the northwest's top gourmet getaways.

ISLE OF MAN

The Isle of Man (Ellan Vannin in the local lingo, Manx) has beautiful scenery in its lush valleys, barren hills and rugged coastlines; in 2016 Unesco designated it a biosphere reserve (one of five in the UK), marking it out as one of the most beautiful spots in Britain to enjoy nature.

Forget what you may have heard on the mainland too: there's nothing odd about the Isle of Man. The island's reputation for oddity is entirely down to its persistent insistence that it do its own thing, rejecting England's warm embrace in favour of a semiautonomous status (it is home to the world's oldest continuous parliament, the Tynwald).

The island's bucolic charm is shattered during the world-famous **Tourist Trophy** (TT) motorbike racing season, which attracts 50,000 punters every May and June. Needless to say, if you want a slice of silence, avoid the high-rev bike fest.

Festivals & Events

Isle of Man
Food & Drink Festival   FOOD & DRINK
(www.gov.im; Villa Marina Gardens, Douglas; £3; ⊙mid-Sep) Over two days in mid-September more than 50 of the island's producers gather to showcase their wares. There's plenty of street food, baked goods, beer and cider, as well as music.

Isle of Man Walking Festival   WALKING
(www.iomevents.com; ⊙Oct) A five-day walking festival held in early October; walks start in different parts of the island and are led by experienced walkers. In the evenings there are plenty of social events generally fuelled by the produce of a Manx brewery.

ⓘ Getting There & Away

AIR
Ronaldsway Airport (www.iom-airport.com) is 10 miles south of Douglas near Castletown. The following airlines have services to the island:
Aer Lingus Regional (www.aerlingus.com; from £25)
British Airways (www.britishairways.com; from £75)
Easyjet (www.easyjet.com; from £25)
Loganair (www.loganair.co.uk; from £60)

BOAT
Isle of Man Steam Packet (www.steam-packet.com; foot passenger single/return from £20/37.50, car & 2 passengers return from £150) offers a car ferry and high-speed catamaran service from Liverpool and Heysham (10 miles west of Lancaster) to Douglas. From mid-April to mid-September there's also a service to Dublin and Belfast.

ⓘ Getting Around

Buses link the airport with Douglas every 30 minutes between 7am and 11pm. Taxis have fixed fares to destinations throughout the island; a cab to Douglas costs from £14, to Peel from £16.

The island has a comprehensive bus service (www.gov.im); the tourist office in Douglas has

timetables and sells tickets. It also sells the Go Explore ticket (one day adult/child £18/10, three day £40/18), which gives you unlimited public-transport use, including the tram to Snaefell and Douglas' horse-trams.

Bicycles can be hired from **Simpsons** (☑01624-842472; www.facebook.com/simpsonsiom; 27 Michael St, Peel; per day/week £15/80; ⊙9am-5pm Mon-Sat) in Peel.

Petrolheads will love the scenic, sweeping bends that make for some exciting driving – and the fact that outside of Douglas town there's no speed limit. Naturally, the most popular drive is along the Tourist Trophy route. Car-hire operators have desks at the airport, and charge from £37 per day.

The 19th-century electric and steam **rail services** (☑01624-663366; www.iombusandrail.info; ⊙Mar-Oct) are a thoroughly satisfying way of getting from A to B:
Douglas–Castletown–Port Erin Steam Train Return £13.40
Douglas–Laxey–Ramsey Electric Tramway Return £12.40
Laxey–Summit Snaefell Mountain Railway Return £12

Douglas

☑01624 / POP 26,218
Douglas is the island's largest town and most important commercial centre. It's a little faded around the edges and a far cry from its Victorian heyday when it was, like Blackpool across the water, a favourite with British holidaymakers. The bulk of the island's hotels and restaurants are still here – as well as most of the finance houses that are frequented so regularly by tax-allergic Brits.

PEEL

Peel is the west coast's most appealing town, with a fine sandy beach. Its big attraction is the ruin of the 11th-century Peel Castle (MH; www.manxnational heritage.im; adult/child £5.50/free; ⏱11am-3pm Thu-Sun Aug-Nov), stunningly positioned atop St Patrick's Island and joined to Peel by a causeway. There's an audio guide available to help you make sense of the ruins, and you're also advised to keep your eyes open for the castle's ghost – a black dog called Moddey Dhoo.

◉ Sights

Manx Museum &
National Art Gallery MUSEUM
(MH; www.manxnationalheritage.im; Kingswood Grove; ⏱10am-4pm) FREE This modern museum (Thie Tashtee Vannin in Manx) begins with an introductory film to the island's 10,000-year history and then races through it, making various stops including Viking gold and silver, the history of the Tynwald, the island's internment camps during WWII and the famous TT races. Also part of the museum is the National Art Gallery, which has works by the island's best-known artists including Archibald Knox and John Miller Nicholson. Overall a fine introduction to the island.

🛏 Sleeping

★ Saba's Glen Yurt YURT ££
(www.sabasglenyurt.com; Close Ny Howin, Main Rd, Union Mills; 2-person yurt from £95) 🌿 In the conservation area of Union Mills you can bed down in a solar-powered eco-yurt that comes equipped with a king-sized bed and a wood burner. Outside are hot tubs filled with steaming water that you can sink into up to your shoulders.

There's a two-night minimum weekend stay between April and September. It's 2.5 miles northwest of town on the road to Peel.

Inglewood BOUTIQUE HOTEL ££
(☑01624-674734; www.inglewood.im; 26 Palace Tce, Queens Promenade; s/d incl breakfast from £42.50/85; P@🛈) Sea-view suites in this beautifully refurbished, friendly hotel have big wooden beds and leather sofas. The homemade breakfasts are superb, and the residents' bar specialises in whisky from all over the world.

Claremont Hotel HOTEL £££
(☑01624-617068; www.claremonthoteldouglas.com; 18-22 Loch Promenade; r from £130; P✳@🛈) The island's fanciest hotel is this classic on the promenade, with huge rooms kitted out with handsome wooden floors, seaside colours and comfortable beds with crisp linen.

✗ Eating

★ Little Fish Cafe SEAFOOD ££
(www.littlefishcafe.com; 31 North Quay; mains £16-24; ⏱11am-9pm) Superb seafood presented in a variety of ways, from hake with mustard and lemon butter to Kerala-style fish curry. For brunch, the Queenie Po'Boy – battered Manx queenies (queen scallops), paprika mayo and avocado on sourdough brioche – is divine. It also does meat dishes, but the real focus is on the sea.

14North MODERN BRITISH ££
(☑01624-664414; www.14north.im; 14 North Quay; 2-/3-course menu £35/39; ⏱6-9.30pm Tue, noon-2.30pm & 6-9.30pm Wed-Fri, noon-5pm & 6-9.30pm Sat) An old timber merchant's house is home to this smart restaurant specialising in local dishes including pickled herring, lamb rump and, of course, queenies (queen scallops) – all sourced locally.

❶ Information

Tourist Office (☑01624-686766; www.visitisleofman.com; Sea Terminal Bldg, Douglas; ⏱9.15am-7pm, closed Sun Oct-Apr)

Northern Isle of Man

North of the capital, the dominant feature is Snaefell (621m), the island's tallest mountain. You can follow the Tourist Trophy circuit up and over the mountain towards Ramsey, or take the alternate route along the coast, going through Laxey, where you can also take the electric tram to near the top of Snaefell, from where it's an easy walk to the summit.

◉ Sights

★ Great Laxey Wheel HISTORIC SITE
(MH; www.manxnationalheritage.im; Mines Rd, Laxey; adult/child £7/free; ⏱10am-4pm Sat-Wed) It's no exaggeration to describe the Lady Isabella Laxey Wheel (Queeyl Vooar Laksey in Manx), built in 1854 to pump water from a mine, as a 'great' wheel: it measures 22m across and can draw 1140L of water per

minute from a depth of 550m. The largest wheel of its kind in the world, it's named after the wife of the then lieutenant-governor.

Grove Museum of Victorian Life   MUSEUM
(MH; www.manxnationalheritage.im; Andreas Rd, Ramsey; adult/child £5.50/free; ⊙11am-3pm Thu-Sun Aug-Nov) This imposing house (Thie Tashtee 'Yn Chell') was built in the mid-19th century by Liverpool shipping merchant Duncan Gibb as a summer retreat for himself and his family. It has been maintained pretty much as it was in its Victorian heyday, and you can wander through its period rooms – and even learn what it was like to be a scullery maid! The house was occupied by the Gibb family until the 1970s. It's on the edge of Ramsey.

❶ Getting There & Away

Bus Vannin services travel the 15 miles between Ramsey and Douglas either via Laxey and the coast (bus 3, 3A) or more directly inland past Snaefell (bus X3). Alternatively, there's the electric tram, which trundles up the coast to Ramsey. Another tram serves Snaefell from Laxey.

Southern Isle of Man

The quiet harbour town of Castletown, at the southern end of the island, was the Isle of Man's original capital. It is home to a fabulous castle and the old parliament.

Port Erin is a smallish Victorian seaside resort that plays host to the small Railway Museum (www.iombusandrail.im; Station Rd; adult/child £2/1; ⊙9.30am-5pm). Port St Mary lies across the headland and is linked to by steam train. The Calf of Man bird sanctuary is accessed from Port St Mary.

⊙ Sights

★Castle Rushen   CASTLE
(MH; www.manxnationalheritage.im; Castletown Sq, Castletown; adult/child £9/free; ⊙10am-4pm Thu-Mon May-Aug) Castletown is dominated by the impressive 13th-century Castle Rushen (Cashtal Rushen), one of the most complete medieval structures in Europe. You can visit the gatehouse, medieval kitchens, dungeons and the Great Hall. The flag tower affords fine views of the town and coast.

Cregneash Village Folk Museum   MUSEUM
(MH; www.manxnationalheritage.im; adult/child £7/free; ⊙10am-2pm Wed, 11am-2.30pm Thu & Fri, open for tours only) Until the early part of the 20th century, most farmers on the island engaged in a practice known as crofting – a social system defined by small-scale communal food production. This folk museum on a raised plateau on the island's southern tip includes a traditional Manx cottage where you can see how crofters lived, while out in the fields you can see four-horned sheep and Manx cats, which you're encouraged to pat.

Old House of Keys   MUSEUM
(MH; www.manxnationalheritage.im; Parliament Sq, Castletown; debate adult/child £6/3, other times free; ⊙10am-4pm Apr-Oct) The former home of the Manx Parliament (Tynwald's lower house; Shenn Thie yn Chiare as Feed in Manx) has been restored to its 1866 appearance – a key date in island history, when the parliament voted to have its members elected by popular mandate. At 11am and 2.45pm visitors can participate in a debate on the hot topics of the day – gaining an insight into how this parliamentary democracy went about its business. You can also learn about the island's struggle for self-determination.

Calf of Man   BIRD SANCTUARY
(www.manxnationalheritage.im; ⊙Apr-Sep) This small island just off Cregneash is on one of western Britain's major bird migration routes, and 33 species breed annually here, including Manx shearwaters, kittiwakes, razorbills and shags. Other species normally observed on the island include peregrines, hen harriers, choughs and ravens. It's been an official bird sanctuary since 1939. Gemini Charter (☎01624-832761; www.geminicharter.co.uk; trips 1-4hr per person £20-35) runs birdwatching trips to the island from Port St Mary.

❶ Getting There & Away

There is a regular Bus Vannin service between Castletown and Douglas (and the airport en route), and between Castletown, Port Erin and Port St Mary (£1.90). There's also the Douglas to Port Erin Steam Train (£13.40 return) which stops in Castletown. A taxi from the airport to Castletown costs around £9.

MANCHESTER, LIVERPOOL & NORTHWEST ENGLAND

AT A GLANCE

POPULATION
499,800

NUMBER OF FELLS
214

BEST BOAT TRIP
Steam Yacht Gondola
(p580)

**BEST
POST-HIKE PUB**
Wasdale Head Inn
(p583)

BEST LAKE VIEW
Crummock Water
from Buttermere
(p589)

WHEN TO GO

Mar–May Spring
in the Lakes brings
green growth,
decent weather and
relatively few
visitors; snow
lingers on high fells.

Jun–Sep Peak
tourist season;
warm weather,
summer festivals,
plentiful traffic,
maximum crowds.
Book everything
well ahead.

Oct–Feb Winter
brings snow, bitter
wind and icy tem-
peratures: perfect
for cosy pub
dinners, but the fells
are for hardcore
hikers only.

Ashness Bridge (p586)
ROBECHIC/SHUTTERSTOCK ©

The Lake District & Cumbria

William Wordsworth mused, 'no part of the country is more distinguished by its sublimity', and two centuries later, his words still ring true. Nowhere in England can compare to the Lake District's natural splendour: poets, painters and perambulators alike have come here for inspiration, and it's still the nation's favourite place to revel in the delights of the landscape.

At 885 square miles, the Lake District is England's largest national park and, since 2017, a Unesco World Heritage Site. With its rugged fells, sheep-flocked valleys, glittering lakes and whitewashed inns, it's many people's idea of the quintessential English view, immortalised in the work of writers including Beatrix Potter, Arthur Ransome and the grandfather of Lakeland hiking, Alfred Wainwright. Don't forget to pack your walking boots.

The Lake District & Cumbria

1 **Helvellyn** (p590) Tackling the most thrilling high-wire ridge walk in England.

2 **Windermere Jetty Museum** (p568) Tracing two centuries of boating history.

3 **Rydal Mount** (p573) Visiting the family home of William Wordsworth.

4 **Borrowdale and Buttermere** (p589) Taking a road trip through the loveliest Lakeland valleys.

5 **Keswick Launch** (p584) Cruising around the wooded shores of Derwentwater.

6 **Castlerigg Stone Circle** (p583) Pondering the mysteries of Lakeland's answer to Stonehenge.

7 **Grizedale Forest** (p579) Cycling woodland trails surrounded by outdoor art.

8 **Great Langdale** (p583) Exploring Lakeland's most dramatic valley – and its hikes.

9 **Carlisle Castle** (p594) Patrolling the battlements of Carlisle's medieval fortress.

10 **Lowther Castle & Gardens** (p596) Visiting a great Cumbrian estate that's slowly being brought back to life.

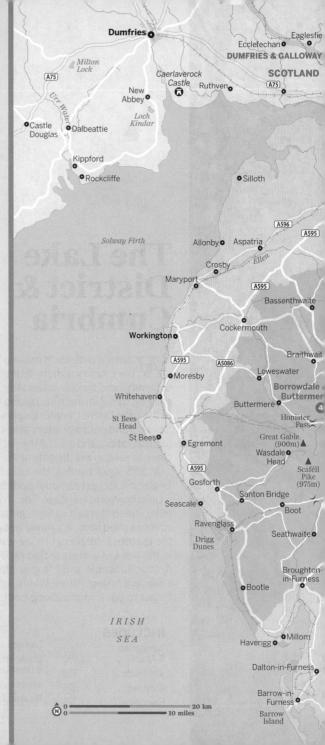

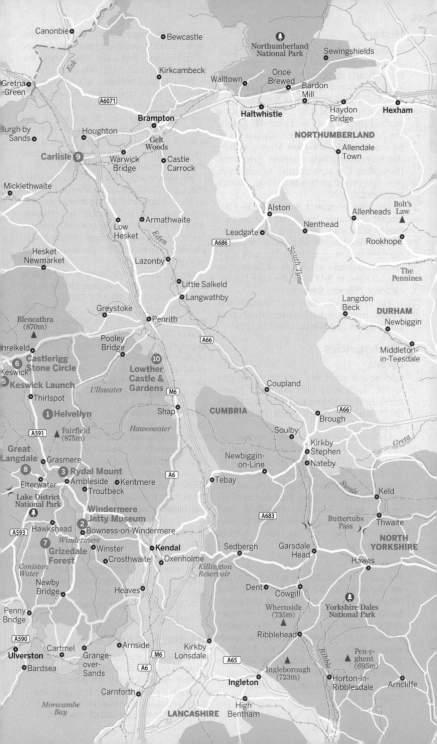

History

Neolithic settlers arrived in the Lake District around 5000 BC. The region was subsequently occupied by Celts, Angles, Vikings and Romans, and later became the centre of the old kingdom of Rheged.

During the Middle Ages, Cumbria marked the start of the 'Debatable Lands', the wild frontier between England and Scotland. Bands of raiders known as Border Reivers regularly plundered the area, prompting the construction of defensive pele towers and castles at Carlisle, Penrith and Kendal.

The area became a centre for the Romantic movement during the 19th century, largely thanks to the Cumbrian-born poet William Wordsworth, who also championed the need to protect the Lake District's landscape from overdevelopment – a dream that was achieved in 1951 when the Lake District National Park was formed.

The present-day county of Cumbria was formed from the neighbouring districts of Cumberland and Westmorland in 1974.

Activities

Cycling

Cycling is a great way to explore, as long as you don't mind hills. For short mountain-bike rides, the trails of Grizedale Forest (p579) and Whinlatter Forest Park (p585) are popular.

Long-distance touring routes include the 70-mile Cumbria Way between Ulverston, Keswick and Carlisle; the 140-mile Sea To Sea Cycle Route (C2C, NCN 7; www.c2c-guide. co.uk), which begins in Whitehaven and cuts east across the northern Pennines to Tynemouth, near Newcastle-upon-Tyne; and the 173-mile Reivers Route (NCN 10; www. reivers-route.co.uk) from the River Tyne to Whitehaven.

Walking

For many people, hiking is the main reason for a visit to the Lake District. Tourist offices and bookshops sell maps and guidebooks, such as Collins' *Lakeland Fellranger* and Ordnance Survey's *Pathfinder Guides*. Purists prefer Alfred Wainwright's seven-volume *Pictorial Guides to the Lakeland Fells* (1955–66) – part walking guides, part illustrated artworks, part philosophical memoirs – with painstakingly hand-penned maps and text.

Maps are essential: the Ordnance Survey's 1:25,000 *Landranger* maps are used by official bodies, while some hikers prefer the Harvey *Superwalker* 1:25,000 maps.

The Lakeland fells may not be huge, but they need to be treated with respect. Trails are often indistinct and sometimes exposed, and it's extremely easy to get lost in bad weather. At minimum, wear good high-ankle boots, carry waterproofs, warm layers, food and water, and let someone know where you're going.

It's also worth noting the devastating effect that millions of footsteps can have on the delicate fells: footpath erosion, habitat damage and soil loss are big problems. Stick to paths wherever possible, and try not to exacerbate 'braiding' (where multiple paths develop as people avoid muddy or slippery sections).

Long-distance trails include the 54-mile Allerdale Ramble from Seathwaite to the Solway Firth, the 70-mile Cumbria Way from Ulverston to Carlisle, and the 191-mile Coast to Coast from St Bees to Robin Hood's Bay in Yorkshire. Door-to-door baggage services such as Coast to Coast Packhorse (☑01768-371777; www.c2cpackhorse. co.uk) and Sherpa Van (☑0871-520 0124; www.sherpavan.com) transport luggage from one destination to the next.

Other Activities

Cumbria is a haven for outdoor activities, including rock climbing, orienteering, horse riding, archery, fell (mountain) running and *ghyll* (waterfall) scrambling. Contact the Outdoor Adventure Company (☑01539-722147; www.theoutdooradventurecompany.co.uk; Old Hutton), Rookin House (☑01768-483561; www.rookinhouse.co.uk) or Keswick Adventure Centre (☑01768-775687; www.keswick adventurecentre.co.uk; Newlands).

The Kendal Wall (☑01539-721766; www. kendalwall.co.uk; unit 27, Lake District Business Park; adult/child £12/7; ⊙10am-10pm Mon-Fri, to 6pm Sat & Sun) is a great place to practice your rock-climbing skills.

Wild camping is not permitted anywhere in the Lake District.

ⓘ Getting There & Away

The nearest major airport is in Manchester, but Carlisle's tiny airport has direct flights to/from London Southend, Belfast and Dublin.

Carlisle is on the main West Coast train line from London Euston to Manchester and Glasgow. To get to the Lake District, change at

ALFRED WAINWRIGHT, THE FELL-WALKERS' FELL-WALKER

Hero to many a Lakeland hiker, Alfred Wainwright (1907–91) – AW to his fans – was an author, artist, cartographer and inveterate hill-walker whose classic seven-volume guidebook series, *The Pictorial Guides to the Lakeland Fells*, remain the choice for many walkers. Filled with hand-illustrated maps, painstaking route descriptions and quirky, sometimes poetic writing, they are the record of a lifelong love affair with the Lakeland landscape.

The first guide was published in 1955, and six decades later they've sold well over a million copies. Second revised editions were published in 2011 by author Chris Jesty, followed by the third updated editions in 2020 by Clive Hutchby.

There are many locations linked with AW: you can see some of his possessions in Kendal Museum (p591), view a plaque dedicated to him in the village church in Buttermere and, most poignantly of all, hike to the top of Haystacks, AW's favourite fell, where his ashes were scattered in 1991.

While nothing beats reading the great man's words, several of his routes have been recorded as podcasts, with AW's voice evocatively brought to life by actor Nik Wood Jones. They can be downloaded from the Visit Lake District website (www.visitlake district.com).

Oxenholme for Kendal and Windermere. The lines around the Cumbrian coast, and between Settle and Carlisle, are particularly scenic.

National Express coaches run direct from London Victoria and Glasgow to Windermere, Carlisle and Kendal.

ℹ️ Getting Around

BOAT

There are round-the-lake ferry services on Windermere, Coniston Water, Ullswater and Derwentwater. Windermere also has cruises and a cross-lake ferry service.

BUS

The main bus operator is **Stagecoach** (www.stagecoachbus.com). Services are reduced in winter. You can download timetables from the Stagecoach website or the Cumbria County Council website (www.cumbria.gov.uk). Bus timetables are also available from tourist offices.

Useful services:

Bus 555 (Lakeslink) Lancaster to Keswick, stopping at all the main towns, including Windermere and Ambleside.

Bus 505 (Coniston Rambler) Kendal, Windermere, Ambleside and Coniston.

Bus X4/X5 Penrith to Workington via Troutbeck, Keswick and Cockermouth.

CAR

Traffic can be a nightmare during peak season and holiday weekends. Many Cumbrian towns use timed parking permits for on-street parking, which you can pick up free from local shops and tourist offices.

If you're driving to the Lake District, National Trust membership is a good idea, as it means

you can park for free at all of the National Trust's car parks (which otherwise charge extortionately high rates).

TRAVEL PASSES

Several travel passes are available in Cumbria. Dayrider tickets can be bought on buses; Ranger tickets can be bought at any staffed train station.

Central Lakes Dayrider (adult/child/family £8.50/6.30/23.50) For bus-only travel, this good-value pass covers Stagecoach buses around Bowness, Ambleside, Grasmere, Langdale and Coniston; it includes buses 599, 505 and 516. You can also buy a combination ticket that includes a boat cruise on Windermere or Coniston.

Lakes Day Ranger (adult/child/family £25.20/12.60/49.40) The best-value one-day ticket, allowing travel on trains and buses in the Lake District. It also includes a boat cruise on Windermere, 10% discount on the Ravenglass & Eskdale and Lakeside & Haverthwaite railways and 20% discount on the Ullswater Steamers.

Cumbria Day Ranger (adult/child £47.20/23.60) This pass provides one day's train travel in Cumbria and parts of Lancashire, North Yorkshire, Northumberland and Dumfries and Galloway. It also includes the Settle to Carlisle line.

Keswick & Honister Dayrider (adult/child/family £8.50/6.30/23.50) Covers buses from Keswick through Borrowdale, Buttermere, Lorton and Whinlatter Forest Park.

North West Megarider Gold (per week £29) Covers seven days' travel on all Stagecoach buses operating in Lancashire, Merseyside, Cumbria, West Cheshire and Newcastle.

THE LAKE DISTRICT

POP 40,478

The Lake District (or Lakeland, as it's commonly known round these parts) is the UK's most popular national park. Every year, some 15 million people pitch up to explore the region's fells and countryside, and it's not hard to see why. Ever since the Romantic poets arrived in the 19th century, its postcard panorama of craggy hilltops, mountain tarns and glittering lakes has been stirring the imaginations of visitors. Since 2017 it has also been a Unesco World Heritage Site, in recognition of its unique hill-farming culture.

ℹ Information

The national park's main visitor centre is at Brockhole (p572), just outside Windermere, and there are tourist offices in Windermere (p572), Bowness (p572), Ambleside (p576), Keswick (p586), Coniston (p581) and Carlisle (p596).

Windermere & Around

☑ 01539 / POP 6180

Stretching for 10.5 glittering miles between Ambleside and Newby Bridge, Windermere is the undisputed queen of Lakeland lakes (and the largest in England, closer in stature to a Scottish loch). Framed by low fells and green fields, it's been a centre for tourism since the first trains chugged into town in 1847, and it's still one of the national park's busiest spots.

Most of the action is located on the eastern shore. Touristy, overdeveloped Bowness-on-Windermere (usually shortened just to Bowness) sits directly beside the lake, with a cluster of shops, restaurants and sights straggling haphazardly along the shoreline, along with cruise boats puttering out from the lake jetties. One and a half miles inland, at the top of the steep Lake Rd, lies Windermere Town, home to the Lake District's main train station and copious B&Bs.

Practically every visitor strays through Windermere at some point during their stay, and accommodation (and parking) can be hard to come by, so plan accordingly.

◉ Sights & Activities

★ **Windermere Jetty Museum** MUSEUM
(☑ 01539-637940; www.lakelandarts.org.uk/windermere-jetty-museum; Rayrigg Rd; adult/child £9/4.50; ⊙ 10am-5pm Mar-Oct, 10.30am-4.30pm Nov-Feb) Two centuries of boating are explored at Windermere's fabulous lakeside museum, opened in 2019 after a long £20 million redevelopment. Housed in a striking wooden structure that resembles a *Grand Designs* take on a traditional boat shed, it contains a collection of gorgeous vintage vessels from the lake's history, including steam launches, lug-sailed boats, racing boats and even a 1936 glider. You can also peek into the restoration workshop, pilot a radio-controlled boat or take a cruise in an Edwardian steam launch.

The centrepiece of the collection is the *Branksome*, an 1896 teak-hulled steam launch originally built for the owner of Langdale Chase; it also has the distinction of twice carrying royal visitors. Also of literary note is the *Esperance*, which provided the inspiration for Captain Flint's houseboat in Arthur Ransome's *Swallows and Amazons*.

WINDERMERE & THE ISLANDS

Windermere gets its name from the old Norse, Vinandr mere (Vinandr's lake; so Lake Windermere is actually tautologous). Encompassing 5.7 sq miles between Ambleside and Newby Bridge, the lake is a mile wide at its broadest point, with a maximum depth of about 220m.

The lake's shoreline is owned by a combination of private landholders, the National Park Authority and the National Trust, but the lakebed (and thus the lake itself) officially belongs to the people of Windermere (local philanthropist Henry Leigh Groves purchased it on their behalf in 1938).

There are 18 islands on Windermere: the largest is Belle Isle, encompassing 16 hectares and an 18th-century Italianate mansion, while the smallest is Maiden Holme, little more than a patch of soil and a solitary tree.

Windermere Lake Cruises (☑ 01539-443360; www.windermere-lakecruises.co.uk; cruises from £9.50) offers sightseeing cruises, departing from Bowness Pier.

Lake District

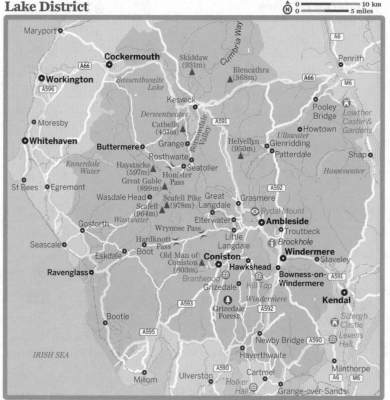

Cruises are provided by the 1902 *Osprey* and the 1930 *Penelope II*: there's no more stylish way to see Windermere.

★ **Blackwell House** HISTORIC BUILDING
(☑ 01539-446139; www.lakelandarts.org.uk/black well; adult/child under 16yr £9/4.50; ⊙10.30am-5pm Apr-Oct, to 4pm Nov-Mar) Two miles south of Bowness on the B5360, Blackwell House is a glorious example of the 19th-century Arts and Crafts movement, which championed handmade goods and craftsmanship over the mass-produced mentality of the Industrial Revolution. Designed by Mackay Hugh Baillie Scott for Sir Edward Holt, a wealthy brewer, the house shimmers with Arts and Crafts details: light, airy rooms, bespoke craftwork, wood panelling, stained glass and delft tiles. The mock-medieval Great Hall and serene White Drawing Room are particularly fine.

The cafe has brilliant views over Windermere.

Wray Castle HISTORIC SITE
(NT; www.nationaltrust.org.uk/wray-castle; adult/child £10.40/5.20; ⊙10am-6pm, cafe 10am-4pm) An impressive sight with its turrets and battlements, this mock-Gothic castle was built in 1840 for James Dawson, a retired doctor from Liverpool, but it has been owned by the National Trust since 1929. Though the interior is largely empty, the lakeside grounds are glorious. It was once used as a holiday home by Beatrix Potter's family. The best way to arrive is by boat from Bowness; there's limited parking and preference is given to non-driving visitors on busy days.

Fell Foot Park GARDENS
(NT; www.nationaltrust.org.uk/fell-foot-park; ⊙10am-6pm Apr-Sep, to 5pm Oct-Mar, cafe 10am-3pm) FREE Located at the southern end of Windermere, 7 miles south of Bowness, this 7-hectare lakeside estate originally belonged to a manor house. It's now owned by the National Trust and its shoreline paths and

Windermere Town

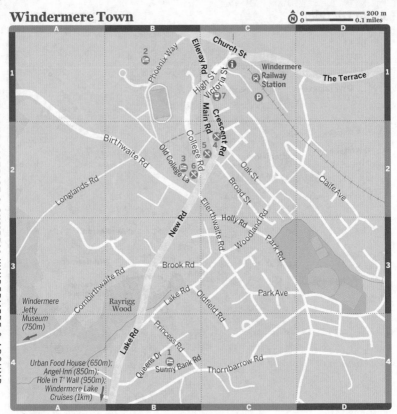

Windermere Town

🛏 Sleeping
1 Rum Doodle	B4
2 The Hideaway	B1
3 Wheatlands Lodge	B2

🍴 Eating
4 Francine's	C2
5 Homeground	C2
6 Hooked	B2

🍷 Drinking & Nightlife
7 Crafty Baa	C1

grassy lawns are ideal for a sunny-day picnic. There's a small cafe, and rowing boats are available for hire.

Lakeland Motor Museum　　　MUSEUM
(☑01539-530400; www.lakelandmotormuseum
.co.uk; Backbarrow; adult/child £9/5.40;
⊙9.30am-5.30pm Apr-Sep, to 4.30pm Oct-Mar)
Two miles south of Newby Bridge on the A590, this museum is a must for petrolheads. Its vintage-car collection ranges from the classic (Minis, Austin Healeys, MGs) to the sporty (DeLoreans, Audi Quattros, Aston Martins) and downright odd (Scootacars, Amphicars). There are also quirky exhibits on the history of caravans and vintage bicycles. A separate building explores Donald and Malcolm Campbell's speed record attempts on Coniston Water, with replicas of the 1935 Bluebird car and 1967 *Bluebird K7* boat.

Lakes Aquarium　　　AQUARIUM
(☑01539-530153; www.lakesaquarium.co.uk;
Lakeside; adult/child £7.95/5.75; ⊙10am-5.30pm)
At the southern end of the lake near Newby Bridge, this aquarium explores underwater habitats from tropical Africa through to Morecambe Bay. Windermere Lake Cruises (p568) and the Lakeside & Haverthwaite Railway stop beside the aquarium, as does bus 6/X6 from Bowness.

Lakeside & Haverthwaite Railway   RAIL
(☑ 01539-531594;   www.lakesiderailway.co.uk;
adult/child return from Haverthwaite to Lakeside
£7.20/3.60; ☺ mid-Mar–Oct) Built to carry ore
and timber to the ports at Ulverston and
Barrow, these dinky steam trains puff their
way between Haverthwaite, near Ulverston,
and Newby Bridge and Lakeside. There are
five to seven trains a day, timed to corre-
spond with the Windermere cruise boats –
combo tickets include an onward lake cruise
to Bowness or Ambleside.

🛌 Sleeping

Windermere YHA   HOSTEL £
(☑ 0845-371 9352; www.yha.org.uk; Bridge Lane;
d/tr/q/f from £49/79/99/119; ☺ reception 7.30-
11.30am & 3-10pm; P @) Slightly misleadingly,
the closest YHA to Windermere is actually
about 1.5 miles from the lake, halfway between Troutbeck Bridge and Troutbeck village. Once a private mansion with grand
lake views, the hostel is at present only open
for exclusive hires, though camping and cabins are available in the grounds.

Inconveniently, buses from Windermere
stop about a mile downhill at Troutbeck
Bridge.

★ Rum Doodle   B&B ££
(☑ 01539-445967;   www.rumdoodlewindermere.
com; Sunny Bank Rd, Windermere Town; d £79-
139; P 🛜) Named after a classic travel novel
about a fictional mountain in the Himalayas,
this B&B zings with imagination. Its rooms
are themed after places and characters in
the book, with details such as book-effect
wallpaper, vintage maps and old suitcases.
Top of the heap is the Summit, snug under
the eaves with a separate sitting room. Two-
night minimum in summer.

The Hideaway   B&B ££
(☑ 01539-443070; www.thehideawayatwindermere
.co.uk; Phoenix Way; d £70-165; P 🛜) There's
a fine range of rooms available at this
much-recommended B&B in a former
schoolmaster's house. There's a choice
for all budgets, from Mini Comfy (simple
decor, not much space) all the way to Ultimate
Comfy (claw-foot tub, split-level mezzanine,
space galore). Regardless which you choose,
you'll be treated to spoils such as homemade
cakes and afternoon tea every day.

Wheatlands Lodge   B&B ££
(☑ 01539-443789; www.wheatlandslodge-winder
mere.co.uk; Old College Lane; d £99-140; P 🛜)
Halfway between Windermere and Bowness, this elegant Victorian B&B is a fine
choice. Rooms vary in size: largest are the
four-poster room 5 (with its own bay window) and the two top-floor suites. Breakfast
is a definite high point, with homemade
bread and granola, locally sourced bacon,
milk and sausages, and jams from Hawkshead Relish company.

Gilpin Hotel   HOTEL £££
(☑ 01539-488818; https://thegilpin.co.uk; Crook
Rd; r £275-465; P) If you really want to push
the Windermere boat out, this famously
posh country-house retreat offers the final
word in lake luxury. The fancy rooms are
named after fells, garden suites have their
own decks and outdoor hot tubs, and the
exclusive Lake House nearby comes with its
own chauffeur.

A Michelin-starred restaurant, lovely spa
and hectares of grounds complete the high-
class package.

🍴 Eating

★ Homeground   CAFE £
(☑ 01539-444863;   www.homegroundcafe.co.uk;
56 Main Rd, Windermere Town; mains £7-10;
☺ 8.30am-5pm Mon-Fri, 9am-5pm Sat & Sun)
Windermere gets its own artisan coffee
house, serving flat whites and cappucinos
garnished with impressive milk art. It's
super for brunch too, with bang-on-trend
options such as pressed tofu and hummus
flatbreads, homemade kedgeree benny and
tahini waffles. All in all, a thoroughly welcome new addition to town.

★ Hooked   SEAFOOD ££
(☑ 01539-448443; www.hookedwindermere.co.uk;
Ellerthwaite Sq, Windermere Town; mains £16-20;
☺ 5-9pm) Fresh fish comes every day direct
from Hartlepool Dock in County Durham,
and this first-class fish restaurant takes full
advantage. From hake with pomme purée to
Cajun swordfish and squid-ink ravioli, it's a
pescatarian's perfect night out. It's small, so
bookings are essential.

Urban Food House   CAFE ££
(☑ 01539-454345;   www.urbanfoodhouse.co.uk;
Lake Rd, Bowness-on-Windermere; lunch mains £8-
12, dinner mains £12-22; ☺ 10am-10pm Mon-Sat,
to 7pm Sun) A peculiar name for a Lakeland
cafe, perhaps, but it makes sense given the
hipsterish design: red-brick walls, rough-
wood tables, bare lightbulbs, casual service. There's range of grub, from fish-finger

LOCAL KNOWLEDGE

CLASSIC PUBS AROUND WINDERMERE

Several super country pubs are within a few miles' drive of Windermere.

Mason's Arms (☑ 01539-568486; www.masonsarmsstrawberrybank.co.uk; Bowland Bridge; mains £12.95-19.95; ⊘ noon-10pm) Three miles east of the lake, near Bowlands Bridge, this marvellous pub is a local secret – particularly for the gorgeous views over fields and fells from the terrace.

Brown Horse Inn (☑ 01539-443443; www.thebrownhorseinn.co.uk; Winster; mains £12.95-17.95; ⊘ lunch noon-2pm, dinner 6-9pm) Also three miles from Windermere in Winster, the Brown Horse is known for its food – much of the produce (including meat and game) comes from its own estate.

Watermill Inn (☑ 01539-821309; www.watermillinn.co.uk; Ings; mains £11-20; ⊘ 11am-11pm Mon-Sat, to 10.30pm Sun) Two miles from Windermere in Ings, this is a resolutely tradition-al Cumbrian inn – beamed ceilings, whitewashed walls, log fires, hand pumps and all. It's renowned for its home-brewed beer.

baps and flatbreads to mussel bowls and herb-crusted lamb (some good veggie options, too).

Francine's
BISTRO ££

(☑ 01539-444088; www.francinesrestaurant windermere.co.uk; 27 Main Rd, Windermere Town; mains £14-18; ⊘ 10am-2.30pm & 6.30-11pm Tue-Sat) 🍽 The definition of a neighbourhood bistro: it's a locals' favourite and if you come more than once you'll probably be greeted by name. It's a tiny space with crammed-in tables, so watch your elbows with your neighbours. Food is solid if not stellar, with tastes tending toward the hearty, such as roast guinea fowl, confit pork belly and chicken supreme.

Angel Inn
PUB FOOD ££

(☑ 01539-444080; www.angelbowness.com; Helm Rd, Bowness-on-Windermere; mains £10.95-16.50; ⊘ 11.30am-4pm & 5-9pm) A decent gastropub on a grassy knoll in Bowness. The menu is nothing fancy – burgers, beer-battered had-dock, Cumberland sausage and mash – but the setting is fantastic, with Windermere views from the front lawn.

🍷 Drinking & Nightlife

★ Crafty Baa
CRAFT BEER

(☑ 01539-488002; https://thecraftybaa.busi-ness.site; 21 Victoria St, Windermere Town; ⊘ 11am-11pm) Brilliant and slightly bonkers, festooned with a mishmash of upcycled materials, this much-loved Windermere craft bar has scooped numerous awards: choose from Czech pilsners, weissbiers, smoked lagers and fruit beers, chalked up on slates

behind the bar and served with accompa-nying snack platters. It's so successful, it's opened a sister pub in Keswick (p586).

Hole in T' Wall
PUB

(☑ 01539-443488; Fallbarrow Rd, Bowness-on-Windermere; ⊘ 11am-11pm) Bowness' oldest boozer, dating back to 1612 and offering lashings of rough-beamed, low-ceilinged atmosphere.

Hawkshead Brewery
BREWERY

(☑ 01539-822644; www.hawksheadbrewery.co.uk; Mill Yard, Staveley; ⊘ noon-11pm) This renowned craft brewery has its own impressive beer hall in Staveley, 3 miles east of Windermere. Core beers include Hawkshead Bitter, dark Brodie's Prime and fruity Red.

ℹ Information

Brockhole National Park Visitor Centre
(☑ 01539-446601; www.brockhole.co.uk; ⊘ 10am-5pm) The lakes' main information centre in a former country house 3 miles north of Windermere along the A591.

Windermere Information Centre
(☑ 01539-446499; www.windermereinfo.co.uk; Victoria St, Windermere Town; ⊘ 8.30am-5.30pm) A small information point in Windermere Town, near the railway station, run by Mountain Goat. It also offers booking services and luggage storage.

Bowness Visitor Information Centre
(☑ 0845-901 0845; bownesstic@lake-district. gov.uk; Glebe Rd, Bowness-on-Windermere; ⊘ 10am-5pm Apr-Oct, to 4.30pm Nov-Mar; 🏢) Basic information point near the Bowness jetty, with a shop and cafe.

ⓘ Getting There & Away

BOAT

To cross Windermere by car, bike or on foot, head south of Bowness to the **Windermere Ferry** (www.cumbria.gov.uk/roads-transport/highways-pavements/windermereferry.asp; car/bicycle/pedestrian £5/2/1; ⊙ 6.50am-9.50pm Mon-Sat, 8.50am-10pm Sun Apr-Oct, to 8.50pm Oct-Mar), which shuttles between Ferry Nab on the east bank to Ferry House on the west bank. Expect car queues in summer.

BUS

Note that if you're travelling any further than Grasmere – or if you're planning on returning from anywhere – you're best to buy a Central Lakes Dayrider (p567) ticket.

Bus 555/556 Lakeslink (£4.90 to £10, at least hourly every day) Starts at the train station, stopping at Troutbeck Bridge (five minutes), Brockhole Visitor Centre (seven minutes), Ambleside (£4.90, 15 minutes), Grasmere (£7.40, 30 minutes) and Keswick (£10, one hour). In the opposite direction it continues to Kendal (£6.50, 25 minutes).

Bus 505 Coniston Rambler (hourly every day) Travels from Bowness to Coniston (£12.60, 50 minutes) via Troutbeck, Brockhole, Ambleside, Skelwith Fold, Hawkshead and Hawkshead Hill. Two buses a day serve Kendal.

Bus 599 Lakes Rider (£4.00 to £7.40, three times hourly every day) Open-top bus between Bowness, Troutbeck, Brockhole, Rydal Church (for Rydal Mount), Dove Cottage and Grasmere. Some buses stop at Windermere train station.

TRAIN

Windermere is the only town inside the national park accessible by train. It's on the branch line to Kendal and Oxenholme, with onward connections to Edinburgh, Manchester and London Piccadilly.

DESTINATION	ONE-WAY FARE (£)	DURATION
Edinburgh	70.80	2½hr
Glasgow	58	2¼-2¾hr
Kendal	5.70	15min
Lancaster	15.50	45min
London Euston	80.90	3½hr
Manchester Piccadilly	25.80	1½hr

Ambleside

🖉 01539 / POP 2529

Once a busy mill and textile centre, Ambleside is an attractive little town at Windermere's northern tip, built from the same slate and stern grey stone so characteristic of Lakeland. Ringed by fells, it's a favourite base for hikers, with a cluster of outdoors shops and plenty of cosy pubs and cafes providing fuel for adventures.

The town's best-known landmark is **Bridge House**, a tiny cottage that spans the clattering brook of Stock Ghyll. Now occupied by a National Trust shop, it's thought to have originally been built as an apple store.

◉ Sights & Activities

★ **Rydal Mount**   HISTORIC BUILDING
(🖉 01539-433002; www.rydalmount.co.uk; adult/child £7.50/4, grounds only £5; ⊙ 9.30am-5pm

---

WORTH A TRIP

TROUTBECK

This out-of-the-way hamlet on the way to Kirkstone Pass is worth a detour – the views of the fells and distant Windermere are fantastic. But it's also home to one of Lakeland's best (and oldest) inns, the **Mortal Man** (🖉 01539-433193; www.themortalman.co.uk; mains £13.95-24.85; 🅿 🐾). Dating from 1689, with a gabled facade, traditional rooms and a cracking outlook from the beer garden, it's a real beauty of a boozer. And if you're wondering about the curious name, have a look at the pub sign on your way in – it's taken from an old Lakeland rhyme.

Troutbeck is also home to the National Trust–owned farmhouse of **Townend** (NT; 🖉 01539-432628; www.nationaltrust.org.uk/townend; adult/child £8.50/4.25; ⊙ garden 10am-5pm Fri-Mon), which belonged to farmer Ben Browne and his family until 1943. The house is brimming with the family's possessions and memorabilia of their rural agricultural life, but its opening hours vary: when it isn't open, the delightful cottage garden is well worth a wander.

Bus 508 from Windermere (£4.90, 25 minutes, five daily) stops in Troutbeck, then continues over Kirkstone Pass to Ullswater and Penrith.

Apr-Oct, 11am-4pm Wed-Sun Nov, Dec, Feb & Mar) The poet William Wordsworth's most famous residence in the Lake District is undoubtedly Dove Cottage (p576), but he actually spent a great deal more time at Rydal Mount, 1.5 miles northwest of Ambleside, off the A591. This was the Wordsworth family's home from 1813 until the poet's death in 1850 and the house contains a treasure trove of Wordsworth memorabilia. Bus 555 (and bus 599 from April to October) stops at the end of the drive.

Downstairs you can wander around the library, dining room and drawing room; upstairs are the family bedrooms and Wordsworth's attic study, containing his encyclopedia and a sword belonging to his brother John, who was lost in a shipwreck in 1805.

There is a plethora of fascinating objects, including recently unveiled exhibits such as the Wordsworth's family Bible (which includes the christening dates of all the Wordsworth children in delicate copperplate) and William's beloved walking sticks (complete with his silver crest). Look closely and you'll also spy gems such as his pen, inkstand and picnic box in the cabinets.

The gardens are lovely, too – Wordsworth fancied himself as a landscape gardener and much of the grounds were laid out according to his designs. Below the house is Dora's Field, a peaceful meadow in which Wordsworth planted daffodils in memory of his eldest daughter, who died from tuberculosis in 1847.

Entry at the time of research was by online bookings only.

Stock Ghyll Force   WALKING

Ambleside's most popular walk is the half-hour stroll up to the 18m-high waterfall of Stock Ghyll Force – the trail is signposted behind the old market hall at the bottom of Stock Ghyll Lane. If you feel energetic, you can follow the trail beyond the falls up Wansfell Pike (482m), a reasonably steep walk of about two hours.

Low Wood Watersports   BOATING

(📞01539-439441; www.englishlakes.co.uk/low-wood-bay/watersports; Low Bay Marina) This water-sports centre offers waterskiing, sailing and kayaking and has rowboats and motorboats for hire. For two hours, kayaks cost £20, canoes £30 and stand-up paddleboards £25.

🛏 Sleeping

⭐ Ambleside YHA   HOSTEL £

(📞0345-371 9620; www.yha.org.uk; Lake Rd; d/f from £39/59; 🅿🛜) This huge lakeside hostel is a fave for activity holidays (everything from kayaking to ghyll scrambling). At the time of research, bookings were for private rooms only (either en suite or with shared bathrooms), and the lounge and kitchen were closed due to Covid-19. It's between Ambleside and Windermere.

Low Wray   CAMPSITE £

(NT; 📞bookings 01539-432733; www.nationaltrust.org.uk/features/lake-district-camping; campsite for 2 adults £18-44, ecopod £30-80; ⊙year-round) One of the most popular of the National Trust's four Lakeland campsites, in a fine spot along Windermere's shores, 3 miles from Ambleside along the B5286. There are 120 tent pitches and nine hard pitches for caravans, plus a handful of camping pods, safari tents and two wacky 'tree tents'. Choose from lake view, woodland, field or water's edge. Bus 505 stops nearby.

Rooms at the Apple Pie   B&B £

(📞01539-433679; www.applepieambleside.co.uk; Rydal Rd; d £55-85; 🅿🛜) Not content with making the best apple pie in town, the eponymous cafe (p575) has expanded its accommodation operations into a separate building next door. There are good-value rooms, plainly furnished and on the small side, but thoroughly comfy. The loft rooms share a landing, so are ideal for families. There's a small car park, too.

Waterwheel   B&B ££

(📞01539-433286; www.waterwheelambleside.co.uk; 3 Bridge St; d £100-120; 🛜) Fall asleep to the sound of the river at this tiny B&B, tucked off the main street. The three rooms are small but sweet: Rattleghyll is cosily Victorian, Loughrigg squeezes under the rafters and Stockghyll features a brass bed and claw-foot bath. The drawback? The only parking is in a public car park 250m away. Two-night minimum.

Gables   B&B ££

(📞01539-433272; www.thegables-ambleside.co.uk; Church Walk; s £60-65, d £95-145; 🅿🛜) One of Ambleside's best-value B&Bs, in a double-gabled house (hence the name) in a quiet spot overlooking the recreation ground. Spotty cushions and colourful prints keep things cheery, but room sizes are variable (in this instance, bigger is definitely better).

FIVE CLASSIC FELL WALKS

The Lake District's most famous fell-walker, the accountant-turned-author Alfred Wainwright, recorded 214 official fells in his seven-volume *Pictorial Guides* (as if that weren't enough, he usually outlined at least two possible routes to the top or, in the case of Scafell Pike, five). If you only have limited time, here are five hikes that offer a flavour of what makes fell-walking in the Lake District so special.

Scafell Pike (p583) The daddy of Lakeland hikes, a six- to seven-hour slog to the top of England's highest peak. The classic route is from Wasdale Head.

Helvellyn (p590) Not for the faint hearted; a vertiginous scramble along the knife-edge ridge of Striding Edge. It takes at least six hours, starting from Glenridding or Patterdale.

Blencathra A mountain on its own, Blencathra (868m) offers a panoramic outlook on Keswick and the northern fells. Count on four hours from Threlkeld.

Haystacks Wainwright's favourite mountain and the place where his ashes were scattered. Haystacks (597m) is a steep, three-hour return hike from Buttermere village.

Catbells The fell for everyone, Catbells (451m) is accessible to six-year-olds and septuagenarians alike. It's on the west side of Derwentwater and takes a couple of hours to climb.

Guests receive discounts at the owner's restaurant, Sheila's Cottage (☑01539-433079; The Slack; mains £12.50-18; ☺noon-9pm). There's a tiny first-come, first-served car park.

Ambleside Townhouse B&B £££
(☑01539-433240; www.amblesidetownhouse.co.uk; Lake Rd; d £94-154; P ☎) Halfway between a B&B and a mini-hotel, this place is handily placed for the town centre. The rooms are simply but smartly decorated in neutral tones; some superior rooms have a full-size wall mural featuring a local beauty spot. Some are in the main building, others in an attached annexe. Breakfast is buffet-style, and there's plenty of parking.

Waterhead Hotel HOTEL £££
(☑08458 504503; www.englishlakes.co.uk; Lake Rd; r £145-360; P ☎☎) For a proper hotel stay in Ambleside (complete with the all-essential Windermere view, of course), the Waterhead is definitely the choice. Outside it's clad in traditional Lakeland stone; inside there are 40-something rooms that, while perfectly comfortable, feel a tad corporate in style. Lake views command a premium, but there are often good online deals.

Eating

★ **Great North Pie** PIES £
(☑01625-522112; www.greatnorthpie.co; unit 2 The Courtyard, Rothay Rd; pies £4-8; ☺9am-5pm) Based in Wilmslow, this much-garlanded pie maker has opened an Ambleside outlet, and it's rightly become a town favourite. Go for a classic such as Swaledale beef mince or

Lancashire cheese and onion, or opt for something on the seasonal pie menu – they're all delicious, and served with lashings of mash and gravy (veggie, should you wish).

Apple Pie CAFE £
(☑01539-433679; www.applepieambleside.co.uk; Rydal Rd; lunches £5-10; ☺9am-5.30pm) For a quick lunch stop, you won't go far wrong at this friendly caff, which serves stuffed sandwiches, hot pies, baked spuds, sausage rolls and yummy cakes (the apple pie is locally legendary). Everything is available either eat in or takeaway.

Zeffirelli's ITALIAN £
(☑01539-433845; www.zeffirellis.com; Compston Rd; pizzas & mains £10-15; ☺11am-10pm) A beloved local landmark, Zeff's is generally packed out for its quality and good-value pizza and pasta. The £24.75 movie deal includes a ticket at Zeffirelli's Cinema (☑01539-433100; Compston Rd).

Kysty BISTRO ££
(☑01539-433647; www.kysty.co.uk; 3/4 Cheapside; lunch mains £14-19, dinner mains £18-26; ☺noon-2pm Wed-Sat, 6-9pm Tue-Sat) Run by the same team behind the Old Stamp House (p576), this town bistro offers a simplified take on its sister restaurant's superb Cumbrian-sourced food. Simple and seasonal, the food is a treat, and the space is lovely, with old-fashioned mullion windows and wooden tables. In case you're wondering, *kysty* is a Cumbrian word for a fussy eater.

Fellini's VEGETARIAN ££
(☑ 01539-432487; www.fellinisambleside.com; Church St; mains £14.95; ⊗ 5.30-10pm; 🍴) Fear not, veggies: even in the land of the Cumberland sausage and the tattie hotpot, you won't go hungry thanks to Fellini's 'vegeterranean' food. The dishes are creative and beautifully presented – think delicate Moroccan filo parcels, stuffed portobello mushrooms and radicchio provolone ravioli.

★**Old Stamp House** BISTRO £££
(☑ 01539-432775; www.oldstamphouse.com; Church St; lunch/dinner menu £45/75; ⊗ 12.30-2pm Wed-Sat, 6.30-10pm Tue-Sat) In the cellar of the building where Wordsworth worked as a distributor of stamps, this fine-dining bistro run by Ryan Blackburn champions Cumbrian produce, much of it raised, caught, shot or cured within a few miles' radius (think Arctic char, Herdwick hogget and roe deer, partnered with foraged ingredients). Outstanding – and now Michelin-starred.

★**Lake Road Kitchen** BISTRO £££
(☑ 01539-422012; www.lakeroadkitchen.co.uk; Lake Rd; 5-/8-course tasting menu £65/90; ⊗ 6-9.30pm Wed-Sun) Quite simply one of the hottest places to dine in the Lakes. Its Noma-trained head chef, James Cross, explores 'cold climate' cooking (think Scandi-inspired, impeccably presented and laced with experimental ingredients aplenty). From shore-sourced seaweed to pickled vegetables and forest-picked mushrooms, the flavours are constantly surprising – and the stripped-back styling feels very appropriate.

❶ Information

Hub (☑ 01539-432582; tic@thehubofambleside.com; Central Buildings, Market Cross; ⊗ 9am-5pm) Ambleside's info centre sells walking guides, local books and also houses the town's post office.

❶ Getting There & Away

Bus 555 Runs at least hourly (including Sundays) to Grasmere (£4.90) and Keswick (£9), and to Bowness, Windermere (£4.90) and Kendal (£7.80) in the opposite direction.

Bus 599 Open-top service that leaves at least hourly (including weekends) to Grasmere, Bowness, Windermere and Brockhole Visitor Centre; four buses daily continue to Kendal. Prices as for bus 555.

Bus 505 To Hawkshead and Coniston (£6.10, hourly each day).

Bus 516 To Elterwater and Langdale (£4.60, six daily).

Grasmere

☑ 01539 / POP 1458

Few corners of the Lake District have such an illustrious literary heritage as little Grasmere. Huddled at the edge of an island-studded lake surrounded by woods, pastures and slate-coloured hills, this was the home of the grand old daddy of the Romantics himself, poet William Wordsworth, who set up home at nearby Dove Cottage in 1799 and spent most of the rest of his life in and around the village. Two of the poet's former homes can be visited, and there's an excellent museum that explores the area's Romantic connections. Most poignantly of all, you can pay your respects at the Wordsworth's family plot in the village churchyard.

Grasmere's literary cachet has its drawbacks: the village's streets are crammed to bursting throughout summer, and the modern-day rash of gift shops, tearooms and coach-tour hotels has done little to preserve the quiet country charm that drew Wordsworth here.

◉ Sights & Activities

Popular hikes starting from Grasmere include **Helm Crag** (404m), often known as the 'Lion and the Lamb', thanks to its distinctive shape; **Silver Howe** (394m); **Loughrigg Fell** (335m); and the multi-peak circuit known as the **Easedale Round** (five to six hours, 8.5 to 9 miles).

A less taxing option is to follow the **Old Coffin Trail** (4 miles) between Grasmere and Rydal Mount, which was once used by pallbearers carrying coffins to St Oswald's Church. The trail begins near Dove Cottage.

★**Dove Cottage & Jerwood Museum** HISTORIC BUILDING
(☑ 01539-435544; www.wordsworth.org.uk; adult/child £9.50/4.50; ⊗ 9.30am-5.30pm Mar-Oct, 10am-4.30pm Nov, Dec & Feb) This tiny, creeper-clad cottage was famously inhabited by William Wordsworth between 1799 and 1808. On the edge of Grasmere, described by Wordsworth as 'the loveliest spot that man hath ever found', the cottage has cramped rooms full of artefacts, including the poet's passport, spectacles, dinner set and a portrait (given to him by Sir Walter Scott) of his dog, Pepper.

Wordsworth lived here happily – initially with his beloved sister Dorothy, and later his wife Mary and first three children, John, Dora and Thomas. Much of his early work was composed at the cottage, often with the help and support of Dorothy, who penned her *Grasmere Journal* while living at the cottage – a fascinating work in its own right for Wordsworth students. In 1808 when the family moved to a nearby house at Allen Bank, the cottage was subsequently rented by Thomas de Quincey (author of *Confessions of an English Opium Eater*).

Around the house is the delightful cottage garden, which Wordsworth described as his own 'little domestic slip of mountain'.

Entry is by prebooked group. Tickets also include admission to the excellent **Jerwood Museum** next door, which houses one of the nation's main collections relating to the Romantic movement, including many original manuscripts, Dorothy's original journal and a huge collection of letters and rare editions by leading Romantic figures.

Grasmere Lake & Rydal Water   LAKE
Quiet paths lead along the shores of Grasmere's twin-set lakes. Rowboats can be hired at the northern end of Grasmere Lake from the **Grasmere Tea Gardens** (☑01539-435590; Stock Lane; ⊙9.30am-5pm), a five-minute walk from the village centre.

St Oswald's Church   CHURCH
(Church Stile) Named after a Viking saint, Grasmere's medieval chapel is where Wordsworth and his family attended service every Sunday for many years. It's also their final resting place – in a corner of the churchyard, the Wordsworth's family graves are under the spreading bows of a great yew tree. A memorial garden to fund the church's restoration has recently been established next door – planted, of course, with daffodils.

Among the tombstones are those belonging to William, his wife Mary, his sister Dorothy and his children Dora, William, Thomas and Catherine. Samuel Taylor Coleridge's son Hartley is also buried here, along with several Quillinans – Edward Quillinan became Wordsworth's son-in-law in 1841, having married his beloved daughter Dora.

The church itself is worth a look. Inside you'll find Wordsworth's own prayer book and his favourite pew, marked by a plaque. The church is one of the oldest in the Lake District, mostly dating from the 13th century, but thought to have been founded sometime in the 7th century. It was restored and re-rendered in 2017.

🛏 Sleeping

Butharlyp How YHA   HOSTEL £
(☑0845 371 9319; www.yha.org.uk; Easedale Rd; r £49-59; ⊙reception 7am-11pm; 🅿🛜) Grasmere's YHA is in a large Victorian house set among grassy grounds within easy walking distance of the village. There's a licensed bar, and camping space in the grounds, plus waterproof 'landpods' for hire.

Thorney How   HOSTEL £
(☑01539-435597; www.thorneyhow.co.uk; Easedale Rd; d from £55) Once a much-loved YHA hostel, this ancient farmhouse off Easedale Rd has been totally renovated since becoming independently run. Snug rooms are available on an en-suite B&B basis, and there's an attached bunkhouse (exclusive hire only at the time of research). Located down a rambling lane, it scores high on Lakeland charm.

Heidi's Grasmere Lodge   B&B ££
(☑07568-333950; www.heidisgrasmerelodge.co.uk; Red Lion Sq; d £99-125; 🛜) Not one for minimalists, this five-room B&B in the centre of the village is awash with frills, puffy cushions and Cath Kidston–style prints. The picks are room 1, with a private balcony offering mountain views, or room 6, reached via a spiral staircase and with its own roof terrace.

How Foot Lodge   B&B ££
(☑01539-435366; www.howfootlodge.co.uk; Town End; d £85-95; 🅿) Just a stroll from Dove Cottage in Town End, this stone house has six rooms finished in fawns and beiges. Nicest are the deluxe doubles, one with a sun terrace, the other with a private sitting room. Rates are a bargain for the location.

⭐ Forest Side   BOUTIQUE HOTEL £££
(☑01539-435250; www.theforestside.com; Keswick Rd; r £189-369; 🅿🛜) This boutique beauty – a former hunting lodge – is hard to top for luxury. Renovated at huge expense by hotelier Andrew Wildsmith, it's a design temple: crushed-velvet sofas, Zoffany fabrics, stag heads and 20 country-chic rooms from 'Cosy' to 'Master'. Its restaurant is Michelin-starred, and the grounds (including a working kitchen garden) are gorgeous.

Daffodil Hotel   BOUTIQUE HOTEL £££
(☑01539-463550; www.daffodilhotel.co.uk; d £160-240, ste £200-320; 🅿🛜) Opened in 2012 this upscale hotel occupies a Victorian building, but the 78 rooms zing with modern style:

swirly carpets, art prints and bold shades of lime, purple and turquoise. There's a choice of lake or valley views and lovely bathrooms with pan-head showers and Molton Brown bath products. A restaurant and spa complete the package.

Eating

Heidi's Cafe   CAFE £

(☑ 01539-435248; www.heidisgrasmerelodge. co.uk; Red Lion Sq; mains £4-8; ⊙9am-5.30pm) This cheery village cafe is the place for homemade soup or an indulgent slice of cake.

Baldry's Tea Room   CAFE £

(☑ 01539-435301; Red Lion Sq; lunch £5-9; ⊙10am-5pm) This old-school tearoom serves a classic cream tea in a bone-china pot, accompanied by buttery scones, flapjacks or Victoria sponge.

Greens   CAFE £

(☑ 01539-435790; www.greensgrasmere.com; College St; mains £4.75-10.50; ⊙9.30am-4pm) A popular little village cafe, good for everything from a Cumbrian fry-up to a lunch of stuffed baguettes, wraps and rarebits.

★ The Yan   BISTRO ££

(☑ 01539-435055; www.theyan.co.uk; Broadrayne Farm; mains £13.95-15.95; ⊙5-10pm Mon-Fri, 3-10pm Sat & Sun) Rustic-meets-refined at the Yan (from an old Cumbrian word for 'one'). Lodged in an ancient farmhouse a mile north of Grasmere, the design marries minimalism with chunky wooden tables, a futuristic fireplace and hefty wood beams, and the food offers a fun, modern spin on traditional classic like fish pie, chicken Kiev and bacon chop. Lovely bedrooms, too.

Jumble Room   MODERN BRITISH ££

(☑ 01539-435188; www.thejumbleroom.co.uk; Langdale Rd; mains £14.50-23; ⊙5-9pm Mon-Wed, Fri & Sat) Grasmere's venerable dining landmark, run for many years by Andy and Crissy Hill. Crissy's eclectic, globetrotting menu spans everything from Malaysian noodles to Turkish lamb, cauliflower and chickpea curry and fish pie.

Shopping

★ Sarah Nelson's Gingerbread Shop   FOOD

(☑ 01539-435428; www.grasmeregingerbread. co.uk; Church Cottage; ⊙9.15am-5.30pm Mon-Sat, 12.30-5pm Sun) In business since 1854, this famous sweet shop next to the village church makes Grasmere's essential souvenir: traditional gingerbread with a half-biscuit, half-cakey texture (six/12 pieces for £3.95/7.50), cooked using the original top-secret recipe.

❶ Getting There & Away

The regular 555 bus (at least hourly, including Sundays) runs from Windermere to Grasmere (15 minutes) via Ambleside, Rydal Church and Dove Cottage, then travels onwards to Keswick.

The open-top 599 (two or three per hour in summer) runs to Grasmere from Windermere and Bowness via Troutbeck Bridge and Ambleside.

Both buses charge the same fares: Grasmere to Ambleside is £4.90; to Bowness and Windermere is £7.40.

Hawkshead

☑ 01539 / POP 1640

Lakeland villages don't come more perfect than pint-sized Hawkshead, a jumble of whitewashed cottages, cobbled lanes and old pubs lost among bottle-green countryside between Ambleside and Coniston. The village has literary cachet, too – Wordsworth went to school here and Beatrix Potter's husband, William Heelis, worked here as a solicitor for many years (his old office is now a National Trust art gallery devoted to Beatrix Potter's work).

Cars are banned in the village centre.

◉ Sights

A number of Hawkshead's sights, including the **Beatrix Potter Gallery** (www.national trust.org.uk/beatrix-potter-gallery) and the **Hawkshead Grammar School** (www.hawks headgrammar.org.uk), which Wordsworth attended, were closed at time of research due to Covid-19. Check their websites for opening times and booking details before you visit.

★ Hill Top   HISTORIC BUILDING

(NT; ☑ 01539-436269; www.nationaltrust.org. uk/hill-top; garden adult/child £5/2.50; ⊙10am-5.30pm Jun-Aug, to 4.30pm Sat-Thu Apr, May, Sep & Oct, weekends only Nov-Mar) Two miles south of Hawkshead, in the tiny village of Near Sawrey, this idyllic farmhouse was purchased in 1905 by Beatrix Potter and inspired many of her tales: the house features in *Samuel Whiskers, Tom Kitten, Pigling Bland* and *Jemima Puddle-Duck,* among others, and you might recognise the kitchen garden

GRIZEDALE FOREST

Stretching for 2428 hectares across the hilltops between Coniston Water and Esthwaite Water is Grizedale Forest, a dense conifer forest whose name derives from the Old Norse 'griss-dale', meaning 'valley of the pigs'. Though it looks lush and unspoilt today, the forest has been largely replanted over the last 100 years – by the late 19th century the original woodland had practically disappeared thanks to the demands of the local logging, mining and charcoal industries.

The forest has nine walking trails and seven cycling trails to explore – some are easy and designed for families, while others are geared towards hardcore hikers and cyclists. Along the way you'll spot more than 40 outdoor sculptures hidden in the undergrowth, created by artists since 1977 (there's a useful online guide at www.grizedalesculpture. org). There's also a **Go Ape** (www.goape.co.uk/locations/grizedale; ⊙9-5pm daily Mar-Oct, Sat & Sun Nov-Feb; ♿) forest adventure centre.

Trail maps of the forest are sold at the **visitors centre** (☑0300 067 4495; www.forestry.gov.uk/grizedale; ⊙10am-1pm & 1.45-4pm), while bikes can be hired from **Grizedale Mountain Bikes** (☑01229-860335; www.grizedalemountainbikes.co.uk; adult/child half-day from £35/20; ⊙9am-5pm).

from *Peter Rabbit*. Check the NT website for the latest opening times, and to prebook.

★**Tarn Hows** LAKE
(NT; www.nationaltrust.org.uk/coniston-and-tarnhows) Two miles off the B5285 from Hawkshead, a winding country lane leads to this famously photogenic artificial lake, now owned by the National Trust. Trails wind their way around the lakeshore and surrounding woodland – keep your eyes peeled for red squirrels in the treetops.

There's a small National Trust car park, but it fills quickly. Several buses, including the 505, stop nearby.

🛏 Sleeping & Eating

Hawkshead YHA HOSTEL £
(☑0845 371 9321; www.yha.org.uk; r £29-49; P@🛜) This impressive YHA is lodged in a Grade II–listed Regency house overlooking Esthwaite Water, a mile from Hawkshead along the Newby Bridge road. It's a fancy spot considering the bargain prices: the rooms are spacious, and there are camping pods outside, as well as bike rentals. The 505 bus stops at the end of the lane.

★**Yewfield** B&B ££
(☑01539-436765; www.yewfield.co.uk; Hawkshead Hill; s £90-115, d £100-145; P🛜) 🍃 This rambling Victorian mansion is one of the best options around Hawkshead, in a tranquil rural spot near Tarn Hows. It's veggie-only and ecofriendly (all heating and hot water comes from a biomass boiler supplied from the hotel's own woodland), and the handsome rooms are stocked with antiques. The spacious landscaped grounds are a highlight.

★**Drunken Duck** PUB FOOD £££
(☑01539-436347; www.drunkenduckinn.co.uk; Barngates; mains £24; ⊙noon-2.30pm & 6-8.45pm; P🛜) Long one of the Lakes' premier dining destinations, the Drunken Duck is a blend of historic pub and fine-dining restaurant. On a wooded crossroads on the top of Hawkshead Hill, it's renowned for its luxurious food and home-brewed ales, and the flagstones and sporting prints conjure a convincing country atmosphere. Book well ahead.

If you fancy staying, you'll find the rooms (£125 to £250) are as fancy as the food. The pub's tricky to find: drive along the B5286 from Hawkshead towards Ambleside and look for the brown signs.

ℹ Getting There & Away

Bus 505 (£4.90 to £6.10, hourly every day) links Hawkshead with Windermere, Ambleside and Coniston.

Coniston

☑01539 / POP 641

Hunkered beneath the pockmarked peak known as the **Old Man of Coniston** (803m), this lakeside village was originally established to support the local mining industry – the surrounding hilltops are littered with the remains of old copper workings. These days most people visit with two things in mind: to cruise on the lovely old

Coniston Launch, or to tramp to the top of the Old Man, a steep but rewarding return hike of around 6 miles.

Coniston's other claim to fame is as the location for a string of world-record speed attempts made by Sir Malcolm Campbell and his son, Donald, between the 1930s and 1960s. Tragically, after beating the record several times, Donald was killed during an attempt in 1967 when his futuristic jetboat *Bluebird* flipped at around 320mph. The boat and its pilot were recovered in 2001, and Campbell was buried in the cemetery of St Andrew's church.

◎ Sights

Coniston Water   LAKE
Coniston's gleaming 5-mile-long lake – the third largest in the Lake District after Windermere and Ullswater – is a half-mile walk from town along Lake Rd. The best way to explore the lake is on one of the two cruise services or, better still, by paddling it yourself. Dinghies, rowing boats, canoes, kayaks and motorboats can be hired from the Coniston Boating Centre.

Along with its connections to the speed attempts made here by Malcolm and Donald Campbell, the lake is famous for inspiring Arthur Ransome's classic children's tale *Swallows and Amazons*. Peel Island, towards the southern end of Coniston Water, supposedly provided the model for Wild Cat Island in the book.

Brantwood   HISTORIC BUILDING
(☑ 01539-441396; www.brantwood.org.uk; gardens only adult/child £6.20/free; ☺10.30am-5pm) John Ruskin (1819–1900) was one of the great thinkers of 19th-century society. A polymath, philosopher, painter and critic, he expounded views on everything from Venetian architecture to lacemaking. In 1871 he purchased this grand house and spent two decades modifying it, championing traditional handmade crafts (he even designed the wallpaper). The house was closed at the time of research, but the cafe and gardens remained open, with fantastic cross-Coniston views. The best way to arrive is on a boat trip from Coniston.

✗ Activities

★ Steam Yacht Gondola   BOATING
(NT; ☑ 01539-0432733; www.nationaltrust.org.uk/steam-yacht-gondola; Coniston Jetty; cruises adult/child/family £17/8.50/38) ✆ Built in 1859 and

restored in the 1980s by the National Trust, this wonderful steam yacht looks like a cross between a Venetian *vaporetto* and an English houseboat, complete with cushioned saloons and polished wood seats. It's a stately way to see the lake, especially if you're visiting Brantwood, and it's ecofriendly – since 2008 it's been powered by waste wood.

Old Man of Coniston   HIKING
Hunkering above Coniston like a benevolent giant, the Old Man (803m) presents an irresistible challenge. The most popular route is up the east side along the Coppermines Valley – a leg-sappingly steep slog, but well worth it for the views at the top. Along the way you'll pass the remains of several slate and copper mines.

Coniston Launch   BOATING
(☑ 01539-436216; www.conistonlaunch.co.uk; Coniston Jetty; Red Route adult/child return £12.50/6.25, Yellow Route £13.75/6.90, Green Route £18.25/9.15) ✆ Coniston's two modern launches have been solar-powered since 2005. The regular 45-minute **Northern Service (Red Route)** calls at the Waterhead Hotel, Torver and Brantwood. The 60-minute **Wild Cat Island Cruise (Yellow Route)** tours the lake's islands.

The 105-minute **Southern Service (Green Route)** is themed: it's *Swallows and Amazons* on Monday and Wednesday, and the Campbell story on Tuesday and Thursday.

Coniston Boating Centre   BOATING
(☑ 01539-441366; www.conistonboatingcentre.co.uk; Coniston Jetty) Hires out rowing boats (£15 per hour), kayaks and stand-up paddleboards (£20 for two hours), Canadian canoes (£25 for two hours) and motorboats (£30 per hour). It also rents out bikes (adult/child £15/5 for two hours).

⌂ Sleeping

Hoathwaite Campsite   CAMPSITE £
(NT; ☑ bookings 01539-463862; www.nationaltrust.org.uk/holidays/hoathwaite-campsite-lakedistrict; adult, tent & car £9-15, extra adult/child £6/3; ☺ Easter-Nov) This back-to-basics National Trust–owned campsite is on the A593 between Coniston and Torver. There's a toilet block, water taps and not much else – but the views over Coniston Water are super.

Lakeland House   B&B ££
(☑ 01539-441303; www.lakelandhouse.co.uk; Tilberthwaite Ave; s £45-85, d £60-114, ste £160-185)

You're smack bang in the centre of Coniston at this good-value, basic B&B above Hollands cafe. The best rooms have views of the Old Man; the Lookout Suite has its own sitting room and in-room bathtub.

Bank Ground Farm   B&B **££**
(☑ 01539-441264; www.bankground.com; East of the Lake Rd; d from £110; P) This lakeside farmhouse has literary cachet: Arthur Ransome used it as the model for Holly Howe Farm in *Swallows and Amazons*. Parts of the house date back to the 15th century, so the rooms are snug. Some have sleigh beds, others exposed beams. The tearoom is a beauty, and there are cottages for longer stays. Two-night minimum.

✖ Eating

Herdwicks   CAFE **£**
(☑ 01539-441141; Yewdale Rd; mains £4-10; ☺10am-4pm) Run by a local family, this bright and cheery cafe makes the perfect stop for lunch, whether you're in the mood for homemade soup, a big chunky sandwich, or a slice of sinful cake. Everything is locally sourced where possible, and the light-filled, large-windowed space is inviting.

Bluebird Cafe   CAFE **£**
(☑ 01539-441649; Lake Rd; mains £4-8; ☺9.30am-5.30pm) This lakeside cafe does a brisk trade from people waiting for the Coniston launches. The usual salads, jacket spuds and sandwiches are on offer and there are lots of tables outside where you can look out on the lake.

Steam Bistro   BISTRO **££**
(☑ 01539-441928; www.steambistro.co.uk; Tilberthwaite Ave; 2-/3-course menu £24.95/29.95; ☺6-11pm Wed-Sun) This swish new bistro has become the go-to address for Coniston dining. Its magpie menu borrows lots of global flavours – you'll find everything from Japanese dumplings to Cajun pulled pork and Greek-style *kleftiko* (slow-cooked lamb) on the specials board. Even better, everything is *prix fixe* (fixed price). At the time of writing, it was operating on a takeaway-only basis.

☕ Drinking & Nightlife

Sun Hotel   PUB
(☑ 01539-441248; www.thesunconiston.com; Sun Hill; ☺10am-11pm) Famously used as a headquarters by Donald Campbell during his fateful campaign, this trad boozer is a good place for a pint, with a fell-view beer garden and cosy crannies in which to hunker down

– look out for Campbell memorabilia. Food (mains £12 to £22) is hit-and-miss at busy times.

Black Bull   PUB
(☑ 01539-441335; www.conistonbrewery.com/black-bull-coniston.htm; Yewdale Rd; ☺10am-11pm) Coniston's main meeting spot, the old Black Bull offers a warren of rooms and a popular outside terrace. The pub grub's good (mains £8 to £18), but it's mainly known for its home-brewed ales: Bluebird Bitter and Old Man Ale are always on tap and there are seasonal ones, too.

ℹ Information

Coniston Tourist Office (☑ 01539-441533; www.conistontic.org; Ruskin Ave; ☺9.30am-4.30pm Mon-Sat, 10am-2pm Sun)

ℹ Getting There & Away

Bus 505 runs to Windermere (£9.80, hourly every day) via Hawkshead and Ambleside. A couple of buses a day go on to Kendal. Note that for most bus journeys, the best value is to buy a 24-hour Central Lakes Dayrider (p567) ticket.

The Coniston Bus-and-Boat ticket (adult/child £19/8.30) includes return bus travel on the 505, plus a trip on the launch and entry to Brantwood.

Elterwater & Great Langdale

☑ 01539
Travelling north from Coniston, the road passes into the wild, empty landscape of Great Langdale, one of Lakeland's iconic hiking valleys. As you pass the pretty village of Elterwater, imposing fells stack up like dominoes along the horizon, looming over a pastoral patchwork of tumbledown barns and lime-green fields.

The circuit around the line-up of fells known as the **Langdale Pikes** – Pike O' Stickle (709m), Loft Crag (682m), Harrison Stickle (736m) and Pavey Ark (700m) – is the valley's most popular hike, allowing you to tick off between three and five Wainwrights depending on your route, and covering around six steep, hard-going miles. Allow a good six hours.

🛏 Sleeping

Great Langdale Campsite   CAMPSITE **£**
(NT; ☑ 01539-463862; www.nationaltrust.org.uk/features/great-langdale-campsite; Great Langdale; sites £12-26, extra adult £6, pods £30-85; ☺year-round; P) Possibly the most

spectacularly positioned campsite in the Lake District, spread over grassy meadows overlooked by Langdale's fells. It gets crowded in high season, so it's best to book in advance. Camping pods and yurts available.

Elterwater Hostel HOSTEL £
(☏ 01539-437245; www.elterwaterhostel.co.uk; Elterwater; s/tw/f £55/63/82.25; ⊗ check-in 4.30-9pm; ＠) Formerly owned by the YHA, this indie hostel, which was once a farmhouse, is near Elterwater's grassy green. Rooms vary in size and scope, but they're attractively decorated. Breakfast is included, and dinner is available on a prebooked basis.

★**Old Dungeon Ghyll** HOTEL ££
(☏ 01539-437272; www.odg.co.uk; Great Langdale; s £62.50, d £116-135; ₱ 🐾 🐕) Affectionately known as the ODG, this inn is awash with Lakeland heritage: many famous walkers have stayed here, including Prince Charles and mountaineer Chris Bonington. It's endearingly olde worlde (well-worn furniture, four-poster beds) and even if you're not staying, the slate-floored, fire-warmed **Hiker's Bar** is a must for a post-hike pint – it's been the hub of Langdale's social life for decades.

★**Eltermere Inn** HOTEL £££
(☏ 01539-437207; www.eltermere.co.uk; Elterwater; r £145-295; ₱ 🐕) This charming inn is one of Lakeland's loveliest boltholes. Rooms are simple and classic, tastefully decorated in fawns and taupes with quirky features such as window seats and free-standing baths. The food's excellent, too, served in the inn's snug bar; afternoon tea is served on the lawn on sunny days.

🍴 Eating & Drinking

Sticklebarn PUB FOOD £
(☏ 01539-437356; Great Langdale; lunch mains £5-8, dinner mains £11-13.50; ⊗ 11am-9pm) Now run by the National Trust, this converted barn is a walkers' favourite, serving wholesome, hearty food and a good ale selection.

Chesters by the River CAFE ££
(☏ 01539-432553; www.chestersbytheriver.co.uk; Skelwith Bridge; lunch mains £8-15; ⊗ 8.30am-5pm) Beside a rattling brook at Skelwith Bridge, halfway between Ambleside and Elterwater, this smart cafe is more gourmet than greasy spoon, serving delicious salads, specials and cakes.

Britannia Inn PUB
(☏ 01539-437210; www.thebritanniainn.com; Elterwater; ⊗ 11am-11pm) On Elterwater's green, this classic whitewashed inn has been serving ale for five centuries: the current line-up includes brews from Coniston Brewery and the nearby Langdale Brewing Company (our pick is the superbly named Neddy Boggle Bitter). Arrive early to bag a table on the grassy lawn on sunny days.

ℹ️ Getting There & Away

Bus 516 (six daily) is the only bus, with stops at Ambleside, Skelwith Bridge, Elterwater and the Old Dungeon Ghyll hotel in Great Langdale. The fare from Ambleside all the way into Great Langdale is £6.10.

WORTH A TRIP

THE STEEPEST ROAD IN ENGLAND

Zigzagging over the fells between the valleys of Little Langdale and Eskdale, an infamous mountain road traverses England's two highest road passes: **Wrynose** and **Hardknott**. In use since ancient times, the old packhorse route was substantially improved by the Romans: at the top of Hardknott Pass, there's a ruined **Roman fort** – you can still see the remains of the walls, parade ground and commandant's house. The views from here to the coast are stunning.

A favourite of TV motoring shows, motorbikers and hardcore cyclists, the road is perfectly drivable if you take things slow and steady, but probably best avoided if you're a hesitant reverser or don't like driving next to steep drops. This is not a road to rush; you'll need to be prepared for plenty of reversing when you meet vehicles coming the opposite way.

To get to the passes from Ambleside, follow road signs on the A593 to Skelwith Bridge, then turn off to Little Langdale. When you reach the Three Shires Inn, the road gets really steep. Alternatively, you can approach from the west: drive along the A595 coast road and turn off towards Eskdale, then follow the road past Boot to the passes.

Parking in Langdale can be a problem in summer. There are National Trust car parks at Stickle Ghyll and the Old Dungeon Ghyll hotel (free for NT members), plus one car park run by the National Park Authority opposite the New Dungeon Ghyll, but all are often full by 10am. Local farmers often open one of their fields to act as an overflow.

Wasdale
☑ 01946

Carving its way for 5 miles from the Cumbrian coast, the craggy, wind-lashed valley of Wasdale is where the Lake District scenery takes a turn for the wild. Ground out by a long-extinct glacier, the valley is home to the Lake District's highest and wildest peaks, as well as the steely grey expanse of Wastwater, England's deepest and coldest lake.

Wasdale's fells are an irresistible draw for hikers, especially those looking to conquer Scafell Pike.

Activities

★ **Scafell Pike**　　　　　　　HIKING
At 978m, England's highest mountain features on every self-respecting hiker's bucket list. The classic route starts from Wasdale Head; it's hard going but achievable for moderately fit walkers, though it's steep and hard to navigate in bad weather. It's a return of around six to seven hours.

Proper gear is essential: raincoat, rucksack (backpack), map, food, water and hiking boots, as is a favourable weather forecast.

It's worth noting that the pressure of people on the top of Scafell Pike can be pretty intense in summer – save it for the shoulder season if you can to minimise damage.

Sleeping

Wasdale Head Campsite　　CAMPSITE £
(NT; ☑ bookings 01539-463862; www.national trust.org.uk/holidays/wasdale-campsite-lake-district; sites £12-26, extra adult £6, pods £30-85) This National Trust campsite is in a fantastically wild spot, nestled beneath the Scafell range. Facilities are basic (laundry room, showers), but the views are out of this world. Camping pods (some with electric hook-ups) provide a bit more shelter in case Wasdale's notorious weather decides to make an appearance.

★ **Wasdale Head Inn**　　　　B&B ££
(☑ 01946-726229; www.wasdale.com; s/d/tr £60/120/180; P 📶) A slice of hill-walking

ENNERDALE

To the north of Wasdale, the remote valley of Ennerdale and its namesake lake were once home to slate mines and timber plantations, but these are slowly being removed and the valley is being returned to nature as part of the Wild Ennerdale (www.wildennerdale.co.uk) project.

The valley is paradise if you prefer your trails quiet. Several popular routes head over the fells to Wasdale, while walking towards Buttermere takes you past the **Black Sail YHA** (☑ 0845-371 9680; www.yha.org.uk; dm from £15) 🍴, a marvellously remote hostel inside a shepherd's bothy, much loved by mountaineers and hikers.

heritage here. Hunkering beneath the brooding bulk of Scafell Pike, this 19th-century hostelry is gloriously old-fashioned and covered in vintage photos and climbing memorabilia. The rooms are cosy, with roomier suites in a converted stable. There's masses of outside seating, and a choice of dining settings in the bar or dining room.

Camping costs £6 a night.

Keswick
☑ 01768 / POP 4821

The most northerly of the Lake District's major towns, Keswick (pronounced kezzick) has perhaps the most beautiful location of all: encircled by cloud-capped fells and nestled alongside the idyllic, island-studded lake of Derwentwater, a silvery curve crisscrossed by puttering cruise boats. It's also brilliantly positioned for further adventures into the nearby valleys of Borrowdale and Buttermere, and a great base for walking.

Sights

★ **Castlerigg Stone Circle**　　MONUMENT
FREE Set on a hilltop a mile east of town, this jaw-dropping stone circle consists of 48 stones that are between 3000 and 4000 years old, surrounded by a dramatic ring of mountain peaks.

Keswick Museum　　　　　　MUSEUM
(☑ 01768-773263; www.keswickmuseum.org.uk; Station Rd; adult/child £4.95/3; ⊙ noon-4pm) Keswick's excellent town museum explores

WORDSWORTH'S BIRTHPLACE

Set at the confluence of the flood-prone Rivers Cocker and Derwent, the Georgian town of Cockermouth has a major claim to literary fame: it's the birthplace of William Wordsworth, who was born on 7 April 1770 in a handsome Georgian house at the end of Main St.

Now known as **Wordsworth House** (NT; ☎ 01900-824805; www.nationaltrust.org.uk/wordsworth-house; Main St; adult/child £8.80/4.40; ⏱ 11am-5pm Sat-Thu Mar-Oct), and run by the National Trust, the house has been meticulously restored based on accounts from the Wordsworth family archive: the kitchen, drawing room, study and bedrooms look much as they would have to a young William. Costumed guides provide added period authenticity.

Bus X4/X5 (half-hourly Monday to Saturday, hourly Sunday) travels from Cockermouth to Keswick (£6.30) and Penrith (£8.20).

the area's history, from ancient archaeology through to the arrival of industry in the Lakes. It's a diverse collection, taking in everything from Neolithic axe heads mined in the Langdale valley to a huge collection of taxidermied butterflies. Its best-known exhibits are a 700-year-old mummified cat and the Musical Stones of Skiddaw, a weird instrument made from hornsfel rock that was once played for Queen Victoria.

Lakes Distillery   DISTILLERY
(☎ 01768-788850; www.lakesdistillery.com; tours £12.50; ⏱ 11am-6pm) The first craft distillery in the Lake District has made a big splash since opening in 2014. It's located on a 'model farm' built during the 1850s and was founded by a team of master distillers. Its range includes several gins, vodkas, blended whiskies and a flagship single malt. Guided tours take you through the process and include a tasting of the three spirits.

The smart bistro (mains £12.50 to £16.50) is well worth a look for lunch, too.

Derwent Pencil Museum   MUSEUM
(☎ 01768-773626; www.derwentart.com; Southy Works; adult/child £4.60/3.70; ⏱ 9.30am-5pm) Only in Britain: a museum dedicated to the pencil, with exhibits including a pencil made for the Queen's Diamond Jubilee,

wartime spy pencils that were hollowed out for secret maps, and the world's largest pencil (a mighty 8m long). It all stems from the discovery of graphite in the Borrowdale valley during the 17th century, after which Keswick became a major pencil manufacturer.

Phone ahead to reserve a ticket.

🏃 Activities

Hiking opportunities abound around Keswick. **Catbells** (451m) is a family-friendly favourite – a mini-mountain on the west shore of Derwentwater, easily reached via the Keswick Launch.

Further afield, the hefty fells of **Skiddaw** (931m) and **Blencathra** (868m) present sterner challenges.

Keswick Launch   BOATING
(☎ 01768-772263; www.keswick-launch.co.uk; round-the-lake pass adult/child/family £11/5.70/27.50) Derwentwater is undoubtedly one of the prettiest of the Lakeland lakes, studded with wooded islands and ringed by craggy fells. The lovely Keswick Launch runs regular cross-lake excursions, and rowboats (£15 per hour) and motor boats (£33) can be hired next to the jetties.

✦ Festivals & Events

Keswick Mountain Festival   OUTDOORS
(www.keswickmountainfestival.co.uk; ⏱ May) This May festival celebrates all things mountainous.

Keswick Beer Festival   BEER
(www.keswickbeerfestival.co.uk; ⏱ Jun) Lots and lots of beer is drunk during Keswick's real-ale fest in June.

🛌 Sleeping

Keswick YHA   HOSTEL £
(☎ 0845 371 9746; www.yha.org.uk; Station Rd; r £49-69; 🛜) Keswick's riverside YHA is one of the best in the Lakes, with cracking views over Fitz Park and the rushing River Greta. The decor is standard YHA, but some rooms have private riverside balconies. What a treat! Food is available from the on-site cafe.

★ Howe Keld   B&B ££
(☎ 01768-772417; www.howekeld.co.uk; 5-7 The Heads; s £80-95, d £120-140; 🅿🛜) A cut above your usual cookie-cutter B&B: the spoils here are numerous, from feather-and-down duvets to glossy wooden floors to furniture made from local materials. The best rooms have views across Crow Park and the golf

course, and the breakfast is a pick-and-mix delight. Free parking is available on The Heads if there's space.

Linnett Hill
B&B **££**

(☑ 01768-744518; www.linnetthillkeswick.co.uk; 4 Penrith Rd; s £53, d £90-100; ☎) Much recommended by travellers, this lovingly run B&B has lots going for it: crisp white rooms, a great location near Fitz Park and keen prices that stay the same year-round. Breakfast is good, too – there's a blackboard of specials to choose from and the dining room has gingham-check tablecloths and a crackling wood burner.

The Mount
B&B **££**

(☑ 01768-773821; www.themountkeswick.co.uk; The Mount, Portinscale; r from £92.50) In the neighbouring hamlet of Portinscale, a mile from town, this super-friendly B&B puts nary a foot wrong, with crisply decorated rooms (some with fell views), an Aga-cooked breakfast (including owner Clive's home-baked bread) and even a shepherd's hut in the garden, should you prefer to sleep al fresco.

✖ Eating

★ Fellpack
CAFE **£**

(☑ 01768-771177; www.fellpack.co.uk; 19 Lake Rd; mains £11-13; ☺ 5-11pm Tue-Sat) This on-trend cafe specialises in 'fell pots' – a Lakeland-style Buddha bowl, incorporating an all-in-one meal such as sweet potato and chickpea curry, chicken ham and leek crumble, or braised chilli beef. It's been a big hit, so the owners have also opened a burger joint, **The Round** (☑ 01768-773991; www.fellpack.co.uk; 21 Main St; burgers £8.50-10; ☺ 4-11pm Tue-Fri, noon-11pm Sat), off Main St.

★ Lingholm Kitchen
CAFE **£**

(☑ 01768-771206; www.thelingholmkitchen.co.uk; mains £6.50-13.50; ☺ 9am-5pm) What a setting this splendid cafe has: in a delightful walled garden on the Lingholme Estate, with a 30m glass wall that presents cinematic views of Skiddaw, plus a dainty old greenhouse. For lunch, expect modern brunch dishes such as poached eggs on sourdough, rarebit, a toasted reuben and (of course) avocado toast.

Jasper's Coffee House
CAFE **£**

(☑ 01768-773366; www.jasperscoffeehouse.com; 20 Station St; mains £6.50-7.50; ☺ 10am-4pm Mon-Thu, 9am-5pm Fri-Sun; 🐾) A canine-themed cafe serving simple salads, wraps and sandwiches named after dogs of legend (the Pongo, the Hooch, the Huckleberry Hound).

Square Orange
CAFE **£**

(☑ 01768-773888; www.thesquareorange.co.uk; 20 St John's St; pizzas £8.65-10.95; ☺ noon-10pm) This lively cafe-bar is an ever-popular hangout for its thin-crust pizzas, cheese platters and tapas. With its big wooden bar and packed-in tables, it all feels rather continental.

Morrel's
BRITISH **££**

(☑ 01768-772666; www.morrels.co.uk; Lake Rd; 2-/3-course menu £20/25; ☺ cafe 9.30am-3.30pm Tue-Sun, restaurant 6-9.30pm Thu-Sat) The best option in Keswick for a sit-down dinner, majoring in British bistro-style food. Glossy wood, spotlights and glass give it a refined feel.

Pheasant Inn
PUB FOOD **££**

(☑ 01768-776234; www.the-pheasant.co.uk; Bassenthwaite Lake; mains £15-22; ☺ 11am-11pm) A short drive along Bassenthwaite Lake is this fine-dining pub. Hunting prints and pewter tankards cover the old bar, which is stocked with vintage whiskies and Lakeland ales, and there's superior pub grub to fill your belly. A bit old-school, perhaps, but big on the Lakeland vibes.

★ Cottage in the Wood
HOTEL **£££**

(☑ 01768-778409; www.thecottageinthewood.co.uk; Braithwaite; lunch/dinner menu £40/55; ☺ lunch 12.30-1.30pm, dinner 6.30-9.30pm; 🅿 ☎) Under chef Ben Wilkinson, this Michelin-starred coaching inn en route to Whinlatter Pass has become Keswick's premier dining destination. The food is

---

WORTH A TRIP

WHINLATTER FOREST PARK

Encompassing 4.6 sq miles of pine, larch and spruce, **Whinlatter** (www.forestry.gov.uk/whinlatter) FREE is England's only true mountain forest, rising to 790m about 5 miles from Keswick. The forest is a red squirrel reserve; you can check out video feeds from squirrel cams at the visitor centre. It's also home to two mountain-bike trails and a tree-top assault course.

Entry to the forest is free, but parking isn't (£2 for one hour, £8 all day).

Bus 77 (four daily) runs from Keswick. If you're driving, head west on the A66 and follow the brown signs near Braithwaite.

seasonal, flavoursome and delicately presented – the Taste Cumbria menu (themed around Stream, Woodland, Coasts and Fells) is an inventive delight. If you fancy making a night of it, sleek rooms survey woods and countryside.

Drinking & Nightlife

Crafty Baa   PUB

(☑01768-785405; https://thecraftybaa.business.site; 13 Bank St; ⊙11am-11pm) This tiny craft-beer bar is decorated with a mishmash of upcycled materials – the ceiling is festooned with Union Jacks, old traffic cones, chandeliers and upside-down lampshades – but it's the fantastic selection of beers and ales that's made it such a hit with Keswick drinkers.

Dog & Gun   PUB

(☑01768-773463; 2 Lake Rd; ⊙11am-11pm) Benches, beams, hearths, rugs: the old Dog is the picture of a Lakeland pub. Order a pint of Thirst Rescue ale, which includes a donation to the Keswick Mountain Rescue Team.

Shopping

★ George Fisher   SPORTS & OUTDOORS

(☑01768-772178; www.georgefisher.co.uk; 2 Borrowdale Rd; ⊙9am-5.30pm Mon-Sat, 10am-4pm Sun) Quite possibly the most famous outdoors shop in the Lake District, founded in 1967 and still the place where discerning hikers go to buy their gear (even if it is a bit more expensive than the chains). There are three floors of boots, tents and gear, and the boot-fitting service is legendarily thorough.

On the top floor, **Abraham's Tea Rooms** (☑01768-772178; www.georgefisher.co.uk/cafe; 2 Borrowdale Rd; mains £6-10; ⊙10am-5pm Mon-Sat, 10.30am-4.30pm Sun) serves a filling lunch.

ℹ Information

Keswick Tourist Office (☑01768-772645; www.keswick.org; Moot Hall, Market Pl; ⊙9.30am-4.30pm; ☎) The town's tourist office is well run and the staff are very informed. It also sells discounted tickets for the Keswick Launch (p584), and has free wi-fi.

ℹ Getting There & Away

The Keswick & Honister Dayrider (p567) is the best-value ticket for buses to Borrowdale and Buttermere (bizarrely, it's cheaper than buying a return).

555/556 Lakeslink Hourly to Grasmere (£8.50, 40 minutes), Ambleside (£9, 45 minutes), Windermere (£10, one hour) and Kendal (£10.80, 1½ hours).

77/77A Circular route (five to seven daily) from Keswick via Portinscale, Catbells, Grange, Seatoller, Honister Pass, Buttermere, Lorton and Whinlatter.

78 (at least hourly Monday to Friday, half-hourly weekends) The main Borrowdale bus, with stops at Lodore, Grange, Rosthwaite and Seatoller.

Borrowdale

☑01768 / POP 417

With their patchwork of craggy hills, broad fields, tinkling streams and drystone walls, Borrowdale and its neighbouring valley of Buttermere are many people's idea of the quintessential Lakeland landscape. Once a centre for mineral mining (especially slate, coal and graphite), this is walkers' country these days and, apart from the odd rickety barn or puttering tractor, there's precious little to spoil the view.

South of Keswick, the B5289 tracks Derwentwater into the heart of Borrowdale, winding past the small farming villages of **Grange-in-Borrowdale**, **Rosthwaite** and **Stonethwaite**.

◉ Sights & Activities

Watendlath Tarn   LAKE

This National Trust–owned tarn is reached via a turn-off on the B5285 south of Keswick. On the way the road passes over one of the Lake District's most photographed packhorse crossings at **Ashness Bridge**. Parking at the tarn is free for NT members, but the road is narrow and has few passing places, so it's more pleasant to walk up in summer (2.3 miles from the B5285 turn-off).

Bowder Stone   NATURAL FEATURE

A mile south of Grange, a turn-off leads up to the geological curiosity known as the Bowder Stone, a 1700-tonne lump of rock left behind by a retreating glacier. A small ladder leads to the top of the rock.

Lodore Falls   WATERFALL

At the southern end of Derwentwater, this waterfall featured in a poem by Robert Southey, but it's only worth visiting after a good spell of rain. It's in the grounds of the Lodore Hotel; there's an honesty box for donations.

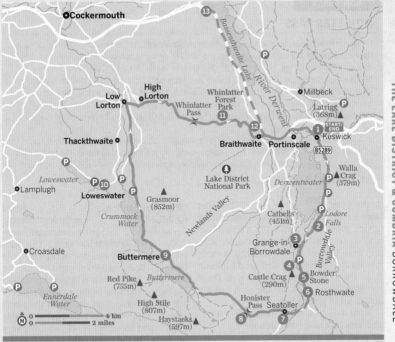

Driving Tour
Borrowdale & Buttermere

START KESWICK
END KESWICK
LENGTH 28 MILES; THREE TO FOUR HOURS

This is one of the Lakes' most beautiful road trips – a perfect day out of Keswick.

Begin with breakfast in ❶ **Keswick**, then head along the B5289 into Borrowdale. First stop is ❷ **Lodore Falls**, a pretty cascade at the southern end of Derwentwater. Next, detour to the little hamlet of ❸ **Grange-in-Borrowdale**, where a trail leads up the slate-strewn sides of ❹ **Castle Crag** (p588), a small fell with great views over Borrowdale.

From Grange carry on to the huge boulder known as the ❺ **Bowder Stone**, shifted into position by the long-gone glacier that carved out the Borrowdale Valley. Pootle on to ❻ **Rosthwaite** for tea and cake at the Flock In Tea-Room, or continue to ❼ **Seatoller** for lunch.

In the afternoon tackle the steep crawl up to ❽ **Honister Pass** (p588), where you can pick up some slate souvenirs, take a tour into the depths of the old slate mine, or venture out onto the hair-raising via ferrata.

From here the road drops into the beautiful valley of ❾ **Buttermere** (p591). Spot the zigzag peaks of High Stile, Haystacks and Red Pike looming on your left-hand side over the lake, stop for a drink at the Fish Inn and remember to pay your respects to hiker and author Alfred Wainwright inside St James' Church.

Continue along the shore of Crummock Water past ❿ **Loweswater**, where you could make an optional but very worthwhile detour to the excellent Kirkstile Inn. When you reach Low Lorton, a right-hand turn carries you over Whinlatter Pass to ⓫ **Whinlatter Forest Park** (p585).

There are a couple of great options for dinner on your way back to Keswick: the ⓬ **Cottage in the Wood** (p585) just before Braithwaite, or the traditional ⓭ **Pheasant Inn** (p585) on the shores of Bassenthwaite Lake.

DON'T MISS

HONISTER PASS

From Borrowdale, a narrow, perilously steep road snakes up the fellside to Honister Pass, home to the last working slate mine in the UK. Though you can still pick up slate souvenirs in the on-site shop, these days the **Honister Slate Mine** (☑01768-777230; www. honister.com; mine tour adult/child £17.50/9.50, all-day pass incl mine tour & classic/extreme via ferrata £55/47; ⊙10am-5pm) has diversified with a range of adventure activities, ranging from subterranean tours to **via ferrata** (classic route £40, Xtreme incl Infinity Bridge £45, all day pass incl mine tour & classic/Xtreme via ferrata £55/60) walks and even a night camping on a cliff face.

In 2019, the slate mine's highly controversial plan to build a zip-line from the summit of nearby Fleetwith Pike was finally approved after more than a decade of wrangling with local campaigners, who believe it will irrevocably damage one of the valley's most prominent peaks.

Castle Crag   HIKING

Once a slate mine, this scree-strewn hillock (290m) provides knockout views across Borrowdale. It's reached along a mainly level trail from Grange, but it gets steep towards the end and the heaps of slate on the hillside make the going slippery in the wet. There are several side trails on the way; bring a map to avoid getting lost.

From the car park in Grange, it's a there-and-back hike of around an hour.

Platty+   BOATING

(☑01768-776572; www.plattyplus.co.uk; kayaks & canoes per hour £8.50-16) Based at the Lodore Boat Landings at the southern end of Derwentwater, this company hires out kayaks, canoes, rowing boats and sailing dinghies. It also runs instruction courses.

🛏 Sleeping & Eating

Seatoller Farm   CAMPSITE £

(☑01768-777232; www.seatollerfarm.co.uk; adult/child £9/3; ⊙Easter-Oct) A lovely, tucked-away site on a 500-year-old farm near Seatoller, with a choice of riverside or woodland pitches. Applejacks, the farm's new on-site food barn, serves wood-fired pizzas and breakfasts.

Derwentwater
Independent Hostel   HOSTEL £

(☑01768-777246; www.derwentwater.org; Barrow House; dm £20, r £60-100; Ⓟ@) Built as a 19th-century mansion, this grand Grade II–listed house is a real stunner. Previously YHA-owned, now private, it's a thing of beauty: many rooms have original features such as plasterwork and fireplaces. The 7-hectare grounds encompass an artificial waterfall.

★ Langstrath Inn   B&B ££

(☑01768-777239; www.thelangstrath.com; Stonethwaite; d £125-140; ⊙restaurant noon-2.30pm & 6-8.30pm Tue-Sun; Ⓟ⊛) This simple country inn makes one of the best little bases in Borrowdale. Its eight rooms are snug and simple, with crimson throws and the occasional roof beam to add character, but it's the views that really sell the place. Hearty, unpretentious food (dinner mains £14.25) and ales from Hawkshead Brewery are served in the restaurant.

Glaramara Hotel   HOTEL ££

(☑01768-777222; www.glaramara.co.uk; Seatoller; s £64, d £79-128; Ⓟ⊛⊛) If your budget won't stretch to Borrowdale's plush country hotels, this activity-focused hotel makes a good-value alternative. The decor is corporate (pine-effect furniture, no-frills furnishings), but the location can't be faulted: on the doorstep of Honister Pass, surrounded by fells and greenery. The hotel has its own outdoor-activities centre for ghyll scrambling, rock climbing, mine exploring and more.

ℹ Getting There & Away

Bus 77/77A (from £3.30, seven daily Monday to Saturday, five on Sunday) makes a circular route from Keswick via Portinscale, the trailhead for Catbells and all the Borrowdale villages, then heads over Honister Pass, through Buttermere and Lorton, over Whinlatter Pass and back to Keswick.

Bus 78 (£6.40 to £8.50, at least hourly, half-hourly on weekends from July to August) shuttles through Borrowdale as far as Seatoller, then heads back the same way to Keswick.

If you're planning on making a return journey the same day, it's nearly always cheaper to buy the Keswick & Honister Dayrider (p567) than a return fare.

Buttermere

☎ 01768 / POP 121

Stretching 1.5 miles northwest of Honister Pass, the deep bowl of Buttermere was gouged out by a steamroller glacier and is backed by a string of impressive peaks and emerald-green hills. The valley's twin lakes, **Buttermere** and **Crummock Water**, were once joined but became separated by glacial silt and rockfall.

The little village of Buttermere sits halfway between the two and provides a wonderfully cosy base for exploring the rest of the valley and the many nearby fells, including **Haystacks** (597m), the favourite mountain and the last resting place of the patron saint of Lakeland walkers, the author Alfred Wainwright.

🛏 Sleeping & Eating

Buttermere YHA HOSTEL £
(☎ 0845 371 9508; www.yha.org.uk; r £29-59; ⏾ mid-Mar–Nov; 🅿🛜) Perched in a perfect position on the Honister–Buttermere road, this excellent slate-fronted hostel (once a hotel) has rooms looking out across the lake. The decor is smart, colourful and surprisingly modern, and there are landpods and tent pitches for al fresco stays.

★ Syke Farm CAMPSITE £
(☎01768-770222; www.sykefarmcampsite. com; adult/child £8/4; ⏾Easter-Oct) Set on a bumpy riverside site, Syke Farm is back-to-basics camping, but you'll wake up to knockout views of Red Pike, High Stile and Haystacks.

Check in at the farm shop in the village first and make sure to sample some of its homemade ice cream.

★ Kirkstile Inn PUB FOOD ££
(☎01900-85219; www.kirkstile.com; mains £13.50-24) A finer country pub you could not hope to find. Hidden away near the little lake of Loweswater, a mile or so north of Buttermere, the Kirkstile is a joy: crackling fires, oak beams, worn carpets, wooden bar and all. It's particularly known for its award-winning ales (try the Loweswater Gold).

Rooms (singles £66 to £95, doubles £121 to £171) are quaint; some have views across Lorton Vale.

Bridge Hotel PUB FOOD ££
(☎01768-770252; www.bridge-hotel.com; mains £10-16; 🅿🛜) As the name suggests, this venerable hostelry is right beside Buttermere's village bridge. There's standard pub food in the walkers' bar, or more upmarket fare in the smart-casual restaurant.

❶ Getting There & Away

Bus 77/77A (£6.40, five to seven daily) serves Buttermere and Honister Pass from Keswick. For same-day return journeys, the Keswick & Honister Dayrider (p567) is cheapest.

Ullswater & Around

☎ 01768

After Windermere, the second-largest lake in the Lake District is Ullswater, stretching for 7.5 miles between **Pooley Bridge** at the northern end and **Glenridding** and **Patterdale** at the southern end. Carved out by a long-gone glacier, the deep valley in which the lake sits is flanked by an impressive string of fells, most notably the razor ridge of **Helvellyn**, England's third-highest mountain at 950m.

The lake's eastern shore is where the three main villages are located. The remote west side is well off the beaten track, and great for crowd-free hiking around the village of **Howtown** and the picturesque valley of **Martindale**.

The area has been badly hit by floods in recent years: the 300-year-old bridge at Pooley Bridge was completely swept away by Storm Desmond in 2015, and was finally replaced by a modern structure in late 2020.

◉ Sights & Activities

The signposted **Ullswater Way** (www.ullswaterway.co.uk) makes a complete 20-mile circuit of the Ullswater shoreline; it's possible to combine sections of the walk with Ullswater 'Steamers' (p590).

Gowbarrow Park & Aira Force PARK
(NT) **FREE** This rolling park stretches across the lakeshore between Pooley Bridge and Glenridding. Well-marked paths lead up to the impressive 20m-high waterfall of Aira Force. Another waterfall, **High Force**, is further up the hillside. South of Gowbarrow Park is **Glencoyne Bay**, where the springtime daffodils inspired William Wordsworth to pen one of his most famous poems.

★ Ullswater 'Steamers'
BOATING

(☎01768-482229; www.ullswater-steamers.co.uk; cruise 'all piers' pass adult/child £16.80/10.10) Ullswater's historic steamers are a memorable way to explore the lake. The various vessels include the stately *Lady of the Lake*, launched in 1877 and supposedly the world's oldest working passenger boat. The boats run east–west from Pooley Bridge to Glenridding via Howtown; tickets should be prebooked online.

★ Helvellyn
HIKING

The Lake District's most famous ridge walk takes in the twin ridges of Striding and Swirral Edges, which are spectacular but very exposed and involve some scrambling and dizzyingly steep drops on either side – if you're at all nervous of heights, Helvellyn is not the fell for you.

The usual routes climb from Glenridding or Patterdale. Always check the weather forecast and take necessary supplies.

The mountain can get crowded in summer, especially at weekends, and queuing on an exposed ridge like this is definitely not ideal; save it for spring or autumn.

Hallin Fell
HIKING

For a quick up-and-down jaunt, this little 388m-high fell on Ullswater's east side is hard to beat – the knockout views from the top are quite out of proportion to its diminutive size. The easiest way up is to catch an Ullswater Steamer to Howtown and follow the trail towards Martindale Church and the summit.

🛏 Sleeping

Quiet Site
CAMPSITE £

(☎07768-727016; www.thequietsite.co.uk; sites £25-45, pods from £65, hobbit holes from £110; ☺year-round; P🅿️) Ecofriendly campsite on the fells above Ullswater, with pre-erected tents and ecopods available as well as fun 'hobbit holes' (timber-lined cabins built into the hillside). Camping is very pricey in summer, but there's plenty of space and the views are outstanding.

Old Water View
B&B ££

(☎01768-482175; www.oldwaterview.co.uk; Patterdale; d £105; P🅿️) Patterdale has several B&Bs, but this one's the pick. It's a simple place focusing on the essentials: friendly service, comfy rooms and value. There's also a little shepherd's hut in the garden (from £85 per night).

Lowthwaite B&B
B&B ££

(☎01768-482343; www.lowthwaiteullswater.com; Matterdale; d £100; P🅿️) This lovely farmhouse in Matterdale is owned by Jim and Tine, who have filled the place with souvenirs from their travels (they previously ran expeditions up Kilimanjaro). Rustic beams meet Tanzanian furniture in the rooms, and breakfast is copious. It's a couple of miles from the lake, off the A5091 to Dockray. Two-night minimum on weekends.

Howtown Hotel
HISTORIC HOTEL ££

(☎01768-486514; www.howtown-hotel.co.uk; Howtown; r £110-210) On Ullswater's eastern shore, this creeper-clad, gabled hotel is a time capsule: charmingly chintzy rooms filled with old-fashioned furniture; a traditional resident's bar complete with ticking grandfather clocks and cosy armchairs; a cute tea room for lunch; and delightfully personal service. Bookings must be confirmed by letter; you'll receive a personal reply from owner Mrs Baldry.

★ Another Place, The Lake
BOUTIQUE HOTEL £££

(☎01768-486442; www.another.place; Watermillock; r £190-370; P🅿️🈲️🈶️) Run by the owners of Cornwall's Watergate Bay Hotel, this lakeshore hotel is one of the national park's most luxurious, family-friendly getaways. A striking new wing has added a wonderful infinity pool and contemporary rooms onto the hotel's original part, which is more classic in feel. There's a restaurant, bar, well-stocked library, lakefront lawns and a wealth of outdoor activities, including SUP and wild swimming.

🍴 Eating

Granny Dowbekin's
CAFE £

(☎01768-486453; www.grannydowbekins.co.uk; Pooley Bridge; mains £6-12; ☺9am-5pm) For a filling all-day brekkie, a ploughman's lunch, chunky sandwich or a slice of something naughty and cake-shaped, this cafe in Pooley Bridge is a favourite. The homemade 'gingerbridge' makes a yummy souvenir.

Fellbites
CAFE ££

(☎01768-482781; www.fellbitescafe.co.uk; Glenridding; lunch mains £4.25-11.50, dinner mains £12-21; ☺11am-8pm Wed-Sun, to 5pm Mon & Tue) Beside the main car park in Glenridding, this cafe is a good bet at any time of day: sandwiches, burgers and rarebits for lunch, rib-eye steaks, battered cod and a roast of the day for dinner.

1863   BISTRO **££**

(☑ 01768-486334; www.1863ullswater.co.uk; High St, Pooley Bridge; 3-course dinner £45; ⊙ dinner 6-9pm, bar 2-10pm, lunch 1-3pm Sat & Sun) A classy addition to Pooley Bridge's dining scene, overseen by head chef Phil Corrie, who has a fondness for the classics: think wood pigeon, saddleback pork and Cumbrian lamb, delicately served and deliciously flavoured. It's now open for lunch at weekends (mains £10 to £15).

There are rooms (doubles £95 to £150) upstairs, too, showcasing some adventurous wallpaper choices.

ⓘ Information

Lake District National Park Ullswater Information Centre (☑ 01768-482414; ullswatertic@lake-district.gov.uk; Glenridding; ⊙ 10am-4pm Apr-Oct, to 3.30pm Sat & Sun Nov-Mar)

ⓘ Getting There & Away

The A592 runs along Ullswater's west side. At the southern end, the road climbs up to **Kirkstone Pass** (which, at 453m, is the highest road pass in the Lake District) before descending via Troutbeck to Windermere.

Bus 508 travels from Penrith to Glenridding and Patterdale (£5.70, nine daily). Five buses continue to Windermere.

Kendal

☑ 01539 / POP 28,586

Often known as the 'Auld Grey Town' thanks to the sombre grey stone used for many of its buildings, Kendal is a historic town that sits just outside the eastern edge of the national park. It's worth visiting for its funky arts centre and intriguing museums, but it'll forever be synonymous in many people's minds with its eponymous mint cake, a teeth-grindingly sweet, calorific hiker's staple that was famously munched by Edmund Hillary and Tenzing Norgay during their ascent of Everest in 1953.

◉ Sights

Kendal's fine-art gallery, **Abbot Hall** (☑ 01539-722464; www.lakelandarts.org.uk/abbot-hall), is currently undergoing major redevelopment, scheduled to reopen in 2022.

Kendal Museum   MUSEUM

(☑ 01539-815597; www.kendalmuseum.org.uk; Station Rd; adult/child £5/2; ⊙ 9.30am-4.30pm Thu-Sat) Founded in 1796 by the inveterate

KIRKBY LONSDALE BREWERY

Established in 2009 high up in the Pennines town of Kirkby Lonsdale, this **brewery** (☑ 01524-271918; www.klbrewery.com; New Rd; ⊙ 10am-9.30pm Mon-Wed, to 11pm Thu-Sat, 11am-10pm Sun) regularly scoops awards as the punters' favourite in Cumbria, and has now opened its own pub, **The Royal Barn**. The house specials are fruity, spicy Ruskin's and the malty, bitter-sweet Pennine Ambler, the official beer of the Pennine Way.

Victorian collector William Todhunter, this mixed-bag museum features everything from stuffed beasts and transfixed butterflies to medieval coin hoards. There's also some interesting memorabilia relating to Alfred Wainwright, who served as honorary curator at the museum from 1945 to 1974: look out for his knapsack and well-chewed pipe.

Levens Hall   HISTORIC BUILDING

(☑ 01539-560321; www.levenshall.co.uk; house & gardens adult/child £14.50/5, gardens only £10.50/4; ⊙ house 10.30am-3.30pm, gardens 10am-5pm Sun-Thu Mar-Oct) This Elizabethan manor is built around a mid-13th-century fortified pele tower, and fine Jacobean furniture litters its interior, though the real draw is the 17th-century topiary garden – a surreal riot of pyramids, swirls, curls, pompoms and peacocks straight out of *Alice in Wonderland*. It's advisable to prebook tickets.

Sizergh Castle   CASTLE

(NT; ☑ 01539-560070; www.nationaltrust.org.uk/sizergh; gardens only £8/4; ⊙ gardens 10am-5pm) Three-and-a-half miles south of Kendal along the A591, this National Trust-owned castle is the feudal seat of the Strickland family. Set around a pele tower, it's worth visiting for its 650-hectare estate encompassing lakes, orchards, woods and pasture.

🛏 Sleeping

Kendal is low on quality sleeping options, and just as easily visited from Windermere.

Sonata Guest House   B&B **££**

(☑ 01539-732290; www.sonataguesthouse.co.uk; 19 Burneside Rd; d £65-90; 🛜) A fairly standard B&B in a Kendal-typical grey-stone terraced house, but it's cosy enough, with feminine

DON'T MISS

CARTMEL

Tiny Cartmel is known for three things: its 12th-century **priory** (☉9am-5.30pm May-Oct, to 3.30pm Nov-Apr) FREE, its small **racecourse** and its world-famous sticky toffee pudding, sold at the **Cartmel Village Shop** (☑01539-536280; www.cartmelvillageshop.co.uk; 1 The Square; ☉9am-5pm Mon-Sat, 10am-4.30pm Sun). The small Cark and Cartmel train station is 2 miles southwest of the village and has regular connections to all stations along the Cumbrian Coast line.

More recently Cartmel has become known as a dining destination: some of Cumbria's top chefs have their restaurants here, notably Simon Rogan (often dubbed Cumbria's answer to Heston Blumenthal) and Kevin Tickle, who has recently taken over the Crown Inn.

Rogan's flagship restaurant, **L'Enclume** (☑01539-536362; www.lenclume.co.uk; Cavendish St; set lunch £65, lunch & dinner menu £159; ☉noon-1.30pm & 6-8.15pm Tue-Sun), showcases his boundary-pushing cuisine and madcap presentation, as well as his passion for foraged ingredients.

He also runs a more relaxed bistro just across the village, **Rogan & Company** (☑01539-535917; www.roganandcompany.co.uk; The Square; 2-/3-course set lunch £29/33, mains £24-28; ☉noon-1.45pm & 6-9pm Mon & Wed-Sat, noon-2pm Sun), which is now Michelin-starred in its own right. Bookings are essential for both.

rooms, floral wallpapers and nice little touches such as goose-down pillows and well-stocked tea trays. Parking is a pain.

★ **Lyth Valley Country Inn** HOTEL £££
(☑01539-568295; https://lythvalleycountryhouse.co.uk; Lyth; r from £125; P🐾) It's seven miles west of Kendal, but there's a reason to head out so far – this hotel sits in a gorgeous spot overlooking the little-visited Lyth Valley, famous locally for its damson plums. Rooms are all named after animals, and they're attractively decorated with solid wooden furniture and patches of exposed brickwork.

✖ Eating

Brew Brothers CAFE £
(☑01539-722237; www.brew-brothers.co.uk; 69 Highgate; mains £6.50-9.25; ☉8.30am-5.30pm Mon-Sat) Hipster coffee culture comes to Kendal: with its scruffy wood furniture and black-aproned baristas, it's got the aesthetic down, but its owners are Lakeland through and through – they previously ran a cafe in Windermere. Smashed avocado, eggs benny in various forms and other on-trend dishes are all on offer if you're hungry.

★ **Yard 46** CAFE £
(☑07585 320522; www.yard46.co.uk; Branthwaite Brow; lunches £3-8; ☉10am-3pm Tue-Sat) This little gem is well worth seeking out. It's down a blink-and-you'll-miss-it alleyway, with a little courtyard and an old white-washed building with cruck-framed attic dining room. Serves delicious soups, imaginative salads and yummy cakes.

Baba Ganoush DELI £
(☑01539-738210; www.facebook.com/pages/Baba-Ganoush-Canteen; 27 Berry's Yard, Finkle St; mains £5-9; ☉10.30am-3pm Tue-Sat) This Mediterranean-inspired cafe has two identities: it's a soup kitchen all week, with veggie cafe dishes served from Thursday onwards. The food is delicious and generous, from crispy falafels to bang-bang cauliflower.

★ **Punch Bowl Inn** PUB FOOD ££
(☑01539-568237; www.the-punchbowl.co.uk; Crosthwaite; mains £14.50-24.50; ☉noon-4pm & 5.30-8.30pm; P) If you don't mind the 5-mile drive from Kendal, this renowned gastropub in the village of Crosthwaite has long been known for its top-notch food. Whitewashed outside, carefully modernised inside, it's a cosy, inviting space in which to dine. Guinea fowl, pork tenderloin, ham hock for mains; blackberry soufflé or elderflower fool for pudding.

The rooms (£135 to £320) are lovely, too: they're all different, but the nicest ones have reclaimed beams, sloping eaves, slate-floored bathrooms and his-and-hers claw-foot tubs.

★ **The Moon Highgate** BISTRO ££
(☑01539-729254; www.themoonhighgate.com; 129 Highgate; 2-/3-course Sunday lunch £20/25, dinner mains £16-21; ☉5-10pm Thu-Sat, noon-6pm Sun) Chef Leon Whitehead has made his bistro Kendal's go-to address for dinner. Seasonal and creative, his food is full of rich, classic flavours, such as pan-roasted Cumbrian chicken with braised barley and chestnut

mushrooms, or roast red leg partridge with celeriac and roast shallots. Sunday lunch is a cracker.

Drinking & Entertainment

Factory Tap   CRAFT BEER
(📞 01539-482541; www.thefactorytap.co.uk; 5 Aynam Rd; ⊙ 4-9pm or 10pm) With nine hand pulls and four keg lines (mostly supplied from one of Cumbria's 40-odd breweries), the Factory Tap is the venue of choice for Kendal's craft-beer connoisseurs. Street food is served in the yard several nights a month.

Brewery Arts Centre   THEATRE, CINEMA
(📞 01539-725133; www.breweryarts.co.uk; Highgate) A cracking arts centre with a gallery, cafe, theatre and two cinemas, hosting the latest films as well as music, theatre, dance and much more.

Shopping

Low Sizergh Barn   FOOD
(📞 01539-560426; www.lowsizerghbarn.co.uk; A590; ⊙ 9am-5.30pm) A prodigious selection of Lakeland goodies is available at this farm shop, just outside Kendal. Look for the raw-milk vending machine beside the shop entrance. Only in Cumbria!

❶ Getting There & Away

The train line from Windermere runs to Kendal (£5.70, 15 minutes, hourly) en route to Oxenholme.

Bus 555/556 Regular bus (half-hourly Monday to Friday, hourly at weekends) to Windermere (£6.70, 30 minutes), Ambleside (£7.80, 40 minutes) and Grasmere (£10, 1¼ hours).

Bus 106 To Penrith (£11.50, one hour 20 minutes, one or two daily Monday to Friday).

CUMBRIAN COAST

📞 01229

While the central lakes and fells pull in a never-ending stream of visitors, surprisingly few make the trek west to explore Cumbria's coastline – and that's a shame. While it might not compare to the wild grandeur of Northumberland, or the rugged splendour of Scotland's shores, Cumbria's coast is well worth exploring – a bleakly beautiful landscape of long sandy bays, grassy headlands, salt marshes and seaside villages stretching from Morecambe Bay to the shores of the Solway Coast. There's an important seabird reserve at St Bees Head, and the grounds of Holker Hall are well worth a wander.

Historically, Cumbria's coast served the local mining, quarrying and shipping industries. Barrow-in-Furness remains a major shipbuilding centre, while the nuclear plant of Sellafield continues to divide local opinion more than half a century from its inception.

◉ Sights & Activities

★ Holker Hall   HISTORIC BUILDING
(📞 01539-558328; www.holker.co.uk; adult/child £18/free, gardens only £9; ⊙ house 10.30am-4pm Wed-Sun) Three miles southwest of Cartmel on the B5278, Holker Hall has been the family seat of the Cavendish family for four centuries. The house was almost entirely rebuilt following a devastating fire in 1871. It's a typically ostentatious Victorian affair: mullioned windows, gables, copper-topped turrets and a warren of rooms. The showstopper is the **Long Gallery**, notable for its plasterwork ceiling and fine English furniture.

Other highlights are the **drawing room**, packed with Chippendale furniture and historic oil paintings, and the **library**, containing an antique microscope belonging to Henry Cavendish (discoverer of nitric acid) and more than 3500 antique books (some of which are fakes, designed to conceal light switches when the house was converted to electric power in 1911).

Holker's grounds sprawl for more than 10 hectares, encompassing a rose garden, woodland, ornamental fountains and a 22m-high lime tree.

There's also a food hall that stocks produce from the estate, including two renowned products: venison and salt marsh lamb.

St Bees Head   WILDLIFE RESERVE
(RSPB; stbees.head@rspb.org.uk) Located 1½ miles north of the tiny town of St Bees, this wind-battered headland is an important reserve for seabirds. Depending on the season, species nesting here include fulmars, kittiwakes and razorbills, as well as Britain's only population of resident black guillemots. There are more than 2 miles of cliff paths to explore.

Muncaster Castle   CASTLE
(📞 01229-717614; www.muncaster.co.uk; adult/child £18/9; ⊙ gardens & owl centre 10.30am-5pm, castle noon-4pm Sun-Fri) This crenellated

castle, 1.5 miles east of Ravenglass, was originally built around a 14th-century pele tower, constructed to resist Reiver raids. Home to the Pennington family for seven centuries, the castle is visitable on a guided tour. The architectural highlights are the great hall and octagonal library. Outside you'll find an ornamental maze and splendid grounds, as well as a hawk and owl centre, which stages several flying displays a day. Tickets can be prebooked online.

Muncaster is also known for its numerous ghosts: keep your eyes peeled for the Muncaster Boggle and a malevolent jester known as Tom Fool (hence 'tomfoolery').

Laurel & Hardy Museum MUSEUM
(☑01229-582292; www.laurel-and-hardy.co.uk; Brogden St, Ulverston; adult/child £6/3; ⊙10am-5pm Easter-Oct) Founded by avid Laurel and Hardy collector Bill Cubin back in 1983, this madcap museum in Ulverston (the birthplace of Stan Laurel) is located in the town's old Roxy cinema. It's crammed with cinematic memorabilia, from original posters to film props, and there's a shoebox-sized cinema showing back-to-back Laurel and Hardy classics. Now run by Bill's grandson, it's a must for movie buffs.

★**Ravenglass & Eskdale Railway** RAIL
(☑01229-717171; www.ravenglass-railway.co.uk; adult/child return £18/12; 🚻) Affectionately known as La'al Ratty, this pocket-sized railway was built to ferry iron ore from the Eskdale mines to the coast. It's now one of Cumbria's most beloved family attractions, with miniature steam trains that chug for 7 miles through the Eskdale valley between Ravenglass and the village of Dalegarth, stopping at stations in between.

ℹ️ **Getting There & Away**

The Furness and Cumbrian Coast railway lines loop 120 miles from Lancaster to Carlisle, stopping at the coastal towns of Grange, Ulverston, Ravenglass, Whitehaven and Workington. The **Cumbria Coast Day Ranger** (adult/child £20.20/10.10) covers a day's unlimited travel on the line and works out cheaper than a return journey from Carlisle or Lancaster.

NORTHERN & EASTERN CUMBRIA

Many visitors speed through the northern and eastern reaches of Cumbria in a headlong dash for the Lake District, but it's worth taking the time to venture inland from the national park. It might not have the big-name fells and chocolate-box villages, but it's full of interest, with traditional towns, crumbling castles, abandoned abbeys and sweeping moors set alongside the magnificent Roman engineering project of Hadrian's Wall.

Carlisle

☑01228 / POP 75,306
Carlisle isn't Britain's prettiest city, but it has history and heritage aplenty. Precariously perched on the frontier between England and Scotland, in the area once ominously dubbed the 'Debatable Lands', Cumbria's capital is a city with a notoriously stormy past: sacked by the Vikings, pillaged by the Scots and plundered by the Border Reivers, the city has been on the front line of England's defences for more than 1000 years.

Reminders of the past are evident in its great crimson castle and cathedral, built from the same rosy-red sandstone as most of the city's houses. On English St, you can also see two massive circular towers that once flanked the city's gateway.

The closest section of Hadrian's Wall begins at nearby Brampton.

◉ Sights

★**Carlisle Castle** CASTLE
(EH; ☑01228-591922; www.english-heritage.org.uk/visit/places/carlisle-castle; Castle Way; adult/child £11.20/6.40; ⊙10am-5pm) Carlisle's brooding, rust-red castle guards the city's north side. Founded around a Celtic and Roman stronghold, the castle's Norman keep was added in 1092 by William Rufus and refortified by Henry II, Edward I and Henry VIII (who added the supposedly cannon-proof towers). From the battlements, the stirring views stretch as far as the Scottish borders. The castle also houses Cumbria's Museum of Military Life, which has military memorabilia associated with the region's regiments. At the time of research tickets had to be prebooked online.

Carlisle Cathedral CHURCH
(☑01228-548151; www.carlislecathedral.org.uk; 7 The Abbey; suggested donation £3; ⊙10am-3pm Mon-Sat, noon-3pm Sun) Built from the same red sandstone as Carlisle Castle, Carlisle's cathedral began life as a priory church in

1122 and became a cathedral when its first abbot, Athelwold, became the first bishop of Carlisle. Among its notable features are the 15th-century choir stalls, the barrel-vaulted roof and the 14th-century East Window, one of the largest Gothic windows in England. Surrounding the cathedral are other priory relics, including the 16th-century fratry and the prior's tower.

A striking wing houses the cathedral's cafe, with views over the cathedral's grounds.

Tullie House Museum   MUSEUM
(☑ 01228-618718; www.tulliehouse.co.uk; Castle St; adult/child £10/free; ⊙10am-3pm Tue-Sat) Carlisle's flagship museum covers 2000 years of the city's past. The Roman Frontier Gallery explores Carlisle's Roman foundations, while the Border Galleries explore the city's past, from prehistoric settlers through to the Vikings and Border Reivers. There are some fascinating artefacts on display, including finds from the Cumwhitton Viking cemetery, which revealed a haul of helmets, swords and grave goods. The top-floor Lookout has cracking views of the castle.

A separate part inside Old Tullie House displays decorative art, sculpture and porcelain.

🛏 Sleeping

Carlisle's accommodation leaves a lot to be desired. The B&Bs in the centre are uninspiring, so you're better off heading further out.

★ Willowbeck Lodge   B&B ££
(☑ 01228-513607; www.willowbeck-lodge.com; Lambley Bank, Scotby; d £115-165; P🖥🛜) If staying in the city centre isn't important, then this palatial B&B is Carlisle's top choice. The four rooms are huge, contemporary and plush, with luxuries such as underfloor heating, Egyptian-cotton bedding and tasteful shades of beige and taupe. Some rooms have balconies overlooking the gardens and pond.

★ Halston Aparthotel   HOTEL £££
(☑ 01228-210240; www.thehalston.com; 20-34 Warwick Rd; 1-bed apt £140-165, 2-bed apt £240-280; P🛜) Housed in the former general post office, this complex of self-catering apartments is Carlisle's best place to stay. While not huge, the apartments are well appointed with small studio kitchens, and the decor combines parquet-style flooring,

OFF THE BEATEN TRACK

HIDDEN RIVER CAFE & CABINS

A piece of Canada comes to Cumbria at this rustic lodge complex (☑ 01228-791318; www.hiddenrivercabins.co.uk; Longtown, Carlisle; cabins from £430), which offers timber-built log cabins that look like something out of *Jeremiah Johnson*. They're very private and quite luxurious, with slate floors, proper bathrooms and outdoor hot tubs. The excellent cafe (mains £10 to £15) is worth the trip even if you're not staying. It's 11 miles north of Carlisle.

sleek furniture and neutral-toned fabrics. For dining, there's Bartons Yard for tapas and bistro dishes, and Penny Blue for light bites and cakes.

Warwick Hall   B&B £££
(☑ 01228-561546; www.warwickhall.co.uk; Warwick-on-Eden; r £128-180) This country house, 2 miles from the centre along Warwick Rd, is a real retreat. With its huge rooms, high ceilings and old-fashioned decor, it feels like staying on an aristocratic friend's estate. There are hectares of grounds and even a private stretch of river for fishing.

🍴 Eating

★ David's   BRITISH ££
(☑ 01228-523578; www.davidsrestaurant.co.uk; 62 Warwick Rd; 2-/3-course menus lunch £17.95/22.95, dinner £22.95/27.95; ⊙noon-1.30pm & 6-9pm Tue-Sat) For many years this town-house restaurant has been the address for formal dining in Carlisle. It majors in rich, traditional dishes with a strong French influence: duo of venison, pan-fried turbot, roast chicken with champ mash. The feel is formal, so dress appropriately. À la carte only on Friday and Saturday evenings.

Coco Mill   GASTROPUB ££
(☑ 01228-318559; www.cocomill.co.uk; 47-49 Lowther St; mains £12-20; ⊙noon-11pm) This shabby-stylish gastropub is a welcome addition to the city centre. Chunky wood, worn sofas and old bits of luggage characterise the decor. There's a good beer and wine selection, and plenty of easy-eating dishes (steaks, chicken katsu, honey salmon and generous platters). The veggie range is good, too.

Thin White Duke BISTRO ££
(📞01228-402334; www.thinwhiteduke.info; 1 Devonshire St; mains £8.95-14.95; ⊙11.45am-11pm)
This central 'eating and drinking abode' is housed in a former monastery. The menu is mainly burgers, wraps and gastropub classics – chicken-in-a-basket, battered haddock, pork belly– and there are some inventively named cocktails (the Tom Hardy – 'slicker than Tom in Inception').

❶ Information

Carlisle Tourist Office (📞01228-598596; www.discovercarlisle.co.uk; Greenmarket; ⊙9.30am-5pm Mon-Sat, 10.30am-4pm Sun)

❶ Getting There & Away

AIR

From Carlisle's tiny **airport** (www.carlisleairport.co.uk), 8 miles northeast of the centre, **Loganair** (www.loganair.co.uk) operates flights to/from London Southend, Dublin and Belfast.

BUS

Bus 554 goes to Keswick (£9.40, one hour 10 minutes, four daily Monday to Saturday, three on Sunday) and bus 104 goes to Penrith (£6.50, 40 minutes, half-hourly Monday to Saturday, nine on Sunday).

TRAIN

Carlisle is on the west-coast line from London to Glasgow. It's also the terminus for the scenic Cumbrian Coast and Tyne Valley lines, as well as the historic **Settle to Carlisle Railway** (www.settle-carlisle.co.uk; adult return £26.90) across the Yorkshire Dales (check the website for steam train trip schedules).

Glasgow £19.10, 1¼ hours
Lancaster £13.40, 45 minutes
London Euston £84.50, 3½ hours
Manchester £43.60, two hours 10 minutes
Newcastle-upon-Tyne £17.50, 1½ hours

Penrith

📞01768 / POP 15,181
Just outside the Lake District National Park, red-brick Penrith perhaps has more in common with the stout market towns of the Yorkshire Dales. It's a solid, traditional place with plenty of cosy pubs and quaint teashops and a lively market on Tuesdays. It's also the main gateway for exploring the picturesque Eden Valley and the remote area around Haweswater, an artificial reservoir created in 1935.

The ruins of Penrith's 14th-century castle loom on the edge of town, opposite the train station.

◉ Sights

★**Lowther Castle & Gardens** HISTORIC SITE
(📞01931-712192; www.lowthercastle.org; adult/child £11/7; ⊙10am-5pm) Six miles south of Penrith, this sprawling country estate, once the ancestral home of the powerful Lowther dynasty, is undergoing a huge, multimillion-pound restoration project. Though the castle itself is to remain a ruin, restoration work is breathing life back into the gardens, which fell into disrepair following WWII. Among the areas to visit are the Iris Garden, the Great Yew Walk, a restored parterre and many hidden follies, lakes and woodland areas. Bikes are available for hire.

A fantasy land of turrets and mock battlements, the house itself was commissioned in 1806 by William, first Earl of Lonsdale, but a combination of chronic mismanagement, debts and death duties meant that in 1957, James Lonsdale, the seventh Earl, stripped it for parts. Practically everything, including all its furnishings and even the castle's roof, was sold. Now an empty shell, it's an atmospheric monument to the plummeting fortunes of one of Cumbria's oldest and most powerful families.

🛏 Sleeping

Lounge HOTEL ££
(📞01768-866395; www.theloungehotelandbar.co.uk; King St; d/f from £88/115; 🛜) For a town-centre hotel at reasonable prices, you can't do any better than this chic little number. Pine furniture, laminate floors and tasteful tints of pistachio, cream and taupe feel a tad generic, but it's chintz-free and central. The three-bed apartment (£180) has its own mini-kitchen. Breakfast and dinner is served in the ground-floor bistro.

Brooklands B&B ££
(📞01768-863395; www.brooklandsguesthouse.com; 2 Portland Pl; s £50-85, d £95-105; 🛜) An upmarket B&B in a terrace of red-brick houses. It's Victorian outside, but inside it has fancy furnishings and posh extras such as White Company toiletries, in-room fridges and chocolates on the tea tray. There's a four-poster room, too.

George Hotel HOTEL £££
(📞01768-862696; www.thegeorgehotelpenrith.co.uk; Devonshire St; d £119-159; 🅿🛜) Penrith's

venerable red-brick coaching inn offers rather old-fashioned rooms, plus a quaint bar and restaurant. It's not quite the heritage beauty it might appear to be at first glance – rooms are comfortable enough, but disappointingly bland.

✖ Eating

Pick up picnic supplies at Penrith's lovely old grocer and victuals shop, **JJ Graham** (☎ 01768-862281; www.jjgraham.co.uk; 6-7 Market Sq; ⊗ 8.30am-5.30pm Mon-Sat).

★ Four & Twenty
BISTRO ££
(☎ 01768-210231; www.fourandtwentypenrith.co.uk; 14 King St; 2-/3-course lunch menu £18/23, dinner menu £20/25; ⊗ noon-2.30pm & 6-9.30pm Tue-Sat) Penrith's top place to eat is this welcoming, surprisingly swish bistro. A spacious dining room filled with wooden furniture, big windows and banquette seats, and a flavoursome menu that goes big on country flavours – things such as slow-cooked lamb, potted wild boar terrine and ale-braised beef. À la carte only on Friday and Saturday night.

George & Dragon
PUB FOOD ££
(☎ 01768-865381; www.georgeanddragonclifton.co.uk; Clifton; mains £14-21; ⊗ food served noon-2.30pm & 5-8.15pm) If you don't mind a drive (3½ miles from Penrith), this pretty pub in the village of Clifton makes a super stop. It's situated on the Lowther Estate (p596) and sources much of its produce (including game) from there. Fires, benches and rafters make for a cosy setting and the food is extremely good.

For something more upmarket, the pub's sister restaurant, **Allium at Askham Hall** (☎ 01931-712350; www.askhamhall.co.uk; Askham; dinner menu £75; ⊗ 6-10pm Tue-Sat), is now Michelin starred.

ℹ Information

Penrith Tourist Office (☎ 01768-867466; pen.tic@eden.gov.uk; Middlegate; ⊗ 10am-4pm Mon & Thu-Sat) Also houses the town's small museum.

ℹ Getting There & Away

There are frequent train connections north to Carlisle (£6.30, 15 minutes) and south to Oxenholme (£7.50, 25 minutes), where you can change for branch trains to Windermere.

The bus station is northeast of the centre, off Sandgate. Bus 104 goes to Carlisle (£6.50, 40 minutes, half-hourly Monday to Saturday, nine on Sunday), and bus X4/X5 goes to the Cumbrian coast (£7 to £11.40, half-hourly Monday to Saturday, hourly Sunday) via Rheged, Keswick and Cockermouth.

598

1. Cyclists on Monsal Trail (p459), Peak District National Park 2. Haystacks (p589), Lake District 3. Horse riding, Dartmoor National Park (p313) 4. Surfer, Devon (p295)

ANDY J BILLINGTON/SHUTTERSTOCK ©

DUNCAN ANDISON/SHUTTERSTOCK ©

2

England's Great Outdoors

The English love the great outdoors. Every weekend sees a mass exodus to the hills, moors and coastline. Walking and cycling are popular pursuits, but there's a huge range of activities. Getting wet and muddy in one of England's beautiful wild places might actually be a highlight of your trip.

Walking

England can seem crowded, but away from the cities there are many beautiful areas, perfect for walking. You can go for a short riverside stroll or a major hike over mountain ranges – or anything in between. The best places include the Cotswolds, Sussex, the Lake District and the Yorkshire Dales.

Cycling

A bike is ideal for getting to know England's countryside. Areas such as Suffolk, Yorkshire and Wiltshire offer a vast network of quiet country roads, disused train lines and marked cycle routes that are ideal for cycle touring. For off-road fun, mountain bikers can go further into the wilds: the Peak District, the North Yorkshire Moors and the South Downs. For the latest cycle adventure, look up King Alfred's Way, which passes Stonehenge.

Horse Riding

If you want to explore the hills and moors at a more leisurely pace, seeing the wilder parts of England from horseback is the way to go. In rural areas and national parks such as Dartmoor and Northumberland there are riding centres catering to all levels of proficiency.

Surfing

England may not be an obvious destination for surfers, but conditions can be surprisingly good at key locations. Top of the list are the west-facing coasts of Cornwall and Devon, while there are smaller scenes on the east coast, notably in Norfolk and Yorkshire.

4

Bamburgh Castle (p629)

Newcastle & Northeast England

Irrepressible Newcastle-upon-Tyne anchors England's northeast. Handsome Victorian buildings adorn the steep hills of this former industrial powerhouse. Galleries, museums, bars and entertainment venues now occupy the city's former factories and warehouses; Newcastle's nightlife is legendary.

Newcastle is also an ideal gateway for exploring the northeast's wild, starkly beautiful countryside. Inland, seek out the Cheviot Hills in brooding Northumberland National Park and the remote North Pennines, or explore spectacular Hadrian's Wall, which cuts a lonely path through the landscape, dotted with dramatic fortress ruins. The stunning coastline is the north's greatest surprise, a little-known succession of long, desolate beaches, windworn castles and magical islands offshore.

INCLUDES

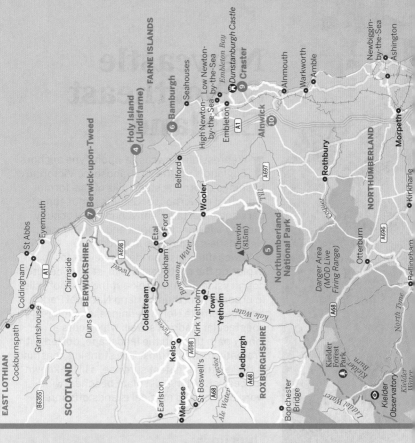

Newcastle & Northeast England Highlights

1 Hadrian's Wall (p617)
Hiking along the remains of Britain's mightiest Roman legacy.

2 Durham (p612)
Exploring the medieval core of one of the north's most atmospheric towns.

3 Newcastle-upon-Tyne (p605)
Falling in love with this gutsy, artsy, style-conscious and vibrant city.

4 Holy Island (Lindisfarne) (p629) Crossing the causeway to reach this other-worldly pilgrimage site.

5 Northumberland National Park (p623)
Exploring the wild back-country of

	20 km
	10 miles

NORTH SEA

FARNE ISLANDS

4 Holy Island (Lindisfarne)

6 Bamburgh

Seahouses

High Newton-by-the-Sea Low Newton-by-the-Sea

Embleton Bay

8 Dunstanburgh Castle

Embleton

9 Craster

A1

10 Alnwick

Alnmouth

Warkworth

Amble

Newbiggin-by-the-Sea

Ashington

7 Berwick-upon-Tweed

St Abbs

Eyemouth

Coldingham

EAST LOTHIAN

Cockburnspath

Grantshouse

SCOTLAND

Chirnside

Duns

B6355

A1

BERWICKSHIRE

Tweed

A698

Etal

Ford

Crookham

Bowmont Water

Wooler

Belford

Till

A697

NORTHUMBERLAND

Rothbury

Coquet

Morpeth

Kirkharle

A696

Earlston

Melrose

Kelso

St Boswell's

A68

A698

Teviot

Town Yetholm

Kirk Yetholm

Kale Water

Cheviot (815m)

5 Northumberland National Park

Danger Area (MOD Live Firing Range)

A68

Otterburn

Ale Water

Jedburgh

A68

ROXBURGHSHIRE

Bonchester Bridge

North Tyne

Bellingham

Kielder Forest Park

Kielder Burn

Liddel Water

Kielder Water

Kielder Observatory

This is a map of the North East England region, showing cities, towns, and points of interest.

Key locations and features include:

National Parks and areas:
- North York Moors National Park
- Yorkshire Dales National Park
- NORTH YORKSHIRE
- DURHAM
- CUMBRIA
- The Pennines

Cities and towns:
Loftus, Danby, Castleton, Saltburn-by-the-Sea, Guisborough, Redcar, Middlesbrough, Hartlepool, Billingham, Stokesley, Eaglescliffe, Stockton-on-Tees, Seaham, Peterlee, Sunderland, South Shields, Tynemouth, Whitley Bay, Darlington, Huworth-on-Tees, Northallerton, Catterick, Sedgefield, Bishop Auckland, Shildon, Croxdale, Summerhouse, Pierce Bridge, Richmond, Bedale, Reeth, Durham, Stanley, Newcastle upon Tyne, Wallsend, Ponteland, Belsay, Corbridge, Hexham, Consett, Knitsley, Crook, West Auckland, Hamsterley Forest, Raby Castle, Barnard Castle, Bowes Castle, Teesdale, Wolsingham, Frosterley, Stanhope, Edmundbyers, Hedley on the Hill, Blanchland, Allendale Town, Allenheads, Killhope, Nenthead, Alston, Ireshopeburn, Langdon Beck, Newbiggin, Middleton-in-Teesdale, Brough, Kirkby Stephen, Coupland, Appleby, Newbiggin-on-Line, Tebay, Haltwhistle, Hawes, Angel of the North, Newcastle International Airport

Rivers and water features:
Seven, Esk, Leven, Tees, Wear, South Tyne, Tyne, Derwent Reservoir, Great, Eden, Ais Gill

Roads:
A171, A174, A19, A1, A67, A68, A686, A66, A683, B6278, B6270, M6, Pennine Way, Buttertubs Pass, Hadrian's Wall

Numbered points of interest:
- 1 Hadrian's Wall
- 2 Durham
- 3 Newcastle-upon-Tyne
- 6 Bamburgh Castle (p629)
- 7 Berwick Walls (p631)
- 8 Bowes Museum (p616)
- 8 Barnard Castle
- 9 Craster (p627)
- 10 Alnwick (p625)

Carlisle (20mi)

6 Bamburgh Castle (p629)
Returning to the past at Northumberland's most spectacular castle.

7 Berwick Walls (p631)
Circumnavigating the Elizabethan walls of England's northernmost city, Berwick-upon-Tweed.

8 Bowes Museum (p616)
Viewing extraordinary objets d'art in the chateau-housed museum at Barnard Castle.

9 Craster (p627)
Walking along the wild and beautiful coast to reach one of the north's most haunting ruins.

10 Alnwick (p625)
Discovering the charming village of Alnwick with its storied bookshop and Harry Potter's Hogwarts, aka Alnwick Castle.

England's last great wilderness.

History

Violent history has shaped this region more than any other in England, primarily because of its frontier position. Hadrian's Wall marked the northern limit of Roman Britain and was the Empire's most heavily fortified line. Following the Romans' departure, the region became part of the Anglian kingdom of Bernicia, which united with the kingdom of Deira (encompassing much of modern-day Yorkshire) to form Northumbria in 604.

The kingdom changed hands and borders shifted several times over the next 500 years as Anglo-Saxons and Danes struggled to seize it. The land north of the River Tweed was finally ceded to Scotland in 1018, while the nascent kingdom of England kept everything below it.

The arrival of the Normans in 1066 saw William I eager to secure his northern borders against the Scots. He commissioned most of the castles you see along the coast, and cut deals with the prince bishops of Durham to ensure their loyalty. The new lords of Northumberland became very powerful because, as Marcher Lords (from 'march' as a synonym of 'border'), they kept the Scots at bay.

Northumberland's reputation as a hotbed of rebellion was well-earned during the Tudor years, when the largely Catholic north, led by the seventh duke of Northumberland, Thomas Percy, rose up against Elizabeth I in the defeated Rising of the North in 1569. The Border Reivers, raiders from both sides of the border in the 16th century, kept the region in a perpetual state of lawlessness that only subsided after the Act of Union between England and Scotland in 1707.

Coal mines were key to the 19th-century industrialisation of the northeast, powering steelworks, shipyards and armament works that rose along the Tyne and Tees. In 1825, the mines also spawned the world's first steam railway, the Stockton & Darlington, built by local engineer George Stephenson. Social strife emerged in the 20th century, however, with mines, shipbuilding, steel production and the railway industries all winding down during the Great Depression and postwar years. Reinventing the northeast has been a mammoth task, but regeneration continues.

Activities

Cycling

The northeast has some of England's most inspiring cycle routes.

Part of the National Cycle Network (NCN), a long-time favourite is the 200-mile **Coast & Castles Cycle Route** (www.coast-and-castles.co.uk), which runs south–north along the glorious Northumberland coast between Newcastle-upon-Tyne and Berwick-upon-Tweed and Edinburgh, Scotland.

The 140-mile **Sea to Sea Cycle Route** (www.c2c-guide.co.uk/route/C2C-Guide) runs across northern England between the Cumbrian coast (St Bees, Whitehaven or Workington) and Tynemouth or Sunderland via the northern Lake District and wild North Pennines' hills.

Another coast-to-coast option is **Hadrian's Cycleway** (www.hadrian-guide.co.uk), a 174-mile route between South Shields or Tynemouth and Ravenglass in Cumbria following the route of Hadrian's Wall.

Also running coast to coast is the 173-mile **Reivers Route** (www.reivers-route.co.uk) from Whitehaven to Tynemouth via Kielder Forest, the Scottish Borders and the Lake District.

Walking

The North Pennines – along with the Cheviots further north – are considered England's last wilderness. Northumberland National Park (p623) in particular has some fine trails.

Long routes through the hills include the famous **Pennine Way** (www.nationaltrail.co.uk/en_GB/trails/pennine-way), Britain's first national trail, established in 1965, which keeps mainly to the high ground between the Yorkshire Dales and the Scottish border, but also crosses sections of river valley and some tedious patches of plantation. The whole route is 268 miles, but the 70-mile section between Bowes and Hadrian's Wall is a fine four-day taster.

Hadrian's Wall has a huge range of easy loop walks taking in forts and other historical highlights. One of the finest walks along the windswept **Northumberland coast**, between the villages of Craster and Bamburgh via Dunstanburgh, includes two of the region's most spectacular castles. Another superb coastal trail is the 30-mile **Berwickshire Coastal Path** (www.walkhighlands.co.uk/borders/berwickshire-coastal-path.shtml) from Berwick-upon-Tweed to Cockburnspath in Scotland.

Getting There & Around

BUS

Bus transport around the region can be sporadic, particularly around the more remote reaches of western Northumberland. Contact **Traveline** (✉ 0871-200 2233; www.travelinenortheast.info; ⏰ 7am-10pm) for information on connections, timetables and prices.

TRAIN

The East Coast Main Line runs north from London King's Cross to Edinburgh via Durham, Newcastle and Berwick; Northern Rail operates local and interurban services in the north, including west to Carlisle.

There are numerous Rover tickets for single-day travel and longer periods; check www.networkonetickets.co.uk.

Newcastle-upon-Tyne

✆ 0191 / POP 293,200

Against a dramatic backdrop of Victorian elegance and industry, this fiercely independent city harbours a spirited mix of heritage and urban grit and sophistication. It's a city with attitude yet filled with culture, excellent art galleries and a magnificent concert hall, along with boutique hotels, some exceptional restaurants and, of course, interesting bars: Newcastle is renowned throughout Britain for its thumping nightlife. The city retains deep-rooted traditions, embodied by the no-nonsense, likeable locals.

Allow at least a couple of days to explore the Victorian city centre and quayside areas along the Tyne and across the river in Gateshead, as well as the rejuvenated Ouseburn Valley to the east, gentrified Jesmond to the north, and, on the coast, the surf beaches of Tynemouth.

◉ Sights

◉ City Centre

Newcastle's grand Victorian centre, a compact area bordered roughly by Grainger St to the west and Pilgrim St to the east, is one of the most compelling examples of urban rejuvenation in England. Down by the quays are the city's most recognisable attractions, including the iconic bridges that span the Tyne and the striking buildings that flank it.

★**Discovery Museum**   MUSEUM
(✆ 0191-232 6789; www.discoverymuseum.org.uk; Blandford Sq; ⏰ 10am-4pm Mon-Fri, 11am-4pm Sat & Sun) FREE Tyneside's rich history is explored at this unmissable museum. Exhibitions spread across three floors of the former Co-operative Wholesale Society building

around the mightily impressive 30m-long *Turbinia*, the fastest ship in the world in 1897 and the first to be powered by steam turbine. Other highlights are a section on shipbuilding on the Tyne, with a scale model of the river in 1929, and the 'Story of Newcastle', spanning the city's history from Pons Aelius (Roman Newcastle) to Cheryl Cole.

★**Life Science Centre**   MUSEUM
(✆ 0191-243 8210; www.life.org.uk; Times Sq; adult/child £15/8; ⏰ 10am-6pm Mon-Sat, 11am-6pm Sun) Part of a sober-minded institute devoted to the study of genetic science, this centre lets you discover the secrets of life through a fascinating series of hands-on exhibits. The highlight is the Motion Ride, a simulator that lets you 'experience' bungee jumping and the like (the 4D film changes every year). There are lots of thought-provoking arcade-style games, and if the information sometimes gets lost along the way, no-one seems to mind. Book ahead at busy times.

Mornings on school days see it filled with groups; visit after 2pm to avoid the crowds.

Great North Museum   MUSEUM
(✆ 0191-208 6765; www.greatnorthmuseum.org.uk; Barras Bridge; general admission free, planetarium adult/child £3.75/2; ⏰ 10am-5pm Mon-Fri, 10am-4pm Sat, 11am-4pm Sun) FREE The contents of Newcastle University's museums and the prestigious Hancock Museum's natural-history exhibits come together in the latter's neoclassical building. The result is a fascinating jumble of dinosaurs, Roman altar stones, Egyptian mummies, samurai warriors and impressive taxidermy. Standout exhibits include a life-size Tyrannosaurus rex recreation and an interactive model of Hadrian's Wall showing every milecastle and fortress. There's also lots of hands-on stuff for kids and a planetarium with screenings throughout the day.

Newcastle Castle   CASTLE
(✆ 0191-230 6300; www.newcastlecastle.co.uk; Castle Garth; adult/child £8.50/5; ⏰ 10am-5pm) The stronghold that put both the 'new' and 'castle' into Newcastle has been largely swallowed up by the train station, leaving only a few remaining fragments including the square Norman keep and the Black Gate. Exhibits inside the two restored buildings cover the history of the city, its castle and its residents from Roman times onwards. The 360-degree city views from the keep's rooftop are the best in town.

Newcastle-upon-Tyne

Map labels:

Boating Lake
Leazes Park
Barras Bridge
B1307 · Jesmond (1mi)
Haymarket
John Dobson St
Durant Rd
Haymarket Bus Station
Eldon Sq Bus Station
New Bridge St
5
Barrack Rd · 21
Strawberry Pl
Percy St
Leazes La
Eldon Sq
Blackett St
Monument
Market St
Central Mwy
St James
Gallowgate
Newgate St
Clayton St
Grainger St
Grey St
Pilgrim St
Worswick St
Carliol Sq · 20
Wellington St
Corporation St
Stowell St
22
18
12
High Bridge
Shakespeare St
Bath La
10 · Friars St
Bigg Market
Groat Market
Grey St
7
Westgate Rd
Clayton St
St Nicholas Sq
Dean St
Castle Garth
Queen St
Blandford Sq
Waterloo St
Clayton St
Neville St
Collingwood St
St Nicholas St
Westgate Rd
6
9
14
Discovery Museum · 2
St James' Blvd
17
16
Central Station
Castle Sq · 15
Sandhill
19
Life Science Centre · 3
National Express Coach Station
Churchill St
Scotswood Rd
Times Sq
Hanover Gardens · 13
Hanover St
The Close
High Level Bridge
Swing Bridge
Forth St
Railway Forth St

Laing Art Gallery GALLERY

(☎0191-278 1611; www.laingartgallery.org.uk; New Bridge St; ⊙10am-4.30pm Mon-Sat) FREE The collection here includes works by Gainsborough, Gauguin and Henry Moore, and an important collection of paintings by Northumberland-born artist John Martin (1789–1854). Check the 'What's On' section of the website for events including talks and tours. Temporary exhibitions may incur a charge.

Biscuit Factory GALLERY

(www.thebiscuitfactory.com; 16 Stoddart St; ⊙10am-5pm Mon-Fri, 10am-6pm Sat, 11am-5pm Sun) FREE No prizes for guessing what this commercial art gallery used to be. These days, it's the UK's biggest contemporary art, craft and design gallery/shop, where you can browse and/or buy works by more than 200 artists each season in a variety of mediums, including painting, sculpture, glassware and furniture, many with a northeast theme. There's an on-site cafe, the Factory Kitchen, and fine-dining restaurant, Artisan.

◉ Ouseburn Valley

Now semi-regenerated, Newcastle's 19th-century industrial heartland, Ouseburn Valley, one mile east of the city centre,

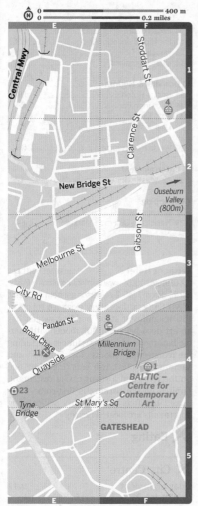

has potteries, glass-blowing studios and other creative workspaces, along with pubs, bars and entertainment venues.

★**Victoria Tunnel**   HISTORIC SITE
(☑0191-230 4210; www.ouseburntrust.org.uk; Victoria Tunnel Visitor Centre, 55 Lime St; tours adult/child £8/4.50; ⊙by reservation) Walking Newcastle's streets, you'd never know this extraordinary tunnel runs for 2.5 miles beneath your feet. Built between 1839 and 1842 as a coal-wagon thoroughfare, it was used as an air-raid shelter during WWII. Volunteer-led two-hour tours take you through an atmospheric 700m-long level section of the tunnel. Book ahead as numbers are limited, and wear good shoes and a washable jacket for the limewashed walls; it's not suitable for kids under seven. Tours finish back at Victoria Visitor Centre.

Special one-hour family tours (including for under-sevens) operate during school holidays.

Seven Stories – The Centre for Children's Books   MUSEUM
(www.sevenstories.org.uk; 30 Lime St; adult/child £7.70/6.60; ⊙10am-5pm Tue-Sat, to 4pm Sun) A marvellous conversion of a handsome Victorian mill has resulted in Seven Stories, a hands-on museum dedicated to the wondrous world of children's literature. Across the seven floors you'll find original manuscripts and artwork from the 1930s onwards, and a constantly changing program of child-oriented exhibitions, activities and events designed to encourage the AA Milnes of the new millennium. There's a bookshop, coffee shop and cafe.

◉ Gateshead

★**BALTIC – Centre for Contemporary Art**   GALLERY
(☑0191-478 1810; www.baltic.art; Gateshead Quays; ⊙10.30am-6pm) FREE Once a huge mustard-coloured grain store, Baltic is now a huge mustard-coloured art gallery rivalling London's Tate Modern. There are no permanent exhibitions; instead, rotating shows feature the work and installations of some of contemporary art's biggest show-stoppers. The complex has artists in residence, a performance space, a cinema, a bar, a spectacular rooftop restaurant (bookings essential) and a ground-floor restaurant with riverside tables.

A 4th-floor outdoor platform and 5th-floor viewing box offer fabulous panoramas of the Tyne.

🛌 Sleeping

Newcastle Jesmond Hotel   HOTEL **£**
(☑0191-239 9943; www.newcastlejesmondhotel. co.uk; 105 Osborne Rd; s/d from £38/45; P🗐) Rooms are smallish at this refurbished red-brick property footsteps from the bars and restaurants of Osborne Rd, but they're cosy, comfy and spotlessly clean, and come with the bonus of free parking (though spaces are limited, so reserve one when you book). Wi-fi can be patchy.

Newcastle-upon-Tyne

Grey Street Hotel　　　　BOUTIQUE HOTEL **£**
(☑️0191-230 6777; www.greystreethotel.co.uk; 2-12 Grey St; d/ste from £49.50/67.50; ✳️🐾🐕) On the city centre's most elegant street, this beautiful Grade II–listed former bank has been adapted for contemporary needs, including triple glazing on the sash windows, wall-sized murals and splashes of colour. Its 49 individually designed rooms have big beds and stylish colour combinations; some have giant black-and-white photographs covering one wall.

★Jesmond Dene House　　BOUTIQUE HOTEL **££**
(☑️0191-212 3000; www.jesmonddenehouse.co.uk; Jesmond Dene Rd; d from £125; 🅿️✳️@🐕) Large bedrooms at this exquisite 40-room property are furnished in a modern interpretation of the Arts and Crafts style and have stunning bathrooms complete with underfloor heating, as well as the latest tech; some have private terraces. The fine-dining restaurant is sublime; dinner, bed and breakfast packages are available.

Malmaison　　　　　　BOUTIQUE HOTEL **££**
(☑️0191-389 8627; www.malmaison.com; 104 Quayside; d/ste from £75/105; 🅿️✳️🐕) The affectedly stylish Malmaison touch has been applied to this former warehouse with considerable success, even down to the French-speaking lifts. Big beds, sleek lighting and designer furniture embellish the 122 plush rooms. The best rooms have views of the Millennium Bridge. There's a spa, gym and on-site brasserie.

Vermont Hotel　　　　　HERITAGE HOTEL **£££**
(☑️0191-233 1010; www.vermont-hotel.com; Castle Garth; d from £145, 2-/4-person apt from £175/199; 🅿️🐕) Early 20th-century elegance reigns at this magnificent stone building, which has an art deco ballroom, 101 rooms with marble bathrooms and glossy timber (including interconnecting rooms for families and sumptuous suites), two bars (including one on the roof) and a smart-casual restaurant. Limited on-site parking is first-come, first-served but free. Its 11 luxury self-catering apartments are located nearby.

🍴 Eating

🍴 City Centre

Quay Ingredient　　　　　　　　CAFE **£**
(☑️0191-447 2327; www.quayingredient.co.uk; 4 Queen St; sandwiches £3-8; ⊙8am-5pm; 🐕) Beneath the Tyne Bridge's soaring steel girders, this chic hole-in-the-wall has a devoted following for cooked breakfasts (scrambled eggs with white truffle oil and toasted brioche, Craster kippers with lemon parsley) served until 11.30am on weekdays and all day on weekends. At lunch there are soups and spectacular sandwiches (think hoisin confit duck wrap or Toulouse sausage with fried onions).

★Broad Chare　　　　　　　GASTROPUB **££**
(☑️0191-211 2144; www.thebroadchare.co.uk; 25 Broad Chare; mains £9-27, bar snacks from £4; ⊙kitchen noon-2.30pm & 5.30-10pm Mon-Sat,

noon-5pm Sun, bar 11am-11pm Mon-Sat, to 10pm Sun) Spiffing English classics and splendid cask ales are served in the dark-wood bar and mezzanine of this perfect gastropub. Starters, such as crispy pig ears, pork pies and venison terrine, are followed by mains that might include a divine grilled pork chop with black pudding and cider sauce.

Blackfriars BRITISH ££

(✆0191-261 5945; www.blackfriarsrestaurant. co.uk; Friars St; mains £15-32; ⊗noon-2.30pm & 5.30-8.30pm Mon-Thu, noon-2.30pm & 5-8.30pm Fri & Sat, noon-4pm Sun; 🖮) 🍴 A 13th-century friary is the atmospheric setting for 'modern medieval' cuisine. Beautiful stained-glass windows frame the dining room; in summer, tables are set up in the cloister garden. Consult the table-mat map for the provenance of your cod, wood pigeon or rare-breed pork. Everything else is made from scratch on site, including breads, pastries, ice creams and sausages. Bookings recommended.

A 'little monk's menu' (mains from £5.50) is available for kids. Check the website for cookery courses.

★House of Tides GASTRONOMY £££

(✆0191-230 3720; www.houseoftides.co.uk; 28-30 The Close; tasting menus lunch £65, incl wines £130, dinner £80, incl wines £150; ⊗6-8.30pm Wed, noon-1.15pm & 6-8.30pm Thu & Fri, noon-1.15pm & 5.30-8.45pm Sat) A 16th-century merchant's house is now the home of Newcastle's most celebrated restaurant, the Michelin-starred House of Tides. Established by acclaimed Newcastle-born chef Kenny Atkinson, it incorporates premium ingredients – Orkney scallops, Norfolk quail, wild blackberries, black truffles and nasturtiums – in regularly changing multicourse tasting menus. Some diners with dietary requirements, including vegetarians, can be catered for by prior arrangement.

✗ Jesmond

Fat Hippo Jesmond BURGERS £

(✆0191-340 8949; www.fathippo.co.uk; 35a St Georges Tce; mains £11-16; ⊗noon-9.30pm Mon-Thu, noon-10pm Fri, 11am-10pm Sat, 11.30am-9.30pm Sun) Humongous burgers arrive on wooden planks with stainless-steel buckets of triple-fried, hand-cut chips at this local success story. Stinky Pete comes with blue cheese, jalapeño peppers and red-onion jam; 4x4 has a whopping four patties. Veggie burgers include spicy bean; sides span

deep-fried gherkins to mac 'n' cheese balls and house-made slaw. There are craft beers, ciders and boozy shakes.

Its city-centre sibling, the **Fat Hippo Underground** (✆0191-447 1161; 2-6 Shakespeare St; burgers £11-16; ⊗noon-10pm Mon-Thu, 11am-10pm Fri & Sat, 11.30am-10pm Sun), occupies a vaulted cellar.

Patricia BISTRO ££

(✆0191-281 4443; www.the-patricia.com; 139 Jesmond Rd; mains £13-24, 6-course dinner menu £55; ⊗5-10pm Wed-Fri, noon-2.30pm & 6-10pm Sat, noon-4pm Sun; 🍴) Named for owner-chef Nick Grieves' grandmother, the Patricia is perpetually busy; book ahead to feast on dishes like raw Orkney scallops with fermented red pepper, and roast quail with chocolate and fennel, all prepared in the semi-open kitchen. Excellent vegetarian choices might include roast leeks with aged feta foam. Many of its old- and new-world wines are available by the glass.

★Jesmond Dene House BRITISH £££

(✆0191-212 5555; www.jesmonddenehouse.co.uk; Jesmond Dene Rd; mains £17-33, 2-/3-course menus £23.50/27.50, afternoon tea £29.50; ⊗7-10am, noon-5pm & 7-9pm Mon-Thu, to 9.30pm Fri, 7.30-10.30am, noon-5pm & 7-9.30pm Sat, 7.30-10.30am & noon-9pm Sun) 🍴 Executive Head Chef Michael Penaluna is the architect of an exquisite regional menu – venison from County Durham, oysters from Lindisfarne and herbs plucked straight from the garden. The result is a gourmet extravaganza.

It's located at the historic hotel Jesmond Dene House.

🍷 Drinking & Nightlife

Central Newcastle can get seriously rowdy on Friday and Saturday nights, especially the areas around Bigg Market (just south of Newgate St) and Newcastle Central Station. Less raucous alternatives include Jesmond's bars and the Ouseburn Valley's pubs, which attract a mellower, arty crowd.

The Crack (www.thecrackmagazine.com) has comprehensive theatre, music, cinema and club listings for the entire northeast.

🍷 City Centre

Lola Jeans COCKTAIL BAR

(✆0191-230 1921; www.lolajeans.co.uk; 1-3 Market St; ⊗noon-midnight Mon-Thu, to 1am Fri-Sun) At this Jazz Age–styled bar with chandeliers, velveteen chairs and dazzling murals, cocktails served in vintage glassware include concoctions such as the Stormy Daniels (Stolichnaya vanilla vodka, sour passion fruit, pineapple shrub and prosecco) or the Shikoku Fizz (hand-batched lychee gin, jasmine syrup, Yuzu puree and tonic water).

World Headquarters   CLUB
(📞 0191-281 3445; www.welovewhq.com; Curtis Mayfield House, Carliol Sq; ⊙ 11pm-5am Fri & Sat, weekday hours vary) Dedicated to the genius of black music – funk, rare groove, dance-floor jazz, northern soul, genuine R&B, lush disco, proper house, reggae and more – this brilliant club is one of the coolest spots in the city centre.

Bridge Hotel   PUB
(📞 0191-232 6400; www.sjf.co.uk/our-pubs/bridge -hotel; Castle Sq; ⊙ 11.30am-11pm Mon-Thu, 11.30am-midnight Fri & Sat, noon-10.30pm Sun) Dating from 1901, this traditional pub retains original features including Victorian snugs, carved woodwork, stained-glass windows and mosaic tiles. At least 10 hand-pulled ales are on tap; there's also a great whisky selection. Its panoramic beer garden overlooking the High Level and Tyne Bridges incorporates part of Newcastle's medieval city walls.

Centurion Bar   BAR
(www.centurion-newcastle.com; Central Station; ⊙ 10am-11pm Mon-Thu, to midnight Fri-Sun) With floor-to-ceiling ornate Victorian tiling, Central Station's former 1st-class waiting room – a Grade I–listed treasure' dating from 1893 – is ideal for a pre-club drink in style.

LGBT+ NEWCASTLE
....

Newcastle's vibrant gay scene centres on the 'Pink Triangle', formed by Waterloo, Neville and Collingwood Sts, though venues stretch south to Scotswood Rd.

Eazy Street (📞 0191-222 0606; 8-10 Westmorland Rd; ⊙ 4pm-3am) Gay and all-welcoming Eazy Street draws a crowd for its nightly feast of cabaret drag shows, karaoke and DJs.

Powerhouse (www.facebook.com/ PowerhouseClub; 9-19 Westmorland Rd; ⊙ 11pm-4am Sun, Mon & Thu, 11.30pm-4am Fri, 11.30pm-5am Sat) Mixed but mainly gay, this massive four-floor club has flashing lights, a pumping sound system and lots of suggestive posing.

🍷 Ouseburn Valley

⭐ Tyne Bar   PUB
(📞 0191-265 2550; www.thetyne.com; 1 Maling St; ⊙ noon-11pm Mon-Thu, to midnight Fri & Sat, to 10.30pm Sun; 🕿) An outdoor stage hosting free gigs, a free jukebox, beer-garden-style seating under one of the brick arches of the Glasshouse Bridge and a sprawling expanse of grass with knockout river views make this tucked-away waterfront pub a magnet for locals. Free bar food is laid on between 7pm and 9pm on Tuesdays (you'll still need to pay for drinks).

Ship Inn   PUB
(📞 0191-222 0878; www.facebook.com/shipouse burn; Stepney Bank; ⊙ 3-10pm Mon & Tue, noon-10pm Wed-Sat, noon-8pm Sun) Spilling onto a small green out front, this red-brick charmer in the Ouseburn Valley has been pouring pints since the early 1800s. Its current owners have breathed new life into its interior, with art on the walls and an excellent vegan kitchen.

🔒 Shopping

Grainger Market   MARKET
(www.facebook.com/GraingerMarketNewcastle; btwn Grainger & Clayton Sts; ⊙ 9am-5.30pm Mon-Sat) Trading since 1835, Newcastle's gorgeous covered market has over 110 stalls selling everything from fish, farm produce, meat and vegetables to clothes, accessories and homewares. Between alleys 1 and 2, look out for the historic Weigh House, where goods were once weighed. There are some fantastic food stalls to pick up lunch on the run.

Newcastle Quayside Market   MARKET
(under the Tyne Bridge; ⊙ 9.30am-4pm Sun) Stalls displaying jewellery, photographic prints, art, clothing, homewares and more set up along the quays around the Tyne Bridge every Sunday (except in adverse weather). Buskers and food stalls add to the street-party atmosphere.

ℹ Information

Information on the city is available at www. newcastlegateshead.com.

ℹ Getting There & Away

Two tollway vehicle tunnels (www.tt2.co.uk; one-way £1.80) travel beneath the Tyne.

AIR
Newcastle International Airport (NCL; 📞 0871 882 1121; www.newcastleairport.com; Woolsington), 7 miles north of the city off the A696,

NEWCASTLE UNITED & THE GEORDIE NATION

Few football clubs in England arouse quite the same passions as Newcastle United (NUFC; ☎ 0844 372 1892; www.nufc.co.uk; St James Park, Strawberry Pl; ☑ box office 10am-5pm Mon-Fri, 9am-4pm Sat, 9am-half-time on match days). NUFC is more than just a football team – it's the collective expression of Geordie hope and pride.

Many NUFC supporters refer to themselves as Geordies, a widely used nickname for people from the Tyneside region. There is no agreement on where the name 'Geordie' comes from. Some sources date it to local support for George II during the 18th-century Jacobite Rebellion, or to miners' use of safety lamps designed by George Stephenson – no one knows for sure. The Geordie dialect is now considered the closest language to 1500-year-old Anglo-Saxon left in England.

Wherever the name comes from, the football club that Geordies traditionally support is an essential part of that identity. NUFC plays its football at the 52,305-seat St James Park and, despite fluctuating fortunes in recent years, the stadium is invariably full on match day. They are the ninth-most-successful club in the history of English football, with four league titles and six FA Cups among their successes. Recent successes have, however, been few. The excitement of finishing runners-up in the Premier League in 1995-96 and again in 1996-97 under manager Kevin Keegan and with local idol Alan Shearer leading the line, gave way to some difficult years: they were relegated from the Premier League in both 2009 and 2016.

Match tickets can be difficult to come by, but you can try online, by phone or at the box office in the Milburn Stand of St James Park. Various stadium tours (stadium tours adult/child £15/8, rooftop tours £20/15; ☑ tours by reservation) include rooftop tours.

has direct services to many UK and European cities as well as long-haul flights to Dubai. Tour operators fly charters to the USA, Middle East and Africa.

The airport is linked to town by the Metro (£3.15, 25 minutes, every 12 minutes).

A taxi to central Newcastle costs around £25.

BUS

Local and regional buses leave from **Haymarket** (Percy St) or Eldon Sq bus stations. National Express buses arrive and depart from the **coach station** (Churchill St). For local buses around the northeast, the excellent-value Explorer North East ticket (adult/child £10.90/5.70) is valid on most services.

Bus X15 runs north along the A1 to Berwick-upon-Tweed (£7.20, 2½ hours, hourly Monday to Saturday, every two hours Sunday). Bus X18 travels along the coast to Berwick (£7.20, four hours, three daily).

National Express operates services to Edinburgh (£14.30, 2¾ hours, three daily), London (£24.60, eight hours, three daily) and Manchester (£19.40, 4½ hours, four daily).

TRAIN

Newcastle is on the main rail line between London and Edinburgh and is the starting point of the scenic Tyne Valley Line west to Carlisle.

Alnmouth (for bus connections to Alnwick) from £2.50, 35 minutes, hourly

Berwick-upon-Tweed £12.70, 45 minutes, up to two per hour

Carlisle from £8.10, 1½ hours, hourly

Durham from £2, 18 minutes, five hourly

Edinburgh from £23.50, 1½ hours, up to two hourly

Hartlepool from £9.10, 50 minutes, hourly

London King's Cross from £49, 3¼ hours, up to four hourly

York from £18.90, 1¼ hours, up to four hourly

ℹ️ Getting Around

There's a large bus network, but the best means of getting around is the excellent Metro (www.nexus.org.uk).

Single fares for public transport start from £1.55.

The DaySaver pass (£3.20 to £5.30) gives unlimited Metro travel for one day for travel after 9am, and the DayRover (adult/child £7.80/3.90) gives unlimited travel on all modes of transport in the Tyne and Wear county for one day for travel any time.

Tynemouth

☎ 0191 / POP 67,520

At the mouth of the Tyne, 9 miles east of Newcastle, Tynemouth is a pretty seaside town with a lovely priory. It's also one of England's best surf spots, with great all-year breaks off the immense, crescent-shaped Blue Flag beach.

⦿ Sights & Activities

Tynemouth Priory & Castle · RUINS
(EH; www.english-heritage.org.uk; Pier Rd; adult/child £6.90/4.10; ⊙10am-5pm) Built by Benedictine monks on a strategic bluff above the mouth of the Tyne in the 11th-century ruins, Tynemouth Priory was ransacked during the Dissolution in 1539. The military took over for four centuries, only leaving in 1960, and today the haunting, ruined remains of the priory church sit alongside the castle's old military installations, their guns aimed out to sea at an enemy that never came.

Tynemouth Surf Company · SURFING
(☑0191-258 2496; www.tynemouthsurf.co.uk; Grand Pde; group surf lesson per person £30; ⊙shop 10am-5pm, surf lesson 1pm Sat & Sun Mar-Nov) For all your surfing needs, call into this surf company, which also provides group lessons for beginners and classes for kids.

🛏 Sleeping & Eating

Grand Hotel · HERITAGE HOTEL ££
(☑0191-293 6666; www.grandhoteltynemouth.co.uk; Grand Pde; d/f incl breakfast from £87/108; 🅿@🛜) Built in 1872, this was the one-time summer residence of the Duke and Duchess of Northumberland. Many of the rooms in the main building and neighbouring town house overlook the beach (sea views cost £10 extra); some have four-poster beds and spa baths. Its Victorian-style real-ale pub, drawing room serving high tea and brasserie are excellent. Book well ahead.

DON'T MISS

NORTHERN ANGEL

Nicknamed the Gateshead Flasher, the **Angel of the North** (www.gateshead.gov.uk; Durham Rd, Low Eighton), an extraordinary 200-tonne, rust-coloured, winged human frame, has loomed over the A1 motorway some 6 miles south of Newcastle since 1998. Sir Antony Gormley's iconic work (which saw him knighted in 2014) stands 20m high, with a wingspan wider than a Boeing 767. Bus 21 from Newcastle's Eldon Sq (£2.50, 20 minutes) stops here. There's a free car park by the base.

★ Riley's Fish Shack · SEAFOOD ££
(☑0191-257 1371; www.rileysfishshack.com; King Edward's Bay; mains £16-27; ⊙9.30am-10pm Mon-Sat, to 5.30pm Sun, hours can vary) 🌱 Steep timber stairs lead from East St to the beach and this rustic, tucked-away shack. Phenomenal local seafood underpins wood-fired dishes from mackerel wraps to empanadas and mains like cod on puy lentils with pancetta and parmesan crumb, served in environmentally friendly wooden boxes. There's a handful of stools outside and deckchairs spread on the sand.

Staith House · GASTROPUB ££
(☑01912-708441; www.thestaithhouse.co.uk; 57 Low Lights; mains £12-27; ⊙kitchen noon-4pm & 5-8pm Wed & Thu, noon-4pm & 5.30-9pm Fri, noon-4pm & 6-9pm Sat, noon-5.30pm Sun, bar noon-1am Mon-Sat, noon-10.30pm Sun; 🛜) 🌱 Opposite the fishing quay where catches are landed daily, gastropub Staith House has a sunny beer garden, a bar made from recycled timbers and an outstanding menu drawing on local, sustainable produce. Seafood is the star (South Shields crab, Lindisfarne oysters, North Sea hake...) but there are also meat dishes such as Northumberland lamb rump.

Reserve ahead for a nine-course seafood tasting menu (£70).

❶ Getting There & Away

From Newcastle, the easiest way to reach Tynemouth is by Metro (£3.60, 25 minutes, every 12 minutes).

Durham

☑0191 / POP 48,070

England's most beautiful Romanesque cathedral, a huge castle, and, surrounding them both, a cobweb of hilly, cobbled streets – welcome to Durham, one of the most beautiful towns in England's north. Throw into the mix a big student population drawn to England's third university of choice (after Oxford and Cambridge) and you have one fine place to visit.

⦿ Sights

★ Durham Cathedral · CATHEDRAL
(☑0191-386 4266; www.durhamcathedral.co.uk; Palace Green; cathedral by donation, guided tours adult/child £5/4.50, tower adult/child £5/2.50; ⊙cathedral 10am-4pm Mon-Sat, 1-3pm Sun, cathedral tours 10.30am, 11am & 2pm Mon-Sat) Monumental Durham Cathedral is the

Durham

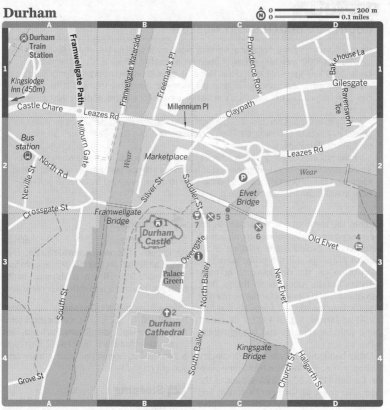

Durham

definitive Anglo-Norman Romanesque structure, a resplendent monument and, since 1986, a Unesco World Heritage Site. Beyond the main door – and the famous **Sanctuary Knocker**, which medieval felons would strike to gain 37 days asylum within the cathedral before standing trial or leaving the country – the interior is spectacular. Highly worthwhile guided tours last one hour. Climb the tower, restored in 2018 and reached by 325 steps, for extraordinary Durham views.

Durham was the first European cathedral to be roofed with stone-ribbed vaulting, which upheld the heavy stone roof and made it possible to build pointed transverse arches – a great architectural achievement. The central tower dates from 1262, but was damaged in a fire caused by lightning in 1429 and unsatisfactorily patched up until it was entirely rebuilt in 1470. The western towers were added in 1217–26.

The northern side of the beautiful, 1175-built **Galilee Chapel** features rare surviving examples of 12th-century wall painting (thought to feature portraits of Sts Cuthbert and Oswald). Galilee Chapel also

WORTH A TRIP

COUNTY DURHAM HISTORY MUSEUM

County Durham's living, breathing, working museum, **Beamish Open-Air Museum** (🖰 0191-370 4000; www.beamish.org.uk; Beamish; adult/child £19.50/11.50; ⊙10am-5pm Easter-Oct, 10am-4pm Nov-Easter, closed Mon & Fri Jan–mid-Feb, last admission 3pm) offers an unflinching glimpse into industrial life in the northeast during the 19th and 20th centuries. Spread over 120 hectares, it is instructive and fun for all ages. Allow at least three hours here.

Beamish is 9 miles northwest of Durham (though there are no useful bus services), and 10 miles south of Newcastle. From Newcastle, take bus 28 or 28A (£5.10, 50 minutes, every 30 minutes).

Highlights include going underground, exploring mine heads, visiting a working farm, school, dentist and pub, and marvelling at how every cramped pit cottage seemed to find room for a piano. Don't miss a ride behind an 1815 Steam Elephant locomotive or a replica of Stephenson's *Locomotion No 1*.

contains the **tomb of the Venerable Bede**, the 8th-century Northumbrian monk turned historian: his *Ecclesiastical History of the English People* is still the prime source of information on the development of early Christian Britain. Among other things, Bede introduced the AD system for the numbering of years from the birth of Jesus. He was first buried at Jarrow, but in 1022 a miscreant monk stole his remains and brought them here.

Other highlights include the 14th-century **Bishop's Throne**; the beautiful stone **Neville Screen** (1372–80), which separates the high altar from **St Cuthbert's tomb**; and the mostly 19th-century **Cloisters** where you'll find the **Monk's Dormitory**, now a library of 30,000 books, with Anglo-Saxon carved stones. There are audiovisual displays on the building of the cathedral and the life of St Cuthbert, and a rolling program of exhibitions.

★**Durham Castle** CASTLE
(🖰 0191-334 2932; www.dur.ac.uk/durham.castle; Palace Green; adult/child £5/4; ⊙guided tours by reservation 1.15pm, 2.15pm, 3.15pm & 4.15pm) Built as a standard motte-and-bailey fort in 1072, Durham Castle was the prince bishops' home until 1837, when it became the University of Durham's first college. It remains a university hall today. Highlights of the 50-minute tour include the 17th-century Black Staircase and the beautifully preserved Norman chapel (1080). Book ahead by phone, or at the Palace Green Library or the World Heritage Site Visitor Centre.

Tours run most days, with additional tours during university holidays.

🏃 Activities

Browns Boathouse BOATING
(🖰 0191-386 3779; www.brownsboats.co.uk; Elvet Bridge; adult/child per hour £7.50/5; ⊙10am-6pm mid-Mar–late Sep) Hire a traditional, hand-built row boat for a romantic river excursion.

Prince Bishop River Cruiser CRUISE
(🖰 0191-386 9525; www.facebook.com/PrinceBishopRiverCruiser; Browns Boathouse, Elvet Bridge; adult/child £10/6; ⊙cruises 12.30pm, 2pm & 3pm Mar-Oct) Scenic one-hour cruises take you out on the Wear.

🛏 Sleeping

Kingslodge Inn INN ££
(🖰 0191-370 9977; www.kingslodgeinn.co.uk; Waddington St, Flass Vale; d/f incl breakfast from £100/130; 🅿🛜🐾) Handily positioned half-a-mile west of the city centre and a quarter of a mile west of the train station, with the bonus of free parking, this comfortable inn is surrounded by woodland woven with walking trails. Its 23 rooms have tartan carpets and furnishings; there's a pub-style restaurant and bar.

Family rooms have pull-out sofa beds; cots are on hand for babies.

★**Lumley Castle** CASTLE £££
(🖰 0191-389 1111; www.lumleycastle.com; Ropery Lane, Chester-le-Street; d £75-180, ste from £210; 🅿🛜) Spiralling stone tower steps and creaking corridors lead to richly decorated rooms with heavy drapes and patterned wallpapers, many with canopied four-poster beds, at this atmosphere-steeped 14th-century castle; there are also more modern courtyard rooms. Within the castle's walls are a fine-dining restaurant and antiquarian book–lined library

bar; regular events include Elizabethan banquets. It's 7 miles northeast of Durham.

The 'Castle State Room' is an extraordinary step back in time.

Guests can wander through the state rooms when they're not being used for private functions.

Townhouse BOUTIQUE HOTEL £££
(☑ 0191-384 1037; www.thetownhousedurham.co.uk; 34 Old Elvet; d from £135; 🗟) Each of the Townhouse's 11 luxurious rooms has a theme, from French-styled Le Jardin to ocean-liner-like Cruise and the Edwardian Express, recreating a night in a yesteryear sleeper compartment. A couple of rooms have private outdoor hot tubs. Aged steaks are the speciality of the Modern British restaurant.

Eating

Tealicious CAFE £
(☑ 0191-340 1393; www.tealicioustearoom.co.uk; 88 Elvet Bridge; dishes £3-7, high tea per person £19.95; ⊙ 10am-4pm Wed-Sat; 🖼) Inside this quaint pastel-blue and white building, homemade cakes (such as white-chocolate cheesecake or ginger and lime), soups and sandwiches are complemented by 24 blends of tea served from individual pots in fine bone china. High tea here is a treat for both adults and kids. It's tiny, so book ahead.

Garden House Inn BRITISH ££
(☑ 0191-386 3395; www.gardenhouseinn.com; Framwellgate; sandwiches £6-12, mains £11-18; ⊙ 5-10pm Mon-Thu, 4-11pm Fri, noon-11pm Sat, noon-10pm Sun; 🗟🖼) Dating from the 18th century, rustic country-style inn Garden House does great lunchtime sandwiches, such as lobster or crab, fennel and nduja (spicy pork salami) and locavore menus at both lunch and dinner (Lindisfarne oysters with wild garlic and smoked chilli, roast Northumberland lamb with hazelnut-crusted beetroot). Its six cosy rooms (four doubles, two for families; from £80/100) have vintage-inspired decor.

Cellar Door Durham BRITISH ££
(☑ 0191-383 1856; www.thecellardoordurham.co.uk; 41 Saddler St; mains £17-25, 2-/3-course lunch menus £14/16; ⊙ noon-5pm) Accessed via an inconspicuous door on Saddler St, this 12th-century building has glorious river views, including from the terrace. The internationally influenced menu features starters such as smoked chicken mousse with

torched gem lettuce followed by mains such as salt-aged striploin or sea bass with feta and mint croquettes (vegetarian and vegan options available). Service is spot on.

Drinking & Nightlife

Shakespeare Tavern PUB
(63 Saddler St; ⊙ 11am-11.30pm) Built in 1190, this authentic-as-it-gets locals' boozer is complete with dartboard, cosy snugs, a terrific selection of beers and spirits, and wise-cracking characters propping up the bar – as well as, allegedly, a resident ghost. Look out for folk-music jam sessions. There's a gin bar on the 1st floor.

ⓘ Information

Durham's **World Heritage Site Visitor Centre** (☑ 0191-334 3805; www.durhamworldheritagesite.com/visit/whs-visitor-centre; 7 Owengate; ⊙ 9.30am-5pm Feb-Dec, to 4.30pm Jan) is in the shadow of the castle.

Comprehensive info on the city and county is available online at www.thisisdurham.com.

ⓘ Getting There & Away

BUS
The bus station is on North Rd, on the western side of the river.

Destinations include:

Hartlepool Bus 57A; £7.80, one hour, two hourly

London National Express; £30, 6¾ hours, two daily

Newcastle Bus 21, X12 and X21; £4.80, 1¼ hours, at least four hourly

LOCAL KNOWLEDGE

A GOURMET FARM SHOP

It's worth stopping off 12 miles northwest of Durham en route to Northumberland National Park and Hadrian's Wall at **Knitsley Farm Shop & Cafe** (☑ 01207-592059; www.knitsleyfarmshop.co.uk; East Knitsley Grange Farm, Knitsley; dishes £5-14; ⊙ shop 10am-5pm Tue-Sat, to 4pm Sun, cafe 10am-5pm Tue-Fri, 9.30am-5pm Sat, 9.30am-4pm Sun) to stock up on its incredible cheeses, meats, fruits, veggies, homemade sweets, biscuits, cakes and breads. It's even better if you can make time to dine at its wonderful cafe on fresh-as-it-gets soups, farmyard sausages, and pulled-pork and crackling baps.

TRAIN

The East Coast Main Line provides speedy connections to destinations including:

Edinburgh from £13.10, 1¾ hours, hourly

London King's Cross from £38.50, three hours, hourly

Newcastle from £2, 18 minutes, five hourly

York from £7.80, 50 minutes, four hourly

Barnard Castle

📞 01833 / POP 5500

The charming market town of Barnard Castle, better known by locals as 'Barney', is a traditionalist's dream, full of antique and craft shops, and atmospheric old pubs. It's a wonderful setting for the town's twin draws: a daunting ruined castle that gives the town its name, and, improbably, an extraordinary French chateau.

👁 Sights

⭐ **Bowes Museum** MUSEUM

(📞 01833-690606; www.thebowesmuseum. org.uk; Newgate; adult/child/family £14/5/30; ☺ 10am-5pm) A monumental chateau half a mile east of the centre contains the lavishly furnished Bowes Museum. Funded by 19th-century industrialist John Bowes, and opened in 1892, this brainchild of his Parisian actress wife, Josephine, was built by French architect Jules Pellechet to display a collection the Bowes had travelled the world to assemble. Serious masterpieces share space with the marvellous 18th-century mechanical silver swan, which performs every day at 2pm. If you miss it, a film shows it in action.

Look for works by Canaletto, El Greco and Goya as well as 55 paintings by Josephine herself. Among the 15,000 other objects d'art are dresses from the 17th century through to the 1970s as part of an exhibit on textiles through the ages, and clocks, watches and tableware in gold and silver in the precious-metals section. It also houses finds unearthed from the nearby Binchester Roman Fort. Tickets are valid for a year, so you can come and go as you please.

Local suppliers provide ingredients for its outstanding cafe. Afterwards, stroll through its formal parterre garden and woodland; there are play areas for kids and events including markets and theatre performances.

Barnard Castle RUINS

(EH; 📞 01833-638212; www.english-heritage.org. uk; Scar Top; adult/child £6.90/4.10; ☺ 10am-6pm daily Easter-Sep, to 5pm daily Oct, 10am-4pm Sat & Sun Nov-Easter) Built on a cliff above the River Tees by Guy de Bailleul and rebuilt around 1150, Barnard Castle was partly dismantled some four centuries later, but its ruins still manage to cover two very impressive hectares, and there are wonderful river views. Inhale the sensory garden.

Raby Castle CASTLE

(📞 01833-660202; www.rabycastle.com; Staindrop; castle, gardens & park adult/child £13/6.50, gardens & park only £8/4; ☺ 11am-4pm Tue-Sun Jul & Aug, 11am-4pm Wed-Sun late Mar-Jun & Sep) Sprawling Raby Castle was a stronghold of the Catholic Neville family until it engaged in ill-judged plotting (the 'Rising of the North') against the Protestant Queen Elizabeth in 1569. Most of the interior dates from the 18th and 19th centuries, but the exterior remains true to the original design, built around a courtyard and surrounded by a moat. It's 6.8 miles northeast of Barnard Castle; take bus 85A (£3.30, 15 minutes, eight daily Monday to Friday, six Saturday and Sunday).

The stables now house tearooms. There are beautiful formal gardens and a deer park; you can hire bikes to explore.

🛏 Sleeping & Eating

Old Well Inn INN ££

(📞 01833-690130; www.theoldwellinn.co.uk; 21 The Bank; s/d incl breakfast from £65/90; 📶) Built over a huge concealed well, this old coaching inn has 10 enormous rooms. No 9 is the most impressive with its own private entrance, flagstone floors and a bath. The pub has regional ales on tap that you can sip in the leafy beer garden in fine weather.

Cross Lanes Organic Farm Shop CAFE £

(📞 01833-630619; www.crosslanesorganics.co.uk; Cross Lanes, Barnard Castle; sandwiches from £5, mains £10-14; ☺ 9am-3.30pm Mon, Wed & Thu, 9am-4pm Fri & Sat, 10am-4pm Sun; 📶🎦) 🖊 Sheep graze on the grass-covered roof of this award-winning farm shop and cafe 1.5 miles south of Barnard Castle, right by the A66. The cavernous interior brims with all-organic produce; breakfasts (home-cured bacon, homemade sausages, and eggs from the farm's chickens) segue into lunches including gourmet sandwiches, steak or veggie burgers and wood-fired pizzas, and 'rustic afternoon tea'.

★ **Raby Hunt**   GASTRONOMY £££

(☑ 01325-374237;   www.rabyhuntrestaurant. co.uk; Summerhouse, Darlington; tasting menu £200, chef's table £240; ☺ 6-9.30pm Wed-Sat, noon-2pm Sun; ☎) A two-century-old, ivy-clad drovers' inn 11 miles east of Barnard Castle is now the staging post for gastronomic expeditions by self-taught chef James Close, who received his first Michelin star in 2012 and second in 2017. Tasting menus (no à la carte) typically feature 16 or more intricate courses, such as in-the-shell razor clams with brown shrimp. Reserve weeks ahead.

In the former stables are three luxurious guest rooms (doubles including breakfast from £180).

★ **Bay Horse**   GASTROPUB £££

(☑ 01325-720663;   www.thebayhorsehurworth. com; The Green, Hurworth-on-Tees; mains dinner £22-33, 2-/3-course set lunch menu from £17/21; ☺ kitchen noon-2.30pm & 6-9.30pm Mon-Sat, noon-4pm Sun, bar 11am-11pm Mon-Sat, noon-10.30pm Sun; ☑) It's worth travelling 19 miles east of Barnard Castle to this 15th-century coaching inn in the pretty riverside village of Hurworth-on-Tees. Book ahead so you don't miss exceptional dishes such as monkfish wrapped in Parma ham, mint raita, prawn risotto, apple dressing, charred cucumber, sweet potato puree, and curried granola. Wild garlic, leeks, nettles and herbs are foraged nearby.

❶ Getting There & Around

Barnard Castle is poorly served by public transport and several of its key draws are outside the town so you really need your own wheels to get here and explore.

Hadrian's Wall

Named in honour of the emperor who ordered it built, Hadrian's Wall was one of Rome's greatest engineering projects. This enormous 73-mile-long wall was built between 122 and 128 CE to separate Romans and Scottish Picts. Today, the sections that remain evoke Roman ambition and tenacity. When completed, the mammoth structure ran across the island's narrow neck, from the Solway Firth in the west almost to the mouth of the Tyne in the east.

Every Roman mile (0.95 miles) there was a gateway guarded by a small fort (milecastle) and between each milecastle were two observation turrets. Milecastles are numbered right across the country, starting with Milecastle 0 at Wallsend – where you can visit the wall's last stronghold, Segedunum – and ending with Milecastle 80 at Bowness-on-Solway.

A series of forts were developed as bases some distance south (and may predate the wall), and a further 16 lie astride it.

Preserved remains of forts and garrisons and intriguing museums punctuate the route, along with sections of the wall you can freely access.

🏃 Activities

The **Hadrian's Wall Path** (www.national trail.co.uk/en_GB/trails/hadrians-wall-path) is an 84-mile national trail that runs the length of the wall from Wallsend in the east to Bowness-on-Solway in the west. The entire route should take about seven days on foot, giving plenty of time to explore the rich archaeological heritage along the way.

❶ Information

There are tourist offices in **Hexham** (☑ 01670-620450; www.visitnorthumberland.com; Queen's Hall, Beaumont St, Hexham; ☺ 9am-5pm Mon-Fri, 9.30am-5pm Sat), Haltwhistle (p623) and Corbridge (p619). The Walltown Visitor Centre (p624), aka the Northumberland National Park Visitor Centre, is located at Greenhead. Tourist information is also available from the **Sill** (☑ 01434-341200; www.thesill.org.uk; Military Rd, Once Brewed; ☺ 10am-5pm Apr-early Nov), aka the National Landscape Discovery Centre, at Once Brewed.

Hadrian's Wall Country (www.hadrianswall-country.co.uk) is the official portal for the entire area.

HEXHAM ABBEY

Bustling Hexham is a handsome if somewhat scuffed market town centred on its grand Augustinian **abbey** (☑ 01434-602031; www.hexhamabbey.org. uk; Beaumont St, Hexham; by donation; ☺ 10am-4pm), a marvellous example of Early English architecture. It cleverly escaped the Dissolution of 1537 by rebranding as Hexham's parish church, a role it still has today. The highlight is the 7th-century Saxon crypt, the only surviving element of St Wilfrid's Church, built with inscribed stones from Corstopitum in 674.

Hadrian's Wall & Northumberland National Park

ℹ Getting There & Around

BUS

The AD122 Hadrian's Wall bus (five daily, Easter to September) is a hail-and-ride service that runs between Hexham and Carlisle, with one bus a day starting and ending at Newcastle's Central Station; not all services cover the entire route. Bikes can be taken aboard AD122 buses, but space is limited.

Bus 10 links Newcastle with Hexham (£5.50, 1½ hours, every 30 minutes Monday to Saturday, hourly on Sunday).

West of Hexham, the wall runs parallel to the A69, which connects Carlisle and Newcastle. Buses X84 and X85 run along the A69 every 30 minutes, passing 2 to 3 miles south of the main sites.

All these services except the X84 and X85 can be used with the **Hadrian's Wall Rover Ticket** (one day adult/child £12.50/6.50, three days £25/13). Show your Rover Ticket to get 10% off admission to all museums and attractions.

The **Hadrian's Frontier Ticket** (one day adult/child £16/8, three day £32/16) provides unlimited transport on all buses throughout Northumberland.

Both tickets are available from bus drivers and tourist offices, where you can also get timetables.

CAR & MOTORCYCLE

Your own wheels are the easiest way to get around, with one fort or garrison usually just a short hop from the next. Parking costs £10 per day; tickets are valid at all sites along the wall.

The B6318 follows the course of the wall from the outskirts of Newcastle to Birdoswald. The main A69 road and the railway line follow 3 or 4 miles to the south.

TRAIN

The railway line between Newcastle and Carlisle (Tyne Valley Line; from £7.50, 1½ hours, hourly) has stations at Corbridge, Hexham, Haydon Bridge, Bardon Mill, Haltwhistle and Brampton, but be aware that not all services stop at all stations.

Corbridge

📞 01434 / POP 3670

Above a green-banked curve in the Tyne, Corbridge's shady, cobbled streets are lined with old-fashioned shops and pubs. Inhabited since Saxon times when there was a substantial monastery here, many of the village's charming buildings feature stones nicked from nearby Corstopitum.

⊙ Sights

**Corbridge
Roman Site & Museum**   HISTORIC SITE

(EH; www.english-heritage.org.uk; Corchester Lane; adult/child £9/5.40; ⊙10am-5pm) What's left of the Roman garrison town of Corstopitum lies about half a mile west of Market Pl on Dere St, once the main road from York to Scotland. It's the oldest fortified site in the area, predating the wall itself by some 40 years. Most of what you see here, though, dates from around 200 CE, when the fort had developed into a civilian settlement and was the main base along the wall.

You get a sense of the domestic heart of the town from the visible remains. Revamped in 2018, the superb museum here displays artefacts unearthed at the site, including Roman sculpture and carvings such as the amazing 3rd-century Corbridge Lion.

🛏 Sleeping & Eating

⭐**Lord Crewe Arms**   INN £££

(📞01434-677100; www.lordcrewearmsblanchland. co.uk; The Square, Blanchland; d from £175; 🅿🛜) An 1165-built abbot's house in the honey-stone North Pennines village of Blanchland, 11 miles south of Corbridge, shelters some of this entrancing inn's 21 rooms, while others are located in former miners' cottages. Rates almost halve outside high season. Non-guests can dine on outstanding Modern British fare and drink in the vaulted bar, the Crypt, with a monumental medieval fireplace.

⭐**Corbridge Larder**   DELI £

(📞01434-632948; www.corbridgelarder.co.uk; 18 Hill St; mains £4-10; ⊙9am-5pm Mon-Sat, 10am-4pm Sun) Gourmet picnic fare at this fabulous deli includes bread, over 100 varieties of cheese, chutneys, cakes, chocolates and wine (you can get hampers made up) as well as made-to-order sandwiches, pies, quiches, tarts, and antipasti and meze delicacies. Upstairs from the wonderland of provisions

there's a small sit-down cafe serving dishes such as Moroccan spiced chicken.

ℹ Information

Tourist Office (📞01434-632815; www.visit northumberland.com; Hill St; ⊙10am-4.30pm Mon-Sat Apr-Sep, 11am-4pm Wed, Fri & Sat Oct-Mar) Occupies a corner of the library.

ℹ Getting There & Away

Buses X84 and X85 between Newcastle (£5.50, 45 minutes, hourly) and Carlisle (£8.10, 2¼ hours, hourly) come through Corbridge, as does bus 10 from Newcastle (£5.50, one hour, every 30 minutes Monday to Saturday, hourly Sunday) to Hexham (£2.40, 12 minutes, every 30 minutes Monday to Saturday, hourly Sunday). At Hexham you can connect with the Hadrian's Wall bus AD122 in summer or bus 185 year-round.

Corbridge is also on the railway line between Newcastle (£6.70, 45 minutes, hourly) and Carlisle (£15.80, 1½ hours, hourly).

Haltwhistle & Around

📞 01434 / POP 3810

The village of Haltwhistle, little more than two intersecting streets, has more key Hadrian's Wall sights in its surrounds than anywhere else along the wall, but tourist infrastructure here is surprisingly (some would say refreshingly) underdeveloped.

Haltwhistle claims to be the geographic centre of the British mainland, although the jury is still out.

⊙ Sights

⭐**Housesteads
Roman Fort & Museum**   HISTORIC SITE

(EH; 📞01434-344363; www.english-heritage.org. uk; Haydon Bridge; adult/child £9/5.40; ⊙10am-6pm Apr-Sep, to 5pm Oct, to 4pm Nov-Mar) The most dramatic site of Hadrian's Wall – and the best-preserved Roman fort in the whole country – is at Housesteads, 4 miles north of Bardon Mill on the B6318, and 6.5 miles northeast of Haltwhistle. Set high on a ridge and covering 2 hectares, from here you can survey the moors of Northumberland National Park and the snaking wall, with a sense of awe at the landscape and the aura of the Roman lookouts.

Up to 800 troops were based at Housesteads at any one time. Its remains include an impressive hospital, granaries with a carefully worked out ventilation system, and barrack blocks. Most memorable are the

Hadrian's Wall

ROME'S FINAL FRONTIER

Of all Britain's Roman ruins, Emperor Hadrian's 2nd-century wall, cutting across northern England from the Irish Sea to the North Sea, is by far the most spectacular; Unesco awarded it World Heritage status in 1987.

We've picked out the highlights, one of which is the prime remaining Roman fort on the wall, Housesteads, which we've reconstructed here.

Housesteads' Granaries
Nothing like the clever underground ventilation system, which kept vital supplies of grain dry in Northumberland's damp and drizzly climate, would be seen again in these parts for 1500 years.

Milecastle

North Gate

Interval Tower

Birdoswald Roman Fort
Explore the longest intact stretch of the wall, scramble over the remains of a large fort then head indoors to wonder at a full-scale model of the wall at its zenith. Great fun for the kids.

Map:
0 — 10 km
0 — 5 miles
N
Birdoswald Roman Fort
Harrow Scar Milecastle
Irthing
Greenhead
Brampton
Roman Army Museum
Once Brewed
Haltwhistle
South Tyne
Housesteads Roman Fort & Museum
B6318
Vindolanda Roman Fort & Museum
Bardon Mill
A69
Sewingshields
Hadrian's Wall
Haydon Bridge
Chesters Roman Fort & Museum
Chollerford
Low Brunton
Acomb
Hexham

Chesters Roman Fort
Built to keep watch over a bridge spanning the River North Tyne, Britain's best-preserved Roman cavalry fort has a terrific bathhouse, essential if you have months of nippy northern winter ahead.

Hexham Abbey
This may be the finest non-Roman sight near Hadrian's Wall, but the 7th-century parts of this magnificent church were built with stone quarried by the Romans for use in their forts.

Housesteads' Hospital
Operations performed at the hospital would have been surprisingly effective, even without anaesthetics; religious rituals and prayers to Aesculapius, the Roman god of healing, were possibly less helpful for a hernia or appendicitis.

Housesteads' Latrines
Communal toilets were the norm in Roman times and Housesteads' are remarkably well preserved – fortunately no traces remain of the vinegar-soaked sponges that were used instead of toilet paper.

ALISON ROSCOE / GETTY IMAGES ©

QUICK WALL FACTS & FIGURES

Latin name Vallum Aelium

Length 73.5 miles (80 Roman miles)

Construction date AD 122–128

Manpower for construction
Three legions (around 16,000 men)

Features At least 16 forts, 80 milecastles, 160 turrets

Did you know Hadrian's wasn't the only Roman wall in Britain – the Antonine Wall was built across what is now central Scotland in the AD 140s, but it was abandoned soon after.

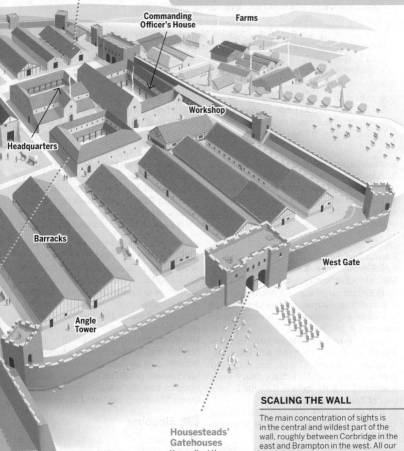

Commanding Officer's House

Farms

Workshop

Headquarters

Barracks

West Gate

Angle Tower

Housesteads' Gatehouses
Unusually at Housesteads neither of the gates faces the enemy, as was the norm at Roman forts; builders aligned them east–west. Ruts worn by cart wheels are still visible in the stone.

FREE GUIDES

At some sites, knowledgeable volunteer heritage guides are on hand to answer questions and add context and interesting details to what you're seeing.

SCALING THE WALL

The main concentration of sights is in the central and wildest part of the wall, roughly between Corbridge in the east and Brampton in the west. All our suggested stops are within this area and follow an east–west route. The easiest way to travel is by car, scooting along the B6318, but special bus AD122 will also get you there. Hiking along the designated Hadrian's Wall Path (84 miles) allows you to appreciate the achievement up close.

HADRIAN'S WALL SITES

Along with key sites such as Housesteads (p619) and Vindolanda, there are numerous other Roman remains stationed along Hadrian's Wall.

Segedunum (☏ 0191-278 4217; www.segedunumromanfort.org.uk; Buddle St, Wallsend; adult/child £4.95/free; ☉ 10am-4pm Jun–mid-Sep, to 3pm mid-Sep–early Dec & mid-Jan–May) was the last strong post of Hadrian's Wall, 5 miles east of Newcastle in the suburb of Wallsend. Beneath the 35m-high tower is an absorbing site that includes a reconstructed Roman bathhouse (with steaming pools and frescos) and a museum.

Chesters Roman Fort (EH; ☏ 01434-681379; www.english-heritage.org.uk; Chollerford; adult/child £9/5.40; ☉ 10am-6pm daily Apr-Sep, 10am-5pm daily Oct, 10am-4pm Sat & Sun Nov–mid-Feb, 10am-4pm Wed-Sun mid-Feb–Mar) near the village of Chollerford housed up to 500 troops from Asturias in northern Spain. It includes part of a bridge (best appreciated from the eastern bank), four gatehouses, a bathhouse and an underfloor heating system.

Birdoswald Roman Fort (EH; ☏ 01697-747602; www.english-heritage.org.uk; Gilsland, Greenhead; adult/child £9/5.50; ☉ 10am-6pm daily Apr-Sep, 10am-5pm daily Oct, 10am-4pm Sat & Sun Nov–mid-Feb, 10am-4pm Wed-Sun mid-Feb–Mar) – Banna to the Romans – has the longest intact stretch of wall, extending from here to Harrow's Scar Milecastle. It overlooks Irthing Gorge, 4 miles west of Greenhead in Cumbria.

Binchester Roman Fort (www.durham.gov.uk/binchester; Bishop Auckland; adult/child £5/3; ☉ 10am-5pm Jul & Aug, 10.30am-4pm Easter-Jun & Sep), or Vinovia, lies 9.6 miles southwest of Durham. First built in wood around AD 80 and refashioned in stone early in the 2nd century, the fort was the largest in County Durham.

spectacularly situated communal flushable latrines. Information boards show what the individual buildings would have looked like in their heyday. There's a scale model of the entire fort in the small museum at the ticket office.

★ Vindolanda

Roman Fort & Museum HISTORIC SITE

(☏ 01434-344277; www.vindolanda.com; Bardon Mill; adult/child/family £8/4.75/22.80; ☉ 10am-5pm) The extensive site of Vindolanda offers a fascinating glimpse into the daily life of a Roman garrison town. The time-capsule museum is just one part of this large, extensively excavated site, which includes impressive parts of the fort and town (excavations continue) and reconstructed turrets and a temple. Extraordinary finds unearthed in 2017 include the only known pair of Roman boxing gloves.

It's 1.5 miles north of Bardon Mill between the A69 and B6318, and 5.8 miles northeast of Haltwhistle.

Highlights of the Vindolanda museum displays include leather sandals, signature Roman toothbrush-flourish helmet decorations, and numerous writing tablets returned from the British Library. These include a student's marked work ('sloppy'), and a parent's note with a present of socks and underpants (things haven't changed – in this climate you can never have too many). Its purpose-built Wooden Underworld Gallery, opened in 2018, displays timber artefacts excavated here (from combs to axles and even a toilet seat) in temperature-controlled cases.

Roman Army Museum MUSEUM

(☏ 01697-747485; www.vindolanda.com/roman-army-museum; Greenhead; adult/child/family £6.89/3.80/19; ☉ 10am-5pm) On the site of the Carvoran Roman Fort a mile northeast of Greenhead, near Walltown Crags, this revamped museum has three galleries covering the Roman army and the expanding and contracting empire; the wall (with a 3D film illustrating what the wall was like nearly 2000 years ago and today); and colourful background detail to Hadrian's Wall life (such as how the soldiers spent their R&R time in this lonely outpost of the empire).

🛏 Sleeping

★ Ashcroft B&B ££

(☏ 01434-320213; www.ashcroftguesthouse.co.uk; Lanty's Lonnen, Haltwhistle; s/d from £77/89; [P] 🛜) British B&Bs don't get better than this elegant Edwardian vicarage surrounded by nearly a hectare of beautifully manicured terraced lawns and gardens. Some rooms open to private balconies and terraces and all have soaring ceilings and 21st-century gadgets. Breakfast (included) is cooked on a cast-iron Aga and served in a grand dining room.

Holmhead Guest House   B&B **££**
(☑ 01697-747402; www.bandb-hadrianswall.co.uk; Greenhead; campsites per 1/2 people £7.50/11, s/d from £70/80; ☺ guesthouse year-round, camping & bunk barn May-Sep; P ☎) Built using recycled bits of the wall on whose foundations it stands, this superb farmhouse half a mile north of Greenhead offers comfy rooms and five unpowered campsites. The Pennine Way and the Hadrian's Wall Path pass through the grounds and Thirlwall Castle's jagged ruins loom above. Ask to see the 3rd-century Roman graffiti.

★**Langley Castle Hotel**   CASTLE **£££**
(☑ 01434-688888; www.langleycastle.com; Langley; d castle view/castle from £175/270; P ☎☎) Soaring above 12 acres of gardens, this 1350-built castle is a beauty, with creaking hallways lined by suits of armour and an alleged resident ghost. Its nine castle rooms are appointed with antique furnishings (many have four-poster beds); there are another 18 'castle view' rooms in the grounds with access to castle facilities. Check for dinner, bed and breakfast packages.

❶ Information

Tourist Office (☑ 01434-321863; www.visit northumberland.com; Mechanics Institute, Westgate; ☺10am-4.30pm Mon-Fri, to 1pm Sat) On Haltwhistle's main street.

❶ Getting There & Around

Bus 185 runs to the Roman Army Museum (£3, 10 minutes, three daily) and Birdoswald Roman Fort (£3.40, 25 minutes, three daily).

Haltwhistle is also linked by train to Hexham (£7.30, 20 minutes, hourly) and Newcastle (£14, one hour, hourly).

Northumberland National Park

England's last great wilderness is the 405 sq miles of natural wonderland that make up the country's least populated national park. The finest sections of Hadrian's Wall run along its southern edge and the landscape is dotted with prehistoric remains and fortified houses – the thick-walled peles were the only solid buildings built here until the mid-18th century.

Adjacent to the national park, the Kielder Water & Forest Park is home to the vast artificial lake Kielder Water, holding 200,000 million litres. Surrounding its 27-mile-long shoreline is England's largest plantation forest, with 150 million spruce and pine trees.

◉ Sights

★**Kielder Observatory**   OBSERVATORY
(☑0191-265 5510; www.kielderobservatory.org; Black Fell, off Shilling Pot; adult/child from £20/15; ☺by reservation) In 2013, Northumberland National Park was awarded dark-sky status by the International Dark Skies Association (www.darksky.org). For the best views of the resulting Northumberland International Dark Sky Park, attend a stargazing session at this state-of-the-art observatory. Its program spans night-time observing sessions to family events and astrophotography. Book well ahead, and dress warmly: it's seriously chilly here at night. At the signs towards Kielder Observatory and Skyspace, turn left; it's a 2-mile drive up the track.

Chillingham Castle   CASTLE
(☑ 01668-215359; www.chillingham-castle.com; Chillingham; castle adult/child £10.50/6.50, Chillingham Wild Cattle £8.50/4, castle & Chillingham Wild Cattle £17.50/6.50; ☺castle noon-5pm Apr-Oct, Chillingham Wild Cattle tours 10am, 11.30am, 1.45pm & 3.15pm Apr-Oct) Steeped in history, warfare, torture and ghosts, 13th-century Chillingham is said to be one of the country's most haunted places, with spectres from a phantom funeral to Lady Mary Berkeley seeking her errant husband. Owner Sir Humphry Wakefield has passionately restored the castle's extravagant medieval staterooms, stone-flagged banquet halls and grisly torture chambers. Chillingham is 6 miles southeast of Wooler. Bus 470 (four daily Monday to Saturday) between Alnwick (£3.30, 25 minutes) and Wooler (£3.30, 20 minutes) stops at Chillingham.

Dates for two-hour evening ghost tours (per person £25), some family-friendly, are listed on the website. Committed ghost hunters can undertake a four-hour hunt (£50) overseen by the castle's dedicated paranormal team.

It's possible to stay at the medieval fortress in one of eight self-catering apartments (doubles from £100) where the likes of Henry III and Edward I once snoozed.

The grounds are home to some 100 Chillingham wild cattle, thought to be the last descendants of the aurochs that once roamed Britain until becoming all but extinct during the Bronze Age, making them one of the world's rarest breeds of any species. Tours lasting one hour are led by a park warden; wear sturdy shoes.

Cragside House,
Garden & Woodland   HISTORIC BUILDING
(NT; ☑ 01669-620333; www.nationaltrust.org.uk; adult/child £15/7.50; ⊙ house 11am-5pm, gardens & woodland 10am-6pm mid-Mar–Oct, hours vary) One mile northeast of Rothbury just off the B6341 is the astonishing country retreat of the first Lord Armstrong. In the 1880s, the house had hot and cold running water, a telephone and alarm system, and was the world's first to be lit by electricity, generated through hydropower. The sprawling Victorian gardens feature lakes, moors and one of Europe's largest rock gardens. Visit late May to mid-June to see Cragside's famous rhododendrons in bloom.

🛏 Sleeping

Wooler YHA   HOSTEL £
(☑ 01668-281365; www.yha.org.uk; 30 Cheviot St, Wooler; d/q from £46/84; ⊙ Apr-Oct; 🅿🛜) In a low, red-brick building above Wooler, this handy hostel contains beds in a variety of rooms (including handcrafted 'shepherds' huts' sleeping two to three people warmed by electric heating), a modern lounge and a small restaurant, as well as a self-catering kitchen, drying room and bike storage.

★ Otterburn Castle
Country House Hotel   CASTLE £££
(☑ 01830-520620; www.otterburncastle.com; Main St, Otterburn; d incl breakfast £140-165, ste £220; 🅿🛜🐾) Founded by William the Conqueror's cousin Robert de Umfraville in 1086 and set in almost 13 hectares of grounds, this story-book castle has 17 classically furnished rooms; some of its suites have four-poster beds and fireplaces. Modern British fare is served in its wood-panelled Oak Room Restaurant (two-/three-course menus £24/30); open fires blaze in its bar.

ℹ Information

For information, contact the **Northumberland National Park information service** (☑ 01434-605555; www.northumberlandnationalpark. org.uk).

As well as tourist offices in towns including **Wooler** (☑ 01668-282123; www.wooler.org. uk; Cheviot Centre, 12 Padgepool Pl, Wooler; ⊙ 10am-4.30pm Mon-Fri, to 1pm Sat) and **Rothbury** (☑ 01669-621979; www.visitnorthumberland.com; Rothbury Library, Front St, Rothbury; ⊙ 10am-4.30pm Mon-Fri, 10.30am-4pm Sat Apr-Oct, reduced hours Nov-Mar), there's a national park office, the **Walltown Visitor Centre** (Northumberland National Park Visitor Centre; ☑ 01434-344396; www. northumberlandnationalpark.org.uk; Greenhead; ⊙ 10am-6pm daily Apr-Sep, to 5pm daily Oct, 10am-4pm Sat & Sun Nov-Mar), near Haltwhistle. Inside Kielder Castle, a hunting lodge built in 1775, the **Forest Park Centre** (☑ 01434-250209; www.visitkielder.com; Forest Dr, Kielder; ⊙ 10am-4pm) has tourist information on the Northumberland National Park, including hiking, mountain biking and watersports in the Kielder area.

ℹ Getting There & Away

Public transport options are limited at best – to explore properly, you really need your own wheels.

Otterburn Bus 808 (£4, one hour, one daily Monday to Saturday) runs between Otterburn and Newcastle.

Wooler Buses 470 and 473 link Wooler and Alnwick (£3.30, 40 minutes, four daily Monday to Saturday). Buses 267 and 464 run between Wooler and Berwick-upon-Tweed (£4.90, one hour, every two hours Monday to Saturday).

WILDLIFE OF NORTHUMBERLAND NATIONAL PARK

Northumberland National Park is a wonderful place to go looking for wildlife as you explore on foot. The park has recorded 169 different bird species, including numerous waders (among them lapwing, snipe, redshank, oystercatcher, golden plover and curlew) and ground-dwellers such as red or black grouse. Mammals include red squirrels, roe deer, and the much-sought-after wild Cheviot goat, a primitive goat species with a long shaggy coat.

DON'T MISS

NORTHUMBERLAND NATIONAL PARK'S BEST HIKES

Northumberland National Park is a wonderful place to walk and the park's website (www.northumberlandnationalpark.org.uk) details 35 hikes of between one and seven hours, from easy to strenuous. These include five with Hadrian's Wall as the focal point, with a further 17 taking you through the Cheviot Hills, frequently passing by prehistoric remnants. Local tourist offices can provide maps, guides and route information.

Our favourites, all of moderate difficulty, include:

Vindolanda & Hadrian's Wall (6 miles or 9.6km, 3½ hours) Among the wall's most rewarding sections with Vindolanda Roman Fort (p622) and stunning views. Begins and ends at the Sill (p617).

Steel Rigg & Crag Lough (4 miles or 6.4km, two hours) One of the prettiest sections of Hadrian's Wall that's especially good for families. The walk begins and ends at the Steel Rigg National Park car park.

Winshield Crags & Cawfields (6 miles or 9.6km, 3½ hours) Some of the loveliest sections of Hadrian's Wall. Starts at the Sill (p617) and ends at Crawfields car park.

Breamish Valley Hillfort Trail (4.5 miles or 7.2km, 3½ hours) Five hillforts and stunning views in the Cheviots.

Harthope Valley (4 miles or 6.4km, two hours) Climb to top of the Cheviots with views that go all the way to the sea. Starts and ends at the Carey Burn bridge southwest of Wooler.

Northumberland Coast

Northumberland's coast is one of the UK's most underrated shores. Instead of glitzy seaside resorts, it's strewn with charming, castle-crowned villages along miles of wide, sand. Like Northumberland's wild and remote interior, the coast is sparsely populated, meaning you might just have all of this beauty to yourself.

Alnwick

01665 / POP 8100

Northumberland's historic ducal town, Alnwick (pronounced 'annick') is an elegant maze of narrow cobbled streets around its colossal medieval castle. Alnwick is also home to a famous bookshop and the spectacular Alnwick Garden.

Sights

★ **Alnwick Castle**   CASTLE

(01665-511178; www.alnwickcastle.com; The Peth; adult/child £8/free; 10am-5pm Apr-Sep, 10am-4pm Oct) Set in parklands designed by Lancelot 'Capability' Brown, the imposing ancestral home of the Duke of Northumberland has changed little since the 14th century. It's a favourite set for filmmakers and starred as Hogwarts for the first couple of *Harry Potter* films. The interior is sumptuous and extravagant; the six rooms open to the public – staterooms, dining room, guard chamber and library – have an incredible display of Italian paintings, including Titian's *Ecce Homo* and many Canalettos.

Various free tours include several focusing on *Harry Potter* (check the website for broomstick training times on weekends) and other productions that have used the castle as a backdrop, including British comedy series *Blackadder* and period drama *Downton Abbey*.

For the best views of the castle's exterior, take The Peth to the River Aln's northern bank and follow the woodland trail east.

Alnwick Garden   GARDENS

(www.alnwickgarden.com; Denwick Lane; adult/child £13/5; 10am-6pm Apr-Oct, hours vary rest of year) This 4.8-hectare walled garden incorporates a series of magnificent green spaces surrounding the breathtaking Grand Cascade – 120 separate jets spurting some 30,000L of water down 21 weirs. Half a dozen other gardens include a Franco-Italian-influenced Ornamental Garden (with over 15,000 plants), a Rose Garden and a fascinating Poison Garden, home to some of the deadliest – and most illegal – plants in the world, including cannabis, magic mushrooms, belladonna

Driving Tour
Northumberland Coast

START NEWBIGGIN-BY-THE-SEA
END BERWICK-UPON-TWEED
LENGTH 78 MILES; ONE DAY

It's possible to shadow the coast to the Scottish border from Tynemouth, but the scenery really picks up at ❶ **Newbiggin-by-the-Sea**. Newbiggin's beach was restored in 2007, when over 500,000 tonnes of Skegness' sand was relocated here to counteract erosion, and Sean Henry's gigantic bronze sculpture *The Couple* was installed offshore.

Continuing north along the A1068 coast road for 13 miles brings you to the fishing port of ❷ **Amble**, with a boardwalk along the seafront and puffin cruises (p630). Less than 2 miles north, biscuit-coloured ❸ **Warkworth** is a cluster of houses around a loop in the River Coquet, dominated by the craggy ruin of 14th-century Warkworth Castle (p629). The castle features in Shakespeare's *Henry IV* Parts I and II, and the 1998 film *Elizabeth* was shot here.

Some 5 miles north of Warkworth is ❹ **Alnmouth**, with brightly painted houses and pretty beaches. It's another 5 miles inland to the bustling town of ❺ **Alnwick** to see its imposing castle (p625) – which starred as Harry Potter's Hogwarts – and glorious Alnwick Garden. Turn back towards the coast and follow the B1339 for 4.7 miles before turning east on Windside Hill to ❻ **Craster**, famed for its smoked kippers, which you can buy direct from the smokery (p628) or taste at its restaurant. From Craster, there are spectacular views of brooding Dunstanburgh Castle. Around 5 miles north at ❼ **Low Newton-by-the-Sea**, on Embleton Bay, pause for a pint brewed at the Ship Inn (p628).

Past the village of Seahouses (the jumping-off point for the Farne Islands), quaint ❽ **Bamburgh** is home to the most dramatic castle (p629) yet. Another 17 miles on, via a tidal causeway (check tide times!), the sacred priory ruins (p630) of otherworldly ❾ **Holy Island (Lindisfarne; p631)** still attract spiritual pilgrims. Return to the mainland where, 14 miles north, you can walk almost the entire length of the Elizabethan walls (p631) encircling England's northernmost city, beautiful ❿ **Berwick-upon-Tweed** (p631).

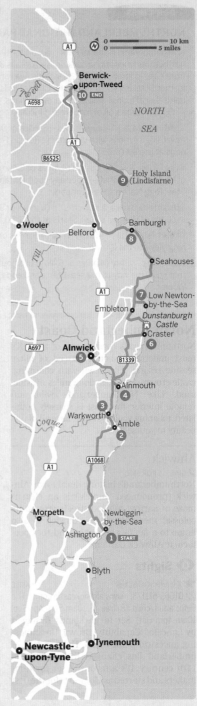

and tobacco. Check the website for opening times, which can change monthly.

Enveloped by – but not in – the treetops, the timber-lined restaurant Treehouse serves Modern British cuisine.

🛏 Sleeping & Eating

★ Alnwick Lodge   B&B, CAMPGROUND ££
(📞 01665-604363; www.alnwicklodge.com; West Cawledge Park, A1; tent sites from £15, glamping incl linen £45-60, B&B s £45-55, d & tw £62-130; 🅿 🛜 🐾) Three miles south of Alnwick's centre, this gorgeous Victorian farmstead has 15 antique-filled rooms with quirky touches like free-standing, lidded baths. Cooked breakfasts are served around a huge circular banqueting table. You can also go 'glamping' in restored gypsy caravans, wagons and shepherds' huts (with shared bathrooms), or pitch up on the sheltered meadow.

White Swan Hotel   HOTEL ££
(📞 01665-602109; www.classiclodges.co.uk; Bondgate Within; d/ste from £105/175; 🅿 🛜 🐾) In the heart of town, this 300-year-old coaching inn has 56 superbly appointed rooms, including family rooms that sleep up to four. Its architectural showpiece is the fine-dining **Olympic restaurant** (mains £13-23, 2-/3-course lunch menus £15/19, 3-course dinner menu £37; ⏰ noon-3pm & 5-9pm).

Treehouse   BRITISH ££
(📞 01665-511852; www.alnwickgarden.com; Alnwick Garden, Denwick Lane; mains £11-18; ⏰ noon-2.30pm Mon & Tue, noon-2.30pm & 6-8.30pm Wed-Sat, noon-4pm Sun) Surrounded by Alnwick Garden's treetops (but not perched up within them as its name would imply), this timber-lined restaurant serves contemporary fare: twice-baked wild garlic soufflé, beetroot- and British gin–cured salmon, and sticky toffee pudding with salted-caramel sauce and honeycomb ice cream. There is often live classical music in the evenings. Bookings are essential.

🛍 Shopping

★ Barter Books   BOOKS
(📞 01665-604888; www.barterbooks.co.uk; Alnwick Station, Wagon Way Rd; ⏰ 9am-6pm) Coal fires, velvet ottomans, reading rooms and a cafe make this secondhand bookshop in Alnwick's Victorian former railway station wonderfully atmospheric and one of Britain's great bookstores. As you browse the crammed bookshelves, the silence is

interrupted only by the tiny toy train that runs along the track above your head.

Taste of Northumbria   FOOD & DRINKS
(📞 01665-602490; www.facebook.com/tasteof northumbria; 4-6 Market Pl; ⏰ 10am-5pm Mon-Sat, 11am-3pm Sun) 🍷 Alnwick-distilled rum and Lindisfarne-made mead along with a range of boutique English gins and Scottish whiskies are sold at this locavore shop in the town centre. Alnwick rum is also used in seasonal Christmas puddings sold here.

ℹ Information

Tourist Office (📞 01670-622152; www.visit alnwick.org.uk; 2 The Shambles; ⏰ 9am-6pm Mon-Sat) Alnwick's friendly tourist office is by Market Pl.

ℹ Getting There & Away

Bus X15 zips along the A1 to Berwick-upon-Tweed (£7.20, one hour, hourly Monday to Saturday, every two hours Sunday) and Newcastle (£7.20, 1½ hours, hourly Monday to Saturday, every two hours Sunday). Bus X18 follows the coast to Berwick-upon-Tweed (£7.20, two hours, three daily) and Newcastle (£7, two hours, hourly).

Craster

📞 01665 / POP 300

Sandy, salty Craster is a small, sheltered fishing village about 6 miles northeast of Alnwick. It stands in the heart of some glorious coastal scenery, and there's a splendid castle nearby. Craster is also famous for its kippers. In the early 20th century, 2500 herring were smoked here daily. The kippers still produced today are said to often grace the Queen's breakfast table.

Dunstanburgh Castle   CASTLE
(EH; www.english-heritage.org.uk; Dunstanburgh Rd; adult/child £5.90/3.50; ⏰ 10am-6pm daily Apr-Aug, to 5pm daily Sep, to 4pm daily Oct, 10am-4pm Sat & Sun Nov-Mar) The dramatic 1.5-mile walk along the coast from Craster (not accessible by car) is the most scenic path to this moody, weather-battered castle. Construction began in 1314 and it was strengthened during the Wars of the Roses, but left to crumble, becoming ruined by 1550. Parts of the original wall and gatehouse keep are still standing and it's a tribute to its builders that so much remains.

You can also reach the castle on foot from Embleton (1.5 miles), but access can be cut off at high tide.

Jolly Fisherman GASTROPUB ££

(📞 016650-576461; www.thejollyfishermancraster. co.uk; Haven Hill; mains lunch £8-15, dinner £12-26; ⏰ 11am-8.30pm Mon-Sat, noon-7pm Sun Apr-Oct, to 5pm Sun Nov-Mar) Crab (in soup, sandwiches, fish platters and more) is the speciality of this gastropub, but it also has a variety of fish dishes, as well as a house burger and steaks served with beef-dripping chips. A strong wine list complements its wonderful real ales. There's a blazing fire in the bar and a beer garden overlooking Dunstanburgh Castle.

⭐ **Robson & Sons** FOOD

(📞 01665-576223; www.kipper.co.uk; Haven Hill; kippers per kg from £9; ⏰ 9am-4.30pm Mon-Fri, 9am-3.30pm Sat, 11am-3.30pm Sun) Four generations have operated this traditional fish smokers; loyal customers include the Royal Family. It's best known for its kippers, but it also smokes salmon and other fish.

❶ Getting There & Away

Bus X18 runs to Alnwick (£5.90, 55 minutes, three daily), Berwick-upon-Tweed (£7.10, 1½ hours, three daily) and Newcastle (£7.10, 2½ hours, three daily). From Monday to Saturday, bus 418 also links Craster to Alnwick (£5.50, 30 minutes, four daily).

Embleton Bay

Beautiful Embleton Bay, a pale wide arc of sand, stretches from Dunstanburgh past the endearing village of Embleton and curves in a broad vanilla-coloured strand around to end at Low Newton-by-the-Sea, a tiny whitewashed, National Trust–preserved village.

Behind the bay is a path leading to the **Newton Pool Nature Reserve**, an important spot for breeding and migrating birds such as black-headed gulls and grasshopper warblers. There are a couple of hides where you can watch them. You can continue walking along the headland beyond Low Newton, where you'll find **Football Hole**, a delightful hidden beach between headlands.

Joiners Arms PUB £££

(📞 01665-576112; www.joiners-arms.com; High Newton-by-the-Sea; d from £155; 🅿🛜🐾) This is a fantastic place to stay: the five contemporary guest rooms here are individually and exquisitely decorated with details like exposed brick, free-standing baths and four-poster beds. Locals also love this gastropub (mains from £9) for its locally sourced ingredients; the seafood and steaks are excellent, and families are warmly welcomed.

Ship Inn PUB FOOD ££

(📞 01665-576262; www.shipinnnewton.co.uk; Low Newton-by-the-Sea; mains lunch £6.50-9, dinner £13-29; ⏰ 11am-7pm Sun-Tue, to 9.30pm Wed-Sat) 🍴 Set around a village green, this idyllic pub brews over two dozen different beers – blond, wheat, rye, bitter, stout and seasonal – using local River Coquet water. The food is first-rate, too, from crab and lobster to regional farm-sourced meat. There is often live music on weekends.

❶ Getting There & Away

Bus X18 to Newcastle (£7.20, 2¾ hours, three daily), Berwick-upon-Tweed (£6.10, 1¼ hours, three daily) and Alnwick (£5.90, 45 minutes, three daily) stops outside the Joiners Arms. From Monday to Saturday, bus 418 (£5.50, 35 minutes, four daily) links the village of Embleton with Alnwick.

KEEP CALM & CARRY ON

Alnwick's Barter Books (p627) is responsible for one of the most unlikely pop culture icons of the early 21st century. At the outbreak of WWII in 1939, the British government produced a series of propaganda posters designed to boost national morale during the difficult days that lay ahead. An estimated 2.5 million posters with the slogan 'Keep Calm and Carry On' were printed but never distributed. They disappeared from view until 2000 when the owners of Barter Books unearthed the poster in a box of books while converting the station. The owners liked it so much that they framed one and put it on the wall. A year later, responding to popular demand, they began to sell the posters, little knowing that the poster and its offshoots would become a successful industry in its own right. The slogan is at once quintessentially British and captures the nation's memories of war-time Britain; the posters are now seen all across the nation. The original is still on the wall behind the till.

Bamburgh

☎ 01668 / POP 410

High up on a basalt crag, Bamburgh's mighty castle looms over the quaint village – a clutch of houses around a pleasant green – which continues to commemorate the valiant achievements of local heroine Grace Darling. In a 2019 study of British seaside resort villages, Bamburgh ranked No.1 in the UK.

★ Bamburgh Castle   CASTLE
(☎01668-214515; www.bamburghcastle.com; Links Rd; adult/child £11.75/5.75; ⊙10am-5pm daily early Feb-early Nov, 11am-4.30pm Sat & Sun early Nov-early Feb) Northumberland's most dramatic castle was built around a powerful 11th-century Norman keep by Henry II. The castle played a key role in the border wars of the 13th and 14th centuries, and in 1464 was the first English castle to fall during the Wars of the Roses. It was restored in the 19th century by the great industrialist Lord Armstrong, and is still home to the Armstrong family.

Its name is a derivative of Bebbanburgh, after the wife of Anglo-Saxon ruler Aedelfrip, whose fortified home occupied this basalt outcrop 500 years earlier. Antique furniture, suits of armour, priceless ceramics and artworks cram the castle's rooms and chambers, but top billing goes to the neo-Gothic King's Hall with wood panelling, leaded windows and hefty beams supporting the roof.

RNLI Grace Darling Museum   MUSEUM
(☎01668-214910; www.rnli.org; 1 Radcliffe Rd; ⊙10am-5pm Mon-Fri & Bank Holiday weekends, Easter-Sep, 10am-4pm Tue-Fri Oct-Easter) FREE Born in Bamburgh, Grace Darling was the lighthouse keeper's daughter on Outer Farne who rowed out to the grounded, flailing SS *Forfarshire* in 1838 and saved its crew in the middle of a dreadful storm. This refurbished museum even has her actual coble (row boat) as well as a film on the events of that stormy night. Grace was born just three houses down from the museum and is buried in the churchyard opposite.

Her ornate wrought-iron and sandstone tomb was built tall so as to be visible to passing ships.

Potted Lobster   SEAFOOD ££
(☎01668-214088; www.thepottedlobster.co.uk; 3 Lucker Rd; mains £14-28, half-/full lobster £22/39, seafood platter for 2 £69; ⊙noon-9pm Jul & Aug, noon-3pm & 6-9pm Sep-Jun) Bamburgh lobster

WARKWORTH CASTLE

Looking like the ultimate sandcastle you'd see at the beach, **Warkworth Castle** (EH; www.english-heritage.org.uk; Castle Tce, Warkworth; adult/child £7.90/4.70, incl Hermitage £11.30/6.80; ⊙10am-5pm), a honey-stone edifice atop a hillock, was built around 1200. From the 14th to 17th centuries, it was home to the Percy family (whose descendants still live at Alnwick Castle), and was pivotal in the Wars of the Roses and the English Civil War. It became a national monument in 1915 but the Duke's Rooms remained under the family's control until 1987. Audio guides give a vivid account of its history.

– served as a creamy egg and brandy thermidor stuffed in the shell, grilled with garlic and parsley butter, or poached and served cold with wild garlic mayo – is the star of this nautical-styled gem. Seafood platters for two, piled high with lobster, Lindisfarne oysters, Craster crab, pickled herring and more, come with hand-cut chips and crusty home-baked bread.

ⓘ Getting There & Away

Take bus X18 north to Berwick-upon-Tweed (£7.20, 50 minutes, three daily) or south to Newcastle (£7.20, 3¼ hours, three daily).

Holy Island (Lindisfarne)

There's something almost other-worldly about this tiny, 2-sq-mile island. Connected to the mainland by a narrow causeway that only appears at low tide, cutting the island off from the mainland for about five hours each day, it's fiercely desolate and isolated, scarcely different from when St Aidan arrived to found a monastery in 635.

As you cross the empty flats, it's easy to imagine the marauding Vikings who repeatedly sacked the settlement between 793 and 875, when the monks finally took the hint and left. They carried with them the illuminated *Lindisfarne Gospels* (now in the British Library in London) and the miraculously preserved body of St Cuthbert, who lived here for a couple of years but preferred the hermit's life on Inner Farne. A priory was re-established in the 11th century, but didn't survive the Dissolution in 1537.

Sights

Lindisfarne Priory RUINS

(EH; www.english-heritage.org.uk; adult/child £7.90/4.70; ⊙10am-5pm, times vary with tides) The skeletal, red and grey ruins of the priory are an eerie sight and give a glimpse into the isolated life of the Lindisfarne monks. The later 13th-century St Mary the Virgin Church is built on the site of the first church between the Tees and the Firth of Forth, and the adjacent museum displays the remains of the first monastery and tells the story of the monastic community before and after the Dissolution.

Lindisfarne Castle CASTLE

(NT; www.nationaltrust.org.uk; adult/child £7.30/3.60; ⊙11am-5pm Tue-Sun late May-Sep, 10am-4pm Easter-late May & Oct) Built atop a rocky bluff in 1550, this tiny, storybook castle was extended and converted by Sir Edwin Lutyens from 1902 to 1910 for Edward Hudson, the owner of *Country Life* magazine – you can imagine some of the glamorous parties that graced its alluring rooms. It's half a mile east of the village. Opening times can vary due to tide times.

🛏 Sleeping & Eating

Lindisfarne Inn INN ££

(☑01289-381223; www.lindisfarneinn.co.uk; Beal Rd, Beal; s/d/f incl breakfast from £71/89/120; P🛜🐕) This mainland inn on the A1 next

to the turn-off to the causeway is a handy alternative to island accommodation and/ or dining if you're cutting it fine with crossing times. Its 23 spotless, modern rooms with tartan carpets are set far back enough that road noise isn't a problem. Well-above-average pub food (such as suet pudding with Northumbrian game) changes seasonally.

Crown & Anchor INN ££

(☑01289-389215; www.holyislandcrown.co.uk; Market Pl; s/d from £60/70; P🐕) A cornerstone of the island's social life, this venerable pub has brightly coloured guest rooms and solid pub food, but the biggest winner is the beer garden with a postcard panorama of the castle, priory and harbour.

Barn @ Beal PUB FOOD ££

(☑01289-540044; www.barnatbeal.com; Beal Farm, Beal; lunch £10-23; ⊙cafe 9am-6pm Mon-Sat, 9am-5pm Sun, bar hours vary seasonally; 🛜♿) You can watch the causeway tides on webcam at this sociable mainland pub 1 mile northeast of the A1 turn-off (2 miles west of the island). Lindisfarne seafood, including lobster, is a menu highlight, as are house-speciality burgers utilising farm produce. There's a kids' play area. It also has 12 tent pitches (from £10) and nine caravan sites (from £25).

🛍 Shopping

St Aidan's Winery FOOD, DRINK

(Lindisfarne Mead; ☑01289-389230; www.lindisfarne-mead.co.uk; Prior Lane; ⊙11am-3.30pm Mon, to 4.30pm Tue, 11.30am-5pm Wed, noon-5pm Thu, 9.30am-5pm Fri & Sat, 10am-5pm Sun, may vary with tides) 🌿 Mead is made here on Lindisfarne by St Aidan's Winery to a traditional Roman recipe using locally drawn water and honey. Free tastings let you try its three varieties – original, blood orange and spiced – as well as its fortified wines, such as ginger, wild strawberry, elderberry, blackberry and cherry. Other products include mead-based chocolate truffles and jams. Check ahead for opening hours.

❶ Getting There & Away

When tides permit, the Holy Island Hopper (www.berwickupontweedtaxis.co.uk; £3, 15 minutes) links the island with the mainland on the corner of Beal Rd and the A1 to connect with buses X15 and X18, serving Berwick-upon-Tweed, Alnwick and Newcastle. If using the

THE PUFFINS OF COQUET ISLAND

For three days in late May to early June, the **Amble Puffin Festival** (www.amblepuffinfest.co.uk) celebrates the hatching of puffin chicks on nearby Coquet Island with events including local history talks, guided birdwatching walks, exhibitions, watersports, a craft fair, a food festival and live music. Festivities occur across town.

During the breeding season, you can also take a boat trip to see the birds with **Dave Gray's Puffin Cruises** (☑01665-711975; www.puffincruises.co.uk; Amble Harbour, Amble; adult/child £10/5; ⊙by reservation Apr-Oct).

THE FARNE ISLANDS

During breeding season (roughly May to July), you can see feeding chicks of 20 seabird species (including puffin, kittiwake, Arctic tern, eider duck, cormorant and gull), and some 6000 grey seals, on this rocky **archipelago** (NT; ☑ 01289-389244; www.national trust.org.uk; adult/child excl boat transport £34.80/17.40, cheaper outside breeding season; ☺ by reservation, season & conditions permitting Mar-Oct) 3 miles offshore from the fishing village of Seahouses. Boat operators, contactable through Seahouses' **tourist office** (☑ 01670-625593; www.visitnorthumberland.com; Seafield car park, Seahouses; ☺ 9.30am-4pm Thu-Tue Apr, 9.30am-4pm daily May-Oct), depart from Seahouses' dock, including **Billy Shiel** (☑ 01665-720308; www.farne-islands.com; Harbour Rd, Seahouses; adult/child excl island landing fees 2½hr tour £20/15, 6hr tour £40/25; ☺ by reservation Apr-Oct).

Crossings can be rough (impossible in bad weather); wear warm, waterproof clothing and an old hat to guard against the birds!

causeway, drivers need to pay close attention to crossing-time information, posted at tourist offices and on notice boards throughout the area, and at www.holy-island.info. Alternatively, call ☑ 01289-330733. Every year drivers are caught midway by the incoming tide and have to abandon their cars.

ℹ Getting Around

Park in the signposted car park (£5.50 per day). A shuttle bus (£2 return) runs from the car park to the castle every 20 minutes from Easter to September; alternatively it's a level 300m walk to the village centre and 1 mile to the castle.

Berwick-upon-Tweed

☑ 01289 / POP 12,400

England's northernmost city is a picturesque fortress town, cleaved by the River Tweed. The Grade I–listed Berwick Bridge (aka Old Bridge), built from sandstone between 1611 and 1624, and the Royal Tweed (1925–28), both span the river.

◎ Sights & Activities

★ **Berwick Walls**   HISTORIC SITE
(EH; www.english-heritage.org.uk; ☺ dawn-dusk) FREE You can walk almost the entire length of Berwick's hefty Elizabethan walls, begun in 1558 to reinforce an earlier set built during the reign of Edward II. The mile-long walk is a must, with wonderful, wide-open views. Only a small fragment remains of the once-mighty border castle, most of the building having been replaced by the train station.

Berwick Barracks   MUSEUM, GALLERY
(EH; www.english-heritage.org.uk; The Parade; adult/child £5.90/3.50; ☺ 10am-5pm Wed-Sun

Apr-Oct) Designed by Nicholas Hawksmoor, Britain's oldest purpose-built barracks (1717) now house an assortment of museums and art galleries, covering a history of the town and British soldiery since the 17th century. The Gymnasium Gallery hosts big-name contemporary art exhibitions.

Berwick Boat Trips   CRUISE
(☑ 07713 170845; www.berwickboattrips.co.uk; Berwick-upon-Tweed Quayside; 2hr North Sea wildlife tour adult/child £18/12, 1hr river tour £10/7; ☺ by reservation) Choose from a North Sea cruise spotting seals, dolphins and sea birds, a river cruise along the Tweed, or a scenic trip along the estuary at sunset. Schedules are posted online.

🛏 Sleeping & Eating

Berwick YHA   HOSTEL £
(☑ 01629-592700; www.yha.org.uk; Dewars Lane; d from £39; [P] [@] [🖤]) A mid-18th-century granary has been converted into a state-of-the-art hostel with private rooms (all with en suite bathrooms). Contemporary facilities include a TV room, a laundry and wi-fi in common areas. Staff are terrifically helpful.

★ **Marshall Meadows
Country House Hotel**   HERITAGE HOTEL ££
(☑ 01289-331133; www.marshallmeadowshotel. co.uk; Marshall Meadows; d/f incl breakfast from £99/119; [P][🖤][🖤]) England's most northerly hotel, just 600m from the Scottish border, sits amid 6 hectares of woodland and ornamental gardens. The Georgian manor's 19 rooms (including a ground-floor family room) have countrified checked and floral fabrics. There are two cosy bars with open fireplaces, a conservatory, and an

ENGLISH OR SCOTTISH?

As you might expect from a town perilously close to one of the continent's most contested borders, Berwick is the most fought-over settlement in European history: between 1174 and 1482 it changed hands 14 times between the Scots and the English. And it's not just about history. Although firmly English since the 15th century, Berwick retains its own identity, with locals south of the border speaking with a noticeable Scottish burr.

Less known (but just as important to many modern locals), the town's football team, Berwick Rangers, is the only English team to play in the Scottish Football League. In 2019, after 114 years in the top three or four tiers of Scottish football (without much success, it must be said), Berwick Rangers were relegated from Scottish League Two. Even so, at the time of writing, Berwick Rangers were still one of very few teams in world football to play in a national league other than that of the country in which they're located: they now play in Scotland's fifth-tier Lowland Football League.

oak-panelled restaurant serving breakfast (including kippers), and evening meals by candlelight.

Audela BRITISH ££
(📞01289-308827; www.audela.co.uk; 64 Bridge St; mains £18-23, 2-/3-course Sunday lunch $20/24.50; ⊙noon-2.30pm & 5.30-9pm Thu-Mon) Named for the last vessel to be built at Berwick Shipyard (in 1979) and set in a former cockle shop, Audela is the town's top table.

Local suppliers provide the ingredients for dishes such as Borders venison loin with, among other ingredients, pickled brambles.

❶ Getting There & Away

On the East Coast Main Line linking London and Edinburgh, Berwick-upon-Tweed is almost exactly halfway between Edinburgh (from £11.60, one hour, up to two per hour) and Newcastle (from £12.70, 45 minutes, up to two per hour).

Buses stop on Golden Sq (where it meets Marygate). National Express coaches between Edinburgh (£17, 1¼ hours, twice daily) and London (£43.50.10, eight hours, twice daily) stop here.

Newcastle is served by the X15 (via Alnwick; £7.20, 2½ hours, hourly Monday to Saturday, every two hours Sunday) and X18 (£7.20, four hours, three daily).

Understand England

History

Tiny geographically, England has been immensely powerful historically. And the extent to which its past shapes its present is profound. To really understand England you must delve into its rich history, packed with drama and intrigue, with characters including incomers and invaders all leaving their mark. The result? A mix of cultures, landscapes and language that shaped a modern nation. For many, this complex heritage – whether seen at Hadrian's Wall, Canterbury Cathedral, Plymouth Dock or the Tower of London – is England's big draw.

Stone Age & Iron Age

Stone tools discovered on a beach in Norfolk suggest the earliest human species habitation in England stretches back to almost a million years ago, with the earliest estimates of homo sapiens at around 40,000 years. These early homo sapiens were nomadic hunter-gatherers, but by around 4000 BCE most had settled down, notably in open areas such as Salisbury Plain in southern England. Alongside fields they built burial mounds (today called barrows), but their most enduring legacies are the great stone circles of Avebury and Stonehenge, still clearly visible today.

Move on a millennium or two and it's the Iron Age. Better tools meant trees could be felled and more land turned over to farming. As landscapes altered, this was also a time of cultural change: a new wave of migrants – the Celts – arrived in Britain from the European mainland. It's not clear if the new arrivals absorbed the indigenous people, or vice versa, but the end result was the widespread adoption of Celtic language and culture, and the creation of a Celtic-British population – today often known as the Britons (or Ancient Britons to distinguish them from today's inhabitants).

By around 100 BCE, the Ancient Britons had separated into about 20 different tribes, including the Cantiaci (in today's county of Kent), the Iceni (in today's Norfolk) and the Brigantes (in northern England). Did you notice the Latin-sounding names? That's because the tribal tags were handed out by the next arrivals on England's shores...

Probably constructed from around 3000 BCE, Stonehenge has stood on Salisbury Plain for more than 5000 years, making it older than the pyramids of Egypt.

TIMELINE	4000 BCE	55 BCE	43 CE
	Neolithic peoples migrate from continental Europe. Differing significantly from previous arrivals, instead of hunting and moving on, they eventually settle in one place and start farming.	Relatively small groups of Roman invaders under the command of General Julius Caesar make forays into southern England from the northern coast of Gaul (today's France).	Emperor Claudius leads the first proper Roman invasion of Britain. His army wages a ruthless campaign, and the Romans control most of southern England by 50 CE.

The Romans

Although there had been some earlier expeditionary campaigns, the main Roman invasion of what is now England began in 43 CE. They called their newly won province Britannia, and within a decade most of southern England was under Roman control. It wasn't a walkover though: some locals fought back, most famously the warrior-queen Boudica, who led a rebel army against Londinium, the Roman port on the present site of London.

Opposition was mostly sporadic, however, and no real threat to Roman military might. By around 80 CE Britannia comprised much of today's England and Wales. Though it's tempting to imagine noble natives battling courageously against occupying forces, Roman control and stability was possibly welcomed by the general population, tired of feuding chiefs and insecure tribal territories.

Roman settlement in Britain continued for almost four centuries, and intermarriage was common between locals and incomers (many from other parts of the Empire – including modern-day Belgium, Spain and Syria – rather than Rome itself). A Romano-British population thus evolved, particularly in the towns, while indigenous Celtic-British culture remained in rural areas.

Along with stability and wealth, the Romans paved the way for another cultural facet: a new religion called Christianity, after it was recognised by Emperor Constantine in the 4th century. Recent research also suggests Celtic Christians may have brought the religion to Britain even earlier. But by this time, although Romano-British culture was thriving in Britannia, back in its Mediterranean heartland the Empire was already in decline.

Boudica was queen of the Iceni, a Celtic-British tribe whose territory was invaded by the Romans around 60 CE. A year later, she led an army against the Roman settlements of Camulodunum (now Colchester) and Londinium (London), but was eventually defeated at the Battle of Watling Street (in today's Shropshire). A statue of the warrior queen stands at the western end of London's Westminster Bridge.

LEGACY OF THE LEGIONS

To control their new territory, the Romans built garrisons across England. Many developed into towns, which can be recognised by names ending in 'chester' or 'caster' (from the Latin *castrum*, meaning military camp) – Lancaster, Winchester, Manchester and, of course, Chester, to name but a few. The Romans also built roads, initially so soldiers could march quickly from place to place, and later so that trade could develop. Wherever possible the roads were straight lines (because it was efficient, not – as the old joke goes – to stop Ancient Britons hiding round corners), such as Ermine St between London and York, Watling St between Kent and Wales, and the Fosse Way between Exeter and Lincoln. As you travel around England, you'll notice many modern highways still follow Roman roads. In a country better known for old lanes and turnpike routes winding through the landscape, these ruler-straight highways stand out on the map.

c 60	c 200	c 410	5th century
The Celtic Iceni warrior queen Boudica (or Boadicea) leads a rebel army against the Romans, destroys the Roman town of Colchester and gets as far as their port at Londinium (now London).	The Romans build a defensive wall around the city of London with four main entrance gates, still reflected today by the districts of Aldgate, Ludgate, Newgate and Bishopsgate.	As the classical world's greatest empire declines after centuries of relative peace and prosperity, Roman rule ends in Britain with more of a whimper than a bang.	Germanic tribes – known today as the Anglo-Saxons – from the area now called Germany migrate to England, and quickly spread across much of the country.

636

HISTORY THE ANGLO-SAXONS

It was an untidy finale. The Romans were not driven out by the Ancient Britons (after more than 300 years, Romano-British culture was so established there was nowhere for many to go 'home' to). In reality, Britannia was simply dumped by the rulers in Rome, and the colony slowly fizzled out. But some historians are tidy folk, and the end of Roman power in England is often dated at 410 CE.

The Anglo-Saxons

When Roman power faded, the province of Britannia went downhill. Romano-British towns were abandoned and rural areas became no-go zones as local warlords fought over fiefdoms. The vacuum didn't go unnoticed, and once again migrants crossed from the European mainland – this time Germanic tribes called Angles and Saxons.

Historians disagree on what happened next; either the Anglo-Saxons largely overcame or absorbed the Romano-British and Celts, or the indigenous tribes simply adopted Anglo-Saxon language and culture. Either way, by the late 6th century much of England was predominantly Anglo-Saxon, divided into separate kingdoms dominated by Wessex (in southern England), Mercia (today's Midlands) and Northumbria (northern England).

Some areas remained unaffected by the incomers, but the overall impact was immense – the name England means 'land of the Angles', and today the core of the English language is Anglo-Saxon, many place names have Anglo-Saxon roots, and the very term 'Anglo-Saxon' has become a (much abused and factually incorrect) byword for 'pure English'.

The Vikings & Alfred the Great

In the 9th century England was yet again invaded by a bunch of pesky Continentals. This time it was the Vikings, from today's Scandinavia. They quickly conquered the eastern and northeastern areas of England, then started to expand into central England. Blocking their route were the Anglo-Saxon armies heading north, led by Alfred the Great, the king of Wessex and one of English history's best-known characters.

Thus England was divided in two: north and east was the Viking land, known as Danelaw, while south and west was Anglo-Saxon territory. Alfred was hailed as king of the English – the first time the Anglo-Saxons regarded themselves as a truly united people. His capital was Winchester; if you come to visit the famous cathedral, look out for the nearby statue of Alfred in the city centre.

Alfred's son and successor was Edward, known as Edward the Elder. After more battles, he gained control of Danelaw, and thus became the first king to rule the whole country – a major milestone in English history.

Despite Anglo-Saxon dominance from around 500 CE, the Celtic language was still being spoken in parts of southern England when the Normans invaded in the 11th century. Irish and Scottish Gaelic, Welsh and Cornish all have their origins in the Celtic tongue.

8th century	9th century	927	1066
King Offa of Mercia orders the construction of a clear border between his kingdom and Wales – that defensive ditch, called Offa's Dyke, is still visible today.	Vikings arrive and conquer east and northeast England. They establish their capital at Jorvik, today's city of York.	Athelstan, grandson of Alfred the Great and son of Edward the Elder, is the first monarch to be crowned king of England, building on his ancestors' success in regaining Viking territory.	Incumbent King Harold II is defeated by an invading Norman army at the Battle of Hastings, and England finds itself with a new monarch: William the Conqueror.

But it was hardly cause for celebration. Later in the 10th century, more raids from Scandinavia threatened the fledgling English unity, and as England came to the end of the 1st millennium CE, the future was anything but certain.

1066 & All That

In 1066 when King Edward the Confessor died, the crown passed to Harold II, his brother-in-law. That should've settled things, but Edward had a cousin in Normandy (in northern France) called William, who thought *he* should have succeeded to the throne of England.

The end result was the Battle of Hastings of 1066, the most memorable of dates for anyone who has studied English history. William sailed from Normandy with an army, the English were defeated, and King Harold II was killed – by an arrow in the eye, according to legend. William became king of England, earning himself the prestigious epithet Conqueror.

In the years after the invasion, the French-speaking Normans and the English-speaking Anglo-Saxons kept pretty much to themselves. At the top of the feudal system came the monarch, and below that came the landowning nobles: barons and baronesses, dukes and duchesses, plus the bishops. Then came earls, knights and lords – and their ladies. At the bottom were landless peasants or serfs, and this strict hierarchy became the basis of a class system that to a certain extent still exists in England today.

Royal & Holy Squabbling

William's successor, William II, was assassinated during a hunting trip and was succeeded by Henry I, then Stephen of Blois, then Henry II who established the House of Plantagenet. This period also established the long-standing English tradition of competition for the throne, and introduced an equally enduring tendency of bickering between royalty and the Church. Things came to a head in 1170 when Henry II had the 'turbulent priest' Thomas Becket murdered in Canterbury Cathedral.

Perhaps the next king, Richard I, wanted to make amends for his forebears' unholy sentiments by fighting against what were then seen as Muslim 'infidels' in the Holy Land (today's Israel and the Palestinian Territories, plus parts of Syria, Jordan and Lebanon). Unfortunately, Richard was too busy crusading to govern England – although his battles earned him the sobriquet Lionheart – and in his absence the country fell into disarray.

Richard was succeeded by his brother John. According to legend, it was during this time that a nobleman named Robert of Loxley, better known as Robin Hood, hid in Sherwood Forest and engaged in a spot of wealth redistribution.

The Year 1000 by Robert Lacey and Danny Danziger looks long and hard at English life a millennium ago. Apparently it was cold and damp then, too.

HISTORY 1066 & ALL THAT

Visitors often get confused about the various names of this part of the world. The country of England is part of the island of Great Britain (along with Wales and Scotland), and part of the United Kingdom of Great Britain and Northern Ireland. Hence 'English' and 'British' mean quite different things.

1085–86	1096	12th century	1215
The Norman invaders compile the Domesday Book – a thorough census of England's stock and future potential; it's still a vital historical document today.	The official start of the First Crusade – a campaign of Christian European armies against the Muslim occupation of Jerusalem and the 'Holy Land'. A series of crusades continues until 1272.	Oxford University founded. There's evidence of teaching in the area since 1096, but King Henry II's 1167 ban on students attending the University of Paris solidifies Oxford's importance.	King John signs the Magna Carta, limiting the monarch's power for the first time in English history: an early step on the path towards constitutional rule.

Plantagenet Progress

By the early 13th century King John's erratic rule was too much for the powerful barons, and they forced him to affirm a document called the Magna Carta (Great Charter), which set limits on the power of the monarch. It was signed at Runnymede, near Windsor; you can still visit the site (basically a field) today.

The next king was Henry III, followed in 1272 by Edward I – a skilled ruler and ambitious general. During a busy 35-year reign, he was unashamedly expansionist, leading campaigns into Wales and Scotland, where his ruthless activities earned him the title 'Hammer of the Scots'.

Edward I was succeeded by Edward II, who lacked his forebear's military success. He failed in the marriage department too, and came to a grisly end when, it's thought, his wife Isabella and her lover Roger Mortimer had him murdered in Berkeley Castle. Today, fans of ghoulish ends can visit the very spot where it happened.

Myths and Legends of the British Isles by Richard Barber is an ideal read if you want a break from firm historical facts. Learn about King Arthur and the Knights of the Round Table, plus much more from the mists of time.

Houses of Lancaster & York

In 1399 Richard II was ousted by a powerful baron called Henry Bolingbroke, who became Henry IV – the first monarch of the House of Lancaster. He was followed, neatly, by Henry V, who decided it was time to end the Hundred Years' War, a long-standing conflict between England and France. Henry's victory at the Battle of Agincourt and the patriotic speech he was given by Shakespeare in his namesake play ('cry God for Harry, England and St George!') ensured his position among the most famous of English monarchs.

Still keeping things neat, Henry V was followed by Henry VI. His main claims to fame were overseeing the building of great places of worship – King's College Chapel, in Cambridge; Eton Chapel, near Windsor – and suffering from great bouts of insanity.

The Hundred Years' War finally ground to a halt in 1453, but just a few years later, England was plunged into a civil conflict dubbed the Wars of the Roses. Briefly it went like this: Henry VI of the House of Lancaster (emblem: a red rose) was challenged by Richard, Duke of York (emblem: a white rose). Henry was weak and it was almost a walkover for Richard, but Henry's wife, Margaret of Anjou, was made of sterner stuff and her forces defeated the challenger. Then Richard's son Edward entered with an army, turned the tables, drove out Henry and became King Edward IV – the first monarch of the House of York.

Today, more than 500 years after the Wars of the Roses, Yorkshire's symbol is still a white rose, while Lancashire's is still a red rose, and rivalry between these two counties is still very strong – especially when it comes to cricket and football.

Dark Deeds in the Tower

Edward IV hardly had time to catch his breath before facing a challenge from the Earl of Warwick, who teamed up with the energetic

1337–1453	1348	1415	1455–85
England battles France in a long conflict known as the Hundred Years' War. It was actually a series of small conflicts. And it lasted for more than a century.	The arrival of the Black Death. Commonly attributed to bubonic plague, the pandemic kills more than 1.5 million people, over a third of the country's population.	The invading English army under Henry V defeats the French army at the Battle of Agincourt – a crucial battle in the Hundred Years' War.	The Wars of the Roses: a conflict between two competing dynasties – the Houses of Lancaster and York. The Yorkists are successful, and King Edward IV gains the throne.

WHO'D WANT TO BE A KING?

The gallop through the story of England's ruling dynasties clearly shows that life is never dull for the person at the top. Despite immense power and privilege, the position of monarch (or, perhaps worse, *potential* monarch) probably ranks as one of history's least safe occupations. English kings to meet an untimely end include Harold II (killed in battle), William II (assassinated), Charles I (beheaded by Republicans), Edward V (allegedly murdered by an uncle), Richard II (probably starved to death), James II (deposed), Edward II (dispatched by his queen and her lover) and William III (died after his horse tripped over a molehill). As you visit the castles and battlefields of England, you may feel a touch of sympathy – but only a touch – for those all-powerful figures continually looking over their shoulders.

Margaret of Anjou to shuttle Edward into exile and bring Henry VI back to the throne. A year later Edward IV came bouncing back, killed Warwick, captured Margaret and had Henry executed in the Tower of London.

Edward IV was succeeded by his 12-year-old son, Edward V. But in 1483 the boy-king was mysteriously murdered, along with his brother, and once again the Tower of London was the scene of the crime.

With the 'little princes' dispatched, the throne was open for their uncle Richard. Whether he was the princes' killer remains the subject of debate, but his rule as Richard III was short-lived: in 1485 he was tumbled from the top job by a Welsh nobleman (from the rival Lancastrian line) named Henry Tudor, who became King Henry VII.

Peace & Dissolution

With the Wars of the Roses only recently ended, Henry VII married Elizabeth of York, so uniting the House of Lancaster and the House of York. He adopted the 'Tudor rose' symbol, which features the flower in both colours. Henry also married off his daughter to James IV of Scotland, linking the Tudor and Stuart lines. The result? A much-welcomed period of peace for England.

The next king, Henry VIII, is one of England's best-known monarchs, mainly thanks to his six wives – the result of a desperate quest for a male heir. He also had a profound impact on England's religious history; his rift with the Pope and the Roman Catholic Church led to the separation of the Church of England from papal rule, and to the 'Dissolution' – the infamous closure of many monasteries, the ruins of which can still be seen today at places such as Fountains Abbey and Rievaulx Abbey in Yorkshire.

Hilary Mantel's Booker Prize–winning *Wolf Hall*, and its sequel *Bring Up the Bodies*, explore the rise to power of Thomas Cromwell and the wider machinations of Henry VIII's court. The third and final instalment, *The Mirror and the Light*, was published in 2020.

1485	1509–47	1558–1603	1605
Henry Tudor defeats Richard III at the Battle of Bosworth to become King Henry VII, establishing the Tudor dynasty and ending York–Lancaster rivalry for the throne.	Reign of King Henry VIII. The Pope's disapproval of Henry's serial marriages and divorces partly prompts the English Reformation – the founding of the Church of England.	Reign of Queen Elizabeth I, a period of boundless English optimism. Enter stage right: playwright William Shakespeare. Exit due west: navigators Walter Raleigh and Francis Drake.	King James' attempts to smooth religious relations are set back by an anti-Catholic outcry following the infamous Gunpowder Plot, a terrorist attempt to blow up parliament led by Guy Fawkes.

The Elizabethan Age

Henry VIII was succeeded by his son Edward VI, and his daughter Mary I (Mary Tudor or 'Bloody Mary'), but their reigns were short. And so Elizabeth, third in line, unexpectedly came to the throne.

The movie *Elizabeth*, directed by Shekhar Kapur (1998) and starring Cate Blanchett, covers the early years of the Virgin Queen's rule, as she graduates from princess to commanding monarch – a time of forbidden love, unwanted suitors, intrigue and death.

Elizabeth I inherited a nasty mess of religious strife and divided loyalties, but after an uncertain start she gained confidence and turned the country around. Refusing marriage, she borrowed biblical motifs and became known as the Virgin Queen – perhaps the first English monarch to create a cult image.

The big moments in her 45-year reign included the naval defeat of the Spanish Armada, the far-flung explorations of English seafarers Walter Raleigh and Francis Drake, and the expansion of England's trading network, including newly established colonies on the east coast of America – not to mention a cultural flourishing, thanks to writers such as William Shakespeare and Christopher Marlowe.

Meanwhile, Elizabeth's Catholic cousin Mary Stuart (daughter of Scottish king James V) had become queen of Scotland. She'd spent her childhood in France, marrying the French dauphin (crown prince), thereby becoming queen of France as well. After her husband's death (so no longer France's queen), Mary returned to Scotland to rule but was eventually forced to abdicate amid claims of infidelity and murder.

She escaped to England and appealed to Elizabeth for help. But Mary had a strong claim to the English throne. That made her a security risk and she was imprisoned by Elizabeth. Historians dispute whether the former Scottish queen then instigated or was simply the focus of numerous Catholic plots to assassinate Protestant Elizabeth and put Mary on the throne. Either way, Elizabeth held Mary under arrest for nearly 19 years, moving her frequently from house to house. As you travel around England today, you can visit many stately homes (and even a few pubs) that proudly claim, 'Mary Queen of Scots slept here'. Elizabeth eventually ordered Mary's execution in 1587.

United & Disunited Britain

The Isles: A History by Norman Davies provides much-acclaimed and highly readable coverage of the past 10,000 years in England, within the broader history of the British Isles.

Elizabeth died in 1603, but despite a bountiful reign, the Virgin Queen had failed to provide an heir. She was succeeded by her closest relative, the Scottish king James, the safely Protestant son of the executed Mary. Thus, he became James I of England and VI of Scotland, the first English monarch of the House of Stuart. James did his best to soothe Catholic–Protestant tensions and united England, Wales and Scotland into one kingdom for the first time – another step towards British unity, at least on paper.

1644–49	1660	1749	1775–83
Civil War. Royalist forces supporting the king are pitted against Oliver Cromwell's army of 'Parliamentarians'. Cromwell is victorious, and England becomes a republic.	After Cromwell's death, conflicting interests beset the republic. The eldest son of Charles I is invited back to take the throne. Charles II is crowned, and the monarchy is restored (the Restoration).	Author and magistrate Henry Fielding founds the Bow Street Runners, London's first professional police force. A 1792 Act of Parliament allowed the Bow Street model to spread across England.	The American War of Independence is the British Empire's first major reversal. William Pitt the Younger becomes the country's youngest-ever prime minister at the age of 24.

But the divide between king and parliament continued to smoulder, and the power struggle worsened during the reign of Charles I, eventually degenerating into the English Civil War. The antiroyalist (or 'Parliamentarian') forces were led by Oliver Cromwell, a Puritan who preached against the excesses of the monarchy and established Church. His army (known as the Roundheads) was pitched against the king's forces (the Cavaliers) in a conflict that tore England apart. It ended with victory for the Roundheads – the king was executed and England declared a republic, with Cromwell hailed as 'Protector'.

The Return of the King

By 1653 Cromwell was finding parliament too restricting and assumed dictatorial powers, much to his supporters' dismay. On his death in 1658, he was followed half-heartedly by his son, but in 1660 parliament decided to re-establish the monarchy, as republican alternatives were proving far worse.

Charles II (the exiled son of Charles I) came to the throne, and his rule – known as 'the Restoration' – saw scientific and cultural activity bursting forth after the strait-laced ethics of Cromwell's time. Exploration and expansion were also on the agenda. Backed by the army and navy (which had been modernised by Cromwell), colonies stretched down the American coast, while the East India Company set up headquarters in Bombay, laying foundations for what was to become the British Empire.

The next king, James II, had a harder time. Attempts to ease restrictive laws on Catholics ended with his overthrow and defeat at the Battle of the Boyne by William III, the Protestant king of Holland, aka William of Orange. William was married to James' daughter Mary. William and Mary had equal rights to the throne, and their joint accession in 1689 was known as the Glorious Revolution.

Empire Building

By 1702, both Mary and William had died. They were succeeded by William's sister-in-law, Anne. During her reign, in 1707, the Act of Union was passed, uniting England, Wales and Scotland under one parliament – based in London – for the first time.

Queen Anne died without an heir in 1714, marking the end of the Stuart line. The throne passed to distant (but still safely Protestant) German relatives – the House of Hanover, commonly known as the Georgians.

Meanwhile, the British Empire continued to grow in the Americas as well as in Asia, while claims were made to Australia after James Cook's epic voyage of 1769.

A History of England in a Nutshell by John Mathew provides exactly what it says on the cover: a quick overview of the nation's key events in less than 200 pages.

HISTORY THE RETURN OF THE KING

At its height, the British Empire covered 20% of the land area of the earth, which contained a quarter of the world's population.

1799–1815	1837–1901	1914	1926
The Napoleonic Wars see a weakened Britain threatened with invasion by Napoleon, whose ambitions are curtailed at the famous battles of Trafalgar (1805) and Waterloo (1815).	Reign of Queen Victoria. The British Empire – 'the Empire where the sun never sets' – expands from Canada through Africa and India to Australia and New Zealand.	Archduke Franz Ferdinand of Austria is assassinated in the Balkan city of Sarajevo – the final spark in a decade-long crisis that starts the Great War, now called WWI.	Increasing mistrust of the government, fuelled by soaring unemployment, leads to the General Strike. Millions of workers – train drivers, miners, shipbuilders – down tools and bring the country to a halt.

The Industrial Era

While the Empire expanded abroad, at home Britain had become the crucible of the Industrial Revolution. Steam power (pioneered by James Watt in the 1760s and 1770s) and steam trains (developed by George Stephenson in the 1820s) transformed methods of production and transport, and the towns of the English Midlands became the first industrial cities.

Industrial growth led to Britain's first major period of internal migration, as vast numbers of people from the countryside came to the cities in search of work. At the same time, medical advances improved life expectancy, creating a sharp population increase. For many ordinary people the effects of Britain's economic blossoming were dislocation and poverty.

But despite the social turmoil of the early 19th century, by the time Queen Victoria took the throne in 1837 Britain's factories and fleets dominated world trade. The rest of the 19th century was seen as Britain's Golden Age – a period of patriotic confidence not seen since the days of Elizabeth I.

The times were optimistic, but it wasn't all tub-thumping jingoism. Education became universal, trade unions were legalised and the right to vote was extended in a series of reform acts, finally being granted to all men over the age of 21 in 1918, and to all women in 1928.

Captain James Cook's voyage to the southern hemisphere was primarily a scientific expedition. His objectives included monitoring the transit of Venus, an astronomical event that happens only twice every 180 years or so (most recently in 2004 and 2012). 'Discovering' Australia was just a sideline.

World War I

When Queen Victoria died in 1901 the country entered a period of decline. Meanwhile, the military powers of Russia, Austria-Hungary, Turkey and Germany were sabre-rattling in the Balkan states, a dispute that eventually started the 'Great War'. By the war's weary end in 1918, over 700,000 British soldiers had died, with hardly a town or village untouched, as the sobering lists of names on war memorials all over England still show.

For the soldiers that did return from WWI, disillusion with the old social order helped strengthen the Labour Party – which represented the working class – as a political force, upsetting the balance long enjoyed by the Liberal and Conservative parties. Labour came to power for the first time, in coalition with the Liberals, in the 1923 election, but by the mid-1920s the Conservatives were back. The world economy was now in decline and industrial unrest had become widespread. The situation worsened in the 1930s as the Great Depression meant another decade of misery and political upheaval, and even the royal family took a knock when Edward VIII abdicated in 1936 so he could marry Wallis Simpson, a woman who was twice divorced and – horror of horrors – American.

One of the finest novels about WWI is *Birdsong* by Sebastian Faulks. Understated, perfectly paced and intensely moving, it tells of passion, fear, waste, incompetent generals and the poor bloody infantry.

World War II

The next monarch was Edward's less charismatic brother, George VI. Britain dithered through the rest of the decade, with mediocre governments failing to confront the country's deep-set problems.

1939–45	1946–48	1948	1952
WWII rages across Europe, and much of Africa and Asia. Britain and Allies, including America, Russia, Australia, India and New Zealand, eventually defeat the armies of Germany, Japan and Italy.	The Labour Party nationalises key industries such as shipyards, coal mines and steel foundries. Britain's 'big four' train companies are combined into British Railways.	Aneurin Bevan, the health minister in the Labour government, launches the National Health Service (NHS): free medical care for all – the core of Britain as a 'welfare state'.	Princess Elizabeth becomes Queen Elizabeth II when her father, George VI, dies. Her coronation takes place in Westminster Abbey in June 1953.

Meanwhile, Adolf Hitler came to power in Germany and in 1939 invaded Poland. Two days later Britain was once again at war. The German army swept through Europe and pushed back British forces to the beaches of Dunkirk, in France. In June 1940 a flotilla of tiny, private vessels (the 'Little Ships') turned total disaster into a brave defeat – and Dunkirk Day is still remembered with pride and sadness in Britain every year.

By mid-1940, most of Europe was controlled by Germany. Russia had negotiated a peace deal and the USA was neutral, leaving Britain virtually isolated. Into this arena came a new prime minister called Winston Churchill.

Between September 1940 and May 1941, the German air force launched 'the Blitz', a series of (mainly night-time) bombing raids on London and other cities. But morale in Britain remained strong, thanks partly to

WINSTON CHURCHILL

More than a century after becoming part of the British government, Winston Churchill is still one of the country's best-known political figures. He was born in 1874 and, although from an aristocratic family, his early years were not auspicious; he was famously a 'dunce' at school, an image he actively cultivated in later life.

As a young man, Churchill joined the British Army and also acted as a newspaper war correspondent, writing several books about his exploits. In 1900 he was elected to parliament as a Conservative MP. In 1904 he defected to the Liberals, the main opposition party. A year later, after a Liberal election victory, he became a government minister. Churchill rejoined the Conservatives in 1924, and held various ministerial positions through the rest of the 1920s. Notable statements during this period included calling Mussolini a 'genius' and Gandhi 'a half-naked fakir'.

Churchill criticised Prime Minister Neville Chamberlain's 1938 'appeasement' of Hitler and called for British rearmament to face a growing German threat, but his political life was generally quiet – so he concentrated on writing. His multi-volume *A History of the English-Speaking Peoples* was drafted during this period; although biased and flawed, it remains his best-known work.

In 1939 Britain entered WWII, and by 1940 Churchill was prime minister, taking additional responsibility as minister of defence. Hitler might have expected an easy victory in the war, but Churchill's extraordinary dedication (not to mention his radio speeches – most famously saying he had 'nothing to offer but blood, toil, tears and sweat' and promising to 'fight on the beaches...') inspired the British people to resist.

Britain's refusal to negotiate terms with Germany and the decision to stand alone against Hitler's forces was an audacious strategy, but it paid off and Churchill was lauded as a national hero – praise that continued beyond his death in 1965 and which continues today (in any survey or poll to find the greatest Englishman or Briton, Churchill inevitably tends to come out on top).

1960–66	1971	1979	1990
The era of African and Caribbean independence brings the freedom of Nigeria, Tanzania, Jamaica, Trinidad and Tobago, Kenya, Malawi, Gambia and Barbados.	Britain adopts the 'decimal' currency (one pound equals 100 pence) and drops the ancient system of 20 shillings or 240 pennies per pound, the centuries-old bane of school maths lessons.	A Conservative government led by Margaret Thatcher wins the general election, a major milestone in Britain's 20th-century history, ushering in a decade of dramatic political and social change.	Thatcher ousted as leader, and the Conservative Party enters a period of decline, but remains in power, partly due to ineffective Labour opposition.

Churchill's regular radio broadcasts. The USA entered the war after the Japanese bombing of Pearl Harbor, and in late 1941 the tide began to turn.

By 1944 Germany was in retreat. Russia pushed back from the east, and Britain, the USA and other Allies were again on the beaches of France. The Normandy landings (D-Day, as it's remembered) marked the start of the liberation of Europe's western side. By 1945 Hitler was dead and the war was over.

Swinging & Sliding

The aftermath of WWII saw an unexpected swing on the political front. An electorate tired of war tumbled Churchill's Conservatives from power in favour of the Labour Party. There was change abroad too, as parts of the British Empire became independent, including India and Pakistan in 1947 and Malaya in 1957, followed by much of Africa and the Caribbean.

But while the Empire's sun may have been setting, Britain's royal family was still going strong. In 1952 George VI was succeeded by his daughter, Elizabeth II. By the late 1950s, postwar recovery was strong enough for Prime Minister Harold Macmillan to famously remind the British people they had 'never had it so good'. Some saw this as a boast for a confident future, others as a warning about difficult times ahead. But many people didn't care either way, as the 1960s had arrived and grey old England was suddenly more fun and lively than it had been for generations.

The '60s may have been swinging, but by the 1970s decline had set in, thanks to a combination of inflation, an oil crisis and international competition revealing the weaknesses of Britain's economy. Britain joined the European Economic Community in 1973, with the country voting in a referendum to remain two years later; 67% were in favour of remaining.

The rest of the '70s were marked by strikes, disputes and general all-round gloom, but neither the Conservatives (also known as the Tories) under Prime Minister Edward Heath, nor Labour, under Prime Ministers Harold Wilson and Jim Callaghan, proved capable of controlling the strife. The elections of May 1979 saw the arrival of a new prime minister: a previously little-known politician named Margaret Thatcher.

The Thatcher Years

Soon everyone had heard of Margaret Thatcher. Love her or hate her, no one could argue that her methods weren't dramatic, and many policies had a lasting impact, one of the most prominent being the privatisation of state-run industries that had been nationalised in the late 1940s.

Some commentators argue that in economic terms the Thatcher government's policies were largely successful. Others claim in social terms they were a failure and created a polarised Britain: on one side were the people who gained from the prosperous wave of opportunities in the

In 2017's *Dunkirk*, British director Christopher Nolan delivered a haunting depiction of the evacuation of British troops from northern France in May 1940. Its stars included Kenneth Branagh, Mark Rylance, Tom Hardy, and pop singer Harry Styles in his first film role.

Stalin's Englishman is a fascinating biography of the 'Cambridge Spy', diplomat Guy Burgess, who passed on state secrets to the Russian secret services between the 1930s and 1950s, and ultimately defected to Russia in 1951.

1992	1997	1998	2003
Labour remains divided between 'traditionalists' and 'modernists'. The Conservatives, under new leader John Major, confound the pundits and unexpectedly win the general election.	The general election sees Tony Blair lead 'New' Labour to victory in the polls, with a record-breaking parliamentary majority, ending 18 years of Conservative rule.	The Good Friday Agreement is signed ending 'the Troubles' an ongoing political conflict in Northern Ireland since the 1960s.	Britain joins the USA in the invasion of Iraq – despite large antiwar demonstrations held in London and other cities – increasing the threat of jihadi terror attacks in England.

'new' industries, while on the other were those who became unemployed and dispossessed as the 'old' industries, such as coal mining and steel production, became an increasingly small part of the country's economy.

Despite policies that were frequently described as uncompromising, by 1988 Margaret Thatcher was the longest-serving British prime minister of the 20th century, although her repeated electoral victories were likely helped considerably by the Labour Party's ineffective campaigns and destructive internal struggles.

From New Labour to Brexit

The pendulum started to swing again in the early 1990s. Margaret Thatcher was replaced as leader by John Major unexpectedly winning the Conservatives the 1992 election. But political fortunes changed in 1997, when 'New' Labour swept to power under a fresh-faced leader called Tony Blair.

Blair and the Labour Party enjoyed an extended honeymoon period, and the next election (in 2001) was another walkover, followed by a historic third term in 2005. A year later Blair became the longest-serving Labour prime minister in British history.

In May 2010, 13 years of Labour rule came to an end, and a coalition government (the first since WWII) was formed between the Conservatives and the Liberal Democrats. This lasted until 2015, when the Conservatives were back in sole charge under David Cameron. But just over a year later, a referendum saw the people of the UK vote, by 52% to 48%, to leave the EU – in defiance of the main parties, which had campaigned to stay in.

Cameron resigned almost immediately after the vote, and was succeeded by the Home Secretary Theresa May, whose premiership was stymied by the challenges of delivering on the Brexit referendum – as well as a misjudged decision to hold a snap general election in 2017, which resulted in her losing her majority in a hung parliament in the House of Commons.

May's plan had been to exploit the apparent unpopularity of the Labour leader, Jeremy Corbyn, whose strongly socialist policies had caused division in his own party. But unexpectedly, Corbyn's leftist agenda proved popular with the public – particularly younger voters. But in 2019 May was replaced by former London Mayor Boris Johnson as the Conservative leader who went on to defeat Corbyn at a pre-Christmas general election.

In his first year, Prime Minister Johnson led the country through the Brexit transition period (trying to hammer out a last-minute trade deal with the EU and find a workable solution to the European border in Ireland) while dealing with a global pandemic that caught many European countries off-guard. At the same time, an increasingly devolved United Kingdom, and growing calls for environmental, social and racial justice in Britain, became key challenges for the Conservatives as the new decade ticked over.

The Iron Lady is a 2011 biographical film based on the life and career of Margaret Thatcher. The sensitive portrayal by Meryl Streep won her the Academy Award for Best Actress.

HISTORY FROM NEW LABOUR TO BREXIT

History Websites

www.royalhistsoc.org

www.bbc.co.uk/history

www.blackbritishhistory.co.uk

2014	2016	2018	2020
Scotland votes in a referendum not to become an independent country (by 55% to 45%), so remaining within the United Kingdom. It sparks a debate on the possibility of a separate English parliament.	The UK votes 52% to 48% to leave the EU in a hotly contested referendum. Scotland and Northern Ireland voted to stay in, re-igniting arguments for devolution.	Prince Harry marries American actress Meghan Markle, becoming the first member of the royal family to wed a person of mixed race.	The Conservative government is blindsided by the Covid-19 pandemic; and, having left the EU in January, Britain ends its Brexit transition period on 31 December, after a trade deal is agreed at the last minute.

Food & Drink

While London is a gastronomic capital, with outstanding dining from any of the world's cuisines, you'll also find good food made with locally sourced ingredients in towns and villages across the country. Wherever you travel you'll find a local pub serving dependable homemade meals like a Sunday roast or bangers (sausages) and mash (creamed potatoes). For something more memorable, or even in the Michelin-starred category, you'll need to do your research and book ahead, including nearby accommodation for those outside the main cities.

Meals

For the locals, the English culinary day is punctuated by the three traditional main meals of breakfast then lunch and dinner (though some call lunch 'dinner', and dinner is sometimes called 'supper' or 'tea').

Breakfast

Many people in England make do with toast or a bowl of cereal before dashing to work, but visitors staying in hotels and B&Bs will undoubtedly encounter a phenomenon called the Full English Breakfast. This usually consists of fried bacon, sausages, eggs, tomatoes, mushrooms, baked beans and fried bread. If you don't feel like eating half a farmyard first thing in the morning, it's OK to ask for just the eggs and tomatoes, for example. Some B&Bs offer other alternatives such as kippers (smoked fish) or a Continental breakfast, which completely omits the cooked stuff and may even add something exotic like croissants.

Lunch

One of the many great inventions that England gave the world is the sandwich, often eaten as a midday meal. Slapping a slice of cheese or ham between two bits of bread may seem a simple concept, but no one apparently thought of it until the 18th century: the Earl of Sandwich (his title comes from a town in southeast England that originally got its name from the Viking word for 'sandy beach') ordered his servants to bring cold meat between bread so he could keep working at his desk or, as some historians claim, keep playing cards late at night.

Another English classic is the ploughman's lunch. Basically it's bread, cheese and pickles, and although hearty yokels probably did carry such food to the fields in the days of yore, the meal was actually invented in the 1960s by the national cheesemakers' organisation to boost consumption, neatly cashing in on public nostalgia and fondness for tradition.

You can still find a basic ploughman's lunch offered in some pubs – and it undeniably goes well with a pint or two of local ale at lunchtime – but these days the meal has usually been smartened up to include butter, salad and dressings. At some pubs you get a selection of cheeses. You'll also find other variations, such as a farmer's lunch (bread and chicken), stockman's lunch (bread and ham), Frenchman's lunch (Brie and baguette) and fisherman's lunch (you guessed it, with fish).

Farmers markets are a feature of most towns and many city neighbourhoods – a chance for food producers large and small to sell direct to the public and made more popular with a growing commitment to food sustainability and buying local.

Dinner

Depending on where you are in England, the evening meal is variously described as dinner, supper or often – and rather confusingly – tea; regardless, it's generally the main meal of the day. While the traditional idea of 'meat and two veg' was an evening staple for many centuries, the English have embraced global cuisine with gusto, and you're just as likely to find a bowl of ramen, curry or linguine on the dinner table as you are a serving of chops, chips and peas. The popularity of cooking shows and celebrity chef cookbooks has expanded the English culinary repertoire and restaurant standards over the last couple of decades.

One tradition that hasn't changed all that much is the Sunday roast, customarily eaten for lunch (or was that dinner?). The classic is roast beef (always 'roast', never 'roasted') accompanied by Yorkshire pudding (portions of crispy baked batter). Another classic dish brings Yorkshire pudding and sausages together, with the delightful name of 'toad-in-the-hole'.

Yorkshire pudding also turns up in another guise, especially in pubs and cafes in northern England, where a big bowl-shaped pudding is filled with stew, gravy or vegetables. You can even find multicultural crossover Yorkshire puddings filled with curry.

Perhaps the best-known classic English meal is fish and chips, often bought from the 'chippie' as a takeaway wrapped in paper to eat on the spot. For visitors, English fish and chips can be an acquired taste. Sometimes the chips can be limp and the fish tasteless, especially once you get away from the sea, but in towns with salt in the air this classic deep-fried delight is a customary meal to partake in.

> In Yorkshire, the eponymous pudding is traditionally a starter, a reminder of days when food was scarce and the pudding was a pre-meal stomach filler.

Dessert

After the main course – usually at an evening meal, or if you're enjoying a hearty lunch – comes dessert or 'pudding'. A classic English pudding is apple or rhubarb crumble, in which the baked fruit is topped with a crunchy 'crumble' made with flour, butter and sugar. It's usually served with custard or ice cream. Other favourites include treacle sponge (sponge cake in a sweet, sticky, caramel-like sauce), sticky toffee (made with dates and a toffee sauce), bread-and-butter pudding (slices of buttered bread cooked with raisins and custard – nicer than it sounds) and plum pudding (a dome-shaped cake with fruit, nuts and brandy or rum, traditionally eaten at Christmas).

> In the 16th century Queen Elizabeth I decreed that mutton could only be served with bitter herbs – intended to stop people eating sheep in order to help the wool trade – but her subjects discovered mint sauce, and it's been a favourite condiment ever since.

Regional Specialities

With the country's large coastline, it's no surprise that seafood is a speciality in many English regions. Yorkshire's seaside resorts are particularly famous for huge servings of cod – certified as sustainable after years

---

THE CORNISH PASTY

A favourite speciality in southwest England is the Cornish pasty: a mix of beef, potato, onion and swede, baked in a pastry casing that's been crimped on the side. Invented long before Tupperware, the pasty was an all-in-one-lunch pack that tin miners carried underground and left on a ledge ready for mealtime. So pasties weren't mixed up, they were marked with their owners' initials – always at one end, so the miner could eat half and safely leave the rest to snack on later without it mistakenly disappearing into the mouth of a workmate. Before going back to the surface, the miners traditionally left the last few crumbs of the pasty as a gift for the spirits of the mine, known as 'knockers', to ensure a safe shift the next day.

In 2011, the pasty was awarded 'protected geographical indication' (PGI) status by the EU, meaning that by law, only pasties made in Cornwall can be called Cornish pasties – the same accolade enjoyed by Champagne and Parma ham.

FOOD & DRINK GLOSSARY

aubergine – large purple-skinned vegetable; 'eggplant' in the USA and Australia

bangers – sausages (colloquial)

bap – a large, wide, flat, soft bread roll

bevvy – drink (slang; originally from northern England)

bill – the total you need to pay after eating in a restaurant ('check' to Americans)

bitter – ale; a type of beer

black pudding – a type of sausage made from dried blood and other ingredients

caff – abbreviated form of cafe

chips – sliced, deep-fried potatoes, eaten hot (what Americans call 'fries')

clotted cream – cream so heavy or rich that it's become almost solid (but not sour)

corkage – a small charge levied by the restaurant when you BYO

courgette – green vegetable ('zucchini' to Americans and Australians)

cream tea – cup of tea and a scone loaded with jam and cream

crisps – thin slices of fried potato bought in a packet, eaten cold; called 'chips' or 'potato chips' in the USA and Australia

dram – whisky measure

greasy spoon – cheap cafe (colloquial)

ice lolly – flavoured ice on a stick; called 'popsicle' in the USA, 'icy pole' in Australia

jam – fruit conserve often spread on bread

jelly – sweet dessert of flavoured gelatine; called 'jello' in the USA

kippers – salted and smoked fish, traditionally herring

Pimm's – popular English spirit; usually drunk mixed with lemonade, mint and fresh fruit

pint – beer measure (as in 'let me buy you a pint')

shandy – beer and lemonade mixed together in equal quantities

shout – to buy a group of people drinks, usually reciprocated (colloquial)

snug – a small room in a pub, usually just inside the door

sweets – what Americans call 'candy' and Australians call 'lollies'

of decline; while restaurants in Devon and Cornwall plate up prawns, oysters, mussels, crab, lobster and scallops. Other local seafood you may encounter elsewhere on your travels includes Norfolk crab and Northumberland kippers.

In northern and central England you'll find the Cumberland sausage – a tasty mix of minced pork and herbs, so large it has to be spiralled to fit on your plate. Look out too for Melton Mowbray pork pies – cooked ham in a casing of pastry, eaten cold. A legal victory in 2005 ensured that only pies from the eponymous Midlands town could carry the Melton Mowbray moniker, in the same way that only fizzy wine from the Champagne region of France can carry that name. Another English speciality that enjoys the same protection is Stilton – a strong white cheese, either plain or in a blue-vein variety. Only five dairies in all of England are allowed to produce cheese with this name.

Perhaps less appealing is black pudding, a large sausage made with pig's blood and oatmeal, and traditionally served for breakfast in northern England.

Eating Out

In England, 'eating out' means simply going to a restaurant or cafe – anywhere away from home. There's a huge choice across the country.

Food Markets & Street Food

When shopping for provisions, local street markets can be a good place for bargains – everything from dented tins of tomatoes to home-baked cakes and organic goats cheese. The English have also embraced street food markets, despite the cold air. Particularly popular with young people and young families because of the informal space and plentiful options.

Caffs, Cafes & Teashops

The traditional English 'caff' (a greasy spoon cafe) is nothing like its continental European namesake. Most are basic, no-frills establishments serving simple meals, such as pies, beans on toast, baked potato or omelette with chips (costing around £4 to £6), and stuff like sandwiches, cakes and other snacks (£3). Quality varies enormously: some cafes definitely earn their 'greasy spoon' handle, while others are neat and clean.

In London and many busier tourist towns, a rearguard of classic cafes (with Formica tables, seats in booths and decor unchanged from their 1950s glory days) are standing up to the onslaught of the international chains – just.

Smarter cafes are called teashops or tearooms (generally found in rural areas), where you pay a bit more for extras such as cosy decor and table service.

As well as the traditional establishments, in most cities and towns you'll also find a growing number of specialist coffee shops (cafes) serving lattes, espressos or cold-drip macchiatos. This was not true a decade ago where a coffee, even in London, was usually tasteless and served too hot.

The experimental chef Heston Blumenthal made his name by taking a 'mad professor' approach to cooking, known as 'molecular cuisine' – resulting in such outlandish dishes as bacon-and-eggs ice cream, snail porridge, lickable wallpaper and edible tableware.

Vegans: Plant-Powered Dining

Vegetarianism of the 20th century has been surpassed by plant-powered dining in England in recent years. With a large market for sustainable animal-free food products, England's cities have seen a surge in vegan spots such as Farmacy (p122), and vegan options on mainstream menus – even at fast-food chains like Nando's – as well as at high-end restaurants. Beyond the city, most supermarkets also stock a decent range of vegan products: ethical eating has never been so easy!

Pubs & Gastropubs

Not so many years ago, a pub was the place to go for a drink. And that was it. If you felt peckish, your choice might be a ham or cheese sandwich, with pickled onions if you were lucky. Today many pubs serve a wide range of food, and it's usually a good-value option, whether you want a toasted sandwich between museum visits in London, or a three-course meal in the evening after touring castles and stately homes in Yorkshire.

NO SMOKING, PLEASE

All restaurants and cafes in England are non-smoking throughout. Pubs have the same rule, which is why there's often a small crowd of smokers standing on the pavement outside. Some pubs provide specific outdoor smoking areas, ranging from a simple yard to elaborate gazebos with canvas walls and the full complement of lighting, heating, piped music and TV screens – you'd never need to know you were 'outside' at all, apart from the pungent clouds of burning tobacco.

While the food in many pubs is good quality and good value, some places raised the bar to such a degree that a whole new genre of eatery – the gastropub – was born. The finest gastropubs are effectively restaurants (with smart decor, neat menus and uniformed table service; a few have won Michelin stars). For visitors relaxing after a hard day's sightseeing, nothing beats the luxury of a wholesome shepherd's pie washed down with a decent ale without the worry of guessing which fork to use.

Drinking

The two beverages most associated with England are probably tea and beer. Both are unlike drinks of the same name found elsewhere in the world, and well worth trying on your travels around the country.

What To Drink

Tea & Coffee

In England, if a local asks 'Would you like a drink?' don't automatically expect a gin and tonic. They may well mean a 'cuppa' (cup of tea), England's favourite beverage. It's usually made with dark tea leaves to produce a strong brown drink, which is partly why it's usually served with a dash of milk here.

Tea is often billed as the national drink and, according to 2019 research, one in 10 tea drinkers in England consume at least six cups a day. The most popular tea is English Breakfast (45%), followed by Earl Grey (19%), Darjeeling (4%) and Assam (4%).

Coffee drinking is a much more serious business in England these days than it used to be. The UK coffee shop market was valued at £10.1b in 2019, across 25,483 outlets. Many are small independently run cafes, but you won't be able to walk far down an English high street without passing a few major coffee chain stores, from Costa (owned by Coca-Cola) to Starbucks.

Beer, Wine & Cider

Among alcoholic drinks, England is probably best known for its beer. As you travel around the country you should definitely try some local brews. English beer typically ranges from dark brown to bright amber in colour, and is usually served at room temperature. Technically it's ale, but it's often called 'bitter'. This is to distinguish it from lager (the drink that most of the rest of the world calls 'beer'), which is generally pale yellow and served cold.

Top Ye Olde Fighting Cocks, St Albans

Bottom Full English Breakfast

Beer that's brewed and served traditionally is called 'real ale' to distinguish it from mass-produced brands, and there are many regional varieties. But be ready! If you're used to the 'amber nectar' or 'king of beers', a traditional British brew may come as a shock – a warm, flat and expensive shock. This is partly to do with Britain's climate, and partly to do with the beer being served by hand pump rather than gas pressure. Most important, though, is the integral flavour: traditional British beer doesn't need to be chilled or fizzed to make it palatable.

A new breed of microbreweries sprung up all over the country in the early 2000s, producing their own varieties of traditional and innovative craft beers. London's 'Bermondsey Beer Mile' has a good concentration of microbreweries, as does Hackney in London. Further afield, beer tourists should head for the East Midlands, Kent or even the Lake District to taste some fine local brews.

On hot summer days, you could go for shandy – beer and lemonade mixed in equal quantities. It may seem an astonishing combination for outsiders, but the English claim it's refreshing and, of course, not too strong, so you can drink for longer.

Since the Normans introduced cider to England in the 13th century, it has grown in popularity and varieties. In fact 56% of apples in the UK are used for ciders. In western and southwestern counties, you might try 'scrumpy', a very strong dry cider traditionally made from local apples.

Many visitors are surprised to learn that wine is produced in England, and has been since the time of the Romans. Today, more than 400 vineyards and wineries produce around two million bottles a year, many winning major awards. English white sparkling wines have been a particular success story, especially those produced in the southeast, where the growing conditions are similar to those of the Champagne region in France.

The Campaign for Real Ale (Camra) promotes the understanding of traditional British beer. Look for endorsement stickers on pub windows, and for more info see www.camra.org.uk.

Where to Drink

In England, the difference between a bar and a pub is sometimes vague, but generally bars are smarter and louder than pubs, and often draw a younger crowd.

As well as beer and wine, pubs and bars offer the usual choice of spirits, often served with a 'mixer', producing English favourites such as gin and tonic, rum and coke or vodka and lime. These drinks are served in measures called 'singles' and 'doubles'. A single is usually 35ml – just over one US fluid ounce.

And finally, two tips: first, if you see a pub called a 'free house' it doesn't mean the booze is free of charge! This term means it doesn't belong to a brewery or pub company, and thus is 'free' to sell any brand of beer.

Second, remember that drinks in English pubs are ordered and paid for at the bar. You can always spot the freshly arrived tourists – they're the ones sitting forlornly at an empty table hoping to spot a server.

When it comes to gratuities, it's not usual to tip pub and bar staff. However, if you're ordering a large round, or the service has been good all evening, you can say to the person behind the bar '...and one for yourself'. They may not have a drink, but they'll add the monetary equivalent to the total you pay and keep it as a tip.

English Architecture

England's architecture spans some five millennia, ranging from the mysterious stone circle of Stonehenge to London's glittering skyscrapers. If you know what to look for, a veritable design timeline can be traced through any of England's villages, towns and cities, and getting to grips with styles from different eras will greatly enhance your stay. Prepare for Roman baths, parish churches, mighty castles, magnificent cathedrals, humble cottages and grand stately homes.

Early Foundations

The oldest surviving structures in England are the grass-covered mounds of earth, called 'tumuli' or 'barrows', used as burial sites by England's prehistoric residents. These mounds – measuring anything from a rough semisphere just 2m high to much larger, elongated semi ovoids 5m high and 10m long – are dotted across the countryside from Cornwall to Cumbria, and are especially common in chalk areas such as Salisbury Plain and the Wiltshire Downs in southern England.

Perhaps the most famous chalk mound – and certainly the largest and most mysterious – is Silbury Hill, near Marlborough. Archaeologists are not sure exactly why this 40m-high conical mound was built – there's no evidence of it actually being used for burial. Theories suggest it was used in cultural ceremonies or as part of the worship of deities, in the style of South American pyramids. Whatever its original purpose, it still remains impressive, more than four millennia after it was built.

Even more impressive than giant tumuli are another legacy of the Neolithic era: menhirs (standing stones), especially when they're set out in rings. These include the iconic stone circle of Stonehenge and the even larger Avebury Stone Circle, both in Wiltshire. Again, their original purpose is a mystery, providing fertile ground for hypotheses and speculation. The most recent theories suggest Stonehenge may have been a place of pilgrimage for the sick, like modern-day Lourdes, though it was also used as a burial ground and as a place of ancestor worship.

Bronze Age & Iron Age

Compared with the large stone circles of the Neolithic era, the surviving architecture of the Bronze Age is on a more domestic scale. Hut circles from this period can still be seen in several parts of England, most notably on Dartmoor.

By the time we reach the Iron Age, the early peoples of England were organising themselves into clans or tribes. Their legacy includes the remains of the forts they built to defend territory and protect themselves from rival tribes or other invaders. Most forts consisted of a large circular or oval ditch, with a steep mound of earth behind. A famous example is Maiden Castle in Dorset.

The Roman Era

Roman remains are found in many English towns and cities, including Chester, Exeter and St Albans – as well as the lavish Roman spa and bathing

The construction of Stonehenge pushed the limits of technology in the Neolithic era. Some giant menhirs were transported a great distance, and many were shaped slightly wider at the top to take account of perspective – a trick used by the Greeks many centuries later.

There are more than a thousand Iron Age hill forts in England. Impressive examples include Danebury Ring, Hampshire; Barbury Castle, Wiltshire; Uffington Castle, Oxfordshire; Carl Wark, Derbyshire; Cadbury Castle, Somerset; and the immense Maiden Castle, Dorset.

complex in Bath. But England's largest and most impressive Roman relic is the 73-mile sweep of Hadrian's Wall, built in the 2nd century CE as a defensive line stretching coast to coast across the neck of northern England, from modern-day Newcastle to Carlisle. Originally built to separate marauding Pictish warriors to the north of the wall (in modern Scotland) from the Empire's territories to the south, it later became as much a symbol of Roman power as a necessary defence mechanism.

Medieval Masterpieces

In the centuries following the Norman Conquest of 1066, the perfection of the mason's art saw an explosion of architecture in stone, inspired by the two most pressing concerns of the day: religion and defence. Early structures of timber and rubble were replaced with churches, abbeys and monasteries built in dressed stone. The round arches, squat towers and chevron decoration of the Norman or Romanesque style (11th to 12th centuries) slowly evolved into the tall pointed arches, ribbed vaults and soaring spires of the Gothic (13th to 16th centuries), a history that can often be seen all in the one church – construction usually took a couple of hundred years to complete. Many cathedrals remain significant landmarks, such as Salisbury, Winchester, Canterbury and York.

Stone was also put to good use in the building of elaborate defensive structures. Castles range from the atmospheric ruins of Tintagel and Dunstanburgh, and the feudal keeps of Lancaster and Bamburgh, to the sturdy fortresses of Warwick and Windsor. And then there's the most impressive of them all: the Tower of London, guarding the capital for more than 900 years.

Stately Homes of England

The medieval period was tumultuous, but by around 1600 life became more settled, and the nobility started to have less need for their castles. While they were excellent for keeping out rivals or the common riff-raff, they were often too dark, cold and draughty to be comfortable. So many castles saw the home improvements of the day – the installation of larger windows, wider staircases and better drainage. Others were simply abandoned for a brand-new dwelling next door; an example of this is Hardwick Hall in Derbyshire.

Following the Civil War, the trend away from castles gathered pace, as through the 17th century the landed gentry developed a taste for fine 'country houses' designed by the most famous architects of the day. Many became the 'stately homes' that are a major feature of the English landscape, celebrated by Noël Coward's famous song 'The Stately Homes of England', and a major attraction for visitors. Among the most extravagant are Holkham Hall in Norfolk, Chatsworth House in Derbyshire and Blenheim Palace in Oxfordshire.

The great stately homes all display the proportion, symmetry and architectural harmony so in vogue during the 17th and 18th centuries, styles later reflected in the fashionable town houses of the Georgian era – most notably in the city of Bath, where the stunning Royal Crescent is the epitome of the genre.

England's Top Castles

Berkeley Castle
(Gloucestershire)

Carlisle Castle
(Cumbria)

Bamburgh Castle
(Northumberland)

Leeds Castle
(Kent)

Skipton Castle
(Yorkshire)

Tintagel Castle
(Cornwall)

Tower of London
(London)

Windsor Castle
(Berkshire)

HOUSE & HOME

It's not all about big houses. Alongside the stately homes, ordinary domestic architecture from the 16th century onwards can also still be seen in rural areas: black-and-white 'half-timbered' houses still characterise counties such as Worcestershire, while brick-and-flint cottages pepper Norfolk and Suffolk, and hardy centuries-old farms built with slate or local gritstone are a feature of areas such as Derbyshire and the Lake District.

Top Avebury Stone Circle (p289)

Bottom Birdoswald Roman Fort (p622), Hadrian's Wall

Victoriana

The Victorian era was a time of great building. A style called Victorian-Gothic developed, echoing the towers and spires that were such a feature of the original Gothic cathedrals. The most famous example of this style is the Palace of Westminster (better known as the Houses of Parliament) and Elizabeth Tower (home to Big Ben), in London. Other highlights include London's Natural History Museum and London's St Pancras station.

Through the early 20th century, as England's cities grew in size and stature, the newly moneyed middle classes built streets and squares of smart town houses. Meanwhile, in other suburbs the first town planners oversaw the construction of endless terraces of red-brick two-up-two-down houses to accommodate the massive influx of workers required to fuel the country's factories – an enduring architectural legacy of the great migration from countryside to town that changed the landscape of England forever.

The Postwar Rebuild

During WWII many of England's cities were damaged by bombing, and the rebuilding that followed showed scant regard for the overall aesthetic of the cities, or for the lives of the people who lived in them. The rows of terraces were swept away in favour of high-rise tower blocks, while the 'brutalist' architects of the 1950s and '60s employed the modern and efficient materials of steel and concrete, leaving legacies such as London's South Bank Centre.

Perhaps this is why, on the whole, the English are conservative in their architectural tastes, and often resent ambitious or experimental designs, especially when they're applied to public buildings, or when form appears more important than function. But a familiar pattern often unfolds: after a few years of resentment, first comes a nickname, then grudging acceptance, and finally – once the locals have got used to it – comes pride and affection for the new building. The English just don't like to be rushed, that's all.

With this attitude in mind, over the following decades, English architecture started to redeem itself, and many big cities now have contemporary buildings their residents can be proud of and enjoy. Highlights in London's financial district include the bulging cone with the official address of 30 St Mary Axe (but widely known by its nickname, the Gherkin), and the former Millennium Dome (now rebranded as simply the O2), which has been transformed from a source of national embarrassment into one of the capital's leading live-music venues.

THE STIRLING PRIZE

The highlight of the year for aficionados of modern architecture is the announcement of the shortlist for the Stirling Prize for the best new building, an annual award for excellence in architecture organised by the Royal Institute of British Architects (RIBA). Established in 1996, this prestigious award is for 'the building that has made the greatest contribution to the evolution of architecture in the past year'.

Famous winners include the Millennium Bridge in Gateshead (2002), the Everyman Theatre in Liverpool (2014), the Burntwood School in London (2015), the redevelopment of Hastings Pier (2017), and Bloomberg's European HQ (2018), credited as the world's most sustainable office.

Imperial War Museum North (p534), Manchester

Twenty-First Century

Through the first decade of the 21st century, many areas of England placed a new importance on progressive, popular architecture as a part of wider regeneration. Top examples include Manchester's Imperial War Museum North, the Deep aquarium in Hull, Cornwall's futuristic Eden Project, and the Sage concert hall in Gateshead, near Newcastle.

From around 2010, development slowed and some plans were shelved, thanks to the global slowdown, but several significant projects continued, including the Turner Contemporary gallery in Margate (opened in 2011) and the futuristic Library of Birmingham (2013).

But England's largest and most high-profile architectural project of recent times was of course Olympic Park, the centrepiece of the 2012 Games, in the London suburb of Stratford. As well as the main Olympic Stadium, other arenas include the Velodrome and the Aquatics Centre – all dramatic structures in their own right, using cutting-edge construction techniques. The Velodrome also won the construction industry's 2011 Better Public Buildings Award.

Meanwhile, in the centre of the capital, the tall, jagged Shard was officially opened in July 2012; at 306m, it's one of Europe's tallest buildings. On the other side of the River Thames, two more giant skyscrapers were completed in 2014: 20 Fenchurch St (nickname: the Walkie-Talkie) and the Leadenhall Building (the Cheesegrater). While in 2015 the Tate Modern unveiled a dramatic new 64.5m pyramid-like extension.

So London continues to grow upwards, and English architecture continues to push new boundaries of style and technology. The buildings may look a little different, but it's great to see the spirit of Stonehenge alive and well after all these years.

GLOSSARY OF ENGLISH ARCHITECTURE

bailey	outermost wall of a castle
bar	fortified gate (in York, and some other northern cities)
barrel vault	semicircular arched roof
brass	memorial consisting of a brass plate set into the side or lid of a tomb, or into the floor of a church to indicate a burial place below
buttress	vertical support for a wall; see also *flying buttress*
campanile	freestanding belfry or bell tower
chancel	eastern end of the church, usually reserved for choir and clergy
choir	area in the church where the choir is seated; see also *quire*
cloister	covered walkway linking the church with adjacent monastic buildings
close	buildings grouped around a cathedral
cob	mixture of mud and straw for building
corbel	stone or wooden projection from a wall supporting a beam or arch
flying buttress	supporting *buttress* in the form of one side of an open arch
lancet	pointed window in Early English style
lierne vault	*vault* containing many tertiary ribs
Martello tower	small, circular tower used for coastal defence
minster	traditionally a church connected to a monastery; now a title signalling a church's importance
nave	main body of the church at the western end, where the congregation gathers
oast house	building containing a kiln for drying hops
pargeting	decorative stucco plasterwork
pele	fortified house
precincts	see *close*
priory	religious house governed by a prior
quire	medieval term for *choir*
rood	archaic word for cross (in churches)
transepts	north–south projections from a church's *nave*, giving church a cruciform (cross-shaped) plan
undercroft	vaulted underground room or cellar
vault	roof with arched ribs, usually in a decorative pattern

The English Landscape

When it comes to landscapes, England is not a place of extremes; there are no Alps or Himalayas here, no Amazon or Sahara. But there are still very diverse environments, and understanding those differences can keep you enthralled. The country may be small, but even a relatively short journey takes you through a surprising mix of scenery. Seeing the change – subtle in some areas, dramatic in others – as you travel is one of this country's great joys.

National Parks & Protected Areas

Back in 1810, English poet and outdoor fan William Wordsworth suggested that the wild landscape of the Lake District in Cumbria should be 'a sort of national property, in which every man has a right'. More than a century later, the Lake District had indeed become a national park, along with parts of the Peak District, Dartmoor, Exmoor, the North York Moors, the Yorkshire Dales and Northumberland. Other national parks (or areas with equivalent status) followed, including the Norfolk and Suffolk Broads, the New Forest and the South Downs.

But the term 'national park' can cause confusion. First, in England the parks are not state-owned: nearly all land is private, belonging to farmers, private estates and conservation organisations. Second, they are *not* areas of wilderness, as in many other countries – most of the national parks have been managed by humans in some way for hundreds of years, whether for agriculture, forestry or other purposes.

In England's national parks you'll see crop fields in lower areas and grazing sheep on the uplands, as well as roads, railways and villages, and even towns, quarries and factories in some parks. It's a reminder of the balance that is struck in this crowded country between protecting the natural environment and catering for the people who live in it.

Despite these apparent anomalies, England's national parks still contain mountains, hills, downs, moors, lakes, woods, river valleys and other areas of quiet countryside, all ideal for enjoying nature however you like to experience it.

In 2017 England's most popular national park, the Lake District, was granted World Heritage status by Unesco.

As well as national parks, other parts of the English countryside are designated as Areas of Outstanding Natural Beauty (AONBs), the second tier of protected landscape after national parks. Some of the finest AONBs in England include the Chilterns, Cornwall, the Cotswolds, the Isles of Scilly, the North Pennines, the Northumberland Coast, the Suffolk Coast and the Wye Valley.

There are also Conservation Areas, Sites of Special Scientific Interest (SSSIs) and many other types of protected landscape that you can enjoy as you travel around.

Since 2015, the Rewilding Britain (www.rewilding britain.org.uk) environmental movement has been advocating for and supporting specific projects – both large and small-scale – which are reintroducing biodiversity to the land by letting nature take care of itself.

FOX HUNTING

The red fox, a doglike animal with a characteristic bushy tail and an anthropomorphic reputation for cunning, is widespread in the English countryside and well adapted to a scavenging life in rural towns and city suburbs. It is a divisive creature in England. The controversy focuses on hunting, and specifically fox hunting with hounds (a type of dog). Supporters say it's been a traditional English rural activity for centuries, and helps control the fox population; opponents say it's a savage blood sport that has little impact on overall numbers. Distaste for this type of hunting is not a new phenomenon; the activity was famously described as 'the unspeakable in pursuit of the inedible' by Oscar Wilde more than a century ago. Fox hunting has been immortalised in thousands of paintings depicting English country life, and in countless rural pub names.

Today, some observers believe the hunting debate has come to represent much bigger issues: town versus country, or the relative limits of privilege, state control and individual freedom. Either way, fox hunting with dogs was banned in 2004 by law – but opinion is still very strongly divided and illegal hunts continue.

Flora & Fauna

For a small country, England has a diverse range of plants and animals. Many native species are hidden away, but there are some undoubted gems, from lowland woods carpeted in shimmering bluebells to stately herds of deer on the high moors. Keeping an eye (and ear) open will enhance your trip enormously.

Animals

Farmland

In rural areas, rabbits are everywhere, but if you're hiking through the countryside be on the lookout for the much larger brown hares, an increasingly rare species. Males who battle for territory by boxing on their hind legs in early spring are, of course, as 'mad as a March hare'.

Common birds of farmland areas (and urban gardens) include the robin, with its instantly recognisable red breast and cheerful whistle; the wren, whose loud trilling song belies its tiny size; and the yellowhammer, with a song that sounds like (if you use your imagination) 'a-little-bit-of-bread-and-no-cheese'. In open fields, the warbling cry of a skylark is another classic, but now threatened, sound of the English outdoors. You're more likely to see a pheasant, a large bird originally introduced from Russia to the nobility's shooting estates, but now considered naturalised. Barn and tawny owls can sometimes be spotted, especially at dawn and dusk.

Alongside rivers, the once rare otter is making a comeback. While in some areas, the black-and-white-striped badger has been the subject of trial culls – some believe it transmits bovine tuberculosis to cattle, others argue the case is far from proven.

Woodland

In woodland areas, mammals include the small white-spotted fallow deer and the even smaller roe deer. Woodland is full of birds too, but you'll hear them more than see them. Listen out for willow warblers (which have a warbling song with a descending cadence), chiffchaffs (which make a repetitive 'chiff chaff' noise) and the rat-a-tat-tat of woodpeckers.

If you hear rustling among the fallen leaves it might be a hedgehog – a spiny-backed insect-eating mammal – but it's an increasingly rare sound these days; conservationists say they'll be extinct in Britain by 2025,

Top Dartmoor National Park (p311)

Bottom Wild ponies, Exmoor

HELEN CRADDUCK/SHUTTERSTOCK ©

ENGLAND'S NATIONAL PARKS

NATIONAL PARK	FEATURES	ACTIVITIES	BEST TIME TO VISIT
Dartmoor	rolling hills, rocky outcrops, serene valleys; Bronze Age relics; wild ponies, deer, peregrine falcons	walking, mountain biking, horse riding, climbing, winter kayaking	May-Jun (wildflowers bloom)
Exmoor	sweeping moors, craggy sea cliffs; red deer, wild ponies, horned sheep	horse riding, walking, mountain biking	Aug-Sep (heather flowering)
Lake District	majestic fells, rugged mountains, shimmering lakes; literary heritage; red squirrels, ospreys	watersports, walking, mountaineering, rock climbing	Sep-Oct (summer crowds departed, autumn colours abound)
New Forest	woodlands, heath; wild ponies, otters, Dartford warblers, southern damselflies	walking, cycling, horse riding	Apr-Sep (lush vegetation)
Norfolk & Suffolk Broads	expansive shallow lakes, rivers, marshlands; windmills; water lilies, wildfowl, otters	walking, cycling, boating	Apr-May (birds most active)
North York Moors	heather-clad hills, deep-green valleys, isolated villages; merlins, curlews, golden plovers	walking, mountain biking	Aug-Sep (heather flowering)
Northumberland	wild rolling moors, heather, gorse; Hadrian's Wall; black grouse, red squirrels	walking, cycling, mountain biking, climbing	Apr-May (lambs) & Sep (heather flowering)
Peak District	high moors, tranquil dales, limestone caves; kestrels, badgers, grouse	walking, cycling, mountain biking, hang-gliding, climbing	Apr-May (even more lambs)
South Downs	rolling grassy chalky hills, chalky sea-cliffs, gorse, heather; Adonis blue butterflies	walking, mountain biking	Aug (heather flowering)
Yorkshire Dales	rugged hills, lush valleys, limestone pavements; red squirrels, hares, curlews, lapwings, buzzards	walking, cycling, mountain biking, climbing	Apr-May (visitors outnumbered by, you guessed it, lambs)

thanks to farming insecticides, decreased habitat and their inability to safely cross roads.

England's native red squirrels are severely endangered thanks to their more aggressive grey cousins, which were originally introduced from North America. As well as being more aggressive and competitive for food, the greys also carry a virus called squirrel pox that is particularly lethal to the reds. Attempts have been made in some areas to limit grey squirrel numbers in order to give the reds a fighting chance: Cumbria is an important stronghold.

Perhaps unexpectedly, England is home to herds of 'wild' ponies, notably in the New Forest, Exmoor and Dartmoor, but although these animals roam free they are privately owned and regularly managed. There's even a pocket of wild goats near Lynmouth in Devon, where they've apparently gambolled merrily for almost 1000 years.

Another recent arrival – or perhaps more accurately returnee – is the beaver, once a native resident of England, but trapped out of existence long ago. The animals have been reintroduced to several locations around England, although the exact sites have been kept secret to ensure their safety.

Mountains & Moors

On some mountains and high moors the most visible mammal is the red deer. Males of the species grow their famous large antlers between April and July, and shed them again in February. Also on the high ground, well-known and easily recognised birds include the red grouse, which often hides in the heather until almost stepped on, then flies away with a loud warning call; and the curlew, with its stately long legs and elegant curved bill. Look hard, and you may see beautifully camouflaged golden plovers, while the spectacular aerial displays of lapwings are impossible to miss.

Birds of prey are also a fairly common sight on the open moors, particularly kestrels and buzzards.

Coastal Areas

By the sea, two seal species frequent English coasts: the larger grey seal, which is more often seen, and the misnamed common seal. In areas such as Norfolk and Northumberland, boat trips to see seal colonies are a popular attraction. Dolphins, porpoises, minke whales and basking sharks can sometimes be seen off the western coasts, especially from about May to September when viewing conditions are better – although you may need to go with someone who knows where to look. Boat trips are available from many coastal resorts.

England's estuaries and mudflats are feeding grounds for numerous migrant wading birds; black-and-white oystercatchers are easily spotted, with their long red bills, while flocks of ringed plovers skitter along the sand. On the coastal cliffs in early summer, particularly in Cornwall and Yorkshire, countless thousands of guillemots, razorbills, kittiwakes and other breeding seabirds fight for space on crowded rock ledges, and the air is thick with their sound – as well as the cries of various types of seagull, now so numerous they've managed to colonise many English cities as well as its coastline.

Plants

In the rolling hills of southern England and the limestone areas further north (such as the Peak District and Yorkshire Dales), the best places to see wildflowers are the areas that evade large-scale farming – many erupt with great profusions of cowslips and primroses in April and May.

For woodland flowers, the best time is also April and May, before the leaf canopy is fully developed and sunlight can still reach plants such as bluebells – a beautiful and internationally rare species. Another classic English plant is gorse: you can't miss this spiky bush in heath areas like Dartmoor, Exmoor and the New Forest. Its vivid yellow flowers show year-round and have a distinctive coconut-like scent.

In contrast, the blooming season for heather is quite short, but no less dramatic; through August and September areas such as the North York Moors and Dartmoor are covered in a riot of purple.

Online Resources

www.nationalparks.gov.uk

www.landscapesforlife.org.uk

www.rspb.org.uk

www.countryfile.com

www.environment-agency.gov.uk

Environmental Issues

With England's long history of human occupation, it's not surprising that the country's appearance is heavily the result of human interaction with the environment. Since the earliest times, trees have been chopped down and fields created for crops or animals, but the really significant changes to rural areas came after WWII in the late 1940s, continuing into the '50s and '60s, when a drive to be self-reliant in food meant new – intensive and large-scale – farming methods. The result was dramatic: in some areas ancient patchworks of small meadows became landscapes of vast prairie-like fields, as walls were demolished, woodlands felled, ponds filled, wetlands drained and, most notably, hedgerows ripped out.

In most cases the hedgerows were lines of dense bushes, shrubs and trees forming a network that stretched across the countryside, protecting fields from erosion, supporting a varied range of flowers, and providing shelter for numerous insects, birds and small mammals. In the rush to improve farm yields, thousands of miles of hedgerows were destroyed in the postwar decades, and between the mid-1980s and the early 2000s another 25% disappeared.

Hedgerows have come to symbolise many other environmental issues in rural areas, and in recent years the destruction has abated, partly because farmers recognise their anti-erosion qualities, and partly because they've been encouraged – with financial incentives from UK or European agencies – to 'set aside' such areas as wildlife havens.

In addition to hedgerow clearance, other farming techniques remain hot environmental issues. Studies suggest the use of pesticides and intensive irrigation results in rivers being contaminated or simply running dry. Meanwhile, monocropping means the fields have one type of grass and not another plant to be seen. These 'green deserts' support no insects, so in turn wild bird populations have plummeted. This picture is not a case of wizened old peasants recalling the idyllic days of their forbears; you only have to be aged about 40 in England to remember a countryside where birds such as skylarks and lapwings were visibly much more numerous.

But all is not lost. In the face of apparently overwhelming odds, England still boasts great biodiversity, and some of the best wildlife habitats are protected (to a greater or lesser extent) by the creation of national parks and similar areas, or private reserves owned by conservation campaign groups such as the Wildlife Trusts (www.wildlifetrusts.org), National Trust (www.nationaltrust.org.uk), Woodland

Although hedgerows around fields have been reduced, new 'hedgerows' have appeared: the long strips of grass and bushes alongside motorways and major roads. These areas support thousands of insect species, plus mice, shrews and other small mammals, so kestrels are often seen hovering nearby, unconcerned by traffic.

WILDLIFE GUIDEBOOKS

Is it a rabbit or a hare? A gull or a tern? Buttercup or cowslip? If you want to know a bit more about England's plant and animal kingdoms, the following field guides are ideal for entry-level naturalists:

➡ *Collins Complete Guide to British Wildlife* by Paul Sterry is portable and highly recommended, covering mammals, birds, fish, plants, snakes, insects and even fungi, with brief descriptions and excellent photos.

➡ If feathered friends are enough, the *Collins Complete Guide to British Birds* by Paul Sterry has clear photos and descriptions, plus when and where each species may be seen.

➡ *Wildlife of the North Atlantic* by world-famous film-maker Tony Soper beautifully covers the animals seen from beach, boat and cliff top in the British Isles and beyond.

➡ The Collins Gem series includes handy little books on wildlife topics such as *Birds, Trees, Fish* and *Wild Flowers*.

Oystercatchers, Isles of Scilly (p347)

Trust (www.woodlandtrust.org.uk) and the Royal Society for the Protection of Birds (www.rspb.org.uk). Many of these areas are open to the public – ideal spots for walking, birdwatching or simply enjoying the peace and beauty of the countryside – and are well worth a visit as you travel around. In 2020, the British government joined the United Nations Summit on Biodiversity commitment by pledging 30% of Britain to be protected nature by 2030.

Arts

England's contributions to literature, drama, comedy, cinema and pop are celebrated around the world. As you travel around England today you'll encounter landscapes made famous as movie sets and literary locations, and places mentioned in songs. Here we've picked some major creative milestones and focused on works with connections to real locations – so your physical journey through England will be one that connects culture with place.

Literature

The roots of England's poetic and story-telling heritage stretch back to Nordic sagas and Early English epics such as *Beowulf*, but modern English literature starts around 1387 (yes, that is 'modern' in history-soaked England) when Geoffrey Chaucer produced *The Canterbury Tales*. This mammoth poem is a collection of fables, stories and morality tales using travelling pilgrims – the Knight, the Wife of Bath and so on – as a narrative hook.

William Shakespeare

The next significant development in English literature came in the 16th century, when John Milton penned *Paradise Lost*, charting the tale of Adam and Eve within the framework of epic poetry. But it was a young playwright by the name of William Shakespeare who left an even greater mark. Best known for his plays, penned in an astonishing burst of creativity between 1590 and 1610, he was also a remarkably prolific and influential poet, writing a series of sonnets that are still quoted to this day ('Shall I compare thee to a summer's day?' is one of Shakespeare's).

His birthplace, Stratford-upon-Avon, is stacked with Shakespearean sights, including the home of the celebrated Royal Shakespeare Company (RSC) – although the debate rages on about precisely how Shakespeare penned his plays. Some academics maintain he was the sole author, while others (including the well-known actor and former director of the RSC, Mark Rylance) maintain that the plays were much more likely to have been written as a collaborative effort. The truth will probably never be known, but the plays will endure.

You can enjoy Shakespeare plays at the rebuilt Globe Theatre in London or at the Royal Shakespeare Company's own theatre in Stratford-upon-Avon.

The Romantics

During the late 18th and early 19th centuries, a new generation of writers drew inspiration from human imagination and the natural world (in some cases helped along by a healthy dose of laudanum). Leading lights of the movement were William Blake, John Keats, Mary and Percy Bysshe Shelley, Lord Byron and Samuel Taylor Coleridge, and perhaps the best-known English poet of all, William Wordsworth. His famous line from 'Daffodils' – 'I wandered lonely as a cloud' – was inspired by a waterside walk in the Lake District in northern England.

Victorian Writers

Industrialisation expanded during the reign of Queen Victoria, and thus many novels of the time explored themes of social change. Charles Dickens tackled many prevailing issues of his day: in *Oliver Twist*, he captures the lives of young pickpockets in the London slums; *Bleak House* is a critique of the English legal system; and *Hard Times* criticises the excesses of capitalism. At around the same time, but choosing a rural setting, George Eliot (the pen name of Mary Ann Evans) wrote *The Mill on the Floss*, where the central character struggles against society's expectations.

Thomas Hardy's classic *Tess of the D'Urbervilles* deals with the peasantry's decline, and *The Trumpet Major* paints a picture of idyllic English country life interrupted by war and encroaching modernity. Many of Hardy's works are based in the fictionalised county of Wessex, largely based on today's Dorset and surrounding counties, where towns such as Dorchester are dotted with literary links.

For extra insight, the *Oxford Guide to Literary Britain and Ireland*, edited by Daniel Hahn and Nicholas Robins, gives details of towns, villages and countryside immortalised by writers, from Geoffrey Chaucer's Canterbury to Jane Austen's Bath.

ARTS LITERATURE

20th Century

The end of WWI and the ensuing social disruption fed into the modernist movement, with DH Lawrence perhaps its finest exponent; *Sons and Lovers* follows the lives and loves of generations in the English Midlands as the country changes from rural idyll to an increasingly industrial landscape, while his controversial exploration of sexuality in *Lady Chatterley's Lover* was originally banned as 'obscene'. Other highlights of this period included Virginia Woolf's fiction and non-fiction, including the seminal *A Room of One's Own;* Daphne du Maurier's romantic suspense novel *Rebecca,* set on the Cornish coast; and Evelyn Waugh's *Brideshead Revisited,* an exploration of moral and social disintegration among the English aristocracy, set partly in Oxford.

The 1970s saw the arrival of two novelists who became prolific for the remainder of the century and beyond. Martin Amis published *The Rachel Papers,* then went on to produce a string of novels where common themes included the absurdity and unappealing nature of modern life, such as *London Fields* (1989) and *Lionel Asbo: State of England* (2012). Meanwhile, Ian McEwan debuted with *The Cement Garden,* and earned critical acclaim for finely observed studies of the English character such as *The Child in Time* (1987), *Atonement* (2001) and *On Chesil Beach* (2007), which is set on the eponymous 18-mile stretch of Dorset shore.

JANE AUSTEN & THE BRONTËS

The beginning of the 19th century saw the emergence of some of English literature's best-known and beloved writers: Jane Austen and the Brontë sisters.

Austen's fame stems from her exquisite observations of love, friendship, intrigues and passions boiling beneath the strait-laced surface of middle-class social convention, and from the endless stream of movies and TV costume dramas based on her works, such as *Pride and Prejudice* and *Sense and Sensibility*. For visitors today, the location most associated with Jane Austen is the city of Bath – a beautiful place even without the literary link. As one of her heroines asked, 'Who can ever be tired of Bath?'.

Of the Brontë sisters' prodigious output, Emily Brontë's *Wuthering Heights* is the best known – an epic tale of obsession and revenge, where the dark and moody landscape plays a role as great as any human character. Charlotte Brontë's *Jane Eyre* and Anne Brontë's *The Tenant of Wildfell Hall* are classics of passion and mystery. Fans still flock to their former home in the Yorkshire town of Haworth, perched on the edge of the wild Pennine moors that inspired so many of their books.

Recent Writers

As the 20th century came to a close, the nation's multicultural landscape proved a rich inspiration for contemporary novelists: Hanif Kureishi sowed the seeds with his groundbreaking *The Buddha of Suburbia,* about a group of British-Asians in suburban London; Zadie Smith published her acclaimed debut *White Teeth* in 2000, followed by a string of bestsellers including *The Autograph Man* and 2012's *NW;* Andrea Levy published *Small Island,* about a Jamaican couple settled in postwar London; Monica Ali's *Brick Lane* was shortlisted for the high-profile Man Booker Prize in 2003; and Bernardine Evaristo won it in 2019 with *Girl, Woman, Other.*

Other contemporary writers include Will Self, known for his surreal, satirical novels, including *The Book of Dave,* and Nick Hornby, best known for novels like *Fever Pitch,* a study of the insecurities of English blokishness. There's also Julian Barnes, whose books include *England, England,* a darkly ironic study of nationalism and tourism among other themes, and *The Sense of An Ending,* winner of the 2011 Man Booker Prize. Not to mention Hilary Mantel, author of many novels on an astoundingly wide range of subjects, and winner of the Man Booker Prize twice, first in 2009 for historical blockbuster *Wolf Hall* (about Henry VIII and his ruthless advisor Thomas Cromwell), and then in 2012 for its sequel *Bring Up the Bodies.* The final of the trilogy, *The Mirror and the Light,* was published in 2020.

England's greatest literary phenomenon of the 21st century is JK Rowling's *Harry Potter* books, a series of otherworldly adventures that have entertained millions of children (and many grown-ups too) since the first book was published in 1996. The magical tales are the latest in a long line of British children's classics enjoyed by adults, stretching back to the works of Lewis Carroll *(Alice's Adventures in Wonderland),* E Nesbit *(The Railway Children),* AA Milne *(Winnie-the-Pooh)* and CS Lewis (The Chronicles of Narnia).

Helen Fielding's book *Bridget Jones's Diary,* originally a series of newspaper articles, is a fond look at the heartache of a modern single woman's blundering search for love, and the epitome of the late-1990s 'chicklit' genre. It's also (very loosely) based on *Pride and Prejudice* by Jane Austen.

Music

The British Invasion

England has been putting the world through its musical paces ever since some mop-haired lads from Liverpool created The Beatles. Elvis may have invented rock and roll, but it was the Fab Four who transformed it into a global phenomenon, backed by the other bands of the 1960s 'British Invasion': The Rolling Stones, The Who, Cream and The Kinks. And the big names have kept coming ever since.

From Glam to Punk

Glam rock arrived in the 1970s, fronted by artists such as the anthemic Queen and the chameleon-like David Bowie (whose passing in 2016 triggered a palpable sense of loss worldwide). Also in the '70s, Led Zeppelin laid down the blueprint for heavy metal, and the psychedelia of the previous decade morphed into the prog rock of Pink Floyd and Yes.

At the end of the decade, it was all swept aside as punk exploded onto the scene, most famously with the Sex Pistols, The Clash, The Damned, the Buzzcocks and The Stranglers. Then punk begat New Wave, with acts including The Jam and Elvis Costello blending spiky tunes and sharp lyrics into a more radio-friendly sound.

The '80s

The conspicuous consumption of the early 1980s influenced the era's pop scene. Big hair and shoulder pads became the uniform of the day, with big names including Wham! (a boyish duo headed by an up-and-coming popster called George Michael) and New Romantic bands such

ROCK & ROLL LOCATIONS

Fans buy the single, then the T-shirt. But true fans visit the location featured on the album cover. The following are a few favourites:

➡ Abbey Rd, St John's Wood, London – *Abbey Road,* The Beatles

➡ Battersea Power Station, London – *Animals,* Pink Floyd (the inflatable pig has gone)

➡ Berwick St, Soho, London – *(What's the Story) Morning Glory,* Oasis

➡ Big Ben plus a corner of plinth under Boudica's statue, London – *My Generation* (US version), The Who

➡ Durdle Door, Dorset – *North Atlantic Drift,* Ocean Colour Scene

➡ Salford Lads' Club, Manchester – *The Queen is Dead,* The Smiths

➡ Thor's Cave, Manifold Valley, near Ashbourne, Peak District National Park – *A Storm In Heaven,* The Verve

➡ Yes Tor, Dartmoor, Devon – *Tomato,* Yes

as Spandau Ballet and Duran Duran. Away from the glitz, fans enjoyed the doom-laden lyrics of The Cure, the heavy metal of Iron Maiden and the 'miserabilism' of The Smiths.

Dance Music & Britpop

The late 1980s and early 1990s saw the rise of ecstasy-fuelled rave culture, centred on famous clubs like Manchester's Haçienda and London's Ministry of Sound. Manchester was also a focus for the burgeoning British 'indie' scene, driven by guitar-based bands such as The Stone Roses, James and the Happy Mondays. Then indie morphed into Britpop, with Oasis, Pulp, Supergrass and Blur, whose distinctively British sound chimed with the country's reborn sense of optimism after the landslide election of New Labour in 1997.

Recent Artists

The new millennium saw no let up in the music scene's continual shifting and reinventing. R&B, hip-hop and drum and bass fused into grime and dubstep, producing acts like Dizzee Rascal, Tinie Tempah and Stormzy. Initially centred on London, both scenes continue to wield an increasing global influence. Dance acts like Calvin Harris and Disclosure have also enjoyed massive international success. Meanwhile the spirit of British indie stays alive thanks to the likes of Arctic Monkeys, Coldplay, Muse, Kasabian and Radiohead.

Pop shows no sign of losing popularity either: boy bands continue to come and go, most notably One Direction, who clocked up the sales before going the way of all boy bands and splitting up in acrimonious fashion. Singer-songwriters are also a strong point – Adele's 2015 album, *25,* won critical acclaim and proved another international blockbuster, while Ed Sheeran has taken the world by storm; his third album, ÷, was released in 2017, and notched up 10 Top 10 hit singles (a British record) as well as two singles in the US Top 10, becoming the first artist in history to do so. To date, Sheeran has sold more than 26 million albums and 100 million singles worldwide, putting him in the top tier of the world's most successful (and richest) artists.

English music-scene movies include: *Backbeat* (1994), The Beatles' early days; *Sid & Nancy* (1986), Sex Pistols' bassist and his girlfriend; *Quadrophenia* (1979), mods and rockers; *Velvet Goldmine* (1998), glam rock; *24 Hour Party People* (2002), Manchester scene; *Control* (2007), biopic of Joy Division singer Ian Curtis; and *Nowhere Boy* (2009), John Lennon pre-Beatles.

Painting & Sculpture

For many centuries, continental Europe – especially the Netherlands, Spain, France and Italy – set the artistic agenda. The first artist with a truly British style and sensibility was arguably William Hogarth, whose riotous canvases exposed the vice and corruption of 18th-century London. His most celebrated work is *A Rake's Progress*, which kick-started a long tradition of British caricatures that can be traced right through to the work of modern-day cartoonists such as Gerald Scarfe and Steve Bell. You can see it at the Sir John Soane's Museum in London.

Portraits

While Hogarth was busy satirising society, other artists were hard at work showing it in its best light. The leading figures of 18th-century English portraiture were Sir Joshua Reynolds, Thomas Gainsborough (you can visit his house in Sudbury, Suffolk) and George Romney, while George Stubbs is best known for his intricate studies of animals (particularly horses). Most of these artists are represented at Tate Britain or the National Gallery in London.

Landscapes & Legends

Some of Henry Moore's work can be seen at the Yorkshire Sculpture Park. Barbara Hepworth is celebrated at the eponymous gallery in Wakefield; her former home and garden are also open to visitors in St Ives, Cornwall.

In the 19th century leading painters favoured the English landscape. John Constable's best-known works include *Salisbury Cathedral* and *The Hay Wain*. The latter is in the National Gallery; you can also visit the setting, a mill at Flatford in Suffolk. JMW Turner, meanwhile, was fascinated by the effects of light and colour on English scenes, with his works becoming almost entirely abstract by the 1840s.

In contrast, the Pre-Raphaelite painters of the late 19th century preferred a figurative style reflecting the Victorian taste for English fables and fairy tales. Key members of the movement included Dante Gabriel Rossetti, John Everett Millais and William Holman Hunt, all represented at London's Tate Britain or the Victoria & Albert Museum.

Sticks & Stones

In the tumultuous 20th century, English art became increasingly experimental. Francis Bacon placed Freudian psychoanalysis on the canvas in his portraits, while pioneering sculptors such as Henry Moore and Barbara Hepworth experimented with natural forms in stone and new materials. At about the same time, the painter LS Lowry was setting his 'matchstick men' among the smokestacks of northern England, and is today remembered by the major art centre that bears his name in Manchester.

Pop Art

The mid-1950s and early '60s saw an explosion of English 'pop art', as artists plundered popular culture for inspiration. Leaders of this new movement included David Hockney. His bold colours and simple lines were groundbreaking at the time, and are still used to great effect half a century later. A contemporary, Peter Blake, codesigned the cut-up collage cover for The Beatles' landmark album *Sgt. Pepper's Lonely Hearts Club Band*. The '60s also saw the rise of sculptor Anthony Caro; creating large abstract works in steel and bronze, he was one of England's most influential sculptors.

ANISH KAPOOR

The sculptor Anish Kapoor has been working in London since the 1970s. He is best known for his large outdoor installations, which often feature curved shapes and reflective materials, such as highly polished steel. You can find one of his major works, *ArcelorMittal Orbit*, in London's 2012 Queen Elizabeth Olympic Park. At over 110m high, it is the largest piece of public art in Britain, and one you can actually slide down, in a hair-raising 40-second glide.

THE TURNER PRIZE

Named after the enduringly popular landscape painter JMW Turner, the Turner Prize is a high-profile and frequently controversial annual award for British visual artists. As well as Damien Hirst, other winners have included Martin Creed (his work was a room with lights going on and off), Mark Wallinger (a collection of anti-war objects), Simon Starling (a shed converted to a boat and back again), Rachel Whiteread (a plaster cast of a house) and Antony Gormley (best known in England for his gigantic *Angel of the North*).

Britart & Beyond

Thanks partly to the support (and money) of advertising tycoon Charles Saatchi, a new wave of British artists came to the fore in the 1990s. The movement was dubbed, inevitably, 'Britart'; its leading members included Damien Hirst, famous (or infamous) for works involving pickled sharks, a cow and calf cut into sections *(Mother and Child Divided)* and a diamond-encrusted skull entitled *For the Love of God.* His pregnant, naked and half-flayed *Verity* towers 20m high beside the harbour mouth at Ilfracombe in north Devon.

A contemporary is Tracey Emin. Once considered an *enfant terrible,* she incurred the wrath of the tabloids for works such as *My Bed* (a messed-up bedroom scene that sold for £2.5 million in 2014), but is now a respected figure and patron of the Turner Contemporary gallery in Margate, named for the famous English artist JMW Turner. Her 20m light sculpture reading *I Want My Time With You,* was installed at London's St Pancras station in 2018 (the terminus for the Eurostar), and has been interpreted by some critics as Emin's response to the Brexit issue.

Cinema

English cinema has a long history, with many early directors cutting their teeth in the silent-film industry. Perhaps the best known of these was Alfred Hitchcock, who directed *Blackmail*, one of the first English 'talkies' in 1929, and who went on to direct a string of films during the 1930s before emigrating to Hollywood in the early 1940s.

War & Postwar

During WWII, films such as *In Which We Serve* (1942) and *We Dive at Dawn* (1943) were designed to raise public morale, while a young director called David Lean produced *Brief Encounter* (1945), the classic tale of buttoned-up English passion, before graduating to Hollywood epics including *Lawrence of Arabia* and *Doctor Zhivago.*

Following the hardships of war, British audiences were in the mood for escape and entertainment. During the late 1940s and early '50s, the domestic film industry specialised in eccentric British comedies epitomised by the output of Ealing Studios: notable titles include *Passport to Pimlico* (1949), *Kind Hearts and Coronets* (1949) and *The Titfield Thunderbolt* (1953).

The '60s

'British New Wave' and 'Free Cinema' explored the gritty realities of British life in semidocumentary style, with directors Lindsay Anderson and Tony Richardson crystallising the movement in films such as *This Sporting Life* (1961) and *A Taste of Honey* (1961). At the other end of the spectrum were the *Carry On* films, the cinematic equivalent of the smutty seaside postcard, packed with bawdy gags and double entendres. The 1960s also saw the birth of another classic English genre: the James Bond films, starring Sean Connery (who is actually Scottish).

The Ladykillers (1955) is a classic Ealing comedy about a band of hapless bank robbers holed up in a London guesthouse, and features Alec Guinness sporting the most outrageous set of false teeth ever committed to celluloid.

WALLACE & GROMIT

One of the great success stories of English TV and cinema has been Bristol-based animator Nick Park and the production company Aardman Animations, best known for the award-winning man-and-dog duo Wallace and Gromit. This lovable pair first appeared in Park's graduation film *A Grand Day Out* (1989) and went on to star in *The Wrong Trousers* (1993), *A Close Shave* (1995) and the full-length feature *The Curse of the Were-Rabbit* (2005). Known for their intricate plots, film homages and amazingly realistic stop-motion animation – as well as their very British sense of humour – the Wallace and Gromit films scooped Nick Park four Oscars. Other Aardman works include *Chicken Run* (2000), *Flushed Away* (2006), *The Pirates!* (2012) and two movies featuring *Shaun the Sheep* (2015 and 2019).

The '70s, '80s & '90s

The 1970s was a tough decade for the British film industry, but the 1980s saw a recovery, thanks partly to David Puttnam's Oscar success with *Chariots of Fire* (1981), and the newly established Channel Four investing in edgy films such as *My Beautiful Laundrette* (1985).

Another minor renaissance occurred in the 1990s, ushered in by the massively successful *Four Weddings and a Funeral* (1994), featuring Hugh Grant in his trademark role as a floppy-haired, self-deprecating Englishman, a character type he reprised in subsequent hits, including *Notting Hill*, *About a Boy* and *Love Actually*.

The British Film Institute (BFI; www.bfi.org.uk) is dedicated to promoting film and cinema in Britain, and publishes the monthly magazine *Sight & Sound*.

The 'Brit Flick' genre – characterised by themes such as irony, social realism and humour in the face of adversity – went on to include *Brassed Off* (1996), about a struggling brass band from a mining colliery; *The Full Monty* (1997), following a troupe of laid-off steelworkers turned male strippers; and *Billy Elliot* (2000), the story of an aspiring young ballet dancer striving to escape the slagheaps and boarded-up factories of the industrial north.

Meanwhile, films such as *East Is East* (1999) and *Bend it like Beckham* (2002) explored the tensions of modern multicultural Britain, while veteran director Mike Leigh, known for his heavily improvised style, found success with *Life Is Sweet* (1991), *Naked* (1993) and the Palme d'Or–winning *Secrets and Lies* (1996).

Recent Cinema

The Brits enjoy a notoriously dark sense of humour. Recent examples of TV shows where tragicomedy has achieved international successes include Phoebe Waller-Bridge's *Fleabag*, Michaela Coel's *Chewing Gum* and David Mitchell and Robert Webb's *Peep Show*.

In the early part of the 21st century, literary adaptations have continued to provide the richest seam of success in the English film industry, including 2012's *Anna Karenina*, directed by Joe Wright and staring Keira Knightley, and of course the blockbuster *Harry Potter* franchise. Biopics are also a perennial favourite: recent big-screen subjects include Elizabeth I (*Elizabeth: The Golden Age*, 2007), Margaret Thatcher (*The Iron Lady*, 2011) and the 19th-century artist JMW Turner (*Mr Turner*, 2014).

Meanwhile, the oldest of English film franchises trundles on: a tough, toned, 21st-century James Bond appeared in 2006 courtesy of Daniel Craig and the blockbuster *Casino Royale* (2006), followed by *Quantum of Solace* (2008), *Skyfall* (2012) and *Spectre* (2015). Craig is set to return as Bond a final time for the 25th instalment, *No Time to Die*, but there is much speculation about who will play the spy next; is it time for the role to go to a Black British actor, or is it high time Bond changed gender, or why not do both? Watch this space.

Theatre

English theatre can trace its roots back to medieval morality plays, court jesters and travelling storytellers, and possibly even to dramas during Roman times in amphitheatres – a few of which still remain, such as at Chester and Cirencester. But most scholars agree that the key milestone in the story is the opening of England's first theatre – called simply The Theatre – in London in 1576. Within 25 years, the Rose and the Globe theatres appeared, and the stage was set for the entrance of England's best-known playwright.

Shakespeare & Co

For most visitors to England (and for most locals), English drama means just one name: William Shakespeare. Born in 1564, in the Midlands town of Stratford-upon-Avon (still rich in Shakespearean sights), Shakespeare made his mark in London between around 1590 and 1610, where most of his plays were performed at the Globe Theatre. His brilliant plots and spectacular use of language, plus the sheer size of his canon of work (including classics such as *Hamlet, Romeo and Juliet, Henry V* and *A Midsummer Night's Dream*), have turned him into a national – and international – icon, so that today, over 400 years after shuffling off this mortal coil, the Bard's plays still pull in big crowds.

Recent Theatre

However you budget your time and money during your visit to England, be sure to see some English theatre. It easily lives up to its reputation as the finest in the world, especially in London, while other big cities also boast their own top-class venues, such as the Birmingham Repertory Theatre, the Bristol Old Vic, Chichester Festival Theatre and the Nottingham Playhouse.

Many accomplished British actors, including Judi Dench, Kristin Scott Thomas, Patrick Stewart, Brenda Blethyn, Jim Broadbent and Simon Callow, juggle high-paying screen roles with appearances on the British stage, while over the last decade or so several American stars have also trodden the London boards, including Glenn Close, Gwyneth Paltrow, Gillian Anderson, Angela Lansbury and Jake Gyllenhaal.

Venues in London include the Donmar Warehouse and the Royal Court Theatre, best known for new and experimental works. For big names, most people head for the West End, where famous spots include the Shaftesbury, the Adelphi Theatre and the Theatre Royal at Drury Lane, or the National Theatre on the South Bank. And then there's *The Mousetrap* – Agatha Christie's legendary whodunit is the world's longest-running play, showing continuously in the West End since 1952, bar a minor interruption during the COVID-19 pandemic.

West End Musicals

As well as drama, London's West End means big musicals, with a long history of crowd-pullers such as *Hamilton, Six* and *The Lion King,* with many of today's shows raiding the pop world for material, such as *We Will Rock You,* inspired by the music of Queen, and Abba-based *Mamma Mia!*

Sporting England

If you want a shortcut to the heart of English culture, watch its people at play. In this sports-mad nation thousands turn out each weekend to cheer on their favourite football team. Events such as Wimbledon (tennis) and the Six Nations (rugby) are big on the calendar, and Tour de France (cycling) and global Test matches (cricket) keep millions of sports-lovers enthralled via the screen. Then there are the efforts of enthusiastic amateurs, be it in pub football leagues or village cricket matches – the English reveal a penchant for rules, hierarchies and playing the game.

Football (Soccer)

The English Premier League (www.premierleague.com) has some of the finest teams in the world, dominated in recent years by six top teams: Liverpool, Manchester United, Manchester City, Chelsea, Arsenal and Tottenham. In 2016, however, unfancied Leicester City stunned the pundits and delighted neutrals by winning the title. Manchester City won back-to-back titles in 2018 and 2019. In 2020 Liverpool won the title for the first time in 30 years.

Down in quality from the Premiership, 72 other teams play in the English divisions called the Championship, League One and League Two.

The football season is the same for all divisions (August to May), so seeing a match can easily be tied into most visitors' itineraries, but tickets for the biggest games are like gold dust – your chances of bagging one are low unless you're a club member, or know someone who is. The exception to this being midweek games for the less prestigious competition, the EFL Cup.

You can often buy tickets on the spot, or at online agencies such as www.ticketmaster.co.uk.

Cricket

Along with Big Ben, The Beatles and a nice cup of tea, cricket is quintessentially English. Dating from the 18th century (although its roots are much older), the sport spread throughout the Commonwealth during

---

THE FA CUP

The Football Association held its first interclub knockout tournament in 1871–72: 15 clubs took part, playing for a nice piece of silverware called the FA Cup – then worth about £20.

Nowadays, around 600 clubs compete for this legendary and priceless trophy. It differs from many other competitions in that every team – from the lowest-ranking part-timers to the stars of the Premier League – is in with a chance. The preliminary rounds begin in August, and the world-famous Cup Final is held in May at the iconic Wembley Stadium in London.

Manchester United and Arsenal have the most FA Cups, but public attention – and affection – is invariably focused on the 'giant-killers': minor clubs that claw their way up through the rounds, unexpectedly beating higher-ranking competitors. One of the best-known giant-killing events occurred in 1992, when Wrexham, then ranked 24th in Division 3, famously came from a goal down to beat league champions Arsenal in the third round.

THE ASHES

The historic Test cricket series between England and Australia known as the Ashes has been played every other year since 1882 (bar a few interruptions during the world wars). It is played alternately in England and Australia, with each of the five matches in the series held at a different cricket ground, always in the summer in the host location.

The contest's name dates back to the landmark Test match of 1882, won (for the very first time) by the Australians. Defeat of the mother country by the colonial upstarts was a source of profound national shock: a mock obituary in the *Sporting Times* lamented the death of English cricket and referred to the sport's ashes being taken to Australia.

Later the name was given to a terracotta urn presented the following year to the English captain Ivo Bligh (later Lord Darnley), purportedly containing the cremated ashes of a stump or bail used in this landmark match. Since 1953 this hallowed relic has resided at the Marylebone Cricket Club (MCC) Museum at Lord's. Despite the vast importance given to winning the series, the urn itself is a diminutive 6in (150mm) high.

The recent history of the Ashes is not without drama. In the 2010–11 series England thrashed Australia, winning on Australian turf for the first time since the 1986–87 series. Then in 2013 Australia thrashed England 5-0, repeating the humiliating clean sweep they had inflicted in 2006–07. But the 2015 Ashes saw England – to national delight – defeat Australia 3-2, only to fail to win a single test in the subsequent 2017–18 series. *Plus ça change* you might think, until Australia managed to break the sequence – retaining the Ashes – holding England to a 2-2 draw on their own turf in 2019.

Britain's colonial era. Australia, the Caribbean and the Indian subcontinent took to the game with gusto, and today the former colonies delight in giving the old country a good spanking on the cricket pitch.

While many English people follow cricket like a religion, to the uninitiated it can be an impenetrable enigma. Spread over one-day games or five-day 'test matches', progress seems so *slow,* and dominated by arcane terminology like 'innings', 'cover drives', 'googlies', 'outswingers', 'leg-byes' and 'silly mid-off'. Nonetheless, at least one cricket match should be a feature of your travels around England. If you're patient and learn the intricacies, you could find cricket as absorbing as it is for all the Brits who remain glued to their radio or computer all summer long, 'just to see how England's getting on'.

Causing ructions is Twenty20 cricket, a relatively new format that limits the number of balls each team has to score off, putting the emphasis on fast, big-batting scores. Traditionalists see it as changing the character of the game, though there's no doubting its popularity – most Twenty20 matches sell out. Grounds include Lord's in London, Edgbaston in Birmingham and Headingley in Leeds.

Tickets cost from £30 to well over £200. The County Championship pits the best teams from around the country against each other; tickets cost £5 to £25, and only the most crucial games tend to sell out. Details are on the website of the English Cricket Board (www.ecb.co.uk).

The easiest way to watch cricket – and often the most enjoyable – is stumbling across a local game on a village green as you travel around the country. There's no charge for spectators, and no one will mind if you nip into the pub during a quiet spell.

Rugby

A wit once said that football was a gentlemen's game played by hooligans, while rugby was a hooligans' game played by gentlemen. That may be true, but rugby is very popular, especially since England became Rugby Union World Champions in 2003, and then hosted the Rugby Union World Cup in 2015. It's worth catching a game for the display of skill (OK,

A highlight of the international rugby calendar is the annual Six Nations Championship (www.sixnationsrugby.com), held in February and March, in which England battles against teams from Wales, Scotland, Ireland, France and Italy.

SPORTING HISTORY

England's intriguing sports have equally fascinating histories. No one can say when football was invented, but the word 'soccer' (the favoured term in countries where 'football' means another game) is held by some to derive from 'sock'. In medieval times this was a tough leather foot-cover worn by peasants – ideal for kicking around a pig's bladder in the park on a Saturday afternoon.

In contrast, rugby can trace its roots to a football match in 1823 at Rugby School in Warwickshire. A player called William Webb Ellis, frustrated at the limitations of mere kicking, reputedly picked up the ball and ran with it towards the goal. True to the sense of English fair play, rather than Ellis being dismissed from the game, a whole new sport was developed around his tactic, and the Rugby Football Union was formally inaugurated in 1871. The Rugby World Cup is named the Webb Ellis Trophy after this enterprising young tearaway.

and brawn), and the fun atmosphere in the grounds. Tickets for games cost around £15 to £50 depending on the club's status and fortunes.

There are two codes of the game: rugby union (www.rfu.com) is played predominantly, but not exclusively, in southern England, Wales and Scotland, and is traditionally thought of as the game of the middle and upper classes. Rugby league (www.therfl.co.uk) is played more in northern England, stereotypically by the 'working classes'. Today, leading rugby union clubs include Leicester Tigers, Bath, Gloucester and current European Rugby Champions Cup holders Exeter Chiefs, while London has a host of good-quality teams (including Wasps and Saracens). In rugby league, teams to watch include the Wigan Warriors, St Helens and Leeds Rhinos.

Tennis

Tennis is widely played at club and regional level, but the best-known tournament is the All England Championships – known to all as Wimbledon (www.wimbledon.com) – when tennis fever sweeps through the country in the last week of June and first week of July. There's something quintessentially English about the combination of grass courts, polite applause and spectators in straw hats, with strawberries and cream devoured by the truckload.

Demand for seats at Wimbledon always outstrips supply, but to give everyone an equal chance tickets are sold through a public ballot. You can also take your chance on the spot; about 5000 tickets are sold at the gate each day, including those – at the earlier stages of the championships – for the show courts. But you'll need to be an early riser: dedicated fans start queuing (how English) the night before. See the website for more information.

Horse Racing

The tradition of horse racing in Britain stretches back centuries, and there's a 'meeting' somewhere pretty much every day. For all but the major events you should be able to get a ticket on the day, or buy in advance from the sport's marketing body Great British Racing (www.greatbritish racing.com).

The top event in the calendar is Royal Ascot (www.ascot.co.uk) at Ascot Racecourse in mid-June, where the rich and famous come to see and be seen, and the fashion is almost as important as the horses.

Other big events include the Grand National steeplechase at Aintree (www.aintree.co.uk) in early April; and the Derby at Epsom (www.epsom downs.co.uk) on the first Saturday in June. The latter is especially popular with the masses so, unlike at Ascot, you won't see so many morning suits or outrageous hats.

Charismatic British long-distance runner – and the most successful British track athlete in modern Olympic Games history – Sir Mohamed Muktar Jama Farah (aka Mo Farah) is no doubt one of the reasons long-distance running has become incredibly popular in England over the last decade.

Survival Guide

Directory A–Z

Accessible Travel

All new buildings have wheelchair access, and even hotels in grand old country houses often have lifts, ramps and other accessibility facilities. Hotels, B&Bs and restaurants in historic buildings are often harder to adapt, so there are fewer options for travellers with extra needs in England.

Modern city buses and trams have low floors for easy access, but few have conductors who can lend a hand when you're getting on or off. London's Tube is busy and there are plenty of stairs, see the Tube map for the limited list of step-free stations (with lifts). Many taxis take wheelchairs but the roof height can be restrictive – seek local advice from Disability Rights UK on your best taxi options.

For long-distance travel, coaches may present problems if you can't walk, but the main operator, National Express (www.national express.com), has wheelchair-friendly coaches on many routes. For details, ring its dedicated Disabled Passenger Travel Helpline (☑0371 781 8181).

On intercity trains there's more room and better facilities, and usually station staff around; just have a word and they'll be happy to help out. A Disabled Persons Railcard (www.disabledpersons-rail card.co.uk) costs £20 and gets you 33% off most train fares.

Useful organisations:

Disability Rights UK (www.disabilityrightsuk.org) Published titles include a *Holiday Guide*. Other services include a key for 7000 public disabled toilets across the UK.

Scope (www.scope.org.uk; ☑0808 800 3333) Helpline if you're having difficulties, for example on public transport.

Tourism For All (www.tourism forall.org.uk)

Download Lonely Planet's free Accessible Travel guides from https://shop.lonelyplanet.com/products/accessible-travel-online-resources-2017.

Customs Regulations

Entering or leaving the UK was straightforward and hassle-free prior to 'Brexit' and the Covid-19 pandemic,

Climate

London

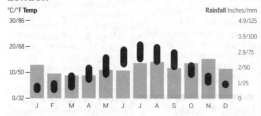

Bath

York

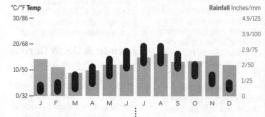

Electricity

Type G
230V/50Hz

save for the occasional inconvenience of long queues at passport control and security.

At the time of research, things had changed with Covid-19 testing and quarantining restrictions. Check www.gov.uk/uk-border-control for up-to-date information from the UK government directly.

Customs Rules & Charges

Britain had a two-tier customs system: one for goods bought duty-free outside the EU; the other for goods bought in another EU country where tax and duty is

paid. After leaving the EU in 2020, changes are expected to these arrangements.

For the latest go to www.gov.uk and search for 'Bringing goods into the UK'.

Duty-free The duty-free limit for goods includes 200 cigarettes or equivalent in cigars, 4L of wine, 1L of spirits and other goods worth up to £390.

Tax and duty on imports Customs officials use the following guidelines to distinguish personal use from commercial imports from the EU: 800 cigarettes, 200 cigars, 10L of spirits, 90L of wine and 110L of beer. Still enough to have one hell of a party.

Emergency & Important Numbers

England (and UK) country code	44
International access code	00
Emergency (police, fire, ambulance, mountain rescue or coastguard)	112 or 999

Health

No vaccinations are currently required to travel to Britain. This may change so check with your GP/medical provider in your own country before you travel.

→ Emergency medical treatment is freely available at National Health Service (NHS) hospitals throughout the country without proof of residence (although this is a contested issue in British politics and thus things may change).

→ For non-emergencies, tourists will need to visit a private medical practice.

→ Chemists (pharmacies) can advise on minor ailments such as sore throats and earaches. In large cities, there's usually at least one 24-hour chemist.

→ For advice that is not an emergency you can call the NHS 111 service (☎111).

Insurance

Although everyone in England receives free emergency medical treatment, regardless of nationality, travel insurance is highly recommended. It will usually cover medical and dental consultation and treatment at private clinics, which can be quicker than NHS places – as well as the cost of any emergency flights – plus all the usual stuff like loss of baggage. Worldwide travel insurance is available at www.lonelyplanet.com/travel-insurance. You can buy, extend and claim online anytime – even if you're already on the road.

Internet Access

→ 3G and 4G mobile broadband coverage is good in large population centres, but limited or nonexistent in rural areas. 5G is now being rolled out across the country.

→ Internet data roaming charges can be very high. Don't get caught out: check with your mobile/cell phone provider before travelling.

→ Most hotels, B&Bs, hostels, stations and coffee shops (even some trains and buses) have wi-fi access, charging anything from nothing to £6 per hour.

Legal Matters

→ Police have the power to detain, for up to six hours, anyone suspected of having committed an offence punishable by imprisonment (including drugs offences). Police have the right to search anyone they suspect of possessing drugs.

→ Illegal drugs are widely available, especially in clubs. Cannabis possession is a criminal offence; punishment for carrying a small amount may be a warning, a fine or imprisonment depending on your luck (and your privilege). Dealers face much stiffer penalties, as do people caught with other drugs.

→ On buses and trains (including the London Underground), people without a valid ticket are fined on the spot (£80, reduced to £40 if you pay within 21 days).

LGBT+ Travellers

England is generally a tolerant place for LGBT+ people. London, Manchester and Brighton have flourishing queer scenes, and in other sizeable cities you'll find communities not entirely in the closet. That said, you'll still find pockets of homophobic hostility in some areas. Local resources include:

Diva (www.divamag.co.uk)

Gay Times (www.gaytimes.co.uk)

Switchboard LGBT+ Helpline (0300 330 0630, open 10am–10pm daily)

Money

The currency of Britain is the pound sterling (£). Paper money (notes) comes in £5, £10, £20 and £50 denominations. Some shops don't accept £50 notes because fakes circulate.

Other currencies are very rarely accepted, except at some gift shops in London, which may take euros, US dollars, yen and other major currencies.

ATMs

ATMs (usually called 'cash points' in England) are common in cities and even small towns. Withdrawals from some ATMs are subject to a small charge, but most are free (look for 'Free Cash'). Check how much your home bank charges for withdrawing money overseas and ask about options. Watch out for tampered ATMs; one ruse by scammers is to attach a card-reader or minicamera.

Credit & Debit Cards

Visa and MasterCard are widely accepted in England. Other cards, including Amex, are not so widely accepted. Most businesses will assume your card is 'Chip and PIN' enabled (using a PIN instead of signing). If it isn't, you should be able to sign instead, but some places may not accept your card so have a back-up plan for payments.

Changing Money

Airports and cities have exchange bureaux for changing your money into pounds. Check rates first; some bureaux offer poor rates or levy outrageous commissions.

Opening Hours

Opening hours may vary throughout the year, especially in rural areas where many places have shorter hours, or close completely, from October or November to March or April.

Banks 9.30am–4pm or 5pm Monday to Friday; some open 9.30am–1pm Saturday

Cafes 9am to 5pm daily

Post Offices 9am to 5pm (5.30pm or 6pm in cities) Monday to Friday. 9am to 12.30pm Saturday; main branches to 5pm

Pubs & bars noon–11pm Monday to Saturday (some till midnight or 1am Friday and Saturday), 12.30pm–11pm Sunday

Restaurants Lunch is noon to 3pm, dinner 6pm to 9pm or 10pm (to midnight or later in cities). Some close Sunday evening or all day Monday.

Shops 9am to 5.30pm (or 6pm in cities) Monday to Saturday, and often 11am to 5pm Sunday. London and other cities have convenience stores open 24/7.

Post

The British postal service is generally efficient and reliable. Information on post-office locations and postage rates can be found at www.postoffice.co.uk.

Public Holidays

Holidays for the whole of Britain:

New Year's Day 1 January

Easter March/April (Good Friday to Easter Monday inclusive)

May Day First Monday in May

Spring Bank Holiday Last Monday in May

Summer Bank Holiday Last Monday in August

Christmas Day 25 December

Boxing Day 26 December

If a public holiday falls on a weekend, the nearest Monday is usually taken instead. Most businesses and banks close on official public holidays (hence the quaint term 'bank holiday').

On public holidays, some small museums and places of interest close, but larger attractions have their busiest times. If a place closes on Sunday, it'll probably be shut on a bank holiday as well.

Virtually everything – attractions, shops, banks, offices – closes on Christmas Day, although pubs are open at lunchtime. There's usually no public transport on Christmas Day, and a very minimal service on Boxing Day.

Safe Travel

England is a remarkably safe country, but crime is not unknown in London and other cities.

➡ Watch out for pickpockets and hustlers in crowded areas popular with tourists, such as around Westminster Bridge in London.

➡ Many town centres can be rowdy on Friday and Saturday nights when pubs and clubs are emptying – which is also a time when tempers may fray.

➡ Try to avoid large crowds especially after a major event – if you don't need to travel on a crowded train of football fans, delay your journey.

➡ Harassment is rare but does happen especially if you do not blend into the crowd: stick to busier streets, train carriages, or the lower deck on a bus – and stay aware of your surroundings.

Telephone
Mobile Phones

The UK uses the GSM 900/1800 network, which covers the rest of Europe, Australia and New Zealand. It's recommended you get a UK SIM card on arrival unless you have a good data roaming plan.

ROAMING CHARGES

The UK's decision to leave the EU (aka 'Brexit') means that British networks will eventually be able to charge for roaming in Europe, and EU network subscribers will have to pay roaming fees once again when visiting the UK. However, the EU roaming agreement should remain in force until at least 2021.

Unless you have a global roaming deal, it will be cheaper to get a UK number. Make sure your phone is unlocked before you depart, then pick up a SIM on arrival. Alternatively, consider a cheap pay-as-you-go phone (aka a 'burner' phone) with a local SIM card (from £20 including calling credit) for local calls, using your own phone where you can access free wi-fi at cafes, museums and your accommodation.

Phone Codes

Dialling to the UK Dial your country's international access code then 44 (the UK country code), then the area code (dropping the first 0) followed by the telephone number.

Dialling from the UK The international access code is 00; dial this, then add the code of the country you wish to dial.

Reverse-charge (Collect) International Call Dial ☑155 for the operator. It's an expensive option, but not for the caller.

Area Codes in the UK No standard format or length, eg Edinburgh 0131, London 020, Ambleside 015394.

Directory assistance A host of agencies offer this service – numbers include ☑118 118, ☑118 500 and ☑118 811 – but fees are extortionate (around £6 for a 45-second call); search online for free at www.thephone book.bt.com.

Mobile phones Codes usually begin with ☑07.

Free calls Numbers starting with ☑0800 or ☑0808 are free.

Call charges Details here: www. gov.uk/call-charges

National Operator ☑100

International Operator ☑155

Time

Britain is on GMT/UTC. The clocks go forward one hour for 'summer time' at the end of March, and go back at the end of October. The 24-hour clock is used for transport timetables.

City	Time Difference with Britain
Los Angeles	8hr behind
Mumbai	5½hr ahead Nov-Feb, 4½hr Mar-Oct
New York	5hr behind
Paris, Berlin, Rome	1hr ahead
Sydney	9hr ahead Apr-Sep, 10hr Oct, 11hr Nov-Mar
Tokyo	9hr ahead Nov-Feb, 8hr Mar-Oct

Toilets

Public toilets in England are generally clean and modern, but cutbacks in public spending mean that many facilities have been closed down. Your best bet is to use the toilets in free-to-enter museums; those in train and bus stations often charge a fee (from 20p to 50p), and most pubs and restaurants stipulate that their toilets are for customers only.

Tourist Information

Most English cities and towns have a tourist information centre or visitor information centre – for ease we've called all these places 'tourist offices'.

Tourist offices have helpful staff, books and maps for sale, leaflets to give away, and advice on things to see or do. Some can also assist with booking accommodation. Some are run by national parks and often have small exhibits about the area.

Most tourist offices keep regular business hours; in quiet areas they close from October to March, while in popular areas they open daily year-round. In recent years cost-cutting has seen many smaller tourist offices close down; some have been replaced with 'tourist information points' – racks of leaflets and maps in locations such as public libraries and town halls.

Before leaving home, check the comprehensive website of England's official tourist board, Visit England (www.visitengland.com), covering all the angles of national tourism, with links to numerous other sites.

Visas

➡ If you're a citizen of the European Economic Area (EEA) nations or Switzerland, you don't need a visa to enter or work in the UK.

➡ Visa regulations are always subject to change, and immigration restriction is big news in the UK, so it's essential to check with www. gov.uk before leaving home.

➡ At the time of research, if you're a citizen of Australia, Canada, New Zealand, Japan, Israel, the USA and several other countries, you can stay for up to six months

HERITAGE ORGANISATIONS

National Trust (NT; www.nationaltrust.org.uk) A charity protecting historic buildings and land with scenic importance across England and Wales. Annual membership is £69 (discounts for under-26s and families). A Touring Pass allows free entry to NT properties for one/two weeks (one person £31/36, two people £55/66, family £61/77).

English Heritage (EH; www.english-heritage.org.uk) State-funded organisation responsible for numerous historic sites. Annual membership is £56 (couples and seniors get discounts). An Overseas Visitors Pass allows free entry to most sites for nine/16 days for £33/39 (couples £57/67, families £62/72).

(no visa required), but are not allowed to work.

➡ Nationals of many countries, including South Africa, will need to obtain a visa: for more info, see www.gov.uk/check-uk-visa.

➡ The Youth Mobility Scheme (www.gov.uk/tier-5-youth-mobility), for Australian, Canadian, Japanese, Hong Kong, New Zealand, South Korean and Taiwanese citizens aged 18 to 30, allows working visits of up to two years, but must be applied for in advance.

➡ Commonwealth citizens with a UK-born parent may be eligible for a Certificate of Entitlement to the Right of Abode, which entitles them to live and work in the UK.

➡ Commonwealth citizens with a UK-born grandparent may qualify for a UK Ancestry Employment Certificate, allowing them to work full time for up to five years in the UK.

➡ British immigration authorities have always been tough; dress neatly and carry proof that you have sufficient funds with which to support yourself. A credit card and/or an onward ticket will help.

BOOK YOUR STAY ONLINE

For more accommodation reviews by Lonely Planet authors, check out http://lonelyplanet.com/hotels. You'll find independent reviews, as well as recommendations on the best places to stay. Best of all, you can book online.

Transport

GETTING THERE & AWAY

Most overseas visitors reach England by air. As London is a global transport hub, it's easy to fly to England from just about anywhere. The massive growth of budget ('no-frills') airlines increased the number of routes – and reduced fares – between England and other countries in Europe.

Another option for travel between England and mainland Europe is by ferry, either port-to-port (eg Dover–Calais) or combined with a long-distance bus trip. The financial savings are not huge compared with budget airfares, so taking a ferry is mainly the choice of cyclists or those travelling with a car and camping equipment.

International trains are much more comfortable and a good low-carbon travel option. There are direct rail services between England, France and Belgium via the Channel Tunnel, with onward connections with many other European destinations.

Air

The national carrier is British Airways (www.britishairways.com).

London Airports

Heathrow (www.heathrow.com) The UK's main airport for international flights; often chaotic and crowded. About 15 miles west of central London.

Gatwick (www.gatwickairport.com) Britain's number-two airport, mainly for international flights, 30 miles south of central London.

Stansted (www.stanstedairport.com) About 35 miles north-east of central London, mainly handling charter and budget European flights.

Luton (www.london-luton.co.uk) Some 35 miles north of central London, well known as a holiday-flight airport.

London City (www.london cityairport.com) Just under nine miles east of central London, specialising in flights to/from European and other UK airports.

London Southend (www.southendairport.com) Close to the coast but with a direct train to Liverpool St Station (one hour).

Regional Airports

Some planes on European and long-haul routes avoid London and use major regional airports including Manchester and Newcastle. Smaller regional airports such as Southampton and Birmingham are served by flights to and from Continental Europe and Ireland.

Land

Bus/Coach

You can easily get between England and other European countries via long-distance

---

CLIMATE CHANGE & TRAVEL

Every form of transport that relies on carbon-based fuel generates CO_2, the main cause of human-induced climate change. Modern travel is dependent on aeroplane, which might use less fuel per kilometre per person than most cars but travel much greater distances. The altitude at which aircraft emit gases (including CO_2) and particles also contributes to their climate change impact. Many websites offer 'carbon calculators' that allow people to estimate the carbon emissions generated by their journey and, for those who wish to do so, to offset the impact of the greenhouse gases emitted with contributions to portfolios of climate-friendly initiatives throughout the world. Lonely Planet offsets the carbon footprint of all staff and author travel.

bus (called 'coach' in England). The international network Eurolines (www.euro lines.com) connects a huge number of destinations; you can buy tickets online via one of the national operators.

Services to/from England are also operated by National Express (www.national express.com). Sample journey times to/from London include Amsterdam (12 hours), Barcelona (24 hours), Dublin (12 hours) and Paris (eight hours).

If you book early, and can be flexible with timings (ie travel when few other people want to), you can get some very good deals. For example, between London and Paris or Amsterdam from about £25 one way (although paying £35 to £45 is more usual).

Train
CHANNEL TUNNEL PASSENGER SERVICE

High-speed Eurostar (www. eurostar.com) passenger services shuttle at least 10 times daily between London and Paris (2½ hours) or Brussels (two hours). Buy tickets from travel agencies, major train stations or the Eurostar website.

The normal one-way fare between London and Paris/Brussels costs around £109; advance booking and off-peak travel gets cheaper fares as low as £29 one way.

CHANNEL TUNNEL CAR SERVICE

Drivers use Eurotunnel (www. eurotunnel.com). At Folkestone in England or Calais in France, you drive onto a train, get carried through the tunnel and drive off at the other end.

Trains run about four times an hour from 6am to 10pm, then hourly through the night. Loading and unloading takes an hour; the journey lasts 35 minutes.

Book in advance online or pay on the spot. The standard one-way fare for a car and up to nine passengers is £75 to

---

As well as Eurostar, many standard trains run between England and mainland Europe. You buy one ticket, but get off the train at the port, walk onto a ferry, then get another train on the other side.

Routes include Amsterdam–London (via Hook of Holland and Harwich). Travelling between Ireland and England, the main train-ferry-train route is Dublin to London, via Dun Laoghaire and Holyhead (Wales). Ferries also run between Rosslare and Fishguard or Pembroke (Wales), with train connections on either side.

£100 depending on time of day; promotional fares often bring it down to £59 or less.

Sea
Ferry Routes
The main ferry routes between England and other countries include the following:

➜ Dover to Calais (France)
➜ Dover to Dunkirk (France)
➜ Harwich to Hook of Holland (Netherlands)
➜ Hull to Rotterdam (Netherlands)
➜ Hull to Zeebrugge (Belgium)
➜ Liverpool to Belfast (Northern Ireland)
➜ Newcastle to Amsterdam (Netherlands)
➜ Newhaven to Dieppe (France)
➜ Plymouth to Roscoff (France)
➜ Poole to Cherbourg (France)
➜ Portsmouth to Bilbao (Spain)
➜ Portsmouth to St Malo (France)
➜ Portsmouth to Santander (Spain)

Ferry Fares
Most ferry operators offer flexible fares, meaning great bargains at quiet times of day or year. For example, short cross-channel routes such as Dover to Calais or Boulogne

---

can be as low as £45 for a car plus two passengers, although around £75 to £105 is more likely. If you're a foot passenger, or cycling, there's less need to book ahead; fares on short crossings cost about £30 to £50 each way.

FERRY BOOKING

You can book directly with one of the ferry operators listed here, or use the very handy www.directferries. co.uk, a single site covering all sea-ferry routes, plus Eurotunnel.

Brittany Ferries (www.brittany-ferries.com)

DFDS Seaways (www.dfdssea ways.co.uk)

P&O Ferries (www.poferries.com)

Stena Line (www.stenaline.com)

GETTING AROUND

Air

England's domestic airline companies include British Airways, Loganair, easyJet and Ryanair. If you're really pushed for time, flights on longer routes across England (eg Exeter or Southampton to Newcastle) are handy, and often very competitive in price – although on shorter routes (eg London to Newcastle, or Manchester to Newquay) trains compare favourably with planes on time, once airport downtime is factored in.

Bicycle

London

The most well-known bike-share scheme in London is from **Santander Cycles** (☎0343 222 6666; www.tfl.gov.uk/modes/cycling/santander-cycles). Nicknamed 'Boris bikes' or 'Sadiq Cycles' after the last two London mayors, these bikes can be hired on the spot from automatic docking stations across the city. Newer options are popping up every year. For more on cycling in London go to www.lcc.org.uk

Around the Country

The nextbike (www.nextbike.co.uk) bike-sharing scheme has stations in Bath, Exeter, Oxford and Coventry, while York and Cambridge also have plentiful bike-rental options. Bikes can also be hired in national parks or forestry sites now primarily used for leisure activities, such as Kielder Water in Northumberland and Grizedale Forest in the Lake District. Rental rates start at about £12 per day, or £20 and up for a top quality model. In some areas, disused railway lines are now bike routes, notably the Peak District in Derbyshire.

Bikes on Trains

Bicycles can be taken free of charge on most local trains (although they may not be allowed at peak times when the trains are crowded with commuters, speak to the local station staff).

Bikes can be carried on long-distance train journeys free of charge, but advance booking is required for most conventional bikes. (Folding bikes can be carried on pretty much any train at any time including in London.)

In theory, this shouldn't be too much trouble as most long-distance rail trips are best bought in advance anyway, but you can go a long way down the path of booking your seat before you start booking your bike – only to find space isn't available.

A final warning: when railways are undergoing repair work, cancelled trains are replaced by buses – and they won't take bikes.

The PlusBike scheme provides all the information you need for travelling by train with a bike. Leaflets are available at major stations, or downloadable from http://plusbike.nationalrail.co.uk.

Bus

If you're on a tight budget, long-distance buses (coaches) are nearly always the cheapest way to get around England, although they're also the slowest – sometimes by a considerable margin. Many towns have separate stations for local buses and long-distance coaches; make sure you go to the right one!

National Express (www.nationalexpress.com) Offers a wide network and frequent services between main centres. Fares vary enormously depending on how far in advance you book and if it is a peak time (ie Friday afternoon).

Megabus (www.megabus.com) Operates a budget coach service serving more than 100 destinations around the country. Go at a quiet time, book early and your ticket will be very cheap. Book later, for a busy time and... You get the picture.

Passes & Discounts

National Express offers discount passes to full-time students and under-26s, called Young Persons Coachcards. They cost £12.50 and give 30% off standard adult fares. Coachcards are also available for people aged over 60, families and travellers with disabilities.

Car & Motorcycle

Travelling by car or motorbike around England means you can be independent and flexible, and reach remote places. Downsides for drivers include motorway traffic jams, the high price of fuel and high parking costs in cities and busy tourist towns.

Rentals

Compared with many countries (especially the USA), hire rates are expensive in Britain; the smallest cars start from about £130 per week, entry-level motorbikes from £215 per week.

Some main players:

Avis (www.avis.co.uk)

Budget (www.budget.co.uk)

Europcar (www.europcar.co.uk)

Sixt (www.sixt.co.uk)

Super Bike Rental (www.superbikerental.co.uk)

Thrifty (www.thrifty.co.uk)

Another option is to look online for small, local car-hire companies that undercut the international franchises. Generally those in cities are cheaper than in rural areas.

Using a rental-broker or comparison site such as UK Car Hire (www.ukcarhire.net) or Rental Cars (www.rentalcars.com) can help you find bargains, for example hiring at airports rather than the city centre can be considerably cheaper.

Campervan Rental

Hiring a campervan or motorhome (£650 to £1100 a week) is more expensive than hiring a car, but saves on accommodation costs and gives almost unlimited freedom. Privately owned campervan hires are also possible for less. Sites to check include the following:

Just Go (www.justgo.uk.com)

Cool Camping (www.coolcamping.com/campervans)

Insurance

It's illegal to drive a car or ride a motorbike in England without (at least) third-party insurance. This will be included with all hire cars as standard, but you will usually be liable for an excess for any damage to the vehicle (sometimes up to £1500).

You can pay an extra fee to the hire company to waive the excess, but it is often quite expensive at around £5 per day; a cheaper, if more convoluted, option (read the fine print!) is to arrange your own excess insurance through a third party such as www.carhireexcess.co.uk.

If you damage the car, you will pay the excess and reclaim it later from the insurance provider; make sure you document any damage and, in the case of a serious accident, get a copy of the police report.

Parking

Many cities have short-stay and long-stay car parks; the latter are cheaper though may be less convenient. 'Park & Ride' systems allow you to park on the edge of the city then ride to the centre on frequent nonstop buses for an all-in-one price.

Yellow lines (single or double) along the edge of the road indicate restrictions. Nearby signs spell out when you can and can't park.

In London and other big cities, traffic wardens operate with efficiency; if you park on the yellow lines at the wrong time, your car will be clamped or towed away, and it'll cost you £130 or more to get driving again. In some cities there are also red lines, which mean no stopping at all. Ever.

Roads

Motorways and main A-roads deliver you quickly from one end of the country to the other. Lesser A-roads, B-roads and minor roads are much more scenic – ideal for car or motorcycle touring. You can't travel fast, but you won't care.

Speed limits vary from 20mph (32km/h) in built-up areas like London; 60mph (96km/h) on main roads; and 70mph (112km/h) on motorways.

Road Rules

A foreign driving licence is valid in Britain for up to 12 months after entering the country.

Drink-driving is taken very seriously; you're allowed a maximum blood-alcohol level of 80mg/100mL (0.08%) – campaigners want it reduced to 50mg/100mL (0.05%), in line with most European countries (including Scotland).

Some other important rules:

➡ Drive on the left (!).

➡ Wear seatbelts in cars.

➡ Wear helmets on motorcycles.

➡ Give way to your right at junctions and roundabouts.

➡ Always use the left lane on motorways and dual carriageways unless overtaking (although so many people ignore this rule, you'd think it didn't exist).

➡ Don't use a mobile phone while driving unless it's fully hands-free (another rule frequently flouted).

Local Transport

English cities usually have good public-transport systems – a combination of bus, train and tram – often run by a confusing number of separate companies. Tourist offices can provide maps and information. See also www.traveline.info.

Bus

There are good local bus networks year-round in cities and towns. Buses also run in some rural areas year-round, although timetables are designed to serve schools and businesses, so there aren't many noon and weekend services (and they may stop running during school holidays), or buses may link local villages to a market town on only one day each week.

In tourist areas (especially national parks) there are frequent services from Easter to September. However, it's always worth double-checking at a tourist office before planning your day's activities around a bus that may not actually be running.

If you're taking a few local bus rides in one area, day passes (with names like Day Rover, Wayfarer or Explorer) are cheaper than buying several single tickets. Often they can be bought on your first bus, and may include local rail services. It's always worth asking ticket clerks or bus drivers about your options, most are happy to help.

Taxi

There are two sorts of taxi in England: those with meters that can be hailed in the street; and minicabs, which are cheaper but can only be called by phone. Unlicensed minicabs operate in some cities.

In London, most taxis are the famous 'black cabs' (some with advertising livery in other colours), which charge by distance and time. Depending on the time of day, a 1-mile journey takes five to 10 minutes and costs £6 to £9. Longer journeys are cheaper per mile.

Ridesharing apps such as Uber (www.uber.com) are an option in most towns and cities, while similar apps like Kabbee (www.kabbee.com) allow you to book a minicab in double-quick time.

In rural areas, taxis need to be called by phone; the best place to find the local taxi's phone number is the local pub. Fares are £3 to £5 per mile.

Traintaxi (www.traintaxi.co.uk) is a portal site that helps 'bridge the final gap' between the train station and your hotel or other final destination.

Train

For long-distance travel around England, trains are generally faster and more comfortable than coaches but are nearly always much more expensive. The English like to moan about their trains, but around 85% run on time. The other 15% that get delayed or cancelled mostly impact commuter services rather than long-distance journeys. The main headache these days is the cost – if you leave booking your ticket to the last minute, fares can be extremely high, so it's always worth booking as far in advance as you can.

Train Operators

About 20 different companies operate train services in England, while Network Rail operates tracks and stations. For some passengers this system can be confusing at first, but information and ticket-buying services are mostly centralised. If you have to change trains, or use two or more train operators, you still buy one ticket – valid for the whole journey. The main railcards and passes are also accepted by all train operators.

Where more than one train operator services the same route, eg York to Newcastle, a ticket purchased from one company may not be valid on trains run by another. So if you miss the train you originally booked, it's worth checking which later services your ticket will be valid for.

Information

Your first stop should be National Rail Enquiries (www.nationalrail.co.uk), the nationwide timetable and fare information service. Its website advertises special offers and has real-time links to station departure boards and downloadable maps of the rail network.

Tickets & Reservations

BUYING TICKETS

Once you've found the journey you need on the National Rail Enquiries website, links take you to the relevant train operator to buy the ticket. This can be mailed to you (UK addresses only) or collected at the station on the day of travel from automatic machines. There's usually no booking fee on top of the ticket price.

You can also use a centralised ticketing service to buy your train ticket. These cover all train services in a single site, and add a small booking fee on top of every ticket price. The main players include the following:

QJump (www.qjump.co.uk)

Rail Easy (www.raileasy.co.uk)

Train Line (www.thetrainline.com)

To use operator or centralised ticketing websites, you always have to state a preferred time and day of travel, even if you don't mind when you go, but you can change it as you go through the process, and with a little delving around you can find some real bargains.

You can also buy train tickets on the spot at stations, which is fine for short journeys (under about 50 miles), but discount tickets for longer trips are usually not available, these must be bought in advance.

Mobile train tickets are gradually becoming more common across the network, but it's a slow process – for now printed tickets are still the norm.

FARES

For longer journeys tickets are much, much cheaper if bought in advance. You can also save if you travel off-peak. Advance purchase usually gets a reserved seat, too.

Whichever operator you travel with and wherever you buy tickets, these are the three main fare types:

Anytime Buy any time, travel any time – always the most expensive option.

Off-peak Travel at off-peak times (what constitutes off-peak depends on the journey). Can be bought at any time up to the point of travel.

Advance These tickets can only be purchased in advance, and travel is only permitted on specific trains. This is usually the cheapest option, as long as you're happy with the restrictions. Note that the cheapest fares are nonrefundable, so if you miss your train you'll have to buy a new ticket.

For an idea of the price difference, an Anytime single ticket from London to York will cost £127 or more, an Off-peak around £56 to £62, with an Advance around £44 to £55, and possibly less if you book early enough or don't mind arriving at midnight.

ONWARD TRAVEL

If the train doesn't get you all the way to your destination, you can add a PlusBus (www.plusbus.info) supplement when making your reservation to validate your train ticket for onward travel by bus. This is more convenient, and usually cheaper, than buying a separate bus ticket.

Classes

There are two classes of rail travel: first and standard. First class costs around 50% more than standard fare (up to double at busy periods) and gets you bigger seats, more legroom, and usually a more peaceful businesslike atmosphere, plus extras such as complimentary drinks and newspapers. At weekends some train operators offer 'upgrades' to 1st class for an extra £5 to £25 on top of your standard-class fare, payable on the spot.

Train Passes
DISCOUNT PASSES

If you're staying in England for a while, passes known as Railcards (www.railcard.co.uk) are available:

16-25 Railcard For those aged 16 to 25, or a full-time UK student.

Family & Friends Railcard Covers up to four adults and four children travelling together.

Two Together Railcard For two specified people travelling together.

Senior Railcard For anyone aged over 60.

Disabled Persons Railcard For people with registered disabilities.

Railcards cost £30 (valid for one year, available from major stations or online) and give a 33% discount on most train fares, except those already heavily discounted. With the Family card, adults get 33% and children get 60% discounts, so the fee is easily repaid in a couple of journeys.

Digital railcards were introduced in 2020, making it even easier to get one before you travel.

NATIONAL PASSES

For countrywide travel, Brit Rail (www.britrail.net) passes are available for visitors from overseas. They must be bought in your country of origin (not in England) from a specialist travel agency. Available in different versions (eg England only; all Britain; UK and the Republic of Ireland) for periods from four to 30 days.

Behind the Scenes

SEND US YOUR FEEDBACK

We love to hear from travellers – your comments keep us on our toes and help make our books better. Our well-travelled team reads every word on what you loved or loathed about this book. Although we cannot reply individually to your submissions, we always guarantee that your feedback goes straight to the appropriate authors, in time for the next edition. Each person who sends us information is thanked in the next edition – the most useful submissions are rewarded with a selection of digital PDF chapters.

Visit **lonelyplanet.com/contact** to submit your updates and suggestions or to ask for help. Our award-winning website also features inspirational travel stories, news and discussions.

Note: We may edit, reproduce and incorporate your comments in Lonely Planet products such as guidebooks, websites and digital products, so let us know if you don't want your comments reproduced or your name acknowledged. For a copy of our privacy policy visit lonelyplanet.com/privacy.

WRITER THANKS

Tasmin Waby

Thank you to Duff Battye for lending me his home in Oxfordshire and his intel on rugby and cycling in England. Cheers to my fellow scribes Oliver Berry and Belinda Dixon, and Dane Waby for your feedback. To all my co-creators on this guidebook, including Sandie Kestell, it's been quite a rollercoaster of a journey this time! And finally to my sometimes companions on the road, Maisie and Willa: you make everything we do magic.

Oliver Berry

Thanks to everyone who helped me put this project together in the crazy circumstances of a global pandemic – especially my fellow authors and my editor Sandie Kestell. On the road, Dan Hinkley, Rebecca Jones, Tom Smith and Hope Delaney deserve a call out. Back home, thanks to Rosie Hillier, Gracie, Susie Berry and Justin Foulkes. Most of all, thanks to all the amazing Lonely Planet people who worked on this title.

Joe Bindloss

I'd like to thank my partner Linda and two boys Benji and Tyler for putting up with me heading off to research at this unsettling time. Thanks to the many helpful staff at tourist offices, bus stations, B&Bs, stately homes and museums who provided local information, and to the pubs and restaurants who were diligent about social distancing to keep everyone safe.

Thanks also to everyone who wrote in with tips – it's great to have extra eyes and ears on the ground!

Fionn Davenport

2020 was a tough year for travel – and travel writing. But in the middle of it all, I was reminded more strongly than ever of the salutary effects of exploring other places – a historic city, a stretch of scenic moorland, the ruins of an ancient castle. A huge thanks to those who kept me going – Andy Parkinson, Joe Keggin and my editor Sandie Kestell, who made the craziest of times that little bit less crazy. Finally, a big thanks to my wife Laura. We'll never forget this particular update!

Belinda Dixon

To all who showed so many kindnesses while I was on the road, thank you; especially at what was such a challenging time.. Sandie and the other Lonely Planet staff, thank you for keeping the ship on course, and to fellow Lonely Planet writers a big 'cheers' for keeping spirits up. And countless thanks to Laura and Midge for making me laugh and keeping me sane.

Anthony Ham

I'm very grateful to everyone at Lonely Planet, for the pleasure of working with you on this book and so many more, especially Sandie Kestell and Darren O'Connell.

Damian Harper

Many thanks to everyone who helped and offered tips, including my co-authors, the ever-helpful staff at the Natural History Museum, Amaya Wang, Polly Bussell, Freya Barry, Tania Patel, Norman MacDonald, Penny Aikens, Bill Moran, Hollie and the excellent staff at Japan House, Shannon and James Peake. And big thanks to Tim Harper for his fine suggestions, and Emma Harper too.

Catherine Le Nevez

Cheers first and foremost to Julian, and to all of the locals and tourism professionals in the Midlands who provided insights, information and inspiration during this project and over the years. Huge thanks too to Sandie Kestell and everyone at Lonely Planet. As ever, *merci encore* to my parents, brother, *belle-sœur, neveu* and *nièce*.

ACKNOWLEDGEMENTS

Climate map data adapted from Peel MC, Finlayson BL & McMahon TA (2007) 'Updated World Map of the Köppen-Geiger Climate Classification', *Hydrology and Earth System Sciences*, 11, 1633–44.

Cover photograph: Church Stairs, Whitby, Martyn Ferry/Getty Images ©

Illustrations: pp80–1 & pp620–1 by Javier Zarracina, pp62–3 by Javier Zarracina and Michael Weldon

THIS BOOK

This 11th edition of Lonely Planet's *England* guidebook was researched and written by Tasmin Waby, Oliver Berry, Joe Bindloss, Fionn Davenport, Belinda Dixon, Anthony Ham, Damian Harper and Catherine Le Nevez. The previous edition was written by Oliver, Fionn, Marc Di Duca, Belinda, Damian, Catherine, Lorna Parkes and Greg Ward. This guidebook was produced by the following:

Senior Product Editor Sandie Kestell

Cartographer Mark Griffiths

Product Editor Ronan Abayawickrema

Book Designer Clara Monitto

Assisting Editors Andrew Bain, Nigel Chin, Andrea Dobbin, Sasha Drew, Carly Hall, Kellie Langdon, Kate Morgan, Angela Tinson, Saralinda Turner, Brana Vladisavljevic

Cover Researcher Fergal Condon

Thanks to Gillian Carass, Francesco Cisternino, Andrea Dobbin, Grace Dobell, Karen Henderson, Genna Patterson

Index

Map Legend

Sights

- Beach
- Bird Sanctuary
- Buddhist
- Castle/Palace
- Christian
- Confucian
- Hindu
- Islamic
- Jain
- Jewish
- Monument
- Museum/Gallery/Historic Building
- Ruin
- Shinto
- Sikh
- Taoist
- Winery/Vineyard
- Zoo/Wildlife Sanctuary
- Other Sight

Activities, Courses & Tours

- Bodysurfing
- Diving
- Canoeing/Kayaking
- Course/Tour
- Sento Hot Baths/Onsen
- Skiing
- Snorkelling
- Surfing
- Swimming/Pool
- Walking
- Windsurfing
- Other Activity

Sleeping

- Sleeping
- Camping
- Hut/Shelter

Eating

- Eating

Drinking & Nightlife

- Drinking & Nightlife
- Cafe

Entertainment

- Entertainment

Shopping

- Shopping

Information

- Bank
- Embassy/Consulate
- Hospital/Medical
- @ Internet
- Police
- Post Office
- Telephone
- Toilet
- Tourist Information
- Other Information

Geographic

- Beach
- Gate
- Hut/Shelter
- Lighthouse
- Lookout
- Mountain/Volcano
- Oasis
- Park
- Pass
- Picnic Area
- Waterfall

Population

- Capital (National)
- Capital (State/Province)
- City/Large Town
- Town/Village

Transport

- Airport
- Border crossing
- Bus
- Cable car/Funicular
- Cycling
- Ferry
- Metro station
- Monorail
- Parking
- Petrol station
- S-Bahn/Subway station
- Taxi
- T-bane/Tunnelbana station
- Train station/Railway
- Tram
- U-Bahn/Underground station
- Other Transport

Routes

- Tollway
- Freeway
- Primary
- Secondary
- Tertiary
- Lane
- Unsealed road
- Road under construction
- Plaza/Mall
- Steps
- Tunnel
- Pedestrian overpass
- Walking Tour
- Walking Tour detour
- Path/Walking Trail

Boundaries

- International
- State/Province
- Disputed
- Regional/Suburb
- Marine Park
- Cliff
- Wall

Hydrography

- River, Creek
- Intermittent River
- Canal
- Water
- Dry/Salt/Intermittent Lake
- Reef

Areas

- Airport/Runway
- Beach/Desert
- Cemetery (Christian)
- Cemetery (Other)
- Glacier
- Mudflat
- Park/Forest
- Sight (Building)
- Sportsground
- Swamp/Mangrove

Note: Not all symbols displayed above appear on the maps in this book

Belinda Dixon

Bristol, Bath & Somerset; Hampshire, Wiltshire & Dorset; Devon, Cornwall & the Isles of Scilly Only happy when her feet are suitably sandy, Belinda has been (gleefully) travelling, researching and writing for Lonely Planet since 2006. It's seen her navigating mountain passes and soaking in hot-pots in Iceland's Westfjords, marvelling at Stonehenge at sunrise; scrambling up Italian mountain paths; horse riding across Donegal's golden sands; gazing at Verona's frescoes; and fossil hunting on Dorset's Jurassic Coast. Belinda is also a podcaster and adventure writer and helps lead wilderness expeditions. See her blog posts at https://belindadixon.com

Anthony Ham

Newcastle & Northeast England Anthony is a freelance writer and photographer who specialises in Spain, East and Southern Africa, the Arctic and the Middle East. When he's not writing for Lonely Planet, Anthony writes about and photographs Spain, Africa and the Middle East for newspapers and magazines in Australia, the UK and US.

Damian Harper

Canterbury & Southeast England With two degrees (one in modern and classical Chinese from SOAS), Damian has been writing for Lonely Planet for over two decades, contributing to titles as diverse as *China, Beijing, Shanghai, Vietnam, Thailand, Ireland, London, Mallorca, Malaysia, Singapore & Brunei, Hong Kong* and *Great Britain*. Damian has also penned articles for numerous newspapers and magazines, including the *Guardian* and the *Daily Telegraph,* and currently makes Surrey, England, his home. A self-taught trumpet novice, his other hobbies include collecting modern first editions, photography and taekwondo. Follow Damian on Instagram (damian.harper).

Catherine Le Nevez

Birmingham & the Midlands Catherine's wanderlust kicked in when she roadtripped across Europe from her Parisian base aged four, and she's been hitting the road at every opportunity since, travelling to some 60 countries and completing her Doctorate of creative arts in writing, Master's in professional writing, and postgrad qualifications in editing and publishing along the way. Over the past decade-and-a-half she's written scores of Lonely Planet guides and articles covering Paris, France, Europe and far beyond. Her work has also appeared in numerous online and print publications. Topping Catherine's list of travel tips is to travel without any expectations.

OUR STORY

A beat-up old car, a few dollars in the pocket and a sense of adventure. In 1972 that's all Tony and Maureen Wheeler needed for the trip of a lifetime – across Europe and Asia overland to Australia. It took several months, and at the end – broke but inspired – they sat at their kitchen table writing and stapling together their first travel guide, *Across Asia on the Cheap*. Within a week they'd sold 1500 copies. Lonely Planet was born.

Today, Lonely Planet has offices in Tennessee, Dublin, Beijing and Delhi, with a network of over 2000 contributors in every corner of the globe. We share Tony's belief that 'a great guidebook should do three things: inform, educate and amuse'.

OUR WRITERS

Tasmin Waby

London; Oxford & the Cotswolds Born in London, Tasmin spent her childhood in Australia before making a home in the UK. When not travelling on assignment, she lives on the Grand Union canal in a narrowboat, raising two tween-aged kids, and a fat Russian Blue cat called Millie.

Oliver Berry

The Lake District & Cumbria Oliver is a writer and photographer from Cornwall. He has worked for Lonely Planet for more than a decade, covering destinations from Cornwall to the Cook Islands, and has worked on more than 30 guidebooks. He is also a regular contributor to many newspapers and magazines, including *Lonely Planet Magazine*. His writing has won several awards, including The Guardian Young Travel Writer of the Year and the TNT Magazine People's Choice Award. His latest work is published at www.oliverberry.com.

Joe Bindloss

Cambridge & East Anglia Joe first got the travel bug from trips around the Med in the family camper van, and he's been travelling ever since, writing more than 100 guidebooks and reference titles for Lonely Planet and other publishers, covering everywhere from India and Nepal to Australia and England. For many years, Joe was Lonely Planet's destination editor for the Indian Subcontinent. He also writes regularly for newspapers, websites and magazines.

Fionn Davenport

Manchester, Liverpool & Northwest England; Yorkshire Irish by birth and conviction, Fionn has spent the last two decades focusing on the country of his birth and its nearest neighbour, England. He's written extensively for Lonely Planet and contributed oodles of travel pieces to a host of newspapers and magazines, including the *Irish Times, Irish Independent, Irish Daily Mail, Lonely Planet Magazine, Cara,* the *Independent* and the *Daily Telegraph*.

OVER PAGE | MORE WRITERS

Published by Lonely Planet Global Limited
CRN 554153
11th edition – Aug 2021
ISBN 978 1 78701 828 0
© Lonely Planet 2021   Photographs © as indicated 2021
10 9 8 7 6 5 4 3 2 1
Printed in China